W9-AWJ-977

University Casebook Series

EDITORIAL BOARD

DAVID L. SHAPIRO
DIRECTING EDITOR
Professor of Law, Harvard University

EDWARD L. BARRETT, Jr.
Professor of Law Emeritus, University of California, Davis

ROBERT C. CLARK
Dean of the School of Law, Harvard University

DANIEL A. FARBER
Professor of Law, University of Minnesota

OWEN M. FISS
Professor of Law, Yale Law School

GERALD GUNTHER
Professor of Law, Stanford University

THOMAS H. JACKSON
President, University of Rochester

HERMA HILL KAY
Dean of the School of Law, University of California, Berkeley

HAROLD HONGJU KOH
Professor of Law, Yale Law School

ROBERT L. RABIN
Professor of Law, Stanford University

CAROL M. ROSE
Professor of Law, Yale Law School

CASS R. SUNSTEIN
Professor of Law, University of Chicago

CASES AND MATERIALS

ON

CORPORATIONS

CONCISE SEVENTH EDITION

By

WILLIAM L. CARY
Late Dwight Professor of Law,
Columbia University

and

MELVIN ARON EISENBERG
Koret Professor of Law,
University of California at Berkeley

Westbury, New York
THE FOUNDATION PRESS, INC.
1995

COPYRIGHT © 1940, 1950, 1951, 1958, 1959, 1970, 1980, 1988 THE FOUNDATION PRESS, INC.

COPYRIGHT © 1995 By THE FOUNDATION PRESS, INC.

             615 Merrick Ave.
             Westbury, N.Y. 11590–6607
             (516) 832–6950

All rights reserved
Printed in the United States of America

ISBN 1–56662–276–X

 TEXT IS PRINTED ON 10% POST CONSUMER RECYCLED PAPER

 PRINTED WITH SOY INK™

PREFACE

In many areas of corporate law, it is difficult to fully understand the issues and the legal rules without some background knowledge of basic accounting and financial concepts. Accordingly, this casebook includes introductory materials on such topics as financial statements, diversification, valuation, the efficient capital market hypothesis, and dividend policy. These materials have been chosen and edited with an eye to ensuring that they are accessibile to students who don't have an accounting and financial background. The materials are introduced gradually, at relevant points throughout the book, so that students are not faced with an onslaught of unfamiliar concepts.

Because of the importance of statutes in corporation law, students should refer to the Statutory Supplement whenever a cross-reference to that Supplement appears. When a cross-referenced statutory provision includes an Official Comment, the Comment should be read as well. Other cross-references to the Statutory Supplement (for example, references to excerpts from the Restatement (Second) of Agency) should be treated the same way.

In the preparation of this casebook, the following conventions have been used: Where a portion of the text of an original source (such as a case) has been omitted, the omission is indicated by ellipses (. . .). The omission of footnotes from original sources is not indicated, but the original footnote numbers are used for those footnotes that are retained. The American Law Institute's Principles of Corporate Governance: Analysis and Recommendations (1994) is cited simply as ALI, Principles of Corporate Governance.

I thank my colleagues Baruch Lev, Eric Rakowski, and Jan Vetter for their very helpful comments on portions of the manuscript, and my Research Assistants Doug Couchman, Matt Forsyth, Christine Kurek, Stu Mackey, Rob Seaver, and Nellwyn Voorhies for their great assistance on all sorts of matters.

MELVIN A. EISENBERG

June, 1995

*

ACKNOWLEDGMENTS

I thank the authors, publishers, and copyrightholders who permitted me to reprint portions of the following works:

Ad Hoc Subcommittee on Merit Regulation of the State Regulation of Securities Committee, Section of Corporations, Banking and Business Law, American Bar Association, Report of State Merit Regulation of Securities Offerings, 41 Business Lawyer 785 (1986). Copyright © 1986 by the American Bar Association.

Alison Grey Anderson, Conflicts of Interest: Efficiency, Fairness and Corporate Structure, 25 U.C.L.A. Law Review 738 (1978) (with permission of Fred B. Rothman & Co.).

William D. Andrews, The Stockholder's Right to Equal Opportunity in the Sale of Shares, 78 Harvard Law Review 505 (1965).

Adolf A. Berle, The Theory of Enterprise Entity, 47 Columbia Law Review 343 (1947). Copyright © 1947 by the Directors of the Columbia Law Review Association, Inc. All rights reserved.

William Bratton, The Economic Structure of the Post-Contractual Corporation 87 Northwestern L.Rev. 180 (1992). Reprinted by special permission of Northwestern University School of Law, Northwestern University Law Review, Volume 87, Issue 1, pp. 180–185 (1992).

Richard Brealy & Stewart C. Myers, Principles of Corporate Finance (McGraw-Hill Book Company 4th ed. 1991).

Thomas W. Briggs, Shareholder Activism and Insurgency Under the New Proxy Rules, 50 Bus.Law. 99 (1994). Copyright © 1994 by the American Bar Association. All rights reserved. Reprinted with the permission of the American Bar Association and its Section of Business Law.

Victor Brudney & William Bratton, Corporate Finance—Cases and Materials (Foundation Press 4th ed. 1993).

Committee on Federal Regulation of Securities, Section of Corporations, Banking and Business Law, American Bar Association, Report of the Task Force on Regulation of Insider Trading, Part I: Regulation under the Antifraud Provisions of the Securities Exchange Act of 1934, 41 Business Lawyer 223 (1985). Copyright © 1985 by the American Bar Association.

Committee on Federal Regulation of Securities, Section of Corporations, Banking and Business Law, American Bar Association, Report of the Task Force on Regulation of Insider Trading, Part II: Reform of Section 16, 42 Business Lawyer 1087 (1987). Copyright © 1987 by the American Bar Association.

Committee on Federal Regulation of Securities, Section of Corporations, Banking and Business Law, American Bar Association, The SEC and

Corporate Disclosure, 36 Business Lawyer 118 (1980). Copyright © 1980 by the American Bar Association.

Dan P. Dobbs, Handbook of the Law of Remedies (West Publishing Co. 2d ed. 1993).

Janet Gamer Feldman & Richard L. Teberg, Beneficial Ownership under Section 16 of the Securities Exchange Act of 1934, 17 Case Western Reserve Law Review 1054 (1966).

Ted Fiflis, Accounting Issues for Lawyers (West Publishing Co. 4th ed. 1991).

William P. Hackney & Tracey G. Benson, Shareholder Liability for Inadequate Capital, 43 University of Pittsburgh Law Review 837 (1982).

Robert W. Hamilton, Fundamentals of Modern Business (Little, Brown 1994).

Harry J. Haynsworth IV, Jr., The Effectiveness of Involuntary Dissolution Suits as a Remedy for Close Corporation Dissension, 35 Clev. State L.Rev. 25 (1987).

James Heard, Esq., Conflicts of Interest in the Proxy Voting System (1987). Copyright © 1987 Investor Responsibility Research Center, Inc.

David R. Herwitz, Materials on Accounting for Lawyers (Foundation Press 1980).

Henry T. C. Hu, New Financial Products, The Modern Process of Financial Innovation, and the Puzzle of Shareholder Welfare, 69 Tex.L. Rev. 1273 (1991).

Henry T. C. Hu, Risk, Time, and Fiduciary Principles in Corporate Investment 38 U.C.L.A. Law Rev. 277 (1990).

George B. Javaras, Equal Opportunity in the Sale of Controlling Shares: A Reply to Professor Andrews, 34 University of Chicago Law Review 420 (1965).

William A. Klein & John C. Coffee, Jr., Business Organization and Finance (Foundation Press 5th ed. 1993).

Robert R. Keatinge, New Gang in Town, Business Law Today, March/April 1995, at 5.

Jensen & Meckling, Theory of the Firm: Managerial Behavior, Agency Costs and Ownership Structure, 3 Journal of Financial Economics 305 (1976).

Park McGinty, What is a Security?, 1993 Wisc.L.Rev. 1033.

Harold Marsh, Jr. and R. Finkle, California Corporation Law (3d ed. 1990). Panel Publishers a division of Aspen Publishers, Inc., 36 W. 44th Suite 1316, New York, NY 10036. All rights reserved.

ACKNOWLEDGMENTS

Geoffrey P. Miller and Jonathan R. Macey, The Plaintiff's Attorney's Role in Class Actions and Derivative Litigations: Economic Analysis and Recommendations for Reform, 58 U.Chi.L.Rev. 1 (1991).

W. Page Keeton, Robert E. Keeton, Dan B. Dobbs & David G. Owen, Prosser & Keeton on The Law of Torts (West Publishing 5th ed. 1984).

Richard O. Kummert, State Statutory Restrictions on Financial Distributions by Corporations to Shareholders (pt. I), 59 Washington Law Review 185 (1984) (with permission of Fred B. Rothman & Co.).

Louis M. Loss, Fundamentals of Securities Regulation (2d ed. 1988) (Little, Brown & Co.).

Bayless Manning & J. Hanks, Jr., Legal Capital (Foundation Press 3d ed. 1993).

F. Hodge O'Neal & Robert B. Thompson, O'Neal's Close Corporations (Clark Boardman Callaghan 3d ed. 1992). Reprinted with permission of Clark Boardman Callaghan, 155 Pfingsten Road, Deerfield, IL 60015.

Harvey L. Pitt, Proxy Reform: A New Era of SEC Activism, Insights, November 1992.

Ross, Westerfeld & Jordan, Fundamentals of Corporate Finance (Richard D. Irwin Inc. 3d ed. 1995)

Carl W. Schneider, Small Business Capital Raising—The Need for Further SEC Initiatives, Insights, February 1993.

Larry W. Sonsini, Regulation A, 16 The Review of Securities Regulation 781 (1983).

A. Gilchrist Sparks III & Theodore Mervis, Recent Developments with Respect to the Demand Requirement in Derivative Actions, Bank & Corporate Governance Law Reporter (1993). Copyright © 1993 Computer Law Reporter, Inc. Reprinted by Permission.

Dan K. Webb, Steven F. Molo & James F. Hurst, Understanding and Avoiding Corporate and Executive Criminal Liability, 49 Bus.Law. 617 (1994). Copyright © 1994 by the American Bar Association. All rights reserved. Reprinted with the permission of the American Bar Association and its Section of Business Law.

Subcommittee on Executive Compensation, Section of Corporations, Banking and Business Law, American Bar Association, Executive Compensation: A Road Map for the Corporate Advisor, 40 Business Lawyer 221 (1984). Copyright © 1984 by the American Bar Association.

*

SUMMARY OF CONTENTS

xi

ANALYTICAL TABLE OF CONTENTS

*

TABLE OF CASES

Principal cases are in italic type. Non-principal cases are in roman type. References are to Pages.

TABLE OF CASES

*

Chapter I

AGENCY

SECTION 1. INTRODUCTION

Courses in corporations or business associations are, in large part, courses in organizational law. Among the most common forms of business organization in this country are the sole proprietorship, the corporation, and the partnership. Based on tax filings, as of 1991 there were 15,181,000 sole proprietorships in the United States, 3,803,000 corporations, and 1,515,000 partnerships. U.S. Bureau of the Census, Statistical Abstract of the United States 540–43 (Tables 835, 837, 840) (1994).

A sole proprietorship is a business owned by one individual. It might be thought that the term "organization" is an inappropriate characterization of a form that involves only a single owner. That terminology can, however, be justified on at least two grounds.

First, a business enterprise owned by an individual is likely to have a degree of psychological and sociological identity separate from that of the individual. This separateness of a sole proprietor's enterprise is often expressed by giving the enterprise its own name, like "Acme Shoe Company." Furthermore, a sole proprietor usually will consider only a certain portion of his property and cash as invested in the business, and will keep a separate set of financial records for the enterprise as if the enterprise's finances were separate from her own.

Thus, if Alice Adams begins a new business in 1995—say, Acme Shoe Company—she is likely to issue a balance sheet for the business that does not show all of her assets and liabilities, but only those assets dedicated to, and those liabilities arising out of, the enterprise's operations. (See Section 4, An Introduction to Financial Statements, infra.) In short, as a psychological matter Adams, and to a certain extent those who deal with her, are likely to regard Acme Shoe Company as an enterprise or firm that has a certain degree of separateness from Adams herself, with a certain amount of capital. As a matter of law, however, a sole proprietorship has no separate identity from its owner. If Adams takes no special legal step, like incorporating the enterprise, all of her wealth will be committed to the enterprise, because an individual who owns a sole proprietorship has unlimited personal liability for obligations incurred in the conduct of the business.

1

The second reason for calling a sole proprietorship an organization is that a sole proprietor typically will not conduct the business by herself, but will engage various people—salespersons, mechanics, managers—to act on her behalf in conducting the business. The employment by one person of another to act on her behalf brings us to the most elementary form of organizational law, known as the law of agency. An *agent* is a person who by mutual assent acts on behalf of another and subject to the other's control. Restatement, Second, Agency § 1. The person for whom the agent acts is a *principal.* Id. Agency law governs the relationship between agents and principals, and among agents, principals, and third parties with whom the agent deals on the principal's behalf. Although agency is a consensual relationship, whether an agency relationship has been created does not turn on whether the parties think of themselves as agent and principal. "Agency is a legal concept which depends upon the existence of required factual elements: the manifestation by the principal that the agent shall act for him, the agent's acceptance of the undertaking and the understanding of the parties that the principal is to be in control of the undertaking. The relation which the law calls agency does not depend upon the intent of the parties to create it, nor their belief that they have done so. To constitute the relation, there must be an agreement, but not necessarily a contract, between the parties; if the agreement results in the factual relation between them to which are attached the legal consequences of agency, an agency exists although the parties did not call it agency and did not intend the legal consequences of the relation to follow. Thus, when one . . . asks a friend to do a slight service for him, such as to return for credit goods recently purchased from a store, [an agency relationship may be created although] neither one may have any realization that they are creating an agency relation or be aware of the legal obligations which would result from performance of the service." Restatement (Second) of Agency § 1, Comment b.

SECTION 2.   AUTHORITY

CROISANT v. WATRUD

Oregon Supreme Court, 1967.
248 Or. 234, 432 P.2d 799.

Before PERRY, Chief Justice, and McALLISTER, O'CONNELL, GOODWIN and DENECKE, Justices.

Reversed and Remanded.

O'CONNELL, J.

This is a suit in equity for an accounting brought against co-partners in a firm of certified public accountants and the executrix of a deceased partner, LaVern Watrud. Plaintiff appeals from a decree in favor of defendants.

We shall refer to the deceased partner, Watrud, as one of the defendants. The defendants engaged in the accounting practice with their principal office in Klamath Falls and their branch office in Medford. Watrud was in charge of the Medford office.

Plaintiff was the owner of a sawmill, timberlands, and other property over which she exercised general control, delegating the details of management of the business to others.

In 1955 plaintiff employed the defendant partnership to advise her on tax matters and to prepare income tax returns for her business enterprises. All of these services were performed by Watrud, who was in charge of the Medford office.

In 1956 plaintiff sold her sawmill. Thereafter her business activities consisted almost entirely of making collections under the contract for the sale of the mill, collections on the sale of timber, collections of rents, and various disbursements from the moneys so collected.

In 1957 plaintiff moved to California. She made arrangements with Watrud to make the collections referred to above, to make certain disbursements, to keep her financial books and records, and to prepare her financial statements and tax returns. The moneys collected by Watrud were deposited in the account of the Lloyd Timber Company (plaintiff's business name in Oregon) in a Grants Pass bank.

In 1957 plaintiff learned that her husband, Glenn Lloyd, had induced Watrud to make unauthorized payments out of the Lloyd Timber Company account to him. Plaintiff instructed Watrud not to make any further payments to her husband, but Watrud violated her instructions. Plaintiff was informed of these subsequent misappropriations by Watrud on behalf of Glenn Lloyd in 1958. She also learned that her husband was unfaithful to her. Plaintiff again excused Watrud's breach of trust and her husband's infidelity. After their reconciliation, plaintiff and her husband took a trip to Europe. When they returned, plaintiff discovered that her husband had forged checks on her California bank account and had also forged her signature upon a $75,000 note and negotiated it. Plaintiff also became aware of the fact that Watrud had continued to pay money to Glenn Lloyd out of plaintiff's Oregon account. In addition, she learned that Watrud, without authorization, had drawn a check payable to himself. When Watrud was confronted with this evidence he finally acknowledged his abuse of his trust. Soon thereafter Watrud died from gunshot wounds while hunting. Plaintiff then filed this suit for an accounting against the surviving partners.

The trial court held that the trust assumed by Watrud in handling plaintiff's business affairs was an "independent trustee employment," separate and distinct from the activities in which the partnership itself was engaged.

 T.C.

It is undisputed that plaintiff's initial business arrangements for tax advice and the preparation of tax returns were with the partnership and not simply with Watrud individually. After the partnership was employed, Watrud individually performed all of the services sought by plaintiff. As time went on plaintiff called upon Watrud to perform additional services in connection with her business including the collection and disbursements of funds. The initial question is whether these subsequent services performed by Watrud are to be regarded as having been performed as a part of the partnership business or under a separate arrangement calling only for the services of Watrud personally.

The record suggests that plaintiff, Watrud, and defendants considered all of Watrud's services to the plaintiff as services performed by a member of a partnership on behalf of that firm. The partnership received a check each month for all of Watrud's services including the services involved in handling plaintiff's business affairs. Had the parties viewed the services in making collections and disbursements for plaintiff as independent activities separate compensation would have been in order. Although the partnership's Medford office was geographically separated from the Klamath Falls office, both operations constituted one autonomous business enterprise and consequently defendants cannot insulate themselves from liability on the ground that the Medford office was a separate business operation. Defendants are liable, therefore, if Watrud can be regarded as the agent of the partnership in performing the fund-handling services for plaintiff.

It is clear that Watrud had no express authority from defendants to perform these services. And there was no evidence from which an authority implied in fact could be derived. If it were common knowledge that accountants frequently act as trustees in the collection and disbursement of funds, we would be in a position to take judicial notice of the common practice and thus find an implied authority or an apparent authority. But we have no basis for saying that accountants commonly or frequently perform fund-handling services. Thus we conclude that liability cannot be rested upon a manifestation by defendants that they assented to be bound for such services. However, an agent can impose liability upon his principal even where there is no actual or apparent authority or estoppel. An agent may have an "inherent agency power" to bind his principal. Such power is defined in Restatement (Second), Agency § 8A as "the power of an agent which is derived not from authority, apparent authority or estoppel, but solely from the agency relation and exists for the protection of persons harmed by or dealing with a servant or other agent." When an agent has acted improperly in entering into a contract the inherent agency power "is based neither upon the consent of the principal nor upon his manifestations."[1] The scope of the principal's liability under an inherent agency power is stated in Section 161:

---

1. Comment to § 8A, p. 37.

> "A general agent for a disclosed or partially disclosed principal subjects his principal to liability for acts done on his account which usually accompany or are incidental to transactions which the agent is authorized to conduct if, although they are forbidden by the principal, the other party reasonably believes that the agent is authorized to do them and has no notice that he is not so authorized." Restatement (Second), Agency § 161, p. 378 (1958).

It will be noted that Section 161 states that the principal is liable only for his agent's acts "which *usually accompany* or are *incidental* to transactions which the agent is authorized to conduct...." (Emphasis added.) As we have previously observed, we have neither evidence nor judicial knowledge of the practice of accountancy from which to decide whether the collection and disbursement of accounts is commonly undertaken by accountants. We cannot say, therefore, that the fund-handling services performed by Watrud in this case were the type which "usually accompany" the transactions which accountants ordinarily conduct viewed from the standpoint of those engaged in accountancy. Upon similar reasoning we are unable to say that the services here were "incidental" to the transactions Watrud was authorized to conduct.

But this does not conclude the matter. Assuming that accountants do not regard the collection and disbursement of funds as a part of the services usually offered by members of their profession, what significance should this have if, in the particular circumstances, a person dealing with a member of an accounting partnership reasonably believes that accountants perform the kind of service which he seeks to have performed? If the phrase "acts ... which usually accompany ... transactions which the agent is authorized to conduct" is to be tested solely from the viewpoint of accountants in describing the kind of services they usually perform then, of course, Section 161 of the Restatement (Second) of Agency would not be applicable even though a client of an accounting firm mistakenly but reasonably believed that the services he requested were not alien to the work of accountants. The basis for the principal's liability under these circumstances is best explained by the comments appended to Section 8A and related sections of the Restatement; whether the theory is categorized as one of apparent authority (treating the circumstances as a manifestation of authority by principal), or as arising out of an inherent agency power is immaterial. The rationale begins with the idea that:

> "The principles of agency have made it possible for persons to utilize the services of others in accomplishing far more than could be done by their unaided efforts.... [The] primary function [of agency] in modern life is to make possible the commercial enterprises which could not exist otherwise.... Partnerships and corporations, through which most of the work of the world is done today, depend for their existence upon agency principles. The rules designed to promote the interests of these enterprises are necessarily accompanied by rules to

police them. It is inevitable that in doing their work, either through negligence or excess of zeal, agents will harm third persons or will deal with them in unauthorized ways. It would be unfair for an enterprise to have the benefit of the work of its agents without making it responsible to some extent for their excesses and failures to act carefully. The answer of the common law has been the creation of special agency powers or, to phrase it otherwise, the imposition of liability upon the principal because of unauthorized or negligent acts of his servants and other agents. . . ." Restatement (Second) Agency, § 8A, comment *a* (1958).

The basis for [a] principal's liability under this section is further explained in the comment as follows:

". . . His liability exists solely because of his relation to the agent. It is based primarily upon the theory that, if one appoints an agent to conduct a series of transactions over a period of time, it is fair that he should bear losses which are incurred when such an agent, although without authority to do so, does something which is usually done in connection with the transactions he is employed to conduct. Such agents can properly be regarded as part of the principal's organization in much the same way as a servant is normally part of the master's business enterprise.* In fact most general agents are also servants, such as managers and other persons continuously employed and subject to physical supervision by the employer. The basis of the extended liability stated in this Section is comparable to the liability of a master for the torts of his servant. See Comment *a* on § 219. In the case of the master, it is thought fair that one who benefits from the enterprise and has a right to control the physical activities of those who make the enterprise profitable, should pay for the physical harm resulting from the errors and derelictions of the servants while doing the kind of thing which makes the enterprise successful. The rules imposing liability upon the principal for some of the contracts and conveyances of a general agent, whether or not a servant, which he is neither authorized nor apparently authorized to make, are based upon a similar public policy. Commercial convenience requires that the principal should not escape liability where there have been deviations from the usually granted authority by persons who are such essential parts of his business enterprise. In the long run it is of advantage to business, and hence to employers as a class, that third persons should not be required to scrutinize too carefully the mandates of permanent or semi-permanent agents who do no more than what is usually done by agents in similar positions." Restatement (Second), Agency § 161 at p. 379–380.

---

* The terms "master" and "servant" have technical meanings in agency law. See the Note on Authority following this case. (Footnote by ed.)

If a third person reasonably believes that the services he has requested of a member of an accounting partnership [are] undertaken as a part of the partnership business, the partnership should be bound for a breach of trust incident to that employment even though those engaged in the practice of accountancy would regard as unusual the performance of such service by an accounting firm.

The reasonableness of a third person's belief in assuming that a partner is acting within the scope of the partnership should not be tested by the profession's own description of the function of its members. Those who seek accounting services may not understand the refinements made by accountants in defining the services they offer to the public. Whether a third person's belief is reasonable in assuming that the service he seeks is within the domain of the profession is a question which must be answered upon the basis of the facts in the particular case.

We are of the opinion that the facts in the present case are sufficient to establish a reasonable belief on the part of plaintiff that Watrud had undertaken all of the work assigned to him by plaintiff as a continuation of the original employment of the partnership firm. The initial work for which defendants were engaged was the preparation of income tax returns. Thereafter plaintiff sought Watrud's advice on tax matters and continued to have him prepare income tax returns for her business ventures. Watrud did not do the actual bookkeeping for plaintiff's business activities when the partnership was first employed, but eventually he prepared and kept in his own custody the financial books and records of plaintiff's enterprises. This service was assumed by Watrud when plaintiff decided to move to California permanently. When plaintiff left Grants Pass she also arranged with Watrud to have him receive all the income from her Oregon and California properties and to make disbursements from the money so collected. Before she employed him to handle her funds she asked him if he was bonded and he assured her that he was. We think it is important to note that the increased responsibilities directed to Watrud coincided with plaintiff's departure for California. Thereafter, Watrud was the only person who drew checks on the account set up pursuant to the arrangement with plaintiff, although the bank signature card included the names of plaintiff and others. Watrud handled a very substantial amount of plaintiff's money during the course of his employment, drawing as many as 1500 checks per year. The bank statements and cancelled checks were sent directly to Watrud; he collected her business mail at her post office box in Grants Pass and in other respects acted in her behalf after her departure for California. As we have already mentioned, the partnership received compensation for these services at the rate of $800 per month.

As plaintiff testified, nothing was ever said or done by Watrud which might have indicated to her that he was acting on his account as distinguished from acting for the partnership. It was reasonable for plaintiff to assume that the added assignment of collecting and disbursing funds delegated to Watrud was an integral part of the function of one employed to keep the accounts reflecting the income and disbursement of those funds. This assumption, we think, is even more likely in circumstances such as we have here where there is trust and confidence reposed in the person employed. This is not a case in which a person deals with an ordinary commercial partnership. Accountants stand in a fiduciary relation to their clients and out of that relationship there is generated a trust and confidence which invites the client to rely upon the advice and guidance of the one she employs. . . .

The trial court also held that since plaintiff, after learning that Watrud was violating his trust continued to allow him to handle her funds [, she] is estopped as against defendants to assert a claim for subsequent breaches of duty by Watrud in paying out money to plaintiff's husband and himself. After a careful reading of the record we are of the opinion that plaintiff did not act unreasonably in further trusting Watrud after the disclosure of his unauthorized payment of funds to plaintiff's husband.

The decree of the trial court is reversed and the cause is remanded for further proceedings not inconsistent with this opinion.[6]

––––––

Contra: Rouse v. Pollard, 130 N.J.Eq. 204, 21 A.2d 801 (E. & A. 1941).

––––––

NOTE ON AUTHORITY

An *agent* is a person who acts on behalf of, and subject to the control of, another. For some purposes, agents are classified as general or special. A *general agent* is an agent who is authorized to conduct a series of transactions involving continuity of service. A *special agent* is an agent authorized to conduct a single transaction or a series of transactions not involving continuity of service.

A *principal* is a person on whose behalf, and subject to whose control, an agent acts. Principals are conventionally divided into three classes: disclosed, partially disclosed, and undisclosed.

A principal is *disclosed* if at the time of the relevant transaction the third party knows that the agent is acting on behalf of a principal and knows the principal's identity.

A principal is *partially disclosed* if at the time of the transaction the third party knows that the agent is acting on behalf of a principal, but does not know the principal's identity.

A principal is *undisclosed* if the agent, in dealing with the third party, purports to be acting on his own behalf. An undisclosed

6. By stipulation the parties agreed to try initially only the issue of defendants' liability and defer the trial of the issue of the extent of defendants' liability, if any.

principal is liable for her agent's authorized activities, even though, because the agent does not disclose his agency, the third party believes the agent is acting strictly on his own behalf. One reason the undisclosed principal is liable is that she set the transaction in motion and stood to gain from it. A second reason is this: Even if the undisclosed principal was not directly liable to the third party, the agent would be. Therefore, the third party could sue the agent, and the agent could then sue the principal for indemnification of the damages he had to pay the third party. See Section 5 of this Note, infra. Accordingly, allowing the third party to sue the undisclosed principal does not materially enlarge the principal's liability, and collapses two lawsuits into one.

A *master* is a principal who controls or has the right to control the physical conduct of an agent in the performance of the agent's services. A *servant* is an agent whose physical conduct in the performance of services for the principal is controlled by or subject to the control of the principal. Restatement (Second) Agency § 2. The terms master and servant are customarily (although not exclusively) used in connection with a principal's liability for the torts of an agent. Both terms are purely technical, and "do not denote menial or manual service. Many servants perform exacting work requiring intelligence rather than muscle. Thus the officers of a corporation or a ship, the [intern] in a hospital ... are servants...." Id, Comment c.

A variety of problems can arise out of an actual or alleged principal-agency relationship. Perhaps the most common problem is that considered in *Croisant*—what liabilities arose out of a certain transaction between the agent and a third party? Most of the issues implicated by that question are addressed by the legal rules governing *authority*. This Note will emphasize the liability of the principal to the third party (Section 1), but will also consider the liability of the third party to the principal (Section 2), the liability of the agent to the third party (Section 3), and the liabilities of the agent and the principal to each other (Sections 4 and 5). Although the law of agency encompasses liabilities in tort as well as in contract, for the most part this Note will address only issues that relate to contractual transactions.

1. *Liability of Principal to Third Party.* Under the law of agency, a principal becomes liable to a third party as a result of an act or transaction by another, A, on the principal's behalf if A had actual or apparent authority, was an agent by estoppel, or had inherent authority, or if the principal ratified the act or transaction.

a. *Actual authority.* An agent has *actual authority* to act in a given way on a principal's behalf if the principal's words or conduct would lead a reasonable person in the agent's position to believe that the principal had authorized him to so act.

> *Restatement (Second) of Agency § 26, Illustration 2:* P goes to an office where, as he knows, several brokers have desks, and leaves upon the desk of A, thinking it to be the desk

of X, a note signed by him, which states: "I authorize you to contract in my name for the purchase of 100 shares of Western Union stock at today's market." A comes in, finds the note and, not knowing of the mistake, immediately makes a contract with T in P's name for the purchase of the shares. A had [actual] authority to make the contract.[1]

Actual authority may be either *implied* or *express:* "It is possible for a principal to specify minutely what the agent is to do. To the extent that he does this, the agent may be said to have express authority. But most authority is created by implication. Thus, in the authorization to 'sell my automobile', the only fully expressed power is to transfer title in exchange for money or a promise to give money. In fact, under some circumstances ... there may ... be power to take or give possession of the automobile or to extend credit or to accept something in partial exchange. These powers are all implied or inferred from the words used, from customs and from the relations of the parties. They are described as 'implied authority.' " Restatement (Second) of Agency § 7, Comment c.[2]

A common type of implied actual authority is *incidental authority,* which is the authority to do incidental acts that are reasonably necessary to accomplish an authorized transaction or that usually accompany it. Incidental authority is a type of implied actual authority, because if the principal has authorized the agent to engage in a given transaction, and certain acts are reasonably necessary to accomplish the transaction, or usually accompany it, a reasonable person in the agent's position would interpret the authority to engage in the transaction as also conferring authority to engage in the incidental acts.

Note that if an agent has actual authority, the principal is bound even if the third party did not know that the agent had actual authority, and indeed even if the third party thought the agent was herself the principal, not merely an agent.

See Restatement (Second) of Agency §§ 26, 32, 33, 35, 39, 43, 144 in the Statutory Supplement.*

b. *Apparent authority.* An agent has *apparent authority* to act in a given way on a principal's behalf in relation to a third party, T, if the words or conduct of the principal would lead a reasonable person in T's position to believe that the principal had authorized the agent to so act.

In most cases, actual and apparent authority go hand in hand, as Restatement (Second) of Agency § 8, Illustration 1, supra, sug-

---

1. Restatement (Second) of Agency uses the term "authority" to mean what is conventionally called "actual authority." The latter terminology is easier to work with, because it sets up a clear opposition between authority of various types.

2. Occasionally, courts use the term "implied authority" to mean apparent authority, but this is bad usage and is not often encountered.

* Corporations and Business Associations—Statutes, Rules, Materials, and Forms (Foundation Press; M. Eisenberg ed.).

gests. For example, if P Bank appoints A as cashier, and nothing more is said, A will reasonably believe she has the authority that cashiers normally have, and third parties who deal with A will reasonably believe the same thing. Apparent authority becomes salient in such a case if P Bank does not actually give A all the authority that cashiers usually have, and T deals with A knowing that A is a cashier, but not knowing that P Bank has placed special limits on A's authority.

The apparent authority of A in the cashier hypothetical is a special type of apparent authority known as *power of position*. "... [A]pparent authority can be created by appointing a person to a position, such as that of manager or treasurer, which carries with it generally recognized duties; to those who know of the appointment there is apparent authority to do the things ordinarily entrusted to one occupying such a position, regardless of unknown limitations which are imposed upon the particular agent.... If a principal puts an agent into, or knowingly permits him to occupy, a position in which according to the ordinary habits of persons in the locality, trade or profession, it is usual for such an agent to have a particular kind of authority, anyone dealing with him is justified in inferring that he has such authority, in the absence of reason to know otherwise." Restatement (Second) of Agency § 27, Comment a, § 49, Comment c.

See Restatement (Second) of Agency §§ 27, 49, 159 in the Statutory Supplement.

c. *Agency by estoppel*. Still another type of authority is known as "agency by estoppel." The core of agency by estoppel is described as follows in Restatement (Second) of Agency § 8B:

> (1) A person who is not otherwise liable as a party to a transaction purported to be done on his account, is nevertheless subject to liability to persons who have changed their positions because of their belief that the transaction was entered into by or for him, if
>
> (a) he intentionally or carelessly caused such belief, or
>
> (b) knowing of such belief and that others might change their positions because of it, he did not take reasonable steps to notify them of the facts.

The concept of agency by estoppel is so close to the concept of apparent authority that for most practical purposes the former concept can be subsumed in the latter.

d. *Inherent authority*. As *Croisant* indicates, under the doctrine of inherent authority an agent may bind a principal even when the agent had neither actual nor apparent authority. Indeed, under this doctrine an agent may bind her principal even when she has no apparent authority and disobeys the principal's instructions.

Although the doctrine of inherent authority is relatively well established, its exact contours are not always clear. Restatement (Second) of Agency § 8A provides that "Inherent agency power is a term used in the restatement of this subject to indicate the power of an agent which is derived not from [actual] authority, apparent authority or estoppel, but solely from the agency relation and exists for the protection of persons harmed by or dealing with a servant or other agent." Section 8A purports to be a definition, but isn't. It states that inherent authority is an agency power that is not derived from actual authority, apparent authority, or estoppel. It states the reason why inherent authority should be recognized. But it doesn't state what inherent authority *is*.

Section 161 of the Restatement concerns the inherent authority of general agents of disclosed or partially disclosed principals. Under Section 161, a disclosed or partially disclosed principal is liable for an act done on his behalf by a general agent, even if the principal had forbidden the agent to do the act, if (i) the act usually accompanies or is incidental to transactions that the agent is authorized to conduct, and (ii) the third party reasonably believes the agent is authorized to do the act. But this leaves open the issue, under what circumstances is a third party reasonable in believing that an agent has authority that by hypothesis is beyond the agent's apparent authority?

Section 194 of the Restatement concerns the inherent authority of agents for undisclosed principals. It provides that "A general agent for an undisclosed principal authorized to conduct transactions subjects his principal to liability for acts done on his account, if usual or necessary in such transactions, although forbidden by the principal to do them." Unlike Section 161, Section 194 does not require that the third party reasonably believes the agent is authorized to act. Indeed, such a requirement could not be imposed, because in the case of an undisclosed principal the third party will not know he is dealing with an agent.

See Restatement (Second) of Agency §§ 3, 8A, 159–161A, 194, 195A in the Statutory Supplement.

e. *Ratification.* Even if an agent has neither actual, apparent, nor inherent authority, the principal will be bound to the third party if the agent purported to act on the principal's behalf and the principal, with knowledge of the material facts, either (1) affirmed the agent's conduct by manifesting an intention to treat the agent's conduct as authorized, or (2) engaged in conduct that was justifiable only if he had such an intention.

Ratification need not be communicated to the third party to be effective, although it must be objectively manifested. Restatement (Second) of Agency § 95. However, to be effective a ratification must occur before either the third party has withdrawn, the agreement has otherwise terminated, or the situation has so materially changed that it would be inequitable to bind the third party and the third party elects not to be bound. See Restatement (Second) of Agency §§ 88, 89.

Ratification should be distinguished from a related concept: the creation of actual or apparent authority by *acquiescence.* "[I]f the agent performs a series of acts of a similar nature, the failure of the principal to object to them is an indication that he consents to the performance of similar acts in the future under similar conditions." Restatement (Second) of Agency § 43, Comment b. Suppose, for example, an agent engages in a series of comparable purchases on the principal's behalf. Prior to the first purchase, a reasonable person in the agent's position would not have thought she had authority to enter into such a transaction. Nevertheless, the principal did not object either to that purchase or to a later such purchase when he learned of them. At that point, a reasonable person in the agent's position would assume that the principal approved the agent's engaging in such purchases. Accordingly, the principal's acquiescence gives rise both to actual authority and, as to third persons who know of the acquiescence, apparent authority.

See Restatement (Second) of Agency §§ 82–85, 87–90, 93, 94, 97–100A, 143 in the Statutory Supplement.

f. *Termination of agent's authority.* A principal normally has the *power* to terminate an agent's authority even if doing so violates a contract between the principal and the agent, and even if the authority is stated to be irrevocable. Accordingly, a contractual provision that an agent's authority cannot be terminated by either party is normally effective only to create *liability* for wrongful termination. This rule rests largely on the ground that contracts relating to personal services will not be specifically enforced.

See Restatement (Second) of Agency § 118 in the Statutory Supplement.

2. *Liability of Third Party to Principal.* Section 1 considered the liability of a principal to a third party. What is the liability of the third party to the principal? The general rule is that if an agent and a third party enter into a contract under which the agent's principal is liable to the third party, then the third party is liable to the principal. Restatement (Second) of Agency § 292. The major exception is that the third party is not liable to an undisclosed principal if the agent or the principal knew that the third party would not have dealt with the principal. Id., Comment c.

3. *Liability of Agent to Third Party.* The liability of an agent to a third party depends in part on whether the principal was disclosed, partially disclosed, or undisclosed.

a. *Undisclosed principal.* If the principal is undisclosed (that is, if at the time of the transaction the agent purported to act on her own behalf), the general rule is that the agent is bound even though the principal is bound too. Restatement (Second) of Agency § 322. The theory is that the third party must have expected the agent to be a party to the contract, because that is how the agent presented the transaction. However, there is a quirk in the law here. Under the majority rule, if the third party, after learning of an undisclosed principal's identity, obtains a judgment against the principal, the agent is discharged from liability even if the judgment is not satisfied. (A counterpart rule discharges the undisclosed principal if the third party obtains a judgment against the agent.)   Under the minority rule, which is sounder, neither the agent nor the principal is discharged by a judgment against the other, but only by satisfaction of the judgment.

   b. *Partially disclosed principal.* If the principal is partially disclosed (that is, if at the time of the transaction the third party knows that the agent is acting on behalf of a principal, but does not know the principal's identity), the general rule is that both the principal and the agent are bound to the third party.   Restatement (Second) of Agency § 321.   The theory is that if the third party did not know the identity of the principal, and therefore could not investigate the principal's credit or reliability, he probably expected that the agent would be liable, either solely or as a co-promisor or surety.   Id., Comment a.

   c. *Disclosed principal.*   Assume now that the principal was disclosed (that is, at the time of the transaction the third party knew that the agent was acting on behalf of a principal and knew the principal's identity).   If the principal is bound by the agent's act, because the agent had actual, apparent, or inherent authority or because the principal ratified the act, the general rule is that the agent is not bound to the third party.   Restatement (Second) of Agency § 320.   The theory is that in such a case the third party does not expect the agent to be bound, does expect the principal to be bound, and gets just what he expects.

   If the principal is *not* bound by the agent's act, because the agent did not have actual, apparent, or inherent authority, the general rule is that the agent is liable to the third party, either for breach of an implied warranty of authority, Restatement (Second) of Agency § 329, or, under some cases, in tort for misrepresentation or on the contract itself.   In principle, the difference between the two theories might lead to a difference in the measure of damages. Under the liability-on-the-contract theory, the third party will recover gains that would have been derived under the contract—essentially, expectation damages.   In contrast, under the implied-warranty theory it might seem that the third party would recover only losses suffered by having entered into the transaction—essentially, reliance damages.   However, Restatement (Second) of Agency § 329, while adopting the implied-warranty theory, provides for an expectation measure of damages, just as if it had adopted the contract theory: "The third person can recover in damages not only for the harm caused to him by the fact that the agent was unauthorized, but also for the amount by which he would have benefitted had the authority existed."   Id., Comment j.

   See Restatement (Second) of Agency §§ 320–322, 328–330 in the Statutory Supplement.

   4. *Liability of Agent to Principal.*   If an agent takes an action that she has no actual authority to perform, but the principal is nevertheless bound because the agent had apparent authority, the agent is liable to the principal for any resulting damages.   Restate-

ment (Second) of Agency § 383, Comment e.   Whether an agent is liable to the principal for an act that binds the principal by virtue of the agent's inherent but not actual authority is an unsettled point.

5.   *Liability of Principal to Agent*.   If an agent has acted within her actual authority, the principal is under a duty to indemnify the agent for payments authorized or made necessary in executing the principal's affairs.   This includes authorized payments made by the agent on the principal's behalf, payments made by the agent to a third party on contracts upon which the agent was authorized to make herself liable (as where the agent acted on behalf of a partially disclosed or undisclosed principal), payments of damages to third parties that the agent incurs because of an authorized act that constituted a breach of contract, and expenses in defending actions brought against the agent by third parties because of the agent's authorized conduct.

See Restatement (Second) of Agency §§ 438–440 in the Statutory Supplement.

SECTION 3.   THE AGENT'S DUTY OF LOYALTY

π = principal
A = agent
sellers

TARNOWSKI v. RESOP

Supreme Court of Minnesota, 1952.
236 Minn. 33, 51 N.W.2d 801.

KNUTSON, Justice.

Plaintiff desired to make a business investment.   He engaged defendant as his agent to investigate and negotiate for the purchase of a route of coin-operated music machines.   On June 2, 1947, relying upon the advice of defendant and the investigation he had made, plaintiff purchased such a business from Phillip Loechler and Lyle Mayer of Rochester, Minnesota, who will be referred to hereinafter as the sellers.   The business was located at LaCrosse, Wisconsin, and throughout the surrounding territory.   Plaintiff alleges that defendant represented to him that he had made a thorough investigation of the route; that it had 75 locations in operation; that one or more machines were at each location; that the equipment at each location was not more than six months old; and that the gross income from all locations amounted to more than $3,000 per month.   As a matter of fact, defendant had made only a superficial investigation and had investigated only five of the locations.   Other than that, he had adopted false representations of the sellers as to the other locations and had passed them on to plaintiff as his own.   Plaintiff was to pay $30,620 for the business.   He paid $11,000 down.   About six weeks after the purchase, plaintiff discovered that the representations made to him by defendant were false, in that there were not more than 47 locations; that at some of the locations there were no machines and at others there were machines more than six months old, some of them being seven years old; and that the gross income was far less than $3,000 per month. Upon discovering the falsity of defendant's representations and those of the sellers, plaintiff rescinded the sale. He offered to return what he had received, and he demanded the return of his money. The sellers refused to comply, and he brought suit against them in the district court of Olmsted county. The action was tried, resulting in a verdict of $10,000 for plaintiff. Thereafter, the sellers paid plaintiff $9,500, after which the action was dismissed with prejudice pursuant to a stipulation of the parties.

In this action, brought in Hennepin county, plaintiff alleges that defendant, while acting as agent for him, collected a secret commission from the sellers for consummating the sale, which plaintiff seeks to recover under his first cause of action. In his second cause of action, he seeks to recover damages for (1) losses suffered in operating the route prior to rescission; (2) loss of time devoted to operation; (3) expenses in connection with rescission of the sale and his investigation in connection therewith; (4) nontaxable expenses in connection with prosecution of the suit against the sellers; and (5) attorneys' fees in connection with the suit. The case was tried to a jury, and plaintiff recovered a verdict of $5,200. This appeal is from the judgment entered pursuant thereto. . . .

1. With respect to plaintiff's first cause of action, the principle that all profits made by an agent in the course of an agency belonging to the principal, whether they are the fruits of performance or the violation of an agent's duty, is firmly established and universally recognized. Smitz v. Leopold, 51 Minn. 455, 53 N.W. 719; Crump v. Ingersoll, 44 Minn. 84, 46 N.W. 141; Kingsley v. Wheeler, 95 Minn. 360, 104 N.W. 543; Goodhue Farmers' Warehouse Co. v. Davis, 81 Minn. 210, 83 N.W. 531; Snell v. Goodlander, 90 Minn. 533, 97 N.W. 421; City of Minneapolis v. Canterbury, 122 Minn. 301, 142 N.W. 812, 48 L.R.A., N.S., 842; Doyen v. Bauer, 211 Minn. 140, 300 N.W. 451; Magee v. Odden, 220 Minn. 498, 20 N.W.2d 87.

It matters not that the principal has suffered no damage or even that the transaction has been profitable to him. Raymond Farmers Elevator Co. v. American Surety Co., 207 Minn. 117, 290 N.W. 231, 126 A.L.R. 1351.

The rule and the basis therefor are well stated in Lum v. McEwen, 56 Minn. 278, 282, 57 N.W. 662, where, speaking through Mr. Justice Mitchell, we said: "Actual injury is not the principle the law proceeds on, in holding such transactions void. Fidelity in the agent is what is aimed at, and, as a means of securing it, the law will not permit him to place himself in a position in which he may be tempted by his own private interests to disregard those of his principal. . . . It is not material that no actual injury to the company [principal] resulted, or that the policy recommended may have been for its best interest. Courts will not inquire into these matters. It is enough to know that the agent in fact placed himself in such relations that he might be tempted by his own interests to disregard those of his principal. The transaction was nothing more or less than the acceptance by the agent of a bribe to perform his duties in the manner desired by the person who gave the bribe. Such a contract is void. This doctrine rests on such plain principles of law, as well as common business honesty, that the citation of authorities is unnecessary."

The right to recover profits made by the agent in the course of the agency is not affected by the fact that the principal, upon discovering a fraud, has rescinded the contract and recovered that with which he parted. Restatement, Agency, § 407(2). Comment e on Subsection (2) reads: "If an agent has violated a duty of loyalty to the principal so that the principal is entitled to profits which the agent has thereby made, the fact that the principal has brought an action against a third person and has been made whole by such action does not prevent the principal from recovering from the agent the profits which the agent has made. Thus, if the other contracting party has given a bribe to the agent to make a contract with him on behalf of the principal, the principal can rescind the transaction, recovering from the other party anything received by him, or he can maintain an action for damages against him; in either event the principal may recover from the agent the amount of the bribe."

It follows that, insofar as the secret commission of $2,000 received by the agent is concerned, plaintiff had an absolute right thereto, irrespective of any recovery resulting from the action against the sellers for rescission.

2. Plaintiff's second cause of action is brought to recover damages for (1) losses suffered in the operation of the business prior to rescission; (2) loss of time devoted to operation; (3) expenses in connection with rescission of the sale and investigation therewith; (4) nontaxable expenses in connection with the prosecution of the suit against the sellers; and (5) attorneys' fees in connection with the suit.

The case comes to us on a bill of exceptions. No part of the testimony of the witnesses is included, so we must assume that the evidence establishes the items of damage claimed by plaintiff. Our inquiry is limited to a consideration of the question whether a principal may recover of an agent who has breached his trust the items of damage mentioned after a successful prosecution of an action for rescission against the third parties with whom the agent dealt for his principal.

The general rule is stated in Restatement, Agency, § 407(1), as follows: "If an agent has received a benefit as a result of violating his duty of loyalty, the principal is entitled to recover from him what he has so received, its value, or its proceeds, and also the amount of damage thereby caused, except that if the violation consists of the wrongful disposal of the principal's property, the principal cannot recover its value and also what the agent received in exchange therefor."

In Comment a on Subsection (1) we find the following: "... In either event, whether or not the principal elects to get back the thing improperly dealt with or to recover from the agent its value or the amount of benefit which the agent has improperly received, he is, in addition, entitled to be indemnified by the agent for any loss which has been caused to his interest by the improper transaction. Thus, if the purchasing agent for a restaurant purchases with the principal's money defective food, receiving a bonus therefor, and the use of the food in the restaurant damages the business, the principal can recover from the agent the amount of money improperly expended by him, the bonus which the agent received, and the amount which will compensate for the injury to the business."

The general rule with respect to damages for a tortious act is that "The wrong-doer is answerable for all the injurious consequences of his tortious act, which according to the usual course of events and the general experience were likely to ensue, and which, therefore, when the act was committed, he may reasonably be supposed to have foreseen and anticipated." 1 Sutherland, Damages (4 ed.) § 45, quoted with approval in Sargent v. Mason, 101 Minn. 319, 323, 112 N.W. 255, 257.

The general rule is given in Restatement, Torts, § 910, as follows: "A person injured by the tort of another is entitled to recover damages from him for all harm, past, present and prospective, legally caused by the tort."

Bergquist v. Kreidler, 158 Minn. 127, 196 N.W. 964, involved an action to recover attorneys' fees expended by plaintiffs in an action seeking to enforce and protect their right to the possession of real estate. Defendant, acting as the owner's agent, had falsely represented to plaintiffs that they could have possession on August 1, 1920. It developed after plaintiffs had purchased the premises that a tenant had a lease running to August 1, 1922, on a rental much lower than the actual value of the premises. Defendant (the agent) conceded that plaintiffs were entitled to recover the loss in rent, but contended that attorneys' fees and disbursements expended by plaintiffs in testing the validity of the tenant's lease were not recoverable. In affirming plaintiffs' right to recover we said, 158 Minn. 132, 196 N.W. 966: "... the litigation in which plaintiffs became involved was the direct, legitimate, and a to be expected result of appellant's misrepresentation. The loss sustained by plaintiffs in conducting that litigation 'is plainly traceable' to appellant's wrong and he should make compensation accordingly."

So far as the right to recover attorneys' fees is concerned, the same may be said in this case. Plaintiff sought to return what had been received and demanded a return of his down payment. The sellers refused. He thereupon sued to accomplish this purpose, as he had a right to do, and was successful. His attorneys' fees and expenses of suit were directly traceable to the harm caused by defendant's wrongful act. As such, they are recoverable.

. . . The general rule applicable here is stated in 15 Am.Jur., Damages, § 144, as follows: "It is generally held that where the wrongful act of the defendant has involved the plaintiff in litigation with others or placed him in such relation with others as makes it necessary to incur expense to protect his interest, such costs and expenses, including attorneys' fees, should be treated as the legal consequences of the original wrongful act and may be recovered as damages."

The same is true of the other elements of damage involved. See, generally, 15 Am.Jur., Damages, § 138. . . .

Affirmed.

RESTATEMENT (SECOND) OF AGENCY §§ 13, 387–396, 401, 403, 404, 407

[See Statutory Supplement]

JENSEN & MECKLING, THEORY OF THE FIRM: MANAGERIAL BEHAVIOR, AGENCY COSTS AND OWNERSHIP STRUCTURE

3 J. Financial Economics 305, 308 (1976).

We define an agency relationship as a contract under which one or more persons (the principal(s)) engage another person (the agent) to perform some service on their behalf which involves delegating some decision making authority to the agent. If both parties to the relationship are utility maximizers there is good reason to believe that the agent will not always act in the best interests of the principal. The *principal* can limit divergences from his interest by establishing appropriate incentives for the agent and by incurring monitoring costs designed to limit the aberrant activities of the agent. In addition in some situations it will pay the *agent* to expend resources (bonding costs) to guarantee that he will not take certain actions which would harm the principal or to ensure that the principal will be compensated if he does take such actions. However, it is generally impossible for the principal or the agent at zero cost to ensure that the agent will make optimal decisions from the principal's viewpoint. In most agency relationships the principal and the agent will incur positive monitoring and bonding costs (non-pecuniary as well as pecuniary), and in addition there will be some divergence between the agent's decisions and those decisions which would maximize the welfare of the principal. The dollar equivalent of the reduction in welfare experienced by the principal due to this divergence is also a cost of the agency relationship, and we refer to this latter cost as the "residual loss". We define *agency costs* as the sum of:

(1) the monitoring expenditures by the principal,

(2) the bonding expenditures by the agent,

(3) the residual loss.

***

SECTION 4. AN INTRODUCTION TO FINANCIAL STATEMENTS

The law of business associations is about enterprises that are organized for profit. Accordingly, issues concerning such matters as accounting, valuation, and portfolio theory are usually lurking behind the legal rules and the cases in this area, and sometimes take center stage. It would be impossible to develop these issues in a really meaningful way in a book like this, which is devoted to explicitly legal materials. However, from time to time in this book, beginning here, materials will be set out that at least provide a vocabulary concerning these issues.

***

D. HERWITZ, MATERIALS ON ACCOUNTING FOR LAWYERS 1–3, 11–12

1980.

. . . THE BALANCE SHEET

The object of bookkeeping is to make it as easy as possible for anyone who understands the language to get a clear and accurate summary of how well a business is doing. Suppose we want a financial picture of E. Tutt, who recently graduated from law school. Certainly one important facet is how much he owns. Since we really are concerned with his business and not his personal affairs, we forget his car, his clothes, and other personal property, and we look to see what he has in his office:

(a) Office furniture

(b) Office equipment

(c) Stationery and supplies

(d) Library

(e) Cash in the bank [of $1,000]

All of these would be understood by laymen to be what the accountant calls them: *assets.*

We would also want some measurement of these assets; i.e., we would want to put a dollar figure on them. And since the price at which the property was bought is ordinarily much easier to ascertain and less subjective than the "present value" of the property, it would make sense to record E. Tutt's assets at *cost.*

If E. Tutt bought all his property out of his own funds and has not yet earned anything, we could simply add up the assets to find out how E. Tutt stands in his business. But if he has borrowed money from a bank to buy some of his assets or, perhaps more likely, has bought some on credit, E. Tutt's personal "stake" in the business would not be as large as if he had bought everything from his own funds. In order to give a true picture of his financial position, we would want to know where the money came from to buy the assets. Suppose we find that he acquired the assets as follows:

(a) Office furniture: bought on credit from Frank Co. for $400;

(b) Office equipment: bought on credit from Elmer Co. for $300;

(c) Stationery and supplies: bought from Stanley for $100 on a promissory note;

(d) Library: purchased for $200 cash, out of Tutt's original "stake" of $1,000;

(e) $800 cash: balance of Tutt's original "stake" remaining.

We could then list, in parallel columns, the assets and their sources:

Assets		Sources	
(a) Office furniture	$ 400	Frank Co.	$ 400 (a)
(b) Office equipment	300	Elmer Co.	300 (b)
(c) Stationery and supplies	100	Stanley	100 (c)
(d) Library	200		
(e) Cash (balance remaining)	800	E. Tutt	1,000 (d, e)
	$1,800		$1,800

This parallel listing of assets and their sources is what the accountant calls a *balance sheet.* It shows, at any point in time, what assets the business now has and where the money came from to acquire them. Since that is all it is, no matter how complicated the business or how long its history the totals of the two columns are always equal.

To give a somewhat clearer picture of how well off E. Tutt himself is, we can separate the sources of assets into two groups: "outside" sources, or here, money owed by the business to outsiders; and "inside" sources, here, what Tutt himself has put into the business. The outside sources, which are usually called "*Liabilities*", may be money owed on open account, usually called an "account payable;" another "outside" source is money advanced on a note, a "note payable". The "inside" source here is E. Tutt's contribution (his "stake" or equity in the business) which is often called "*Proprietorship*". We might also rearrange the assets, listing them in the order in which they are likely to be used up. The result would be a somewhat more refined balance sheet that might look like this:

Assets		**Liabilities & Proprietorship**		
		Liabilities:		
(e) Cash	$ 800	Accounts Payable		
(c) Supplies	100	Frank Co.	$ 400	(a)
(a) Furniture	400	Elmer Co.	300	(b)
(b) Equipment	300	Notes Payable		
		Stanley	100	(c)
(d) Library	200	Proprietorship	1,000	(d, e)
	$1,800		$1,800	

Note that no change has been made except a change in presentation. The essential meaning is the same. But because clear disclosure is one of the accountant's main concerns, matters of presentation are important....

... THE INCOME STATEMENT

The balance sheet shows the present status of the assets and the "sources of assets" resulting from all transactions since the business was formed. It is drawn up at regular intervals which will vary with the needs of the business. There is another, and increasingly more important, basic financial statement: the *income statement*. The income statement is a statement for a period of time, giving a summary of earnings between balance sheet dates. A fundamental distinction between the two is that the balance sheet speaks as of a particular date, while the income statement covers a period of time between successive balance sheet dates....

It may be easiest to start by drawing up an income statement for E. Tutt, say for the month of June. Suppose that during the month he receives legal fees of $600 and $400.

(1) Professional Income		$600
(2) Professional Income		$400

To find his net income, we have to subtract his expenses for the month. Suppose that the operating expenses were as follows:

(3) Rent		$200
(4) Secretary		$230
(5) Telephone		$ 15
(6) Heat & Light		$ 5
(7) Miscellaneous		$ 5

In addition, during the month Tutt suffered a loss when a thief broke into his office and stole $20 cash. This loss is treated as just another expense:

(8) Theft loss		$ 20

There is no particular form required for an income statement, so long as it is a clear and fair statement of the information. An acceptable one might look like this:

INCOME STATEMENT—E. TUTT, JUNE

(1 & 2)	Professional Income........................		$1,000
	Less: Expenses		
(3)	Rent	$200	
(4)	Secretary	230	
(5)	Telephone	15	
(6)	Heat & Light	5	
(7)	Miscellaneous	5	
(8)	Theft Loss	20	
	Total Expenses		475
	NET INCOME		$525

To get started on seeing how the income statement fits into the balance sheet we might ask where "net income" shows up on a balance sheet. In lay terms, it is an increase in the owner's stake in the business, which we call "Proprietorship". Hence, if no other change in Proprietorship occurs, the balance sheet figure for Proprietorship on June 30 should be $525 larger than on June 1.

––––––

R. HAMILTON, FUNDAMENTALS OF MODERN BUSINESS 154–55

1989.

... *[E]very transaction entered into by a business must be recorded in at least two ways if the balance sheet is to continue to balance.* This last point underlies the concept of that mysterious subject, *double entry bookkeeping*, and is the cornerstone on which modern accounting is built.

Assume that we have a new business, just starting out, in which the owner has invested $10,000 in cash .... The opening balance sheet will look like this:

Assets:		Liabilities	–0–
Cash	10,000	Owner's Equity	10,000

Now let us assume that the owner buys a used truck for $3,000 cash. The effect of this transaction is to reduce cash by $3,000 and create a new asset on the balance sheet:

Assets:		Liabilities	–0–
Cash	7,000	Owner's Equity	10,000
Used Truck	3,000		
	10,000		10,000

Voila! The balance sheet still balances. Let us assume next that the owner goes down to the bank and borrows an additional $1,000. This also has a dual effect: it increases cash by $1,000 (since the business is receiving the proceeds of the loan) and increases liabilities by $1,000 (since the business thereafter has to repay the loan). Yet another balance sheet can be created showing the additional effect of this second transaction:

Assets:		Liabilities	
Cash	8,000	Debt to Bank	1,000
Used Truck	3,000	Owner's Equity	10,000
	11,000		11,000

Chapter II

PARTNERSHIP

INTRODUCTORY NOTE

Although partnership had a rich history under the common law, it has long been governed by statute. Until recently, the relevant statute was the Uniform Partnership Act ("the UPA"), which was promulgated by the Commissioners on Uniform State Laws in 1914 and was adopted in every state except Louisiana.

In 1994, the Commissioners on Uniform State Laws adopted the Revised Uniform Partnership Act ("RUPA"), which is intended to supersede the UPA. As of early 1995, RUPA had been enacted in several states, and undoubtedly it will be enacted by additional states in the future. Under RUPA § 1006, RUPA normally applies not only to all partnerships formed after RUPA is adopted in any given state, but, after a transition period, to all partnerships, even those formed before RUPA was adopted.

Because RUPA is so new, because it has yet to be adopted in most states, and because RUPA continues many of the rules of the UPA, the cases and materials in this Section will largely concern the UPA. In general, however, where RUPA changes a relevant UPA rule the changes will be set out and discussed in a Note.

SECTION 1. PARTNERSHIP FORMATION

UNIFORM PARTNERSHIP ACT §§ 6, 7
Revised Uniform Partnership Act § 202

[See Statutory Supplement]

MARTIN v. PEYTON

New York Court of Appeals, 1927.
246 N.Y. 213, 158 N.E. 77.

Appeal from Supreme Court, Appellate Division, First Department.

Action by Charles S. Martin against William C. Peyton and others. A judgment of the Special Term, entered on the report of a referee in favor of the defendants was affirmed by the Appellate Division (219 App.Div. 287, 220 N.Y.S. 29), and plaintiff appeals. Affirmed.

ANDREWS, J. Much ancient learning as to partnership is obsolete. Today only those who are partners between themselves may be charged for partnership debts by others. (Partnership Law [Cons. Laws, ch. 39], sec. 11.) There is one exception. Now and then a recovery is allowed where in truth such relationship is absent. This is because the debtor may not deny the claim. (Sec. 27.)

Partnership results from contract, express or implied. If denied it may be proved by the production of some written instrument; by testimony as to some conversation; by circumstantial evidence. If nothing else appears the receipt by the defendant of a share of the profits of the business is enough. (Sec. 11.)

Assuming some written contract between the parties the question may arise whether it creates a partnership. If it be complete; if it expresses in good faith the full understanding and obligation of the parties, then it is for the court to say whether a partnership exists. It may, however, be a mere sham intended to hide the real relationship. Then other results follow. In passing upon it effect is to be given to each provision. Mere words will not blind us to realities. Statements that no partnership is intended are not conclusive. If as a whole a contract contemplates an association of two or more persons to carry on as co-owners a business for profit a partnership there is. (Sec. 10.) On the other hand, if it be less than this no partnership exists. Passing on the contract as a whole, an arrangement for sharing profits is to be considered. It is to be given its due weight. But it is to be weighed in connection with all the rest. It is not decisive. It may be merely the method adopted to pay a debt or wages, as interest on a loan or for other reasons.

An existing contract may be modified later by subsequent agreement, oral or written. A partnership may be so created where there was none before. And again, that the original agreement has been so modified may be proved by circumstantial evidence—by showing the conduct of the parties.

In the case before us the claim that the defendants became partners in the firm of Knauth, Nachod & Kuhne, doing business as bankers and brokers, depends upon the interpretation of certain instruments. There is nothing in their subsequent acts determinative of or indeed material upon this question. And we are relieved of questions that sometimes arise. "The plaintiff's position is not," we are told, "that the agreements of June 4, 1921, were a false expression or incomplete expression of the intention of the parties. We say that they express defendants' intention and that that intention was to create a relationship which as a matter of law constitutes a partnership." Nor may the claim of the plaintiff be rested on any question of estoppel. "The plaintiff's claim," he stipulates, "is a claim of actual partnership, not of partnership by estoppel. . . ."

Remitted then, as we are, to the documents themselves, we refer to circumstances surrounding their execution only so far as is necessary to make them intelligible. And we are to remember that although the intention of the parties to avoid liability as partners is clear, although in language precise and definite they deny any design to then join the firm of K.N. & K.; although they say their interests in profits should be construed merely as a measure of compensation for loans, not an interest in profits as such; although they provide that they shall not be liable for any losses or treated as partners, the question still remains whether in fact they agree to so associate themselves with the firm as to "carry on as co-owners a business for profit."

In the spring of 1921 the firm of K.N. & K. found itself in financial difficulties. John R. Hall was one of the partners. He was a friend of Mr. Peyton. From him he obtained the loan of almost $500,000 of Liberty bonds, which K.N. & K. might use as collateral to secure bank advances. This, however, was not sufficient. The firm and its members had engaged in unwise speculations, and it was deeply involved. Mr. Hall was also intimately acquainted with George W. Perkins, Jr., and with Edward W. Freeman. He also knew Mrs. Peyton and Mrs. Perkins and Mrs. Freeman. All were anxious to help him. He, therefore, representing K.N. & K., entered into negotiations with them. While they were pending a proposition was made that Mr. Peyton, Mr. Perkins and Mr. Freeman or some of them should become partners. It met a decided refusal. Finally an agreement was reached. It is expressed in three documents, executed on the same day, all a part of the one transaction. They were drawn with care and are unambiguous. We shall refer to them as "the agreement," "the indenture" and "the option."

We have no doubt as to their general purpose. The respondents were to loan K.N. & K. $2,500,000 worth of liquid securities, which were to be returned to them on or before April 15, 1923. The firm might hypothecate them to secure loans totalling $2,000,-000, using the proceeds as its business necessities required. To insure respondents against loss K.N. & K. were to turn over to them a large number of their own securities which may have been valuable, but which were of so speculative a nature that they could not be used as collateral for bank loans. In compensation for the loan the respondents were to receive 40 per cent of the profits of the firm until the return was made, not exceeding, however, $500,-000 and not less than $100,000. Merely because the transaction involved the transfer of securities and not of cash does not prevent its being a loan within the meaning of section 11. The respondents also were given an option to join the firm if they or any of them expressed a desire to do so before June 4, 1923.

Many other detailed agreements are contained in the papers. Are they such as may be properly inserted to protect the lenders?

Or do they go further? Whatever their purpose, did they in truth associate the respondents with the firm so that they and it together thereafter carried on as co-owners a business for profit? The answer depends upon an analysis of these various provisions.

As representing the lenders, Mr. Peyton and Mr. Freeman are called "trustees." The loaned securities when used as collateral are not to be mingled with other securities of K.N. & K., and the trustees at all times are to be kept informed of all transactions affecting them. To them shall be paid all dividends and income accruing therefrom. They may also substitute for any of the securities loaned securities of equal value. With their consent the firm may sell any of its securities held by the respondents, the proceeds to go, however, to the trustees. In other similar ways the trustees may deal with these same securities, but the securities loaned shall always be sufficient in value to permit of their hypothecation for $2,000,000. If they rise in price the excess may be withdrawn by the defendants. If they fall they shall make good the deficiency.

So far there is no hint that the transaction is not a loan of securities with a provision for compensation. Later a somewhat closer connection with the firm appears. Until the securities are returned the directing management of the firm is to be in the hands of John R. Hall, and his life is to be insured for $1,000,000, and the policies are to be assigned as further collateral security to the trustees. These requirements are not unnatural. Hall was the one known and trusted by the defendants. Their acquaintance with the other members of the firm was of the slightest. These others had brought an old and established business to the verge of bankruptcy. As the respondents knew, they also had engaged in unsafe speculation. The respondents were about to loan $2,500,000 of good securities. As collateral they were to receive others of problematical value. What they required seems but ordinary caution. Nor does it imply an association in the business.

The trustees are to be kept advised as to the conduct of the business and consulted as to important matters. They may inspect the firm books and are entitled to any information they think important. Finally they may veto any business they think highly speculative or injurious. Again we hold this but a proper precaution to safeguard the loan. The trustees may not initiate any transaction as a partner may do. They may not bind the firm by any action of their own. Under the circumstances the safety of the loan depended upon the business success of K.N. & K. This success was likely to be compromised by the inclination of its members to engage in speculation. No longer, if the respondents were to be protected, should it be allowed. The trustees, therefore, might prohibit it, and that their prohibition might be effective, information was to be furnished them. Not dissimilar agreements have been held proper to guard the interests of the lender.

As further security each member of K.N. & K. is to assign to the trustees their interest in the firm. No loan by the firm to any member is permitted and the amount each may draw is fixed. No other distribution of profits is to be made. So that realized profits may be calculated the existing capital is stated to be $700,000, and profits are to be realized as promptly as good business practice will permit. In case the trustees think this is not done, the question is left to them and to Mr. Hall, and if they differ then to an arbitrator. There is no obligation that the firm shall continue the business. It may dissolve at any time. Again we conclude there is nothing here not properly adapted to secure the interest of the respondents as lenders. If their compensation is dependent on a percentage of the profits still provision must be made to define what these profits shall be.

The "indenture" is substantially a mortgage of the collateral delivered by K.N. & K. to the trustees to secure the performance of the "agreement." It certainly does not strengthen the claim that the respondents were partners.

Finally we have the "option." It permits the respondents or any of them or their assignees or nominees to enter the firm at a later date if they desire to do so by buying 50 per cent or less of the interests therein of all or any of the members at a stated price. Or a corporation may, if the respondents and the members agree, be formed in place of the firm. Meanwhile, apparently with the design of protecting the firm business against improper or ill-judged action which might render the option valueless, each member of the firm is to place his resignation in the hands of Mr. Hall. If at any time he and the trustees agree that such resignation should be accepted, that member shall then retire, receiving the value of his interest calculated as of the date of such retirement.

This last provision is somewhat unusual, yet it is not enough in itself to show that on June 4, 1921, a present partnership was created nor taking these various papers as a whole do we reach such a result. It is quite true that even if one or two or three like provisions contained in such a contract do not require this conclusion, yet it is also true that when taken together a point may come where stipulations immaterial separately cover so wide a field that we should hold a partnership exists. As in other branches of the law a question of degree is often the determining factor. Here that point has not been reached. . . .

The judgment appealed from should be affirmed, with costs.

CARDOZO, Ch. J., POUND, CRANE, LEHMAN, KELLOGG and O'BRIEN, JJ., concur.

Judgment affirmed, etc.

———

LUPIEN v. MALSBENDEN

Supreme Judicial Court of Maine, 1984.
477 A.2d 746.

Before McKUSICK, C.J., and NICHOLS, ROBERTS, WATHEN, GLASSMAN and SCOLNIK, JJ.

McKUSICK, Chief Justice.

Defendant Frederick Malsbenden appeals a judgment of the Superior Court (York County) holding him to partnership liability on a written contract entered into between plaintiff Robert Lupien and one Stephen Cragin doing business as York Motor Mart.[1] The sole issue asserted on appeal is whether the Superior Court erred in its finding that Malsbenden and Cragin were partners in the pertinent part of York Motor Mart's business. We affirm.

On March 5, 1980, plaintiff entered into a written agreement with Stephen Cragin, doing business in the town of York as York Motor Mart, for the construction of a Bradley automobile.[2] Plaintiff made a deposit of $500 towards the purchase price of $8,020 upon signing the contract, and made a further payment of $3,950 one week later on March 12. Both the purchase order of March 5, 1980, and a later bill of sale, though signed by Cragin, identified the seller as York Motor Mart. At the jury-waived trial, plaintiff testified that after he signed the contract he made visits to York Motor Mart on an average of once or twice a week to check on the progress being made on his car. During those visits plaintiff generally dealt with Malsbenden because Cragin was seldom present. On one such visit in April, Malsbenden told plaintiff that it was necessary for the latter to sign over ownership of his pickup truck, which would constitute the balance of the consideration under the contract, so that the proceeds from the sale of the truck could be used to complete construction of the Bradley. When plaintiff complied, Malsbenden provided plaintiff with a rental car, and later with a "demo" model of the Bradley, for his use pending the completion of the vehicle he had ordered. When it was discovered that the "demo" actually belonged to a third party who had entrusted it to York Motor Mart for resale, Malsbenden purchased the vehicle for plaintiff's use. Plaintiff never received the Bradley he had contracted to purchase.

In his trial testimony, defendant Malsbenden asserted that his interest in the Bradley operation of York Motor Mart was only that of a banker. He stated that he had loaned $85,000 to Cragin, without interest, to finance the Bradley portion of York Motor

---

1. Cragin "disappeared" several months before this action was commenced. Plaintiff Lupien originally named Cragin as a co-defendant. However, since Cragin was never served with process, the Superior Court at the behest of both Lupien and defendant Malsbenden dismissed the claim against Cragin.

2. A Bradley automobile is a "kit car" constructed on a Volkswagen chassis.

Mart's business.[3] The loan was to be repaid from the proceeds of each car sold. Malsbenden acknowledged that Bradley kits were purchased with his personal checks and that he had also purchased equipment for York Motor Mart. He also stated that after Cragin disappeared sometime late in May 1980, he had physical control of the premises of York Motor Mart and that he continued to dispose of assets there even to the time of trial in 1983.

The Uniform Partnership Act, adopted in Maine at 31 M.R.S.A. §§ 281–323 (1978 & Supp.1983–1984), defines a partnership as "an association of 2 or more persons . . . to carry on as co-owners[4] a business for profit." 31 M.R.S.A. § 286 (1978). Whether a partnership exists is an inference of law based on established facts. *See Dalton v. Austin,* 432 A.2d 774, 777 (Me.1981); *Roux v. Lawand,* 131 Me. 215, 219, 160 A. 756, 757 (1932); *James Bailey Co. v. Darling,* 119 Me. 326, 328, 111 A. 410, 411 (1920). A finding that the relationship between two persons constitutes a partnership may be based upon evidence of an agreement, either express or implied,

> to place their money, effects, labor, and skill, or some or all of them, in lawful commerce or business with the understanding that a community of profits will be shared. . . . No one factor is alone determinative of the existence of a partnership. . . .

Dalton v. Austin, 432 A.2d at 777; *Cumberland County Power & Light Co. v. Gordon,* 136 Me. 213, 218, 7 A.2d 619, 622 (1939). *See James Bailey Co. v. Darling,* 119 Me. at 328, 111 A. at 411. If the arrangement between the parties otherwise qualifies as a partnership, it is of no matter that the parties did not expressly agree to form a partnership or did not even intend to form one:

> It is possible for parties to intend no partnership and yet to form one. If they agree upon an arrangement which is a partnership in fact, it is of no importance that they call it something else, or that they even expressly declare that they are not to be partners. The law must declare what is the legal import of their agreements, and names go for nothing when the substance of the arrangement shows them to be inapplicable.

James Bailey Co. v. Darling, 119 Me. at 328, 111 A. at 411 (quoting *Beecher v. Bush,* 45 Mich. 188, 193–94, 7 N.W. 785, 785–86 (1881)).

Here the trial justice concluded that, notwithstanding Malsbenden's assertion that he was only a "banker," his "total involvement" in the Bradley operation was that of a partner. The testimony at trial, both respecting Malsbenden's financial interest in the enterprise and his involvement in day-to-day business operations, amply supported the Superior Court's conclusion. Malsbenden had a

---

3. Malsbenden's testimony indicated that Cragin carried on an automotive repair business at the York Motor Mart that was unrelated to the Bradley operation. Malsbenden testified, without contradiction, that he had no involvement with that other business.

4. As we made clear in *Dalton v. Austin,* 432 A.2d 774, 777 (Me.1981), the term "co-owners" as used in the statute does not necessarily mean joint title to all assets. On the contrary, "the right to participate in control of the business is the essence of co-ownership." *Id.*

financial interest of $85,000 in the Bradley portion of York Motor Mart's operations. Although Malsbenden termed the investment a loan, significantly he conceded that the "loan" carried no interest. His "loan" was not made in the form of a fixed payment or payments, but was made to the business, at least in substantial part, in the form of day-to-day purchases of Bradley kits, other parts and equipment, and in the payment of wages. Furthermore, the "loan" was not to be repaid in fixed amounts or at fixed times, but rather only upon the sale of Bradley automobiles.

The evidence also showed that, unlike a banker, Malsbenden had the right to participate in control of the business and in fact did so on a day-to-day basis.[5] According to Urbin Savaria, who worked at York Motor Mart from late April through June 1980, Malsbenden during that time opened the business establishment each morning, remained present through part of every day, had final say on the ordering of parts, paid for parts and equipment, and paid Savaria's salary. On plaintiff's frequent visits to York Motor Mart, he generally dealt with Malsbenden because Cragin was not present. It was Malsbenden who insisted that plaintiff trade in his truck prior to the completion of the Bradley because the proceeds from the sale of the truck were needed to complete the Bradley. When it was discovered that the "demo" Bradley given to plaintiff while he awaited completion of his car actually belonged to a third party, it was Malsbenden who bought the car for plaintiff's use. As of three years after the making of the contract now in litigation, Malsbenden was still doing business at York Motor Mart, "just disposing of property."

Malsbenden and Cragin may well have viewed their relationship to be that of creditor-borrower, rather than a partnership. At trial Malsbenden so asserts, and Cragin's departure from the scene in the spring of 1980 deprives us of the benefit of his view of his business arrangement with Malsbenden. In any event, whatever the intent of these two men as to their respective involvements in the business of making and selling Bradley cars, there is no clear error in the Superior Court's finding that the Bradley car operation represented a pooling of Malsbenden's capital and Cragin's automotive skills, with joint control over the business and intent to share the fruits of the enterprise. As a matter of law, that arrangement amounted to a partnership under 31 M.R.S.A. § 286.

The entry is:

Judgment affirmed.

All concurring.

---

5. Thus its facts clearly distinguish the case at bar from *James Bailey Co. v. Darling,* 119 Me. 326, 332, 111 A. 410, 413 (1920), where although the defendant advanced money for the purchase of automobiles that was to be repaid upon the sale of individual automobiles, the defendant had no control over the business.

NOTE ON THE FORMATION OF PARTNERSHIPS

Corporations and limited partnerships can be organized (formed) only if certain formalities are complied with and certain filings are made. In contrast, general partnerships can be organized with no formalities and no filings. The absence of a filing requirement reflects in part a conception that partnership status depends on the factual characteristics of a relationship between two or more persons, not on whether the persons think of themselves as having entered into a partnership.

Although no filings are *required* under either the UPA or RUPA, RUPA *permits* certain filings. See, e.g., Note on the Authority of Partners Under RUPA, p. 41, infra.

––––––

SECTION 2. THE LEGAL NATURE OF A PARTNERSHIP

––––––

UNIFORM PARTNERSHIP ACT § 6
REVISED UNIFORM PARTNERSHIP ACT §§ 101(4), 201

[See Statutory Supplement]

––––––

NOTE ON THE LEGAL NATURE OF A PARTNERSHIP: ENTITY OR AGGREGATE STATUS

1. Individuals may associate in a wide variety of forms, and the issue often arises whether a given form of association has a legal status separate from that of its members. Frequently, this issue is stated in terms of whether or not a form of association is a "separate entity" or a "legal person" (as opposed to a natural person, that is, an individual). A variety of issues may turn on the answer to this question—for example, whether the association can sue and be sued in its own name, and whether it can hold property in its own right.

In the history of English and American law this issue arose in the context of many different kinds of associations, such as universities, charitable institutions, and even municipalities. In most cases the issue was eventually resolved in a straightforward way, but in the case of partnerships it continued to be vexing. The predominant although not exclusive view under the common law was that a partnership was not an entity, but merely an aggregate of its members, so that a partnership was no more a legal person than was a friendship.

In 1902, when the Conference of Commissioners on Uniform State Laws determined to promulgate a Uniform Partnership Act, Dean James Barr Ames of Harvard Law School was appointed to draft the Act. Subsequently, the Commissioners instructed Dean Ames, at his own urging, to draft the Act on the theory that a partnership is a legal entity. Accordingly, in the drafts submitted by Dean Ames a partnership was defined as "a legal person formed by the association of two or more individuals for the purpose of carrying on business with a view to profit," and various provisions of the drafts reflected the entity theory. Dean Ames died before the work was completed, however, and his successor, Dean William Draper Lewis of the University of Pennsylvania Law School, was distinctly unfriendly to the entity view. Ultimately, Dean Lewis convinced the Commissioners to instruct him to draft the Act on the aggregate theory. UPA Section 6 therefore provides that "A partnership is an association of two or more persons to carry on as co-owners a business for profit." Although the language of this provision does not in itself render the issue free from doubt, it is clear that the Act was intended to adopt the aggregate theory.

That is not, however, the end of the story. Having adopted the aggregate theory, the UPA nevertheless deals with a number of issues *as if* the partnership were an entity. This may seem to be a pragmatic solution, and for many purposes the UPA does work pretty well. On the whole, however, the use of an aggregate theory in the UPA was unfortunate. Generally speaking, the entity theory of a partnership is much more functional than the aggregate theory. In those cases where the UPA does not treat the partnership as if it were an entity, the result tends to be bad, and in need of legislative revision. In those cases where the UPA does treat the partnership as if it were an entity, the result is good, but the statutory approach is often made needlessly complex by the mechanics of reconciling the entity result with the aggregate theory.[1]

2. The question often arises whether a partnership is to be treated as an aggregate or an entity for the purpose of some statute other than the UPA. This question is a matter of legislative intent under the particular statute. As in all such matters, the answer will depend on the language employed and the purposes manifested in the statute at hand. The fact that the UPA adopted the aggregate theory will be relevant, but not dispositive, in answering that question. A legislature may choose to treat a partnership as an entity for purposes of another statute even though a partnership is defined as an association under the U.P.A. See, e.g., United States v. A & P Trucking Co., 358 U.S. 121, 79 S.Ct. 203, 3 L.Ed.2d 165 (1958).

1. On the common law background and the statutory history of the entity/aggregate debate, see Commissioners' Prefatory Note to the Uniform Partnership Act, 6 Uniform Laws Ann. 5 (1969); Lewis, The Uniform Partnership Act, 24 Yale L.J. 617 (1915); Crane, The Uniform Partnership Act—A Criticism, 28 Harv.L.Rev. 762 (1915); Crane, The Uniform Partnership Act and Legal Persons, 29 Harv.L.Rev. 838 (1916); Jensen, Is a Partnership Under the Uniform Partnership Act an Aggregate or an Entity?, 16 Vand.L.Rev. 377 (1963).

3. In contrast to the UPA, RUPA confers entity status on partnerships. RUPA § 101 (Definitions) defines a partnership as "an association of two or more persons to carry on as co-owners a business for profit." RUPA § 201 then squarely provides that "A partnership is an entity."

————

SECTION 3. THE ONGOING OPERATION OF PARTNERSHIPS

————

(a) MANAGEMENT

————

UNIFORM PARTNERSHIP ACT §§ 18(a), (e), (g), (h), 19, 20

REVISED UNIFORM PARTNERSHIP ACT §§ 401(f), (i), (j), 403

[See Statutory Supplement]

————

SUMMERS v. DOOLEY

Supreme Court of Idaho, 1971.
94 Idaho 87, 481 P.2d 318.

DONALDSON, Justice.

This lawsuit, tried in the district court, involves a claim by one partner against the other for $6,000. The complaining partner asserts that he has been required to pay out more than $11,000 in expenses without any reimbursement from either the partnership funds or his partner. The expenditure in question was incurred by the complaining partner (John Summers, plaintiff-appellant) for the purpose of hiring an additional employee. The trial court denied him any relief except for ordering that he be entitled to one half $966.72 which it found to be a legitimate partnership expense.

The pertinent facts leading to this lawsuit are as follows. Summers entered a partnership agreement with Dooley (defendant-respondent) in 1958 for the purpose of operating a trash collection business. The business was operated by the two men and when either was unable to work, the non-working partner provided a replacement at his own expense. In 1962, Dooley became unable to work and, at his own expense, hired an employee to take his place. In July, 1966, Summers approached his partner Dooley regarding the hiring of an additional employee but Dooley refused. Nevertheless, on his own initiative, Summers hired the man and paid him out of his own pocket. Dooley, upon discovering that Summers had hired an additional man, objected, stating that he did not feel additional labor was necessary and refused to pay for the new employee out of the partnership funds. Summers continued to operate the business using the third man and in October of 1967 instituted suit in the district court for $6,000 against his partner, the gravamen of the complaint being that Summers has been required to pay out more than $11,000 in expenses, incurred in the hiring of the additional man, without any reimbursement from either the partnership funds or his partner. After trial before the court, sitting without a jury, Summers was granted only partial relief[1] and he has appealed. He urges in essence that the trial court erred by failing to conclude that he should be reimbursed for expenses and costs connected in the employment of extra help in the partnership business.

The principal thrust of appellant's contention is that in spite of the fact that one of the two partners refused to consent to the hiring of additional help, nonetheless, the non-consenting partner retained profits earned by the labors of the third man and therefore the non-consenting partner should be estopped from denying the need and value of the employee, and has by his behavior ratified the act of the other partner who hired the additional man.

The issue presented for decision by this appeal is whether an equal partner in a two man partnership has the authority to hire a new employee in disregard of the objection of the other partner and then attempt to charge the dissenting partner with the costs incurred as a result of his unilateral decision.

The State of Idaho has enacted specific statutes with respect to the legal concept known as "partnership." Therefore any solution of partnership problems should logically begin with an application of the relevant code provision.

In the instant case the record indicates that although Summers requested his partner Dooley to agree to the hiring of a third man, such requests were not honored. In fact Dooley made it clear that he was "voting no" with regard to the hiring of an additional employee.

An application of the relevant statutory provisions and pertinent case law to the factual situation presented by the instant case indicates that the trial court was correct in its disposal of the issue since a majority of the partners did not consent to the hiring of the third man. I.C. § 53–318(8) provides:

"Any difference arising as to ordinary matters connected with the partnership business may be decided by a *majority of the partners*...." (emphasis supplied)

It is the opinion of this Court that the preceding statute is of a mandatory rather than permissive nature. This conclusion is based upon the following reasoning. Whether a statute is mandatory or

1. The trial court did award Summers one half of $966.72 which it found to be a   legitimate partnership expense.

directory does not depend upon its form, but upon the intention of the legislature, to be ascertained from a consideration of the entire act, its nature, its object, and the consequences that would result from construing it one way or the other. In re McQuistons Adoption, 238 Pa. 304, 86 A. 205 (1913).

The intent of the legislature may be implied from the language used, or inferred on grounds of policy or reasonableness. See Barnett v. Prairie Oil & Gas Co. et al., 19 F.2d 504 (8th Cir.1927); Motorcoach Operators Ass'n v. Board of Street Railway Commissioners of the City of Detroit, 267 Mich. 568, 255 N.W. 391 (1934); 3 Sutherland, Statutory Construction, § 5803, p. 79. A careful reading of the statutory provision indicates that subsection 5 bestows *equal rights in the management and conduct of the partnership business* upon all of the partners. The concept of equality between partners with respect to management of business affairs is a central theme and recurs throughout the Uniform Partnership law, I.C. § 53–301 et seq., which has been enacted in this jurisdiction. Thus the only reasonable interpretation of I.C. § 53–318(8) is that business differences must be decided by a majority of the partners provided no other agreement between the partners speaks to the issues.

A noted scholar has dealt precisely with the issue to be decided.

" . . . if the partners are equally divided, those who forbid a change must have their way." Walter B. Lindley, A Treatise on the Law of Partnership, Ch. II, § III, ¶ 24–8, p. 403 (1924). See also, W. Shumaker, A Treatise on the Law of Partnership, § 97, p. 266.

See also, Clarke et al. v. Slate Valley R. Co., 136 Pa. 408, 20 A. 562 (1890) for a discussion of this rule.

In the case at bar one of the partners continually voiced objection to the hiring of the third man. He did not sit idly by and acquiesce in the actions of his partner. Under these circumstances it is manifestly unjust to permit recovery of an expense which was incurred individually and not for the benefit of the partnership but rather for the benefit of one partner.

Judgment affirmed. Costs to respondent.

McQUADE, C.J., and McFADDEN, SHEPARD and SPEAR, JJ., concur.

––––––––

QUESTION

Suppose that A, B, and C form a partnership. A contributes 90% of the capital, and by agreement is entitled to 90% of any profits and is responsible for 90% of any losses. B and C each contribute 5% of the capital and by agreement are each entitled to 5% of any profits and are responsible for 5% of any losses. Nothing is said in the agreement concerning how decisions will be made. If, on an ordinary matter connected with the partnership, A votes one way, and B and C another, who prevails?

———

NOTE ON THE MANAGEMENT OF PARTNERSHIPS

1. The cases and authorities are divided on the issue raised in Summers v. Dooley. In accord with *Summers* is Covalt v. High, 100 N.M. 700, 675 P.2d 999 (App.1983). But see National Biscuit Co. v. Stroud, 249 N.C. 467, 106 S.E.2d 692 (1959), noted, 1960 Duke L.J. 150 (where one of two partners transacts with a third party on a matter that is otherwise within the ordinary business of the partnership, the other partner is liable even though he had put the third party on notice that the partners were divided on the matter).

2. Because UPA Section 18(h) provides that partnership action requires a majority vote, what is added by UPA Section 18(e), which provides that all partners have equal rights in the management and conduct of the partnership business? Presumably, the effect of this Section is to require that, absent contrary agreement, every partner be provided on an ongoing basis with information concerning the partnership business and be consulted in partnership decisions. See Hillman, Power Shared and Power Denied: A Look at Participatory Rights in the Management of General Partnerships, 1984 U.Ill. L.Rev. 865 (1984); E. Scamell & R. Banks, Lindley on the Law of Partnership, 427 (14th ed. 1979).

> For a majority of partners to say; We do not care what one partner may say, we, being the majority, will do what we please, is, I apprehend what this Court will not allow. So, again, with respect to making Mr. *Robertson* the treasurer, Mr. *Const* had a right to be consulted; his opinion might be overruled, and honestly over-ruled, but he ought to have had the question put to him and discussed: In all partnerships ... the partners are bound to be true and faithful to each other: They are to act upon the joint opinion of all, and the discretion and judgment of anyone cannot be excluded: What weight is to be given to it is another question....

Const v. Harris, 37 Eng.Rep. 1191, 1202 (Ch.1824) (Lord Chancellor Eldon). Thus a majority of partners who made decisions without consulting a minority partner would violate § 18(e), absent contrary agreement.

3. RUPA § 401(f) continues the rule of UPA § 18(e), conferring on each partner the right to participate in management. The Comment to § 401(f) notes that UPA § 18(e) "has been interpreted broadly to mean that, absent contrary agreement, each partner has a continuing right to participate in the management of the partnership and to be informed about the partnership business, even if his assent ... is not required."

RUPA § 401(j) generally follows the voting rules of UPA § 18(h), although there are several differences between the sections.   Under UPA § 18(h):

> Any difference arising as to ordinary matters connected with the partnership business may be decided by a majority of the partners; but no act in contravention of any agreement between the partners may be done rightfully without the consent of all the partners.

Under RUPA § 401(j):

> A difference arising as to a matter in the ordinary course of business of a partnership may be decided by a majority of the partners.   An act outside the ordinary course of business of a partnership and an amendment to the partnership agreement may be undertaken only with the consent of all of the partners.

(b) DISTRIBUTIONS, REMUNERATION, INDEMNIFICATION, AND CONTRIBUTION

UNIFORM PARTNERSHIP ACT §§ 18(b), (c), (d), (f)
REVISED UNIFORM PARTNERSHIP ACT § 401(a)–(e), (h)

[See Statutory Supplement]

QUESTION

Suppose A, B, and C form a partnership.   A contributes 90% of the capital, and B and C each contribute 5%.   All work full-time in the partnership business, with roughly equal responsibilities.   Nothing is said in the partnership agreement concerning how partnership profits will be divided.   If the partnership makes a profit in a given year, how is it to be divided?

NOTE ON INDEMNIFICATION AND CONTRIBUTION

As shown in Section 5, infra, each partner is individually liable to a partnership creditor for partnership obligations.   As between the partners, however, each partner is liable only for his share of a partnership obligation.   Thus if one partner pays off a partnership obligation in full (or, for that matter, if he simply pays more than his share), he is entitled to indemnification from the partnership for the difference between what he paid and his share of the liability.

Indemnification should be distinguished from contribution. A *partner* has a right to be indemnified in a proper case by the partnership. Correspondingly, the obligation to indemnify a partner is a partnership liability. In contrast, the *partnership* has a right to require contribution in a proper case from one or more partners. Correspondingly, the obligation to make contribution is a liability of a partner. Contribution may be required to fund indemnification, so that all partners share a burden initially placed on only one. Contribution may also be required for other purposes—in particular, paying off partnership creditors and equalizing capital losses.

SECTION 4. THE AUTHORITY OF A PARTNER

UNIFORM PARTNERSHIP ACT §§ 3, 4(3), 9, 10, 11, 12, 13, 14

REVISED UNIFORM PARTNERSHIP ACT §§ 301, 302, 303, 304, 305, 306, 308

[See Statutory Supplement]

CROISANT v. WATRUD

See p. 2, supra.

BURNS v. GONZALEZ, 439 S.W.2d 128 (Tex.Civ.App.1969). Bosquez and Gonzalez were partners in a business that sold broadcast time on a radio station located in Mexico. The station was owned and operated by a Mexican corporation, Radiodifusora. Bosquez and Gonzalez each owned 50% of Radiodifusora's stock, and Bosquez was its president. In 1957, Radiodifusora made a contract with Burns, which it failed to perform. Subsequently, Bosquez, purporting to act on his own behalf and on behalf of the partnership, executed a $40,000 promissory note payable to Burns, partly in exchange for Burns's promise not to sue Radiodifusora. Burns sued Bosquez and Gonzalez on the note, as partners, and Gonzalez argued that Bosquez had no authority to execute the note on the partnership's behalf. In reviewing a jury verdict in favor of defendants, the court stated:

> [Because the] express limitation on the authority of Bosquez was unknown to Burns, then, under the language of Sec. 9(1), his act in executing the note would bind the

partnership if such act can be classified as an act "for apparently carrying on in the usual way the business of the partnership."

As we interpret Sec. 9(1), the act of a partner binds the firm, absent an express limitation of authority known to the party dealing with such partner, if such act is for the purpose of "apparently carrying on" the business of the partnership in the way in which other firms engaged in the same business in the locality usually transact business, or in the way in which the particular partnership usually transacts its business. In this case, [however,] there is no evidence relating to the manner in which firms engaged in the sale of advertising time on radio stations usually transact business.

NOTE ON THE AUTHORITY OF PARTNERS UNDER RUPA

For most practical purposes, the major difference between the UPA and RUPA concerning a partner's authority is that RUPA § 301(1) makes clear, as the UPA did not, that a partnership is bound by an act of the partner for apparently carrying on in the usual way the partnership business or business *of the kind* carried on by the partnership. The Comment to § 301(1) states:

Section 301(1) .... clarifies that a partner's apparent authority includes acts for carrying on in the ordinary course "business of the kind carried on by the partnership," not just the business of the particular partnership in question. The UPA is ambiguous on this point, but there is some authority for an expanded construction.... See, e.g., Burns v. Gonzalez, 439 S.W.2d 128, 131 (Tex.Civ.App. 1969) (dictum)....

The treatment of authority under RUPA also differs from the UPA in certain other respects. For example, RUPA § 302 provides elaborate rules concerning when a transfer of partnership property is binding. RUPA § 303 enables a partnership to file a "Statement of Partnership Authority." Under § 303, a *grant* of authority set forth in such a Statement is normally conclusive in favor of third persons, even if they have no actual knowledge of the Statement, unless they have actual knowledge that the partner has no such authority. However, a *limitation* on a partner's authority that is contained in such a Statement, other than a limitation on the partner's authority to transfer real property, will not be effective unless the third party knows of the limitation or the Statement has been delivered to him. The Comment states:

Under Section 301, only a third party who knows or has *received* a notification of a partner's lack of authority in an ordinary course transaction is bound [by a limitation in the notification]. Thus, a limitation on a partner's authority to transfer personal property or to enter into other non-real property transactions on behalf of the partnership, contained in a filed statement of partnership authority, is effective only against a third party who knows or has received a notification of it. The fact of the statement being filed has no legal significance in those transactions, although the filed statement is a potential source of actual knowledge to third parties. (Emphasis added.)

In contrast to other types of limitations, a limitation in a Statement of Partnership Authority of a partner's authority to transfer real property held in the name of the partnership is effective against all third persons if a certified copy of the Statement is filed in the real-property recording office.

SECTION 5.   LIABILITY FOR PARTNERSHIP OBLIGATIONS

UNIFORM PARTNERSHIP ACT §§ 9, 13, 14, 15, 16, 17, 36

REVISED UNIFORM PARTNERSHIP ACT §§ 305, 306, 307, 308

[See Statutory Supplement]

NOTE ON LIABILITY FOR PARTNERSHIP OBLIGATIONS

1. The provisions of the Uniform Partnership Act governing liability for partnership obligations reflect an amalgam of the entity and aggregate theories. On the one hand, UPA §§ 9, 13, and 14 make "the partnership" liable for defined acts of the partners. It might seem to follow that this liability could be enforced by a suit against the partnership. However, the UPA does not authorize such a suit, since it does not recognize a partnership as an entity, and unless authorized by statute, suit normally cannot be brought against an association that is not an entity. Indeed, the UPA goes to the opposite extreme. Under UPA § 15(a), partners are *jointly and severally* liable for wrongful acts and omissions of the partnership (such as torts) and breaches of trust. Under UPA § 15(b), however, partners are only *jointly* liable "for all other debts and obligations of the partnership." At common law, if an obligation is "joint and several" the obligors can be sued either jointly or separately. If, however, an obligation is only "joint" the obligee must join all the obligors, subject to a few exceptions where jurisdiction over all the obligors cannot be obtained. See C. Clark, Handbook of the Law of Code Pleading 373–74 (2d ed. 1947). Thus under the UPA, not

only must an action on a partnership's contractual obligation be brought against all the partners, but if one partner is not joined the action can be dismissed on motion by the partners who were joined.   (If the partners who were joined don't move to dismiss, the defense is waived.   However, the plaintiff's cause of action is usually considered to be merged into the judgment, thereby extinguishing his claim against unjoined partners.)

2.   The inability of a partnership creditor to sue a partnership in its own name under the UPA is obviously undesirable, and many states have statutorily patched up the UPA rule by adopting Common Name Statutes, which explicitly allow a partnership to be sued in its own name.   An example is N.Y.Civ.Prac.L. & R. § 1025: "Two or more persons conducting a business as a partnership may sue or be sued in the partnership name...."

3.   The need of a partnership contract creditor to join all the partners in a suit to establish individual liability on a contract claim is also undesirable.   Some states address this issue by making all partnership liabilities joint and several.   Other states have adopted Joint Debtor Statutes, which provide that a suit against joint obligors can proceed even if some of the obligors are not joined.   An example is Cal.Civ.Proc.Code § 410.70: "In an action against two or more persons who are jointly, jointly and severally, or severally liable on a contract, the court in which the action is pending has jurisdiction to proceed against such of the defendants as are served as if they were the only defendants."

4.   Unlike the UPA, RUPA § 307(a) specifically provides that a partnership may both sue and be sued in its own name.   Furthermore, RUPA § 306 provides that partners are jointly and severally *liable* for *all* obligations of the partnership.   However, RUPA adds a new barrier to *collecting* against an individual partner on such a liability.   RUPA § 307 provides that a judgment against a partner based on a claim against the partnership normally cannot be satisfied against the partner's individual assets unless and until a judgment on the same claim has been rendered against the partnership and a writ of execution on the judgment has been returned unsatisfied.   To put this differently, RUPA § 307 adopts an exhaustion rule, under which partnership assets must be exhausted before a partner's individual assets can be reached.   (The exhaustion rule is made subject to certain exceptions, one of which is that the rule does not apply if the partnership is in bankruptcy.)   Thus as the Comment to RUPA § 306 points out:

> Joint and several liability under RUPA differs ... from the classic model [of joint and several liability outside partnership law], which permits a judgment creditor to proceed immediately against any of the joint and several judgment debtors.

In effect, RUPA takes an aggregate-like approach to a partner's liability, but an entity-like approach to collecting judgments based on that liability.

SECTION 6. PARTNERSHIP INTERESTS AND PARTNERSHIP PROPERTY

UNIFORM PARTNERSHIP ACT §§ 8, 18, 24, 25, 26, 27, 28

REVISED UNIFORM PARTNERSHIP ACT §§ 203, 204, 501, 502, 503, 504

[See Statutory Supplement]

NOTE ON PARTNERSHIP PROPERTY

1. Whether property that is used by a partnership is partnership property or the property of the individual partners may be important for several different reasons. The issue may be important to determine who has the power to use and transfer the property. The issue may be important if creditors of the partnership are competing with creditors of an individual partner. The issue may also be important if the partnership is dissolved. If property used by the partnership is partnership property, on dissolution the property must be sold for cash, along with other partnership assets, and the proceeds of the sale must be distributed among the partners. In contrast, if property used by the partnership is the individual property of a partner, on dissolution the property must normally be returned directly to that partner, rather than sold for the account of all the partners.[1] This third issue may be especially important if the property is crucial to the partnership's business, so that as a practical matter whoever owns the property has the ability to continue the business.

If the aggregate theory of the UPA were strictly applied, a partnership could not own property. Rather, the property that the partners think of as partnership property would as a matter of law be held by the individual partners as joint tenants or tenants in common. For a variety of reasons, such a regime would be wholly impracticable. Accordingly, in the matter of partnership property, as in several other matters, the UPA lays down rules that effectively treat the partnership *as if* it were an entity. This objective is accomplished largely with mirrors. UPA Section 8 recognizes the concept of "partnership property," and explicitly permits real property to be held in the partnership's name. (Even before the UPA it was well settled that personal property could be so held.) However, UPA Section 25(1) provides that "partnership property" is owned by the *partners,* under the ingenuous nomenclature, "ten-

---

1. But see Pav–Saver Corp. v. Vasso Corp., 143 Ill.App.3d 1013, 97 Ill.Dec. 760, 493 N.E.2d 423 (1986) (wrongfully dissolv- ing partner held not entitled to return of property).

an[cy] in partnership." UPA Section 25(2) then systematically strips from the individual partners every incident normally associated with ownership. Under Section 25(2)(a), a partner has no right to possess partnership property as an individual. Under Section 25(2)(b), a partner cannot individually assign his rights in specific partnership property. Under Section 25(2)(c), a partner's rights in specific partnership property cannot be subject to attachment or execution by a creditor of the partner in the latter's individual capacity. Under Section 25(2)(d), when the partner dies his right in specific partnership property does not devolve on his heirs or legatees. Under Section 25(2)(e), widows, heirs, and next of kin cannot claim dower, curtesy, or allowances in the partner's right to specific partnership property.

In short, under the UPA individual partners own the partnership property in theory, but all the incidents of ownership are vested in the partnership, so that the "tenan[cy] in partnership" rule of the UPA has no real-world significance.

2. RUPA, which confers entity status on partnerships, drops the elaborate tenancy-in-partnership apparatus of the UPA. RUPA § 203 provides that "Property acquired by a partnership is property of the partnership and not the partners individually." RUPA § 204 then sets out a series of rules and presumptions concerning whether any given property is partnership property or the separate property of a partner. These provisions are supplemented by § 501, which provides that "A partner is not a co-owner of partnership property and has no interest in partnership property which can be transferred, either voluntarily or involuntarily." The purpose of § 501 is to explicitly abolish the UPA concept of tenancy-in-partnership.

NOTE ON PARTNERSHIP INTERESTS

1. Although a partner does not own partnership property under the UPA, except in some metaphysical sense, he does own his interest in the partnership, that is, his share of the partnership. The net result is a functional two-level ownership structure somewhat comparable to the legal two-level ownership structure in a corporation. A corporation is the owner of corporate property and a shareholder is the owner of his shares in the corporation. A partnership is the functional owner of partnership property and a partner is the owner of his interest in the partnership.

As compared to ordinary property interests, a partnership interest is conditioned in one very important respect. Normally, the owner of a property interest can freely sell it, and a creditor can freely levy on it. Under UPA § 18(g), however, no person can become a partner without the consent of all the partners. It follows that unless the partnership agreement otherwise provides, a partner cannot make a transfer of his partnership interest that would substitute the transferee as a partner in the transferor's place. Correspondingly, a creditor can neither levy on a partnership interest in such a way as to be substituted as a partner, nor recover his debt by selling the interest to a third party who will be substituted as a partner. Nevertheless, a partnership interest is assignable. As pointed out in *Rapoport,* the assignee does not become a partner (unless all the other partners consent), and has no right to information about the partnership and no right to inspect the partnership books. However, while the partnership continues the assignee has a right to receive the profits to which the assigning partner would otherwise be entitled, and on dissolution the assignee has a right to receive the assigning partner's interest. According to A. Bromberg, supra, at 240, partnership interests have a fairly high degree of assignability despite the limitations on the rights of an assignee.

2. The creditor of a partner in the partner's individual capacity is in a position very similar to the assignee of a partnership interest. Under UPA § 28, if such a creditor obtains a judgment, he can get a "charging order" on the partner's partnership interest. Such an order will effectively permit him to get the share of profits to which the indebted partner would be otherwise entitled. If the creditor forecloses on the partnership interest under § 28, and thereby causes its sale, the buyer of the interest will have the right to compel dissolution if the term of the partnership has expired or the partnership is at will. Alternatively, the creditor may put the individual partner into bankruptcy, which results in dissolution of the partnership under UPA § 31(5).

RUPA § 504 continues UPA § 28 largely unchanged in substance. RUPA § 504 does add some details that are not found in UPA § 28, but for the most part these details are consistent with the case law under § 28. RUPA § 801(a), like the UPA, provides that a transferee of a partner's transferable interest is entitled to judicial dissolution of the partnership (i) at any time, in a partnership at will, and (ii) after the expiration of the partnership's term or completion of the undertaking, in a partnership for a definite term or particular undertaking.

———

FARMERS STATE BANK & TRUST CO. v. MIKESELL, 51 Ohio App.3d 69, 554 N.E.2d 900, 909 (1988). "The rule we derive from [the] cases is that a partner's interest in the partnership, his right to share in profits and surplus, is assignable. However, a partner may not assign his interest in particular assets of the partnership. If the creditor of an individual partner has obtained a judgment against a partner, his sole means of attaching the partner's interest in the partnership is the charging order...."

———

SECTION 7. THE PARTNER'S DUTY OF LOYALTY

UNIFORM PARTNERSHIP ACT §§ 20, 21
REVISED UNIFORM PARTNERSHIP ACT §§ 103, 104, 403, 404, 405

[See Statutory Supplement]

MEINHARD v. SALMON

New York Court of Appeals, 1928.
249 N.Y. 458, 164 N.E. 545.

Appeal from a judgment of the Appellate Division of the Supreme Court in the first judicial department, entered June 28, 1928, modifying and affirming as modified a judgment in favor of plaintiff entered upon the report of a referee.

CARDOZO, Ch. J. On April 10, 1902, Louisa M. Gerry leased to the defendant Walter J. Salmon the premises known as the Hotel Bristol at the northwest corner of Forty-second street and Fifth avenue in the city of New York. The lease was for a term of twenty years, commencing May 1, 1902, and ending April 30, 1922. The lessee undertook to change the hotel building for use as shops and offices at a cost of $200,000. Alterations and additions were to be accretions to the land.

Salmon, while in course of treaty with the lessor as to the execution of the lease, was in course of treaty with Meinhard, the plaintiff, for the necessary funds. The result was a joint venture with terms embodied in a writing. Meinhard was to pay to Salmon half of the moneys requisite to reconstruct, alter, manage and operate the property. Salmon was to pay to Meinhard 40 per cent of the net profits for the first five years of the lease and 50 per cent for the years thereafter. If there were losses, each party was to bear them equally. Salmon, however, was to have sole power to "manage, lease, underlet and operate" the building. There were to be certain pre-emptive rights for each in the contingency of death.

The two were coadventurers, subject to fiduciary duties akin to those of partners (King v. Barnes, 109 N.Y. 267). As to this we are all agreed. The heavier weight of duty rested, however, upon Salmon. He was a coadventurer with Meinhard, but he was manager as well. During the early years of the enterprise, the building, reconstructed, was operated at a loss. If the relation had then ended, Meinhard as well as Salmon would have carried a heavy burden. Later the profits became large with the result that for each of the investors there came a rich return. For each, the venture had its phases of fair weather and of foul. The two were in it jointly, for better or for worse.

When the lease was near its end, Elbridge T. Gerry had become the owner of the reversion. He owned much other property in the neighborhood, one lot adjoining the Bristol Building on Fifth avenue and four lots on Forty-second street. He had a plan to lease the entire tract for a long term to some one who would destroy the buildings then existing, and put up another in their place. In the latter part of 1921, he submitted such a project to several capitalists and dealers. He was unable to carry it through with any of them. Then, in January, 1922, with less than four months of the lease to run, he approached the defendant Salmon. The result was a new lease to the Midpoint Realty Company, which is owned and controlled by Salmon, a lease covering the whole tract, and involving a huge outlay. The term is to be twenty years, but successive covenants for renewal will extend it to a maximum of eighty years at the will of either party. The existing buildings may remain unchanged for seven years. They are then to be torn down, and a new building to cost $3,000,000 is to be placed upon the site. The rental, which under the Bristol lease was only $55,000, is to be from $350,000 to $475,000 for the properties so combined. Salmon personally guaranteed the performance by the lessee of the covenants of the new lease until such time as the new building had been completed and fully paid for.

The lease between Gerry and the Midpoint Realty Company was signed and delivered on January 25, 1922. Salmon had not told Meinhard anything about it. Whatever his motive may have been, he had kept the negotiations to himself. Meinhard was not informed even of the bare existence of a project. The first that he knew of it was in February when the lease was an accomplished fact. He then made demand on the defendants that the lease be held in trust as an asset of the venture, making offer upon the trial to share the personal obligations incidental to the guaranty. The demand was followed by refusal, and later by this suit. A referee gave judgment for the plaintiff, limiting the plaintiff's interest in the lease, however, to 25 per cent. The limitation was on the theory that the plaintiff's equity was to be restricted to one-half of so much of the value of the lease as was contributed or represented by the occupation of the Bristol site. Upon cross-appeals to the Appellate Division, the judgment was modified so as to enlarge the equitable interest to one-half of the whole lease. With this enlargement of plaintiff's interest, there went, of course, a corresponding enlargement of his attendant obligations. The case is now here on an appeal by the defendants.

Joint adventurers, like copartners, owe to one another, while the enterprise continues, the duty of the finest loyalty. Many forms of conduct permissible in a workaday world for those acting at arm's length, are forbidden to those bound by fiduciary ties. A trustee is held to something stricter than the morals of the market place. Not honesty alone, but the punctilio of an honor the most sensitive is then the standard of behavior. As to this there has developed a tradition that is unbending and inveterate. Uncompromising rigidity has been the attitude of courts of equity when petitioned to undermine the rule of undivided loyalty by the "disintegrating erosion" of particular exceptions (Wendt v. Fischer, 243 N.Y. 439, 444). Only thus has the level of conduct for fiduciaries been kept at a level higher than that trodden by the crowd. It will not consciously be lowered by any judgment of this court.

The owner of the reversion, Mr. Gerry, had vainly striven to find a tenant who would favor his ambitious scheme of demolition and construction. Baffled in the search, he turned to the defendant Salmon in possession of the Bristol, the keystone of the project. He figured to himself beyond a doubt that the man in possession would prove a likely customer. To the eye of an observer, Salmon held the lease as owner in his own right, for himself and no one else. In fact he held it as a fiduciary, for himself and another, sharers in a common venture. If this fact had been proclaimed, if the lease by its terms had run in favor of a partnership, Mr. Gerry, we may fairly assume, would have laid before the partners, and not merely before one of them, his plan of reconstruction. The pre-emptive privilege, or, better, the pre-emptive opportunity, that was thus an incident of the enterprise, Salmon appropriated to himself in secrecy and silence. He might have warned Meinhard that the plan had been submitted, and that either would be free to compete for the award. If he had done this, we do not need to say whether he would have been under a duty, if successful in the competition, to hold the lease so acquired for the benefit of a venture then about to end, and thus prolong by indirection its responsibilities and duties. The trouble about his conduct is that he excluded his coadventurer from any chance to compete, from any chance to enjoy the opportunity for benefit that had come to him alone by virtue of his agency. This chance, if nothing more, he was under a duty to concede. The price of its denial is an extension of the trust at the option and for the benefit of the one whom he excluded.

No answer is it to say that the chance would have been of little value even if seasonably offered. Such a calculus of probabilities is beyond the science of the chancery. Salmon, the real estate operator, might have been preferred to Meinhard, the woolen merchant. On the other hand, Meinhard might have offered better terms, or reinforced his offer by alliance with the wealth of others. Perhaps he might even have persuaded the lessor to renew the Bristol lease alone, postponing for a time, in return for higher rentals, the improvement of adjoining lots. We know that even under the lease as made the time for the enlargement of the building was delayed for seven years. All these opportunities were cut away from him through another's intervention. He knew that Salmon was the manager. As the time drew near for the expiration of the lease, he would naturally assume from silence, if from nothing else, that the lessor was willing to extend it for a term of years, or at least to let it stand as a lease from year to year. Not impossibly the lessor would have done so, whatever his protestations of unwillingness, if Salmon had not given assent to a project more attractive. At all events, notice of termination, even if not necessary, might seem, not unreasonably, to be something to be looked for, if the business was over and another tenant was to enter. In the absence of such notice, the matter of an extension was one that would naturally be attended to by the manager of the enterprise, and not neglected altogether. At least, there was nothing in the situation to give warning to any one that while the lease was still in being, there had come to the manager an offer of extension which he had locked within his breast to be utilized by himself alone. The very fact that Salmon was in control with exclusive powers of direction charged him the more obviously with the duty of disclosure, since only through disclosure could opportunity be equalized. If he might cut off renewal by a purchase for his own benefit when four months were to pass before the lease would have an end, he might do so with equal right while there remained as many years (cf. Mitchell v. Reed, 61 N.Y. 123, 127). He might steal a march on his comrade under cover of the darkness, and then hold the captured ground. Loyalty and comradeship are not so easily abjured.

Little profit will come from a dissection of the precedents. None precisely similar is cited in the briefs of counsel. What is similar in many, or so it seems to us, is the animating principle. Authority is, of course, abundant that one partner may not appropriate to his own use a renewal of a lease, though its term is to begin at the expiration of the partnership (Mitchell v. Read, 61 N.Y. 123; 84 N.Y. 556). The lease at hand with its many changes is not strictly a renewal. Even so, the standard of loyalty for those in trust relations is without the fixed divisions of a graduated scale. There is indeed a dictum in one of our decisions that a partner, though he may not renew a lease, may purchase the reversion if he acts openly and fairly (Anderson v. Lemon, 8 N.Y. 236; cf. White & Tudor, Leading Cases in Equity [9th ed.], vol. 2, p. 642; Bevan v. Webb, 1905, 1 Ch. 620; Griffith v. Owen, 1907, 1 Ch. 195, 204, 205). It is a dictum, and no more, for on the ground that he had acted slyly he was charged as a trustee. The holding is thus in favor of the conclusion that a purchase as well as a lease will succumb to the infection of secrecy and silence. Against the dictum in that case, moreover, may be set the opinion of DWIGHT, C., in Mitchell v. Read, where there is a dictum to the contrary (61 N.Y. at p. 143). To say that a partner is free without restriction to buy in the reversion of the property where the business is conducted is to say in effect that he may strip the good will of its chief element of value, since good will is largely dependent upon continuity of possession (Matter of Brown, 242 N.Y. 1, 7.) Equity refuses to confine within the bounds of classified transactions its precept of a loyalty that is undivided and unselfish. . . .

We have no thought to hold that Salmon was guilty of a conscious purpose to defraud. Very likely he assumed in all good

faith that with the approaching end of the venture he might ignore
his coadventurer and take the extension for himself. He had given
to the enterprise time and labor as well as money. He had made it
a success. Meinhard, who had given money, but neither time nor
labor, had already been richly paid. There might seem to be
something grasping in his insistence upon more. Such recrim-
inations are not unusual when coadventurers fall out. They are not
without their force if conduct is to be judged by the common
standards of competitors. That is not to say that they have perti-
nency here. Salmon had put himself in a position in which thought
of self was to be renounced, however hard the abnegation. He was
much more than a coadventurer. He was a managing coadventurer
(Clegg v. Edmondson, 8 D.M. & G. 787, 807). For him and for
those like him, the rule of undivided loyalty is relentless and
supreme (Wendt v. Fischer, supra; Munson v. Syracuse, etc., R.R.
Co., 103 N.Y. 58, 74). A different question would be here if there
were lacking any nexus of relation between the business conducted
by the manager and the opportunity brought to him as an incident
of management (Dean v. MacDowell, 8 Ch.D. 345, 354; Aas v.
Benham, 1891, 2 Ch. 244, 258; Latta v. Kilbourn, 150 U.S. 524).
For this problem, as for most, there are distinctions of degree. If
Salmon had received from Gerry a proposition to lease a building at
a location far removed, he might have held for himself the privilege
thus acquired, or so we shall assume. Here the subject-matter of
the new lease was an extension and enlargement of the subject-
matter of the old one. A managing coadventurer appropriating the
benefit of such a lease without warning to his partner might fairly
expect to be reproached with conduct that was underhand, or
lacking, to say the least, in reasonable candor, if the partner were to
surprise him in the act of signing the new instrument. Conduct
subject to that reproach does not receive from equity a healing
benediction.

A question remains as to the form and extent of the equitable
interest to be allotted to the plaintiff. The trust as declared has
been held to attach to the lease which was in the name of the
defendant corporation. We think it ought to attach at the option of
the defendant Salmon to the shares of stock which were owned by
him or were under his control. The difference may be important if
the lessee shall wish to execute an assignment of the lease, as it
ought to be free to do with the consent of the lessor. On the other
hand, an equal division of the shares might lead to other hardships.
It might take away from Salmon the power of control and management which under the plan of the joint venture he was to have from
first to last. The number of shares to be allotted to the plaintiff
should, therefore, be reduced to such an extent as may be necessary
to preserve to the defendant Salmon the expected measure of
dominion. To that end an extra share should be added to his half.

Subject to this adjustment, we agree with the Appellate Division
that the plaintiff's equitable interest is to be measured by the value
of half of the entire lease, and not merely by half of some undivided

part. A single building covers the whole area. Physical division is impracticable along the lines of the Bristol site, the keystone of the whole. Division of interests and burdens is equally impracticable. Salmon, as tenant under the new lease, or as guarantor of the performance of the tenant's obligations, might well protest if Meinhard, claiming an equitable interest, had offered to assume a liability not equal to Salmon's, but only half as great. He might justly insist that the lease must be accepted by his coadventurer in such form as it had been given, and not constructively divided into imaginary fragments. What must be yielded to the one may be demanded by the other. The lease as it has been executed is single and entire. If confusion has resulted from the union of adjoining parcels, the trustee who consented to the union must bear the inconvenience (Hart v. Ten Eyck, 2 Johns. Ch. 62)....

[Three judges dissented. Andrews, J., who wrote the dissenting opinion, agreed that "(w)ere this a general partnership I should have little doubt as to the correctness of this result assuming the new lease to be an offshoot of the old," but concluded that the parties' joint venture "had in view a very limited object and was to end at a limited time."]

SECTION 8. DISSOLUTION (I): DISSOLUTION BY RIGHTFUL ELECTION

UNIFORM PARTNERSHIP ACT §§ 29, 30, 31(1), 38(1), 40

REVISED UNIFORM PARTNERSHIP ACT §§ 601, 603, 701, 801, 802, 803, 804, 807

[See Statutory Supplement]

DREIFUERST v. DREIFUERST

Wisconsin Court of Appeals, 1979.
90 Wis.2d 566, 280 N.W.2d 335.

Before BROWN, P.J., BODE, J., and ROBERT W. HANSEN, Reserve Judge.

BROWN, P.J. The plaintiffs and the defendant, all brothers, formed a partnership. The partnership operated two feed mills, one located at St. Cloud, Wisconsin and one located at Elkhart Lake, Wisconsin. There were no written Articles of Partnership governing this partnership.

On October 4, 1975, the plaintiffs served the defendant with a notice of dissolution and wind-up of the partnership. The action for dissolution and wind-up was commenced on January 27, 1976. The dissolution complaint alleged that the plaintiffs elected to dissolve the partnership. There was no allegation of fault, expulsion or contravention of an alleged agreement as grounds for dissolution. The parties were unable, however, to agree to a winding-up of the partnership.

Hearings on the dissolution were held on October 18, 1976 and March 4, 1977. Testimony was presented regarding the value of the partnership assets and each partner's equity. At the March 4, 1977 hearing, the defendant requested that the partnership be sold pursuant to sec. 178.33(1), Stats., and that the court allow a sale, at which time the partners would bid on the entire property. By such sale, the plaintiffs could continue to run the business under a new partnership, and the defendant's partnership equity could be satisfied in cash.

On February 20, 1978, the trial court, by written decision, denied the defendant's request for a sale and instead divided the partnership assets in-kind according to the valuation presented by the plaintiffs. The plaintiffs were given the physical assets from the Elkhart Lake mill, and the defendant was given the physical assets from the St. Cloud mill. The defendant appeals this order and judgment dividing the assets in-kind.

Under sec. 178.25(1), Stats., a partnership is dissolved when any partner ceases to be associated in the carrying on of the business. The partnership is not terminated, but continues, until the winding-up of the partnership is complete. Sec. 178.25(2), Stats. The action started by the plaintiffs, in this case, was an action for dissolution and wind-up. The plaintiffs were not continuing the partnership and, therefore, secs. 178.36 and 178.37, Stats.,[3] do not apply. The sole question in this case is whether, in the absence of a written agreement to the contrary, a partner, upon dissolution and wind-up of the partnership, can force a sale of the partnership assets.

At the outset, we note, and the parties agree, that the appellant was not in contravention of the partnership agreement since there was no partnership agreement. The partnership was a partnership at will. They also agree there was no written agreement governing distribution of partnership assets upon dissolution and wind-up. The dispute, in this case, is over the authority of the trial court to order in-kind distribution in the absence of any agreement of the partners.

Section 178.33(1), Stats., provides:

3. Sections 178.36 and 178.37 deal with cases where the partnership is not wound up, but continues after one partner leaves.

When dissolution is caused in any way, except in contravention of the partnership agreement, each partner, as against his copartners and all persons claiming through them in respect to their interests in the partnership, *unless otherwise agreed,* may have the partnership property applied to discharge its liabilities, and the surplus applied to pay *in cash* the net amount owing to the respective partners. [Emphasis supplied.]

The appellant contends this statute grants him the right to force a sale of the partnership assets in order to obtain his fair share of the partnership assets in cash upon dissolution. He claims that in the absence of an agreement of the partners to in-kind distribution, the trial court had no authority to distribute the assets in-kind. He is entitled to an in-cash settlement after judicial sale.

The respondents contend the statute does not entitle the appellant to force a sale and grants the trial court the power to distribute the assets in-kind if in-kind distribution is equitably possible and doesn't jeopardize the rights of creditors.

We do not believe that the statute can be read in any way to permit in-kind distribution unless the partners agree to in-kind distribution or unless there is a partnership agreement calling for in-kind distribution at the time of dissolution and wind-up.

A partnership at will is a partnership which has no definite term or particular undertaking and can rightfully be dissolved by the express will of any partner. Sec. 178.26(1)(b), Stats.; J. Crane and A. Bromberg, Law of Partnership § 74(b) (1968) [hereinafter cited as Crane and Bromberg]. In the present case, the respondents wanted to dissolve the partnership. This being a partnership at will, they could rightfully dissolve this partnership with or without the consent of the appellant. In addition, the respondents have never claimed the appellant was in violation of any partnership agreement. Therefore, neither the appellant nor the respondents have wrongfully dissolved the partnership.

Unless otherwise agreed, partners who have not wrongfully dissolved a partnership have a right to wind up the partnership. Sec. 178.32, Stats. Winding-up is the process of settling partnership affairs after dissolution. Winding-up is often called liquidation and involves reducing the assets to cash to pay creditors and distribute to partners the value of their respective interests. Crane and Bromberg, supra, §§ 73 and 80(c). Thus, lawful dissolution (or dissolution which is caused in any way except in contravention of the partnership agreement) gives each partner the right to have the business liquidated and his share of the surplus paid *in cash*. Young v. Cooper, 30 Tenn.App. 55, 203 S.W.2d 376 (1947); sec. 178.33(1), Stats.; Crane and Bromberg, supra, § 83A. In-kind distribution is permissible only in very limited circumstances. If the partnership agreement permits in-kind distribution upon dissolution or wind-up or if, at any time prior to wind-up, all partners agree to in-kind distribution, the court may order in-kind distribution.   Logoluso v. Logoluso, 43 Cal.Rptr. 678 (1965); Gathright v. Fulton, 122 Va. 17, 94 S.E. 191, 194 (1917).   While at least one court has permitted in-kind distribution, absent an agreement by all partners, Rinke v. Rinke, 330 Mich. 615, 48 N.W.2d 201 (1951), the court's holding in that case was limited.   In *Rinke,* the court stated:

> The decree of the trial court provided for dividing the assets of the partnerships rather than for the sale thereof and the distribution of cash proceeds.   Appellants insist that such method of procedure is erroneous and [not] contemplated by the uniform partnership act.   Attention is directed to Section 38 of said act, C.L. 1948, § 449.38, Stat.Ann. § 20.38.   Construing together pertinent provisions of the statute leads to the conclusion that it was not the intention of the legislature in the enactment of the Uniform Partnership Act to impose a mandatory requirement that, under all circumstances, the assets of a dissolved partnership shall be sold and the money received therefor divided among those entitled to it, particularly so, as in the case at bar, where there are no debts to be paid from the proceeds.   *The situation disclosed by the record in the present case is somewhat unusual in that no one other than the former partners is interested in the assets of the businesses.   In view of this situation and of the nature of the assets,* we think that the trial court was correct in apportioning them to the partners.   There is no showing that appellants have been prejudiced thereby.   [Emphasis supplied.]   330 Mich. at 628, 48 N.W.2d at 207.

The Michigan court's holding was limited to situations where: (1) there were no creditors to be paid from the proceeds, (2) ordering a sale would be senseless since no one other than the partners would be interested in the assets of the business, and (3) an in-kind distribution was fair to all partners.

That is not the case here.   There was no showing that there were no creditors who would be paid from the proceeds, nor was there a showing that no one other than the partners would be interested in the assets.   These factors are important if an in-kind distribution is to be allowed.   Section 178.33(1) and § 38 of the Uniform Partnership Act are intended to protect creditors as well as partners.   In-kind distributions may affect a creditor's right to collect the debt owed since the assets of the partnership, as a whole, may be worth more than the assets once divided up.   Thus, the creditor's ability to collect from the individual partners may be jeopardized.   Secondly, if others are interested in the assets, a sale provides a more accurate means of establishing the market value of the assets and, thus, better assuring each partner his share in the value of the assets.   Where only the partners are interested in the assets, a fair value can be determined without the necessity of a sale.   The sale would be merely the partners bidding with each other without any competition.   This process could be accomplished through negotiations or at trial with the court as a final arbitrator of the value of the assets.   With these policy considerations in mind, we think the Michigan court's holding in *Rinke* was limited to the facts of that case. Those facts not being present in this case, we do not feel an in-kind distribution in this case was proper.

However, even assuming the respondents in this case can show that there are no creditors to be paid, no one other than the partners are interested in the assets, and in-kind distribution would be fair to all partners, we cannot read § 38 of the Uniform Partnership Act or sec. 178.33(1), Stats. (the Wisconsin equivalent), as permitting an in-kind distribution under any circumstances, unless all partners agree. The statute and § 38 of the Uniform Partnership Act are quite clear that if a partner may force liquidation, he is entitled to his share of the partnership assets, after creditors are paid *in cash*. To the extent that Rinke v. Rinke, supra, creates an exception to cash distribution, we decline to adopt that exception. We, therefore, must hold the trial court erred in ordering an in-kind distribution of the assets of the partnership.

The last question that arises is whether the appellant can force an actual sale of the assets or whether the trial court can determine the fair market value of the assets and order the respondents to pay the appellant in cash an amount equal to his share in the assets.

As discussed above, a sale is the best means of determining the true fair market value of the assets. Generally, liquidation envisions some form of sale. Since the statutes provide that, unless otherwise agreed, any partner who has not wrongfully dissolved the partnership has the right to wind up the partnership and force liquidation, he likewise has a right to force a sale, unless otherwise agreed. Fortugno v. Hudson Manure Co., 51 N.J.Super. 482, 144 A.2d 207, 218–19 (1958); Young v. Cooper, 30 Tenn.App. 55, 203 S.W.2d 376 (1947). See also Crane and Bromberg, supra, § 83A; 4 Vill.L.Rev. 457 (1959). While judicial sales in some instances may cause economic hardships, these hardships can be avoided by the use of partnership agreements.

By the Court.—Judgment reversed and cause remanded for further proceedings not inconsistent with this opinion.

––––––––

NOTE ON NICHOLES v. HUNT

Nicholes v. Hunt, 273 Or. 255, 541 P.2d 820 (1975) was a case of rightful dissolution of a partnership between Nicholes and Hunt. Hunt had contributed an operating business to the partnership and Nicholes had contributed cash and services. The trial court refused to order a sale of the partnership's assets, and instead awarded the operating assets to Hunt and ordered that Nicholes be paid the value of his partnership interest in cash. Affirmed. "We conclude, as defendant contends and as the trial court found, that the equities lie with the defendant in this case. . . . The defendant conceived and designed the machinery and the method of operation, which was successfully operated for a number of years before formation of the partnership at will." The court relied in part on Rinke v. Rinke, which was mentioned but distinguished in *Dreirfurst.* See also Swann v. Mitchell, 435 So.2d 797 (Fla.1983); Wiese v. Wiese, 107 So.2d 208 (Fla.App.1958); Schaefer v. Bork, 413 N.W.2d 873 (Minn. App.1987).

NOTE ON PARTNERSHIP BREAKUP UNDER THE UPA

One of the most difficult issues in partnership law is how to treat cases in which a person's status as a partner is terminated, the partnership is to be terminated as a going concern, or both. (The complexity of these issues is illustrated by the fact that they occupy about a third of the text and comment of RUPA.) The difficult substantive issues raised by these issues have been made even more complex by the nomenclature that partnership law has employed. The UPA and RUPA take different strategies toward both the nomenclature and the underlying substantive issues. This Note will focus on dissolution under the UPA. A Note in Section 9, infra, will focus on dissolution under RUPA.

Before getting directly into the legal issues, it is useful to outline the business economics involved.

Assume that a partnership is to be terminated as a going concern. Typically, the termination process will fall into three phases.

(i) The first phase consists of an event—which may be a decision of a partner or a court—that sets the termination in motion.

(ii) Inevitably, some period of time must elapse between the moment at which that event occurs and the time at which termination of the partnership is completed. The second phase consists of the process of actually terminating the partnership's business. For example, if the partnership is in the manufacturing business, to terminate the business the partnership will need to pay off its debts, settle its contracts with employees and suppliers, find a purchaser for the factory, and so forth. All this will take time.

(iii) The final phase consists of the completion of the second phase and an end to the partnership as a going concern.

Under the UPA, the first phase is referred to as "dissolution," the second phase is referred to as "winding up," and the third phase is referred to as "termination." As the Official Comment states, "dissolution designates the point in time when the partners cease to carry on the business together; ... winding up, the process of settling partnership affairs after dissolution [; and termination, the point in time when all the partnership affairs are wound up]." Similarly, the principal draftsman of the UPA explained as follows the manner in which that statute uses the term "dissolution":

> [The term "dissolution" is used in the UPA to designate] a change in the relation of the partners caused by any partner ceasing to be associated in the carrying on of the business. As thus used "dissolution" does not terminate the partnership, it merely ends the carrying on of the business in that partnership. The partnership continues until the winding up of partnership affairs is completed.

Lewis, The Uniform Partnership Act, 24 Yale L.J. 617, 626–27 (1915).

To put all of this somewhat differently, "dissolution" is used in the UPA to describe a change in the *legal status* of the partners and the partnership. "Winding-up" is used to describe the *economic* event of liquidation that follows dissolution.

Under the UPA, any termination of a person's status as a partner effects a dissolution of the partnership. It's not easy to see why this should be so when, as often happens, the remaining partners rightfully carry on the partnership's business after one partner has departed. Basically, the UPA's treatment of this issue seems to have been driven by a form of conceptualism. The UPA defines a partnership as an aggregation of persons to carry on business for profit as co-owners, rather than as an entity. Because the UPA treats a partnership as an aggregation, the drafters seemed to have believed that it followed "logically" that any change in the identity of the partners "necessarily" worked a dissolution of the partnership. If a partnership is conceptualized as an aggregation of the partners, and if the partners in Partnership P are A, B, C, and D, then it may have seemed to the drafters of the UPA that if D ceases to be a partner, Partnership P "must be" dissolved, because there is no longer an aggregation of A, B, C, and D. Following this line, UPA § 29 defines dissolution as "the change in the relation of partners caused by any partner ceasing to be associated in the carrying on" of the partnership's business.

The law, however, should not be built on deductive logic, but on policy, morality, and experience. We make rules because they are desirable, not because they are deducible. If a person ceases to be a partner, the law can treat the partnership as either dissolved or not dissolved. Which course the law takes should depend on which treatment better protects the parties' expectations and best reflects social policy. This, in turn, depends on what consequences the law should and does attach to dissolution.

Broadly speaking, the law may attach consequences to dissolution: (1) among the partners themselves; (2) between the partners as a group, and third persons such as individuals or firms with whom the partnership has contracted; and (3) for tax purposes. The remainder of this Note will consider each of these areas.

(1) *Consequences among the partners.* Under the UPA, upon the occurrence of dissolution—which, remember, under the UPA

means simply that any partner ceases to be a partner—then unless otherwise agreed, the partnership normally must sell its assets for cash and distribute the proceeds of the sale among all the partners. See Dreifuerst v. Dreifuerst, supra. (If, however, a partner, D, *wrongfully* causes dissolution, UPA § 38(2)(b) provides that notwithstanding the occurrence of dissolution the remaining partners can continue the partnership's business. To do so, however, the remaining partners must either (i) pay D the value of his partnership interest (but without counting the value of the partnership's good will), minus any damages caused by the dissolution, or (ii) put up a bond to secure that payment, and indemnify D against present and future partnership liabilities. See Section 9, infra.)

Furthermore, UPA § 38(1) provides that "[w]hen dissolution is [rightfully] caused ... each partner ... *unless otherwise agreed,* may have the partnership property applied to discharge its liabilities, and the surplus applied to pay in cash the net amount owing to the respective partners." (Emphasis added.) It is well accepted, under the "unless" clause, that the partnership agreement can provide that after the termination of a person's status as a partner (and, therefore, after the dissolution of the partnership under the UPA) the remaining partners can continue the partnership business, even if the partnership has been "dissolved" and the dissolution is rightfully caused. See, e.g., Meehan v. Shaughnessy, 404 Mass. 419, 535 N.E.2d 1255 (1989); Adams v. Jarvis, 23 Wis.2d 453, 127 N.W.2d 400 (1964).

Agreements under which the remaining partners can continue the business after dissolution are common, especially in large partnerships, such as law partnerships. Such agreements are usually known as business-continuation agreements or, more simply, continuation agreements. Typically, continuation agreements include not only the right of the remaining partners to continue the partnership's business, but also the terms on which the partner who causes dissolution (or his estate) will be compensated for his partnership interest.

(2) *Effect of dissolution on the relationship between the partnership and third parties.* As among the partners, it often won't matter very much whether the withdrawal of a partner does or does not cause dissolution, because as among the partners a continuation agreement can override the substantive effects that dissolution would otherwise have. However, dissolution may also affect the relationship of the partnership to third persons.

For example, suppose that Partnership P, consisting of partners A, B, C, and D, is dissolved by the withdrawal of D, but the business of the partnership is continued by A, B, and C under a continuation agreement. Because P has been dissolved, the partnership of A, B, and C may be deemed a "new" partnership for legal purposes, so that P's assets and agreements, such as leases, licenses, or franchises, must be "transferred" to the new partnership. See Report of the ABA Subcommittee on the Revision of the U.P.A., 43 Bus.Law.

121, 160–62 (1987). In a much remarked-on case, Fairway Development Co. v. Title Insurance Co., 621 F.Supp. 120 (N.D.Ohio 1985), Fairway, a partnership, sued Title Insurance Co. under a title guarantee policy. The policy had been issued at a time when the partners in Fairway were B, S, and W. Subsequently, B and S transferred their partnership interests to W and a third party, V. W and V apparently continued Fairway's business under the Fairway name. The court nevertheless held that Title Insurance was not bound under its policy because the partnership to which it had issued the policy had been legally dissolved.

A debated point under the UPA is whether a partnership agreement can provide not only that the partnership business may be continued after dissolution, but also that the withdrawal of a partner will not cause dissolution, so that the partnership's relation with third parties will not be affected by a partner's withdrawal, as happened in the *Fairway* case. The prevailing (but not unanimous) answer is no, on the ground that UPA § 31 expressly states that "[d]issolution is caused" by the withdrawal of a partner.

(3) *Tax consequences.* The tax-law treatment of dissolution is relatively straightforward, and largely unimpeded by conceptualism. Internal Revenue Code § 708 provides that a partnership's existence does not terminate for tax purposes until either "(A) no part of any business, financial operation, or venture of the partnership continues to be carried on by any of [the] partners in a partnership, or (B) within a twelve-month period there is a sale or exchange of fifty percent or more of the total interest in partnership capital and profits." Accordingly, dissolution under partnership law is normally a non-event for federal income tax purposes. (Warning: Despite IRC § 708, dissolution may have tax effects on a partner who does not continue, or on his estate. Even these effects, however, can normally be avoided by a continuation agreement.)

————

SECTION 9. DISSOLUTION (II): DISSOLUTION BY JUDICIAL DECREE AND WRONGFUL DISSOLUTION

————

UNIFORM PARTNERSHIP ACT §§ 31(2), 32, 38

REVISED UNIFORM PARTNERSHIP ACT §§ 601, 602, 603, 701, 802, 803, 804, 807

[See Statutory Supplement]

————

DRASHNER v. SORENSON

Supreme Court of South Dakota, 1954.
75 S.D. 247, 63 N.W.2d 255.

SMITH, P.J. In January 1951 the plaintiff, C.H. Drashner, and defendants, A.D. Sorenson and Jacob P. Deis, associated themselves as co-owners in the real estate, loan and insurance business at Rapid City. For a consideration of $7500 they purchased the real estate and insurance agency known as J. Schumacher Co. located in an office room on the ground floor of the Alex Johnson Hotel building. The entire purchase price was advanced for the partnership by the defendants, but at the time of trial $3,000 of that sum had been repaid to them by the partnership. Although, as will appear from facts presently to be outlined, their operations were not unsuccessful, differences arose and on June 15, 1951 plaintiff commenced this action in which he sought an accounting, dissolution and winding up of the partnership. The answer and counterclaim of defendants prayed for like relief.

The cause came on for trial September 4, 1951. The court among others made the following findings. VII. "That thereafter the plaintiff violated the terms of said partnership agreement, in that he demanded a larger share of the income of the said partnership than he was entitled to receive under the terms of said partnership agreement; that the plaintiff was arrested for reckless driving and served a term in jail for said offense; that the plaintiff demanded that the defendants permit him to draw money for his own personal use out of the moneys held in escrow by the partnership; that the plaintiff spent a large amount of time during business hours in the Brass Rail Bar in Rapid City, South Dakota, and other bars, and neglected his duties in connection with the business of the said partnership. ... That the plaintiff, by his actions hereinbefore set forth, has made it impossible to carry on the partnership." The conclusions adopted read as follows: I "That the defendants are entitled to continue the partnership and have the value of the plaintiff's interest in the partnership business determined, upon the filing and approval of a good and sufficient bond, conditioned upon the release of the plaintiff from any liability arising out of the said partnership, and further conditioned upon the payment by the defendants to the plaintiff of the value of plaintiffs' interest in the partnership as determined by the Court." II "That in computing the value of the plaintiff's interest in the said partnership, the value of the good will of the business shall not be considered." III "That the value of the partnership shall be finally determined upon a hearing before this Court, ..." and IV "That the plaintiff shall be entitled to receive one-third of the value of the partnership property owned by the partnership on the 12th day of September, 1951, not including the good will of the business, after the payment of the liabilities of the partnership and the payment to the defendants of the invested capital in the sum of $4,500.00." Judgment was accordingly entered dissolving the partnership as of September 12, 1951.

After hearing at a later date the court found: I "That the value of the said partnership property on the 12th day of September, 1951, was the sum of Four Thousand Four Hundred Ninety-eight and 90/100 Dollars ($4498.90), and on said date there was due and owing by the partnership for accountant's services the sum of Four Hundred Eighty Dollars ($480.00), and that on said date the sum of Four Thousand Five Hundred Dollars ($4500.00) of the capital invested by the defendants had not been returned to the defendants." and II "That there is not sufficient partnership property to reimburse the defendants for their invested capital." Thereupon the court decreed "that the plaintiff had no interest in the property of the said partnership", and that the defendants were the sole owners thereof.

The assignments of error are predicated upon insufficiency of the evidence to support the findings and conclusions. Of these assignments, only those which question whether the court was warranted in finding that (a) the plaintiff caused the dissolution wrongfully, and (b) the value of the partnership property, exclusive of good will, was $4498.90 on the 12th day of September, 1951, merit discussion. A preliminary statement is necessary to place these issues in their framework.

The agreement of the parties contemplated an association which would continue at least until the $7500 advance of defendants had been repaid from the gross earnings of the business. Hence, it was not a partnership at will. Vangel v. Vangel, 116 Cal.App.2d 615, 254 P.2d 919; Zeibak v. Nasser, 12 Cal.2d 1, 82 P.2d 375. In apparent recognition of that fact, both plaintiff and defendants sought dissolution in contravention of the partnership agreement, see SDC 49.0603(2) under SDC 49.0604(1)(d) on the ground that the adverse party had caused the dissolution wrongfully by willfully and persistently committing a breach of the partnership agreement, and by so conducting himself in matters relating to the partnership business as to render impracticable the carrying on of the business in partnership with him.

[The court here quoted U.P.A. Section 38(2)].

From this background we turn to a consideration of the evidence from which the trial court inferred that plaintiff caused the dissolution wrongfully.

The breach between the parties resulted from a continuing controversy over the right of plaintiff to withdraw sufficient money from the partnership to defray his living expenses. Plaintiff was dependent upon his earnings for the support of his family. The defendants had other resources. Plaintiff claimed that he was to be permitted to draw from the earnings of the partnership a sufficient amount to support himself and family. The defendants asserted that there was a definite arrangement for the allocation of the income of the partnership and there was no agreement for withdrawal by plaintiff of more than his allotment under that plan. Defendants' version of the facts was corroborated by a written admission of plaintiff offered in evidence. From evidence thus sharply in conflict, the trial court made a finding, reading as follows: "That the oral partnership agreement between the parties provided that each of the three partners were to draw as compensation one-third of one-half of the commissions earned upon sales made by the partners; that the other one-half of the commissions earned on sales made by the partners and one-half of the commissions earned upon sales made by salesmen employed by the partnership, together with the earnings from the insurance business carried on by the partnership, was to be placed in a fund to be used for the payment of the operating expenses of the partnership, and after the payment of such operating expenses to be used to reimburse the defendants for the capital advanced in the purchase of the Julius Schumacher business and the capital advanced in the sum of Eight Hundred Dollars ($800.00) for the operating expenses of the business."

As an outgrowth of this crucial difference, there was evidence from which a court could reasonably believe that plaintiff neglected the business and spent too much time in a nearby bar during business hours. At a time when plaintiff had overdrawn his partners and was also indebted to one of defendants for personal advances, he requested $100 and his request was refused. In substance he then said, according to the testimony of the defendant Deis, that he would see that he "gets some money to run on", if they "didn't give it to him he was going to dissolve the partnership and see that he got it." Thereafter plaintiff pressed his claims through counsel, and eventually brought this action to dissolve the partnership. The claim so persistently asserted was contrary to the partnership agreement found by the court.

The foregoing picture of the widening breach between the parties is drawn almost entirely from the evidence of defendants. Of course, plaintiff's version of the agreement of the parties, and of the ensuing differences, if believed, would have supported findings of a different order by the trier of the fact. It cannot be said, we think, that the trial court acted unreasonably in believing defendants, and we think it equally clear the court could reasonably conclude that the insistent and continuing demands of the plaintiff and his attendant conduct rendered it reasonably impracticable to carry on the business in partnership with him. It follows, we are of the opinion, the evidence supports the finding that plaintiff caused the dissolution wrongfully. Zeibak v. Nasser, 12 Cal.2d 1, 82 P.2d 375; Owen v. Cohen, 19 Cal.2d 147, 119 P.2d 713; Meherin v. Meherin, 93 Cal.App.2d 459, 209 P.2d 36; and Vangel v. Vangel, 116 Cal.App.2d 615, 254 P.2d 919.

This brings us to a consideration of the sufficiency of the evidence to support the finding of the court that the property of the partnership was of the value of $4498.90 as of the date of dissolution.

Bitter complaint is made because the trial court refused to consider the good will of this business in arriving at its conclusion. The feeling of plaintiff is understandable. These partners must have placed a very high estimate upon the value of the good will of this agency because they paid Mr. Schumacher $7500 to turn over that office with its very moderate fixtures and its listing of property, together with an agreement that he would not engage in the business in Rapid City for at least two years. No doubt they attached some of this good will value to the location of the business which was under only a month to month letting. Cf. 38 C.J.S., Good Will, § 3, page 951; In re Brown's Will, 242 N.Y. 1, 150 N.E. 581, 44 A.L.R. 510, at page 513. Their estimate of value was borne out by the subsequent history of the business. Its real estate commissions, earned but only partly received, grossed $21,528.25 and its insurance commissions grossed $661.21 in the period January 15 to August 31, 1951. In that period the received commissions paid all expenses, including the commissions of salesmen, retired $3,000 of the $7500 purchase price advanced by defendants, and all of $800 of working capital so advanced, allowed the parties to withdraw $1453.02 each, and accumulated a cash balance of $2221.43. In addition the partnership has commissions due. . . . Notwithstanding this indication of the great value of the good will of this business, the statute does not require the court to take it into consideration in valuing the property of the business in these circumstances. The statute provides such a sanction for causing the dissolution of a partnership wrongfully. SDC 49.0610(2)(c)(2) quoted supra. The court applied the statute. . . .

That the $1500 value placed on [the assets other than good will] was conservative we do not question. However, after mature study and reflection we have concluded that the court's finding is not against the clear weight of the evidence appearing in this record. Hence we are not at liberty to disturb it.

The brief of plaintiff includes some discussion of his right to a share in the profits from the date of the dissolution until the final judgment. It does not appear from the record that this claim was presented to the trial court, or that the net profit of the business during that period was evidenced. Because that issue was not presented below, it is not before us.

The judgment of the trial court is affirmed.

All the Judges concur.

———

NOTE ON WRONGFUL DISSOLUTION

Drashner v. Sorenson illustrates that rather drastic consequences can befall a wrongfully dissolving partner in the form of damages, a valuation of his interest that does not reflect its real value because goodwill is not taken into account, and a continuation of the business without him. These consequences may have a special impact in a partnership without a stated term. Suppose one of the partners, A, elects to dissolve such a partnership on the theory that the partnership is at will. If the court finds that as a matter of implication the partnership is for a specified term, A will presumably have dissolved in contravention of the partnership agreement under UPA § 38(2). The penalties for guessing wrong on whether the court will make such a finding "may act as significant disincentives to dissolution [and may therefore] tend to stabilize the partnership." Hillman, The Dissatisfied Participant in the Solvent Business Venture: A Consideration of the Relative Permanence of Partnerships and Close Corporations, 67 Minn.L.Rev. 1, 34 (1982). For comparable reasons, a partner is normally ill-advised to try to dissolve a partnership, based on a claim of wrongful conduct, through some sort of self-help election, as opposed to going to court for a decree under UPA Section 32. (The other side of the coin, of course, is the delay that judicial proceedings normally entail.)

NOTE ON PARTNERSHIP BREAKUP UNDER RUPA

RUPA's provisions on partnership breakup are even more complex than those of the UPA. To begin with nomenclature, RUPA continues to use the terms "dissolution," "winding up," and "termination." However, RUPA adds a new term, "dissociation," to describe the termination of a person's status as a partner.

1. *Events of dissociation.* Although the term "dissociation" is new, the concept is not. Even under the UPA, a variety of events result in the termination of a person's status as a partner, and there is a very substantial overlap between the UPA and RUPA concerning the description of those events. For example, RUPA § 602(a) continues the rule of the UPA that every partner has the right to dissociate (withdraw) from the partnership at any time, rightfully or wrongfully, by express will.[1] RUPA § 602(c) provides that a partner who wrongfully dissociates is liable to the partnership and to the other partners for damages cased by the dissociation. Furthermore, if a partner wrongfully dissociates, the partnership can continue without him.

The events that result in dissociation under RUPA, other than voluntary withdrawal, are set out in RUPA § 601(2)–(10).

2. *Rightful and wrongful dissociation.* RUPA § 602 distinguishes between events of dissociation that involve rightful conduct by the dissociated partner and events of dissociation that involve

---

1. RUPA § 103(b)(6) provides that the partnership agreement cannot vary the power of a partner to dissociate under § 602(a), except to require that the notice of dissociation must be in writing. RUPA § 103(b)(8) provides that the partnership agreement may not vary the rights of partners to have the partnership dissolved under specified provisions of RUPA § 801.

wrongful conduct. An event of dissociation is rightful unless it is specified as wrongful in § 602(b). The major types of wrongful dissociation are (i) a dissociation that is in breach of an express provision of the partnership agreement; (ii) a withdrawal of a partner by the partner's express will before the expiration of the partnership term or the completion of an undertaking for which the partnership was formed; and (iii) a dissociation that results from an expulsion of the partner by judicial order under § 601(5). The grounds for expulsion under § 601(5) are that: the partner engaged in wrongful conduct that adversely and materially affected the partnership business; the partner willfully or persistently committed a material breach of the partnership agreement or of a duty of care, loyalty, good faith, and fair dealing owed to the partnership or the other partners under § 404; or the partner engaged in conduct relating to the partnership business that makes it not reasonably practicable to carry on the business in partnership with the partner.

The Comment to RUPA § 602 states:

> [Under 602(a)] . . . a partner has the power to dissociate at any time by expressing a will to withdraw, even in contravention of the partnership agreement. The phrase "rightfully or wrongfully" reflects the distinction between a partner's *power* to withdraw in contravention of the partnership agreement and a partner's *right* to do so. In this context, although a partner can not be enjoined from exercising the power to dissociate, the dissociation may be wrongful under subsection (b). . . .

> . . . The significance of a wrongful dissociation is that it may give rise to damages under subsection (c) and, if it results in the dissolution of the partnership, the wrongfully dissociating partner is not entitled to participate in winding up the business. . . .

3. *Consequences of dissociation.* Unlike the UPA, the partnership-breakup provisions of RUPA are driven by functional considerations rather than by the "nature" of a partnership (although the Comments occasionally lapse into conceptual justifications based on the entity theory). Along these lines, RUPA, unlike the UPA, does not provide that every termination of a person's status as a partner—every dissociation—causes dissolution. In fact, the breakup provisions of RUPA do not even pivot on whether dissolution occurs. Instead, the key issue is whether *dissociation* has occurred.

Under RUPA, a dissociation normally leads to one of two alternatives: winding up of the partnership or mandatory buyout of the dissociated partner. (Depending on the nature of the dissociation, a mandatory buyout may be required to be made immediately or only at some later date. See p. 68, infra.) Accordingly, although the term "dissolution" is used in RUPA, nothing really turns on whether there is a dissolution, and the term could have been left out. As stated by the Reporters for RUPA:

> The term *dissolution* has no independent operative significance under RUPA. Stated somewhat differently, RUPA's provi-

sions are redundant when they state that "a partnership is dissolved, *and* its business must be wound up." Section 801 simply is a list of those situations in which the business of the partnership must begin to be wound up. The word *dissolution* is nothing more than a shorthand term for the occurrence of one of those situations.[2]

In short, under RUPA, dissociation leads to two forks in the statutory road: winding up under Article 8, or mandatory buyout under Article 7. Which fork must be taken depends on the nature of the event of dissociation. Thus as stated in the Comment to RUPA § 601:

> RUPA dramatically changes the law governing partnership breakups and dissolution. An entirely new concept, "dissociation," is used in lieu of the UPA term "dissolution" to denote the change in the relationship caused by a partner's ceasing to be associated in the carrying on of the business.... The entity theory of partnership [adopted in RUPA] provides a conceptual basis of continuing the firm itself despite a partner's withdrawal from the firm.

> Under RUPA, unlike the UPA, the dissociation of a partner does not necessarily cause a dissolution and winding up of the business of the partnership. Section 801 identifies the situations in which the dissociation of a partner causes a winding up of the business. Section 701 provides that in all other situations there is a buyout of the partner's interest in the partnership, rather than a windup of the partnership business. In those other situations, the partnership entity continues, unaffected by the partner's dissociation.

First Fork: Winding Up. The events of dissociation that require the partnership to be wound up under RUPA are described in § 801. The Official Comment adds:

> ... Under RUPA, not every partner dissociation causes a dissolution of the partnership. Only certain departures trigger a dissolution. The basic rule is that a partnership is dissolved, and its business must be wound up, only upon the occurrence of one of the events listed in Section 801. All other dissociations result in a buyout of the partner's interest under Article 7

---

2. Earlier, the Reporter had commented:

> Initially, RUPA's new rules on breakups were forged without the use of the term "dissolution." After more than two years of work, the Drafting Committee put the word dissolution back in the statute. Yet an examination of RUPA's breakup provisions indicates that the word as reinstated is surplusage.

> Throughout the project, there have been those who have urged the Drafting Committee to reinstate the word dissolution. They were asked to defer discussion of this suggestion to give the Committee a chance to draft a statute without "the D word." They finally had a chance to state their case, and the Drafting Committee in the Spring of 1990 decided to reinstate the word without changing either the basic structure we had drafted or the substantive decisions we had hung on that structure....

Weidner, Three Policy Decisions [that] Animate [the] Revision of the Uniform Partnership Act, 46 Bus.Law. 427 (1991).

and a continuation of the partnership entity and business by the remaining partners.

Section 801 continues two basic rules from the UPA. First, it continues the rule that any member of an *at-will* partnership has the right to force a liquidation. Second, by negative implication, it continues the rule that the partners who wish to continue the business of a *term* partnership can not be forced to liquidate the business by a partner who withdraws prematurely in violation of the partnership agreement.

Second Fork: Buyout. If, upon the dissociation of a partner, winding up is not required under § 801, then RUPA § 701 requires a mandatory buyout of the dissociated partner's interest by the partnership. However, if the dissociation was wrongfully caused by the dissociated partner, § 701(c) provides that the buyout price under § 701(b) is to be reduced by damages for the wrongful dissociation. Furthermore, under § 701(h) a partner who wrongfully dissociates before the expiration of a definite term, or the completion of a particular undertaking, is not entitled to payment of any portion of the buyout price until the expiration of the term or completion of the undertaking, unless the partner establishes to the satisfaction of the court that earlier payment will not cause undue hardship to the business of the partnership. A deferred payment must be adequately secured and bear interest. Under § 701(b), the buyout price of a dissociated partner's interest is the amount that would have been distributable to the dissociating partner if, on the date of dissociation, the assets of the partnership were sold at a price equal to the greater of the liquidation value or the value based on a sale of the entire business as a going concern, without the dissociated partner, and the partnership was wound up as of that date.

SECTION 10. LIMITED PARTNERSHIPS

(a) THE UNIFORM LIMITED PARTNERSHIP ACTS

Over the course of time, the Commissioners on Uniform State Laws have promulgated several uniform limited partnership acts.

In 1916, the Commissioners promulgated the original Uniform Limited Partnership Act. It was adopted in every state except Louisiana.

In 1976, the Commissioners promulgated a replacement for the Uniform Limited Partnership Act, called the Revised Uniform Partnership Act. The new Act modernized the prior Act, picked up some modifications of the original Act that had been made in adopting states, and generally reflected the influence of the corporate model. It has been widely but not universally adopted.

In 1985, the Commissioners amended the Revised Uniform Limited Partnership Act in a number of important respects. The states are still in the process of adopting these amendments.

In the balance of this Section, the 1916 Act, and the 1976 Act as amended in 1985, will be referred to as the ULPA and the RULPA, respectively.

(b) FORMATION OF A LIMITED PARTNERSHIP

REVISED UNIFORM LIMITED PARTNERSHIP ACT §§ 101, 201

[See Statutory Supplement]

Unlike general partnerships, limited partnerships are basically creatures of statute, although they have nonstatutory historical antecedents. Section 1 of the ULPA defined a limited partnership as "a partnership formed by two or more persons under the provisions of Section 2, having as members one or more general partners and one or more limited partners." Section 2, in turn, provided that persons who desire to form a limited partnership must execute a certificate setting forth the name of the partnership, the names and residences of each member (including the limited partners), the contributions of the partners, and much other information, and must file the certificate in a designated state or county office.

RULPA § 101 carries forward the substance of ULPA Section 1. However, Section 201 drastically reduces the amount of information that must be contained in the certificate. Under Section 201, as amended, the certificate need only state the name of the limited partnership, the name and business address of each general partner, the latest date upon which the limited partnership is to dissolve, and the name and address of the agent for service of process. Thus under the RULPA, as amended, neither the identity of the limited partners nor the partnership's capitalization need be stated in the certificate.

(c) LIABILITY OF LIMITED PARTNERS; CORPORATION AS A SOLE GENERAL PARTNER

REVISED UNIFORM LIMITED PARTNERSHIP ACT §§ 302, 303

[See Statutory Supplement]

NOTE ON RULPA § 303(a)

Prior to the 1985 amendments to the RULPA, § 303(a) of that Act read as follows:

> ... [A] limited partner is not liable for the obligations of a limited partnership unless he is also a general partner or, in addition to the exercise of his rights and powers as a limited partner, he takes part in the control of the business. However, if the limited partner's participation in the control of the business is not substantially the same as the exercise of the powers of a general partner, he is liable only to persons who transact business with the limited partnership with actual knowledge of his participation in control.

This provision, or a close counterpart, is still in force in states that adopted the RULPA but have not yet adopted the 1985 amendments.

––––––––

NOTE ON CORPORATE GENERAL PARTNERS

Although a limited partnership must have at least one general partner, and a general partner has unlimited liability for the partnership's obligations, it is common for a limited partnership to have a corporation as its sole general partner. In principle, a corporate general partner has unlimited liability for the partnership's obligations, but in practice, recovery against the corporate partner is limited to the net worth of the corporation, which may be much less than the partnership's debts. Under the doctrine of limited liability, which will be considered in Chapter 3, the shareholders of a corporate general partner normally will not themselves be liable for the corporate general partner's obligations. Therefore, the practical effect of creating a limited partnership with a corporate general partner is that the liability of all partners is limited. The liability of limited partners is limited under limited-partnership law; the liability of the corporate general partner is limited to the amount of its assets.

––––––––

(d) NOTE ON LIMITED PARTNERSHIPS

1. Approximately 1.5 million partnerships filed federal income tax returns for 1992. Of these, approximately 270,000 were limited

partnerships.   The general partnerships had an average of approximately 4 partners.   The limited partnerships had an average of approximately 41 partners.   Wheeler, Partnership Returns, 1992, Internal Revenue Service, Statistics of Income Bulletin, Fall 1994, at 75, 77 (Figure E).

2.   Under Internal Revenue Code § 7701(a)(3), the term "corporation" is defined for income-tax purposes to include "associations."   The latter term is not defined, but can include organizations like limited partnerships.   In Morrissey v. Commissioner, 296 U.S. 344, 56 S.Ct. 289, 80 L.Ed. 263 (1935), the Supreme Court held that whether a given partnership was an "association" within the meaning of the Code depended on how closely the partnership resembled a corporation.   Subsequently, the Internal Revenue Service adopted Regulations—known as the Kintner Regulations—that identify four critical "characteristics of corporations" for tax-law purposes: continuity of life, centralized management, limited liability, and free transferability of interests.   The Kintner Regulations indicate that a limited partnership will be treated as an association (and will therefore be taxed like a corporation) if, but only if, it has more than two of these characteristics.   See Treas.Reg. § 301.7701–2(a).

However, the Kintner Regulations and related Revenue Procedures define the relevant characteristics in such a restrictive manner that a limited partnership will normally not have the characteristics. For example, although in fact limited partnerships always have centralized management, vested in the hands of the general partners, under the Regulations and Procedures a limited partnership is deemed *not* to have centralized management as long as the general partners have a defined minimum interest in the firm—normally, 1%.   Similarly, a limited partnership is treated as if it has unlimited liability even if the only general partner is a corporation with limited liability, as long as the corporation meets certain net worth standards.[1]   Furthermore, although the Kintner Regulations purport to adopt the *Morrissey* resemblance test, in fact the test under the Regulations depends on a by-the-numbers count of the relevant characteristics.

As a result of the artificial nature of the definitions in the Regulations and Procedures, a limited partnership will normally not be deemed to have more than two of the four critical characteristics. As a result of the mechanical nature of the by-the-numbers test, as a practical matter a limited partnership that is not publicly held is unlikely to be taxed as a corporation under § 7701.

3.   In the last thirty years, many publicly held limited partnerships have been organized.   The limited partnership interests in these limited partnerships were initially offered to the public through underwriters, and in some cases were publicly traded on organized markets.   These partnerships are known as "master limited partnerships."   That term arose "as a description of the method

---

1.   See Rev.Proc. 92–88, 1992–42 I.R.B. 39 (safe harbor guidelines).

by which these large publicly traded partnerships were first developed. An independent oil company formed the first master limited partnership in 1981. The company consolidated thirty pre-existing drilling and exploration limited partnerships into one 'master' limited partnership. The partners of the drilling and exploration partnerships contributed their partnership interests to a new limited partnership in return for limited partnership interests in the new entity. This method of forming a master limited partnership is called a 'roll up' and is generally used to combine several smaller limited partnerships into one large partnership. The definition of master limited partnerships [was later expanded, and the term] now refers more generally to large partnerships that are widely held and whose ownership interests are frequently traded." Adler, Master Limited Partnerships, 21 U.Fla.L.Rev. 755, 756–57.

A major incentive for forming master limited partnerships is to combine the economic advantages of publicly traded ownership interests and limited liability, on the one hand (advantages that are normally associated with corporations) with the tax treatment accorded to partnerships, on the other. However, the Internal Revenue Code was amended in 1987 to treat any partnership with interests that are "traded on an established securities market," or that "are readily tradeable on a secondary market (or the substantial equivalent thereof)" as "publicly traded partnerships," and to tax such partnerships as corporations. See IRC § 7704.

This tax treatment is subject to certain exceptions. In particular, a publicly traded limited partnership will not be taxed as a corporation if 90 percent of its income consists of interest, dividends, real property rents, gain from the sale of real property or certain other types of "passive income," or gains derived from the exploration, development, mining or production, processing, refining, transportation, or marketing of any minerals or natural resources. "Because master limited partnerships have most often been used in the oil and gas and real estate industries, these exceptions substantially limit the effect of the recharacterization of publicly traded partnerships. For example, of the existing exchange-traded partnerships listed in [a] statement of the Treasury, 66 percent ... are either involved in the natural resource or real estate industry and would likely fit within the passive-type income exception." Adler, supra at 757.

————

SECTION 11. LIMITED LIABILITY
PARTNERSHIPS

————

DELAWARE LIMITED LIABILITY PARTNERSHIP ACT

[See Statutory Supplement]

————

TEXAS LIMITED LIABILITY PARTNERSHIP ACT

[See Statutory Supplement]

———

NOTE ON LIMITED LIABILITY PARTNERSHIPS

An important new form of business organization is the limited liability partnership ("LLP"). Essentially, LLPs are general partnerships with one core difference and several ancillary differences. The core difference is that, as the name indicates, the liability of general partners of a limited liability partnership is less extensive than the ordinary liability of a general partner. Although the statutes vary, generally speaking a partner in an LLP is not personally liable for *all* partnership obligations arising from negligence, wrongful acts, and misconduct, but only for obligations arising (1) from the partner's own negligence, wrongful acts; (2) from the negligence, wrongful acts, or misconduct of those under the partner's supervision and control; and, (3) under some statutes, from the negligence, wrongful acts, or misconduct of those engaged in a specific activity (as opposed to the general partnership business) in which the partner was involved. This core idea is articulated differently under different LLP statutes, and the precise liability of a partner in an LLP will depend on the statute.

The LLP statutes apparently are generally not intended to exclude a partner's liability for contractual obligations (although that result could sometimes be achieved by a provision in the relevant contract). Furthermore, under the statutes the liability of a partner in an LLP is "limited" only in the sense that the partner is not personally liable for *all* of the LLP's obligations. A partner in an LLP *is* personally liable for certain obligations, and as to those obligations a partner's liability is unlimited—that is, a partner is personally liable for those obligations to the entire extent of her wealth.

An ancillary difference between ordinary general partnerships and LLPs is that under some LLP statutes there is a tradeoff for limited liability, in the form of a requirement of a minimum amount of liability insurance or segregated funds. Another ancillary difference between LLPs and ordinary general partnerships is that LLPs must be registered.

Chapter III

THE CORPORATE FORM

SECTION 1.   DECIDING WHETHER
TO INCORPORATE

NOTE ON THE CHARACTERISTICS OF THE CORPORATION

1.   Traditionally, corporations have been characterized by five substantive attributes and a tax attribute.   The substantive attributes are limited liability, free transferability of ownership interests, continuity of existence, centralized management, and entity status.   The tax attribute is taxation of enterprise income at the entity (corporate) level rather than directly to the shareholders-owners.

a.   Free transferability of ownership interests.   A transferee of a general partnership interest normally cannot be substituted as a partner without the unanimous consent of the remaining partners. In contrast, ownership (or "equity") interests in corporations—represented by shares of stock—are freely transferable.

b.   Limited liability.   General partners are personally liable for obligations that arise out of the conduct of their business.   In contrast, shareholders of a corporation are not personally liable for corporate obligations.   This legal rule is conventionally expressed by the statement that shareholders have limited liability.   Furthermore, the *managers* of a corporation are also normally not personally liable for corporate obligations.   As long as corporate managers act on the corporation's behalf, and within their authority, they are treated like agents, not principals, for liability purposes—even if they are shareholders as well as managers.

c.   Continuity of existence.   Unlike partnerships, which are typically for a limited term, the legal existence of a corporation is perpetual, unless a shorter term is stated in the certificate of incorporation.

d.   Centralized management.   Under partnership law, all partners have a right to participate in management.   In contrast, under the corporate statutes a corporation is normally managed by or under the direction of a board of directors, and a shareholder, as such, has no right to participate in management.   This characteristic of corporations is known as centralized management.   A byproduct of centralized management is that, unlike a general partner, a

74

shareholder, as such, has no power to bind the corporation to a contract or to place the corporation under other types of obligation.

e. Entity status. At least in the past, corporations had the status of "legal persons," or entities, while partnerships did not. (However, under the Revised Uniform Partnership Act—RUPA— partnerships are also treated as entities.)

f. Taxation. A corporation is normally taxed as an entity— that is, a corporation's income is taxed to the corporation, rather than to the shareholders. If the corporation's after-tax income is later distributed as a dividend, the dividend is taxed to the share- holders as part of their income. This effect is sometimes referred to as "double taxation." In contrast, partnership income is treated on a conduit, or pass-through, basis. Under the pass-through ap- proach, partnership income and losses are taxable as if they had been realized by the partners, rather than by the partnership. The partnership therefore pays no tax, and there is no "double taxation" effect. If the partnership has a tax loss, the partners can utilize the loss on their individual returns.

Whether corporate or partnership taxation is preferable in any given case depends on the tax rates and the circumstances. If maximum corporate tax rates are lower than maximum individual rates, capital gains are taxed at lower rates than ordinary income, and income is to be retained by the corporation rather than distributed to the shareholders, corporate-tax treatment may be more attractive than partnership-tax treatment. When income is to be distributed rather than retained, or initial losses are expected, partnership-tax treatment may be more attractive than corporate-tax treatment.

2. Although in any given case, any single corporate character- istic may be an important factor in choosing or rejecting the corporate form, in practice the choice of a form for a business organization tends to be driven by considerations of liability, taxa- tion, and, to a certain extent, cost (corporations tend to be more costly to organize and maintain than other forms).

Until recently, the process of making such a choice was relative- ly straightforward. Where a business enterprise was to be publicly held (that is, where ownership interests were to be held by mem- bers of the public, as opposed to owner-managers and their affili- ates), the corporation was almost always the form of choice. Al- though limited partnerships shared many of a corporation's substan- tive attributes, most publicly held investors were probably uncom- fortable with that form, if only because of a lack of familiarity and, perhaps, the residual threat of personal liability. Historically, there- fore, where public ownership was contemplated, limited partner- ships were a less attractive form than corporations. Where the business was to have more than one owner, but was not to be publicly held, as a practical matter the choice had to be made between three forms—general partnership, limited partnership, or corporation. Indeed, the effective choice often was between only two forms. Either the choice was between a corporation and a limited partnership, because not all the owners were to be active in the business, or the choice was between a corporation and a general partnership, because all the owners were to be active in the business.

Today, however, the choice of form has become more complex. For business enterprises that are to be publicly held, limited partnerships are no longer uncommon, although their use has undoubtedly been made much less attractive by an amendment to the Internal Revenue Code under which "publicly traded limited partnerships" are normally treated like corporations for tax purposes. (See Chapter 2, Section 10.)

For business enterprises that are not to be publicly held, the choice is much more difficult. Even if the choice were confined to the traditional forms of business organization, more flexible statutes and sophisticated drafting usually can eliminate many of the substantive differences between forms, and economic reality often minimizes the remaining differences. For example: (i) Limited partners can achieve limited liability for all members by utilizing a corporate general partner. Even partners in a general partnership can reduce their exposure to liability by purchasing insurance for the partnership. (ii) Limited partnerships automatically have centralized management, and general partnerships can be structured to have centralized management. (iii) A general or limited partnership can be structured so that even if the partnership is technically dissolved, its business can be continued by non-withdrawing partners. In any event, as a business matter corporations that are not publicly held are likely to run their course over a limited term regardless of their legally perpetual duration. (iv) Shares in such corporations are usually not easy to transfer as a practical matter, and often the transferability of such shares is limited by contract. (v) Even under the UPA, partnerships are treated as if they were entities for so many purposes that the difference between the partnership and corporate forms in this regard is inconsequential. Furthermore, RUPA formally confers entity status on partnerships.

The tax comparison of the traditional forms has also blurred. On the one hand, publicly traded limited partnerships are now normally taxed like corporations. On the other, the Internal Revenue Code provides a route through which partnership-tax treatment can be achieved by certain corporate enterprises. Subchapter S of the Code (I.R.C. §§ 1361–1379) permits the owners of qualifying corporations to elect a special tax status under which the corporation and its shareholders receive conduit-type taxation that is comparable (although not identical) to partnership taxation. The taxable income of an S corporation is computed essentially as if the corporation were an individual. I.R.C. § 1363(b). Items of income, loss, deduction, and credit, with some exceptions, are then passed through to the shareholders on a pro rata basis, and added to or subtracted from each shareholder's gross income. I.R.C. § 1366. Among the conditions for making and maintaining a

Subchapter S election are the following: (1) The corporation may not have more than thirty-five shareholders. (2) The corporation may not have more than one class of stock. (3) All the shareholders must be individuals or qualified estates or trusts. (4) No shareholder may be a nonresident alien. (5) The corporation may not be a member of an affiliated group of corporations.[1] I.R.C. § 1361. The amount of the corporation's assets and income is immaterial under Subchapter S. In 1991, 3,803,000 corporate returns were filed in the United States. Of these, 1,695,000 were filed by S corporations. U.S. Bureau of the Census, Statistical Abstract of the United States 543 (Table 840) (1994).

3. The complications caused by a blurring at the edges between the traditional forms has been compounded by the invention in recent years of two new forms. One of these new forms, the limited liability partnership, has already been considered. (See pp. 72–73, supra.) Another, the limited liability company, will be considered in the materials that follow.

DELAWARE LIMITED LIABILITY COMPANY ACT

[See Statutory Supplement]

UNIFORM LIMITED LIABILITY COMPANY ACT

[See Statutory Supplement]

FORM OF LIMITED LIABILITY COMPANY
OPERATING AGREEMENT

[See Statutory Supplement]

NOTE ON LIMITED LIABILITY COMPANIES

Limited Liability Companies ("LLCs") are a relatively new form of business organization. An LLC has been described as "a noncorporate business that provides its owners ('members') with limit-

---

1. The term *affiliated groups* refers primarily to corporations in a parent-subsidiary relationship where the parent possesses 80% of the voting power and the stock value of the subsidiary. See I.R.C. § 1504.

ed liability and allows them to participate actively in the entity's management." Keatinge, et al., The Limited Liability Company: A Study of the Emerging Entity, 47 Bus.Law. 375, 384 (1992). Some characteristics of the LLC resemble those of partnerships; other characteristics resemble those of corporations.

Although the LLC has historical precursors, essentially the form began with a 1977 Wyoming statute. For a while, the Internal Revenue Service took the position that LLCs would be treated as corporations for tax purposes, on the ground that an enterprise in which no member had unlimited liability could not be treated as a corporation. Eventually, however, the IRS concluded that limited liability for all members of an LLC would not in itself preclude partnership-tax status. Instead, the IRS will apply the "majority of characteristics" test developed in connection with limited partnerships. (See Note on Limited Partnerships, p. 70, supra.) Under that test a business organization that is not in form a corporation will be taxed as a partnership if the organization has no more than three of the following characteristics: limited liability, free transferability of interests, unlimited life, and centralized management. Because the members of an LLC will by definition have limited liability, as a practical matter an LLC will be accorded partnership tax status only if it has no more than two of the other three characteristics.

The need to avoid those characteristics shapes both the LLC statutes and the formation of individual LLCs. Some statutes limit the characteristics of an LLC in such a way that an LLC formed under these statutes will necessarily have enough noncorporate characteristics to ensure that it will be treated as a partnership for tax purposes. These statutes are sometimes called "bulletproof" statutes. Other statutes allow much more flexibility. These are sometimes called "flexible" statutes. An LLC organized under a flexible statute may or may not be treated as a partnership for tax purposes, depending on the characteristics it is given in its organizational documents.

KEATINGE, NEW GANG IN TOWN
Business Law Today, March/April 1995, at 5.*

History is the progression of revolution becoming orthodoxy. The limited liability company (LLC) is at the transition point between being a revolutionary idea and being an established alternative that must be considered in analyzing any business organization. Forty-seven states and the District of Columbia have LLC legislation, and bills have been introduced in the other three. Now that LLCs have attained virtually universal legislative acceptance, business lawyers and their clients need to understand their organization and use.

* Copyright American Bar Association.
Reprinted with permission.

Several definitions are helpful: A **limited liability company** is an organization in which the owners, known as members, are not individually liable for the obligations and liabilities of the organization.

A **member** is the owner of an interest in the LLC and a party to the contract (generally known as an operating agreement). The **operating agreement** (sometimes known as "regulations," "limited liability company agreement," or "member control agreement") is the agreement among the members setting forth their rights and duties. State statutes vary on whether the operating agreement or some provisions of it must be in writing. Some require that the entire agreement be in writing. Others, following partnership laws, permit nonwritten operating agreements to govern all, or all but a few, of the relationships among the members and between the members and the LLC. The **articles of organization** is a filed document that creates the LLC, provides certain information about it, and, under some statutes, constitutes a superagreement among the members.

There are two types of LLCs: **member-managed**, in which members have statutorily granted agency and the authority to make management decisions; and **manager-managed**, in which members are not agents of the LLC and, generally, have the authority to make only major decisions, and in which **managers** (who are not necessarily members) exercise statutorily granted agency authority, and, in some cases, authority to make most ordinary management decisions.

To a far greater extent than is true of the corporation, an LLC may be organized in accordance with the agreement of the members. Most statutes (known as **flexible statutes**) permit the members to enter into any agreement they desire to govern the internal relationships, limited only by certain broad public policy restrictions. Others (**bulletproof statutes**) limit the ability of members to vary certain provisions that are considered essential to federal tax classification [as partnerships]. Because the flexible statutes permit organizers to waive many corporate characteristics, there is both a maximum of flexibility and a requirement that the most care [be exercised] to ensure that partnership classification is attained.

With these exceptions, the principle of freedom of contract underlies all LLCs. As such, some statutes expressly refer to the public policy favoring the enforcement of the operating agreement among the members.

The concept of a contractual arrangement that affords limited liability like a corporation but also provides the freedom to establish ownership and management relationships based on the contract of the parties and that is treated as a partnership for tax purposes has long been considered to be the ideal business vehicle. . . .

An LLC is a separate legal entity. It acts through its statutorily authorized agents (members in a member-managed LLC and managers in a manager-managed LLC), and any other agents the LLC chooses to designate. A member-managed LLC is similar to a partnership in this respect since its owners are agents of the organization for carrying on its usual business. In this respect, a manager-managed LLC in which the managers are periodically elected resembles a corporation.

No member of an LLC, simply by virtue of being a member, is liable for its obligations. In this respect the LLC is similar to a corporation, in which ownership of an interest in the organization does not impose personal liability on the owners, and unlike a partnership, there is no owner who has unlimited individual liability for its obligations. Of course each member is personally liable under that member's guarantee [if any,] and for damages resulting from that member's wrongful act.

This lack of individual liability also extends to the relationships among members. In a partnership, general partners have an obligation to contribute to the partnership and to indemnify other partners for losses and obligations incurred in carrying on the business.

While an LLC is generally required to indemnify a member for obligations incurred by the member in carrying on the business of the LLC, no such individual contribution obligations exist for members. To the extent that the LLC does not have sufficient assets to fully indemnify the member, the member may not look to the individual assets of other members for contribution, as may a partner in a general partnership.

The dissociation of a member (death, bankruptcy, dissolution or other event that causes a person to cease to be a member) will cause a dissolution of the LLC unless the remaining members consent to continue the business, in which case the LLC continues.

Members generally have the right to transfer their economic rights to third parties, but the transferees do not have the right to take part in the management of the LLC, demand information or exercise other powers of members unless admitted by the consent of the nontransferring members.

Under flexible statutes, these rules are subject to modification by agreement of the members. Such modifications should be done carefully to avoid jeopardizing the tax classification.

Under most LLC statutes, members have the right to withdraw at any time and demand payment for their interest. This right to "put" an interest back into the LLC is similar to the rule that applies to partnerships. Recent amendments to some statutes have changed this rule to limit members' rights to withdraw or to demand that the LLC purchase their interests unless the members have agreed otherwise. . . .

In comparison to the corporation, an LLC has the advantages of flexibility and directness. Rather than setting forth the relationship among the owners and employees of a small business in articles of incorporation, bylaws, buy-sell agreements and employment contracts as is the case with a corporation, the members of an LLC may deal with all of these matters in a single consistent document—the operating agreement.

As an established business organization, a corporation enjoys the advantages of wider recognition, simplicity and economy of formation. Corporations tend to be less expensive to form than LLCs and partnerships because fewer decisions have to be made to create them. Articles of incorporation and bylaws are far more standard than operating agreements, which should be designed to address the client's specific needs.

On the other hand, an operating agreement is more likely to accurately represent the full agreement of the parties than simply drafted corporate documents, and if corporate documents sufficient to address all of the issues that must be covered in an operating agreement are drafted, the cost and time involved will probably meet or exceed the cost of an operating agreement.

Recent developments in corporate law, such as the elimination of the concept of par value with all its related trappings and the advent of the statutory close corporation show a movement toward simpler, more flexible, corporations. The LLC, however, attains that simplicity directly, rather than through the modification of a more complex corporate structure.

In comparison with partnerships, an LLC has the advantage of not requiring any owner to be personally liable for its debts and obligations. With the recent development of limited liability partnerships (LLPs) and limited liability limited partnerships (LLLPs), this advantage may diminish over time. In addition, in comparison with general partnerships organized under most versions of the Uniform Partnership Act, an LLC does not necessarily dissolve on the dissociation of a member. This is particularly helpful where the organization holds real estate or other rights, the title to which might be adversely affected by the dissolution and reformation that technically accompanies the dissociation of a partner from a general partnership. For example, see *Fairway Development Co. v. Title Insurance Co. of Minnesota,* 621 F.Supp. 120 (N.D.Ohio 1985).

The LLC offers the advantage of allowing members to participate in the control of the business without the risk of the loss of liability protection. In this respect, members have an advantage over limited partners.

While LLCs if properly organized are partnerships for tax purposes, the application of the partnership tax rules to LLCs is not yet clear, although recently issued guidance has significantly reduced this concern. Thus, partnerships, like corporations, offer greater certainty as to tax treatment. This same novelty may cause some concern in the application of nontax laws to LLCs. This concern should diminish over the next few years as people become familiar with LLCs and develop rules to deal with them . . . .

———

For an exposition of the relative tax advantages and disadvantages of LLCs, "C" (ordinary) corporations, and S Corporations, see Jelsma, How do LLCs Stack Up?, Business Law Today, March/April 1995, at 32.

SECTION 2.   SELECTING A STATE OF INCORPORATION

NOTE ON COMPETITION AMONG THE STATES FOR INCORPORATIONS

1.   Once the owners of a business decide to incorporate, they must determine in which state they should incorporate.   Under traditional choice-of-law rules, a corporation's internal affairs are governed by the law of its state of incorporation even if the corporation has no other contact with that state.[1]   A corporation with only a few owners—a "close corporation"—will almost invariably incorporate locally, that is, in the state where it has its principal place of business.   Incorporation in some other state—"out-of-state incorporation"—will usually be unnecessary, because for most practical purposes the various state statutes now offer fairly comparable legal regimes to close corporations.   Out-of-state incorporation may also increase costs.   A corporation normally must pay taxes to the state of incorporation for the privilege of organizing within that state and maintaining its corporate status.   It must also pay taxes to the local state for the privilege of doing business in that state.   Elements of the manner in which these two taxes are measured may overlap, so that total taxes will be less if the corporation is incorporated in the state in which it does most of its business.   Furthermore, local attorneys, familiar with local corporate law, may be hesitant about rendering formal opinions on the laws of other states.   The attorney for a close corporation is therefore likely to be more comfortable if the business is incorporated locally, and legal costs may be less because the attorney will not need to regularly consult with out-of-state counsel.

In the case of a publicly held corporation, a different calculus prevails.   On the corporation's side of the equation, the legal regimes offered by various states may differ significantly.   The rules governing such issues as what transactions require shareholder approval and trigger appraisal rights, and how are the fiduciary duties of directors and officers enforced, may vary dramatically across state lines.   The extra costs attendant on out-of-state incorpo-

---

1. Statutes in some states vary this rule under limited circumstances. See, e.g., Cal. Corp.Code § 2115 (subjecting certain for-

eign corporations to the state's corporate laws); N.Y.Bus.Corp.Law §§ 1317–1320.

ration may be inconsequential in comparison with the corporation's total revenues and the comparative advantages of a particular state's legal regime.

On the state's side of the equation, franchise-tax revenues represent a potentially enormous source of revenue to a state, like Delaware, with a small fiscal base. Such a state therefore has a great economic incentive to tailor its corporation-law regime in a way that will attract incorporation.

2. Delaware is far and away the preeminent state in terms of the number of publicly held corporations incorporated there. Many states have striven to match or outmatch Delaware in attracting publicly held corporations. What accounts for Delaware's continued success? First, Delaware is reliable. Both history and structural political factors help to assure corporations that Delaware, more than most states, will be responsive to corporate needs on a continuing basis. Second, Delaware offers corporations more than a statute. It also has an unusually well-developed case law in the corporate area. Its law is therefore much more predictable than that of many states.[2] Third, a Delaware corporate address is accepted, perhaps even prestigious. The investment community does not look askance when a corporation reincorporates in Delaware to take advantage of some new provision of the Delaware statute. In contrast, reincorporation in another tiny state for the same purpose might raise eyebrows.

Because the law of the state of incorporation normally governs internal corporate affairs, and because Delaware is preeminent for publicly held corporations, the Delaware statute provides a major axis of this book. A second major axis is provided by the Revised Model Business Corporation Act, promulgated by the Committee on Corporate Laws of the ABA's Section of Business Law. Although the Model Act itself has no official status, it has served as a template for the statutes of many states.

———

SECTION 3.   ORGANIZING A CORPORATION

Once a decision has been made to incorporate, and the state of incorporation has been selected, the next step is to create or "organize" the corporation. The first stage of the organization process, and the most critical from a legal perspective, is to file a "certificate of incorporation" or "articles of incorporation" or "charter" (the nomenclature varies from state to state) with the relevant state official—usually the secretary of state.

———

2. As Romano points out, this also gives attorneys an incentive to advise Delaware incorporation. Romano, The State Compe-tition Debate in Corporate Law, 8 Cardozo L.Rev. 709, 723 (1987).

DEL. GEN. CORP. LAW §§ 101, 102, 103, 106, 107, 108, 109

[See Statutory Supplement] *

REV. MODEL BUS. CORP. ACT §§ 2.01, 2.02, 2.03(a), 2.05, 2.06

[See Statutory Supplement]

FORM OF CERTIFICATE OF INCORPORATION

[See Statutory Supplement]

NOTE ON AUTHORIZED AND ISSUED STOCK AND ON PREEMPTIVE RIGHTS

An important function of a certificate of incorporation is to designate the classes of stock, and the number of shares of each class, that the corporation is *authorized* to issue. If the corporation's authorized stock consists of one class of common stock, the certificate need only designate the number of authorized shares. If there is to be more than one class of stock, and particularly if there is to be one or more classes of preferred stock (that is, stock that carries a preference as to dividends, on liquidation, or both, over common stock), the certificate of incorporation must either (i) designate the terms of each class or (ii) authorize the board to issue portions of the authorized class in series from time to time and to designate the terms of each series as it is issued. In either event, the power to *issue* authorized stock, and the price at which the stock will be issued, is in the hands of the board, subject only to certain very limited constraints.

At common law, one of these constraints was that each existing shareholder had the right to subscribe to her proportionate part of a new issue of stock of the class she held. This is known as the "preemptive right." The right was riddled with exceptions—for example, it did not apply to stock that was issued for property rather than cash. Modern statutes provide that shareholders have no preemptive rights unless the certificate of incorporation provides such a right. Few do.

Even where shareholders have no preemptive rights, the board may not issue stock for the purpose of reallocating or perpetuating

---

* Corporations and Business Associations, Statutes, Rules, and Forms (M. Eisenberg, ed.).

control. See, e.g., Schwartz v. Marien, 37 N.Y.2d 487, 373 N.Y.S.2d 122, 335 N.E.2d 334 (1975). And under basic fiduciary principles, the board cannot issue stock to individual directors at an unfairly low price. The right to prohibit a non-pro-rata stock issuance for an improper purpose is sometimes referred to as the "quasi-preemptive right."

NOTE ON THE BASIC MODES OF CORPORATE FINANCE

The three major modes of corporate finance are common stock, preferred stock, and debt. The basic concepts and underlying elements of these modes may be mixed and matched to create further modes.

Common stock. The basic concept of common stock is that of ultimate or residual ownership. "Common shareholders are often thought of as the owners of the firm or as the holders of the equity interest in the firm.... The equity interest is sometimes usefully thought of as the residual interest—the claim to what is left after all senior elements have been satisfied." W. Klein & J. Coffee, Business Organization and Finance 271 (5th ed. 1993).

The "senior elements" to which Coffee & Klein refer are debt and preferred stock.

Debt. The basic concept of debt is a fixed claim against the corporation for principal and interest. The major forms of corporate debt are described as follows by Professors Brudney and Bratton in V. Brudney & W. Bratton, Corporate Finance—Cases and Materials 150–152 (4th ed. 1993).

1. *Bonds, Debentures, and Notes.*

All of these are long term promissory notes. No inherent or legally recognized definition distinguishes one from the other. As a matter of historical practice, bonds and debentures are long term obligations issued under indentures, bonds generally being secured obligations and debentures being unsecured obligations. Under the historical practice, notes may be long term or short term obligations, but in either case are not issued pursuant to an indenture. Recent practice has changed this. Today, "notes" often are issued pursuant to indentures as unsecured long term obligations. But they tend to be intermediate term securities, coming due in ten years or less, where "debentures" tend to mature in ten years or more.

A bond, debenture or note is simply a promise by the borrower to pay a specified amount on a specified date, together with interest at specified times, on the terms and subject to the conditions spelled out in a governing indenture or note agreement. Bonds, debentures and notes are, then, promissory notes issued pursuant to and governed by longer contracts. Some of the governing terms and conditions will be set out on the face of the promissory note itself. Most terms, however, will be in the contract that governs the instrument and will be merely referred to on its face. The note incorporates the contract by reference.

It is the practice in both financial and legal writing to use "bond" as a generic term for all long term debt securities. . . .

2. *Indentures.*

An indenture is a contract entered into between the borrowing corporation and a trustee. The trustee administers the payments of interest and principal, and monitors and enforces compliance with other obligations on behalf of the bondholders as a group. The indenture defines the assorted obligations of the borrower, the rights and remedies of the holders of the bonds, and the role of the trustee.

The borrower contracts with a trustee rather than directly with the holders of the bonds so as to permit the bonds to be sold in small denominations to large numbers of scattered investors. Given widespread ownership in small amounts, unilateral monitoring and enforcement by each holder is not cost effective. The device of the trust solves this problem. . . .

The student should keep in mind a distinction between the "bonds" and the "indenture." The bonds set out a promise to pay that runs to the holders of the bonds. The indenture is a bundle of additional promises (including a backup promise to pay) that run to the trustee. The holders of the bonds are third party beneficiaries of the promises in the indenture. Even though the promises in the bonds run directly to the holders, the bonds are subject to the indenture, and therefore may be enforced directly by the holders only to the extent that the indenture allows. Indentures generally constrain the unilateral enforcement rights of small holders, channelling enforcement through the central agency of the trustee. The device of the trust indenture, then, not only facilitates enforcement by the widely scattered holders, but also restrains such enforcement. It facilitates borrowing in small amounts from large numbers of widely scattered lenders not only by constraining the issuer as against the holders, but by protecting the issuer from the holders.

Preferred stock. The basic concept of preferred stock is a hybridization of the ownership element of common stock and the senior nature of debt. The basic elements of such stock are described as follows in Hunt, Williams & Donaldson, Basic Business Finance 358–61 (5th ed. 1974):

From the purely legal point of view . . . preferred stock is a type of ownership and thus takes a classification similar to that of the common stock. Accounting practice recognizes this by placing preferred stock along with common stock in the net worth section of the balance sheet, and tax laws interpret preferred dividends as a distribution of net profits to the owners rather than a cost of the business, as in the case of bond interest.... Unlike [a] bond, ... preferred stock does not contain any promise of repayment of the original investment; and as far as the shareholders are concerned, this must be considered as a permanent investment for the life of the company. Further, there is no legal obligation to pay a fixed rate of return on the investment.

The special character of the preferred stock lies in its relationship to the common stock. When a preferred stock is used as a part of the corporate capital structure, the rights and responsibilities of the owners as the residual claimants to the asset values and earning power of the business no longer apply equally to all shareholders. Two types of owners emerge, representing a voluntary subdivision of the overall ownership privileges. Specifically, the common shareholders agree that the preferred shareholder shall have "preference" or first claim in the event that the directors are able and willing to pay a dividend. In the case of what is termed a nonparticipating or *straight preferred stock*, which is the most frequent type, the extent of this priority is a fixed percentage of the par value of the stock or a fixed number of dollars per share in the case of stock without a nominal or par value....

In most cases the prior position of preferred stock also extends to the disposition of assets in the event of liquidation of the business. Again, the priority is only with reference to the common stock and does not affect the senior position of creditors in any way....[1]

Typically, preferred stock carries a dividend that is payable periodically—say, quarterly—in the board's discretion. Thus the most obvious difference between debt and preferred stock is that debt holders have a fixed claim on the corporation for interest and principal, while preferred shareholders normally have no fixed claims for distributions. Instead, the claims of preferred stock for distributions are only contingent. *If* the corporation proposes to pay a dividend on common, then it must first pay a designated dividend to the preferred. *If* the corporation liquidates, then before it distributes anything to the common it must satisfy the preferred's liquidation preference.

Often, preferred is given the right to vote on the election of directors if, but only if, preferred dividends are in default for a designated number of periods. Often too, the preferred's dividend preference is "cumulative"—that is, no dividend can be paid on common unless all prior dividends on the preferred have been paid.

---

1. As quoted in V. Brudney & W. Bratton, Corporate Finance—Cases and Materials 335–36 (4th ed. 1993).

(If a preferred is noncumulative, a dividend can be paid on common as long as the current dividend on the preferred is paid.)

There are very important tax differences between preferred stock and debt. Dividends paid to preferred are not an "expense" to the corporation, and therefore do not reduce the corporation's income for tax purposes. In contrast, interest payable on debt is an expense, and therefore reduces the corporation's taxable income. On the other hand, interest is normally taxable to the recipient. In contrast, while dividends are normally taxable to the recipient, dividends may not be fully taxable to the recipient, or may even be nontaxable, if the recipient-owner of the stock is a corporation and certain conditions are met.

3. *Convertibles, classified stock, and derivatives.* In the modern world, the basic elements of common stock, preferred stock, and debt are often just ingredients for designing more exotic corporate securities. For example, many preferred stocks, and some bonds, are made convertible into common, at the option of the holder, on specified terms. Preferred is often issued in several classes, and common may be issued in several classes as well ("classified common"). In such cases, each class enjoys somewhat different rights than the others, usually in respect of voting, dividend, or liquidation rights, or all three. (It is not unusual, in the case of classified common, for one class to be more desirable than another class in some respects and less desirable in others.) Furthermore, securities may be designed that are "derived" from common, in the sense that although the securities are not themselves common stocks, their value largely depends on the value of common and on the terms of their relationship to the common. The simplest example is a "right" or "warrant," which is a security issued by the corporation that gives the holder a right or option to purchase common on stated terms.

––––––

NOTE ON INITIAL DIRECTORS

Once a corporation is under way, its board of directors is elected by the shareholders. However, there can be no shareholders until stock is issued, and the function of issuing stock is normally committed to the board. Accordingly, there must be a mechanism for either naming directors before stock is issued, or for issuing stock before directors are elected by the shareholders. There are two basic statutory patterns for solving this problem. Under the law of some states, like New York, the corporation's incorporators have the powers of shareholders until stock is issued, and the powers of directors until directors are elected. N.Y.Bus. Corp.Law §§ 404(a), 615(c). Under such a statute, the incorporators will typically adopt by-laws, fix the number of directors, and elect directors to serve until the first annual meeting of sharehold-

ers.   See N.Y.Bus.Corp.Law § 404(a).   Under the law of other
states, like Delaware, the incorporators have the powers of shareholders and directors unless initial directors are named in the
corporation's   certificate   of   incorporation.   Del.Gen.Corp.Law
§§ 107, 108.   If the initial directors are named in the certificate of
incorporation, the functions of the incorporators pass to the directors when the certificate is filed and recorded.   Del.Gen.Corp.
Law §§ 107, 108(a).

Once the initial directors are named, either by the incorporators or by the certificate of incorporation, they will hold an
organization meeting.   A typical agenda for such a meeting is
reflected in the Form of Minutes that follows.

———

FORM OF MINUTES OF ORGANIZATION MEETING

[See Statutory Supplement]

———

NOTE ON SUBSCRIPTIONS FOR SHARES

Normally, stock is issued by a corporation in a simultaneous
exchange for cash or property.   In some cases, however, a would-be
shareholder enters into a "subscription agreement," under which
he agrees to purchase a corporation's stock when it is issued to him
at some future date.   Typically, in such cases, the corporation has
not yet been formed.   (The agreement is then made on the would-
be corporation's behalf by incorporators, agents, or trustees.)
Agreements of this type are called pre-incorporation subscription
agreements.

There is a good deal of old law on various aspects of such
agreements.   The general rule was that a pre-incorporation subscription was only a continuing offer by the subscriber, and that a
subscriber therefore was not bound if he made a timely revocation.
Under this rule, a subscriber could revoke until the moment of
incorporation or, in the alternative, until some kind of effective
action had been taken by the corporation after it was formed.
(There was an exception where the mutual promises of subscribers
were expressed as consideration for each other.   In that case, a
contract was formed immediately.   In addition, subscription agreements entered into after the corporation was formed were treated
as ordinary contracts, and raised no special problems of enforceabil-
ity.)

This treatment of pre-incorporation subscription agreements
has been changed by the modern corporate statutes.   Most statutes
now provide that pre-incorporation subscriptions are irrevocable for
a specified period of time, unless all the subscribers consent to a

revocation or the agreement otherwise provides. See, e.g., Del. Gen.Corp.Law § 165 (preincorporation subscription agreements irrevocable for six months except with the consent of all other subscribers); RMBCA § 6.20(a) (same). As a practical matter, because of these statutory changes the law relating to subscriptions is of greatly diminished importance today, and current cases on the subject are rare.

―――――

FORM OF BY–LAWS

[See Statutory Supplement]

―――――

FORM OF STOCK CERTIFICATE

[See Statutory Supplement]

―――――

DEL. GEN. CORP. LAW § 109

[See Statutory Supplement]

―――――

REV. MODEL BUS. CORP. ACT §§ 2.06, 10.20–10.22

[See Statutory Supplement]

―――――

SECTION 4.   PREINCORPORATION TRANSACTIONS BY PROMOTERS

―――――

INTRODUCTORY NOTE

The term *promoter* has an invidious sound to most of us. To quote Professor L.C.B. Gower:

> If, in a psycho-analyst's consulting room, we were asked to say what picture formed in our minds at the mention of the expression "company promoter," most of us would probably confess that we envision a character of dubious repute and antecedents who infests the commercial *demi-monde* with a

menagerie of bulls, bears, stags, and sharks as his familiars, and who, after rising to affluence by preying on the susceptibilities of a gullible public, finally retires from the scene in the blaze of a sensational suicide or Old Bailey trial. In other words, we should envisage someone whose profession it was to form bogus companies and foist them off on the public to the latter's detriment and his own profit. Such figures have existed and it is probably too much to hope that they will ever be entirely eradicated, but even in their Edwardian heyday they formed only the minutest fraction of those whom the law classifies as promoters.

L. Gower, J. Cronin, A. Easson, & Lord Wedderburn of Charlton, Gower's Principles of Modern Company Law 324 (4th Ed.1979) (footnotes omitted). See also A. Dewing, Financial Policy of Corporations 402–11 (5th ed. 1953).

The promoter, however, performs a necessary and useful economic service. He is the person who transforms an idea into a business capable of generating a profit, who brings and holds together the persons needed, and who superintends the various steps required to bring the new business into existence. He contributes business imagination, plus the judgment and skill to execute the idea. As noted by Justice Rugg in Old Dominion Copper Mining & Smelting Co. v. Bigelow, 203 Mass. 159, 177, 89 N.E. 193, 201 (1909):

> In a comprehensive sense promoter includes those who undertake to form a corporation and to procure for it the rights, instrumentalities and capital by which it is to carry out the purposes set forth in its charter, and to establish it as fully able to do its business. Their work may begin long before the organization of the corporation, in seeking the opening for a venture and projecting a plan for its development, and it may continue after the incorporation by attracting the investment of capital in its securities and providing it with the commercial breath of life.

A corporate promotion includes three stages: discovery, investigation, and assembly. H. Guthmann & H. Dougall, Corporate Financial Policy 248 (4th ed. 1962). The discovery stage involves the generation of an idea, such as the perception of a need for a new product or service or for another company in an existing line of business. The investigation stage involves an analysis of what resources will be required to turn the idea into a business and whether the estimated earnings will justify the costs. The assembly stage involves bringing property, money, and personnel together into an organization.

Often, as part of the assembly stage, contracts are made for the benefit of the corporation even before the corporation has been formed. If, as is usually the case, the corporation is later formed, and benefits from such a contract, issues may arise regarding whether the corporation becomes liable under the contract, and whether the promoter remains liable. This Section addresses those issues.

––––––

(a) LIABILITY OF THE PROMOTER

––––––

GOODMAN v. DARDEN, DOMAN & STAFFORD ASSOCIATES

Supreme Court of Washington, En Banc, 1983.
100 Wash.2d 476, 670 P.2d 648.

DIMMICK, Justice.

John Goodman signed a contract as president of a corporation "in formation." The narrow issue in the instant appeal is whether Goodman, as an individual, is a party to arbitration proceedings brought under the contract. The trial court held he was not. The Court of Appeals reversed, holding the evidence was insufficient to support the trial court's conclusion. We affirm the Court of Appeals.

Goodman, a real estate salesman, sold an apartment building to Darden, Doman & Stafford Associates (hereafter DDS), a general partnership. The apartments needed extensive renovation and Goodman represented that he personally had experience in renovation work. During the course of negotiations on a renovation contract, Goodman informed Don Doman, managing partner of DDS, that he would be forming a corporation in order to limit his personal liability.

A contract was executed in August 1979 between DDS and "BUILDING DESIGN AND DEVELOPMENT INC. (In Formation) John A. Goodman, President." The partners of DDS knew that the corporation was not yet in existence and they testified at trial that they never agreed to look solely to the corporation for performance of the contract. The contract required that work be completed by October 15 and contained an arbitration clause. Goodman immediately subcontracted the work. The work was not completed by October 15 and the work which was done was allegedly of poor quality. On November 1, after this apparent default, Goodman filed articles of incorporation. A corporate license was issued the next day. The first meeting of the board of directors was not held until February 1980.

Between August and December 1979 DDS made five progress payments on the contract. The first check was made out to "Building Design and Development [*Sic*] Inc.—John Goodman." Goodman struck out his name and endorsed the check "Bldg. Design & Dev. Inc., John A. Goodman, Pres." He instructed DDS to make further payments to the corporation only.

In May 1980, after attempts to remedy the alleged breaches, DDS served Goodman with a demand for arbitration. The demand named both the corporation and Goodman. The record is not clear as to the present status of the corporation although it shows some effort on Goodman's part to sell the corporation. Goodman moved for a stay of arbitration and an order dismissing him from the arbitration proceedings. The trial court entered an order dismissing Goodman, as an individual, from the arbitration. The Court of Appeals reversed. *Goodman v. Darden, Doman & Stafford Assocs.,* 33 Wash.App. 278, 653 P.2d 1371 (1982).

The issue in this appeal is whether Goodman, as a promoter, is a party to the preincorporation contract and as such whether he is required to take part in the arbitration. As a general rule

> where a corporation is contemplated but has not yet been organized at the time when a promoter makes a contract for the benefit of the contemplated corporation, the promoter is personally liable on it, even though the contract will also benefit the future corporation.

Harding v. Will, 81 Wash.2d 132, 139, 500 P.2d 91 (1972); *Heintze Corp., Inc. v. Northwest Tech–Manuals, Inc.,* 7 Wash.App. 759, 760, 502 P.2d 486 (1972)[3]; *Refrigeration Eng'g Co. v. McKay,* 4 Wash. App. 963, 972, 486 P.2d 304 (1971); 18 Am.Jur.2d *Corporations* § 127 (1965); Annot., *Personal Liability of Promoter to Third Person on or With Respect to Contract Made for Corporation or in Aid of Promotion,* 41 A.L.R.2d 477 (1955). There is a "strong inference that a person intends to make a present contract with an existing person." *White & Bollard, Inc. v. Goodenow,* 58 Wash.2d 180, 184, 361 P.2d 571 (1961).

An exception to the general rule is that if the contracting party knew that the corporation was not in existence at the time of contracting but nevertheless agreed to look solely to the corporation for performance, the promoter is not a party to the contract. *Heintze Corp.* See also *Frazier v. Ash,* 234 F.2d 320 (5th Cir.1956); *Sherwood & Roberts–Oregon, Inc. v. Alexander,* 269 Or. 389, 525 P.2d 135 (1974); 18 Am.Jur.2d *Corporations* § 127 (1965); Annot., 41 A.L.R.2d 477.

As the proponent of the alleged agreement to look solely to the corporation, Goodman has the burden of proving the agreement. *Johnson v. Nasi,* 50 Wash.2d 87, 309 P.2d 380 (1957). As with any

---

3. The *Heintze* court held that RCW 23A.44.100 codified this rule. That statute states: "All persons who assume to act as a corporation without authority so to do shall be jointly and severally liable for all debts and liabilities incurred or arising as a result thereof." The Supreme Court of Oregon has criticized this reasoning, stating that RCW 23A.44.100 was only intended to abolish the doctrine of de facto corporations and not to alter the liability of promoters. *Sherwood & Roberts–Oregon, Inc. v. Alex-* ander, 269 Or. 389, 525 P.2d 135 (1974). *Roberts* nonetheless held that the common law rule is the same as that applied in *Heintze.* Because the common law in this state is well settled as to promoter liability and the parties rely on that common law, we expressly decline at this time to decide whether the purpose of RCW 23A.44.100 is to codify these common law principles on promoter liability or to abolish de facto corporations.

agreement, release of the promoter depends on the intent of the parties. The parties did not manifest their intentions in the contract. Goodman argues that the language indicating that the corporation was "in formation" was an expression by the parties of their intent to make the corporation alone a party to the contract. Some courts do look to such language in the contract and contemporaneous documents to determine intent to release the promoter. *See Stap v. Chicago Aces Tennis Team, Inc.,* 63 Ill.App.3d 23, 20 Ill.Dec. 230, 379 N.E.2d 1298 (1978); *H.F. Philipsborn & Co. v. Suson,* 59 Ill.2d 465, 322 N.E.2d 45 (1974); *Schwedtman v. Burns,* 11 S.W.2d 348 (Tex.Civ.App.1928). Those cases and others cited by Goodman do not analyze the agreements in light of a "strong inference" that one intends to contract with an existing party—an inference we must keep in mind. The mere signing of a contract with a corporation "in formation" does not suffice to show an agreement to look solely to the corporation. It simply begs the question to say that such language in a contract with a promoter in and of itself constitutes an agreement to release the promoter from the contract. Rather, the language raises the question of the parties' intent. Given the "strong inference" that DDS intended to contract with an existing party, the "in formation" language drafted by Goodman is at best ambiguous as to the parties' intentions.

Courts of other jurisdictions differ in their approach as to how specific the agreement must be to release a promoter from a contract and what evidence they will consider in determining the parties' intent. *See generally* Annot., 41 A.L.R.2d 447. As noted by the Court of Appeals:

> Some jurisdictions require that the contract show clearly on its face that there is *no* intent to hold the promoter liable before he is released. *Vodopich v. Collier Cy. Developers, Inc.,* 319 So.2d 43, 45 (Fla.App.1975). The agreement must be "specific" or "express." *Malisewski v. Singer,* 123 Ariz. 195, 598 P.2d 1014 (Ct.App.1979); *Spence v. Huffman,* 15 Ariz.App. 99, 486 P.2d 211 (1971). In *RKO–Stanley Warner Theatres, Inc. v. Graziano,* 467 Pa. 220, 223, 355 A.2d 830, 832 (1976), the contract stated:

>> "It is understood by the parties hereto that it is the intention of the Purchaser to incorporate. Upon condition that such incorporation be completed by closing, all agreements, covenants, and warranties contained herein shall be construed to have been made between Seller and the resultant corporation and all documents shall reflect same."

The court held that "while [this paragraph] does make provision for recognition of the resultant corporation as to the closing documents, it makes no mention of any release of personal liability." 467 Pa. at 226. Since the paragraph did not expressly provide for release on closing, the court found it ambiguous and construed it to hold the promoter liable until the corporation actually ratified the contract.

33 Wash.App., at 281–82, 653 P.2d 1371.

We do not believe the agreement to release a promoter from liability must say in so many words, "I agree to release." Where the promoter cannot show an express agreement, existence of the agreement to release him from liability may be shown by circumstances. Of course, where circumstantial evidence is relied on, the circumstances must be such as to make it reasonably certain that the parties intended to and did enter into the agreement. *Kellogg v. Gleeson,* 27 Wash.2d 501, 178 P.2d 969 (1947).

Goodman cites *Quaker Hill, Inc. v. Parr,* 148 Colo. 45, 364 P.2d 1056 (1961) and *Sherwood & Roberts–Oregon, Inc. v. Alexander, supra,* as cases similar to this one. The courts in those cases found that the promoter had been released from liability. Among the circumstances considered by those courts was the fact that the parties seeking personal liability on the part of the promoter actually urged that the contract be made in the name of the proposed corporation. DDS did not so urge Goodman or even suggest incorporation to him.

The trial court did not make a written finding that the parties intended to look solely to the corporation for performance. Thus we may look to the oral decision to clarify the theory on which the trial court decided the case. *Heikkinen v. Hansen,* 57 Wash.2d 840, 360 P.2d 147 (1961). From its oral opinion it is clear that the trial court relied on three considerations in holding that the parties agreed to release Goodman from the contract: (1) DDS knew of the corporation's nonexistence; (2) Goodman told Doman that he was forming a corporation to limit his personal liability; and (3) the progress payments were made to the corporation.

The fact that DDS knew of the corporation's nonexistence is not dispositive in any way of its intent. The rule is that the contracting party may know of the nonexistence of the corporation *but nevertheless* may agree to look solely to the corporation. The fact that a contracting party knows that the corporation is nonexistent does not indicate any agreement to release the promoter. To the contrary, such knowledge alone would seem to indicate that the members of DDS intended to make Goodman a party to the contract. They could not hold the corporation, a nonexistent entity, responsible and of course they would expect to have recourse against someone (Goodman) if default occurred. This consideration also relates to another factor the trial court apparently had in mind—that the members of DDS were all educated people. Goodman argues that as such they should have expressly requested that he be personally liable. This was unnecessary because under the law as set out above, Goodman was liable until the partners of DDS agreed otherwise. Thus, they were not required to specify personal liability.

The fact that Goodman expressed a desire to form the corporation to limit his liability also is not dispositive of the intentions of the members of DDS. No one from DDS objected to his incorporating but this failure to object does not indicate an affirmative assent to limit Goodman's personal liability. Apparently Goodman believed that incorporation would automatically limit his liability thus misunderstanding the rules regarding promoter liability. The Court of Appeals correctly held in this regard:

> Even if the expression of desire constituted an offer to make release a term of the contract, silence is acceptance only when there is a duty to speak. *American Aviation, Inc. v. Hinds,* 1 Wash.App. 959, 465 P.2d 676 (1970). DDS had no duty to correct, or even perceive, Goodman's mistaken interpretation of the promoter liability rules.

33 Wash.App. at 282, 653 P.2d 1371.

The only other evidence of the parties' intent to make the corporation the sole party to the contract is that the progress payments were made payable to the corporation. However, they were so written only at the instruction of Goodman and in fact the first check written by DDS after the signing of the contract was written to the corporation *and* Goodman as an individual. This evidence does not show by reasonable certainty that DDS intended to contract only with the corporation. *See Wolfe v. Warfield,* 266 Md. 621, 296 A.2d 158 (1972).

Goodman argues that we should not examine the evidence in this manner because in doing so we improperly reweigh it. We acknowledge appellate review is limited to determining whether a trial court's findings are supported by substantial evidence and, if so, whether the findings in turn support the conclusions of law. *Holland v. Boeing Co.,* 90 Wash.2d 384, 390, 583 P.2d 621 (1978). From the oral decision it is clear that the court made a finding that DDS intended to look solely to the corporation as a party to the contract based on the items of evidence discussed above. We can uphold this finding of intent only if the evidence supporting it is substantial; we find that it is not.

The trial court erred in dismissing Goodman from the arbitration proceedings. We therefore remand.

WILLIAM H. WILLIAMS, C.J., ROSELLINI, BRACHTENBACH and PEARSON, JJ., and HAMILTON, J. Pro Tem., concur.

DORE, Justice (dissenting).

The trial court found that Darden, Doman and Stafford Associates (DDS) intended to look solely to the corporation as the party of the contract. There is substantial evidence in the record to substantiate this finding. I would affirm the trial court and dismiss Goodman from the arbitration proceedings....

Doman made all checks out to the corporate name, Building Design and Development, Inc., at Goodman's request. The original check had been made out to both the corporation and Goodman individually, but Goodman had his name deleted and a new check issued in the name of the corporation only. Doman had no objection to this and impliedly acknowledged that he would look to the corporation and not to Goodman as an individual. All of such checks were deposited in the corporation's bank account at Rainier National Bank, Westlake branch. Neither Goodman nor the corporation profited from the Suncrest Apartments contract, and there was no commingling of the personal assets and liabilities of Goodman with the corporation.

On November 1, 1979, a certificate of incorporation was issued to Goodman. The court found that at that time the corporate entity was fully capitalized and operating. DDS was aware of the incorporation and continued to make the checks payable to the corporation. Subsequently, Goodman had the corporation ratify the contract as an action of the corporation. . . .

I would affirm the order of the trial court staying arbitration proceedings as to John Goodman individually.

DOLLIVER and UTTER, JJ., concur.

————

REV. MODEL BUS. CORP. ACT § 2.04

[See Statutory Supplement]

————

QUAKER HILL, INC. v. PARR, 148 Colo. 45, 364 P.2d 1056 (1961). Quaker Hill sold a large quantity of nursery stock to "Denver Memorial Nursery, Inc." A sales contract was executed together with a promissory note. The form of the signature on the note was as follows:

"Denver Memorial Nursery, Inc.

"E.D. Parr, Pres.

"James P. Presba, Sc'y.–Treas."

The signature on the contract was comparable.

As Quaker Hill knew, Denver Memorial Nursery, Inc. had not yet been formed when the contract was signed. Quaker Hill had insisted that the deal be consummated even before the corporation was formed, because the growing season was rapidly passing. About a week after the contract was signed, the corporation that was originally to be called Denver Memorial Nurseries, Inc. was formed under the name "Mountain View Nurseries, Inc." A new note and contract, prepared by Quaker Hill's Division Manager, and containing the name Mountain View Nurseries, Inc. as contracting party, was then submitted to Parr and Presba, signed in Mountain View's name, and returned to Quaker Hill. Quaker Hill thereafter used the designation Mountain View Nurseries in its communications.

Mountain View never functioned as a going concern, and Quaker Hill brought suit under the contract and note against Parr and Presba, in their individual capacities. Held, for defendants.

"The general principle which plaintiff urges as applicable here is that promoters are personally liable on their contracts, though made on behalf of a corporation to be formed. . . . A well recognized exception to this general rule, however, is that if the contract is made on behalf of the corporation and the other party agrees to look to the corporation and not to the promoters for payment, the promoters incur no personal liability.

"In the present case, according to the trial court's findings, the plaintiff, acting through its agent, was well aware of the fact that the corporation was not formed and nevertheless urged that the contract be made in the name of the proposed corporation. There is but little evidence indicating intent on the part of the plaintiff to look to the defendants for performance or payment. The single fact supporting plaintiff's theory is the obtaining of an individual balance sheet. On the contrary, the entire transaction contemplated the corporation as the contracting party. Personal liability does not arise under such circumstances. See 41 A.L.R.2d 477, where the annotation recognizes the noted exception that personal liability does not attach where the contracting party is shown to be looking solely to the corporation for payment and not to the promoters or officers."

RESTATEMENT (SECOND) OF AGENCY § 326

[See Statutory Supplement]

(b) LIABILITY OF THE CORPORATION

CLIFTON v. TOMB, 21 F.2d 893 (4th Cir.1927). ". . . Since a corporation before its organization cannot have agents, and is unable to contract or be contracted with, it is not liable upon any contract which a promoter attempts to make for it, unless it becomes so by its own act after its incorporation is completed. . . . But there are cases where a corporation becomes bound for the contracts of its promoters. While there are many decisions holding corporations liable in such cases, the courts have had great difficulty in finding a scientific or rational basis for sustaining such liability. The usual grounds that have been suggested are ratification, adoption, novation, and that the proposition made to the promoters is a continuing offer to be accepted or rejected by the corporation when it comes into being, and upon acceptance becomes an original contract on its part; and the liability has also been sustained on the ground that the corporation, by accepting the benefits of a contract, takes it cum onere, and is estopped to deny its liability on the contract."

SECTION 5. CONSEQUENCES OF DEFECTIVE INCORPORATION

CANTOR v. SUNSHINE GREENERY, INC.

Superior Court of New Jersey, Appellate Division, 1979.
165 N.J.Super. 411, 398 A.2d 571.

LARNER, J.

This appeal involves the propriety of a personal judgment against defendant William J. Brunetti for the breach of a lease between plaintiffs and a corporate entity known as Sunshine Greenery, Inc., and more particularly whether there was a *de facto* corporation in existence at the time of the execution of the lease.

Plaintiffs brought suit for damages for the breach of the lease against Sunshine Greenery, Inc. and Brunetti. Default judgment was entered against the corporation and a nonjury trial was held as to the liability of the individual. The trial judge in a letter opinion determined that plaintiffs were entitled to judgment against Brunetti individually on the theory that as of the time of the creation of the contract he was acting as a promoter and that his corporation, Sunshine Greenery, Inc., was not a legal or *de facto* corporation.

The undisputed facts reveal the following: Plaintiffs prepared the lease naming Sunshine Greenery, Inc. as the tenant, and it was signed by Brunetti as president of that named entity. Mr. Cantor, acting for plaintiffs, knew that Brunetti was starting a new venture as a newly formed corporation known as Sunshine Greenery, Inc. Although Cantor had considerable experience in ownership and leasing of commercial property to individuals and corporations, he did not request a personal guarantee from Brunetti, nor did he make inquiry as to his financial status or background. Without question, he knew and expected that the lease agreement was undertaken by the corporation and not by Brunetti individually, and that the corporation would be responsible thereunder.

At the time of the signing of the lease on December 16, 1974 in Cantor's office, Brunetti was requested by Cantor to give him a check covering the first month's rent and the security deposit. When Brunetti stated that he was not prepared to do so because he had no checks with him, Cantor furnished a blank check which was filled out for $1,200, with the name of Brunetti's bank and signed by him as president of Sunshine Greenery, Inc. The lease was repudiated by a letter from counsel for Sunshine Greenery, Inc. dated December 17, 1974, which in turn was followed by a response from Cantor to the effect that he would hold the "client" responsible for all losses. The check was not honored because Brunetti stopped payment, and in any event because Sunshine Greenery, Inc. did not have an account in the bank.

The evidence is clear that on November 21, 1974 the corporate name of Sunshine Greenery, Inc. had been reserved for Brunetti by the Secretary of State, and that on December 3, 1974 a certificate of incorporation for that company was signed by Brunetti and Sharyn N. Sansoni as incorporators. The certificate was forwarded by mail to the Secretary of State on that same date with a check for the filing fee, but for some unexplained reason it was not officially filed until December 18, 1974, two days after the execution of the lease.[1]

In view of the late filing, Sunshine Greenery, Inc. was not a *de jure* corporation on December 16, 1974 when the lease was signed. See N.J.S.A. 14A:2–7(2). Nevertheless, there is ample evidence of the fact that it was a *de facto* corporation in that there was a *bona fide* attempt to organize the corporation some time before the consummation of the contract and there was an actual exercise of the corporate powers by the negotiations with plaintiffs and the execution of the contract involved in this litigation. When this is considered in the light of the concession that plaintiffs knew that they were dealing with that corporate entity and not with Brunetti individually, it becomes evident that the *de facto* status of the corporation suffices to absolve Brunetti from individual liability. Plaintiffs in effect are estopped from attacking the legal existence of the corporation collaterally because of the nonfiling in order to impose liability on the individual when they have admittedly contracted with a corporate entity which had *de facto* status.... In fact, their prosecution of the claim against the corporation to default judgment is indicative of their recognition of the corporation as the true obligor and theoretically inconsistent with the assertion of the claim against the individual.

The trial judge's finding that Sunshine Greenery, Inc. was not a *de facto* corporation is unwarranted under the record facts herein. The mere fact that there were no formal meetings or resolutions or issuance of stock is not determinative of the legal or *de facto* existence of the corporate entity, particularly under the simplified New Jersey Business Corporation Act of 1969, which eliminates the necessity of a meeting of incorporators. See N.J.S.A. 14A:2–6 and Commissioners' Comment thereunder. The act of executing the certificate of incorporation, the *bona fide* effort to file it and the dealings with plaintiffs in the name of that corporation fully satisfy

---

1. We note that the letter enclosing the certificate of incorporation is addressed to "Mortimer G. Newman, Jr., Secretary of State, State House Annex, Trenton, New Jersey." Whether this misidentification of the person holding the office of Secretary of State accounts for the filing delay we are unable to say from the record.

the requisite proof of the existence of a *de facto* corporation. To deny such existence because of a mere technicality caused by administrative delay in filing runs counter to the purpose of the *de facto* concept, and would accomplish an unjust and inequitable result in favor of plaintiffs contrary to their own contractual expectations. . . .

In view of the foregoing, the judgment entered against defendant William J. Brunetti is reversed and set aside, and the matter is remanded to the Law Division to enter judgment on the complaint in favor of William J. Brunetti.

————

McLEAN BANK v. NELSON, 232 Va. 420, 350 S.E.2d 651 (1986). "It is the corporate form that provides limited liability. Without the corporation . . . personal liability exists. The limited liability provided by a de jure corporation is the exception, not the rule. . . . [I]f a group of individuals have not done the things necessary to secure or retain de jure corporate status, then they will not have corporate protection. They will be exposed to personal liability. . . ."

————

McCHESNEY, DOCTRINAL ANALYSIS AND STATISTICAL MODELING IN LAW: THE CASE OF DEFECTIVE INCORPORATION, 71 Wash. U. L.Q. 493, 498–99 (1993). "Three requirements are typically cited for application of the de facto corporation doctrine. There must have been: (1) a statute in existence by which incorporation was legally possible; (2) a 'colorable' attempt to comply with the statute; and (3) some actual use or exercise of corporate privileges. Because every state has a corporation statute and defendants ordinarily have been acting under the aegis of a supposed corporation, the three factors typically dissolve into one: whether defendants' attempts to incorporate had gone far enough to be deemed 'colorable compliance.' For example, an attempt to file the articles of incorporation, albeit unsuccessful, has frequently sufficed as the necessary attempt at statutory compliance. 'In addition, some cases and commentators have added good faith of corporation or associates as a fourth element. [The good faith requirement] is often omitted, however, because a colorable compliance with the incorporation statute usually encompasses a good faith attempt to incorporate.' "

————

TIMBERLINE EQUIPMENT CO. v. DAVENPORT

Supreme Court of Oregon, 1973.
267 Or. 64, 514 P.2d 1109.

DENECKE, Justice.

Plaintiff brought this action for equipment rentals against the defendant Dr. Bennett and two others. In addition to making a general denial, Dr. Bennett alleged as a defense that the rentals were to a de facto corporation, Aero–Fabb Corp., of which Dr. Bennett was an incorporator, director and shareholder. He also alleged plaintiff was estopped from denying the corporate character of the organization to whom plaintiff rented the equipment. The trial court held for plaintiff. Dr. Bennett, only, appeals.

On January 22, 1970, Dr. Bennett signed articles of incorporation for Aero–Fabb Co. The original articles were not in accord with the statutes and, therefore, no certificate of incorporation was issued for the corporation until June 12, 1970, after new articles were filed. The leases were entered into and rentals earned during the period between January 22nd and June 12th.

Prior to 1953 Oregon had adopted the common-law doctrine that prohibited a collateral attack on the legality of a defectively organized corporation which had achieved the status of a de facto corporation. See, for example, Marsters v. Umpqua Oil Co., 49 Or. 374, 377, 90 P. 151, 12 LRA(ns) 825 (1907).

In 1953 the legislature adopted the Oregon Business Corporation Act. Oregon Laws 1953, ch. 549. The Model Business Corporation Act was used as a working model for the Oregon Act. 1952 Oregon State Bar Committee Reports, p. 5.

ORS 57.321 of the Oregon Business Corporation Act provides:

"Upon the issuance of the certificate of incorporation, the corporate existence shall begin, and such certificate of incorporation shall be conclusive evidence that all conditions precedent required to be performed by the incorporators have been complied with and that the corporation has been incorporated under the Oregon Business Corporation Act, except as against this state in a proceeding to cancel or revoke the certificate of incorporation or for involuntary dissolution of the corporation."

This section is virtually identical to § 56 of the Model Act. The Comment to the Model, prepared as a research project by the American Bar Foundation and edited by the American Bar Association Committee on Corporate Laws, states:

* * *

"Under the unequivocal provisions of the Model Act, any steps short of securing a certificate of incorporation would not constitute apparent compliance.   Therefore a de facto corporation cannot exist under the Model Act.

"Like provisions are made throughout the Model Act in respect of the conclusiveness of the issuance by the secretary of state of the appropriate certificate in connection with filings made in his office. . . .

"In some states, however, issuance of the certificate of incorporation and compliance with any additional requirements for filing, recording or publication is not conclusive evidence of incorporation.   In those states, such action is stated to be only prima facie evidence of incorporation, and in others the effect is merely one of estoppel preventing any question of due incorporation being raised in legal actions by or against the corporation."   Model Business Corporation Act Annotated § 56, p. 205 (2d ed. 1971).

ORS 57.793 provides:

"All persons who assume to act as a corporation without the authority of a certificate of incorporation issued by the Corporation Commissioner, shall be jointly and severally liable for all debts and liabilities incurred or arising as a result thereof."

This is merely an elaboration of § 146 of the Model Act.   The Comment states:

"This section is designed to prohibit the application of any theory of de facto incorporation.   The only authority to act as a corporation under the Model Act arises from completion of the procedures prescribed in sections 53 to 55 inclusive.   The consequences of those procedures are specified in section 56 as being the creation of a corporation.   No other means being authorized, the effect of section 146 is to negate the possibility of a de facto corporation.

"Abolition of the concept of de facto incorporation, which at best was fuzzy, is a sound result.   No reason exists for its continuance under general corporate laws, where the process of acquiring de jure incorporation is both simple and clear. The vestigial appendage should be removed."   2 Model Business Corporation Act Annotated § 146, pp. 908–909 (2d ed. 1971).

In Robertson v. Levy, 197 A.2d 443 (D.C.Ct. of App.1964), the court held the president of a defectively organized corporation personally liable to a creditor of the "corporation."   The applicable legislation was similar to Oregon's.   The court held the legislation ended the common-law doctrine of de facto corporation.

The Alaska court upheld the cancellation of a special land-use permit upon the ground that the applicant had not yet been issued its certificate of incorporation at the time the permit was issued. Swindel v. Kelly, 499 P.2d 291 (Alaska 1972).   Alaska has a statute similar to Oregon's.   The court commented: "The concept of de facto corporations has been increasingly disfavored, and Alaska is among the states whose corporation statutes are designed to eliminate the concept." 499 P.2d at 299, n. 28.

Vincent Drug Co. v. Utah State Tax Com'n, 17 Utah 2d 202, 407 P.2d 683 (1965), cited by defendant, involved a statute similar to that of Oregon; however, the court held the de facto corporation doctrine continued to exist. No reasoning is stated and we find the case unpersuasive.

We hold the principle of de facto corporation no longer exists in Oregon.

The defendant also contends that the plaintiff is estopped to deny that it contracted with a corporation.[1]

The doctrine of "corporation by estoppel" has been recognized by this court but never fully dissected.... Corporation by estoppel is a difficult concept to grasp and courts and writers have "gone all over the lot" in attempting to define and apply the doctrine. One of the better explanations of the problem and the varied solutions is contained in Ballantine, Manual of Corporation Law and Practice §§ 28–30 (1930):

> "The so-called estoppel that arises to deny corporate capacity does not depend on the presence of the technical elements of equitable estoppel, viz., misrepresentations and change of position in reliance thereon, but on the nature of the relations contemplated, that one who has recognized the organization as a corporation in business dealings should not be allowed to quibble or raise immaterial issues on matters which do not concern him in the slightest degree or affect his substantial rights." Ballantine, supra, at 92.

As several writers have pointed out, in order to apply the doctrine correctly, the cases must be classified according to who is being charged with estoppel. Ballantine, supra, at 91; 1 Hornstein, Corporation Law and Practice § 30, p. 31, n. 6 (1959).

When a defendant seeks to escape liability to a corporation plaintiff by contending that the plaintiff is not a lawful corporate entity, courts readily apply the doctrine of corporation by estoppel. Thompson Optical Institute v. Thompson [119 Or. 252, 237 P. 965 (1925)], well illustrates the equity of the doctrine in this class of cases. R.A. Thompson carried on an optical business for years. He

1. Robertson v. Levy, supra (197 A.2d 443), held the adoption of the provisions of the Model Business Corporation Act eliminated the concept of corporations by estoppel as well as de facto corporations. Fletcher follows this view. Fletcher, supra, § 3890. However, the same court that decided Robertson v. Levy, with the same panel, held a party was estopped to deny the existence of the corporation. Namerdy v. Generalcar, 217 A.2d 109 (D.C.Ct. of App. 1966). Robertson v. Levy was not mentioned.

In view of our decision that the defense of estoppel was not established, we do not need to decide the effect of the new Business Corporation Act on the doctrine of estoppel. We observe, however, that "[a]lthough some cases tend to assimilate the doctrines of incorporation de facto and by estoppel, each is a distinct theory and they are not dependent on one another in their application." Cranson v. International Business Machine Corp., 234 Md. 477, 200 A.2d 33, 38 (1964).

then organized a corporation to buy his optical business and subscribed to most of the stock in this corporation. He chaired the first meeting at which the Board resolved to purchase the business from him. The corporation and Thompson entered into a contract for the sale of the business which included a covenant by Thompson not to compete. Thereafter, Thompson sold all of his stock to another individual. Some years later Thompson re-entered the optical business in violation of the covenant not to compete. The corporation brought suit to restrain Thompson from competing. Thompson defended upon the ground that the corporation had not been legally organized. We held, "The defendant cannot be heard to challenge the validity of the contract or the proper organization of the corporation." [2]   119 Or. at 260, 237 P. at 968.

The fairness of estopping a defendant such as Thompson from denying the corporate existence of his creation is apparent.

On the other hand, when individuals such as the defendants in this case seek to escape liability by contending that the debtor is a corporation, Aero–Fabb Co., rather than the individual who purported to act as a corporation, the courts are more reluctant to estop the plaintiff from attacking the legality of the alleged debtor corporation. Ballantine, supra, at 96; 8 Fletcher, Cyclopedia of the Law of Private Corporations (perm. ed.) § 3914, p. 228.

The most appealing explanation of why the plaintiff may be estopped is based upon the intention of the parties. The creditor-plaintiff contracted believing it could look for payment only to the corporate entity. The associates, whatever their relationship to the supposed corporate entity, believed their only potential liability was the loss of their investment in the supposed corporate entity and that they were not personally liable. . . .

From the plaintiff-creditor's viewpoint, such reasoning is somewhat tenuous. The creditor did nothing to create the appearance that the debtor was a legal corporate entity. The creditor formed its intention to contract with a debtor corporate entity because someone associated with the debtor represented, expressly or impliedly, that the debtor was a legal corporate entity.

We need not decide whether the doctrine of corporation by estoppel would apply in such a case as this. The trial court found that if this doctrine was still available under the Business Corporation Act defendants did not prove all the elements necessary for its application, and, moreover, it would be inequitable to apply the doctrine.[3]

Under the explanation stated above for the application of the doctrine of estoppel in this kind of case, it is necessary that the plaintiff believe that it was contracting with a corporate entity. The

2. The court also based its decision upon a finding that the plaintiff was a de facto corporation.

3. The trial court made these as conclusions of law, but these statements are in effect general findings of fact.

evidence on this point is contradictory and the trial court apparently found against defendants.

The trial court found, and its findings are supported by the evidence, that all the defendants were partners prior to January 1970 and did business under the name "Aero–Fabb Co." Not until June 1970 were the interests in this partnership assigned to the corporation "Aero–Fabb Co." and about the same time the assumed business name "Aero–Fabb Co." was cancelled. . . .

Plaintiff's bookkeeper testified that she thought it was a corporation because, "This was the way the information was given to me." It is uncertain whether the information was given to her by someone employed by plaintiff or by a company with whom she made a credit check. In any event, plaintiff's salesman said Mr. Davenport, speaking for the organization, stated several times that he was in a partnership with Drs. Gorman and Bennett. The salesman was dubious and checked the title to the land on which the debtors' operation was being conducted and found it was in the name of the three defendants as individuals.

A final question remains: Can the plaintiff recover against Dr. Bennett individually?

In the first third of this century the liability of persons associated with defectively organized corporations was a controversial and well-documented legal issue. The orthodox view was that if an organization had not achieved de facto status and the plaintiff was not estopped to attack the validity of the corporate status of the corporation, all shareholders were liable as partners. This court, however, rejected the orthodox rule. In Rutherford v. Hill, 22 Or. 218, 29 P. 546, 29 Am.St.R. 596, 17 L.R.A. 549 (1892), we held that a person could not be held liable as a partner merely because he signed the articles of incorporation though the corporation was so defectively formed as to fall short of de facto status. The court stated that under this rule a mere passive stockholder would not be held liable as a partner. We went on to observe, however, that if the party actively participated in the business he might be held liable as a partner.

This controversy subsided 30 or 40 years ago probably because the procedure to achieve de jure corporate status was made simpler; so the problem did not arise.

The Model Act and the Oregon Business Corporation Act, ORS 57.793, solve the problem as follows:

> "All persons who assume to act as a corporation without the authority of a certificate of incorporation issued by the Corporation Commissioner, shall be jointly and severally liable for all debts and liabilities incurred or arising as a result thereof."

We have found no decisions, comments to the Model Act, or literature attempting to explain the intent of this section.

We find the language ambiguous. Liability is imposed on "[a]ll persons who assume to act as a corporation." Such persons shall be liable "for all debts and liabilities incurred or arising as a result thereof."

We conclude that the category of "persons who assume to act as a corporation" does not include those whose only connection with the organization is as an investor. On the other hand, the restriction of liability to those who personally incurred the obligation sued upon cannot be based upon logic or the realities of business practice. When several people carry on the activities of a defectively organized corporation, chance frequently will dictate which of the several active principals directly incurs a certain obligation or whether an employee, rather than an active principal, personally incurs the obligation.

We are of the opinion that the phrase, "persons who assume to act as a corporation" should be interpreted to include those persons who have an investment in the organization and who actively participate in the policy and operational decisions of the organization. Liability should not necessarily be restricted to the person who personally incurred the obligation.

The trial court found that Dr. Bennett "acted in the business venture which was subsequently incorporated on June 12, 1970."

The proposed business of the corporation which was to be formed was to sell airplanes, recondition airplanes and give flying lessons. Land was leased for this purpose. Equipment was rented from plaintiff to level and clear for access and for other construction.

There is evidence from which the trial court could have found that while Drs. Bennett and Gorman, another defendant, entrusted the details of management to Davenport, they endeavored to and did retain some control over his management. All checks required one of their signatures. Dr. Bennett frequently visited the site and observed the activity and the presence of the equipment rented by plaintiff. He met with the organization's employees to discuss the operation of the business. Shortly after the equipment was rented and before most of the rent had accrued, Dr. Bennett was informed of the rentals and given an opinion that they were unnecessary and ill-advised. Drs. Bennett and Gorman thought they had Davenport and his management "under control."

This evidence all supports the finding that Dr. Bennett was a person who assumed to act for the organization and the conclusion of the trial court that Dr. Bennett is personally liable.

Affirmed.

———

NOTE ON CANTOR

At the time *Cantor,* supra, was decided, the New Jersey statute had a counterpart of old Model Act § 56, but did not have a counterpart of old Model Act § 146, both of which are discussed in *Timberline.*

————

REV. MODEL BUS. CORP. ACT §§ 2.03, 2.04

[See Statutory Supplement]

————

DEL. GEN. CORP. LAW §§ 106, 329, 392

[See Statutory Supplement]

————

NOTE ON INDIVIDUAL LIABILITY IN CASES OF DEFECTIVE INCORPORATION

As *Timberline* indicates, de facto corporation cases raise two kinds of questions. The first question is whether the business enterprise in question is a de facto corporation. The second question is, who is liable if the enterprise is not a de facto corporation.

One possible answer to the second question is that if the business organization is not a corporation, and there are several owners, the organization must be a partnership. For example, in Partnership Liability of Stockholders in Defective Corporations, 40 Harv.L.Rev. 521 (1927), Professor Dodd argued that "a defective corporation must be either a partnership or a sort of legal waif," and that it was therefore not "possible to escape the conclusion that the members [of a defective corporation] are partners." Id. at 530, 532.

This position—which is rejected in *Timberline*—reflects the concept, discussed in Chapter 2, Section 1, that partnerships are the default form of organization. For the reasons discussed in that section, this concept is inaccurate. The point is nicely put in a reply to Dodd by then-Professor (later Judge) Calvert Magruder in A Note on Partnership Liability of Stockholders in Defective Corporations, 40 Harv.L.Rev. 733, at 733 (1927):

> [A]s a teacher of the law of partnership, I feel rather imposed upon when I am told that the legal waifs and strays which have been rejected from the corporation fold must be

embraced within the partnership family. . . .   [I]t would never occur to me to go to my colleague who teaches the law of corporations, and insist that the association must be a corporation because it isn't a partnership.

NOTE ON ESTOPPEL

The court in *Timberline* pointed out that the estoppel theory is sometimes used as an alternative to the de facto corporation theory. Neither the precise contours of the estoppel theory nor its relationship to the de facto theory has ever been entirely clear.   It is sometimes said that the estoppel theory differs from the de facto theory in that it is effective for only a specific transaction.   However, the de facto theory also may be effective only for a specific transaction: A decision in one suit that a corporation has de facto status will normally not be res judicata in a suit brought by an unrelated plaintiff on an unrelated transaction.   As a practical matter, however, there is likely to be a difference between the precedential effect of decisions based on estoppel theory and decisions based on de facto theory.   A decision based on estoppel theory will normally turn heavily on the facts of the plaintiff's transaction, and therefore may have only a limited precedential effect on future cases involving other plaintiffs and other transactions.   In contrast, a decision based on de facto theory will normally turn on the defendant's conduct in attempting to organize a corporation.   Because the same conduct will be the focus of any future de facto case involving those defendants, the initial decision will have a stare decisis effect on such future cases in the same jurisdiction, and will have a precedential effect on future cases in other jurisdictions.

A problem with the estoppel theory is that in fact it is not a single theory, but a cluster of very different rules covering cases that fall into very different categories, only one of which involves a true estoppel, that is, reliance by one party on the other's representation.

1.   First is the case in which an association, or its owners, having claimed corporate status in an earlier transaction with a third party, T, later denies that status in a suit brought by T.   This is a true estoppel case, at least if T relied on the initial claim.

2.   Another category consists of cases in which the question of corporate status is raised in a technical procedural context.   For example, the defendant in a suit brought by a would-be corporation may seek to raise the defense that the plaintiff is not really a corporation, and therefore cannot sue in a corporate name.   The courts tend to regard such defenses as nonmeritorious, and to brush them off, using "estoppel" as a handy tool.

3.   In the most important category of cases, a third party who has dealt with a business as a corporation seeks to impose personal

liability on would-be shareholders who in turn raise estoppel as a defense.   Here the issue is whether, as a matter of equity, the claimant, having dealt with a business as if it were a corporation, should be prevented—"estopped"—from treating it as anything else.   A leading case in this category is Cranson v. International Business Mach. Corp., 234 Md. 477, 200 A.2d 33 (1964).   I.B.M. had sold typewriters to Real Estate Service Bureau on credit.   I.B.M. dealt with Bureau as if Bureau were a corporation.   In fact, it wasn't, because, without the knowledge of the would-be shareholders, their attorney had negligently failed to file the certificate of incorporation before the transaction with the third party.   The court held that the estoppel doctrine could be applied even when a corporation did not have de facto existence, and that although the organizational defects in the case might have prevented the Bureau from being a de facto corporation, "we think that I.B.M. having dealt with the Bureau as if it were a corporation and relied on its credit rather than that of [the would-be shareholders], is estopped to assert that the Bureau was not incorporated at the time the typewriters were purchased."

In this third category of cases the estoppel theory is comparable in its function to the de facto theory, but the two theories differ in two important ways in their application:

First, the nub of the estoppel theory in such cases is that the third party has dealt with the business as if it were a corporation. Presumably, therefore, the theory would not apply to a tort claimant, or other involuntary creditor, who was a stranger to the business before his claim arose.   In contrast, the de facto theory can be applied to such claimants.

Second, the would-be shareholders would not need to resort to the estoppel theory if they could establish that their business had de facto corporate status.   Presumably, therefore, less in the way of corporateness must be shown to establish a corporation by estoppel than to establish a de facto corporation.   (Thus in Cranson v. International Business Mach., supra, the court applied the estoppel theory only after observing that since the certificate of incorporation had not been filed at the time of the transaction, the de facto theory might not be applicable.)

There is an obvious relationship between the first and second points.   A tort claimant or other involuntary creditor has a stronger claim against would-be shareholders than a contract creditor, because a contract creditor who transacts with a would-be corporation expects only limited liability, while the expectation of a typical tort or other involuntary creditor is usually not so limited.

———

NOTE ON QUO WARRANTO

1. A traditional method for testing corporate status is through a quo warranto proceeding brought by the state. This proceeding derives from an ancient prerogative writ issued on behalf of the King against one who falsely claimed an office or franchise. Such a proceeding can be maintained even against a de facto corporation, because the de facto theory is a defense only against a "collateral attack" on corporate status—in effect, only against a challenge raised by private actors—not against a challenge by the state itself.

Most states now provide by statute for proceedings in the nature of quo warranto, often without using that name. See, e.g., New York § 109; California § 1801(a).

2. An association that fails to meet all the requirements for incorporation may nevertheless be a corporation "de jure" if the noncompliance is extremely insubstantial. De jure status, unlike de facto status, is a good defense even to a quo warranto proceeding. For example, in People v. Ford, 294 Ill. 319, 128 N.E. 479 (1920), the Attorney General filed an information in the nature of quo warranto against three incorporators who had failed to comply with a statute providing that the statement of incorporation be sealed. The incorporators had filed on the Secretary of State's forms, which neither contained nor mentioned a seal. The court concluded that de jure status had been attained: the provision for a seal was only "directory," because the purpose of the statute was to make a public record, and a seal did not further that purpose.

———

SECTION 6.   DISREGARD OF THE CORPORATE ENTITY

———

DEL. GEN. CORP. LAW § 102(b)(6)

[See Statutory Supplement]

———

REV. MODEL BUS. CORP. ACT § 6.22

[See Statutory Supplement]

———

INTRODUCTORY NOTE ON LIMITED LIABILITY

This Section concerns the concepts of limited liability, the entity status of corporations, and disregard of the corporate entity. These concepts raise issues at three levels. The first level is conceptual and terminological: what exactly does "limited liability" mean, and what is the relevance, for these purposes, of the corporation's entity status? The second issue is one of fairness and policy: how and when is limited liability justified? The third issue is, when should exceptions to limited liability be made? The three issues are related—sometimes loosely, sometimes very closely. The first issue will be considered in this Note. The second and third issues are addressed in the materials that follow.

Several terminological and conceptual points need to be confronted before considering limited liability directly.

First, the term "limited" liability is a misnomer, because under modern corporate statutes a shareholder ordinarily has *no* liability for corporate debts and other obligations. A more accurate description of the rule is that a shareholder's *risk* is limited to his *investment*—that is, the most the shareholder stands to lose, even if the corporation fails, is the amount he paid for his shares. Having said that, it is nevertheless the case that the term "limited liability" is universally used to refer to the no-liability rule, and will therefore be used in this Note as well.

Second, although it is sometimes said that shareholders are not liable for corporate debts because the corporation is a separate entity—a legal person—in fact the entity status of corporations has almost nothing to do with shareholder limited liability. For example, English law conferred entity status on corporations long before it afforded limited liability to shareholders. Similarly, the Revised Uniform Partnership Act (RUPA) confers entity status on partnerships, and makes a partnership responsible for partnership obligations, but also provides that the partners are individually liable for all partnership obligations once the partnership's assets are exhausted. See Chapter 2, Sections 2, 5. Accordingly, it does not require "disregard of the corporate entity" to make shareholders personally liable for corporate debts. Rather, it requires the courts to conclude that in a given case the normal statutory rule that provides that shareholders will not have such liability should not be applied.

Third, in considering the rules concerning shareholder liability, it should be borne in mind that corporate managers, as well as corporate shareholders, are ordinarily not responsible for corporate obligations. Shareholders are not responsible for corporate obligations by statute. In contrast, managers are not liable for corporate obligations on straightforward agency principles. In the case of a contract made by a corporate agent within his authority, the agent is not liable as long as the corporation's status as a principal is disclosed. (See Chapter 1, Section 2, supra.) In the case of a tort by a corporate employee, the employee may be liable, and the corporation may be liable as the employee's principal, but a manager will normally not be vicariously liable simply because the employee was a subordinate of the manager. (However, a corporate manager may be liable if he personally commits or perhaps orders the tort.) The general rules, and special exceptions, concerning the liability of corporate managers, will be considered in Chapter 7, Section 1.

————

WARNING: The principal cases in this Chapter are not representative of the population of limited-liability cases. The basic rule of corporate law is the statutory rule of limited liability. Accordingly, the law reports are filled with cases that quickly and routinely conclude either that the facts do not justify a departure from the basic rule, or that the applicability of the basic rule is an issue to be determined by the factfinder. Cases like these are not represented in this Chapter, because the object of this Chapter is to explore the reasons for and limits on the basic rule. Accordingly, the principal cases have been selected not because they are representative, but either because they are difficult, and therefore force the court to articulate those reasons and limits, or because they illustrate or suggest important categories of limits.

————

WALKOVSZKY v. CARLTON

Court of Appeals of New York, 1966.
18 N.Y.2d 414, 276 N.Y.S.2d 585, 223 N.E.2d 6.

FULD, Judge.   This case involves what appears to be a rather common practice in the taxicab industry of vesting the ownership of a taxi fleet in many corporations, each owning only one or two cabs.

The complaint alleges that the plaintiff was severely injured four years ago in New York City when he was run down by a taxicab owned by the defendant Seon Cab Corporation and negligently operated at the time by the defendant Marchese. The individual defendant, Carlton, is claimed to be a stockholder of 10 corporations, including Seon, each of which has but two cabs registered in its name, and it is implied that only the minimum automobile liability insurance required by law (in the amount of $10,000) is carried on any one cab. Although seemingly independent of one another, these corporations are alleged to be "operated . . . as a single entity, unit and enterprise" with regard to financing, supplies, repairs, employees and garaging, and all are named as defendants.[1]   The plaintiff asserts that he is also entitled to hold their stockholders personally liable for the damages sought because the

————

1. The corporate owner of a garage is also included as a defendant.

multiple corporate structure constitutes an unlawful attempt "to defraud members of the general public" who might be injured by the cabs.

The defendant Carlton has moved, pursuant to CPLR 3211(a)7, to dismiss the complaint on the ground that as to him it "fails to state a cause of action". The court at Special Term granted the motion but the Appellate Division, by a divided vote, reversed, holding that a valid cause of action was sufficiently stated. The defendant Carlton appeals to us, from the nonfinal order, by leave of the Appellate Division on a certified question.

The law permits the incorporation of a business for the very purpose of enabling its proprietors to escape personal liability (see, e.g., Bartle v. Home Owners Co-op., 309 N.Y. 103, 106, 127 N.E.2d 832, 833) but, manifestly, the privilege is not without its limits. Broadly speaking, the courts will disregard the corporate form, or, to use accepted terminology, "pierce the corporate veil", whenever necessary "to prevent fraud or to achieve equity". (International Aircraft Trading Co. v. Manufacturers Trust Co., 297 N.Y. 285, 292, 79 N.E.2d 249, 252.) In determining whether liability should be extended to reach assets beyond those belonging to the corporation, we are guided, as Judge Cardozo noted, by "general rules of agency". (Berkey v. Third Ave. Ry. Co., 244 N.Y. 84, 95, 155 N.E. 58, 61, 50 A.L.R. 599.) In other words, whenever anyone uses control of the corporation to further his own rather than the corporation's business, he will be liable for the corporation's acts "upon the principle of *respondeat superior* applicable even where the agent is a natural person".... Such liability, moreover, extends not only to the corporation's commercial dealings ... but to its negligent acts as well....

In the Mangan case (247 App.Div. 853, 286 N.Y.S. 666, mot. for lv. to app. den. 272 N.Y. 676, 286 N.Y.S. 666, supra), the plaintiff was injured as a result of the negligent operation of a cab owned and operated by one of four corporations affiliated with the defendant Terminal. Although the defendant was not a stockholder of any of the operating companies, both the defendant and the operating companies were owned, for the most part, by the same parties. The defendant's name (Terminal) was conspicuously displayed on the sides of all of the taxis used in the enterprise and, in point of fact, the defendant actually serviced, inspected, repaired and dispatched them. These facts were deemed to provide sufficient cause for piercing the corporate veil of the operating company—the nominal owner of the cab which injured the plaintiff—and holding the defendant liable. The operating companies were simply instrumentalities for carrying on the business of the defendant without imposing upon it financial and other liabilities incident to the actual ownership and operation of the cabs....

In the case before us, the plaintiff has explicitly alleged that none of the corporations "had a separate existence of their own" and, as indicated above, all are named as defendants. However, it is one thing to assert that a corporation is a fragment of a larger corporate combine which actually conducts the business.   (See Berle, The Theory of Enterprise Entity, 47 Col.L.Rev. 343, 348–350.) It is quite another to claim that the corporation is a "dummy" for its individual stockholders who are in reality carrying on the business in their personal capacities for purely personal rather than corporate ends.   (See African Metals Corp. v. Bullowa, 288 N.Y. 78, 85, 41 N.E.2d 366, 469.)   Either circumstance would justify treating the corporation as an agent and piercing the corporate veil to reach the principal but a different result would follow in each case.   In the first, only a larger *corporate* entity would be held financially responsible . . . while, in the other, the stockholder would be personally liable. . . .   Either the stockholder is conducting the business in his individual capacity or he is not.   If he is, he will be liable; if he is not, then it does not matter—insofar as his personal liability is concerned—that the enterprise is actually being carried on by a larger "enterprise entity".   (See Berle, The Theory of Enterprise Entity, 47 Col.L.Rev. 343.)

At this stage in the present litigation, we are concerned only with the pleadings and, since CPLR 3014 permits causes of action to be stated "alternatively or hypothetically", it is possible for the plaintiff to allege both theories as the basis for his demand for judgment.   In ascertaining whether he has done so, we must consider the entire pleading, educing therefrom " 'whatever can be imputed from its statements by fair and reasonable intendment.' " (Condon v. Associated Hosp. Serv., 287 N.Y. 411, 414, 40 N.E.2d 230, 231. . . .)   Reading the complaint in this case most favorably and liberally, we do not believe that there can be gathered from its averments the allegations required to spell out a valid cause of action against the defendant Carlton.

The individual defendant is charged with having "organized, managed, dominated and controlled" a fragmented corporate entity but there are no allegations that he was conducting business in his individual capacity.   Had the taxicab fleet been owned by a single corporation, it would be readily apparent that the plaintiff would face formidable barriers in attempting to establish personal liability on the part of the corporation's stockholders.   The fact that the fleet ownership has been deliberately split up among many corporations does not ease the plaintiff's burden in that respect.   The corporate form may not be disregarded merely because the assets of the corporation, together with the mandatory insurance coverage of the vehicle which struck the plaintiff, are insufficient to assure him the recovery sought.   If Carlton were to be held individually liable on those facts alone, the decision would apply equally to the thousands of cabs which are owned by their individual drivers who conduct their businesses through corporations organized pursuant to section 401 of the Business Corporation Law, Consol.Laws, c. 4 and carry the minimum insurance required by subdivision 1 (par. [a]) of section 370 of the Vehicle and Traffic Law, Consol.Laws, c. 71.   These taxi owner-operators are entitled to form such corporations (cf. Elenkrieg v. Siebrecht, 238 N.Y. 254, 144 N.E. 519, 34 A.L.R. 592), and we agree with the court at Special Term that, if the insurance coverage required by statute "is inadequate for the protection of the public, the remedy lies not with the courts but with the Legislature." It may very well be sound policy to require that certain corporations must take out liability insurance which will afford adequate compensation to their potential tort victims. However, the responsibility for imposing conditions on the privilege of incorporation has been committed by the Constitution to the Legislature (N.Y. Const., art. X, § 1) and it may not be fairly implied, from any statute, that the Legislature intended, without the slightest discussion or debate, to require of taxi corporations that they carry automobile liability insurance over and above that mandated by the Vehicle and Traffic Law.

This is not to say that it is impossible for the plaintiff to state a valid cause of action against the defendant Carlton. However, the simple fact is that the plaintiff has just not done so here. While the complaint alleges that the separate corporations were undercapitalized and that their assets have been intermingled, it is barren of any "sufficiently particular[ized] statements" (CPLR 3013; see 3 Weinstein–Korn–Miller, N.Y.Civ.Prac., par. 3013.01 et seq., pp. 30–142 et seq.) that the defendant Carlton and his associates are actually doing business in their individual capacities, shuttling their personal funds in and out of the corporations "without regard to formality and to suit their immediate convenience." (Weisser v. Mursam Shoe Corp., 2 Cir., 127 F.2d 344, 345, 145 A.L.R. 467, supra.) Such a "perversion of the privilege to do business in a corporate form" (Berkey v. Third Ave. Ry. Co., 244 N.Y. 84, 95, 155 N.E. 58, 61, 50 A.L.R. 599, supra) would justify imposing personal liability on the individual stockholders. (See African Metals Corp. v. Bullowa, 288 N.Y. 78, 41 N.E.2d 466, supra.) Nothing of the sort has in fact been charged, and it cannot reasonably or logically be inferred from the happenstance that the business of Seon Cab Corporation may actually be carried on by a larger corporate entity composed of many corporations which, under general principles of agency, would be liable to each other's creditors in contract and in tort.[3]

---

3. In his affidavit in opposition to the motion to dismiss, the plaintiff's counsel claimed that corporate assets had been "milked out" of, and "siphoned off" from the enterprise. Quite apart from the fact that these allegations are far too vague and conclusory, the charge is premature. If the plaintiff succeeds in his action and becomes a judgment creditor of the corporation, he may then sue and attempt to hold the individual defendants accountable for any dividends and property that were wrongfully distributed (Business Corporation Law, §§ 510, 719, 720).

[By ed.: Cf. R. Clark, Corporate Law 84 n. 14 (1986):

The court overlooked the possibility of suit under New York's version of the [Uniform Fraudulent Conveyance Act], it having been held long before that a prior judgment is *not* a procedural prerequisite to suit under that statute. American Surety Co. v. Connor, 166 N.E. 783 (N.Y. 1929). (This has also been the consistent interpretation in other states of the UFCA. . . .) Furthermore, New York fraudulent conveyance law has been applied to remedy milking and diversion of corporate assets, even where one of the devices was payment of dividends. United States v. 58th Street Plaza Theatre, Inc., 287 F.Supp. 475, 498 (S.D.N.Y. 1968). (Emphasis in original.)]

In point of fact, the principle relied upon in the complaint to sustain the imposition of personal liability is not agency but fraud. Such a cause of action cannot withstand analysis. If it is not fraudulent for the owner-operator of a single cab corporation to take out only the minimum required liability insurance, the enterprise does not become either illicit or fraudulent merely because it consists of many such corporations. The plaintiff's injuries are the same regardless of whether the cab which strikes him is owned by a single corporation or part of a fleet with ownership fragmented among many corporations. Whatever rights he may be able to assert against parties other than the registered owner of the vehicle come into being not because he has been defrauded but because, under the principle of *respondeat superior,* he is entitled to hold the whole enterprise responsible for the acts of its agents.

In sum, then, the complaint falls short of adequately stating a cause of action against the defendant Carlton in his individual capacity.

The order of the Appellate Division should be reversed, with costs in this court and in the Appellate Division, the certified question answered in the negative and the order of the Supreme Court, Richmond County, reinstated, with leave to serve an amended complaint.

KEATING, Judge (dissenting).

The defendant Carlton, the shareholder here sought to be held for the negligence of the driver of a taxicab, was a principal shareholder and organizer of the defendant corporation which owned the taxicab. The corporation was one of 10 organized by the defendant, each containing two cabs and each cab having the "minimum liability" insurance coverage mandated by section 370 of the Vehicle and Traffic Law. The sole assets of these operating corporations are the vehicles themselves and they are apparently subject to mortgages.*

From their inception these corporations were intentionally undercapitalized for the purpose of avoiding responsibility for acts which were bound to arise as a result of the operation of a large taxi fleet having cars out on the street 24 hours a day and engaged in public transportation. And during the course of the corporations' existence all income was continually drained out of the corporations for the same purpose.

The issue presented by this action is whether the policy of this State, which affords those desiring to engage in a business enterprise the privilege of limited liability through the use of the corporate devise, is so strong that it will permit that privilege to continue no matter how much it is abused, no matter how irresponsibly the corporation is operated, no matter what the cost to the public. I do not believe that it is.

---

* It appears that the medallions, which are of considerable value, are judgment proof. (Administrative Code of City of New York, § 436–2.0.) [Footnote by the court.]

Under the circumstances of this case the shareholders should all be held individually liable to this plaintiff for the injuries he suffered. (See Mull v. Colt Co., D.C., 31 F.R.D. 154, 156; Teller v. Clear Serv. Corp., 9 Misc.2d 495, 173 N.Y.S.2d 183.) At least, the matter should not be disposed of on the pleadings by a dismissal of the complaint. "If a corporation is organized and carries on business without substantial capital in such a way that the corporation is likely to have no sufficient assets available to meet its debts, it is inequitable that shareholders should set up such a flimsy organization to escape personal liability. The attempt to do corporate business without providing any sufficient basis of financial responsibility to creditors is an abuse of the separate entity and will be ineffectual to exempt the shareholders from corporate debts. It is coming to be recognized as the policy of law that shareholders should in good faith put at the risk of the business unincumbered capital reasonably adequate for its prospective liabilities. If capital is illusory or trifling compared with the business to be done and the risks of loss, this is a ground for denying the separate entity privilege." (Ballantine, Corporations [rev. ed., 1946], § 129, pp. 302–303.) . . .

The policy of this State has always been to provide and facilitate recovery for those injured through the negligence of others. The automobile, by its very nature, is capable of causing severe and costly injuries when not operated in a proper manner. The great increase in the number of automobile accidents combined with the frequent financial irresponsibility of the individual driving the car led to the adoption of section 388 of the Vehicle and Traffic Law which had the effect of imposing upon the owner of the vehicle the responsibility for its negligent operation. It is upon this very statute that the cause of action against both the corporation and the individual defendant is predicated.

In addition the Legislature, still concerned with the financial irresponsibility of those who owned and operated motor vehicles, enacted a statute requiring minimum liability coverage for all owners of automobiles. The important public policy represented by both these statutes is outlined in section 310 of the Vehicle and Traffic Law. That section provides that: "The legislature is concerned over the rising toll of motor vehicle accidents and the suffering and loss thereby inflicted. The legislature determines that it is a matter of grave concern that motorists shall be financially able to respond in damages for their negligent acts, so that innocent victims of motor vehicle accidents may be recompensed for the injury and financial loss inflicted upon them."

The defendant Carlton claims that, because the minimum amount of insurance required by the statute was obtained, the corporate veil cannot and should not be pierced despite the fact that the assets of the corporation which owned the cab were "trifling compared with the business to be done and the risks of loss" which were certain to be encountered. I do not agree.

The Legislature in requiring minimum liability insurance of $10,000, no doubt, intended to provide at least some small fund for recovery against those individuals and corporations who just did not have and were not able to raise or accumulate assets sufficient to satisfy the claims of those who were injured as a result of their negligence. It certainly could not have intended to shield those individuals who organized corporations, with the specific intent of avoiding responsibility to the public, where the operation of the corporate enterprise yielded profits sufficient to purchase additional insurance. . . .

The defendant, however, argues that the failure of the Legislature to increase the minimum insurance requirements indicates legislative acquiescence in this scheme to avoid liability and responsibility to the public. In the absence of a clear legislative statement, approval of a scheme having such serious consequences is not to be so lightly inferred.

The defendant contends that the court will be encroaching upon the legislative domain by ignoring the corporate veil and holding the individual shareholder. This argument was answered by Mr. Justice DOUGLAS in Anderson v. Abbot, [321 U.S. 349], 366–367, 64 S.Ct. p. 540, where he wrote that: "In the field in which we are presently concerned, judicial power hardly oversteps the bounds when it refuses to lend its aid to a promotional project which would circumvent or undermine a legislative policy. To deny it that function would be to make it impotent in situations where historically it has made some of its most notable contributions. If the judicial power is helpless to protect a legislative program from schemes for easy avoidance, then indeed it has become a handy implement of high finance. *Judicial interference to cripple or defeat a legislative policy is one thing; judicial interference with the plans of those whose corporate or other devices would circumvent that policy is quite another.* Once the purpose or effect of the scheme is clear, once the legislative policy is plain, we would indeed forsake a great tradition to say we were helpless to fashion the instruments for appropriate relief." (Emphasis added.)

The defendant contends that a decision holding him personally liable would discourage people from engaging in corporate enterprise.

What I would merely hold is that a participating shareholder of a corporation vested with a public interest, organized with capital insufficient to meet liabilities which are certain to arise in the ordinary course of the corporation's business, may be held personally responsible for such liabilities. Where corporate income is not sufficient to cover the cost of insurance premiums above the statutory minimum or where initially adequate finances dwindle under the pressure of competition, bad times or extraordinary and unexpected liability, obviously the shareholder will not be held liable (Henn, Corporations, p. 208, n. 7).

The only types of corporate enterprises that will be discouraged as a result of a decision allowing the individual shareholder to be sued will be those such as the one in question, designed solely to abuse the corporate privilege at the expense of the public interest.

For these reasons I would vote to affirm the order of the Appellate Division.

DESMOND, C.J., and VAN VOORHIS, BURKE and SCILEPPI, JJ., concur with FULD, J.

KEATING, J., dissents and votes to affirm in an opinion in which BERGAN, J., concurs.

Order reversed, etc.

NOTE ON FURTHER PROCEEDINGS IN WALKOVSZKY v. CARLTON

Following the decision in *Walkovszky,* the plaintiff amended his complaint. The Appellate Division held that "the amended complaint sufficiently alleges a cause of action against appellant, i.e., that he and the other individual defendants were conducting the business of the taxicab fleet in their individual capacities." Walkovszky v. Carlton, 29 A.D.2d 763, 287 N.Y.S.2d 546 (1968). That decision was affirmed by the Court of Appeals, 23 N.Y.2d 714, 296 N.Y.S.2d 362, 244 N.E.2d 55 (1968), noting that the amended complaint "now meets the pleading requirements set forth in [our prior] opinion and states a valid cause of action." Neither opinion stated the particulars in which the amended complaint differed from the original.

BERKEY v. THIRD AVE. RY. CO., 244 N.Y. 84, 155 N.E. 58 (1926) (Cardozo, J.). "The whole problem of the relation between parent and subsidiary corporations is one that is still enveloped in the mists of metaphor. Metaphors in law are to be narrowly watched, for starting as devices to liberate thought, they end often by enslaving it. We say at times that the corporate entity will be ignored when the parent corporation operates a business through a subsidiary which is characterized as an 'alias' or a 'dummy.' All this is well enough if the picturesqueness of the epithets does not lead us to forget that the essential term to be defined is the act of operation. Dominion may be so complete, interference so obtrusive, that by the general rules of agency the parent will be a principal and the subsidiary an agent. Where control is less than this, we are remitted to the tests of honesty and justice. Ballentine, Parent and Subsidiary Corporations, 14 Cal.Law Review, 12, 18, 19, 20. The logical consistency of a juridical conception will indeed be sacrificed at times, when the sacrifice is essential to the end that some accepted public policy may be defended or upheld. This is so, for illustration, though agency in any proper sense is lacking, where the attempted separation between parent and subsidiary will work a fraud upon the law. . . . At such times unity is ascribed to parts which, at least for many purposes, retain an independent life, for the reason that only thus can we overcome a perversion of the privilege to do business in a corporate form."

––––––––

MINTON v. CAVANEY

Supreme Court of California, In Bank, 1961.
56 Cal.2d 576, 15 Cal.Rptr. 641, 364 P.2d 473.

TRAYNOR, Justice. The Seminole Hot Springs Corporation, hereinafter referred to as Seminole, was duly incorporated in California on March 8, 1954. It conducted a public swimming pool that it leased from its owner. On June 24, 1954 plaintiffs' daughter drowned in the pool, and plaintiffs recovered a judgment for $10,000 against Seminole for her wrongful death. The judgment remains unsatisfied.

On January 30, 1957, plaintiffs brought the present action to hold defendant Cavaney personally liable for the judgment against Seminole. Cavaney died on May 28, 1958 and his widow, the executrix of his estate, was substituted as defendant. The trial court entered judgment for plaintiffs for $10,000. Defendant appeals.

Plaintiffs introduced evidence that Cavaney was a director and secretary and treasurer of Seminole and that on November 15, 1954, about five months after the drowning, Cavaney as secretary of Seminole and Edwin A. Kraft as president of Seminole applied for permission to issue three shares of Seminole stock, one share to be issued to Kraft, another to F.J. Wettrick and the third to Cavaney. The commissioner of corporations refused permission to issue these shares unless additional information was furnished. The application was then abandoned and no shares were ever issued. There was also evidence that for a time Seminole used Cavaney's office to keep records and to receive mail. Before his death Cavaney answered certain interrogatories. He was asked if Seminole "ever had any assets?" He stated that "insofar as my own personal knowledge and belief is concerned said corporation did not have any assets." Cavaney also stated in the return to an attempted execution that "[I]nsofar as I know, this corporation had no assets of any kind or character. The corporation was duly organized but never functioned as a corporation."

Defendant introduced evidence that Cavaney was an attorney at law, that he was approached by Kraft and Wettrick to form Seminole, and that he was the attorney for Seminole. Plaintiffs introduced Cavaney's answer to several interrogatories that he held the post of secretary and treasurer and director in a temporary capacity and as an accommodation to his client.

Defendant contends that the evidence does not support the court's determination that Cavaney is personally liable for Seminole's debts and that the "alter ego" doctrine is inapplicable because plaintiffs failed to show that there was " '(1) . . . such unity of interest and ownership that the separate personalities of the corporation and the individual no longer exist and (2) that, if the acts are treated as those of the corporation alone, an inequitable result will follow.' "

Riddle v. Leuschner, 51 Cal.2d 574, 580, 335 P.2d 107, 110; Automotriz Del Golfo De California S.A. De C.V. v. Resnick, 47 Cal.2d 792, 796, 306 P.2d 1, 63 A.L.R.2d 1042; Minifie v. Rowley, 187 Cal. 481, 487, 202 P. 673.

The figurative terminology "alter ego" and "disregard of the corporate entity" is generally used to refer to the various situations that are an abuse of the corporate privilege. . . . The equitable owners of a corporation, for example, are personally liable when they treat the assets of the corporation as their own and add or withdraw capital from the corporation at will . . .; when they hold themselves out as being personally liable for the debts of the corporation . . .; or when they provide inadequate capitalization and actively participate in the conduct of corporate affairs. . . .

In the instant case the evidence is undisputed that there was no attempt to provide adequate capitalization. Seminole never had any substantial assets. It leased the pool that it operated, and the lease was forfeited for failure to pay the rent. Its capital was " 'trifling compared with the business to be done and the risks of loss . . .' " Automotriz Del Golfo De California S.A. De C.V. v. Resnick, supra, 47 Cal.2d 792, 797, 306 P.2d 1, 4. The evidence is also undisputed that Cavaney was not only the secretary and treasurer of the corporation but was also a director. The evidence that Cavaney was to receive one-third of the shares to be issued supports an inference that he was an equitable owner (see Riddle v. Leuschner, supra, 51 Cal.2d 574, 580, 335 P.2d 107), and the evidence that for a time the records of the corporation were kept in Cavaney's office supports an inference that he actively participated in the conduct of the business. The trial court was not required to believe his statement that he was only a "temporary" director and officer "for accommodation." In any event it merely raised a conflict in the evidence that was resolved adversely to defendant. Moreover, section 800 of the Corporations Code provides that " . . . the business and affairs of every corporation shall be controlled by a board of not less than three directors." Defendant does not claim that Cavaney was a director with specialized duties (see 5 U.Chi. L.Rev. 668). It is immaterial whether or not he accepted the office of director as an "accommodation" with the understanding that he would not exercise any of the duties of a director. A person may not in this manner divorce the responsibilities of a director from the statutory duties and powers of that office.

There is no merit in defendant's contentions that the "alter ego" doctrine applies only to contractual debts and not to tort claims . . .; that plaintiffs' cause of action abated when Cavaney died . . . or that the judgment in the action against the corporation bars plaintiffs from bringing the present action. . . .

In this action to hold defendant personally liable upon the judgment against Seminole plaintiffs did not allege or present any evidence on the issue of Seminole's negligence or on the amount of damages sustained by plaintiffs. They relied solely on the judgment against Seminole. Defendant correctly contends that Cavaney or his estate cannot be held liable for the debts of Seminole without an opportunity to relitigate these issues. . . . Cavaney was not a party to the action against the corporation, and the judgment in that action is therefore not binding upon him unless he controlled the litigation leading to the judgment. . . .

The judgment is reversed.

GIBSON, C.J., and PETERS, WHITE and DOOLING, JJ., concur.

SCHAUER, Justice (concurring and dissenting).

I concur in the judgment of reversal on the ground . . . stated in [the last paragraph of] the majority opinion. . . .

I dissent from any implication that *mere professional activity by an attorney at law, as such,* in the organization of a corporation, can constitute any basis for a finding that the corporation is the attorney's alter ego or that he is otherwise personally liable for *its* debts, whether based on contract or tort. . . .

In the process of developing an idea of a person or persons into an embryonic corporation and finally to full legal entity status with a permit issued, directors and officers elected, and assets in hand ready to begin business, there may often be delays. In such event a qualifying share of stock may stand in the name of the organizing attorney for substantial periods of time. In none of the activities indicated is the corporation actually engaging in business. And the lawyer who handles the task of determining and directing and participating in the steps appropriate to transforming the idea into a competent legal entity *ready to engage in business* is not an alter ego of the corporation. By his professional acts he has not been engaging in business in the name of the corporation; he has been merely practicing law.

McCOMB, J., concurs.

————

ARNOLD v. BROWNE, 27 Cal.App.3d 386, 396, 103 Cal.Rptr. 775, 783 (1972). "Evidence of inadequate capitalization is, at best, merely a factor to be considered by the trial court in deciding whether or not to pierce the corporate veil (Harris v. Curtis, 8 Cal.App.3d 837, 841, 87 Cal.Rptr. 614). To be sure, it is an important factor, but no case has been cited, nor have any been found, where it has been held that this factor alone *requires* invoking the equitable doctrine prayed for in the instant case."

————

NILSSON, ROBBINS v. LOUISIANA HYDROLEC, 854 F.2d 1538, 1544 (9th Cir.1988). "The unity of interest required under California law does not require a demonstration of complete ownership. California considers a host of factors relevant to finding a unity of interest. . . .   One highly relevant factor in determining a unity of interest is undercapitalization.   In fact, the California Supreme Court has held that undercapitalization alone will justify piercing the corporate veil.   See Minton v. Cavaney, 56 Cal.2d 576, 364 P.2d 473, 15 Cal.Rptr. 641 (1961).   In this case, Aqualec's undercapitalization is clear.   In addition, Ethridge failed to treat Aqualec as a separate entity.   He guaranteed loans for the corporation, and paid some of its bills from his own bank account.   These facts, together with his control over the activities of the corporation, are more than enough evidence to support a finding of a unity of interests."

————

NOTE ON FRAUDULENT TRANSFERS

Under a legal rule that is closely related to piercing based on undercapitalization, a transfer by a corporation to a shareholder without an equivalent exchange can be recovered on the corporation's behalf if the transfer left the corporation with unreasonably small capital to engage in its business. See Note on Transfers Made by a Corporation Without an Equivalent Exchange, at p. 137, infra.

————

FURTHER NOTE ON LIMITED LIABILITY

What justifies the rule that shareholders are not liable for the obligations of their corporation? A distinction must be drawn here between shareholder liability for the corporation's obligations to voluntary creditors and to involuntary creditors. The paradigm case of the voluntary creditor is a person who has given the corporation credit or otherwise contracted with the corporation. Call such creditors *contract creditors.* The paradigm case of the involuntary creditor is a person who has been injured by the corporation's tortious or other wrongful conduct that does not grow out of a contractual or other voluntary transaction. Call such creditors *tort creditors.*

In the case of contract creditors, limited liability is often easy to justify. Most non-lawyers don't know much law, but they do know some. One legal rule that is probably known to most businesspersons is that shareholders have limited liability. Therefore, when a person voluntarily contracts with a valid corporation, she is likely to know that she can look for relief only to the corporation, not to its shareholders. (Indeed, under the doctrine of corporation by estoppel (Section 5, supra), a contract creditor may be taken to implicitly agree to limited liability even in some cases where the corporation is not validly formed.)

In short, limited liability to contract creditors can often be justified simply on the ground that once limited liability is established by statute, contract creditors know what they are getting. Therefore, a contract creditor who deals with a corporation can often "contract around" limited liability by making any adjustments in her contract with the corporation that she thinks limited liability requires—like requiring security for the corporation's debt, getting personal guarantees from the corporation's shareholders, getting covenants (promises) from the corporation that it will not take designated steps that might impair its financial condition, or charging a price that impounds (reflects) the cost of taking the extra risk entailed.

This contracting-around justification completely fails in the case of a tort creditor, like a pedestrian who is run over by a corporation's taxi. Furthermore, at least in the case of a publicly held corporation, the large body of shareholders may be better risk-bearers than an injured tort victim. See Leebron, Limited Liability, Tort Victims, and Creditors, 91 Colum.L.Rev. 1565, at 1601–02 (1992).

Moreover, it's pretty clear that in most or all tort contexts limited liability is inefficient. Modern conceptions of policy suggest that an enterprise should internalize—should be made to bear—the costs that the enterprise entails, including costs from injuries to third persons. Limited liability therefore seems to provide exactly the *wrong* incentive. Under a regime of limited liability, the owners of a corporation will reap all the benefits of the risks the corporation takes, but will not suffer all the costs of those risks. Accordingly, limited liability provides corporations with an incentive to take risks that are economically undue: managers who desire to advance the interests of their shareholders may make investments that they should not make, because the investment would be inefficient if all externalities had to be taken into account. As Henry Hansmann and Reiner Kraakman put it:

> The most familiar inefficiency created by limited liability is the incentive it provides for the shareholder to direct the corporation to spend too little on precautions to avoid accidents. In contrast, a rule of unlimited liability induces the socially efficient level of expenditure on precautions by making the shareholder personally liable for any tort damages that the corporation cannot pay.

Further, limited liability encourages overinvestment in hazardous industries. Since limited liability permits cost externalization, a corporation engaged in highly risky activities can have positive value for its shareholder, and thus can be an attractive investment, even when its net present value to society as a whole is negative. Consequently, limited liability encourages excessive entry and aggregate overinvestment in unusually hazardous industries.

Hansmann & Kraakman, Toward Unlimited Shareholder Liability for Corporate Torts, 100 Yale L.J. 1879, 1882–83 (1991).

Given all these factors, what might justify limited liability in the tort context? One possible argument is that the grounds for *imposing* liability on shareholders are not compelling. The normal predicate for making a principal vicariously liable for a tort committed by his agent is that the principal had control over the agent's physical activities and stood to benefit from those activities. In publicly held corporations, however, management is vested in the board and the officers, not in the shareholders. In that context, therefore, the normal predicate of vicarious liability for torts is missing.

This argument, however, does not justify limited liability to tort creditors in corporations that are not publicly held, in which control and ownership are usually intertwined. Two classes of corporations normally fall into this category: corporations whose shares are owned by only a few shareholders ("close corporations"), and subsidiaries that are wholly or mostly owned by a parent corporation. Moreover, even in publicly held corporations, shareholder liability to tort creditors could be supported on the theory (often referred to as enterprise liability) that those persons who stand to benefit from the activities of an enterprise should shoulder the costs that those activities inflict.

A very different argument for limited liability in the tort context is that in the absence of limited liability, the market for publicly held stock would be less efficient. The essential points of this argument, made by Halpern, Trebilcock & Turnbull, An Economic Analysis of Limited Liability in Corporation Law, 30 U. Toronto L.J. 117 (1980) and by F. Easterbrook & D. Fischel, The Economic Structure of Corporate Law 40–44 (1991), are as follows: A requirement of an efficient capital market is that the relevant capital assets (here, corporate stock) can be quickly and easily converted into cash. This characteristic is known as liquidity. A condition of liquidity, in turn, is that the asset be worth the same amount to all potential investors. As a practical matter, however, if shareholders had unlimited liability for tort claims, tort creditors would sue only very wealthy shareholders, like banks and pension funds, because non-wealthy shareholders would be unable to satisfy a judgment. As a result, the market for stock would not function efficiently because the value of shares would vary inversely with the wealth of the shareholder. Furthermore, if a tort creditor sued only, say, one wealthy shareholder, and collected the entire amount of his claim from that shareholder, that shareholder would seek contribution, but because of transaction costs she would seek contribution only from other wealthy shareholders. Because the right of contribution would be very important under an unlimited-liability rule, wealthy shareholders would need to continually incur costs to monitor the wealth of other shareholders, and the need to incur those costs would make the market even less efficient.

The stock-market-efficiency argument, like the argument based on lack of control, does not apply to closely held corporations and wholly owned subsidiaries, which have no publicly traded stock. Even in the case of publicly held corporations, the real-world weight of the stock-market-efficiency argument is difficult to judge. A rule that shareholders were liable to tort creditors would presumably be coupled with a rule, similar to that of the Revised Uniform Partnership Act, that required exhaustion of corporate assets before suit was brought against a shareholder. Based on past history, the likelihood that any shareholder in a publicly held corporation would be required to make any payments to tort creditors under an exhaustion regime would be only slightly more than zero, because very few publicly held corporations have faced tort claims that exceeded their ability to pay.

Furthermore, under a rule of shareholder liability for tort claims, wealthy shareholders would avoid investment in corporations that did not make adequate provision for tort claims through insurance. This would be a powerful incentive to corporations to adequately insure. That, in turn, would not only be a socially desirable result, but would further minimize the likelihood that liability would actually be imposed on shareholders. Leebron concludes that the market effects of making shareholders of publicly held corporations liable to tort creditors would probably be too small to affect the efficiency of stock markets.

The analysis of limited liability against tort creditors was moved forward in 1991, when both Leebron and Hansmann & Kraakman made notable contributions to the debate (in their articles cited above) by elaborating the concept that shareholders should be liable to tort creditors, but only on a pro rata basis, rather than on a joint and several basis. Under *joint and several* shareholder liability, each shareholder would be unlimitedly liable for all of a corporation's debts to tort creditors. Thus a shareholder who held only one share in a publicly held corporation could in theory be liable for the corporation's entire tort debts—in the worst case, hundreds of millions of dollars or more. In contrast, under *pro rata* shareholder liability each shareholder would be liable to a corporation's tort creditors only for that portion of the creditors' claims that equalled the shareholder's pro rata holding of the corporation's shares. Thus shareholders would have *individual* liability to tort creditors, but not *unlimited* liability.

To see how these rules differ, suppose that a wealthy investor holds five percent of a hotel company, while two impecunious hoteliers hold the remaining ninety-five percent. If a fire causes tort damages that exceed the company's assets by $200 million, the wealthy investor is potentially liable for $200 million under the joint and several rule but only $10 million under the pro rata rule.

Hansmann & Kraakman, supra, at 1892–93.[1]

Shareholder pro rata liability to tort creditors would have several advantages over joint liability. One advantage is that pro rata liability would be more closely tailored to the benefits that a shareholder stands to gain by the corporation's activities:

The basic justification for shareholder liability is that an enterprise should bear all its costs. As applied to shareholders, this means that costs of the enterprise are viewed as costs caused by investments. It would seem appropriate to view these costs as proportional to the amount of the investment. Each investor makes her own decision about the investment; she is unconcerned about the returns to other investors. Furthermore, the amount invested by any one investor is unlikely to be able to produce the total amount of risk and injury resulting from the entire enterprise. If we force each investor potentially to bear the costs "caused" by other investors, then inefficient investment decisions will be made.

Leebron, supra, at 1582–83. In addition, pro rata liability would largely undercut the stock-market-efficiency argument. Because each shareholder would bear only her own pro rata portion of liability, different wealth would not normally cause different shareholders to value the same shares differently. Furthermore, under a regime of pro rata liability a shareholder would have no need to monitor the wealth of other shareholders, because there would be no need for, and therefore no right to, contribution. See Leebron, supra, at 1607.

Some objections to pro rata liability can be made. Janet Cooper Alexander has shown that for jurisdictional reasons, ground-

---

1. Even under a joint-liability regime, a shareholder who was successfully sued by corporate creditors could seek contribution from the remaining shareholders, presumably on a pro rata basis in a publicly held corporation. However, in a publicly held corporation the transaction costs of suing all the other shareholders for contribution would be crushing (unless, at least, all the shareholders could be joined as involuntary class-action defendants).

Since contribution on a pro rata basis is generally available under the joint and several rule, the joint and several and pro rata rules converge when all shareholders can pay their pro rata portions of the

firm's tort damages. In this situation, the chief difference between the rules is that the pro rata rule assigns the full costs of collection to the plaintiff, while the joint and several rule assigns the bulk of these costs to the wealthiest defendant shareholder. Yet, because the joint and several rule also assigns the risk of failing to collect to the wealthiest defendant, the two rules produce dramatically different results when, as in the hypothetical in the text, some shareholders are judgment proof.

Hansmann & Kraakman, supra, at 1893, n. 36. See also Leebron, supra, at 1579–80.

ed on due process concerns, pro rata liability for tort claims could be effectively imposed only under the law of the state of incorporation or by the federal government.   Alexander, Unlimited Shareholder Liability Through a Procedural Lens, 106 Harv.L.Rev. 387 (1992).   However, that is not an argument against imposing such liability.   Joe Grundfest has argued that capital markets would undercut a regime of pro rata liability by generating a clientele of investors, such as offshore shareholders, who would be de facto attachment-proof.   Grundfest, The Limited Future of Unlimited Liability: A Capital Markets Perspective, 102 Yale L.J. 387 (1992). This objection is inapplicable to closely held corporations and wholly owned subsidiaries.   Furthermore, the discounted risk of liability might be too small to make it worthwhile for investors to allocate their resources on that basis.   Whether the risk of pro rata liability would be sufficiently large to produce a clientele effect has not been established.

A somewhat different problem with pro rata liability is that such liability might lead investors to purchase smaller shareholdings in individual corporations than they otherwise would, partly to reduce and diversify their exposure to tort claims, and partly because the smaller the shareholder's exposure, the higher are the transaction costs of bringing suit against the shareholder.   This might lead to inefficient degree of diversification, and might also reduce the likelihood of shareholder monitoring of corporate management, because the likelihood of such monitoring is partly a function of the size of a shareholder's holding.   See Leebron, supra, at 1612.

SEA–LAND SERVICES, INC. v. PEPPER SOURCE

United States Court of Appeals, Seventh Circuit, 1991.
941 F.2d 519.

Before BAUER, Chief Judge, WOOD, Jr., and POSNER, Circuit Judges.

BAUER, Chief Judge.

This spicy case finds its origin in several shipments of Jamaican sweet peppers.   Appellee Sea–Land Services, Inc. ("Sea–Land"), an ocean carrier, shipped the peppers on behalf of The Pepper Source ("PS"), one of the appellants here.   PS then stiffed Sea–Land on the freight bill, which was rather substantial.   Sea–Land filed a federal diversity action for the money it was owed.   On December 2, 1987, the district court entered a default judgment in favor of Sea–Land and against PS in the amount of $86,767.70.   But PS was nowhere to be found; it had been "dissolved" in mid–1987 for failure to pay the annual state franchise tax.   Worse yet for Sea–Land, even had it not been dissolved, PS apparently had no assets.   With the well empty, Sea–Land could not recover its judgment against PS.   Hence the instant lawsuit.

In June 1988, Sea–Land brought this action against Gerald J. Marchese and five business entities he owns: PS, Caribe Crown, Inc., Jamar Corp., Salescaster Distributors, Inc., and Marchese Fegan Associates. Marchese also was named individually. Sea–Land sought by this suit to pierce PS's corporate veil and render Marchese personally liable for the judgment owed to Sea–Land, and then "reverse pierce" Marchese's other corporations so that they, too, would be on the hook for the $87,000. Thus, Sea–Land alleged in its complaint that all of these corporations "are alter egos of each other and hide behind the veils of alleged separate corporate existence for the purpose of defrauding plaintiff and other creditors." Count I, ¶ 11. Not only are the corporations alter egos of each other, alleged Sea–Land, but also they are alter egos of Marchese, who should be held individually liable for the judgment because he created and manipulated these corporations and their assets for his own personal uses. Count III, ¶¶ 9–10. (Hot on the heels of the filing of Sea–Land's complaint, PS took the necessary steps to be reinstated as a corporation in Illinois.)

In early 1989, Sea–Land filed an amended complaint adding Tie–Net International, Inc., as a defendant. Unlike the other corporate defendants, Tie–Net is not owned solely by Marchese: he holds half of the stock, and an individual named George Andre owns the other half. Sea–Land alleged that, despite this shared ownership, Tie–Net is but another alter ego of Marchese and the other corporate defendants, and thus it also should be held liable for the judgment against PS.

. . . In December 1989, Sea–Land moved for summary judgment. . . .

In an order dated June 22, 1990, the court granted Sea–Land's motion. The court discussed and applied the test for corporate veil-piercing explicated in *Van Dorn Co. v. Future Chemical and Oil Corp.*, 753 F.2d 565 (7th Cir.1985). Analyzing Illinois law, we held in *Van Dorn* that

> a corporate entity will be disregarded and the veil of limited liability pierced when two requirements are met:
>
>> [F]irst, there must be such unity of interest and ownership that the separate personalities of the corporation and the individual [or other corporation] no longer exist; and second, circumstances must be such that adherence to the fiction of separate corporate existence would sanction a fraud or promote injustice.

753 F.2d at 569–70. As for determining whether a corporation is so controlled by another to justify disregarding their separate identities, the Illinois cases, as we summarized them in *Van Dorn,* focus on four factors: "(1) the failure to maintain adequate corporate records or to comply with corporate formalities, (2) the commingling of funds or assets, (3) undercapitalization, and (4) one corporation treating the assets of another corporation as its own." 753 F.2d at 570 (citations omitted). *See also Main Bank,* 427 N.E.2d at

102; *Pederson,* 214 Ill.App.3d at 820, 158 Ill.Dec. at 374, 574 N.E.2d at 168.

Following the lead of the parties, the district court in the instant case laid the template of *Van Dorn* over the facts of this case. Dist.Ct.Op. at 3–12.   The court concluded that both halves and all features of the test had been satisfied, and, therefore, entered judgment in favor of Sea–Land and against PS, Caribe Crown, Jamar, Salescaster, Tie–Net, and Marchese individually.   These defendants were held jointly liable for Sea–Land's $87,000 judgment, as well as for post-judgment interest under Illinois law.   From that judgment Marchese and the other defendants brought a timely appeal....

The first and most striking feature that emerges from our examination of the record is that these corporate defendants are, indeed, little but Marchese's playthings.   Marchese is the sole shareholder of PS, Caribe Crown, Jamar, and Salescaster.   He is one of the two shareholders of Tie–Net.   Except for Tie–Net, none of the corporations ever held a single corporate meeting.   (At the handful of Tie–Net meetings held by Marchese and Andre, no minutes were taken.)   During his deposition, Marchese did not remember any of these corporations ever passing articles of incorporation, bylaws, or other agreements.   As for physical facilities, Marchese runs all of these corporations (including Tie–Net) out of the same, single office, with the same phone line, the same expense accounts, and the like.   And how he does "run" the expense accounts!   When he fancies to, Marchese "borrows" substantial sums of money from these corporations—interest free, of course. The corporations also "borrow" money from each other when need be, which left at least PS completely out of capital when the Sea–Land bills came due.   What's more, Marchese has used the bank accounts of these corporations to pay all kinds of personal expenses, including alimony and child support payments to his ex-wife, education expenses for his children, maintenance of his personal automobiles, health care for his pet—the list goes on and on. Marchese did not even have a personal bank account!   (With "corporate" accounts like these, who needs one?)

And Tie–Net is just as much a part of this as the other corporations.   On appeal, Marchese makes much of the fact that he shares ownership of Tie–Net, and that Sea–Land has not been able to find an example of funds flowing from PS to Tie–Net to the detriment of Sea–Land and PS's other creditors.   So what?   The record reveals that, in all material senses, Marchese treated Tie–Net like his other corporations: he "borrowed" over $30,000 from Tie–Net; money and "loans" flowed freely between Tie–Net and the other corporations; and Marchese charged up various personal expenses (including $460 for a picture of himself with President Bush) on Tie–Net's credit card.   Marchese was not deterred by the fact that he did not hold all of the stock of Tie–Net; why should his creditors be?[2]

2. We note that the record evidence in this case, if true, establishes that for years   Marchese flagrantly has disregarded the tax code concerning the treatment of corporate

In sum, we agree with the district court that [there] can be no doubt that the "shared control/unity of interest and ownership" part of the *Van Dorn* test is met in this case: corporate records and formalities have not been maintained; funds and assets have been commingled with abandon; PS, the offending corporation, and perhaps others have been undercapitalized; and corporate assets have been moved and tapped and "borrowed" without regard to their source. Indeed, Marchese basically punted this part of the inquiry before the district court by coming forward with little or no evidence in response to Sea–Land's extensively supported argument on these points. That fact alone was enough to do him in; opponents to summary judgment motions cannot simply rest on their laurels, but must come forward with specific facts showing that there is a genuine issue for trial. Regarding the elements that make up the first half of the *Van Dorn* test, Marchese and the other defendants have not done so. Thus, Sea–Land is entitled to judgment on these points.

The second part of the *Van Dorn* test is more problematic, however. "Unity of interest and ownership" is not enough; Sea–Land also must show that honoring the separate corporate existences of the defendants "would sanction a fraud or promote injustice." *Van Dorn*, 753 F.2d at 570. This last phrase truly is disjunctive:

> Although an intent to defraud creditors would surely play a part if established, the Illinois test does not require proof of such intent. Once the first element of the test is established, *either* the sanctioning of a fraud (intentional wrongdoing) or the promotion of injustice, will satisfy the second element.

Id. (emphasis in original). Seizing on this, Sea–Land has abandoned the language in its two complaints that make repeated references to "fraud" by Marchese, and has chosen not to attempt to *prove* that PS and Marchese intended to defraud it—which would be quite difficult on summary judgment. Instead, Sea–Land has argued that honoring the defendants' separate identities would "promote injustice."

But what, exactly, does "promote injustice" mean, and how does one establish it on summary judgment? These are the critical, troublesome questions in this case. To start with, as the above passage from *Van Dorn* makes clear, "promote injustice" means something less than an affirmative showing of fraud—but how much less? In its one-sentence treatment of this point, the district court held that it was enough that "Sea–Land would be denied a judicially-imposed recovery." Dist.Ct.Op. at 11–12. Sea–Land defends this

funds. Yet, when we inquired at oral argument whether Marchese currently is under investigation by the IRS, his counsel informed us that to his knowledge he is not. Marchese also stated in his deposition that he never has been audited by the IRS. If these statements are true, and the IRS has so far shown absolutely no interest in Marchese's financial shenanigans with his "corporations," how and why that has occurred may be the biggest puzzles in this litigation.

reasoning on appeal, arguing that "permitting the appellants to hide behind the shield of limited liability would clearly serve as an injustice against appellee" because it would "impermissibly deny appellee satisfaction." Appellee's Brief at 14–15. But that cannot be what is meant by "promote injustice." The prospect of an unsatisfied judgment looms in every veil-piercing action; why else would a plaintiff bring such an action? Thus, if an unsatisfied judgment is enough for the "promote injustice" feature of the test, then *every* plaintiff will pass on that score, and *Van Dorn* collapses into a one-step "unity of interest and ownership" test. . . .

Generalizing from [the Illinois] cases, we see that the courts that properly have pierced corporate veils to avoid "promoting injustice" have found that, unless [they] did so, some "wrong" beyond a creditor's inability to collect would result: the common sense rules of adverse possession would be undermined; former partners would be permitted to skirt the legal rules concerning monetary obligations; a party would be unjustly enriched; a parent corporation that caused a sub's liabilities and its inability to pay for them would escape those liabilities; or an intentional scheme to squirrel assets into a liability-free corporation while heaping liabilities upon an asset-free corporation would be successful. Sea–Land, although it alleged in its complaint the kind of intentional asset- and liability-shifting found in *Van Dorn,* has yet to come forward with evidence akin to the "wrongs" found in these cases. Apparently, it believed, as did the district court, that its unsatisfied judgment was enough. That belief was in error, and the entry of summary judgment premature. We, therefore, reverse the judgment and remand the case to the district court.

On remand, the court should require that Sea–Land produce, if it desires summary judgment, evidence and argument that would establish the kind of additional "wrong" present in the above cases. For example, perhaps Sea–Land could establish that Marchese, like Roth in *Van Dorn,* used these corporate facades to avoid its responsibilities to creditors; or that PS, Marchese, or one of the other corporations will be "unjustly enriched" unless liability is shared by all. Of course, Sea–Land is not required fully to prove intent to defraud, which it probably could not do on summary judgment anyway. But it is required to show the kind of injustice to merit the evocation of the court's essentially equitable power to prevent "injustice." It may well be that, after more of such evidence is adduced, no genuine issue of fact exists to prevent Sea–Land from reaching Marchese's other pet corporations for PS's debt. Or it may be that only a finder of fact will be able to determine whether fraud or "injustice" is involved here. In any event, the record as it currently stands is insufficient to uphold the entry of summary judgment.

Reversed and Remanded with instructions.

———

SEA–LAND SERVICES, INC. v. PEPPER SOURCE

United States Court of Appeals, Seventh Circuit, 1993.
993 F.2d 1309.

Before BAUER, Chief Judge, ROVNER, Circuit Judge, and TIMBERS, Senior Circuit Judge.*

TIMBERS, Senior Circuit Judge.

Appellants appeal from a judgment entered after a bench trial in the Northern District of Illinois, James F. Holderman, *District Judge,* piercing the corporate veil and awarding appellee $118,132.61 in damages. . . .

On remand, additional discovery was permitted. The issues raised by the second prong of *Van Dorn* were tried on July 6 and 7, 1992. On July 9, 1992, the court entered judgment for Sea–Land, awarding it $118,132.61 in damages. The court concluded that Sea–Land satisfied the second prong of *Van Dorn* by establishing wrongs beyond its inability to collect on its judgment.

On the instant appeal, appellants contend that the evidence presented by Sea–Land at trial was insufficient to satisfy the second prong of *Van Dorn.* They also assert that the court misapplied Illinois law in reaching its decision. . . .

. . . Sea–Land adduced sufficient evidence at trial to establish additional wrongs to justify piercing the corporate veil. First, Sea–Land demonstrated that Marchese and his corporations were unjustly enriched. We have defined "unjust enrichment" as the receipt of money or its equivalent under circumstances that, in equity and good conscience, suggest that it ought not to be retained because it belongs to someone else. *Midcoast Aviation, Inc. v. General Elec. Credit Corp.,* 907 F.2d 732, 737 (7th Cir.1990). At trial, Sea–Land demonstrated that Marchese obtained countless benefits at the expense of not only Sea–Land, but the Internal Revenue Service (IRS) and other creditors as well. Indeed, Marchese used PS funds to pay his personal expenses as well as expenses incurred by his other corporations. As a result, PS was left without sufficient funds to satisfy Sea–Land or PS's other creditors. *American Trade Partners v. A1 Int'l Importing Enter.,* 770 F.Supp. 273, 278 (E.D.Pa. 1991) (corporate veil pierced on basis of unjust enrichment where managing shareholder, with knowledge of debt to creditor, used corporation's funds to pay personal expenses). Since Marchese was enriched unjustly by his intentional manipulation and diversion of funds from his corporate entities, to allow him to use these same entities to avoid liability "would be to sanction an injustice." *Gromer, Wittenstrom & Meyer, P.C. v. Strom,* 140 Ill.App.3d 349, 354, 489 N.E.2d 370, 374 (1986).

Sea–Land also satisfied the second prong of *Van Dorn* by demonstrating at trial that Marchese used his corporate entities as

* The Honorable William H. Timbers, Senior Circuit Judge, United States Court of Appeals for the Second Circuit, sitting by designation.

"playthings" to avoid his responsibilities to creditors. An accountant testified that Marchese's payment of personal expenses with corporate funds enabled those corporations to avoid their monetary obligations to vendors, creditors, and federal and state tax authorities. One example was Marchese's withdrawal of $19,000 as salary from Jamar Corporation. This withdrawal rendered Jamar insolvent and thus unable to satisfy liabilities in excess of $450,000. Marchese also frequently took "shareholder loans" from the corporations to pay personal expenses, leaving the corporations with insufficient funds to satisfy liabilities as they became due. Further, a tax accountant testified that Marchese's business practices were replete with illegal transactions. Indeed, as we previously recognized, "for years Marchese flagrantly has disregarded the tax code concerning the treatment of corporate funds." *Sea–Land, supra,* 941 F.2d at 522 n. 2.

Marchese's practice of avoiding liability to Sea–Land and other creditors by insuring that his corporations had insufficient funds with which to pay their debts, is ground for piercing the corporate veil. *Van Dorn, supra,* 753 F.2d at 572–73 (piercing of corporate veil allowed where subsidiary was stripped by parent corporation of its assets and rendered insolvent to the prejudice of creditor). Further, as the district court here properly recognized, Marchese was the "dominant force" behind all of the corporations and was responsible for the manipulation and diversion of corporate funds without regard for creditors or the law. *B. Kreisman & Co. v. First Arlington Nat'l Bank,* 91 Ill.App.3d 847, 415 N.E.2d 1070 (1980) (piercing corporate veil proper where defendant was the dominant force behind corporation). On the basis of the facts adduced at trial, the court properly concluded that Sea–Land satisfied the second-prong of *Van Dorn* and therefore was entitled to pierce the corporate veil. . . .

Appellants further assert that Sea–Land fails to satisfy the requirement that a nexus exist between its injuries and the fraud or injustice committed by appellants. *South Side Bank v. T.S.B. Corp.,* 94 Ill.App.3d 1006, 419 N.E.2d 477 (1981). This claim fails, however, in view of the fact that Marchese assured Sea–Land in 1987 that it would receive payment from PS as long as there were sufficient funds. The court's findings that Marchese knew at that time that he would manipulate the funds of PS so as to insure that Sea–Land would not be paid, and that he eventually did manipulate those funds, were not clearly erroneous. Since Marchese's intentional and improper financial maneuvering caused Sea–Land's inability to collect on its default judgment, the required nexus existed here. . . .

Affirmed.

———

SECTION 7. EQUITABLE SUBORDINATION OF SHAREHOLDER CLAIMS

NOTE ON EQUITABLE SUBORDINATION OF SHAREHOLDER CLAIMS

1. Under the doctrine of equitable subordination, when a corporation is in bankruptcy the claim of a controlling shareholder may be subordinated to other claims, including the claims of preferred shareholders, on various equitable grounds. The doctrine of equitable subordination is often referred to as the "Deep Rock" doctrine, named after the subsidiary corporation in the seminal case of Taylor v. Standard Gas & Electric Co., 306 U.S. 307, 59 S.Ct. 543, 83 L.Ed. 669 (1939). The Court in this case subordinated a parent's claim as a creditor of the subsidiary to the claims of other creditors and of preferred stockholders, because of the improper management of the subsidiary by the parent for the benefit of the parent and because the subsidiary had been inadequately capitalized.

See also Pepper v. Litton, 308 U.S. 295, 310, 60 S.Ct. 238, 246, 84 L.Ed. 281 (1939); Hackney & Benson, Shareholder Liability for Inadequate Capital, 43 U.Pitt.L.Rev. 837 (1982).

2. "As compared with denying to a shareholder his privilege of limited liability, the equitable remedy of subordination is much less drastic: it simply takes an investment already made, and denies it the status of a creditor's claim on a parity with outside creditors, whereas imposing liability for corporate debts undermines the essential premise of limited liability—that a shareholder's risk is limited to the amount of his investment.... It is logical, therefore, for the courts to have found it fair to subordinate a controlling person's claim based upon a lesser evidence of misuse of the corporate form than what is required to impose affirmative personal liability for all corporate obligations. Furthermore, if actual shareholder capital were so small as to result in treating a shareholder loan as equity, then the equity as supplemented by the subordinated loan may be deemed an adequate cushion to support limited liability. Accordingly, inadequate capitalization may result in subordination when it does not necessarily require imposition of affirmative liability." Hackney & Benson, supra, at 882.

UNIFORM FRAUDULENT TRANSFER ACT § 4(a)

[See Statutory Supplement]

BANKRUPTCY ACT § 548

[See Statutory Supplement]

NOTE ON TRANSFERS MADE BY A CORPORATION
WITHOUT AN EQUIVALENT EXCHANGE

Under the Bankruptcy Act, a transfer by a corporation to its shareholders without an equivalent exchange—for example, a dividend—can be recovered on the corporation's behalf, even if the corporation was solvent at the time of the transfer, if the corporation "was engaged in business or a transaction, or was about to engage in business or a transaction, for which any property remaining with the debtor was an unreasonably small capital." Similarly, under the Uniform Fraudulent Transfer Act such a transfer can be recovered if the corporation "was engaged or was about to engage in a business or a transaction for which the remaining assets of the debtor were unreasonably small in relation to the business or transaction." The Reporter's Note to UFTA § 4 states that the term "assets," rather than the term "capital," was used in § 4 to avoid confusing the concept of working capital with the legal concept of capital under corporate law.

SECTION 8. THE CORPORATE ENTITY AND THE INTERPRETATION OF STATUTES AND CONTRACTS

The questions often arise (1) whether a statute or contract that applies to a corporation also applies by implication to the corporation's shareholders, or (2) whether a statute or contract that applies to an individual also applies by implication to a corporation that the individual owns. If a statute prohibits aliens from owning ships that ply the U.S. coastal trade, does it also prohibit corporations from owning ships where all of the stock is held by aliens? If Corporation A agrees with X not to compete with X, may A's sole shareholder compete with X?

These are not questions concerning whether individual liability should be imposed despite the general rule of limited liability. Rather, they are questions of interpretation. In making such an interpretation, it must be borne in mind that, on the one hand, the law normally treats a corporation and its shareholders as distinct, but on the other, the legislature or contracting parties may not intend to treat a corporation and its shareholders as distinct for all purposes. Two of the leading cases in this area are United States v. Milwaukee Refrigerator Transit Co., 142 Fed. 247, 255 (E.D.Wis. 1905), and Anderson v. Abbott, 321 U.S. 349, 64 S.Ct. 531, 88 L.Ed. 793 (1944). In the *Milwaukee* case, a statute prohibited railroads from giving rebates to shippers. The statute was held applicable to a corporation that was not itself a shipper, but had been formed by a shipper's officers and principal shareholders for the purpose of obtaining what were in substance rebates. "[A] corporation will be looked upon as a legal entity as a general rule, and until sufficient reason to the contrary appears; but, when the notion of legal entity is used to defeat public convenience ... the law will regard the corporation as an association of persons." In the *Anderson* case, a statute made a shareholder in a national bank liable for the debts of the bank "to the amount of his stock therein, at the par value thereof in addition to the amount invested in such stock." The question was whether this statute applied to shareholders of a parent corporation with a national bank subsidiary, although technically only the parent was a shareholder in the bank. The Supreme Court concluded that the parent's shareholders would be deemed shareholders of the bank for the purpose of the statute, on the ground that to hold otherwise would permit that purpose to be undercut:

> It has often been held that the interposition of a corporation will not be allowed to defeat a legislative policy, whether that was the aim or only the result of the arrangement. . . .

> To allow this holding company device to succeed would be to put the policy of double liability at the mercy of corporation finance.

321 U.S. at 362–63, 64 S.Ct. at 537–38. See also Reich v. Gateway Press, Inc., 13 F.3d 685 (3d Cir.1994); Kavanaugh v. Ford Motor Co., 353 F.2d 710, 716–17 (7th Cir.1965); Note, Efficacy of the Corporate Entity in Evasion of Statutes, 26 Iowa L.Rev. 350 (1941).

SECTION 9.   THE CLASSICAL ULTRA VIRES DOCTRINE

INTRODUCTORY NOTE

1. Under the classical theory of corporate existence, the corporation is regarded as a fictitious person, endowed with life and capacity only insofar as provided in its charter. Early corporate charters tended to narrowly circumscribe the activities in which a corporation could permissibly engage. Transactions outside that sphere were characterized by the courts as "ultra vires" (beyond the corporation's power) and unenforceable—unenforceable *against*

the corporation because beyond the corporation's powers, and unenforceable *by* the corporation on the ground of lack of mutuality.[1] A leading example is Ashbury Railway Carriage & Iron Co. v. Riche, 7 L.R.–Eng. & Ir.App. 653, 33 L.T.R. 450 (1875). Ashbury was authorized by its charter "to make and sell, or lend on hire, railway-carriages and wagons, and all kinds of railway plant, fittings, machinery, and rolling-stock; to carry on the business of mechanical engineers and general contractors; to purchase and sell, as merchants, timber, coal, metals, or other materials; and to buy and sell any such materials on commission, or as agents." 7 L.R.–Eng. & Ir.App. at 654. Ashbury purchased a concession to construct and operate a railway line in Belgium, and Riche contracted to do the construction. After Riche had done some of the work, Ashbury repudiated the contract. Riche brought suit. The House of Lords held for Ashbury on the ground that it lacked the power under its charter to build a railroad, and therefore lacked the power to contract for that purpose.

The original purpose of the ultra vires doctrine seems to have been to protect the public or the state from unsanctioned corporate activity. Accordingly, under classical English law even unanimous shareholder ratification would not be a bar to an ultra vires defense if the transaction was outside the objects of the corporation. See *Ashbury,* supra; Frommel, Reform of the Ultra Vires Rule: A Personal View, 8 The Company Lawyer 11 (1987).

2.   In theory, the classical ultra vires doctrine was applicable to two somewhat different kinds of questions. The first question was whether a corporation had acted beyond its *purposes,* that is, had engaged in a type of business activity not permitted under its certificate. The second question was whether the corporation had exercised a *power* not specified in its certificate. In practice, the two questions tended to merge. For example, certificates of incorporation commonly contained clauses describing the corporation's purposes and powers with a provision to the effect that they were to be deemed both purposes and powers. Similarly, judicial opinions

1. The term "ultra vires" is best reserved for the question whether a corporation is empowered to take an action, but it is often loosely used in other contexts:

(i) In some cases, an action the corporation is empowered to take is lawful only if consent has been obtained from a public official. Corporate action without having secured such consent is sometimes labeled ultra vires. See, e.g., Texas & Pacific Ry. Co. v. Pottorff, 291 U.S. 245, 54 S.Ct. 416, 78 L.Ed. 777 (1934). However, failure to secure the consent does not make the action ultra vires; the action, if consented to, would be within the corporation's powers, and if not consented to, would be unlawful even if taken by an individual.

(ii) In other cases, a corporation can take certain action only if the action has been approved by a prescribed shareholder vote. Action without such approval is sometimes labeled ultra vires. Here too the label is inappropriate, because the action is within the corporation's powers, and the only issue is which corporate organ must authorize it.

(iii) In still other cases, an action, although within the scope of permissible corporate activity, is outside the scope of authority of the officer or agent who took it. Such an action may be "ultra vires" the officer, but it is not ultra vires the corporation.

would often say that a corporation had no "power" to engage in a type of business activity not permitted under the certificate.

3. A number of problems concerning specific types of powers tended to recur. See 1 Model Business Corporation Act Annotated 190–91 (3d ed. 1985). One of these recurring problems concerned the power of a corporation to guarantee a third party's debts. Early cases often held such guarantees ultra vires in the absence of a certificate provision explicitly conferring the power to guarantee. See, e.g., Brinson v. Mill Supply Co., 219 N.C. 498, 14 S.E.2d 505 (1941).[2] Present-day statutes explicitly empower a corporation to make guarantees, even without a provision to that effect in the certificate of incorporation. See, e.g., Del. Gen. Corp. Law § 123.

Another recurring issue concerned the power of a corporation to be a general partner. Early cases often held that a corporation had no power to enter into a partnership unless that power was explicitly granted by a statute or by the certificate. See, e.g., Whittenton Mills v. Upton, 76 Mass. (10 Gray) 582 (1858); Central R.R. Co. v. Collins, 40 Ga. 582 (1869). The concern was that a corporate partner would be bound by the acts and decisions of copartners who were not its duly appointed officers, thereby improperly impinging on the board's power and duty to manage the corporation.[3] Present-day statutes make this problem moot by explicitly empowering corporations to become partners. See, e.g., Del. Gen. Corp. Law § 122(11); N.Y.Bus.Corp.Law § 202(15); Rev. Model Bus. Corp. Act § 3.02(9).

4. Ultra vires was always regarded by the commentators as an unsound doctrine. For example, Ballantine, writing in 1927, argued:

> The practical question ... is not what power or capacity or authority has the state granted to an imaginary person, but rather what authority has the group of stockholders granted to their representatives, the directors, to do business on their behalf.
>
> ... [I]n general the objects and purposes clause of the articles should operate simply like by-laws or articles of partnership, as limitations on the actual authority of the directors and officers to bind the corporation, but not upon their ostensible or apparent authority, unless reasonably to be inferred or actually known.

Ballantine, Proposed Revision of the Ultra Vires Doctrine, 12 Cornell L.Q. 453, 455 (1927). Neither the courts nor, for the most part, the legislatures, ever went quite that far, but the history of the doctrine is one of steady erosion by the courts and the bar, resulting in large

---

2. Where the corporation received a direct benefit from making the guarantee, the courts often found that the guarantee was within the corporation's implied powers. See Kriedmann, The Corporate Guaranty, 13 Vand.L.Rev. 229 (1959).

3. The cases did permit corporations to enter into joint ventures, which are usually temporary in nature and created for a limited purpose.

part from the widespread view that the doctrine was unsound. This erosion proceeded along a variety of fronts:

(i) It was established even in early cases that corporate powers could be implied as well as explicit. See Sutton's Hospital Case, 10 Coke 23a (1613). The courts eventually became very liberal in finding implied powers, including implied powers to enter into business activities not specified in the certificate. Thus in Jacksonville Mayport, Pablo Ry. & Navigation Co. v. Hooper, 160 U.S. 514, 526, 16 S.Ct. 379, 40 L.Ed. 515 (1896), the Supreme Court held that a Florida company, whose purpose, under its charter, was to run a railroad, could also engage in leasing and running a resort hotel. "Undoubtedly the main business of a corporation is to be confined to that class of operations which properly appertain to the general purposes for which its charter was granted. But it may also enter into and engage in transactions which are auxiliary or incidental to its main business." See also, e.g., John B. Waldbillig, Inc. v. Gottfried, 22 A.D.2d 997, 254 N.Y.S.2d 924 (1964), aff'd 16 N.Y.2d 773, 209 N.E.2d 818, 262 N.Y.S.2d 498 (1965) (corporation organized to "engage in the business of building, construction, and contracting" could have incidental or implied power to practice engineering).

(ii) Generally speaking, ultra vires was not a defense at all to tort or criminal liability, and in areas where it was a defense it could not be used to reverse completed transactions. Accordingly, the major impact of the doctrine was confined to executory contracts.

(iii) Even as applied to executory contracts, the ambit of the doctrine was limited. If both parties to a contract had fully performed, ultra vires could not be used to undo the transaction. If neither had performed, ultra vires was a defense to both the corporation and the third party. The difficult case occurred where only one party had performed, and the nonperforming party then sought to assert ultra vires as a defense for its nonperformance. Under the majority view, the nonperforming party, having received a benefit under the contract, was "estopped" from asserting the ultra vires defense. See, e.g., Joseph Schlitz Brewing Co. v. Missouri Poultry & Game Co., 297 Mo. 400, 229 S.W. 813 (1921). Under the minority view—known as the "federal rule"—part performance did not raise an estoppel, on the theory that an ultra vires contract was prohibited by law and therefore void. Even the cases taking this view, however, usually permitted the performing party to recover in quasi-contract for the value of any benefit conferred. See Central Transportation Co. v. Pullman's Palace–Car Co., 139 U.S. 24, 11 S.Ct. 478, 35 L.Ed. 55 (1891).

(iv) Under American law, at least, unanimous shareholder approval barred the ultra vires defense unless creditors would be injured. See Note, 83 U.Pa.L.Rev. 479, 488–92 (1935).

(v) The final source of erosion of the ultra vires doctrine was the decreasing significance of the certificate of incorporation as a limit on the corporation's purposes and powers. Draftsmen began writing seemingly endless and crushingly boring certificate provisions that enumerated every possible business purpose and power imaginable. Eventually, most statutes made this kind of draftsmanship unnecessary by stating that the certificate of incorporation could provide simply that the corporation could engage in any lawful business, and by setting out a laundry list of powers that are conferred on every corporation without enumeration in the certificate.

DEL. GEN. CORP. LAW §§ 101(b), 102(a)(3), 121, 122, 124

[See Statutory Supplement]

REV. MODEL BUS. CORP. ACT §§ 3.01(a), 3.02, 3.04

Statutes comparable to Del. Gen. Corp. Law § 124 and Rev. Model Bus. Corp. Act § 3.04 have been adopted in all but a few states. See Schaeftler, Ultra Vires—Ultra Useless: The Myth of State Interest in Ultra Vires Acts of Business Corporations, 9 J.Corp.Law 81, 81–83 & n. 6 (1983).

GOODMAN v. LADD ESTATE CO.

Supreme Court of Oregon, 1967.
224 Or. 621, 427 P.2d 102.

Before McALLISTER, C.J., and SLOAN, GOODWIN, HOLMAN * and LUSK, JJ.

LUSK, Justice.

Plaintiffs brought this suit to enjoin the defendant Ladd Estate Company, a Washington corporation, from enforcing a guaranty agreement executed by Westover Tower, Inc., a corporation, in favor of Ladd Estate. From a decree dismissing the suit plaintiffs appeal.

In 1961 the defendant Walter T. Liles[1] held all the common shares of Westover and he, Dr. Edmond F. Wheatley and Samuel H. Martin were its directors.

On September 8, 1961, Dr. Wheatley borrowed $10,000 from Citizens Bank of Oregon and gave his promissory note therefor,

---

* Did not participate in this decision. (Footnote by the court.)

1. Pursuant to stipulation, the suit was dismissed as to Liles and Westover. The stipulation provided that "this suit may proceed in the same manner as if the said Walter T. Liles and Westover Tower, Inc. were parties hereto."

which was endorsed by Ladd Estate. Contemporaneously with this transaction Liles, individually, and Westover, by Liles as president, and Martin, as secretary, executed an agreement in writing by which they unconditionally guaranteed Ladd Estate against loss arising out of the latter's endorsement of the Wheatley note to Citizens Bank. The agreement was also signed by Ladd Estate. It recited that it was made at the request of Liles and Westover and that Ladd Estate would not have guaranteed payment of the Wheatley note without the guarantee of Liles and Westover to Ladd Estate.

Wheatley defaulted on his note, Ladd Estate paid to Citizens Bank the amount owing thereon, $9,583.61, and demanded reimbursement from Westover. Upon the latter's rejection of the demand Ladd filed an action at law upon the guaranty agreement against Liles and Westover.

The plaintiffs Morton J. Goodman and Edith Goodman, husband and wife, came into the case in this manner: On September 27, 1963, plaintiffs purchased all the common shares of Westover from a receiver appointed by the Circuit Court for Multnomah County who was duly authorized to make such sale. At the time of such purchase, plaintiffs were fully aware of the guaranty agreement given by Westover and Liles to Ladd Estate. It is conceded that the guaranty agreement was ultra vires the corporation. Plaintiffs, as stockholders, brought this suit pursuant to the provisions of ORS 57.040. [ORS 57.040 is comparable to Del.G.C.L. § 124, supra]. . . .

It will be noticed that the court may set aside and enjoin the performance of the ultra vires contract if it deems such a course equitable. Plaintiffs argue that to deny them the relief they seek would be "shocking," because Westover executed the guaranty agreement in order to enable one of its directors, Wheatley, to obtain a loan of money to be used for purposes entirely foreign to any corporate purpose. We see nothing shocking or even inequitable about it. The corporation was organized for the purposes, among others, to engage in the business of providing housing for rent or sale and to obtain contracts of mortgage insurance from the Federal Housing Commissioner, pursuant to the provisions of the National Housing Act, 12 U.S.C.A. § 1701 et seq. Authorized capital stock comprised 30,100 shares of which 100 shares, having a par value of $1 per share and designated preferred stock, were issued to the Commissioner, pursuant to § 1743(b)(1), U.S.C.A. and 30,000 shares, having a par value of $1 per share and designated common stock, were issued to Liles. Voting rights of the shareholders were vested exclusively in the holders of the common stock. The guaranty agreement recites that, at the request of Liles and Westover, Ladd Estate guaranteed payment of the Wheatley note. Ladd Estate made good on its endorsement when Wheatley defaulted and now calls upon Westover to honor its obligation. The agent of the plaintiffs, who purchased the shares for them, testified that he considered the question whether the guaranty was a valid obligation of the corporation before making the purchase and concluded that it was not.

The fact that he guessed wrong does not in any way enhance plaintiffs' claim to equitable consideration.

Neither would it be inequitable to enforce the agreement because of the purpose which the guaranty was intended to serve. Even before the enactment of ORS 57.040 a corporation might properly enter into a guaranty agreement in the legitimate furtherance of its business or purposes: Depot R. Syndicate v. Enterprise B. Co., 87 Or. 560, 562, 170 P. 294, 171 P. 223, L.R.A. 1918C, 1001; 19 Am.Jur.2d 493, Corporations § 1030; that the agreement does not further such purposes is what makes it ultra vires. But the statute says the agreement is enforceable even though ultra vires, and to accept the plaintiffs' argument would be to say that because it is ultra vires the agreement is inequitable and, therefore, unenforceable. This would effectually emasculate the statute.

Moreover, plaintiffs are in no position to invoke the aid of a court of equity. Liles, the former holder of their shares—all the voting shares of Westover—induced Ladd Estate to endorse Wheatley's note by procuring Westover to execute the guaranty agreement. If a shareholder himself has participated in the ultra vires act he cannot thereafter attack it as ultra vires: 7 Fletcher, Cyc. of Corporations (perm. ed., 1964 rev.) 613, § 3453. This would seem to be emphatically so of a shareholder who exercises the entire voting power of the corporation. Plaintiffs, as purchasers of Liles' shares, are in no better position than he would have been to raise the question: McCampbell v. Fountain Head R. Co., 111 Tenn. 55, 75, 77 S.W. 1070, 102 Am.St.Rep. 731; 7 Fletcher, op. cit. 614, § 3456.

It should be added that no rights of creditors of Westover are involved and there is nothing to indicate that the security of any mortgage guaranteed by the Federal Housing Commissioner would be impaired by enforcement of the agreement here in question. . . .

We are of the opinion that plaintiffs are not entitled to equitable relief. The decree is affirmed.

––––––––

INTER–CONTINENTAL CORP. v. MOODY, 411 S.W.2d 578 (Tex.Civ.App.1966). Inter–Continental Corp., a Texas corporation, guaranteed a note given by Shively, its president, to Moody. Moody knew or should have known that the guarantee was given for Shively's personal benefit. Shively lost control of Inter–Continental and Moody brought suit on the guarantee. Texas had a statute comparable to Del.Gen.Corp.Law § 124. Inter–Continental defended on the ground of ultra vires, and also arranged for a minority shareholder to intervene for the purpose of enjoining payment of the note on the same ground. (Inter–Continental's attorney drafted the shareholder's petition, promised to pay his legal expenses, and contacted his lawyer, who testified that he had never talked to the shareholder.) The court held that a defense of ultra vires by the corporation is barred under the statute even if the third party actually knew that the corporation lacked authority to enter into the transaction. However, the court continued, a shareholder can intervene to enjoin an ultra vires act even if he has been solicited to do so by the corporation, provided the shareholder is not the corporation's agent. (On a rehearing, the court added that if on remand "it is determined that on the facts the stockholder is entitled to some relief ... [the other party] will be entitled to a judgment against the corporation, not for the full amount of the note, but only to the extent that the stockholder is held not to be entitled to relief.") See Note, 45 Tex.L.Rev. 1422 (1967).

––––––––

711 KINGS HIGHWAY CORP. v. F.I.M.'S MARINER REPAIR SERV. INC., 51 Misc.2d 373, 273 N.Y.S.2d 299 (Spec.Term 1966). Kings Highway leased a theater to Mariner Repair for fifteen years, beginning July 1, 1966. Before July 1, Kings Highway brought an action for a declaratory judgment to invalidate the lease, on the ground that it was void because it would be ultra vires for Mariner Repair to conduct a motion-picture theater business. The New York statute, Bus.Corp.Law § 203, was comparable to Del.Gen. Corp.Law § 124. Held, for Mariner Repair. "It is undisputed that the present case does not fall within the stated exceptions contained in Section 203. . . . Neither is there merit to the plaintiff's contention that Section 203 applies only where ultra vires is raised as a defense. Notwithstanding the fact that this section is entitled 'Defense of ultra vires' it seems that except in the three stated situations set forth in the section, which are not applicable to the instant case, ultra vires may not be invoked as a sword in support of a cause of action any more than it can be utilized as a defense. . . ."

––––––––

SECTION 10. THE OBJECTIVE AND CONDUCT OF THE CORPORATION

––––––––

The question considered in this Section is, to what extent may a corporation act in a manner that is not intended to maximize corporate profits. This question is often put in terms of whether a given act would be "ultra vires," but it penetrates much more deeply into the nature of the corporate institution, and its place in society, than does the classical ultra vires issue.

––––––––

(a) THE SHAREHOLDERS' INTERESTS

HU, NEW FINANCIAL PRODUCTS, THE MODERN PROCESS OF FINANCIAL INNOVATION, AND THE PUZZLE OF SHAREHOLDER WELFARE

69 Tex.L.Rev. 1273, 1278–1283 (1991).

The most basic principle of corporate law is that a corporation is to be primarily run for the pecuniary benefit of its shareholders. Apart from the impact of nonstockholder constituency statutes and notions of social responsibility generally, few would disagree with this principle as a general matter.

But what does this principle mean in the usual day-to-day operation of publicly held corporations?   . . .

The traditional conception of the basic pecuniary goals of a corporation is based on the simple premise that what is good for the corporation is good for the shareholder. If corporate welfare is furthered, as through the maximization of earnings or earnings per share, shareholder welfare is presumed to be furthered as well. . . .

The traditional conception is based on two related assumptions. First, accounting-based measures such as earnings or earnings per share are appropriate indicators of corporate performance. Second, the welfare of a shareholder is largely coincident with the welfare of the corporation.

Unfortunately, both of these classic assumptions are of limited validity. Financial theorists have long argued—and corporate managers are starting to realize—that maximization of total corporate earnings or even earnings per share does not necessarily maximize shareholder wealth. Earnings growth as a sole measure of corporate performance fails to measure the risk characteristics of corporate investments, the extent of investments in working and fixed capital needed to sustain the firm, dividend policy, and the time value of money. . . .

The second assumption underlying the traditional conception, that the welfare of the corporation is coincident with the welfare of its shareholder, is also fundamentally flawed. For example, there may be a conflict of interest concerning risk between the corporation and its shareholders. . . . [M]odern financial theory suggests that corporations concerned about the well-being of shareholders will generally take more risks than corporations concerned about the entity's own well-being; shareholders can, by holding a portfolio of stocks, diversify away much of the risk that a corporation might itself find daunting. Similarly, there may be a conflict of interest as to time. For example, from the point of view of shareholders, the best thing to do with the typical company in a dying industry may be to liquidate the company immediately, pay the net proceeds to shareholders, and allow shareholders to put the money to better use. From the point of view of the company itself—and its managers and employees—long-term decline may be preferable.

[A second, competing] conception of the pecuniary goals of a corporation is directly focused on the welfare of the shareholder. Under this view, shareholder wealth maximization is sought directly, rather than as a by-product of corporate welfare. Managers should seek to take those actions that maximize the wealth of shareholders through a combination of maximizing the actual short- or long-term trading price of each share of common stock and the dividends they actually receive. There is no focus on measures of corporate performance like accounting earnings and no concern for the corporation independent of the welfare of its shareholders.

The shift to this second conception has been gradual but discernible. Most academics now believe that shareholder wealth maximization is the basic pecuniary objective of the modern publicly held corporation. Judges have typically subscribed to this standard only in the most limited of circumstances, typically in the context of a sale of the entire company.

———

HU, RISK, TIME, AND FIDUCIARY PRINCIPLES IN CORPORATE INVESTMENT
38 U.C.L.A. L.Rev. 277, 291–94, 299–300 (1990).

. . . *The Paramount Importance of Nondiversifiable Risk*

Assume that . . . a corporation is trying to decide between Project B and Project C. [Project B has a projected return of 10%. Project C has a projected return of 15%.] The variability of returns on the two projects suggests that Project C is riskier than Project B. Thus, it follows that management should choose Project C only if it believes that the additional return [on Project C] is somehow worth the additional risk.

This view ignores diversification effects. If a shareholder invests exclusively in one corporation and that corporation invests in Project C, the shareholder would be intensely interested in what happens in a year; the one "flip of the coin" would determine whether the shareholder makes money or loses it. In a close corporation setting, the shareholder may well have all or a substantial part of his wealth in shares of one corporation. That corporation's financial welfare can be equated to the shareholder's; if the corporation does badly, the shareholder does badly.

In the typical publicly held corporation setting, however, a shareholder is usually able to avoid keeping all his eggs in one basket. Assume that the publicly held corporation ("Corporation I") invests in Project C and the economy has other publicly held corporations (Corporations II, III, IV, and so forth), each of which also invests in projects with risks and returns similar to Project C. If the shareholder can invest half his funds in Corporation I and half his funds in Corporation II, and if the economic forces affecting Corporation I and those affecting Corporation II are completely unrelated, then the chances of both such companies ending up with a loss is only 25%, not 50%; there are two flips of the coin, and there is only a 25% chance both coins would end up tails. By the simple act of investing in two companies, the investor will cut in half the possibility of disaster.

The investor could extend this diversification further. Intuition and statistics suggest that the investor who invests in 100 such corporations that in turn invest in projects with characteristics like Project C (all with flips of the coin which are completely independent of each other) is virtually certain to receive a return very close to 15%. Under these circumstances, because of diversification, Project C is really no riskier than Project B. Thus, if all of the risk associated with Projects B and C can be diversified away—if both have zero "systematic" or "nondiversifiable" risk—a corporation should invest in Project C because it provides a higher expected return than Project B.

What does this first type of diversification effect suggest to managers dedicated to maximizing shareholder wealth? If shareholders are diversified and the risk associated with a project can be diversified away, managers can concentrate on expected returns and pay relatively little attention to such "diversifiable," "unique," or "unsystematic" risk. Stated more generally, if shareholders hold diversified portfolios (as is usually presumed for publicly held corporations), corporate managers dedicated to acting consistently with shareholder optimality should pay relatively little attention to unsystematic risk in judging among investment alternatives....

(b) INTERESTS OTHER THAN MAXIMIZATION OF THE SHAREHOLDERS' ECONOMIC WEALTH

NOTE ON DODGE v. FORD MOTOR CO.

One of the most famous of all corporation law cases is Dodge v. Ford Motor Co., 204 Mich. 459, 170 N.W. 668 (1919). The case is unusual in its early consideration of the issue (or at least one aspect of the issue) that is now known as corporate social responsibility.

Ford had been incorporated in 1903 with a capital of $150,000, and in 1908 the capital was increased to $2 million. Henry Ford owned 58% of Ford's stock and controlled the board; the two Dodge brothers owned 10%, and five other shareholders owned the balance. From 1908 on, Ford Motor had paid a regular annual dividend of $1.2 million, and between December 1911 and October 1915 it paid special dividends totaling $41 million. At the close of its July 31, 1916, fiscal year, Henry Ford, who controlled the board, declared it to be the settled policy of the company not to pay in the future any special dividends, but to put back into the business for the future all of the earnings of the company, other than the regular dividend of $1.2 million. "My ambition," declared Mr. Ford, "is to employ still more men; to spread the benefits of this industrial system to the greatest possible number, to help them build up their lives and their homes. To do this, we are putting the greatest share of our profits back into the business." At the time of the announcement, Ford Motor had a surplus of $112 million, including $52.5 million in cash and $1.3 million in municipal bonds. The Dodge brothers then brought an action, whose objects included compelling a dividend equal to 75% of the accumulated cash surplus, and restraining a proposed expansion of Ford Motor's facilities. The trial court ordered Ford Motor to declare a dividend of $19.3 million—equal to half its cash surplus as of July 31, 1916, minus special dividends paid between the time the complaint was filed and July 31, 1917. The Michigan Supreme Court affirmed this portion of the trial court's decree:

When plaintiffs made their complaint and demand for further dividends the Ford Motor Company had concluded its most prosperous year of business. The demand for its cars at the price of the preceding year continued. It could make and could market in the year beginning August 1, 1916, more than 500,000 cars. Sales of parts and repairs would necessarily increase. The cost of materials was likely to advance, and perhaps the price of labor, but it reasonably might have expected a profit for the year of upwards of $60,000,000. . . . Considering [the facts of this case] a refusal to declare and pay further dividends appears to be not an exercise of discretion on the part of the directors, but an arbitrary refusal to do what the circumstances required to be done. These facts and others call upon the directors to justify their action, or failure or refusal to act. In justification, the defendants have offered testimony tending to prove, and which does prove, the following facts. [Ford Motor had a general policy to reduce the price of its cars every year while maintaining or improving quality. In June 1915, it adopted a general plan under which it would double productive capacity and also erect a smelter. In furtherance of this plan, the price of cars was not reduced for the year beginning August 1, 1915, so that a large surplus could be accumulated to pay for the expansion. Even without expansion, Ford Motor could have produced 600,000 cars in the year beginning August 1, 1916, and sold them for $440 each. However, the policy of reducing prices called for the cars to be sold at $360 each, a difference of $48 million.]

The plan, as affecting the profits of the business for the year beginning August 1, 1916, and thereafter, calls for a reduction in the selling price of the cars.... In short, the plan does not call for and is not intended to produce immediately a more profitable business but a less profitable one; not only less profitable than formerly but less profitable than it is admitted it might be made. The apparent immediate effect will be to diminish the value of shares and the returns to shareholders.

It is the contention of plaintiffs that the apparent effect of the plan is intended ... to continue the corporation henceforth as a semieleemosynary institution and not as a business institution. In support of this contention they point to the attitude and to the expressions of Mr. Henry Ford....

The record, and especially the testimony of Mr. Ford, convinces that he has to some extent the attitude towards shareholders of one who has dispensed and distributed to them large gains and that they should be content to take what he chooses to give. His testimony creates the impression, also, that he thinks the Ford Motor Company has made too much money, has had too large profits, and that although large profits might be still earned, a sharing of them with the public, by reducing the price of the output of the company, ought to be undertaken. We have no doubt that certain sentiments, philanthropic and altruistic, creditable to Mr. Ford, had large influence in determining the policy to be pursued by the Ford Motor Company—the policy which has been herein referred to.

It is said by his counsel that—

"Although a manufacturing corporation cannot engage in humanitarian works as its principal business, the fact that it is organized for profit does not prevent the existence of implied powers to carry on with humanitarian motives such charitable works as are incidental to the main business of the corporation."...

The difference between an incidental humanitarian expenditure of corporate funds for the benefit of the employees, like the building of a hospital for their use and the employment of agencies for the betterment of their condition, and a general purpose and plan to benefit mankind at the expense of others, is obvious. There should be no confusion (of which there is evidence) of the duties which Mr. Ford conceives that he and the stockholders owe to the general public and the duties which in law he and his codirectors owe to protesting, minority stockholders. A business corporation is organized and carried on primarily for the profit of the stockholders. The powers of the directors are to be employed for that end. The discretion of directors is to be exercised in the choice of means to attain that end and does not extend to a change in the end itself, to the reduction of profits or to the nondistribution of profits among stockholders in order to devote them to other purposes.

... As we have pointed out, and the proposition does not require argument to sustain it, it is not within the lawful powers of a board of directors to shape and conduct the affairs of a corporation for the merely incidental benefit of shareholders and for the primary purpose of benefiting others, and no one will contend that if the avowed purpose of the defendant directors was to sacrifice the interests of shareholders it would not be the duty of the courts to interfere.

We are not, however, persuaded that we should interfere with the proposed expansion of the business of the Ford Motor Company. In view of the fact that the selling price of products may be increased at any time, the ultimate results of the larger business cannot be certainly estimated. The judges are not business experts.... We are not satisfied that the alleged motives of the directors, in so far as they are reflected in the conduct of the business, menace the interests of shareholders. It is enough to say, perhaps, that the court of equity is at all times open to complaining shareholders having a just grievance....

A.P. SMITH MFG. CO. v. BARLOW

Supreme Court of New Jersey, 1953.
13 N.J. 145, 98 A.2d 581, appeal dismissed, 346 U.S. 861, 74 S.Ct. 107, 98 L.Ed. 373 (1953).

JACOBS, J. The Chancery Division, in a well-reasoned opinion by Judge Stein, determined that a donation by the plaintiff The A.P. Smith Manufacturing Company to Princeton University was *intra vires*. Because of the public importance of the issues presented, the appeal duly taken to the Appellate Division has been certified directly to this court under Rule 1:5–1(*a*).

The company was incorporated in 1896 and is engaged in the manufacture and sale of valves, fire hydrants and special equipment, mainly for water and gas industries. Its plant is located in East Orange and Bloomfield and it has approximately 300 employees. Over the years the company has contributed regularly to the local community chest and on occasions to Upsala College in East Orange and Newark University, now part of Rutgers, the State University. On July 24, 1951 the board of directors adopted a resolution which set forth that it was in the corporation's best interests to join with others in the 1951 Annual Giving to Princeton University, and appropriated the sum of $1,500 to be transferred by the corporation's treasurer to the university as a contribution towards its maintenance. When this action was questioned by stockholders the corporation instituted a declaratory judgment action in the Chancery Division and trial was had in due course.

Mr. Hubert F. O'Brien, the president of the company, testified that he considered the contribution to be a sound investment, that the public expects corporations to aid philanthropic and benevolent institutions, that they obtain good will in the community by so doing, and that their charitable donations create favorable environment for their business operations. In addition, he expressed the thought that in contributing to liberal arts institutions, corporations were furthering their self-interest in assuring the free flow of properly trained personnel for administrative and other corporate employment. Mr. Frank W. Abrams, chairman of the board of the Standard Oil Company of New Jersey, testified that corporations are expected to acknowledge their public responsibilities in support of the essential elements of our free enterprise system. He indicated that it was not "good business" to disappoint "this reasonable and justified public expectation," nor was it good business for corporations "to take substantial benefits from their membership in the economic community while avoiding the normally accepted obligations of citizenship in the social community." Mr. Irving S. Olds, former chairman of the board of the United States Steel Corporation, pointed out that corporations have a self-interest in the maintenance of liberal education as the bulwark of good government. He stated that "Capitalism and free enterprise owe their survival in no small degree to the existence of our private, independent universities" and that if American business does not aid in their maintenance it is not "properly protecting the long-range interest of its stockholders, its employees and its customers." Similarly, Dr. Harold W. Dodds, President of Princeton University, suggested that if private institutions of higher learning were replaced by governmental institutions our society would be vastly different and private enterprise in other fields would fade out rather promptly. Further on he stated that "democratic society will not long endure if it does not nourish within itself strong centers of non-governmental fountains of knowledge, opinions of all sorts not governmentally or politically originated. If the time comes when all these centers are absorbed into government, then freedom as we know it, I submit, is at an end."

The objecting stockholders have not disputed any of the foregoing testimony nor the showing of great need by Princeton and other private institutions of higher learning and the important public service being rendered by them for democratic government and industry alike. Similarly, they have acknowledged that for over two decades there has been state legislation on our books which expresses a strong public policy in favor of corporate contributions such as that being questioned by them. Nevertheless, they have taken the position that (1) the plaintiff's certificate of incorporation does not expressly authorize the contribution and under common-law principles the company does not possess any implied or incidental power to make it, and (2) the New Jersey statutes which expressly authorize the contribution may not constitutionally be applied to the plaintiff, a corporation created long before their enactment. See *R.S.* 14:3–13; *R.S.* 14:3–13.1 *et seq.*

In his discussion of the early history of business corporations Professor Williston refers to a 1702 publication where the author stated flatly that "The general intent and end of all civil incorporations is for better government." And he points out that the early corporate charters, particularly their recitals, furnish additional support for the notion that the corporate object was the public one of managing and ordering the trade as well as the private one of profit for the members. See 3 *Select Essays on Anglo–American Legal History* 201 (1909); 1 *Fletcher, Corporations* (*rev. ed.* 1931), 6. See also *Currie's Administrators v. The Mutual Assurance Society,* 4 *Hen. & M.* 315, 347 (*Va.Sup.Ct.App.* 1809), where Judge Roane referred to the English corporate charters and expressed the view that acts of incorporation ought never to be passed "but in consideration of services to be rendered to the public." However, with later economic and social developments and the free availability of the corporate device for all trades, the end of private profit became generally accepted as the controlling one in all businesses other than those classed broadly as public utilities. *Cf. Dodd, For Whom Are Corporate Managers Trustees?,* 45 *Harv.L.Rev.* 1145, 1148 (1932). As a concomitant the common-law rule developed that those who managed the corporation could not disburse any corporate funds for philanthropic or other worthy public cause unless the expenditure would benefit the corporation. *Hutton v. West Cork Railway Company,* 23 *Ch.D.* 654 (1883); *Dodge v. Ford Motor Co.,* 204 *Mich.* 459, 170 *N.W.* 668, 3 *A.L.R.* 413 (*Sup.Ct.* 1919). *Ballantine, Corporations* (*rev. ed.* 1946), 228; 6A *Fletcher, supra,* 667. During the 19th Century when corporations were relatively few and small and did not dominate the country's wealth, the common-law rule did not significantly interfere with the public interest. But the 20th Century has presented a different climate. *Berle and Means, The Modern Corporation and Private Property* (1948). Control of economic wealth has passed largely from individual entrepreneurs to dominating corporations, and calls upon the corporations for reasonable philanthropic donations have come to be made with increased public support. In many instances such contributions have been sustained by the courts within the common-law doctrine upon liberal findings that the donations tended reasonably to promote the corporate objectives. See *Cousens, How Far Corporations May Contribute to Charity,* 35 *Va.L.Rev.* 401 (1949)....

[C]ourts, while adhering to the terms of the common-law rule, have applied it very broadly to enable worthy corporate donations with indirect benefits to the corporations. In *State ex rel. Sorensen v. Chicago B. & Q.R. Co.,* 112 *Neb.* 248, 199 *N.W.* 534, 537 (1924), the Supreme Court of Nebraska, through Justice Letton, went even further and without referring to any limitation based on economic benefits to the corporation said that it saw "no reason why if a railroad company desires to foster, encourage and contribute to a charitable enterprise, or to one designed for the public weal and welfare, it may not do so"; later in its opinion it repeated this view with the expression that it saw "no reason why a railroad corporation may not, to a reasonable extent, donate funds or services to aid in good works." ...

When the wealth of the nation was primarily in the hands of individuals they discharged their responsibilities as citizens by donating freely for charitable purposes. With the transfer of most of the wealth to corporate hands and the imposition of heavy burdens of individual taxation, they have been unable to keep pace with increased philanthropic needs. They have therefore, with justification, turned to corporations to assume the modern obligations of good citizenship in the same manner as humans do. Congress and state legislatures have enacted laws which encourage corporate contributions, and much has recently been written to indicate the crying need and adequate legal basis therefor. . . . In actual practice corporate giving has correspondingly increased. Thus, it is estimated that annual corporate contributions throughout the nation aggregate over 300 million dollars with over 60 million dollars thereof going to universities and other educational institutions. Similarly, it is estimated that local community chests receive well over 40% of their contributions from corporations; these contributions and those made by corporations to the American Red Cross, to Boy Scouts and Girl Scouts, to 4–H Clubs and similar organizations have almost invariably been unquestioned.

During the first world war corporations loaned their personnel and contributed substantial corporate funds in order to insure survival; during the depression of the '30s they made contributions to alleviate the desperate hardships of the millions of unemployed; and during the second world war they again contributed to insure survival. They now recognize that we are faced with other, though nonetheless vicious, threats from abroad which must be withstood without impairing the vigor of our democratic institutions at home and that otherwise victory will be pyrrhic indeed. More and more they have come to recognize that their salvation rests upon sound economic and social environment which in turn rests in no insignificant part upon free and vigorous nongovernmental institutions of learning. It seems to us that just as the conditions prevailing when corporations were originally created required that they serve public as well as private interests, modern conditions require that corporations acknowledge and discharge social as well as private responsibilities as members of the communities within which they operate. Within this broad concept there is no difficulty in sustaining, as incidental to their proper objects and in aid of the public welfare, the power of corporations to contribute corporate funds within reasonable limits in support of academic institutions. But even if we confine ourselves to the terms of the common-law-rule in its application to current conditions, such expenditures may likewise readily be justified as being for the benefit of the corporation; indeed, if need be the matter may be viewed strictly in terms of actual survival of the corporation in a free enterprise system. The genius of our common law has been its capacity for growth and its adaptability to the needs of the times. Generally courts have accomplished the desired result indirectly through the molding of old forms. Occasionally they have done it directly through frank rejection of the old and recognition of the new. But whichever path the common law has taken it has not been found wanting as

the proper tool for the advancement of the general good. *Cf.*
Holmes, The Common Law, 1, 5 (1951); *Cardozo, Paradoxes of*
Legal Science, Hall, Selected Writings, 253 (1947).

In 1930 a statute was enacted in our State which expressly
provided that any corporation could cooperate with other corporations and natural persons in the creation and maintenance of
community funds and charitable, philanthropic or benevolent instrumentalities conducive to public welfare, and could for such
purposes expend such corporate sums as the directors "deem
expedient and as in their judgment will contribute to the protection
of the corporate interests." ... In 1950 a more comprehensive
statute was enacted. *L.* 1950, *c.* 220; *N.J.S.A.* 14:3–13.1 *et seq.* In
this enactment the Legislature declared that it shall be the public
policy of our State and in furtherance of the public interest and
welfare that encouragement be given to the creation and maintenance of institutions engaged in community fund, hospital, charitable, philanthropic, educational, scientific or benevolent activities or
patriotic or civic activities conducive to the betterment of social and
economic conditions; and it expressly empowered corporations
acting singly or with others to contribute reasonable sums to such
institutions, provided, however, that the contribution shall not be
permissible if the donee institution owns more than 10% of the
voting stock of the donor and provided, further, that the contribution shall not exceed 1% of capital and surplus unless the excess is
authorized by the stockholders at a regular or special meeting. To
insure that the grant of express power in the 1950 statute would
not displace preexisting power at common law or otherwise, the
Legislature provided that the "act shall not be construed as directly
or indirectly minimizing or interpreting the rights and powers of
corporations, as heretofore existing, with reference to appropria-
tions, expenditures or contributions of the nature above specified."
N.J.S.A. 14:3–13.3. It may be noted that statutes relating to charitable contributions by corporations have now been passed in 29
states. See *Andrews, supra,* 235.

The appellants contend that the foregoing New Jersey statutes
may not be applied to corporations created before their passage.
Fifty years before the incorporation of The A.P. Smith Manufacturing
Company our Legislature provided that every corporate charter
thereafter granted "shall be subject to alteration, suspension and
repeal, in the discretion of the legislature." L.1846, p. 16; *R.S.*
14:2–9. A similar reserved power was placed into our State Constitution in 1875 (Art. IV, Sec. VII, par. 11), and is found in our
present Constitution....

... We are entirely satisfied that within the orbit of above
authorities the legislative enactments found in *R.S.* 14:3–13 and
N.J.S.A. 14:3–13.1 *et seq.* and applied to pre-existing corporations
do not violate any constitutional guarantees afforded to their stockholders.

... And since in our view the corporate power to make reasonable charitable contributions exists under modern conditions, even apart from express statutory provision, its enactments simply constitute helpful and confirmatory declarations of such power, accompanied by limiting safeguards.

In the light of all of the foregoing we have no hesitancy in sustaining the validity of the donation by the plaintiff. There is no suggestion that it was made indiscriminately or to a pet charity of the corporate directors in furtherance of personal rather than corporate ends. On the contrary, it was made to a preeminent institution of higher learning, was modest in amount and well within the limitations imposed by the statutory enactments, and was voluntarily made in the reasonable belief that it would aid the public welfare and advance the interests of the plaintiff as a private corporation and as part of the community in which it operates. We find that it was a lawful exercise of the corporation's implied and incidental powers under common-law principles and that it came within the express authority of the pertinent state legislation. As has been indicated, there is now widespread belief throughout the nation that free and vigorous non-governmental institutions of learning are vital to our democracy and the system of free enterprise and that withdrawal of corporate authority to make such contributions within reasonable limits would seriously threaten their continuance. Corporations have come to recognize this and with their enlightenment have sought in varying measures, as has the plaintiff by its contribution, to insure and strengthen the society which gives them existence and the means of aiding themselves and their fellow citizens. Clearly then, the appellants, as individual stockholders whose private interests rest entirely upon the well-being of the plaintiff corporation, ought not be permitted to close their eyes to present-day realities and thwart the long-visioned corporate action in recognizing and voluntarily discharging its high obligations as a constituent of our modern social structure.

The judgment entered in the Chancery Division is in all respects

Affirmed.

For affirmance—Chief Justice VANDERBILT, and Justices HEHER, OLIPHANT, WACHENFELD, BURLING and JACOBS—6.

For reversal—None.

———

DEL. GEN. CORP. LAW § 122(9), (12)

[See Statutory Supplement]

———

REV. MODEL BUS. CORP. ACT § 3.02(12)–(14)

[See Statutory Supplement]

———

MILTON FRIEDMAN, THE SOCIAL RESPONSIBILITY OF BUSINESS IS TO INCREASE ITS PROFITS, N.Y. Times, Sept. 13, 1970, § 6 (magazine) at 32. "In a free-enterprise, private-property system, a corporate executive is an employee of the owners of the business. He has direct responsibility to his employers. That responsibility is to conduct the business in accordance with their desires, which generally will be to make as much money as possible while conforming to the basic rules of the society, both those embodied in law and those embodied in ethical custom."

———

AMERICAN LAW INSTITUTE, PRINCIPLES OF CORPORATE GOVERNANCE §§ 2.01, 6.02

[See Statutory Supplement]

———

CONN. GEN. STATS. ANN. §§ 33–313

[See Statutory Supplement]

———

INDIANA CODE ANN. § 23–1–35–1

[See Statutory Supplement]

———

N.Y. BUS. CORP. LAW § 717

[See Statutory Supplement]

———

PENNSYLVANIA CONSOL. STATS. ANN. TITLE 15, §§ 1711, 1715, 1716, 1717, 2502

[See Statutory Supplement]

———

CREDIT LYONNAIS BANK NEDERLAND, N.V. v. PATHE COMMUNICATIONS CORP., 1991 WL 277613 (Del.Ch.1991). In this case, Chancellor Allen stated that "At least where a corporation is operating in the vicinity of insolvency, a board of directors is not merely the agent of the residual risk bearers [that is, the shareholders], but owes its duty to the corporate enterprise." He elaborated on this observation as follows:

> The possibility of insolvency can do curious things to incentives, exposing creditors to risks of opportunistic behavior and creating complexities for directors. Consider, for example, a solvent corporation having a single asset, a judgment for $51 million against a solvent debtor. The judgment is on appeal and thus subject to modification or reversal. Assume that the only liabilities of the company are to bondholders in the amount of $12 million. Assume that the array of probable outcomes of the appeal is as follows:

	Expected Value
25% chance of affirmance ($51mm)	$12.75
70% chance of modification ($4mm)	2.8
5% chance of reversal ($0)	0
Expected Value of Judgment on Appeal	$15.55

> Thus, the best evaluation is that the current value of the equity is $3.55 million. ($15.55 million expected value of judgment on appeal [minus] $12 million liability to bondholders). Now assume an offer to settle at $12.5 million (also consider one at $17.5 million). By what standard do the directors of the company evaluate the fairness of these offers? The creditors of this solvent company would be in favor of accepting either a $12.5 million offer or a $17.5 million offer. In either event they will avoid the 75% risk of insolvency and default. The stockholders, however, will plainly be opposed to acceptance of a $12.5 million settlement (under which they get practically nothing). More importantly, they very well may be opposed to acceptance of the $17.5 million offer under which the residual value of the corporation would increase from $3.5 to $5.5 million. This is so because the litigation alternative, with its 25% probability of a $39 million outcome to them ($51 million—$12 million [=] $39 million) has an expected value to the residual risk bearer of $9.75 million ($39 million × 25% chance of affirmance), substantially greater than the $5.5 million available to them in the settlement. While in fact the stockholders' preference would reflect their appetite for risk, it is possible (and with diversified shareholders likely) that shareholders would prefer rejection of both settlement offers.

> But if we consider the community of interests that the corporation represents it seems apparent that one should in this hypothetical accept the best settlement offer available pro-

viding it is greater than $15.55 million, and one below that amount should be rejected. But that result will not be reached by a director who thinks he owes duties directly to shareholders only. It will be reached by directors who are capable of conceiving of the corporation as a legal and economic entity. Such directors will recognize that in managing the business affairs of a solvent corporation in the vicinity of insolvency, circumstances may arise when the right (both the efficient and the fair) course to follow for the corporation may diverge from the choice that the stockholders (or the creditors, or the employees, or any single group interested in the corporation) would make if given the opportunity to act.

Id. at 31, n. 55.

SECTION 11. THE NATURE OF CORPORATE LAW

M. EISENBERG, THE STRUCTURE OF THE CORPORATION 1 (1976). "Corporate law is constitutional law; that is, its dominant function is to regulate the manner in which the corporate institution is constituted, to define the relative rights and duties of those participating in the institution, and to delimit the powers of the institution vis-à-vis the external world."

M. EISENBERG, THE STRUCTURE OF CORPORATION LAW, 89 Colum.L.Rev. 1461 (1989). "A corporation is a profit-seeking enterprise of persons and assets organized by rules. Most of these rules are determined by the unilateral action of corporate organs or officials. Some of [the] rules are determined by market forces. Some are determined by contract or other forms of agreement. Some are determined by law.

" . . . Viewed in terms of their form, [the rules that concern the internal organization of the corporation and the conduct of corporate actors] fall into three basic categories. *Enabling rules* give legal effect to rules that corporate actors adopt in a specified manner. *Suppletory* or *default rules* govern defined issues unless corporate actors adopt other rules in a specified manner. *Mandatory rules* govern defined issues in a manner that cannot be varied by corporate actors.

" . . . [Viewed in terms of their subject matter, these rules also fall into three categories.] *Structural rules* govern the allocation of decisionmaking power among various corporate organs and agents and the conditions for the exercise of decisionmaking power; the allocation of control over corporate organs and agents; and the flow of information concerning the actions of corporate organs and agents. *Distributional rules* govern the distribution of assets (including earnings) to shareholders. *Fiduciary rules* govern the duties of managers and controlling shareholders. These three types of rules [may] be referred to collectively as *constitutive rules* [since taken together they make up the constitution of the corporation]."

BRATTON, THE ECONOMIC STRUCTURE OF THE POST–CONTRACTUAL CORPORATION

87 Northwestern L.Rev. 180 (1992).

I. Introduction

The political economics of corporate law changed abruptly during the 1980s. At the decade's start, the prevailing economics counseled that excess management power needed to be curbed for productivity's sake. Law reform was assumed to be an appropriate means to this end. But this antimanagerialist paradigm fell from favor, and by the time the takeover market became white-hot in 1984 and 1985, a "contract paradigm" had taken its place. The large American corporation [was reconceived] as a nexus for a set of contracts among individual factors of production. Corporate governance followed suit, and reappeared as a field well suited to microeconomic modeling. . . . Credit for this change goes in the first instance to Professor (later Judge) Frank Easterbrook and Professor Daniel Fischel, the leading exponents of the new "contractarian" view. . . .

Now Easterbrook and Fischel summarize their enterprise with *The Economic Structure of Corporate Law.* This long-awaited book collects, highlights, and integrates their foundational pieces so as to give us a touchstone volume. This book provides a corporate law counterpart to Judge Posner's *Economic Analysis of Law,* and a counter to Professor Eisenberg's positivist account, *The Structure of the Corporation.* No other contemporary book about corporate doctrine approaches its theoretical force. It may be that no comparable integration of corporate law and economics has appeared since 1934, when Berle and Means published *The Modern Corporation and Private Property. . . .*

. . . True to the Chicago tradition of law and neoclassical microeconomics, [Easterbrook & Fischel] tend to accord determinative force to the triumvirate of investor self-protection, market price, and market constraint. The corporate law mainstream, in contrast, holds open a door to the proposition that contract can fail. It follows an economic model of the contractual firm, drawn from the work of Oliver Williamson and built around a recognition of contract failure. In this model the failure sometimes occurs because the pursuit of rational self-interest goes overboard, becoming sub-optimal opportunism. At other times, the failure occurs because of intrinsic limits on the problem-solving abilities of contracting parties. Either way, contract failure causes economic actors to build compensating governance structures, and sometimes even justifies government regulation.

Review of the works collected in *The Economic Structure of Corporate Law* prompts reappraisal of Easterbrook and Fischel's reputation as neoclassical critics of the rest of the legal academy. They prove quite sensitive to the flow of the corporate law mainstream. When the moment for concrete decision arrives, they tend to find a way to join it. Much of the talk to the effect that market and other contracting processes achieve pricing solutions to every problem in corporate governance turns out to be just talk. They often conclude that the market or other contract process in question has failed or arguably failed, and that regulation by statute or judicial intervention may be justifiable. As applied, if not as stated, their model is thoroughly Williamsonian.

Easterbrook and Fischel are so astute that they keep a safe distance from the assertion that the corporation is a nexus of contracts. The book delimits and subordinates this once foundational proposition. This is an appropriate step. The claim that everything in corporate life and law is contract at some deep structural level has outlived its usefulness. The idea never worked all that well as it was. Its shortcomings have been exhaustively discussed. It had heuristic value ten years ago, when microeconomic models of corporate structure were new to law. At that time the nexus-of-contracts assertion taught the lesson that the models have a valid bearing on legal corporate governance. Now that the lesson has been learned and, indeed, now that the rhetoric and politics of the entire field have been captured and tamed, the nexus-of-contracts theory no longer needs emphasis. Its heuristic value has been spent. Economic analysis can proceed without it on the uncontroverted assumption that the corporation has significant contractual aspects.

II.   THE GOING CONCERN ...

B.   *The Disappearing Nexus of Contracts* ...

1. Containing the Nexus of Contracts.—Easterbrook and Fischel pause at the book's start to "step back and ask whether corporation-as-contract is a satisfying way of looking at things even in theory." To all appearances the proposition survives inspection. But the process drains off much of the content.

Easterbrook and Fischel make an uncharacteristically half-hearted case. The corporation, they say, is contractual in nature because it is a "voluntary" and "adaptive" "complex [of] arrangements." This statement is true, but it does not support the old paradigm. Today's United States Army is also a "voluntary" complex of arrangements. Yet the Army's norm of sacrifice and structure of command make a contractual description unhelpful. As to "adaptive" capacity, the Delaware courts and legislature perform better in a dynamic economic environment than do, for instance, the car companies. Yet few would find it useful to describe state government as a nexus of contracts.

Easterbrook and Fischel do not bother to pursue the claim that corporate law is contractual at a deep structural level even when mandatorily phrased. It is just, they say, that the voluntary is more important than the mandatory to everyday operation and ultimate welfare. This is another true statement. But it is a statement no observer would have bothered to dispute back in 1968.... Nor do Easterbrook and Fischel claim that agency-cost analysis leads to some necessarily contractual bottom line. Instead, they look for the balance of advantages among the various devices that control agency costs, and not all of these are contractual.

Easterbrook and Fischel do continue to employ a "contractual" normative yardstick. The law, they say, should replicate the contract the parties would have reached if left to themselves in a low-cost world. But deciding to bring a hypothetical contract norm to bear on corporate law questions does not, as a positive proposition, make the corporation a nexus of contracts. Hypothetical contract is a welfare norm asserted by an academic. It is not a transactional artifact. In Easterbrook and Fischel's construct, the "contractual" analytical product is imposed without regard to whether the real-world actors in a situation of higher cost and bounded rationality would have employed it themselves if offered the chance. Here, if the issue ever is joined, welfare trumps choice....

Given all of this, what was that nexus-of-contracts corporation all about in its day? The book provides an accurate answer:

> The arrangements among [corporate actors] usually depend on contracts and on positive law, not on corporate law or the status of the corporation as an entity. More often than not a reference to the corporation as an entity will hide the essence of the transaction. So we often speak of the corporation as a "nexus of contracts" or a set of implicit and explicit contracts....

The nexus-of-contracts assertion, then, deflects attention from the shop-worn juridical corporation, with its shareholder "owners," and its long history of conceptual concern for the role and meaning of the "corporate entity." Clearing out this juridical clutter frees us to concentrate on economic fundamentals. We demystify the shareholders, now seeing them as investors who happen to have agency cost problems in their relationship with another group of corporate participants, the managers. Thus described, the "nexus of contracts" is not a positive and normative foundation for corporate legal theory, nor even much of an heuristic. It is a point of critique.

2. The Containment Explained.—Easterbrook and Fischel have stepped back from the nexus-of-contracts corporation because developments in both theory and practice made manifest its inadequacy as a foundation for any plausible legal theory. The theoretical development was the "mandatory/enabling" discussion of the late 1980s. This showed that shareholder-manager relationships did not, in the main, lie within the zone of free contract. The practical development was the failure of crucial subject matter—the law addressed to takeovers—to develop in conformity to the model's predictions. This showed emphatically that corporate law does not always instantiate contractual norms. The fact that these two topics had been the principal focus of corporate legal scholarship for a number of years made these developments doubly debilitating for the proposition that corporations are comprised of a nexus of contracts.

(a) Mandatory corporate law affirmed.—The mandatory/enabling discussion was an extended consideration of the implications of the nexus-of-contracts proposition. The proposition on the table was this: If the firm is contract, then the parties in interest should be able to "opt-out" of the terms provided by state law and substitute their own terms. Discussion of this proposition iterated contract law's "overreaching" analysis. It turned out that process defects make the corporate charter amendment an inappropriate context for complete freedom of contract, even when viewed through the lens of an economic model. Shareholders have a collective action problem when managers propose charter amendments. Small stakes make it irrational for individual holders to invest in information acquisition. Moreover, managers, by virtue of their control of the structure and timing of the amendment process, can easily turn the shareholders' disadvantaged negotiating position to their own advantage. The upshot is a contract failure: the shareholders rationally vote to approve an amendment that decreases value to them.

A consensus of sorts emerged from the discussion. The amendment process is deemed reliable as to amendments such as poison pills or stock option plans that are company-specific and transaction-specific. But, as to general, open-ended proposals such as a broad-brush abolition of director and officer fiduciary duties, contract failure is probable. Therefore, according to the consensus, charter amendments sometimes should be subject to mandatory regulation even under a contract paradigm.

The appearance of this consensus against universal "opting-out" had paradigmatic implications. The consensus confirmed the legitimacy of legal intervention in corporate affairs from an economic perspective. In other words, corporate law and economics would go forward under the Williamsonian paradigm. Although no one mentioned it at the time, this also began a process of disassociation between corporate law and economics and the nexus-of-contracts concept of the corporation. The process continues today.

Easterbrook and Fischel joined the mandatory/enabling consensus, albeit with qualifications. Their book iterates this position. In taking this position they do not, of course, expunge contract from their theory of the firm.... But, since contract turns out to be a matter of degree, the issue goes to the dimensions of the zone of contract freedom provided for by a particular model. Easterbrook and Fischel's zone is rhetorically expansive, but more compact as a practical matter. A blank contracting slate occurs only in respect to recent and prospective initial public offerings. Since most Fortune 500 companies went public long ago, the critical questions respecting most corporations remain legitimate subject matter for legal mandates.

(b) Takeovers reversed.—Takeovers made a contractual picture of the public corporation plausible in the first place. Under the managerialist paradigm of the corporation, managers had unassailable and excessive power. As hostile tender offers proliferated, market actors broke the power of target managers through the simple expedient of purchasing shares. In effect, what was thought unassailable was assailed successfully through the medium of the discrete contract. As discrete contracts came to alter the flow of corporate power, the nexus-of-contracts corporation came into economic and legal theory.

Fittingly, developments begun in the late 1980s in response to takeovers are prompting the nexus-of-contracts corporation's subsequent departure. Shark repellant charter amendments and poison pill plans—"contractual" modifications that entrench management and devalue the shareholders' investment—retained the support of the courts even as they became more widespread and effective. In addition, state legislatures came down emphatically on the side of defending managers. Their antitakeover statutes imposed significant costs on hostile control transfers. Viewed cumulatively, these changes open up a rift between the contract paradigm's implicit normative structure, on the one hand, and that of actual corporate contracts and state corporate law, on the other.

To their credit, Easterbrook and Fischel not only admit, but explore the negative implications of these developments for the contractual corporation. They conclude that takeover law has developed in an inefficient direction. Managers exploit the collective action problem in getting shareholders to assent to shark repellant provisions. And, in the "last period," when managers defend their jobs from attack, the ordinary controls of the capital and labor markets do not operate. Judicial intervention becomes the only available means to the end of [efficient] deployment of assets.

Furthermore, Easterbrook and Fischel abandon the "race to the top" story of state corporate law. This tale had it that a market for charters operated among the states, with the most efficient state getting the most business. It was first formulated to counter the assertion that the state corporate law system was a corrupt "race for the bottom." But the "race to the top" assertion was more than a point of critique. It threw the development of state corporate law into an evolutionary context determined by economic competition, thereby fusing positive law and contract. Legal mandate was reinterpreted as form; the substance was contract.

Today, Easterbrook and Fischel speak of the performance of state corporate law with less confidence. In their opinion, while survival still is the best measure of success, state corporate law is a process of satisfying rather than optimizing. No one, moreover, knows what the market wants. Easterbrook and Fischel do find a contractual term to describe the proliferation of antitakeover statutes. In a rare resort to Williamsonian terminology, they ascribe the legislation to management "opportunism." But this is bravado. Their model no longer fuses state law together with contract so as to make economics the sole determinant of the law's evolution.

Chapter IV

CORPORATE STRUCTURE

SECTION 1. SHAREHOLDERSHIP IN PUBLICLY HELD CORPORATIONS

NOTE ON SHAREHOLDERSHIP IN PUBLICLY HELD CORPORATIONS

1. *The Traditional Model.* Until recently, corporation law reflected what might be called the traditional model of formal corporate decisionmaking. Under this model, the board of directors manages the corporation's business and makes business policy; the officers act as agents of the board and execute its decisions; and the shareholders elect the board and decide on "major corporate actions" or "fundamental" changes. The model is an inverted pyramid in form. At the top of the inverted pyramid are the shareholders, whose vote is required to elect the board of directors and to pass on other major corporate actions. The next level down is represented by the directors, who constitute the policymaking body of the corporation and select the officers. At the bottom of the inverted pyramid are the officers, who have some discretion but in general are limited to the execution of policies formulated by the board.

2. *Berle and Means.* This model was first called into drastic question in 1932, with the publication of Berle & Means' classic work, *The Modern Corporation and Private Property.* One of this book's principal conclusions, almost revolutionary at the time, was that as corporate ownership had come to be widely dispersed, control had come to be divorced from ownership:

> Frequently . . . ownership is so widely scattered that working control can be maintained with but a minority interest. . . . Separation of ownership and control becomes almost complete when not even a substantial minority interest exists, as in the American Telephone and Telegraph Company. . . . Under such conditions control may be held by the directors or titular managers who can employ the proxy machinery to become a self-perpetuating body, even though as a group they own but a small fraction of the stock outstanding.

> . . . [A] large body of security holders has been created who exercise virtually no control over the wealth which they or

their predecessors in interest have contributed to the enterprise. In the case of management control, the ownership interest held by the controlling group amounts to but a very small fraction of the total ownership. . . .

. . . [T]he position of ownership has changed from that of an active to that of a passive agent. In place of actual physical properties over which the owner could exercise direction and for which he was responsible, the owner now holds a piece of paper representing a set of rights and expectations with respect to an enterprise. But over the enterprise and over the physical property—the instruments of production—in which he has an interest, the owner has little control. . . .

. . . [I]n the corporate system, the "owner" of industrial wealth is left with a mere symbol of ownership while the power, the responsibility and the substance which have been an integral part of ownership in the past are being transferred to a separate group in whose hands lies control.

Id. at 4–5, 66, 68.

The separation of ownership from control that Berle & Means documented did not result from the fact that the modern corporation has a huge *number* of shareholders—often, hundreds of thousands—but that in the large corporations that Berle & Means observed, shareholdings were highly *dispersed,* so that no single individual, firm, or compact group owned more than a tiny fraction of a corporation's stock. Where shareholdership is highly dispersed, the corporation will be controlled not by the shareholders, but by management; that is what Berle & Means meant by the separation of ownership (which still lay with the shareholders) and control (which had shifted to management). As a result, the inherent conflict between principal and agent (the agency cost problem) is compounded, because when the principal consists of a highly dispersed group it faces not only an agency problem but coordination costs (the collective action problem). See Rock, The Logic and (Uncertain) Significance of Institutional Shareholder Activism, 79 Geo.L.Rev. 445, 453 (1991).

Why does control shift to management when shareholdings are highly dispersed? First, if all shareholders own only tiny amounts of a corporation's stock, it is not cost effective for a shareholder to spend a significant amount of time on the corporation's affairs. Such a shareholder, therefore, will be "rationally apathetic," and management will fill the vacuum. Second, when a corporation's stock is held by thousands of shareholders living across the country, voting must be done by proxy rather than in person. Typically, in such a corporation, management controls the corporate proxy machinery and has cost-free access to that machinery. In contrast, shareholders who want to oppose a management action must find a way to coordinate, which will itself be difficult, and then must pay the expense of a proxy contest out of their own pockets. If a proxy contest does occur, management has in its favor not only cost-free access to the corporate proxy machinery, but the legitimacy that goes along with being management. Moreover, shareholders who are extremely dissatisfied often prefer "exit" to "voice"—that is, will prefer to sell rather than to vote against management—so that the market siphons off many potential anti-management shareholders. As a result of these various factors, where shareholdings are highly dispersed, incumbent management rather than shareholders will normally have control.

Berle & Means's analyses of control in the very largest corporations is impressive and important, but it must be kept in perspective. To begin with, shareholdings will normally become less dispersed—more concentrated—as the number of shareholders in a corporation diminishes. There are approximately three million corporations in this country. Although there are no definitive data on the distribution of corporations by number of shareholders, Table 1 (based on 1970s data) probably gives a fair approximation and shows that only a tiny percentage of all corporations are large publicly held corporations that have so many shareholders that great dispersion of shareholdership is likely.

Table 1

Number of Shareholders	Percentage of Corporations
1–10	93.94
11–99	4.03
100–499	1.53
500–1499	.29
1500–2999	.10
3000–10,000	.07
Over 10,000	.03

Furthermore, many of the corporations with only a small number of shareholders are very large in terms of employees and assets:

A look at the one thousand largest privately held companies makes the point.... Cargill Inc., the largest close corporation in the country, boasts sales of $42 billion and employs nearly 54,000 workers. United Parcel Service, the fifth largest, has more than $13.5 billion in sales and more than 250,000 employees.

The one hundred largest privately held companies include a litany of household names—corporate providers of goods like Publix Super Markets, Montgomery Ward, Bechtel, ... Hallmark Cards, Levi Strauss, Amway, SC Johnson and Son, Land O'Lakes, Domino's Pizza, Borg–Warner, Ace Hardware, Estee Lauder, and Dow Corning.

Brickey, Close Corporations and the Criminal Law: On "Mom and Pop" and a Curious Rule, 71 Wash.U.L.Q. 189 (1993).

Nevertheless, it remains true that a very high proportion of total corporate wealth is concentrated in just those large publicly held corporations that do have a great number of shareholders. Professor Merritt Fox has concluded that about 75% of the nation's industrial assets are controlled by the largest five hundred industrial corporations, and that these firms are responsible for a roughly comparable proportion of new investment. M. Fox, Finance and Industrial Performance in a Dynamic Economy 117 (1987).

3. *The Rise of Institutional Shareholders.* Since Berle & Means wrote, there has been a major shift in the patterns of shareholdings in large publicly held corporations. The modern data suggest that shareholdings are now somewhat concentrated even in such corporations. For example, in connection with its 1963 *Special Study,* the SEC found that in more than half of the sampled corporations with 1000 to 1999 shareholders, the ten largest record shareholders held at least 40 percent of the stock. In more than half of the sampled corporations with 2000 to 4999 shareholders, the ten largest record shareholders, held at least 30 percent of the stock. In about 30 percent of the sampled corporations with 5000 or more shareholders, the ten largest record shareholders held over 30 percent of the stock. SEC, Report of Special Study of the Securities Markets, H.R.Doc. No. 95, 88th Cong., 1st Sess., pt. 3, at 30 (1963).

This increased level of concentration is principally due to the rise and dramatic growth in shareholdings of institutional investors (that is, institutions that hold large amounts of stock, usually on others' behalf), such as pension funds and mutual funds. This growth is based on two elements. First, the amount of assets held by such investors has increased very dramatically since Berle & Means wrote. Second, because of changing concepts of financial analysis, there has been a major shift in the holdings of certain kinds of institutions, from fixed-income securities, like bonds, to stock.

Data on institutional shareholdings varies somewhat from source to source, primarily because of differences in the corporate populations studied, databases, years, or all three. In 1994, Business Week reported that 56% of the shares of the 1,000 largest American corporations were held by institutions. The Business Week 1000, Business Week, March 28, 1994, at 72. The same year, the New York Stock Exchange reported that in 1992, 44% of all equities were owned by American institutions. New York Stock Exchange, Fact Book 90 (1994). (Another 6% was owned by the foreign sector, which undoubtedly included foreign institutions.) In 1993, the Brancato Report on Institutional Investment reported the following data for 1992:

Equity Holdings as a Percentage of the Total
U.S. Equity Market by Category: 1992

TYPE OF INSTITUTION	1992	
	Equity Holdings ($ Bil) [1]	Percentage of Total Equity Market
Pension Funds	1,585	28.6%
Private Trustee Funds	1,023	18.5
Private Insured Funds	106	1.9
State & Local Funds	456	8.2
Investment Companies	392	7.1
Open End Mutual Fund	374	6.7
Closed End Investment Cos.	18	0.3
Insurance Companies	136	2.4
Life Insurance Companies	31	0.6
Property & Casualty Companies	105	1.9
Bank & Trust Companies	403	7.3
Foundations	74	1.3
All Institutions	2,591	46.8

Source: The Brancato Report on Institutional Investment, Volume 1, Edition 1, December
1993

Moreover, most of the shareholdings held by institutional investors are held by a relatively small percentage of all such institutions. The SEC's *Institutional Investor Study* reported in 1971 that the 50 largest bank trust departments accounted for 72 percent of the common stock managed by all bank trust departments. The 71 investment advisers managing the largest investment-company complexes accounted for 64 percent of all common stock managed by all investment advisers. The 26 largest life insurance companies accounted for 82 percent of all common stock held by such companies. The 25 largest property-and-liability insurance companies accounted for 71 percent of all common stock held by such insurers. SEC Institutional Investor Study Report, H.R.Doc. No. 64, 922 Cong., 1st Sess. pt. 3, at 1309. The net result is that a very substantial proportion of the stock of many or most of the country's very largest corporations is held by a limited number of institutional investors.

The increased concentration of shareholdings in publicly held corporations, due to the dramatic increase of shareholdings by institutional investors, has set the stage for a dramatic increase in the shareholder role in the modern publicly held corporation. As shareholders get more sophisticated, the costs of playing the shareholder role decreases. As shareholdings get larger, the cost-benefit ratio for investing time in the corporation improves. As shareholdings become more concentrated, coordination becomes easier.

However, setting the stage is one thing; putting on the play is another. Until very recently, a number of social and legal factors

1. The figures in this column have been
rounded.

have combined to limit the role played by institutional investors as active shareholders.

Paramount among the social constraints on institutional investors is the problem of conflicts of interest. Many institutional investors have ties to management that inhibit voting against managements' wishes. For example, if the trust department of Bank B holds the stock of Corporation C in a pension portfolio, and C is also a client of Bank B's commercial department, a trust officer of Bank B will think long and hard before voting against a proposal made by C's management, or in favor of a proposal C's management opposes. Insurance companies, like banks, often have extensive commercial contacts with corporations whose stock they hold in their investment portfolios. Mutual funds may want to stay on management's good side, to keep open their lines of access for getting information about a corporation's business. Managers of private pension funds can be and have been bullied into pro-management votes by threats that if they fail to vote that way, the fund will be switched to another manager. Apart from these specific conflicts of interest, at least until recently there seems to have been a club culture shared by many institutional investors, under which voting against management "wasn't done." A governing rule was the so-called Wall Street rule—if you don't like management, sell. The corollary of that Rule was, if you don't sell, support management.

On the legal side, the most important—although not the only—constraint was the SEC's Proxy Rules, which made it very expensive for institutional shareholders to communicate with each other to determine whether it was in their mutual interests to combine forces in connection with voting on a management proposal or initiating a proposal of their own. That constraint was significantly reduced, although not entirely eliminated, by significant amendments to the Proxy Rules in 1992. See Chapter 5, Section 3. As a result of these amendments, in 1994 The Economist reported that "in this year's lone battle of any consequence [the fight to separate the jobs of chief executive and chairman at Sears, Roebuck, the] United Shareholders Association, a group of small shareholders, plans to contact the company's 1,000 largest shareholders, who have around 70% of the votes. This will cost $5,000–10,000. Under the old SEC rules, which obliged the association to contact all shareholders if it lobbied more than ten, the exercise would have cost [$1 million]." American Corporate Governance: The Shareholders Call the Plays, The Economist, April 24, 1993, at 83.[2]

These economic, cultural, and legal shifts over the last ten years or so are evidenced by the following data based on a table prepared by the Investor Responsibility Research Center, which shows the average votes on shareholder proposals relating to corporate governance in 1994:

---

2. Other legal constraints remain. For example, a voting consortium of several large institutional shareholders may be deemed to be a "group" within the meaning of Section 13(d) of the Securities Exchange Act. If beneficial ownership by the group exceeds five percent of a company's stock, disclosure obligations will be triggered. If the "group's" ownership reaches 10%, members of the group may face potential liability under Section 16(b) of the Exchange Act.

Proposal Type	Number of Proposals	Average Vote
Redeem or vote on poison pill	12	53.7
Confidential voting	13	39.9
Targeted share placements	2	36.0
Vote on future golden parachutes	4	30.7
Repeal classified board	39	35.8
Restrict director compensation	6	29.1
Provide for cumulative voting	35	25.1
Separate CEO & chairman	6	20.1
Independent nominating committee	6	16.0
Restrict executive comp.	37	14.2
Majority of independent directors	3	12.8
Minimum stock ownership	6	12.6
Disclose executive compensation	15	9.8
Board diversity	3	7.7
Shareholder advisory committees	2	6.0

Despite the recent legal and cultural changes concerning the role of institutional investors, there are still very important constraints on the extent of which institutional investors can be expected to be active monitors of the corporations in which they hold stock. To begin with, under modern portfolio theory an institutional investor should diversify its portfolio. That objective will normally prevent the investor from putting too many eggs in any single corporate basket, particularly given the huge capitalization of many large American publicly held corporations. In addition, certain kinds of institutional investors are statutorily forbidden to hold more than a fixed percentage of the stock of any given corporation. As a result of these economic and legal constraints, typically any one institutional investor will hold only a relatively small percentage of stock in any one corporation.

The significance of limited holdings by any given institution in any given portfolio corporation is that it leads to a free rider problem: Any expenses the institution incurs for beyond-the-ordinary course shareholder activities may mainly benefit the other shareholders. Suppose, for example, Corporation C has a governance rule that diminishes C's value, like an anti-takeover defense. A proxy contest to repeal the rule, and thereby increase the value of S stock, would cost $500,000. Institution S holds 1% of Corporation C's stock. Assume that if S runs the contest by itself, it will derive no economic benefit except the increased value of its C stock. In that case, if S does run the contest it will in effect spend $5,000 on itself and $495,000 on behalf of the other shareholders, who will free ride at S's expense.

One solution to this problem is for institutional investors to form coalitions, so that costs can be shared. Non-coalition shareholders would still free ride, but the reduction in each institution's costs might bring those costs to a level that is lower than each institution's potential gains. "When it is collectively rational for a subgroup to provide a good, and when the critical members can organize themselves into an efficacious subgroup, the fact that a nonmember takes a free ride does not make the provision of the good any less collectively rational.... This is an example of what Olson called the 'exploitation of the great by the small.' " Rock, supra, at 461–62.

As Professor Coffee has pointed out, however, it may not be easy to form such coalitions. Most institutional shareholders remain subject to conflicts of interest that militate against activism on their part. The major exception consists of publicly held pension funds, and it is no accident that these funds have been the most activist type of institutional shareholder. Furthermore, a significant portion of the voting authority over stock held by institutional investors is vested in external fund managers (that is, managers, external to the institutional investor, who are paid to manage some portion of the investor's assets). An external manager may have less incentive to expend costs than an internal manager:

> ... [T]he external fund manager is compensated under a contractual formula that typically requires it to "perform normal proxy activity" and to bear the costs thereof. The concept of "normal proxy activity" is, of course, changing, but the larger point here goes beyond the drafting question. Whatever the contractual formula, there is a potential conflict of interest between the interests of the money manager and those of the pension fund: proxy activism that could produce gains to the pension fund's beneficiaries may yet result in a net loss to the fund manager. ...

Coffee, The SEC and the Institutional Investor: A Half–Time Report, 15 Cardozo L.Rev. 837, 863–64 (1994).

It is important to bear in mind what the analysis of collective action and free rider problems does and does not show. It does show that institutional investors are not likely to engage in monitoring or voting activity if the activity (i) would go beyond the monitoring and voting activity in which the investor can be expected to engage in the normal course of its shareholding capacity; (ii) would require significant expenditures; (iii) would increase the value of the institution's holdings in the portfolio corporation by less than the costs of the activity; and (iv) would result in no private economic benefit to the investor beyond the increased value of its holding. If, however, all four of these conditions are not satisfied, institutional investors will engage in monitoring if they are economically rational. And in fact, these four conditions frequently aren't satisfied, for a variety of reasons:

1. Much voting activity requires very little effort. In many cases, the same issue recurs in a number of corporations—for example, how to deal with anti-takeover provisions of various kinds—so that the investor need only make a one-time expenditure of effort to determine its general position, and can then amortize the expenditure over a number of votes.

2.   A vote on a recurring issue, like a certain type of corporate governance rule, may send a message to all portfolio corporations, and may therefore have an economic benefit to the investor beyond its impact on the immediate portfolio corporation.

3.   Many institutional investors can no longer easily get in and out of investments in stock, either because the blocks they hold are so large that a sale of the block would depress the market price, or because they follow the investment strategy known as indexing, which requires the investor's portfolio to mimic the entire market. For example, in some stocks the Fidelity family of mutual funds has holdings equal to 100–150 days' average trading volume.   Some Magellan Holdings Are Target of Short Sellers, The Wall Street Journal, Friday, October 7, 1994, p. C1.   "In terms of [Albert] Hirchman's framework, as the exit option becomes less attractive or available, the voice option . . . becomes comparatively more attractive."   Rock, supra, at 463.

4.   Unless an investor has adopted an indexing or buy-and-hold strategy, it must monitor its portfolio corporations continually to determine whether to hold or sell.

5.   The costs of playing a shareholder role have been dramatically reduced by the development of firms like Institutional Shareholders Services and Investors Responsibility Research Center. These firms analyze a huge number of proxy materials, and report those analyses in bulletins that are distributed regularly to institutional-investor clients.   In effect, the clients of these services form a sort of research coalition, by pooling their funds through the subscription prices they pay for the costs of the services' analyses.

6.   If there are financial costs to playing the shareholder role, there are also financial costs to getting in and out of equity investments.

7.   In many cases a voting decision has a very obvious and dramatic effect on the value of a portfolio stock, as where the vote concerns a merger or a value-decreasing anti-takeover provision.   In such cases, beyond-ordinary-course activity may be cost-justified.

8.   Even in less dramatic cases there has been an increasing acceptance of the idea that changes in a corporation's governance rules, and often in its management, can increase the value of the corporation's stock, so that it may be more cost effective to hold and vote than to sell and buy a new stock.

––––––

SECTION 2.   THE ALLOCATION OF LEGAL POWER BETWEEN MANAGEMENT AND SHAREHOLDERS

DEL. GEN. CORP. LAW § 141(a)

[See Statutory Supplement]

REV. MODEL BUS. CORP. ACT § 8.01(b)

[See Statutory Supplement]

CHARLESTOWN BOOT & SHOE CO. v. DUNSMORE

New Hampshire Supreme Court, 1880.
60 N.H. 85.

CASE.   Demurrer to the declaration in which the following facts were alleged:—The plaintiffs are a manufacturing corporation having for its object a dividend of profits, and commenced business in 1871.   Dunsmore was elected director in 1871 and Willard in 1873, and entered upon the discharge of their duties, and have continued so to act by virtue of successive elections until the present time. December 10, 1874, the corporation * voted to choose a committee to act with the directors to close up its affairs, and chose one Osgood for such committee.   Osgood tendered his services, but the defendants refused to act with him, and contracted new debts to a larger extent than allowed by law.   By their negligence, debts due to the corporation to the amount of $2,161.23 have been wholly lost.   By their negligence in disposing of the goods of the corporation, a loss has accrued of $3,300.40.   By their neglect to sell the buildings and machinery of the corporation when they might and ought, and were urged by Osgood to sell, the same depreciated in value to the extent of $20,000.

Also for that the plaintiffs owned and possessed a certain shop of the value of $10,000, and a large amount of machinery and fixtures of the value of $10,000; "and whereas it was the duty of said defendants, directors as aforesaid, to procure sufficient and proper insurance against fire to be made on said property, and keep the same so sufficiently insured, of all which the said defendants had notice, yet they did not and would not keep the said property so insured, and afterwards, to wit, on the 28th day of April, 1878, while the said property was so remaining without insurance, the same was wholly consumed by fire and wholly lost to the plaintiff, whereby the plaintiff suffered great loss and damage, to wit, $20,-000."

* By "the corporation," in this phrase and some others, the court seems to mean the body of shareholders.   (Footnote by ed.)

SMITH, J.   The provision of the statute is, that the business of a dividend paying corporation shall be managed by the directors. The statute reads, "The business of every such corporation shall be managed by the directors thereof, subject to the by-laws and votes of the corporation, and under their direction by such officers and agents as shall be duly appointed by the directors or by the corporation." G.L., *c.* 148, *s.* 3; Gen.Stats., *c.* 134, *s.* 3. The only limitation upon the judgment or discretion of the directors is such as the corporation by its by-laws and votes shall impose. It may define its business, its nature and extent, prescribe rules and regulations for the government of its officers and members, and determine whether its business shall be wound up or continued; but when it has thus acted, the business as thus defined and limited is to be managed by its directors, and by such officers and agents under their direction as the directors or the corporation shall appoint. The statute does not authorize a corporation to join another officer with the directors, nor compel the directors to act with one who is not a director. They are bound to use ordinary care and diligence in the care and management of the business of the corporation, and are answerable for ordinary negligence. *March v. Railroad,* 43 N.H. 516, 529; *Scott v. Depeyster,* 1 Edw. Ch. 513, 543; Ang. & Ames Corp., *s.* 314. There is no difference in this respect between the agents of corporations and those of natural persons, unless expressly made by the charter or by-laws. *Id., s.* 315. It would be unreasonable to hold them responsible for the management of the affairs of the corporation if compelled to act with one who to a greater or less extent could control their acts. The statute not only entrusts the management of the business of the corporation to the directors, but places its other officers and agents under their direction. When a statute provides that powers granted to a corporation shall be exercised by any set of officers or any particular agents, such powers can be exercised only by such officers or agents, although they are required to be chosen by the whole corporation; and if the whole corporation attempts to exercise powers which by the charter are lodged elsewhere, its action upon the subject is void. *Insurance Co. v. Keyser,* 32 N.H. 313, 315. The vote choosing Osgood a committee to act with the directors in closing up the affairs of the plaintiff corporation was inoperative and void.

The declaration also alleges that it was the duty of the defendants, as directors, to keep the property of the corporation insured. There is no statute that makes it the duty of the directors of a corporation to keep its property insured, and there are no facts alleged from which we can say, as matter of law, that it was the duty of the defendants to insure the property of the corporation.

Demurrer sustained.

STANLEY, J., did not sit: the others concurred.

———

PEOPLE EX REL. MANICE v. POWELL, 201 N.Y. 194, 200–01, 94 N.E. 634, 637 (1911). " 'The board of directors of a corporation do not stand in the same relation to the corporate body which a private agent holds towards his principal. . . .   In corporate bodies the powers of the board of directors are, in a very important sense, original and undelegated.'   (*Hoyt v. Thompson's Executors,* 19 N.Y. 207, 216; *Beveridge v. N.Y.E.R.R. Co.,* 112 N.Y. 1, 22, 23.)

"While the ordinary rules of law relating to an agent are applicable in considering the acts of a board of directors in behalf of a corporation when dealing with third persons, the individual directors making up the board are not mere employees, but a part of an elected body of officers constituting the executive agents of the corporation. They hold such office charged with the duty to act for the corporation according to their best judgment, and in so doing they cannot be controlled in the reasonable exercise and performance of such duty. As a general rule the stockholders cannot act in relation to the ordinary business of the corporation, nor can they control the directors in the exercise of the judgment vested in them by virtue of their office.

"The relation of the directors to the stockholders is essentially that of trustee and *cestui que trust.* The peculiar relation that they bear to the corporation and the owners of its stock grows out of the inability of the corporation to act except through such managing officers and agents. The corporation is the owner of the property, but the directors in the performance of their duty possess it, and act in every way as if they owned it."

———

DEL. GEN. CORP. LAW § 141(k)

[See Statutory Supplement]

———

REV. MODEL BUS. CORP. ACT §§ 8.08–8.09

[See Statutory Supplement]

———

CAL. CORP. CODE §§ 303, 304

[See Statutory Supplement]

———

N.Y. BUS. CORP. LAW § 706

[See Statutory Supplement]

———

NOTE ON REMOVAL OF DIRECTORS

1.   Under the common law:

(i) The shareholders can remove a director for cause.

(ii) Shareholders cannot remove a director without cause, absent specific authority in the certificate of incorporation or by-laws. See, e.g., Frank v. Anthony, 107 So.2d 136 (Fla.App.1958); Toledo Traction, Light & Power Co. v. Smith, 205 Fed. 643, 645–646 (N.D.Ohio 1913); People ex rel. Manice v. Powell, 201 N.Y. 194, 94 N.E. 634 (1911).   However, a certificate or by-law provision can permit the removal without cause of directors elected after the provision has been adopted.   Everett v. Transnation Development Corp., 267 A.2d 627 (Del.Ch.1970); In re Singer, 189 Misc. 150, 70 N.Y.S.2d 550 (1947), aff'd without opinion 273 App.Div. 755, 75 N.Y.S.2d 514.

(iii) The board cannot remove a director, with or without cause.   See, e.g., Bruch v. National Guarantee Credit Corp., 13 Del.Ch. 180, 116 A. 738 (1922); cf. Stott v. Stott Realty Co., 246 Mich. 267, 224 N.W. 623 (1929).   It is doubtful whether the certificate of incorporation can change this rule.   See Dillon v. Berg, 326 F.Supp. 1214 (D.Del.1971), aff'd 453 F.2d 876 (3d Cir.); Bruch v. National Guarantee Credit Corp., supra.

(iv) The cases are split on whether a court can remove directors for cause.   Compare Webber v. Webber Oil Co., 495 A.2d 1215 (Me.1985) and Harkey v. Mobley, 552 S.W.2d 79 (Mo.App. 1977) (courts do not have power to remove directors) with Brown v. North Ventura Road Development Co., 216 Cal.App.2d 227, 30 Cal.Rptr. 568 (1963); Ross v. 311 North Central Avenue Building Corp., 130 Ill.App.2d 336, 264 N.E.2d 406 (1970) and Feldman v. Pennroad Corp., 60 F.Supp. 716 (D.Del.1945), aff'd 155 F.2d 773 (3d Cir.1946), cert. denied 329 U.S. 808, 67 S.Ct. 621, 91 L.Ed. 690 (1947) (courts have power to remove directors, at least for fraud or the like).

2.   The common law rules have been significantly altered by statute in a number of states:

(i) Some statutes permit the shareholders to remove a director without cause.   See, e.g., Cal.Corp.Code § 303(a); Rev.Model Bus. Corp.Act § 8.08.   A few statutes permit the shareholders to remove a director without cause if the certificate or by-laws so provide. See, e.g., N.Y.Bus.Corp.Law § 706(b).

(ii) Some statutes permit the board to remove a director for cause, see, e.g., Mass.Gen.Laws ch. 156B, § 51(c), or for specified reasons such as conviction of a felony, see, e.g., Calif.Corp.Code § 302.   A few statutes permit the board to remove a director for cause or for specified reasons if the certificate of incorporation so provides.   See, e.g., N.J.Stat.Ann. § 14A:6–6.

(iii) Some statutes permit the courts to remove a director for specified reasons, such as fraudulent or dishonest acts. These statutes usually provide that a petition for such removal can be brought only by a designated percentage of the shareholders (most commonly 10%), by the attorney general, or in some cases, by either. See, e.g., Calif.Corp.Code § 304; N.Y.Bus.Corp.Law § 706(d); Rev.Model Bus.Corp.Act § 8.09.

————

SCHNELL v. CHRIS–CRAFT INDUSTRIES, INC.

Supreme Court of Delaware, 1971.
285 A.2d 437.

HERRMANN, Justice (for the majority of the Court):

This is an appeal from the denial by the Court of Chancery of the petition of dissident stockholders for injunctive relief to prevent management * from advancing the date of the annual stockholders' meeting from January 11, 1972, as previously set by the by-laws, to December 8, 1971.

The opinion below is reported at 285 A.2d 430. This opinion is confined to the frame of reference of the opinion below for the sake of brevity and because of the strictures of time imposed by the circumstances of the case.

It will be seen that the Chancery Court considered all of the reasons stated by management as business reasons for changing the date of the meeting; but that those reasons were rejected by the Court below in making the following findings:

> "I am satisfied, however, in a situation in which present management has disingenuously resisted the production of a list of its stockholders to plaintiffs or their confederates and has otherwise turned a deaf ear to plaintiffs' demands about a change in management designed to lift defendant from its present business doldrums, management has seized on a relatively new section of the Delaware Corporation Law for the purpose of cutting down on the amount of time which would otherwise have been available to plaintiffs and others for the waging of a proxy battle. Management thus enlarged the scope of its scheduled October 18 directors' meeting to include the by-law amendment in controversy after the stockholders committee had filed with the S.E.C. its intention to wage a proxy fight on October 16.

> "Thus plaintiffs reasonably contend that because of the tactics employed by management (which involve the hiring of two established proxy solicitors as well as a refusal to produce a list of its stockholders, coupled with its use of an amendment to the Delaware Corporation Law to limit the time for contest),

———

* We use this word as meaning "managing directors".

they are given little chance, because of the exigencies of time, including that required to clear material at the S.E.C., to wage a successful proxy fight between now and December 8...."

In our view, those conclusions amount to a finding that management has attempted to utilize the corporate machinery and the Delaware Law for the purpose of perpetuating itself in office; and, to that end, for the purpose of obstructing the legitimate efforts of dissident stockholders in the exercise of their rights to undertake a proxy contest against management. These are inequitable purposes, contrary to established principles of corporate democracy. The advancement by directors of the by-law date of a stockholders' meeting, for such purposes, may not be permitted to stand. Compare Condec Corporation v. Lunkenheimer Company, Del.Ch., 230 A.2d 769 (1967).

When the by-laws of a corporation designate the date of the annual meeting of stockholders, it is to be expected that those who intend to contest the reelection of incumbent management will gear their campaign to the by-law date. It is not to be expected that management will attempt to advance that date in order to obtain an inequitable advantage in the contest.

Management contends that it has complied strictly with the provisions of the new Delaware Corporation Law in changing the by-law date. The answer to that contention, of course, is that inequitable action does not become permissible simply because it is legally possible.

Management relies upon American Hardware Corp. v. Savage Arms Corp., 37 Del.Ch. 10, 135 A.2d 725, aff'd 37 Del.Ch. 59, 136 A.2d 690 (1957). That case is inapposite for two reasons: it involved an effort by stockholders, engaged in a proxy contest, to have the stockholders' meeting adjourned and the period for the proxy contest enlarged; and there was no finding there of inequitable action on the part of management. We agree with the rule of *American Hardware* that, in the absence of fraud or inequitable conduct, the date for a stockholders' meeting and notice thereof, duly established under the by-laws, will not be enlarged by judicial interference at the request of dissident stockholders solely because of the circumstance of a proxy contest. That, of course, is not the case before us.

We are unable to agree with the conclusion of the Chancery Court that the stockholders' application for injunctive relief here was tardy and came too late. The stockholders learned of the action of management unofficially on Wednesday, October 27, 1971; they filed this action on Monday, November 1, 1971. Until management changed the date of the meeting, the stockholders had no need of judicial assistance in that connection. There is no indication of any prior warning of management's intent to take such action; indeed, it appears that an attempt was made by management to conceal its action as long as possible. Moreover, stockholders may not be charged with the duty of anticipating inequitable action by management, and of seeking anticipatory injunctive relief to foreclose such action, simply because the new Delaware Corporation Law makes such inequitable action legally possible.

Accordingly, the judgment below must be reversed and the cause remanded, with instructions to nullify the December 8 date as a meeting date for stockholders; to reinstate January 11, 1972 as the sole date of the next annual meeting of the stockholders of the corporation; and to take such other proceedings and action as may be consistent herewith regarding the stock record closing date and any other related matters.

WOLCOTT, Chief Justice (dissenting):

I do not agree with the majority of the Court in its disposition of this appeal. The plaintiff stockholders concerned in this litigation have, for a considerable period of time, sought to obtain control of the defendant corporation. These attempts took various forms.

In view of the length of time leading up to the immediate events which caused the filing of this action, I agree with the Vice Chancellor that the application for injunctive relief came too late.

I would affirm the judgment below on the basis of the Vice Chancellor's opinion.

———

A.A. BERLE & G. MEANS, THE MODERN CORPORATION AND PRIVATE PROPERTY 220 (rev. ed. 1967). "[A]n underlying thesis in corporation law ... could be applied to each and every power in the whole corporate galaxy. Succinctly stated, the thesis [is] that all powers granted to a corporation or to the management of a corporation, or to any group within the corporation, whether derived from statute or charter or both, are necessarily and at all times exercisable only for the ratable benefit of all the shareholders as their interest appears. That, in consequence, the *use* of the power is subject to equitable limitation when the power has been exercised to the detriment of their interest, however absolute the grant of power may be in terms, and however correct the technical exercise of it may have been."

———

BLASIUS INDUSTRIES, INC. v. ATLAS CORP.

Court of Chancery of Delaware, 1988.
564 A.2d 651.

OPINION

ALLEN, Chancellor.

Two cases pitting the directors of Atlas Corporation against that company's largest (9.1%) shareholder, Blasius Industries, have been consolidated and tried together. Together, these cases ultimately require the court to determine who is entitled to sit on Atlas' board of directors....

The first of the cases was filed on December 30, 1987. As amended, it challenges the validity of board action taken at a telephone meeting of December 31, 1987 that added two new members to Atlas' seven member board. That action was taken as an immediate response to the delivery to Atlas by Blasius the previous day of a form of stockholder consent that, if joined in by holders of a majority of Atlas' stock, would have increased the board of Atlas from seven to fifteen members and would have elected eight new members nominated by Blasius.

As I find the facts of this first case, they present the question whether a board acts consistently with its fiduciary duty when it acts, in good faith and with appropriate care, for the primary purpose of preventing or impeding an unaffiliated majority of shareholders from expanding the board and electing a new majority. For the reasons that follow, I conclude that, even though defendants here acted on their view of the corporation's interest and not selfishly, their December 31 action constituted an offense to the relationship between corporate directors and shareholders that has traditionally been protected in courts of equity. As a consequence, I conclude that the board action taken on December 31 was invalid and must be voided....

The facts set forth below represent findings based upon a preponderance of the admissible evidence, as I evaluate it.

I.

Blasius Acquires a 9% Stake in Atlas.

Blasius is a new stockholder of Atlas. It began to accumulate Atlas shares for the first time in July, 1987. On October 29, it filed a Schedule 13D with the Securities Exchange Commission disclosing that, with affiliates, it then [owned] 9.1% of Atlas' common stock. It stated in that filing that it intended to encourage management of Atlas to consider a restructuring of the Company or other transaction to enhance shareholder values. It also disclosed that Blasius was exploring the feasibility of obtaining control of Atlas, including instituting a tender offer or seeking "appropriate" representation on the Atlas board of directors.

Blasius has recently come under the control of two individuals, Michael Lubin and Warren Delano, who after experience in the commercial banking industry, had, for a short time, run a venture capital operation for a small investment banking firm. Now on their own, they apparently came to control Blasius with the assistance of Drexel Burnham's well noted junk bond mechanism. Since then, they have made several attempts to effect leveraged buyouts, but without success....

The prospect of Messrs. Lubin and Delano involving themselves in Atlas' affairs, was not a development welcomed by Atlas' management. Atlas had a new CEO, defendant Weaver, who had, over the course of the past year or so, overseen a business restructuring of a sort. Atlas had sold three of its five divisions. It had just announced (September 1, 1987) that it would close its once important domestic uranium operation. The goal was to focus the Company on its gold mining business. By October, 1987, the structural changes to do this had been largely accomplished. Mr. Weaver was perhaps thinking that the restructuring that had occurred should be given a chance to produce benefit before another restructuring (such as Blasius had alluded to in its Schedule 13D filing) was attempted, when he wrote in his diary on October 30, 1987:

> 13D by Delano & Lubin came in today. Had long conversation w/MAH & Mark Golden [of Goldman Sachs] on issue. All agree we must dilute these people down by the acquisition of another Co. w/stock, or merger or something else.

The Blasius Proposal of A Leverage Recapitalization Or Sale.

Immediately after filing its 13D on October 29, Blasius' representatives sought a meeting with the Atlas management. Atlas dragged its feet. A meeting was arranged for December 2, 1987 following the regular meeting of the Atlas board. Attending that meeting were Messrs. Lubin and Delano for Blasius, and, for Atlas, Messrs. Weaver, Devaney (Atlas' CFO), Masinter (legal counsel and director) and Czajkowski (a representative of Atlas' investment banker, Goldman Sachs).

At that meeting, Messrs. Lubin and Delano suggested that Atlas engage in a leveraged restructuring and distribute cash to shareholders. In such a transaction, which is by this date a commonplace form of transaction, a corporation typically raises cash by sale of assets and significant borrowings and makes a large one time cash distribution to shareholders. The shareholders are typically left with cash and an equity interest in a smaller, more highly leveraged enterprise. Lubin and Delano gave the outline of a leveraged recapitalization for Atlas as they saw it.

Immediately following the meeting, the Atlas representatives expressed among themselves an initial reaction that the proposal was infeasible. On December 7, Mr. Lubin sent a letter detailing the proposal. In general, it proposed the following: (1) an initial special cash dividend to Atlas' stockholders in an aggregate amount equal to (a) $35 million, (b) the aggregate proceeds to Atlas from the exercise of option warrants and stock options, and (c) the proceeds from the sale or disposal of all of Atlas' operations that are not related to its continuing minerals operations; and (2) a special non-cash dividend to Atlas' stockholders of an aggregate $125 million principal amount of 7% Secured Subordinated Gold–Indexed Debentures. The funds necessary to pay the initial cash dividend were to principally come from (i) a "gold loan" in the amount of $35,625,000, repayable over a three to five year period and secured by 75,000 ounces of gold at a price of $475 per ounce, (ii) the proceeds from the sale of the discontinued Brockton Sole and Plastics and Ready–Mix Concrete businesses, and (iii) a then expected January, 1988 sale of uranium to the Public Service Electric & Gas Company....

The proposal met with a cool reception from management....

On December 30, 1987, Blasius caused Cede & Co. (the registered owner of its Atlas stock) to deliver to Atlas a signed written consent (1) adopting a precatory resolution recommending that the board develop and implement a restructuring proposal, (2) amending the Atlas bylaws to, among other things, expand the size of the board from seven to fifteen members—the maximum number under Atlas' charter, and (3) electing eight named persons to fill the new directorships....

The reaction was immediate. Mr. Weaver conferred with Mr. Masinter, the Company's outside counsel and a director, who viewed the consent as an attempt to take control of the Company. They decided to call an emergency meeting of the board, even though a regularly scheduled meeting was to occur only one week hence, on January 6, 1988. The point of the emergency meeting was to act on their conclusion (or to seek to have the board act on their conclusion) "that we should add at least one and probably two directors to the board ..." (Tr. 85, Vol. II). A quorum of directors, however, could not be arranged for a telephone meeting that day. A telephone meeting was held the next day. At that meeting, the board voted to amend the bylaws to increase the size of the board from seven to nine and appointed John M. Devaney and Harry J. Winters, Jr. to fill those newly created positions. Atlas' Certificate of Incorporation creates staggered terms for directors; the terms to which Messrs. Devaney and Winters were appointed would expire in 1988 and 1990, respectively.

The Motivation of the Incumbent Board In Expanding the Board and Appointing New Members.

In increasing the size of Atlas' board by two and filling the newly created positions, the members of the board realized that they were thereby precluding the holders of a majority of the Company's shares from placing a majority of new directors on the board through Blasius' consent solicitation, should they want to do so. Indeed the evidence establishes that that was the principal motivation in so acting.

The conclusion that, in creating two new board positions on December 31 and electing Messrs. Devaney and Winters to fill those positions the board was principally motivated to prevent or delay the shareholders from possibly placing a majority of new members on the board, is critical to my analysis of the central issue posed by the first filed of the two pending cases. If the board in fact was not so motivated, but rather had taken action completely independently of the consent solicitation, which merely had an incidental impact upon the possible effectuation of any action authorized by the shareholders, it is very unlikely that such action would be subject to judicial nullification. See, e.g., Frantz Manufacturing Company v. EAC Industries, Del.Supr., 501 A.2d 401, 407 (1985); Moran v. Household International, Inc., Del.Ch., 490 A.2d 1059, 1080, aff'd, Del.Supr., 500 A.2d 1346 (1985). The board, as a general matter, is under no fiduciary obligation to suspend its active management of the firm while the consent solicitation process goes forward....

... I conclude that, while the addition of these qualified men would, under other circumstances, be clearly appropriate as an independent step, such a step was in fact taken in order to impede or preclude a majority of the shareholders from effectively adopting the course proposed by Blasius....

II.

Plaintiff attacks the December 31 board action as a selfishly motivated effort to protect the incumbent board from a perceived threat to its control of Atlas. Their conduct is said to constitute a violation of the principle, applied in such cases as Schnell v. Chris Craft Industries, Del.Supr., 285 A.2d 437 (1971), that directors hold legal powers [subject] to a supervening duty to exercise such powers in good faith pursuit of what they reasonably believe to be in the corporation's interest. The December 31 action is also said to have been taken in a grossly negligent manner, since it was designed to preclude the recapitalization from being pursued, and the board had no basis at that time to make a prudent determination about the wisdom of that proposal, nor was there any emergency that required it to act in any respect regarding that proposal before putting itself in a position to do so advisedly.

Defendants, of course, contest every aspect of plaintiffs' claims. They claim the formidable protections of the business judgment rule. See, e.g., Aronson v. Lewis, Del.Supr., 473 A.2d 805 (1983); Grobow v. Perot, Del.Supr., 539 A.2d 180 (1988); In re J.P. Stevens & Co., Inc. Shareholders Litigation, Del.Ch., 542 A.2d 770 (1988).

They say that, in creating two new board positions and filling them on December 31, they acted without a conflicting interest (since the Blasius proposal did not, in any event, challenge *their* places on the board), they acted with due care (since they well knew the persons they put on the board and did not thereby preclude later consideration of the recapitalization), and they acted in good faith (since they were motivated, they say, to protect the shareholders from the threat of having an impractical, indeed a dangerous, recapitalization program foisted upon them). Accordingly, defendants assert there is no basis to conclude that their December 31 action constituted any violation of the duty of the fidelity that a director owes by reason of his office to the corporation and its shareholders.

Moreover, defendants say that their action was fair, measured and appropriate, in light of the circumstances. Therefore, even should the court conclude that some level of substantive review of it is appropriate under a legal test of fairness, or under the intermediate level of review authorized by *Unocal Corp. v. Mesa Petroleum Co.*, Del.Supr., 493 A.2d 946 (1985), defendants assert that the board's decision must be sustained as valid in both law and equity.

III. . . .

On balance, I cannot conclude that the board was acting out of a self-interested motive in any important respect on December 31. I conclude rather that the board saw the "threat" of the Blasius recapitalization proposal as posing vital policy differences between itself and Blasius. It acted, I conclude, in a good faith effort to protect its incumbency, not selfishly, but in order to thwart implementation of the recapitalization that it feared, reasonably, would cause great injury to the Company.

The real question the case presents, to my mind, is whether, in these circumstances, the board, even if it *is* acting with subjective good faith (which will typically, if not always, be a contestable or debatable judicial conclusion), may validly act for the principal purpose of preventing the shareholders from electing a majority of new directors. The question thus posed is not one of intentional wrong (or even negligence), but one of authority *as between the fiduciary and the beneficiary* (not simply legal authority, *i.e.*, as between the fiduciary and the world at large).

IV.

It is established in our law that a board may take certain steps— such as the purchase by the corporation of its own stock—that have the effect of defeating a threatened change in corporate control, when those steps are taken advisedly, in good faith pursuit of a corporate interest, and are reasonable in relation to a threat to legitimate corporate interests posed by the proposed change in control. See Unocal Corp. v. Mesa Petroleum Co., Del.Supr., 493 A.2d 946 (1985); Kors v. Carey, Del.Ch., 158 A.2d 136 (1960); Cheff v. Mathes, Del.Supr., 199 A.2d 548 (1964); Kaplan v. Goldsamt, Del.Ch., 380 A.2d 556 (1977). Does this rule—that the reasonable exercise of good faith and due care generally validates, in equity, the exercise of legal authority even if the act has an entrenchment effect—apply to action designed for the primary purpose of interfering with the effectiveness of a stockholder vote? Our authorities, as well as sound principles, suggest that the central importance of the franchise to the scheme of corporate governance, requires that, in this setting, that rule not be applied and that closer scrutiny be accorded to such transaction.

1. *Why the deferential business judgment rule does not apply to board acts taken for the primary purpose of interfering with a stockholder's vote, even if taken advisedly and in good faith.*

A. *The question of legitimacy.*

The shareholder franchise is the ideological underpinning upon which the legitimacy of directorial power rests. Generally, shareholders have only two protections against perceived inadequate business performance. They may sell their stock (which, if done in sufficient numbers, may so affect security prices as to create an incentive for altered managerial performance), or they may vote to replace incumbent board members.

It has, for a long time, been conventional to dismiss the stockholder vote as a vestige or ritual of little practical importance. It may be that we are now witnessing the emergence of new institutional voices and arrangements that will make the stockholder vote a less predictable affair than it has been. Be that as it may, however, whether the vote is seen functionally as an unimportant formalism, or as an important tool of discipline, it is clear that it is critical to the theory that legitimates the exercise of power by some (directors and officers) over vast aggregations of property that they do not own. Thus, when viewed from a broad, institutional perspective, it can be seen that matters involving the integrity of the shareholder voting process involve [considerations] not present in any other context in which directors exercise delegated power.

B. *Questions of this type raise issues of the allocation of authority as between the board and the shareholders.*

The distinctive nature of the shareholder franchise context also appears when the matter is viewed from a less generalized, doctrinal point of view. From this point of view, as well, it appears that the ordinary considerations to which the business judgment rule originally responded are simply not present in the shareholder voting context. That is, a decision by the board to act for the primary purpose of preventing the effectiveness of a shareholder vote inevitably involves the question who, as between the principal and the agent, has authority with respect to a matter of internal corporate governance. That, of course, is true in a very specific way in this case which deals with the question who should constitute the board of directors of the corporation, but it will be true in every instance in which an incumbent board seeks to thwart a shareholder majority. A board's decision to act to prevent the shareholders from creating a majority of new board positions and filling them does not involve the exercise of *the corporation's power* over its property, or with respect to *its* rights or obligations; rather, it involves allocation, between shareholders as a class and the board, of effective power with respect to governance of the corporation. This need not be the case with respect to other forms of corporate action that may have an entrenchment effect—such as the stock buybacks present in *Unocal, Cheff* or *Kors v. Carey.* Action designed principally to interfere with the effectiveness of a vote inevitably involves a conflict between the board and a shareholder majority. Judicial review of such action involves a determination of the legal and equitable obligations of an agent towards his principal. This is not, in my opinion, a question that a court may leave to the agent finally to decide so long as he does so honestly and competently; that is, it may not be left to the agent's business judgment.

2. *What rule does apply: per se invalidity of corporate acts intended primarily to thwart effective exercise of the franchise or is there an intermediate standard?*

Plaintiff argues for a rule of *per se* invalidity once a plaintiff has established that a board has acted for the primary purpose of thwarting the exercise of a shareholder vote. Our opinions in Canada Southern Oils, Ltd. v. Manabi Exploration Co., Del.Ch., 96 A.2d 810 (1953) and Condec Corporation v. Lunkenheimer Company, Del.Ch., 230 A.2d 769 (1967) could be read as support for such a rule of *per se* invalidity. . . .

. . . A *per se* rule that would strike down, in equity, any board action taken for the primary purpose of interfering with the effectiveness of a corporate vote would have the advantage of relative clarity and predictability.[4] It also has the advantage of most vigorously enforcing the concept of corporate democracy. The disadvantage it brings along is, of course, the disadvantage a *per se* rule always has: it may sweep too broadly. . . .

In my view, our inability to foresee now all of the future settings in which a board might, in good faith, paternalistically seek to thwart a shareholder vote, counsels against the adoption of a *per se* rule invalidating, in equity, every board action taken for the sole or primary purpose of thwarting a shareholder vote, even though I recognize the transcending significance of the franchise to the claims to legitimacy of our scheme of corporate governance. It may be that some set of facts would justify such extreme action. This, however, is not such a case.

3. *Defendants have demonstrated no sufficient justification for the action of December 31 which was intended to prevent an unaffiliated majority of shareholders from effectively exercising their right to elect eight new directors.*

The board was not faced with a coercive action taken by a powerful shareholder against the interests of a distinct shareholder constituency (such as a public minority). It was presented with a consent solicitation by a 9% shareholder. Moreover, here it had time (and understood that it had time) to inform the shareholders of its views on the merits of the proposal subject to stockholder vote. The only justification that can, in such a situation, be offered for the action taken is that the board knows better than do the shareholders what is in the corporation's best interest. While that premise is no doubt true for any number of matters, it is irrelevant (except insofar as the shareholders wish to be guided by the board's recommendation) when the question is who should comprise the

---

4. While it must be admitted that any rule that requires for its invocation the finding of a subjective mental state (*i.e.,* a primary purpose) necessarily will lead to controversy concerning whether it applies or not, nevertheless, once it is determined to apply, this *per se* rule would be clearer than the alternative discussed below.

board of directors. The theory of our corporation law confers power upon directors as the agents of the shareholders; it does not create Platonic masters. It may be that the Blasius restructuring proposal was or is unrealistic and would lead to injury to the corporation and its shareholders if pursued. Having heard the evidence, I am inclined to think it was not a sound proposal. The board certainly viewed it that way, and that view, held in good faith, entitled the board to take certain steps to evade the risk it perceived. It could, for example, expend corporate funds to inform shareholders and seek to bring them to a similar point of view. See, e.g. Hall v. Trans–Lux Daylight Picture Screen Corporation, Del.Ch., 171 A. 226, 227 (1934); Hibbert v. Hollywood Park, Inc., Del.Supr., 457 A.2d 339 (1982). But there is a vast difference between expending corporate funds to inform the electorate and exercising power for the primary purpose of foreclosing effective shareholder action. A majority of the shareholders, who were not dominated in any respect, could view the matter differently than did the board. If they do, or did, they are entitled to employ the mechanisms provided by the corporation law and the Atlas certificate of incorporation to advance that view. They are also entitled, in my opinion, to restrain their agents, the board, from acting for the principal purpose of thwarting that action.

I therefore conclude that, even finding the action was taken in good faith, it constituted an unintended violation of the duty of loyalty that the board owed to the shareholders. I note parenthetically that the concept of an unintended breach of the duty of loyalty is unusual but not novel.... That action will, therefore, be set aside by order of this court....

[During the pendency of the case involving Blasius's attack on the action of the directors in adding two members to the board, Blasius presented Atlas with shareholder consents purporting to show that a majority of Atlas's shareholders had adopted Blasius's proposals to enlarge the board from seven to fifteen, elect eight new directors nominated by Blasius, and take certain other actions. Atlas appointed Manufacturers Hanover Trust Company to act as judge of the shareholders' "vote." Manufacturers reported that the vote had been extremely close, but that none of Blasius's proposals had succeeded. Blasius then brought a second case, in which it challenged certain of Manufacturers' determinations. That case was consolidated with Blasius's attack on the action of the directors in adding two members to the board. The court upheld most of Manufacturers' determinations and Manufacturers' conclusion that Blasius had lost the vote, and rendered judgment in the second case for the defendants.]

————

NOTE ON STROUD v. GRACE

In Stroud v. Grace, 606 A.2d 75 (Del.1992), the Delaware Supreme Court approved both Schnell and Blasius, although holding that the principles established in those cases were not applicable on the facts of the case before the Court:

> In Schnell v. Chris–Craft Industries, Inc., Del.Supr., 285 A.2d 437 (1971), this Court recognized that management may not inequitably manipulate corporate machinery to perpetuate "itself in office" and disenfranchise the shareholders. Id. at 439. The crux of *Schnell* is that:
>
> > [I]nequitable action does not become permissible simply because it is legally possible.
>
> Id.
>
> *Schnell's* broad holding spawned an entirely new line of Court of Chancery decisions. Lerman v. Diagnostic Data, Inc., Del.Ch., 421 A.2d 906 (1980); *Aprahamian*, 531 A.2d at 1208; *Blasius*, 564 A.2d at 659–60; Centaur Partners, IV, v. National Intergroup, Inc., Del.Supr., 582 A.2d 923, 927 (1990); Stahl v. Apple Bancorp, Inc., Del.Ch., 579 A.2d 1115, 1122–23 (1990).
>
> While we accept the basic legal tenets of *Stahl* and *Blasius,* certain principles emerge from those cases which are inextricably related to their specific facts. Almost all of the post-*Schnell* decisions involved situations where boards of directors deliberately employed various legal strategies either to frustrate or completely disenfranchise a shareholder vote. As *Blasius* recognized, in those circumstances, board action was intended to thwart free exercise of the franchise. There can be no dispute that such conduct violates Delaware law.. . .

_____

DELAWARE GEN. CORP. LAW § 109

[See Statutory Supplement]

_____

REVISED MODEL BUS. CORP. ACT §§ 10.20–10.22

[See Statutory Supplement]

_____

NOTE ON WEIGHTED VOTING IN PUBLICLY HELD CORPORATIONS

In the majority of publicly held corporations, only common shareholders have voting rights, and each share of common stock carries one vote. However, voting rights can be conferred on preferred stock or even on bonds, and corporations may have two or more classes of common, each with different voting rights. Often when there are two or more classes of common, one class has voting power all out of proportion to its equity interests. Such structures are sometimes referred to as dual-class common, super-voting stock, or weighted voting. Although not new, the incidence of such structures increased during the takeover movement in the 1980s, when they were often installed as an antitakeover device.

In theory, the creation of such a structure affects only the relative rights of different shareholders, not the allocation of power between managers and shareholders. As the use of such structures to defend against takeovers suggests, however, in practice these structures usually involve the issuance of super-voting stock to managers or members of a control group with the objective of allowing control to be maintained with a minimum investment.

In Stroh v. Blackhawk Holding Corp., 48 Ill.2d 471, 272 N.E.2d 1 (1971), noted, 85 Harv.L.Rev. 1676 (1972), 26 Sw.L.J. 618 (1972), Blackhawk's certificate authorized a Class A and a Class B stock. Class B voted share for share with Class A, but was entitled neither to dividends nor to a share in the proceeds of liquidation. After Blackhawk's formation, its promoters purchased 500,000 shares of Class B at a quarter of a cent per share, and 87,868 shares of Class A at $3.40 per share, and thereafter sold Class A stock to the public at $4 per share. As of June 1968, Blackhawk had outstanding 1,237,-681 Class A shares and 500,000 Class B shares, the latter representing an investment of $1250 but carrying 28.78% of the total vote. The court upheld the validity of the B stock.

> ... Section 14 of the Business Corporation Act ... provides that shares of stock in an Illinois corporation may be divided into classes,
>
>> "with such designations, preferences, qualifications, limitations, restrictions and such special or relative rights as shall be stated in the articles of incorporation. The articles of incorporation shall not limit or deny the voting power of the shares of any class...."
>
> Section 14 ... clearly expresses the intent of the legislature to be that parties to a corporate entity may create whatever restrictions and limitations they may want with regard to their corporate stock by expressing such restrictions and limitations in the articles of incorporation....
>
> ... It has long been the common practice in Illinois to classify shares of stock such that one may invest less than another in a corporation, and yet have control. One of two shareholders may purchase ten shares of a class of stock issued at its par value of $1,000 per share, and his business partner may purchase 100 shares of another class of the corporate stock issued at its par value of $10 per share. The parties, for varying reasons, may be very willing that the party investing the $1,000

have control of the management of the corporation, as opposed to the party having the investment of $10,000....

In this case the parties went one step further than is customary. The stock which could be bought cheaper, and yet carry the same voting power per share, was not permitted to share at all in the dividends or assets of the corporation. This additional step did not invalidate the stock.

In Providence & Worcester Co. v. Baker, 378 A.2d 121 (Del. 1977), a form of weighted voting was achieved by limiting the number of votes that could be cast by any one shareholder. P & W's certificate provided that each holder of common stock had one vote per share for his first 50 shares, but only one vote per 20 shares for all shares over 50. The validity of these limitations was challenged by the trustees in bankruptcy of Penn Central, who held 28% of P & W's stock, but were effectively restricted to 3% of the total voting power. The court upheld the restrictions under Del. § 212(a), which states that "[u]nless otherwise provided in the certificate of incorporation ... each stockholder shall be entitled to 1 vote for each share of capital stock held by such stockholder." The court concluded that "if the General Assembly intended to bar the type of restriction on stockholders' voting rights here under review, such prohibition would appear in § 212.... Under § 212(a), voting rights of stockholders may be varied from the 'one share-one vote' standard by the certificate of incorporation...." See also Lacos Land Co. v. Arden Group Co., 517 A.2d 271 (Del.Ch. 1986); 1 F.H. O'Neal & R. Thompson, O'Neal's Close Corporations § 3.16 (3d ed. 1992).

In a few states, weighted voting in publicly held corporations is controlled to varying extents by the Blue Sky administrator, and in several situations Congress has acted to prevent abuses in this area. For example, § 18 of the Investment Company Act of 1940, 15 U.S.C.A. § 80a–18, forbids the issuance of nonvoting stock by companies subject to that Act, except in a few special cases.

The rules of the New York Stock Exchange, the American Stock Exchange and NASDAQ, set certain limits on weighted voting in listed corporations.

See generally Gordon, Ties that Bond: Dual Class Common Stock and the Problem of Shareholder Choice, 76 Calif.L.Rev. 1 (1988); Gilson, Evaluating Dual Class Common Stock: The Relevance of Substitutes, 73 Va.L.Rev. 807 (1987).

————

NEW YORK STOCK EXCHANGE, LISTED COMPANY MANUAL § 313.00

[See Statutory Supplement]

————

SECTION 3.   THE LEGAL STRUCTURE OF MANAGEMENT (I): THE BOARD OF DIRECTORS AND THE OFFICERS

NOTE ON THE LEGAL STRUCTURE OF THE CORPORATION

Perhaps the most striking aspect of the traditional legal model of the corporation described at p. 166, supra, is the distinctive position of the board.   Simple business organizations are managed either by the owners or by persons who are legally agents of the owners.   Under the traditional legal model of the corporation, however, the officers are agents not of the shareholders but of the board, while the board itself is conceived of not strictly as an agent of the shareholders but as an independent institution.   For example, although the authority of an agent can normally be terminated by his principal at any time, directors are normally removable by shareholders only for good cause.   Similarly, although an agent must normally follow his principal's instructions, shareholders have no legal power to give binding instructions to the board on matters within its power.   Any study of corporate structure must therefore consider two very different interfaces: that between the shareholders and the managerial organs taken together, and that between the managerial organs themselves.

In recent times, it has become obvious that the traditional legal model is inadequate.   Under that model, the board of directors manages the corporation's business and sets business policy.   This aspect of the model was reflected in a central provision of the traditional corporate statutes: "The business and affairs of a corporation shall be managed by a board of directors."   It has become increasingly clear, however, that in practice the board rarely performs either the management or the policymaking functions.   It has always been understood that in closely held corporations the business is typically managed by owner-managers, pretty much without any regard to formal capacities.   All serious students of corporate affairs also now recognize that in the typical large publicly held corporation the management function is vested not in the board but in the executives.   "Under the system of directorates which has developed in this country among large, listed companies, directors are unable to 'manage' corporations in any narrow interpretation of the word. . . .   Directors do not and cannot 'direct' corporations in the sense of operating them."   J. Baker, *Directors and Their Functions* 12 (1945).   See also R. Gordon, *Business Leadership in the Large Corporation* 79–90, 114–115, 128–134, 143–146 (2d ed. 1961).   It is often said, however, that the board *does* make business policy, and it is frequently implied that by making business policy the board fulfills the statutory command.   In fact, of course, policymaking is not equivalent to management: civilians may make policy for the Army; they certainly do not manage the Army. In any event, the typical board no more makes business policy than it manages the business. In the publicly held corporation, policymaking, like management, is an executive function. As early as 1945 the economist Robert Aaron Gordon reported in *Business Leadership in the Large Corporation* that in both financial and nonfinancial matters there was little or no indication that the boards of large companies initiated decisions on either specific matters or broad policies. Although the board's approval function was more important than its function of initiating activities, Gordon found that "even with respect to approval, many boards in these large companies are almost completely passive," and that the final approval function was usually exercised by the chief executive in conjunction with either his immediate subordinates, an executive or finance committee of the board, or a few influential directors acting as his informal advisors. Gordon, supra, at 128–129, 131. See also id. at 114. Similarly, John C. Baker of the Harvard Business School reported the same year that major policies in production, marketing, finance, and personnel were usually formulated by the executives and not even formally confirmed by the board (although there was often consultation with individual directors). In such matters as addition of new products, preparation of operating budget, and negotiation of collective bargaining agreements, the board's role was limited to receipt and consideration of after-the-fact reports. Baker, supra, at 18. More recent studies, particularly that of Professor Myles Mace, have confirmed these earlier findings. M. Mace, *Directors: Myth and Reality* 47–48 and passim (1971).

In short, under what might be called the modern legal model of management structure—that is, the model that embodies actual corporate practice—most of the powers supposedly vested in the board are actually vested in the executives.

————

AMERICAN LAW INSTITUTE, PRINCIPLES OF CORPORATE GOVERNANCE §§ 5.03, 5.05

[See Statutory Supplement]

————

SECTION 4. THE LEGAL STRUCTURE OF MANAGEMENT (II): COMPOSITION AND COMMITTEES OF THE BOARD IN PUBLICLY HELD CORPORATIONS

————

DEL. GEN. CORP. LAW § 141(c)

[See Statutory Supplement]

REV. MODEL BUS. CORP. ACT § 8.25

[See Statutory Supplement]

AMERICAN LAW INSTITUTE, PRINCIPLES OF CORPORATE GOVERNANCE §§ 3.05, 3A.01–3A.05

[See Statutory Supplement]

SECTION 5.　FORMALITIES REQUIRED FOR ACTION BY THE BOARD

DEL. GEN. CORP. LAW §§ 141(b), (f), (i), 229

[See Statutory Supplement]

REV. MODEL BUS. CORP. ACT §§ 8.20, 8.21, 8.22, 8.23, 8.24

[See Statutory Supplement]

NOTE ON FORMALITIES REQUIRED FOR ACTION BY THE BOARD

The validity of an action by the board of directors is governed by rules concerning the formalities required for meeting, notice, quorum, and voting.

Before turning to these rules, a preliminary question should be addressed. In the most typical case involving the validity of a board action, a third party claims to have a right against the corporation based on a contract executed by an officer and purportedly approved by the board. The corporation defends on the ground that the purported board approval was invalid because a requisite formality was not satisfied. In such a case, the third party could have foreclosed this defense by demanding, when he made the contract, that the corporation produce a certificate from its secretary attesting that the board, at a duly held meeting, duly adopted resolutions authorizing the contract. A corporate secretary normally has at least apparent authority to provide such certified resolutions, and in the normal case the corporation is bound by the secretary's certificate. See p. 206, infra. Why then should problems concerning the validity of board action ever arise? There are several reasons. Sometimes it is awkward to demand such a certificate. Sometimes the third party does not realize he is best protected by such a certificate. Sometimes the third party doesn't know about the board approval at the time of the transaction (relying, instead, on the action by the officer), and only later learns of the purported board approval. And often problems concerning the validity of board action do not involve a third party, but instead grow out of a contest between inside factions.

Let us now turn directly to the rules concerning the validity of board action. These rules can be stratified at three levels. At the first level are rules that lay down a basic model of board action. At the second level are rules that explicitly permit variations in the basic model. At the third level are rules that govern the conse-quence of noncompliance with rules at the first two levels. The rules at all three levels originated in the common law, but most of the issues on the first two levels are now governed by statute. Unless otherwise indicated, the following account is based on predominant statutory patterns.

Level 1: The Basic Model.

(i) *Meetings.* Under the basic model the board of directors is conceived as a collegial body. Therefore, directors can act only at a duly convened meeting at which a quorum is present. As a corollary, directors have no power to act on the corporation's behalf except at such a meeting. The theory behind the basic model is that someone—presumably, the body of shareholders—is entitled to a collegial interchange among all the directors before a board decision is made, or, at least, is entitled to insist that all the directors be given the opportunity to attend a meeting affording the opportunity for such interchange, and that a majority of the di-rectors actually do attend.

(ii) *Notice.* Formal notice is not required for a regular board meeting; since the meeting is regular, the directors are already on notice of its date, time, and place. In the case of a special meeting, however, notice of date, time, and place must be given to every director. The notice need not state the purpose of a meeting unless the certificate of incorporation or the bylaws otherwise provide. The statutes usually provide that notice must be given a stated number of days in advance of the meeting, but then add that the stated period may be made shorter or longer by the certificate of incorporation or by-laws.

(iii) *Quorum.* A quorum consists of a majority of the full board (that is, a majority of the authorized number of directors)—not a majority of the directors then in office, which may be less than the authorized number because of board vacancies.

(iv) *Voting.* Assuming that a quorum is present when a vote is taken, the affirmative vote of a majority of those present—not a majority of those voting—is required.

Level 2: Explicitly Approved Variations.

(i) *Meetings.* Most statutes provide that a meeting of the board can be conducted by conference telephone, or by any other means of communication through which all participating directors can simultaneously hear each other. Of more importance, most permit board action to be accomplished by unanimous written consent, without a meeting of any kind.

(ii) *Notice.* Most statutes provide that notice can be waived in writing before or after a meeting, and that attendance at a meeting constitutes a waiver unless the director attends merely to protest against holding the meeting.

(iii) *Quorum.* A majority of statutes permit the certificate of incorporation or bylaws to require a greater number for a quorum than a majority of the full board. A substantial minority of the statutes, including the Delaware statute and the Model Act, permit the certificate or bylaws to set a lower number, but usually no less than one-third of the full board.

(iv) *Voting.* Most statutes provide that the articles or bylaws can require a greater-than-majority vote for board action.

Level 3: Consequences of Noncompliance.

The rules at Levels 1 and 2 are relatively clear. The consequences of noncompliance with those rules are not always clear. In a publicly held corporation, where bureaucratic order usually prevails and the statutory rules stand surrogate for fair shareholder expectations concerning corporate procedure, lack of a quorum, lack of the requisite affirmative vote, or an uncured lack of notice to even one director will usually render board action ineffective. In closely held corporations, where formalities are seldom followed and the shareholders tend to make their own rules, the results of a failure to observe proper formalities are much less clear-cut. Unless otherwise indicated, the balance of this Note concerns cases involving closely held corporations.

(i) *Unanimous informal approval.* Some cases, most of which are quite old, have held that informal approval by directors is ineffective even if the approval is explicit and unanimous. For example, in Baldwin v. Canfield, 26 Minn. 43, 54, 1 N.W. 261, 270 (1879), the court said:

> [T]he general rule that [is] the governing body of a corporation, as such, are agents of the corporation only as a board, and

not individually. Hence it follows that they have no authority to act, save when assembled at a board meeting. The separate action, individually, of the persons composing such governing body, is not the action of the constituted body of men clothed with corporate powers.

Cases like *Baldwin* are of doubtful validity today. More characteristic of modern authority is Gerard v. Empire Square Realty Co., 195 App.Div. 244, 187 N.Y.S. 306 (1921). Plaintiff brought an action against several related corporations to recover damages for breach of an employment contract. The corporations' shares were owned by five persons, all of whom were directors. Owing to dissension, no shareholders' or directors' meetings were held, but there was evidence that each director had separately agreed to hire plaintiff. The court held that on these facts the corporations would be bound:

> I think that under the circumstances of the case we are considering, where the directors own all the capital stock of the corporations, where they are members of the same family but so at variance that directors' and stockholders' meetings are not held, their action, concurred in by all, although separately and not as a body, binds the corporation. We must recognize the fact that to a greater and greater degree all business, great and small, is being brought under the management of corporations instead of partnerships; that they are, in perhaps the majority of instances, conducted by officers and directors little informed in the law of corporations, who often act informally, sometimes without meetings or even by-laws. To hold that in all instances technical conformity to the requirements of the law of corporations is a condition to a valid action by the directors, would be to lay down a rule of law which could be used as a trap for the unwary who deal with corporations, and to permit corporations sometimes to escape liability to which an individual in the same circumstances would be subjected.

The results in this area are too disparate to be captured by a single clear rule. In general, however, it is fair to say that at a minimum, most modern courts would hold informal but explicit approval by all the directors to be effective where, as in *Gerard*, a person who has contracted with a corporate officer has been led to regard his transaction with the corporation as valid, and all the shareholders are directors or have acquiesced in the transaction or in a past practice of informal board action. See Anderson v. K.G. Moore, Inc., 6 Mass.App.Ct. 386, 376 N.E.2d 1238 (1978), cert. denied 439 U.S. 1116, 99 S.Ct. 1020, 59 L.Ed.2d 74 (1979); Myhre v. Myhre, 170 Mont. 410, 422, 554 P.2d 276, 282 (1976) ("Where the directors of a corporation are the only stockholders, they may act for the corporation without formal meetings. Formal meetings can also be waived by custom or general consent"); Leslie, Semple & Garrison, Inc. v. Gavit & Co., 81 A.D.2d 950, 439 N.Y.S.2d 707 (1981); Remillong v. Schneider, 185 N.W.2d 493 (N.D.1971); cf. Rowland v. Rowland, 102 Idaho 534, 633 P.2d 599 (1981). In the balance of this Note, the concept that informal board action should be valid at least under these circumstances will be referred to as the shareholder-acquiescence model.

Where a case falls within the shareholder-acquiescence model, corporate liability is consistent with the rules at Levels 1 and 2. Those rules are designed to protect shareholder interests. Under the conditions of the shareholder-acquiescence model, all the shareholders have acquiesced, in their directorial or shareholder capacities, either to the transaction or to a practice of informal action. As stated in Lake Motel, Inc. v. Lowery, 224 Va. 553, 559–60, 299 S.E.2d 496, 500 (1983):

> Lake. . . . rests its case for reversal upon the bald proposition that, in the absence of a formal resolution of the board of directors authorizing the sale to the Lowerys, the deed effectuating the sale is void. We considered a similar argument in *Moore v. Aetna Co.,* 155 Va. 556, 155 S.E. 707 (1930):
>
>> . . . Certainly a corporation should act through its board of directors, and in accordance with the limitations imposed by its charter and by-laws; but when, with the knowledge and acquiescence of all of its stockholders, it declines so to do, it must accept the consequences. It cannot be permitted to accept all the benefits of such irregular contracts without assuming all of the resulting liabilities.
>
> 155 Va. at 570, 155 S.E. at 711. . . .
>
> . . . [This rule] is designed to protect parties who deal in good faith with close corporations that conduct their internal affairs informally.

Furthermore, where a third person has been led to regard a transaction with the corporation as valid, it is typically because he has dealt with an officer who purported to have either authority to consummate the transaction or board approval of the transaction. In such cases there is something to be said for a rule that the corporation, which appointed the officer, ought to be bound by his conduct, particularly if the third person has relied on the transaction. True, the usual rule is that a corporation is not bound by an officer's conduct in the absence of actual or apparent authority. However, the question is close enough that adding the element of informal board approval may appropriately tip the balance, particularly when reliance is present. See Morris v. Y. & B. Corp., 198 N.C. 705, 153 S.E. 327 (1930).[1]

---

1. An example of a modern case in which the corporation was not bound by the informal approval of all the directors is Fradkin v. Ernst, 571 F.Supp. 829 (N.D.Ohio 1983). This case did not fall within the shareholder-acquiescence model. There were a number of shareholders; the shareholders were not shown to have ac- quiesced; and the transaction did not involve a party who had been led reasonably to regard the transaction as valid (the defendant-directors were seeking to uphold the questioned transaction, and they were in a position to know of the lack of necessary formalities). See also Greenberg v. Harrison, 143 Conn. 519, 124 A.2d 216

Today, many cases involving unanimous informal approval probably fall under the statutory rule that such approval is effective if it is in writing. (Indeed, Baldwin v. Canfield, supra, which involved a form of written consent, would probably be decided differently under the modern statutes.[2]) It might be argued that these statutes by negative implication preclude the courts from giving effect to informal unanimous approval that is not in writing. In Village of Brown Deer v. City of Milwaukee, 16 Wis.2d 206, 114 N.W.2d 493 (1962), cert. denied 371 U.S. 902, 83 S.Ct. 205, 9 L.Ed.2d 164, the court held, "The legislature has said that the corporation could act informally, without a meeting, by obtaining the consent in writing of all of the directors. In our opinion, this pronouncement has preempted the field and prohibits corporations from acting informally without complying with" the statute. In *Brown Deer*, however, apparently only a majority of the directors knew of the transaction in question, so there was no unanimous approval, formal or informal. Other cases decided in jurisdictions that have unanimous-written-consent statutes have held the corporation bound by unanimous oral consent. See Note, Corporations: When Informal Action by Corporate Directors Will Be Permitted to Bind the Corporation, 53 B.U.L.Rev. 101, 120 (1973). The intent of the statutes seems to be to protect persons dealing with a corporation, not to weaken the rights of such persons. The preferable construction of these statutes, therefore, is that they provide a safe harbor and leave the balance of the field to judicial development. Indeed, the statutes can be read to support liability under the shareholder-acquiescence model, because they manifest a legislative policy that undermines the basic model's emphasis on collegial interchange.

(ii) *Unanimous acquiescence.* In the type of case just considered, all the directors informally but explicitly approve a transaction. Suppose that a majority of the directors explicitly approve a transaction, and the remaining directors know of the transaction and take no steps to disavow it, so that although they do not explicitly approve, they may be said to acquiesce. The difference between this case and the case in which all the directors explicitly approve is not terribly significant—even in the latter case the approval is only informal—and the courts will normally treat the two cases alike. See, e.g., Winchell v. Plywood Corp., 324 Mass. 171, 85 N.E.2d 313 (1949). The same result will normally follow even if there is no explicit approval by a majority of the directors but all the directors acquiesce. See Juergens v. Venture Capital Corp., 1 Mass.App.Ct. 274, 295 N.E.2d 398 (1973); Wuerderman v. J.O. Lively Const. Co., 602 S.W.2d 215 (Mo.App.1980); Pierce v. Astoria Fish Factors, Inc., 31 Wash.App. 214, 640 P.2d 40 (1982).

(1956), in which the transaction in question was a preferential transfer to an insider.

2. However, Baldwin v. Canfield may not quite fit within the shareholder-acquiescence model. In that case, one director, who was the moving force in the transaction, owned all the shares, but he had pledged his shares to a bank. Therefore, while all the shareholders had acquiesced, all parties with an economic interest in the corporation's stock had not.

(iii) *Majority acquiescence.* Suppose, finally, that a majority of the directors approve a transaction, explicitly or by acquiescence, but the remaining directors lack knowledge of the transaction. Some courts have refused to hold the corporation liable under these circumstances. See, e.g., Hurley v. Ornsteen, 311 Mass. 477, 42 N.E.2d 273 (1942). Other courts have held the corporation liable, at least if the shareholders acquiesced in the transaction or the shareholders or the remaining directors acquiesced in a practice of informal action by the directors. One theory is that the remaining directors would have known of the transaction if they had been properly active. Another is that the shareholders, if they have tolerated informal action by the directors over a period of time, have by that acquiescence authorized the directors to act in this manner. See, e.g., Holy Cross Gold Mining & Milling Co. v. Goodwin, 74 Colo. 532, 223 P. 58 (1924):

> Ballard, the president, and Peck, the secretary, who execut-
> ed or signed the contract sued on, were directors of the
> defendant. They constituted a majority of the board of
> directors, because there were but three directors, G.E.
> Stearns being the third. The directors had never held a
> meeting, except on October 10, 1918. Peck and Ballard
> came to the office of plaintiff's attorney and signed the
> contract involved herein on January 14, 1922. The evi-
> dence shows that it was the customary usage of the corpo-
> ration to act through its directors individually. In the
> instant case a majority of the directors acted. The case of
> Longmont S.D. Co. v. Coffman, 11 Colo. 551, 19 Pac. 508,
> is authority for the proposition that a board of directors
> may act individually and the act be binding on the corpora-
> tion if it has become a practice of the directors to act that
> way.

In some cases involving informal approval by only a majority of the directors, the courts have held the corporation liable simply because a majority of the shareholders had approved or acquiesced in the transaction. See Phillips Petroleum Co. v. Rock Creek Mining Co., 449 F.2d 664 (9th Cir.1971); Mannon v. Pesula, 59 Cal.App.2d 597, 139 P.2d 336 (1943); Mickshaw v. Coca Cola Bottling Co., Inc., of Sharon, Pennsylvania, 166 Pa.Super. 148, 70 A.2d 467 (1950).

———

SECTION 6. AUTHORITY OF CORPORATE OFFICERS

———

DEL. GEN. CORP. LAW § 142

[See Statutory Supplement]

———

REV. MODEL BUS. CORP. ACT §§ 8.40, 8.41

[See Statutory Supplement]

NOTE ON AUTHORITY, pp. 8–15, supra

NOTE ON THE AUTHORITY OF CORPORATE OFFICERS

Legal questions concerning the authority of a corporate officer typically arise out of a transaction between a third person and the corporation in which an officer acted on the corporation's behalf. The major concepts relevant to determining such questions are the agency principles of actual and apparent authority. The application of these principles in the corporate context often rests on the officer's position, that is, his title. Apparent authority will often rest largely on position, because a third party can normally assume that an officer has the authority customarily vested in persons holding the position in question. Even actual authority may rest partly on position, because the authority an officer reasonably believes he possesses may depend in part on the authority customarily possessed by persons holding the position in question.

1. *The President.* There are a great number of cases concerning the apparent authority of a president by virtue of his position. Some cases—most but not all of them early—hold that a president does not have any apparent authority by virtue of his position; that he has only the actual authority the board confers upon him. For example, in Federal Services Finance Corp. v. Bishop Nat. Bank of Hawaii at Honolulu, 190 F.2d 442 (9th Cir.1951), supplemented 205 F.2d 11 (9th Cir.1953), the court held that the president of an ordinary trading corporation had no presumed power by virtue of his office to cash checks payable to the company's order. See also Har–Bel Coal Co. v. Asher Coal Mining Co., 414 S.W.2d 128 (Ky.1966); Lucey v. Hero Int'l Corp., 361 Mass. 569, 281 N.E.2d 266 (1972); Nelms v. A & A Liquor Stores, Inc., 445 S.W.2d 256 (Tex.Civ.App.1969).

Some cases avoided the force of this rather unrealistic rule by holding that a special rule applies where the president also serves as general manager. See, e.g., Memorial Hospital Ass'n of Stanislaus County v. Pacific Grape Products Co., 45 Cal.2d 634, 637, 290 P.2d 481, 483 (1955): "Where the president of a corporation is also its general manager, having the power to superintend and conduct its business, he has implied authority to make any contract or do any other act appropriate in the ordinary course of its business. In such case his powers are greater than he would have as president alone." See also Fletcher Oil Co. v. City of Bay City, 346 Mich. 411, 78

N.W.2d 205 (1956); cf. Gillian v. Consolidated Foods Corp., 424 Pa. 407, 227 A.2d 858 (1967). The title "general manager" is rarely used today; its closest modern counterpart is "chief executive officer" (CEO), although the CEO title may carry more weight now than the GM title did in the past. The title is not inevitably conferred on the president. In many corporations, the chairman of the board is the CEO. In a few corporations, there is an "office of the chief executive" shared by several persons. There is little or no case law on the implications of the CEO title.

The prevalent modern rule is discussed as follows in Lee v. Jenkins Bros., 268 F.2d 357 (2d Cir.1959), cert. denied 361 U.S. 913, 80 S.Ct. 257, 4 L.Ed.2d 183:

> The rule most widely cited is that the president only has authority to bind his company by acts arising in the usual and regular course of business but not for contracts of an "extraordinary" nature. The substance of such a rule lies in the content of the term "extraordinary" which is subject to a broad range of interpretation.

> The growth and development of this rule occurred during the late nineteenth and early twentieth centuries when the potentialities of the corporate form of enterprise were just being realized. As the corporation became a more common vehicle for the conduct of business it became increasingly evident that many corporations, particularly small closely held ones, did not normally function in the formal ritualistic manner hitherto envisaged. While the boards of directors still nominally controlled corporate affairs, in reality officers and managers frequently ran the business with little, if any, board supervision. The natural consequence of such a development was that third parties commonly relied on the authority of such officials in almost all the multifarious transactions in which corporations engaged. The pace of modern business life was too swift to insist on the approval by the board of directors of every transaction that was in any way "unusual."

> The judicial recognition given to these developments has varied considerably. Whether termed "apparent authority" or an "estoppel" to deny authority, many courts have noted the injustice caused by the practice of permitting corporations to act commonly through their executives and then allowing them to disclaim an agreement as beyond the authority of the contracting officer, when the contract no longer suited its convenience. Other courts, however, continued to cling to the past with little attempt to discuss the unconscionable results obtained or the doctrine of apparent authority. Such restrictive views have been generally condemned by the commentators.

In a footnote, the court summarized holdings pro on the subject of what are and what are not "extraordinary," with the objective of showing that the application of that test has tended to be unpredictable:

[T]he following acts have been held to be within either the implied or apparent authority of a corporate president or manager: borrowing money and executing a corporate note; pledging security for a loan; guaranteeing the note of another corporation; purchasing merchandise; making a tax closing agreement; executing a time limitations waiver; pledging a substantial contribution to a hospital; licensing a factory spur track; sale of the corporation's only property; of all its merchandise and fixtures; or its real estate.

Other courts have left the question to the jury when the matter involved was: execution of a corporate note; a promise to pay a stale debt; entering a joint venture; oral waiver of written contract provisions . . ., and sale of the corporation's sole asset.

On the other hand authority has been found lacking in the following instances: sale of all the company's assets or its major asset; a brokerage contract to effectuate a merger; employing an architect in a major construction project; giving away corporate property; postponing a mortgage foreclosure; guaranteeing the debt of another; and contracts deemed unconscionable from the corporation's point of view. (Citations omitted.)

The difficulty lies in drawing a line between what is "ordinary" and what is "extraordinary." Some cases have been restrictive in determining the apparent authority of a president, perhaps influenced by statutory language that the business of the corporation shall be managed by the board. See Sacks v. Helene Curtis Industries, 340 Ill.App. 76, 91 N.E.2d 127 (1950); Parks v. Midland Ford Tractor Co., 416 S.W.2d 22, 29 (Mo.App.1967); Liebermann v. Princeway Realty Corp., 17 A.D.2d 258, 233 N.Y.S.2d 1001 (1962), aff'd 13 N.Y.2d 999, 245 N.Y.S.2d 390, 195 N.E.2d 57 (1963). Other cases, like Lee v. Jenkins Brothers, interpret the president's apparent authority in a more expansive manner. See Three Sisters, Inc. v. Vertigo West, Inc., 18 Ill.App.3d 400, 309 N.E.2d 400 (1974); Yucca Mining & Petroleum Co. v. Howard C. Phillips Oil Co., 69 N.M. 281, 365 P.2d 925 (1961). The decisions that give the authority of officers an expansive interpretation in cases involving third persons reflect both the reality that the management of the business of the corporation is normally conducted by or under the supervision of its executives rather than its board, and a sound understanding of the normal expectations of third persons in such cases.

Any attempt at precision in determining the apparent authority of a president would almost certainly be futile, because the issue is highly dependent on the context in which it arises, and the types of business transactions that may arise are endlessly variable. Nevertheless, certain boundaries can be identified. To begin with, some matters, such as the declaration of dividends, are required by statute to be decided by the board. Typically, the statutes also enumerate certain matters that the board cannot delegate to a committee, such as approval of an action that requires approval by both the board and the shareholders pursuant to statute. By analogy, it would normally not be within the authority of the president or other senior executives to take binding action on these matters.

Beyond these boundaries, among the elements to be taken into account for purposes of determining what constitutes an "extraordinary" action, that would normally be outside the apparent authority of the president, are the economic magnitude of the action in relation to corporate assets and earnings, the extent of risk involved, the timespan of the action's effect, and the cost of reversing the action. Examples of the kinds of actions that would normally be "extraordinary" include the creation of long-term or other significant debt, the reacquisition of equity or debt securities, significant capital investments, business combinations (including those effected for cash), the disposition of significant businesses, entry into important new lines of business, significant acquisitions of stock in other corporations, and actions that would foreseeably expose the corporation to significant litigation or significant new regulatory problems. A useful generalization is that decisions that would make a significant change in the structure of the business enterprise, or the structure of control over the enterprise, are extraordinary corporate actions and therefore normally outside the president's apparent authority.[1]

Of course, the president, or any other officer, may have actual authority greater than his apparent authority. The president's actual authority may be found in the certificate of incorporation, the by-laws, or board resolutions, see, e.g., Missouri Valley Steel Co. v. New Amsterdam Casualty Co., 275 Minn. 433, 148 N.W.2d 126 (1966), or may derive from a pattern of past acquiescence by the board, see, e.g., Buxton v. Diversified Resources Corp., 634 F.2d 1313 (10th Cir.1980), cert. denied 454 U.S. 821, 102 S.Ct. 105, 70 L.Ed.2d 93 (1981); Juergens v. Venture Capital Corp., 1 Mass.App. Ct. 274, 295 N.E.2d 398 (1973); A. Schulman, Inc. v. Baer Co., 197 Pa.Super. 429, 178 A.2d 794 (1962), or from the board's acquiescence in or ratification of a specific transaction, see, e.g., De Pova v. Camden Forge Co., 254 F.2d 248 (3d Cir.1958), cert. denied 358 U.S. 816, 79 S.Ct. 26, 3 L.Ed.2d 59; Rachelle Enterprises, Inc. v. United States, 169 F.Supp. 266 (Ct.Cl.1959); Wuerderman v. J.O. Lively Const. Co., 602 S.W.2d 215 (Mo.App.1980); Pierce v. Astoria Fish Factors, Inc., 31 Wash.App. 214, 640 P.2d 40 (1982); Coastal Pharmaceutical Co. v. Goldman, 213 Va. 831, 195 S.E.2d 848 (1973).[2]

---

1. The last two paragraphs are adapted from ALI, Principles of Corporate Governance § 3.01, Reporter's Note.

2. In Boston Athletic Ass'n v. International Marathons, Inc., 392 Mass. 356, 363–365, 467 N.E.2d 58, 62–63 (1984), the court held that despite a board delegation of certain authority to the corporation's president, he did not have the authority to make an exclusive contract with an independent company to promote the Boston Marathon, stating the board cannot "delegate authority which is so broad that it enables the officer to bind the corporation to extraordi-

2. *Chairman of the Board.* There is little case-law on the apparent authority of a chairman of the board by virtue of his position, in part because the actual authority of the chairman varies enormously. "It is an office in evolution assuming different roles in different corporations. In some it is held by a chief executive officer who has relinquished day-by-day operations to a younger man while still holding the reins of power; in others it is held by a retired chief executive officer whose counsel and advice are still valued; in still others it provides a formula for dividing up between two relatively equal principals the control of the corporation." American Express Co. v. Lopez, 72 Misc.2d 648, 340 N.Y.S.2d 82 (Civ.Ct.1973).

3. *Vice-presidents.* The case-law on the apparent authority of vice-presidents is also sparse. Under the relatively strict outlook of the earlier cases, a vice-president had little or no apparent authority. See James F. Monaghan, Inc. v. M. Lowenstein & Sons, 290 Mass. 331, 195 N.E. 101 (1935). There is some indication that the more expansive approach reflected in Lee v. Jenkins Brothers may carry over to vice-presidents, at least if they have the appearance of standing close to the top of the corporate hierarchy. Kanavos v. Hancock Bank & Trust Co., 14 Mass.App.Ct. 326, 439 N.E.2d 311 (1982).

4. *Secretary.* The secretary has apparent authority to certify the records of the corporation, including resolutions of the board. Accordingly, a secretary's certificate that a given resolution was duly adopted by the board is conclusive in favor of third party relying on the certificate.

SECTION 7. FORMALITIES REQUIRED FOR SHAREHOLDER ACTION

DEL. GEN. CORP. LAW §§ 211, 213, 214, 216, 222, 228

[See Statutory Supplement]

REV. MODEL BUS. CORP. ACT §§ 7.01, 7.02, 7.03–7.07, 7.21, 7.25–7.28

[See Statutory Supplement]

---

nary commitments.... Certain transactions require specific authorization by the board in order to be valid." This case involved a charitable organization, and special reasons of policy may be applicable to such corporations. It seems doubtful that the same result could properly be reached in the case of a business corporation.

NOTE ON FORMALITIES REQUIRED
FOR SHAREHOLDER ACTION

1. *Meeting and notice.* All of the statutes contemplate that a corporation will hold an annual meeting of shareholders. Notice of place, time, and date is required for the annual meeting and for any special meeting. The notice of a special meeting must also describe the purpose for which the meeting is called. Some state statutes, and the federal Proxy Rules, also require a description of purpose in the notice of an annual meeting. However, the Proxy Rules apply to only a small fraction of all corporations, and under most of the state statutes the notice of an annual meeting must describe the matters to be acted upon only in certain cases—for example, when it is proposed to amend the certificate of incorporation, sell substantially all of the corporation's assets, engage in a merger, or dissolve.

Because the identity of the shareholders in a publicly held corporation constantly undergoes change, notice of a meeting is given not to those persons who are beneficial owners of stock on the date of the meeting, but to those persons who are shareholders of record on a designated record date prior to the meeting. Correspondingly, only those persons who were record holders on the record date are entitled to vote at the meeting. The record date is normally fixed in the by-laws, or by the board, within prescribed statutory limits. If a record date is not fixed in this manner, the statutes usually provide that the record date will be the day of, or the business day preceding, the day on which the notice of meeting is sent. (Under an older, alternative procedure that is still sanctioned in many statutes, but is generally regarded as archaic, the corporation can close its share-transfer books as of a given date, and give notice only to those persons who were record holders at the time the transfer books were closed.)

2. *Quorum.* Under most of the statutes a majority of the shares entitled to vote is necessary for a quorum, unless the certificate of incorporation sets a higher or lower figure. A substantial majority of the statutes provide that the certificate cannot set a quorum lower than one-third of the shares entitled to vote. Most of the balance of the statutes set no minimum.

3. *Voting.* (i) *Ordinary matters.* Under most statutes, the affirmative vote of a majority of the shares represented at a meeting is required for shareholder action on ordinary matters. Under some statutes, however, only the affirmative vote of a majority of those voting is required. If a statute requires the affirmative vote of a majority of those present, an abstention affectively counts as a negative vote.

Virtually all the statutes permit the certificate of incorporation to set a higher vote than would otherwise be required. Under some of the statutes, a certificate amendment that adds a provision requiring a higher-than-normal vote may be adopted only by the same vote as is required under the amendment.

(ii) *Structural changes.*   Structural changes, such as certificate amendment, merger, sale of substantially all assets, and dissolution, usually require approval by a majority or two-thirds of the outstanding voting shares, rather than a majority of those present or voting at the meeting.   See Chapter 11, infra.

(iii) *Election of directors.*   The election of directors requires only a plurality vote—that is, those candidates who receive the highest number of votes are elected, up to the maximum number to be chosen at the election, even if they receive less than a majority of the votes present at the meeting.   Some states require cumulative voting in the election of directors.   See infra.

(iv) *Written consent.*   The statutes typically permit the shareholders to act by written consent in lieu of a meeting.   Most of the statutes permit shareholder action by written consent only if the consent is unanimous.

4. *Cumulative voting.*   Cumulative voting for directors is required by some states, and is sometimes voluntarily adopted even when not required.   The mechanics of cumulative voting are described in the material that follows.

———

2 H. MARSH & R. FINKLE, MARSH'S CALIFORNIA CORPORATION LAW § 11.2*

3d ed. 1990.

In voting cumulatively, a shareholder casts for any one or more candidates a number of votes greater than the number of his shares. The number of votes a shareholder is entitled to cast cumulatively is calculated by multiplying the number of votes to which his shares are entitled by the number of directors to be elected.   In other words, if there is a five-man board and the shareholder owns 100 shares (each entitled to one vote per share), then the shareholder has 100 times five or 500 votes which he may cast in the election. He may cast the entire sum, 500 votes, for one candidate or he may allocate the votes among more than one or all of the candidates.   If he votes an equal number of votes for five candidates, however, he has not "cumulated" his votes; if all shareholders do this, the effect is the same as though cumulate voting did not exist.

The significant calculation in cumulative voting is the determination of the number of shares needed to elect a specified number of directors.   Such a calculation may be made according to the following formula:

* Reprinted by permission of Panel Publishers, a division of Aspen Publishers, Inc., 36 W. 44th, Suite 1316, New York, NY 10036. All rights reserved.

$$X = \frac{S \times D}{N + 1} + 1 \text{ (vote)}$$

In this formula X is the number of shares required to elect a specified number of directors (D); S is the number of shares which are voted at an election of directors; N is the total number of directors who will be elected. In an election for the entire five-man board of a corporation having 1,000 shares outstanding entitled to vote, if all of such shares are present and are voted at the meeting, the number of shares entitled to elect two directors may be calculated as follows:

$$S = 1,000; \quad N = 5; \quad D = 2.$$

$$X = \frac{1000 \times 2}{5 + 1} + .2 = \frac{2,000}{6} + .2 = 334 \text{ [16]}$$

Therefore, in the example, assuming all shares which are entitled to vote do so, 334 shares are required to elect two directors. To illustrate, assume there are 1,000 shares outstanding entitled to vote in an election of directors and two shareholders, one holding 334 shares and the other holding 666 shares. In the election, the shareholders would be entitled to cast a number of votes equal to the number of shares they hold times the number of directors to be elected or, respectively, 1,670 votes and 3,330 votes. If the majority shareholder distributed his votes equally among four candidates, each candidate would receive 832 + votes. Since the minority shareholder is able to cast 1,670 votes, he would cast 835 votes for each of two candidates, resulting in the election of both of his candidates and the election of only three of those of the majority shareholder. The majority shareholder could not cumulate his votes in any manner that would produce more than 835 votes for more than three of his candidates.

On the other hand, if the majority shareholder held 667 shares (or one more) he could distribute his 3,335 votes by giving each of four candidates 833 + votes; whereas, the minority shareholder with 333 shares and 1,665 votes could give each of two candidates only 832 + votes, which would mean that he could elect only one . . . .

The formula may easily be rearranged to determine the number of directors one could elect given the ownership of a specified number of voting shares. If an individual owns 350 of the 1,000 outstanding shares entitled to vote in an election for directors, the calculation of the number of directors he could elect to a nine man board would require rearrangement of the formula to determine the value for D. The resultant formula would be expressed as follows:

16. The 1 *vote* in the formula is translated here into .2 share since there are *five* directors and .2 share in this particular case equals 1 *vote*. The calculation produces the figure 333.53, but this must be rounded off to the next higher integer, since normally no fractional shares are outstanding.

$$D = \frac{(X - 1)\ (N + 1)}{S}$$

The calculation of the number of directors that could be elected with 350 shares would be as follows:

$$D = \frac{(350 - 1)\ (9 + 1)}{1,000} = \frac{349(10)}{1,000} = \frac{3,490}{1,000} = 3.49$$

Rounding off to the lower integer, since a fractional director cannot be elected, the number of directors that could be elected by a proper cumulation of the votes of 350 shares at an election at which all of the 1,000 outstanding shares voted would be three out of a total of nine.

The general formula assumes that all shares entitled to vote in an election of directors are voted and are properly cumulated. If the total number of shares entitled to vote in an election are not voted, the number of shares necessary to elect a director is obviously less. Therefore, a particular faction at a shareholders' meeting may be able to elect a number of directors greater than that which would ordinarily result upon the proper cumulation of votes at a meeting at which all voting shares are present and voting. Furthermore, errors in calculation and in cumulating of votes may give unexpected results.

In Pierce v. Commonwealth [19] inadvertence by the holders of a majority of the voting shares in cumulating their votes resulted in the election of a majority of the directors by a minority of the shareholders. In that case the majority held 3,396 shares to the 3,037 shares held by the minority, in an election of six directors. The majority cumulated its votes (3,396 × 6 = 20,376) equally over six candidates (each candidate receiving 3,396 votes). The minority group cumulated its votes (3,037 × 6 = 18,222) over four candidates (each candidate receiving approximately 4,555 votes). The minority group elected all four of its candidates and gained control of the board. The election was upheld by the Supreme Court of Pennsylvania.*

NOTE ON CUMULATIVE VOTING

The percentage of stock that minority shareholders must hold to elect at least one director under cumulative voting varies inversely with the number of directors to be elected. Accordingly, a 12% minority (for example) can elect one director if nine directors are to be elected, but cannot elect any directors if three directors are to be

---

19. 104 Pa.St.Rep. 150 (1883).

* For qualifications on the general formulas, see Glazer, Glazer & Grofman, Cumulative Voting in Corporate Elections; Introducing Strategy Into the Equation, 35 S.C.L.Rev. 295 (1984). (Footnote by ed.)

elected. This can give rise to various problems in a state in which cumulative voting is mandatory.

One problem is whether, in a state in which cumulative voting is required, a corporation can have a classified board, in which the directors are divided into classes and each class serves for a term of years. Where a board is classified the minority must hold more stock, to elect a single director, than if a board of the same size was unclassified. In Wolfson v. Avery, 6 Ill.2d 78, 126 N.E.2d 701 (1955), the Illinois court held that a constitutional requirement of cumulative voting prohibited classified boards. In Bohannan v. Corporation Commission, 82 Ariz. 299, 313 P.2d 379 (1957), the Arizona court held to the contrary. Subsequently, the Arizona legislature enacted a statutory provision that permitted classification if a board had nine or more directors.

Still another issue concerns the removal of directors. If a director who is elected by a minority under cumulative voting could be removed without cause by majority vote (as was held permissible, at least where the removal was for cause, in Campbell v. Loew's, Inc., 36 Del.Ch. 563, 134 A.2d 852 (Ch. 1957)), a requirement of cumulative voting could be undercut. Accordingly, some statutes provide that under cumulative voting a director cannot be removed if the number of shares voting against her removal would be sufficient to elect her. See, e.g., Cal.Corp. Code § 303(a)(1).

Chapter V

SHAREHOLDER INFORMATIONAL RIGHTS AND PROXY VOTING

SECTION 1. SHAREHOLDER INFORMATIONAL RIGHTS UNDER STATE LAW

(a) INSPECTION OF BOOKS AND RECORDS

DEL. GEN. CORP. LAW §§ 219, 220

[See Statutory Supplement]

REV. MODEL BUS. CORP. ACT §§ 7.20, 16.01–16.04

[See Statutory Supplement]

CAL. CORP. CODE §§ 1600, 1601

[See Statutory Supplement]

N.Y. BUS. CORP. LAW §§ 624, 1315

[See Statutory Supplement]

COMPAQ COMPUTER CORP. v HORTON
Delaware Supreme Court, 1993.
631 A.2d 1.

MOORE, Justice.

This is a stocklist case arising under 8 *Del.C.* § 220(b) of our General Corporation Law. The issue is whether a shareholder states a proper purpose for inspection under our statute in seeking to solicit the participation of other shareholders in legitimate non-derivative litigation against the defendant corporation. The Court of Chancery found that the litigation concerned alleged corporate wrongdoing that affected the value of the plaintiff's stock. Accordingly, the trial court concluded that plaintiff's desire to contact other stockholders, and solicit their involvement in the litigation, was a purpose reasonably related to one's interest as a stockholder. We agree and affirm.

I.

Compaq Computer Corporation's ("Compaq") refused to permit Charles E. Horton ("Horton"), a Compaq stockholder, to inspect its stock ledger and other related materials. Horton has beneficially owned 112 shares of Compaq common stock continuously since December 6, 1990. Cede & Co., a nominal party to this action, is the record holder of these shares.

On July 22, 1991, Horton and seventy-eight other parties sued Compaq, fifteen of its advisors and certain management personnel (the "Texas litigation"). Horton and the other plaintiffs allege that Compaq and its co-defendants violated the Texas Security Act and the Texas Deceptive Trade Practices Consumer Protection Act. Plaintiffs also charge defendants with a continuing pattern of misconduct involving common law fraud, conspiracy, aiding and abetting, fraudulent concealment and breach of fiduciary duty. All these claims arise from the contention that Compaq misled the public as to the true value of its stock at a time when members of management were selling their own shares. The plaintiffs seek individual damages.

On September 22, 1992, Horton, through counsel, delivered a letter demanding to inspect Compaq's stock ledger and related information for the period from October 1, 1990 to June 30, 1991, to the extent such information is available and in the possession or control of Compaq. The demand letter stated that the purpose of the request was:

> [T]o enable Mr. Horton to communicate with other Compaq shareholders to inform them of the pending shareholders' suit of *Charles E. Horton, et al. v. Compaq Computer Corporation and Joseph R. Canion* and to ascertain whether any of them would desire to become associated with that suit or bring similar actions against Compaq, and assume a pro rata share of the litigation expenses.

On September 30, 1992, Compaq refused the demand, stating that the purpose described in the letter was not a "proper purpose" under Section 220(b) of the General Corporation Law of the State of Delaware. After this action was filed in the Court of Chancery, the parties presented cross-motions for summary judgment. Compaq conceded that Horton had met all of the technical requirements for making a demand under 8 *Del.C.* § 220, and that the only issue remaining for the trial court to resolve was whether Horton stated a proper purpose for inspecting the various documents.

On November 12, 1992, the Court of Chancery ordered Compaq to permit Horton and Cede to inspect and copy the stockholder lists and related stockholder information requested in their demand letter.   The Vice Chancellor ruled that even though the Texas litigation is neither derivative, nor brought for the benefit of Compaq, it concerns alleged corporate wrongdoing that affected the value of Horton's Compaq stock. *Horton & Cede Co. v. Compaq Computer Corporation,* Del.Ch., C.A. No. 12,741, Berger, V.C. (November 12, 1992) (ORDER).   Accordingly, Horton stated a proper purpose reasonably related to his interest as a Compaq stockholder.

II.

The question of a "proper purpose" under Section 220(b) of our General Corporation Law is an issue of law and equity which this Court reviews *de novo.* *Oberly v. Kirby,* Del.Supr., 592 A.2d 445, 462 (1991); *see, e.g., Western Air Lines, Inc. v. Kerkorian,* Del.Supr., 254 A.2d 240 (1969) (court reviewed proper purpose determination in stocklist case *de novo*).

A.

In Delaware, a shareholder's common law right to inspect the stock ledger is codified in 8 *Del.C.* § 220(b).   It provides in pertinent part:

> Any stockholder ... shall, upon written demand under oath stating the purpose thereof, have the right during the usual hours for business to inspect for any proper purpose the corporation's stock ledger....   A proper purpose shall mean a *purpose reasonably related to such person's interest as a stockholder.*

8 *Del.C.* § 220(b) (emphasis added).   Under Section 220, when a stockholder complies with the statutory requirements as to form and manner of making a demand, then the corporation bears the burden of proving that the demand is for an improper purpose. 8 *Del.C.* § 220(c); *Loew's Theaters, Inc. v. Commercial Credit Co.,* Del.Ch., 243 A.2d 78, 81 (1968).   If there is any doubt, it must be resolved in favor of the statutory right of the stockholder to have an inspection. *State ex rel. Foster v. Standard Oil Co. of Kansas,* Del.Super., 18 A.2d 235, 238 (1941).

B.

Horton contends that this purpose is not only proper, but was earlier approved in *State ex rel. Foster v. Standard Oil Co. of Kansas,* 18 A.2d at 239.   The holding in *Standard Oil* has been interpreted by a number of authoritative treatises for the proposition Horton advances—that shareholders may inspect stocklists for the purpose of communicating with fellow shareholders, not only about pending litigation, but to solicit their interest in joining it.

See 1 WILLIAM M. FLETCHER, FLETCHER CYCLOPEDIA OF THE LAW OF PRIVATE CORPORATIONS § 2225 (PERM.ED.REV.VOL. 1992); ERNEST L. FOLK ET AL., FOLK ON THE DELAWARE GENERAL CORPORATION LAW § 220.7.3 AT 490–91 (2ND ED. 1990); HENN AND ALEXANDER, CORPORATIONS § 199, AT 537 (3D ED. 1986). Most of the cases cited, however, involved derivative suits. Under the circumstances here, we consider that to be a distinction without a difference. *See, e.g., Standard Oil of Kansas,* 18 A.2d at 238; *State ex rel. Bloch v. Sentry Safety Control Corp.,* Del.Supr., 24 A.2d 587 (1942); *Baker v. Macfadden Publications, Inc.,* N.Y.Ct.App., 300 N.Y. 325, 90 N.E.2d 876 (1950). *But see Trans World Airlines, Inc. v. State ex rel. Porterie,* Del.Supr., 183 A.2d 174 (1962) (implying that an individual claimant could have bought shares in his own name and then filed a personal claim for damages).

Essentially, Horton alleges that it is in the interests of Compaq's shareholders to know that acts of mismanagement and fraud are continuing and cannot be overlooked. Thus, it is assumed that the resultant filing of a large number of individual damage claims might well discourage further acts of misconduct by the defendants. In this specific context, the antidotal effect of the Texas litigation may indeed serve a purpose reasonably related to Horton's current interest as a Compaq stockholder.

C.

We recognize that even though a purpose may be reasonably related to one's interest as a stockholder, it cannot be adverse to the interests of the corporation. *CM & M Group, Inc. v. Carroll,* Del.Supr., 453 A.2d 788, 792 (1982); *Skoglund v. Ormand Industries, Inc.,* Del.Ch., 372 A.2d 204, 207 (1976); *State ex rel. Miller v. Loft, Inc.,* Del.Super., 156 A. 170, 172 (1931). In this respect, it becomes clear that a stockholder's right to inspect and copy a stockholder list is not absolute. Rather, it is a qualified right depending on the facts presented. *Loft,* 156 A. at 172.

Horton's ultimate objective, to solicit additional parties to the Texas litigation, may impose substantial expenses upon the company. Compaq argues, therefore, that such a purpose is per se improper as adverse to the interests of the corporation. Significantly, however, Compaq conceded at oral argument that it could cite no authority in support of its proposition that the purpose behind a demand must benefit the defendant corporation.

Horton, as a current stockholder of Compaq, has nothing to gain by harming the legitimate interests of the company. Moreover, as he argues, the prospect of the Texas litigation poses no legitimate threat to Compaq's interests. The Texas litigation is already pending with seventy-nine plaintiffs. The inclusion of more plaintiffs will not substantially increase Compaq's costs of defending the action. The real risk to Compaq is that any additional plaintiffs, who may join the suit, potentially increase the damage award against the company. Yet, insofar as law and policy require corporations and their agents to answer for the breaches of their duties to shareholders, Compaq has no legitimate interest in avoiding the payment of compensatory damages which it, its management or advisors may owe to those who own the enterprise. *See Standard Oil,* 18 A.2d at 239 (noting that "where litigation is brought in apparent good faith against a corporation for the purpose of redressing supposed corporate wrongs, public policy would be on the side of those who have invested their money in the enterprise"). Thus, common sense and public policy dictate that a proper purpose may be stated in these circumstances, notwithstanding the lack of a direct benefit flowing to the corporation.

Equally important is the fact that if damages are assessed against Compaq in the Texas litigation, the company is entitled to seek indemnification from its co-defendant managers and advisors or to pursue its own claims against them. The availability of this diminishes the possibility that Compaq will suffer any harm at all. It is well-settled that the mere prospect of harm to a corporate defendant is insufficient to deny relief under Section 220. *Skouras v. Admiralty Enterprises, Inc.,* Del.Ch., 386 A.2d 674, 682–83 (1978). Any doubt on the issue must be resolved in favor of the statutory right of the stockholder to an inspection. *Standard Oil,* 18 A.2d at 235, 238. This is especially true where the burden is on the corporation to show an improper purpose. 8 *Del.C.* § 220(c); *Loew's Theaters, Inc. v. Commercial Credit Co.,* Del.Ch., 243 A.2d 78, 81 (1968). Accordingly, we are satisfied that the purpose for which Horton seeks to inspect the stock ledger and related materials is not adverse to the legitimate interests of the company.

D.

This conclusion does not suggest that Compaq's burden of showing an improper purpose is impossible to bear. Previous cases provide valuable examples of the degree to which a stated purpose is so indefinite, doubtful, uncertain or vexatious as to warrant denial of the right of inspection. In *State ex rel. Linihan v. United Brokerage Co.,* Del.Super., 101 A. 433, 437 (1917), the trial court held that instituting annoying or harassing litigation against the corporation was an improper purpose. In *Carpenter v. Texas Air Corp.,* Del.Ch., C.A. No. 7976, Hartnett, V.C., slip op. at 9, 1985 WL 11548 (April 18, 1985), the court ruled improper the stockholder's plan to use a stocklist in furtherance of a scheme to bring pressure on a third corporation. In *General Time Corp. v. Talley Indus., Inc.,* Del.Supr., 240 A.2d 755, 756 (1968), it was recognized that obtaining a list for purposes of selling the stockholder's names was also improper. Finally, in *Insuranshares Corp. of Delaware v. Kirchner,* Del.Supr., 5 A.2d 519, 521 (1939), the Court stated that neither conducting a "fishing expedition" nor satisfying idle curiosity were proper purposes to justify inspection. On the whole, a fair reading of these cases leads to the conclusion that where the person making demand is acting in bad faith or for reasons wholly unrelated to his or her role as a stockholder, access to the ledger will be denied. That simply is not the case here.

Horton seeks in good faith to solicit the support of other similarly situated Compaq stockholders, not only to seek monetary redress for their individual economic injuries, but also *to prevent further acts of fraud or mismanagement* from disrupting the fair market value of Compaq's stock.[1] These goals are consistent with at least two different, but analogous purposes that have been previously upheld by our courts, *regardless* of whether the purpose benefitted the corporation or just the claimant alone.

First, in *Weiss v. Anderson, Clayton & Co.,* Del.Ch., C.A. No. 8488, 1986 WL 5970, Allen, C., (May 22, 1986), the Chancellor held that a stockholder's desire to contact other stockholders for the purpose of encouraging them to dissent from a merger and seek their appraisal rights was proper. *Weiss* is analogous to this case insofar as both claimants seek to solicit other stockholders to bring actions against the corporation which may ultimately protect the value of its stock. Second, in *Nodana Petroleum Corp. v. State ex rel. Brennan,* Del.Supr., 123 A.2d 243, 246 (1956), this Court upheld a stockholder's right to inspect the ledger for the purposes of investigating allegedly improper transactions or mismanagement. *Nodana* is similar to this case because Horton also seeks to curb managerial fraud and mismanagement.

III.

We find, therefore, that Compaq's arguments simply fail to meet the burden imposed on it by law to show that Horton acts from an improper purpose. First, Compaq's contention that Horton's demand is not connected to his status as a stockholder is unsubstantiated. Horton's demand is connected to his status as a stockholder because he seeks to bring an end to injuries sustained, past and present, that directly, and adversely, affect his stock ownership. Second, Compaq's complaint that Horton seeks an historical stocklist is inconsequential. Many cases recognize a stockholder's right to investigate past acts of mismanagement. Furthermore, Section 220(b) expressly grants the right to inspect not only a corporation's list of present stockholders, but also the stock ledger. Third, Compaq's accusation that Horton only seeks inspection for his personal gain is immaterial. So long as Horton establishes a single proper purpose *related to his role as a stockholder,* all other purposes are irrelevant. *Mite Corp. v. Heli–Coil Corp.,* Del.Ch., 256 A.2d 855, 856 (1969).

Finally, Compaq's contention that Horton's purpose is contrary to the best interests of the corporation and its current stockholders is both speculative and specious. Any harm that may accrue to the corporation as a result of releasing the list is too remote and uncertain to warrant denial of the stockholder's statutory right to

---

1. This is not champerty because Horton does not seek a bargain with a third party to carry on the litigation in Horton's absence at the third party's own risk and expense in consideration of receiving a part of the proceeds. Nor is it maintenance because Horton is not soliciting others as improper and officious intermeddlers who as non-parties would help maintain the costs of the suit.

inspection. If anything, the corporation and its stockholders, as well as public policy, will best be served by exposure of the fraud, if that is the case, and restoration of the stock to a value set by a properly informed market.

The judgment of the Court of Chancery is AFFIRMED.

––––––––

RALES v. BLASBAND, 634 A.2d 927, 934 n. 10 (Del.1993). "[Potential plaintiffs in derivative actions] have many avenues available to obtain information bearing on the subject of their claims. For example, . . . a stockholder who has met the procedural requirements and has shown a specific proper purpose may use the summary procedure embodied in 8 *Del.C.* § 220 to investigate the possibility of corporate wrongdoing. *Compaq Computer Corp. v. Horton,* Del.Supr., 631 A.2d 1 (1993). Surprisingly, little use has been made of section 220 as an information-gathering tool in the derivative context."

––––––––

NOTE ON THE SHAREHOLDER'S INSPECTION RIGHTS

1. At common law, a shareholder "acting in good faith for the purpose of advancing the interests of the corporation and protecting his own interest as a stockholder" has a right to examine the corporate books and records at reasonable times. Albee v. Lamson & Hubbard Corp., 320 Mass. 421, 424, 69 N.E.2d 811, 813 (1946). The general rule is that the shareholder has the burden of alleging and proving good faith and proper purpose. Id. But see Bennett v. Mack's Supermarkets, Inc., 602 S.W.2d 143 (Ky.1979).

Many or most legislatures have now enacted statutes governing the right of inspection. Many of these statutes are more limited in their coverage than the common law rule. For example, a statute may apply only to certain kinds of shareholders (such as those who are record holders of at least 5% of the corporation's stock or who have been record holders for at least six months) or only to certain kinds of books and records. A common problem of interpretation is whether the statutes (i) preserve the common law rule that the shareholder must prove a proper purpose; (ii) discard the proper purpose test, or (iii) preserve the proper purpose test, but place on the corporation the burden of proving that the shareholder's purpose is improper. Generally, the last interpretation is followed, at least if the language is ambiguous. Crane Co. v. Anaconda Co., 39 N.Y.2d 14, 382 N.Y.S.2d 707, 346 N.E.2d 507 (1976); Carter v. Wilson Const. Co., Inc., 83 N.C.App. 61, 348 S.E.2d 830 (1986); Rosentool v. Bonanza Oil and Mine Corp., 221 Or. 520, 352 P.2d 138 (1960). But see Riser v. Genuine Parts Co., 150 Ga.App. 502, 258 S.E.2d 184 (1979). A second common problem of interpretation, under those statutes that are more limited in their coverage than the common law rule, is whether the statutes replace or supplement that rule. The general answer is that the statutes supplement the common law, so that a suit for inspection that does not fall within the statute can still be brought under the common law. See Tucson Gas & Electric Co. v. Schantz, 5 Ariz.App. 511, 428 P.2d 686 (1967); Bank of Heflin v. Miles, 294 Ala. 462, 318 So.2d 697 (1975); State ex rel. Lowell Wiper Supply Co. v. Helen Shop, Inc., 211 Tenn. 107, 362 S.W.2d 787 (1962). But see Caspary v. Louisiana Land & Exploration Co., 707 F.2d 785 (4th Cir.1983).

2. Among the purposes the courts have recognized as "proper" for purposes of exercising the shareholder's inspection right are: (i) To determine whether the corporation is being properly managed or whether there has been managerial misconduct (at least if the shareholder alleges some specific concerns). Helmsman Management Services, Inc. v. A & S Consultants, Inc., 525 A.2d 160 (Del.Ch.1987); Skouras v. Admiralty Enterprises, Inc., 386 A.2d 674 (Del.Ch.1978); Briskin v. Briskin Manufacturing Co., 6 Ill.App.3d 740, 286 N.E.2d 571 (1972); State ex rel. Watkins v. Cassell, 294 S.W.2d 647 (Mo.App.1956); Hagy v. Premier Mfg. Corp., 404 Pa. 330, 172 A.2d 283 (1961). (ii) To determine the condition of the corporation. Riser v. Genuine Parts Co., 150 Ga.App. 502, 258 S.E.2d 184 (1979). (iii) To ascertain the value of the petitioner's shares. Friedman v. Altoona Pipe and Steel Supply Co., 460 F.2d 1212 (3d Cir.1972); CM & M Group, Inc. v. Carroll, 453 A.2d 788 (Del.1982); E.I.F.C., Inc. v. Atnip, 454 S.W.2d 351 (Ky.1970); Tatko v. Tatko Bros. Slate Co., 173 A.D.2d 917, 569 N.Y.S.2d 783 (1991).

––––––––

NOTE ON PROPER PURPOSE

1. In State ex rel. Pillsbury v. Honeywell, Inc., 291 Minn. 322, 191 N.W.2d 406 (1971), Pillsbury was a shareholder of Honeywell, Inc. Pillsbury opposed the Vietnam war, and asked Honeywell to produce its shareholder ledger and all corporate records dealing with weapons and munitions manufacture. Pillsbury admitted that his sole motive in purchasing Honeywell stock was to persuade Honeywell to cease producing munitions, but argued that the desire to communicate with fellow shareholders was per se a proper purpose. Honeywell argued that a proper purpose contemplates a concern with investment return. Held, for Honeywell:

> Several courts agree with petitioner's contention that a mere desire to communicate with other shareholders is, per se, a proper purpose.... This would seem to confer an almost absolute right to inspection. We believe that a better rule would allow inspections only if the shareholder has a proper purpose for such communication....

> Petitioner had utterly no interest in the affairs of Honeywell before he learned of Honeywell's production of fragmenta-

tion bombs. Immediately after obtaining this knowledge, he purchased stock in Honeywell for the sole purpose of asserting ownership privileges in an effort to force Honeywell to cease such production. . . . Such a motivation can hardly be deemed a proper purpose germane to his economic interest as a shareholder.

Honeywell was a Delaware corporation, and the Minnesota Court apparently assumed for purposes of the case that Delaware law applied, or in any event was no different than Minnesota law insofar as relevant. In Credit Bureau Reports, Inc. v. Credit Bureau of St. Paul, Inc., 290 A.2d 691 (Del.1972), however, the Delaware Supreme Court repudiated the *Pillsbury* case insofar as it applied to requests for stockholder lists:

> [In] General Time Corporation v. Talley Industries, Inc., Del. Supr., 240 A.2d 755 (1968). . . . we stated that, under [Del.Gen. Corp.Law] § 220, "the desire to solicit proxies for a slate of directors in opposition to management is a purpose reasonably related to the stockholder's interest as a stockholder"; and we held that "any further or secondary purpose in seeking the list is irrelevant." Those rulings are dispositive. . . . The defendant corporation . . . relies upon Pillsbury v. Honeywell, Inc., Minn., 191 N.W.2d 406 (1971). Insofar as the *Pillsbury* case is inconsistent herewith, it is inconsistent with [§ 220] as properly applied.

See also The Conservative Caucus Research, Analysis & Education Foundation, Inc. v. Chevron Corp., 525 A.2d 569 (Del.Ch.1987).

2. As a practical matter, the courts are understandably much readier to grant access to stockholder lists and the like than to grant access to otherwise-confidential financial and business information, such as internal data and contracts. In the case of business and financial information, the shareholder will normally have to show the court a specific and plausible reason why the information is needed. In contrast, in the case of stockholder lists a statement by a shareholder that he wants the list to communicate with other shareholders is usually, although not always, a talismanic phrase whose utterance will suffice. (*Honeywell* may be an exception, although in that case the plaintiff requested not only a stockholder list, but all corporate records dealing with weapons and munitions manufacture.) This distinction is understandable. The production of a stockholder list imposes only a minimum burden on the corporation, usually cannot injure the business of the corporation, and is almost invariably necessary for the shareholders to exercise their role in corporate governance. In contrast, other kinds of information may be costly to produce, may have the potential to injure the corporation's business if misused, and (depending on the information) may not be necessary for the normal exercise of the shareholder's role.

In some cases, the statutes themselves distinguish between different types of corporate books and records. See, e.g., Del.Gen. Corp.Law § 220; see also Model Act §§ 7.20(b), 16.02.

3.   Suppose the shareholder has mixed purposes, one proper and one not.   In Helmsman Management Services, Inc. v. A & S Consultants, Inc., 525 A.2d 160, 164, 166 (Del.Ch.1987), the court held that "Once it is determined that a shareholder has a proper purpose that is primary, any secondary purpose or ulterior motive that the stockholder might have is irrelevant."   Accordingly, "even if [the shareholder] does have an ulterior (*i.e.,* a non-shareholder-related) purpose, it would still not be barred from relief under [Del.Gen.Corp.Law] § 220, unless the ulterior purpose is also its primary purpose."

4.   Suppose the corporation claims that although the shareholder appears to have a proper purpose for obtaining the information he requests, in fact he intends to misuse confidential information by disclosing it.   In Tatko v. Tatko Bros. Slate Co., 173 A.D.2d 917, 569 N.Y.S.2d 783, 785 (1991) the court dealt with such a claim by prohibiting the shareholder from making such disclosure, rather than refusing to give the shareholder access to the information.

––––––

(b) REPORTING UNDER STATE LAW

––––––

REV. MODEL BUS. CORP. ACT §§ 16.20, 16.21

[See Statutory Supplement]

––––––

CAL. CORP. CODE § 1501

[See Statutory Supplement]

––––––

N.Y. BUS. CORP. LAW § 624

[See Statutory Supplement]

––––––

SECTION 2.   SHAREHOLDER INFORMATIONAL RIGHTS UNDER FEDERAL LAW AND STOCK EXCHANGE RULES

––––––

INTRODUCTORY NOTE

Given the limitations of the shareholder's inspection right, not the least of which is the cost of going to court, it was probably inevitable that corrective action would be taken to ensure that shareholders are provided with adequate information at the corporation's expense. Two major bodies of rules evolved to alleviate the deficiencies in the inspection right—(i) the Securities Exchange Act of 1934 and the Rules promulgated by the SEC thereunder, and (ii) the rules for listed companies issued by various stock exchanges, particularly the New York Stock Exchange. To put these rules in context, this Section will begin with overviews of the Securities Exchange Act and the stock markets.

(a) AN OVERVIEW OF THE SEC AND THE SECURITIES EXCHANGE ACT

SECURITIES AND EXCHANGE COMMISSION, THE WORK OF THE SEC

3–4, 9–13 (1986).

The U.S. Securities and Exchange Commission's mission is to administer Federal securities laws that seek to provide protection for investors. The purpose of these laws is to ensure that the securities markets are fair and honest and to provide the means to enforce the securities laws through sanctions where necessary. Laws administered by the Commission are the:

- Securities Act of 1933;

- Securities Exchange Act of 1934;

- Public Utility Holding Company Act of 1935;

- Trust Indenture Act of 1939;

- Investment Company Act of 1940; and

- Investment Advisers Act of 1940....

The Commission is composed of five members: a Chairman and four Commissioners. Commission members are appointed by the President, with the advice and consent of the Senate, for five-year terms. The Chairman is designated by the President. Terms are staggered; one expires on June 5th of every year. Not more than three members may be of the same political party.

Under the direction of the Chairman and Commissioners, the staff ensures that publicly held entities, broker-dealers in securities, investment companies and advisers, and other participants in the securities markets comply with Federal securities laws. These laws were designed to facilitate informed investment analyses and decisions by the investing public, primarily by ensuring adequate disclosure of material (significant) information. Conformance with Federal securities laws and regulations does not imply merit. If information essential to informed investment analysis is properly disclosed, the Commission cannot bar the sale of securities which analysis may show to be of questionable value. It is the investor, not the Commission, who must make the ultimate judgment of the worth of securities offered for sale.

The Commission's staff is composed of lawyers, accountants, financial analysts and examiners, engineers, and other professionals. The staff is divided into divisions and offices (including fourteen regional and branch offices), each directed by officials appointed by the Chairman. . . .

SECURITIES EXCHANGE ACT OF 1934

By this act, Congress extended the "disclosure" doctrine of investor protection to securities listed and registered for public trading on our national securities exchanges. Thirty years later, the Securities Act Amendments of 1964 extended disclosure and reporting provisions to equity securities in the over-the-counter market. This included hundreds of companies with . . . shareholders numbering 500 or more. (Today, securities of thousands of companies are traded over the counter.) The act seeks to ensure fair and orderly securities markets by prohibiting certain types of activities and by setting forth rules regarding the operation of the markets and participants. . . .

———

SECURITIES EXCHANGE ACT § 12(a), (b), (g)

[See Statutory Supplement]

———

SECURITIES EXCHANGE ACT RULE 12g–1

[See Statutory Supplement]

———

(b) AN OVERVIEW OF THE STOCK MARKETS

S. ROSS, R. WESTERFIELD & B. JORDAN, FUNDAMENTALS OF CORPORATE FINANCE 14–17

3d ed. 1995.

A financial market, like any market, is just a way of bringing buyers and sellers together. In financial markets, it is debt and equity securities that are bought and sold. Financial markets differ in detail, however. The most important differences concern the types of securities that are traded, how trading is conducted, and who the buyers and sellers are. . . .

[Money versus Capital Markets

Financial markets can be classified as either **money markets** or **capital markets.** Short-term debt securities of many varieties are bought and sold in money markets. These short-term debt securities are often called money market "instruments" and are essentially IOUs. For example, *commercial paper* represents short-term borrowing by large corporations and is a money market instrument. Capital markets are the markets for long-term debt and shares of stock, so the New York Stock Exchange, for example, is a capital market.

The money market is a *dealer market.* Generally speaking, dealers buy and sell something for themselves, at their own risk. A car dealer, for example, buys and sells automobiles. In contrast, brokers and agents match buyers and sellers, but they do not actually own the commodity. A real estate agent or broker, for example, does not normally buy and sell houses] . . .

Primary versus Secondary Markets

Financial markets function as both primary and secondary markets for debt and equity securities. The term *primary market* refers to the original sale of securities by governments and corporations. The *secondary markets* are where these securities are bought and sold after the original sale. . . .

Primary Markets. In a primary market transaction, the corporation is the seller, and the transaction raises money for the corporation. . . .

Secondary Markets. A secondary market transaction involves one owner or creditor selling to another. It is therefore the secondary markets that provide the means for transferring ownership of corporate securities.

Dealer Versus Auction Markets. There are two kinds of secondary markets: *auction* markets and *dealer* markets. . . .

Dealer markets in stocks and long-term debt are called *over-the-counter* (OTC) markets. Most trading in debt securities takes place over the counter. The expression *over the counter* refers to days of old when securities were literally bought and sold at counters in offices around the country. Today, a significant fraction of the market for stocks and almost all of the market for long-term debt have no central location; the many dealers are connected electronically.

Auction markets differ from dealer markets in two ways. First, an auction market or exchange, unlike a dealer market, has a physical location (like Wall Street). Second, in a dealer market most of the buying and selling is done by the dealer. The primary purpose of an auction market, on the other hand, is to match those who wish to sell with those who wish to buy. Dealers play a limited role.

... The equity shares of most ... large firms in the United States trade in organized auction markets. The largest such market is the New York Stock Exchange (NYSE ...), which accounts for more than 85 percent of all the shares traded in auction markets. Other auction exchanges include the American Stock Exchange (AMEX) and regional exchanges such as the Midwest Stock Exchange.

... [I]n addition to the stock exchanges, there is a large OTC market for stocks. In 1971, the National Association of Securities Dealers (NASD) made available to dealers and brokers an electronic quotation system called NASDAQ (NASD Automated Quotation system, pronounced "naz-dak"). There are roughly three times as many companies on NASDAQ as there are on NYSE, but they tend to be much smaller in size and trade less actively. There are exceptions, of course. Both Microsoft and Intel trade OTC, for example.*
...

Listing. Stocks that trade on an organized exchange are said to be *listed* on that exchange. In order to be listed, firms must meet certain minimum criteria concerning, for example, asset size and number of shareholders. These criteria differ for different exchanges.

NYSE has the most stringent requirements of the exchanges in the United States. For example, to be listed on NYSE, a company is expected to have a market value for its publicly held shares of at least $18 million and a total of at least 2,000 shareholders with at least 100 shares each. There are additional minimums on earnings, assets, and number of shares outstanding.

----

* By 1992, NASDAQ accounted for 42% of trading in share volume, and 29 percent of trading by dollar volume, in the U.S. equity market. See SEC, Market 2000—An Examination of Current Equity Market Developments (1992). (Footnote by ed.)

(c) PERIODIC DISCLOSURE UNDER THE SECURITIES EXCHANGE ACT

SECURITIES EXCHANGE ACT § 13(a)

[See Statutory Supplement]

SECURITIES EXCHANGE ACT RULES 13a–1, 13a–11, 13a–13
SECURITIES EXCHANGE ACT FORMS 8–K, 10–K, 10–Q

[See Statutory Supplement]

NOTE ON REPORTING BY REGISTERED CORPORATIONS

1. The Securities Exchange Act addresses the informational deficiencies in state law by imposing reporting requirements on corporations registered under section 12. Under section 13 of the Act, and the rules promulgated thereunder, such corporations must file a Form 10–K annually, a Form 10–Q quarterly, and a Form 8–K within 15 days after the occurrence of certain specified events. Form 10–K must include audited financial statements; management's discussion of the corporation's financial condition and results of operations; and disclosure concerning legal proceedings, developments in the corporation's business, executive compensation, conflict-of-interest transactions, and other specified issues. Form 10–Q must include quarterly financial data prepared in accordance with generally accepted accounting principles; a management report; and disclosure concerning legal proceedings, defaults on senior securities, and other specified issues. Among the matters that trigger an 8–K Report are a change in control of the corporation, the acquisition or disposition of a significant amount of assets, and a change of accountants.

A limitation on the usefulness of the reporting requirements under the Securities Exchange Act is that the required reporting is not both comprehensive and timely. The 8–K, which is the most timely form, need be filed in only very limited cases and may be filed as late as 15 days after the event. The 10–Q is also limited in its coverage, and much less timely. The 10–K is more comprehensive, but not timely at all. See Brown, Corporate Communications and the Federal Securities Laws, 53 Geo.Wash.L.Rev. 741 (1985).

The disclosure required by the Securities Exchange Act's reporting requirements is sometimes called "structured" disclosure, because what must be disclosed and how it must be disclosed is structured by the relevant SEC rules. Another example of structured disclosure is the disclosure required under the Securities Act when a corporation makes a public offering of securities.

2.   Generally speaking, neither the Exchange Act nor the Securities Act require timely disclosure of material corporate developments, as such. Instead, disclosure is required only (1) periodically, to the extent required by the Security Exchange Act's reporting requirements, and (2) when some triggering event occurs. The most significant of these triggering events is a public offering as defined by the Securities Act, but disclosure may also be required whenever the corporation or an insider purchases or sells stock, whether or not in a public offering. See Chapter 9. In addition, a corporation that has made a prior disclosure or has allowed information to leak out may be under a duty to correct or update the disclosure. See Note on the Obligations of a Nontrading Corporation Under Rule 10b–5, Chapter 9, Section 2, infra. It has been said, "A principal shortcoming [of Securities Exchange Act disclosure] is the fact that the information required to be filed is always substantially behind the event and, hence, fails to fulfill the function of informing investors in a market which tends to be hypersensitive rather than reflective. Disclosure under the 1934 Act also suffers from the fact that the express civil liability provisions of that Act in contrast to those under the 1933 Act are largely ineffective." 3B H. Bloomenthal, Securities and Federal Corporate Law § 9.11 at 9–97 (1993).

Of course, a corporation may make voluntary timely disclosure of material corporate developments, even if not required to do so by law. Furthermore, the rules of the major stock exchanges and of NASDAQ often require listed corporations to make timely disclosure of material developments.

———

(d) DISCLOSURE UNDER STOCK EXCHANGE RULES

———

NEW YORK STOCK EXCHANGE, LISTED COMPANY MANUAL §§ 202.01, 202.03, 202.05, 202.06[1]

[See Statutory Supplement]

———

1.   For similar rules, see American Stock Exchange, AMEX Company Guide, §§ 401–405 (Disclosure Policies), 2 CCH, American Stock Exchange Guide ¶ 10,121–10,125; Nat'l Ass'n Sec. Dealers Manual (CCH) § 5, Schedule D, Part II, ¶ 1806A, at 1571–72.

SECTION 3. THE PROXY RULES
(I): AN INTRODUCTION

NOTE ON TERMINOLOGY

This and the next two Sections concern the Proxy Rules, which are promulgated by the SEC.   The following terms are important in considering these Rules:

Proxy holder.   A person authorized to vote shares on a shareholder's behalf.

Proxy, or *form of proxy.*   The instrument in which such an authorization is embodied.   (The term "proxy" is also sometimes used to mean a proxy holder, but for purposes of clarity that usage will be avoided in the Notes in this Chapter.)

Proxy solicitation.   The process by which shareholders are asked to give their proxies.

Proxy statement.   The written statement sent to shareholders as a means of proxy solicitation.

Proxy materials.   The proxy statement and form of proxy.

SECURITIES EXCHANGE ACT § 14(a), (c)

SECURITIES EXCHANGE ACT RULES 14a–1—14a–6, 14c–2, 14c–3, SCHEDULE 14A, SCHEDULE 14C

[See Statutory Supplement]

NOTE—AN OVERVIEW OF THE PROXY RULES

1. *Background.*   Proxy voting is the dominant mode of shareholder decisionmaking in publicly held corporations.   There are a number of reasons for this.   Shareholders in such corporations are often geographically dispersed, so that a given shareholder may not live near the site of the meeting.   Shareholders often have some principal business other than investing, so that a given shareholding may not represent a substantial proportion of a shareholder's total wealth.   And whether a shareholder supports or opposes the matters scheduled for action at a meeting, he may not wish to speak on the issues.   Physical attendance at a shareholders's meeting is normally an uneconomical use of a shareholder's time when he can vote by proxy.

A natural outgrowth of the preference for proxy voting is proxy solicitation—the process of systematically contacting shareholders and urging them to execute and return proxy forms that authorize named proxyholders to cast the shareholder's votes, either in a manner designated in the proxy form or according to the proxy-holder's discretion.

Despite these developments, as of the 1930's state law hardly regulated proxy voting, except in the extreme case in which proxies had been fraudulently solicited. Abuses were notorious and wide-spread. Accordingly, Congress entered the field in 1934 through Section 14(a) of the Securities Exchange Act. In itself, Section 14(a) has no effect on private conduct: its only effect is to authorize the SEC to promulgate rules that will govern private conduct. Pursuant to Section 14(a), the SEC has promulgated a set of Proxy Rules that serve a variety of purposes.

2. *Coverage.* Rule 14a–2 provides that the Proxy Rules "apply to every solicitation of a proxy with respect to securities registered pursuant to section 12 of the Act," with certain exceptions, such as "[a]ny solicitation made otherwise than on behalf of the registrant where the total number of persons solicited is not more than ten." The definitions of "proxy" and "solicitation" are extremely broad. Under Rule 14a–1(f), the term "proxy" means "every proxy, consent, or authorization within the meaning of section 14a of the Act. The consent or authorization may take the form of failure to object or to dissent." Under Rule 14a–1(l)(1), the term "solicitation" includes "(i) [a]ny request for a proxy ...; (ii) [a]ny request to execute or not to execute, or to revoke, a proxy; or (iii) [t]he furnishing of a form of proxy or other communication to security holders under circumstances reasonably calculated to result in the procurement, withholding or revocation of a proxy." This language has been given a very expansive interpretation. For example, in Studebaker Corp. v. Gittlin, 360 F.2d 692 (2d Cir.1966), Gittlin, a shareholder in Studebaker, had solicited authorizations from other Studebaker shareholders to inspect Studebaker's shareholders list, for the purpose of meeting the five percent test under the relevant New York inspection statute. Judge Friendly said:

> ... The assistant general counsel of the SEC ... stated at the argument that the Commission believes § 14(a) should be construed, in all its literal breadth, to include authorizations to inspect stockholders lists, even in cases where obtaining the authorizations was not a step in a planned solicitation of proxies.

> We need not go that far to uphold the order of the district court. In SEC v. Okin, 132 F.2d 784 (2d Cir.1943), this court ruled that a letter which did not request the giving of any authorization was subject to the Proxy Rules if it was part of "a continuous plan" intended to end in solicitation and to prepare the way for success. This was

the avowed purpose of Gittlin's demand for inspection of the stockholders list. . . .

Id. at 695–96.

3. *Transactional disclosure.*   One purpose of the Proxy Rules is to require full disclosure in connection with transactions that shareholders are being asked to approve, such as mergers, certificate amendments, or election of directors.   This purpose is accomplished in the first instance by Rule 14a–3 and Schedule 14A.   Rule 14a–3 provides that no solicitation of proxies that is subject to the Proxy Rules shall be made unless the person being solicited "is concurrently furnished or has previously been furnished with a written proxy statement containing the information specified in Schedule 14A."   Schedule 14A, in turn, lists in detail the information that must be furnished when specified types of transactions are to be acted upon by the shareholders.   Rule 14a–3 and Schedule 14A are backed up by Rule 14a–9, which provides that no solicitation subject to the Proxy Rules shall contain any statement that is false or misleading with respect to any material fact or omits a material fact.

4. *Periodic disclosure.*   The Proxy Rules also require certain forms of annual disclosure.   Much of this disclosure is only very loosely related to any specific action the shareholders are asked to vote upon.   For example, Rule 14a–3 provides that the proxy statement for an annual meeting at which directors are to be elected must be accompanied by an annual report that includes audited balance sheets for each of the corporation's two most recent fiscal years, audited income statements for its three most recent fiscal years, and certain other information.   Under Items 7 and 8 of Schedule 14A, the proxy statement for an annual meeting at which directors are being elected must disclose the compensation of the five most highly paid executives and the executive officers as a group (including not only salary, but bonuses, deferred compensation, stock options, and the like), and significant conflict-of-interest transactions during the corporation's last fiscal year involving, among others, directors, executive officers, and five percent beneficial owners.   Under Item 7, the proxy statement for such a meeting must also disclose whether the corporation has audit, nominating, and compensation committees, and if so, the number of meetings each committee held during the last fiscal year and the functions it performs.   And under Section 14(c), Regulation 14C, and Schedule 14C, a corporation that is registered under Section 12 must distribute, in connection with an annual meeting at which directors are to be elected, an annual report and certain other information (such as information relating to conflict-of-interest transactions and compensation), even if the corporation is *not* soliciting proxies.

5. *Proxy contests.*   Proxy Rule 14a–11 regulates proxy contests, in which insurgents try to oust incumbent directors.   Basically, Rule 14a–11 is an adaptation of the salient concepts of other

Proxy Rules to the special circumstances of a proxy fight. Its main bite is to require the filing of certain information by insurgents.

6. *Access to the body of shareholders.* Two Proxy Rules, 14a–7 and 14a–8, provide mechanisms through which the stockholders can communicate with each other. See Section 5, infra.

7. *Mechanics of proxy voting.* Still another purpose of the Proxy Rules is to regulate the mechanics of proxy voting itself. This is done, somewhat indirectly, through Rule 14a–4, which governs the form of proxy.

FORM OF PROXY

[See Statutory Supplement]

NOTE ON THE 1992 REVISIONS OF THE PROXY RULES

In 1992, the SEC radically revised the Proxy Rules, principally to make it easier for shareholders—especially institutional shareholders—to communicate with each other. A great number of revisions were made; the most significant are summarized as follows by Professor John C. Coffee:

1. The Release [adopting the 1992 revisions] created a new safe harbor rule (Rule 14a–2(b)(1)) to exclude from the definition of "solicitation" communications between shareholders that did not solicit proxy voting authority and that were sent by persons who had no material economic interest in the solicitation (other than their interest as shareholders). This safe harbor was intended and expected to encourage and permit broad communication among shareholder activists and institutional investors, which communications would formerly have fallen within the definition of solicitation in Rule 14a–1(*l*)(iii).

2. The Release amended Rules 14a–11(d) and 14a–12, to permit a person to contest an election of directors or to oppose a nonelection matter prior to the delivery of a definitive proxy statement. To use this procedure, a preliminary proxy statement must be filed with the SEC, no form of proxy may be provided by the person relying on the exemption, and such person has to provide a definitive proxy statement to those persons actually solicited as soon as practicable.

3. The Release adopted new Rule 14a–3(f), which permits a party who has filed a definitive proxy statement with the SEC to broadcast or publish its communications in advertisements, speeches, or columns, without preceding such communications with copies of the definitive proxy statement. . . .

5.   The Release also eliminated the prior requirement of a preliminary filing of soliciting materials (except for the preliminary filing of the proxy and the proxy statement).   This effectively eliminated any SEC prior restraint over newspaper ads and similar soliciting materials (although, of course, the antifraud rules continued to apply to all such materials).

Coffee, The SEC and the Institutional Investor: A Half–Time Report, 15 Cardozo L.Rev. 837, 840–41 n. 17 (1994).

The most important of the 1992 revisions were those that freed shareholders—particularly institutional investors—to communicate with each other about proxy voting without the risk that those communications would be deemed a solicitation under the sweeping definition of that term in the Proxy Rules. See Securities Exchange Act Release No. 34–31326 (1992).

SECTION 4.   THE PROXY RULES (II): PRIVATE ACTIONS UNDER THE PROXY RULES

SECURITIES EXCHANGE ACT RULE 14a–9

[See Statutory Supplement]

NOTE ON J.I. CASE CO. v. BORAK

In J.I. Case Co. v. Borak, 377 U.S. 426, 84 S.Ct. 1555, 12 L.Ed.2d 423 (1964), the Supreme Court held that a shareholder could bring either a direct or a derivative action for violation of the Proxy Rules, although neither the 1934 Act nor the Proxy Rules themselves explicitly provide for such an action.

The injury which a stockholder suffers from corporate action pursuant to a deceptive proxy solicitation ordinarily flows from the damage done the corporation, rather than from the damage inflicted directly upon the stockholder. The damage suffered results not from the deceit practiced on him alone but rather from the deceit practiced on the stockholders as a group. To hold that derivative actions are not within the sweep of the section would therefore be tantamount to a denial of private relief. Private enforcement of the proxy rules provides a necessary supplement to Commission action. As in antitrust treble damage litigation, the possibility of civil damages or injunctive relief serves as a most effective weapon in the enforcement of the proxy requirements. The Commission advises that it examines over 2,000 proxy statements annually and each of them must necessarily be expedited. Time does not permit an independent examination of the facts set out in the proxy material and this results in the Commission's acceptance of the representations contained therein at their face value, unless contrary to other material on file with it. Indeed, on the allegations of respondent's complaint, the proxy material failed to disclose alleged unlawful market manipulation of the stock of ATC, and this unlawful manipulation would not have been apparent to the Commission until after the merger.

We, therefore, believe that under the circumstances here it is the duty of the courts to be alert to provide such remedies as are necessary to make effective the congressional purpose.

Id. at 432–33, 84 S.Ct. at 1560.

————

NOTE ON MILLS v. ELECTRIC AUTO–LITE CO.

In Mills v. Electric Auto–Lite Co., 396 U.S. 375, 90 S.Ct. 616, 24 L.Ed.2d 593 (1970), the Supreme Court held that:

Where the misstatement or omission in a proxy statement has been shown to be "material," as it was found to be here, that determination itself indubitably embodies a conclusion that the defect was of such a character that it might have been considered important by a reasonable shareholder who was in the process of deciding how to vote. This requirement that the defect have a significant *propensity* to affect the voting process is found in the express terms of Rule 14a–9, and it adequately serves the purpose of ensuring that a cause of action cannot be established by proof of a defect so trivial, or so unrelated to the transaction for which approval is sought, that correction of the defect or imposition of liability would not further the interests protected by § 14(a).

There is no need to supplement this requirement, as did the Court of Appeals, with a requirement of proof of whether the defect actually had a decisive effect on the voting. Where there has been a finding of materiality, a shareholder has made a sufficient showing of causal relationship between the violation and the injury for which he seeks redress if, as here, he proves that the proxy solicitation itself, rather than the particular defect in the solicitation materials, was an essential link in the accomplishment of the transaction. This objective test will avoid the impracticalities of determining how many votes were affected, and, by resolving doubts in favor of those the statute is designed to protect, will effectuate the congressional policy of ensuring that the shareholders are able to make an informed choice when they are consulted on corporate transactions.

Mills v. Electric Auto–Lite Co. leaves no doubt that a materially false or misleading proxy statement must be deemed to be the cause of a shareholder vote the proxy statement solicits. Accordingly, where a shareholder seeks to set aside or enjoin a transaction approved by the shareholders on the ground that the approval was solicited by a proxy statement that involved misstatements or omissions, he need do nothing more to prove causation than to prove materiality. See Gaines v. Haughton, 645 F.2d 761, 773–74 (9th Cir.1981), cert. denied 454 U.S. 1145, 102 S.Ct. 1006, 71 L.Ed.2d 297 (1982); Weisberg v. Coastal States Gas Corp., 609 F.2d 650, 653 (2d Cir.1979), cert. denied 445 U.S. 951, 100 S.Ct. 1600, 63 L.Ed.2d 786 (1980).

NOTE ON TSC INDUSTRIES v. NORTHWAY, INC.

In TSC Industries, Inc. v. Northway, Inc., 426 U.S. 438, 96 S.Ct. 2126, 48 L.Ed.2d 757 (1976), the Supreme Court addressed the issue of how materiality was to be defined, as follows:

> . . . [I]n *Mills,* we attempted to clarify to some extent the elements of a private cause of action for violation of § 14(a). In a suit challenging the sufficiency under § 14(a) and Rule 14a–9 of a proxy statement soliciting votes in favor of a merger, we held that there was no need to demonstrate that the alleged defect in the proxy statement actually had a decisive effect on the voting. So long as the misstatement or omission was material, the causal relation between violation and injury is sufficiently established, we concluded, if "the proxy solicitation itself . . . was an essential link in the accomplishment of the transaction." 396 U.S., at 385, 90 S.Ct., at 622. After *Mills,* then, the content given to the notion of materiality assumes heightened significance.[7] . . .

> The question of materiality, it is universally agreed, is an objective one, involving the significance of an omitted or misrepresented fact to a reasonable investor. Variations in the formulation of a general test of materiality occur in the articulation of just how significant a fact must be or, put another way, how certain it must be that the fact would affect a reasonable investor's judgment.

> The Court of Appeals in this case concluded that material facts include "all facts which a reasonable shareholder *might* consider important." 512 F.2d, at 330 (emphasis added). This

7. Our cases have not considered, and we have no occasion in this case to consider, what showing of culpability is required to establish the liability under § 14(a) of a corporation issuing a materially misleading proxy statement, or of a person involved in the preparation of a materially misleading proxy statement. See Gerstle v. Gamble-Skogmo, Inc., 478 F.2d 1281, 1298, 1301 (C.A.2 1973); Richland v. Crandall, 262 F.Supp. 538, 553 n. 12 (S.D.N.Y.1967); Jennings & Marsh, Securities Regulation: Cases and Materials 1358–1359 (3d ed. 1972). See also Ernst & Ernst v. Hochfelder, 425 U.S. 185, 207–209, 96 S.Ct. 1375, 1388, 47 L.Ed.2d 668 (1976).

formulation of the test of materiality has been explicitly rejected by at least two courts as setting too low a threshold for the imposition of liability under Rule 14a–9. Gerstle v. Gamble–Skogmo, Inc., 478 F.2d 1281, 1301–1302 (C.A.2 1973); Smallwood v. Pearl Brewing Co., 489 F.2d 579, 603–604 (C.A.5 1974). In these cases, panels of the Second and Fifth Circuits opted for the conventional tort test of materiality—whether a reasonable man *would* attach importance to the fact misrepresented or omitted in determining his course of action. See Restatement (Second) of Torts § 538(2)(a) (Tent.Draft No. 10, 1964). See also ALI Federal Securities Code § 256(a) (Tent. Draft No. 2, 1973). Gerstle v. Gamble–Skogmo, supra, at 1302, also approved the following standard, which had been formulated with reference to statements issued in a contested election: "whether, taking a properly realistic view, there is a substantial likelihood that the misstatement or omission may have led a stockholder to grant a proxy to the solicitor or to withhold one from the other side, whereas in the absence of this he would have taken a contrary course." General Time Corp. v. Talley Industries, Inc., 403 F.2d 159, 162 (C.A.2 1968), cert. denied, 393 U.S. 1026, 89 S.Ct. 631, 21 L.Ed.2d 570 (1969)....

In formulating a standard of materiality under Rule 14a–9, we are guided, of course, by the recognition in *Borak* and *Mills* of the Rule's broad remedial purpose. That purpose is not merely to ensure by judicial means that the transaction, when judged by its real terms, is fair and otherwise adequate, but to ensure disclosures by corporate management in order to enable the shareholders to make an informed choice. See *Mills,* supra, at 381, 90 S.Ct., at 620. As an abstract proposition, the most desirable role for a court in a suit of this sort, coming after the consummation of the proposed transaction, would perhaps be to determine whether in fact the proposal would have been favored by the shareholders and consummated in the absence of any misstatement or omission. But as we recognized in *Mills,* supra, at 382 n. 5, 90 S.Ct., at 620, such matters are not subject to determination with certainty. Doubts as to the critical nature of information misstated or omitted will be commonplace. And particularly in view of the prophylactic purpose of the Rule and the fact that the content of the proxy statement is within management's control, it is appropriate that these doubts be resolved in favor of those the statute is designed to protect. *Mills,* supra, at 385, 90 S.Ct., at 622.

We are aware, however, that the disclosure policy embodied in the proxy regulations is not without limit. See id., at 384, 90 S.Ct., at 621. Some information is of such dubious significance that insistence on its disclosure may accomplish more harm than good. The potential liability for a Rule 14a–9 violation can be great indeed, and if the standard of materiality is unnecessarily low, not only may the corporation and its management be subjected to liability for insignificant omissions or misstatements, but also management's fear of exposing itself to substantial liability may cause it simply to bury the shareholder in an avalanche of trivial information—a result that is hardly conducive to informed decisionmaking. Precisely these dangers are presented, we think, by the definition of a material fact adopted by the Court of Appeals in this case—a fact which a reasonable shareholder *might* consider important. We agree with Judge Friendly, speaking for the Court of Appeals in *Gerstle,* that the "might" formulation is "too suggestive of mere possibility, however unlikely." 478 F.2d, at 1302.

The general standard of materiality that we think best comports with the policies of Rule 14a–9 is as follows: an omitted fact is material if there is a substantial likelihood that a reasonable shareholder would consider it important in deciding how to vote. This standard is fully consistent with *Mills* general description of materiality as a requirement that "the defect have a significant *propensity* to affect the voting process." It does not require proof of a substantial likelihood that disclosure of the omitted fact would have caused the reasonable investor to change his vote. What the standard does contemplate is a showing of a substantial likelihood that, under all the circumstances, the omitted fact would have assumed actual significance in the deliberations of the reasonable shareholder. Put another way, there must be a substantial likelihood that the disclosure of the omitted fact would have been viewed by the reasonable investor as having significantly altered the "total mix" of information made available.

VIRGINIA BANKSHARES, INC. v. SANDBERG

Supreme Court of the United States, 1991.
501 U.S. 1083, 111 S.Ct. 2749, 115 L.Ed.2d 929.

SOUTER, J., delivered the opinion of the Court, in Part I of which REHNQUIST, C.J., and WHITE, MARSHALL, BLACKMUN, O'CONNOR, SCALIA, and KENNEDY, JJ., joined, in Part II of which REHNQUIST, C.J., and WHITE, MARSHALL, BLACKMUN, O'CONNOR, and KENNEDY, JJ., joined, and in Parts III and IV of which REHNQUIST, C.J., and WHITE, O'CONNOR, and SCALIA, JJ., joined. SCALIA, J., filed an opinion concurring in part and concurring in the judgment. STEVENS, J., filed an opinion concurring in part and dissenting in part, in which MARSHALL, J., joined. KENNEDY, J., filed an opinion concurring in part and dissenting in part, in which MARSHALL, BLACKMUN, and STEVENS, JJ., joined.

Justice SOUTER delivered the opinion of the Court.

Section 14(a) of the Securities Exchange Act of 1934, 48 Stat. 895, 15 U.S.C. § 78n(a), authorizes the Securities and Exchange

Commission to adopt rules for the solicitation of proxies, and prohibits their violation.   In J.I. Case Co. v. Borak, 377 U.S. 426, 84 S.Ct. 1555, 12 L.Ed.2d 423 (1964), we first recognized an implied private right of action for the breach of § 14(a) as implemented by SEC Rule 14a–9, which prohibits the solicitation of proxies by means of materially false or misleading statements.[2]

The questions before us are whether a statement couched in conclusory or qualitative terms purporting to explain directors' reasons for recommending certain corporate action can be materially misleading within the meaning of Rule 14a–9, and whether causation of damages compensable under § 14(a) can be shown by a member of a class of minority shareholders whose votes are not required by law or corporate bylaw to authorize the corporate action subject to the proxy solicitation.   We hold that knowingly false statements of reasons may be actionable even though conclusory in form, but that respondents have failed to demonstrate the equitable basis required to extend the § 14(a) private action to such shareholders when any indication of congressional intent to do so is lacking.

I

In December 1986, First American Bankshares, Inc., (FABI), a bank holding company, began a "freeze-out" merger, in which the First American Bank of Virginia (Bank) eventually merged into Virginia Bankshares, Inc., (VBI), a wholly owned subsidiary of FABI. VBI owned 85% of the Bank's shares, the remaining 15% being in the hands of some 2,000 minority shareholders.   FABI hired the investment banking firm of Keefe, Bruyette & Woods (KBW) to give an opinion on the appropriate price for shares of the minority holders, who would lose their interests in the Bank as a result of the merger.   Based on market quotations and unverified information from FABI, KBW gave the Bank's executive committee an opinion that $42 a share would be a fair price for the minority stock.   The executive committee approved the merger proposal at that price, and the full board followed suit.

Although Virginia law required only that such a merger proposal be submitted to a vote at a shareholders' meeting, and that the meeting be preceded by circulation of a statement of information to the shareholders, the directors nevertheless solicited proxies for voting on the proposal at the annual meeting set for April 21, 1987.[3] In their solicitation, the directors urged the proposal's adoption and stated they had approved the plan because of its opportunity for the

2. . . .

The Federal Deposit Insurance Corporation (FDIC) administers and enforces the securities laws with respect to the activities of federally insured and regulated banks. See Section 12(i) of the Exchange Act, 15 U.S.C. § 78*l*(i). An FDIC rule also prohibits materially misleading statements in the solicitation of proxies, 12 CFR § 335.206 (1991), and is essentially identical to Rule 14a–9. See generally Brief for SEC et al. as Amici Curiae 4, n. 5.

3. Had the directors chosen to issue a statement instead of a proxy solicitation, they would have been subject to an SEC antifraud provision analogous to Rule 14a–9. See 17 CFR 240.14c–6 (1990). See also 15 U.S.C. § 78n(c).

minority shareholders to achieve a "high" value, which they else-where described as a "fair" price, for their stock.

Although most minority shareholders gave the proxies request-ed, respondent Sandberg did not, and after approval of the merger she sought damages in the United States District Court for the Eastern District of Virginia from VBI, FABI, and the directors of the Bank. She pleaded two counts, one for soliciting proxies in viola-tion of § 14(a) and Rule 14a–9, and the other for breaching fiduciary duties owed to the minority shareholders under state law. Under the first count, Sandberg alleged, among other things, that the directors had not believed that the price offered was high or that the terms of the merger were fair, but had recommended the merger only because they believed they had no alternative if they wished to remain on the board. At trial, Sandberg invoked lan-guage from this Court's opinion in Mills v. Electric Auto–Lite Co., 396 U.S. 375, 385, 90 S.Ct. 616, 622, 24 L.Ed.2d 593 (1970), to obtain an instruction that the jury could find for her without a showing of her own reliance on the alleged misstatements, so long as they were material and the proxy solicitation was an "essential link" in the merger process.

The jury's verdicts were for Sandberg on both counts, after finding violations of Rule 14a–9 by all defendants and a breach of fiduciary duties by the Bank's directors. The jury awarded Sand-berg $18 a share, having found that she would have received $60 if her stock had been valued adequately.

While Sandberg's case was pending, a separate action on similar allegations was brought against petitioners in the United States District Court for the District of Columbia by several other minority shareholders including respondent Weinstein, who, like Sandberg, had withheld his proxy. This case was transferred to the Eastern District of Virginia. After Sandberg's action had been tried, the Weinstein respondents successfully pleaded collateral estoppel to get summary judgment on liability.

On appeal, the United States Court of Appeals for the Fourth Circuit affirmed the judgments, holding that certain statements in the proxy solicitation were materially misleading for purposes of the Rule, and that respondents could maintain their action even though their votes had not been needed to effectuate the merger. 891 F.2d 1112 (1989).[4] We granted certiorari because of the importance of the issues presented. 495 U.S. 903, 110 S.Ct. 1921, 109 L.Ed.2d 285 (1990).

II

The Court of Appeals affirmed petitioners' liability for two statements found to have been materially misleading in violation of

---

4. The Court of Appeals reversed the District Court, however, on its refusal to certify a class of all minority shareholders in Sandberg's action. Consequently, it ruled that petitioners were liable to all of the Bank's former minority shareholders for $18 per share. 891 F.2d, at 1119.

§ 14(a) of the Act, one of which was that "The Plan of Merger has been approved by the Board of Directors because it provides an opportunity for the Bank's public shareholders to achieve a high value for their shares." App. to Pet. for Cert. 53a. Petitioners argue that statements of opinion or belief incorporating indefinite and unverifiable expressions cannot be actionable as misstatements of material fact within the meaning of Rule 14a–9, and that such a declaration of opinion or belief should never be actionable when placed in a proxy solicitation incorporating statements of fact sufficient to enable readers to draw their own, independent conclusions.

A

We consider first the actionability per se of statements of reasons, opinion or belief. Because such a statement by definition purports to express what is consciously on the speaker's mind, we interpret the jury verdict as finding that the directors' statements of belief and opinion were made with knowledge that the directors did not hold the beliefs or opinions expressed, and we confine our discussion to statements so made.[5] That such statements may be materially significant raises no serious question. The meaning of the materiality requirement for liability under § 14(a) was discussed at some length in TSC Industries, Inc. v. Northway, Inc., 426 U.S. 438, 96 S.Ct. 2126, 48 L.Ed.2d 757 (1976), where we held a fact to be material "if there is a substantial likelihood that a reasonable shareholder would consider it important in deciding how to vote." Id., at 449, 96 S.Ct., at 2132. We think there is no room to deny that a statement of belief by corporate directors about a recommended course of action, or an explanation of their reasons for recommending it, can take on just that importance. Shareholders know that directors usually have knowledge and expertness far exceeding the normal investor's resources, and the directors' perceived superiority is magnified even further by the common knowledge that state law customarily obliges them to exercise their judgment in the shareholders' interest. Cf. Day v. Avery, 179 U.S.App.D.C. 63, 71, 548 F.2d 1018, 1026 (1976) (action for misrepresentation). Naturally, then, the share owner faced with a proxy request will think it important to know the directors' beliefs about the course they recommend, and their specific reasons for urging the stockholders to embrace it.

B

1

But, assuming materiality, the question remains whether statements of reasons, opinions, or beliefs are statements "with respect to . . . material fact[s]" so as to fall within the strictures of the Rule. Petitioners argue that we would invite wasteful litigation of amor-

---

5. In TSC Industries, Inc. v. Northway, Inc., 426 U.S. 438, 444, n. 7, 96 S.Ct. 2126, 2130, n. 7, 48 L.Ed.2d 757 (1976), we re- served the question whether scienter was necessary for liability generally under § 14(a). We reserve it still.

phous issues outside the readily provable realm of fact if we were to recognize liability here on proof that the directors did not recommend the merger for the stated reason. . . .

Attacks on the truth of directors' statements of reasons or belief, however, need carry no such threats. Such statements are factual in two senses: as statements that the directors do act for the reasons given or hold the belief stated and as statements about the subject matter of the reason or belief expressed. In neither sense does the proof or disproof of such statements implicate the concerns expressed in Blue Chip Stamps [v. Manor Drug Stores, 421 U.S. 723, 95 S.Ct. 1917, 44 L.Ed. 539 (1975)]. The root of those concerns was a plaintiff's capacity to manufacture claims of hypothetical action, unconstrained by independent evidence. Reasons for directors' recommendations or statements of belief are, in contrast, characteristically matters of corporate record subject to documentation, to be supported or attacked by evidence of historical fact outside a plaintiff's control. Such evidence would include not only corporate minutes and other statements of the directors themselves, but circumstantial evidence bearing on the facts that would reasonably underlie the reasons claimed and the honesty of any statement that those reasons are the basis for a recommendation or other action, a point that becomes especially clear when the reasons or beliefs go to valuations in dollars and cents.

It is no answer to argue, as petitioners do, that the quoted statement on which liability was predicated did not express a reason in dollars and cents, but focused instead on the "indefinite and unverifiable" term, "high" value, much like the similar claim that the merger's terms were "fair" to shareholders.[6] The objection ignores the fact that such conclusory terms in a commercial context are reasonably understood to rest on a factual basis that justifies them as accurate, the absence of which renders them misleading. Provable facts either furnish good reasons to make a conclusory commercial judgment, or they count against it, and expressions of such judgments can be uttered with knowledge of truth or falsity just like more definite statements, and defended or attacked through the orthodox evidentiary process that either substantiates their underlying justifications or tends to disprove their existence. In addressing the analogous issue in an action for misrepresenta-

---

6. Petitioners are also wrong to argue that construing the statute to allow recovery for a misleading statement that the merger was "fair" to the minority shareholders is tantamount to assuming federal authority to bar corporate transactions thought to be unfair to some group of shareholders. It is, of course, true that we said in Santa Fe Industries, Inc. v. Green, 430 U.S. 462, 479, 97 S.Ct. 1292, 1304, 51 L.Ed.2d 480 (1977), that " '[c]orporations are creatures of state law, and investors commit their funds to corporate directors on the understanding that, except where federal law *expressly* requires certain responsibilities of directors with respect to stockholders, state law will govern the internal affairs of the corporation,' " quoting Cort v. Ash, 422 U.S. 66, 84, 95 S.Ct. 2080, 2091, 45 L.Ed.2d 26 (1975). But § 14(a) does impose responsibility for false and misleading proxy statements. Although a corporate transaction's "fairness" is not, as such, a federal concern, a proxy statement's claim of fairness presupposes a factual integrity that federal law is expressly concerned to preserve. Cf. Craftmatic Securities Litigation v. Kraftsow, 890 F.2d 628, 639 (CA3 1989).

tion, the court in Day v. Avery, 179 U.S.App.D.C. 63, 548 F.2d 1018 (1976), for example, held that a statement by the executive committee of a law firm that no partner would be any "worse off" solely because of an impending merger could be found to be a material misrepresentation. Id., at 70–72, 548 F.2d at 1025–1027. Cf. Vulcan Metals Co. v. Simmons Mfg. Co., 248 F. 853, 856 (CA2 1918) (L. Hand, J.) ("An opinion is a fact. . . . When the parties are so situated that the buyer may reasonably rely upon the expression of the seller's opinion, it is no excuse to give a false one"); W. Keeton, D. Dobbs, R. Keeton, & D. Owen, Prosser and Keeton on Law of Torts § 109, pp. 760–762 (5th ed. 1984). In this case, whether $42 was "high," and the proposal "fair" to the minority shareholders depended on whether provable facts about the Bank's assets, and about actual and potential levels of operation, substantiated a value that was above, below, or more or less at the $42 figure, when assessed in accordance with recognized methods of valuation.

Respondents adduced evidence for just such facts in proving that the statement was misleading about its subject matter and a false expression of the directors' reasons. Whereas the proxy statement described the $42 price as offering a premium above both book value and market price, the evidence indicated that a calculation of the book figure based on the appreciated value of the Bank's real estate holdings eliminated any such premium. The evidence on the significance of market price showed that KBW had conceded that the market was closed, thin and dominated by FABI, facts omitted from the statement. There was, indeed, evidence of a "going concern" value for the Bank in excess of $60 per share of common stock, another fact never disclosed. However conclusory the directors' statement may have been, then, it was open to attack by garden-variety evidence, subject neither to a plaintiff's control nor ready manufacture, and there was no undue risk of open-ended liability or uncontrollable litigation in allowing respondents the opportunity for recovery on the allegation that it was misleading to call $42 "high."

This analysis comports with the holding that marked our nearest prior approach to the issue faced here, in *TSC Industries,* 426 U.S., at 454–55, 96 S.Ct., at 2135. There, to be sure, we reversed summary judgment for a *Borak* plaintiff who had sued on a description of proposed compensation for minority shareholders as offering a "substantial premium over current market values." But we held only that on the case's undisputed facts the conclusory adjective "substantial" was not materially misleading as a necessary matter of law, and our remand for trial assumed that such a description could be both materially misleading within the meaning of Rule 14a–9 and actionable under § 14(a). See *TSC Industries,* supra, at 458–460, 463–464, 96 S.Ct., at 2136–2138, 2139.

2

Under § 14(a), then, a plaintiff is permitted to prove a specific statement of reason knowingly false or misleadingly incomplete, even when stated in conclusory terms. In reaching this conclusion we have considered statements of reasons of the sort exemplified here, which misstate the speaker's reasons and also mislead about the stated subject matter (e.g., the value of the shares). A statement of belief may be open to objection only in the former respect, however, solely as a misstatement of the psychological fact of the speaker's belief in what he says. In this case, for example, the Court of Appeals alluded to just such limited falsity in observing that "the jury was certainly justified in believing that the directors did not believe a merger at $42 per share was in the minority stockholders' interest but, rather, that they voted as they did for other reasons, e.g., retaining their seats on the board." 891 F.2d, at 1121.

The question arises, then, whether disbelief, or undisclosed belief or motivation, standing alone, should be a sufficient basis to sustain an action under § 14(a), absent proof by the sort of objective evidence described above that the statement also expressly or impliedly asserted something false or misleading about its subject matter. We think that proof of mere disbelief or belief undisclosed should not suffice for liability under § 14(a), and if nothing more had been required or proven in this case we would reverse for that reason.

On the one hand, it would be rare to find a case with evidence solely of disbelief or undisclosed motivation without further proof that the statement was defective as to its subject matter. While we certainly would not hold a director's naked admission of disbelief incompetent evidence of a proxy statement's false or misleading character, such an unusual admission will not very often stand alone, and we do not substantially narrow the cause of action by requiring a plaintiff to demonstrate something false or misleading in what the statement expressly or impliedly declared about its subject.

On the other hand, to recognize liability on mere disbelief or undisclosed motive without any demonstration that the proxy statement was false or misleading about its subject would authorize § 14(a) litigation confined solely to what one skeptical court spoke of as the "impurities" of a director's "unclean heart." *Stedman v. Storer,* 308 F.Supp. 881, 887 (SDNY 1969) (dealing with § 10(b)). This, we think, would cross the line that *Blue Chip Stamps* sought to draw. While it is true that the liability, if recognized, would rest on an actual, not hypothetical, psychological fact, the temptation to rest an otherwise nonexistent § 14(a) action on psychological enquiry alone would threaten just the sort of strike suits and attrition by discovery that *Blue Chip Stamps* sought to discourage. We therefore hold disbelief or undisclosed motivation, standing alone, insufficient to satisfy the element of fact that must be established under § 14(a).

C

Petitioners' fall-back position assumes the same relationship between a conclusory judgment and its underlying facts that we described in Part II–B–1, supra. Thus, citing Radol v. Thomas, 534 F.Supp. 1302, 1315, 1316 (SD Ohio 1982), petitioners argue that even if conclusory statements of reason or belief can be actionable under § 14(a), we should confine liability to instances where the proxy material fails to disclose the offending statement's factual basis. There would be no justification for holding the shareholders entitled to judicial relief, that is, when they were given evidence that a stated reason for a proxy recommendation was misleading, and an opportunity to draw that conclusion themselves.

The answer to this argument rests on the difference between a merely misleading statement and one that is materially so. While a misleading statement will not always lose its deceptive edge simply by joinder with others that are true, the true statements may discredit the other one so obviously that the risk of real deception drops to nil. Since liability under § 14(a) must rest not only on deceptiveness but materiality as well (i.e., it has to be significant enough to be important to a reasonable investor deciding how to vote, see *TSC Industries,* 426 U.S., at 449, 96 S.Ct., at 2132), petitioners are on perfectly firm ground insofar as they argue that publishing accurate facts in a proxy statement can render a misleading proposition too unimportant to ground liability.

But not every mixture with the true will neutralize the deceptive. If it would take a financial analyst to spot the tension between the one and the other, whatever is misleading will remain materially so, and liability should follow. Gerstle v. Gamble–Skogmo, Inc., 478 F.2d 1281, 1297 (CA2 1973) ("[I]t is not sufficient that overtones might have been picked up by the sensitive antennae of investment analysts"). Cf. Milkovich v. Lorain Journal Co., 497 U.S. ——, ——, 110 S.Ct. 2695, 2708, 111 L.Ed.2d 1 (1990) (a defamatory assessment of facts can be actionable even if the facts underlying the assessment are accurately presented). The point of a proxy statement, after all, should be to inform, not to challenge the reader's critical wits. Only when the inconsistency would exhaust the misleading conclusion's capacity to influence the reasonable shareholder would a § 14(a) action fail on the element of materiality.

Suffice it to say that the evidence invoked by petitioners in the instant case fell short of compelling the jury to find the facial materiality of the misleading statement neutralized. The directors claim, for example, to have made an explanatory disclosure of further reasons for their recommendation when they said they would keep their seats following the merger, but they failed to mention what at least one of them admitted in testimony, that they would have had no expectation of doing so without supporting the proposal, App. at 281–82.[7] And although the proxy statement did

---

7. Petitioners fail to dissuade us from recognizing the significance of omissions such as this by arguing that we effectively require them to accuse themselves of breach of fiduciary duty. Subjection to liability for misleading others does not raise a duty of self-accusation; it enforces a duty to refrain from misleading. We have no occa-

speak factually about the merger price in describing it as higher than share prices in recent sales, it failed even to mention the closed market dominated by FABI. None of these disclosures that the directors point to was, then, anything more than a half-truth, and the record shows that another fact statement they invoke was arguably even worse. The claim that the merger price exceeded book value was controverted, as we have seen already, by evidence of a higher book value than the directors conceded, reflecting appreciation in the Bank's real estate portfolio. Finally, the solicitation omitted any mention of the Bank's value as a going concern at more than $60 a share, as against the merger price of $42. There was, in sum, no more of a compelling case for the statement's immateriality than for its accuracy.

III

The second issue before us, left open in Mills v. Electric Auto-Lite Co., 396 U.S., at 385, n. 7, 90 S.Ct., at 622, n. 7, is whether causation of damages compensable through the implied private right of action under § 14(a) can be demonstrated by a member of a class of minority shareholders whose votes are not required by law or corporate bylaw to authorize the transaction giving rise to the claim.

[The Court held that the answer to this question was, no. The plaintiffs argued that such a claim could be supported by two theories: that the proxy statement was an essential link between the director's proposal and the merger (1) because VBI and FABI would have been unwilling to proceed with the merger unless the minority approved, and (2) because the vote of the minority was the means to satisfy a state statutory requirement of minority shareholder approval as a condition for saving the merger from voidability resulting from a conflict of interest. The court rejected the first theory on the ground that acceptance of the concept would give rise to speculative claims. As to the second theory, the court said:]

This case does not ... require us to decide whether § 14(a) provides a cause of action for lost state remedies, since there is no indication in the law or facts before us that the proxy solicitation resulted in any such loss. The contrary appears to be the case. Assuming the soundness of respondents' characterization of the proxy statement as materially misleading, the very terms of the Virginia statute indicate that a favorable minority vote induced by the solicitation would not suffice to render the merger invulnerable to later attack on the ground of the conflict. The statute bars a shareholder from seeking to avoid a transaction tainted by a director's conflict if, inter alia, the minority shareholders ratified the

---

sion to decide whether the directors were obligated to state the reasons for their support of the merger proposal here, but there can be no question that the statement they did make carried with it no option to deceive. Cf. Berg v. First American Bank-

shares, Inc., 254 U.S.App.D.C. 198, 205, 796 F.2d 489, 496 (1986) ("Once the proxy statement purported to disclose the factors considered ..., there was an obligation to portray them accurately").

transaction following disclosure of the material facts of the transaction and the conflict. Va.Code § 13.1–691(A)(2) (1989). Assuming that the material facts about the merger and Beddow's interests were not accurately disclosed, the minority votes were inadequate to ratify the merger under state law, and there was no loss of state remedy to connect the proxy solicitation with harm to minority shareholders irredressable under state law. Nor is there a claim here that the statement misled respondents into entertaining a false belief that they had no chance to upset the merger, until the time for bringing suit had run out.[14]

IV

The judgment of the Court of Appeals is reversed.

It is so ordered.

[Justice Scalia wrote a separate opinion in which he concurred in the judgment and joined in the opinion except for Part II. Justice Stevens, with whom Justice Marshall joined, wrote a separate opinion in which he agreed in substance with Parts I and II, but dissented from the reasoning in Part III. Justice Kennedy, with whom Justice Marshall, Justice Blackman, and Justice Stevens joined, wrote a separate opinion which expressed general agreement with Parts I and II but dissented from Part III.]

––––––––

NOTE ON THE STANDARD OF FAULT IN PRIVATE ACTIONS UNDER THE PROXY RULES

Under *Borak* and *Mills,* shareholders have standing to bring an action under Rule 14a–9, which prohibits false or misleading proxy statements. Does a plaintiff-shareholder prevail if he shows that a proxy statement was false or misleading by virtue of a material misstatement or omission, or must he also show that the misstatement or omission resulted from the defendant's fault? If the plaintiff must show fault, does negligence suffice?

In the leading case of Gerstle v. Gamble–Skogmo, Inc., 478 F.2d 1281 (2d Cir.1973), where the proxy statement was issued in connection with a proposed merger, the Second Circuit, in an opinion written by Judge Friendly, held that negligence sufficed to establish liability under Rule 14a–9. The opinion is particularly striking because Judge Friendly was a leading advocate for imposing a higher scienter standard in private actions under Rule 10b–5, which relates to misstatements or omissions in connection with the purchase or sale of stock:

> We thus hold that in a case like this, where the plaintiffs represent the very class who were asked to approve a merger

14. Respondents do not claim that any other application of a theory of lost state remedies would avail them here. It is clear, for example, that no state appraisal remedy was lost through a § 14(a) violation in this case. . . .

on the basis of a misleading proxy statement and are seeking compensation from the beneficiary who is responsible for the preparation of the statement, they are not required to establish any evil motive or even reckless disregard of the facts. Whether in situations other than that here presented "the liability of the corporation issuing a materially false or misleading proxy statement is virtually absolute, as under Section 11 of the 1933 Act with respect to a registration statement," Jennings & Marsh, Securities Regulation: Cases and Materials 1358 (3d ed. 1972), we leave to another day. 478 F.2d at 1298–1301. Accord: Herskowitz v. Nutri/System, Inc., 857 F.2d 179 (3d Cir.1988), cert. denied 489 U.S. 1054, 109 S.Ct. 1315, 103 L.Ed.2d 584 (1989); Gould v. American–Hawaiian Steamship Co., 535 F.2d 761 (3d Cir.1976).

But see Adams v. Standard Knitting Mills, Inc., 623 F.2d 422 (6th Cir.1980), cert. denied 449 U.S. 1067, 101 S.Ct. 795, 66 L.Ed.2d 611. ("scienter should be an element of liability in private suits under the proxy provisions as they apply to outside accountants").

In Shidler v. All American Life & Financial Corp., 775 F.2d 917, 927 (8th Cir.1985), the Eighth Circuit addressed the issue that Judge Friendly left to another day in *Gerstle,* and held there was no liability without fault in an action under Section 14(a):

> The purpose of section 14(a) is "to prevent management or others from obtaining authorization for corporate action by means of deceptive or inadequate disclosure in proxy solicitation." J.I. Case Co. v. Borak, 377 U.S. 426, 431, 84 S.Ct. 1555, 1559, 12 L.Ed.2d 423 (1964). A strict liability rule would impose liability for fully innocent misstatements. It is too blunt a tool to ferret out the kind of deceptive practices Congress sought to prevent in enacting section 14(a).

The Supreme Court has three times explicitly taken note of the position of *Gerstle* and other cases that scienter is not an element of liability under § 14(a), and has each time declined to address the issue. See Ernst & Ernst v. Hochfelder, 425 U.S. 185, 209 n. 28, 96 S.Ct. 1375, 1388 n. 28, 47 L.Ed.2d 668 (1976); TSC Indus., Inc. v. Northway, 426 U.S. 438, 444 n. 7, 96 S.Ct. 2126, 2130 n. 7, 48 L.Ed.2d 757 (1976); *Virginia Bankshares,* supra, at note 5.

SECTION 5. THE PROXY RULES (III): SHAREHOLDER PROPOSALS

SECURITIES EXCHANGE ACT RULE 14a–7

[See Statutory Supplement]

SECURITIES EXCHANGE ACT RULE 14a–8

[See Statutory Supplement]

NOTE ON NO–ACTION LETTERS INTERPRETING
RULE 14a–8(c)(7)

Rule 14a–8(d) provides that if management believes a shareholder proposal can be excluded from the corporation's proxy statement under Rule 14a–8, it must submit to the SEC staff a statement of the reasons why it deems omission of the proposal to be proper. If the staff agrees with management's statement, it sends management a "no-action letter"—that is, a letter stating that if the shareholder proposal is omitted, no action will be taken by the SEC. If the staff disagrees with management's statement, it sends a letter stating why the proposal should be included. Such letters are also referred to as no-action letters, although in fact they are just the opposite—that is, they implicitly threaten legal proceedings if management omits the shareholder proposal. In such cases management may still omit the shareholder proposal and run the risk of legal proceedings by the SEC, but that option is seldom if ever exercised.

ROOSEVELT v. E.I. DUPONT de NEMOURS & CO.

United States Court of Appeals, District of Columbia Circuit, 1992.
958 F.2d 416.

Before EDWARDS, RUTH BADER GINSBURG, and SENTELLE, Circuit Judges.

Opinion for the Court filed by Circuit Judge RUTH BADER GINSBURG.

RUTH BADER GINSBURG, Circuit Judge.

Amelia Roosevelt appeals the district court's judgment that E.I. Du Pont de Nemours & Co. ("Du Pont") could omit her shareholder proposal from its proxy materials for the 1992 annual meeting. The district court concluded that Roosevelt's proposal "deals with a matter relating to the conduct of [Du Pont's] ordinary business operations," and is therefore excludable under Securities and Exchange Commission ("SEC") Rule 14a–8(c)(7), 17 C.F.R. § 240.14a–8(c)(7). We affirm the district court's judgment and deal first with a threshold question. Consistent with congressional intent and Supreme Court case law, we hold, a private right of action is properly implied from section 14(a) of the Securities Exchange Act of 1934 (the "Act"), 15 U.S.C. § 78n(a), to enforce a company's obligation to include shareholder proposals in annual meeting proxy materials.

Reaching the merits, we uphold the district court's determination that Roosevelt's two-part proposal is excludable under Rule 14a–8(c)(7).

I.   Background

Prior to Du Pont's 1991 annual shareholder meeting, Friends of the Earth Oceanic Society ("Friends of the Earth") submitted a proposal, on behalf of Roosevelt, regarding: (1) the timing of Du Pont's phase out of the production of chlorofluorocarbons ("CFCs") and halons; and (2) the presentation to shareholders of a report detailing (a) research and development efforts to find environmentally sound substitutes, and (b) marketing plans to sell those substitutes.[1] Du Pont opposed inclusion of the proposal in its proxy materials; as required by SEC rule, see 17 C.F.R. § 240.14a–8(d), the company notified the SEC staff of its intention to omit the proposal and its reasons for believing the omission proper. Friends of the Earth filed with the staff a countersubmission on Roosevelt's behalf urging that the proposal was not excludable.

The SEC staff issued a "no-action letter"; citing the Rule 14a–8(c)(7) exception for matters "relating to the conduct of the [company's] ordinary business operations," the staff stated that it would not recommend Commission enforcement action against Du Pont if the company excluded the proposal. Du Pont, SEC No–Action Letter (available March 8, 1991). Roosevelt did not seek Commission review of the staff's disposition.

Instead, with the 1991 meeting weeks away, Roosevelt filed a complaint and a motion for a temporary restraining order in federal district court. Denying the motion, the motions judge stated preliminarily that "[t]he Supreme Court has recognized an implied private right of action for alleged violations of Rule 14a–8." She found, however, that Roosevelt had not shown the requisite irreparable harm. If Du Pont mailed its proxy materials on March 18, as

---

1. Roosevelt's proposal consists of twelve "whereas" clauses followed by two resolutions. In relevant part, the proposal states:

> Whereas, The international scientific community has determined that synthetic chemicals—including chlorofluorocarbons (CFCs), halons, carbon tetrachloride, methyl chloroform, and hydrochlorofluorocarbons (HCFCs)—are destroying the Earth's protective ozone layer at an alarming rate;

> * * *

> Whereas, Many governments are taking action beyond the Montreal Protocol [the international ozone protection treaty, including an agreement to stop CFC production in the year 2000]; for example, Germany plans to stop CFC and halon production in 1995, and German CFC producers Hoechst AG and Kali–Chemie

have announced they will stop making CFCs in 1995;

> * * *

> Resolved, That the shareholders of the Du Pont Company, assembled in annual meeting in person and by proxy, request that the Board of Directors:

> 1. Rapidly accelerate plans to phase out CFC and halon production, surpassing our global competitors which have set a 1995 target date;

> 2. Present a report to shareholders within six months detailing (a) research and development program expenditures which dramatically increase efforts to find CFC and halon substitutes which do not harm the ozone layer or contribute significantly to global warning; and (b) a marketing plan to sell those environmentally safe alternatives to present customers.

scheduled, without Roosevelt's proposal, the motions judge observed, a supplemental mailing containing the proposal could still be made in advance of the April 24 annual meeting date. C.A. No. 91–556, Memorandum Order (March 18, 1991) at 1, 3. The trial judge held an expedited trial on the morning of April 2, 1991; in a Memorandum Opinion filed two days later, he ruled that, based on the "ordinary business operations" exception in Rule 14a–8(c)(7), Du Point could omit Roosevelt's proposal. C.A. No. 91–556, Memorandum Opinion (April 4, 1991) ("Mem.Op.").

We expedited Roosevelt's appeal when she informed us that she sought inclusion of her proposal in the proxy materials for Du Pont's 1992 annual meeting. C.A. No. 91–5087, Order (April 9, 1991) (per curiam). Before the appeal was heard, Du Pont had again advised the SEC that it intended to exclude the proposal, and the SEC staff had issued a second no-action letter, once more concluding that "[t]here appears to be some basis for [Du Pont's] view that the proposal may be excluded ... pursuant to rule 14a–8(c)(7)." Du Pont, SEC No–Action Letter (available Sept. 11, 1991).[3] Neither Roosevelt nor the SEC staff requested the Commission's view on the applicability of the "ordinary business operations" exception to Roosevelt's proposal.

II. The Implied Private Right of Action and Shareholder Proposals

Before reviewing the district court's application of Rule 14a–8(c)(7), we resolve a preliminary question: Does a shareholder have an implied right of action under section 14(a) of the Act and Commission Rule 14a–8 when a company refuses to include the shareholder's proposal in proxy materials? ...

[The court held that a shareholder did have such a right of action.]

III. Roosevelt's Proposals and the Rule 14a–8(c)(7) Exception for "Ordinary Business Operations"

Reaching the merits, we restate the district court's ruling: "Roosevelt's proposal deals with matters relating to the conduct of the ordinary business operations of Du Pont. Therefore, [under Rule 14a–8(c)(7)], Du Pont properly omitted her proposal from its proxy statement." Mem.Op. at 1. In reviewing this ruling, we emphasize that Roosevelt's disagreement with Du Pont's current policy is not about whether to eliminate CFC production or even whether to do so at once. The former is an end to which Du Pont is committed, and immediate cessation, before environmentally safe alternatives are available, is not what Roosevelt proposes.

3. The staff reasoned in September 1991, as it had the previous March, that "the thrust of the proposal appears directed at those questions concerning the timing, research and marketing decisions that involve matters relating to the conduct of the Company's ordinary business operations." Id.

Roosevelt differs with Du Pont on a less fundamental matter—the rapidity with which the near-term phase out should occur. Roosevelt seeks a target no later than 1995 ("surpassing [Du Pont's] global competitors which have set a 1995 target date"). In contrast, when this litigation began, Du Pont had set a target of "as soon as possible, but at least by the year 2000." Mem.Op. at 4.

In recent months and days, the "at least by" year has moved ever closer to Roosevelt's target. Prior to oral argument, Roosevelt informed the court, pursuant to Fed.R.App.P. 28(j) and D.C.Cir.R. 11(h), that Du Pont had issued a press release reiterating its "as soon as possible" policy, but "advancing the end point to year-end 1994 for Halons and 1996 for CFCs." Du Pont Corporate News, Oct. 22, 1991, at 1 (citing "scientific data released today by the United Nations Environment Programme . . . and World Meteorological Organization"). Following oral argument, Du Pont informed the court that, "[i]n response to an announcement issued by the White House today regarding an accelerated phaseout of CFCs and Halons," the company "will accelerate its CFC end date to no later than December 31, 1995 in developed countries." Du Pont Statement on Accelerated CFC Phaseout, Feb. 12, 1992.

Although the regulation necessary to give effect to the President's announcement has not yet been adopted, Du Pont immediately reported that it "supports the Administration's position," id., and that it will phase out CFC production by December 31, 1995. We accept that public statement as the company's current timetable. While the SEC staff and the district court considered Roosevelt's proposal with the company's year–2000 end point in view, we think it proper to take account of the current reality: Roosevelt's proposal would have Du Pont surpass its global competitors' target of 1995; Du Pont projects completion of the phase out "as soon as possible," but no later than year-end 1995.

Roosevelt has confirmed that the first, or phase-out portion of her proposal is the "core issue" and that, if necessary, she would withdraw the second, or report-to-shareholders portion, so that the first portion could be included in Du Pont's 1992 proxy materials. Plaintiff–Appellant's Reply to Brief of the Securities and Exchange Commission, Amicus Curiae, at 4–5. We therefore consider separately the two portions of Roosevelt's proposal.

Because both parts of Roosevelt's proposal must be measured against the Rule 14a–8(c)(7) "ordinary business operations" exception, we set out here the Commission's general understanding of that phrase. When the Commission adopted the current version of the "ordinary business operations" exception, it announced its intention to interpret the phrase both "more restrictive[ly]" and "more flexibly than in the past." *Adoption of Amendments Relating to Proposals by Security Holders,* Exchange Act Release No. 12,999, 41 Fed.Reg. 52,994, 52,998 (Dec. 3, 1976) ("*1976 Rule 14a–8 Amendments* "). Specifically, the Commission explained:

[T]he term "ordinary business operations" has been deemed on occasion to include certain matters which have significant policy, economic or other implications inherent in them. For instance, a proposal that a utility company not construct a proposed nuclear power plant has in the past been considered excludable under [the predecessor of (c)(7)]. In retrospect, however, it seems apparent that the economic and safety considerations attendant to nuclear power plants are of such magnitude that a determination whether to construct one is not an "ordinary" business matter. Accordingly, proposals of that nature, as well as others that have major implications, will in the future be considered beyond the realm of an issuer's ordinary business operations. . . .

Id.; see *Grimes*, 909 F.2d at 531 (observing that, "[u]nfortunately, the phrase [ordinary business operations] has no precise definition"). The Commission contrasted with matters of such moment as a decision not to build a nuclear power plant, "matters . . . mundane in nature [that] do not involve any substantial policy . . . considerations." *1976 Rule 14a–8 Amendments,* 41 Fed.Reg. at 52,998. Proposals of that genre, the Commission said, may be safely omitted from proxy materials.

In its brief as amicus curiae, the SEC stated that it regarded the first portion of Roosevelt's proposal, on the timing of the CFC phase out, as not excludable under Rule 14a–8(c)(7), but the second part, on research and development programs and marketing plans, as fitting within the "ordinary business operations" exception. Brief of the Securities and Exchange Commission, Amicus Curiae, at 31. The Commission noted that "[its] staff, in contrast, viewed the timing of the phase-out as an ordinary business matter." Id. at 32 n. 23. We agree with the Commission on the second part of Roosevelt's proposal but not on the first.

A. The Phase Out Target Date

It is not debated in this case that CFCs contribute intolerably to depletion of the ozone layer and that their manufacture has caused a grave environmental hazard. However, Roosevelt's proposal, we emphasize again, relates not to *whether* CFC production should be phased out, but *when* the phase out should be completed. Cf. Loews Corporation, SEC No–Action Letter (available Feb. 22, 1990) (shareholder proposal for eventual cessation of manufacture of tobacco products; company unsuccessfully urged that what products it makes is a matter of "ordinary business operations").

Timing questions no doubt reflect "significant policy" when large differences are at stake. That would be the case, for example, if Du Pont projected a phase-out period extending into the new century. On the other hand, were Roosevelt seeking to move up Du Pont's target date by barely a season, the matter would appear much more of an "ordinary" than an extraordinary business judgment. In evaluating the Commission's classification of the timing question here as extraordinary, *i.e.,* one involving "fundamental business strategy" or "long-term goals," see Brief of the Securities and Exchange Commission, Amicus Curiae, at 31, we are mindful that the SEC focused on a five-year interval, see id. at 32 n. 25, not an interval cut down to one year. See supra pp. 425–26.[19]

We are furthermore mindful that we sit in this case as a court of review and owe respect to the findings made by the district court. The trial judge concluded from the record that "Du Pont's 'as soon as possible' policy," contrary to Roosevelt's argument, "does not lack definition." Mem.Op. at 5. The judge found the policy genuine based on evidence that Du Pont had already spent more than $240 million developing alternatives to CFCs and had just announced the shutdown of the facility that had been the largest CFC plant in the world. Id. Du Pont, the district court also observed, continues to work "toward a global policy of phasing out CFCs" and "with CFC consumers to phase out their use of CFCs." Id.

Stressing the undisputed need for the responsible development of safe substitutes, and the acknowledged irresponsibility of suddenly cutting off all CFC production, the trial judge highlighted the essential difference between this case and the nuclear power plant in the Commission's *1976 Rule 14a–8 Amendments* example. See supra p. 426. Phasing out CFC production is not a go/no go matter. Cf. *Medical Comm.,* 432 F.2d at 663 (proposal to halt immediately all production of napalm). The phase out takes work "day-to-day . . . with equipment manufacturers to help develop the technology needed for alternative compounds." Mem.Op. at 6. It takes careful planning "in sensitive areas, such as the storage of perishable food and medical products (like vaccines and transfusable blood)," and expertise "in technical fields, such as the sterilization of temperature-sensitive surgical instruments." Id.

We recognize that "ordinary business operations" ordinarily do not attract the interest of both the executive and legislative branches of the federal government. See supra notes 15, 18. But government regulation of the CFC phase out, even the President's headline-attracting decision to accelerate the schedule initially set by Congress, does not automatically elevate shareholder proposals on timing to the status of "significant policy." See supra p. 427. What the President and Congress have said about CFCs is not the subject of our closest look. Instead, Rule 14a–8(c)(7) requires us to home in on Roosevelt's proposal, to determine whether her request dominantly implicates ordinary business matters. The gap between her proposal and the company's schedule is now one year, not five. The steps to be taken to accomplish the phase out are complex; as

19. As Roosevelt correctly points out, the principle of deference described in Chevron U.S.A. Inc. v. NRDC, Inc., 467 U.S. 837, 104 S.Ct. 2778, 81 L.Ed.2d 694 (1984), is not applicable here, for neither the staff's no-action letter nor the Commis-sion's brief ranks as an agency adjudication or rulemaking. See Reply Brief at 12–14. Nonetheless, we value the SEC's presentation; the Commission's brief has clarified several points and thereby aided our analysis considerably.

the district court found, the company, having agreed on the essential policy, must carry it out safely, using "business and technical skills" day-to-day that are not meant for "shareholder debate and participation." Mem.Op. at 5, 6.

In sum, the parties agree that CFC production must be phased out, that substitutes must be developed, and that both should be achieved sooner rather than later. Du Pont has undertaken to eliminate the products in question by year-end 1995, and has pledged to do so sooner if "possible." The trial judge has found Du Pont's "as soon as possible" pledge credible. In these circumstances, we conclude that what is at stake is the "implementation of a policy," "the timing for an agreed-upon action," see Brief of the Securities and Exchange Commission, Amicus Curiae, at 31, and we therefore hold the target date for the phase out a matter excludable under Rule 14a–8(c)(7).

B. The Report to Shareholders

The second part of Roosevelt's proposal solicits a report from management within six months detailing research and development efforts on environmentally safe substitutes and a marketing plan to sell those substitutes. See supra note 1. This portion of the proposal, the SEC concluded in agreement with its staff, "requires detailed information about the company's day-to-day business operations [and] is subject to exclusion pursuant to [Rule 14a–8(c)(7)]." Brief of the Securities and Exchange Commission, Amicus Curiae, at 31. Roosevelt concedes that the report is not central to her proposal, see supra p. 426, and we find no cause to place the matter outside the "ordinary business operations" exception.

For a time, the Commission staff "ha[d] taken the position that proposals requesting issuers to prepare reports on specific aspects of their business or to form [study committees] would not be excludable under Rule 14a–8(c)(7)." *Amendments to Rule 14a–8 Under the Securities Exchange Act of 1934 Relating to Proposals by Security Holders,* Exchange Act Release No. 20,091, 48 Fed.Reg. 38,218, 38,221 (Aug. 23, 1983). The Commission has changed that position. Pointing out that the staff's interpretation "raise[d] form over substance," the Commission instructed the staff to "consider whether the subject matter of the [requested] report or [study] committee involves a matter of ordinary business: where it does, the proposal [is] excludable under Rule 14a–8(c)(7)." Id.

We need not linger over the report issue. The staff's no-action letters in this respect are unremarkable and entirely in keeping with current practice. See, e.g., Carolina Power & Light Co., SEC No–Action Letter (available Mar. 8, 1990) (shareholder proposal requesting preparation of a report on specific aspects of company's nuclear operations, covering, *inter alia,* safety, regulatory compliance, emissions problems, hazardous waste disposal and related cost information, may be omitted as relating to ordinary business operations).

Just as the Commission has clarified that requests for special reports or committee studies are not automatically includable in proxy materials, we caution that such requests are not inevitably excludable. But Roosevelt has not shown that the detailed research and development or marketing information she seeks implicates significant policy issues, and not merely implementation arrangements. She does not, for example, suggest that Du Pont is developing or planning to market hazardous substitutes. Cf. Lovenheim v. Iroquois Brands, Ltd., 618 F.Supp. 554, 556, 561 (D.D.C.1985) (in light of "ethical and social significance" of proposal, court granted preliminary injunction barring corporation from excluding from its proxy materials shareholder proposal that requested formation of committee to study, and submission of report to shareholders about, whether company's supplier produced pate de foie gras in a manner involving undue pain or suffering to animals and whether distribution of product should be discontinued pending development of a more humane method).

In agreement with the district judge, the Commission, and the staff, we hold that the second part of Roosevelt's proposal falls within the "ordinary business operations" exception.

Conclusion

A private right of action is properly implied from section 14(a) of the Act, and Commission Rule 14a–8 thereunder, to enforce a registrant's obligation to include a shareholder's proposal in proxy materials mailed out in advance of the annual meeting. Roosevelt's proposal, however, may be excluded by Du Pont because, in both of its parts, the proposal falls within the exception furnished by Rule 14a–8(c)(7) for matters relating to "ordinary business operations." Accordingly, the judgment of the district court is

Affirmed.

NOTE ON EMPIRICAL DATA CONCERNING SHAREHOLDER PROPOSALS

Shareholder resolutions are conventionally divided into social-policy resolutions and corporate-governance resolutions. At one time, the most celebrated issues for shareholder proposals were social-policy issues, such as the propriety of investing in apartheid South Africa. Although these issues still play an important role, the most celebrated issues today tend to concern corporate governance.

Not surprisingly, the emphasis of social policy resolutions tends to shift over time. Prior to the 1994 proxy season, South Africa had dominated. In the 1994 season, the social policy issue that drew the largest number of proposals was the environment. Other leading issues concerned tobacco and equal employment opportunities. In the 1994 proxy season, 232 social policy resolutions were presented to corporations, and of these 118 were voted upon. (Many of the balance were ruled improper under Rule 14a–8 by the SEC staff.) None of the 1994 social-policy proposals were adopted, although ten received votes of 15 percent or more and several received votes of 20 percent or more. See A. Bradley, How Institutions Voted on Social Policy Shareholder Resolutions (Institutional Responsibility Research Center 1994).

The proportion of votes cast for many governance proposals, as well as the rate of success, was considerably higher. For example, according to Institutional Shareholder Services, Inc., in 1994 shareholder proposals to redeem poison pills, or put them to a vote, were adopted in five out of nine cases, and received an average of 37% of the vote even in the four corporations in which the proposals were defeated. Proposals to institute confidential voting were adopted in two out of nine cases, and received more than 40% of the vote in three others. Almost 30 corporations received proposals to require the annual election of directors. Two of the proposals were adopted, and about half of the proposals received at least 30% of the vote. See Institutional Shareholder Services, Inc., The 1994 Proxy Season: Shareholders Maintain Their Edge 35–37 (Tables 3, 4, 5). See also p. 172, supra.

SECTION 6. PROXY CONTESTS

SECURITIES EXCHANGE ACT RULE 14a–11, SCHEDULE 14B

[See Statutory Supplement]

ROSENFELD v. FAIRCHILD ENGINE AND AIRPLANE CORP.

Court of Appeals of New York, 1955.
309 N.Y. 168, 128 N.E.2d 291.

FROESSEL, Judge. In a stockholder's derivative action brought by plaintiff, an attorney, who owns 25 out of the company's over 2,300,000 shares, he seeks to compel the return of $261,522, paid out of the corporate treasury to reimburse both sides in a proxy contest for their expenses. The Appellate Division, 284 App.Div. 201, 132 N.Y.S.2d 273, has unanimously affirmed a judgment of an Official Referee, Sup., 116 N.Y.S.2d 840, dismissing plaintiff's complaint on the merits, and we agree. Exhaustive opinions were written by both courts below, and it will serve no useful purpose to review the facts again.

Of the amount in controversy $106,000 was spent out of corporate funds by the old board of directors while still in office in defense of their position in said contest; $28,000 [was] paid to the old board by the new board after the change of management following the proxy contest, to compensate the former directors for such of the remaining expenses of their unsuccessful defense as the new board found was fair and reasonable; payment of $127,000, representing reimbursement of expenses to members of the prevailing group, was expressly ratified by a 16 to 1 majority vote of the stockholders.

The essential facts are not in dispute, and, since the determinations below are amply supported by the evidence, we are bound by the findings affirmed by the Appellate Division. The Appellate Division found that the difference between plaintiff's group and the old board "went deep into the policies of the company", and that among these Ward's contract was one of the "main points of contention". The Official Referee found that the controversy "was based on an understandable difference in policy between the two groups, at the very bottom of which was the Ward employment contract".

By way of contrast with the findings here, in Lawyers' Advertising Co. v. Consolidated Ry., Lighting & Refrigerating Co., 187 N.Y. 395, at page 399, 80 N.E. 199, at page 200, which was an action to recover for the cost of publishing newspaper notices not authorized by the board of directors, it was expressly found that the proxy contest there involved was "by one faction in its contest with another for the control of the corporation . . . a contest for the perpetuation of their offices and control." We there said by way of *dicta* that under *such* circumstances the publication of certain notices on behalf of the management faction was not a corporate expenditure which the directors had the power to authorize.

Other jurisdictions and our own lower courts have held that management may look to the corporate treasury for the reasonable expenses of soliciting proxies to defend its position in a bona fide policy contest. . . .

It should be noted that plaintiff does not argue that the aforementioned sums were fraudulently extracted from the corporation; indeed, his counsel conceded that "the charges were fair and reasonable", but denied "they were legal charges which may be reimbursed for". This is therefore not a case where a stockholder challenges specific items, which, on examination, the trial court may find unwarranted, excessive or otherwise improper. Had plaintiff made such objections here, the trial court would have been required to examine the items challenged.

If directors of a corporation may not in good faith incur reasonable and proper expenses in soliciting proxies in these days of giant corporations with vast numbers of stockholders, the corporate business might be seriously interfered with because of stockholder indifference and the difficulty of procuring a quorum, where there is no contest. In the event of a proxy contest, if the directors may not freely answer the challenges of outside groups and in good faith defend their actions with respect to corporate policy for the information of the stockholders, they and the corporation may be at the mercy of persons seeking to wrest control for their own purposes, so long as such persons have ample funds to conduct a proxy contest. The test is clear. When the directors act in good faith in a contest over policy, they have the right to incur reasonable and proper expenses for solicitation of proxies and in defense of their corporate policies, and are not obliged to sit idly by. The courts are entirely competent to pass upon their *bona fides* in any given case, as well as the nature of their expenditures when duly challenged.

It is also our view that the members of the so-called new group could be reimbursed by the corporation for their expenditures in this contest by affirmative vote of the stockholders. With regard to these ultimately successful contestants, as the Appellate Division below has noted, there was, of course, "no duty ... to set forth the facts, with corresponding obligation of the corporation to pay for such expense". However, where a majority of the stockholders chose—in this case by a vote of 16 to 1—to reimburse the successful contestants for achieving the very end sought and voted for by them as owners of the corporation, we see no reason to deny the effect of their ratification nor to hold the corporate body powerless to determine how its own moneys shall be spent.

The rule then which we adopt is simply this: In a contest over policy, as compared to a purely personal power contest, corporate directors have the right to make reasonable and proper expenditures, subject to the scrutiny of the courts when duly challenged, from the corporate treasury for the purpose of persuading the stockholders of the correctness of their position and soliciting their support for policies which the directors believe, in all good faith, are in the best interests of the corporation. The stockholders, moreover, have the right to reimburse successful contestants for the reasonable and bona fide expenses incurred by them in any such policy contest, subject to like court scrutiny. That is not to say, however, that corporate directors can, under any circumstances, disport themselves in a proxy contest with the corporation's moneys to an unlimited extent. Where it is established that such moneys have been spent for personal power, individual gain or private advantage, and not in the belief that such expenditures are in the best interests of the stockholders and the corporation, or where the fairness and reasonableness of the amounts allegedly expended are duly and successfully challenged, the courts will not hesitate to disallow them.

The judgment of the Appellate Division should be affirmed, without costs.

DESMOND, Judge (concurring). We granted leave to appeal in an effort to pass, and in the expectation of passing, on this question, highly important in modern-day corporation law: is it lawful for a corporation, on consent of a majority of its stockholders, to pay, out of its funds, the expenses of a "proxy fight", incurred by competing candidates for election as directors? Now that the appeal has been argued, I doubt that the question is presented by this record. The defendants served were Allis who was on the old board but was reelected to the new board, McComas and Wilson, defeated members of the old board, and Fairchild, leader of the victorious group and largest stockholder in the corporation. The expenses of the old board, or management group, in the proxy fight, were about $134,000, and those of the victorious Fairchild group amounted to about $127,500. In the end, the corporation paid both those sums, and it is for the reimbursement thereof, to the corporation, that this stockholder's derivative action is brought. Of the proxy fight expenses of the management slate, about $106,-000 was paid out on authorization of the old board while the old directors were still in office. The balance of those charges, as well as the whole of the expenses of the new and successful ... Fairchild group, was paid by the corporation after the new directors had taken over and after a majority of stockholders had approved such expenditures. The election had been fought out on a number of issues, chief of which concerned a contract which Ward (a defendant not served), who was a director and the principal executive officer of the company, had obtained from the corporation, covering compensation for, and other conditions of, his own services. Each side, in the campaign for proxies, charged the other with seeking to perpetuate, or grasp, control of the corporation. The Fairchild group won the election by a stock vote of about two-to-one, and obtained, at the next annual stockholders' meeting and by a much larger vote, authorization to make the payments above described.

Plaintiff asserts that it was illegal for the directors (unless by unanimous consent of stockholders) to expend corporate moneys in the proxy contest beyond the amounts necessary to give to stockholders bare notice of the meeting and of the matters to be voted on thereat. Defendants say that the proxy contest revolved around disputes over corporate policies and that it was, accordingly, proper not only to assess against the corporation the expense of serving formal notices and of routine proxy solicitation, but to go further and spend corporate moneys, on behalf of each group, thoroughly to inform the stockholders. The reason why that important question is, perhaps, not directly before us in this lawsuit is because, as the Appellate Division properly held, [284 App.Div. 201, 132 N.Y.S.2d 280] plaintiff failed "to urge liability as to specific expenditures". The cost of giving routinely necessary notice is, of course, chargeable to the corporation. It is just as clear, we think, that payment by a corporation of the expense of "proceedings by one faction in its contest with another for the control of the corporation" is *ultra vires,* and unlawful. Lawyers' Advertising Co. v. Consolidated Ry., Lighting & Refrigerating Co., 187 N.Y. 395, 399, 80 N.E. 199, 200. Approval by directors or by a majority stock vote could not validate such gratuitous expenditures. Continental Securities Co. v. Belmont, 206 N.Y. 7, 99 N.E. 138, 51 L.R.A.,N.S., 112.

Some of the payments attacked in this suit were, on their face, for lawful purposes and apparently reasonable in amount but, as to others, the record simply does not contain evidentiary bases for a determination as to either lawfulness or reasonableness. Surely, the burden was on plaintiff to go forward to some extent with such particularization and proof. It failed to do so, and so failed to make out a prima facie case.

We are, therefore, reaching the same result as did the Appellate Division but on one only of the grounds listed by that court, that is, failure of proof. We think it not inappropriate, however, to state our general views on the question of law principally argued by the parties, that is, as to the validity of corporate payments for proxy solicitations and similar activities in addition to giving notice of the meeting, and of the questions to be voted on. For an answer to that problem we could not do better than quote from this court's opinion in the Lawyers' Advertising Co. case, 187 N.Y. 395, 399, 80 N.E. 199, 200, supra: "The remaining notices were not legally authorized and were not legitimately incidental to the meeting or necessary for the protection of the stockholders. They rather were proceedings by one faction in its contest with another for the control of the corporation, and the expense thereof, as such, is not properly chargeable to the latter. This is so apparent as to the last two notices that nothing need be said in reference to them; but a few words may be said in regard to the first one, calling for proxies. It is to be noted that this is not the case of an ordinary circular letter sent out with and requesting the execution of proxies. The custom has become common upon the part of corporations to mail proxies to their respective stockholders, often accompanied by a brief circular of directions, and such custom when accompanied by no unreasonable expenditure, is not without merit in so far as it encourages voting by stockholders, through making it convenient and ready at hand. The notice in question, however, was not published until after proxies had been sent out. It simply amounted to an urgent solicitation that these proxies should be executed and returned for use by one faction in its contest, and we think there is no authority for imposing the expense of its publication upon the company. . . . it would be altogether too dangerous a rule to permit directors in control of a corporation and engaged in a contest for the perpetuation of their offices and control, to impose upon the corporation the unusual expense of publishing advertisements or, by analogy, of dispatching special messengers for the purpose of procuring proxies in their behalf."

A final comment: since expenditures which do not meet that test of propriety are intrinsically unlawful, it could not be any answer to such a claim as plaintiff makes here that the stockholder vote which purported to authorize them was heavy or that the change in management turned out to be beneficial to the corporation.

The judgment should be affirmed, without costs.

VAN VOORHIS, Judge (dissenting). The decision of this appeal is of far-reaching importance insofar as concerns payment by corporations of campaign expenses by stockholders in proxy contests for control. This is a stockholder's derivative action to require directors to restore to a corporation moneys paid to defray expenses of this nature, incurred both by an incumbent faction and by an insurgent faction of stockholders. The insurgents prevailed at the annual meeting, and payments of their own campaign expenses were attempted to be ratified by majority vote. It was a large majority, but the stockholders were not unanimous. Regardless of the merits of this contest, we are called upon to decide whether it was a corporate purpose (1) to make the expenditures which were disbursed by the incumbent or management group in defense of their acts and to remain in control of the corporation, and (2) to defray expenditures made by the insurgent group, which succeeded in convincing a majority of the stockholders. The Appellate Division held that stockholder authorization or ratification was not necessary to reasonable expenditures by the management group, the purpose of which was to inform the stockholders concerning the affairs of the corporation, and that, although these incumbents spent or incurred obligations of $133,966 (the previous expenses of annual meetings of this corporation ranging between $7,000 and $28,000), plaintiff must fail for having omitted to distinguish item by item between which of these expenditures were warranted and which ones were not; and the Appellate Division held that the insurgents also should be reimbursed, but subject to the qualification that "The expenses of those who were seeking to displace the management should not be reimbursed by the corporation except upon approval by the stockholders." It was held that the stockholders had approved.

No resolution was passed by the stockholders approving payment to the management group. It has been recognized that not all of the $133,966 in obligations paid or incurred by the management group was designed merely for information of stockholders. This outlay included payment for all of the activities of a strenuous campaign to persuade and cajole in a hard-fought contest for control of this corporation. It included, for example, expenses for entertainment, chartered airplanes and limousines, public relations counsel and proxy solicitors. However legitimate such measures may be on behalf of stockholders themselves in such a controversy, most of them do not pertain to a corporate function but are part of the familiar apparatus of aggressive factions in corporate contests. In Lawyers' Advertising Co. v. Consolidated Ry., Lighting & Refrigerating Co., 187 N.Y. 395, 399, 80 N.E. 199, 201, this court said: "This notice in question, however, was not published until after proxies had been sent out. It simply amounted to an urgent solicitation that these proxies should be executed and returned for use by one faction in its contest, and we think there is no authority for imposing the expense of its publication upon the company. It may be conceded that the directors who caused this publication acted in good faith, and felt that they were serving the best interests of the stockholders; but it would be altogether too dangerous a rule to permit directors in control of a corporation and engaged in a contest for the perpetuation of their offices and control, to impose upon the corporation the unusual expense of publishing advertisements, or, by analogy, of dispatching special messengers for the purpose of procuring proxies in their behalf."

The Appellate Division acknowledged in the instant case that "It is obvious that the management group here incurred a substantial amount of needless expense which was charged to the corporation," but this conclusion should have led to a direction that those defendants who were incumbent directors should be required to come forward with an explanation of their expenditures under the familiar rule that where it has been established that directors have expended corporate money for their own purposes, the burden of going forward with evidence of the propriety and reasonableness of specific items rests upon the directors.... The complaint should not have been dismissed as against incumbent directors due to failure of plaintiff to segregate the specific expenditures which are *ultra vires,* but, once plaintiff had proved facts from which an inference of impropriety might be drawn, the duty of making an explanation was laid upon the directors to explain and justify their conduct.

The second ground assigned by the Appellate Division for dismissing the complaint against incumbent directors is stockholder ratification of reimbursement to the insurgent group. Whatever effect or lack of it this resolution had upon expenditures by the insurgent group, clearly the stockholders who voted to pay the insurgents entertained no intention of reimbursing the management group for their expenditures. The insurgent group succeeded as a result of arousing the indignation of these very stockholders against the management group; nothing in the resolution to pay the expenses of the insurgent group purported to authorize or ratify payment of the campaign expenses of their adversaries, and certainly no inference should be drawn that the stockholders who voted to pay the insurgents intended that the incumbent group should also be paid. Upon the contrary, they were removing the incumbents from control mainly for the reason that they were charged with having mulcted the corporation by a long-term salary and pension contract to one of their number, J. Carlton Ward, Jr. If these stockholders had been presented with a resolution to pay the expenses of that group, it would almost certainly have been voted down. The stockholders should not be deemed to have authorized or ratified reimbursement of the incumbents.

There is no doubt that the management was entitled and under a duty to take reasonable steps to acquaint the stockholders with essential facts concerning the management of the corporation, and it may well be that the existence of a contest warranted them in circularizing the stockholders with more than ordinarily detailed information....

What expenses of the incumbent group should be allowed and what should be disallowed should be remitted to the trial court to ascertain, after taking evidence, in accordance with the rule that the incumbent directors were required to assume the burden of going forward in the first instance with evidence explaining and justifying their expenditures. Only such as were reasonably related to informing the stockholders fully and fairly concerning the corporate affairs should be allowed. The concession by plaintiff that such expenditures as were made were reasonable in amount does not decide this question. By way of illustration, the costs of entertainment for stockholders may have been, and it is stipulated that they were, at the going rates for providing similar entertainment. That does not signify that entertaining stockholders is reasonably related to the purposes of the corporation. The Appellate Division, as above stated, found that the management group incurred a substantial amount of needless expense. That fact being established, it became the duty of the incumbent directors to unravel and explain these payments.

Regarding the $127,556 paid by the new management to the insurgent group for their campaign expenditures, the question immediately arises whether that was for a corporate purpose. . . .

In considering this issue, as in the case of the expenses of the incumbents, we begin with the proposition that this court has already held that it is beyond the power of a corporation to authorize the expenditure of mere campaign expenses in a proxy contest. Lawyers' Advertising Co. v. Consolidated Ry., Lighting & Refrigerating Co., supra. . . .

. . . The case most frequently cited and principally relied upon from among [the] Delaware decisions is Hall v. Trans–Lux Daylight Picture Screen Corp. [20 Del.Ch. 78]. There the English case was followed of Peel v. London & North Western Ry. Co. . . . which distinguished between expenses merely for the purpose of maintaining control, and contests over policy questions of the corporation. In the Hall case the issues concerned a proposed merger, and a proposed sale of stock of a subsidiary corporation. These were held to be policy questions, and payment of the management campaign expenses was upheld.

In our view, the impracticability [of distinguishing between expenses incurred merely for the purpose of maintaining control, and expenses in contests over policy questions] is illustrated by the statement in the Hall case, supra, 20 Del.Ch. at page 85, 171 A. at page 229, that "It is impossible in many cases of intracorporate contests over directors, to sever questions of policy from those of persons". This circumstance is stressed in Judge Rifkind's opinion in [Steinberg v. Adams, 90 F.Supp. 604] at page 608: "The simple fact, of course, is that generally policy and personnel do not exist in separate compartments. A change in personnel is sometimes indispensable to a change of policy. A new board may be the symbol of the shift in policy as well as the means of obtaining it."

That may be all very well, but the upshot of this reasoning is that inasmuch as it is generally impossible to distinguish whether "policy" or "personnel" is the dominant factor, any averments must be accepted at their face value that questions of policy are dominant. Nowhere do these opinions mention that the converse is equally true and more pervasive, that neither the "ins" nor the "outs" ever say that they have no program to offer to the shareholders, but just want to acquire or to retain control, as the case may be. In common experience, this distinction is unreal. It was not mentioned by this court in Lawyers' Advertising Co. v. Consolidated Ry., Lighting & Refrigerating Co., supra. As in political contests, aspirations for control are invariably presented under the guise of policy or principle. . . .

The main question of "policy" in the instant corporate election, as is stated in the opinions below and frankly admitted, concerns the long-term contract with pension rights of a former officer and director, Mr. J. Carlton Ward, Jr. The insurgents' chief claim of benefit to the corporation from their victory consists in the termination of that agreement, resulting in an alleged actuarial saving of $350,000 to $825,000 to the corporation, and the reduction of other salaries and rent by more than $300,000 per year. The insurgents had contended in the proxy contest that these payments should be substantially reduced so that members of the incumbent group would not continue to profit personally at the expense of the corporation. If these charges were true, which appear to have been believed by a majority of the shareholders, then the disbursements by the management group in the proxy contest fall under the condemnation of the English and the Delaware rule.

These circumstances are mentioned primarily to illustrate how impossible it is to distinguish between "policy" and "personnel", as Judge Rifkind expressed it, but they also indicate that personal factors are deeply rooted in this contest. That is certainly true insofar as the former management group is concerned. . . .

Some expenditures may concededly be made by a corporation represented by its management so as to inform the stockholders, but there is a clear distinction between such expenditures by management and by mere groups of stockholders. The latter are under no legal obligation to assume duties of managing the corporation. They may endeavor to supersede the management for any reason, regardless of whether it be advantageous or detrimental to the corporation but, if they succeed, that is not a determination that the company was previously mismanaged or that it may not be mismanaged in the future. A change in control is in no sense analogous to an adjudication that the former directors have been guilty of misconduct. The analogy of allowing expenses of suit to minority stockholders who have been successful in a derivative action based on misconduct of officers or directors, is entirely without foundation.

Insofar as a management group is concerned, it may charge the corporation with any expenses within reasonable limits incurred in giving widespread notice to stockholders of questions affecting the welfare of the corporation.   Lawyers' Advertising Co. v. Consolidated Ry., Lighting & Refrigerating Co., supra.   Expenditures in excess of these limits are *ultra vires.*   The corporation lacks power to defray them.   The corporation lacks power to defray the expenses of the insurgents in their entirety.   The insurgents were not charged with responsibility for operating the company.   No appellate court case is cited from any jurisdiction holding otherwise.   No contention is made that such disbursements could be made, in any event, without stockholder ratification; they could not be ratified except by unanimous vote if they were *ultra vires.*   The insurgents, in this instance, repeatedly announced to the stockholders in their campaign literature that their proxy contest was being waged at their own personal expense.   If reimbursement of such items were permitted upon majority stockholder ratification, no court or other tribunal could pass upon which types of expenditures were "needless", to employ the characterization of the Appellate Division in this case.   Whether the insurgents should be paid would be made to depend upon whether they win the stockholders election and obtain control of the corporation.   It would be entirely irrelevant whether the corporation is "benefitted" by their efforts or by the outcome of such an election.   The courts could not indulge in a speculative inquiry into that issue.   That would truly be a matter of business judgment.   In some instances corporations are better governed by the existing management and in others by some other group which supersedes the existing management.   Courts of law have no jurisdiction to decide such questions, and successful insurgent stockholders may confidently be relied upon to reimburse themselves whatever may be the real merits of the controversy.   The losers in a proxy fight may understand the interests of the corporation more accurately than their successful adversaries, and agitation of this character may ultimately result in corporate advantage even if there be no change in management.   Nevertheless, under the judgment which is appealed from, success in a proxy contest is the indispensable condition upon which reimbursement of the insurgents depends.   Adventurers are not infrequent who are ready to take advantage of economic recessions, reduction of dividends or failure to increase them, or other sources of stockholder discontent to wage contests in order to obtain control of well-managed corporations, so as to divert their funds through legal channels into other corporations in which they may be interested, or to discharge former officers and employees to make room for favored newcomers according to the fashion of political patronage, or for other objectives that are unrelated to the sound prosperity of the enterprise.   The way is open and will be kept open for stockholders and groups of stockholders to contest corporate elections, but if the promoters of such movements choose to employ the costly modern media of mass persuasion, they should look for reimbursement to themselves and to the stockholders who are aligned with them.   If the law be that they can be recompensed by the corporation in case of success, and only in that event, it will operate as a powerful incentive to persons accustomed to taking calculated risks to increase this form of high-powered salesmanship to such a degree that, action provoking reaction, stockholders' meetings will be very costly. To the financial advantages promised by control of a prosperous corporation, would be added the knowledge that the winner takes all insofar as the campaign expenses are concerned. To the victor, indeed, would belong the spoils.

The questions involved in this case assume mounting importance as the capital stock of corporations becomes more widely distributed. To an enlarged extent the campaign methods consequently come more to resemble those of political campaigns, but, as in the latter, campaign expenses should be borne by those who are waging the campaign and their followers, instead of being met out of the corporate or the public treasury. Especially is this true when campaign promises have been made that the expenses would not be charged to the corporation. . . .

The judgment appealed from should be reversed so as to direct respondent Fairchild to pay to the corporation the sum of $118,-448.78, with appropriate interest, representing the moneys reimbursed to him by the corporation and, upon his default, the respondent, Allis should be required to pay said sum; respondents Fairchild and Allis should be required to pay to the corporation the sum of $9,107.10, with appropriate interest, representing the amount reimbursed to L.M. Bolton by the corporation; and an interlocutory judgment should be entered for an accounting to determine what part of the $133,966, representing expenses incurred by the old board, was improperly charged to the corporation and requiring the respondents Wilson and McComas to pay to the corporation the sum thereof, and the respondents Allis and Fairchild such amounts thereof as were paid out after July 15, 1949, with costs of the action to the plaintiff in all courts.

CONWAY, C.J., and BURKE, J., concur with FROESSEL, J.; DESMOND, J., concurs in part in a separate opinion; VAN VOORHIS, J., dissents in an opinion in which DYE and FULD, JJ., concur.

Judgment affirmed.

J. HEARD & H. SHERMAN
CONFLICTS OF INTEREST IN THE PROXY
VOTING SYSTEM 84–85
(1987).

Very few contested elections are run without the aid of professional proxy solicitors. Because of their experience and personal contacts in the investment community and at proxy departments of brokerage houses and banks, professional solicitors usually are able to generate a higher vote turnout than issuer companies can do by themselves. For this reason, both management and the dissident side usually engage their own solicitors during contested elections. Even for uncontested elections, companies that are worried about not reaching a quorum count employ the services of a solicitor to guarantee a high turnout. Companies also use solicitors when they expect significant opposition to uncontested management proposals, such as antitakeover charter amendments or defensive recapitalizations.

The leading proxy solicitation firms include Georgeson and Co., the Carter Organization, D.F. King and Co., Morrow and Co. and the Kissel–Blake Organization.

By virtue of their years of experience in the business, solicitors often know how a particular shareholder, or a particular type of shareholder, will vote on different issues. For this reason, firms trying to pass proposals that they fear will be met with strong opposition often engage solicitors to determine whether or not the proposal should even be included on the ballot. For example, Georgeson and Co. prepares a best case/worst case voting scenario for clients on various types of proposals. If the likely outcome seems to be a defeat for management, based on Georgeson's analysis, the issuer company will often decide to exclude the proposal from its ballot. John Wilcox, a principal at Georgeson, told IRRC that this explains why so few antitakeover proposals are defeated. According to Wilcox, most antitakeover proposals that are likely to be defeated, based on Georgeson's or another solicitor's analysis, are never put on a ballot in the first place.

When engaged by management or a dissident during a contested election, a solicitor's services are invaluable. The solicitor handles all the physical requirements of the proxy campaign. It identifies beneficial owners, mails the proxy material to recordholders, makes sure that beneficial owners have received proxy material from the recordholder bank or broker, rounds up late votes with phone calls or follow-up mailings, and tabulates the vote for management or the dissident.

The first of these functions, identifying beneficial owners, is among the most important services a solicitor can offer. . . . [R]egistration in bank nominee name often enables a beneficial owner to hide its identity and security position from the issuer company. When votes come in to a solicitor from a bank client, the proxy is signed by the bank, and the owner is identified only by an account number assigned to the client by his bank. The owner's name does not appear on the proxy card. When such votes are cast against management or a dissident, the interested party has no way of knowing who is behind the shares being voted against him. But proxy solicitors have developed their own data bases over the years that match bank account numbers with the identity of their owners. This enables a solicitor to tell a client who is behind the bank votes being cast during the proxy campaign. When the proxy vote is going against the solicitor's client, this ability becomes very important, for it allows the solicitor or the solicitor's client to contact the shareowner and ask him to reconsider his vote.

During a proxy campaign, a solicitor keeps in close contact with the proxy clerks at brokerage firms and with appropriate bank officers to make sure that their client's proxy material is being forwarded to beneficial owners. A solicitor can therefore decide if a second mailing is necessary. Such contact also enables a solicitor to tell his client how the vote is progressing, since brokers and banks usually tally votes as they are received but wait until shortly before a meeting to submit their proxies. If a solicitor determines that the final voting results may go against its client, advance information gives the solicitor's client time to exert more pressure on important shareholders to influence their vote, to resolicit shareholders who may have voted against the client, or to redouble efforts to reach shareholders who have not responded.

When final proxies arrive, the solicitor checks them to make sure that they are valid proxies, that they have been signed correctly, that they represent the appropriate number of shares, and that they are not duplicate or replacement proxies. Once done, the solicitor usually also participates in the actual tabulation at the annual meeting. The solicitor's experience can save a company much time when counting the vote, since the solicitor knows which way of sorting and collating the proxies will be the most expedient. When proxy votes are challenged by the opposing side in a proxy contest, the solicitor's knowledge of the technical requirements of valid proxies can prove invaluable....

———

WARREN & ABRAMS, EVOLVING STANDARDS OF JUDICIAL REVIEW OF PROCEDURAL DEFENSES IN PROXY CONTESTS, 47 Bus.Law. 647, 648 n. 9 (1992). "According to a report commissioned by the Business Roundtable and prepared by Georgeson & Company, Inc., 41 proxy contests were conducted in 1989 (the highest number ever recorded), 35 proxy contests were conducted in 1990, and 20 proxy contests had been announced through June 1, 1991.... [I]ncumbents prevailed in 40% of the election contests for corporate control, dissidents won 28% of such elections, dissidents acquired control through negotiated settlements or related developments in 7% of the control contests, and dissidents obtained minority representation in 16% of the control contests.... In addition, Georgeson found that, based on the same sample of contests for corporate control, the company was sold in 16% of the contests, the company was restructured in 5% of the contests, and the dissidents achieved other concessions in 3% of the contests. The Georgeson study concluded that, considering 'contests in which challengers won the vote, together with negotiated settlements during or after the contest and other developments within one year, challengers achieved significant advances toward their objectives or gained other benefits for themselves and other shareholders in 80% of all control contests.'   ..."

———

INSTITUTIONAL SHAREHOLDER SERVICES, THE 1994 PROXY SEASON 21 (1994).   "Proxy contests and consent solicitation activity remained relatively light in 1994 for the third consecutive year.   Of the 6,500 domestic companies that ISS covered from November 1993 through the end of the 1994 proxy season, only eight were the subject of contested solicitations where control of the board was directly or indirectly challenged.   The small number of contests is somewhat of a mystery, because dissident shareholders have had two full proxy seasons to devise strategies to exploit the SEC's new shareholder communications rules, which make solicitations easier for dissidents in some circumstances.   However, some speculate that the same environment of unfettered communications compels managements to respond to shareholder concerns before an eruption occurs.   An alternative explanation is that companies have adequately protected themselves against contests by staggering boards and adopting other entrenchment devices that make the ousting of a standing board more difficult."

———

Chapter VI

THE SPECIAL PROBLEMS OF CLOSE CORPORATIONS

SECTION 1. INTRODUCTION

(a) A BRIEF LOOK BACK AT PARTNERSHIP

NOTE ON PARTNERSHIP LAW AND CORPORATE LAW

The title of this chapter refers to "close corporations." Exactly what constitutes a close corporation is often a matter of theoretical dispute. Some authorities emphasize the number of shareholders, some the presence of owner-management, some the lack of a market for the corporation's stock, and some the existence of formal restrictions on the transferability of the corporation's shares. For present purposes, a close corporation can be regarded as one whose shares are held by a relatively small number of persons: given that element, the remaining incidents normally follow. Viewed from this perspective, the close corporation resembles the partnership, which is also typically characterized by a small number of owners, as well as owner-management and nontransferability of ownership interests. Indeed, certain aspects of partnership law form an important backdrop to the study of close corporations, not only because the practitioner must have some acquaintance with partnership law to render intelligent advice to clients who must decide between the two forms, but also because in recent years legislators and courts have increasingly looked to partnership-law norms in solving close-corporation-law problems.

The most striking aspect of partnership law is its heavily contractual nature. For many purposes, both the Uniform Partnership Act (the "UPA") and the Revised Uniform Partnership Act ("RUPA") operate only in the absence of an agreement by the partners on a given issue. The following is a highly generalized summary of the partnership-law rules most salient to the ongoing conduct of the firm:

(1) As concerns internal decisionmaking, partnership law is essentially *suppletory,* that is, both the UPA and RUPA impliedly validate whatever arrangements the partners make between them-

selves, and provides rules to govern only those situations that the owners' arrangements fail to cover. The two basic rules are:

(a) Absent contrary agreement, all partners have equal rights in the management and conduct of the partnership business. UPA § 18(e), RUPA § 401(F).

(b) Absent contrary agreement, differences among the partners "as to ordinary matters connected with the partnership business" are determined by a majority of the partners, but differences as to matters that are outside the scope of the partnership business, would be in conflict with the partnership agreement, or would make it impossible to carry on the ordinary business of the partnership, require unanimous consent. UPA §§ 9(3)(c), 18(h). (Under the counterpart provision of RUPA, § 401(h), differences arising as to a matter in the ordinary course of business are settled by a majority of the partners, but acts outside the ordinary course of business and amendments to partnership agreement require unanimous consent.)

(2) Any partner has power to bind the partnership on a matter in the ordinary course of business, even if he has no authority in fact by virtue of the partnership's internal arrangements, unless the third party with whom he deals knows that the partner has no authority in fact. UPA § 9(1); RUPA § 301.

(3) Absent contrary agreement, partnership profits are shared per capita, and no partner is entitled to a salary. UPA §§ 18(a), (f); RUPA §§ 401(b), (h).

(4) Absent contrary agreement, no person can become a member of a partnership without the consent of all the partners. UPA § 18(g); RUPA § 401(i).

(5) Partnerships are normally created for a limited term— frequently a relatively short term—and dissolution is easy. If the partnership is not for a specified term (express or implied) any partner may cause dissolution at any time. If the partnership is for a specified term, dissolution occurs at the end of the term or on the death or incapacity of any partner, and may also be caused by any partner during the term, although in that case the dissolving partner will have acted wrongfully and will be liable to the remaining partners in damages. See Chapter 2, Sections 8, 9.

(6) Partners stand in a fiduciary relationship to each other. See, e.g., Meinhard v. Salmon, 249 N.Y. 458, 164 N.E. 545 (1928).

(7) The Internal Revenue Code generally taxes a partnership's profits and losses to the individual partners, rather than to the partnership.

Although it is often said that a close corporation is an "incorporated partnership," it will readily be seen that ordinary corporation-law norms are diametrically opposed to almost every one of these partnership-law rules:

(1) As to many aspects of internal decisionmaking, traditional corporate statutes are *regulatory* rather than suppletory. For example, under traditional corporate-law norms, shareholders, as such, have no right to participate in the management of the corporation's business.

(2) Because shareholders as such have no right to participate in the management of the corporation's business, they also have no apparent authority to bind the corporation.

(3) Corporate profits are not shared except to the extent dividends are declared, and at that point are not shared per capita, but in proportion to stock ownership.

(4) Absent contrary agreement, shares of stock—and the shareholder status they carry—are freely transferable.

(5) Corporations are normally created for a perpetual term, and dissolution is relatively difficult.

(6) The traditional view (now changing in certain important respects) was that, shareholders do not stand in a direct fiduciary relationship to each other.

(7) The Internal Revenue Code generally taxes profits and losses to the corporation, rather than to the individual shareholders.

These norms were essentially designed with an eye to the publicly held corporation, and as will be seen, their application to close corporations often leads to the frustration of legitimate expectations.

(b) AN INTRODUCTION TO THE CLOSE CORPORATION

DONAHUE v. RODD ELECTROTYPE CO.

Supreme Judicial Court of Massachusetts, 1975.
367 Mass. 578, 328 N.E.2d 505.

TAURO, Chief Justice.

The plaintiff, Euphemia Donahue, a minority stockholder in the Rodd Electrotype Company of New England, Inc. (Rodd Electrotype), a Massachusetts corporation, brings this suit against the directors of Rodd Electrotype, Charles H. Rodd, Frederick I. Rodd and Mr. Harold E. Magnuson, against Harry C. Rodd, a former director, officer, and controlling stockholder of Rodd Electrotype and against Rodd Electrotype (hereinafter called defendants). The plaintiff seeks to rescind Rodd Electrotype's purchase of Harry Rodd's shares in Rodd Electrotype and to compel Harry Rodd "to repay to the corporation the purchase price of said shares, $36,000, together with interest from the date of purchase." The plaintiff alleges that the defendants caused the corporation to purchase the shares in violation of their fiduciary duty to her, a minority stockholder of Rodd Electrotype.[4]

The trial judge, after hearing oral testimony, dismissed the plaintiff's bill on the merits. He found that the purchase was without prejudice to the plaintiff and implicitly found that the transaction had been carried out in good faith and with inherent fairness. The Appeals Court affirmed with costs. Donahue v. Rodd Electrotype Co. of New England, Inc., 1 Mass.App. 876, 307 N.E.2d 8 (1974). The case is before us on the plaintiff's application for further appellate review. . . .

[Briefly, the facts were as follows: In the mid–1930's Harry Rodd and Joseph Donahue had become employees of Royal Electrotype (the predecessor of Rodd Electrotype). Donahue's duties were confined to operational matters within the plants, and he never participated in the management aspect of the business. In contrast, Rodd's advancement within the company was rapid, and in 1946 he became general manager and treasurer. Subsequently Rodd acquired 200 of the corporation's 1000 shares and Donahue (at Rodd's suggestion) acquired 50 shares. In 1955 Rodd became president and general manager, and later that year Royal itself purchased the remaining 750 shares, so that Rodd and Donahue became Royal's sole shareholders, owning 80% and 20% of its stock, respectively. In 1960 the corporation was renamed Rodd Electrotype, and in the early 60's Harry Rodd's two sons, Charles and Frederick, took important positions with the company. In 1965 Charles succeeded his father as president and general manager.

In 1970 Harry Rodd was seventy-seven years old and not in good health, and his sons wished him to retire. Prior to 1967 Harry had distributed 117 of his 200 shares equally among his sons and his daughter, and had returned 2 shares to the corporate treasury. Harry insisted that as a condition to his retirement some financial arrangement be made with respect to his remaining 81 shares. Accordingly, Charles, acting on the corporation's behalf, negotiated for the purchase of 45 of Harry's shares for $800/share—a price which, Charles testified, reflected book and liquidating value. At a special board meeting in July 1970, the corporation's board (then consisting of Charles and Frederick Rodd and a lawyer) voted to have the corporation make the purchase at this price. Subsequently Harry Rodd sold 2 shares to each of his three children at $800/share, and gave each child 10 shares as a gift.[7] Meanwhile Donahue

---

4. In form, the plaintiff's bill of complaint presents, at least in part, a derivative action, brought on behalf of the corporation, and, in the words of the bill, "on behalf of . . . [the] stockholders" of Rodd Electrotype. Yet . . . the plaintiff's bill, in substance, was one seeking redress because of alleged breaches of the fiduciary duty owed *to her,* a minority stockholder, by the controlling stockholders.

We treat the bill of complaint (as have the parties) as presenting a proper cause of suit in the personal right of the plaintiff. . . .

7. An inference is permissible that the "gift" of these shares was a part of the "deal" for the stock purchase.

had died and his 50 shares had passed to his wife and son. When the Donahues learned that the corporation had purchased Harry Rodd's shares, they offered their shares to the corporation on the terms given to Harry but the offer was rejected.[10] This suit followed.]

In her argument before this court, the plaintiff has characterized the corporate purchase of Harry Rodd's shares as an unlawful distribution of corporate assets to controlling stockholders. She urges that the distribution constitutes a breach of the fiduciary duty owed by the Rodds, as controlling stockholders, to her, a minority stockholder in the enterprise, because the Rodds failed to accord her an equal opportunity to sell her shares to the corporation. The defendants reply that the stock purchase was within the powers of the corporation and met the requirements of good faith and inherent fairness imposed on a fiduciary in his dealings with the corporation. They assert that there is no right to equal opportunity in corporate stock purchases for the corporate treasury. For the reasons hereinafter noted, we agree with the plaintiff and reverse the decree of the Superior Court. However, we limit the applicability of our holding to "close corporations," as hereinafter defined. Whether the holding should apply to other corporations is left for decision in another case, on a proper record.

A. *Close Corporations.* In previous opinions, we have alluded to the distinctive nature of the close corporation . . . but have never defined precisely what is meant by a close corporation. There is no single, generally accepted definition. Some commentators emphasize an "integration of ownership and management" (Note, Statutory Assistance for Closely Held Corporations, 71 Harv.L.Rev. 1498 [1958]), in which the stockholders occupy most management positions. . . . Others focus on the number of stockholders and the nature of the market for the stock. In this view, close corporations have few stockholders; there is little market for corporate stock. The Supreme Court of Illinois adopted this latter view in Galler v. Galler, 32 Ill.2d 16, 203 N.E.2d 577 (1965). . . . We accept aspects of both definitions. We deem a close corporation to be typified by: (1) a small number of stockholders; (2) no ready market for the corporate stock; and (3) substantial majority stockholder participation in the management, direction and operations of the corporation.

As thus defined, the close corporation bears striking resemblance to a partnership. . . . Just as in a partnership, the relationship among the stockholders must be one of trust, confidence and absolute loyalty if the enterprise is to succeed. . . .

In Helms v. Duckworth, 101 U.S.App.D.C. 390, 249 F.2d 482 (1957) . . . Judge Burger, now Chief Justice Burger, writing for the court, emphasized the resemblance of the two-man close corpora-

---

10. Between 1965 and 1969, the company offered to purchase the Donahue shares for amounts between $2,000 and $10,000 ($40 to $200 a share). The Donahues rejected these offers.

tion to a partnership: "In an intimate business venture such as this, stockholders of a close corporation occupy a position similar to that of joint adventurers and partners. While courts have sometimes declared stockholders 'do not bear toward each other that same relation of trust and confidence which prevails in partnerships,' this view ignores the practical realities of the organization and functioning of a small 'two-man' corporation organized to carry on a small business enterprise in which the stockholders, directors, and managers are the same persons" (footnotes omitted). Id. at 486.

Although the corporate form provides ... advantages for the stockholders (limited liability, perpetuity, and so forth), it also supplies an opportunity for the majority stockholders to oppress or disadvantage minority stockholders. The minority is vulnerable to a variety of oppressive devices, termed "freeze-outs," which the majority may employ.... An authoritative study of such "freeze-outs" enumerates some of the possibilities: "The squeezers ... may refuse to declare dividends; they may drain off the corporation's earnings in the form of exorbitant salaries and bonuses to the majority shareholder-officers and perhaps to their relatives, or in the form of high rent by the corporation for property leased from majority shareholders ...; they may deprive minority shareholders of corporate offices and of employment by the company...."

The minority can, of course, initiate suit against the majority and their directors. Self-serving conduct by directors is proscribed by the director's fiduciary obligation to the corporation.... However, in practice, the plaintiff will find difficulty in challenging dividend or employment policies. Such policies are considered to be within the judgment of the directors ... [G]enerally, plaintiffs who seek judicial assistance against corporate dividend or employment policies do not prevail....

Thus, when these types of "freeze-outs" are attempted by the majority stockholders, the minority stockholders, cut off from all corporation-related revenues, must either suffer their losses or seek a buyer for their shares. Many minority stockholders will be unwilling or unable to wait for an alteration in majority policy. Typically, the minority stockholder in a close corporation has a substantial percentage of his personal assets invested in the corporation. The stockholder may have anticipated that his salary from his position with the corporation would be his livelihood. Thus, he cannot afford to wait passively. He must liquidate his investment in the close corporation in order to reinvest the funds in income-producing enterprises.

At this point, the true plight of the minority stockholder in a close corporation becomes manifest. He cannot easily reclaim his capital. In a large public corporation, the oppressed or dissident minority stockholder could sell his stock in order to extricate some of his invested capital. By definition, this market is not available for shares in the close corporation. In a partnership, a partner who feels abused by his fellow partners may cause dissolution by his

"express will ... at any time" ... and recover his share of partnership assets and accumulated profits.... By contrast, the stockholder in the close corporation or "incorporated partnership" may
achieve dissolution and recovery of his share of the enterprise assets
only by compliance with the rigorous terms of the applicable
chapter of the General Laws....

Thus, in a close corporation, the minority stockholders may be
trapped in a disadvantageous situation. No outsider would knowingly assume the position of the disadvantaged minority. The
outsider would have the same difficulties. To cut losses, the
minority stockholder may be compelled to deal with the majority.
This is the capstone of the majority plan. Majority "freeze-out"
schemes which withhold dividends are designed to compel the
minority to relinquish stock at inadequate prices.... When the
minority stockholder agrees to sell out at less than fair value, the
majority has won.

Because of the fundamental resemblance of the close corporation to the partnership, the trust and confidence which are essential
to this scale and manner of enterprise, and the inherent danger to
minority interests in the close corporation, we hold that stockholders [17] in the close corporation owe one another substantially the
same fiduciary duty in the operation of the enterprise [18] that partners owe to one another. In our previous decisions, we have
defined the standard of duty owed by partners to one another as the
"utmost good faith and loyalty." Cardullo v. Landau, 329 Mass. 5,
8, 105 N.E.2d 843 (1952); DeCotis v. D'Antona, 350 Mass. 165, 168,
214 N.E.2d 21 (1966). Stockholders in close corporations must
discharge their management and stockholder responsibilities in
conformity with this strict good faith standard. They may not act
out of avarice, expediency or self-interest in derogation of their duty
of loyalty to the other stockholders and to the corporation.

We contrast this strict good faith standard with the somewhat
less stringent standard of fiduciary duty to which directors and
stockholders of all corporations must adhere in the discharge of
their corporate responsibilities. Corporate directors are held to a
good faith and inherent fairness standard of conduct (Winchell v.
Plywood Corp., 324 Mass. 171, 177, 85 N.E.2d 313 [1949]) and are
not "permitted to serve two masters whose interests are antagonis-
tic." Spiegel v. Beacon Participations, Inc., 297 Mass. 398, 411, 8

---

17. We do not limit our holding to majority stockholders. In the close corporation, the minority may do equal damage
through unscrupulous and improper "sharp
dealings" with an unsuspecting majority.
See Helms v. Duckworth, 101 U.S.App.D.C.
390, 249 F.2d 482 (1957).

18. We stress that the strict fiduciary
duty which we apply to stockholders in a
close corporation in this opinion governs
only their actions relative to the operations
of the enterprise and the effects of that
operation on the rights and investments of

other stockholders. We express no opinion
as to the standard of duty applicable to
transactions in the shares of the close corporation when the corporation is not a party to the transaction. Cf. Andrews, The
Stockholder's Right to Equal Opportunity
in the Sale of Shares, 78 Harv.L.Rev. 505
(1965). Compare Perlman v. Feldmann,
219 F.2d 173 (2d Cir.), cert. den. 349 U.S.
952, 75 S.Ct. 880, 99 L.Ed. 1277 (1955) with
Zahn v. Transamerica Corp., 162 F.2d 36
(3d Cir.1947).

N.E.2d 895, 904 (1937). "Their paramount duty is to the corporation, and their personal pecuniary interests are subordinate to that duty." Durfee v. Durfee & Canning, Inc., 323 Mass. 187, 196, 80 N.E.2d 522, 527 (1948).

The more rigorous duty of partners and participants in a joint adventure, here extended to stockholders in a close corporation, was described by then Chief Judge Cardozo of the New York Court of Appeals in Meinhard v. Salmon, 249 N.Y. 458, 164 N.E. 545 (1928): "Joint adventurers, like co-partners, owe to one another, while the enterprise continues, the duty of the finest loyalty. Many forms of conduct permissible in a workaday world for those acting at arm's length, are forbidden to those bound by fiduciary ties. . . . Not honesty alone, but the punctilio of an honor the most sensitive, is then the standard of behavior." Id. at 463–464, 164 N.E. at 546. . . .

B. *Equal Opportunity in a Close Corporation.* Under settled Massachusetts law, a domestic corporation, unless forbidden by statute, has the power to purchase its own shares. . . . An agreement to reacquire stock "[is] enforceable, subject, at least, to the limitations that the purchase must be made in good faith and without prejudice to creditors and stockholders." . . . When the corporation reacquiring its own stock is a close corporation, the purchase is subject to the additional requirement, in the light of our holding in this opinion, that the stockholders, who, as directors or controlling stockholders, caused the corporation to enter into the stock purchase agreement, must have acted with the utmost good faith and loyalty to the other stockholders.

To meet this test, if the stockholder whose shares were purchased was a member of the controlling group, the controlling stockholders must cause the corporation to offer each stockholder an equal opportunity to sell a ratable number of his shares to the corporation at an identical price. Purchase by the corporation confers substantial benefits on the members of the controlling group whose shares were purchased. These benefits are not available to the minority stockholders if the corporation does not also offer them an opportunity to sell their shares. The controlling group may not, consistent with its strict duty to the minority, utilize its control of the corporation to obtain special advantages and disproportionate benefit from its share ownership. See Jones v. H.F. Ahmanson & Co., 1 Cal.3d 93, 108, 81 Cal.Rptr. 592, 460 P.2d 464 (1969); Note, 83 Harv.L.Rev. 1904, 1908 (1970). Cf. Brudney and Chirelstein, Fair Shares in Corporate Mergers and Takeovers, 88 Harv.L.Rev. 297, 334 (1974).

The benefits conferred by the purchase are twofold: (1) provision of a market for shares; (2) access to corporate assets for personal use. By definition, there is no ready market for shares of a close corporation. The purchase creates a market for shares which previously had been unmarketable. It transforms a previously illiquid investment into a liquid one. If the close corporation purchases shares only from a member of the controlling group, the controlling stockholder can convert his shares into cash at a time when none of the other stockholders can. Consistent with its strict fiduciary duty, the controlling group may not utilize its control of the corporation to establish an exclusive market in previously unmarketable shares from which the minority stockholders are excluded. See Jones v. H.F. Ahmanson & Co. . . .

The purchase also distributes corporate assets to the stockholder whose shares were purchased. Unless an equal opportunity is given to all stockholders, the purchase of shares from a member of the controlling group operates as a *preferential* distribution of assets. In exchange for his shares, he receives a percentage of the contributed capital and accumulated profits of the enterprise. The funds he so receives are available for his personal use. The other stockholders benefit from no such access to corporate property and cannot withdraw their shares of the corporate profits and capital in this manner unless the controlling group acquiesces. Although the purchase price for the controlling stockholder's shares may seem fair to the corporation and other stockholders under the tests established in the prior case law (see Spiegel v. Beacon Participations, Inc., 297 Mass. 398, 429, 8 N.E.2d 895 [1937]; Winchell v. Plywood Corp., 324 Mass. 171, 178, 85 N.E.2d 313 [1949]), the controlling stockholder whose stock has been purchased has still received a relative advantage over his fellow stockholders, inconsistent with his strict fiduciary duty—an opportunity to turn corporate funds to personal use.

The rule of equal opportunity in stock purchases by close corporations provides equal access to these benefits for all stockholders. We hold that, in any case in which the controlling stockholders have exercised their power over the corporation to deny the minority such equal opportunity, the minority shall be entitled to appropriate relief. To the extent that language in Spiegel v. Beacon Participations, Inc., 297 Mass. 398, 431, 8 N.E.2d 895 (1937), and other cases suggests that there is no requirement of equal opportunity for minority stockholders when a close corporation purchases shares from a controlling stockholder, it is not to be followed.

C. *Application of the Law to this Case.* We turn now to the application of the learning set forth above to the facts of the instant case.

The strict standard of duty is plainly applicable to the stockholders in Rodd Electrotype. Rodd Electrotype is a close corporation [under the test set out above] . . . .

. . . In testing the stock purchase from Harry Rodd against the applicable strict fiduciary standard, we treat the Rodd family as a single controlling group . . . . From the evidence, it is clear that the Rodd family was a close-knit one with strong community of interest . . . .

Moreover, a strong motive of interest requires that the Rodds be considered a controlling group. When Charles Rodd and Frederick Rodd were called on to represent the corporation in its dealings with their father, they must have known that further advancement within the corporation and benefits would follow their father's retirement and the purchase of his stock. . . .

On its face, then, the purchase of Harry Rodd's shares by the corporation is a breach of the duty which the controlling stockholders, the Rodds, owed to the minority stockholders, the plaintiff and her son. The purchaser distributed a portion of the corporate assets to Harry Rodd, a member of the controlling group, in exchange for his shares. The plaintiff and her son were not offered an equal opportunity to sell their shares to the corporation. In fact, their efforts to obtain an equal opportunity were rebuffed by the corporate representative. As the trial judge found, they did not, in any manner, ratify the transaction with Harry Rodd.

Because of the foregoing, we hold that the plaintiff is entitled to relief. Two forms of suitable relief are set out hereinafter. The judge below is to enter an appropriate judgment. The judgment may require Harry Rodd to remit $36,000 with interest at the legal rate from July 15, 1970, to Rodd Electrotype in exchange for forty-five shares of Rodd Electrotype treasury stock. This, in substance, is the specific relief requested in the plaintiff's bill of complaint. Interest is manifestly appropriate. A stockholder, who, in violation of his fiduciary duty to the other stockholders, has obtained assets from his corporation and has had those assets available for his own use, must pay for that use. See Silversmith v. Sydeman, 305 Mass. 65, 74, 25 N.E.2d 215 (1940). Cf. Spiegel v. Beacon Participations, Inc., 297 Mass. 398, 420, 8 N.E.2d 895 (1937). In the alternative, the judgment may require Rodd Electrotype to purchase all of the plaintiff's shares for $36,000 without interest. In the circumstances of this case, we view this as the equal opportunity which the plaintiff should have received. Harry Rodd's retention of thirty-six shares, which were to be sold and given to his children within a year of the Rodd Electrotype purchase, cannot disguise the fact that the corporation acquired one hundred per cent of that portion of his holdings (forty-five shares) which he did not intend his children to own. The plaintiff is entitled to have one hundred per cent of her forty-five shares similarly purchased.[30]

The final decree, in so far as it dismissed the bill as to Harry C. Rodd, Frederick I. Rodd, Charles H. Rodd, Mr. Harold E. Magnuson and Rodd Electrotype Company of New England, Inc., and awarded costs, is reversed. The case is remanded to the Superior Court for entry of judgment in conformity with this opinion.

30. If there has been a significant change in corporate circumstances since this case was argued, this is a matter which can be brought to the attention of the court below and may be considered by the judge

So ordered.*

WILKINS, Justice (concurring).

I agree with much of what the Chief Justice says in support of granting relief to the plaintiff. However, I do not join in any implication (see, e.g., footnote 18 and the associated text) that the rule concerning a close corporation's purchase of a controlling stockholder's shares applies to all operations of the corporation as they affect minority stockholders. That broader issue, which is apt to arise in connection with salaries and dividend policy, is not involved in this case. The analogy to partnerships may not be a complete one.

NOTE

One response to the kinds of problems described in Donahue v. Rodd Electrotype Co. is to plan around them, by making special arrangements designed to suit the needs of the parties. In a partnership, this would be a relatively simple matter: as regards internal arrangements, partnership law is highly contractual in nature—that is, it gives the parties wide scope to determine the rules by which their relationship will be governed. In contrast, corporation law has not in the past been as attuned to contractualization, and in the corporate context there has often been serious question whether such arrangements will be deemed valid. This remains a serious question; but as courts and legislatures have shown themselves increasingly ready to enforce internal arrangements, the close corporation has become increasingly contractual in nature, and eventually close corporation law may become as contractualized as partnership law.

The materials in Sections 2–5, infra, will be concerned to a large extent with the role of *planning* in the close corporation. Section 6 will then consider the remedies available when planning has been inadequate or the problems are of a kind that resist advance solution.

NOTE ON LEGISLATIVE STRATEGIES TOWARD THE CLOSE CORPORATION

As noted at the outset of this chapter, many of the problems raised by the early close-corporation case law reflects the fact that traditional statutory norms were drafted with publicly held corpora-

in granting appropriate relief in the form of a judgment.

* See also Comolli v. Comolli, 241 Ga. 471, 246 S.E.2d 278 (1978); cf. Schwartz v. Marien, 37 N.Y.2d 487, 335 N.E.2d 334, 373 N.Y.S.2d 122 (1975). For additional cases and materials on the fiduciary obligations of shareholders in close corporations, see Section 7(a), infra. (Footnote by ed.)

tions in mind. Accordingly, one of the major responses to these problems has been the enactment of new statutory provisions aimed primarily or exclusively at close corporations. The substantive content of such provisions will be considered throughout this chapter. The purpose of this Note is to lay the groundwork for that consideration by examining several different strategies, and clarifying the applicability of the principal statutes referred to in this chapter. The principal strategies to be examined are those exemplified by the California, Delaware, and New York statutes, and the Model Act. Almost all other close-corporation legislation either derives from or closely parallels one of these statutes.

(1) A Unified Strategy. One legislative strategy is to make no special provision for close corporations as such, but to modify traditional statutory norms so that they will meet the needs of close corporations, although applicable to publicly held corporations as well. This kind of "unified" approach was at one time a very common strategy, but the tide has turned against it.

(2) New York and the Model Act. A second strategy, exemplified by the New York statute, is to follow the unified approach up to a point, but to add one or two important provisions that are applicable only to those corporations with defined shareholding characteristics. Thus while N.Y.Bus.Corp.Law § 620(a) takes a unified approach by authorizing voting agreements in all corporations, N.Y.Bus.Corp.Law § 620(c) takes a definitional approach by authorizing certain kinds of certificate provisions "so long as no shares of the corporation are listed on a national securities exchange or regularly quoted in an over-the-counter market by one or more members of a national or affiliated securities association." Similarly, Model Act § 7.32 authorizes certain kinds of shareholder agreements in corporations that are not listed on a national securities exchange or traded in a market maintained by one or more members of a national securities association. (In 1982, the ABA's Committee on Corporate Laws approved a Model Statutory Close Corporation Supplement, which is, as the title indicates, a close corporation statute. However, as the title also indicates, this statute is not part of the Model Act itself, and has been adopted in very few states.) [1]

(3) Statutory Close Corporations—Delaware and California.

(a) Delaware. Like the New York statute, the Delaware statute follows the unified approach up to a point, through various provisions that modify traditional statutory norms so that they will meet the needs of close corporations, although applicable to publicly held corporations as well. Thus, Delaware provides considerable flexibility for close corporations even without special provisions applicable only to a limited class of corporations. The Delaware statute also contains, however, an integrated set of provisions,

---

1. For other provisions that authorize certain types of arrangements so long as the corporation's shares are not traded on a securities market, see Mich. § 450.1463; N.C. § 55–73(b); N.J. § 14A:5–21; S.C. § 33–11–220(b), (c).

Subchapter XIV (§§ 341–356), which are explicitly made applicable *only* to corporations that both qualify for and elect statutory close-corporation status. In effect, therefore, the statute contemplates a special subclass of close corporations, which may be called statutory close corporations. Under Del. Gen. Corp. Law § 342, a corporation can *qualify* for statutory close-corporation status if its certificate provides that:

> (1) All of the corporation's issued stock of all classes, exclusive of treasury shares, shall be represented by certificates and shall be held of record by not more than a specified number of persons, not exceeding 30; and

> (2) All of the issued stock of all classes shall be subject to 1 or more of the restrictions on transfer permitted by § 202 of this title; and

> (3) The corporation shall make no offering of any of its stock of any class which would constitute a "public offering" within the meaning of the United States Securities Act of 1933. . . .

Under § 343, a corporation that qualifies for statutory close-corporation status can *elect* such status by adopting a heading in its certificate that states the name of the corporation and the fact that it is a close corporation.[2]

Most of the substantive provisions of Del.Gen.Corp.Law Subchapter XIV are enabling—that is, most of the provisions do not regulate the conduct of the shareholders or managers of such corporations, but simply authorize shareholders in statutory close corporations to enter into arrangements that would otherwise be unenforceable or of doubtful validity. As will be seen below, Subchapter XIV provides enormous flexibility—so much so, that for a well-advised corporation that elects to qualify under this Subchapter, almost everything will turn on the lawyer's drafting, rather than on corporate law. At the same time, the remaining provisions of the Delaware statute are sufficiently flexible so that much the same may be true even for close corporations which do not qualify under Subchapter XIV.

(b) California. The California strategy is comparable to that of Delaware—that is, it involves a combination of (i) unified provisions that are particularly useful for close corporations but are not

---

2. Since the heading must be in the certificate, as a practical matter election of close-corporation status by an about-to-be organized corporation requires unanimous consent of all the organizers. However, where a corporation has already been organized as a nonelecting corporation, § 344 provides that it "may become a close corporation . . . by amending its certificate to conform to §§ 342 and 343 by a two-thirds class vote." Taken by itself, § 344 would therefore enable a two-thirds majority to adopt statutory close-corporation status over the objections of a one-third minority. Under § 342(2), however, a corporation cannot qualify unless all of its issued stock is subject to a transfer restriction authorized by § 202, and under § 202(b), no such restriction will bind securities issued prior to its adoption unless the holders of the securities assent. Arguably, the result is that unless the corporation has already adopted § 202(b) restrictions, a minority shareholder can block election of statutory close-corporation status by refusing to consent to the adoption of such restrictions.

restricted to such corporations, and (ii) a systematic set of provisions applicable only to statutory close corporations. In contrast to the Delaware legislation, however, California's statutory-close-corporation provisions are scattered throughout the statute, rather than integrated in a single subchapter. In addition, there are important definitional differences. California does not require the articles of a statutory close corporation to either restrict stock transfers or prohibit public offerings. Instead, the articles need only provide that all of the corporation's issued shares "shall be held of record by not more than a specified number of persons, not exceeding 35"; state that "This corporation is a close corporation"; and include the words "corporation," "incorporated," or "limited" in the corporate name. Cal. §§ 158(a), 202(a).[3] As in Delaware, most of the California statutory close corporation provisions are enabling rather than regulatory.

———

In considering the statutory provisions referred to throughout this chapter, it is important to keep in mind the following questions: (1) Is the provision applicable to all corporations or only to certain corporations? (2) If it is applicable only to certain corporations, what attributes must a corporation have to qualify under the provision? (3) Is the provision *regulatory* (one that governs corporate and shareholder conduct regardless of the parties' arrangements); *suppletory* (one that governs corporate or shareholder conduct unless the parties specifically make another arrangement); or *enabling* (one that serves principally to validate specific types of arrangements the parties may make)? (4) If the provision is *enabling,* what requirements must be met to adopt the arrangements it validates? (5) If the provision is applicable only to statutory close corporations, does it permit shareholders to accomplish objectives that could not be accomplished under the provisions of the statute applicable to all corporations?

———

NOTE ON CLOSE CORPORATION STATUTES

Modern statutes governing close corporations mark a considerable advance over close corporation law as it stood thirty or forty years ago. In general, however, the statutes still leave a lot to be desired.

The major problem can be simply stated: Most of the statutes are, for most purposes, applicable only to corporations that opt in, by an explicit election, for special statutory treatment. However, the data convincingly shows that only a tiny fraction of newly

---

3. Election of statutory close-corporation status requires a unanimous vote of   the outstanding shares.

formed corporations elect such treatment. See Blunk, Analyzing Texas Articles of Incorporation: Is the Statutory Close Corporation Format Viable, 34 Sw.L.J. 941 (1980); 1 F.H. O'Neal & R. Thompson, O'Neal's Close Corporations § 1.18 (3d ed. 1987). The number of previously existing corporations that make such an election is undoubtedly even smaller. The result is that for many practical purposes, these statutes are much ado about nothing. Most of the modern statutes continue to leave close corporations in the lurch in important ways.

How did the law get into such a situation? The legislatures may have adopted elective statutes on the premise that it is impossible to statutorily define the close corporation in a rigorous manner. However, such a definition is unnecessary. What the legislatures could do is draw a line, however arbitrary, based on number of shareholders—say, all corporations with ten shareholders or less—and adopt special provisions that are applicable to all corporations that fall under the line, subject, in most cases, to the corporation's right to opt out. In drawing that line, the legislature would not have to determine that all corporations with more shareholders should not receive special treatment. It would only say, "We know that all corporations that are under the line should receive special treatment; we will leave it to the courts to determine whether special treatment is available for other corporations." (Such an approach is reflected in some statutory provisions. For example, California makes special provision for dissolution in corporations with thirty-five or less shareholders. See Section 6, infra.) Special provisions that were available on an elective basis could stand side-by-side with this kind of legislation. In contrast, under the current regime, in which elective legislation constitutes the predominant statutory response, in most close corporations the shareholders must look to the courts, rather than the legislatures, for realistic rules to govern their enterprise and validate their self-government.

See Bradley, An Analysis of the Model Close Corporation Act and a Proposed Legislative Strategy, 10 J.Corp.Law 817 (1985); Elfin, A Critique of the Proposed Statutory Close Corporation Supplement to the Model Business Corporation Act, 8 J.Corp.Law 439 (1983).

---

1 O'NEAL & THOMPSON, CLOSE CORPORATIONS § 1.19*

3d ed. 1992.

Evaluation of special close corporation [statutes] should include consideration of the numbers of eligible corporations that are electing to come under the special rules provided by these laws.

* Reprinted with permission from *O'Neal's Close Corporations*, 3rd Edition,   published by Clark Boardman Callaghan, 155 Pfingsten Road, Deerfield, IL 60015.

The evidence to date suggests that the great majority of corporations eligible for statutory close corporation coverage do not elect to be covered, probably five percent or less in most states.

Of the 15 states or so that have special close corporation laws that require the corporation to make an election or designation, only a minority keep a record of close corporation filings. Even where a precise number of close corporation filings is known, the number of close corporations that could have elected that status within the statutory definition is not certain. A vast majority of corporations in this country, probably ninety percent or more, fall within the definition of close corporations used in this treatise and in the various statutes. To the extent that as many as ten percent of all corporations would not be eligible to elect statutory close corporation status, using the number of statutory close corporations as a percentage of all corporations filings, as this section does, understates the percentage of eligible corporations choosing statutory close corporation status. Yet these figures probably offer a reasonable approximation of the use of the statutes and certainly support the general conclusion that only a fraction of the corporations which could use these statutes are electing to do so.

Several states report elections around the five percent mark. Wisconsin notes 5,101 statutory close corporations and 98,602 total incorporations. Alabama reports 5,324 close corporations out of 155,198 total corporations; Pennsylvania reports approximately 24,-000 close corporations out of approximately 580,000 total corporations. Delaware reported 16,684 close corporations in 1985. The Kansas Secretary of State's office reported less than 5 percent close corporations and "probably a lot less," adding that observations of attorneys and experienced people indicate that the number has been declining. Four states enacting close corporations supplements most recently report a smaller number, 863 of 82,694 total corporations in Missouri, 828 of 97,009 in Montana, 742 of 63,172 in Nevada and 753 of 12,422 in Wyoming.

In those states without official numbers, the most comprehensive studies have been done in Texas. A review of all corporate articles processed by the secretary of state during a one-week period in 1978 and a similar period in 1979 showed that 3.71 percent of the filing corporations elected close corporation status in the 1978 period and 5.59 percent in the 1979 period. A study done for this treatise of Texas filings for a similar week in 1985 revealed that 43 of 727 for-profit corporations (5.91%) elected close corporation status. A parallel study examining random filings during a 12–month period from June 1984 to June 1985 showed a similar result—6.09 percent of for-profit corporations elected close corporation statutes.

The greatest use of statutory close corporation status appears to be in California. A 1978 survey of 300 articles of incorporation filed in California showed 28 percent filed as statutory close corporations. A 1985 survey of 200 California incorporations found 19 percent to be statutory close corporations. The attorney who conducted the California surveys suggests, however, that the number is "entirely misleading" because many corporations electing to become statutory close corporations are organized by nonlawyers using printed forms who do not understand the reasons they are electing statutory close corporation status. He states further that many lawyers mistakenly believe they have to elect close corporation status to be eligible to elect the tax status provided by Subchapter S of the Internal Revenue Code or believe they have to elect such status to come within the "short form" exemption of the California securities law. After excluding corporations formed by nonlawyers, those formed by lawyers under erroneous beliefs, and one-person corporations seeking to avoid corporate formalities while retaining corporate limited liability, the attorney conducting the surveys concluded that "the number of 'real' situations for the use of the statutory close corporation would be extremely small but also undeterminable."

SECTION 2. SPECIAL VOTING ARRANGEMENTS AT THE SHAREHOLDER LEVEL

(a) VOTING AGREEMENTS

DEL. GEN. CORP. LAW §§ 212(c), 342

[See Statutory Supplement]

REV. MODEL BUS. CORP. ACT §§ 7.22(d), 7.31, 7.32

[See Statutory Supplement]

CAL. CORP. CODE §§ 158(a), 705(e), 706

[See Statutory Supplement]

N.Y. BUS. CORP. LAW §§ 609, 620

[See Statutory Supplement]

RINGLING BROS.–BARNUM & BAILEY COMBINED SHOWS v. RINGLING

Supreme Court of Delaware, 1947.
29 Del.Ch. 610, 53 A.2d 441.

Suit by Edith Conway Ringling against Ringling Brothers–Barnum & Bailey Circus Combined Shows, Inc., and others to determine the right of individual defendants to hold office as directors or officers of the corporation and to determine the validity of election of directors at the 1946 annual stockholders' meeting. From a decree for complainant entered in conformity with opinion of the Vice Chancellor, 49 A.2d 603, the defendants appeal....

PEARSON, Judge.

The Court of Chancery was called upon to review an attempted election of directors at the 1946 annual stockholders meeting of the corporate defendant. The pivotal questions concern an agreement between two of the three present stockholders, and particularly the effect of this agreement with relation to the exercise of voting rights by these two stockholders. At the time of the meeting, the corporation had outstanding 1000 shares of capital stock held as follows: 315 by petitioner Edith Conway Ringling; 315 by defendant Aubrey B. Ringling Haley (individually or as executrix and legatee of a deceased husband); and 370 by defendant John Ringling North. The purpose of the meeting was to elect the entire board of seven directors. The shares could be voted cumulatively. Mrs. Ringling asserts that by virtue of the operation of an agreement between her and Mrs. Haley, the latter was bound to vote her shares for an adjournment of the meeting, or in the alternative, for a certain slate of directors. Mrs. Haley contends that she was not so bound for reason that the agreement was invalid, or at least revocable.

The two ladies entered into the agreement in 1941. It makes like provisions concerning stock of the corporate defendant and of another corporation, but in this case, we are concerned solely with the agreement as it affects the voting of stock of the corporate defendant. The agreement recites that each party was the owner "subject only to possible claims of creditors of the estates of Charles Ringling and Richard Ringling, respectively" (deceased husbands of the parties), of 300 shares of the capital stock of the defendant corporation; that in 1938 these shares had been deposited under a voting trust agreement which would terminate in 1947, or earlier, upon the elimination of certain liability of the corporation; that each party also owned 15 shares individually; that the parties had "entered into an agreement in April 1934 providing for joint action by them in matters affecting their ownership of stock and interest in" the corporate defendant; that the parties desired "to continue to act jointly in all matters relating to their stock ownership or interest in" the corporate defendant (and the other corporation). The agreement then provides as follows:

"Now, Therefore, in consideration of the mutual covenants and agreements hereinafter contained the parties hereto agree as follows:

"1.   Neither party will sell any shares of stock or any voting trust certificates in either of said corporations to any other person whosoever, without first making a written offer to the other party hereto of all of the shares or voting trust certificates proposed to be sold, for the same price and upon the same terms and conditions as in such proposed sale, and allowing such other party a time of not less than 180 days from the date of such written offer within which to accept same.

"2.   In exercising any voting rights to which either party may be entitled by virtue of ownership of stock or voting trust certificates held by them in either of said corporation, each party will consult and confer with the other and the parties will act jointly in exercising such voting rights in accordance with such agreement as they may reach with respect to any matter calling for the exercise of such voting rights.

"3.   In the event the parties fail to agree with respect to any matter covered by paragraph 2 above, the question in disagreement shall be submitted for arbitration to Karl D. Loos, of Washington, D.C. as arbitrator and his decision thereon shall be binding upon the parties hereto.   Such arbitration shall be exercised to the end of assuring for the respective corporations good management and such participation therein by the members of the Ringling family as the experience, capacity and ability of each may warrant.   The parties may at any time by written agreement designate any other individual to act as arbitrator in lieu of said Loos.

"4.   Each of the parties hereto will enter into and execute such voting trust agreement or agreements and such other instruments as, from time to time they may deem advisable and as they may be advised by counsel are appropriate to effectuate the purposes and objects of this agreement.

"5.   This agreement shall be in effect from the date hereof and shall continue in effect for a period of ten years unless sooner terminated by mutual agreement in writing by the parties hereto.

"6.   The agreement of April 1934 is hereby terminated.

"7.   This agreement shall be binding upon and inure to the benefit of the heirs, executors, administrators and assigns of the parties hereto respectively."

The Mr. Loos mentioned in the agreement is an attorney and has represented both parties since 1937, and, before and after the voting trust was terminated in late 1942, advised them with respect to the exercise of their voting rights. At the annual meetings in 1943 and the two following years, the parties voted their shares in accordance with mutual understandings arrived at as a result of discussions. In each of these years, they elected five of the seven directors. Mrs. Ringling and Mrs. Haley each had sufficient votes, independently of the other, to elect two of the seven directors. By both voting for an additional candidate, they could be sure of his election regardless of how Mr. North, the remaining stockholder, might vote.[1]

Some weeks before the 1946 meeting, they discussed with Mr. Loos the matter of voting for directors. They were in accord that Mrs. Ringling should cast sufficient votes to elect herself and her son; and that Mrs. Haley should elect herself and her husband; but they did not agree upon a fifth director. The day before the meeting, the discussions were continued, Mrs. Haley being represented by her husband since she could not be present because of illness. In a conversation with Mr. Loos, Mr. Haley indicated that he would make a motion for an adjournment of the meeting for sixty days, in order to give the ladies additional time to come to an agreement about their voting. On the morning of the meeting, however, he stated that because of something Mrs. Ringling had done, he would not consent to a postponement. Mrs. Ringling then made a demand upon Mr. Loos to act under the third paragraph of the agreement "to arbitrate the disagreement" between her and Mrs. Haley in connection with the manner in which the stock of the two ladies should be voted. At the opening of the meeting, Mr. Loos read the written demand and stated that he determined and directed that the stock of both ladies be voted for an adjournment of sixty days. Mrs. Ringling then made a motion for adjournment and voted for it. Mr. Haley, as proxy for his wife, and Mr. North voted against the motion. Mrs. Ringling (herself or through her attorney, it is immaterial which), objected to the voting of Mrs. Haley's stock in any manner other than in accordance with Mr. Loos' direction. The chairman ruled that the stock could not be voted contrary to such direction, and declared the motion for adjournment had carried. Nevertheless, the meeting proceeded to the election of directors. Mrs. Ringling stated that she would continue in the meeting "but without prejudice to her position with respect to the voting of the stock and the fact that adjournment had not been taken." Mr. Loos directed Mrs. Ringling to cast her votes 882 for Mrs. Ringling, 882 for her son, Robert, and 441 for a Mr. Dunn, who had been a member of the board for several years. She

---

1. Each lady was entitled to cast 2205 votes (since each had the cumulative voting rights of 315 shares, and there were 7 vacancies in the directorate). The sum of the votes of both is 4410, which is sufficient to allow 882 votes for each of 5 persons. Mr. North, holding 370 shares, was entitled to cast 2590 votes, which obviously cannot be divided so as to give to more than two candidates as many as 882 votes each. It will be observed that in order for Mrs. Ringling and Mrs. Haley to be sure to elect five directors (regardless of how Mr. North might vote) they must act together in the sense that their combined votes must be divided among five different candidates and at least one of the five must be voted for by both Mrs. Ringling and Mrs. Haley.

complied. Mr. Loos directed that Mrs. Haley's votes be cast 882 for Mrs. Haley, 882 for Mr. Haley, and 441 for Mr. Dunn. Instead of complying, Mr. Haley attempted to vote his wife's shares 1103 for Mrs. Haley, and 1102 for Mr. Haley. Mr. North voted his shares 864 for a Mr. Woods, 863 for a Mr. Griffin, and 863 for Mr. North. The chairman ruled that the five candidates proposed by Mr. Loos, together with Messrs. Woods and North, were elected. The Haley–North group disputed this ruling insofar as it declared the election of Mr. Dunn; and insisted that Mr. Griffin, instead, had been elected. A directors' meeting followed in which Mrs. Ringling participated after stating that she would do so "without prejudice to her position that the stockholders' meeting had been adjourned and that the directors' meeting was not properly held." Mr. Dunn and Mr. Griffin, although each was challenged by an opposing faction, attempted to join in voting as directors for different slates of officers. Soon after the meeting, Mrs. Ringling instituted this proceeding.

The Vice Chancellor determined that the agreement to vote in accordance with the direction of Mr. Loos was valid as a "stock pooling agreement" with lawful objects and purposes, and that it was not in violation of any public policy of this state. He held that where the arbitrator acts under the agreement and one party refuses to comply with his direction, "the Agreement constitutes the willing party . . . an implied agent possessing the irrevocable proxy of the recalcitrant party for the purpose of casting the particular vote." It was ordered that a new election be held before a master, with the direction that the master should recognize and give effect to the agreement if its terms were properly invoked. [In reaching this result, Vice Chancellor Seitz stated, "Here an implied agency based on an irrevocable proxy is fully justified to implement the Agreement without doing violence to its terms. Moreover, the provisions of the Agreement make it clear that the proxy may be treated as one coupled with an interest so as to render it irrevocable under the circumstances. . . . Obviously, to deny specific performance here would be tantamount to declaring the Agreement invalid. Since petitioner's rights in this respect were properly preserved at the stockholders' meeting, the meeting was a nullity to the extent that it failed to give effect to the provisions of the Agreement here involved. However, I believe it preferable to hold a new election rather than attempt to reconstruct the contested meeting. In this way the parties will be acting with explicit knowledge of their rights."]

Before taking up defendants' objections to the agreement, let us analyze particularly what it attempts to provide with respect to voting, including what functions and powers it attempts to repose in Mr. Loos, the "arbitrator". The agreement recites that the parties desired "to continue to act jointly in all matters relating to their stock ownership or interest in" the corporation. The parties agreed to consult and confer with each other in exercising their voting rights and to act jointly—that is, concertedly; unitedly; towards unified courses of action—in accordance with such agreement as they might reach. Thus, so long as the parties agree for whom or for what their shares shall be voted, the agreement provides no function for the arbitrator. His role is limited to situations where the parties fail to agree upon a course of action. In such cases, the agreement directs that "the question in disagreement shall be submitted for arbitration" to Mr. Loos "as arbitrator and his decision thereon shall be binding upon the parties". These provisions are designed to operate in aid of what appears to be a primary purpose of the parties, "to act jointly" in exercising their voting rights, by providing a means for fixing a course of action whenever they themselves might reach a stalemate.

Should the agreement be interpreted as attempting to empower the arbitrator to carry his directions into effect? Certainly there is no express delegation or grant of power to do so, either by authorizing him to vote the shares or to compel either party to vote them in accordance with his directions. The agreement expresses no other function of the arbitrator than that of deciding questions in disagreement which prevent the effectuation of the purpose "to act jointly". The power to enforce a decision does not seem a necessary or usual incident of such a function. Mr. Loos is not a party to the agreement. It does not contemplate the transfer of any shares or interest in shares to him, or that he should undertake any duties which the parties might compel him to perform. They provided that they might designate any other individual to act instead of Mr. Loos. The agreement does not attempt to make the arbitrator a trustee of an express trust. What the arbitrator is to do is for the benefit of the parties, not for his own benefit. Whether the parties accept or reject his decision is no concern of his, so far as the agreement or the surrounding circumstances reveal. We think the parties sought to bind each other, but to be bound only to each other, and not to empower the arbitrator to enforce decisions he might make.

From this conclusion, it follows necessarily that no decision of the arbitrator could ever be enforced if both parties to the agreement were unwilling that it be enforced, for the obvious reason that there would be no one to enforce it. Under the agreement, something more is required after the arbitrator has given his decision in order that it should become compulsory: at least one of the parties must determine that such decision shall be carried into effect. Thus, any "control" of the voting of the shares, which is reposed in the arbitrator, is substantially limited in action under the agreement in that it is subject to the overriding power of the parties themselves.

The agreement does not describe the undertaking of each party with respect to a decision of the arbitrator other than to provide that it "shall be binding upon the parties". It seems to us that this language, considered with relation to its context and the situations to which it is applicable, means that each party promised the other to exercise her own voting rights in accordance with the arbitrator's decision. The agreement is silent about any exercise of the voting rights of one party by the other. The language with reference to situations where the parties arrive at an understanding as to voting plainly suggests "action" by each, and "exercising" voting rights by each, rather than by one for the other. There is no intimation that this method should be different where the arbitrator's decision is to be carried into effect.

Assuming that a power in each party to exercise the voting rights of the other might be a relatively more effective or convenient means of enforcing a decision of the arbitrator than would be available without the power, this would not justify implying a delegation of the power in the absence of some indication that the parties bargained for that means. The method of voting actually employed by the parties tends to show that they did not construe the agreement as creating powers to vote each other's shares; for at meetings prior to 1946 each party apparently exercised her own voting rights, and at the 1946 meeting, Mrs. Ringling, who wished to enforce the agreement, did not attempt to cast a ballot in exercise of any voting rights of Mrs. Haley. We do not find enough in the agreement or in the circumstances to justify a construction that either party was empowered to exercise voting rights of the other.

Having examined what the parties sought to provide by the agreement, we come now to defendants' contention that the voting provisions are illegal and revocable. They say that the courts of this state have definitely established the doctrine "that there can be no agreement, or any device whatsoever, by which the voting power of stock of a Delaware corporation may be irrevocably separated from the ownership of the stock, except by an agreement which complies with Section 18" of the Corporation Law, Rev.Code 1935, § 2050, and except by a proxy coupled with an interest....*

In our view, neither the cases nor the statute sustain the rule for which the defendants contend. Their sweeping formulation would impugn well-recognized means by which a shareholder may effectively confer his voting rights upon others while retaining various other rights. For example, defendants' rule would apparently not permit holders of voting stock to confer upon stockholders of another class by the device of an amendment of the certificate of incorporation, the exclusive right to vote during periods when dividends are not paid on stock of the latter class. The broad prohibitory meaning which defendants find in Section 18 seems inconsistent with their concession that proxies coupled with an interest may be irrevocable, for the statute contains nothing about such proxies. The statute authorizes, among other things, the deposit or transfer of stock in trust for a specified purpose, namely, "vesting" in the transferee "the right to vote thereon" for a limited period; and prescribes numerous requirements in this connection.

---

* Section 18 was the precursor of Del. Gen.Corp.Law § 218, relating to voting trusts. Proxies coupled with an interest are discussed in the background note following Ringling. (Footnote by ed.)

Accordingly, it seems reasonable to infer that to establish the relationship and accomplish the purpose which the statute authorizes, its requirements must be complied with.

But the statute does not purport to deal with agreements whereby shareholders attempt to bind each other as to how they shall vote their shares. Various forms of such pooling agreements, as they are sometimes called, have been held valid and have been distinguished from voting trusts.... We think the particular agreement before us does not violate Section 18 or constitute an attempted evasion of its requirements, and is not illegal for any other reason.

Generally speaking, a shareholder may exercise wide liberality of judgment in the matter of voting, and it is not objectionable that his motives may be for personal profit, or determined by whims or caprice, so long as he violates no duty owed his fellow shareholders. Heil v. Standard G. & E. Co., 17 Del.Ch. 214, 151 A. 303. The ownership of voting stock imposes no legal duty to vote at all. A group of shareholders may, without impropriety, vote their respective shares so as to obtain advantages of concerted action. They may lawfully contract with each other to vote in the future in such way as they, or a majority of their group, from time to time determine.

Reasonable provisions for cases of failure of the group to reach a determination because of an even division in their ranks seem unobjectionable. The provision here for submission to the arbitrator is plainly designed as a deadlock-breaking measure, and the arbitrator's decision cannot be enforced unless at least one of the parties (entitled to cast one-half of their combined votes) is willing that it be enforced. We find the provision reasonable. It does not appear that the agreement enables the parties to take any unlawful advantage of the outside shareholder, or of any other person. It offends no rule of law or public policy of this state of which we are aware.

Legal consideration for the promises of each party is supplied by the mutual promises of the other party. The undertaking to vote in accordance with the arbitrator's decision is a valid contract. The good faith of the arbitrator's action has not been challenged and, indeed, the record indicates that no such challenge could be supported.

Accordingly, the failure of Mrs. Haley to exercise her voting rights in accordance with his decision was a breach of her contract. It is no extenuation of the breach that her votes were cast for two of the three candidates directed by the arbitrator. His directions to her were part of a single plan or course of action for the voting of the shares of both parties to the agreement, calculated to utilize an advantage of joint action by them which would bring about the election of an additional director. The actual voting of Mrs. Haley's shares frustrates that plan to such an extent that it should not be treated as a partial performance of her contract.

Throughout their argument, defendants make much of the fact that all votes cast at the meeting were by the registered shareholders. The Court of Chancery may, in a review of an election, reject votes of a registered shareholder where his voting of them is found to be in violation of rights of another person. Compare: In re Giant Portland Cement Co., 26 Del.Ch. 32, 21 A.2d 697; In re Canal Construction Co., 21 Del.Ch. 155, 182 A. 545. It seems to us that upon the application of Mrs. Ringling, the injured party, the votes representing Mrs. Haley's shares should not be counted. Since no infirmity in Mr. North's voting has been demonstrated, his right to recognition of what he did at the meeting should be considered in granting any relief to Mrs. Ringling; for her rights arose under a contract to which Mr. North was not a party.

With this in mind, we have concluded that the election should not be declared invalid, but that effect should be given to a rejection of the votes representing Mrs. Haley's shares. No other relief seems appropriate in this proceeding. Mr. North's vote against the motion for adjournment was sufficient to defeat it. With respect to the election of directors, the return of the inspectors should be corrected to show a rejection of Mrs. Haley's votes, and to declare the election of the six persons for whom Mr. North and Mrs. Ringling voted.

This leaves one vacancy in the directorate. The question of what to do about such a vacancy was not considered by the court below and has not been argued here. For this reason, and because an election of directors at the 1947 annual meeting (which presumably will be held in the near future) may make a determination of the question unimportant, we shall not decide it on this appeal. If a decision of the point appears important to the parties, any of them may apply to raise it in the Court of Chancery, after the mandate of this court is received there.

An order should be entered directing a modification of the order of the Court of Chancery in accordance with this opinion.

NOTE ON IRREVOCABLE PROXIES

Even if a proxy is expressly conferred in connection with a voting agreement, a further problem remains. Classically a proxy has been treated as an agency, in which the shareholder is the principal and the proxyholder is the agent. It is a rule of agency, however, that a principal can terminate an agent's authority at will, even if the termination is in breach of contract (although in such cases the principal may be liable to the agent in damages). See Restatement, Second, of Agency § 118, in the Statutory Supplement. There is an exception to this rule in cases where the agent holds a "power coupled with an interest," or, as Restatement (Second) of Agency § 138 calls it, a "power given as security." See Restatement, Second, of Agency §§ 138, 139. Generally speaking, this exception is applicable to arrangements in which it is understood that the "agent" or power-holder has an interest in the subject-matter to which the power relates, and is therefore expected not to execute the power solely on the power-giver's behalf—the crux of the normal agency relationship—but on his own behalf as well. Obviously, the safest way to insure that a proxy will be irrevocable is to confer it upon a proxyholder who has an "interest" in the shares to which the proxy relates. Relatively clear examples are cases where the proxyholder is a pledgee of the shares, or has agreed to purchase the shares. See N.Y.Bus.Corp.Law § 609(f)(1), (2).

If the general agency rules are applied to a proxy given pursuant to a voting agreement, the proxy would be revocable notwithstanding the agreement, unless it is deemed to be coupled with an interest. It is often unclear at common law, however, what constitutes a sufficient interest to make a proxy irrevocable. The problem is that where a proxy is given pursuant to a voting agreement, normally the proxyholder is either an arbitrator, who has no proprietary interest in the shares or the corporation, or a shareholder, who has a proprietary interest in the corporation but not in the shares that are the subject-matter of the proxy. In In re Chilson, 19 Del.Ch. 398, 409, 168 A. 82, 86 (1933), the court held that where the proxyholder has "some recognizable property or financial interest in the stock" the proxy would be validly irrevocable. However, the court held, where the proxyholder has only "an interest in the corporation generally," or "an interest in the bare voting power or the results to be accomplished by the use of" the proxy, the proxy would be revocable. On the other hand, in Deibler v. Chas. H. Elliott Co., 368 Pa. 267, 81 A.2d 557 (1951), the Supreme Court of Pennsylvania, construing Delaware law, upheld the irrevocability of a proxy given to secure payment of the purchase price of stock in a Delaware corporation and the seller's continued employment by the corporation. See generally Comment, Irrevocable Proxies, 43 Tex. L.Rev. 733 (1965).

———

(b) VOTING TRUSTS

———

DEL. GEN. CORP. LAW § 218

[See Statutory Supplement]

———

REV. MODEL BUS. CORP. ACT § 7.30

[See Statutory Supplement]

———

CAL. CORP. CODE § 706

[See Statutory Supplement]

———

NOTE ON VOTING TRUSTS

1.   A voting trust is a device by which shareholders separate voting rights in, and legal title to, their shares from beneficial ownership, by conferring the voting rights and legal title on one or more voting trustees, while retaining the ultimate right to distributions and appreciation.   Usually, two or more shareholders are involved, so that the voting trust is a type of pooling agreement. Sometimes, however, only one shareholder is involved—for example, where a sole shareholder creates a voting trust to satisfy creditors, or to vest control of his business in managers.   The creation of a voting trust normally involves (i) the execution of a written trust agreement between participating shareholders and the voting trustees, and (ii) a transfer to the trustee, for a specified period, of the shareholders' stock certificates and the legal title to their stock.   The voting trustee then registers the transfer on the corporation's books, so that during the term of the trust the trustee is the record owner of the shares, entitled to vote in the election of directors and often on other matters as well.   Dividends are paid by the corporation to the trustee, but are almost invariably then paid over by the trustee to the beneficial owners.   Several statutes require the trustee to issue certificates of beneficial interest to participating shareholders, and frequently such certificates are issued even where not statutorily required, to facilitate trading in the beneficial interests.

Voting trusts are an effective and a moderately simple way to separate control and beneficial ownership for a limited period of time.   The separation is self-executing, because the trustee is the legal owner and is registered as such on the corporation's books. The separation survives transfers by the beneficial owners, since they can transfer only their retained equitable interests (essentially, most ownership rights except the right to vote during the term of the trust).   Upon termination of the voting trust, the beneficial owners receive stock certificates which reinstate them as complete owners, registered as such on the corporation's books.

2.   In the context of close corporations, voting trusts may sometimes be used, like voting agreements, to allocate voting control in other than a pro rata manner, or to preserve the solidarity of a faction consisting of less than all the shareholders.   Because voting trusts and voting agreements may have substantially overlapping purposes, the substantive legal rules applicable to one of these two legal forms have sometimes been applied to an arrangement that was nominally cast in the other form.   Thus in Abercrom-

bie v. Davies, 36 Del.Ch. 371, 130 A.2d 338 (1957), the Delaware Supreme Court held that an "Agent's Agreement" that was in form a voting agreement was in substance a voting trust.

(c) CLASSIFIED STOCK AND WEIGHTED VOTING

DEL. GEN. CORP. LAW § 212

[See Statutory Supplement]

REV. MODEL BUS. CORP. ACT §§ 6.01, 7.21, 8.04

[See Statutory Supplement]

NOTE ON CLASSIFIED STOCK AND WEIGHTED VOTING

"One of the simplest and most effective ways of assuring that all the participants or that particular minority shareholders will have representation on the board of directors is to set up two or more classes of stock, provide that each class is to vote for and elect a specified number or a stated percentage of the directors, and then issue each class or a majority of shares in each class to a different shareholder or faction of shareholders.... Class A common stock might be given power, for instance, to elect three directors and Class B common stock power to elect two." 1 F.H. O'Neal & R. Thompson, O'Neal's Close Corporations § 3.23 (3d ed. 1991). A few statutes validate this technique explicitly (e.g., N.Y.Bus.Corp. Law § 703), and most of the remaining statutes validate it implicitly by providing that a corporation may have one or more classes of stock with such voting powers as shall be stated in the certificate (e.g., Del.Gen.Corp.Law § 151(a)). In its simplest version, the use of classified common does not necessarily involve voting power for any class that is disproportionate to the investment made by that class. Often, however, separate classes carry voting power whose weight differs considerably from the relative investment made by their holders. At the extremes a class of stock may have proprietary rights but no voting power, or voting power but no proprietary rights.[1] The possible utility of nonvoting stock in that context has been illustrated as follows by Professor Hecker:

---

1. Use of this technique may have adverse tax consequences: a corporation cannot elect Subchapter S status under the Internal Revenue Code if it has more than one class of stock, unless the characteristics of the stock of all classes are identical and

[A] common situation is for parties making unequal capital contributions to desire an equal voice in matters properly the subject of shareholder action.... [T]heir needs may be accommodated by use of voting and nonvoting stock. One class of voting stock with relatively few authorized shares and low par value can be allocated equally among the parties. A second class of nonvoting stock, which will represent the bulk of each party's investment, can be allocated among them in accordance with the capital contribution of each. The total of each shareholder's voting and nonvoting stock will then equal the amount of his capital contribution. Thus an arrangement roughly approximating a partnership will be created under which each party will have an equal voice in the election of directors and other shareholder matters but will share in corporate assets in proportion to his capital investment.[2]

SECTION 3. AGREEMENTS CONTROLLING MATTERS WITHIN THE BOARD'S DISCRETION

Voting arrangements of the kind discussed in Section 2, supra, control only those matters that are decided on a shareholder level. Typically, however, the issues that are most important to shareholders in a close corporation are determined on a board level—for example, managerial positions, managerial compensation, and dividends. If the shareholders attempt to also control these matters by agreement, the problem arises whether (or under what conditions) such an agreement is valid, in the face of the normal statutory provision that the business of the corporation shall be managed by or under the direction of the board. That question is addressed by the materials in this section.

McQUADE v. STONEHAM & McGRAW

Court of Appeals of New York, 1934.
263 N.Y. 323, 189 N.E. 234.

Appeal, by permission of Court of Appeals, from judgment of Appellate Division, First Department, unanimously affirming judgment for plaintiff for $42,827.38 and other relief.

POUND, Ch. J. The action is brought to compel specific performance of an agreement between the parties, entered into to

the voting power is proportionate to the number of shares owned. See Section 5, infra.

2. Hecker, Close Corporations and the Kansas General Corporations Code of 1972, 22 Kan.L.Rev. 489, 509 (1974).

secure the control of National Exhibition Company, also called the baseball club (New York Nationals or "Giants"). This was one of Stoneham's enterprises which used the New York Polo Grounds for its home games. McGraw was manager of the Giants. McQuade was, at the time the contract was entered into, a city magistrate. He resigned December 8, 1930.

Defendant Stoneham became the owner of 1,306 shares, or a majority of the stock of National Exhibition Company (there being then 2,500 shares outstanding). Plaintiff and defendant McGraw each purchased seventy shares of his stock. Plaintiff paid Stoneham $50,338.10 for the stock he purchased. As a part of the transaction the agreement in question was entered into. It was dated May 21, 1919. Some of its pertinent provisions are:

"VIII.   The parties hereto will use their best endeavors for the purpose of continuing as directors of said company and as officers thereof the following:

"Directors: Charles A. Stoneham, John J. McGraw, Francis X. McQuade, with right to the party of the first part (Stoneham) to name all additional directors as he sees fit.

"Officers: Charles A. Stoneham, president; John J. McGraw, vice-president; Francis X. McQuade, treasurer.

"IX.   No salaries are to be paid to any of the above officers or directors, except as follows: President, $45,000; vice-president, $7,500; treasurer, $7,500.

"X.   There shall be no change in said salaries, no change in the amount of capital, or the number of shares, no change or amendment of the by-laws of the corporation or any matters regarding the policy of the business of the corporation or any matters which may in anywise affect, endanger or interfere with the rights of minority stockholders, excepting upon the mutual and unanimous consent of all . . . of the parties hereto.

"XIV.   This agreement shall continue and remain in force so long as the parties or any of them or the representative of any own the stock referred to in this agreement, to wit, the party of the first part, 1,166 shares, the party of the second part 70 shares and the party of the third part 70 shares, except as may otherwise appear by this agreement. . . ."

In pursuance of this contract Stoneham became president and McGraw vice-president of the corporation. McQuade became treasurer. In June, 1925, his salary was increased to $10,000 a year. He continued to act until May 2, 1928, when Leo J. Bondy was elected to succeed him. The board of directors consisted of seven men. The four outside of the parties hereto were selected by Stoneham and he had complete control over them. At the meeting of May 2, 1928, Stoneham and McGraw refrained from voting, McQuade voted for himself and the other four voted for Bondy. Defendants did not keep their agreement with McQuade to use their best efforts to continue him as treasurer. On the contrary, he was dropped with their entire acquiescence. At the next stockholders' meeting he was dropped as a director, although they might have elected him.

The courts below have refused to order the reinstatement of McQuade, but have given him damages for wrongful discharge, with a right to sue for future damages.

The cause for dropping McQuade was due to the falling out of friends. McQuade and Stoneham had disagreed. The trial court has found in substance that their numerous quarrels and disputes did not affect the orderly and efficient administration of the business of the corporation; that plaintiff was removed because he had antagonized the dominant Stoneham by persisting in challenging his power over the corporate treasury and for no misconduct on his part. The court also finds that plaintiff was removed by Stoneham for protecting the corporation and its minority stockholders. We will assume that Stoneham put him out when he might have retained him, merely in order to get rid of him.

Defendants say that the contract in suit was void because the directors held their office charged with the duty to act for the corporation according to their best judgment and that any contract which compels a director to vote to keep any particular person in office and at a stated salary is illegal. Directors are the exclusive executive representatives of the corporation, charged with administration of its internal affairs and the management and use of its assets. They manage the business of the corporation (Gen.Corp. Law, Cons.Laws, c. 23, sec. 27). "An agreement to continue a man as president is dependent upon his continued loyalty to the interests of the corporation" (Fells v. Katz, 256 N.Y. 67, 72, 175 N.E. 516, 517). So much is undisputed.

Plaintiff contends that the converse of this proposition is true and that an agreement among directors to continue a man as an officer of a corporation is not to be broken so long as such officer is loyal to the interests of the corporation and that, as plaintiff has been found loyal to the corporation, the agreement of defendants is enforceable.

Although it has been held that an agreement among stockholders whereby it is attempted to divest the directors of their power to discharge an unfaithful employee of the corporation is illegal as against public policy (Fells v. Katz, supra), it must be equally true that the stockholders may not, by agreement among themselves, control the directors in the exercise of the judgment vested in them by virtue of their office to elect officers and fix salaries. Their motives may not be questioned so long as their acts are legal. The bad faith or the improper motives of the parties does not change this rule (Manson v. Curtis, 223 N.Y. 313, 324, 119 N.E. 559). Directors may not by agreements entered into by stockholders abrogate their independent judgment (Creed v. Copps, 103 Vt. 164, 71 A.L.R.Ann. 1287).

Stockholders may, of course, combine to elect directors. That rule is well settled. As Holmes, Ch. J., pointedly said (Brightman v. Bates, 175 Mass. 105, 110, 55 N.E. 809, 811): "If stockholders want to make their power felt, they must unite. There is no reason why a majority should not agree to keep together." The power to unite is, however, limited to the election of directors and is not extended to contracts whereby limitations are placed on the power of directors to manage the business of the corporation by the selection of agents at defined salaries.

The minority shareholders whose interests McQuade says he has been punished for protecting, are not, aside from himself, complaining about his discharge. He is not acting for the corporation or for them in this action. It is impossible to see how the corporation has been injured by the substitution of Bondy as treasurer in place of McQuade. As McQuade represents himself in this action and seeks redress for his own wrongs, "we prefer to listen to [the corporation and the minority stockholders] before any decision as to their wrongs" (Faulds v. Yates, 57 Ill. 416).

It is urged that we should pay heed to the morals and manners of the market place to sustain this agreement, and that we should hold that its violation gives rise to a cause of action for damages, rather than base our decision on any outworn notions of public policy. Public policy is a dangerous guide in determining the validity of a contract, and courts should not interfere lightly with the freedom of competent parties to make their own contracts. We do not close our eyes to the fact that such agreements, tacitly or openly arrived at, are not uncommon, especially in close corporations where the stockholders are doing business for convenience under a corporate organization. We know that majority stockholders, united in voting trusts, effectively manage the business of a corporation by choosing trustworthy directors to reflect their policies in the corporate management. Nor are we unmindful that McQuade has, so the court has found, been shabbily treated as a purchaser of stock from Stoneham. We have said: "A trustee is held to something stricter than the morals of the market place" (Meinhard v. Salmon, 249 N.Y. 458, 464, 164 N.E. 545, 546), but Stoneham and McGraw were not trustees for McQuade as an individual. Their duty was to the corporation and its stockholders, to be exercised according to their unrestricted lawful judgment. They were under no legal obligation to deal righteously with McQuade if it was against public policy to do so.

The courts do not enforce mere moral obligations, nor legal ones either, unless someone seeks to establish rights which may be waived by custom and for convenience. We are constrained by authority to hold that a contract is illegal and void so far as it precludes the board of directors, at the risk of incurring legal liability, from changing officers, salaries or policies or retaining individuals in office, except by consent of the contracting parties. On the whole, such a holding is probably preferable to one which would open the courts to pass on the motives of directors in the lawful exercise of their trust. . . .

The judgment of the Appellate Division and that of the Trial Term should be reversed and the complaint dismissed, with costs in all courts.*

[The opinion of Lehman, J., concurring in the result, is omitted.]

GALLER v. GALLER

Supreme Court of Illinois, 1964, reh. denied 1965.
32 Ill.2d 16, 203 N.E.2d 577.

UNDERWOOD, Justice.   Plaintiff, Emma Galler, sued in equity for an accounting and for specific performance of an agreement made in July, 1955, between plaintiff and her husband, of one part, and defendants, Isadore A. Galler and his wife, Rose, of the other. Defendants appealed from a decree of the superior court of Cook County granting the relief prayed.   The First District Appellate Court reversed the decree and denied specific performance, affirming in part the order for an accounting, and modifying the order awarding master's fees.   (45 Ill.App.2d 452, 196 N.E.2d 5.)   That decision is appealed here on a certificate of importance.

There is no substantial dispute as to the facts in this case. From 1919 to 1924, Benjamin and Isadore Galler, brothers, were equal partners in the Galler Drug Company, a wholesale drug concern.   In 1924 the business was incorporated under the Illinois Business Corporation Act, each owning one half of the outstanding 220 shares of stock.   In 1945 each contracted to sell 6 shares to an employee, Rosenberg, at a price of $10,500 for each block of 6 shares, payable within 10 years.   They guaranteed to repurchase the shares if Rosenberg's employment were terminated, and further agreed that if they sold their shares, Rosenberg would receive the same price per share as that paid for the brothers' shares.   Rosenberg was still indebted for the 12 shares in July, 1955, and continued to make payments on account even after Benjamin Galler died in 1957 and after the institution of this action by Emma Galler in 1959.   Rosenberg was not involved in this litigation either as a party or as a witness, and in July of 1961, prior to the time that the master in chancery hearings were concluded, defendants Isadore and Rose Galler purchased the 12 shares from Rosenberg.   A supplemental complaint was filed by the plaintiff, Emma Galler, asserting an equitable right to have 6 of the 12 shares transferred to her and

---

* The court also held that the agreement violated the Inferior Criminal Courts Act, which provided that "[n]o city magistrate shall engage in any other business or profession . . ., but each of said justices and magistrates shall devote his whole time and capacity, so far as the public interest demands, to the duties of his office. . . ." At the date of the agreement McQuade was a city magistrate, and he did not resign his position until after commencement of the action. (Footnote by ed.)

offering to pay the defendants one half of the amount that the defendants paid Rosenberg. The parties have stipulated that pending disposition of the instant case, these shares will not be voted or transferred. For approximately one year prior to the entry of the decree by the chancellor in July of 1962, there were no outstanding minority shareholder interests.

In March, 1954, Benjamin and Isadore, on the advice of their accountant, decided to enter into an agreement for the financial protection of their immediate families and to assure their families, after the death of either brother, equal control of the corporation. [The agreement was executed in July 1955, after Benjamin had fallen ill. In September 1956, Emma agreed to permit Isadore's son Aaron to become president for one year and agreed that she would not interfere with the business during that year. In December 1957, Benjamin died.] The evidence is undisputed that defendants had decided prior to Benjamin's death they would not honor the agreement, but never disclosed their intention to plaintiff or her husband. . . .

Shortly after Benjamin's death, Emma went to the office and demanded the terms of the 1955 agreement be carried out. Isadore told her that anything she had to say could be said to Aaron, who then told her that his father would not abide by the agreement. He offered a modification of the agreement by proposing the salary continuation payment but without her becoming a director. When Emma refused to modify the agreement and sought enforcement of its terms, defendants refused and this suit followed.

During the last few years of Benjamin's life both brothers drew an annual salary of $42,000. Aaron, whose salary was $15,000 as manager of the warehouse prior to September, 1956, has since the time that Emma agreed to his acting as president drawn an annual salary of $20,000. In 1957, 1958, and 1959 a $40,000 annual dividend was paid. Plaintiff has received her proportionate share of the dividend.

The July, 1955, agreement in question here, entered into between Benjamin, Emma, Isadore and Rose, recites that Benjamin and Isadore each own 47½% of the issued and outstanding shares of the Galler Drug Company, an Illinois corporation, and that Benjamin and Isadore desired to provide income for the support and maintenance of their immediate families. No reference is made to the shares then being purchased by Rosenberg. The essential features of the contested portions of the agreement are substantially as set forth in the opinion of the Appellate Court: (2) that the bylaws of the corporation will be amended to provide for a board of four directors; that the necessary quorum shall be three directors; and that no directors' meeting shall be held without giving ten days notice to all directors. (3) The shareholders will cast their votes for the above named persons (Isadore, Rose, Benjamin and Emma) as directors at said special meeting and at any other meeting held for the purpose of electing directors. (4, 5) In the event of the death of either brother his wife shall have the right to nominate a director in place of the decedent. (6) Certain annual dividends will be declared by the corporation. The dividend shall be $50,000 payable out of the accumulated earned surplus in excess of $500,000. If 50% of the annual net profits after taxes exceeds the minimum $50,000 then the directors shall have discretion to declare a dividend up to 50% of the annual net profits. If the net profits are less than $50,000 nevertheless the minimum $50,000 annual dividend shall be declared, providing the $500,000 surplus is maintained. Earned surplus is defined. (9) The certificates evidencing the said shares of Benjamin Galler and Isadore Galler shall bear a legend that the shares are subject to the terms of this agreement. (10) A salary continuation agreement shall be entered into by the corporation which shall authorize the corporation upon the death of Benjamin Galler or Isadore Galler, or both, to pay a sum equal to twice the salary of such officer, payable monthly over a five-year period. Said sum shall be paid to the widow during her widowhood, but should be paid to such widow's children if the widow remarries within the five-year period. (11, 12) The parties to this agreement further agree and hereby grant to the corporation the authority to purchase, in the event of the death of either Benjamin or Isadore, so much of the stock of Galler Drug Company held by the estate as is necessary to provide sufficient funds to pay the federal estate tax, the Illinois inheritance tax and other administrative expenses of the estate. If as a result of such purchase from the estate of the decedent the amount of dividends to be received by the heirs is reduced, the parties shall nevertheless vote for directors so as to give the estate and heirs the same representation as before (2 directors out of 4, even though they own less stock), and also that the corporation pay an additional benefit payment equal to the diminution of the dividends. In the event either Benjamin or Isadore decides to sell his shares he is required to offer them first to the remaining shareholders and then to the corporation at book value, according each six months to accept the offer.

The Appellate Court found the 1955 agreement void because "the undue duration, stated purpose and substantial disregard of the provisions of the Corporation Act outweigh any considerations which might call for divisibility" and held that "the public policy of this state demands voiding this entire agreement".

While the conduct of defendants towards plaintiff was clearly inequitable, the basically controlling factor is the absence of an objecting minority interest, together with the absence of public detriment....

At this juncture it should be emphasized that we deal here with a so-called close corporation.... For our purposes, a close corporation is one in which the stock is held in a few hands, or in a few families, and wherein it is not at all, or only rarely, dealt in by buying or selling. (Brooks v. Willcuts, 8th Cir.1935, 78 F.2d 270, 273.) Moreover, it should be recognized that shareholder agreements similar to that in question here are often, as a practical consideration, quite necessary for the protection of those financially interested in the close corporation. While the shareholder of a public-issue corporation may readily sell his shares on the open market should management fail to use, in his opinion, sound business judgment, his counterpart of the close corporation often has a large total of his entire capital invested in the business and has no ready market for his shares should he desire to sell. He feels, understandably, that he is more than a mere investor and that his voice should be heard concerning all corporate activity. Without a shareholder agreement, specifically enforceable by the courts, insuring him a modicum of control, a large minority shareholder might find himself at the mercy of an oppressive or unknowledgeable majority. Moreover, as in the case at bar, the shareholders of a close corporation are often also the directors and officers thereof. With substantial shareholding interests abiding in each member of the board of directors, it is often quite impossible to secure, as in the large public-issue corporation, independent board judgment free from personal motivations concerning corporate policy. For these and other reasons too voluminous to enumerate here, often the only sound basis for protection is afforded by a lengthy, detailed shareholder agreement securing the rights and obligations of all concerned. For a discussion of these and other considerations, see Note, "A Plea for Separate Statutory Treatment of the Close Corporation", 33 N.Y.U.L.Rev. 700 (1958).

As the preceding review of the applicable decisions of this court points out, there has been a definite, albeit inarticulate, trend toward eventual judicial treatment of the close corporation as *sui generis*. Several shareholder-director agreements that have technically "violated" the letter of the Business Corporation Act have nevertheless been upheld in the light of the existing practical circumstances, i.e., no apparent public injury, the absence of a complaining minority interest, and no apparent prejudice to creditors. However, we have thus far not attempted to limit these decisions as applicable only to close corporations and have seemingly implied that general considerations regarding judicial supervision of all corporate behavior apply.

The practical result of this series of cases, while liberally giving legal efficacy to particular agreements in special circumstances notwithstanding literal "violations" of statutory corporate law, has been to inject much doubt and uncertainty into the thinking of the bench and corporate bar of Illinois concerning shareholder agreements. See e.g., Cary, "How Illinois Corporations May Enjoy Partnership Advantages: Planning for the Closely Held Firm." 48 N.W.U.L.Rev. 427; Note, "The Validity of Stockholders' Voting Agreements in Illinois," 3 U.Chi.L.Rev. 640.

It is therefore necessary, we feel, to discuss the instant case with the problems peculiar to the close corporation particularly in mind. . . .

This court has recognized, albeit *sub silentio,* the significant conceptual differences between the close corporation and its public-issue counterpart in, among other cases, Kantzler v. Bensinger, 214 Ill. 589, 73 N.E. 874, where an agreement quite similar to the one under attack here was upheld. Where, as in Kantzler and here, no complaining minority interest appears, no fraud or apparent injury to the public or creditors is present, and no clearly prohibitory statutory language is violated, we can see no valid reason for precluding the parties from reaching any arrangements concerning the management of the corporation which are agreeable to all. . . .

Since the question as to the duration of the agreement is a principal source of controversy, we shall consider it first. The parties provided no specific termination date, and while the agreement concludes with a paragraph that its terms "shall be binding upon and shall inure to the benefits of" the legal representatives, heirs and assigns of the parties, this clause is, we believe, intended to be operative only as long as one of the parties is living. It further provides that it shall be so construed as to carry out its purposes, and we believe these must be determined from a consideration of the agreement as a whole. Thus viewed, a fair construction is that its purposes were accomplished at the death of the survivor of the parties. While these life spans are not precisely ascertainable, and the Appellate Court noted Emma Galler's life expectancy at her husband's death was 26.9 years, we are aware of no statutory or public policy provision against stockholders' agreements which would invalidate this agreement on that ground. . . . While defendants argue that the public policy evinced by the legislative restrictions upon the duration of voting trust agreements (Ill.Rev.Stat. 1963, chap. 32, par. 157.30a) should be applied here, this agreement is not a voting trust, but as pointed out by the dissenting justice in the Appellate Court, is a straight contractual voting control agreement which does not divorce voting rights from stock ownership. That the policy against agreements in which stock ownership and voting rights are separated, indicated in Luthy v. Ream, 270 Ill. 170, 110 N.E. 373, is inapplicable to voting control agreements was emphasized in Thompson wherein a control agreement was upheld as not attempting to separate ownership and voting power. While limiting voting trusts in 1947 to a maximum duration of 10 years, the legislature has indicated no similar policy regarding straight voting agreements although these have been common since prior to 1870. In view of the history of decisions of this court generally upholding, in the absence of fraud or prejudice to minority interests or public policy, the right of stockholders to agree among themselves as to the manner in which their stock will be voted, we do not regard the period of time within which this agreement may remain effective as rendering the agreement unenforceable.

The clause that provides for the election of certain persons to specified offices for a period of years likewise does not require invalidation. In Kantzler v. Bensinger, 214 Ill. 589, 73 N.E. 874, this court upheld an agreement entered into by all the stockholders providing that certain parties would be elected to the offices of the corporation for a fixed period. In Faulds v. Yates, 57 Ill. 416, we upheld a similar agreement among the majority stockholders of a corporation, notwithstanding the existence of a minority which was not before the court complaining thereof. See also Hornstein, "Judicial Tolerance of the Incorporated Partnership," 18 Law and Contemporary Problems 435 at page 444.

We turn next to a consideration of the effect of the stated purpose of the agreement upon its validity. The pertinent provision is: "The said Benjamin A. Galler and Isadore A. Galler desire to provide income for the support and maintenance of their immediate families." Obviously, there is no evil inherent in a contract entered into for the reason that the persons originating the terms desired to so arrange their property as to provide post-death support for those dependent upon them. Nor does the fact that the subject property is corporate stock alter the situation so long as there exists no detriment to minority stock interests, creditors or other public injury. It is, however, contended by defendants that the methods provided by the agreement for implementation of the stated purpose are, as a whole, violative of the Business Corporation Act (Ill.Rev.Stat.1963, chap. 32, pars. 157.28, 157.30a, 157.33, 157.34, 157.41) to such an extent as to render it void *in toto*.

The terms of the dividend agreement require a minimum annual dividend of $50,000, but this duty is limited by the subsequent provision that it shall be operative only so long as an earned surplus of $500,000 is maintained. It may be noted that in 1958, the year prior to commencement of this litigation, the corporation's net earnings after taxes amounted to $202,759 while its earned surplus was $1,543,270, and this was increased in 1958 to $1,680,-079 while earnings were $172,964. The minimum earned surplus requirement is designed for the protection of the corporation and its creditors, and we take no exception to the contractual dividend requirements as thus restricted. Kantzler v. Bensinger, 214 Ill. 589, 73 N.E. 874.

The salary continuation agreement is a common feature, in one form or another, of corporate executive employment. It requires that the widow should receive a total benefit, payable monthly over a five-year period, aggregating twice the amount paid her deceased husband in one year. This requirement was likewise limited for the protection of the corporation by being contingent upon the payments being income tax-deductible by the corporation. The charge made in those cases which have considered the validity of payments to the widow of an officer and shareholder in a corporation is that a gift of its property by a noncharitable corporation is in violation of the rights of its shareholders and *ultra vires*. Since there are no shareholders here other than the parties to the contract, this objection is not here applicable, and its effect, as limited, upon the corporation is not so prejudicial as to require its invalidation.

Having concluded that the agreement, under the circumstances here present, is not vulnerable to the attack made on it, we must consider the accounting feature of this action. The trial court allowed the relief prayed, an action we deem proper except as to the master's fees which were modified by the Appellate Court. Since no question is here raised regarding them, we affirm the action of that court in this respect. The questions as to salary which the Appellate Court correctly held were improperly increased became ones of fact to be determined by the trial court.

We hold defendants must account for all monies received by them from the corporation since September 25, 1956, in excess of that theretofore authorized.

Accordingly, the judgment of the Appellate Court is reversed except insofar as it relates to fees, and is, as to them affirmed. The cause is remanded to the circuit court of Cook County with directions to proceed in accordance herewith.

Affirmed in part and reversed in part, and remanded with directions.

NOTE ON FURTHER PROCEEDINGS IN GALLER v. GALLER

The decree in *Galler* became effective on February 11, 1965. It ordered Isadore and Rose to "account for all monies received by them from the company since September 25, 1956 [up to the time of the decree], in excess of that theretofore authorized," but provided that Isadore and Aaron be allowed "fair compensation . . . for services rendered by them to the corporation during said period." On remand, defendants argued that the salaries of Aaron and Isadore during the relevant period represented the fair market value of their services, and in any event since Isadore's $42,000 salary after Benjamin's death was a continuation of his salary under the agreement, it had been "theretofore authorized" within the meaning of the decree. The Appellate Court rejected both arguments. As to the former issue the court adopted the findings of a master who valued Isadore's services at $10,000/year and Aaron's at $15,000/year. As to whether continuation of Isadore's $42,000 salary was authorized by the agreement, the court said

> . . . Isadore's continued receipt of the same salary upon the death of Benjamin without the *quid pro quo* for his brother's family, is an alteration of the past arrangement, and was without authorization.

> Furthermore, the clear import of the 1955 shareholders' agreement is that the partnership-like arrangement was intended to remain after the death of either Benjamin or Isadore. While not specifically addressing itself to salaries, the agreement provides that upon the death of either Benjamin or Isadore, four directors are to be elected; two from Isadore's

family and two from Benjamin's family. The officers and their salaries are voted upon by the directors. Dividends are required to be paid provided $500,000 earned surplus is maintained. It may be inferred that this agreement sought to replace a deceased brother's position as an officer with members of his family, thereby permitting them to share equally in the company's earnings, including salaries, a significant means of distributing the corporate profits. This inference is not negated by the fact that no provision in the 1955 agreement requires equality of salaries between the family branches.

For other disputes among the Gallers after the Supreme Court's decree, see Galler v. Galler, 69 Ill.App.2d 397, 217 N.E.2d 111 (1966); Galler v. Galler, 95 Ill.App.2d 340, 238 N.E.2d 274 (1968).

DEL. GEN. CORP. LAW §§ 102(b)(1), 141(a), 142(b), 350, 351, 354

[See Statutory Supplement]

REV. MODEL BUS. CORP. ACT §§ 2.02(b), 2.06, 7.31, 7.32, 8.01(b)

N.Y. BUS. CORP. LAW § 620

[See Statutory Supplement]

CAL. CORP. CODE §§ 186, 300, 312

[See Statutory Supplement]

SECTION 4. SUPERMAJORITY VOTING AND QUORUM REQUIREMENTS AT THE SHAREHOLDER AND BOARD LEVELS

BENINTENDI v. KENTON HOTEL

Court of Appeals of New York, 1945.
294 N.Y. 112, 60 N.E.2d 829.

DESMOND, J. Two men who owned, in inequal amounts, all the stock of a domestic business corporation, made an agreement to vote for, and later did vote for and adopt at a stockholders' meeting, by-laws of the corporation, providing as follows: 1. That no action should be taken by the stockholders except by unanimous vote of all of them; if, however, thirty days' notice of the meeting had been given, unanimous vote of the stockholders present in person or by proxy should be sufficient; 2. That the directors of the corporation should be the three persons receiving, at the annual stockholders' meeting, the unanimous vote of all the stockholders; 3. That no action should be taken by the directors except by unanimous vote of all of them; 4. That the by-laws should not be amended except by unanimous vote of all the stockholders. The minority stockholder brought this suit to have those by-laws adjudged valid and to enjoin the other stockholder from doing anything inconsistent therewith. Special Term and the Appellate Division held that the two by-laws first above described were invalid and the other two valid. [181 Misc. 897, 45 N.Y.S.2d 705; 268 App.Div. 857, 50 N.Y.S.2d 843]. Both sides have appealed to this court.

In striking down the by-law (No. 2 above) which requires unanimous stock vote for election of directors, Special Term properly relied upon Matter of Boulevard Theatre & Realty Co., 195 App.Div. 518, 186 N.Y.S. 430, affirmed 231 N.Y. 615, 132 N.E. 910. This court wrote no opinion in that case. The Appellate Division had ruled, however, that a provision in the Boulevard Theatre's certificate of incorporation requiring unanimous vote of all stockholders to elect directors, violated section 55 of the Stock Corporation Law, Consol. Laws, c. 59, which says that directors shall be chosen "by a plurality of the votes at such election." We think it unimportant that the condemned provision was found in the certificate of incorporation in the Boulevard Theatre case, and in a by-law in the present case. . . .

The device is intrinsically unlawful because it contravenes an essential part of the State policy, as expressed in the Stock Corporation Law. An agreement by a stockholder to vote for certain persons as directors is not unlawful (Clark v. Dodge, 269 N.Y. 410, 415, 199 N.E. 641) since the directors are still, under such an agreement, elected by a plurality of votes, as the statute mandates. But a requirement, wherever found, that there shall be no election of directors at all unless every single vote be cast for the same nominees, is in direct opposition to the statutory rule—that the receipt of a plurality of the votes entitles a nominee to election.

Although not covered by the Boulevard Theatre case, or any other decision we have found, the by-law (No. 1 above) which requires unanimous action of stockholders to pass any resolution or take any action of any kind, is equally obnoxious to the statutory scheme of stock corporation management. The State, granting to individuals the privilege of limiting their individual liabilities for business debts by forming themselves into an entity separate and distinct from the persons who own it, demands in turn that the entity take a prescribed form and conduct itself, procedurally, according to fixed rules. As Special Term pointed out in this case, the Legislature, for reasons thought by it to be sufficient, has specified the various percentages of stock vote necessary to pass different kinds of resolutions. For instance, sections 36 and 37 of the Stock Corporation Law require an affirmative two-thirds vote for changing the capitalization, while section 102 of the General Corporation Law empowers the holders of a majority of the stock to force the directors to dissolve the corporation, and section 103 of that law gives the same power to holders of half the stock, if there be a deadlock on the question of dissolution. Any corporation may arrive at a condition where dissolution is the right and necessary course. The Legislature has decided that a vote of a majority of the shares, or half of them in case of a deadlock, is sufficient to force a dissolution. Yet under the by-laws of this corporation, the minority stockholder could prevent dissolution until such time as he should decide to vote for it.

Those who own all the stock of a corporation may, so long as they conduct the corporate affairs in accordance with the statutory rules, deal as they will with the corporation's property (always assuming nothing is done prejudicial to creditors' rights). They may, individually, bind themselves in advance to vote in a certain way or for certain persons. But this State has decreed that every stock corporation chartered by it must have a representative government, with voting conducted conformably to the statutes, and the power of decision lodged in certain fractions, always more than half, of the stock. That whole concept is destroyed when the stockholders, by agreement, by-law or certificate of incorporation provision as to unanimous action, give the minority interest an absolute, permanent, all-inclusive power of veto. We do not hold that an arrangement would necessarily be invalid, which, for particular decisions, would require unanimous consent of all stockholders. See for instance, Ripin v. United States Woven Label Co., 205 N.Y. 442, 98 N.E. 855; Tompkins v. Hale, 284 N.Y. 675, 30 N.E.2d 721. In Tompkins v. Hale, supra, the stockholders of a "cooperative apartment house" had agreed in writing that such leases could be canceled and surrendered only if all the stockholder-tenants concurred. That is a far cry from a by-law which prohibits any nonunanimous determination on any corporate question.

The by-law numbered 3 in our list above makes it impossible for the directors to act on any matter except by unanimous vote of all of them. Such a by-law, like the others already discussed herein, is, almost as a matter of law, unworkable and unenforcible for the reason given by the Court of King's Bench in Hascard v. Somany, 1 Freeman 504, in 1693: "primâ facie in all acts done by a corporation, the major number must bind the lesser, or else differences could never be determined."

The directors of a corporation are a select body, chosen by the stockholders. By Section 27 of the General Corporation Law, the board as such is given the power of management of the corporation. At common law only a majority thereof were needed for a quorum and a majority of that quorum could transact business. Ex parte Willcocks, 7 Cow. 402, 17 Am.Dec. 525. Section 27 modifies that common-law rule only to the extent of permitting a corporation to enact a by-law fixing "the number of directors necessary to constitute a quorum at a number less than a majority of the board, but not less than one-third of its number." Every corporation is thus given the privilege of enacting a by-law fixing its own quorum requirement at any fraction not less than one-third, nor more than a majority, of its directors. But the very idea of a "quorum" is that, when that required number of persons goes into session as a body, the votes of a majority thereof are sufficient for binding action. See for example, Harroun v. Brush Electric Light Co., 152 N.Y. 212, 46 N.E. 291, 38 L.R.A. 615, as to a quorum of the Appellate Division. Thus, while by-law No. 3 is not in explicit terms forbidden by Section 27, supra, it seems to flout the plain purpose of the Legislature in passing that statute.

We have not overlooked Section 28 of the General Corporation Law, the first sentence of which is as follows: "Whenever, under the provisions of any corporate law a corporation is authorized to take any action by its directors, action may be taken by the directors, regularly convened as a board, and acting by a majority of a quorum, except when otherwise expressly required by law or the by-laws and any such action shall be executed in behalf of the corporation by such officers as shall be designated by the board." Reading together Sections 27 and 28 and examining their legislative history (see L.1890, Ch. 563; L.1892, Ch. 687; L.1904, Ch. 737), we conclude that there never was a legislative intent so to change the common-law rule as to quorums as to authorize a by-law like the one under scrutiny in this paragraph. A by-law requiring for every action of the board not only a unanimous vote of a quorum of the directors, but of all the directors, sets up a scheme of management utterly inconsistent with Sections 27 and 28.

Before passing to a consideration of the fourth disputed by-law, we comment here on a view expressed in the dissenting opinion herein. The dissenting Judges conclude that, while the two by-laws first herein discussed are invalid as such because violative of statutes, the courts should, nevertheless, enforce as against either stockholder the agreement made by both of them and which finds expression in those by-laws. The substance of that stockholders' agreement was, as the dissenting opinion says, that neither stockholder would vote his stock in opposition to the stock of the other. Each stockholder thus agreed that he would conform his opinion to that of his associate on every occasion, or, absent such accord, that neither would vote at all on any occasion. We are at a loss to understand how any court could entertain a suit, or frame a judgment, to enforce such a compact. . . .

The fourth by-law here in dispute, requiring unanimity of action of all stockholders to amend the by-laws, is not, so far as we can find, specifically or impliedly authorized or forbidden by any statute of this State. Nor do we think it involves any public policy or interest. Every corporation is empowered to make by-laws, General Corporation Law, § 14, subd. 5, and by-laws of some sort or other are usually considered to be essential to the organization of a corporation. But a corporation need not provide any machinery at all for amending its by-laws—and for such an omission it could not be accused of an attempt to escape from the regulatory framework set up by law. . . . [O]nce proper by-laws have been adopted, the matter of amending them is, we think, no concern of the State. We, therefore, see no invalidity in by-law numbered 4 above.

The judgment should be modified in accordance with this opinion, and, as so modified, affirmed, without costs.

CONWAY, Judge (dissenting) . . . [The dissent described the negotiations between Dondero, who owned two-thirds of the shares (part of which were held in his wife's name), and Benintendi, which resulted in an agreement that neither would vote his shares in opposition to the shares of the other.]

. . . The question presented to us is whether the two owners of the entire stock in Kenton Hotel, Inc. (Dondero being the beneficial owner of the stock standing in his wife's name) had the power to amend the by-laws as they did.

The owners of 100% of the stock of a corporation may do with it as they will, even to giving it away, provided the rights of creditors are not involved and the public policy of the State is not offended. . . .

Despite that power of 100% of the stockholders, they may not write into a certificate of incorporation nor adopt in by-laws provisions contrary to applicable statutes. Since corporations are creatures of statute, their charters and by-laws must conform to the will of the creating power. Ripin v. United States Woven Label Co., supra; Matter of Boulevard Theatre & Realty Co., 195 App.Div. 518, 186 N.Y.S. 430, affirmed 231 N.Y. 615, 132 N.E. 910; Lorillard v. Clyde et al., 86 N.Y. 384. For that reason we think that the amendments to article I, section 4, and article II, section 2,* were beyond the power of the stockholders since they contravene General Corporation Law, sections 102 and 103, and Stock Corporation Law, sections 35, subd. c, 36, 55, 86(b), 105, subd. c.

The amendment to article II, section 10, appears to be proper

* These are the by-laws referred to in the majority opinion as by-laws (1) and (2). (Footnote by ed.)

under General Corporation Law, sections 27 and 28.** Those sections are in part as follows and show clearly by the portions we have italicized that the amendment was permissible.

"27. Directors; Qualifications; Powers of Majority.

"The business of a corporation shall be managed by its board of directors, all of whom shall be of full age and at least one of whom shall be a citizen of the United States and a resident of this state. *Unless otherwise provided* a majority of the board at a meeting duly assembled shall be necessary to constitute a quorum for the transaction of business and the act of a majority of the directors present at such a meeting shall be the act of the board. The by-laws may fix the number of directors necessary to constitute a quorum at a number less than a majority of the board, but not less than one-third of its number. . . ." (Emphasis supplied.)

"28. Acts of Directors.

"Whenever, under the provisions of any corporate law a corporation is authorized to take any action by its directors, action may be taken by the directors, regularly convened as a board, and acting by a majority of a quorum, *except when otherwise expressly required by law or the by-laws and any such action* shall be executed in behalf of the corporation by such officers as shall be designated by the board. Any business may be transacted by the board at a meeting at which every member of the board is present, though held without notice." (Emphasis supplied.)

The amendment to article VIII, section 1, is not forbidden by any statute.

The question is then presented whether the *agreement* between the parties as to the manner in which they would vote their stock may be specifically enforced through the injunctive process of an equity court *in forbidding a breach of it by Dondero* even though validity may not be accorded to the first two attempted amendments. We think it may. Benintendi and Dondero agreed together as to the manner in which they would vote their respective stock interests. To implement their agreement they chose a method forbidden by statute. The agreement, however, was valid without the method chosen. Both of the parties have lived up to and under that agreement for more than a year. We granted specific performance of an agreement in Clark v. Dodge, supra, to vote for a single-named director—certainly a more drastic limitation upon the power of a stockholder than the limitation here. . . .

There are here no rights of creditors involved. A totality of stockholders may agree among themselves as to how they shall or shall not vote shares of stock owned by them. They may by

---

** This is the by-law referred to in the majority opinion as by-law (3). (Footnote by ed.)

agreement waive or relinquish as between themselves statutory rights where such waiver or abandonment is not contrary to the public interest. There is here no question of public policy. The State does not need the assistance or leadership of Dondero in vindicating its public policy. . . .

The order should be modified in accordance herewith, with costs to the plaintiffs in the Appellate Division and in this court.

————

N.Y. BUS. CORP. LAW §§ 616, 709

[See Statutory Supplement]

————

DEL. GEN. CORP. LAW §§ 102(b)(4), 141(b), 216

[See Statutory Supplement]

————

CAL. CORP. CODE §§ 204, 307, 602

[See Statutory Supplement]

————

REV. MODEL BUS. CORP. ACT §§ 7.27, 7.32, 8.24

[See Statutory Supplement]

————

SECTION 5. FIDUCIARY OBLIGATIONS OF SHAREHOLDERS IN CLOSE CORPORATIONS: IMPLIED UNDERSTANDINGS

————

DONAHUE v. RODD ELECTROTYPE CO.

[See page 271, supra.]

————

WILKES v. SPRINGSIDE NURSING HOME, INC.

Supreme Judicial Court of Massachusetts, 1976.
370 Mass. 842, 353 N.E.2d 657.

HENNESSEY, Chief Justice.

[The plaintiff (Wilkes) filed a bill in equity for declaratory judgment, naming as defendants T. Edward Quinn,[3] Leon L. Riche, the executors of Lawrence R. Connor, and the Springside Nursing Home, Inc. Wilkes sought, among other forms of relief, damages in the amount of the salary he would have received had he continued as a director and officer of Springside subsequent to March, 1967. The court referred the suit to a master. The master's report was confirmed, a judgment was entered dismissing Wilkes's action on the merits, and the Massachusetts Supreme Court granted direct appellate review.] On appeal, Wilkes argued in the alternative that (1) he should recover damages for breach of the alleged partnership agreement; and (2) he should recover damages because the defendants, as majority stockholders in Springside, breached their fiduciary duty to him as a minority stockholder by their action in February and March, 1967.

... [W]e reverse so much of the judgment as dismisses Wilkes's complaint and order the entry of a judgment substantially granting the relief sought by Wilkes under the second alternative set forth above.

A summary of the pertinent facts as found by the master is set out in the following pages. . . .

In 1951 Wilkes acquired an option to purchase a building and lot located on the corner of Springside Avenue and North Street in Pittsfield, Massachusetts, the building having previously housed the Hillcrest Hospital. Though Wilkes was principally engaged in the roofing and siding business, he had gained a reputation locally for profitable dealings in real estate. Riche, an acquaintance of Wilkes, learned of the option, and interested Quinn (who was known to Wilkes through membership on the draft board in Pittsfield) and Pipkin (an acquaintance of both Wilkes and Riche) in joining Wilkes in his investment. The four men met and decided to participate jointly in the purchase of the building and lot as a real estate investment which, they believed, had good profit potential on resale or rental.

The parties later determined that the property would have its greatest potential for profit if it were operated by them as a nursing home. Wilkes consulted his attorney, who advised him that if the four men were to operate the contemplated nursing home as planned, they would be partners and would be liable for any debts incurred by the partnership and by each other. On the attorney's suggestion, and after consultation among themselves, ownership of

---

3. T. Edward Quinn died while this action was sub judice. The executrix of his estate has been substituted as a party-defendant. . . .

the property was vested in Springside, a corporation organized under Massachusetts law.

Each of the four men invested $1,000 and subscribed to ten shares of $100 par value stock in Springside.[6] At the time of incorporation it was understood by all of the parties that each would be a director of Springside and each would participate actively in the management and decision making involved in operating the corporation.[7] It was, further, the understanding and intention of all the parties that, corporate resources permitting, each would receive money from the corporation in equal amounts as long as each assumed an active and ongoing responsibility for carrying a portion of the burdens necessary to operate the business.

The work involved in establishing and operating a nursing home was roughly apportioned, and each of the four men undertook his respective tasks.[8] Initially, Riche was elected president of Springside, Wilkes was elected treasurer, and Quinn was elected clerk.[9] Each of the four was listed in the articles of organization as a director of the corporation.

At some time in 1952, it became apparent that the operational income and cash flow from the business were sufficient to permit the four stockholders to draw money from the corporation on a regular basis. Each of the four original parties initially received $35 a week from the corporation. As time went on the weekly return to each was increased until, in 1955, it totalled $100.

In 1959, after a long illness, Pipkin sold his shares in the corporation to Connor, who was known to Wilkes, Riche and Quinn through past transactions with Springside in his capacity as president of the First Agricultural National Bank of Berkshire County. Connor received a weekly stipend from the corporation equal to that received by Wilkes, Riche and Quinn. He was elected a director of the corporation but never held any other office. He was assigned no specific area of responsibility in the operation of the nursing home but did participate in business discussions and deci-

---

6. On May 2, 1955, and again on December 23, 1958, each of the four original investors paid for and was issued additional shares of $100 par value stock, eventually bringing the total number of shares owned by each to 115.

7. Wilkes testified before the master that, when the corporate officers were elected, all four men "were ... guaranteed directorships." Riche's understanding of the parties' intentions was that they all wanted to play a part in the management of the corporation and wanted to have some "say" in the risks involved; that, to this end, they all would be directors; and that "unless you [were] a director and officer you could not participate in the decisions of [the] enterprise."

8. Wilkes took charge of the repair, upkeep and maintenance of the physical plant and grounds; Riche assumed supervision over the kitchen facilities and dietary and food aspects of the home; Pipkin was to make himself available if and when medical problems arose; and Quinn dealt with the personnel and administrative aspects of the nursing home, serving informally as a managing director. Quinn further coordinated the activities of the other parties and served as a communication link among them when matters had to be discussed and decisions had to be made without a formal meeting.

9. Riche held the office of president from 1951 to 1963; Quinn served as president from 1963 on, as clerk from 1951 to 1967, and as treasurer from 1967 on; Wilkes was treasurer from 1951 to 1967.

sions as a director and served additionally as financial adviser to the corporation.

In 1965 the stockholders decided to sell a portion of the corporate property to Quinn who, in addition to being a stockholder in Springside, possessed an interest in another corporation which desired to operate a rest home on the property. Wilkes was successful in prevailing on the other stockholders of Springside to procure a higher sale price for the property than Quinn apparently anticipated paying or desired to pay. After the sale was consummated, the relationship between Quinn and Wilkes began to deteriorate.

The bad blood between Quinn and Wilkes affected the attitudes of both Riche and Connor. As a consequence of the strained relations among the parties, Wilkes, in January of 1967, gave notice of his intention to sell his shares for an amount based on an appraisal of their value. In February of 1967 a directors' meeting was held and the board exercised its right to establish the salaries of its officers and employees.[10] A schedule of payments was established whereby Quinn was to receive a substantial weekly increase and Riche and Connor were to continue receiving $100 a week. Wilkes, however, was left off the list of those to whom a salary was to be paid. The directors also set the annual meeting of the stockholders for March, 1967.

At the annual meeting in March,[11] Wilkes was not reelected as a director, nor was he reelected as an officer of the corporation. He was further informed that neither his services nor his presence at the nursing home was wanted by his associates.

The meetings of the directors and stockholders in early 1967, the master found, were used as a vehicle to force Wilkes out of active participation in the management and operation of the corporation and to cut off all corporate payments to him. Though the board of directors had the power to dismiss any officers or employees for misconduct or neglect of duties, there was no indication in the minutes of the board of directors' meeting in February, 1967, that the failure to establish a salary for Wilkes was based on either ground. The severance of Wilkes from the payroll resulted not from misconduct or neglect of duties, but because of the personal desire of Quinn, Riche and Connor to prevent him from continuing to receive money from the corporation. Despite a continuing deterioration in his personal relationship with his associates, Wilkes had consistently endeavored to carry on his responsibilities to the corporation in the same satisfactory manner and with the same

10. The by-laws of the corporation provided that the directors, subject to the approval of the stockholders, had the power to fix the salaries of all officers and employees. This power, however, up until February, 1967, had not been exercised formally; all payments made to the four participants in the venture had resulted from the informal but unanimous approval of all the parties concerned.

11. Wilkes was unable to attend the meeting of the board of directors in February or the annual meeting of the stockholders in March, 1967. He was represented, however, at the annual meeting by his attorney, who held his proxy.

degree of competence he had previously shown. Wilkes was at all times willing to carry on his responsibilities and participation if permitted so to do and provided that he receive his weekly stipend.

1.   We turn to Wilkes's claim for damages based on a breach of the fiduciary duty owed to him by the other participants in this venture.   In light of the theory underlying this claim, we do not consider it vital to our approach to this case whether the claim is governed by partnership law or the law applicable to business corporations.   This is so because, as all the parties agree, Springside was at all times relevant to this action, a close corporation as we have recently defined such an entity in Donahue v. Rodd Electrotype Co. of New England, Inc..... [where] we held that "stockholders in the close corporation owe one another substantially the same fiduciary duty in the operation of the enterprise that partners owe to one another." ...

In the *Donahue* case we recognized that one peculiar aspect of close corporations was the opportunity afforded to majority stockholders to oppress, disadvantage or "freeze out" minority stockholders....

... One ... device which has proved to be particularly effective in accomplishing the purpose of the majority is to deprive minority stockholders of corporate offices and of employment with the corporation ...   This "freeze-out" technique has been successful because courts fairly consistently have been disinclined to interfere in those facets of internal corporate operations, such as the selection and retention or dismissal of officers, directors and employees, which essentially involve management decisions subject to the principle of majority control....

The denial of employment to the minority at the hands of the majority is especially pernicious in some instances. A guaranty of employment with the corporation may have been one of the "basic reason[s] why a minority owner has invested capital in the firm." ... The minority stockholder typically depends on his salary as the principal return on his investment, since the "earnings of a close corporation ... are distributed in major part in salaries, bonuses, and retirement benefits." 1 F.H. O'Neal, Close Corporations § 1.07 (1971).[13] Other noneconomic interests of the minority stockholder are likewise injuriously affected by barring him from corporate office. See F.H. O'Neal, "Squeeze–Outs" of Minority Shareholders 79 (1975). Such action severely restricts his participation in the management of the enterprise, and he is relegated to enjoying those benefits incident to his status as a stockholder. See Symposium— The Close Corporation, 52 Nw.U.L.Rev. 345, 386 (1957). In sum, by terminating a minority stockholder's employment or by severing him from a position as an officer or director, the majority effectively frustrate the minority stockholder's purposes in entering on the

---

13. We note here that the master found that Springside never declared or paid a   dividend to its stockholders.

corporate venture and also deny him an equal return on his investment.

The *Donahue* decision acknowledged, as a "natural outgrowth" of the case law of this Commonwealth, a strict obligation on the part of majority stockholders in a close corporation to deal with the minority with the utmost good faith and loyalty.   On its face, this strict standard is applicable in the instant case.   The distinction between the majority action in *Donahue* and the majority action in this case is more one of form than of substance.   Nevertheless, we are concerned that untempered application of the strict good faith standard enunciated in *Donahue* to cases such as the one before us will result in the imposition of limitations on legitimate action by the controlling group in a close corporation which will unduly hamper its effectiveness in managing the corporation in the best interests of all concerned.   The majority, concededly, have certain rights to what has been termed "selfish ownership" in the corporation which should be balanced against the concept of their fiduciary obligation to the minority.   See Hill, The Sale of Controlling Shares, 70 Harv.L.Rev. 986, 1013–1015 (1957); Note, 44 Iowa L.Rev. 734, 740–741 (1959); Symposium—The Close Corporation, 52 Nw. U.L.Rev. 345, 395–396 (1957).

Therefore, when minority stockholders in a close corporation bring suit against the majority alleging a breach of the strict good faith duty owed to them by the majority, we must carefully analyze the action taken by the controlling stockholders in the individual case.   It must be asked whether the controlling group can demonstrate a legitimate business purpose for its action.   See Bryan v. Brock & Blevins Co., 343 F.Supp. 1062, 1068 (N.D.Ga.1972), aff'd, 490 F.2d 563, 570–571 (5th Cir.1974); Schwartz v. Marien, 37 N.Y.2d 487, 492, 373 N.Y.S.2d 122, 335 N.E.2d 334 (1975). . . .   In asking this question, we acknowledge the fact that the controlling group in a close corporation must have some room to maneuver in establishing the business policy of the corporation.   It must have a large measure of discretion, for example, in declaring or withholding dividends, deciding whether to merge or consolidate, establishing the salaries of corporate officers, dismissing directors with or without cause, and hiring and firing corporate employees.

When an asserted business purpose for their action is advanced by the majority, however, we think it is open to minority stockholders to demonstrate that the same legitimate objective could have been achieved through an alternative course of action less harmful to the minority's interest.   See Schwartz v. Marien, supra. . . .   If called on to settle a dispute, our courts must weigh the legitimate business purpose, if any, against the practicability of a less harmful alternative.

Applying this approach to the instant case it is apparent that the majority stockholders in Springside have not shown a legitimate business purpose for severing Wilkes from the payroll of the corporation or for refusing to reelect him as a salaried officer and director. . . .

It is an inescapable conclusion from all the evidence that the action of the majority stockholders here was a designed "freeze out" for which no legitimate business purpose has been suggested. Furthermore, we may infer that a design to pressure Wilkes into selling his shares to the corporation at a price below their value well may have been at the heart of the majority's plan.[14]

In the context of this case, several factors bear directly on the duty owed to Wilkes by his associates. At a minimum, the duty of utmost good faith and loyalty would demand that the majority consider that their action was in disregard of a long-standing policy of the stockholders that each would be a director of the corporation and that employment with the corporation would go hand in hand with stock ownership; that Wilkes was one of the four originators of the nursing home venture; and that Wilkes, like the others, had invested his capital and time for more than fifteen years with the expectation that he would continue to participate in corporate decisions. Most important is the plain fact that the cutting off of Wilkes's salary, together with the fact that the corporation never declared a dividend (see note 13 supra), assured that Wilkes would receive no return at all from the corporation.

2. The question of Wilkes's damages at the hands of the majority has not been thoroughly explored on the record before us. Wilkes, in his original complaint, sought damages in the amount of the $100 a week he believed he was entitled to from the time his salary was terminated up until the time this action was commenced. However, the record shows that, after Wilkes was severed from the corporate payroll, the schedule of salaries and payments made to the other stockholders varied from time to time. In addition, the duties assumed by the other stockholders after Wilkes was deprived of his share of the corporate earnings appear to have changed in significant respects.[15] Any resolution of this question must take into account whether the corporation was dissolved during the pendency of this litigation.

Therefore our order is as follows: So much of the judgment as dismisses Wilkes's complaint and awards costs to the defendants is reversed.[16] The case is remanded . . . for further proceedings concerning the issue of damages. Thereafter a judgment shall be entered declaring that Quinn, Riche and Connor breached their

14. This inference arises from the fact that Connor, acting on behalf of the three controlling stockholders, offered to purchase Wilkes's shares for a price Connor admittedly would not have accepted for his own shares.

15. In fairness to Wilkes, who, as the master found, was at all times ready and willing to work for the corporation, it should be noted that neither the other stockholders nor their representatives may be heard to say that Wilkes's duties were performed by them and that Wilkes's damages should, for that reason, be diminished.

16. We do not disturb the judgment in so far as it dismissed a counterclaim by Springside against Wilkes arising from the payment of money by Quinn to Wilkes after the sale in 1965 of certain property of Springside to a corporation owned at that time by Quinn and his wife. . . .

fiduciary duty to Wilkes as a minority stockholder in Springside, and awarding money damages therefor. Wilkes shall be allowed to recover from Riche, the estate of T. Edward Quinn and the estate of Lawrence R. Connor, ratably, according to the inequitable enrichment of each, the salary he would have received had he remained an officer and director of Springside. In considering the issue of damages the judge on remand shall take into account the extent to which any remaining corporate funds of Springside may be diverted to satisfy Wilkes's claim.

NIXON v. BLACKWELL

Supreme Court of Delaware, 1993.
626 A.2d 1366.

Upon appeal from the Court of Chancery. REVERSED AND REMANDED.

Before VEASEY, C.J., HORSEY, MOORE, and WALSH, JJ., and RIDGELY, President Judge (sitting by designation pursuant to art. IV, § 12), constituting the Court en Banc.

VEASEY, Chief Justice ...

I. FACTS ...

A. The Parties

Plaintiffs are 14 minority stockholders of Class B, non-voting, stock of E.C. Barton & Co. (the "Corporation"). The individual defendants are the members of the board of directors (the "Board" or the "directors"). The Corporation is also a defendant. Plaintiffs collectively own only Class B stock, and own no Class A stock. Their total holdings comprise approximately 25 percent of all the common stock outstanding as of the end of fiscal year 1989.

At all relevant times, the Board consisted of ten individuals who either are currently employed, or were once employed, by the Corporation. At the time this suit was filed, these directors collectively owned approximately 47.5 percent of all the outstanding Class A shares. The remaining Class A shares were held by certain other present and former employees of the Corporation.

B. Mr. Barton's Testamentary Plan

The Corporation is a non-public, closely-held Delaware corporation headquartered in Arkansas. It is engaged in the business of selling wholesale and retail lumber in the Mississippi Delta. The Corporation was formed in 1928 by E.C. Barton ("Mr. Barton") and has two classes of common stock: Class A voting stock and Class B non-voting stock. Substantially all of the Corporation's stock was held by Mr. Barton at the time of his death in 1967. Mr. Barton was survived by his second wife, Martha K. Barton ("Mrs. Barton") who died in 1985, and by Dorothy B. Rebsamen and Mary Lee Marcom, his daughter and granddaughter, respectively, from his first marriage. Pursuant to Mr. Barton's testamentary plan, 49 percent of the Class A voting stock was bequeathed outright to eight of his loyal employees. The remaining 51 percent, along with 14 percent of the Class B non-voting stock, was placed into an independently managed 15–year trust for the same eight people. Sixty-one percent of the Class B non-voting stock was bequeathed outright to Mrs. Barton. Mr. Barton's daughter and granddaughter received 21 percent of the Class B stock in trust. The non-voting Class B shares Mr. Barton bequeathed to his family represented 75 percent of the Corporation's total equity.

Ownership interests in the Corporation began to change in the early 1970s following the distribution of Mr. Barton's estate. Mrs. Barton gave certain shares of Class B non-voting stock to her three children, Guy C. Blackwell, Owen G. Blackwell and Martha G. Hestand (the "children"). In 1973 the Corporation purchased all of the Class B stock held in trust for Mr. Barton's daughter and granddaughter at a price of $45 per share. Mrs. Barton sold the remainder of her Class B shares to the Corporation in January 1975 at a price of $45 per share. These transactions left Mrs. Barton's three children collectively with 30 percent of the outstanding Class B non-voting stock. The children have no voting rights despite their substantial equity interest in the Corporation. The children are also the only non-employee Class B stockholders.

There is no public market for, or trading in, either class of the Corporation's stock. This creates problems for stockholders, particularly the Class B minority stockholders, who wish to sell or otherwise realize the value of their shares. The corporation purported to address this problem in several ways over the years.

C. The Self–Tenders

The Corporation occasionally offered to purchase the Class B stock of the non-employee stockholders through a series of self-tender offers. [One of the self-tender offers was accepted by Martha Hestand, but otherwise the offers were rejected by the remaining children and the other plaintiffs.]

D. The Employee Stock Ownership Plan ("ESOP")

In November 1975 the Corporation established an ESOP designed to hold Class B non-voting stock for the benefit of eligible employees of the Corporation.... Under the plan, terminating and retiring employees are entitled to receive their interest in the ESOP by taking Class B stock or cash in lieu of stock. It appears from the record that most terminating employees and retirees elect to receive cash in lieu of stock.... Thus, the ESOP provides employee Class B stockholders with a substantial measure of liquidity not available to non-employee stockholders....

E.   The Key Man Insurance Policies

The Corporation also purchased certain key man life insurance policies with death benefits payable to the Corporation. [These policies provided a further degree of liquidity to the employee-shareholders.]

II.   PROCEEDINGS IN THE COURT OF CHANCERY ...

At trial, the plaintiffs charged the defendants with ... breaching their fiduciary duties by pursuing a discriminatory liquidity policy that favors employee stockholders over non-employee stockholders through the ESOP and key man life insurance policies. The plaintiffs sought money damages for past dividends, a one-time liquidity dividend, and a guarantee of future dividends at a specified rate....

[The Vice Chancellor found for the plaintiffs.] The finding for the plaintiffs and the form of the relief granted to the plaintiffs ... are set forth in paragraphs 4 and 5 of the Order and Final Judgment of March 10, 1992:

> 4.   On the claim of the plaintiffs presented at trial that the individual defendants breached their fiduciary duty as directors and treated the plaintiffs unfairly as the non-employee, minority Class B stockholders of the Company by providing no method by which plaintiffs might liquidate their stock at fair value while providing a means through the ESOP and key-man life insurance whereby the stock of terminating employees could be purchased from them, judgment is entered in favor of the plaintiffs.

> 5.   Pursuant to the judgment entered in paragraph 4 above, defendants shall take the following steps in order to remedy the unfair treatment of Class B stockholders:

>> a.   An amount equal to the total of all key man life insurance premiums paid to date, together with interest from the date of payment shall be used to repurchase Class B stock other than shares held by the ESOP or defendants, at a price to be set by an independent appraiser.

>> b.   Hereafter, neither the ESOP nor the company shall purchase or repurchase any stock without offering to purchase the same number of shares, on the same terms and conditions, from the Class B stockholders other than defendants and the ESOP.

Plaintiffs were awarded attorneys' fees and costs in a subsequent order entered on May 20, 1992....

The following portions of the opinion of the trial court are crucial to the determination of the issues on appeal....

> All Barton stockholders face the same liquidity problem. If they are to sell their shares, they must persuade defendants to authorize a repurchase by the company. The stockholders have no bargaining power and must accept whatever terms are

dictated by defendants or retain their stock. If the stockholder is pressed for cash to pay estate taxes, for example, as has happened more than once, the stockholder is entirely at defendants' mercy. Defendants recognized their employee stockholders' liquidity needs when they established the ESOP. As noted previously, employees have the option of taking cash in lieu of the shares allocated to their accounts. Moreover, the disparity in bargaining position is eliminated for employee stockholders because the cash payment is determined on the basis of an annual valuation made by an independent party. *No similar plan or arrangement has been put into place with respect to the Class B stockholders. There is no point in time at which they can be assured of receiving cash for all or any portion of their holdings at a price determined by an independent appraiser.*

Defendants have gone one step farther in addressing their own liquidity problems. Their ESOP allocation may be handled in the same manner as other employees. However, defendants are substantial stockholders independent of their ESOP holdings. *In order to solve defendants' own liquidity problem, the company has been purchasing key man life insurance since at least 1982. The proceeds will help assure that Barton is in a position to purchase all of defendants' stock at the time of death.* In 1989, the premium cost for the key man insurance was slightly higher than the total amount paid in dividends for the year. . . .

I find it inherently unfair for defendants to be purchasing key man life insurance in order to provide liquidity for themselves while providing no method by which plaintiffs may liquidate their stock at fair value. By this ruling, I am not suggesting that there is some generalized duty to purchase illiquid stock at any particular price. However, the needs of all stockholders must be considered and addressed when decisions are made to provide some form of liquidity. Both the ESOP and the key man insurance provide some measure of liquidity, but only for a select group of stockholders. Accordingly, I find that relief is warranted.

Blackwell v. Nixon, Del.Ch., C.A. No. 9041, Berger, V.C. (Sept. 26, 1991) at pp. 10–13, 1991 WL 194725 (footnotes omitted; emphasis supplied). . . .

V. APPLICABLE PRINCIPLES OF SUBSTANTIVE LAW

Defendants contend that the trial court erred in not applying the business judgment rule. Since the defendants benefited from the ESOP and could have benefited from the key man life insurance beyond that which benefited other stockholders generally, the defendants are on both sides of the transaction. For that reason, we agree with the trial court that the entire fairness test applies to this aspect of the case. Accordingly, defendants have the burden of showing the entire fairness of those transactions....

The trial court in this case, however, appears to have adopted the novel legal principle that Class B stockholders had a right to "liquidity" equal to that which the court found to be available to the defendants. It is well established in our jurisprudence that stockholders need not always be treated equally for all purposes.... To hold that fairness necessarily requires precise equality is to beg the question:

> Many scholars, though few courts, conclude that one aspect of fiduciary duty is the equal treatment of investors. Their argument takes the following form: fiduciary principles require fair conduct; equal treatment is fair conduct; hence, fiduciary principles require equal treatment. The conclusion does not follow. The argument depends on an equivalence between *equal* and *fair* treatment. To say that fiduciary principles require equal treatment is to beg the question whether investors would contract for equal or even equivalent treatment.

Frank H. Easterbrook and Daniel R. Fischel, The Economic Structure of Corporate Law 110 (1991) (emphasis in original). This holding of the trial court overlooks the significant facts that the minority stockholders were not: (a) employees of the Corporation; (b) entitled to share in an ESOP; (c) qualified for key man insurance; or (d) protected by specific provisions in the certificate of incorporation, by-laws, or a stockholders' agreement.

There is support in this record for the fact that the ESOP is a corporate benefit and was established, at least in part, to benefit the Corporation. Generally speaking, the creation of ESOPs is a normal corporate practice and is generally thought to benefit the corporation. The same is true generally with respect to key man insurance programs. If such corporate practices were necessarily to require equal treatment for non-employee stockholders, that would be a matter for legislative determination in Delaware. There is no such legislation to that effect. If we were to adopt such a rule, our decision would border on judicial legislation. See Providence & Worcester Co. v. Baker, Del.Supr., 378 A.2d 121, 124 (1977).

Accordingly, we hold that the Vice Chancellor erred as a matter of law in concluding that the liquidity afforded to the employee stockholders by the ESOP and the key man insurance required substantially equal treatment for the non-employee stockholders. Moreover, the Vice Chancellor failed to evaluate and articulate, for example, whether or not and to what extent (a) corporate benefits flowed from the ESOP and the key man insurance; (b) the ESOP and key man insurance plans are novel, extraordinary, or relatively routine business practices; (c) the dividend policy was even relevant; (d) Mr. Barton's plan for employee management and benefits should be honored; and (e) the self-tenders showed defendants' willingness to provide an exit opportunity for the plaintiffs....

We hold on this record that defendants have met their burden of establishing the entire fairness of their dealings with the non-employee Class B stockholders, and are entitled to judgment. The record is sufficient to conclude that plaintiffs' claim that the defendant directors have maintained a discriminatory policy of favoring Class A employee stockholders over Class B non-employee stockholders is without merit. The directors have followed a consistent policy originally established by Mr. Barton, the founder of the Corporation, whose intent from the formation of the Corporation was to use the Class A stock as the vehicle for the Corporation's continuity through employee management and ownership.

Mr. Barton established the Corporation in 1928 by creating two classes of stock, not one, and by holding 100 percent of the Class A stock and 82 percent of the Class B stock. Mr. Barton himself established the practice of purchasing key man life insurance with funds of the Corporation to retain in the employ of the Corporation valuable employees by assuring them that, following their retirement or death, the Corporation will have liquid assets which could be used to repurchase the shares acquired by the employee, which shares may otherwise constitute an illiquid and unsalable asset of his or her estate. Another rational purpose is to prevent the stock from passing out of the control of the employees of the Corporation into the hands of family or descendants of the employee.

The directors' actions following Mr. Barton's death are consistent with Mr. Barton's plan. An ESOP, for example, is normally established for employees. Accordingly, there is no inequity in limiting ESOP benefits to the employee stockholders. Indeed, it makes no sense to include non-employees in ESOP benefits. The fact that the Class B stock represented 75 percent of the Corporation's total equity is irrelevant to the issue of fair dealing. The Class B stock was given no voting rights because those stockholders were not intended to have a direct voice in the management and operation of the Corporation. They were simply passive investors—entitled to be treated fairly but not necessarily to be treated equally. The fortunes of the Corporation rested with the Class A employee stockholders and the Class B stockholders benefited from the multiple increases in value of their Class B stock. Moreover, the Board made continuing efforts to buy back the Class B stock.

We hold that paragraphs 4 and 5 of the March 10, 1992 order of the trial court and the order of May 20, 1992, awarding fees and costs to plaintiffs, are reversed and remanded with instructions to conform the judgment to the findings and conclusions in this opinion...

Accordingly, we REVERSE the judgment of the Court of Chancery and REMAND the matter for proceedings not inconsistent with this opinion.

———

SECTION 6. THE VALUATION
OF A BUSINESS

Many issues of corporate law are intimately related to problems of valuation. That is particularly true of the issues raised in sections 7, 8 and 10, infra, concerning restrictions on the transferability of shares, mandatory sales of shares, and dissolution. Now is therefore an appropriate time to provide an introduction to the general problem of valuing a business, and the special problem of valuing a business in corporate form.

The present Section includes two selections. The first selection is a case that illustrates the traditional methods that courts have used in corporate law for valuing stock. (Note that unlike most of the cases in this Chapter, the case in this Section involves a publicly held corporation.) The second selection provides a more sophisticated treatment of valuation methods, written in a highly accessible way. Many courts continue to use the more traditional valuation methods, but increasingly courts are using, or at least are open to using, more sophisticated methods.

It may be useful, before studying the materials in this section, to review the materials on the present-value rule in Chapter 3, Section 10.

PIEMONTE v. NEW BOSTON GARDEN CORP.[1]

Supreme Judicial Court of Massachusetts, 1979.
377 Mass. 719, 387 N.E.2d 1145.

WILKINS, Justice.

The plaintiffs were stockholders in Boston Garden Arena Corporation (Garden Arena), a Massachusetts corporation whose stockholders voted on July 19, 1973, to merge with the defendant corporation in circumstances which entitled each plaintiff to "demand payment for his stock from the resulting or surviving corporation and an appraisal in accordance with the provisions of [G.L. c. 156B, §§ 86–98]." G.L. c. 156B, § 85, as amended by St.1969, c. 392, § 22. The plaintiffs commenced this action under G.L. c. 156B, § 90, seeking a judicial determination of the "fair value" of their shares "as of the day preceding the date of the vote approving the proposed corporate action."[2] G.L. c. 156B, § 92, inserted by St.1964, c. 723, § 1. Each party has appealed from a judgment

---

1. The fifteen plaintiffs collectively owned 6,289 shares in Garden Arena Corporation, representing approximately 2.8% of its 224,892 shares of outstanding stock.

2. The plaintiffs took all the necessary, preliminary steps to preserve their rights. Each plaintiff objected in writing to the proposed merger; none of their shares was voted in favor of the proposed corporate

determining the fair value of the plaintiffs' stock. We granted the defendant's application for direct appellate review.

On July 18, 1973, Garden Arena owned all the stock in a subsidiary corporation that owned both a franchise in the National Hockey League (NHL), known as the Boston Bruins, and a corporation that held a franchise in the American Hockey League (AHL), known as the Boston Braves. Garden Arena also owned and operated Boston Garden Sports Arena (Boston Garden), an indoor auditorium with facilities for the exhibition of sporting and other entertainment events, and a corporation that operated the food and beverage concession at the Boston Garden. A considerable volume of documentary material was introduced in evidence concerning the value of the stock of Garden Arena on July 18, 1973, the day before Garden Arena's stockholders approved the merger. Each side presented expert testimony. The judge gave consideration to the market value of the Garden Arena stock, to the value of its stock based on its earnings, and to the net asset value of Garden Arena's assets. Weighting these factors, the judge arrived at a total, per share value of $75.27.[3]

In this appeal, the parties raise objections to certain of the judge's conclusions. We will expand on the facts as necessary when we consider each issue. We conclude that the judge followed acceptable procedures in valuing the Garden Arena stock; that his determinations were generally within the range of discretion accorded a fact finder; but that, in three instances, the judge's treatment of the evidence was or may have been in error and, accordingly, the case should be remanded to him for further consideration of those three points.

General Principles of Law

The statutory provisions applicable to this case were enacted in 1964 as part of the Massachusetts Business Corporation Law. St.1964, c. 723, § 1. The appraisal provisions (G.L. c. 156B, §§ 86–98) were based on a similar, but not identical, Delaware statute (Del.Code tit. 8, § 262). See Notes by Boston Bar Committee—1964, M.G.L.A. c. 156B, §§ 86–92, 94–97 (West). In these circumstances, consideration of the Delaware law, including judicial decisions, is appropriate, but in no sense should we feel compelled to adhere without question to that law, which has been in the process of development since our enactment of G.L. c. 156B in 1964. We

action (see G.L. c. 156B, § 86); each plaintiff seasonably demanded in writing payment from the defendant for the fair value of his stock (see G.L. c. 156B, § 89); and no agreement as to that fair value was reached within thirty days of the demand (see G.L. c. 156B, § 90).

3. The judge determined the market value, earnings value, and net asset value of the stock and then weighted these values as follows:

	Value	Weight		Result
Market Value:	$ 26.50	×	10% =	$ 2.65
Earnings Value:	$ 52.60	×	40% =	$21.04
Net Asset Value:	$103.16	×	50% =	$51.58

Total Value Per Share: $75.27

do not perceive a legislative intent to adopt judicial determinations of Delaware law made prior to the enactment of G.L. c. 156B and certainly no such intent as to judicial interpretations made since that date.[4]

The Delaware courts have adopted a general approach to the appraisal of stock which a Massachusetts judge might appropriately follow, as did the judge in this case. The Delaware procedure, known as the "Delaware block approach," calls for a determination of the market value, the earnings value, and the net asset value of the stock, followed by the assignment of a percentage weight to each of the elements of value. See generally, Note, Valuation of Dissenters' Stock under Appraisal Statutes, 79 Harv.L.Rev. 1453, 1456–1471 (1966).

There have been no appellate decisions in this State concerning the appraisal of stock since the present appraisal statute was enacted, and there were few under the previously applicable, somewhat similar, statute.[5] See Martignette v. Sagamore Mfg. Co., 340 Mass. 136, 163 N.E.2d 9 (1959); Cole v. Wells, 224 Mass. 504, 113 N.E. 189 (1916). In the *Martignette* case, the court held that, even where stock had an established market, market price was not determinative and that "it is for the appraisers in the particular case to determine the weight of the relevant factors." Martignette v. Sagamore Mfg. Co., supra, 340 Mass. at 142, 163 N.E.2d at 13. If the corporation is solvent or has significant earnings prospects, "the earnings and worth of the corporation as a going concern are important." Id. at 142–143, 163 N.E.2d at 13 (overruling in this respect Cole v. Wells, supra, 224 Mass. at 513, 113 N.E. 189, which had held that the value of a dissenting stockholder's shares should be ascertained "as if liquidation had been voted"). We perceive no legislative intention to overrule these cases by the enactment of the new appraisal provisions in 1964.

With these considerations in mind, we turn to the specific issues that have been argued on appeal, considering, in order, the judge's determination of market value, earnings value and net asset value of the stock; his decision concerning the weighting of these components; the defendant's objection to the consideration of certain evidence; and, finally, the judge's decision on the rate of interest to be allowed to the plaintiffs.

Market Value

The judge was acting within reasonable limits when he determined that the market value of Garden Arena stock on July 18, 1973, was $26.50 a share. Each party challenges this determination.

---

4. This is not a case in which the statute of another jurisdiction was subsequently enacted here. . . . The Massachusetts appraisal provisions differ somewhat from the Delaware appraisal provisions. Compare G.L. c. 156B, §§ 86–98, with Del.Code tit. 8, § 262.

5. Under the previously applicable statute, a panel of three appraisers (rather than a judge) valued the stock. See G.L. c. 156, § 46.

The plaintiffs' contention is that market value should be disregarded because it was not ascertainable due to the limited trading in Garden Arena stock.[6] The defendant argues that the judge was obliged to reconstruct market value based on comparable companies, and, in doing so, should have arrived at a market value of $22 a share.

Market value may be a significant factor, even the dominant factor, in determining the "fair value" of shares of a particular corporation under G.L. c. 156B, § 92. Shares regularly traded on a recognized stock exchange are particularly susceptible to valuation on the basis of their market price, although even in such cases the market value may well not be conclusive. See Martignette v. Sagamore Mfg. Co., 340 Mass. 136, 141–142, 163 N.E.2d 9 (1959). On the other hand, where there is no established market for a particular stock, actual market value cannot be used. In such cases, a judge might undertake to "reconstruct" market value, but he is not obliged to do so.[7] Indeed, the process of the reconstruction of market value may actually be no more than a variation on the valuation of corporate assets and corporate earnings.

In this case, Garden Arena stock was traded on the Boston Stock Exchange, but rarely. Approximately ninety per cent of the company's stock was held by the controlling interests and not traded. Between January 1, 1968, and December 4, 1972, 16,741 shares were traded. During this period, an annual average of approximately 1.5% of the outstanding stock changed hands. In 1972, 4,372 shares were traded at prices ranging from $20.50 a share to $29 a share. The public announcement of the proposed merger was made on December 7, 1972. The last prior sale of 200 shares on December 4, 1972, was made at $26.50 a share. The judge accepted that sale price as the market price to be used in his determination of value.

The judge concluded that the volume of trading was sufficient to permit a determination of market value and expressed a preference for the actual sale price over any reconstruction of a market value, which he concluded would place "undue reliance on corporations, factors, and circumstances not applicable to Garden Arena stock." The decision to consider market value and the market value selected were within the judge's discretion.

Valuation Based on Earnings

The judge determined that the average per share earnings of Garden Arena for the five-fiscal-year period which ended June 30,

---

6. This argument also bears on the relative weight to be assigned to market value as against net asset value and earnings value, a subject we shall consider subsequently.

7. The Delaware cases require the reconstruction of market value only when the actual market value cannot be determined and a hypothetical market value can be reconstructed. Compare Application of Del. Racing Ass'n, 213 A.2d 203, 211–212 (Del. 1965), with Universal City Studios, Inc. v. Francis I. duPont & Co., 334 A.2d 216, 222 (Del.1975).

1973, was $5.26. To this amount he applied a factor, or multiplier, of 10 to arrive at $52.60 as the per share value based on earnings.

Each party objects to certain aspects of this process. We reject the plaintiffs' argument that the judge could not properly use any value based on earnings, and also reject the parties' various challenges to the judge's method of determining value based on earnings.

Delaware case law, which, as we have said, we regard as instructive but not binding, has established a method of computing value based on corporate earnings. The appraiser generally starts by computing the average earnings of the corporation for the past five years.[8] Universal City Studios, Inc. v. Francis I. duPont & Co., 334 A.2d 216, 218 (Del.1975); Application of Del. Racing Ass'n, 213 A.2d 203, 212 (Del.1965). Extraordinary gains and losses are excluded from the average earnings calculation. Gibbons v. Schenley Indus., Inc., 339 A.2d 460, 468–470 (Del.Ch.1975); Felder v. Anderson, Clayton & Co., 39 Del.Ch. 76, 86–87, 159 A.2d 278 (1960). The appraiser then selects a multiplier (to be applied to the average earnings) which reflects the prospective financial condition of the corporation and the risk factor inherent in the corporation and the industry. Universal City Studios, Inc. v. Francis I. duPont & Co., supra. In selecting a multiplier, the appraiser generally looks to other comparable corporations. Universal City Studios, Inc. v. Francis I. duPont & Co., supra at 219–221 (averaging price-earnings ratios of nine other motion picture companies as of date of merger); Gibbons v. Schenley Indus., Inc., supra at 471 (using Standard & Poor's Distiller's Index as of date of merger); Felder v. Anderson, Clayton & Co., supra, 39 Del.Ch. at 87, 159 A.2d 278 (averaging price-earnings ratios of representative stocks over previous five-year period because of recent boom in industry). The appraiser's choice of a multiplier is largely discretionary and will be upheld if it is "within the range of reason." Universal City Studios, Inc. v. Francis I. duPont & Co., supra at 219 (approving multiplier of 16.1); Application of Del. Racing Ass'n, supra at 213 (approving multiplier of 10); Swanton v. State Guar. Corp., 42 Del.Ch. 477, 483, 215 A.2d 242 (1965) (approving multiplier of 14).[9]

The judge chose not to place "singular reliance on comparative data preferring to choose a multiplier based on the specific situation and prospects of the Garden Arena." He weighed the favorable financial prospects of the Bruins: the popularity and success of the team, the relatively low average age of its players, the popularity of Bobby Orr and Phil Esposito, the high attendance record at home

8. A 1976 amendment to the Delaware statute requires the court to appraise the stock rather than appoint an appraiser. 60 Del.Laws, c. 371, Del.Code tit. 8, § 262(f).

9. Although Delaware courts have relied on, and continue to rely on, Professor Dewing's capitalization chart (see 1 A.S. Dewing, The Financial Policy of Corporations 390–391 [5th ed. 1953]), they have recognized that it is somewhat outdated and no longer the "be-all and end-all" on the subject of earnings value. See Universal City Studios, Inc. v. Francis I. duPont & Co., supra at 219; Swanton v. State Guar. Corp., 42 Del.Ch. 477, 483–484, 215 A.2d 242 (1965).

games (each home team retained all gate receipts), and the advantageous radio and television contracts. On the other hand, he recognized certain risks, the negative prospects: the existence of the World Hockey Association with its potential, favorable impact on players' bargaining positions, and legal threats to the players' reserve clause. He concluded that a multiplier of 10 was appropriate. There was ample evidentiary support for his conclusion. He might have looked to and relied on price-earnings ratios of other corporations, but he was not obliged to.

The judge did not have to consider the dividend record of Garden Arena, as the defendant urges. Dividends tend to reflect the same factors as earnings and, therefore, need not be valued separately. See Felder v. Anderson, Clayton & Co., 39 Del.Ch. 76, 88–89, 159 A.2d 278 (1960). And since dividend policy is usually reflected in market value, the use of market value as a factor in the valuation process permitted the low and sporadic dividend rate to be given some weight in the process. Beyond that, the value of the plaintiffs' stock should not be depreciated because the controlling interests often chose to declare low dividends or none at all.

The judge did not abuse his discretion in including expansion income (payments from teams newly admitted to the NHL) received during two of the five recent fiscal years. His conclusion was well within the guidelines of decided cases. See Gibbons v. Schenley Indus., Inc., 339 A.2d 460, 470 (Del.Ch.1975) (gain from sale of real estate not extraordinary where corporation often sold such assets); Felder v. Anderson, Clayton & Co., 39 Del.Ch. 76, 86–87, 159 A.2d 278 (1960) (loss attributable to a drought not extraordinary). The Bruins first received expansion income ($2,000,000) during the fiscal year which ended on June 30, 1967, a year not included in the five-year average. The franchise received almost $1,000,000 more in 1970 and approximately $860,000 in 1972. This 1970 and 1972 income was reflected in the computation of earnings. Expansion income did not have to be treated as extraordinary income. The judge concluded that it did not distort "an accurate projection of the earnings value of Garden Arena" and noted, as of July 18, 1973, an NHL expansion plan for the admission of two more teams in 1974–1975 and for expansion thereafter.

Valuation Based on Net Asset Value

The judge determined total net asset value by first valuing the net assets of Garden Arena apart from the Bruins franchise and the concession operations at Boston Garden. He selected $9,400,000 (the June 30, 1973, book value of Garden Arena) as representing that net asset value. Then, he added his valuations of the Bruins franchise ($9,600,000) and the concession operation ($4,200,000) to arrive at a total asset value of $23,200,000, or $103.16 a share.[10]

The parties raise various objections to these determinations. The defendant argues that the judge included certain items twice in

---

10. $23,200,000 ÷ 224,892 (the number of outstanding shares).

his valuation of the net assets of Garden Arena and that he should have given no separate value to the concession operation. The plaintiff argues that the judge undervalued both the Boston Garden and the value of the Bruins franchise.

The defendant objects to the judge's refusal to deduct $1,116,-000 from the $9,400,000 that represented the net asset value of Garden Arena (exclusive of the net asset value of the Bruins franchise and the concession operation). The defendant's expert testified that the $9,400,000 figure included $1,116,000 attributable to the goodwill of the Bruins, net player investment, and the value of the AHL franchise. The judge recognized that the items included in the $1,116,000 should not be valued twice and seemingly agreed that they would be more appropriately included in the value of the Bruins franchise than in the $9,400,000. He was not plainly wrong, however, in declining to deduct them from the $9,400,000, because, as is fully warranted from the testimony of the defendant's expert, the judge concluded that the defendant's expert did not include these items in his determination of the value of the Bruins franchise.[11] The defendant's expert, whose determination the judge accepted, arrived at his value of the Bruins franchise by adding certain items to the cost of a new NHL franchise, but none of those items included goodwill, net player investment, or the value of an AHL franchise. Acceptance of the defendant's argument would have resulted in these items being entirely omitted from the net asset valuation of Garden Arena.[12]

The plaintiffs object that the judge did not explicitly determine the value of the Boston Garden and implicitly undervalued it. Garden Arena had purchased the Boston Garden on May 25, 1973, for $4,000,000, and accounted for it on the June 30, 1973, balance sheet as a $4,000,000 asset with a corresponding mortgage liability of $3,437,065. Prior to the purchase, Garden Arena had held a long-term lease which was unfavorable to the owner of the Boston Garden.[13] The existence of the lease would tend to depress the purchase price.

The judge stated that the $9,400,000 book value "*includes* a reasonable value for Boston Garden" (emphasis supplied). He did not indicate whether, if he had meant to value the Boston Garden at its purchase price (with an adjustment for the mortgage liabilities), he had considered the effect the lease would have had on that price.

---

11. The defendant makes no special argument concerning the judge's failure to deduct certain relatively minor, intangible assets, including merger costs.

12. One of the points on which we will remand this case is the valuation of the Bruins franchise. Since, as discussed below, the judge need not have felt constrained to accept the defendant's expert's opinion on this issue, on remand he will be free to determine the value of the franchise based on such evidence as he chooses to accept. Assignment of a different value to the franchise may require an adjustment in the net asset value of Garden Arena if the franchise value determined by the judge includes some or all of the items supposedly included in the $1,116,000.

13. The lease, which ran until June 1, 1986, contained a fixed maximum rent and an obligation on the lessee to pay only two-thirds of any increase in local real estate taxes. In a period of inflation and rising local real estate taxes, the value of the lease to the lessor was decreasing annually.

While we recognize that the fact-finding role of the judge permits him to reject the opinions of the various experts,[14] we conclude, in the absence of an explanation of his reasons, that it is possible that the judge did not give adequate consideration to the value of the Garden property. The judge should consider this subject further on remand.

A major area of dispute was the value of the Bruins franchise. The judge rejected the value advanced by the plaintiffs' expert ($18,000,000), stating that "[a]lthough the defendant's figure of [$9,600,000] seems somewhat low in comparison with the cost of expansion team franchises, *the Court is constrained* to accept defendant's value as it is the more creditable and legally appropriate expert opinion in the record" (emphasis supplied). Although the choice of the word "constrained" may have been inadvertent, it connotes a sense of obligation. As the trier of fact, the judge was not bound to accept the valuation of either one expert or the other. He was entitled to reach his own conclusion as to value. . . .

Because the judge may have felt bound to accept the value placed on the Bruins franchise by the defendant's expert, we shall remand this case for him to arrive at his own determination of the value of the Bruins franchise. He would be warranted in arriving at the same valuation as that advanced on behalf of the defendant, but he is not obliged to do so.

The defendant argues that, in arriving at the value of the assets of Garden Arena, the judge improperly placed a separate value on the right to operate concessions at the Boston Garden. We agree with the judge. The fact that earnings from concessions were included in the computation of earnings value, one component in the formula, does not mean that the value of the concessions should have been excluded from the computation of net asset value, another such component.

The value of the concession operation was not reflected in the value of the real estate. Real estate may be valued on the basis of rental income, but it is not valued on the basis of the profitability of business operations within the premises. . . . Moreover, it is manifest that the value of the concession operation was not included in the value placed on the Boston Garden. The record indicates that Garden Arena already owned the concession rights when it purchased the Boston Garden. The conclusion that the value of the concession operation was not reflected in the value of the Boston Garden is particularly warranted because the determined value of the right to operate the concessions ($4,200,000) was higher than the May 25, 1973, purchase price ($4,000,000) of the Boston Garden.

We do conclude, however, that the judge may have felt unnecessarily bound to accept the plaintiffs' evidence of the value of the

14. The lowest value expressed by any expert for the plaintiffs was $8,250,000 (exclusive of mortgage liabilities), based on depreciated reproduction cost. The defendant offered no testimony concerning the value of the property on July 18, 1973.

concession operation.   He stated that "since the defendant did not submit evidence on this issue, the Court will accept plaintiffs' expert appraisal of the value of the concession operation."   Although the judge did not express the view that he was "constrained" to accept the plaintiffs' valuation, as he did concerning the defendant's valuation of the Bruins franchise, he may have misconstrued his authority on this issue.   The judge was not obliged to accept the plaintiffs' evidence at face value merely because no other evidence was offered. . . .

On remand, the judge should reconsider his determination of the value of the concession operation and exercise his own judgment concerning the bases for the conclusion arrived at by the plaintiffs' expert.   However, the evidence did warrant the value selected by the judge, and no reduction in that value is required on this record.

Weighting of Valuations

The judge weighted the three valuations as follows:

Market Value	—	10%
Earnings Value	—	40%
Net Asset Value	—	50%

We accept these allocations as reasonable and within the range of the judge's discretion.

Any determination of the weight to be given the various elements involved in the valuation of a stock must be based on the circumstances.   Heller v. Munsingwear, Inc., 33 Del.Ch. 593, 598, 98 A.2d 774 (1953).   The decision to weight market value at only 10% was appropriate, considering the thin trading in the stock of Garden Arena.   The decision to attribute 50% weight to net asset value was reasonably founded.   The judge concluded that, because of tax reasons, the value of a sports franchise, unlike many corporate activities, depends more on its assets than on its earnings;   that Garden Arena had been largely a family corporation in which earnings were of little significance;   that Garden Arena had approximately $5,000,000 in excess liquid assets;   and that the Garden property was a substantial real estate holding in an excellent location.

The judge might have reached different conclusions on this record.   He was not obliged, however, to reconstruct market value and, as the defendant urges, attribute 50% weight to it.   Nor was he obliged, as the plaintiffs argue, to consider only net asset value. See Martignette v. Sagamore Mfg. Co., 340 Mass. 136, 142, 163 N.E.2d 9 (1959).   Market value and earnings value properly could be considered in these circumstances.

Although we would have found no fault with a determination to give even greater weight to the price per share based on the net asset value of Garden Arena, the judge was acting within an acceptable range of discretion in selecting the weights he gave to the various factors.

Evidentiary Objections

The defendant objects to the introduction and consideration of evidence of events arising after the statutory valuation date. The judge carefully noted his statutory obligation to value the shares "as of the day preceding the date of the vote approving the proposed corporate action" and "exclusive of any element of value arising from the expectation or accomplishment of the proposed corporate action." G.L. c. 156B, § 92.... Even more significant is the plain fact that there is no showing that the judge relied on any evidence of events occurring after July 18, 1973, or on any expert opinion that was based on any such events.

Interest Allowance

The defendant objects to the judge's determination to award interest at 8% per annum. It does not object to the judge's decision to award interest, a matter within his discretion (see G.L. c. 156B, §§ 92 and 95), nor to his decision to compound interest annually.... [T]he judge reasonably could have concluded that 8% per annum reflected "the rate of interest at which a prudent investor could have invested money." Universal City Studios, Inc. v. Francis I. duPont & Co., 334 A.2d 216, 222 (Del.1975)....

Conclusion

We have concluded that the judge's method of valuing the Garden Arena stock was essentially correct. In this opinion, we have indicated, however, that the case should be remanded to him for clarification and further consideration on the record of three matters: his valuation of the Boston Garden, the Bruins franchise, and the concession operation.

So ordered.

L. SOLOMON, D. SCHWARTZ, J. BAUMAN & E. WEISS, CORPORATIONS—LAW AND POLICY 96–102

3d ed. 1994.

THE OLD MAN AND THE TREE: A PARABLE OF VALUATION

Once there was a wise old man who owned an apple tree. The tree was a fine tree, and with little care it produced a crop of apples each year which he sold for $100. The man was getting old, wanted to retire to a different climate and he decided to sell the tree. He enjoyed teaching a good lesson, and he placed an advertisement in the Business Opportunities section of the Wall Street Journal in which he said he wanted to sell the tree for "the best offer."

The first person to respond to the ad offered to pay the $50 which, the offeror said, was what he would be able to get for selling the apple tree for firewood after he had cut it down. "You are a very foolish person," said the old man. "You are offering to pay only the salvage value of this tree. That might be a good price for a pine tree or perhaps even this tree if it had stopped bearing fruit or if the price of apple wood had gotten so high that the tree was more valuable as a source of wood than as a source of fruit. But my tree is worth much more than $50."

The next person to come to see the old man offered to pay $100 for the tree. "For that," said she, "is what I would be able to get for selling this year's crop of fruit which is about to mature."

"You are not quite so foolish as the first one," responded the old man. "At least you see that this tree has more value as a producer of apples than it would as a source of firewood. But $100 is not the right price. You are not considering the value of next year's crop of apples, nor that of the years after. Please take your $100 and go elsewhere."

The next person to come along was a young man who had just started business school. "I am going to major in marketing," he said. "I figure that the tree should live for at least another fifteen years. If I sell the apples for $100 a year, that will total $1,500. I offer you $1,500 for your tree."

"You, too, are foolish," said the man. "Surely the $100 you would earn by selling the apples from the tree fifteen years from now cannot be worth $100 to you today. In fact, if you placed $41.73 today in a bank account paying 6% interest, compounded annually, that small sum would grow to $100 at the end of fifteen years. Therefore the present value of $100 worth of apples fifteen years from now, assuming an interest rate of 6%, is only $41.73, not $100. Pray," said the old man, "take your $1,500 and invest it safely in high-grade corporate bonds until you have graduated from business school and know more about finance."

Before long, there came a wealthy physician, who said, "I don't know much about apple trees, but I know what I like. I'll pay the market price for it. The last fellow was willing to pay you $1,500 for the tree, and so it must be worth that."

"Doctor," advised the old man, "you should get yourself a knowledgeable investment adviser. If there were truly a market in which apple trees were traded with some regularity, the prices at which they were sold would be a good indication of their value. But there is no such market. And the isolated offer I just received tells very little about how much my tree is really worth—as you would surely realize if you had heard the other foolish offers I have heard today. Please take your money and buy a vacation home."

The next prospective purchaser to come along was an accounting student. When the old man asked "What price are you willing to give me?" the student first demanded to see the old man's books.

The old man had kept careful records and gladly brought them out. After examining them the accounting student said, "Your books show that you paid $75 for this tree ten years ago. Furthermore, you have made no deductions for depreciation. I do not know if that conforms with generally accepted accounting principles, but assuming that it does, the book value of your tree is $75. I will pay that."

"Ah, you students know so much and yet so little," chided the old man. "It is true that the book value of my tree is $75, but any fool can see that it is worth far more than that. You had best go back to school and see if you can find some books that will show you how to use your numbers to better effect."

The next prospective purchaser was a young stockbroker who had recently graduated from business school. Eager to test her new skills she, too, asked to examine the books. After several hours she came back to the old man and said she was now prepared to make an offer that valued the tree on the basis of the capitalization of its earnings.

For the first time the old man's interest was piqued and he asked her to go on.

The young woman explained that while the apples were sold for $100 last year, that figure did not represent profits realized from the tree. There were expenses attendant to the tree, such as the cost of fertilizer, the expense of pruning the tree, the cost of the tools, expenses in connection with picking the apples, carting them into town and selling them. Somebody had to do these things, and a portion of the salaries paid to those persons ought to be charged against the revenues from the tree. Moreover, the purchase price, or cost, of the tree was an expense. A portion of the cost is taken into account each year of the tree's useful life. Finally, there were taxes. She concluded that the profit from the tree was $50 last year.

"Wow!" exclaimed the old man. "I thought I made $100 off that tree."

"That's because you failed to match expenses with revenues, in accordance with generally accepted accounting principles," she explained. "You don't actually have to write a check to be charged with what accountants consider to be your expenses. For example, you bought a station wagon some time ago and you used it part of the time to cart apples to market. The wagon will last a while and each year some of the original cost has to be matched against revenues. A portion of the amount has to be spread out over the next several years even though you expended it all at one time. Accountants call that depreciation. I'll bet you never figured that in your calculation of profits."

"I'll bet you're right," he replied. "Tell me more."

"I also went back into the books for a few years and I saw that in some years the tree produced fewer apples than in other years, the prices varied and the costs were not exactly the same each year. Taking an average of only the last three years, I came up with a figure of $45 as a fair sample of the tree's earnings. But that is only half of what we have to do so as to figure the value."

"What's the other half?" he asked.

"The tricky part," she told him. "We now have to figure what percentage of the value of the tree is represented by its fair average earnings for a single year. If I believed that the tree was a one year wonder, I would say 100% of its value—as a going business—was represented by one year's earnings. But if I believe, as both you and I do, that the earnings from a single year are but a fraction of what the tree will produce, then the key is to figure out that fraction. In other words, the tree is capital, and to compute its value we must capitalize the earnings. We must divide them by the right fraction."

"Do you have something in mind?" he asked.

"I'm getting there. If this tree could produce steady and predictable earnings each year, it would be like a U.S. Treasury bond. But its earnings are not guaranteed. So we have to take into account risk and uncertainty. If the risk of its ruin is high, I will insist that a single year's earnings represent a higher percentage of the value of the tree. After all, apples could become a glut on the market one day and you would have to cut the price and increase the costs of selling them. Or some doctor could discover a link between eating an apple a day and heart disease. A drought could cut the yield of the tree. Or, heaven forbid, the tree could become diseased and die. These are all risks. And of course we do not know what will happen to costs that we know we have to bear."

"You are a gloomy one," reflected the old man. "There are treatments, you know, that could be applied to increase the yield of the tree. This tree could help spawn a whole orchard."

"I am aware of that," she assured him. "We will include that in the calculus. The fact is, we are talking about risk, and investment analysis is a cold business. We don't know with certainty what's going to happen. You want your money now and I'm supposed to live with the risk. That's fine with me, but then I have to look through a cloudy crystal ball, and not with 20/20 hindsight. And my resources are limited. I have to choose between your tree and the strawberry patch down the road. I cannot do both and the purchase of your tree will deprive me of alternative investments. That means I have to compare the opportunities and the risks. To determine the proper rate at which we should capitalize earnings, I have looked at investment opportunities that are comparable to the apple tree, particularly in the agribusiness industry, where these factors have been taken into account. I have concluded that it is appropriate to use a capitalization rate of 20%. In other words, average earnings over the last three years (which seems to be a representative period) represent 20% of the value of the tree. And that is the risk I am willing to take. I am not willing to take any greater risk, because I don't have to since I can buy the strawberry patch instead. Now, to figure the price, we simply divide 45 by .20.''

"Long division was never my long suit. Is there a simpler way of doing the figuring?'' he asked hopefully.

"There is,'' she assured him. "The reciprocal of .20 is 5. If you don't want to divide by the capitalization rate, you can multiply by its reciprocal, which is what we Wall Street types prefer. We call that reciprocal the price-earnings (or P–E) ratio. Any way you do the math, the answer is $225. That's my offer.''

The old man sat back and said he greatly appreciated the lesson. He would have to think about her offer, and he asked if she could come by the next day.

When the young woman returned she found the old man emerging from a sea of work sheets, small print columns of numbers and a calculator. "Glad to see you,'' he said. "I think we can do some business.''

"It's easy to see how you Wall Street smarties make so much money, buying people's property for a fraction of the value. I think my tree is worth more than you figured, and I think I can get you to agree to that.''

"I'm open minded,'' she assured him.

"The number you worked so hard over my books to come up with was something you called profits, or earnings that I earned in the past. I'm not so sure it tells you anything that important.''

"Of course it does,'' she protested. "Profits measure efficiency and economic utility.''

"Maybe,'' he mused, "but it sure doesn't tell you how much money you've got. I looked in my safe yesterday after you left and I saw I had some stocks that hadn't ever paid much of a dividend to me. And I kept getting reports each year telling me how great the earnings were, but I sure couldn't spend them. It's just the opposite with the tree. You figured the earnings were lower because of some amounts I'll never have to spend. It seems to me these earnings are an idea worked up by the accountants. Now I'll grant you that ideas, or concepts as you call them, are important and give you lots of useful information, but you can't fold them up, and put them in your pocket.''

Surprised, she asked, "What is important, then?''

"Cash flow,'' he answered. "I'm talking about dollars you can spend, or save or give to your children. This tree will go on for years yielding revenues after costs. And it is the future, not the past, that we're trying to figure out.''

"Don't forget the risks,'' she reminded him. "And the uncertainties.''

"Quite right," he observed. "I think we can deal with that. Chances are that you and I could agree, after a lot of thought, on the possible range of future revenues and costs. I suspect we would estimate that for the next five years, there is a 25% chance that the cash flow will be $40, a 50% chance it will be $50 and a 25% chance it will be $60. That makes $50 our best guess, if you average it out. Then let us figure that for ten years after that the average will be $40. And that's it. The tree doctor tells me it can't produce any longer than that. Now all we have to do is figure out what you pay today to get $50 a year from now, two years from now, and so on for the first five years until we figure what you would pay to get $40 a year for each of the ten years after that. Then, throw in the 20 bucks we can get for firewood at that time, and that's that."

"Simple," she said. "You want to discount to the present value of future receipts including salvage value. Of course you need to determine the rate at which you discount."

"Precisely," he noted. "That's what all these charts and the calculator are doing." She nodded knowingly as he showed her discount tables that revealed what a dollar received at a later time is worth today, under different assumptions of the discount rate. It showed, for example, that at an 8% discount rate, a dollar delivered a year from now is worth $.93 today, simply because $.93 today, invested at 8%, will produce $1 a year from now.

"You could put your money in a savings bank or a savings and loan association and receive 5% interest, insured. But you could also put your money into obligations of the United States Government and earn 8% interest. That looks like the risk free rate of interest to me. Anywhere else you put your money deprives you of the opportunity to earn 8% risk free. Discounting by 8% will only compensate you for the time value of the money you invest in the tree rather than in government securities. But the cash flow from the apple tree is not riskless, sad to say, so we need to use a higher discount rate to compensate you for the risk in your investment. Let us agree that we discount the receipt of $50 a year from now by 15%, and so on with the other deferred receipts. That is about the rate that is applied to investments with this magnitude of risk. You can check that out with my cousin who just sold his strawberry patch yesterday. According to my figures, the present value of the anticipated annual net revenues is $268.05, and today's value of the firewood is $2.44, making a grand total of $270.49. I'll take $270 even. You can see how much I'm allowing for risk because if I discounted the stream at 8%, it would come to $388.60."

After a few minutes reflection, the young woman said to the old man, "It was a bit foxy of you yesterday to let me appear to be teaching you something. Where did you learn so much about finance as an apple grower?"

"Don't be foolish, my young friend," he counseled her. "Wisdom comes from experience in many fields. Socrates taught us how to learn. I'll tell you a little secret; I spent a year in law school.''

The young woman smiled at this last confession. ''I have enjoyed this little exercise but let me tell you something that some of the financial whiz kids have told me. Whether we figure value on the basis of the discounted cash flow method or the capitalization of earnings, so long as we apply both methods perfectly we should come out at exactly the same point.''

''Of course!'' the old man exclaimed. ''Some of the wunder-kinds are catching on. But the clever ones are looking not at old earnings, but doing what managers are doing and projecting earn-ings into the future. The question is, however, which method is more likely to be misused. I prefer to calculate by my method because I don't have to monkey around with depreciation. You have to make these arbitrary assumptions about useful life and how fast you're going to depreciate. Obviously that's where you went wrong in your figuring.''

''You are a crafty old devil,'' she rejoined. ''There are plenty of places for your calculations to go off. It's easy to discount cash flows when they are nice and steady, but that doesn't help you when you've got some lumpy expenses that do not recur. For example, several years from now that tree will require some exten-sive pruning and spraying operations that simply do not show up in your flow. The labor and chemicals for that once-only occasion throw off the evenness of your calculations. But I'll tell you what, I'll offer you $250. My cold analysis tells me I'm overpaying, but I really like that tree. I think the psychic rewards of sitting in its shade must be worth something.''

''It's a deal,'' said the old man. ''I never said I was looking for the *perfect* offer, but only the *best* offer.''

MORAL: There are several. Methods are useful as tools, but good judgment comes not from methods alone, but from experi-ence. And experience comes from bad judgment.

Listen closely to the experts, and hear those things they don't tell you. Behind all the sweet sounds of their confident notes, there is a great deal of discordant uncertainty. One wrong assump-tion can carry you pretty far from the truth.

Finally, you are never too young to learn.

———

SECTION 7. RESTRICTIONS ON THE TRANSFERABILITY OF SHARES AND MANDATORY–SALE PROVISIONS

INTRODUCTORY NOTE

This Section concerns two linked but separate issues. The first issue is the extent to which restrictions on transferability can be imposed on the stock of close corporations. The second issue is under what circumstances a close corporation can mandate a shareholder to sell his stock back to the corporation (or to the other shareholders) against his wishes at the time. The two issues are linked in several ways.

First, both issues concern limits on what a shareholder in a close corporation can do with his stock.

Second, the issues may be linked mechanically, because an attempt by a shareholder to sell his stock may not only be subject to a restriction on transferability, but may trigger a right in the corporation to repurchase the stock.

Finally, the two issues are linked by the problem of valuation. In theory, a shareholder might object to a restriction on transferability simply because as a matter of principle he wants to be free to sell to whoever he wants, on whatever conditions he wants, or free to remain a shareholder. In practice, however, problems with a restriction on transferability usually arise where the restriction precludes the shareholder from realizing any value through a transfer of his shares, or limits the shareholder from realizing the full value of his shares on a transfer. If a restriction on transferability is coupled with some mechanism that provides a shareholder who wants to transfer his shares with the same economic value he could have realized in the absence of the restriction, he would be unlikely to complain.

Mandatory-sale provisions are more complex. To start with, more than economics may be involved, because a shareholder in a close corporation may place a psychological value on his position as a participant in an enterprise. Moreover, if the event that triggers a mandatory sale of one shareholder's stock is wholly or partly within the control of the other shareholders, the other shareholders may have an incentive to manipulate the corporation's affairs in a way that will trigger the buyout. Finally, if a restriction on transferability requires a shareholder to either retain his stock or sell it to the corporation at a price less than fair value, the shareholder can opt to retain the stock. In contrast, if a mandatory sale provision requires a shareholder to sell his stock to the corporation at less than fair value, the shareholder cannot opt to retain his stock if the conditions of the provision are satisfied.

ALLEN v. BILTMORE TISSUE CORP.

New York Court of Appeals, 1957.
2 N.Y.2d 534, 161 N.Y.S.2d 418, 141 N.E.2d 812.

FULD, Judge.

The by-laws of defendant corporation give it an option to purchase, in case of the death of a stockholder, his shares of the corporate stock. The enforcibility of this option is one of the questions for decision.

Biltmore Tissue Corporation was organized under the Stock Corporation Law, Consol.Laws, c. 59, § 1 et seq., in 1932, with an authorized capitalization of 1,000 shares without par value, to manufacture and deal in paper and paper products. The by-laws, adopted by the incorporators-directors, contain provisions limiting the number of shares (originally 5, later 20) available to each stockholder (§ 28) and restricting stock transfers both during the life of the stockholder and in case of his death (§§ 29, 30). Whenever a stockholder desires to sell or transfer his shares, he must, according to one by-law (§ 29), give the corporation or other stockholders "an opportunity to repurchase the stock at the price that was paid for the same to the Corporation at the time the Corporation issued the stock"; if, however, the option is not exercised, "then, after the lapse of sixty days, the stock may be sold by the holder to such person and under such circumstances as he sees fit." The by-law, dealing with the transfer of stock upon the death of a stockholder (§ 30)—the provision with which we are here concerned—is almost identical. It recites that the corporation is to have the right to purchase its late stockholder's shares for the price it originally received for them:

> "Stock Transfer in Case of Death. In case of the death of any stockholder, the Corporation shall have the right to purchase the stock from the legal representative of the deceased for the same price that the Corporation received therefor originally. If the Corporation does not, or cannot, purchase such stock, the Board of Directors shall have the right to empower such of its existing stockholders as it sees fit to make such purchase from such legal representative at the same price. Should the option provided for in this section not be exercised, then, after the lapse of ninety days, the legal representative may dispose of said stock as he sees fit."

Harry Kaplan, a paper jobber, was one of Biltmore's customers and some months after its incorporation purchased 5 shares of stock from the corporation at $5 a share. In 1936, Kaplan received a stock dividend of 5 more shares, and two years later purchased an additional 10 shares for $100. On the face of each of the three certificates, running vertically along the left-hand margin, appeared the legend,

"Issued subject to restrictions in sections 28, 29, and 30 of the By-laws."

On October 20, 1953, Kaplan wrote to the corporation stating that he was "interested in selling" his 20 shares of stock and requesting that he be given the "price" which the board of directors "will consider, so that I may come to a decision." He died five days later. Some months thereafter, in February, 1954, his son, who was also one of his executors, addressed a letter to Biltmore, inquiring whether it was "still interested in acquiring shares and at what price." By another letter, dated the same day, the attorney for the executors sent to the corporation the three stock certificates, representing the 20 shares, and requested that a new certificate be issued in the name of the estate or the executors. Within 30 days, on March 4, 1954, Biltmore's board of directors voted to exercise its option to purchase the stock, pursuant to section 30 of the by-laws, and about three weeks later the executors' attorney was advised of the corporation's action. He was also informed, that although the by-law provision permitted purchase at "the same price that the company received therefor from the stockholder originally," the corporation had, nevertheless, decided to pay $20 a share, "considerably more than the original purchase price", based on the prices at which it had acquired shares from other stockholders.

Kaplan's executors declined to sell to the corporation, insisting that the stock which had been in the decedent's name be transferred to them. When their demand was refused, they brought this action to compel Biltmore to accept surrender of the decedent's stock certificate and to issue a new certificate for 20 shares to them. They contended ... that the by-law is void as an unreasonable restraint. The corporation interposed a counterclaim for specific performance based on the exercise of its option to purchase the shares under by-law section 30. The court at Special Term granted judgment to the corporation on its counterclaim and dismissed the complaint. The Appellate Division reversed, rendered judgment directing the transfer of the stock to the plaintiffs and dismissed the defendant's counterclaim upon the ground that the by-law in question is void.

Section 176 of the Personal Property Law, which is identical with section 15 of the Uniform Stock Transfer Act, provides that "there shall be no restriction upon the transfer of shares" represented by a stock certificate "by virtue of any by-law of such corporation, or otherwise, unless the ... restriction is *stated* upon the certificate." (Emphasis supplied.) In order to comply with this statutory mandate, the corporation printed the words, "Issued subject to restrictions in sections 28, 29, and 30 of the By-laws," on the side of the certificate....

Since ... the legend on the certificate meets the statute's requirements, we turn to the validity of the by-law restriction.

The validity of qualifications on the ownership of corporate shares through restrictions on the right to transfer has long been a source of confusion in the law.   The difficulties arise primarily from the clash between the concept of the shares as "creatures of the company's constitution and therefore ... essentially contractual choses in action" (Gower, Some Contrasts between British and American Corporation Law, 69 Harv.L.Rev. 1369, 1377) and the concept of the shares as personal property represented so far as possible by the certificate itself and, therefore, subject to the time-honored rule that there be no unreasonable restraint upon alienation.   While the courts of this state and of many other jurisdictions, as opposed to those of England and of Massachusetts (Gower, supra, 69 Harv.L.Rev. 1369, 1377–1378; O'Neal, Restrictions on Transfer of Stock in Closely Held Corporations, 65 Harv.L.Rev. 773, 778), have favored the "property" concept (see O'Neal, supra, 65 Harv.L.Rev. 773, 779), the tendency is, as section 176 of the Personal Property Law implies, to sustain a restriction imposed on the transfer of stock if "reasonable" and if the stockholder acquired such stock with requisite notice of the restriction.

The question posed, therefore, is whether the provision, according the corporation a right or first option to purchase the stock at the price which it originally received for it, amounts to an unreasonable restraint.   In our judgment, it does not.

The courts have almost uniformly held valid and enforcible the first option provision, in charter or by-law, whereby a shareholder desirous of selling his stock is required to afford the corporation, his fellow stockholders or both an opportunity to buy it before he is free to offer it to outsiders....   The courts have often said that this first option provision is "in the nature of a contract" between the corporation and its stockholders and, as such, binding upon them. Hassel v. Pohle, ... 214 App.Div. 654, 658, 212 N.Y.S.2d 561, 565; see, also, 8 Fletcher, ... § 4194, p. 736.   In Doss v. Yingling, ... 95 Ind.App. 494, 172 N.E. 801, a leading case on the subject and one frequently cited throughout the country, a by-law provision against transfer by any stockholder—there were three—of any shares until they had first been offered for sale to other stockholders at *book value,* was sustained as reasonable and valid, 95 Ind.App. at page 500, 172 N.E. at page 803: "The weight of authority is to the effect that a corporate by-law which requires the owner of the stock to give the other stockholders of the corporation ... *an option to purchase the same at an agreed price or the then-existing book value before offering the stock for sale to an outsider, is a valid and reasonable restriction* and binding upon the stockholders." (Emphasis supplied.)   And in the Penthouse Properties case, ... 256 App.Div. 685, 690–691, 11 N.Y.S.2d 417, 422, the court declared that "The general rule that ownership of property cannot exist in one person and the right of alienation in another ... has in this State been frequently applied to shares of corporate stock ... and cognizance has been taken of the principle that 'the right of transfer is a right of property, and if another has the arbitrary power to forbid a transfer of property by the owner that amounts to annihilation of property'....   But restrictions against the sale of shares of stock, unless other stockholders or the corporation have first been accorded an opportunity to buy, are not repugnant to that principle. . . . The weight of authority elsewhere is to the same effect." [2]

As the cases thus make clear, what the law condemns is, not a *restriction* on transfer, a provision merely postponing sale during the option period, but an effective *prohibition* against transferability itself. Accordingly, if the by-law under consideration were to be construed as rendering the sale of the stock impossible to anyone except to the corporation at whatever price it wished to pay, we would, of course, strike it down as illegal. But that is not the meaning of the provision before us. The corporation had its option only for a 90–day period. If it did not exercise its privilege within that time, the deceased stockholder's legal representative was at liberty to "dispose of said stock as he [saw] fit" (§ 30), and, once so disposed of, it would thereafter be free of the restriction. In a very real sense, therefore, the primary purpose of the by-laws was to enable a particular party, the corporation, to buy the shares, not to prevent the other party, the stockholder, from selling them. (See 3 Simes & Smith on Law of Future Interests [2d ed., 1956], § 1154, p. 61.)

The Appellate Division, however, was impressed with what it deemed the "unreasonableness," that is, "unfairness," of the price specified in the by-law, namely, a price at which the shares had originally been purchased from the corporation. Carried to its logical conclusion, such a rationale would permit, indeed, would encourage, expensive litigation in every case where the price specified in the restriction, or the formula for fixing the price, was other than a recognized and easily ascertainable fair market value. This would destroy part of the social utility of the first option type of restriction which, when imposed, is intended to operate *in futuro* and must, therefore, include some formula for future determination of the option price.

Generally speaking, these restrictions are employed by the so-called "close corporation" as part of the attempt to equate the corporate structure to a partnership by giving the original stockholders a sort of pre-emptive right through which they may if they choose, veto the admission of a new participant. See Bloomingdale v. Bloomingdale, supra, 107 Misc. 646, 651–652, 177 N.Y.S. 873, 875; Model Clothing House v. Dickinson, 146 Minn. 367, 370–371, 178 N.W. 957; see, also, Israels, The Close Corporation and the Law, 33 Corn.L.Q. 488, 492–493. Obviously, the case where there is an easily ascertainable market value for the shares of a closely held corporate enterprise is the exception, not the rule, and, consequently, various methods or formulae for fixing the option

---

2. The court went further in the Penthouse Properties case than we are called upon to go here; in view of the special purposes of a corporation owning a cooperative apartment house, it sustained a restriction actually requiring the "consent" of the directors to a proposed transfer. 256 App. Div. 685, 689, 11 N.Y.S.2d 416, 420. The present case involves no such "consent" restriction.

price are employed in practice—e.g., book or appraisal value, often exclusive of good will, see, e.g., Lawson v. Household Finance Corp., 17 Del.Ch. 343, 152 A. 723, affirming 17 Del.Ch. 1, 147 A. 312; Doss v. Yingling, supra, 95 Ind.App. 494, 172 N.E. 801, or a fixed price, Scruggs v. Cotterill, 67 App.Div. 583, 73 N.Y.S. 882, or the par value of the stock. See, e.g., Boston Safe Dep. & Tr. Co. v. North Attleborough Chapt. of American Red Cross, 330 Mass. 114, 111 N.E.2d 447; Chaffee v. Farmers' Co–Op. Elevator Co., 39 N.D. 585, 590, 168 N.W. 616; O'Neal, supra, 65 Harv.L.Rev. 773, 798 et seq.[3]

In sum, then, the validity of the restriction on transfer does not rest on any abstract notion of intrinsic fairness of price. To be invalid, more than mere disparity between option price and current value of the stock must be shown. See Palmer v. Chamberlin, supra, 191 F.2d 532, 541, 27 A.L.R.2d 416. Since the parties have in effect agreed on a price formula which suited them, and provision is made freeing the stock for outside sale should the corporation not make, or provide for, the purchase, the restriction is reasonable and valid.

The further argument made by the plaintiffs, that the defendant corporation, in any event, waived its right by failing to exercise its option within the prescribed 90 days, cannot avail them. Section 30 of the by-laws provides that the corporation has the right "to purchase the stock from the legal representative of the deceased" and that, if the option is not exercised, "then, after the lapse of ninety days, the legal representative may dispose of said stock as he sees fit." The section is patently deficient in omitting to specify the date upon which the 90–day period is to commence. It cannot mean the date of death (here it was October 25, 1953) or even the date on which the corporation learned of the death (shortly thereafter), for, until letters testamentary or letters of administration are issued, the "legal representative" of the deceased is not ascertainable and there is no one from whom the corporation could purchase the stock. Cf. Motyka v. City of Oswego, 309 N.Y. 881, 131 N.E.2d 291. In the present case, letters testamentary were issued to the plaintiffs on December 17, 1953, but the corporation was not informed of this until February 10, 1954. Consequently, since the corporation's board of directors voted on March 4 to purchase the shares and apprised counsel for the plaintiffs, the legal representatives of the deceased stockholder, of their desire to do so on March 23, the option was clearly exercised within the permitted period.

The judgment of the Appellate Division dismissing the defendant's counterclaim and sustaining the plaintiff's complaint should be reversed, and that of Special Term reinstated, with costs in this court and in the Appellate Division.

3. In the case of no-par shares, it should be noted, the figure usually most comparable to par value is issue price.

CONWAY, C.J., and DESMOND, DYE, FROESSEL, VAN VOO-RHIS and BURKE, JJ., concur.

Judgment of Appellate Division reversed and that of Special Term reinstated, with costs in this court and in the Appellate Division.

———

EVANGELISTA v. HOLLAND, 27 Mass.App.Ct. 244, 537 N.E.2d 589 (1989). A shareholders' agreement allowed the corporation to buy out, for $75,000, the estate of any deceased shareholder. The corporation brought suit against the estate of a deceased sharehold-er to enforce the agreement. There was strong evidence that the decedent's stock was worth at least $191,000. Held, for the corpo-ration:

> The executors suggest that to require them to part with their interest in the business for so much less than the [value of the stock] violates the duty of good faith and loyalty owed one another by stockholders in a closely held corporation.... Questions of good faith and loyalty do not arise when all the stockholders in advance enter into an agreement for the pur-chase of stock of a withdrawing or deceased stockholder.... That the price established by a stockholders' agreement may be less than the appraised or market value is unremarkable. Such agreements may have as their purpose: the payment of a price for a decedent's stock which will benefit the corporation or surviving stockholders by not unduly burdening them; the payment of a price tied to life insurance; or fixing a price which assures the beneficiaries of the deceased stockholder of a predetermined price for stock which might have little market value.... When the agreement was entered into in 1984, the order and time of death of stockholders was an unknown. There was a "mutuality of risk."

———

DEL. GEN. CORP. LAW §§ 202, 342, 347, 349

[See Statutory Supplement]

———

CAL. CORP. CODE §§ 204(a)(3), (b), 418

[See Statutory Supplement]

———

REV. MODEL BUS. CORP. ACT § 6.27

MODEL STAT. CLOSE CORP. SUPP. §§ 10–17

[See Statutory Supplement]

NOTE ON RESTRICTIONS ON TRANSFERABILITY
AND MANDATORY SALES

1.   Although some of the earlier cases held that all restrictions on the transferability of shares constituted illegal restraints on alienation, the modern cases hold that "reasonable" restrictions are valid and enforceable.   Three basic types of restrictions are commonly used in the context of the close corporation: (1) First refusals, which prohibit a sale of stock unless the shares have been first offered to the corporation, the other shareholders, or both, on the terms offered by the third party;   (2) First options, which prohibit a transfer of stock unless the shares have been first offered to the corporation, the other shareholders, or both, at a price fixed under the terms of the option;   and (3) Consent restraints, which prohibit a transfer of stock without the permission of the corporation's board of shareholders.

Of these three basic types, the *first refusal* is obviously least restrictive in its impact on a shareholder who wants to sell his stock, and such provisions are widely upheld.   See, e.g., Groves v. Prickett, 420 F.2d 1119 (9th Cir.1970);   Tu–Vu Drive–In Corp. v. Ashkins, 61 Cal.2d 283, 38 Cal.Rptr. 348, 391 P.2d 828 (1964);   State ex rel. Hudelson v. Clarks Hill Tel. Co., 139 Ind.App. 507, 218 N.E.2d 154 (1966).

The restrictiveness of a *first option* depends largely on the relationship between the option price and a fair price at the time the option is triggered.   As Allen v. Biltmore suggests, the courts have been giving increasing latitude to this type of provision.   See, e.g., Lawson v. Household Finance Corp., 17 Del.Ch. 343, 152 A. 723 (1930);   In re Mather's Estate, 410 Pa. 361, 189 A.2d 586 (1963), noted, 48 Minn.L.Rev. 808 (1964), 16 Stan.L.Rev. 449 (1964), 49 Va.L.Rev. 1211 (1963) (agreement setting price at $1 per share enforced although actual value was $1,060 per share).

A *consent restraint* is obviously the most restrictive of the three basic types, and at one time such a restraint was almost certain to be deemed invalid.   However, some recent statutes specifically contemplate the validity of such restraints (see, e.g., Del. § 202), and the courts have also begun to be more tolerant.   Thus in Colbert v. Hennessey, 351 Mass. 131, 217 N.E.2d 914 (1966), three shareholders owning 55% of Bay State's stock agreed that none would transfer his stock without the others' consent.   The court held the agreement valid. "The agreement was a means of securing corporate control of Bay State to those whose enterprise sponsored it and who contributed to the daily operation of the business. This was not a 'palpably unreasonable' purpose." The court cited Holmes's dictum, in Barrett v. King, 181 Mass. 476, 479, 63 N.E. 934, 935 (1902), that "there seems to be no greater objection to retaining the right of choosing one's associates in a corporation than in a firm." See also Irwin v. West End Development Co., 342 F.Supp. 687 (D.Colo.1972), rev'd in part 481 F.2d 34 (10th Cir. 1973); Longyear v. Hardman, 219 Mass. 405, 106 N.E. 1012 (1914); Fayard v. Fayard, 293 So.2d 421, 69 A.L.R.3d 1322 (Miss.1974).

In spite of the increasingly tolerant climate, however, the validity of consent restraints remains uncertain in the absence of statute or authoritative precedent. In Rafe v. Hindin, 29 A.D.2d 481, 288 N.Y.S.2d 662 (1968), P and D each owned 50% of the stock of Bil Cy Realty, which they had organized in 1963. A legend on each stock certificate made the stock nontransferable except to the other shareholder, and written permission from the other shareholder was required to record a transfer of the stock on Bil Cy's books. P brought an action for a judgment that the legend on the certificate was void and the stock was transferable without D's consent. The court so held:

> In New York certificates of stock are regarded as personal property and are subject to the rule that there be no unreasonable restraint on alienation. . . .

> The legend on the stock certificate at bar contains no provision that the individual defendant's consent may not be unreasonably withheld. Since the individual defendant is thus given the arbitrary power to forbid a transfer of the shares of stock by the plaintiff, the restriction amounts to annihilation of property. The restriction is not only not reasonable, but it is against public policy and, therefore, illegal. It is an unwarrantable and unlawful restraint on the sale of personal property, the sale and interchange of which the law favors, and in restraint of trade.

See also, e.g., Tracey v. Franklin, 31 Del.Ch. 477, 67 A.2d 56 (1949).[1]

2. The three basic types of restraints discussed above limit the shareholders' power of transfer. Other types of arrangements go further, and give the corporation or the remaining shareholders an option to purchase shares upon the occurrence of designated contingencies, even if the shareholder wants to retain the stock. A common example is an arrangement under which the corporation is given an option to repurchase stock that it has issued to an

---

1. Provisions in the certificate of incorporation, or even in shareholder agreements, that restrict the transferability of shares or impose buy-out rights may be subject not only to the general principles of corporation law, but to state securities acts. In particular, California has elaborate rules concerning such provisions. See generally Berger, Protection of Shareholder Interests in California Closely Held and Statutory Close Corporations: A Practitioner's Guide, 20 Pac.L.J. 1127 (1989).

employee, if the employment relationship is terminated. The courts have tended to enforce such arrangements even when the option price is quite low in relation to the value of the stock at the time the buyback right is triggered. See, e.g., St. Louis Union Trust Co. v. Merrill Lynch, Pierce, Fenner & Smith Inc., 562 F.2d 1040 (8th Cir.1977), cert. denied 435 U.S. 925, 98 S.Ct. 1490, 55 L.Ed.2d 519 (1978); State ex rel. Howeth v. D.A. Davidson & Co., 163 Mont. 355, 517 P.2d 722 (1973); Georesearch, Inc. v. Morriss, 193 F.Supp. 163 (W.D.La.1961), aff'd per curiam 298 F.2d 442 (5th Cir.1962). Another example is the buy-sell or survivor-purchase agreement, which provides that on the death or retirement of a shareholder in a close corporation, his estate has an obligation to sell its shares to the corporation or the remaining shareholders at a price fixed under the agreement, and the corporation or the remaining share-holders have an obligation (rather than an option) to purchase the shares. The major purpose of such agreements is to provide liquidity to the seller or his estate. Since the corporation is by hypothesis closely held, any market for the shares is negligible, and in the absence of the agreement the retiring shareholder or his estate might be in a helpless bargaining position if more liquid or higher-yielding assets are needed to meet tax liabilities or other needs. The corporation's obligation is often "funded" in whole or in part by insurance on the shareholders' lives. It is beyond the scope of this Note to treat in detail buy-sell agreements and their insurance and tax implications.

3. Another kind of problem concerns the pricing clause in first-option, repurchase, or buy-sell arrangements. Where shares are closely held, price cannot realistically be set on the basis of market value, and some alternative pricing provision is therefore required. Even where shares are not closely held, an alternative to market value may be employed for substantive reasons.

(a) One common approach is to use a pricing formula based on book value. Book value, however, may be an unreliable guide to a concern's real worth: it reflects the historical cost of assets rather than their present value, and usually ignores goodwill or going-concern value. As a general proposition, the courts have tended to hold that a large disparity between book value and real value is not in itself sufficient to avoid the operation of a book-value pricing provision. Thus in Palmer v. Chamberlin, 191 F.2d 532 (5th Cir.1951), the court, quoting New England Trust Co. v. Abbott, 162 Mass. 148, 38 N.E. 432 (1894) stated, " '. . . specific performance of an agreement to convey will not be refused merely because the price is inadequate or excessive. The difference must be so great as to lead to a reasonable conclusion of fraud, mistake, or concealment in the nature of fraud, and to render it plainly inequitable and against conscience that the contract should be enforced.' " See also, e.g., In re Estate of Brown, 130 Ill.App.2d 514, 264 N.E.2d 287 (1970). Accordingly, a book value formula may be disastrous where goodwill represents the most valuable component of the business—as is typical in non-capital-intensive enterprises, see, e.g., Jones v.

Harris, 63 Wash.2d 559, 388 P.2d 539 (1964)—or where there is a significant disparity between historical costs and present values. See, e.g., S.C. Pohlman Co. v. Easterling, 211 Cal.App.2d 466, 27 Cal.Rptr. 450 (1962).

(b) A second common approach is to fix the price on the basis of capitalized earnings. This approach is less likely than a book-value formula to produce an unfair price, but involves a number of drafting or interpretation problems, such as (1) defining earnings, (2) over what period, (3) with or without salaries paid to shareholder-officers, and (4) considering the possible impact of the transferor's withdrawal on the value of the business.

(c) A third common approach is to agree on a dollar price when the provision is adopted, subject to periodic revision at agreed-upon intervals. This approach may lead to trouble when the parties fail to make periodic revision, through carelessness or inability to agree. In Helms v. Duckworth, 249 F.2d 482 (D.C.Cir.1957), Easterday, age 70, and Duckworth, age 37, formed a corporation and agreed that when one died his stock would be sold to the other at $10 a share, which was then a fair price, "provided, however, that such sale and purchase price may, from time to time, be redetermined . . . [annually] by an instrument in writing signed by the parties. . . ." When Easterday died six years later the price had never been adjusted, although the actual value of the stock had risen to $80 a share. Easterday's administratrix brought suit to declare the agreement void, and Duckworth submitted an affidavit in which he stated that it was never his intention to consent to any change in the price provision. The district court granted summary judgment to Duckworth, but the Court of Appeals reversed.

> . . . Plainly [the agreement] implied a periodic bargaining or negotiating process in which each party must participate in good faith. . . .

> . . . We believe that the holders of closely held stock in a corporation such as shown here bear a fiduciary duty to deal fairly, honestly, and openly with their fellow stockholders and to make disclosure of all essential information.

> . . . [T]he very nature of Duckworth's secret intent was such that it had to be kept secret and undisclosed or it would fail of its purpose. . . . [Duckworth's] failure to disclose to his corporate business "partner" his fixed intent never to alter the original price constitutes a flagrant breach of a fiduciary duty. Standing alone this warrants cancellation of the agreement by a court of equity.

(d) A fourth approach is to provide for appraisal at the time the option is triggered. See, e.g., Ginsberg v. Coating Products, Inc., 152 Conn. 592, 210 A.2d 667 (1965); Lawson v. Household Finance Corp., 17 Del.Ch. 343, 152 A. 723 (1930). This approach has the advantage of flexibility, but unless the parties are willing to give the appraisers free rein, it too may involve the use of an agreed-upon standard of valuation that can turn out to have unforeseen and undesired results.

GALLAGHER v. LAMBERT

New York Court of Appeals, 1989.
74 N.Y.2d 562, 549 N.Y.S.2d 945, 549 N.E.2d 136.

OPINION OF THE COURT

BELLACOSA, Judge.

Plaintiff Gallagher purchased stock in the defendant close corporation with which he was employed. The purchase of his 8.5% interest was subject to a mandatory buy-back provision: if the employment ended for any reason before January 31, 1985, the stock would return to the corporation for book value. The corporation fired plaintiff prior to the fulcrum date, after which the buy-back price would have been higher.

We must decide whether plaintiff's dismissed causes of action, seeking the higher repurchase price based on an alleged breach of a fiduciary duty, should be reinstated. We think not and affirm, concluding that the Appellate Division did not err in dismissing these causes of action by summary judgment because there was no cognizable breach of any fiduciary duty owed to plaintiff under the plain terms of the parties' repurchase agreement.

Gallagher was employed by defendant Eastdil Realty as a mortgage broker from 1968 to 1973. Three years later, in 1976, he returned to the company as a broker, officer and director, serving additionally as president and chief executive officer of defendant's wholly owned subsidiary, Eastdil Advisors, Inc. Gallagher was at all times an employee at will. Still later, in 1981, Eastdil offered all its executive employees an opportunity to purchase stock subject to a mandatory buy-back provision, which provided that upon "voluntary resignation or other termination" prior to January 31, 1985, an employee would be required to return the stock for book value. After that date, the formula for the buy-back price was keyed to the company's earnings. Plaintiff accepted the offer and its terms.

On January 10, 1985, Gallagher was fired by Eastdil Realty. He did not and does not now contest the firing. But he demanded payment for his shares calculated on the post-January 31, 1985 buy-back formula. Eastdil refused and Gallagher sued, asserting eight causes of action. Only three claims, based on an alleged breach of fiduciary duty of good faith and fair dealing, are before us. The trial court denied defendants' motion for summary judgment on these claims, stating that factual issues were raised relating to defendants' motive in firing plaintiff. The Appellate Division, by divided vote, reversed, dismissed those claims and ordered payment for the shares at book value. 143 A.D.2d 313, 532 N.Y.S.2d 255. That court then granted leave and certified the following question to us:

"Was the order of this Court, which modified the order of the Supreme Court, properly made?"

The parties negotiated a written contract containing a common and plain buy-back provision. Plaintiff got what he bargained for— book value for his minority shares if his employment in the corporation ended before January 31, 1985. There being no basis presented for the courts to interfere with the operation and consequences of this agreement between the parties, the order of the Appellate Division granting summary judgment to defendants, dismissing the first three causes of action, should be affirmed and the certified question answered in the affirmative.

Earlier this year, in *Ingle v. Glamore Motor Sales,* 73 N.Y.2d 183, 538 N.Y.S.2d 771, 535 N.E.2d 1311, we expressly refrained from deciding the precise issue presented by this case. There, the challenge was directed to the at-will discharge from employment and was predicated on a claimed fiduciary obligation flowing from the shareholder relationship. Relying principally on *Sabetay v. Sterling Drug,* 69 N.Y.2d 329, 335–336, 514 N.Y.S.2d 209, 506 N.E.2d 919, and *Murphy v. American Home Prods. Corp.,* 58 N.Y.2d 293, 300, 461 N.Y.S.2d 232, 448 N.E.2d 86, we held that "[a] minority shareholder in a close corporation, by that status alone, who contractually agrees to the repurchase of his shares upon termination of his employment for any reason, *acquires no right from the corporation or majority shareholders against at-will discharge.*" (*Ingle v. Glamore Motor Sales,* 73 N.Y.2d, *supra,* at 188, 538 N.Y.S.2d 771, 535 N.E.2d 1311 [emphasis added].) However, we cautioned that "[i]t is necessary * * * to appreciate and keep distinct the duty a corporation owes to a minority shareholder *as a shareholder* from any duty it might owe him as an *employee.*" (*Id.,* at 188, 538 N.Y.S.2d 771, 535 N.E.2d 1311.)

The causes before us on this appeal are based on an alleged departure from a fiduciary duty of fair dealing existing independently of the employment and arising from the plaintiff's simultaneous relationship as a minority shareholder in the corporation. Plaintiff claims entitlement to the higher price based on a breach flowing from Eastdil's premature "bad faith" termination of his at-will employment because, he asserts, the sole purpose of the firing at that time was to acquire the stock at a contractually and temporally measured lower buy-back price formula.

The claim seeking a higher price for the shares cannot be neatly divorced, as the dissent urges, from the employment because the buy-back provision links them together as to timing and consequences. Plaintiff not only agreed to the particular buy-back formula, he helped write it and he reviewed it with his attorney during the negotiation process, before signing the agreement and purchasing the minority interest. These provisions, which require an employee shareholder to sell back stock upon severance from corporate employment, are designed to ensure that ownership of all of the stock, especially of a close corporation, stays within the control of the remaining corporate owners-employees; that is, those who will continue to contribute to its successes or failures (*see,* Kessler, *Share Repurchases Under Modern Corporation Laws,* 28 Fordham L.Rev. 637, 648 [1959–1960]). These agreements define the scope of the relevant fiduciary duty and supply certainty of obligation to each side. They should not be undone simply upon an allegation of unfairness. This would destroy their very purpose, which is to provide a certain formula by which to value stock in the future (*Allen v. Biltmore Tissue Corp.,* 2 N.Y.2d 534, 542–543, 161 N.Y.S.2d 418, 141 N.E.2d 812). Indeed, the dissenters in *Ingle* itself acknowledged that employee shareholders would be precluded from complaining about the terms of an otherwise enforceable buyback provision (*Ingle v. Glamore Motor Sales,* 73 N.Y.2d, *supra,* at 192, n. 1, 538 N.Y.S.2d 771, 535 N.E.2d 1311).

Gallagher accepted the offer to become a minority stockholder, but only for the period during which he remained an employee. The buy-back price formula was designed for the benefit of both parties precisely so that they could know their respective rights on certain dates and avoid costly and lengthy litigation on the "fair value" issue (*see, Coleman v. Taub,* 3d Cir., 638 F.2d 628, 637). Permitting these causes to survive would open the door to litigation on both the value of the stock and the date of termination, and hinder the employer from fulfilling its contractual rights under the agreement. This would frustrate the agreement and would be disruptive of the settled principles governing like agreements where parties contract between themselves in advance so that there may be reliance, predictability and definitiveness between themselves on such matters. There being no dispute that the employer had the unfettered discretion to fire plaintiff at any time, we should not redefine the precise measuring device and scope of the agreement. Defendant agreed to abide by these terms and thus fulfilled its fiduciary duty in that respect.

The dissenting opinion uses a number of rhetorical characterizations about the defendant and about what we are deciding or avoiding to decide, none of which, we believe, require response, because our holding and rationale rest on the application of fundamental contractual principles to the plain terms in the parties' own stock repurchase agreement.

Accordingly, the order of the Appellate Division should be affirmed, with costs, and the certified question answered in the affirmative.

HANCOCK, Judge (concurring).

I agree that the complaint should be dismissed. I believe that this court's *holding* in *Ingle v. Glamore Motor Sales,* 73 N.Y.2d 183, 538 N.Y.S.2d 771, 535 N.E.2d 1311, and an analysis of the *Ingle* complaint which the court dismissed require dismissal of the claim asserted here (*see, id.,* at 192–193, 538 N.Y.S.2d 771, 535 N.E.2d 1311 [Hancock, Jr., J., dissenting]; *see also,* verified complaint in *Ingle,* appellant's appx., at A37–A38; appellant's brief, at 28 ff).

KAYE, Judge (dissenting).

By proceeding, as if inexorably, from *Sabetay* to *Ingle* to *Gallagher,* the court avoids confronting plaintiff's true claims and unnecessarily weakens traditional protections afforded minority shareholders in close corporations. I therefore respectfully dissent.

I.

To begin at a point of agreement, this case is significantly different from *Ingle v. Glamore Motor Sales,* 73 N.Y.2d 183, 538 N.Y.S.2d 771, 535 N.E.2d 1311. As the majority acknowledges, this case presents "an alleged departure from a fiduciary duty of fair dealing existing independently of the employment" that was not present in *Ingle* (majority opn., at 566, at 946 of 549 N.Y.S.2d, at 137 of 549 N.E.2d).

In *Ingle* we reached only the corporation's duty to plaintiff as *an employee,* carving out and reserving for another day any question of the duty a corporation might owe an employee as *a shareholder,* which was not in issue. The court was careful to note that Mr. Ingle had already accepted full payment for his shares without reservation; while his complaint referred to a fiduciary duty owed him as a shareholder, the only interest he asserted in the litigation was in his job. In its succinct opinion the court took pains to emphasize at least six separate times that its concern was only with Mr. Ingle's employment, not in any sense with the duty a corporation owes to a minority shareholder, or with undervaluation of shares (73 N.Y.2d, at 187, 188, 189, 538 N.Y.S.2d 771, 535 N.E.2d 1311).

Here, plaintiff *does* question the duty the corporation owes him as a shareholder. He *does* contend that the corporation undervalued his shares and that it did not offer a fair price for his equity interest. Indeed, that is the only question he raises; he does not challenge defendant's absolute right to terminate his employment. Yet despite careful identification and recognition in *Ingle* of the different considerations such a question would present, now that the question is before us the court finds that the very same answer and the very same rationale are wholly dispositive, with no analysis of the fiduciary obligation owed plaintiff.

The court's insistence that the rationale of *Ingle* and the other at-will employment cases must be carried over—lock, stock and barrel—even to the fiduciary obligations owed minority shareholders in close corporations, plainly represents an extension of the law to a different jural relationship. I believe this is wholly unwarranted.

II.

A fuller statement of the facts portrays both plaintiff's true claims and the error of summary dismissal of his complaint.

Before he was dismissed on January 10, 1985, plaintiff (James V. Gallagher) was an officer and director of both defendant Eastdil

Realty, Inc. and its wholly owned subsidiary, Eastdil Advisers, Inc. Eastdil Realty is a closely held real estate investing banking firm. Defendant Lambert is its founder, principal shareholder and chief executive officer. The other defendants are officers and shareholders of the corporation.

Gallagher was first employed by Eastdil Realty as vice-president, from 1968 to 1973, when he left to start his own firm. He returned as a consultant in 1976, and was soon offered a full-time position as vice-president at a base salary of $60,000. In 1978, Gallagher was appointed president and chief executive officer of the newly created Eastdil Advisors, and he was elected to Eastdil's board of directors in 1980. As Gallagher's responsibilities increased, his salary and bonuses rose commensurately and steadily—from $135,000 in 1979 to more than a million dollars for the fiscal year ending on January 31, 1984.

In 1981, a number of executives of Eastdil Realty were offered the opportunity to purchase shares of class B nonvoting stock in the company. Gallagher bought 4%—40 shares—at $100 a share. Lambert continued to own all of the voting stock. In connection with his purchase of shares, Gallagher executed a stockholders' agreement that contained a mandatory repurchase provision. For a period of two years "commencing with the voluntary resignation or other termination of any class B stockholder's employment with the company," the company had a right to reacquire the shares. The agreement set the repurchase price at book value.

In mid–1983, Eastdil implemented a recapitalization plan. All of the voting stock was to be retired, and the nonvoting shares increased and redistributed, and then converted into voting common stock. As Gallagher alleges, the recapitalization was no act of charity by the corporation; it was a response to a mass exodus of valued employees, and an effort to forestall further defections by offering financial incentives to continue with the corporation at least to year-end.

In summer 1984, Gallagher received 8.5% of Eastdil's stock, becoming the third largest shareholder, and he executed an amended stockholders' agreement. The agreement continued to provide for mandatory repurchase at book value upon "voluntary resignation or other termination" of employment. But it also stipulated that after January 31, 1985, the buy-out price would be calculated by an escalating formula based on the company's earnings and the length of the shareholder's employment. According to Gallagher, the new buy-out price represented "golden handcuffs" designed to induce employees to remain on, at least until January 31, 1985.

On January 10, 1985—just 21 days before the new valuation formula became effective—Gallagher was fired and Eastdil invoked its right to repurchase his stock at book value. According to Gallagher, book value for the shares was $89,000; the price under the new valuation formula would have been around $3,000,000.

After Gallagher's refusal to deliver his shares at book value, and defendants' refusal to pay the higher value, Gallagher began this damages action for breach of contract, breach of fiduciary duty, breach of a duty of good faith and fair dealing, and other alleged wrongdoing. For nearly a year defendants conducted discovery of plaintiff—including a very extensive deposition—and then sought summary judgment; plaintiff had no discovery whatever. The trial court denied defendants' motion, noting factual issues concerning defendants' motive for firing plaintiff, and that it "would clearly be an injustice to grant * * * defendants' motion, when plaintiff has had no disclosure at all." A divided Appellate Division reversed; dismissed plaintiff's causes of action for breach of contract, breach of fiduciary duty, and breach of a duty of good faith and fair dealing; granted defendants specific performance of the amended stockholders' agreement; and granted plaintiff leave to appeal to this court on a certified question.

III.

Gallagher alleges that defendants had no bona fide, business-related reason to terminate his employment when they did—assertions we must accept as true on this summary judgment motion. He charges that defendants fired him for the sole purpose of recapturing his shares at an unfairly low price and redistributing them among themselves.

These claims put in issue an aspect of the employee-shareholder relationship that we have not previously considered in our at-will employment cases. Plaintiff claims that defendants, the holders of a majority of the corporate stock, breached distinctly different duties to him by manipulating his termination so as to deprive him of the opportunity to reap the benefits of a "golden handcuffs" agreement, and for no other reason than to effect repurchase of his shares at less than their fair value. In short, plaintiff claims defendants breached two duties related to each other but conceptually unrelated to his at-will employment status: (1) a duty of good faith in the performance of the shareholders' agreement, and (2) a fiduciary obligation owed to him as a minority shareholder by the controlling shareholders to refrain from purely self-aggrandizing conduct. Neither claim is foreclosed by plaintiff's status as an at-will employee.

If plaintiff were a minority shareholder, but not an employee, defendants would be barred from acting selfishly and opportunistically, for no corporate purpose, as he alleges they did. The controlling stockholders in a close corporation stand, in relation to minority owners, in the same fiduciary position as corporate directors generally, and are held "to the extreme measure of candor, unselfishness and good faith." (*Kavanaugh v. Kavanaugh Knitting Co.*, 226 N.Y. 185, 193, 123 N.E. 148.) Although, without more, the courts will not interfere when parties have set the repurchase price at book value (*Allen v. Biltmore Tissue Corp.*, 2 N.Y.2d 534, 542–543, 161 N.Y.S.2d 418, 141 N.E.2d 812), here plaintiff asserts there was more. The corporation agreed, commencing January 31, 1985, to pay a higher price, said to be more reflective of the true value of defendant's shares.* Defendants' invocation of the pre-January 31 repurchase price was adverse to plaintiff's interests as a minority stockholder, and therefore subject to a standard of good faith under the foregoing principles.

Directors and majority shareholders may not act "for the aggrandizement or undue advantage of the fiduciary to the exclusion or detriment of the [minority] stockholders." (*Alpert v. 28 Williams St. Corp.*, 63 N.Y.2d 557, 569, 483 N.Y.S.2d 667, 473 N.E.2d 19 [citing cases].) Nor is it considered a legitimate corporate interest if the sole purpose is reduction of the number of profit-sharers, or ultimately "to increase the individual wealth of the remaining shareholders" (*id.*, at 573, 483 N.Y.S.2d 667, 473 N.E.2d 19). Yet that is precisely what we must assume defendants' motive was, and this court now sanctions such conduct.

Defendants' broad interpretation of the "other termination" language of the repurchase clause amounts to an assertion that plaintiff agreed to waive substantial rights he might otherwise have possessed as a minority shareholder. However, in the absence of evidence that plaintiff knowingly assented to such a waiver, I cannot agree that the general language of the clause unambiguously expresses an understanding that the option could be exploited for the sole personal gain of the controlling shareholders in derogation of their fiduciary obligations to minority shareholders. Notably, the repurchase clause contains no reference to plaintiff's at-will employment status and no reservation of defendant's right to discharge plaintiff for any reason at all.

Moreover, defendants' interpretation denies that defendants themselves had any duty of good faith in connection with the shareholders' agreement. We have said that "there is an implied covenant that neither party shall do anything which will have the effect of destroying or injuring the right of the other party to receive the fruits of the contract, which means that in every contract there exists an implied covenant of good faith and fair dealing." (*Kirke La Shelle Co. v. Armstrong Co.*, 263 N.Y. 79, 87, 188 N.E. 163.) This general rule does not apply to at-will employment relationships, as "it would be incongruous to say that an inference may be drawn that the employer impliedly agreed to a provision which would be destructive of his right of termination." (*Murphy v. American Home Prods. Corp.*, 58 N.Y.2d 293, 304–305, 461 N.Y.S.2d 232, 448 N.E.2d 86.) It does not follow, however, that there can be no covenant of good faith implicit in the shareholders' agreement that gives rise to obligations surviving termination of the employment relationship.

---

* The majority's premise that certainty would be undermined, and "costly and lengthy litigation on the 'fair value' issue" would ensue (majority opn., at 567, at 946 of 549 N.Y.S.2d, at 137 of 549 N.E.2d) simply is without basis. No one proposes a valuation proceeding, or any other uncertainty. The only issue is which of the two values fixed in the agreement should apply.

Assuming plaintiff's claims about the purpose of the amendments to be true, the expectations and relationship of the parties, as structured by the shareholders' agreement, dictate an implied contractual obligation of good faith, notwithstanding that there is none in their employment relationship (*see, Wakefield v. Northern Telecom*, 769 F.2d 109 [2d Cir.]). A covenant of good faith is anomalous in the context of at-will employment because performance and entitlement to benefits are simultaneous. Termination even without cause does not operate to deprive the employee of the benefits promised in return for performance.

But the alleged "golden handcuffs" agreement is different. An implied covenant of good faith *is* necessary to enable the employee to receive the benefits promised for performance. As one court noted, "an unfettered right to avoid payment * * * creates incentives counterproductive to the purpose of the contract itself in that the better the performance by the employee, the greater the temptation to terminate." (*Wakefield v. Northern Telecom, supra*, at 112–113; Note, *Exercising Options to Repurchase Employee–Held Stock: A Question of Good Faith*, 68 Yale L.J. 773, 779 [1959].) . . .

IV.

Denial of summary judgment would deprive defendants of no legitimate expectation or right, contractual or otherwise. Under the law, they remain free to terminate plaintiff's employment as agreed; they remain free to buy back his stock at book value as agreed—so long as there is a corporate purpose for their conduct. What controlling shareholders cannot do to a minority shareholder is take action against him solely for the self-aggrandizing, opportunistic purpose of themselves acquiring his shares at the low price, and they cannot do this because in the law it means something to be a shareholder, particularly a minority shareholder.

Because the majority gives no credence whatever to plaintiff's independent status as a shareholder, and because the majority now needlessly extends the at-will employment doctrine yet another notch, to diminish the long-recognized duties owed minority shareholders, I must dissent.

SIMONS, ALEXANDER and TITONE, JJ., concur with BELLACOSA, J.

HANCOCK, J., concurs in a separate opinion.

KAYE, J., dissents and votes to reverse in another opinion in which WACHTLER, C.J., concurs.

Order affirmed, etc.

———

SECTION 8.   DISSOLUTION FOR DEADLOCK

DEL. GEN. CORP. LAW §§ 273, 355

[See Statutory Supplement]

REV. MODEL BUS. CORP. ACT §§ 14.30, 14.34

[See Statutory Supplement]

N.Y. BUS. CORP. LAW §§ 1002, 1104, 1111

[See Statutory Supplement]

WOLLMAN v. LITTMAN

New York Supreme Court, Appellate Div., First Dept., 1970.
35 A.D.2d 935, 316 N.Y.S.2d 526.

PER CURIAM . . .

The stock of the corporation is held, fifty percent each, by two distinct groups, one of which, the Nierenberg sisters, are plaintiffs, and the other, the Littmans, defendants, each group having equal representation on the board of directors.   The corporation's business is the selling of artificial fur fabrics to garment manufacturers. Defendants, the Littmans, allegedly had the idea for the business and developed a market for the fabrics among its manufacturing customers.   Plaintiffs are the daughters of Louis Nierenberg, the main stockholder of Louis Nierenberg, Inc., who procures the fabrics and sells them to the corporation.   The Littmans, in a separate action in which they are plaintiffs, charge the plaintiffs here (the Nierenberg sisters) and Louis Nierenberg Corporation with seeking to lure away the corporation's customers for Louis Nierenberg Corporation and with doing various acts to affect the corporation's business adversely.   The Nierenberg faction countered with this suit, claiming that the bringing of the other action indicates that the corporate management is at such odds among themselves that effective management is impossible.   Special Term agreed, but we do not.   Irreconcilable differences even among an evenly divided board of directors do not in all cases mandate dissolution. . . . Here, two factors would require further exploration.   The first is that the functions of the two disputing interests are distinct, one selling and the other procuring, and each can pursue its own without need for collaboration.   The second is that a dissolution which will render nugatory the relief sought in the representative action would actually accomplish the wrongful purpose that defendants (Nierenberg) are charged with in that action. It would not only squeeze the Littmans out of the business but would require the receiver to dispose of the inventory with the Nierenbergs the only interested purchaser financially strong enough to take advantage of the situation. Such a result, if supported by the facts, would be intolerable to a court of equity. A trial of the issues is necessitated. On that trial it has been agreed by both counsel it would be advantageous to have the representative action and the action for dissolution tried together, though not consolidated (for a discussion of the distinction, see the comprehensive opinion in Padilla v. Greyhound Lines, 29 A.D.2d 495, 288 N.Y.S. 641), and it is so directed.

We affirm the appointment of a receiver. His function, however, should be limited to the necessities indicated, namely, to the orderly functioning of the regular course of business of the corporation until the further order of the court.

NOTE ON DISSOLUTION FOR DEADLOCK

1. A number of statutes provide for involuntary dissolution on a showing of deadlock. A few of the statutes define deadlock in terms of an "equally divided" board or body of shareholders, see, e.g., Mass. § 50; Cook v. Cook, 270 Mass. 534, 170 N.E. 455 (1930), but most are phrased broadly enough to include deadlock brought about by supermajority or veto arrangements.

2. The deadlock statutes are generally interpreted to make dissolution discretionary even when deadlock as defined in the statute is shown to exist, and the courts have often been reluctant to order the dissolution of a profitable corporation on deadlock grounds. However, profitability is not a bar to dissolution for deadlock. In Weiss v. Gordon, 32 A.D.2d 279, 301 N.Y.S.2d 839 (1969), the court stated, "The earlier thinking stressed the distinction between the corporation as an entity and the shareholders, and as long as the former could continue to function profitably the relationship between the shareholders was of no moment (cf. Matter of Radom & Neidorff, Inc., 307 N.Y. 1, 119 N.E.2d 563 (1954)). It is being increasingly realized that the relationship between the stockholders in a close corporation vis-a-vis each other in practice closely approximates the relationship between partners (see Application of Surchin, 55 Misc.2d 888, 890, 286 N.Y.S.2d 580, 583 (1967)). As a consequence, when a point is reached where the shareholders who are actively conducting the business of the corporation cannot agree, it becomes in the best interests of those shareholders to order a dissolution. . . ." [1]

---

1. See also Application of Pivot Punch & Die Corp., 15 Misc.2d 713, 182 N.Y.S.2d 459 (1959), modified 9 A.D.2d 861, 193 N.Y.S.2d 34; cf. Laskey v. L. & L. Manches-

SECTION 9. PROVISIONAL DIRECTORS AND CUSTODIANS

DEL. GEN. CORP. LAW §§ 226, 352, 353

[See Statutory Supplement]

CAL. CORP. CODE §§ 308, 1802

[See Statutory Supplement]

THOMPSON, THE SHAREHOLDER'S CAUSE OF ACTION FOR OPPRESSION, 48 Bus.Law. 699, 723 (1993). "[More than half of the states have added to the remedies available in shareholder disputes by providing for the appointment of a custodian. About twenty states authorize a court to appoint a provisional director to help resolve shareholder disputes.] . . . Despite their widespread inclusion in statutes, these remedies are not used often. [The remedy is more important in states like Delaware, where it is the only effective remedy for shareholder dissension.] There is a cost to an additional layer of management, which would unduly burden a small enterprise, and the appointment of an outside party may not address the underlying differences among the participants." *

SECTION 10. DISSOLUTION FOR OPPRESSION AND MANDATORY BUY–OUT

REV. MODEL BUS. CORP. ACT § 14.30, 14.34

[See Statutory Supplement]

---

ter Drive–In, Inc., 216 A.2d 310 (Me.1966); Ellis v. Civic Improvement, Inc., 24 N.C.App. 42, 209 S.E.2d 873 (1974), cert. denied 286 N.C. 413, 211 S.E.2d 794 (1975); Application of Surchin, 55 Misc.2d 888, 286 N.Y.S.2d 580 (1967).

* The material in brackets has been transposed from footnotes to text. (Footnote by ed.)

CAL. CORP. CODE §§ 1800, 1804, 2000

[See Statutory Supplement]

––––––

N.Y. BUS. CORP. LAW §§ 1104–a, 1111, 1118

[See Statutory Supplement]

––––––

NOTE ON HETHERINGTON AND DOOLEY

In 1977, John Hetherington & Michael Dooley published a celebrated article, Illiquidity and Exploitation: A Proposed Statutory Solution to the Remaining Close Corporation Problem, 63 Va.L.Rev. 1 (1977). In this article, the authors marshalled empirical evidence to show that a judicial order to dissolve a corporation was not likely to lead to the breakup of a solvent business, because if it is advantageous to continue a business rather than break it up, then after such an order is issued, either one or more of the shareholders or a third party would normally purchase and continue the business. Hetherington & Dooley analyzed the 54 reported dissolution cases decided between 1960 and 1976. In half the cases, the plaintiff had been successful; in half, unsuccessful. Of the twenty-seven cases in which the plaintiff had been successful, in only six cases was the corporation actually liquidated. In seventeen cases one party bought out the other; in three cases, the business was sold to an outsider; and in one case there was no buyout or other change. (Of the twenty-seven cases in which plaintiff was unsuccessful, in fourteen cases one party bought out the other; in two cases the business was sold to a third party; in three cases the business was liquidated; in six cases there was no change in ownership; and in two cases the result was unknown.) Id. at 30–31.

Furthermore, Hetherington & Dooley argued, dissolution, or something like it, was a central remedy for disaffected shareholders in close corporations because, given the limits of reasonable foreseeability, shareholders who organized such corporations could not possibly plan in advance to deal with all the interpersonal problems that might occur between them. Therefore, Hetherington & Dooley concluded, in the case of a close corporation a remedy comparable to dissolution—specifically, free exit through a mandatory buyout of the minority's interest—should be available on demand.

> The emphasis on contractual arrangements [in close corporations] reveals a fundamental misunderstanding of the nature of close corporations. Whether the parties adopt special contractual arrangements is much less important than their ability

to sustain a close, harmonious relationship over time. The continuance of such a relationship is crucial because it reflects what is perhaps the fundamental assumption made by those who decide to invest in a close corporation: they expect that during the life of the firm the shareholders will be in substantial agreement as to its operation.

Time and human nature may cause a divergence of interests and a breakdown in consensus, however. . . .

Our thesis is that the problem of exploitation is uniquely related to liquidity and, for that reason, it is resistant to solution by ex ante contractual arrangements or by ex post judicial relief for breach of fiduciary duty. Accordingly, we [propose that the law should require] the majority to repurchase the minority's interest at the request of the latter and subject to appropriate safeguards.

Id. at 2–3, 6. This insight, as well as the authors' data, form a backdrop to the materials in this section.

MATTER OF KEMP & BEATLEY, INC.

Court of Appeals of New York, 1984.
64 N.Y.2d 63, 484 N.Y.S.2d 799, 473 N.E.2d 1173.

COOKE, Chief Judge.

When the majority shareholders of a close corporation award *de facto* dividends to all shareholders except a class of minority shareholders, such a policy may constitute "oppressive actions" and serve as a basis for an order made pursuant to section 1104–a of the Business Corporation Law dissolving the corporation. In the instant matter, there is sufficient evidence to support the lower courts' conclusion that the majority shareholders had altered a long-standing policy to distribute corporate earnings on the basis of stock ownership, as against petitioners only. Moreover, the courts did not abuse their discretion by concluding that dissolution was the only means by which petitioners could gain a fair return on their investment.

I

The business concern of Kemp & Beatley, incorporated under the laws of New York, designs and manufactures table linens and sundry tabletop items. The company's stock consists of 1,500 outstanding shares held by eight shareholders. Petitioner Dissin had been employed by the company for 42 years when, in June 1979, he resigned. Prior to resignation, Dissin served as vice-president and a director of Kemp & Beatley. Over the course of his employment, Dissin had acquired stock in the company and currently owns 200 shares.

Petitioner Gardstein, like Dissin, had been a long-time employee of the company. Hired in 1944, Gardstein was for the next 35 years involved in various aspects of the business including material procurement, product design, and plant management. His employment was terminated by the company in December 1980. He currently owns 105 shares of Kemp & Beatley stock.

Apparent unhappiness surrounded petitioners' leaving the employ of the company. Of particular concern was that they no longer received any distribution of the company's earnings. Petitioners considered themselves to be "frozen out" of the company; whereas it had been their experience when with the company to receive a distribution of the company's earnings according to their stockholdings, in the form of either dividends or extra compensation, that distribution was no longer forthcoming.

Gardstein and Dissin, together holding 20.33% of the company's outstanding stock, commenced the instant proceeding in June 1981, seeking dissolution of Kemp & Beatley pursuant to section 1104–a of the Business Corporation Law. Their petition alleged "fraudulent and oppressive" conduct by the company's board of directors such as to render petitioners' stock "a virtually worthless asset." Supreme Court referred the matter for a hearing, which was held in March 1982.

Upon considering the testimony of petitioners and the principals of Kemp & Beatley, the referee concluded that "the corporate management has by its policies effectively rendered petitioners' shares worthless, and ... the only way petitioners can expect any return is by dissolution". Petitioners were found to have invested capital in the company expecting, among other things, to receive dividends or "bonuses" based upon their stock holdings. Also found was the company's "established buyout policy" by which it would purchase the stock of employee shareholders upon their leaving its employ.

The involuntary-dissolution statute (Business Corporation Law, § 1104–a) permits dissolution when a corporation's controlling faction is found guilty of "oppressive action" toward the complaining shareholders. The referee considered oppression to arise when "those in control" of the corporation "have acted in such a manner as to defeat those expectations of the minority stockholders which formed the basis of [their] participation in the venture." The expectations of petitioners that they would not be arbitrarily excluded from gaining a return on their investment and that their stock would be purchased by the corporation upon termination of employment, were deemed defeated by prevailing corporate policies. Dissolution was recommended in the referee's report, subject to giving respondent corporation an opportunity to purchase petitioners' stock.

Supreme Court confirmed the referee's report. It, too, concluded that due to the corporation's new dividend policy petitioners had been prevented from receiving any return on their investments.

Liquidation of the corporate assets was found the only means by which petitioners would receive a fair return. The court considered judicial dissolution of a corporation to be "a serious and severe remedy." Consequently, the order of dissolution was conditioned upon the corporation's being permitted to purchase petitioners' stock. The Appellate Division affirmed, without opinion. 99 A.D.2d 445, 471 N.Y.S.2d 245.

At issue in this appeal is the scope of section 1104–a of the Business Corporation Law. Specifically, this court must determine whether the provision for involuntary dissolution when the "directors or those in control of the corporation have been guilty of . . . oppressive actions toward the complaining shareholders" was properly applied in the circumstances of this case. We hold that it was, and therefore affirm.

II

Judicially ordered dissolution of a corporation at the behest of minority interests is a remedy of relatively recent vintage in New York. Historically, this State's courts were considered divested of equity jurisdiction to order dissolution, as statutory prescriptions were deemed exclusive (see Hitch v. Hawley, 132 N.Y. 212, 217, 30 N.E. 401). Statutes permitting judicial dissolution of corporations either limited the types of corporations under their purview (see L. 1817, ch. 146, §§ 1–4; see, also, Matter of Niagara Ins. Co., 1 Paige Ch. 258) or restricted the parties who could petition for dissolution to the Attorney–General, or the directors, trustees, or majority shareholders of the corporation (see Hitch v. Hawley, 132 N.Y., at pp. 218–219, 30 N.E. 401, supra; see, generally, Business Corporation Law, §§ 1101–1104).

Minority shareholders were granted standing in the absence of statutory authority to seek dissolution of corporations when controlling shareholders engaged in certain egregious conduct (see Leibert v. Clapp, 13 N.Y.2d 313, 247 N.Y.S.2d 102, 196 N.E.2d 540; Fontheim v. Walker, 282 App.Div. 373, 122 N.Y.S.2d 642, affd. no opn. 306 N.Y. 926, 119 N.E.2d 605). Predicated on the majority shareholders' fiduciary obligation to treat all shareholders fairly and equally, to preserve corporate assets, and to fulfill their responsibilities of corporate management with "scrupulous good faith," the courts' equitable power can be invoked when "it appears that the directors and majority shareholders 'have so palpably breached the fiduciary duty they owe to the minority shareholders that they are disqualified from exercising the exclusive discretion and the dissolution power given to them by statute.' " (Leibert v. Clapp, 13 N.Y.2d, at p. 317, 247 N.Y.S.2d 102, 196 N.E.2d 540, supra, quoting Hoffman, New Horizons for the Close Corporation, 28 Brooklyn L.Rev. 1, 14.) True to the ancient principle that equity jurisdiction will not lie when there exists a remedy at law (see Brady v. McCosker, 1 N.Y. 214, 217), the courts have not entertained a minority's petition in equity when their rights and interests could be adequately protected in a legal action, such as by a shareholder's derivative suit (see Matter of Nelkin v. H.J.R. Realty Corp., 25 N.Y.2d 543, 550, 307 N.Y.S.2d 454, 255 N.E.2d 713; cf. Leibert v. Clapp, 13 N.Y.2d, at p. 317, 247 N.Y.S.2d 102, 196 N.E.2d 540, supra).

Supplementing this principle of judicially ordered equitable dissolution of a corporation, the Legislature has shown a special solicitude toward the rights of minority shareholders of closely held corporations by enacting section 1104–a of the Business Corporation Law. That statute provides a mechanism for the holders of at least 20% of the outstanding shares of a corporation whose stock is not traded on a securities market to petition for its dissolution "under special circumstances" (see Business Corporation Law, § 1104–a, subd. [a]). The circumstances that give rise to dissolution fall into two general classifications: mistreatment of complaining shareholders (subd. [a], par. [1]), or misappropriation of corporate assets (subd. [a], par. [2]) by controlling shareholders, directors or officers.

Section 1104–a (subd. [a], par. [1]) describes three types of proscribed activity: "illegal", "fraudulent", and "oppressive" conduct. The first two terms are familiar words that are commonly understood at law. The last, however, does not enjoy the same certainty gained through long usage. As no definition is provided by the statute, it falls upon the courts to provide guidance (see Goncalves v. Regent Int. Hotels, 58 N.Y.2d 206, 218, 460 N.Y.S.2d 750, 447 N.E.2d 693).

The statutory concept of "oppressive actions" can, perhaps, best be understood by examining the characteristics of close corporations and the Legislature's general purpose in creating this involuntary-dissolution statute. It is widely understood that, in addition to supplying capital to a contemplated or ongoing enterprise and expecting a fair and equal return, parties comprising the ownership of a close corporation may expect to be actively involved in its management and operation. . . . The small ownership cluster seeks to "contribute their capital, skills, experience and labor" toward the corporate enterprise. . . .

As a leading commentator in the field has observed: "Unlike the typical shareholder in a publicly held corporation, who may be simply an investor or a speculator and cares nothing for the responsibilities of management, the shareholder in a close corporation is a co-owner of the business and wants the privileges and powers that go with ownership. His participation in that particular corporation is often his principal or sole source of income. As a matter of fact, providing employment for himself may have been the principal reason why he participated in organizing the corporation. He may or may not anticipate an ultimate profit from the sale of his interest, but he normally draws very little from the corporation as dividends. In his capacity as an officer or employee of the corporation, he looks to his salary for the principal return on his capital investment, because earnings of a close corporation, as is well known, are distributed in major part in salaries, bonuses and retirement benefits." (O'Neal, Close Corporations [2d ed.], § 1.07, at pp. 21–22 [n. omitted].)

Shareholders enjoy flexibility in memorializing these expectations through agreements setting forth each party's rights and obligations in corporate governance (see, generally, Kessler, Shareholder–Managed Close Corporation Under the New York Business Corporation Law, 43 Fordham L.Rev. 197; Davidian, op. cit., 56 St. John's L.Rev. 24, 29–30, and nn. 21–22). In the absence of such an agreement, however, ultimate decision-making power respecting corporate policy will be reposed in the holders of a majority interest in the corporation (see, e.g., Business Corporation Law, §§ 614, 708). A wielding of this power by any group controlling a corporation may serve to destroy a stockholder's vital interests and expectations.

As the stock of closely held corporations generally is not readily salable, a minority shareholder at odds with management policies may be without either a voice in protecting his or her interests or any reasonable means of withdrawing his or her investment. This predicament may fairly be considered the legislative concern underlying the provision at issue in this case; inclusion of the criteria that the corporation's stock not be traded on securities markets and that the complaining shareholder be subject to oppressive actions supports this conclusion.

Defining oppressive conduct as distinct from illegality in the present context has been considered in other forums. The question has been resolved by considering oppressive actions to refer to conduct that substantially defeats the "reasonable expectations" held by minority shareholders in committing their capital to the particular enterprise (see, e.g., Mardikos v. Arger, 116 Misc.2d 1028, 457 N.Y.S.2d 371; Matter of Barry One Hour Photo Process, 111 Misc.2d 559, 444 N.Y.S.2d 540. . . . This concept is consistent with the apparent purpose underlying the provision under review. A shareholder who reasonably expected that ownership in the corporation would entitle him or her to a job, a share of corporate earnings, a place in corporate management, or some other form of security, would be oppressed in a very real sense when others in the corporation seek to defeat those expectations and there exists no effective means of salvaging the investment.

Given the nature of close corporations and the remedial purpose of the statute, this court holds that utilizing a complaining shareholder's "reasonable expectations" as a means of identifying and measuring conduct alleged to be oppressive is appropriate. A court considering a petition alleging oppressive conduct must investigate what the majority shareholders knew, or should have known, to be the petitioner's expectations in entering the particular enterprise. Majority conduct should not be deemed oppressive simply because the petitioner's subjective hopes and desires in joining the venture are not fulfilled. Disappointment alone should not necessarily be equated with oppression.

Rather, oppression should be deemed to arise only when the majority conduct substantially defeats expectations that, objectively viewed, were both reasonable under the circumstances and were central to the petitioner's decision to join the venture. It would be inappropriate, however, for us in this case to delineate the contours of the courts' consideration in determining whether directors have been guilty of oppressive conduct. As in other areas of the law, much will depend on the circumstances in the individual case.

The appropriateness of an order of dissolution is in every case vested in the sound discretion of the court considering the application (see Business Corporation Law, § 1111, subd. [a]). Under the terms of this statute, courts are instructed to consider both whether "liquidation of the corporation is the only feasible means" to protect the complaining shareholder's expectation of a fair return on his or her investment and whether dissolution "is reasonably necessary" to protect "the rights or interests of any substantial number of shareholders" not limited to those complaining (Business Corporation Law, § 1104–a, subd. [b], pars. [1], [2]). Implicit in this direction is that once oppressive conduct is found, consideration must be given to the totality of circumstances surrounding the current state of corporate affairs and relations to determine whether some remedy short of or other than dissolution, constitutes a feasible means of satisfying both the petitioner's expectations and the rights and interests of any other substantial group of shareholders (see, also, Business Corporation Law, § 1111, subd. [b], par. [1]).

By invoking the statute, a petitioner has manifested his or her belief that dissolution may be the only appropriate remedy. Assuming the petitioner has set forth a prima facie case of oppressive conduct, it should be incumbent upon the parties seeking to forestall dissolution to demonstrate to the court the existence of an adequate, alternative remedy (cf. Baker v. Commercial Body Bldrs., 264 Or. 614, 507 P.2d 387, supra; White v. Perkins, 213 Va. 129, 189 S.E.2d 315). A court has broad latitude in fashioning alternative relief, but when fulfillment of the oppressed petitioner's expectations by these means is doubtful, such as when there has been a complete deterioration of relations between the parties, a court should not hesitate to order dissolution. Every order of dissolution, however, must be conditioned upon permitting any shareholder of the corporation to elect to purchase the complaining shareholder's stock at fair value (see Business Corporation Law, § 1118).

One further observation is in order. The purpose of this involuntary dissolution statute is to provide protection to the minority shareholder whose reasonable expectations in undertaking the venture have been frustrated and who has no adequate means of recovering his or her investment. It would be contrary to this remedial purpose to permit its use by minority shareholders as merely a coercive tool (see Davidian, op. cit., 56 St. John's L.Rev. 24, 59–60, and nn. 159–160). Therefore, the minority shareholder whose own acts, made in bad faith and undertaken with a view toward forcing an involuntary dissolution, give rise to the complained-of oppression should be given no quarter in the statutory protection (cf. Mardikos v. Arger, 116 Misc.2d 1028, 1032, 457 N.Y.S.2d 371, supra).

III

There was sufficient evidence presented at the hearing to support the conclusion that Kemp & Beatley had a long-standing policy of awarding *de facto* dividends based on stock ownership in the form of "extra compensation bonuses." Petitioners, both of whom had extensive experience in the management of the company, testified to this effect. Moreover, both related that receipt of this compensation, whether as true dividends or disguised as "extra compensation", was a known incident to ownership of the company's stock understood by all of the company's principals. Finally, there was uncontroverted proof that this policy was changed either shortly before or shortly after petitioners' employment ended. Extra compensation was still awarded by the company. The only difference was that stock ownership was no longer a basis for the payments; it was asserted that the basis became services rendered to the corporation. It was not unreasonable for the fact finder to have determined that this change in policy amounted to nothing less than an attempt to exclude petitioners from gaining any return on their investment through the mere recharacterization of distributions of corporate income. Under the circumstances of this case, there was no error in determining that this conduct constituted oppressive action within the meaning of section 1104–a of the Business Corporation Law.[2]

Nor may it be said that Supreme Court abused its discretion in ordering Kemp & Beatley's dissolution, subject to an opportunity for a buy-out of petitioners' shares. After the referee had found that the controlling faction of the company was, in effect, attempting to "squeeze-out" petitioners by offering them no return on their investment and increasing other executive compensation, respondents, in opposing the report's confirmation, attempted only to controvert the factual basis of the report. They suggested no feasible, alternative remedy to the forced dissolution. In light of an apparent deterioration in relations between petitioners and the governing shareholders of Kemp & Beatley, it was not unreasonable for the court to have determined that a forced buy-out of petitioners' shares or liquidation of the corporation's assets was the only

2. Respondent is correct in arguing that there is no basis in the record for the referee's conclusion that the corporation had an established policy to buy-out the shares of employees when they left the company. Although the record reflects that petitioners intended to offer proof on this issue, the referee erroneously concluded that the issue was beyond the scope of the reference. He considered such evidence only as "background." In light of this limitation of the issues under consideration, which neither side objected to, the referee could not then properly ground his decision on a failure by respondent to abide by any buy-out policy. The referee's reliance on this ground is irrelevant for the purposes of this appeal, however, as Supreme Court's confirmation of the report was based solely on the principal ground for the finding of oppression, the company's failure to award dividends.

means by which petitioners could be guaranteed a fair return on their investments.

Accordingly, the order of the Appellate Division should be modified, with costs to petitioners-respondents, by affirming the substantive determination of that court but extending the time for exercising the option to purchase petitioners-respondents' shares to 30 days following this court's determination.

JASEN, JONES, WACHTLER, MEYER and SIMONS, JJ., concur.

KAYE, J., taking no part.

Order modified, with costs to petitioners-respondents, in accordance with the opinion herein and, as so modified, affirmed.

————

MEISELMAN v. MEISELMAN, 309 N.C. 279, 307 S.E.2d 551 (1983). "Professor O'Neal, perhaps the foremost authority on close corporations, points out that many close corporations are companies based on personal relationships that give rise to certain 'reasonable expectations' on the part of those acquiring an interest in the close corporation. Those 'reasonable expectations' include, for example, the parties' expectation that they will participate in the management of the business or be employed by the company. O'Neal, *Close Corporations: Existing Legislation and Recommended Reform,* 33 Bus.Law 873, 885 (1978)....

"Thus, when personal relations among the participants in a close corporation break down, the 'reasonable expectations' the participants had, for example, an expectation that their employment would be secure, or that they would enjoy meaningful participation in the management of the business—become difficult if not impossible to fulfill. In other words, when the personal relationships among the participants break down, the majority shareholder, because of his greater voting power, is in a position to terminate the minority shareholder's employment and to exclude him from participation in management decisions.

"Some may argue that the minority shareholder should have bargained for greater protection before agreeing to accept his minority shareholder position in a close corporation. However, the practical realities of this particular business situation oftentimes do not allow for such negotiations....

"Apparently in response to these commentators' uniform calls for reform in this area of corporate law, many state legislatures have enacted statutes giving the tribunals in their states the power to grant relief to minority shareholders under more liberal circumstances....

"In helping to establish this growing trend toward enactment of more liberal grounds under which dissolution will be granted to a complaining shareholder, the legislature in this State enacted in 1955 N.C.G.S. § 55–125(a)(4), the statute granting superior court judges the 'power to liquidate the assets and business of a corporation in an action by a shareholder when it is established' that '[l]iquidation is reasonably necessary for the protection of the rights or interests of the complaining shareholder.' . . .

"[B]efore it can be determined whether, in any given case, it has been 'established' that liquidation is 'reasonably necessary' to protect the complaining shareholder's 'rights or interest,' the particular 'rights or interests' of the complaining shareholder must be articulated.   This is so because N.C.G.S. § 55–125(a)(4) refers to the 'rights or interests' of *the complaining shareholder';* the statute does not refer to the 'rights or interests' of shareholders generally. . . .   [W]e hold that a complaining shareholder's 'rights or interests' in a close corporation include the 'reasonable expectations' the complaining shareholder has in the corporation.   These 'reasonable expectations' are to be ascertained by examining the entire history of the participants' relationship.   That history will include the 'reasonable expectations' created at the inception of the participants' relationship; those 'reasonable expectations' as altered over time; and the 'reasonable expectations' which develop as the participants engage in a course of dealing in conducting the affairs of the corporation.   The interests and views of the other participants must be considered in determining 'reasonable expectations.' The key is *'reasonable.'*   In order for plaintiff's expectations to be reasonable, they must be known to or assumed by the other shareholders and concurred in by them.   Privately held expectations which are not made known to the other participants are not 'reasonable.'   Only expectations embodied in understandings, express or implied, among the participants should be recognized by the court. . . .

"Defendants argue, however, that . . . [a shareholder] is only entitled to relief if his traditional shareholder rights have been infringed.   They contend that those traditional shareholder rights include the right to notice of stockholders' meetings, the right to vote cumulatively, the right of access to the corporate offices and to corporate financial information, and the right to compel the payment of dividends. . . .

"While it may be true that a shareholder in, for example, a publicly held corporation may have 'rights or interests' defined as defendants argue, a shareholder's rights in a closely held corporation may not necessarily be so narrowly defined. . . ."

———

HAYNSWORTH, THE EFFECTIVENESS OF INVOLUNTARY DISSOLUTION SUITS AS A REMEDY FOR CLOSE CORPORATION DISSENSION, 35 Clev.St. L.Rev. 25 (1987).   "In recent years courts have increasingly focused on developing the concept of oppression, and proof of oppressive conduct is rapidly becoming the most likely avenue for minority shareholder relief in close corporations.   Three definitions of oppression have been used in the cases.

"The first, drawn from English case law is:

> burdensome, harsh and wrongful conduct ... a lack of probity and fair dealing in the affairs of a company to the prejudice of some portion of its members; or a visual departure from the standards of fair dealing, and a violation of fair play on which every shareholder who entrusts his money to a company is entitled to rely.

Under this definition, oppression is basically a breach of the general fiduciary duty of good faith and fair dealing that majority shareholders in a corporation owe to the minority shareholders.

"The second definition, first enunciated in the now famous case of *Donahue v. Rodd Electrotype Company of New England, Inc.,* is conduct that constitutes a violation of the strict fiduciary duty of 'utmost good faith and loyalty' owed by partners *inter se.* This standard, which is based on the analogy of close corporation shareholders who are active in management to general partners in a partnership, is theoretically higher than the 'good faith and inherent fairness' standard normally applicable in a corporation.

"The third definition of oppression, initially derived from English case law, and long advocated by Dean F. Hodge O'Neal as well as other leading close corporation experts, is conduct which frustrates the reasonable expectations of the investors. The reasonable expectations doctrine has been gaining wide acceptance in the past few years. Decisions in at least eight states have explicitly adopted this concept, and decisions in at least nine additional states have implicitly recognized it. The approval of the reasonable expectations doctrine by the New York Court of Appeals in the 1984 case of *In re Kemp & Beatley, Inc.* is quite significant and will undoubtedly influence other courts."

NOTE ON THE DUTY OF CARE AND THE DUTY OF LOYALTY IN THE CLOSELY HELD CORPORATION

Two major legal bulwarks for minority shareholders in publicly held corporations are the duty of care and the duty of loyalty imposed by law on corporate directors and officers. These duties are extremely complex in their details, and are the subject of Chapters VII–IX. To oversimplify somewhat, the duty of care renders a director or officer liable for certain types of managerial negligence, and the duty of loyalty renders a director or officer liable for unfair self-interested transactions with the corporation. However, under the business judgment rule, a decision by an officer or director will not subject him to liability for violation of the duty of care, even if the decision is unreasonable, if it was taken in good faith, there was no self-interest, the director or officer properly informed himself before making the decision, and the decision was not so unreasonable as to be irrational. Under the duty of loyalty, a self-interested transaction will not subject a director or officer to liability if he made full disclosure and the transaction was objectively fair.

The duties of care and loyalty protect minority shareholders in closely held as well as publicly held corporations, but in the closely held context they are often an insufficient protection. For example, the discharge of a minority shareholder from corporate office might qualify for protection under the business judgment rule. A purchase of stock from majority shareholders might not violate the duty of loyalty if the price paid for the stock was fair. The real vice of such actions lies in the fact that they treat shareholders unequally, defeat legitimate expectations of a sort found in closely but not publicly held corporations, or both. Accordingly, the "reasonable expectations" analysis that is made explicit in cases like Meiselman v. Meiselman, that is implicit in cases like Donahue v. Rodd, and that in part underlies the concept of dissolution for oppression, fills a major gap in corporate law. It would be a mistake, however, to believe that analysis based on expectations can be separated from the concept of fairness. One way in which a court determines that reasonable expectations have been defeated by majority shareholders is by asking itself what similarly situated shareholders would have probably expected. Often the only way to answer that question is to ask what similarly situated shareholders would have regarded as fair.

––––––

MICH. COMP. LAWS § 450.1825

[See Statutory Supplement]

––––––

MINN. STAT. ANN. § 302A.751

[See Statutory Supplement]

––––––

NOTE ON DISSOLUTION

The evolution of the legal treatment of dissolution can, with some oversimplification, be divided into four stages.

1. *First stage: dissolution granted only for deadlock and even then granted very sparingly.* In the first, original stage, which lasted until about the early 1960s, the courts typically granted dissolution only on the ground of deadlock. Furthermore, the courts were often reluctant to grant dissolution of a profitable corporation even on that ground, partly on the theory that there was a public interest in preserving economically viable businesses.

2. *Second stage: dissolution on the ground of the majority's fault.* Partly under the influence of scholarship, like that of Hetherington & Dooley, supra, and of F. Hodge O'Neal, who wrote extensively to show that dissolution was often a highly desirable remedy to resolve the problems of minority shareholders, and partly based on a wave of dissolution-for-oppression statutes, courts in the second stage became more willing to grant dissolution, even of profitable corporations, not only on the ground of deadlock but also on the ground of oppression.[1]

3. *Third stage: dissolution on the ground of defeat of the minority's reasonable expectations.* In the third stage, the emphasis shifted from an inquiry into whether there was fault on the part of majority shareholders, to an inquiry into whether the reasonable expectations of the minority shareholders were being defeated. Often, this shift simply involved a reconstruction of the meaning of "oppression," as in *Kemp & Beatley, supra.*

4. *Fourth stage: dissolution converted into mandatory buy-out.* In the fourth, present stage, there has been a marked tendency to grant relief even more freely to minority shareholders who petition for dissolution, but to cast that relief not in the form of dissolution, but in the form of a mandatory buy-out of the petitioner's shares at fair value. In many cases, the dissolution statutes give the majority a right to buy out the minority. In other cases, the courts order buy-out rather than dissolution as a matter of discretion.

At present, therefore, a petition by a minority shareholder for dissolution is commonly a trigger for requiring a mandatory buy-out of the minority shareholder's stock—that is, the courts, with increasing frequency, hold that grounds for dissolution exist, but then substitute mandatory buy-out for dissolution as the appropriate remedy. This development has several implications.

First, the power to order a mandatory buy-out in lieu of dissolution serves to alleviate the persistent, if questionable, view of the courts that liquidation of a profitable corporation is against the public interest, because under a mandatory buy-out, liquidation is not required. As a result, the courts may be more ready to find in favor of a minority shareholder in a dissolution proceeding, just because they know that such a finding will not necessarily result in an actual liquidation of the corporation's business.

The power to order a mandatory buy-out in lieu of dissolution also obviates a concern, expressed by some commentators, that freely granting dissolution may enable minority shareholders to opportunistically use a petition for dissolution, or the threat of such a petition, to put undue pressure on the majority shareholders by

---

1. As the Introduction to this Note states, the evolution described in this Note is somewhat oversimplified. For example, even some very recent cases contain expressions of concern about dissolution of profitable corporations. See, e.g., Struckhoff v. Echo Ridge Farm, Inc., 833 S.W.2d 463 (Mo.App.1992); Application of Ng, 174 A.D.2d 523, 572 N.Y.S.2d 295, 297 (1991).

making them fear that they will lose control of the business, and thereby extort an unduly high settlement from the majority. (This possibility is sometimes referred to as "oppression by the minority.")

Second, the easier it is to convert a dissolution proceeding into mandatory buy-out, the less likely the courts are to set at a very high level the standard of proof that minority shareholders must satisfy. That is, the less drastic the remedy, the readier the courts will be to set a standard that minority shareholders can often meet. This, indeed, has been the trend of the law in the area of dissolution: over time, as the remedy has been diluted from dissolution to buy-out, the standard for granting relief has been diluted and the frequency of relief to minority shareholders has increased.

Third, to the extent that petitions for dissolution have become triggering events for mandatory buy-outs, and the courts grant such petitions without a showing of fault by the majority, in effect the law is edging toward the position advocated by Hetherington & Dooley, that minority shareholders in close corporations should be allowed exit on demand. (This position also moves close corporation law toward partnership law, which already allows dissolution on very free terms. See Chapter 2, Sections 8, 9.)

Chapter VII

THE DUTY OF CARE

SECTION 1.   THE BASIC STANDARD OF CARE; THE DUTY TO MONITOR

FRANCIS v. UNITED JERSEY BANK

Supreme Court of New Jersey, 1981.
87 N.J. 15, 432 A.2d 814.

POLLOCK, J.   The primary issue on this appeal is whether a corporate director is personally liable in negligence for the failure to prevent the misappropriation of trust funds by other directors who were also officers and shareholders of the corporation.

Plaintiffs are trustees in bankruptcy of Pritchard & Baird Intermediaries Corp. (Pritchard & Baird), a reinsurance broker or intermediary.   Defendant Lillian P. Overcash is the daughter of Lillian G. Pritchard and the executrix of her estate.   At the time of her death, Mrs. Pritchard was a director and the largest single shareholder of Pritchard & Baird.   Because Mrs. Pritchard died after the institution of suit but before trial, her executrix was substituted as a defendant. United Jersey Bank is joined as the administrator of the estate of Charles Pritchard, Sr., who had been president, director and majority shareholder of Pritchard & Baird.

This litigation focuses on payments made by Pritchard & Baird to Charles Pritchard, Jr. and William Pritchard, who were sons of Mr. and Mrs. Charles Pritchard, Sr., as well as officers, directors and shareholders of the corporation.   Claims against Charles, Jr. and William are being pursued in bankruptcy proceedings against them.

The trial court, sitting without a jury, characterized the payments as fraudulent conveyances within N.J.S.A. 25:2–10 and entered judgment of $10,355,736.91 plus interest against the estate of Mrs. Pritchard.   162 N.J.Super. 355, 392 A.2d 1233 (Law Div.1978). The judgment includes damages from her negligence in permitting payments from the corporation of $4,391,133.21 to Charles, Jr. and $5,483,799.02 to William.   The trial court also entered judgment for payments of other sums plus interest: (1) against the estate of Lillian Pritchard for $33,000 accepted by her during her lifetime; (2) against the estate of Charles Pritchard, Sr. for $189,194.17 paid to him during his lifetime and $168,454 for payment of taxes on his estate; and (3) against Lillian Overcash individually for $123,156.51 for payments to her.

The Appellate Division affirmed, but found that the payments were a conversion of trust funds, rather than fraudulent conveyances of the assets of the corporation. 171 N.J.Super. 34, 407 A.2d 1253 (1979). We granted certification limited to the issue of the liability of Lillian Pritchard as a director. 82 N.J. 285, 412 A.2d 791 (1980).

Although we accept the characterization of the payments as a conversion of trust funds, the critical question is not whether the misconduct of Charles, Jr. and William should be characterized as fraudulent conveyances or acts of conversion. Rather, the initial question is whether Mrs. Pritchard was negligent in not noticing and trying to prevent the misappropriation of funds held by the corporation in an implied trust. A further question is whether her negligence was the proximate cause of the plaintiffs' losses. Both lower courts found that she was liable in negligence for the losses caused by the wrongdoing of Charles, Jr. and William. We affirm.

I

The matrix for our decision is the customs and practices of the reinsurance industry and the role of Pritchard & Baird as a reinsurance broker. Reinsurance involves a contract under which one insurer agrees to indemnify another for loss sustained under the latter's policy of insurance. Insurance companies that insure against losses arising out of fire or other casualty seek at times to minimize their exposure by sharing risks with other insurance companies. Thus, when the face amount of a policy is comparatively large, the company may enlist one or more insurers to participate in that risk. Similarly, an insurance company's loss potential and overall exposure may be reduced by reinsuring a part of an entire class of policies (e.g., 25% of all of its fire insurance policies). The selling insurance company is known as a ceding company. The entity that assumes the obligation is designated as the reinsurer.

The reinsurance broker arranges the contract between the ceding company and the reinsurer. In accordance with industry custom before the Pritchard & Baird bankruptcy, the reinsurance contract or treaty did not specify the rights and duties of the broker. Typically, the ceding company communicates to the broker the details concerning the risk. The broker negotiates the sale of portions of the risk to the reinsurers. In most instances, the ceding company and the reinsurer do not communicate with each other, but rely upon the reinsurance broker. The ceding company pays premiums due a reinsurer to the broker, who deducts his commission and transmits the balance to the appropriate reinsurer. When a loss occurs, a reinsurer pays money due a ceding company to the broker, who then transmits it to the ceding company.

The reinsurance business was described by an expert at trial as having "a magic aura around it of dignity and quality and integrity."

A telephone call which might be confirmed by a handwritten memorandum is sufficient to create a reinsurance obligation. Though separate bank accounts are not maintained for each treaty, the industry practice is to segregate the insurance funds from the broker's general accounts. Thus, the insurance fund accounts would contain the identifiable amounts for transmittal to either the reinsurer or the ceder. The expert stated that in general three kinds of checks may be drawn on this account: checks payable to reinsurers as premiums, checks payable to ceders as loss payments and checks payable to the brokers as commissions.

Messrs. Pritchard and Baird initially operated as a partnership. Later they formed several corporate entities to carry on their brokerage activities. The proofs supporting the judgment relate only to one corporation, Pritchard & Baird Intermediaries Corp. (Pritchard & Baird), and we need consider only its activities. When incorporated under the laws of the State of New York in 1959, Pritchard & Baird had five directors: Charles Pritchard, Sr., his wife Lillian Pritchard, their son Charles Pritchard, Jr., George Baird and his wife Marjorie. William Pritchard, another son, became director in 1960. Upon its formation, Pritchard & Baird acquired all the assets and assumed all the liabilities of the Pritchard & Baird partnership. The corporation issued 200 shares of common stock. Charles Pritchard, Sr. acquired 120 shares, his sons Charles Pritchard, Jr., 15 and William 15; Mr. and Mrs. Baird owned the remaining 50. In June 1964, Baird and his wife resigned as directors and sold their stock to the corporation. From that time on the corporation operated as a close family corporation with Mr. and Mrs. Pritchard and their two sons as the only directors. After the death of Charles, Sr. in 1973, only the remaining three directors continued to operate as the board. Lillian Pritchard inherited 72 of her husband's 120 shares in Pritchard & Baird, thereby becoming the largest stockholder in the corporation with 48% of the stock.

The corporate minute books reflect only perfunctory activities by the directors, related almost exclusively to the election of officers and adoption of banking resolutions and a retirement plan. None of the minutes for any of the meetings contain a discussion of the loans to Charles, Jr. and William or of the financial condition of the corporation. Moreover, upon instructions of Charles, Jr. that financial statements were not to be circulated to anyone else, the company's statements for the fiscal years beginning February 1, 1970, were delivered only to him.

Charles Pritchard, Sr. was the chief executive and controlled the business in the years following Baird's withdrawal. Beginning in 1966, he gradually relinquished control over the operations of the corporation. In 1968, Charles, Jr. became president and William became executive vice president. Charles, Sr. apparently became ill in 1971 and during the last year and a half of his life was not involved in the affairs of the business. He continued, however, to serve as a director until his death on December 10, 1973. Notwithstanding the presence of Charles, Sr. on the board until his death in

1973, Charles, Jr. dominated the management of the corporation and the board from 1968 until the bankruptcy in 1975.

Contrary to the industry custom of segregating funds, Pritchard & Baird commingled the funds of reinsurers and ceding companies with its own funds. All monies (including commissions, premiums and loss monies) were deposited in a single account. Charles, Sr. began the practice of withdrawing funds from the commingled account in transactions identified on the corporate books as "loans." As long as Charles, Sr. controlled the corporation, the "loans" correlated with corporate profits and were repaid at the end of each year. Starting in 1970, however, Charles, Jr. and William begin to siphon ever-increasing sums from the corporation under the guise of loans. As of January 31, 1970, the "loans" to Charles, Jr. were $230,932 and to William were $207,329. At least by January 31, 1973, the annual increase in the loans exceeded annual corporate revenues. By October 1975, the year of bankruptcy, the "shareholders' loans" had metastasized to a total of $12,-333,514.47.

The trial court rejected the characterization of the payments as "loans." 162 N.J.Super. at 365, 392 A.2d 1233. No corporate resolution authorized the "loans," and no note or other instrument evidenced the debt. Charles, Jr. and William paid no interest on the amounts received. The "loans" were not repaid or reduced from one year to the next; rather, they increased annually.

The designation of "shareholders' loans" on the balance sheet was an entry to account for the distribution of the premium and loss money to Charles, Sr., Charles, Jr. and William. As the trial court found, the entry was part of a "woefully inadequate and highly dangerous bookkeeping system." 162 N.J.Super. at 363, 392 A.2d 1233.

The "loans" to Charles, Jr. and William far exceeded their salaries and financial resources. If the payments to Charles, Jr. and William had been treated as dividends or compensation, then the balance sheets would have shown an excess of liabilities over assets. If the "loans" had been eliminated, the balance sheets would have depicted a corporation not only with a working capital deficit, but also with assets having a fair market value less than its liabilities. The balance sheets for 1970–1975, however, showed an excess of assets over liabilities. This result was achieved by designating the misappropriated funds as "shareholders' loans" and listing them as assets offsetting the deficits. Although the withdrawal of the funds resulted in an obligation of repayment to Pritchard & Baird, the more significant consideration is that the "loans" represented a massive misappropriation of money belonging to the clients of the corporation.

The "loans" were reflected on financial statements that were prepared annually as of January 31, the end of the corporate fiscal year. Although an outside certified public accountant prepared the 1970 financial statement, the corporation prepared only internal financial statements from 1971–1975. In all instances, the statements were simple documents, consisting of three or four 8½ × 11 inch sheets.

The statements of financial condition from 1970 forward demonstrated:

	Working Capital Deficit	Shareholders' Loans	Net Brokerage Income
1970	$ 389,022	$ 509,941	$ 807,229
1971	not available	not available	not available
1972	$ 1,684,289	$ 1,825,911	$1,546,263
1973	$ 3,506,460	$ 3,700,542	$1,736,349
1974	$ 6,939,007	$ 7,080,629	$ 876,182
1975	$10,176,419	$10,298,039	$ 551,598.

Those financial statements showed working capital deficits increasing annually in tandem with the amounts that Charles, Jr. and William withdrew as "shareholders' loans." In the last complete year of business (January 31, 1974, to January 31, 1975), "shareholders' loans" and the correlative working capital deficit increased by approximately $3,200,000.

The funding of the "loans" left the corporation with insufficient money to operate. Pritchard & Baird could defer payment on accounts payable because its clients allowed a grace period, generally 30 to 90 days, before the payment was due. During this period, Pritchard & Baird used the funds entrusted to it as a "float" to pay current accounts payable. By recourse to the funds of its clients, Pritchard & Baird not only paid its trade debts, but also funded the payments to Charles, Jr. and William. Thus, Pritchard & Baird was able to meet its obligations as they came due only through the use of clients' funds.

The pattern that emerges from these figures is the substantial increase in the monies appropriated by Charles Pritchard, Jr. and William Pritchard after their father's withdrawal from the business and the sharp decline in the profitability of the operation after his death. This led ultimately to the filing in December, 1975, of an involuntary petition in bankruptcy and the appointments of the plaintiffs as trustees in bankruptcy of Pritchard & Baird.

Mrs. Pritchard was not active in the business of Pritchard & Baird and knew virtually nothing of its corporate affairs. She briefly visited the corporate offices in Morristown on only one occasion, and she never read or obtained the annual financial statements. She was unfamiliar with the rudiments of reinsurance and made no effort to assure that the policies and practices of the corporation, particularly pertaining to the withdrawal of funds, complied with industry custom or relevant law. Although her husband had warned her that Charles, Jr. would "take the shirt off my back," Mrs. Pritchard did not pay any attention to her duties as a director or to the affairs of the corporation. 162 N.J.Super. at 370, 392 A.2d 1233.

After her husband died in December 1973, Mrs. Pritchard became incapacitated and was bedridden for a six-month period. She became listless at this time and started to drink rather heavily. Her physical condition deteriorated, and in 1978 she died. The trial court rejected testimony seeking to exonerate her because she "was old, was grief-stricken at the loss of her husband, sometimes consumed too much alcohol and was psychologically overborne by her sons." 162 N.J.Super. at 371, 392 A.2d 1233. That court found that she was competent to act and that the reason Mrs. Pritchard never knew what her sons "were doing was because she never made the slightest effort to discharge any of her responsibilities as a director of Pritchard & Baird." 162 N.J.Super. at 372, 392 A.2d 1233.

II

A preliminary matter is the determination of whether New Jersey law should apply to this case. Although Pritchard & Baird was incorporated in New York, the trial court found that New Jersey had more significant relationships to the parties and the transactions than New York. The shareholder, officers and directors were New Jersey residents. The estates of Mr. and Mrs. Pritchard are being administered in New Jersey, and the bankruptcy proceedings involving Charles, Jr., William and Pritchard & Baird are pending in New Jersey. Virtually all transactions took place in New Jersey. Although many of the creditors are located outside the state, all had contacts with Pritchard & Baird in New Jersey. Consequently, the trial court applied New Jersey law. 162 N.J.Super. at 369, 392 A.2d 1233. The parties agree that New Jersey law should apply. We are in accord.

III

Individual liability of a corporate director for acts of the corporation is a prickly problem. Generally directors are accorded broad immunity and are not insurers of corporate activities. The problem is particularly nettlesome when a third party asserts that a director, because of nonfeasance, is liable for losses caused by acts of insiders, who in this case were officers, directors and shareholders. Determination of the liability of Mrs. Pritchard requires findings that she had a duty to the clients of Pritchard & Baird, that she breached that duty and that her breach was a proximate cause of their losses.

The New Jersey Business Corporation Act, which took effect on January 1, 1969, was a comprehensive revision of the statutes relating to business corporations. One section, N.J.S.A. 14A:6–14, concerning a director's general obligation had no counterpart in the old Act. That section makes it incumbent upon directors to

> discharge their duties in good faith and with that degree of diligence, care and skill which ordinarily prudent men would exercise under similar circumstances in like positions. [N.J.S.A. 14A:6–14]

This provision was based primarily on section 43 of the Model Business Corporation Act and is derived also from section 717 of the New York Business Corporation Law (L.1961, c. 855, effective September 1, 1963). Commissioners' Comments—1968 and 1972, N.J.S.A. 14A:6–14. Before the enactment of N.J.S.A. 14A:6–14, there was no express statutory authority requiring directors to act as ordinarily prudent persons under similar circumstances in like positions. Nonetheless, the requirement had been expressed in New Jersey judicial decisions.

A leading New Jersey opinion is Campbell v. Watson, 62 N.J.Eq. 396, 50 A. 120 (Ch.1901), which, like many early decisions on director liability, involved directors of a bank that had become insolvent. A receiver of the bank charged the directors with negligence that allegedly led to insolvency. In the opinion, Vice Chancellor Pitney explained that bank depositors have a right to

> rely upon the character of the directors and officers [and upon the representation] that they will perform their sworn duty to manage the affairs of the bank according to law and devote to its affairs the same diligent attention which ordinary, prudent, diligent men pay to their own affairs; and ... such diligence and attention as experience has shown it is proper and necessary that bank directors should give to that business in order to reasonably protect the bank and its creditors against loss. [Id. at 406]

Because N.J.S.A. 14A:6–14 is modeled in part upon section 717 of the New York statute, N.Y.Bus.Corp.Law § 717 (McKinney), we consider also the law of New York in interpreting the New Jersey statute. See Suter v. San Angelo Foundry & Machine Co., 81 N.J. 150, 161–162, 406 A.2d 140 (1979) (approving the propriety of examining as an interpretative aid the law of a state, the statute of which has been copied).

Prior to the enactment of section 717, the New York courts, like those of New Jersey, had espoused the principle that directors owed that degree of care that a businessman of ordinary prudence would exercise in the management of his own affairs. Kavanaugh v. Gould, 223 N.Y. 103, 105, 119 N.E. 237, 238 (Ct.App.1918); Hun v. Cary, 82 N.Y. 65, 72 (Ct.App.1880); McLear v. McLear, 265 App.Div. 556, 560, 266 App.Div. 702, 703, 40 N.Y.S.2d 432, 436 (Sup.Ct. 1943), aff'd 291 N.Y. 809, 53 N.E.2d 573, 292 N.Y. 580, 54 N.E.2d 694 (Ct.App.1944); Simon v. Socony–Vacuum Oil Co., 179 Misc. 202, 203, 38 N.Y.S.2d 270, 273 (Sup.Ct.1942), aff'd 267 App.Div. 890, 47 N.Y.S.2d 589 (Sup.Ct.1944); Van Schaick v. Aron, 170 Misc. 520, 534, 10 N.Y.S.2d 550, 563 (Sup.Ct.1938). In addition to requiring that directors act honestly and in good faith, the New York courts recognized that the nature and extent of reasonable care depended upon the type of corporation, its size and financial resources. Thus, a bank director was held to stricter accountability than the director of an ordinary business.[1] Hun v. Cary, supra, 82 N.Y. at 72; Litwin v. Allen, 25 N.Y.S.2d 667, 678 (Sup.Ct.1940).

In determining the limits of a director's duty, section 717 continued to recognize the individual characteristics of the corporation involved as well as the particular circumstances and corporate role of the director. Significantly, the legislative comment to section 717 states:

> The adoption of the standard prescribed by this section will allow the court to envisage the director's duty of care as a relative concept, depending on the kind of corporation involved, the particular circumstances and the corporate role of the director. [N.Y.Bus.Corp.Law § 717, comment (McKinney)]

This approach was consonant with the desire to formulate a standard that could be applied to both publicly and closely held entities. The report of the Chairman and chief counsel of the New York Joint Legislative Committee to Study Revision of Corporation Laws stated that the statute "reflects an attempt to merge the interests of public issue corporations and closely held corporations." Anderson & Lesher, The New Business Corporation Law, xxvii, reprinted in N.Y.Bus.Corp.Law §§ 1 to 800 xxv (McKinney).[2]

Underlying the pronouncements in section 717, Campbell v. Watson, supra, and N.J.S.A. 14A:6–14 is the principle that directors must discharge their duties in good faith and act as ordinarily prudent persons would under similar circumstances in like positions. Although specific duties in a given case can be determined only after consideration of all of the circumstances, the standard of ordinary care is the wellspring from which those more specific duties flow.

As a general rule, a director should acquire at least a rudimentary understanding of the business of the corporation. Accordingly, a director should become familiar with the fundamentals of the business in which the corporation is engaged. *Campbell*, supra, 62 N.J.Eq. at 416, 50 A. 120. Because directors are bound to exercise ordinary care, they cannot set up as a defense lack of the knowledge needed to exercise the requisite degree of care. If one "feels that he has not had sufficient business experience to qualify him to perform the duties of a director, he should either acquire the knowledge by inquiry, or refuse to act." Ibid.

1. The obligations of directors of banks involve some additional consideration because of their relationship to the public generally and depositors in particular. Statutes impose certain requirements on bank directors. For example, directors of national banks must take an oath that they will diligently and honestly administer the affairs of the bank and will not permit violation of the banking laws. Moreover, they must satisfy certain requirements such as residence, citizenship, stockholdings and not serving as an investment banker. 12 U.S.C.A. §§ 77–78. See generally R. Bar-

nett, Responsibilities & Liabilities of Bank Directors (1980).

2. Section 717 was amended in 1977 (L.1977, c. 432, § 4, effective September 1, 1977) to provide that directors must exercise a "degree of care" in place of a "degree of diligence, care and skill." The report of the Association of the Bar of the City of New York Committee on Corporation Law states the amendment did not alter but clarified and reaffirmed existing law. Report No. 178 on S254–A and A245–A, 544.

Directors are under a continuing obligation to keep informed about the activities of the corporation. Otherwise, they may not be able to participate in the overall management of corporate affairs. Barnes v. Andrews, 298 F. 614 (S.D.N.Y.1924) (director guilty of misprision of office for not keeping himself informed about the details of corporate business); Atherton v. Anderson, 99 F.2d 883, 889–890 (6 Cir.1938) (ignorance no defense to director liability because of director's "duty to know the facts"); *Campbell,* supra, 62 N.J.Eq. at 409, 50 A. 120 (directors "bound to acquaint themselves with ... extent ... of supervision exercised by officers"); Williams v. McKay, 46 N.J.Eq. 25, 36, 18 A. 824 (Ch.1889) (director under duty to supervise managers and practices to determine whether business methods were safe and proper). Directors may not shut their eyes to corporate misconduct, and then claim that because they did not see the misconduct, they did not have a duty to look. The sentinel asleep at his post contributes nothing to the enterprise he is charged to protect. Wilkinson v. Dodd, 42 N.J.Eq. 234, 245, 7 A. 327 (Ch.1886), aff'd 42 N.J.Eq. 647, 9 A. 685 (E. & A.1887).

Directorial management does not require a detailed inspection of day-to-day activities, but rather a general monitoring of corporate affairs and policies. Williams v. McKay, supra, at 37, 18 A. 824. Accordingly, a director is well advised to attend board meetings regularly. Indeed, a director who is absent from a board meeting is presumed to concur in action taken on a corporate matter, unless he files a "dissent with the secretary of the corporation within a reasonable time after learning of such action." N.J.S.A. 14A:6–13 (Supp.1981–1982). Regular attendance does not mean that directors must attend every meeting, but that directors should attend meetings as a matter of practice. A director of a publicly held corporation might be expected to attend regular monthly meetings, but a director of a small, family corporation might be asked to attend only an annual meeting. The point is that one of the responsibilities of a director is to attend meetings of the board of which he or she is a member. That burden is lightened by N.J.S.A. 14A:6–7(2) (Supp.1981–1982), which permits board action without a meeting if all members of the board consent in writing.

While directors are not required to audit corporate books, they should maintain familiarity with the financial status of the corporation by a regular review of financial statements. *Campbell,* supra, 62 N.J.Eq. at 415, 50 A. 120; *Williams,* supra, 46 N.J.Eq. at 38–39, 18 A. 824; see Section of Corporation, Banking and Business Law, American Bar Association, "Corporate Director's Guidebook," 33 Bus.Law. 1595, 1608 (1978) (Guidebook); N. Lattin, The Law of Corporations 280 (2 ed. 1971). In some circumstances, directors may be charged with assuring that bookkeeping methods conform to industry custom and usage. Lippitt v. Ashley, 89 Conn. 451, 464, 94 A. 995, 1000 (Sup.Ct.1915). The extent of review, as well as the nature and frequency of financial statements, depends not only on the customs of the industry, but also on the nature of the corporation and the business in which it is engaged. Financial statements of some small corporations may be prepared internally and only on an annual basis; in a large publicly held corporation, the statements may be produced monthly or at some other regular interval. Adequate financial review normally would be more informal in a private corporation than in a publicly held corporation.

Of some relevance in this case is the circumstance that the financial records disclose the "shareholders' loans". Generally directors are immune from liability if, in good faith,

> they rely upon the opinion of counsel for the corporation or upon written reports setting forth financial data concerning the corporation and prepared by an independent public accountant or certified public accountant or firm of such accountants or upon financial statements, books of account or reports of the corporation represented to them to be correct by the president, the officer of the corporation having charge of its books of account, or the person presiding at a meeting of the board. [N.J.S.A. 14A:6–14]

The review of financial statements, however, may give rise to a duty to inquire further into matters revealed by those statements. Corsicana Nat'l Bank v. Johnson, 251 U.S. 68, 71, 40 S.Ct. 82, 84, 64 L.Ed. 141 (1919); *Atherton,* supra, 99 F.2d at 890; LaMonte v. Mott, 93 N.J.Eq. 229, 239, 107 A. 462 (E. & A.1921); see *Lippitt,* supra, 89 Conn. at 457, 94 A. at 998. Upon discovery of an illegal course of action, a director has a duty to object and, if the corporation does not correct the conduct, to resign. See Dodd v. Wilkinson, 42 N.J.Eq. 647, 651, 9 A. 685 (E. & A.1887); Williams v. Riley, 34 N.J.Eq. 398, 401 (Ch.1881).

In certain circumstances, the fulfillment of the duty of a director may call for more than mere objection and resignation. Sometimes a director may be required to seek the advice of counsel. *Guidebook,* supra, at 1631. One New Jersey case recognized the duty of a bank director to seek counsel where doubt existed about the meaning of the bank charter. Williams v. McKay, supra, 46 N.J.Eq. at 60, 18 A. 824. The duty to seek the assistance of counsel can extend to areas other than the interpretation of corporation instruments. Modern corporate practice recognizes that on occasion a director should seek outside advice. A director may require legal advice concerning the propriety of his or her own conduct, the conduct of other officers and directors or the conduct of the corporation. In appropriate circumstances, a director would be "well advised to consult with regular corporate counsel (or his own legal adviser) at any time in which he is doubtful regarding proposed action...." *Guidebook,* supra, at 1618. Sometimes the duty of a director may require more than consulting with outside counsel. A director may have a duty to take reasonable means to prevent illegal conduct by co-directors; in an appropriate case, this may include threat of suit. See Selheimer v. Manganese Corp., 423 Pa. 563, 572, 584, 224 A.2d 634, 640, 646 (Sup.Ct.1966) (director exonerated when he objected, resigned, organized shareholder action group, and threatened suit).

A director is not an ornament, but an essential component of corporate governance. Consequently, a director cannot protect himself behind a paper shield bearing the motto, "dummy director." *Campbell*, supra, 62 N.J.Eq. at 443, 50 A. 120 ("The directors were not intended to be mere figure-heads without duty or responsibility"); Williams v. McKay, supra, 46 N.J.Eq. at 57–58, 18 A. 824 (director voluntarily assuming position also assumes duties of ordinary care, skill and judgment). The New Jersey Business Corporation Act, in imposing a standard of ordinary care on all directors, confirms that dummy, figurehead and accommodation directors are anachronisms with no place in New Jersey law. See N.J.S.A. 14A:6–14. Similarly, in interpreting section 717, the New York courts have not exonerated a director who acts as an "accommodation." Barr v. Wackman, 36 N.Y.2d 371, 381, 329 N.E.2d 180, 188, 368 N.Y.S.2d 497, 507 (Ct.App.1975) (director "does not exempt himself from liability by failing to do more than passively rubber-stamp the decisions of the active managers"). See Kavanaugh v. Gould, supra, 223 N.Y. at 111–117, 119 N.E. at 240–241 (the fact that bank director never attended board meetings or acquainted himself with bank's business or methods held to be no defense, as a matter of law, to responsibility for speculative loans made by the president and acquiesced in by other directors). Thus, all directors are responsible for managing the business and affairs of the corporation. N.J.S.A. 14A:6–1 (Supp.1981–1982); 1 G. Hornstein, Corporation Law and Practice § 431 at 525 (1959).

The factors that impel expanded responsibility in the large, publicly held corporation may not be present in a small, close corporation.[3] Nonetheless, a close corporation may, because of the nature of its business, be affected with a public interest. For example, the stock of a bank may be closely held, but because of the nature of banking the directors would be subject to greater liability than those of another close corporation. Even in a small corporation, a director is held to the standard of that degree of care that an ordinarily prudent director would use under the circumstances. M. Mace, The Board of Directors of Small Corporations 83 (1948).

---

3. Our decision is based on directorial responsibilities arising under state statutory and common law as distinguished from the Securities Act of 1933, 15 U.S.C. § 77a et seq., and the Securities Exchange Act of 1934, 15 U.S.C. § 78a et seq. Nonetheless, we recognize significant developments in directorial liability under both Acts and related rules and regulations of the Securities and Exchange Commission. For example, an outside director may be liable in negligence under section 11 of the 1933 Act for the failure to make a reasonable investigation before signing a registration statement. Escott v. Barchris Constr. Corp., 283 F.Supp. 643, 687–689 (S.D.N.Y.1968); see also Feit v. Leasco Data Processing Equip. Corp., 332 F.Supp. 544, 575–576 (E.D.N.Y. 1971) (outside director who was partner in law firm for corporation considered an insider). The Securities and Exchange Commission has made it clear that outside directors should become knowledgeable about a company's business and accounting practices so that they may make "an informed judgment of its more important affairs or the abilities and integrity of the officers." Securities Exchange Act of 1934, Release No. 11,516 (July 2, 1975)....

A director's duty of care does not exist in the abstract, but must be considered in relation to specific obligees. In general, the relationship of a corporate director to the corporation and its stockholders is that of a fiduciary. Whitfield v. Kern, 122 N.J.Eq. 332, 341, 192 A. 48 (E. & A.1937). Shareholders have a right to expect that directors will exercise reasonable supervision and control over the policies and practices of a corporation. The institutional integrity of a corporation depends upon the proper discharge by directors of those duties.

While directors may owe a fiduciary duty to creditors also, that obligation generally has not been recognized in the absence of insolvency. *Whitfield*, supra, 122 N.J.Eq. at 342, 345, 192 A. 48. With certain corporations, however, directors are [deemed] to owe a duty to creditors and other third parties even when the corporation is solvent. Although depositors of a bank are considered in some respects to be creditors, courts have recognized that directors may owe them a fiduciary duty. See Campbell, supra, 62 N.J.Eq. at 406–407, 50 A. 120. Directors of nonbanking corporations may owe a similar duty when the corporation holds funds of others in trust. Cf. McGlynn v. Schultz, 90 N.J.Super. 505, 218 A.2d 408 (Ch.Div.1966), aff'd 95 N.J.Super. 412, 231 A.2d 386 (App.Div.), certif. den. 50 N.J. 409, 235 A.2d 901 (1967) (directors who did not insist on segregating trust funds held by corporation liable to the *cestuis que trust*).

In three cases originating in New Jersey, directors who did not participate actively in the conversion of trust funds were found not liable. In each instance, the facts did not support the conclusion that the director knew or could have known of the wrongdoing even if properly attentive. *McGlynn*, supra, 90 N.J.Super. at 509, 511, 218 A.2d 408 (director from Chicago not "in a position to know the details of the corporation's business" not liable for conversions that occurred over four month period); General Films, Inc. v. Sanco Gen. Mfg. Corp., 153 N.J.Super. 369, 371, 379 A.2d 1042 (App.Div.1977), certif. den. 75 N.J. 614, 384 A.2d 843 (1978) (director and sole shareholder not liable for conversion by dominant principal, her husband, in misappropriating proceeds of single check); Ark–Tenn Distrib. Corp. v. Breidt, 209 F.2d 359, 360 (3 Cir.1954) (president who was not active in corporation not liable for conversion of trust funds received in single transaction). To the extent that the cases support the proposition that directors are not liable unless they actively participate in the conversion of trust funds, they are disapproved.

Courts in other states have imposed liability on directors of nonbanking corporations for the conversion of trust funds, even though those directors did not participate in or know of the conversion. Preston–Thomas Constr. Inc. v. Central Leasing Corp., 518 P.2d 1125 (Okl.Ct.App.1973) (director liable for conversion of funds entrusted to corporation for acquisition of stock in another corporation); Vujacich v. Southern Commercial Co., 21 Cal.App. 439, 132 P. 80 (Dist.Ct.App.1913) (director of wholesale grocery business personally liable for conversion by corporation of worker's funds deposited for safekeeping). The distinguishing circumstances in regard to banks and other corporations holding trust funds is that the depositor or beneficiary can reasonably expect the director to act with ordinary prudence concerning the funds held in a fiduciary capacity. Thus, recognition of a duty of a director to those for whom a corporation holds funds in trust may be viewed as another application of the general rule that a director's duty is that of an ordinary prudent person under the circumstances.

The most striking circumstances affecting Mrs. Pritchard's duty as a director are the character of the reinsurance industry, the nature of the misappropriated funds and the financial condition of Pritchard & Baird. The hallmark of the reinsurance industry has been the unqualified trust and confidence reposed by ceding companies and reinsurers in reinsurance brokers. Those companies entrust money to reinsurance intermediaries with the justifiable expectation that the funds will be transmitted to the appropriate parties. Consequently, the companies could have assumed rightfully that Mrs. Pritchard, as a director of a reinsurance brokerage corporation, would not sanction the commingling and the conversion of loss and premium funds for the personal use of the principals of Pritchard & Baird.

As a reinsurance broker, Pritchard & Baird received annually as a fiduciary millions of dollars of clients' money which it was under a duty to segregate.[4] To this extent, it resembled a bank rather than a small family business. Accordingly, Mrs. Pritchard's relationship to the clientele of Pritchard & Baird was akin to that of a director of a bank to its depositors. All parties agree that Pritchard & Baird held the misappropriated funds in an implied trust. That trust relationship gave rise to a fiduciary duty to guard the funds with fidelity and good faith. Ellsworth Dobbs, Inc. v. Johnson, 50 N.J. 528, 553, 236 A.2d 843 (1967); General Films, Inc. v. Sanco Gen. Mfg. Corp., supra, 153 N.J.Super. at 372–373, 379 A.2d 1042.

As a director of a substantial reinsurance brokerage corporation, she should have known that it received annually millions of dollars of loss and premium funds which it held in trust for ceding and reinsurance companies. Mrs. Pritchard should have obtained and read the annual statements of financial condition of Pritchard & Baird. Although she had a right to rely upon financial statements prepared in accordance with N.J.S.A. 14A:6–14, such reliance would not excuse her conduct. The reason is that those statements disclosed on their face the misappropriation of trust funds.

From those statements, she should have realized that, as of January 31, 1970, her sons were withdrawing substantial trust funds under the guise of "Shareholders' Loans." The financial statements

---

4. Following the Pritchard & Baird bankruptcy, New York, a reinsurance center, adopted legislation regulating reinsurance intermediaries. One statute codified the industry standard by prohibiting reinsurance intermediaries from commingling their funds with funds of their principals. N.Y.Ins.Law § 122–a(9) (McKinney Supp. 1980–1981).

for each fiscal year commencing with that of January 31, 1970, disclosed that the working capital deficits and the "loans" were escalating in tandem.   Detecting a misappropriation of funds would not have required special expertise or extraordinary diligence; a cursory reading of the financial statements would have revealed the pillage.   Thus, if Mrs. Pritchard had read the financial statements, she would have known that her sons were converting trust funds. When financial statements demonstrate that insiders are bleeding a corporation to death, a director should notice and try to stanch the flow of blood.

In summary, Mrs. Pritchard was charged with the obligation of basic knowledge and supervision of the business of Pritchard & Baird.   Under the circumstances, this obligation included reading and understanding financial statements, and making reasonable attempts at detection and prevention of the illegal conduct of other officers and directors.   She had a duty to protect the clients of Pritchard & Baird against policies and practices that would result in the misappropriation of money they had entrusted to the corporation.   She breached that duty.

IV

Nonetheless, the negligence of Mrs. Pritchard does not result in liability unless it is a proximate cause of the loss.   Kulas v. Public Serv. Elec. and Gas Co., 41 N.J. 311, 317, 196 A.2d 769 (1964). Analysis of proximate cause requires an initial determination of cause-in-fact.   Causation-in-fact calls for a finding that the defendant's act or omission was a necessary antecedent of the loss, i.e., that if the defendant had observed his or her duty of care, the loss would not have occurred.   Ibid., W. Prosser, Law of Torts § 41 at 238 (4 ed. 1971).   Further, the plaintiff has the burden of establishing the amount of the loss or damages caused by the negligence of the defendant.   H. Henn, Law of Corporations § 234 at 456 (2 ed. 1970).   Thus, the plaintiff must establish not only a breach of duty, "but in addition that the performance by the director of his duty would have avoided loss, and the amount of the resulting loss."   1 Hornstein, supra, § 446 at 566.

Cases involving nonfeasance present a much more difficult causation question than those in which the director has committed an affirmative act of negligence leading to the loss.   Analysis in cases of negligent omissions calls for determination of the reasonable steps a director should have taken and whether that course of action would have averted the loss.

Usually a director can absolve himself from liability by informing the other directors of the impropriety and voting for a proper course of action.   Dyson, "The Director's Liability for Negligence," 40 Ind.L.J. 341, 365 (1965).   Conversely, a director who votes for or concurs in certain actions may be "liable to the corporation for the benefit of its creditors or shareholders, to the extent of any injuries suffered by such persons, respectively, as a result of any such action." N.J.S.A. 14A:6–12 (Supp.1981–1982). A director who is present at a board meeting is presumed to concur in corporate action taken at the meeting unless his dissent is entered in the minutes of the meeting or filed promptly after adjournment. N.J.S.A. 14A:6–13. In many, if not most, instances an objecting director whose dissent is noted in accordance with N.J.S.A. 14A:6–13 would be absolved after attempting to persuade fellow directors to follow a different course of action. Cf. McGlynn, supra, 90 N.J.Super. at 520–521, 529, 218 A.2d 408 (receiver had no case against director who advised president that certain funds should be escrowed, wrote to executive committee to that effect, and objected at special meeting of board of directors); Selheimer v. Manganese Corp., supra, 423 Pa. at 572, 584, 224 A.2d at 640, 646 (dissenting minority director in publicly held corporation absolved because he did all he could to divert majority directors from their course of conduct by complaining to management, threatening to institute suit and organizing a stockholders' committee).

Even accepting the hypothesis that Mrs. Pritchard might not be liable if she had objected and resigned, there are two significant reasons for holding her liable. First, she did not resign until just before the bankruptcy. Consequently, there is no factual basis for the speculation that the losses would have occurred even if she had objected and resigned. Indeed, the trial court reached the opposite conclusion: "The actions of the sons were so blatantly wrongful that it is hard to see how they could have resisted any moderately firm objection to what they were doing." 162 N.J.Super. at 372, 392 A.2d 1233. Second, the nature of the reinsurance business distinguishes it from most other commercial activities in that reinsurance brokers are encumbered by fiduciary duties owed to third parties. In other corporations, a director's duty normally does not extend beyond the shareholders to third parties.

In this case, the scope of Mrs. Pritchard's duties was determined by the precarious financial condition of Pritchard & Baird, its fiduciary relationship to its clients and the implied trust in which it held their funds. Thus viewed, the scope of her duties encompassed all reasonable action to stop the continuing conversion. Her duties extended beyond mere objection and resignation to reasonable attempts to prevent the misappropriation of the trust funds. *Campbell*, supra, 62 N.J.Eq. at 427, 50 A. 120.

A leading case discussing causation where the director's liability is predicated upon a negligent failure to act is Barnes v. Andrews, 298 F. 614 (S.D.N.Y.1924). In that case the court exonerated a figurehead director who served for eight months on a board that held one meeting after his election, a meeting he was forced to miss because of the death of his mother. Writing for the court, Judge Learned Hand distinguished a director who fails to prevent general mismanagement from one such as Mrs. Pritchard who failed to stop an illegal "loan":

When the corporate funds have been illegally lent, it is a fair inference that a protest would have stopped the loan, and that the director's neglect caused the loss. But when a business fails from general mismanagement, business incapacity, or bad judgment, how is it possible to say that a single director could have made the company successful, or how much in dollars he could have saved? [Id. at 616–617]

Pointing out the absence of proof of proximate cause between defendant's negligence and the company's insolvency, Judge Hand also wrote:

The plaintiff must, however, go further than to show that [the director] should have been more active in his duties. This cause of action rests upon a tort, as much though it be a tort of omission as though it had rested upon a positive act. The plaintiff must accept the burden of showing that the performance of the defendant's duties would have avoided loss, and what loss it would have avoided. [Id. at 616]

Other courts have refused to impose personal liability on negligent directors when the plaintiffs have been unable to prove that diligent execution of the directors' duties would have precluded the losses. Briggs v. Spaulding, 141 U.S. 132, 11 S.Ct. 924, 35 L.Ed. 662 (1891) (no causal relationship because discovery of defalcations could have resulted only from examination of books beyond duty of director); ... Virginia–Carolina Chem. Co. v. Ehrich, 230 F. 1005 (E.D.S.C.1916) (close supervision of daily corporate affairs necessary to notice wrongdoing; failure to attend meetings not causally related to loss); ... Sternberg v. Blaine, 179 Ark. 448, 17 S.W.2d 286 (Sup.Ct.1929) ("[n]o ordinary examination usually made by directors of a country bank, however careful, would have discovered" misappropriations); ___ Allied Freightways, Inc. v. Cholfin, 325 Mass. 630, 91 N.E.2d 765 (Sup.Jud.Ct.1950) (director not liable where losses resulted from general mismanagement and director, in the reasonable exercise of her duties, could not have discovered illegal payments from examination of corporate books) . . . .

Other courts have held directors liable for losses actively perpetrated by others because the negligent omissions of the directors were considered a necessary antecedent to the defalcations. Ringeon v. Albinson, 35 F.2d 753 (D.Minn.1929) (negligent director not excused from liability for losses that could have been prevented by supervision and prompt action); Heit v. Bixby, 276 F.Supp. 217, 231 (E.D.Mo.1967) (directors liable for 40% commissions taken by co-directors because directors' "lackadaisical attitude" proximately caused the loss); Ford v. Taylor, 176 Ark. 843, 4 S.W.2d 938 (1928) (bank directors liable for losses due to misappropriations of cashier who "felt free to pursue [misconduct] without fear of detection by the directors through their failure to discharge the functions of their office"); ... Coddington v. Canaday, 157 Ind. 243, 61 N.E. 567 (Sup.Ct.1901) (directors liable for losses resulting from bank insolvency due to improper supervision and concomitant acceptance of worthless notes); ... Neese v. Brown, 218 Tenn. 686, 405 S.W.2d 577 (Sup.Ct.1964) (directors who abdicate control liable for losses caused by breach of trust by those left in control if due care on part of inactive directors could have avoided loss).

In assessing whether Mrs. Pritchard's conduct was a legal or proximate cause of the conversion, "[l]egal responsibility must be limited to those causes which are so closely connected with the result and of such significance that the law is justified in imposing liability." Prosser, supra, § 41 at 237. Such a judicial determination involves not only considerations of causation-in-fact and matters of policy, but also common sense and logic. Caputzal v. The Lindsay Co., 48 N.J. 69, 77–78 (1966). The act or the failure to act must be a substantial factor in producing the harm. Prosser, supra, § 41 at 240; Restatement (Second) of Torts, §§ 431, 432 (1965).

Within Pritchard & Baird, several factors contributed to the loss of the funds: comingling of corporate and client monies, conversion of funds by Charles, Jr. and William and dereliction of her duties by Mrs. Pritchard. The wrongdoing of her sons, although the immediate cause of the loss, should not excuse Mrs. Pritchard from her negligence which also was a substantial factor contributing to the loss. Restatement (Second) of Torts, supra, § 442B, comment b. Her sons knew that she, the only other director, was not reviewing their conduct; they spawned their fraud in the backwater of her neglect. Her neglect of duty contributed to the climate of corruption; her failure to act contributed to the continuation of that corruption. Consequently, her conduct was a substantial factor contributing to the loss.

Analysis of proximate cause is especially difficult in a corporate context where the allegation is that nonfeasance of a director is a proximate cause of damage to a third party. Where a case involves nonfeasance, no one can say "with absolute certainty what would have occurred if the defendant had acted otherwise." Prosser, supra, § 41 at 242. Nonetheless, where it is reasonable to conclude that the failure to act would produce a particular result and that result has followed, causation may be inferred. Ibid. We conclude that even if Mrs. Pritchard's mere objection had not stopped the depredations of her sons, her consultation with an attorney and the threat of suit would have deterred them. That conclusion flows as a matter of common sense and logic from the record. Whether in other situations a director has a duty to do more than protest and resign is best left to case-by-case determinations. In this case, we are satisfied that there was a duty to do more than object and resign. Consequently, we find that Mrs. Pritchard's negligence was a proximate cause of the misappropriations.

To conclude, by virtue of her office, Mrs. Pritchard had the power to prevent the losses sustained by the clients of Pritchard & Baird. With power comes responsibility. She had a duty to deter the depredation of the other insiders, her sons.   She breached that duty and caused plaintiffs to sustain damages.

The judgment of the Appellate Division is affirmed.

For affirmance—Justices SULLIVAN, PASHMAN, CLIFFORD, SCHREIBER, HANDLER and POLLOCK—6.

For reversal—none.

————

REV. MODEL BUS. CORP. ACT § 8.30

[See Statutory Supplement]

————

CAL. CORP. CODE § 309(a)

[See Statutory Supplement]

————

NEW JERSEY STAT. ANN. § 14A:6–14

[See Statutory Supplement]

————

NEW YORK BUS. CORP. LAW § 717

[See Statutory Supplement]

————

NOTE ON STATUTORY FORMULATIONS
OF THE DUTY OF CARE

1.   Twenty-two states have enacted statutory due-care provisions comparable to those of the RMBCA, California, New Jersey, and New York. See ALI, Principles of Corporate Governance § 4.01, Reporters' Note 1 (1994). A few of these statutes use a phrase like "[with that care which] ordinarily prudent men would exercise under similar circumstances in their personal affairs."   In Selheimer v. Manganese Corp. of America, 423 Pa. 563, 224 A.2d 634 (1966), the court held, perhaps questionably, that the phrase "in their personal affairs" imposed a higher standard of care than the more usual phrase, "in a like position."

2.   About half the statutes refer to officers as well as directors. It is not clear why the remaining statutes omit officers.   Is the

implication that the level of care owed by officers is to be determined under general principles of agency law? See Restatement, Agency, Second § 379: "Unless otherwise agreed, a paid agent is subject to a duty to the principal to act with standard care and with the skill which is standard in the locality for the kind of work which he is employed to perform and, in addition, to exercise any special skill that he has."

———

ALI, PRINCIPLES OF CORPORATE GOVERNANCE
§§ 4.01(a), (b), 4.02, 4.03

[See Statutory Supplement]

———

ARONSON v. LEWIS, 473 A.2d 805, 812 (Del.1984). "[D]irectors have a duty to inform themselves, prior to making a business decision, of all material information reasonably available to them. Having become so informed, they must then act with requisite care in the discharge of their duties. While the Delaware cases use a variety of terms to describe the applicable standard of care, our analysis satisfies us that under the business judgment rule director liability is predicated upon concepts of gross negligence."

———

QUILLEN, *TRANS UNION*, BUSINESS JUDGMENT, AND NEUTRAL PRINCIPLES, 10 Del.J.Corp.L. 465, 497–98 (1985). "Even if one assumes that negligence law is the proper pigeonhole for director liability—a most questionable assumption at least at the decisional level—the concept of 'gross negligence' has been expressly rejected by the better tort scholarship as practically meaningless. Therefore its recent adoption in corporate law would appear, in some respects, to be an analytical step backwards. . . .

"Perhaps we should say straight out that, on the threshold duty of care issue, the standard should be 'reasonable care under the circumstances' as some argued all along. If that flexible standard includes all factors, e.g., director expertise, time pressures, price, and cash, as well as depth of inquiry, then one suspects the results probably would not radically change, but the judicial focus would be to a keener negligence standard and emphasis more on the qualitative nature of the varying circumstances."

———

NOTE ON GRAHAM v. ALLIS–CHALMERS MFG. CO.

In Graham v. Allis–Chalmers Manufacturing Co., 41 Del.Ch. 78, 188 A.2d 125 (1963), Allis–Chalmers and four employees had pleaded guilty to indictments based on price-fixing and other violations of federal antitrust laws. FTC consent decrees, entered some twenty years earlier against Allis and nine other companies, had enjoined Allis from making agreements to fix uniform prices on products similar to those involved in the indictments. The plaintiff brought a derivative action against Allis's directors and the four employees for damages to Allis resulting from the conduct that was the subject of the indictments. Plaintiff claimed that the directors were liable under various theories, one of which was that the board should have taken action to learn about and prevent antitrust violations. Allis's operations were extensive and complex, and decentralized management was encouraged. The board formulated general policy, but did not deal with the details of corporate affairs. Held, for the directors:

> The duties of the Allis–Chalmers Directors were fixed by the nature of the enterprise which employed in excess of 30,000 persons, and extended over a large geographical area. By force of necessity, the company's Directors could not know personally all the company's employees. The very magnitude of the enterprise required them to confine their control to the board policy decisions. That they did this is clear from the record. At the meetings of the Board in which all Directors participated, these questions were considered and decided on the basis of summaries, reports and corporate records. These they were entitled to rely on, not only, we think, under general principles of the common law, but by reason of 8 Del.C. § 141(f) as well, which in terms fully protects a director who relies on such in the performance of his duties.

Id. at 85, 188 A.2d at 130.

Allis–Chalmers, although perhaps correctly decided on its facts (at least as concerns the outside directors) seems to envision a passive role for the board that would not be consistent with the modern view of the board's monitoring obligation. As stated in the Comment to § 4.01 of the ALI's Principles of Corporate Governance:

> The *Allis–Chalmers* case was decided over twenty years ago and a basic theme of the commentaries in Part IV has been that the "obligation" component of duty of care provisions is a flexible and dynamic concept. Today, an ordinarily prudent person serving as the director of a corporation of any significant scale or complexity should recognize the need to be reasonably concerned with the existence and effectiveness of procedures, programs, and other techniques to assist the board in its oversight role.

In contrast to the passive implications of the *Allis–Chalmers* reasoning (e.g., "no duty ... to install and operate a corporate system ... to ferret out wrongdoing"), the *Corporate Director's Guidebook* (p. 1610) states:

"The corporate director should be concerned that the corporation has programs looking toward compliance with applicable laws and regulations, both foreign and domestic, that it circulates (as appropriate) policy statements to this effect to its employees, and that it maintains procedures for monitoring such compliance."

A comparable view is expressed in Veasey & Manning, Codified Standard—Safe Harbor or Uncharted Reef?, 35 Bus.Law. 919 (1980):

... [A] final "core function" of the board identified by the Business Roundtable (compliance with the law) was discussed by the Roundtable in the following terms:

Some recent lapses in corporate behavior have emphasized the need for policies and implementing procedures on corporate law compliance. These policies should be designed to promote such compliance on a sustained and systematic basis by all levels of operating management.

Certain requirements are of major importance from both business and public points of view. Examples of these are antitrust compliance.... It is appropriate in these cases for the board to assure itself that there are policy directives and compliance procedures designed to prevent breaches of the law.

... [A] comparison of the results of *Graham* and ... [The position reflected in the Business Roundtable Statement] exposes not a philosophical difference between Delaware courts and the Business Roundtable; rather, it shows a natural development in the role of an "ordinarily prudent director" since 1963, the year in which *Graham* was decided.

NOTE ON CORPORATE CRIMINAL LIABILITY, THE SENTENCING GUIDELINES, AND COMPLIANCE PROGRAMS

The monitoring function of the board of directors has been given a substantial push by the Sentencing Guidelines issued by the United States Sentencing Commission. A corporation can be found guilty of a crime by imputing to the corporation the acts and intent of agents who acted within the scope of their authority. See Corporate Criminal Liability for Acts In Violation of Company Policy, 50 Geo.L.J. 547, 547–51 (1962). Determinations of corporate criminal liability, for such crimes as violation of the antitrust law or environmental laws, have become increasingly common. In the last two decades, the number of federal criminal convictions has gone from a few dozen per year to more than 300 per year. Penalties have also been increasing. From 1988 to 1989–1990, for all sentenced corporations, excluding antitrust offenders, the mean criminal fine rose from under $100,000 to over $800,000; the median criminal fine rose from $10,000 to $200,000; the mean total sanction rose from over $300,000 to almost $2.4 million; and the median total sanction rose from $22,000 to $500,000. If a corporation does violate the law, the fact that it had an "effective compliance program" drastically lowers its fine and allows the corporation to avoid probation. The Sentencing Guidelines therefore serve to reinforce the board's duty to monitor.

To constitute an "effective program to prevent and detect violations of the law," a compliance program must be reasonably designed, implemented, and enforced. Sentencing Guidelines § 8A1.2, commentary (n. 3(k)). The hallmark of an effective program is whether the corporation exercised due diligence in seeking to prevent and detect criminal conduct by its employees and other agents. *Id.* At a minimum, due diligence requires that the corporation must have taken the following seven steps: (1) Establish standards and procedures, reasonably capable of reducing the prospect of criminal conduct, to be followed by employees and other agents of the corporation. (2) Assign specific high-level individuals overall responsibility to oversee compliance with the standards and procedures. (3) Exercise due care to not delegate substantial discretionary authority to those individuals whom the corporation knew or should have known have a propensity to engage in illegal activities. (4) Effectively communicate corporate standards and procedures to all employees and other agents through training programs or dissemination of written information. (5) Attempt to achieve compliance through the use of monitoring and auditing systems to detect criminal conduct by employees and agents and by having in place and publicizing a reporting system whereby employees and agents can report criminal conduct by others within the organization without fear of retribution. (6) Enforce standards to achieve compliance through appropriate disciplinary mechanisms. (7) Respond appropriately if an offense is detected and take steps to prevent additional similar offenses. Sentencing Guidelines § 8A1.2, commentary (n. 3(k)).

A corporation that installs a compliance program will characteristically promulgate (i) a code of ethical conduct for its employees; (ii) procedures to ensure that the employees read, understand, and keep current on the code; and (iii) procedures to satisfy the due diligence inquiry requirement.

———

SECTION 2. THE DUTY TO MAKE INQUIRY

BATES v. DRESSER

Supreme Court of the United States, 1920.
251 U.S. 524, 40 S.Ct. 247, 64 L.Ed. 388.

Mr. Justice HOLMES delivered the opinion of the court.

This is a bill in equity brought by the receiver of a national bank to charge its former president and directors with the loss of a great part of its assets through the thefts of an employee of the bank while they were in power. The case was sent to a master who found for the defendants; but the District Court entered a decree against all of them. 229 Fed.Rep. 772. The Circuit Court of Appeals reversed this decree, dismissed the bill as against all except the administrator of Edwin Dresser, the president, cut down the amount with which he was charged and refused to add interest from the date of the decree of the District Court. 250 Fed.Rep. 525. 162 C.C.A. 541. Dresser's administrator and the receiver both appeal, the latter contending that the decree of the District Court should be affirmed with interest and costs.

The bank was a little bank at Cambridge with a capital of $100,000 and average deposits of somewhere about $300,000. It had a cashier, a bookkeeper, a teller and a messenger. Before and during the time of the losses Dresser was its president and executive officer, a large stockholder, with an inactive deposit of from $35,000 to $50,000. From July, 1903, to the end, Frank L. Earl was cashier. Coleman, who made the trouble, entered the service of the bank as messenger in September, 1903. In January, 1904, he was promoted to be bookkeeper, being then not quite eighteen but having studied bookkeeping. In the previous August an auditor employed on the retirement of a cashier had reported that the daily balance book was very much behind, that it was impossible to prove the deposits, and that a competent bookkeeper should be employed upon the work immediately. Coleman kept the deposit ledger and this was the work that fell into his hands. There was no cage in the bank, and in 1904 and 1905 there were some small shortages in the accounts of three successive tellers that were not accounted for, and the last of them, Cutting, was asked by Dresser to resign on that ground. Before doing so he told Dresser that someone had taken the money and that if he might be allowed to stay he would set a trap and catch the man, but Dresser did not care to do that and thought that there was nothing wrong. From Cutting's resignation on October 7, 1905, Coleman acted as paying and receiving teller, in addition to his other duty, until November, 1907. During this time there were no shortages disclosed in the teller's accounts. In May, 1906, Coleman took $2,000 cash from the vaults of the bank, but restored it the next morning. In November of the same year he began the thefts that come into question here. Perhaps in the beginning he took the money directly. But as he ceased to have charge of the cash in November, 1907, he invented another way. Having a small account at the bank, he would draw checks for the amount he wanted, exchange checks with a Boston broker, get cash for the broker's check, and, when his own check came to the bank through the clearing house, would abstract it from the envelope, enter the others on his book and conceal the difference by a charge to some other account or a false addition in the column of drafts or deposits in the depositors' ledger. He handed to the cashier only the slip from the clearing house that showed the totals. The cashier paid whatever appeared to be due and thus Coleman's checks were honored. So far as Coleman thought it necessary, in view of the absolute trust in him on the part of all concerned, he took care that his balances should agree with those in the cashier's book.

By May 1, 1907, Coleman had abstracted $17,000, concealing the fact by false additions in the column of total checks, and false balances in the deposit ledger. Then for the moment a safer concealment was effected by charging the whole to Dresser's account. Coleman adopted this method when a bank examiner was expected. Of course when the fraud was disguised by overcharging a depositor it could not be discovered except by calling in the pass-books, or taking all the deposit slips and comparing them with the depositors' ledger in detail. By November, 1907, the amount taken by Coleman was $30,100, and the charge on Dresser's account was $20,000. In 1908 the sum was raised from $33,000 to $49,671. In 1909 Coleman's activity began to increase. In January he took $6,829.26; in March, $10,833.73; in June, his previous stealings amounting to $83,390.94, he took $5,152.06; in July, $18,050; in August, $6,250; in September, $17,350; in October, $47,277.08; in November, $51,847; in December, $46,956.44; in January, 1910, $27,395.53; in February, $6,473.97; making a total of $310,143.02, when the bank closed on February 21, 1910. As a result of this the amount of the monthly deposits seemed to decline noticeably and the directors considered the matter in September, 1909, but concluded that the falling off was due in part to the springing up of rivals, whose deposits were increasing, but was parallel to a similar decrease in New York. An examination by a bank examiner in December, 1909, disclosed nothing wrong to him.

In this connection it should be mentioned that in the previous semi-annual examinations by national bank examiners nothing was discovered pointing to malfeasance. The cashier was honest and everybody believed that they could rely upon him, although in fact he relied too much upon Coleman, who also was unsuspected by all. If Earl had opened the envelopes from the clearing house, and had seen the checks, or had examined the deposit ledger with any care he would have found out what was going on. The scrutiny of anyone accustomed to such details would have discovered the false additions and other indicia of fraud that were on the face of the book. But it may be doubted whether anything less than a continuous pursuit of the figures through pages would have done so except by a lucky chance.

The question of the liability of the directors in this case is the question whether they neglected their duty by accepting the cashier's statement of liabilities and failing to inspect the depositors' ledger. The statements of assets always were correct. A by-law that had been allowed to become obsolete or nearly so is invoked as establishing their own standard of conduct. By that a committee was to be appointed every six months "to examine into the affairs of the bank, to count its cash, and compare its assets and liabilities with the balances on the general ledger, for the purpose of ascertaining whether or not the books are correctly kept, and the condition of the bank is in a sound and solvent condition." Of course liabilities as well as assets must be known to know the condition and, as this case shows, peculations may be concealed as well by a false understatement of liabilities as by a false show of assets. But the former is not the direction in which fraud would have been looked for, especially on the part of one who at the time of his principal abstractions was not in contact with the funds. A debtor hardly expects to have his liability understated. Some animals must have given at least one exhibition of dangerous propensities before the owner can be held. This fraud was a novelty in the way of swindling a bank so far as the knowledge of any experience had reached Cambridge before 1910. We are not prepared to reverse the finding of the master and the Circuit Court of Appeals that the directors should not be held answerable for taking the cashier's statement of liabilities to be as correct as the statement of assets always was. If he had not been negligent without their knowledge it would have been. Their confidence seemed warranted by the semi-annual examinations by the government examiner and they were encouraged in their belief that all was well by the president, whose responsibility, as executive officer; interest, as large stockholder and depositor; and knowledge, from long daily presence in the bank, were greater than theirs. They were not bound by virtue of the office gratuitously assumed by them to call in the pass-books and compare them with the ledger, and until the event showed the possibility they hardly could have seen that their failure to look at the ledger opened a way to fraud. See *Briggs v. Spaulding,* 141 U.S. 132; *Warner v. Penoyer,* 91 Fed.Rep. 587. We are not laying down general principles, however, but confine our decision to the circumstances of the particular case.*

---

* Compare the opinion in the same case in the District Court, 229 F. 772, 796 (1915): "The directors knew that the national bank examiners examined the bank twice a year. They knew that only one examiner at a time made the examination, and Mr. Edwin Dresser knew that the time allotted to the examination of the depositors' ledger was very brief. The other directors had no knowledge of the time allotted to the depositors' ledger, but in a general way knew that the time consumed in making the entire examination was but a portion of a day. Mr. Edwin Dresser, Sumner Dresser, and Mr. Gale must have known that the examination made by the bank examiner was not the equivalent of an audit, for they were directors in 1903 when they caused an audit to be made, and that it took from 12 to 14 days for two men to make it, and, while the directors, as a board, were not aware of the warnings regarding Mr. Coleman, which were brought to the attention of Mr. Edwin Dresser and Mr. Barber, and their knowledge that examinations were made by national bank examiners may have been a sufficient justification for their not causing an audit to be made, it was not a justification for their failure to perform their duty to examine the bank twice a year before declaring dividends. And it would seem very doubtful whether it should be regarded as a justifica-

The position of the president is different.   Practically he was the master of the situation.   He was daily at the bank for hours, he had the deposit ledger in his hands at times and might have had it at any time.   He had had hints and warnings in addition to those that we have mentioned, warnings that should not be magnified unduly, but still that taken with the auditor's report of 1903, the unexplained shortages, the suggestion of the teller, Cutting, in 1905, and the final seeming rapid decline in deposits, would have induced scrutiny but for an invincible repose upon the *status quo.* In 1908 one Fillmore learned that a package containing $150 left with the bank for safe keeping was not to be found, told Dresser of the loss, wrote to him that he could but conclude that the package had been destroyed or removed by someone connected with the bank, and in later conversation said that it was evident that there was a thief in the bank.   He added that he would advise the president to look after Coleman, that he believed he was living at a pretty fast pace, and that he had pretty good authority for thinking that he was supporting a woman.   In the same year or the year before, Coleman, whose pay was never more than twelve dollars a week, set up an automobile, as was known to Dresser and commented on unfavorably, to him.   There was also some evidence of notice to Dresser that Coleman was dealing in copper stocks.   In 1909 came the great and inadequately explained seeming shrinkage in the deposits.   No doubt plausible explanations of his conduct came from Coleman and the notice as to speculations may have been slight, but taking the whole story of the relations of the parties, we are not ready to say that the two courts below erred in finding that Dresser had been put upon his guard.   However little the warnings may have pointed to the specific facts, had they been accepted they would have led to an examination of the depositors' ledger, a discovery of past and a prevention of future thefts.

We do not perceive any ground for applying to this case the limitations of liability *ex contractu* adverted to in *Globe Refining Co. v. Landa Cotton Oil Co.,* 190 U.S. 540.   In accepting the presidency Dresser must be taken to have contemplated responsibility for losses to the bank, whatever they were, if chargeable to his fault. Those that happened were chargeable to his fault, after he had warnings that should have led to steps that would have made fraud impossible, even though the precise form that the fraud would take hardly could have been foreseen.   We accept with hesitation the date of December 1, 1908, as the beginning of Dresser's liability. . . .

> *Decree modified by charging the estate of Dresser with interest from February 1, 1916, to June 1, 1918, upon the sum found to be due, and affirmed.*

Mr. Justice McKENNA and Mr. Justice PITNEY dissent, upon the ground that not only the administrator of the president of the bank

tion for their failure to cause an audit to be made in September, 1909, when they were aware the shrinkage in their deposits was abnormal."   (Footnote by ed.)

but the other directors ought to be held liable to the extent to which they were held by the District Court, 229 Fed.Rep. 772.

Mr. Justice VAN DEVANTER and Mr. Justice BRANDEIS took no part in the decision.

SECTION 3. THE BUSINESS JUDGMENT RULE

KAMIN v. AMERICAN EXPRESS CO.

Supreme Court, Special Term, N.Y. County, Part 1, 1976.
86 Misc.2d 809, 383 N.Y.S.2d 807, aff'd on opinion below
54 A.D.2d 654, 387 N.Y.S.2d 993 (1st Dept.1976).

EDWARD J. GREENFIELD, Justice:

In this stockholders' derivative action, the individual defendants, who are the directors of the American Express Company, move for an order dismissing the complaint for failure to state a cause of action pursuant to CPLR 3211(a)(7), and alternatively, for summary judgment pursuant to CPLR 3211(c).

The complaint is brought derivatively by two minority stockholders of the American Express Company, asking for a declaration that a certain dividend in kind is a waste of corporate assets, directing the defendants not to proceed with the distribution, or, in the alternative, for monetary damages. The motion to dismiss the complaint requires the Court to presuppose the truth of the allegations. It is the defendants' contention that, conceding everything in the complaint, no viable cause of action is made out.

After establishing the identity of the parties, the complaint alleges that in 1972 American Express acquired for investment 1,954,418 shares of common stock of Donaldson, Lufken and Jenrette, Inc. (hereafter DLJ), a publicly traded corporation, at a cost of $29.9 million. It is further alleged that the current market value of those shares is approximately $4.0 million. On July 28, 1975, it is alleged, the Board of Directors of American Express declared a special dividend to all stockholders of record pursuant to which the shares of DLJ would be distributed in kind. Plaintiffs contend further that if American Express were to sell the DLJ shares on the market, it would sustain a capital loss of $25 million, which could be offset against taxable capital gains on other investments. Such a sale, they allege, would result in tax savings to the company of approximately $8 million, which would not be available in the case of the distribution of DLJ shares to stockholders. It is alleged that on October 8, 1975 and October 16, 1975, plaintiffs demanded that the directors rescind the previously declared dividend in DLJ shares and take steps to preserve the capital loss which would result from selling the shares. This demand was rejected by the Board of Directors on October 17, 1975.

It is apparent that all the previously-mentioned allegations of the complaint go to the question of the exercise by the Board of Directors of business judgment in deciding how to deal with the DLJ shares. The crucial allegation which must be scrutinized to determine the legal sufficiency of the complaint is paragraph 19, which alleges:

"19. All of the defendant Directors engaged in or acquiesced in or negligently permitted the declaration and payment of the Dividend in violation of the fiduciary duty owed by them to Amex to care for and preserve Amex's assets in the same manner as a man of average prudence would care for his own property."

Plaintiffs never moved for temporary injunctive relief, and did nothing to bar the actual distribution of the DLJ shares. The dividend was in fact paid on October 31, 1975. Accordingly, that portion of the complaint seeking a direction not to distribute the shares is deemed to be moot, and the Court will deal only with the request for declaratory judgment or for damages.

Examination of the complaint reveals that there is no claim of fraud or self-dealing, and no contention that there was any bad faith or oppressive conduct. The law is quite clear as to what is necessary to ground a claim for actionable wrongdoing.

"In actions by stockholders, which assail the acts of their directors or trustees, courts will not interfere unless the powers have been illegally or unconscientiously executed; or unless it be made to appear that the acts were fraudulent or collusive, and destructive of the rights of the stockholders. Mere errors of judgment are not sufficient as grounds for equity interference, for the powers of those entrusted with corporate management are largely discretionary." Leslie v. Lorillard, 110 N.Y. 519, 532, 18 N.E. 363, 365. . . .

More specifically, the question of whether or not a dividend is to be declared or a distribution of some kind should be made is exclusively a matter of business judgment for the Board of Directors.

". . . Courts will not interfere with such discretion unless it be first made to appear that the directors have acted or are about to act in bad faith and for a dishonest purpose. It is for the directors to say, acting in good faith of course, when and to what extent dividends shall be declared . . . The statute confers upon the directors this power, and the minority stockholders are not in a position to question this right, so long as the directors are acting in good faith . . ."

Thus, a complaint must be dismissed if all that is presented is a decision to pay dividends rather than pursuing some other course of conduct. Weinberger v. Quinn, 264 App.Div. 405, 35 N.Y.S.2d 567, affd. 290 N.Y. 635, 49 N.E.2d 131. A complaint which alleges merely that some course of action other than that pursued by the

Board of Directors would have been more advantageous gives rise to no cognizable cause of action. Courts have more than enough to do in adjudicating legal rights and devising remedies for wrongs. The directors' room rather than the courtroom is the appropriate forum for thrashing out purely business questions which will have an impact on profits, market prices, competitive situations, or tax advantages. As stated by Cardozo, J., when sitting at Special Term, the substitution of someone else's business judgment for that of the directors "is no business for any court to follow." Holmes v. St. Joseph Lead Co., 84 Misc. 278, 283, 147 N.Y.S. 104, 107, quoting from Gamble v. Queens County Water Co., 123 N.Y. 91, 99, 25 N.E. 201, 208.

It is not enough to allege, as plaintiffs do here, that the directors made an imprudent decision, which did not capitalize on the possibility of using a potential capital loss to offset capital gains. More than imprudence or mistaken judgment must be shown.

> "Questions of policy of management, expediency of contracts or action, adequacy of consideration, lawful appropriation of corporate funds to advance corporate interests, are left solely to their honest and unselfish decision, for their powers therein are without limitation and free from restraint, and the exercise of them for the common and general interests of the corporation may not be questioned, although the results show that what they did was unwise or inexpedient." Pollitz v. Wabash Railroad Co., 207 N.Y. 113, 124, 100 N.E. 721, 724.

Section 720 of the Business Corporation Law permits an action against directors for "the neglect of, or failure to perform, or other violations of his duties in the management and disposition of corporate assets committed to his charge." This does not mean that a director is chargeable with ordinary negligence for having made an improper decision, or having acted imprudently. The "neglect" referred to in the statute is neglect of duties (i.e., malfeasance or nonfeasance) and not misjudgment. To allege that a director "negligently permitted the declaration and payment" of a dividend without alleging fraud, dishonesty or nonfeasance, is to state merely that a decision was taken with which one disagrees.

Nor does this appear to be a case in which a potentially valid cause of action is inartfully stated.... The affidavits of the defendants and the exhibits annexed thereto demonstrate that the objections raised by the plaintiffs to the proposed dividend action were carefully considered and unanimously rejected by the Board at a special meeting called precisely for that purpose at the plaintiffs' request. The minutes of the special meeting indicate that the defendants were fully aware that a sale rather than a distribution of the DLJ shares might result in the realization of a substantial income tax saving. Nevertheless, they concluded that there were countervailing considerations primarily with respect to the adverse effect such a sale, realizing a loss of $25 million, would have on the net income figures in the American Express financial statement. Such a reduction of net income would have a serious effect on the market value of the publicly traded American Express stock. This was not a situation in which the defendant directors totally overlooked facts called to their attention. They gave them consideration, and attempted to view the total picture in arriving at their decision. While plaintiffs contend that according to their accounting consultants the loss on the DLJ stock would still have to be charged against current earnings even if the stock were distributed, the defendants' accounting experts assert that the loss would be a charge against earnings only in the event of a sale, whereas in the event of distribution of the stock as a dividend, the proper accounting treatment would be to charge the loss only against surplus. While the chief accountant for the SEC raised some question as to the appropriate accounting treatment of this transaction, there was no basis for any action to be taken by the SEC with respect to the American Express financial statement.

The only hint of self-interest which is raised, not in the complaint but in the papers on the motion, is that four of the twenty directors were officers and employees of American Express and members of its Executive Incentive Compensation Plan. Hence, it is suggested, by virtue of the action taken earnings may have been overstated and their compensation affected thereby. Such a claim is highly speculative and standing alone can hardly be regarded as sufficient to support an inference of self-dealing. There is no claim or showing that the four company directors dominated and controlled the sixteen outside members of the Board. Certainly, every action taken by the Board has some impact on earnings and may therefore affect the compensation of those whose earnings are keyed to profits. That does not disqualify the inside directors, nor does it put every policy adopted by the Board in question. All directors have an obligation, using sound business judgment, to maximize income for the benefit of all persons having a stake in the welfare of the corporate entity. See, Amdur v. Meyer, 15 A.D.2d 425, 224 N.Y.S.2d 440, appeal dismissed 14 N.Y.2d 541, 248 N.Y.S.2d 639, 198 N.E.2d 30. What we have here as revealed both by the complaint and by the affidavits and exhibits, is that a disagreement exists between two minority stockholders and a unanimous Board of Directors as to the best way to handle a loss already incurred on an investment. The directors are entitled to exercise their honest business judgment on the information before them, and to act within their corporate powers. That they may be mistaken, that other courses of action might have differing consequences, or that their action might benefit some shareholders more than others presents no basis for the superimposition of judicial judgment, so long as it appears that the directors have been acting in good faith. The question of to what extent a dividend shall be declared and the manner in which it shall be paid is ordinarily subject only to the qualification that the dividend be paid out of surplus (Business Corporation Law Section 510, subd. b). The

Court will not interfere unless a clear case is made out of fraud, oppression, arbitrary action, or breach of trust.

Courts should not shrink from the responsibility of dismissing complaints or granting summary judgment when no legal wrongdoing is set forth. . . .

In this case it clearly appears that the plaintiffs have failed as a matter of law to make out an actionable claim. Accordingly, the motion by the defendants for summary judgment and dismissal of the complaint is granted.

————

ALI, PRINCIPLES OF CORPORATE GOVERNANCE § 4.01(d)

[See Statutory Supplement]

————

NOTE ON THE DIVERGENCE OF STANDARDS OF CONDUCT AND STANDARDS OF REVIEW IN CORPORATE LAW

A *standard of conduct* states how an actor should conduct a given activity or play a given role. A *standard of review* states the test a court should apply when it reviews an actor's conduct to determine whether to impose liability or grant injunctive relief. In many or most areas of law, standards of conduct and standards of review are identical. For example, the standard of conduct that governs an automobile driver is that he should drive carefully. Correspondingly, the standard of review in a liability claim against a driver is whether he drove carefully. The standard of conduct that governs an agent who engages in a transaction with his principal that involves the subject matter of the agency is that the agent must deal fairly. Correspondingly, the standard of review in a liability claim by the principal against an agent based on such a transaction is whether the agent dealt fairly.

An identity between standards of conduct and standards of review is so common that it is easy to overlook the fact that the two kinds of standards may diverge in any given area—that is, the standard of conduct that states how an actor should conduct himself may differ from the standard of review by which courts determine whether to impose liability on the basis of the actor's conduct. A divergence of standards of conduct and standards of review is particularly common in corporation law.

The duty of care is a leading example of this divergence. The general *standard of conduct* applicable to directors and officers in the performance of their functions, in relation to matters in which they are not interested, varies somewhat in its formulation, but the basic standard is set forth in Section 4.01(a) of the ALI's *Principles of Corporate Governance.* "A director or officer has a duty to the corporation to perform the director's or officer's functions in good faith, in a manner that he or she reasonably believes to be in the best interests of the corporation, and with the care that an ordinarily prudent person would reasonably be expected to exercise in a like position and under similar circumstances." The application of this standard of conduct to the functions of directors results in several distinct duties—in particular, the duty to monitor, the duty of inquiry, the duty to make prudent or reasonable decisions on matters that the board is obliged or chooses to act upon, and the duty to employ a reasonable process to make decisions.

Officers have comparable duties, although for most officers decisionmaking is likely to be more important than monitoring.

On their face, the elements of these duties are fairly demanding. This is particularly true of the elements of prudence or reasonableness. In practice, however, the *standards of review* applied to the performance of these duties are less stringent, especially when the substance or quality of a decision—as opposed to the quality of the decisionmaking process—is called into question. In such cases, a much less demanding standard of review may apply where the business judgment rule is applicable. If the conditions of that rule (such as disinterestedness) are met, then under the rule the substance or quality of the director's or officer's decision will be reviewed, not under the basic standard of conduct to determine whether the decision was prudent or reasonable, but only under a much more limited standard.

There is some difference of opinion as to how that limited standard should be formulated. A few courts have stated that the standard is whether the director or officer acted in good faith. See, e.g., In re RJR Nabisco, Inc. Shareholders Litigation, Fed.Sec.L.Rep. ¶ 94,194(CCH), 1989 WL 7036 at n. 13 (1994). However, it is often unclear whether good faith, as used in this context, is purely subjective or also has an objective element. In Sam Wong & Son, Inc. v. New York Mercantile Exchange, 735 F.2d 653 (2d Cir.1984), Judge Friendly held (in a non-corporate context) that in determining whether a person made a decision in good faith, it was relevant whether the decision had rationality. "By this," he stated, "we mean . . . a minimal requirement of some basis in reason. . . . Absent some basis in reason, action could hardly be in good faith even apart from ulterior motive." Id. at 678 n. 32. Furthermore, even courts that seem to use the term "good faith" in a relatively subjective way nevertheless almost always review the quality of decisions under the guise of a rule that the irrationality of a decision *shows* bad faith.

Most courts, in applying the business judgment rule, have employed a standard that is much less searching than a reasonability standard, but nevertheless does involve some objective review of the quality of the decision, however limited. As William Quillen, a leading Delaware judge prior to his retirement from the bench, has stated: "[T]here can be no question that for years the courts have in fact reviewed directors' business decisions to some extent from a quality of judgment point of view. Businessmen do not like it, but courts do it and are likely to continue to do it because directors are fiduciaries." Quillen, *Trans Union,* Business Judgment, and Neutral Principles, 10 Del.J.Corp.L. 465, 492 (1985).

Accordingly, the prevalent formulation of the standard of review of a substantive decision under the business-judgment rule is that the decision must be "rational." See Principles of Corporate Governance § 4.01(c)(3). See also Meyers v. Moody, 693 F.2d 1196, 1211 (5th Cir.1982), cert. denied 464 U.S. 920, 104 S.Ct. 287, 78 L.Ed.2d 264 (1983); McDonnell v. American Leduc Petroleums, Ltd., 491 F.2d 380, 384 (2d Cir.1974); Arsht & Hinsey, Codified Standard—Same Harbor But Charted Channel: A Response, 35 Bus.Law. 947 (1980). The rationality standard of review is much easier for a defendant to satisfy than a prudence or reasonability standard. To see how exceptional a rationality standard is, one need only think about the judgments we make in everyday life. It is common to characterize a person's conduct as imprudent or unreasonable, but it is very uncommon to characterize a person's conduct as irrational.

An obvious example of a decision that fails to satisfy the rationality standard is a decision that cannot be coherently explained. For example, in Selheimer v. Manganese Corp. of America, 423 Pa. 563, 224 A.2d 634 (1966), managers poured a corporation's funds into the development of a single plant, even though they knew that the plant could not be operated profitably because of various factors, including lack of a railroad siding and lack of proper storage areas. The court imposed liability because the managers' conduct "defie[d] explanation; in fact, the defendants have failed to give any satisfactory explanation or advance any justification for [the] expenditures." Id. at 584, 224 A.2d at 646. Another type of conduct that would fail to satisfy the rationality standard of review is conduct that is reckless.

The duty to monitor, the duty of inquiry, and the duty to employ a reasonable decisionmaking process are normally not protected by the business-judgment rule. Even in the case of these duties, however, the standard of review may depart somewhat from the relevant standard of conduct. A few courts have expressed this difference by adopting a rule that the standard of review in such cases is whether the director was "grossly negligent." See, e.g., Smith v. Van Gorkom. The concept of gross negligence, however, is notoriously ambiguous, and in practice it is common to find that courts that purport to apply that standard actually apply a standard that is either more or less demanding. For example, a gross-negligence standard of review is often associated with Delaware, but in Smith v. Van Gorkom, infra, the Delaware court, although purporting to apply that standard of review, in fact held outside directors to be liable for conduct that many observers believe did not constitute even ordinary negligence. Conversely, in Rabkin v. Philip A. Hunt Chemical Corp., 13 Del.J.Corp.L. 1210, 1987 WL

28436 (Del.Ch.1987), decided after Smith v. Van Gorkom, Vice–Chancellor Berger stated that the gross-negligence test did not apply across the board:

> The Hunt [directors] argue that [in] a claim of director neglect . . . the gross negligence standard should be applied for legal and practical reasons.
>
> I conclude that ordinary negligence is the appropriate standard of liability in director neglect claims. I am satisfied that . . . *Van Gorkom* did not adopt the gross negligence standard in [such] claims. . . .

Id. at 1216–17.

Courts that purport to adopt a gross-negligence standard to review the duty to monitor, the duty of inquiry, or the duty to employ a reasonable decisionmaking process, probably do so because the performance of these duties seldom presents a cut-and-dried issue, and the gross-negligence standard of review emphasizes the importance of leaving a play in the joints in determining whether the relevant standard of conduct was satisfied in such cases. A play in the joints, however, is built into the very concept of due care. In *Rabkin,* for example, Vice–Chancellor Berger stated that even under an ordinary-negligence standard, "corporate directors will face no liability for the failure to focus on an isolated bit of information." 13 Del.J.Corp.L. at 1216–17.

The same point can be made, without using the problematic gross-negligence standard, by employing the terminology of due care, rather than the terminology of negligence, and by making clear that in determining whether directors or officers acted with due care, courts should consider the complexities of the corporate context and give directors and officers a certain amount of running room. As stated by William Quillen, "in *information gathering,* a negligence standard . . . may be appropriate so long as courts recognize that 'circumstances' vary. Such a standard would not be materially different in result than the 'gross negligence' standard of *Trans Union* and would certainly be a more accurate description of the test on the *Trans Union* facts." Quillen, *Trans Union,* Business Judgment, and Neutral Principles, 10 Del.J.Corp.L. 465, 500 (1985) (emphasis added).

SMITH v. VAN GORKOM

Supreme Court of Delaware, 1985.
488 A.2d 858.

Before HERRMANN, C.J., and McNEILLY, HORSEY, MOORE and CHRISTIE, JJ., constituting the Court en banc.

HORSEY, Justice (for the majority):

This appeal from the Court of Chancery involves a class action brought by shareholders of the defendant Trans Union Corporation

("Trans Union" or "the Company"), originally seeking rescission of a cash-out merger of Trans Union into the defendant New T Company ("New T"), a wholly-owned subsidiary of the defendant, Marmon Group, Inc. ("Marmon"). Alternate relief in the form of damages is sought against the defendant members of the Board of Directors of Trans Union, New T, and Jay A. Pritzker and Robert A. Pritzker, owners of Marmon.[1]

Following trial, the former Chancellor granted judgment for the defendant directors by unreported letter opinion dated July 6, 1982.[2] Judgment was based on two findings: (1) that the Board of Directors had acted in an informed manner so as to be entitled to protection of the business judgment rule in approving the cash-out merger; and (2) that the shareholder vote approving the merger should not be set aside because the stockholders had been "fairly informed" by the Board of Directors before voting thereon. The plaintiffs appeal.

Speaking for the majority of the Court, we conclude that both rulings of the Court of Chancery are clearly erroneous. Therefore, we reverse and direct that judgment be entered in favor of the plaintiffs and against the defendant directors for the fair value of the plaintiffs' stockholdings in Trans Union, in accordance with Weinberger v. UOP, Inc., Del.Supr., 457 A.2d 701 (1983).

We hold: (1) that the Board's decision, reached September 20, 1980, to approve the proposed cash-out merger was not the product of an informed business judgment; (2) that the Board's subsequent efforts to amend the Merger Agreement and take other curative action were ineffectual, both legally and factually; and (3) that the Board did not deal with complete candor with the stockholders by failing to disclose all material facts, which they knew or should have known, before securing the stockholders' approval of the merger.

I.

The nature of this case requires a detailed factual statement. The following facts are essentially uncontradicted....

Trans Union was a publicly-traded, diversified holding company, the principal earnings of which were generated by its railcar leasing business. During the period here involved, the Company

---

1. The plaintiff, Alden Smith, originally sought to enjoin the merger; but, following extensive discovery, the Trial Court denied the plaintiff's motion for preliminary injunction by unreported letter opinion dated February 3, 1981. On February 10, 1981, the proposed merger was approved by Trans Union's stockholders at a special meeting and the merger became effective on that date. Thereafter, John W. Gosselin was permitted to intervene as an additional plaintiff; and Smith and Gosselin were certified as representing a class consisting of all persons, other than defendants, who

held shares of Trans Union common stock on all relevant dates. At the time of the merger, Smith owned 54,000 shares of Trans Union stock, Gosselin owned 23,600 shares, and members of Gosselin's family owned 20,000 shares.

2. Following trial, and before decision by the Trial Court, the parties stipulated to the dismissal, with prejudice, of the Messrs. Pritzker as parties defendant. However, all references to defendants hereinafter are to the defendant directors of Trans Union, unless otherwise noted.

had a cash flow of hundreds of millions of dollars annually. However, the Company had difficulty in generating sufficient taxable income to offset increasingly large investment tax credits (ITCs)....

B.

[Jerome Van Gorkom, Trans Union's Chairman and Chief Executive Officer, met with senior management on August 27, 1980, to discuss Trans Union's difficulty in producing sufficient taxable income to offset its increasing investment-tax credits and accelerated-depreciation deductions.] Donald Romans, Chief Financial Officer of Trans Union, stated that his department had done a "very brief bit of work on the possibility of a leveraged buy-out." ... The work consisted of a "preliminary study" of the cash which could be generated by the Company if it participated in a leveraged buy-out. As Romans stated, this analysis "was very first and rough cut at seeing whether a cash flow would support what might be considered a high price for this type of transaction."

On September 5, at another Senior Management meeting which Van Gorkom attended, Romans again brought up the idea of a leveraged buy-out as a "possible strategic alternative" to the Company's acquisition program. Romans and Bruce S. Chelberg, President and Chief Operating Officer of Trans Union, had been working on the matter in preparation for the meeting. According to Romans: They did not "come up" with a price for the Company. They merely "ran the numbers" at $50 a share and at $60 a share with the "rough form" of their cash figures at the time. Their "figures indicated that $50 would be very easy to do but $60 would be very difficult to do under those figures." This work did not purport to establish a fair price for either the Company or 100% of the stock. It was intended to determine the cash flow needed to service the debt that would "probably" be incurred in a leveraged buy-out, based on "rough calculations" without "any benefit of experts to identify what the limits were to that, and so forth." These computations were not considered extensive and no conclusion was reached.

At this meeting, Van Gorkom stated that he would be willing to take $55 per share for his own 75,000 shares. He vetoed the suggestion of a leveraged buy-out by Management, however, as involving a potential conflict of interest for Management. Van Gorkom, a certified public accountant and lawyer, had been an officer of Trans Union for 24 years, its Chief Executive Officer for more than 17 years, and Chairman of its Board for 2 years. It is noteworthy in this connection that he was then approaching 65 years of age and mandatory retirement.

For several days following the September 5 meeting, Van Gorkom pondered the idea of a sale....

Van Gorkom decided to meet with Jay A. Pritzker, a well-known corporate takeover specialist and a social acquaintance. However, rather than approaching Pritzker simply to determine his interest in acquiring Trans Union, Van Gorkom assembled a proposed per share price for sale of the Company and a financing structure by which to accomplish the sale. Van Gorkom did so without consulting either his Board or any members of Senior Management except one: Carl Peterson, Trans Union's Controller. Telling Peterson that he wanted no other person on his staff to know what he was doing, but without telling him why, Van Gorkom directed Peterson to calculate the feasibility of a leveraged buy-out at an assumed price per share of $55. Apart from the Company's historic stock market price,[5] and Van Gorkom's long association with Trans Union, the record is devoid of any competent evidence that $55 represented the per share intrinsic value of the Company....

Van Gorkom arranged a meeting with Pritzker at the latter's home on Saturday, September 13, 1980. Van Gorkom prefaced his presentation by stating to Pritzker: "Now as far as you are concerned, I can, I think, show how you can pay a substantial premium over the present stock price and pay off most of the loan in the first five years.... If you could pay $55 for this Company, here is a way in which I think it can be financed."

Van Gorkom then reviewed with Pritzker his calculations based upon his proposed price of $55 per share. Although Pritzker mentioned $50 as a more attractive figure, no other price was mentioned. However, Van Gorkom stated that to be sure that $55 was the best price obtainable, Trans Union should be free to accept any better offer. Pritzker demurred, stating that his organization would serve as a "stalking horse" for an "auction contest" only if Trans Union would permit Pritzker to buy 1,750,000 shares of Trans Union stock at market price which Pritzker could then sell to any higher bidder. After further discussion on this point, Pritzker told Van Gorkom that he would give him a more definite reaction soon.

On Monday, September 15, Pritzker advised Van Gorkom that he was interested in the $55 cash-out merger proposal and requested more information on Trans Union....

On Thursday, September 18, Van Gorkom met again with Pritzker. At that time, Van Gorkom knew that Pritzker intended to make a cash-out merger offer at Van Gorkom's proposed $55 per share. Pritzker instructed his attorney, a merger and acquisition specialist, to begin drafting merger documents. There was no further discussion of the $55 price. However, the number of shares of Trans Union's treasury stock to be offered to Pritzker was negotiated down to one million shares; the price was set at $38— 75 cents above the per share price at the close of the market on September 19. At this point, Pritzker insisted that the Trans Union Board act on his merger proposal within the next three days, stating to Van Gorkom: "We have to have a decision by no later than

---

5. The common stock of Trans Union was traded on the New York Stock Exchange. Over the five year period from 1975 through 1979, Trans Union's stock had traded within a range of a high of $39½ and a low of $24¼. Its high and low range for 1980 through September 19 (the last trading day before announcement of the merger) was $38¼–$29½.

Sunday [evening, September 21] before the opening of the English stock exchange on Monday morning." Pritzker's lawyer was then instructed to draft the merger documents, to be reviewed by Van Gorkom's lawyer, "sometimes with discussion and sometimes not, in the haste to get it finished."

On Friday, September 19, Van Gorkom, Chelberg, and Pritzker consulted with Trans Union's lead bank regarding the financing of Pritzker's purchase of Trans Union. The bank indicated that it could form a syndicate of banks that would finance the transaction. On the same day, Van Gorkom retained James Brennan, Esquire, to advise Trans Union on the legal aspects of the merger. Van Gorkom did not consult with William Browder, a Vice–President and director of Trans Union and former head of its legal department, or with William Moore, then the head of Trans Union's legal staff.

On Friday, September 19, Van Gorkom called a special meeting of the Trans Union Board for noon the following day. He also called a meeting of the Company's Senior Management to convene at 11:00 a.m., prior to the meeting of the Board. No one, except Chelberg and Peterson, was told the purpose of the meetings. Van Gorkom did not invite Trans Union's investment banker, Salomon Brothers or its Chicago-based partner, to attend.

Of those present at the Senior Management meeting on September 20, only Chelberg and Peterson had prior knowledge of Pritzker's offer. Van Gorkom disclosed the offer and described its terms, but he furnished no copies of the proposed Merger Agreement. Romans announced that his department had done a second study which showed that, for a leveraged buy-out, the price range for Trans Union stock was between $55 and $65 per share. Van Gorkom neither saw the study nor asked Romans to make it available for the Board meeting.

Senior Management's reaction to the Pritzker proposal was completely negative. No member of Management, except Chelberg and Peterson, supported the proposal. Romans objected to the price as being too low [6] . . . .

Ten directors served on the Trans Union Board, five inside (defendants Bonser, O'Boyle, Browder, Chelberg, and Van Gorkom) and five outside (defendants Wallis, Johnson, Lanterman, Morgan and Reneker). All directors were present at the meeting, except O'Boyle who was ill. Of the outside directors, four were corporate chief executive officers and one was the former Dean of the University of Chicago Business School. None was an investment banker or trained financial analyst. All members of the Board were well informed about the Company and its operations as a going concern. They were familiar with the current financial condition of the

---

6. Van Gorkom asked Romans to express his opinion as to the $55 price. Romans stated that he "thought the price was too low in relation to what he could derive for the company in a cash sale, particularly one which enabled us to realize the values of certain subsidiaries and independent entities."

Company, as well as operating and earnings projections reported in the recent Five Year Forecast. The Board generally received regular and detailed reports and was kept abreast of the accumulated investment tax credit and accelerated depreciation problem.

Van Gorkom began the Special Meeting of the Board with a twenty-minute oral presentation. Copies of the proposed Merger Agreement were delivered too late for study before or during the meeting.[7] He reviewed the Company's ITC and depreciation problems and the efforts theretofore made to solve them. He discussed his initial meeting with Pritzker and his motivation in arranging that meeting. Van Gorkom did not disclose to the Board, however, the methodology by which he alone had arrived at the $55 figure, or the fact that he first proposed the $55 price in his negotiations with Pritzker.

Van Gorkom outlined the terms of the Pritzker offer as follows: Pritzker would pay $55 in cash for all outstanding shares of Trans Union stock upon completion of which Trans Union would be merged into New T Company, a subsidiary wholly-owned by Pritzker and formed to implement the merger; for a period of 90 days, Trans Union could receive, but could not actively solicit, competing offers; the offer had to be acted on by the next evening, Sunday, September 21; Trans Union could only furnish to competing bidders published information, and not proprietary information; the offer was subject to Pritzker obtaining the necessary financing by October 10, 1980; if the financing contingency were met or waived by Pritzker, Trans Union was required to sell to Pritzker one million newly-issued shares of Trans Union at $38 per share.

Van Gorkom took the position that putting Trans Union "up for auction" through a 90–day market test would validate a decision by the Board that $55 was a fair price. He told the Board that the "free market will have an opportunity to judge whether $55 is a fair price." Van Gorkom framed the decision before the Board not as whether $55 per share was the highest price that could be obtained, but as whether the $55 price was a fair price that the stockholders should be given the opportunity to accept or reject.[8]

Attorney Brennan advised the members of the Board that they might be sued if they failed to accept the offer and that a fairness opinion was not required as a matter of law.

Romans attended the meeting as chief financial officer of the Company. He told the Board that he had not been involved in the negotiations with Pritzker and knew nothing about the merger proposal until the morning of the meeting; that his studies did not indicate either a fair price for the stock or a valuation of the

---

7. The record is not clear as to the terms of the Merger Agreement. The Agreement, as originally presented to the Board on September 20, was never produced by defendants despite demands by the plaintiffs. Nor is it clear that the directors were given an opportunity to study the Merger Agreement before voting on it. All that can be said is that Brennan had the Agreement before him during the meeting.

8. In Van Gorkom's words: The "real decision" is whether to "let the stockholders decide it" which is "all you are being asked to decide today."

Company; that he did not see his role as directly addressing the fairness issue; and that he and his people "were trying to search for ways to justify a price in connection with such a [leveraged buy-out] transaction, rather than to say what the shares are worth." Romans testified:

> I told the Board that the study ran the numbers at 50 and 60, and then the subsequent study at 55 and 65, and that was not the same thing as saying that I have a valuation of the company at X dollars. But it was a way—a first step towards reaching that conclusion.

Romans told the Board that, in his opinion, $55 was "in the range of a fair price," but "at the beginning of the range." . . .

The Board meeting of September 20 lasted about two hours. Based solely upon Van Gorkom's oral presentation, Chelberg's supporting representations, Romans' oral statement, Brennan's legal advice, and their knowledge of the market history of the Company's stock, the directors approved the proposed Merger Agreement. However, the Board later claimed to have attached two conditions to its acceptance: (1) that Trans Union reserved the right to accept any better offer that was made during the market test period; and (2) that Trans Union could share its proprietary information with any other potential bidders. While the Board now claims to have reserved the right to accept any better offer received after the announcement of the Pritzker agreement (even though the minutes of the meeting do not reflect this), it is undisputed that the Board did not reserve the right to actively solicit alternate offers.

The Merger Agreement was executed by Van Gorkom during the evening of September 20 at a formal social event that he hosted for the opening of the Chicago Lyric Opera. Neither he nor any other director read the agreement prior to its signing and delivery to Pritzker. . . .

On Monday, September 22, the Company issued a press release announcing that Trans Union had entered into a "definitive" Merger Agreement with an affiliate of the Marmon Group, Inc., a Pritzker holding company. Within 10 days of the public announcement, dissent among Senior Management over the merger had become widespread. Faced with threatened resignations of key officers, Van Gorkom met with Pritzker who agreed to several modifications of the Agreement. Pritzker was willing to do so provided that Van Gorkom could persuade the dissidents to remain on the Company payroll for at least six months after consummation of the merger.

Van Gorkom reconvened the Board on October 8 and secured the directors' approval of the proposed amendments—sight unseen. The Board also authorized the employment of Salomon Brothers, its investment banker, to solicit other offers for Trans Union during the proposed "market test" period.

The next day, October 9, Trans Union issued a press release announcing: (1) that Pritzker had obtained "the financing commitments necessary to consummate" the merger with Trans Union; (2) that Pritzker had acquired one million shares of Trans Union common stock at $38 per share; (3) that Trans Union was now permitted to actively seek other offers and had retained Salomon Brothers for that purpose; and (4) that if a more favorable offer were not received before February 1, 1981, Trans Union's shareholders would thereafter meet to vote on the Pritzker proposal.

It was not until the following day, October 10, that the actual amendments to the Merger Agreement were prepared by Pritzker and delivered to Van Gorkom for execution. As will be seen, the amendments were considerably at variance with Van Gorkom's representations of the amendments to the Board on October 8; and the amendments placed serious constraints on Trans Union's ability to negotiate a better deal and withdraw from the Pritzker agreement. Nevertheless, Van Gorkom proceeded to execute what became the October 10 amendments to the Merger Agreement without conferring further with the Board members and apparently without comprehending the actual implications of the amendments....

Salomon Brothers' efforts over a three-month period from October 21 to January 21 produced only one serious suitor for Trans Union—General Electric Credit Corporation ("GE Credit"), a subsidiary of the General Electric Company. However, GE Credit was unwilling to make an offer for Trans Union unless Trans Union first rescinded its Merger Agreement with Pritzker. When Pritzker refused, GE Credit terminated further discussions with Trans Union in early January.

In the meantime, in early December, the investment firm Kohlberg, Kravis, Roberts & Co. ("KKR"), the only other concern to make a firm offer for Trans Union, withdrew its offer under circumstances hereinafter detailed.

On December 19, this litigation was commenced and, within four weeks, the plaintiffs had deposed eight of the ten directors of Trans Union, including Van Gorkom, Chelberg and Romans, its Chief Financial Officer. On January 21, Management's Proxy Statement for the February 10 shareholder meeting was mailed to Trans Union's stockholders. On January 26, Trans Union's Board met and, after a lengthy meeting, voted to proceed with the Pritzker merger. The Board also approved for mailing, "on or about January 27," a Supplement to its Proxy Statement. The Supplement purportedly set forth all information relevant to the Pritzker Merger Agreement, which had not been divulged in the first Proxy Statement....

On February 10, the stockholders of Trans Union approved the Pritzker merger proposal. Of the outstanding shares, 69.9% were voted in favor of the merger; 7.25% were voted against the merger; and 22.85% were not voted.

II.

We turn to the issue of the application of the business judgment rule to the September 20 meeting of the Board.

The Court of Chancery concluded from the evidence that the Board of Directors' approval of the Pritzker merger proposal fell within the protection of the business judgment rule. The Court found that the Board had given sufficient time and attention to the transaction, since the directors had considered the Pritzker proposal on three different occasions, on September 20, and on October 8, 1980 and finally on January 26, 1981. On that basis, the Court reasoned that the Board had acquired, over the four-month period, sufficient information to reach an informed business judgment on the cash-out merger proposal. The Court ruled:

> ... that given the market value of Trans Union's stock, the business acumen of the members of the board of Trans Union, the substantial premium over market offered by the Pritzkers and the ultimate effect on the merger price provided by the prospect of other bids for the stock in question, that the board of directors of Trans Union did not act recklessly or improvidently in determining on a course of action which they believed to be in the best interest of the stockholders of Trans Union.

The Court of Chancery made but one finding; i.e., that the Board's conduct over the entire period from September 20 through January 26, 1981 was not reckless or improvident, but informed. This ultimate conclusion was premised upon three subordinate findings, one explicit and two implied. The Court's explicit finding was that Trans Union's Board was "free to turn down the Pritzker proposal" not only on September 20 but also on October 8, 1980 and on January 26, 1981. The Court's implied, subordinate findings were: (1) that no legally binding agreement was reached by the parties until January 26; and (2) that if a higher offer were to be forthcoming, the market test would have produced it, and Trans Union would have been contractually free to accept such higher offer. However, the Court offered no factual basis or legal support for any of these findings; and the record compels contrary conclusions....

Under Delaware law, the business judgment rule is the offspring of the fundamental principle, codified in 8 Del.C. § 141(a), that the business and affairs of a Delaware corporation are managed by or under its board of directors.... The rule itself "is a presumption that in making a business decision, the directors of a corporation acted on an informed basis, in good faith and in the honest belief that the action taken was in the best interests of the company." ... [Aronson v. Lewis, 473 A.2d 805, 812 (Del.1984)]. Thus, the party attacking a board decision as uninformed must rebut the presumption that its business judgment was an informed one. Id.

The determination of whether a business judgment is an informed one turns on whether the directors have informed themselves "prior to making a business decision, of all material information reasonably available to them." Id.

Under the business judgment rule there is no protection for directors who have made "an unintelligent or unadvised judgment."

Mitchell v. Highland–Western Glass, Del.Ch., 167 A. 831, 833 (1933). A director's duty to inform himself in preparation for a decision derives from the fiduciary capacity in which he serves the corporation and its stockholders. Lutz v. Boas, Del.Ch., 171 A.2d 381 (1961). See Weinberger v. UOP, Inc., supra; Guth v. Loft, supra. . . .   [F]ulfillment of the fiduciary function requires more than the mere absence of bad faith or fraud. Representation of the financial interests of others imposes on a director an affirmative duty to protect those interests and to proceed with a critical eye in assessing information of the type and under the circumstances present here. . . .

The standard of care applicable to a director's duty of care has also been recently restated by this Court. In Aronson, supra, we stated:

> While the Delaware cases use a variety of terms to describe the applicable standard of care, our analysis satisfies us that under the business judgment rule director liability is predicated upon concepts of gross negligence. (footnote omitted)

473 A.2d at 812.

We again confirm that view. We think the concept of gross negligence is also the proper standard for determining whether a business judgment reached by a board of directors was an informed one.[13]

In the specific context of a proposed merger of domestic corporations, a director has a duty under 8 Del.C. 251(b),[14] along with his fellow directors, to act in an informed and deliberate manner in determining whether to approve an agreement of merger before submitting the proposal to the stockholders. Certainly in the merger context, a director may not abdicate that duty by leaving to the shareholders alone the decision to approve or disapprove the agreement. See Beard v. Elster, Del.Supr., 160 A.2d 731, 737 (1960). Only an agreement of merger satisfying the requirements of 8 Del.C. § 251(b) may be submitted to the shareholders under § 251(c). See generally Aronson v. Lewis, supra at 811–13; see also Pogostin v. Rice, supra.

13. Compare Mitchell v. Highland–Western Glass, supra, where the Court posed the question as whether the board acted "so far without information that they can be said to have passed an unintelligent and unadvised judgment." 167 A. at 833. Compare also Gimbel v. Signal Companies, Inc., 316 A.2d 599, aff'd per curiam Del. Supr., 316 A.2d 619 (1974), where the Chancellor, after expressly reiterating the *Highland–Western Glass* standard, framed the question, "Or to put the question in its legal context, did the Signal directors act without the bounds of reason and recklessly in approving the price offer of Burmah?" Id.

14. 8 Del.C. § 251(b) provides in pertinent part:

(b) The board of directors of each corporation which desires to merge or consolidate *shall adopt a resolution approving an agreement of merger* or consolidation. . . .   Any of the terms of the agreement of merger or consolidation may be made dependent upon facts ascertainable outside of such agreement, provided that the manner in which such facts shall operate upon the terms of the agreement is clearly and expressly set forth in the agreement of merger or consolidation. (underlining added [by the court] for emphasis)

It is against those standards that the conduct of the directors of Trans Union must be tested, as a matter of law and as a matter of fact, regarding their exercise of an informed business judgment in voting to approve the Pritzker merger proposal.

III.

The defendants argue that the determination of whether their decision to accept $55 per share for Trans Union represented an informed business judgment requires consideration, not only of that which they knew and learned on September 20, but also of that which they subsequently learned and did over the following four-month period before the shareholders met to vote on the proposal in February, 1981. The defendants thereby seek to reduce the significance of their action on September 20 and to widen the time frame for determining whether their decision to accept the Pritzker proposal was an informed one. Thus, the defendants contend that what the directors did and learned subsequent to September 20 and through January 26, 1981, was properly taken into account by the Trial Court in determining whether the Board's judgment was an informed one. We disagree with this *post hoc* approach.

The issue of whether the directors reached an informed decision to "sell" the Company on September 20, 1980 must be determined only upon the basis of the information then reasonably available to the directors and relevant to their decision to accept the Pritzker merger proposal. This is not to say that the directors were precluded from altering their original plan of action, had they done so in an informed manner. What we do say is that the question of whether the directors reached an informed business judgment in agreeing to sell the Company, pursuant to the terms of the September 20 Agreement presents, in reality, two questions: (A) whether the directors reached an informed business judgment on September 20, 1980; and (B) if they did not, whether the directors' actions taken subsequent to September 20 were adequate to cure any infirmity in their action taken on September 20. We first consider the directors' September 20 action in terms of their reaching an informed business judgment.

–A–

On the record before us, we must conclude that the Board of Directors did not reach an informed business judgment on September 20, 1980 in voting to "sell" the Company for $55 per share pursuant to the Pritzker cash-out merger proposal. Our reasons, in summary, are as follows:

The directors (1) did not adequately inform themselves as to Van Gorkom's role in forcing the "sale" of the Company and in establishing the per share purchase price; (2) were uninformed as to the intrinsic value of the Company; and (3) given these circumstances, at a minimum, were grossly negligent in approving the "sale" of the Company upon two hours' consideration, without prior notice, and without the exigency of a crisis or emergency.

As has been noted, the Board based its September 20 decision to approve the cash-out merger primarily on Van Gorkom's representations. None of the directors, other than Van Gorkom and Chelberg, had any prior knowledge that the purpose of the meeting was to propose a cash-out merger of Trans Union. . . .

Without any documents before them concerning the proposed transaction, the members of the Board were required to rely entirely upon Van Gorkom's 20–minute oral presentation of the proposal. No written summary of the terms of the merger was presented; the directors were given no documentation to support the adequacy of $55 price per share for sale of the Company; and the Board had before it nothing more than Van Gorkom's statement of his understanding of the substance of an agreement which he admittedly had never read, nor which any member of the Board had ever seen.

Under 8 Del.C. § 141(e), "directors are fully protected in relying in good faith on reports made by officers." Michelson v. Duncan, Del.Ch., 386 A.2d 1144, 1156 (1978); aff'd in part and rev'd in part on other grounds, Del.Supr., 407 A.2d 211 (1979). See also Graham v. Allis–Chalmers Mfg. Co., Del.Supr., 188 A.2d 125, 130 (1963); Prince v. Bensinger, Del.Ch., 244 A.2d 89, 94 (1968). The term "report" has been liberally construed to include reports of informal personal investigations by corporate officers, Cheff v. Mathes, Del.Supr., 199 A.2d 548, 556 (1964). However, there is no evidence that any "report," as defined under § 141(e), concerning the Pritzker proposal, was presented to the Board on September 20. Van Gorkom's oral presentation of his understanding of the terms of the proposed Merger Agreement, which he had not seen, and Romans' brief oral statement of his preliminary study regarding the feasibility of a leveraged buy-out of Trans Union do not qualify as § 141(e) "reports" for these reasons: The former lacked substance because Van Gorkom was basically uninformed as to the essential provisions of the very document about which he was talking. Romans' statement was irrelevant to the issues before the Board since it did not purport to be a valuation study. At a minimum for a report to enjoy the status conferred by § 141(e), it must be pertinent to the subject matter upon which a board is called to act, and otherwise be entitled to good faith, not blind, reliance. Considering all of the surrounding circumstances—hastily calling the meeting without prior notice of its subject matter, the proposed sale of the Company without any prior consideration of the issue or necessity therefor, the urgent time constraints imposed by Pritzker, and the total absence of any documentation whatsoever—the directors were duty bound to make reasonable inquiry of Van Gorkom and Romans, and if they had done so, the inadequacy of that upon which they now claim to have relied would have been apparent.

The defendants rely on the following factors to sustain the Trial Court's finding that the Board's decision was an informed one: (1) the magnitude of the premium or spread between the $55 Pritzker offering price and Trans Union's current market price of $38 per share; (2) the amendment of the Agreement as submitted on September 20 to permit the Board to accept any better offer during the "market test" period; (3) the collective experience and expertise of the Board's "inside" and "outside" directors; and (4) their reliance on Brennan's legal advice that the directors might be sued if they rejected the Pritzker proposal. We discuss each of these grounds *seriatim:*

(1)

A substantial premium may provide one reason to recommend a merger, but in the absence of other sound valuation information, the fact of a premium alone does not provide an adequate basis upon which to assess the fairness of an offering price. Here, the judgment reached as to the adequacy of the premium was based on a comparison between the historically depressed Trans Union market price and the amount of the Pritzker offer. Using market price as a basis for concluding that the premium adequately reflected the true value of the Company was a clearly faulty, indeed fallacious, premise. . . .

The record is clear that before September 20, Van Gorkom and other members of Trans Union's Board knew that the market had consistently undervalued the worth of Trans Union's stock. . . .

The parties do not dispute that a publicly-traded stock price is solely a measure of the value of a minority position and, thus, market price represents only the value of a single share. Nevertheless, on September 20, the Board assessed the adequacy of the premium over market, offered by Pritzker, solely by comparing it with Trans Union's current and historical stock price. . . .

Indeed, as of September 20, the Board had no other information on which to base a determination of the intrinsic value of Trans Union as a going concern. As of September 20, the Board had made no evaluation of the Company designed to value the entire enterprise, nor had the Board ever previously considered selling the Company or consenting to a buy-out merger. Thus, the adequacy of a premium is indeterminate unless it is assessed in terms of other competent and sound valuation information that reflects the value of the particular business.

Despite the foregoing facts and circumstances, there was no call by the Board, either on September 20 or thereafter, for any valuation study or documentation of the $55 price per share as a measure of the fair value of the Company in a cash-out context. It is undisputed that the major asset of Trans Union was its cash flow. Yet, at no time did the Board call for a valuation study taking into account that highly significant element of the Company's assets.

We do not imply that an outside valuation study is essential to support an informed business judgment; nor do we state that fairness opinions by independent investment bankers are required as a matter of law. Often insiders familiar with the business of a going concern are in a better position than are outsiders to gather relevant information; and under appropriate circumstances, such directors may be fully protected in relying in good faith upon the valuation reports of their management. See 8 Del.C. § 141(e)....

Here, the record establishes that the Board did not request its Chief Financial Officer, Romans, to make any valuation study or review of the proposal to determine the adequacy of $55 per share for sale of the Company. On the record before us: The Board rested on Romans' elicited response that the $55 figure was within a "fair price range" within the context of a leveraged buy-out. No director sought any further information from Romans. No director asked him why he put $55 at the bottom of his range. No director asked Romans for any details as to his study, the reason why it had been undertaken or its depth. No director asked to see the study; and no director asked Romans whether Trans Union's finance department could do a fairness study within the remaining 36–hour period available under the Pritzker offer.

Had the Board, or any member, made an inquiry of Romans, he presumably would have responded as he testified: that his calculations were rough and preliminary; and, that the study was not designed to determine the fair value of the Company, but rather to assess the feasibility of a leveraged buy-out financed by the Company's projected cash flow, making certain assumptions as to the purchaser's borrowing needs. Romans would have presumably also informed the Board of his view, and the widespread view of Senior Management, that the timing of the offer was wrong and the offer inadequate.

The record also establishes that the Board accepted without scrutiny Van Gorkom's representation as to the fairness of the $55 price per share for sale of the Company—a subject that the Board had never previously considered. The Board thereby failed to discover that Van Gorkom had suggested the $55 price to Pritzker and, most crucially, that Van Gorkom had arrived at the $55 figure based on calculations designed solely to determine the feasibility of a leveraged buy-out. No questions were raised either as to the tax implications of a cash-out merger or how the price for the one million share option granted Pritzker was calculated.

We do not say that the Board of Directors was not entitled to give some credence to Van Gorkom's representation that $55 was an adequate or fair price. Under § 141(e), the directors were entitled to rely upon their chairman's opinion of value and adequacy, provided that such opinion was reached on a sound basis. Here, the issue is whether the directors informed themselves as to all information that was reasonably available to them. Had they done so, they would have learned of the source and derivation of the $55 price and could not reasonably have relied thereupon in good faith.

None of the directors, Management or outside, were investment bankers or financial analysts. Yet the Board did not consider recessing the meeting until a later hour that day (or requesting an extension of Pritzker's Sunday evening deadline) to give it time to elicit more information as to the sufficiency of the offer, either from inside Management (in particular Romans) or from Trans Union's own investment banker, Salomon Brothers, whose Chicago specialist in merger and acquisitions was known to the Board and familiar with Trans Union's affairs.

Thus, the record compels the conclusion that on September 20 the Board lacked valuation information adequate to reach an informed business judgment as to the fairness of $55 per share for sale of the Company.

(2)

This brings us to the post-September 20 "market test" upon which the defendants ultimately rely to confirm the reasonableness of their September 20 decision to accept the Pritzker proposal. In this connection, the directors present a two-part argument: (a) that by making a "market test" of Pritzker's $55 per share offer a condition of their September 20 decision to accept his offer, they cannot be found to have acted impulsively or in an uninformed manner on September 20; and (b) that the adequacy of the $17 premium for sale of the Company was conclusively established over the following 90 to 120 days by the most reliable evidence available—the marketplace. Thus, the defendants impliedly contend that the "market test" eliminated the need for the Board to perform any other form of fairness test either on September 20, or thereafter.

Again, the facts of record do not support the defendants' argument. There is no evidence: (a) that the Merger Agreement was effectively amended to give the Board freedom to put Trans Union up for auction sale to the highest bidder; or (b) that a public auction was in fact permitted to occur. The minutes of the Board meeting make no reference to any of this. Indeed, the record compels the conclusion that the directors had no rational basis for expecting that a market test was attainable, given the terms of the Agreement as executed during the evening of September 20. We rely upon the following facts which are essentially uncontradicted:

The Merger Agreement, specifically identified as that originally presented to the Board on September 20, has never been produced by the defendants, notwithstanding the plaintiffs' several demands for production before as well as during trial. No acceptable explanation of this failure to produce documents has been given to either the Trial Court or this Court. . . .

Van Gorkom states that the Agreement as submitted incorporated the ingredients for a market test by authorizing Trans Union to receive competing offers over the next 90–day period. However, he concedes that the Agreement barred Trans Union from actively soliciting such offers and from furnishing to interested parties any information about the Company other than that already in the public domain. Whether the original Agreement of September 20 went so far as to authorize Trans Union to receive competitive proposals is arguable. The defendants' unexplained failure to produce and identify the original Merger Agreement permits the logical inference that the instrument would not support their assertions in this regard. . . .

The defendant directors assert that they "insisted" upon including two amendments to the Agreement, thereby permitting a market test: (1) to give Trans Union the right to accept a better offer; and (2) to reserve to Trans Union the right to distribute proprietary information on the Company to alternative bidders. Yet, the defendants concede that they did not seek to amend the Agreement to permit Trans Union to solicit competing offers.

Several of Trans Union's outside directors resolutely maintained that the Agreement as submitted was approved on the understanding that, "if we got a better deal, we had a right to take it." Director Johnson so testified; but he then added, "And if they didn't put that in the agreement, then the management did not carry out the conclusion of the Board. And I just don't know whether they did or not." The only clause in the Agreement as finally executed to which the defendants can point as "keeping the door open" is the following underlined statement found in subparagraph (a) of section 2.03 of the Merger Agreement as executed:

> The Board of Directors shall recommend to the stockholders of Trans Union that they approve and adopt the Merger Agreement ("the stockholders' approval") and to use its best efforts to obtain the requisite votes therefor. *GL acknowledges that Trans Union directors may have a competing fiduciary obligation to the shareholders under certain circumstances.*

Clearly, this language on its face cannot be construed as incorporating either of the two "conditions" described above: either the right to accept a better offer or the right to distribute proprietary information to third parties. . . . No reference to either of the so-called "conditions" or of Trans Union's reserved right to test the market appears in any notes of the Board meeting or in the Board Resolution accepting the Pritzker offer or in the Minutes of the meeting itself. That evening, in the midst of a formal party which he hosted for the opening of the Chicago Lyric Opera, Van Gorkom executed the Merger Agreement without he or any other member of the Board having read the instruments.

The defendants attempt to downplay the significance of the prohibition against Trans Union's actively soliciting competing offers by arguing that the directors "understood that the entire financial community would know that Trans Union was for sale upon the announcement of the Pritzker offer, and anyone desiring to make a better offer was free to do so." Yet, the press release issued on September 22, with the authorization of the Board, stated that Trans Union had entered into "definitive agreements" with the Pritzkers; and the press release did not even disclose Trans Union's limited right to receive and accept higher offers. Accompanying this press release was a further public announcement that Pritzker had been granted an option to purchase at any time one million shares of Trans Union's capital stock at 75 cents above the then-current price per share.

Thus, notwithstanding what several of the outside directors later claimed to have "thought" occurred at the meeting, the record compels the conclusion that Trans Union's Board had no rational basis to conclude on September 20 or in the days immediately following, that the Board's acceptance of Pritzker's offer was conditioned on (1) a "market test" of the offer; and (2) the Board's right to withdraw from the Pritzker Agreement and accept any higher offer received before the shareholder meeting.

(3)

The directors' unfounded reliance on both the premium and the market test as the basis for accepting the Pritzker proposal undermines the defendants' remaining contention that the Board's collective experience and sophistication was a sufficient basis for finding that it reached its September 20 decision with informed, reasonable deliberation.[21] Compare Gimbel v. Signal Companies, Inc., Del.Ch., 316 A.2d 599 (1974), aff'd per curiam, Del.Supr., 316 A.2d 619 (1974). There, the Court of Chancery preliminarily enjoined a board's sale of stock of its wholly-owned subsidiary for an alleged grossly inadequate price. It did so based on a finding that the business judgment rule had been pierced for failure of management to give its board "the opportunity to make a reasonable and reasoned decision." 316 A.2d at 615. The Court there reached this result notwithstanding the board's sophistication and experience; the company's need of immediate cash; and the board's need to act promptly due to the impact of an energy crisis on the value of the underlying assets being sold—all of its subsidiary's oil and gas interests. The Court found those factors denoting competence to be outweighed by evidence of gross negligence; that management in effect sprang the deal on the board by negotiating the asset sale without informing the board; that the buyer intended to "force a quick decision" by the board; that the board meeting was called on only one-and-a-half days' notice; that its outside directors were not notified of the meeting's purpose; that during a meeting spanning "a couple of hours" a sale of assets worth $480 million was approved; and that the Board failed to obtain a *current* appraisal of

---

21. Trans Union's five "inside" directors had backgrounds in law and accounting, 116 years of collective employment by the Company and 68 years of combined experience on its Board. Trans Union's five "outside" directors included four chief executives of major corporations and an economist who was a former dean of a major school of business and chancellor of a university. The "outside" directors had 78 years of combined experience as chief executive officers of major corporations and 50 years of cumulative experience as directors of Trans Union. Thus, defendants argue that the Board was eminently qualified to reach an informed judgment on the proposed "sale" of Trans Union notwithstanding their lack of any advance notice of the proposal, the shortness of their deliberation, and their determination not to consult with their investment banker or to obtain a fairness opinion.

its oil and gas interests. The analogy of *Signal* to the case at bar is significant.

(4) ...

We conclude that Trans Union's Board was grossly negligent in that it failed to act with informed reasonable deliberation in agreeing to the Pritzker merger proposal on September 20; and we further conclude that the Trial Court erred as a matter of law in failing to address that question before determining whether the directors' later conduct was sufficient to cure its initial error. . . .

–B–

We now examine the Board's post-September 20 conduct for the purpose of determining first, whether it was informed and not grossly negligent; and second, if informed, whether it was sufficient to legally rectify and cure the Board's derelictions of September 20.[23]

(1)

First, as to the Board meeting of October 8. . . .

The public announcement of the Pritzker merger resulted in an "en masse" revolt of Trans Union's Senior Management. The head of Trans Union's tank car operations (its most profitable division) informed Van Gorkom that unless the merger were called off, fifteen key personnel would resign.

Instead of reconvening the Board, Van Gorkom again privately met with Pritzker, informed him of the developments, and sought his advice. Pritzker then made the following suggestions for overcoming Management's dissatisfaction: (1) that the Agreement be amended to permit Trans Union to solicit, as well as receive, higher offers; and (2) that the shareholder meeting be postponed from early January to February 10, 1981. In return, Pritzker asked Van Gorkom to obtain a commitment from Senior Management to remain at Trans Union for at least six months after the merger was consummated.

Van Gorkom then advised Senior Management that the Agreement would be amended to give Trans Union the right to solicit competing offers through January, 1981, if they would agree to remain with Trans Union. Senior Management was temporarily mollified; and Van Gorkom then called a special meeting of Trans Union's Board for October 8.

Thus, the primary purpose of the October 8 Board meeting was to amend the Merger Agreement, in a manner agreeable to Pritzker, to permit Trans Union to conduct a "market test." [24] Van Gorkom

23. As will be seen, we do not reach the second question.

24. As previously noted, the Board mistakenly thought that it had amended the

September 20 draft agreement to include a market test.

A secondary purpose of the October 8 meeting was to obtain the Board's approval

understood that the proposed amendments were intended to give the Company an unfettered "right to openly solicit offers down through January 31." Van Gorkom presumably so represented the amendments to Trans Union's Board members on October 8. In a brief session, the directors approved Van Gorkom's oral presentation of the substance of the proposed amendments, the terms of which were not reduced to writing until October 10. But rather than waiting to review the amendments, the Board again approved them sight unseen and adjourned, giving Van Gorkom authority to execute the papers when he received them.[25] . . .

The next day, October 9, and before the Agreement was amended, Pritzker moved swiftly to off-set the proposed market test amendment. First, Pritzker informed Trans Union that he had completed arrangements for financing its acquisition and that the parties were thereby mutually bound to a firm purchase and sale arrangement. Second, Pritzker announced the exercise of his option to purchase one million shares of Trans Union's treasury stock at $38 per share—75 cents above the current market price. Trans Union's Management responded the same day by issuing a press release announcing: (1) that all financing arrangements for Pritzker's acquisition of Trans Union had been completed; and (2) Pritzker's purchase of one million shares of Trans Union's treasury stock at $38 per share.

The next day, October 10, Pritzker delivered to Trans Union the proposed amendments to the September 20 Merger Agreement. Van Gorkom promptly proceeded to countersign all the instruments on behalf of Trans Union without reviewing the instruments to determine if they were consistent with the authority previously granted him by the Board. The amending documents were apparently not approved by Trans Union's Board until a much later date, December 2. The record does not affirmatively establish that Trans Union's directors ever read the October 10 amendments.[26]

The October 10 amendments to the Merger Agreement did authorize Trans Union to solicit competing offers, but the amendments had more far-reaching effects. The most significant change was in the definition of the third-party "offer" available to Trans Union as a possible basis for withdrawal from its Merger Agreement with Pritzker. Under the October 10 amendments, a better *offer*

for Trans Union to employ its investment advisor, Salomon Brothers, for the limited purpose of assisting Management in the solicitation of other offers. Neither Management nor the Board then or thereafter requested Salomon Brothers to submit its opinion as to the fairness of Pritzker's $55 cash-out merger proposal or to value Trans Union as an entity. . . .

25. We do not suggest that a board must read *in haec verba* every contract or legal document which it approves, but if it is to successfully absolve itself from charges of the type made here, there must be some credible contemporary evidence demonstrating that the directors knew what they were doing, and ensured that their purported action was given effect. That is the consistent failure which cast this Board upon its unredeemable course.

26. There is no evidence of record that Trans Union's directors ever raised any objections, procedural or substantive, to the October 10 amendments or that any of them, including Van Gorkom, understood the opposite result of their intended effect—until it was too late.

was no longer sufficient to permit Trans Union's withdrawal. Trans Union was now permitted to terminate the Pritzker Agreement and abandon the merger only if, prior to February 10, 1981, Trans Union had either consummated a merger (or sale of assets) with a third party or had entered into a "definitive" merger agreement more favorable than Pritzker's and for a greater consideration— subject only to stockholder approval. Further, the "extension" of the market test period to February 10, 1981 was circumscribed by other amendments which required Trans Union to file its preliminary proxy statement on the Pritzker merger proposal by December 5, 1980 and use its best efforts to mail the statement to its shareholders by January 5, 1981. Thus, the market test period was effectively reduced, not extended. . . .

In our view, the record compels the conclusion that the directors' conduct on October 8 exhibited the same deficiencies as did their conduct on September 20. The Board permitted its Merger Agreement with Pritzker to be amended in a manner it had neither authorized nor intended. . . .

We conclude that the Board acted in a grossly negligent manner on October 8; and that Van Gorkom's representations on which the Board based its actions do not constitute "reports" under § 141(e) on which the directors could reasonably have relied. Further, the amended Merger Agreement imposed on Trans Union's acceptance of a third party offer conditions more onerous than those imposed on Trans Union's acceptance of Pritzker's offer on September 20. After October 10, Trans Union could accept from a third party a better offer only if it were incorporated in a definitive agreement between the parties, and not conditioned on financing or on any other contingency.

The October 9 press release, coupled with the October 10 amendments, had the clear effect of locking Trans Union's Board into the Pritzker Agreement. Pritzker had thereby foreclosed Trans Union's Board from negotiating any better "definitive" agreement over the remaining eight weeks before Trans Union was required to clear the Proxy Statement submitting the Pritzker proposal to its shareholders.

(2)

Next, as to the "curative" effects of the Board's post-September 20 conduct, we review in more detail the reaction of Van Gorkom to the KKR proposal and the results of the Board-sponsored "market test."

The KKR proposal was the first and only offer received subsequent to the Pritzker Merger Agreement. The offer resulted primarily from the efforts of Romans and other senior officers to propose an alternative to Pritzker's acquisition of Trans Union. In late September, Romans' group contacted KKR about the possibility of a leveraged buy-out by all members of Management, except Van Gorkom. By early October, Henry R. Kravis of KKR gave Romans written notice of KKR's "interest in making an offer to purchase 100%" of Trans Union's common stock.

Thereafter, and until early December, Romans' group worked with KKR to develop a proposal. It did so with Van Gorkom's knowledge and apparently grudging consent. On December 2, Kravis and Romans hand-delivered to Van Gorkom a formal letter-offer to purchase all of Trans Union's assets and to assume all of its liabilities for an aggregate cash consideration equivalent to $60 per share. The offer was contingent upon completing equity and bank financing of $650 million, which Kravis represented as 80% complete. . . .

Van Gorkom's reaction to the KKR proposal was completely negative; he did not view the offer as being firm because of its financing condition. It was pointed out, to no avail, that Pritzker's offer had not only been similarly conditioned, but accepted on an expedited basis. Van Gorkom refused Kravis' request that Trans Union issue a press release announcing KKR's offer, on the ground that it might "chill" any other offer.[27] . . .

Within a matter of hours and shortly before the scheduled Board meeting, Kravis withdrew his letter-offer. He gave as his reason a sudden decision by the Chief Officer of Trans Union's rail car leasing operation to withdraw from the KKR purchasing group. Van Gorkom had spoken to that officer about his participation in the KKR proposal immediately after his meeting with Romans and Kravis. However, Van Gorkom denied any responsibility for the officer's change of mind. . . .

GE Credit Corporation's interest in Trans Union did not develop until November; and it made no written proposal until mid-January. Even then, its proposal was not in the form of an offer. Had there been time to do so, GE Credit was prepared to offer between $2 and $5 per share above the $55 per share price which Pritzker offered. But GE Credit needed an additional 60 to 90 days; and it was unwilling to make a formal offer without a concession from Pritzker extending the February 10 "deadline" for Trans Union's stockholder meeting. As previously stated, Pritzker refused to grant such extension. . . .

In the absence of any explicit finding by the Trial Court as to the reasonableness of Trans Union's directors' reliance on a market test and its feasibility, we may make our own findings based on the record. Our review of the record compels a finding that confirmation of the appropriateness of the Pritzker offer by an unfettered or free market test was virtually meaningless in the face of the terms and time limitations of Trans Union's Merger Agreement with Pritzker as amended October 10, 1980.

. . . Under [Del.] § 251(b), the Board had but two options: (1) to proceed with the merger and the stockholder meeting, with the

---

27. This was inconsistent with Van Gorkom's espousal of the September 22 press release following Trans Union's acceptance of Pritzker's proposal. Van Gorkom had then justified a press release as encouraging rather than chilling later offers.

Board's recommendation of approval; *or* (2) to rescind its agreement with Pritzker, withdraw its approval of the merger, and notify its stockholders that the proposed shareholder meeting was cancelled. There is no evidence that the Board gave any consideration to these, its only legally viable alternative courses of action....

... [W]e hold that the defendants' post-September conduct did not cure the deficiencies of their September 20 conduct; and that, accordingly, the Trial Court erred in according to the defendants the benefits of the business judgment rule....

V.

The defendants ultimately rely on the stockholder vote of February 10 for exoneration. The defendants contend that the stockholders' "overwhelming" vote approving the Pritzker Merger Agreement had the legal effect of curing any failure of the Board to reach an informed business judgment in its approval of the merger....

[The court rejected this defense on the ground that Trans Union's stockholders were not fully informed of all facts material to their vote on the Pritzker Merger, and that the Trial Court's ruling to the contrary was clearly erroneous.] ...

VI.

... We hold, therefore, that the Trial Court committed reversible error in applying the business judgment rule in favor of the director defendants in this case.

On remand, the Court of Chancery shall conduct an evidentiary hearing to determine the fair value of the shares represented by the plaintiffs' class, based on the intrinsic value of Trans Union on September 20, 1980. Such valuation shall be made in accordance with Weinberger v. UOP, Inc., supra.... Thereafter, an award of damages may be entered to the extent that the fair value of Trans Union exceeds $55 per share.

Reversed and Remanded for proceedings consistent herewith.

McNEILLY, Justice, dissenting ...

Following the October 8 board meeting of Trans Union, the investment banking firm of Salomon Brothers was retained by the corporation to search for better offers than that of the Pritzkers, Salomon Brothers being charged with the responsibility of doing "whatever possible to see if there is a superior bid in the marketplace over a bid that is on the table for Trans Union". In undertaking such project, it was agreed that Salomon Brothers would be paid the amount of $500,000 to cover its expenses as well as a fee equal to ⅜ths of 1% of the aggregate fair market value of the consideration to be received by the company in the case of a merger or the like, which meant that in the event Salomon Brothers should find a buyer willing to pay a price of $56.00 a share instead of

$55.00, such firm would receive a fee of roughly $2,650,000 plus disbursements.

As the first step in proceeding to carry out its commitment, Salomon Brothers had a brochure prepared, which set forth Trans Union's financial history, described the company's business in detail and set forth Trans Union's operating and financial projections. Salomon Brothers also prepared a list of over 150 companies which it believed might be suitable merger partners, and while four of such companies, namely, General Electric, Borg–Warner, Bendix, and Genstar, Ltd. showed some interest in such a merger, none made a firm proposal to Trans Union and only General Electric showed a sustained interest. As matters transpired, no firm offer which bettered the Pritzker offer of $55 per share was ever made. . . .

I have no quarrel with the majority's analysis of the business judgment rule. It is the application of that rule to these facts which is wrong. An overview of the entire record, rather than the limited view of bits and pieces which the majority has exploded like popcorn, convinces me that the directors made an informed business judgment which was buttressed by their test of the market.

At the time of the September 20 meeting the 10 members of Trans Union's Board of Directors were highly qualified and well informed about the affairs and prospects of Trans Union. These directors were acutely aware of the historical problems facing Trans Union which were caused by the tax laws. They had discussed these problems *ad nauseam.* In fact, within two months of the September 20 meeting the board had reviewed and discussed an outside study of the company done by The Boston Consulting Group and an internal five year forecast prepared by management. At the September 20 meeting Van Gorkom presented the Pritzker offer, and the board then heard from James Brennan, the company's counsel in this matter, who discussed the legal documents. Following this, the Board directed that certain changes be made in the merger documents. These changes made it clear that the Board was free to accept a better offer than Pritzker's if one was made. The above facts reveal that the Board did not act in a grossly negligent manner in informing themselves of the relevant and available facts before passing on the merger. To the contrary, this record reveals that the directors acted with the utmost care in informing themselves of the relevant and available facts before passing on the merger. . . .

CHRISTIE, Justice, dissenting:

I respectfully dissent.

Considering the standard and scope of our review under Levitt v. Bouvier, Del.Supr., 287 A.2d 671, 673 (1972), I believe that the record taken as a whole supports a conclusion that the actions of the defendants are protected by the business judgment rule. Aronson v. Lewis, Del.Supr., 473 A.2d 805, 812 (1984); Pogostin v. Rice, Del.Supr., 480 A.2d 619, 627 (1984)....

———

It is reported that after the decision of the Delaware Supreme Court, an agreement was reached to settle *Van Gorkom* by the payment of $23.5 million to the plaintiff class. Of that amount, $10 million, the policy limit, was provided by Trans Union's directors' and officers' liability-insurance carrier. Nearly all of the $13.5 million balance was paid by the Pritzker group on behalf of the Trans Union defendant directors, although the Pritzker group was not a defendant. See Manning, Reflections and Practical Tips on Life in the Boardroom After *Van Gorkom,* 41 Bus.Law. 1 (1985).

———

NOTE ON SUBSTANCE AND PROCESS IN THE DUTY OF CARE

In many areas of law, a distinction is drawn between substance and process. The duty of care may be understood in that way too. In effect, the business judgment rule gives wide latitude to a substantive decision of a director or senior executive if the *process* elements of the duty of care are satisfied. Under this distinction, the process elements of the duty of care, which involve such matters as preparing to make a decision, general monitoring, and following up suspicious circumstances, are governed by a standard of reasonability. However, if the process by which a decision was made satisfies the reasonability standard, the substantive decision itself will be reviewed only under the much looser standard of rationality.

———

SECTION 4. LIMITS ON LIABILITY; DIRECTORS' AND OFFICERS' LIABILITY INSURANCE

———

In assessing the duties of directors and officers to act with care and lawfully, account must be taken of three elements that may serve to reduce or eliminate civil liability for breach of those duties: direct limits of liability; insurance; and indemnification. The first two elements are addressed in this Section. Indemnification is addressed in Chapter 10, Section 10.

———

(a) LIMITS ON LIABILITY

———

VIRGINIA CORPORATIONS CODE § 13.1–690

[See Statutory Supplement]

———

OHIO GEN. CORP. LAW § 1701.59

[See Statutory Supplement]

———

DEL. GEN. CORP. LAW § 102(b)(7)

[See Statutory Supplement]

———

REV. MODEL BUSINESS CORP. ACT § 2.02(b)(4)

[See Statutory Supplement]

———

(b) DIRECTORS' AND OFFICERS' LIABILITY INSURANCE

———

FORM OF DIRECTORS' AND OFFICERS' LIABILITY INSURANCE

[See Statutory Supplement]

———

Chapter VIII

THE DUTY OF LOYALTY

SECTION 1. SELF–INTERESTED TRANSACTIONS

MARSH, ARE DIRECTORS TRUSTEES?—CONFLICTS OF INTEREST AND CORPORATE MORALITY

22 Bus.Law. 35, 36–43 (1966).

a. *Prohibition.*

In 1880 it could have been stated with confidence that in the United States the general rule was that any contract between a director and his corporation was voidable at the instance of the corporation or its shareholders, without regard to the fairness or unfairness of the transaction. This rule was stated in powerful terms by a number of highly regarded courts and judges in cases which arose generally out of the railroad frauds of the 1860's and 1870's.

In *Wardell v. Union Pacific R.R. Co.*[4] Mr. Justice Field stated that:

> It is among the rudiments of the law that the same person cannot act for himself and at the same time, with respect to the same matter, as agent for another, whose interests are conflicting.... The two positions impose different obligations, and their union would at once raise a conflict between interest and duty; and 'Constituted as humanity is, in the majority of cases duty would be overborne in the struggle.' ... Hence, all arrangements by directors of a railroad company, to secure an undue advantage to themselves at its expense, by the formation of a new company as an auxiliary to the original one, with an understanding that they or some of them shall take stock in it, and then, that valuable contracts shall be given to it, in the profits of which they, as stockholders in the new company, are to share, are so many unlawful devices to enrich themselves to the detriment of the stockholders and creditors of the original company, and will be condemned whenever properly brought before the courts for consideration.[5]

---

4. 103 U.S. 651 (1880). **5.** 103 U.S. at 658.

437

Under this rule it mattered not the slightest that there was a majority of so-called disinterested directors who approved the contract. The courts stated that the corporation was entitled to the unprejudiced judgment and advice of all of its directors and therefore it did no good to say that the interested director did not participate in the making of the contract on behalf of the corporation. "... the very words in which he asserts his right declare his wrong; he ought to have participated...."[6] Furthermore, the courts said that it was impossible to measure the influence which one director might have over his associates, even though ostensibly abstaining from participation in the discussion or vote. "... a corporation, in order to defeat a contract entered into by directors, in which one or more of them had a private interest, is not bound to show that the influence of the director or directors having the private interest determined the action of the board. The law cannot accurately measure the influence of a trustee with his associates, nor will it enter into the inquiry...."[7]

Perhaps the strongest reason for this inflexibility of the law was given by the Maryland Supreme Court which stated that, when a contract is made with even one of the directors, "the remaining directors are placed in the embarrassing and invidious position of having to pass upon, scrutinize and check the transactions and accounts of one of their *own body, with* whom they are associated on terms of equality in the general management of all the affairs of the corporation."[8] Or, as Justice Davies of the New York Supreme Court expressed the same thought: "The moment the directors permit one or more of their number to deal with the property of the stockholders, they surrender their own independence and self control."[9]

This rule applied not only to individual contracts with directors, but also to the situation of interlocking directorates where even a minority of the boards were common to the two contracting corporations. Not only that, it was also applied to the situation where one corporation owned a majority of the stock of another and appointed its directors, even though they might not be the same men as sat on the board of the parent corporation....

This principle, absolutely inhibiting contracts between a corporation and its directors or any of them, appeared to be impregnable in 1880. It was stated in ringing terms by virtually every decided case, with arguments which seemed irrefutable, and it was sanctioned by age. As Justice Davies stated:

> To hold otherwise, would be to overturn principles of equity which have been regarded as well settled since the days of Lord Keeper Bridgman, in the 22nd of Charles Second, to

6. Stewart v. Lehigh Valley R.R. Co., 38 N.J.Law 505, at 523 (Ct.Err. & App.1875).

7. Munson v. Syracuse, G. & C. Ry. Co., 103 N.Y. 58, at 74, 8 N.E. 355, at 358 (1886).

8. Cumberland Coal and Iron Co. v. Parish, 42 Md. 598, at 606 (1875).

9. Cumberland Coal and Iron Co. v. Sherman, 30 Barb. 553, at 573 (N.Y.Sup.Ct. 1859).

the present time—principles enunciated and enforced by Hard-wicke, Thurlow, Loughborough, Eldon, Cranworth, Story and Kent, and which the highest courts in our country have declared to be founded on immutable truth and justice, and to stand upon our great moral obligation to refrain from placing ourselves in relations which excite a conflict between self interest and integrity.

Thirty years later this principle was dead.

b.   *Approval by a disinterested majority of the board.*

It could have been stated with reasonable confidence in 1910 that the general rule was that a contract between a director and his corporation was valid if it was approved by a disinterested majority of his fellow directors and was not found to be unfair or fraudulent by the court if challenged; but that a contract in which a majority of the board was interested was voidable at the instance of the corporation or its shareholders without regard to any question of fairness.

One searches in vain in the decided cases for a reasoned defense of this change in legal philosophy, or for the slightest attempt to refute the powerful arguments which had been made in support of the previous rule. Did the courts discover in the last quarter of the Nineteenth Century that greed was no longer a factor in human conduct? If so, they did not share the basis of this discovery with the public; nor did they humbly admit their error when confronted with the next wave of corporate frauds arising out of the era of the formation of the "trusts" during the 1890's and early 1900's. . . .

The only explanation which seems to have been given for this change in position was the technical one that a trustee, while forbidden to deal with himself in connection with the trust property, could deal directly with the cestui que trust if he made full disclosure and took no unfair advantage; and that the case of a director who abstained from representing the corporation but dealt in his personal capacity with a majority of disinterested directors was properly analogized to a trustee dealing with the cestui que trust. As the Texas court said: [19]

> . . . we think it is not true that one who holds the position of director is incapable, under all circumstances, of divesting himself of his representative character in a particular transaction, and dealing with the corporation through others competent to represent it, as other trustees may deal directly with the beneficiaries. . . . [T]he company is represented by those who alone can act for it, and, if they are disinterested, he can, we think, deal with them as any other trustee can deal with the cestui que trust, if he makes a full disclosure of all facts known to him about the subject, takes no advantage of his position,

19. Tennison v. Patton, 95 Tex. 284, at 292–93, 67 S.W. 92, at 95 (1902).

deals honestly and openly, and concludes a contract fair and beneficial to the company.

But in no case is there any discussion or attempted refutation of the reasons previously given by the courts as to why it is impossible, in such a situation, for any director to be disinterested. Some courts seem simply to admit that the practice has grown too widespread for them to cope with. In *South Side Trust Co. v. Washington Tin Plate Co.* the Supreme Court of Pennsylvania said: [20] "The interests of corporations are sometimes so interwoven that it is desirable to have joint representatives in their respective managements, and at any rate it is a not uncommon and [therefore?] not unlawful practice." . . .

Under the rule that a disinterested majority of the directors must approve a transaction with one of their number, the question arose whether this meant a disinterested quorum (i.e., normally a majority of the whole board) or merely a disinterested majority of a quorum, so that the interested director or directors could be counted to make up the quorum. Virtually all of the cases held that the interested director could not be counted for quorum purposes. As the California court said, the interested director for this purpose was "as much a stranger to the board as if he had never been elected a director. . . ." [28]

c. *Judicial review of the fairness of the transaction.*

By 1960 it could be said with some assurance that the general rule was that no transaction of a corporation with any or all of its directors was automatically voidable at the suit of a shareholder, whether there was a disinterested majority of the board or not; but that the courts would review such a contract and subject it to rigid and careful scrutiny, and would invalidate the contract if it was found to be unfair to the corporation. . . .

LEWIS v. S.L. & E., INC.

United States Court of Appeals, Second Circuit, 1980.
629 F.2d 764.

Before TIMBERS and KEARSE, Circuit Judges, and LASKER, District Judge.

KEARSE, Circuit Judge:

This case arises out of an intra-family dispute over the management of two closely-held affiliated corporations. Plaintiff Donald E. Lewis ("Donald"), a shareholder of S.L. & E., Inc. ("SLE"), appeals from judgments entered against him in the United States District

---

20. 252 Pa. 237 at 241, 97 A. 450 at 451 (1916).

28. Curtis v. Salmon River Hydraulic Gold–Mining & Dutch Co., . . . 10 Cal. at 349, 62 P. at 554.

Court for the Western District of New York, Harold P. Burke, Judge, after a bench trial of his derivative claim against directors of SLE, and of a claim asserted against him by the other corporation, Lewis General Tires, Inc. ("LGT"), which intervened in the suit.   The defendants Alan E. Lewis ("Alan"), Leon E. Lewis, Jr. ("Leon, Jr."), and Richard E. Lewis ("Richard"), are the brothers of Donald; they were, at pertinent times herein, directors of SLE and officers, directors and shareholders of LGT.   Donald charged that his brothers had wasted the assets of SLE by causing SLE to lease business premises to LGT from 1966 to 1972 at an unreasonably low rental. LGT was permitted to intervene in the action, and filed a complaint seeking specific performance of an agreement by Donald to sell his SLE stock to LGT in 1972.   The district court held that Donald had failed to prove waste by the defendant directors, and entered judgment in their favor.   The court also awarded attorneys' fees to the defendant directors and to SLE, and granted LGT specific performance of Donald's agreement to sell his SLE stock.

On appeal, Donald argues that the district court improperly allocated to him the burden of proving his claims of waste, and that since defendants failed to prove that the transactions in question were fair and reasonable, he was entitled to judgment.   Donald also argues that the awards of attorneys' fees were improper.   We agree with each of these contentions, and therefore reverse and remand.

I

For many years Leon Lewis, Sr., the father of Donald and the defendant directors, was the principal shareholder of SLE and LGT. LGT, formed in 1933, operated a tire dealership in Rochester, New York.   SLE, formed in 1943, owned the land and complex of buildings at 260 East Avenue in Rochester.   This property was SLE's only significant asset.   Prior to 1956 LGT occupied SLE's premises without benefit of a lease; the rent paid was initially $200 per month, and had increased over the years to $800 per month by 1956, when additional parcels were added.   On February 28, 1956, SLE granted LGT a 10–year lease on the newly expanded property ("the Property"), for a rent of $1200 per month, or $14,400 per year.   Under the terms of the lease, SLE was responsible for payment of real estate taxes on the Property, while all other current expenses were to be borne by the tenant, LGT.[1]

In 1962, Leon Lewis, Sr., transferred his SLE stock, 90 shares in all, to his six children (defendants Richard, Alan and Leon, Jr., plaintiff Donald, and two daughters, Margaret and Carol), giving 15 shares to each.[2]   At that time Richard, Alan and Leon, Jr., were already shareholders, officers and directors of LGT.   Contemporane-

---

1. It appears that SLE was also responsible for payments due on a mortgage on the Property.   In addition, LGT charged SLE for the costs of certain capital improvements, such as the major structural repairs to the principal building's facade, carried out in 1969.

2. SLE had 150 shares outstanding, and each child thus received a ten percent interest.   At the same time LGT purchased the remaining 60 outstanding shares from the elder Lewis's business partner, Henry Etsberger.

ously with their receipt of SLE stock, all six of the children entered into a "shareholders' agreement" with LGT, under which each child who was not a shareholder of LGT on June 1, 1972 would be required to sell his or her SLE shares to LGT, within 30 days of that date, at a price equal to the book value of the SLE stock as of June 1, 1972.[3]

LGT's lease on the SLE property expired on February 28, 1966. At that time the directors of SLE were Richard, Alan, Leon, Jr., Leon, Sr., and Henry Etsberger; these five were also the directors of LGT. In 1966 Alan owned 44% of LGT, Richard owned 30%, Leon, Jr., owned 19%, and Leon, Sr., owned 7%. From 1967 to 1972 Richard owned 61% of LGT and Leon, Jr., owned the remaining 39%. When the lease expired in 1966, no new lease was entered into. LGT nonetheless continued to occupy the property and to pay SLE at the old rate, $14,400 per year. According to the defendants' testimony at trial, there was never any thought or discussion among the SLE directors of entering into a new lease or of increasing the rent. Richard testified: "We never gave consideration to a new lease." From all that appears, the defendant directors viewed SLE as existing purely for the benefit of LGT. Richard testified, for example, that although real estate taxes rose sharply during the period 1966–1971, from approximately $7,800 to more than $11,000, to be paid by SLE out of its constant $14,400 rental income, raising the rent was never mentioned. He testified that SLE was "only a shell to protect the operating company [LGT]." When this suit was commenced there had not been a formal meeting of either the shareholders or the directors of SLE since 1962. Richard, Alan and Leon, Jr., had largely ignored SLE's separate corporate existence[4] and disregarded the fact that SLE had shareholders who were not shareholders of LGT and who therefore could not profit from actions that used SLE solely for the benefit of LGT.

Neither Donald nor his sisters ever owned LGT stock. As the June 1972 date approached for the required sale of their SLE stock to LGT, Donald apparently came to believe that SLE's book value was lower than it should have been. He sought SLE financial information from Richard, who had been president of SLE since

3. The agreement specified procedures by which the book value, and hence the price of the shares, would be determined.

4. For example, Richard's testimony includes the following statements:

Q Mr. Lewis, you have always looked at these two corporations as being one and the same, haven't you, Lewis General Tires and S.L. & E.?

A Yes.

* * *

I never really got into S.L. & E. at all. (Tr. 6/21/78, at 972–73.)

* * *

I don't think I ever looked at an operating statement of S.L. & E. seriously. (*Id.* at 991.)

* * *

I had very little to do with S.L. & E. (Tr. 7/28/78, at 80.)

Alan testified that at no time after 1964 did he participate in any discussions of any increase in rent for SLE. (*Id.* at 160, 164.)

And Leon, Jr., testified, "I didn't have anything to do with running S.L. & E....." (*Id.* at 230.)

1967.[5]   Richard refused to provide information.   Donald therefore refused to sell his SLE shares in 1972,[6] and commenced this shareholders' derivative action in the district court in August 1973, basing jurisdiction on diversity of citizenship.[7]   The sole claim raised in the complaint was that the defendant directors[8] had wasted the assets of SLE by "grossly undercharging" LGT for the latter's occupancy and use of the Property.   Although the complaint charged such mismanagement for the period 1962 to 1973, plaintiff subsequently limited this claim to the period between February 28, 1966, the date on which the lease expired,[9] and June 1, 1972, the date contractually set for valuation of the SLE shares which plaintiff had agreed to sell to LGT.   LGT intervened and demanded specific performance of Donald's agreement to sell his SLE stock.   Donald did not contest his ultimate obligation to sell, but took the position that since the book value of the shares would be increased if he prevailed on his derivative claim, specific performance should be granted only after adjudication of that claim.

There ensured an eight-day bench trial, at which plaintiff sought to prove, by the testimony of several expert witnesses, that the fair rental value of the Property was greater than the $14,400 per year that SLE had been paid by LGT.   Defendants sought to show that the rental paid was reasonable, by offering evidence concerning the financial straits of LGT, the cost to LGT of operating the Property, the general economic decline of the East Avenue neighborhood, and rentals paid on two other properties in that neighborhood.   LGT presented expert testimony that the value of plaintiff's stock as of June 1972, assuming a successful defense of the derivative claims, was $15,650.

The district court subsequently filed lengthy and detailed findings of fact and conclusions of law.   Many of the court's findings went to the validity and probative value of the testimony given by plaintiff's expert witnesses, and the court ultimately declined to credit that testimony.   On this basis, the court held that Donald had failed to establish the rental value of the Property during the period at issue, and that defendants were therefore entitled to judgment on the derivative claims.   Implicit in the district court's ruling, granting judgment for defendants upon plaintiff's failure to prove waste, was a determination that plaintiff bore the burden of proof on that

---

5. It does not appear that SLE paid salaries to any of its officers or directors.

6. Donald's sisters Carol and Margaret sold their SLE shares to LGT in 1972 and 1973 respectively.   Alan, who had sold his LGT stock in 1967, sold his SLE stock to LGT in 1972.

7. When suit was commenced, plaintiff was a citizen of Ohio, Alan was a citizen of Florida and all of the other individual defendants were citizens of New York.   SLE is a New York corporation and has its principal place of business in New York.

8. Leon E. Lewis, Sr., also was originally named as a defendant in this action. When he died in 1975 his executor was substituted as a defendant; subsequently the parties stipulated to dismissal of the executor.   Etsberger died in about 1969, and his estate was not named as a defendant.

9. Donald was not a shareholder of SLE in 1956 when the lease was entered into and hence had no standing to challenge its terms.   BCL § 626(b); *Bernstein v. Polo Fashions, Inc.*, 55 A.D.2d 530, 389 N.Y.S.2d 368 (1st Dep't 1976).

issue. The court also ruled that LGT was entitled to specific performance of Donald's agreement to sell his SLE stock, and that Donald was not entitled to recover attorneys' fees from SLE, but that SLE and the individual defendants were entitled to attorneys' fees from Donald. This appeal followed.

II

Turning first to the question of burden of proof, we conclude that the district court erred in placing upon plaintiff the burden of proving waste. Because the directors of SLE were also officers, directors and/or shareholders of LGT, the burden was on the defendant directors to demonstrate that the transactions between SLE and LGT were fair and reasonable. New York Business Corporation Law ("BCL") § 713(b) (McKinney Supp.1979) (eff. September 1, 1971); BCL § 713(a)(3) (McKinney 1963) (repealed as of September 1, 1971); *see Cohen v. Ayers,* 596 F.2d 733, 739–40 (7th Cir.1979) (construing current BCL § 713); *Remillard Brick Co. v. Remillard–Dandini Co.,* 109 Cal.App.2d 405, 241 P.2d 66, 75 (1952) (construing California Corporations Code § 820, upon which the prior BCL § 713 was patterned).

Under normal circumstances the directors of a corporation may determine, in the exercise of their business judgment, what contracts the corporation will enter into and what consideration is adequate, without review of the merits of their decisions by the courts. The business judgment rule places a heavy burden on shareholders who would attack corporate transactions. *Galef v. Alexander,* 615 F.2d 51, 57–58 (2d Cir.1980); *Auerbach v. Bennett,* 47 N.Y.2d 619, 629, 419 N.Y.S.2d 920, 926, 393 N.E.2d 994, 1000 (1979); 3A Fletcher, *Cyclopedia of the Law of Private Corporations* § 1039 (perm. ed. 1975). But the business judgment rule presupposes that the directors have no conflict of interest. When a shareholder attacks a transaction in which the directors have an interest other than as directors of the corporation, the directors may not escape review of the merits of the transaction. At common law such a transaction was voidable unless shown by its proponent to be fair, and reasonable to the corporation.[11] BCL § 713, in both its current and its prior versions, carries forward this common law principle, and provides special rules for scrutiny of a transaction between the corporation and an entity in which its directors are directors or officers or have a substantial financial interest.

The current version of § 713,[12] which became effective on September 1, 1971, and governs at least so much of the dealing

---

11. *E.g., Geddes v. Anaconda Copper Co.,* 254 U.S. 590, 599 (1921); *Sage v. Culver,* 147 N.Y. 241, 41 N.E. 513 (1895); *Kaminsky v. Kahn,* 23 App.Div.2d 231, 240, 259 N.Y.S.2d 716, 725 (1st Dep't 1965); *Tomarkin v. Vitron Research Corp.,* 12 App. Div.2d 496, 206 N.Y.S.2d 869 (2d Dep't 1960). *See also* 3 Fletcher, *supra* § 921.

12. BCL § 713 (McKinney Supp.1979) provides in pertinent part:

(a) No contract or other transaction between a corporation and one or more of its directors, or between a corporation and any other corporation, firm, association or other entity in which one or more of its directors are directors or officers, or

between SLE and LGT as occurred after that date, expressly provides that a contract between a corporation and an entity in which its directors are interested may be set aside unless the proponent of the contract "shall establish affirmatively that the contract or transaction was fair and reasonable as to the corporation at the time it was approved by the board...." § 713(b). Thus when the transaction is challenged in a derivative action against the interested directors, they have the burden of proving that the transaction was fair and reasonable to the corporation. *Cohen v. Ayers, supra.*

The same was true under the predecessor to § 713(b), former § 713(a)(3), which was in effect prior to September 1, 1971.[13] Section 713(a)(3) was not explicit as to the burden of proof, but simply stated that a transaction with interested directors would not be voidable "If the contract or transaction is fair and reasonable as to the corporation at the time it is approved by the board ..." The

have a substantial financial interest, shall be either void or voidable for this reason alone or by reason alone that such director or directors are present at the meeting of the board, or of a committee thereof, which approves such contract or transaction, or that his or their votes are counted for such purpose:

(1) If the material facts as to such director's interest in such contract or transaction and as to any such common directorship, officership or financial interest are disclosed in good faith or known to the board or committee, and the board or committee approves such contract or transaction by a vote sufficient for such purpose without counting the vote of such interested director or, if the votes of the disinterested directors are insufficient to constitute an act of the board as defined in section 708 (Action by the board), by unanimous vote of the disinterested directors; or

(2) If the material facts as to such director's interest in such contract or transaction and as to any such common directorship, officership or financial interest are disclosed in good faith or known to the shareholders entitled to vote thereon, and such contract or transaction is approved by vote of such shareholders.

(b) If such good faith disclosure of the material facts as to the director's interest in the contract or transaction and as to any such common directorship, officership or financial interest is made to the directors or shareholders, or known to the board or committee or shareholders approving such contract or transaction, as provided in paragraph (a), the contract or transaction may not be avoided by the corporation for the reasons set forth in paragraph (a). If there was no such disclosure or knowledge, or if the vote of such interested director was necessary for

the approval of such contract or transaction at a meeting of the board or committee at which it was approved, the corporation may avoid the contract or transaction unless the party or parties thereto shall establish affirmatively that the contract or transaction was fair and reasonable as to the corporation at the time it was approved by the board, a committee or the shareholders.

13. BCL § 713 (McKinney 1963) (repealed) provided in pertinent part:

(a) No contract or other transaction between a corporation and one or more of its directors, or between a corporation and any other corporation, firm, association or other entity in which one or more of its directors are directors or officers, or are financially interested, shall be either void or voidable for this reason alone or by reason alone that such director or directors are present at the meeting of the board, or of a committee thereof, which approves such contract or transaction, or that his or their votes are counted for such purpose:

(1) If the fact of such common directorship, officership or financial interest is disclosed or known to the board or committee, and the board or committee approves such contract or transaction by a vote sufficient for such purpose without counting the vote or votes of such interested director or directors;

(2) If such common directorship, officership or financial interest is disclosed or known to the shareholders entitled to vote thereon, and such contract or transaction is approved by vote of the shareholders; or

(3) If the contract or transaction is fair and reasonable as to the corporation at

consensus among the commentators was that § 713(a)(3) carried
forward the common law rule, which placed the burden of proof as
to fairness on the interested directors. *E.g.,* Hoffman, The Status of
Shareholders and Directors Under New York's Business Corporation
Law: A Comparative View, 11 Buff.L.Rev. 496, 566 (1962); Note,
"Interested Director's" Contracts—Section 713 of the New York
Business Corporation Law and the "Fairness" Test, 41 Fordham
L.Rev. 639, 648–49 (1973); *see also* Note, The Status of the Fairness
Test Under Section 713 of the New York Business Corporation Law,
76 Colum.L.Rev. 1156, 1167–74 (1976) (discussing legislative histo-
ry). We agree with this construction. *Cf. Remillard Brick Co. v.
Remillard–Dandini Co., supra* (burden of proof allocated to inter-
ested directors under California Corporations Code § 820, upon
which § 713(a)(3) was modeled).

During the entire period 1966–1972, Richard, Alan and Leon,
Jr., were directors of both SLE and LGT;[14] there were no SLE
directors who were not also directors of LGT. Richard, Alan and
Leon, Jr., were all shareholders of LGT in 1966, and from 1967 to
1972 Richard and Leon, Jr., were the sole shareholders of LGT.
Under BCL § 713, therefore, Richard, Alan and Leon, Jr., had the
burden of proving that $14,400 was a fair and reasonable annual
rent for the SLE property for the period February 28, 1966 through
June 1, 1972.

Our review of the record convinces us that defendants failed to
carry their burden. At trial, there was no direct testimony as to
what would have been a fair rental during the relevant period, *i.e.,*
1966 to 1972, and the evidence that was introduced fell far short of
establishing that $14,400 was a fair annual rental value for those
years.

Quite clearly Richard, Alan and Leon, Jr., had made no effort to
determine contemporaneously what rental would be fair during the
years 1966–1972. Their view was that the rent should simply cover
expenses and that SLE existed for the benefit of LGT.[15] During this
period no appraisals were made; no attempts were made to sell or
rent the Property; no thought whatever was given to whether
$14,400 was a fair and reasonable rent even when real estate taxes
had risen to consume nearly all of that amount.

Defendants offered instead evidence of rents paid on other
properties. Among their best evidence was the expert testimony of
Harvey Rosenbloom, a real estate appraiser. Rosenbloom testified
that two other East Avenue buildings, which the district court found
to be comparable to the 260 East Avenue premises, were leased at
lower per-square-foot rentals than was paid by LGT to SLE. However, as to one of these properties, Rosenbloom testified only to rent
paid in 1973 and 1974, and did not consider the 1966–1972 period.

the time it is approved by the board, a
committee or the shareholders.

14. Alan ceased to be a director in November 1972; Leon, Jr., ceased to be a

director in 1977. Richard remains a director.

15. *See* footnote 4 *supra,* and accompanying text.

As to the other property, Rosenbloom described a fifteen year lease that was entered into in 1961. This testimony, while perhaps not wholly irrelevant to the issues in this suit, fell far short of demonstrating what rental the Property could have fetched in 1966, or in any other of the relevant years. Indeed, Rosenbloom himself testified that rental value could well be different for each year of the period. Thus, rentals that Rosenbloom testified were agreed to in 1961 or 1973 might well have been unfair in 1966 or 1967. This evidence thus could not support a finding that defendants acted fairly in maintaining an annual rental of $14,400 during the years from 1966 to 1972.[16]

Defendants also produced considerable evidence that over the relevant period, the East End neighborhood had been on an economic decline; that businesses had been leaving the area; that urban renewal projects and increased crime had depressed property values there; and that the area had, in general, become a less desirable place to do business. There was also evidence of specific developments that had an adverse effect on the Property: for example, the street running along one side of the Property was made a one-way street, thus limiting customers' access to LGT's premises. The district court credited all of this testimony, and it is fair to say that defendants proved that there was a general downward trend in the value of the Property. However, as noted above, defendants did not establish what was a fair rental value for the Property in 1966. Absent such a point of reference, a general downward trend in value is of no assistance in determining whether the rental actually paid was fair and reasonable during the ensuing years.

Moreover, working in reverse, some of defendants' own evidence as to the value of the Property at the end of the relevant period suggested that $14,400 was less than a fair rental in 1966, and that the figure of $38,099, estimated by plaintiff's expert, was perhaps not far off the mark.[17] First, there was a variety of evidence suggesting that in 1972 the Property was worth more than $200,-000. An appraisal by defense witness Harold Grunert in 1972 set the fair market value of the Property as of June 30, 1972, at $220,000. In 1972 Leon, Jr., had offered personally to buy the Property for $200,000, an offer which Richard had rejected.[18] And in 1971, Richard had informed Donald that evaluations by another appraiser, Harold Galloway, had set the value of the Property at $200,000 and $236,000. Second, defendants' expert witness Rosenbloom, asked what he would consider a fair rent for the property,

---

16. Defendant Richard E. Lewis testified that defendants tried, without success, to sell the Property in 1975, listing it with a realtor for $200,000. In addition he testified that an effort was made to rent the Property in 1973, and that only one offer, for $700 per month, was forthcoming. Since these efforts were made in 1973 and 1975, this evidence, like the evidence as to rentals of other property, was too remote in time to establish a fair rental value, especially as to the earlier years of the 1966–1972 period.

17. Plaintiff's expert made his evaluation as of February 1973. He did not make any evaluation for the period 1966–1972.

18. Leon, Jr., had just been fired from LGT by Richard.

given Grunert's 1972 valuation of $220,000, stated that ten percent of the value would be inadequate and that fifteen to seventeen percent would be closer to adequate. Fifteen percent of $220,000 would have yielded a rent of $33,000 on the basis of the 1972 valuation. Grunert's own expert testimony was entirely consistent with this. While he had made no estimate as to the fair rental value of the property for 1966–1972, he opined that a fair rental as of June 30, 1972, would be $20–21,000 with the tenant paying all expenses including real estate taxes. According to Richard, SLE's real estate taxes in 1972 were about $12,000. Thus Grunert's testimony, too, suggests about $33,000 as the fair rental value in 1972. Finally, consistent with their view of the general downward economic trend, Richard and Alan conceded that, whatever the Property was worth in 1972, it was worth more in 1966.[19] Thus the evidence presented by defendants, far from carrying their burden of showing that $14,400 was a fair and reasonable annual rental in 1966–1972, suggested that the fair rental value of the Property throughout that period exceeded $33,000 per year.

The defendants argued, however, that LGT could not have afforded to pay SLE rent higher than $14,400. They produced evidence designed to show that LGT had made little profit; that this low profitability was due to the expenses of maintenance and upkeep of the 260 East Avenue property; and that LGT therefore would not have been able to pay a higher rent to SLE. The district court credited this evidence, finding that LGT had "experienced a number of years of very severe losses," that during the period from 1962–1973, LGT's overall profit was only $53,876, and that payment of rent at the rate of $39,099 per year during this period could have led to the "demise" of LGT. These findings have only a distorted relationship to this lawsuit.

The period in issue here is 1966–1972. The only "severe" losses shown, totaling nearly $83,000, occurred in 1963 and 1973. Their inclusion in the computation of what LGT could afford to pay in 1966–1972 was patently unfair. In fact LGT's only unprofitable year during the period in issue was 1969 when its loss was small: $1,168. LGT's after-tax profits in 1966–1972 in fact totaled $102,-963, or an average of $14,709 per year. Thus, even on paper, LGT could have "afforded" to double its rent payments to SLE during the period in question.

Moreover, the proposition that LGT could not afford to pay as rent more than what its own books showed as profits ignores the fact that LGT was owned and managed by members of the Lewis family, some of whom were also employees of that corporation. It is entirely possible that these family members granted to themselves unusually high salaries or other perquisites, thus reducing LGT's paper profits. For example, in 1966 Richard's salary was approxi-

---

19. Leon, Jr., did not know whether the value had decreased from 1966 to 1972, but did not believe it had risen.

mately $21,000; Leon, Jr.'s compensation was $3,000 salary plus commissions. In 1967, LGT acquired all of Alan's LGT stock; and Richard and Leon, Jr., acquired all of the LGT stock of their father, agreeing to pay the purchase price over a ten-year period. Richard and Leon, Jr., thus became LGT's only shareholders, and their LGT salaries were immediately increased by a total of $23,000 per year (Richard's salary went from $21,000 to $36,000; Leon, Jr.'s went from $3,000 to $11,000), to cover the cost of the LGT stock they had just acquired.[20] Defendants bore the burden of proof on the question of a fair and reasonable rental; if they would rely on the proposition that LGT was unable to pay more, it was incumbent on them to demonstrate the fairness of the management and the reasonableness of the conduct of LGT's affairs. It does not appear that they made any effort to do so.

Finally, even if we were to assume that LGT's financial records provided a fair basis for evaluating the SLE–LGT transactions, defendants would not have carried their burden of proof. Defendants did not demonstrate that SLE could not have found some other tenant, stronger financially than LGT, which would have been willing and able to pay a higher rental. Even given the general downward trend of the East Avenue neighborhood, it is entirely possible that at least during the early years of the 1966–1972 period, such a tenant might have been secured. No effort was made during that period to rent to anyone other than LGT.

We conclude, therefore, that defendants failed to prove that the rental paid by LGT to SLE for the years 1966–1972 was fair and reasonable. Thus, Donald is not required to sell his SLE shares to LGT without such upward adjustment in the June 1, 1972, book value of SLE as may be necessary to reflect the amount by which the fair rental value of the Property exceeded $14,400 in any of the years 1966–1972....

We remand to the district court (a) for the entry of judgment in favor of SLE against Richard, Alan and Leon, Jr., jointly and severally, in such amount as the district court shall determine to be equal to the amounts by which the annual fair rental value of the Property exceeded $14,400 in the period February 28, 1966–June 1, 1972, (b) for an accounting as to the value of Donald's SLE shares as of June 1, 1972, in light of such judgment, (c) for an order, following such accounting, of specific performance of the shareholders' agreement, and (d) for such other proceedings as are not inconsistent with this opinion.

---

20. Richard had no doubt he could have paid for his newly acquired shares without the increase in his LGT salary. Leon, Jr., apparently lacked other resources from which to pay for the LGT stock (at least after he was fired from LGT in 1972).

NOTE ON REMEDIES FOR VIOLATION
OF THE DUTY OF LOYALTY

The traditional remedies for violation of the duty of loyalty are restitutionary in nature. For example, if a director has engaged in improper self-dealing with the corporation, normally the remedy is rescission—or, if rescission is not feasible, an accounting for the difference between the contract price and a fair price. Similarly, if an officer has improperly appropriated a corporate opportunity (see Section 4, infra), normally the remedy is to impose a constructive trust in the corporation's favor, conditioned on reimbursement by the corporation of the officer's outlay in acquiring the opportunity.

The result of this restitutionary theory of remedies is that as a practical matter, the legal sanctions for violation of the duty of loyalty are much less severe than the legal sanctions for violation of the duty of care. If D, a director or officer, violates his duty of care, he must pay damages although he made no gain from his wrongful action. This leaves D much worse off than he was before the wrong. In contrast, if D violates his duty of fair dealing, under a restitutionary remedy he need only return a gain to which he was not entitled in the first place. This simply places D where he was before the wrong.

Indeed, putting aside important nonlegal remedies such as discharge and negative publicity, if D is totally immoral, he would conclude that under a strictly restitutionary regime it normally paid to engage in a course of wrongful self-interested transactions. Some of the transactions may remain undiscovered. Where D's wrongdoing is discovered, he will only be required to surrender his wrongful gains. Where D's wrongdoing is not discovered, he will retain his wrongful gains. If D engages in enough transactions, he will come out ahead.

In some cases, however, the remedies for violation of the duty of loyalty may make the director or officer worse off than he was before the wrong. For example:

(i) Where the director or officer sells property to the corporation at an unfairly high price, and the value of the property later drops below its fair value at the time of the transaction, rescission may leave him worse off than if he had sold the property to a third party. For example, suppose that in 1985, D sells property to his corporation, without full disclosure, at $110,000, when it had a fair value of $100,000. In 1986, the corporation discovers the wrong and rescinds. Meanwhile, the market has fallen and the property is only worth $70,000. If D had sold the property to a third party to whom he owed no duty of disclosure, the third party would (let us assume) not be able to rescind. Thus D is $30,000 worse off than if he had not engaged in wrongful self-dealing. A comparable result may obtain where D buys property from the corporation, the market rises, and the corporation rescinds.

(ii) A director or officer who violates the duty of fair dealing may be required to repay the corporation any salary he earned during the relevant period in addition to making restitution of his wrongful gain. This remedy was granted, for example, in American Timber & Trading Co. v. Niedermeyer, 276 Or. 1135, 558 P.2d 1211 (1976), a case in which the fiduciary had depleted the corporation's assets by a series of unfair deals. The court there said:

> The remedy of restoration of compensation is an equitable principle and its applicability is dependent upon the individual facts of each case. *See, e.g., Lawson v. Baltimore Paint & Chem. Corp.,* 347 F.Supp. 967 (D.Md.1972); *Lydia E. Pinkham Med. Co. v. Gove,* 303 Mass. 1, 20 N.E.2d 482 (1939); 5 Fletcher, supra § 2145 at 635 (rev. ed. 1967). The general rule, however, is that a corporate officer who engages in activities which constitute either a breach of his duty of loyalty or a wilful breach of his contract of employment is not entitled to any compensation for services rendered during that period of time even though part of those services may have been properly performed....

Id. at 1155–56, 558 P.2d 1223.

(iii) Courts have sometimes awarded punitive damages against directors or officers who have breached their duty of loyalty. See, e.g., Holden v. Construction Machinery Co., 202 N.W.2d 348 (Iowa 1972); Rowen v. Le Mars Mutual Insurance Co. of Iowa, 282 N.W.2d 639, 662 (Iowa 1979). In Goben v. Barry, 234 Kan. 721, 728, 676 P.2d 90, 97–98 (1984), the court said, "Punitive damages may be awarded in the trial court's discretion whenever there is proof of fraud.... Fraud itself is difficult to define, but it has been held [that] fraud 'in its general sense, is deemed to comprise anything calculated to deceive, including all acts, omissions, and concealments involving a breach of legal or equitable duty, trust, or confidence justly reposed, resulting in damage to another....' Barry [the defendant] concealed his withdrawals [from the company], denied Goben [the plaintiff] had any interest in the company and ousted him, all to Goben's damage. That is sufficient evidence of fraud. The trial court did not err in awarding punitive damages."

(iv) ALI, Principles of Corporate Governance § 7.18(d) provides that a director or officer who violates the duty of fair dealing should normally be required to pay the counsel fees and other expenses incurred by the corporation in establishing the violation:

> (d) The losses deemed to be legally caused by a knowing violation of [the duty of loyalty] ... include the costs and expenses to which the corporation was subjected as a result of the violation, including the counsel fees and expenses of a successful plaintiff in a derivative action, except to the extent the court determines that inclusion of some or all of such costs and expenses would be inequitable in the circumstances.

The categories described in (i)–(iv) are illustrative, not exhaustive. In considering the remaining cases in this Chapter, you should be alert to remedies in general, and in particular to whether the remedy granted in a given case is more than restitutionary.

———

TALBOT v. JAMES

Supreme Court of South Carolina, 1972.
259 S.C. 73, 190 S.E.2d 759.

MOSS, Chief Justice:

This equitable action was brought by C.N. Talbot and Lula E. Talbot, appellants herein, against W.A. James, individually, and as President of Chicora Apartments, Inc., and Chicora Apartments, Inc., respondents herein, for an accounting. In the complaint it is alleged that W.A. James, as an officer and director of the Corporation, violated his fiduciary relationship to the Corporation and the appellants as stockholders thereof, by diverting specific funds to himself.

The respondents, by answer, denied the allegations of the complaint and alleged that W.A. James had received no funds from the Corporation except for the sums paid for the erection of Chicora Apartments, pursuant to a contract between Chicora Apartments, Inc., and the said W.A. James.

The case was referred to the Master in Equity for Horry County, who after taking the testimony, filed a report in which he found that W.A. James was not entitled to general overhead expense and profits arising out of the construction contract with Chicora Apartments, Inc., and recommended judgment in favor of Chicora Apartments, Inc., against him in the amount of $25,025.31.

The respondents timely appealed from the recommendations contained in the Report of the Master. The appeal was heard by the Honorable Dan F. Laney, Jr., presiding judge, and he issued his order reversing the findings of the Master and ordered judgment in favor of the respondents. This appeal followed.

1. This being an equity case and the Master and the Circuit Judge having disagreed and made contrary findings on the material issues in the case, this Court has jurisdiction to consider the evidence and make findings in accordance with our view of the preponderance or greater weight of the evidence. *Gantt v. Van Der Hoek*, 251 S.C. 307, 162 S.E.(2d) 267.

Lula E. Talbot owned a tract of land fronting on U.S. Highway 17, in Myrtle Beach, South Carolina. The title thereto was conveyed to her by her husband, C.N. Talbot. The appellants were approached by W.A. James with a proposal that the tract of land be used for the erection thereon of an apartment complex. After preliminary talks and negotiations, the parties on January 12, 1963, entered into a written agreement thereabout. Basically, the parties agreed to form a Corporation to construct and operate an apartment complex. Lula E. Talbot was to convey to said Corporation the tract of land owned by her and W.A. James agreed, as set forth in paragraph 5, of said contract,

"To promote the project aforementioned and shall be responsible for the planning, architectural work, construction, landscaping, legal fees, and loan processing of the entire project, same to contain at least fifty (50) one, two and three room air conditioned apartments for customer as approved by FHA appraisers."

It was further agreed that upon the formation of the Corporation that the appellants were to receive 50% of the stock of the Corporation in consideration for their transfer of the land to it. This was to be the absolute limit of the contribution of the appellants. W.A. James was to receive 50% of the stock of the Corporation in consideration of his efforts on its behalf.

It appears, that after the aforementioned contract was entered into, that W.A. James obtained the services of an architectural firm on a contingency basis and preliminary plans and sketches of the proposed apartment complex were made by such firm. James was also successful in obtaining commitments from the Federal Housing Administration and from an acceptable mortgagee with regard to financing. These commitments having been obtained, a corporation was formed to be known as Chicora Apartments, Inc., and a charter was duly issued by the Secretary of State on November 5, 1963.

Pursuant to the terms of the agreement dated January 12, 1963, 20 shares of no par value capital stock were issued, with W.A. James receiving 10 shares, C.N. Talbot one share and Lula E. Talbot 9 shares. At an organizational meeting of the corporation W.A. James was elected president, his wife, B.N. James, was elected secretary, C.N. Talbot was elected vice president, and Lula E. Talbot was elected treasurer. W.A. James and C.N. Talbot were elected as directors of the Corporation.

At a meeting of the Board of Directors held on November 5, 1963, a resolution was adopted accepting the offer of Lula E. Talbot to transfer the tract of land in question to Chicora Apartments, Inc., in exchange for 10 shares of the no par value capital stock thereof. In the said resolution, it was declared that the said property, to be so transferred, was of a value of $44,000.00. At the same meeting, a resolution was adopted accepting the offer of W.A. James to transfer to Chicora Apartments, Inc., in exchange for 10 shares of the no par value stock thereof, at a valuation of $44,000.00 the following:

"1. FHA Commitment issued pursuant to Title 2, Section 207 of the National Housing Act, whereby the FHA agrees to insure a mortgage loan in the amount of $850,700.00, on a parcel of land in Myrtle Beach, South Carolina, more particularly described in Schedule 'A' hereto attached, provided 66 apartment units are constructed thereon in accordance with plans and specifications as prepared by Lyles, Bissett, Carlisle & Wolff, Architects–Engineers, of Columbia, South Carolina.

"2. Commitment from United Mortgagee Servicing Corp. agreeing to make a mortgage loan on said property in the amount of $850,700.00 and also commitment from said mortgagee to make an interim construction loan in an identical amount.

"3. Certain contracts and agreements which W.A. James over the past two years have worked out and developed in connection with the architectural and construction services required for said project.

"4. The use of the finances and credit of W.A. James during the past two years (and including the construction period) in order to make it possible to proceed with the project."

The day following the election of the officers and the issuance of the capital stock, the Board of Directors of Chicora Apartments, Inc., met in Columbia, South Carolina, and passed a resolution authorizing the Corporation to borrow from United Mortgagee Servicing Corporation of Norfolk, Virginia, the sum of $850,700.00, upon the terms stated, said loan to be insured with the Federal Housing Administration. It was further resolved:

"That the President of the corporation, W.A. James, be authorized, empowered and directed to make, execute and deliver such documents and instruments as are required by the F.H.A. and the lender, in order to close the loan transaction; said documents including but not limited to, note, mortgage, Building Loan Agreement, Construction Contract, Architect's Agreement, Mortgagor's Certificate, Regulatory Agreement, Mortgagor's Oath and Agreement and Certificate."

The record shows that on November 6, 1963, James Construction Company entered into a construction contract with Chicora Apartments, Inc. This contract was executed by W.A. James, as president, and attested by B.N. James, secretary, on behalf of Chicora Apartments, Inc., and by W.A. James, sole proprietor, for James Construction Company. The contract sum was to be the actual cost of construction plus a fee equal to $20,000.00 but in no event was the contract price, including the fee, to exceed $736,-000.00. Attached to the contract was a "Trade Payment Breakdown" which made an allowance for overhead expenses in the amount of $31,589.00, but, this said sum was to be paid by means other than cash. The aforementioned loan was obtained and the apartment complex was constructed. All funds from the mortgage loan were received and disbursed by W.A. James and the renting of the apartments was begun, such being conducted by a resident manager, who was an employee of the Corporation.

It appears... that in 1968, an accountant, who was employed by the corporation, advised James and C.N. Talbot that it was in financial straits. It was at this time that the appellants questioned the disbursement of the mortgage funds by W.A. James. Their demands to examine the corporate records were refused by James. Thereafter, an order was obtained from the Honorable James B. Morrison, Resident Judge of the Fifteenth Judicial Circuit, making available the corporate records to the appellants. This action was thereafter instituted.

The record in this case clearly shows that W.A. James personally received or there was paid for his benefit the sum of $25,025.31 from the proceeds of the mortgage loan. He received this directly or by payments of his own personal debts by the corporation. He contends that he was entitled to these funds and more under the construction contract which he had with Chicora Apartments, Inc. This raises the question of whether James, who was a stockholder, officer, and director of Chicora Apartments, Inc., could enter into a contract with himself as an individual and [make] a profit therefrom for himself.

The Master found that Chicora Apartments, Inc., through W.A. James as president thereof, entered into a contract with himself, as sole proprietor of James Construction Company, without disclosing his identity of interest to the other officers or stockholders of the corporation, and that such contract has not been acquiesced in or ratified by the other director, officers or stockholders. He further found that the initial agreement between the parties required W.A. James to perform the same duties that he later contracted with the corporation to perform and for which he now seeks to justify the payment to him from the mortgage funds of the corporation. It was also found that according to the initial agreement these services were to be performed and, in consideration of such performance, James was to receive one-half of the shares of the capital stock of Chicora Apartments, Inc. The trial judge, upon exceptions to the Master's Report, made contrary findings of fact and reversed the Master and entered judgment in favor of the respondents.

The first question for determination is whether the fiduciary relationship existing between W.A. James as a stockholder, officer and director of Chicora Apartments, Inc., prevented him from contracting with the said corporation for his profit without first having disclosed the terms of the contract to the disinterested officers and directors of the corporation.

2. The officers and directors of the corporation stand in a fiduciary relationship to the individual stockholders and in every instance must make a full disclosure of all relevant facts when entering into a contract with said corporation. *Jacobson v. Yaschik,* 249 S.C. 577, 155 S.E.(2d) 601. The object of this rule is to prevent directors from secretly using their fiduciary positions to their own advantage and to the detriment of the corporation and of the stockholders.

3. The cases of *Peurifoy v. Loyal,* 154 S.C. 267, 151 S.E. 579, and *Fidelity Fire Ins. Co. v. Harby,* 156 S.C. 238, 153 S.E. 141, firmly establish the ineligibility of a director to participate in corporate action with respect to a transaction in which he has an interest adverse to the corporation. He may not even be counted to make a quorum at a meeting where the matter is acted upon, which is the general rule.

The case of *Gilbert v. McLeod Infirmary*, 219 S.C. 174, 64 S.E.(2d) 524, contains a good statement of the law relating to personal dealings of an officer or director with his corporation or its property. We quote the following from this case:

"From the extensive review of the authorities there is extracted the rule that when a director, in selling corporate property to himself, represents or joins in the representation of the corporation, the transaction is voidable at the option of the corporation, or others suing in its behalf, merely upon proof of the fact stated; but when the purchasing director abstains from participation in behalf of the corporation and it is properly represented by others who are personally disinterested, the transaction will stand under attack if the director made full disclosure, paid full value, and the corporation has not been imposed upon; and the burden is upon the director to establish these requisites by evidence."

We quote again from the *Gilbert* case the following:

"A director or officer of a corporation is not absolutely precluded by his official position from dealing or entering into a contract with the corporation, nor is such a transaction void *per se*. While it is true, on the one hand, that where the directors or officers of a corporation deal with themselves as individuals, the transactions are subject to the closest scrutiny, under the most searching light of truth, and must be characterized by absolute good faith, it is also true, on the other hand, that where persons holding positions of trust and confidence in a corporation deal with the corporation, which is also represented by others, in entire good faith, fairness, and honesty, such transactions are not invalid and will be upheld. It would also seem that the mere fact that a director with whom the contract was made voted at the directors' meeting authorizing the same would not necessarily invalidate the contract, where the disinterested directors, who themselves constituted a quorum, were unanimous in the action." 13 Am.Jur. 958, sec. 1005.

4. We point out that in the *Gilbert* case a director of a corporation was purchasing from it corporate property. The rationale of the rule stated in *Gilbert* is applicable to the situation where a director is entering into a contract individually with the corporation.

We examined the evidence in this case in the light of the foregoing rules. The testimony of C.N. Talbot is that he discussed with James as to who was going to construct the Chicora Apartments and was told that Dargan Construction Company was going to take the contract. He further testified that during the period of construction he saw Dargan Construction Company signs on the premises and also trucks bearing its name. This witness further testified that James never discussed with him or his wife the matter of his constructing the apartments. Talbot denied that he knew that James was to be the contractor.

James testified that he explained to C.N. Talbot that the only possible way that the apartments could be built without putting in money was that he be the building contractor.   James further testified that the only way the project could survive and the only way that "we" could get the builder's equity was that he should be the builder.   He says that everybody understood that because his attorney had explained it at a meeting of the directors.

5, 6.   Assuming that James revealed to Talbot that he was to be the building contractor for the Chicora Apartments complex, his testimony does not show that he disclosed his entitlement to a fee of $20,000.00 and an allowance for overhead expenses in the amount of $31,589.00.   It is thus apparent that he did not make a full disclosure of the profits or monetary benefits that he was to receive under the terms of the contract.   It was his duty to make such full disclosure and the burden of proof was upon him to show that such had been done.

We have carefully examined the minutes of the several meetings of the stockholders and directors of the corporation.   We find from such examination that they reflect each and every detail and transaction looking toward the construction of the apartment complex but nowhere in said minutes is there any mention that James was to be the building contractor.   The minutes reflect that there was a meeting of the directors of the corporation on November 6, 1963, and a resolution adopted at such meeting authorizing the borrowing of the sum of $850,700.00 from the United Mortgagee Servicing Corporation, and authorizing James, as president, to make, execute and deliver such documents and instruments as were required by the FHA and the lender.   If James was to be the building contractor and such was discussed at this meeting, as he contends, the minutes should have reflected such, particularly in view of the fact that the building contract was being awarded to him when he was a director and president of the corporation.   There is no explanation of why such a resolution or authorization was not considered or passed at this meeting of the Board of Directors.

7.   The record shows that the appellants were stockholders and officers of the corporation.   As such, they were entitled to inspect the books of the corporation at any and all times.   Section 12–263 of the Code.   When they demanded their right to exercise this privilege, such was refused by James and they only obtained the right to inspect the records and books of the corporation by an order of the court.   James' only explanation was that the Talbots were not entitled to see the books.   It is inferable from this action on the part of James that he did not want the appellants to discover how the funds of the corporation had been disbursed and see that he had received benefit in such disbursement.

8.   It appears that at the meeting of the directors of the corporation held on November 6, 1963, W.A. James, as president, was authorized to execute and deliver several documents including a "construction contract."   The respondents argue that this gave W.A. James the authority to make the construction contract here involved.   It is true that he was authorized to sign a "construction

contract" on behalf of the corporation but such resolution did not authorize him to sign one on behalf of the corporation in favor of himself individually.

9.   The respondents contend and place great emphasis on the fact that the construction contract was approved by the Federal Housing Administration and the fees provided therein were allowed by it.   This has no relevancy to the issue here.

10.   Considering the entire record in this case, it is our conclusion that W.A. James, as president of Chicora Apartments, Inc., entered into a contract with himself as sole proprietor of James Construction Company without making full disclosure of his identity of interest to the other officers and stockholders of the corporation.   In this conclusion, we agree with the findings of the Master. It follows that the Chicora Apartments, Inc., is entitled to judgment against the said W.A. James in the amount of $25,025.31, this being the amount of the corporate funds received by or paid in behalf of W.A. James.

The Master found that under the language in paragraph 5 of the pre-incorporation agreement, hereinbefore quoted, that W.A. James was to be responsible for overseeing, supervising and generally managing all aspects of the construction of the apartment complex. He found that W.A. James, as sole proprietor of James Construction Company, performed the contract obligations and for such he received one-half of the shares of the capital stock of Chicora Apartments, Inc.   The trial judge reversed this finding of the Master. The appellants allege error.

11.   James testified that he was the general contractor for the construction of the apartment complex.   He testified further that the apartment complex was constructed by some eighteen to twenty subcontractors with whom he negotiated contracts.   The record reveals that the only service that James rendered in connection with the construction of the apartment complex was supervisory.   These duties were those contemplated by the pre-incorporation agreement of the parties.   He was compensated for these services when he received one-half of the capital stock in the corporation.   He was not entitled to any other compensation for the services rendered. We think the trial judge was in error in not so holding.

The order of the trial judge is reversed and this case remanded to the Court of Common Pleas for Horry County for an appropriate order to effectuate the views herein expressed.

Reversed and remanded.

LEWIS and LITTLEJOHN, JJ., concur.

BUSSEY and BRAILSFORD, JJ., dissent.

BUSSEY, Justice (dissenting):

While admittedly there is some evidence tending to support the findings of fact by the master, adopted in the majority opinion, I have concluded after considerable study of the record and exhibits that the clear weight of the evidence preponderates in favor of the findings of fact by the circuit judge rather than those of the master. Being of this view, I am compelled to dissent.

The apartment complex was completed in July 1964, whereupon the plaintiff, C.N. Talbot, with the help of a resident manager, selected by him but approved by James, took charge of the management and operation of the apartment complex, all receipts being deposited by Talbot and all checks being written by Talbot. In 1968, after Talbot and his manager had been in charge of the apartment complex for nearly four years, the corporation was virtually insolvent and the recommendation of Talbot's auditor was that the project be surrendered to FHA as a failure. To this James did not agree; instead he took charge of the operation of the apartment complex himself for the corporation, and a little more than a year later the corporation had seventeen to eighteen thousand dollars in the bank with all current bills paid.

Talbot was obviously chagrined at this course of events and it was not until after he was ousted from management that he actively asserted any claim on behalf of the corporation against James. While he denied knowing that James Construction Company was the general contractor on the project, by his own testimony about January or February 1965 he knew that a check for more than fifteen thousand dollars had been drawn on the construction account for the benefit of James. There is no suggestion that he then made any issue thereabout; instead, he waited until nearly four years later and until after he had been ousted from the active management of the operation. . . .

The resolution of the Board of Directors at the meeting on November 5, 1963, unanimously confirmed by the meeting of the stockholders on the same date, as evidenced by their written signatures, clearly shows that all parties agreed that James' efforts over a two year period and the contracts and commitments thereby produced plus the continued use of the finances and credit of James during the actual construction period represented a value of $44,-000, which was accepted in full payment for James' ten shares of stock. According to the literal terms of this resolution, nothing remained to be done by James to fully earn his ten shares except allow the use of his credit throughout the construction period. As president of the corporation, he would have been expected to at least reasonably supervise the construction of the project in the interest of the corporation, whether or not required to do so by either the resolution of November 5 or the pre-incorporation agreement between the parties. The general supervisory duties of a corporation president or a pre-incorporation promoter are a far cry from the arduous, time consuming and expensive duties of a general contractor.

Supervising a general contractor is one thing; while acting as a general contractor, engaging, supervising, and following up eighteen or twenty subcontractors is an entirely different thing. There is uncontradicted evidence of voluminous paper work, record keeping, reports, etc., on the part of James and his personnel in the performance of the general construction contract. The record leaves no doubt whatever, to my mind, that James Construction Company performed services to the corporation subsequent to November 5, 1963 far over and above the service contemplated by either the aforesaid resolution or the pre-incorporation agreement.

As mentioned in the majority opinion, the "Trade Payment Breakdown" attached to the approved FHA construction contract made an allowance for overhead expenses in the amount of $31,-589, payable by means other than cash. Apparently from the evidence, this amount, otherwise drawable, as overhead by James, was to form a part of the equity of the corporation required for the FHA loan and, of course, not actually received by James. Aside, however, from this item, the record reflects that where, as here, there was an identity of interest between the contractor and the sponsor, FHA, within certain limitations, permitted the contractor to include in his certification of the actual cost of a project a reasonable allocation of his general overhead expense, *i.e.*, the proportion of his actual general overhead expense attributable to the particular contract job.

In his cost certification to FHA James showed the entire overhead of James Construction Company during the period that the apartment project was under construction, and represented that 88.98% thereof, or $22,817.34, was attributable to the construction of Chicora Apartments. Of this amount, FHA allowed only $21,-231.90 (3% of other costs) as a portion of the actual cost of Chicora Apartments. James' figures as to his overhead and the portion thereof attributable to the construction of Chicora Apartments may or may not have been accurate, but he was not even cross-examined thereabout. Assuming the accuracy of his figures it follows that his net profit from this general construction contract was the sum of $25,025.31 less $22,817.34 overhead, or $2,207.97. Even Talbot had to frankly admit that he did not know of any loss suffered by the Talbots or the corporation as a result of the general contract being let to James. He tacitly, if not expressly, conceded that Dargan, or any other reputable contractor, would have cost the corporation some twenty-five or thirty thousand dollars more. . . .

For the foregoing reasons, I would affirm the judgment of the lower court, but at the very least, if the corporation is to recover at all from James, its recovery should be limited to any profit actually received, as opposed to his overhead expense. If the judgment below be not affirmed, the cause should be remanded for the purpose of determining the amount of actual overhead which James should equitably be allowed to retain.

BRAILSFORD, J., concurs.

———

NOTE ON THE DUTY OF DISCLOSURE BY CONTROLLING SHAREHOLDERS UNDER DELAWARE LAW

[See p. 744, supra]

NOTE ON THE DUTY OF LOYALTY

Fairness requires not only that the terms of a self-interested transaction be fair, but that entering into the transaction, even on fair terms, is in the corporation's interest. For example, in Fill Buildings, Inc. v. Alexander Hamilton Life Ins. Co. of America, 396 Mich. 453, 241 N.W.2d 466 (1976), Fill Buildings, Inc., which had leased premises to Wayne National Life Insurance Co., brought suit under the lease for past-due rent. Leon Fill was the principal shareholder and a director of Wayne National and the sole shareholder and president of Fill Buildings. Wayne's corporate successor sought to avoid liability under the lease, on the ground that the lease was unfair. The trial court held that Fill Buildings had not borne its burden of establishing that the lease was in the interests of Wayne National:

> Given an instance of alleged director enrichment at corporate expense such as in this case, the burden to establish fairness resting on the director requires not only a showing of "fair price" but also a showing of the fairness of the bargain to the interests of the corporation. Only when a convincing showing is made in both respects can "fairness" under the statute be said to have been established.

> We are inclined to agree with Fill Buildings' position that that corporation was entitled to make a profit on its lease and that a "fair price" for the leasehold agreement was established. The costs of extensive renovations and the thrust of expert testimony adduced at trial support this conclusion. The proofs respecting the showing that entry into the lease served the interests of Wayne National are, however, unconvincing. Evidence adduced at trial indicated that Wayne National was a corporation in trouble. The corporation had been warned against over-expansion. Yet here we have entry into a long-term lease (*i.e.*, expansion) at a time when the corporate future was in question....

ALI, PRINCIPLES OF CORPORATE GOVERNANCE
§§ 1.09, 1.20, 5.02, 5.07

[See Statutory Supplement]

SECTION 2.　STATUTORY APPROACHES

CAL. CORP. CODE § 310

[See Statutory Supplement]

DEL. GEN. CORP. LAW § 144

[See Statutory Supplement]

REV. MODEL BUS. CORP. ACT § 8.31

[See Statutory Supplement]

N.Y. BUS. CORP. LAW § 713

[See Statutory Supplement]

COOKIES FOOD PRODUCTS v. LAKES WAREHOUSE

Supreme Court of Iowa, 1988.
430 N.W.2d 447.

NEUMAN, Justice.

This is a shareholders' derivative suit brought by the minority shareholders of a closely held Iowa corporation specializing in barbeque sauce, Cookies Food Products, Inc. (Cookies). The target of the lawsuit is the majority shareholder, Duane "Speed" Herrig and two of his family-owned corporations, Lakes Warehouse Distributing, Inc. (Lakes) and Speed's Automotive Co., Inc. (Speed's). Plaintiffs alleged that Herrig, by acquiring control of Cookies and executing self-dealing contracts, breached his fiduciary duty to the company and fraudulently misappropriated and converted corporate funds. Plaintiffs sought actual and punitive damages. Trial to the court resulted in a verdict for the defendants, the district court finding that Herrig's actions benefited, rather than harmed, Cookies. We affirm.

I. *Background.*

We review decisions in shareholders' derivative suits de novo, deferring especially to district court findings where the credibility of witnesses is a factor in the outcome. *Midwest Management Corp. v. Stephens,* 353 N.W.2d 76, 78 (Iowa 1984). To better understand this dispute, and the issues this appeal presents, we shall begin by recounting in detail the facts surrounding the creation and growth of this corporation.

L.D. Cook of Storm Lake, Iowa, founded Cookies in 1975 to produce and distribute his original barbeque sauce. Searching for a plant site in a community that would provide financial backing, Cook met with business leaders in seventeen Iowa communities, outlining his plans to build a growth-oriented company. He selected Wall Lake, Iowa, persuading thirty-five members of that community, including Herrig and the plaintiffs, to purchase Cookies stock. All of the investors hoped Cookies would improve the local job market and tax base. The record reveals that it has done just that.

Early sales of the product, however, were dismal. After the first year's operation, Cookies was in dire financial straits. At that time, Herrig was one of thirty-five shareholders and held only two hundred shares. He was also the owner of an auto parts business, Speed's Automotive, and Lakes Warehouse Distributing, Inc., a company that distributed auto parts from Speed's. Cookies' board of directors approached Herrig with the idea of distributing the company's products. It authorized Herrig to purchase Cookies' sauce for twenty percent under wholesale price, which he could then resell at full wholesale price. Under this arrangement, Herrig began to market and distribute the sauce to his auto parts customers and to grocery outlets from Lakes' trucks as they traversed the regular delivery routes for Speed's Automotive.

In May 1977, Cookies formalized this arrangement by executing an exclusive distribution agreement with Lakes. Pursuant to this agreement, Cookies was responsible only for preparing the product; Lakes, for its part, assumed all costs of warehousing, marketing, sales, delivery, promotion, and advertising. Cookies retained the right to fix the sales price of its products and agreed to pay Lakes thirty percent of its gross sales for these services.

Cookies' sales have soared under the exclusive distributorship contract with Lakes. Gross sales in 1976, the year prior to the agreement, totaled only $20,000, less than half of Cookies' expenses that year. In 1977, however, sales jumped five-fold, then doubled in 1978, and have continued to show phenomenal growth every year thereafter. By 1985, when this suit was commenced, annual sales reached $2,400,000.

As sales increased, Cookies' board of directors amended and extended the original distributorship agreement. In 1979, the board amended the original agreement to give Lakes an additional two percent of gross sales to cover freight costs for the ever-expanding market for Cookies' sauce. In 1980, the board extended the amended agreement through 1984 to allow Herrig to make long-term advertising commitments. Recognizing the role that Herrig's personal strengths played in the success of their joint endeavor, the board also amended the agreement that year to allow Cookies to cancel the agreement with Lakes if Herrig died or disposed of the corporation's stock.

In 1981, L.D. Cook, the majority shareholder up to this time, decided to sell his interest in Cookies. He first offered the directors an opportunity to buy his stock, but the board declined to purchase any of his 8100 shares. Herrig then offered Cook and all other shareholders $10 per share for their stock, which was twice the original price. Because of the overwhelming response to these offers, Herrig had purchased enough Cookies stock by January 1982 to become the majority shareholder. His investment of $140,000 represented fifty-three percent of the 28,700 outstanding shares. Other shareholders had invested a total of $67,500 for the remaining forty-seven percent.

Shortly after Herrig acquired majority control he replaced four of the five members of the Cookies' board with members he selected. This restructuring of authority, following on the heels of an unsuccessful attempt by certain stockholders to prevent Herrig from acquiring majority status, solidified a division of opinion within the shareholder ranks. Subsequent changes made in the corporation under Herrig's leadership formed the basis for this lawsuit.

First, under Herrig's leadership, Cookies' board has extended the term of the exclusive distributorship agreement with Lakes and expanded the scope of services for which it compensates Herrig and his companies. In April 1982, when a sales increase of twenty-five percent over the previous year required Cookies to seek additional short-term storage for the peak summer season, the board accepted Herrig's proposal to compensate Lakes at the "going rate" for use of its nearby storage facilities. The board decided to use Lakes' storage facilities because building and staffing its own facilities would have been more expensive. Later, in July 1982, the new board approved an extension of the exclusive distributorship agreement. Notably, this agreement was identical to the 1980 extension that the former board had approved while four of the plaintiffs in this action were directors.

Second, Herrig moved from his role as director and distributor to take on an additional role in product development. This created a dispute over a royalty Herrig began to receive. Herrig's role in product development began in 1982 when Cookies diversified its product line to include taco sauce. Herrig developed the recipe because he recognized that taco sauce, while requiring many of the same ingredients needed in barbeque sauce, is less expensive to produce. Further, since consumer demand for taco sauce is more consistent throughout the year than the demand for barbeque sauce, this new product line proved to be a profitable method for increasing year-round utilization of production facilities and staff. In August 1982, Cookies' board approved a royalty fee to be paid to Herrig for this taco sauce recipe. This royalty plan was similar to royalties the board paid to L.D. Cook for the barbeque sauce recipe. That plan gives Cook three percent of the gross sales of barbeque sauce; Herrig receives a flat rate per case. Although Herrig's rate is equivalent to a sales percentage slightly higher than what Cook receives, it yields greater profit to Cookies because this new product line is cheaper to produce.

Third, since 1982 Cookies' board has twice approved additional compensation for Herrig. In January 1983, the board authorized payment of a $1000 per month "consultant fee" in lieu of salary, because accelerated sales required Herrig to spend extra time managing the company. Averaging eighty-hour work weeks, Herrig devoted approximately fifteen percent of his time to Cookies and eighty percent to Lakes business. In August, 1983, the board authorized another increase in Herrig's compensation. Further, at the suggestion of a Cookies director who also served as an accountant for Cookies, Lakes, and Speed's, the Cookies board amended the exclusive distributorship agreement to allow Lakes an additional two percent of gross sales as a promotion allowance to expand the market for Cookies products outside of Iowa. As a direct result of this action, by 1986 Cookies regularly shipped products to several states throughout the country.

As we have previously noted, however, Cookies' growth and success has not pleased all its shareholders. The discontent is motivated by two factors that have effectively precluded shareholders from sharing in Cookies' financial success: the fact that Cookies is a closely held corporation, and the fact that it has not paid dividends. Because Cookies' stock is not publicly traded, shareholders have no ready access to buyers for their stock at current values that reflect the company's success. Without dividends, the shareholders have no ready method of realizing a return on their investment in the company. This is not to say that Cookies has improperly refused to pay dividends. The evidence reveals that Cookies would have violated the terms of its loan with the Small Business Administration had it declared dividends before repaying that debt. That SBA loan was not repaid until the month before the plaintiffs filed this action.

Unsatisfied with the status quo, a group of minority shareholders commenced this equitable action in 1985. Based on the facts we have detailed, the plaintiffs claimed that the sums paid Herrig and his companies have grossly exceeded the value of the services rendered, thereby substantially reducing corporate profits and shareholder equity. Through the exclusive distributorship agreements, taco sauce royalty, warehousing fees, and consultant fee, plaintiffs claimed that Herrig breached his fiduciary duties to the corporation and its shareholders because he allegedly negotiated for these arrangements without fully disclosing the benefit he would gain. The plaintiffs sought recovery for lost profits, an accounting to determine the full extent of the damage, attorneys fees, punitive damages, appointment of a receiver to manage the company properly, removal of Herrig from control, and sale of the company in order to generate an appropriate return on their investment.

Having heard the evidence presented on these claims at trial, the district court filed a lengthy ruling that reflected careful attention to the testimony of the twenty-two witnesses and myriad of exhibits admitted. The court concluded that Herrig had breached no duties owed to Cookies or to its minority shareholders, and found that Herrig's compensation was fair and reasonable for each of the four challenged categories of service. In summary, the court found that: (1) the exclusive distributorship arrangement has been the "key to corporate growth and expansion" and the fees under the agreement were appropriate for the diverse services Lakes provided; (2) the warehousing agreement was fair because it allowed Cookies to store its goods at the "going rate" and the board had considered and rejected the idea of constructing its own warehouse as storage at the Lakes facility would be less expensive; (3) the taco sauce royalty agreement appropriately compensated Herrig for the value of his recipe; and (4) the consultant fee "is actually a management fee for services rendered seven days a week" and is "well within reason, considering the success of the business." Additionally, the district court found that Herrig had withheld no information from directors or other shareholders that he was obligated to provide. The court concluded its findings with the following observation:

> The Court believes that the plaintiffs' complaint is not that they have been damaged but that they have not been paid a profit for their investment yet. There is a vast difference. Plaintiffs have made a profit. That profit is in the form of increased value of their stocks rather than in the form of dividends because of the capital considerations of operating the company.

On appeal from this ruling, the plaintiffs challenge: (1) the district court's allocation of the burden of proof with regard to the four claims of self-dealing; (2) the standard employed by the court to determine whether Herrig's self-dealing was fair and reasonable to Cookies; (3) the finding that any self-dealing by Herrig was done in good faith, and with honesty and fairness; (4) the finding that Herrig breached no duty to disclose crucial facts to Cookies' board before it completed deliberations on Herrig's self-dealing transactions; and (5) the district court's denial of restitution and other equitable remedies as compensation for Herrig's alleged breach of his duty of loyalty. After a brief review of the nature and source of Herrig's fiduciary duties, we will address the appellants' challenges in turn.

II. *Fiduciary Duties.*

Herrig, as an officer and director of Cookies, owes a fiduciary duty to the company and its shareholders. *See* Iowa Code § 496A.34 (1985) (director must serve in manner believed in good faith to be in best interest of corporation); *see also Schildberg Rock Prods. Co. v. Brooks,* 258 Iowa 759, 766–67, 140 N.W.2d 132, 136 (1966) (officers and directors occupy fiduciary relation to corporation and its stockholders). Herrig concedes that Iowa law imposed the same fiduciary responsibilities based on his status as majority stockholder. *See Des Moines Bank & Trust Co. v. George M. Bechtel & Co.,* 243 Iowa 1007, 1082–83, 51 N.W.2d 174, 217 (1952) (hereinafter *Bechtel*); *see also* 12B W. Fletcher, *Cyclopedia on the Law of Private Corporations* § 5810, at 149 (1986). Conversely, before acquiring majority control in February 1982, Herrig owed no fiduciary duty to Cookies or plaintiffs. *See* Fletcher § 5713, at 13 (stockholders not active in management of corporation owe duties radically different from director, and vote at shareholder's meetings merely for own benefit). Therefore, Herrig's conduct is subject to scrutiny only from the time he began to exercise control of Cookies. . . .

Appellants . . . claim that Herrig violated his duty of loyalty to Cookies. That duty derives from "the prohibition against self-dealing that inheres in the fiduciary relationship." *Norlin,* 744 F.2d at 264. As a fiduciary, one may not secure for oneself a business opportunity that "in fairness belongs to the corporation." *Rowen v. LeMars Mut. Ins. Co. of Iowa,* 282 N.W.2d 639, 660 (Iowa 1979). As we noted in *Bechtel:*

> Corporate directors and officers may under proper circumstances transact business with the corporation including the purchase or sale of property, but it must be done in the strictest good faith and with full disclosure of the facts to, and the consent of, all concerned. And the burden is upon them to establish their good faith, honesty and fairness. Such transactions are scanned by the courts with skepticism and the closest scrutiny, and may be nullified on slight grounds. It is the policy of the courts to put such fiduciaries beyond the reach of temptation and the enticement of illicit profit.

243 Iowa 1007, 1081, 51 N.W.2d 174, 216 (1952). We have repeatedly applied this standard, including the burden of proof and level of scrutiny, when a corporate director engages in self-dealing with another corporation for which he or she also serves as a director. *See Holden v. Construction Mach. Co.,* 202 N.W.2d 348, 356–57 (Iowa 1972).

Against this common law backdrop, the legislature enacted section 496A.34, quoted here in pertinent part, that establishes three sets of circumstances under which a director may engage in self-dealing without clearly violating the duty of loyalty:

> No contract or other transaction between a corporation and one or more of its directors or any other corporation, firm, association or entity in which one or more of its directors are directors or officers or are financially interested, shall be either void or voidable because of such relationship or interest . . . if any of the following occur:

1.   The fact of such relationship or interest is disclosed or known to the board of directors or committee which authorizes, approves, or ratifies the contract or transaction ... without counting the votes ... of such interested director.

2.   The fact of such relationship or interest is disclosed or known to the shareholders entitled to vote [on the transaction] and they authorize ... such contract or transaction by vote or written consent.

3.   The contract or transaction is fair and reasonable to the corporation.

Some commentators have supported the view that satisfaction of any *one* of the foregoing statutory alternatives, in and of itself, would prove that a director has fully met the duty of loyalty. *See* Hansell, Austin, & Wilcox, *Director Liability Under Iowa Law— Duties and Protections,* 13 J.Corp.L. 369, 382. We are obliged, however, to interpret statutes in conformity with the common law wherever statutory language does not directly negate it. *See Hardwick v. Bublitz,* 253 Iowa 49, 59, 111 N.W.2d 309, 314 (1961); Iowa Code § 4.2 (1987). Because the common law and section 496A.34 require directors to show "good faith, honesty, and fairness" in self-dealing, we are persuaded that satisfaction of any one of these three alternatives under the statute would merely preclude us from rendering the transaction void or voidable *outright* solely on the basis "of such [director's] relationship or interest." Iowa Code § 496A.34; *see Bechtel,* 243 Iowa at 1081–82, 51 N.W.2d at 216. To the contrary, we are convinced that the legislature did not intend by this statute to enable a court, in a shareholder's derivative suit, to rubber stamp *any* transaction to which a board of directors or the shareholders of a corporation have consented. Such an interpretation would invite those who stand to gain from such transactions to engage in improprieties to obtain consent. We thus require directors who engage in self-dealing to establish the additional element that they have acted in good faith, honesty, and fairness. *Holi–Rest, Inc. v. Treloar,* 217 N.W.2d 517, 525 (Iowa 1974).

III.   *Burden of Proof.*

[The court held that the district court had appropriately placed the burden of proof on Herrig.]

IV.   *Standard of Law.*

Next, appellants claim the district court applied an inappropriate standard of law to determine whether Herrig's conduct was fair and reasonable to Cookies. Appellants correctly assert that self-dealing transactions must have the earmarks of arms-length transactions before a court can find them to be fair or reasonable. *See Bechtel,* 243 Iowa at 1023, 51 N.W.2d at 184. The crux of appellants' claim is that the court should have focused on the fair market value of Herrig's services to Cookies rather than on the success Cookies achieved as a result of Herrig's actions.

We agree with appellants' contention that corporate profitability should not be the sole criteria by which to test the fairness and reasonableness of Herrig's fees. In this connection, appellants cite authority from the Michigan Supreme Court that we find persuasive:

> Given an instance of alleged director enrichment at corporate expense . . . the burden to establish fairness resting on the director requires not only a showing of "fair price" but also a showing of the fairness of the bargain to the interests of the corporation.

Fill Bldgs., Inc. v. Alexander Hamilton Life Ins. Co., 396 Mich. 453, 241 N.W.2d 466, 469 (1976). Applying such reasoning to the record before us, however, we cannot agree with appellants' assertion that Herrig's services were either unfairly priced or inconsistent with Cookies corporate interest.

There can be no serious dispute that the four agreements in issue—for exclusive distributorship, taco sauce royalty, warehousing, and consulting fees—have all benefited Cookies, as demonstrated by its financial success. Even if we assume Cookies could have procured similar services from other vendors at lower costs, we are not convinced that Herrig's fees were therefore unreasonable or exorbitant. Like the district court, we are not persuaded by appellants' expert testimony that Cookies' sales and profits would have been the same under agreements with other vendors. As Cookies' board noted prior to Herrig's takeover, he was the driving force in the corporation's success. Even plaintiffs' expert acknowledged that Herrig has done the work of at least five people—production supervisor, advertising specialist, warehouseman, broker, and salesman. While eschewing the lack of internal control, for accounting purposes, that such centralized authority may produce, the expert conceded that Herrig may in fact be underpaid for all he has accomplished. We believe the board properly considered this source of Cookies' success when it entered these transactions, as did the district court when it reviewed them. . . .

V. *Denial of Equitable Relief.*

. . . [T]he record before us aptly demonstrates that all members of Cookies' board were well aware of Herrig's dual ownership in Lakes and Speed's. We are unaware of any authority supporting plaintiffs' contention that Herrig was obligated to disclose to Cookies' board or shareholders the extent of his profits resulting from these distribution and warehousing agreements; nevertheless, the exclusive distribution agreement with Lakes authorized the board to ascertain that information had it so desired. Appellants cannot reasonably claim that Herrig owed Cookies a duty to render such services at no profit to himself or his companies. Having found that the compensation he received from these agreements was fair and reasonable, we are convinced that Herrig furnished sufficient pertinent information to Cookies' board to enable it to make prudent decisions concerning the contracts. . . .

We concur in the trial court's assessment of the evidence presented and affirm its dismissal of plaintiffs' claims.

AFFIRMED.

All Justices concur except SCHULTZ, J., who dissents.

SCHULTZ, Justice (dissenting) . . . .

Much of Herrig's evidence concerned the tremendous success of the company. I believe that the trial court and the majority opinion have been so enthralled by the success of the company that they have failed to examine whether these matters of self-dealing were fair to the stockholders. While much credit is due to Herrig for the success of the company, this does not mean that these transactions were fair to the company.

I believe that Herrig failed on his burden of proof by what he did not show. He did not produce evidence of the local going rate for distribution contracts or storage fees outside of a very limited amount of self-serving testimony. He simply did not show the fair market value of his services or expense for freight, advertising and storage cost. He did not show that his taco sauce royalty was fair. This was his burden. He cannot succeed on it by merely showing the success of the company.

The shareholders, on the other hand, produced testimony of what the fair market value of Herrig's services were. The majority discounts this testimony and chooses instead to focus on the success Cookies achieved as a result of Herrig's actions. They focus on the success of the company rather than whether his self-dealing actions were arms-length transactions that were fair and reasonable to the stockholders. The appellants have put forth convincing testimony that Herrig has been grossly over compensated for his services based on their fair market value. Appellant's expert witness, a CPA, performed an analysis to show what the company would have earned if it had hired a $65,000 a year executive officer, paid a marketing supervisor and an advertising agency a commission of five percent of the sales each, built a new warehouse and hired a warehouseman. It was compared with what the company actually did make under Herrig's management. The analysis basically shows what the operating cost of this company should be on the open market when hiring out the work to experts. In 1985 alone, the company's income would have doubled what it actually made were these changes made. The evidence clearly shows that the fair market value of those services is considerably less than what Herrig actually has been paid.

Similarly, appellant's food broker expert witness testified that for $110,865, what the CPA analysis stated was the fair market value for brokerage services, his company would have provided all of the services that Herrig had performed. The company actually paid $730,637 for the services, a difference of $620,000 in one year.

In summary, I believe the majority was dazzled by the tales of Herrig's efforts and Cookies' success in these difficult economic times. In the process, however, it is forgotten that Herrig owes a fiduciary duty to the corporation to deal fairly and reasonably with it in his self-dealing transactions. Herrig is not entitled to skim off the majority of the profits through self-dealing transactions unless they are fair to the minority stockholders. At trial, he failed to prove how his charges were in line with what the company could have gotten on the open market. Because I cannot ignore this inequity to the company and its shareholders, I must respectfully dissent.

NEW YORK STOCK EXCHANGE LISTED COMPANY MANUAL § 312.03(b)

[See Statutory Supplement]

SECTION 3.   COMPENSATION AND THE DOCTRINE OF WASTE

NOTE ON THE AMERICAN TOBACCO LITIGATION *

In 1911, the Supreme Court held that The American Tobacco Company was a monopoly in violation of the Sherman Antitrust Act. United States v. American Tobacco Co., 221 U.S. 106, 31 S.Ct. 632, 55 L.Ed. 663 (1911). As a result, American Tobacco was broken up into a number of new companies, one of which retained the American Tobacco name. In 1912, the shareholders of the new American Tobacco Company adopted the following by-law, Article XII:

> Section 1.   As soon as practicable after the end of the year 1912 and of each year of the Company's operations thereafter, the Treasurer of the Company shall ascertain the net profits, as hereinafter defined, earned by the Company during such year, and if such net profits exceed the sum of $8,222,245.82, which is the estimated amount of such net profits earned during the year 1910 by the businesses that now belong to the Company, the Treasurer shall pay an amount equal in the aggregate to ten per cent of such excess to the President and five Vice–Presi-

---

* Except as otherwise indicated, the facts in this Note are drawn from Rogers v. Hill, 289 U.S. 582, 53 S.Ct. 731, 77 L.Ed. 1385 (1933), *reversing,* 60 F.2d 109 (2d Cir.1932); Heller v. Boylan, 29 N.Y.S.2d 653 (1941), aff'd without opinion 263 App.Div. 815, 32 N.Y.S.2d 131; Rogers v. Guaranty Trust Co. of New York, 288 U.S. 123, 53 S.Ct. 295, 77 L.Ed. 652 (1933); Rogers v. Hill, 34 F.Supp. 358 (S.D.N.Y.1940); J. Baker, Directors and Their Functions (1945); and 2 G. Washington & V. Rothschild, Compensating the Corporate Executive, 880–89 (3d ed. 1962).

dents of the Company in the following proportions, to wit: One-fourth thereof, or 2½ per cent of such amount, to the President; one-fifth of the remainder thereof or 1½ per cent of such amount, to each of the five Vice–Presidents as salary for the year, in addition to the fiscal salary of each of said officers. . . .

Section 5.   This By–Law may be modified or repealed only by the action of the stockholders of the Company and not by the directors.

Rogers v. Hill, 289 U.S. 582, 584 n. 1, 53 S.Ct. 731, 732 n. 1, 77 L.Ed. 1385 (1933).

The background of this by-law was later explained as follows by George Washington Hill, the second president of American Tobacco after it was reconstituted under the 1911 decree:

... Under the plan of dissolution, Mr. Duke was to be a large stockholder in the new companies, as he had been in the old.   He felt it advisable that he himself should have no part in the management of these new competitive companies, *and from a personal point of view he was greatly concerned about providing a real incentive for the men who were to run them.*

I remember, as if it were yesterday, how Mr. Duke explained his plan to me the day he told me I had been selected to be one of the Vice Presidents of the new The American Tobacco Company.   He called me into his office—the very room that is my office today—he sat in the place that I now occupy, and I sat opposite him—he wagged two fingers of his hand at me in the gesture that was typical of him, and he said:

"George, I've worked it out: this is it.   If I sat here, and there was a procession of men coming in through that door, each bringing me $100, I'd be glad to give each of them $10, because there would be $90 out of every hundred for me.   If I own a business, and somebody else runs it for me, and I want additional profits, the smart thing for me to do is to make a deal with him that I'll pay him $10 out of every $100 *of the additional profit he earns for me.*   If he brings me enough additional profit, he'll profit too—but I won't mind that, because I'll be getting $90 out of every hundred.   Well, that's the idea I'm going to propose to the stockholders of every one of these companies.   Now if you fellows sit back and are satisfied with what your business is earning now, you'll have to get along with a salary.   But if you stir your stumps and increase the profits, you'll gain with the stockholders by the increase, and *your stockholders will be glad to pay it to you, because they'll get 90% of the result of your work.*"

That was Mr. Duke's plan, and the stockholders of all the resulting tobacco companies were quick to adopt it.   In our Company—The American Tobacco Company—it took the form of Article XII of the By-laws and was adopted by 621,047 shares, with only 35 shares voting against it.

J. Baker, Directors and Their Functions 49–50 (1945) (emphasis in original).

By the late 1920's, the compensation of American Tobacco's top executives had reached great heights. For example, George W. Hill, American Tobacco's president, received the following salary, "cash credits," and By-law XII bonuses in 1929 and 1930:

Year	Salary	Special Cash Credits	Bonus Under By–Law XII
1929	144,500	$136,507.71	447,870.30
1930	168,000	273,470.76	842,507.72

Hill received amounts in 1931 and 1932 comparable to his 1930 compensation. He also received certain very large stock allotments; his 1931 allotment alone was worth $1,169,280, and was in addition to all other compensation. American Tobacco's vice-presidents received lesser but nevertheless extremely large amounts during this period. For example, two vice-presidents each received bonuses of more than $400,000 in 1930, 1931, and 1932.

Shareholders filed several suits attacking these compensation arrangements. One of these suits, Rogers v. Hill, claimed that By-law XII was invalid, and that, even if valid, the amounts paid under it were unreasonably large. The Second Circuit dismissed Rogers' complaint 2–1, with a ringing dissent by Judge Swan. 60 F.2d 109 (2d Cir.1932). The majority opinion was written by Judge Manton. On appeal, the Supreme Court reversed. It held that the by-law was valid when adopted, but that

> the payments under the by-law have by reason of increase of profits become so large as to warrant investigation in equity in the interest of the company. Much weight is to be given to the action of the stockholders, and the by-law is supported by the presumption of regularity and continuity. But the rule pre-scribed by it cannot, against the protest of a shareholder, be used to justify payments of sums as salaries so large as in substance and effect to amount to spoliation or waste of corporate property. The dissenting opinion of Judge Swan [below] indicates the applicable rule: "If a bonus payment has no relation to the value of services for which it is given, it is in reality a gift in part and the majority stockholders have no power to give away corporate property against the protest of the minority." 60 F.(2d) 109, 113. The facts alleged by plaintiff are sufficient to require that the district court, upon a consideration of all the relevant facts brought forward by the parties, determine whether and to what extent payments to the individual defendants under the by-law constitute misuse and waste of the money of the corporation.

289 U.S. at 591–92, 53 S.Ct. at 735. (It was later learned that Judge Manton, who wrote the Second Circuit's majority opinion in Rogers v. Hill, had been paid $250,000 by American Tobacco's lawyer. Manton was convicted and the lawyer was disbarred.)

————

AMERICAN LAW INSTITUTE, PRINCIPLES OF CORPORATE GOVERNANCE § 5.03

[See Statutory Supplement]

————

NEW YORK STOCK EXCHANGE LISTED COMPANY MANUAL § 312.03(a)

[See Statutory Supplement]

————

SUBCOMMITTEE ON EXECUTIVE COMPENSATION OF THE ABA SECTION ON CORPORATION, BANKING AND BUSINESS LAW, EXECUTIVE COMPENSATION: A 1987 ROAD MAP FOR THE CORPORATE ADVISOR

43 Bus.Law. 185 (1987).

CHAPTER 3: STOCK–RELATED LONG–TERM INCENTIVE PROGRAMS

I. NON–QUALIFIED (NONSTATUTORY) STOCK OPTIONS

. . .

As used in the context of an executive compensation program, the term "non-qualified stock option" means a right granted to one or more employees or executives by a corporation (or by a parent or subsidiary corporation) to acquire shares of the corporation's stock (or stock of a parent or subsidiary). Non-qualified stock options derive their name from the fact that neither the options nor the shares issued upon exercise of the options satisfy the criteria of, or "qualify" for, the special, and heretofore generally favorable, income tax treatment provided under the Code for incentive stock options (formerly "statutory" or "qualified" options). Since non-qualified stock options are neither afforded special tax treatment under nor defined in the Code, by way of contrast to the old statutory stock options, such options are also sometimes referred to as "nonstatutory options."

Stock options often constitute an important part of the compensation and incentive program of a corporation. They may be offered pursuant to a plan applicable to one or more executives, or they may represent part of the premium offered to attract new executives or retain the services of valued existing executives.   By obtaining the right to acquire an equity interest in the corporation, whether at a discount or at market value, the executive acquires a stake in the long-term growth of the corporation, benefits from the capital appreciation of the corporation's stock, and therefore presumably will work diligently for the success of the venture.   However, there is little empirical evidence to prove that corporate performance can be improved by granting stock options. . . .

Neither grant nor vesting of a non-qualified stock option would ordinarily result in recognition of taxable income.   First, the grant of an option does not constitute a transfer of the underlying stock. Second, the option itself is not treated as "property" for federal income tax purposes unless the option has a readily ascertainable fair market value.   According to the regulations, an option has a readily ascertainable fair market value where either: (i) the option itself is actively traded on an established market, or (ii) if not so traded, the option is transferable, immediately exercisable in full, and subject to no restrictions which would affect the fair market value of the option, and the option privilege has a readily ascertainable fair market value. . . .

At the time of exercise of a non-qualified stock option, if the stock received on exercise is not restricted, the executive will recognize income immediately [equal to the difference between the option price and the market value of the stock when the option is exercised] . . . .

II.   INCENTIVE STOCK OPTIONS

One of the most significant developments in the area of executive compensation prior to the passage of the 1986 Tax Act was the reinstatement by the Economic Recovery Tax Act of 1981 ("ERTA") of a special class of statutory stock options known as "incentive stock options."   Incentive stock options provided several advantages for executives over nonstatutory stock options and were generally well received by major employers. . . .

[To qualify for incentive-stock-option (ISO) treatment, a number of conditions must be satisfied, including the following: (1) The option must be issued pursuant to a written plan which specifies the total number of employees, or the class of employees, who are eligible to receive the options.   (2) The written plan must restrict the maximum aggregate fair market value of the stock, with respect to which any employee may exercise options, to no more than $100,000 during any calendar year.   (3) The plan must be approved by the shareholders, within twelve months before or after it is adopted by the board.   (4) The option must be granted within ten years after the plan has been adopted by the board or approved by the shareholders, whichever is earlier.   (5) The option must be exercisable only during the executive's employment, or within three months after termination of employment, and may not be exercisable for more than ten years from the date of grant.   (6) The option price must equal or exceed the fair market value of the stock on the date that the option is granted.]

If the requirements for incentive stock option treatment are satisfied, the executive is not subject to federal income tax either at the time of grant of the option or at the time of its exercise.... Upon disposition of stock acquired pursuant to an incentive stock option, the executive will be taxed at long-term capital gains rates, provided certain holding period requirements are satisfied....

[Stock acquired pursuant to an ISO cannot be disposed of until at least two years has elapsed since the option was granted, and one year has elapsed since the stock was acquired by the employee pursuant to exercise of the option.]

III. STOCK APPRECIATION RIGHTS

A stock appreciation right is the right to be paid an amount equal to the increase in value or spread between the value (or a fraction of the value) of a share of employer stock on the date the SAR is granted and the value (or a fraction of the value) of the share on the date the SAR is exercised. SARs are distinguishable from "phantom stock" ... units (discussed in the next section) because SARs are usually granted in tandem or in conjunction with another right, usually a stock option, and SARs generally do not include (as phantom stock often does) a right to receive the value of dividends payable on the underlying stock while the SAR is outstanding.

SARs can be granted in conjunction with stock options in order to allow the executive to realize the increase in market value of the underlying stock without having to expend cash or otherwise raise capital to pay the option exercise price. In that case, the executive usually may choose to exercise either the option or the SAR, and the exercise of one extinguishes the right to exercise the other. If the executive chooses to exercise the SAR in lieu of the stock option, he may also sometimes choose whether the value of the SAR will be paid to him in cash or in stock. If the executive chooses to receive stock, he will have the opportunity to enjoy future appreciation in the value of the stock, although he will have fewer shares than if he had exercised the option. If the executive chooses cash, future growth in value will obviously depend on how the cash is invested.

Alternatively, SARs may be granted in connection with stock options in order to provide a source of cash with which to pay taxes upon exercise of the associated option. In that case the SAR is usually exercisable (or automatically exercised) in addition to, rather than in lieu of, the associated option, and the SAR is usually payable in cash. However, the executive may be given the right to elect to have some or all of the SAR paid in stock....

SARs also may be granted independently of the grant of any option. When granted in this manner, so-called "naked SARs" take the form of stock-related performance units, entitling the holder to a form of deferred compensation that may be made conditional on continued services, noncompetition, or other conduct not adverse to the employer during or after the executive's termination of employment. . . .

Upon the exercise of an SAR, the executive will normally have to include in gross income (and thus subject to federal income tax) compensation in an amount equal to the cash and/or the fair market value of the shares of stock received pursuant to such exercise. . . .

The principal advantage of SARs to the executive is that they permit the executive to realize the appreciation in the value of employer stock without making an investment, or provide cash with which to pay taxes on exercise of non-qualified stock options. . . .

IV. PHANTOM STOCK . . .

The term "phantom stock" can be used to describe any form of long-term executive incentive arrangement using units that are equivalent to, but are not, actual shares of employer stock. Thus, a phantom stock plan might provide outright grants of phantom "shares" or options based on phantom stock.

Under a phantom stock arrangement, the value of a unit of phantom stock typically equals the appreciation in the market value of the underlying stock between the date the unit is acquired by the executive and its settlement date. In that case, a phantom stock unit is substantially similar to a "naked SAR" discussed in the preceding section of this report. . . .

Phantom stock units can be settled in cash, stock, or some combination of the two forms. Furthermore, dividend equivalents are sometimes paid or accrued on phantom stock.

Phantom stock plans are among the least common forms of long-term incentive compensation plans, particularly among large publicly-held companies. For example, in 1986, only three Fortune 100 companies reported offering such plans. By contrast, ninety-five percent of these companies reported the use of stock option plans that year. . . .

V. RESTRICTED STOCK . . .

"Restricted stock" is a term that defies brief definition. It is capital stock, generally the common stock of an employer, issued pursuant to a plan or agreement to an executive in connection with the performance of services to the employer. The shares may be issued without cost or for a nominal price. The ownership of the stock is subject to certain conditions or "restrictions." The executive's right to ownership in some or all of the shares of the stock, "vesting," is generally made contingent upon the executive's continued employment by the employer for a certain period. Furthermore, the stock may vest ratably over a period of time, or nonratably, according to a prearranged schedule. The plan or agreement typically requires forfeiture of unvested shares upon the participant's termination of employment during the restriction period. Occasionally vested shares may also be subject to repurchase. The repurchase price for the nonvested stock is likely to be the price, if any, paid by the executive, while the repurchase price for the vested stock may be its fair market value as determined by the board of directors, its book value, or the price offered by a third party. . . .

. . . [U]nder Section 83 of the Code and relevant regulations, if [stock] is transferred to an executive in connection with the performance of services, the executive must include in gross [taxable] income the excess of the then fair market value of the [stock] over the amount, if any, paid for it in the first taxable year in which his beneficial interest in the [stock] is either transferable or is not subject to a substantial risk of forfeiture, [but can defer taxation on the stock until that time]. The rights of the executive in restricted stock are treated as transferable for purposes of Section 83 if and when the executive can sell, assign, pledge, or otherwise transfer any interest in the stock to any person (other than the party from whom the executive received the stock) provided that the third-party transferee is not required to surrender the property or an amount equal to its value if the substantial risk of forfeiture materializes. [Accordingly, the executive will recognize ordinary income when the restrictions on transferability expire, but not until then.]

————

SEC REGULATION S–K, ITEM 402

[See Statutory Supplement]

————

INTERNAL REVENUE CODE § 161(m) AND REGULATIONS THEREUNDER

[See Statutory Supplement]

————

SECTION 4. THE CORPORATE OPPORTUNITY DOCTRINE

————

AMERICAN LAW INSTITUTE, PRINCIPLES OF CORPORATE GOVERNANCE § 5.04

[See Statutory Supplement]

————

RESTATEMENT (SECOND) OF AGENCY § 388

[See Statutory Supplement]

AMERICAN LAW INSTITUTE, PRINCIPLES OF CORPORATE GOVERNANCE § 5.05

[See Statutory Supplement]

KLINICKI v. LUNDGREN

Supreme Court of Oregon, In Banc, 1985.
298 Or. 662, 695 P.2d 906.

JONES, Justice.

The factual and legal background of this complicated litigation was succinctly set forth by Chief Judge Joseph in the Court of Appeals opinion as follows:

"In January, 1977, plaintiff Klinicki conceived the idea of engaging in the air transportation business in Berlin, West Germany. He discussed the idea with his friend, defendant Lundgren. At that time, both men were furloughed Pan American pilots stationed in West Germany. They decided to enter the air transportation business, planning to begin operations with an air taxi service and later to expand into other service, such as regularly scheduled flights or charter flights. In April, 1977, they incorporated Berlinair, Inc., as a closely held Oregon corporation. Plaintiff was a vice-president and a director. Lundgren was the corporation's president and a director. Each man owned 33 percent of the company stock. Lelco, Inc., a corporation owned by Lundgren and members of his family, owned 33 percent of the stock. The corporation's attorney owned the remaining one percent of the stock. Berlinair obtained the necessary governmental licenses, purchased an aircraft and in November, 1977, began passenger service.

"As president, Lundgren was responsible, in part, for developing and promoting Berlinair's transportation business. Plaintiff was in charge of operations and maintenance. In November, 1977, plaintiff and Lundgren, as representatives of Berlinair, met with representatives of the Berliner Flug Ring (BFR), a consortium of Berlin travel agents that contracts for charter flights to take sallow German tourists to sunnier climes. The BFR contract was considered a lucrative business opportunity by those familiar with the air transportation business, and plaintiff and defendant had contemplated pursuing the contract when they formed Berlinair. After the initial meeting, all subsequent contacts with BFR were made by Lundgren or other Berlinair employes acting under his directions.

"During the early stages of negotiations, Lundgren believed that Berlinair could not obtain the contract because BFR was then satisfied with its carrier. In early June, 1978, however, Lundgren learned that there was a good chance that the BFR contract might be available. He informed a BFR representative that he would make a proposal on behalf of a new company. On July 7, 1978, he incorporated Air Berlin Charter Company (ABC) and was its sole owner. On August 20, 1978, ABC presented BFR with a contract proposal, and after a series of discussions it was awarded the contract on September 1, 1978. Lundgren effectively concealed from plaintiff his negotiations with BFR and his diversion of the BFR contract to ABC, even though he used Berlinair working time, staff, money and facilities.

"Plaintiff, as a minority stockholder in Berlinair, brought a derivative action against ABC for usurping a corporate opportunity of Berlinair. He also brought an individual claim against Lundgren for compensatory and punitive damages based on breach of fiduciary duty.[1]

"The trial court found that ABC, acting through Lundgren, had wrongfully diverted the BFR contract, which was a corporate opportunity of Berlinair. The court imposed a constructive trust on ABC in favor of Berlinair, ordered an accounting by ABC and enjoined ABC from transferring its assets. The trial court also found that Lundgren, as an officer and director of Berlinair, had breached his fiduciary duties of good faith, fair dealing and full disclosure owed to plaintiff individually and to Berlinair. The court did not award plaintiff any actual damages on the breach of fiduciary duty claim. All the issues were tried

---

1. The named plaintiff in the complaint is F.R. Klinicki. The named defendants are Kim Lundgren, Berlinair, Inc., an Oregon corporation, and Air Berlin Charter Company, an Oregon corporation. The complaint set forth four causes of suit summarized as follows:

(A) The first cause of suit was brought by plaintiff as a derivative stockholders suit in his own behalf and on behalf of all other stockholders of Berlinair, Inc. "and in the right of Berlinair, Inc. and for its benefit" seeking a constructive trust against Lundgren and ABC jointly and severally, an accounting by all defendants and an injunction and attorney fees.

(B) The second cause of suit involves a personal claim by Klinicki requesting the court to require Lundgren to purchase the stock of plaintiff in Berlinair after the BFR corporate opportunity held by ABC is restored to Berlinair, Inc.

(C) The third cause of suit—Count I— is an individual claim of Klinicki for an accounting from Lundgren and ABC.

(D) The third cause of suit—Count II—is plaintiff's individual claim for unjust enrichment against Lundgren.

(E) The third cause of suit—Count III—is a personal claim by plaintiff against Lundgren for breach of implied covenant of good faith and fair dealing to plaintiff. For the third cause of suit plaintiff sought a constructive trust and accounting decree against Lundgren and ABC covering any "monies, funds, assets, facilities and properties received and acquired as a result of Lundgren's breach of fiduciary duty."

(F) The fourth cause of action is an individual suit by Klinicki solely against Lundgren for breach of fiduciary duty seeking general damages of $50,000 and $1 million in punitive damages.

to the court, except that a jury was empaneled to try the punitive damages issue.   It returned a verdict in favor of plaintiff and assessed punitive damages against Lundgren in the amount of $750,000.   Lundgren then moved to dismiss plaintiff's claim for punitive damages.   The court granted the motion to dismiss and, *sua sponte,* entered judgment in favor of Lundgren notwithstanding the verdict on the punitive damages claim."   Klinicki v. Lundgren, 67 Or.App. 160, 162–63, 678 P.2d 1250, 1251–52 (1984) (footnote omitted).

ABC appealed to the Court of Appeals contending that it did not usurp a corporate opportunity of Berlinair. . . .

ABC petitions for review to this court contending that the concealment and diversion of the BFR contract was not a usurpation of a corporate opportunity, because Berlinair did not have the financial ability to undertake that contract.   ABC argues that proof of financial ability is a necessary part of a corporate opportunity case and that plaintiff had the burden of proof on that issue and did not carry that burden.

There is no dispute that the corporate opportunity doctrine precludes corporate fiduciaries from diverting to themselves business opportunities in which the corporation has an expectancy, property interest or right, or which in fairness should otherwise belong to the corporation.   See Henn & Alexander, Laws of Corporations 632–37, § 237 (3rd ed. 1983).   The doctrine follows from a corporate fiduciary's duty of undivided loyalty to the corporation. ABC agrees that, unless Berlinair's financial inability to undertake the contract makes a difference, the BFR contract was a corporate opportunity of Berlinair.[3]

We first address the issue, resolved by the Court of Appeals in Berlinair's favor, of the relevance of a corporation's financial ability to undertake a business opportunity to proving a diversion of corporate opportunity claim.   This is an issue of first impression in Oregon.

The Court of Appeals held that a corporation's financial ability to undertake a business opportunity is not a factor in determining the existence of a corporate opportunity unless the defendant demonstrates that the corporation is technically or de facto insolvent.   Without defining these terms, the Court of Appeals specifically placed the burden of proof as to this issue on the fiduciary by saying: "To avoid liability for usurping a corporate opportunity on the basis that the corporation was insolvent, the fiduciary must prove insolvency."   67 Or.App. at 165, 678 P.2d at 1254.   The Court of Appeals then concluded "that ABC usurped a corporate opportunity belonging to Berlinair when, acting through Lundgren,

---

3. ABC asserts in its brief that the single issue in the corporate opportunity portion of this appeal is the financial ability of Berlinair to undertake the BFR contract. It makes no point of the fact that the trial court found Kim Lundgren usurped the corporate opportunity for himself, yet ABC was controlled and owned by Kim Lundgren, his father, Leonard Lundgren, and their attorney.

the BFR contract was diverted" because nothing in Lundgren's
testimony or otherwise in the record suggested that Berlinair was
insolvent or was no longer a viable corporate entity. 67 Or.App. at
166, 678 P.2d at 1254. Accordingly, the Court of Appeals held that
the constructive trust, injunction, duty to account and other relief
granted by the trial court against ABC were appropriate remedies. . . .

Before proceeding further our initial task must be to define
what is meant by "corporate opportunity," and to determine when,
if ever, a corporate fiduciary may take personal advantage of such an
opportunity. Our resolution of this case will be limited to announcing a rule to be applied when allegations of usurpation of a
corporate opportunity are made against a director of a close corporation. The determination of a rule to apply to similar situations
arising between a director and a publicly held corporation presents
problems and concepts which may not necessarily require us to
apply an identical rule in that similar but distinguishable context.

As we mentioned at the outset, this issue is a matter of first
impression in this state. While courts universally stress the high
standard of fiduciary duty owed by directors and officers to their
corporation, there are distinct schools of thought on the circumstances in which business opportunities may be taken for personal
advantage. One group of jurisdictions severely restricts the corporate official's freedom to take advantage of opportunities by saying
that the ability to undertake the opportunity is irrelevant and
usurpation is essentially prohibited; other jurisdictions use a test
which gives relatively wide latitude to the corporate official on the
theory that financial ability to undertake a corporate opportunity is
a prerequisite to the existence of a corporate opportunity.

A rigid rule was applied in Irving Trust Co. v. Deutsch, 73 F.2d
121 (2nd Cir.1934). In that case a syndicate made up of directors
of Acoustic Products Co. purchased for themselves from another
corporation the rights to manufacture under certain radio patents
which were concededly essential to Acoustic. They justified this on
the ground that Acoustic was not financially able to purchase the
patents on which the defendants later made very substantial profits.
The court refused to inquire whether the conclusion of financial
inability was justified. Referring to the facts which raised a question
whether Acoustic actually did lack the funds or credit necessary to
make the acquisition, the court said:

> ". . . Nevertheless, they [the facts in the case concerning
> whether Acoustic lacked funds to carry out the contract] tend to
> show the wisdom of a rigid rule forbidding directors of a
> solvent corporation to take over for their own profit a corpo-
> rate contract on the plea of the corporation's financial inability
> to perform. If the directors are uncertain whether the corpora-
> tion can make the necessary outlays, they need not embark it
> upon the venture; if they do, they may not substitute them-

selves for the corporation any place along the line and divert possible benefits into their own pockets. . . ."   73 F.2d at 124.

An oft-cited Harvard Law Review note discussed executive appropriation of corporate opportunities and the *Irving Trust* case as follows:

> "Where an opportunity is within the corporation's line of business, the executive seems normally required to offer it for consideration by the board of directors and to await rejection— should it be forthcoming—before seizing it himself.   There are, however, some exceptions to this disclosure requirement, all of which rest immediately on the proposition that the circumstances clearly evidence corporate inability . . . to seize the opportunity. . . .   [An] exception to the requirement of tender arises where the corporation is insolvent and nearly defunct. [Jasper v. Appalachian Gas Co., 152 Ky. 68, 153 S.W. 50 (1913).]   The problem with this exception is the difficulty of its extension to cases where the corporation is in serious financial difficulty or lacks liquid assets but may still be a going concern. [In Hannerty v. Standard Theatre Co., 109 Mo. 297, 19 S.W. 82 (1891), a finding of absence of corporate opportunity was based on the financial inability of the corporation.   But see Irving Trust Co. v. Deutsch, 73 F.2d 121 (2d Cir.1934), and Electronic Dev. Co. v. Robson, 148 Neb. 526, 28 N.W.2d 130 (1947), where mere financial inability was held inadequate to exonerate an executive who appropriated an opportunity.]   In neither case will it ordinarily be entirely clear that, given knowledge of the opportunity, the corporation will be unable to secure needed financing with reasonable rapidity.   The very existence of a prospective profitmaking venture may generate additional financial backing and may convince creditors to be less importunate in their demands.   Every major executive, including the one who has discovered the opportunity, would seem obligated to make a genuine effort to enable the corporation to secure the anticipated profit. . . .

> "Fearing that anything less than a prophylactic rule would discourage executives from expending their full efforts to obtain financing for the corporation, at least one court has articulated the rule that the executive is precluded from appropriating the opportunity where the corporation is allegedly unable to obtain the required funds.   [Citing Irving Trust Co. v. Deutsch, supra.] . . ."   Note, Corporate Opportunity, 74 (Vol. I) Harv.L.Rev. 765, 772–73 (1961) (brackets contain text of footnotes; other footnotes omitted). . . .

Representing a more relaxed view of a corporate official's responsibility, in Guth v. Loft, Inc., 23 Del.Ch. 255, 272–73, 5 A.2d 503, 511 (1939), the Supreme Court of Delaware said:

> ". . . [I]f there is presented to a corporate officer or director a business opportunity *which the corporation is financially able to undertake,* is, from its nature, in the line of the

corporation's business and is of practical advantage to it, is one in which the corporation has an interest or a reasonable expectancy, and, by embracing the opportunity, the self-interest of the officer or director will be brought into conflict with that of his corporation, the law will not permit him to seize the opportunity for himself. . . . "   (Emphasis added.)

The language in *Guth* implies that financial ability to undertake a corporate opportunity is not only relevant, but perhaps a condition precedent to the existence of a corporate opportunity.   But the language in *Guth* was dictum because that famous case, involving the creation of the Pepsi–Cola enterprise, did not involve the issue of financial ability to undertake the opportunity.   The court may have thought that a lack of funds short of insolvency was relevant because it discussed Guth's defense in this area, finding that "Loft's net asset position at that time was amply sufficient to finance the enterprise." [6]   But other language in *Guth* raises the question whether the terms "ability to undertake" and "ability to take advantage of" have broader concerns than mere financial capacity or incapacity:

> " . . . Where a corporation is engaged in a certain business, and an opportunity is presented to it embracing an activity as to which it has *fundamental knowledge, practical experience and ability to pursue, which, logically and naturally is adaptable to its business having regard for its financial position, and is one that is consonant with its reasonable needs and aspirations for expansion,* it may be properly said that the opportunity is in the line of the corporation's business."   23 Del.Ch. at 279, 5 A.2d at 514 (emphasis added).

On the other end of the legal spectrum from Irving Trust Co. v. Deutsch, supra, are two Minnesota cases: Miller v. Miller, 301 Minn. 207, 222 N.W.2d 71, 77 A.L.R.3d 941 (1974), and A.C. Petters v. St. Cloud Enterprises, Inc., 301 Minn. 261, 222 N.W.2d 83 (1974).   In *Miller,* the Minnesota Supreme Court stated a two-step test to be applied in corporate opportunity cases.   The first step, the "line of business" part of the test, was described as follows:

---

6.   In Guth v. Loft, Inc., 23 Del.Ch. 255, 270, 5 A.2d 503, 510 (1939), the court held that determination of the issue of breach of duty should be made from a consideration of all the circumstances of the transactions, noting the accepted rule that corporate officers and directors are not permitted to use their position of trust and confidence to further their private interests:

" . . . The standard of loyalty is measured by no fixed scale.

"If an officer or director of a corporation, in violation of his duty as such, acquires gain or advantage for himself, the law charges the interest so acquired with a trust for the benefit of the corporation, at its election, while it denies to

the betrayer all benefit and profit.   The rule, inveterate and uncompromising in its rigidity, does not rest upon the narrow ground of injury or damage to the corporation resulting from a betrayal of confidence, but upon a broader foundation of a wise public policy that, for the purpose of removing all temptation, extinguishes all possibility of profit flowing from a breach of the confidence imposed by the fiduciary relation.   Given the relation between the parties, a certain result follows; and a constructive trust is the remedial device through which precedence of self is compelled to give way to the stern demands of loyalty.   [Citations omitted.]"

"... The threshold question to be answered is whether a business opportunity presented is also a 'corporate' opportunity, i.e., whether the business opportunity is of sufficient importance and is so closely related to the existing or prospective activity of the corporation as to warrant judicial sanctions against its personal acquisition by a managing officer or director of the corporation. This question, necessarily one of fact, can best be resolved, we believe, by resort to a flexible application of the 'line of business' test set forth in Guth v. Loft, Inc., supra. The inquiry of the factfinder should be directed to all facts and circumstances relevant to the question, the most significant being: Whether the business opportunity presented is one in which the complaining corporation has an interest or an expectancy growing out of an existing contractual right; the relationship of the opportunity to the corporation's business purposes and current activities—whether essential, necessary, or merely desirable to its reasonable needs and aspirations—; whether within or without its corporate powers, the opportunity embraces areas adaptable to its business and into which the corporation might easily, naturally, or logically expand; the competitive nature of the opportunity—whether prospectively harmful or unfair—; *whether the corporation, by reason of insolvency or lack of resources, has the financial ability to acquire the opportunity;* and whether the opportunity includes activities as to which the corporation has a fundamental knowledge, practical experience, facilities, equipment, personnel, and the ability to pursue. The fact that the opportunity is not within the scope of the corporation's powers, while a factor to be considered, should not be determinative, especially where the corporate fiduciary dominates the board of directors or is the majority shareholder." 301 Minn. at 224–25, 222 N.W.2d at 81 (emphasis added).*

* The Court in Miller v. Miller went on to delineate the second step in its two-step test as follows:

Absent any evidence of fraud or a breach of fiduciary duty, if it is determined that a business opportunity is not a corporate opportunity, the corporate officer should not be held liable for its acquisition. If, however, the opportunity is found to be a corporate one, liability should not be imposed upon the acquiring officer if the evidence establishes that his acquisition did not violate his fiduciary duties of loyalty, good faith, and fair dealing toward the corporation. Thus the second step in the two-step process leading to the determination of the ultimate question of liability involves close scrutiny of the equitable considerations existing prior to, at the time of, and following the officer's acquisition. Resolution will necessarily depend upon a consideration of all the facts and circumstances of each case considered in the light of those factors which control the decision that the opportunity was in fact a corporate opportunity. Significant factors which should be considered are the nature of the officer's relationship to the management and control of the corporation; whether the opportunity was presented to him in his official or individual capacity; his prior disclosure of the opportunity to the board of directors or shareholders and their response; whether or not he used or exploited corporate facilities, assets, or personnel in acquiring the opportunity; whether his acquisition harmed or benefited the corporation; and all other facts and circumstances bearing on the officer's good faith and whether he exercised the diligence, devotion, care, and fairness toward the corporation which ordinarily prudent men would exercise under similar circumstances in like positions....

In other words, the court found that financial ability is a prerequisite to establishing a corporate opportunity. The court went on to hold that, where the facts were in dispute, the burden of proof on the financial issue rests upon the "party attacking the acquisition":

> "If the facts are undisputed that the business opportunity presented bears no logical or reasonable relation to the existing or prospective business activities of the corporation *or that it lacks either the financial or fundamental practical or technical ability to pursue it,* then such opportunity would have to be found to be noncorporate as a matter of law. If the facts are disputed or reasonable minds functioning judicially could disagree as to whether the opportunity is closely associated with the existing or prospective activities of the corporation or its financial or technical ability to pursue it, *the question is one of fact with the burden of proof resting upon the party attacking the acquisition.*" 301 Minn. at 225, 222 N.W.2d at 81 (emphasis added).

The companion case of A.C. Petters v. St. Cloud Enterprises, Inc., supra, applied the rule of Miller v. Miller, supra. See also Ellzey v. Fyr–Pruf, Inc. 376 So.2d 1328 (Miss.1979).

Counsel for defendant, relying on *Miller,* contends there is no corporate opportunity if there is no capacity to take advantage of the corporate opportunity. We reject this argument. By the same token, we reject plaintiff's contention, relying on *Irving Trust,* that financial ability is totally irrelevant in an unlawful taking of a corporate opportunity. . . .

On April 13, 1984, the American Law Institute published its "Tentative Draft No. 3" concerning "Principles of Corporate Governance: Analysis and Recommendations." The draft, of course, does not represent the position of the ALI, but it does contain definitions and rules which we find helpful in resolving the main issue in this case. Section 5.12 of the draft, which contains the proposed general rule and definition, reads as follows:

> "(a) *General Rule:*

> "A director or principal senior executive may not take a corporate opportunity for himself or an associate unless:

> (1) The corporate opportunity has first been offered to the corporation, and disclosure has been made to the corporate

---

We are not to be understood, by adopting this two-step process, as suggesting that a finding of bad faith is essential to impose liability upon the acquiring officer. Nor, conversely, that good faith alone, apart from the officer's fiduciary duty requiring loyalty and fair dealing toward the corporation, will absolve him from liability. And it must be acknowledged, in adopting corporate opportunity doctrine expanded beyond the narrow preexisting property interest or expectancy standard, that there can be cases where the officer's personal seizure of an opportunity so clearly essential to the continuance of a corporation or so intimately related to its activities as to amount to a direct interference with its existing activities would negate any attempt by the officer to prove his good faith, loyalty, and fair dealing.

301 Minn. at 225–27; 222 N.W.2d at 81–82.

decisionmaker of all material facts known to the director or principal senior executive concerning his conflict of interest and the corporate opportunity (unless the corporate decisionmaker is otherwise aware of such material facts); and

(2) The corporate opportunity has been rejected by the corporation in a manner that meets one of the following standards:

(A) In the case of a rejection of a corporate opportunity that was authorized by disinterested directors following such disclosure, the directors who authorized the rejection acted in a manner that meets the standards of the business judgment rule set forth in § 4.01(d); [8]

(B) In the case of a rejection that was authorized or ratified by disinterested shareholders following such disclosure, the rejection was not equivalent to a waste of corporate assets; and

(C) In the case of a rejection that was not authorized or ratified in the manner contemplated in § 5.12(a)(2)(A) or (B) or permitted by the terms of a [validly adopted] standard of the corporation . . ., the taking of the opportunity was fair to the corporation.

"(b) *Definition of a Corporate Opportunity:*

"A corporate opportunity means any opportunity to engage in a business activity (including acquisition or use of any contract right or other tangible or intangible property) that:

(1) In the case of a principal senior executive or any director, is an opportunity that is communicated or otherwise made available to him either:

(A) in connection with the performance of his obligations as a principal senior executive or director or under circumstances that should reasonably lead him to believe that the person offering the opportunity expects him to offer it to the corporation, or

(B) through the use of corporate information or property, if the resulting opportunity is one that the principal senior executive or director should reasonably be expected to believe would be of interest to the corporation; or

(2) In the case of a principal senior executive or a director who is a full-time employee of the corporation, is an opportunity that he knows or reasonably should know

---

8. Section 4.01 provides in pertinent part:

"A director has a duty to his corporation to perform his functions in good faith, in a manner that he reasonably believes to be in the best interests of the corporation * * * and with the care that an ordinarily prudent person would reasonably be expected to exercise in a like profession and under similar circumstances."

See, Devlin v. Moore, 64 Or. 433, 462, 130 P. 35, 45 (1913).

is closely related to the business in which the corporation is engaged or may reasonably be expected to engage." (Bracketed section references omitted.) *

Section 5.12 presents an approach very similar to that suggested by Chief Judge Joseph in the Court of Appeals decision rendered in this case. Section 5.12 generally would require an opportunity that could be advantageous to the corporation to be offered to the corporation by a director or principal senior executive before he takes it for himself. Section 5.12 declines to adopt the rigid rule expressed in Irving Trust Co. v. Deutsch, supra, which precludes a person subject to the duty of loyalty from pursuing a rejected opportunity. The proposed rule permits a director or principal senior executive to deal with his corporation so long as he deals fairly with full disclosure and bears the burden of proving fairness unless the corporate opportunity was rejected by disinterested directors or shareholders.

The comment to Section 5.12(a) reads:

"Section 5.12(a) sets forth the general rule requiring a director or principal senior executive to first offer an opportunity to the corporation before taking it for himself. If the opportunity is not offered to the corporation, the director or principal senior executive will have violated § 5.12(a).

"Section 5.12(a) contemplates that a corporate opportunity will be promptly offered to the corporation, and that the corporation will promptly accept or reject the opportunity. Failure to accept the opportunity promptly will be considered tantamount to a rejection. . . ."

and that

". . . Rejection in the context of § 5.12(a)(2) may be based on one or more of a number of factors, such as lack of interest of the corporation in the opportunity, *its financial inability to acquire the opportunity,* legal restrictions on its ability to accept the opportunity, or unwillingness of a third party to deal with the corporation. . . ." (Emphasis added.)

The comment to Section 5.12(b) reads:

"Section 5.12(b) defines a corporate opportunity broadly as including any proposed acquisition of contract rights or other tangible or intangible property which falls into one of the categories set forth in §§ 5.12(b)(1) or 5.12(b)(2). . . ."

Section 5.12(c) would allocate the burden of proof in corporate opportunity cases as follows:

"(c) *Burden of Proof:*

"In any proceeding in which there is a challenge under § 5.12(a), the challenging party has the burden of proof, except

---

* Section 5.12 of ALI, Principles of Corporate Governance was renumbered as § 5.05 and somewhat revised in the final version of the *Principles*. (Footnote by ed.)

if the rejection of a corporate opportunity was not authorized or ratified in the manner contemplated in § 5.12(a)(2)(A) or (B) or permitted by the terms of a [validly adopted] standard of the corporation ..., the director or principal senior executive has the burden of proving that his taking of the opportunity was fair to the corporation.... *If the challenging party satisfies the burden of proving that a corporate opportunity was taken without being offered to the corporation, the challenging party will prevail.*"   (Emphasis added.)

The comment to Section 5.12(c) reads in part:

"The burden of coming forward with evidence and the ultimate burden of proof will be upon the person attacking a director's or principal senior executive's conduct to prove that (1) the director or principal senior executive acquired a corporate opportunity....   The complainant will also have the burden of proof with respect to all other aspects of the transaction, including lack of disclosure to the corporate decisionmaker and establishing that the requisite number of directors or shareholders who approved or ratified the transaction were not disinterested.   *However, if disinterested directors or shareholders have not approved or ratified the rejection of the opportunity, the director or principal senior executive will have the burden of proving that his taking of the opportunity was fair and that the rejection of the opportunity was fair to the corporation at the time of the rejection....*"   (Emphasis added.)

Whether the rejection was fair or not includes consideration of whether the corporation was financially or otherwise incapacitated from undertaking the corporate opportunity.   We agree with the proposed ALI Principles of Corporate Governance, supra, as to the following rules for application in close corporation corporate opportunity cases.

Where a director or principal senior executive of a close corporation wishes to take personal advantage of a "corporate opportunity," as defined by the proposed rule, the director or principal senior executive must comply strictly with the following procedure:

(1) the director or principal senior executive must promptly offer the opportunity and disclose all material facts known regarding the opportunity to the disinterested directors or, if there is no disinterested director, to the disinterested shareholders.   If the director or principal senior executive learns of other material facts after such disclosure, the director or principal senior executive must disclose these additional facts in a like manner before personally taking the opportunity.

(2) The director or principal senior executive may take advantage of the corporate opportunity only after full disclosure and only if the opportunity is rejected by a majority of the disinterested directors or, if there are no disinterested directors, by a majority of the disinterested shareholders.   If, after full disclosure, the disinter-

ested directors or shareholders unreasonably fail to reject the offer,[13] the interested director or principal senior executive may proceed to take the opportunity if he can prove the taking was otherwise "fair" to the corporation. Full disclosure to the appropriate corporate body is, however, an absolute condition precedent to the validity of any forthcoming rejection as well as to the availability to the director or principal senior executive of the defense of fairness.

(3) An appropriation of a corporate opportunity may be ratified by rejection of the opportunity by a majority of disinterested directors or a majority of disinterested shareholders, after full disclosure subject to the same rules as set out above for prior offer, disclosure and rejection. Where a director or principal senior executive of a close corporation appropriates a corporate opportunity without first fully disclosing the opportunity and offering it to the corporation, absent ratification, that director or principal senior executive holds the opportunity in trust for the corporation.

Applying these rules to the facts in this case, we conclude:

(1) Lundgren, as director and principal executive officer of Berlinair, owed a fiduciary duty to Berlinair.

(2) The BFR contract was a "corporate opportunity" of Berlinair.

(3) Lundgren formed ABC for the purpose of usurping the opportunity presented to Berlinair by the BFR contract.

(4) Lundgren did not offer Berlinair the BFR contract.

(5) Lundgren did not attempt to obtain the consent of Berlinair to his taking of the BFR corporate opportunity.

(6) Lundgren did not fully disclose to Berlinair his intent to appropriate the opportunity for himself and ABC.

(7) Berlinair never rejected the opportunity presented by the BFR contract.

(8) Berlinair never ratified the appropriation of the BFR contract.

(9) Lundgren, acting for ABC, misappropriated the BFR contract.

Because of the above, the defendant may not now contend that Berlinair did not have the financial ability to successfully pursue the BFR contract. As stated in proposed Section 5.12(c) of the Principles of Corporate Governance, supra, "If the challenging party satisfies the burden of proving that a corporate opportunity was

---

13. A valid acceptance of the offer by the disinterested directors or shareholders would bar the fiduciary from appropriating the opportunity. An acceptance of the offer by the disinterested directors which failed to meet the standards of the business judgment rule, or an acceptance by the disinterested shareholders which was the equivalent of a waste of corporate assets would have the same effect as an unreasonable failure to reject. The corporate fiduciary could appropriate the opportunity only upon a showing that the taking was fair to the corporation. See ALI, Principles of Corporate Governance and Structure § 5.12(a)(2) (Tent.Draft No. 3 1984).

taken without being offered to the corporation, the challenging party will prevail." ...

The Court of Appeals is affirmed.

———

KERRIGAN v. UNITY SAVINGS ASS'N, 58 Ill.2d 20, 28, 317 N.E.2d 39, 43–44 (1974). "[I]f the doctrine of business opportunity is to possess any vitality, the corporation ... must be given the opportunity to decide, upon full disclosure of the pertinent facts, whether it wishes to enter into a business that is reasonably incident to its present or prospective operations. If directors fail to make such a disclosure and to tender the opportunity, the prophylactic purpose of the rule imposing a fiduciary obligation requires that the directors be foreclosed from exploiting that opportunity on their own behalf."

———

ALI, PRINCIPLES OF CORPORATE GOVERNANCE § 5.06

[See Statutory Supplement]

———

NOTE ON THE APPLICATION OF THE CORPORATE OPPORTUNITY DOCTRINE

A variety of tests have been utilized to determine whether a director or officer has wrongfully appropriated a corporate opportunity.

1. Under one test, often associated with Lagarde v. Anniston Lime & Stone Co., 126 Ala. 496, 502, 28 So. 199, 201 (1900), the corporate opportunity doctrine applies only when the director or officer has acquired property in which "the corporation has an interest already existing or in which it has an expectancy growing out of an existing right," or his "interference will in some degree balk the corporation in effecting the purposes of its creation."

The application of the first branch of the *Lagarde* test is uncertain, because the terms "interest" and "expectancy" have no fixed meaning in this context. See, e.g., Abbott Redmont Thinlite Corp. v. Redmont, 475 F.2d 85, 88–89 (2d Cir.1973). In *Lagarde* itself, the court held that real estate in which the corporation was a tenant constituted a corporate expectancy, but real estate in which the corporation owned an undivided one-third interest did not.

The application of the second branch of the *Lagarde* test is also uncertain. Presumably, it would cover cases in which the corporation's need for the property is very substantial. See, e.g., Harmony

Way Bridge Co. v. Leathers, 353 Ill. 378, 187 N.E. 432 (1933) (a director purchased a right of way that was needed as an approach to his corporation's bridge); News–Journal Corp. v. Gore, 147 Fla. 217, 2 So.2d 741 (1941) (a director purchased a tract of land that the corporation leased for its building, and immediately increased the rent).

Insofar as the meaning of the *Lagarde* test can be determined, it is unduly narrow. Even the Alabama Supreme Court may now be seeking more leeway, by broadening the second branch:

> The last restriction in *Lagarde*, that which prohibits "balking the corporate purpose," is really quite broad in its formulation, although the case has often been described as restrictive.... We think that *Lagarde* when properly read enforces responsibilities for the corporate officer or director comparable to those outlined in *Guth v. Loft, Inc.*, 23 Del.Ch. 255, 5 A.2d 503 (1939), where the Delaware Supreme Court employed the doctrine of corporate opportunity and observed that it
>
> > ". . . demands of a corporate officer or director, peremptorily and inexorably, the most scrupulous observance of his duty, not only affirmatively to protect the interests of the corporation committed to his charge, but also to refrain from doing anything that would work injury to the corporation, or to deprive it of profit or advantage which his skill and ability might properly bring to it, or to enable it to make in the reasonable and lawful exercise of its powers. . . .

Morad v. Coupounas, 361 So.2d 6, 8–9 (Ala.1978).

2. A second test is whether the opportunity was in the corporation's "line of business." This test was adopted in the leading case of Guth v. Loft, Inc., 23 Del.Ch. 255, 5 A.2d 503 (1939), relied on in *Morad*. Guth was the president and chief executive of Loft, Inc., which was engaged in the manufacture and sale of beverages. Guth became dissatisfied with Loft's existing business arrangements with Coca–Cola Company. National Pepsi–Cola Company was then bankrupt, and Guth and an associate organized Pepsi–Cola Company to acquire National's secret formula and trademark. The opportunity came to Guth as a result of his connection with Loft, Guth used Loft's funds and facilities to acquire and develop Pepsi–Cola Company's business, and Loft purchased large quantities of Pepsi–Cola. Partly by these means, and partly by his own efforts, Pepsi–Cola's shares became very valuable. The court required Guth to transfer those shares to Loft.

> Where a corporation is engaged in a certain business, and an opportunity is presented to it embracing an activity as to which it has fundamental knowledge, practical experience and ability to pursue, which, logically and naturally, is adaptable to its business having regard for its financial position, and is one that is consonant with its reasonable needs and aspirations for

expansion, it may be properly said that the opportunity is in the line of the corporation's business.

Id. at 279, 5 A.2d at 514.   The opinion clearly implied that Guth would have been liable even if he had not used Loft funds and facilities, because Pepsi–Cola was so closely related to Loft's existing business.

Delaware also appears to place weight on how the opportunity comes to the corporate director or officer.   If the offer is made to the director or officer as an agent of the corporation, the "line of business" test is employed.   If the opportunity is offered to the director or officer as an individual, however, liability will apparently arise only if the opportunity is "essential" to the corporation, or is subject to an "interest or expectancy" of the corporation, or if the director or officer uses corporate resources to exploit the opportunity.   Kaplan v. Fenton, 278 A.2d 834, 836 (Del.1971).   See Carrad, The Corporate Opportunity Doctrine in Delaware: A Guide to Corporate Planning and Anticipatory Defensive Measures, 2 Del. J.Corp.L. 1, 5 (1977).

3.   A third test is the "fairness" test.   A typical example is Durfee v. Durfee & Canning, Inc., 323 Mass. 187, 199, 80 N.E.2d 522, 529 (1948), in which the court approved a statement in H. Ballantine, Corporations 204–05 (rev. ed. 1946) that "the true basis of the doctrine should not be found in any 'expectancy' or property interest concept, but in the unfairness on the particular facts of a fiduciary taking advantage of an opportunity when the interests of the corporation justly call for protection.   This calls for the application of ethical standards of what is fair and equitable to particular sets of facts."

4.   Still another test, calling for a two-step line-of-business and fairness analysis, was adopted in Miller v. Miller, 301 Minn. 207, 222 N.W.2d 71 (1974).   This test is discussed in Klinicki v. Lundgren, supra, which reflects yet another approach.

5.   Pat K. Chew conducted a comprehensive analysis of corporate opportunity cases reported between April 1977 and April 1988. Chew, Competing Interests in the Corporate Opportunity Doctrine, 67 N.C. L.Rev. 436 (1989).   She found that these disputes usually occur in close corporations and that the opportunities were often directly competitive to the business of the corporation.

———

NOTE ON CORPORATE OPPORTUNITIES

Traditionally, the body of law governing corporate opportunities has lacked clarity in two important respects.   To begin with, that body of law has tended to lump all corporate opportunities together.   In fact, however, there are two very different kinds of reasons why an opportunity that a corporate fiduciary took for herself may have been a *corporate* opportunity.   Call an individual who is a director, officer, employee, or agent of a corporation, *A,* and call the Corporation *C.* One reason that an opportunity that *A* took may have been a corporate opportunity is that *A* became aware of the opportunity through the use of corporate property, corporate information, or *A* 's corporate position—that is, through the use of corporate assets. In such cases, the opportunity seems to be Corporation *C* 's property. If *A* took such an opportunity for herself without offering it to Corporation *C* she seems to be stealing it, just as much as if she had taken or used any other kind of corporate property for her own personal benefit.

A second, very different kind of reason why an opportunity can constitute a corporate opportunity is that it is closely related to the corporation's business. If that is the *only* reason why an opportunity constitutes a corporate opportunity, then by hypothesis *A* will have found the opportunity on her own, rather than through the use of corporate property, information, or position. If an opportunity that *A* finds on her own constitutes a corporate opportunity, it is not because the discovery of the opportunity is a product of the use of corporate assets—it isn't—but because for some other reason *A* owes Corporation *C* a duty to turn over the opportunity to it.

If *A* is an officer of Corporation *C,* the reason why she might owe *C* the duty to turn over an opportunity, simply because the opportunity is closely related to the corporation's business, is that *A* owes *C* not only the duty not to take advantage of *C* by using *C* 's assets for her own personal benefit, but also the duty to advance *C* 's legitimate interests when a chance to do so arises. Whether a given individual owes such a duty may depend in part on the individual's position. The higher up in the corporate hierarchy the individual is, the more plausible it is that she owes such a duty, and the more demanding the duty will normally be. Indeed, in the case of opportunities that are closely related to the corporation's business, a high-ranking executive like a CEO may not have an "individual" capacity—that is, the CEO may reasonably be expected to give all of her business efforts, and certainly any business efforts that are within the penumbra of the corporation's business, to the corporation. Moreover, as an administrative matter it might be good policy to conclusively presume that any opportunity that is closely related to the corporation's business comes to a high-ranking officer as a result of the fact that she is a high-ranking officer, because it may be too difficult to prove otherwise.

In short, an opportunity that is discovered through the use of corporate property, information, or position should be a corporate opportunity regardless of *A* 's position, but whether an opportunity is a corporate opportunity simply because it is closely related to the corporation's business may partly depend on *A* 's position. Although a high-ranking executive can fairly be expected to turn over to the corporation any opportunity that is closely related to the corporation's business, solely because it is so related, the same expectation may not apply to a blue-collar or clerical worker, and perhaps not even to a low-level manager.

Another area in which the traditional law of corporate opportunities has lacked clarity concerns the issue whether and to what extent an individual who takes an opportunity can raise, as a defense to a suit based on the taking, that the corporation was unable to take the opportunity. This issue usually, although not always, arises in the context of whether the corporation had the financial ability to take the relevant opportunity. The courts are all over the lot on this issue. At one extreme, some cases, like Irving Trust v. Deutsch (discussed in Klinicki v. Lundgren, supra) hold that the corporation's financial ability should be irrelevant, because it is too easy for executives who take a corporate opportunity to create a financial-inability excuse through manipulation of the corporation's financial picture. At the other extreme, some cases hold that not only is the corporation's financial ability relevant, but that a plaintiff who claims that a corporate opportunity has been taken has the burden of pleading and proving that the corporation had the financial ability to take the opportunity. See, e.g., Miller v. Miller, p. 733, supra. Still other courts take some intermediate position between these two extremes. See, e.g., Klinicki v. Lundgren, p. 716, supra. Furthermore, there are a number of shadings on the issue how the corporation's financial ability should be measured in this context. See, e.g., Yiannatisis v. Stephanis, 653 A.2d 275 (Del.1995).

More importantly, the courts have failed to disentangle two very different scenarios in which a corporate-inability defense may play a role. In one scenario, *A* first offers the opportunity to Corporation *C*; *C* decides to reject the opportunity; and *A* then takes it for herself. A shareholder then brings a derivative action against *A*, and *A* raises as a defense that she did not take the opportunity until the corporation had rejected it. If, in such a case, the plaintiff puts into issue the fairness or reasonability of Corporation *C*'s rejection of the opportunity, *C*'s inability to take the opportunity is relevant because it may justify the rejection.

In the second scenario, *A* takes an opportunity *without* having first offered it to Corporation *C*. Then, when *A* is sued for taking the opportunity, she raises as a defense that *C* did not have the ability to take the opportunity. In this scenario, *C*'s inability to take the opportunity should not be a defense, because if an opportunity is a corporate opportunity, a fiduciary should always be obliged to offer the opportunity to the corporation in the first instance, and let the *corporation* decide whether it is, or can make itself, able to take the opportunity. This is essentially the position taken in cases like *ERCO*, supra, and in ALI, Principles of Corporate Governance § 5.05.

———

SECTION 5. DUTIES OF CONTROLLING SHAREHOLDERS

SINCLAIR OIL CORPORATION v. LEVIEN
Supreme Court of Delaware, 1971.
280 A.2d 717.

WOLCOTT, Chief Justice. This is an appeal by the defendant, Sinclair Oil Corporation (hereafter Sinclair), from an order of the Court of Chancery, 261 A.2d 911, in a derivative action requiring Sinclair to account for damages sustained by its subsidiary, Sinclair Venezuelan Oil Company (hereinafter Sinven), organized by Sinclair for the purpose of operating in Venezuela, as a result of dividends paid by Sinven, the denial to Sinven of industrial development, and a breach of contract between Sinclair's wholly-owned subsidiary, Sinclair International Oil Company, and Sinven.

Sinclair, operating primarily as a holding company, is in the business of exploring for oil and of producing and marketing crude oil and oil products. At all times relevant to this litigation, it owned about 97% of Sinven's stock. The plaintiff owns about 3000 of 120,000 publicly held shares of Sinven. Sinven, incorporated in 1922, has been engaged in petroleum operations primarily in Venezuela and since 1959 has operated exclusively in Venezuela.

Sinclair nominates all members of Sinven's board of directors. The Chancellor found as a fact that the directors were not independent of Sinclair. Almost without exception, they were officers, directors, or employees of corporations in the Sinclair complex. By reason of Sinclair's domination, it is clear that Sinclair owed Sinven a fiduciary duty. Getty Oil Company v. Skelly Oil Co., 267 A.2d 883 (Del.Supr.1970); Cottrell v. Pawcatuck Co., 35 Del.Ch. 309, 116 A.2d 787 (1955). Sinclair concedes this.

The Chancellor held that because of Sinclair's fiduciary duty and its control over Sinven, its relationship with Sinven must meet the test of intrinsic fairness. The standard of intrinsic fairness involves both a high degree of fairness and a shift in the burden of proof. Under this standard the burden is on Sinclair to prove, subject to careful judicial scrutiny, that its transactions with Sinven were objectively fair. Guth v. Loft, Inc., 23 Del.Ch. 255, 5 A.2d 503 (1939); Sterling v. Mayflower Hotel Corp., 33 Del.Ch. 293, 93 A.2d 107, 38 A.L.R.2d 425 (Del.Supr.1952); Getty Oil Co. v. Skelly Oil Co., supra.

Sinclair argues that the transactions between it and Sinven should be tested, not by the test of intrinsic fairness with the accompanying shift of the burden of proof, but by the business judgment rule under which a court will not interfere with the judgment of a board of directors unless there is a showing of gross and palpable overreaching. Meyerson v. El Paso Natural Gas Co., 246 A.2d 789 (Del.Ch.1967). A board of directors enjoys a presumption of sound business judgment, and its decisions will not be disturbed if they can be attributed to any rational business purpose. A court under such circumstances will not substitute its own notions of what is or is not sound business judgment.

We think, however, that Sinclair's argument in this respect is misconceived. When the situation involves a parent and a subsidiary, with the parent controlling the transaction and fixing the terms, the test of intrinsic fairness, with its resulting shifting of the burden of proof, is applied. Sterling v. Mayflower Hotel Corp., supra; David J. Greene & Co. v. Dunhill International, Inc., 249 A.2d 427 (Del.Ch.1968); Bastian v. Bourns, Inc., 256 A.2d 680 (Del.Ch.1969) aff'd. Per Curiam (unreported) (Del.Supr.1970). The basic situation for the application of the rule is the one in which the parent has received a benefit to the exclusion and at the expense of the subsidiary.

Recently, this court dealt with the question of fairness in parent-subsidiary dealings in Getty Oil Co. v. Skelly Oil Co., supra. In that case, both parent and subsidiary were in the business of refining and marketing crude oil and crude oil products. The Oil Import Board ruled that the subsidiary, because it was controlled by the parent, was no longer entitled to a separate allocation of imported crude oil. The subsidiary then contended that it had a right to share the quota of crude oil allotted to the parent. We ruled that the business judgment standard should be applied to determine this contention. Although the subsidiary suffered a loss through the administration of the oil import quotas, the parent gained nothing. The parent's quota was derived solely from its own past use. The past use of the subsidiary did not cause an increase in the parent's quota. Nor did the parent usurp a quota of the subsidiary. Since the parent received nothing from the subsidiary to the exclusion of the minority stockholders of the subsidiary, there was no self-dealing. Therefore, the business judgment standard was properly applied.

A parent does indeed owe a fiduciary duty to its subsidiary when there are parent-subsidiary dealings. However, this alone will not evoke the intrinsic fairness standard. This standard will be applied only when the fiduciary duty is accompanied by self-dealing—the situation when a parent is on both sides of a transaction with its subsidiary. Self-dealing occurs when the parent, by virtue of its domination of the subsidiary causes the subsidiary to act in such a way that the parent receives something from the subsidiary to the exclusion of, and detriment to, the minority stockholders of the subsidiary.

We turn now to the facts. The plaintiff argues that, from 1960 through 1966, Sinclair caused Sinven to pay out such excessive dividends that the industrial development of Sinven was effectively prevented, and it became in reality a corporation in dissolution.

From 1960 through 1966, Sinven paid out $108,000,000 in dividends ($38,000,000 in excess of Sinven's earnings during the same period). The Chancellor held that Sinclair caused these dividends to be paid during a period when it had a need for large amounts of cash. Although the dividends paid exceeded earnings, the plaintiff concedes that the payments were made in compliance with 8 Del.C. § 170, authorizing payment of dividends out of surplus or net profits. However, the plaintiff attacks these dividends on the ground that they resulted from an improper motive— Sinclair's need for cash. The Chancellor, applying the intrinsic fairness standard, held that Sinclair did not sustain its burden of proving that these dividends were intrinsically fair to the minority stockholders of Sinven.

Since it is admitted that the dividends were paid in strict compliance with 8 Del.C. § 170, the alleged excessiveness of the payments alone would not state a cause of action. Nevertheless, compliance with the applicable statute may not, under all circumstances, justify all dividend payments. If a plaintiff can meet his burden of proving that a dividend cannot be grounded on any reasonable business objective, then the courts can and will interfere with the board's decision to pay the dividend.

Sinclair contends that it is improper to apply the intrinsic fairness standard to dividend payments even when the board which voted for the dividends is completely dominated. In support of this contention, Sinclair relies heavily on American District Telegraph Co. [ADT] v. Grinnell Corp., (N.Y.Sup.Ct.1969) aff'd. 33 A.D.2d 769, 306 N.Y.S.2d 209 (1969). Plaintiffs were minority stockholders of ADT, a subsidiary of Grinnell. The plaintiffs alleged that Grinnell, realizing that it would soon have to sell its ADT stock because of a pending anti-trust action, caused ADT to pay excessive dividends. Because the dividend payments conformed with applicable statutory law, and the plaintiffs could not prove an abuse of discretion, the court ruled that the complaint did not state a cause of action. Other decisions seem to support Sinclair's contention. In Metropolitan Casualty Ins. Co. v. First State Bank of Temple, 54 S.W.2d 358 (Tex.Civ.App.1932), rev'd. on other grounds, 79 S.W.2d 835 (Sup.Ct.1935), the court held that a majority of interested directors does not void a declaration of dividends because all directors, by necessity, are interested in and benefited by a dividend declaration. See, also, Schwartz v. Kahn, 183 Misc. 252, 50 N.Y.S.2d 931 (1944); Weinberger v. Quinn, 264 A.D. 405, 35 N.Y.S.2d 567 (1942).

We do not accept the argument that the intrinsic fairness test can never be applied to a dividend declaration by a dominated board, although a dividend declaration by a dominated board will not inevitably demand the application of the intrinsic fairness standard. Moskowitz v. Bantrell, 41 Del.Ch. 177, 190 A.2d 749 (Del. Supr.1963). If such a dividend is in essence self-dealing by the parent, then the intrinsic fairness standard is the proper standard. For example, suppose a parent dominates a subsidiary and its board of directors. The subsidiary has outstanding two classes of stock, X and Y. Class X is owned by the parent and Class Y is owned by minority stockholders of the subsidiary. If the subsidiary, at the direction of the parent, declares a dividend on its Class X stock only, this might well be self-dealing by the parent. It would be receiving something from the subsidiary to the exclusion of and detrimental to its minority stockholders. This self-dealing, coupled with the parent's fiduciary duty, would make intrinsic fairness the proper standard by which to evaluate the dividend payments.

Consequently it must be determined whether the dividend payments by Sinven were, in essence, self-dealing by Sinclair. The dividends resulted in great sums of money being transferred from Sinven to Sinclair. However, a proportionate share of this money was received by the minority shareholders of Sinven. Sinclair received nothing from Sinven to the exclusion of its minority stockholders. As such, these dividends were not self-dealing. We hold therefore that the Chancellor erred in applying the intrinsic fairness test as to these dividend payments. The business judgment standard should have been applied.

We conclude that the facts demonstrate that the dividend payments complied with the business judgment standard and with 8 Del.C. § 170. The motives for causing the declaration of dividends are immaterial unless the plaintiff can show that the dividend payments resulted from improper motives and amounted to waste. The plaintiff contends only that the dividend payments drained Sinven of cash to such an extent that it was prevented from expanding.

The plaintiff proved no business opportunities which came to Sinven independently and which Sinclair either took to itself or denied to Sinven. As a matter of fact, with two minor exceptions which resulted in losses, all of Sinven's operations have been conducted in Venezuela, and Sinclair had a policy of exploiting its oil properties located in different countries by subsidiaries located in the particular countries.

From 1960 to 1966 Sinclair purchased or developed oil fields in Alaska, Canada, Paraguay, and other places around the world. The plaintiff contends that these were all opportunities which could have been taken by Sinven. The Chancellor concluded that Sinclair had not proved that its denial of expansion opportunities to Sinven was intrinsically fair. He based this conclusion on the following findings of fact. Sinclair made no real effort to expand Sinven. The excessive dividends paid by Sinven resulted in so great a cash drain as to effectively deny to Sinven any ability to expand. During this same period Sinclair actively pursued a company-wide policy of developing through its subsidiaries new sources of revenue, but Sinven was not permitted to participate and was confined in its activities to Venezuela.

However, the plaintiff could point to no opportunities which came to Sinven. Therefore, Sinclair usurped no business opportunity belonging to Sinven. Since Sinclair received nothing from Sinven to the exclusion of and detriment to Sinven's minority stockholders, there was no self-dealing. Therefore, business judgment is the proper standard by which to evaluate Sinclair's expansion policies.

Since there is no proof of self-dealing on the part of Sinclair, it follows that the expansion policy of Sinclair and the methods used to achieve the desired result must, as far as Sinclair's treatment of Sinven is concerned, be tested by the standards of the business judgment rule. Accordingly, Sinclair's decision absent fraud or gross overreaching, to achieve expansion through the medium of its subsidiaries, other than Sinven, must be upheld.

Even if Sinclair was wrong in developing these opportunities as it did, the question arises, with which subsidiaries should these opportunities have been shared? No evidence indicates a unique need or ability of Sinven to develop these opportunities. The decision of which subsidiaries would be used to implement Sinclair's expansion policy was one of business judgment with which a court will not interfere absent a showing of gross and palpable overreaching. Meyerson v. El Paso Natural Gas Co., 246 A.2d 789 (Del.Ch.1967). No such showing has been made here.

Next, Sinclair argues that the Chancellor committed error when he held it liable to Sinven for breach of contract.

In 1961 Sinclair created Sinclair International Oil Company (hereafter International), a wholly owned subsidiary used for the purpose of coordinating all of Sinclair's foreign operations. All crude purchases by Sinclair were made thereafter through International.

On September 28, 1961, Sinclair caused Sinven to contract with International whereby Sinven agreed to sell all of its crude oil and refined products to International at specified prices. The contract provided for minimum and maximum quantities and prices. The plaintiff contends that Sinclair caused this contract to be breached in two respects. Although the contract called for payment on receipt, International's payments lagged as much as 30 days after receipt. Also, the contract required International to purchase at least a fixed minimum amount of crude and refined products from Sinven. International did not comply with this requirement.

Clearly, Sinclair's act of contracting with its dominated subsidiary was self-dealing. Under the contract Sinclair received the products produced by Sinven, and of course the minority shareholders of Sinven were not able to share in the receipt of these products. If the contract was breached, then Sinclair received these products to the detriment of Sinven's minority shareholders. We agree with the Chancellor's finding that the contract was breached by Sinclair, both as to the time of payments and the amounts purchased.

Although a parent need not bind itself by a contract with its dominated subsidiary, Sinclair chose to operate in this manner. As Sinclair has received the benefits of this contract, so must it comply with the contractual duties.

Under the intrinsic fairness standard, Sinclair must prove that its causing Sinven not to enforce the contract was intrinsically fair to the minority shareholders of Sinven. Sinclair has failed to meet this burden. Late payments were clearly breaches for which Sinven should have sought and received adequate damages. As to the quantities purchased, Sinclair argues that it purchased all the products produced by Sinven. This, however, does not satisfy the standard of intrinsic fairness. Sinclair has failed to prove that Sinven could not possibly have produced or some way have obtained the contract minimums. As such, Sinclair must account on this claim.

Finally, Sinclair argues that the Chancellor committed error in refusing to allow it a credit or setoff of all benefits provided by it to Sinven with respect to all the alleged damages. The Chancellor held that setoff should be allowed on specific transactions, e.g., benefits to Sinven under the contract with International, but denied an overall setoff against all damages claimed. We agree with the Chancellor, although the point may well be moot in view of our holding that Sinclair is not required to account for the alleged excessiveness of the dividend payments.

We will therefore reverse that part of the Chancellor's order that requires Sinclair to account to Sinven for damages sustained as a result of dividends paid between 1960 and 1966, and by reason of the denial to Sinven of expansion during that period. We will affirm the remaining portion of that order and remand the cause for further proceedings.

———

Accord: Ripley v. International Railways of Central America, 8 N.Y.2d 430, 209 N.Y.S.2d 289, 171 N.E.2d 443 (1960) (controlling shareholder of railroad was liable for the difference between (i) the transportation rates it paid for shipping commodities over the railroad and (ii) the fair and reasonable value of the transportation services).

———

KAHN v. LYNCH COMMUNICATION SYSTEMS

Supreme Court of Delaware, 1994.
638 A.2d 1110.

Before MOORE, WALSH, and HOLLAND, JJ.

HOLLAND, Justice:

This is an appeal by the plaintiff-appellant, Alan R. Kahn ("Kahn"), from a final judgment of the Court of Chancery which was entered after a trial. The action, instituted by Kahn in 1986, originally sought to enjoin the acquisition of the defendant-appellee, Lynch Communication Systems, Inc. ("Lynch"), by the defendant-appellee, Alcatel U.S.A. Corporation ("Alcatel"), pursuant to a tender offer and cash-out merger.[1] Kahn amended his complaint to

---

1. In his capacity as custodian for Amanda and Kimberly Kahn, Kahn held 525 shares of Lynch common stock.

seek monetary damages after the Court of Chancery denied his request for a preliminary injunction. The Court of Chancery subsequently certified Kahn's action as a class action on behalf of all Lynch shareholders, other than the named defendants, who tendered their stock in the merger, or whose stock was acquired through the merger.

A three-day trial was held April 13–15, 1993. Kahn alleged that Alcatel was a controlling shareholder of Lynch and breached its fiduciary duties to Lynch and its shareholders. According to Kahn, Alcatel dictated the terms of the merger; made false, misleading, and inadequate disclosures; and paid an unfair price.

The Court of Chancery concluded that Alcatel was, in fact, a controlling shareholder that owed fiduciary duties to Lynch and its shareholders. It also concluded that Alcatel had not breached those fiduciary duties. Accordingly, the Court of Chancery entered judgment in favor of the defendants.

Kahn has raised three contentions in this appeal. Kahn's first contention is that the Court of Chancery erred by finding that "the tender offer and merger were negotiated by an independent committee," and then placing the burden of persuasion on the plaintiff, Kahn. Kahn asserts the uncontradicted testimony in the record demonstrated that the committee could not and did not bargain at arm's length with Alcatel. Kahn's second contention is that Alcatel's Offer to Purchase was false and misleading because it failed to disclose threats made by Alcatel to the effect that if Lynch did not accept its proposed price, Alcatel would institute a hostile tender offer at a lower price. Third, Kahn contends that the merger price was unfair. Alcatel contends that the Court of Chancery was correct in its findings, with the exception of concluding that Alcatel was a controlling shareholder.

This Court has concluded that the record supports the Court of Chancery's finding that Alcatel was a controlling shareholder. However, the record does not support the conclusion that the burden of persuasion shifted to Kahn. Therefore, the burden of proving the *entire* fairness of the merger transaction remained on Alcatel, the controlling shareholder. Accordingly, the judgment of the Court of Chancery is reversed. The matter is remanded for further proceedings in accordance with this opinion.

Facts

Lynch, a Delaware corporation, designed and manufactured electronic telecommunications equipment, primarily for sale to telephone operating companies. Alcatel, a holding company, is a subsidiary of Alcatel (S.A.), a French company involved in public telecommunications, business communications, electronics, and optronics. Alcatel (S.A.), in turn, is a subsidiary of Compagnie Generale d'Electricite ("CGE"), a French corporation with operations in energy, transportation, telecommunications and business systems.

In 1981, Alcatel acquired 30.6 percent of Lynch's common stock pursuant to a stock purchase agreement. As part of that agreement, Lynch amended its certificate of incorporation to require an 80 percent affirmative vote of its shareholders for approval of any business combination. In addition, Alcatel obtained proportional representation on the Lynch board of directors and the right to purchase 40 percent of any equity securities offered by Lynch to third parties. The agreement also precluded Alcatel from holding more than 45 percent of Lynch's stock prior to October 1, 1986. By the time of the merger which is contested in this action, Alcatel owned 43.3 percent of Lynch's outstanding stock; designated five of the eleven members of Lynch's board of directors; two of three members of the executive committee; and two of four members of the compensation committee.

In the spring of 1986, Lynch determined that in order to remain competitive in the rapidly changing telecommunications field, it would need to obtain fiber optics technology to complement its existing digital electronic capabilities. Lynch's management identified a target company, Telco Systems, Inc. ("Telco"), which possessed both fiber optics and other valuable technological assets. The record reflects that Telco expressed interest in being acquired by Lynch. Because of the supermajority voting provision, which Alcatel had negotiated when it first purchased its shares, in order to proceed with the Telco combination Lynch needed Alcatel's consent. In June 1986, Ellsworth F. Dertinger ("Dertinger"), Lynch's CEO and chairman of its board of directors, contacted Pierre Suard ("Suard"), the chairman of Alcatel's parent company, CGE, regarding the acquisition of Telco by Lynch. Suard expressed Alcatel's opposition to Lynch's acquisition of Telco. Instead, Alcatel proposed a combination of Lynch and Celwave Systems, Inc. ("Celwave"), an indirect subsidiary of CGE engaged in the manufacture and sale of telephone wire, cable and other related products.

Alcatel's proposed combination with Celwave was presented to the Lynch board at a regular meeting held on August 1, 1986. Although several directors expressed interest in the original combination which had been proposed with Telco, the Alcatel representatives on Lynch's board made it clear that such a combination would not be considered before a Lynch/Celwave combination. According to the minutes of the August 1 meeting, Dertinger expressed his opinion that Celwave would not be of interest to Lynch if Celwave was not owned by Alcatel.

At the conclusion of the meeting, the Lynch board unanimously adopted a resolution establishing an Independent Committee, consisting of Hubert L. Kertz ("Kertz"), Paul B. Wineman ("Wineman"), and Stuart M. Beringer ("Beringer"), to negotiate with Celwave and to make recommendations concerning the appropriate terms and conditions of a combination with Celwave. On October 24, 1986,

Alcatel's investment banking firm, Dillon, Read & Co., Inc. ("Dillon Read") made a presentation to the Independent Committee. Dillon Read expressed its views concerning the benefits of a Celwave/Lynch combination and submitted a written proposal of an exchange ratio of 0.95 shares of Celwave per Lynch share in a stock-for-stock merger.

However, the Independent Committee's investment advisors, Thomson McKinnon Securities Inc. ("Thomson McKinnon") and Kidder, Peabody & Co., Inc. ("Kidder Peabody"), reviewed the Dillon Read proposal and concluded that the 0.95 ratio was predicated on Dillon Read's overvaluation of Celwave. Based upon this advice, the Independent Committee determined that the exchange ratio proposed by Dillon Read was unattractive to Lynch. The Independent Committee expressed its unanimous opposition to the Celwave/Lynch merger on October 31, 1986.

Alcatel responded to the Independent Committee's action on November 4, 1986, by withdrawing the Celwave proposal. Alcatel made a simultaneous offer to acquire the entire equity interest in Lynch, constituting the approximately 57 percent of Lynch shares not owned by Alcatel. The offering price was $14 cash per share.

On November 7, 1986, the Lynch board of directors revised the mandate of the Independent Committee. It authorized Kertz, Wineman, and Beringer to negotiate the cash merger offer with Alcatel. At a meeting held that same day, the Independent Committee determined that the $14 per share offer was inadequate. The Independent's Committee's own legal counsel, Skadden, Arps, Slate, Meagher & Flom ("Skadden Arps"), suggested that the Independent Committee should review alternatives to a cash-out merger with Alcatel, including a "white knight" third party acquiror, a repurchase of Alcatel's shares, or the adoption of a shareholder rights plan.

On November 12, 1986, Beringer, as chairman of the Independent Committee, contacted Michiel C. McCarty ("McCarty") of Dillon Read, Alcatel's representative in the negotiations, with a counteroffer at a price of $17 per share. McCarty responded on behalf of Alcatel with an offer of $15 per share. When Beringer informed McCarty of the Independent Committee's view that $15 was also insufficient, Alcatel raised its offer to $15.25 per share. The Independent Committee also rejected this offer. Alcatel then made its final offer of $15.50 per share.

At the November 24, 1986 meeting of the Independent Committee, Beringer advised its other two members that Alcatel was "ready to proceed with an unfriendly tender at a lower price" if the $15.50 per share price was not recommended by the Independent Committee and approved by the Lynch board of directors. Beringer also told the other members of the Independent Committee that the alternatives to a cash-out merger had been investigated but were impracticable.[3] After meeting with its financial and legal advisors, the Independent Committee voted unanimously to recommend that the Lynch board of directors approve Alcatel's $15.50 cash per share price for a merger with Alcatel. The Lynch board met later that day. With Alcatel's nominees abstaining, it approved the merger.

Alcatel Dominated Lynch
Controlling Shareholder Status

This Court has held that "a shareholder owes a fiduciary duty only if it owns a majority interest in or *exercises control* over the business affairs of the corporation." *Ivanhoe Partners v. Newmont Mining Corp.*, Del.Supr., 535 A.2d 1334, 1344 (1987) (emphasis added). With regard to the exercise of control, this Court has stated:

> [A] shareholder who owns less than 50% of a corporation's outstanding stocks does not, without more, become a controlling shareholder of that corporation, with a concomitant fiduciary status. For a dominating relationship to exist in the absence of controlling stock ownership, a plaintiff must allege domination by a minority shareholder through actual control of corporation conduct.

Citron v. Fairchild Camera & Instrument Corp., Del.Supr., 569 A.2d 53, 70 (1989) (quotations and citation omitted).

Alcatel held a 43.3 percent minority share of stock in Lynch. Therefore, the threshold question to be answered by the Court of Chancery was whether, despite its minority ownership, Alcatel exercised control over Lynch's business affairs. Based upon the testimony and the minutes of the August 1, 1986 Lynch board meeting, the Court of Chancery concluded that Alcatel did exercise control over Lynch's business decisions.

The standard of appellate review with regard to the Court of Chancery's factual findings is deferential. *Cede & Co. v. Technicolor, Inc.*, Del.Supr., 634 A.2d 345, 360 (1993). Those findings will not be set aside by this Court unless they are clearly erroneous or not the product of a logical and orderly deductive reasoning process. *Id.* The record supports the Court of Chancery's factual finding that Alcatel dominated Lynch. . . .

Entire Fairness Requirement
Dominating Interested Shareholder

A controlling or dominating shareholder standing on both sides of a transaction, as in a parent-subsidiary context, bears the burden of proving its entire fairness. *Weinberger v. UOP, Inc.*, Del.Supr., 457 A.2d 701, 710 (1983). *See Rosenblatt v. Getty Oil Co.*, Del.

---

3. The minutes reflect that Beringer told the Committee the "white knight" alternative "appeared impractical with the 80% approval requirement"; the repurchase of Alcatel's shares would produce a "highly leveraged company with a lower book value" and was an alternative "not in the least encouraged by Alcatel"; and a shareholder rights plan was not viable because of the increased debt it would entail.

Supr., 493 A.2d 929, 937 (1985). The demonstration of fairness that is required was set forth by this Court in *Weinberger:*

> The concept of fairness has two basic aspects: fair dealing and fair price. The former embraces questions of when the transaction was timed, how it was initiated, structured, negotiated, disclosed to the directors, and how the approvals of the directors and the stockholders were obtained. The latter aspect of fairness relates to the economic and financial considerations of the proposed merger, including all relevant factors: assets, market value, earnings, future prospects, and any other elements that affect the intrinsic or inherent value of a company's stock. However, the test for fairness is not a bifurcated one as between fair dealing and price. All aspects of the issue must be examined as a whole since the question is one of entire fairness.

Weinberger v. UOP, Inc., 457 A.2d at 711 (citations omitted).

The logical question raised by this Court's holding in *Weinberger* was what type of evidence would be reliable to demonstrate entire fairness. That question was not only anticipated but also initially addressed in the *Weinberger* opinion. *Id.* at 709–10 n. 7. This Court suggested that the result "could have been entirely different if UOP had appointed an independent negotiating committee of its outside directors to deal with Signal at arm's length," because "fairness in this context can be equated to conduct by a theoretical, wholly independent, board of directors." *Id.* Accordingly, this Court stated, "a showing that the action taken was as though each of the contending parties had in fact exerted its bargaining power against the other at arm's length is strong *evidence* that the transaction meets the test of fairness." *Id.* (emphasis added).

In this case, the Vice Chancellor noted that the Court of Chancery has expressed "differing views" regarding the effect that an approval of a cash-out merger by a special committee of disinterested directors has upon the controlling or dominating shareholder's burden of demonstrating entire fairness. One view is that such approval shifts to the plaintiff the burden of proving that the transaction was unfair.... The other view is that such an approval renders the business judgment rule the applicable standard of judicial review....

"It is often of critical importance whether a particular decision is one to which the business judgment rule applies or the entire fairness rule applies." *Nixon v. Blackwell,* Del.Supr., 626 A.2d 1366, 1376 (1993). The definitive ... answer with regard to the Court of Chancery's "differing views" is [that] in the context of a ... proceeding involving a parent-subsidiary merger, ... the "approval of a merger ... by an informed vote of a majority of the minority stockholders, while not a legal prerequisite, shifts the burden of proving the unfairness of the merger entirely to the plaintiffs." ...

Entire fairness remains the proper focus of judicial analysis in examining an interested merger, irrespective of whether the burden of proof remains upon or is shifted away from the controlling or dominating shareholder, because the unchanging nature of the underlying "interested" transaction requires careful scrutiny. *See Weinberger v. UOP, Inc.*, 457 A.2d at 710 (citing *Sterling v. Mayflower Hotel Corp.*, Del.Supr., 93 A.2d 107, 110 (1952)). The policy rationale for the exclusive application of the entire fairness standard to interested merger transactions has been stated as follows:

> Parent subsidiary mergers, unlike stock options, are proposed by a party that controls, and will continue to control, the corporation, whether or not the minority stockholders vote to approve or reject the transaction. The controlling stockholder relationship has the potential to influence, however subtly, the vote of [ratifying] minority stockholders in a manner that is not likely to occur in a transaction with a noncontrolling party.
>
> Even where no coercion is intended, shareholders voting on a parent subsidiary merger might perceive that their disapproval could risk retaliation of some kind by the controlling stockholder. For example, the controlling stockholder might decide to stop dividend payments or to effect a subsequent cash out merger at a less favorable price, for which the remedy would be time consuming and costly litigation. At the very least, the potential for that perception, and its possible impact upon a shareholder vote, could never be fully eliminated. Consequently, in a merger between the corporation and its controlling stockholder—even one negotiated by disinterested, independent directors—no court could be certain whether the transaction terms fully approximate what truly independent parties would have achieved in an arm's length negotiation. Given that uncertainty, a court might well conclude that even minority shareholders who have ratified a . . . merger need procedural protections beyond those afforded by full disclosure of all material facts. One way to provide such protections would be to adhere to the more stringent entire fairness standard of judicial review.

Citron v. E.I. Du Pont de Nemours & Co., 584 A.2d at 502.

Once again, this Court holds that the exclusive standard of judicial review in examining the propriety of an interested cash-out merger transaction by a controlling or dominating shareholder is entire fairness. *Weinberger v. UOP, Inc.*, 457 A.2d at 710–11. The initial burden of establishing entire fairness rests upon the party who stands on both sides of the transaction. *Id.* However, an approval of the transaction by an independent committee of directors or an informed majority of minority shareholders shifts the burden of proof on the issue of fairness from the controlling or dominating shareholder to the challenging shareholder-plaintiff. *See Rosenblatt v. Getty Oil Co.*, 493 A.2d at 937–38. Nevertheless, even when an interested cash-out merger transaction receives the informed approval of a majority of minority stockholders or an independent committee of disinterested directors, an entire fairness analysis is the only proper standard of judicial review. *See id.*

Independent Committees
Interested Merger Transactions

It is a now well-established principle of Delaware corporate law that in an interested merger, the controlling or dominating shareholder proponent of the transaction bears the burden of proving its entire fairness. *Weinberger v. UOP, Inc.,* Del.Supr., 457 A.2d 701, 710–11 (1983). It is equally well-established in such contexts that any shifting of the burden of proof on the issue of entire fairness must be predicated upon this Court's decisions in *Rosenblatt v. Getty Oil Co.,* Del.Supr., 493 A.2d 929 (1985) and *Weinberger v. UOP, Inc.,* Del.Supr., 457 A.2d 701 (1983). In *Weinberger,* this Court noted that "[p]articularly in a parent-subsidiary context, a showing that the action taken was as though each of the contending parties had *in fact* exerted its bargaining power against the other at arm's length is strong evidence that the transaction meets the test of fairness." 457 A.2d at 709–10 n. 7 (emphasis added). *Accord Rosenblatt v. Getty Oil Co.,* 493 A.2d at 937–38 & n. 7. In *Rosenblatt,* this Court pointed out that "[an] independent bargaining structure, while not conclusive, is strong evidence of the fairness" of a merger transaction. *Rosenblatt v. Getty Oil Co.,* 493 A.2d at 938 n. 7.

The same policy rationale which requires judicial review of interested cash-out mergers exclusively for entire fairness also mandates careful judicial scrutiny of a special committee's real bargaining power before shifting the burden of proof on the issue of entire fairness. A recent decision from the Court of Chancery articulated a two-part test for determining whether burden shifting is appropriate in an interested merger transaction. *Rabkin v. Olin Corp.,* Del.Ch., C.A. No. 7547 (Consolidated), Chandler, V.C., 1990 WL 47648, slip op. at 14–15 (Apr. 17, 1990), *reprinted in* 16 Del.J.Corp.L. 851, 861–62 (1991), *aff'd,* Del.Supr., 586 A.2d 1202 (1990). In *Olin,* the Court of Chancery stated:

> The mere existence of an independent special committee . . . does not itself shift the burden. At least two factors are required. First, the majority shareholder must not dictate the terms of the merger. *Rosenblatt v. Getty Oil Co.,* Del.Ch., 493 A.2d 929, 937 (1985). Second, the special committee must have real bargaining power that it can exercise with the majority shareholder on an arms length basis.

Id., slip op. at 14–15, 16 Del.J.Corp.L. at 861–62. This Court expressed its agreement with that statement by affirming the Court of Chancery decision in *Olin* on appeal.

Lynch's Independent Committee

In the case *sub judice,* the Court of Chancery observed that although "Alcatel did exercise control over Lynch with respect to the decisions made at the August 1, 1986 board meeting, it does not necessarily follow that Alcatel also controlled the terms of the merger and its approval." This observation is theoretically accurate, as this opinion has already stated. *Weinberger v. UOP, Inc.,* 457 A.2d at 709–10 n. 7. However, the performance of the Independent Committee merits careful judicial scrutiny to determine whether Alcatel's demonstrated pattern of domination was effectively neutralized so that "each of the contending parties had in fact exerted its bargaining power against the other at arm's length." *Id.* The fact that the same independent directors had submitted to Alcatel's demands on August 1, 1986 was part of the basis for the Court of Chancery's finding of Alcatel's domination of Lynch. Therefore, the Independent Committee's ability to bargain at arm's length with Alcatel was suspect from the outset.

The Independent Committee's original assignment was to examine the merger with Celwave which had been proposed by Alcatel. The record reflects that the Independent Committee effectively discharged that assignment and, in fact, recommended that the Lynch board reject the merger on Alcatel's terms. Alcatel's response to the Independent Committee's adverse recommendation was not the pursuit of further negotiations regarding its Celwave proposal, but rather its response was an offer to buy Lynch. That offer was consistent with Alcatel's August 1, 1986 expressions of an intention to dominate Lynch, since an acquisition would effectively eliminate once and for all Lynch's remaining vestiges of independence.

The Independent Committee's second assignment was to consider Alcatel's proposal to purchase Lynch. The Independent Committee proceeded on that task with full knowledge of Alcatel's demonstrated pattern of domination. The Independent Committee was also obviously aware of Alcatel's refusal to negotiate with it on the Celwave matter.

Burden of Proof Shifted
Court of Chancery's Finding

The Court of Chancery began its factual analysis by noting that Kahn had "attempted to shatter" the image of the Independent Committee's actions as having "appropriately simulated" an arm's length, third-party transaction. The Court of Chancery found that "to some extent, [Kahn's attempt] was successful." The Court of Chancery gave credence to the testimony of Kertz, one of the members of the Independent Committee, to the effect that he did not believe that $15.50 was a fair price but that he voted in favor of the merger because he felt there was no alternative.

The Court of Chancery also found that Kertz understood Alcatel's position to be that it was ready to proceed with an unfriendly tender offer at a lower price if Lynch did not accept the $15.50 offer, and that Kertz perceived this to be a threat by Alcatel. The Court of Chancery concluded that Kertz ultimately decided that, "although $15.50 was not fair, a tender offer and merger at that price would be better for Lynch's stockholders than an unfriendly tender offer at a significantly lower price." The Court of Chancery determined that "Kertz failed either to satisfy himself that the offered price was fair or oppose the merger."

In addition to Kertz, the other members of the Independent Committee were Beringer, its chairman, and Wineman. Wineman did not testify at trial.[7] Beringer was called by Alcatel to testify at trial. Beringer testified that at the time of the Committee's vote to recommend the $15.50 offer to the Lynch board, he thought "that *under the circumstances,* a price of $15.50 was fair and should be accepted" (emphasis added).

Kahn contends that these "circumstances" included those referenced in the minutes for the November 24, 1986 Independent Committee meeting: "Mr. Beringer added that Alcatel is 'ready to proceed with an unfriendly tender at a lower price' if the $15.50 per share price is not recommended to, and approved by, the Company's Board of Directors." In his testimony at trial, Beringer verified, albeit reluctantly, the accuracy of the foregoing statement in the minutes: "[Alcatel] *let us know* that they were giving serious consideration to making an unfriendly tender" (emphasis added).

The record reflects that Alcatel was "ready to proceed" with a hostile bid. This was a conclusion reached by Beringer, the Independent Committee's chairman and spokesman, based upon communications to him from Alcatel. Beringer testified that although there was no reference to a particular price for a hostile bid during his discussions with Alcatel, or even specific mention of a "lower" price, "the implication was clear to [him] that it probably would be at a lower price."[8]

According to the Court of Chancery, the Independent Committee rejected three lower offers for Lynch from Alcatel and then accepted the $15.50 offer "after being advised that [it] was fair and after considering the absence of alternatives." The Vice Chancellor expressly acknowledged the impracticability of Lynch's Independent Committee's alternatives to a merger with Alcatel:

> Lynch was not in a position to shop for other acquirors, since Alcatel could block any alternative transaction. Alcatel also made it clear that it was not interested in having its shares

---

7. Based upon inferences from Kertz's testimony, the Court of Chancery noted that "Wineman apparently agreed" that $15.50 was a fair price. However, the record also reflects that it was Wineman who urged the other independent directors to yield to Alcatel's demands at the August 1, 1986 meeting.

Wineman's failure to testify also permits both this Court and the Court of Chancery to draw the inference adverse to Alcatel, that Alcatel dictated the outcome of the November 24, 1986 meeting. As we have

previously noted, the production of weak evidence when strong is, or should have been, available can lead only to the conclusion that the strong would have been adverse. *See Smith v. Van Gorkom,* Del. Supr., 488 A.2d 858, 878 (1985).

8. On the other hand, Dertinger, an officer and director of Lynch, testified that he was informed by Alcatel that the price of an unfriendly tender offer would indeed be lower and would in fact be $12 per share.

repurchased by Lynch. The Independent Committee decided that a stockholder rights plan was not viable because of the increased debt it would entail.

Nevertheless, based upon the record before it, the Court of Chancery found that the Independent Committee had "appropriately simulated a third-party transaction, where negotiations are conducted at arms-length and there is no compulsion to reach an agreement." The Court of Chancery concluded that the Independent Committee's actions "as a whole" were "sufficiently well informed ... and aggressive to simulate an arms-length transaction," so that the burden of proof as to entire fairness shifted from Alcatel to the contending Lynch shareholder, Kahn. The Court of Chancery's reservations about that finding are apparent in its written decision.

The Power to Say No, The Parties' Contentions, Arm's Length Bargaining

The Court of Chancery properly noted that limitations on the alternatives to Alcatel's offer did not mean that the Independent Committee should have agreed to a price that was unfair:

> The power to say no is a significant power. It is the duty of directors serving on [an independent] committee to approve only a transaction that is in the best interests of the public shareholders, to say no to any transaction that is not fair to those shareholders and is not the best transaction available. It is not sufficient for such directors to achieve the best price that a fiduciary will pay if that price is not a fair price.

(Quoting *In re First Boston, Inc. Shareholders Litig.*, Del.Ch., C.A. 10338 (Consolidated), Allen, C., 1990 WL 78836, slip op. at 15–16 (June 7, 1990)). . . .

In [*American Gen. Corp. v. Texas Air Corp.*, Del.Ch., C.A. Nos. 8390, 8406, 8650 & 8805, Hartnett, V.C., 1987 WL 6337 (Feb. 5, 1987), *reprinted in* 13 Del.J.Corp.L. 173 (1988)] in the context of an application for injunctive relief, the Court of Chancery found that the members of the Special Committee were "truly independent and ... performed their tasks in a proper manner," but it also found that "at the end of their negotiations with [the majority shareholder] the Committee members were issued an ultimatum and told that they must accept the $16.50 per share price or [the majority shareholder] would proceed with the transaction without their input." *Id.,* slip op. at 11–12, 13 Del.J.Corp.L. at 181. The Court of Chancery concluded based upon this evidence that the Special Committee had thereby lost "its ability to negotiate in an arms-length manner" and that there was a reasonable probability that the burden of proving entire fairness would remain on the defendants if the litigation proceeded to trial. *Id.,* slip op. at 12, 13 Del.J.Corp.L. at 181.

Alcatel's efforts to distinguish *American General* are unpersuasive. . . .

Alcatel's Entire Fairness Burden Did Not Shift to Kahn

A condition precedent to finding that the burden of proving entire fairness has shifted in an interested merger transaction is a careful judicial analysis of the factual circumstances of each case. Particular consideration must be given to evidence of whether the special committee was truly independent, fully informed, and had the freedom to negotiate at arm's length. . . . "Although perfection is not possible," unless the controlling or dominating shareholder can demonstrate that it has not only formed an independent committee but also replicated a process "as though each of the contending parties had in fact exerted its bargaining power at arm's length," the burden of proving entire fairness will not shift. *Weinberger v. UOP, Inc.,* 457 A.2d at 709–10 n. 7. *See also Rosenblatt v. Getty Oil Co.,* Del.Supr., 493 A.2d 929, 937–38 (1985).

Subsequent to *Rosenblatt,* this Court pointed out that "the use of an independent negotiating committee of outside directors may have significant advantages to the majority stockholder in defending suits of this type," but it does not *ipso facto* establish the procedural fairness of an interested merger transaction. *Rabkin v. Philip A. Hunt Chem. Corp.,* Del.Supr., 498 A.2d 1099, 1106 & n. 7 (1985). In reversing the granting of the defendants' motion to dismiss in *Rabkin,* this Court implied that the burden on entire fairness would not be shifted by the use of an independent committee which concluded its processes with "what could be considered a quick surrender" to the dictated terms of the controlling shareholder. *Id.* at 1106. This Court concluded in *Rabkin* that the majority stockholder's "attitude toward the minority," coupled with the "apparent absence of any meaningful negotiations as to price," did not manifest the exercise of arm's length bargaining by the independent committee. *Id.* . . .

The Court of Chancery's determination that the Independent Committee "appropriately simulated a third-party transaction, where negotiations are conducted at arm's-length and there is no compulsion to reach an agreement," is not supported by the record. Under the circumstances present in the case *sub judice,* the Court of Chancery erred in shifting the burden of proof with regard to entire fairness to the contesting Lynch shareholder-plaintiff, Kahn. The record reflects that the ability of the Committee effectively to negotiate at arm's length was compromised by Alcatel's threats to proceed with a hostile tender offer if the $15.50 price was not approved by the Committee and the Lynch board. The fact that the Independent Committee rejected three initial offers, which were well below the Independent Committee's estimated valuation for Lynch and were not combined with an explicit threat that Alcatel was "ready to proceed" with a hostile bid, cannot alter the conclusion that any semblance of arm's length bargaining ended when the Independent Committee surrendered to the ultimatum that accompanied Alcatel's final offer. *See Rabkin v. Philip A. Hunt Chem. Corp.,* Del.Supr., 498 A.2d 1099, 1106 (1985).

Conclusion

Accordingly, the judgment of the Court of Chancery is reversed. This matter is remanded for further proceedings consistent herewith, including a redetermination of the entire fairness of the cashout merger to Kahn and the other Lynch minority shareholders with the burden of proof remaining on Alcatel, the dominant and interested shareholder.

———

JONES v. H.F. AHMANSON & CO.

Supreme Court of California, 1969.
1 Cal.3d 93, 81 Cal.Rptr. 592, 460 P.2d 464.

TRAYNOR, C.J.—June K. Jones, the owner of 25 shares of the capital stock of United Savings and Loan Association of California brings this action on behalf of herself individually and of all similarly situated minority stockholders of the Association. The defendants are United Financial Corporation of California, fifteen individuals, and four corporations, all of whom are present or former stockholders or officers of the Association. Plaintiff seeks damages and other relief for losses allegedly suffered by the minority stockholders of the Association because of claimed breaches of fiduciary responsibility by defendants in the creation and operation of United Financial, a Delaware holding company that owns 87 percent of the outstanding Association stock.

Plaintiff appeals from the judgment entered for defendants after an order sustaining defendants' general and special demurrers to her third amended complaint without leave to amend. Defendants have filed a protective cross-appeal. We have concluded that the allegations of the complaint and certain stipulated facts sufficiently state a cause of action and that the judgment must therefore be reversed.

The following facts appear from the allegations of the complaint and stipulation.

United Savings and Loan Association of California is a California chartered savings and loan association that first issued stock on April 5, 1956. Theretofore it had been owned by its depositors, who, with borrowing members, elected the board of directors. No one depositor had sufficient voting power to control the Association.

The Association issued 6,568 shares of stock on April 5, 1956. No additional stock has been issued. Of these shares, 987 (14.8 percent) were purchased by depositors pursuant to warrants issued in proportion to the amount of their deposits. Plaintiff was among these purchasers. The shares allocated to unexercised warrants were sold to the then chairman of the board of directors who later resold them to defendants and others. The stockholders have the right to elect a majority of the directors of the Association.

The Association has retained the major part of its earnings in tax-free reserves with the result that the book value of the outstanding shares has increased substantially.[2] The shares were not actively traded. This inactivity is attributed to the high book value, the closely held nature of the Association,[3] and the failure of the management to provide investment information and assistance to shareholders, brokers, or the public. Transactions in the stock that did occur were primarily among existing stockholders. Fourteen of the nineteen defendants comprised 95 percent of the market for Association shares prior to 1959.

In 1958 investor interest in shares of savings and loan associations and holding companies increased. Savings and loan stocks that were publicly marketed enjoyed a steady increase in market price thereafter until June 1962, but the stock of United Savings and Loan Association was not among them. Defendants determined to create a mechanism by which they could participate in the profit taking by attracting investor interest in the Association. They did not, however, undertake to render the Association shares more readily marketable. Instead, the United Financial Corporation of California was incorporated in Delaware by all of the other defendants except defendant Thatcher on May 8, 1959. On May 14, 1959, pursuant to a prior agreement, certain Association stockholders who among them owned a majority of the Association stock exchanged their shares for those of United Financial, receiving a "derived block" of 250 United Financial shares for each Association share.[4]

After the exchange, United Financial held 85 percent of the outstanding Association stock. More than 85 percent of United Financial's consolidated earnings[5] and book value of its shares reflected its ownership of this Association stock. The former majority stockholders of the Association had become the majority shareholders of United Financial and continued to control the Association through the holding company. They did not offer the minority stockholders of the Association an opportunity to exchange their shares.

The first public offering of United Financial stock was made in June 1960. To attract investor interest, 60,000 units were offered, each of which comprised two shares of United Financial stock and one $100, 5 percent interest-bearing, subordinated, convertible debenture bond. The offering provided that of the $7,200,000 return from the sale of these units, $6,200,000 would be distributed immediately as a return of capital to the original shareholders of

2. Between 1959 and 1966 the book value of each share increased from $1,131 to $4,143.70.

3. H.F. Ahmanson & Co. acquired a majority of the shares in May 1958. On May 14, 1959, the company owned 4,171 of the outstanding shares.

4. The number of shares in these derived blocks of United Financial stock was later modified by pro-rata surrenders and stock dividends in a series of transactions not pertinent here.

5. The balance reflected United Financial's ownership of three insurance agencies and stock in a fourth.

United Financial, *i.e.,* the former majority stockholders of the Association.[6] To obtain a permit from the California Corporations Commissioner for the sale, United Financial represented that the financial reserve requirement for debenture repayment established by Commissioner's Rules 480 subdivision (a) and 486 would be met by causing the Association to liquidate or encumber its income producing assets for cash that the Association would then distribute to United Financial to service and retire the bonds.

In the Securities and Exchange Commission prospectus accompanying this first public offering, United Financial acknowledged that its prior earnings were not sufficient to service the debentures and noted that United Financial's direct earnings would have to be augmented by dividends from the Association.

A public offering of 50,000 additional shares by United Financial with a secondary offering of 600,000 shares of the derived stock by the original investors was made in February 1961 for a total price of $15,275,000. The defendants sold 568,190 shares of derived stock in this secondary offering. An underwriting syndicate of 70 brokerage firms participated. The resulting nationwide publicity stimulated trading in the stock until, in mid–1961, an average of 708.5 derived blocks were traded each month. Sales of Association shares decreased during this period from a rate of 170 shares per year before the formation of United Financial to half that number. United Financial acquired 90 percent of the Association shares that were sold.

Shortly after the first public offering of United Financial shares, defendants caused United Financial to offer to purchase up to 350 shares of Association stock for $1,100 per share. The book value of each of these shares was $1,411.57, and earnings were $301.15 per share. The derived blocks of United Financial shares then commanded an aggregate price of $3,700 per block exclusive of the $927.50 return of capital. United Financial acquired an additional 130 shares of Association stock as a result of this offer.

In 1959 and 1960 extra dividends of $75 and $57 per share had been paid by the Association, but in December 1960, after the foregoing offer had been made, defendants caused the Association's president to notify each minority stockholder by letter that no dividends other than the regular $4 per share annual dividend would be paid in the near future. The Association president, defendant M.D. Jameson, was then a director of both the Association and United Financial.

Defendants then proposed an exchange of United Financial shares for Association stock. Under this proposal each minority stockholder would have received approximately 51 United Financial shares of a total value of $2,400 for each Association share. When the application for a permit was filed with the California Corpora-

---

6. This distribution was equivalent to a $927.50 return of capital on each derived block of shares.

tions Commissioner on August 28, 1961, the value of the derived blocks of United Financial shares received by defendants in the initial exchange had risen to approximately $8,800.[9] The book value of the Association stock was in excess of $1,700 per share, and the shares were earning at an annual rate of $615 per share. Each block of 51 United Financial shares had a book value of only $210 and earnings of $134 per year, 85 percent of which reflected Association earnings. At the hearings held on the application by the Commissioner, representatives of United Financial justified the higher valuation of United Financial shares on the ground that they were highly marketable, whereas Association stock was unmarketable and poor collateral for loans. Plaintiff and other minority stockholders objected to the proposed exchange, contending that the plan was not fair, just, and equitable. Defendants then asked the Commissioner to abandon the application without ruling on it.

Plaintiff contends that in following this course of conduct defendants breached the fiduciary duty owed by majority or controlling shareholders to minority shareholders. She alleges that they used their control of the Association for their own advantage to the detriment of the minority when they created United Financial, made a public market for its shares that rendered Association stock unmarketable except to United Financial, and then refused either to purchase plaintiff's Association stock at a fair price or exchange the stock on the same basis afforded to the majority. She further alleges that they also created a conflict of interest that might have been avoided had they offered all Association stockholders the opportunity to participate in the initial exchange of shares. Finally, plaintiff contends that the defendants' acts constituted a restraint of trade in violation of common law and statutory antitrust laws.

I

Plaintiff's Capacity to Sue

We are faced at the outset with defendants' contention that if a cause of action is stated, it is derivative in nature since any injury suffered is common to all minority stockholders of the Association. Therefore, defendants urge, plaintiff may not sue in an individual capacity or on behalf of a class made up of stockholders excluded from the United Financial exchange, and in any case may not maintain a derivative action without complying with Financial Code section 7616.[10]

It is clear from the stipulated facts and plaintiff's allegations that she does not seek to recover on behalf of the corporation for injury

---

9. The derived block sold for as much as $13,127.41 during 1960–1961. On January 30, 1962, the date upon which plaintiff commenced this action, the mean value was $9,116.08.

10. Section 7616 provides: "No action may be instituted or maintained in the right of any savings and loan association ... by a stockholder of any association,

unless ... [the banking] commissioner shall have determined, after a hearing upon at least 20 days' written notice to such association and each of its directors, that such action (a) is proposed in good faith and (b) there is reasonable possibility that the prosecution of such action will benefit the association and its stockholders...."

done to the corporation by defendants. Although she does allege that the value of her stock has been diminished by defendants' actions, she does not contend that the diminished value reflects an injury to the corporation and resultant depreciation in the value of the stock. Thus the gravamen of her cause of action is injury to herself and the other minority stockholders [and her action is individual rather than derivative]....

II
Majority Shareholders' Fiduciary Responsibility

Defendants take the position that as shareholders they owe no fiduciary obligation to other shareholders, absent reliance on inside information, use of corporate assets, or fraud. This view has long been repudiated in California. The Courts of Appeal have often recognized that majority shareholders, either singly or acting in concert to accomplish a joint purpose, have a fiduciary responsibility to the minority and to the corporation to use their ability to control the corporation in a fair, just, and equitable manner. Majority shareholders may not use their power to control corporate activities to benefit themselves alone or in a manner detrimental to the minority. Any use to which they put the corporation or their power to control the corporation must benefit all shareholders proportionately and must not conflict with the proper conduct of the corporation's business. (*Brown v. Halbert,* 271 Cal.App.2d 252 [76 Cal.Rptr. 781]; *Burt v. Irvine Co.,* 237 Cal.App.2d 828 [47 Cal.Rptr. 392]; *Efron v. Kalmanovitz,* 226 Cal.App.2d 546 [38 Cal.Rptr. 148]; *Remillard Brick Co. v. Remillard–Dandini Co.,* 109 Cal.App.2d 405 [241 P.2d 66].)

The extensive reach of the duty of controlling shareholders and directors to the corporation and its other shareholders was described by the Court of Appeal in *Remillard Brick Co. v. Remillard–Dandini Co., supra,* 109 Cal.App.2d 405, where, quoting from the opinion of the United States Supreme Court in *Pepper v. Litton,* 308 U.S. 295 [84 L.Ed. 281, 60 S.Ct. 238], the court held: " 'A director is a fiduciary ... So is a dominant or controlling stockholder or group of stockholders ... Their powers are powers of trust ... Their dealings with the corporation are subjected to rigorous scrutiny and where any of their contracts or engagements with the corporation is challenged the burden is on the director or stockholder not only to prove the good faith of the transaction but also to show its inherent fairness from the viewpoint of the corporation and those interested therein ...' " ...

... The rule that has developed in California is a comprehensive rule of "inherent fairness from the viewpoint of the corporation and those interested therein." (*Remillard Brick Co. v. Remillard–Dandini Co., supra,* 109 Cal.App.2d 405, 420. See also, *In re Security Finance Co., supra,* 49 Cal.2d 370; *Brown v. Halbert, supra,* 271 Cal.App.2d 252; *Burt v. Irvine Co., supra,* 237 Cal. App.2d 828; *Efron v. Kalmanovitz, supra,* 226 Cal.App.2d 546.) The rule applies alike to officers, directors, and controlling shareholders in the exercise of powers that are theirs by virtue of their position and to transactions wherein controlling shareholders seek to gain an advantage in the sale or transfer or use of their controlling block of shares. . . .

The increasingly complex transactions of the business and financial communities demonstrate the inadequacy of the traditional theories of fiduciary obligation as tests of majority shareholder responsibility to the minority. These theories have failed to afford adequate protection to minority shareholders and particularly to those in closely held corporations whose disadvantageous and often precarious position renders them particularly vulnerable to the vagaries of the majority. Although courts have recognized the potential for abuse or unfair advantage when a controlling shareholder sells his shares at a premium over investment value (*Perlman v. Feldmann*, 219 F.2d 173 [50 A.L.R.2d 1134] [premium paid for control over allocation of production in time of shortage]; *Gerdes v. Reynolds*, 28 N.Y.S.2d 622 [sale of control to looters or incompetents]; *Porter v. Healy*, 244 Pa. 427 [91 A. 428]; *Brown v. Halbert, supra*, 271 Cal.App.2d 252 [sale of only controlling shareholder's shares to purchaser offering to buy assets of corporation or all shares]) or in a controlling shareholder's use of control to avoid equitable distribution of corporate assets (*Zahn v. Transamerica Corp.* (3rd Cir.1946) 162 F.2d 36 [172 A.L.R. 495] [use of control to cause subsidiary to redeem stock prior to liquidation and distribution of assets]), no comprehensive rule has emerged in other jurisdictions. Nor have most commentators approached the problem from a perspective other than that of the advantage gained in the sale of control. Some have suggested that the price paid for control shares over their investment value be treated as an asset belonging to the corporation itself (Berle and Means, The Modern Corporation and Private Property (1932) p. 243), or as an asset that should be shared proportionately with all shareholders through a general offer (Jennings, *Trading in Corporate Control* (1956) 44 Cal.L.Rev. 1, 39), and another contends that the sale of control at a premium is always evil (Bayne, *The Sale-of-Control Premium: the Intrinsic Illegitimacy* (1969) 47 Texas L.Rev. 215).

The additional potential for injury to minority shareholders from majority dealings in its control power apart from sale has not gone unrecognized, however. The ramifications of defendants' actions here are not unlike those described by Professor Gower as occurring when control of one corporation is acquired by another through purchase of less than all of the shares of the latter: "The [acquired] company's existence is not affected, nor need its constitution be altered; all that occurs is that its shareholders change. From the legal viewpoint this methodological distinction is formidable, but commercially the two things may be almost identical. If . . . a controlling interest is acquired, the [acquired] company . . . will become a subsidiary of the acquiring company . . . and cease, in fact though not in law, to be an independent entity.

"This may produce the situation in which a small number of dissentient members are left as a minority in a company intended to be operated as a member of a group. As such, their position is likely to be unhappy, for the parent company will wish to operate the subsidiary for the benefit of the group as a whole and not necessarily for the benefit of that particular subsidiary." (Gower, The Principles of Modern Company Law (2d ed. 1957) p. 561.) Professor Eisenberg notes that as the purchasing corporation's proportionate interest in the acquired corporation approaches 100 percent, the market for the latter's stock disappears, a problem that is aggravated if the acquiring corporation for its own business purposes reduces or eliminates dividends. (Eisenberg, *The Legal Role of Shareholders and Management in Modern Corporate Decision–Making* (1969) 57 Cal.L.Rev. 1, 132. See also, O'Neal and Derwin, Expulsion or Oppression of Business Associates (1961) *passim;* Leech, *Transactions in Corporate Control* (1956) 104 U.Pa.L.Rev. 725, 728; Comment, *The Fiduciary Relation of the Dominant Shareholder to the Minority Shareholders* (1958) 9 Hastings L.J. 306, 314.) The case before us, in which no sale or transfer of actual control is directly involved, demonstrates that the injury anticipated by these authors can be inflicted with impunity under the traditional rules and supports our conclusion that the comprehensive rule of good faith and inherent fairness to the minority in any transaction where control of the corporation is material properly governs controlling shareholders in this state.

We turn now to defendants' conduct to ascertain whether this test is met.

III

Formation of United Financial and Marketing its Shares

Defendants created United Financial during a period of unusual investor interest in the stock of savings and loan associations. They then owned a majority of the outstanding stock of the Association. This stock was not readily marketable owing to a high book value, lack of investor information and facilities, and the closely held nature of the Association. The management of the Association had made no effort to create a market for the stock or to split the shares and reduce their market price to a more attractive level. Two courses were available to defendants in their effort to exploit the bull market in savings and loan stock. Both were made possible by defendants' status as controlling stockholders. The first was either to cause the Association to effect a stock split (Corp.Code, § 1507) and create a market for the Association stock or to create a holding company for Association shares and permit all stockholders to exchange their shares before offering holding company shares to the public. All stockholders would have benefited alike had this been done, but in realizing their gain on the sale of their stock the majority stockholders would of necessity have had to relinquish some of their control shares. Because a public market would have been created, however, the minority stockholders would have been able to extricate themselves without sacrificing their investment had they elected not to remain with the new management.

The second course was that taken by defendants. A new corporation was formed whose major asset was to be the control block of Association stock owned by defendants, but from which minority shareholders were to be excluded. The unmarketable Association stock held by the majority was transferred to the newly formed corporation at an exchange rate equivalent to a 250 for 1 stock split. The new corporation thereupon set out to create a market for its own shares. Association stock constituted 85 percent of the holding company's assets and produced an equivalent proportion of its income. The same individuals controlled both corporations. It appears therefrom that the market created by defendants for United Financial shares was a market that would have been available for Association stock had defendants taken the first course of action.[13]

After United Financial shares became available to the public it became a virtual certainty that no equivalent market could or would be created for Association stock. United Financial had become the

---

13. The situation of minority stockholders and the difficulties they faced in attempting to market their savings and loan stock were described in The Savings and Loan Industry in California, a report prepared by the Stanford Research Institute for the California Savings and Loan Commissioner, and published by the Commissioner in 1960. The attractiveness of the holding company as a device to enhance liquidity was recognized: "The majority and minority stockholders in the original associations often found that they had difficulties in selling their shares at a price approximating their book value. Their main difficulties arose from the fact that book values and prices of shares often ran into many thousands of dollars, a price not generally suitable for wide public sale. These shares were usually owned by a relatively small number of stockholders. When one of them, or his heirs, wished to sell his shares, he had to negotiate with a buyer in this small group or attempt to find an outside purchaser. Minority stockholders had a special problem, because they could not sell control with their stock.

"The holding company was regarded by many stockholders as an attractive device to solve the problem of the marketability of their shares. Through this method, the control of one, two, or several associations could be consolidated and offered to the investing public in a single large stock issue at relatively low prices, either over the counter or through a stock exchange. The wide public ownership of holding company shares would thus provide a more active market and more protection against large

capital losses in the event the original owners or their heirs wished to sell their holding company stock.

" * * *

"Large capital gains on the sale of holding company stock to the public have been an important incentive and consequence of this form of organization. The issuance of holding company stock to the general public usually found an enthusiastic demand which made it possible to sell the stock for as much as two to three times book value. In many but not all cases the majority stockholders in the original associations have offered less than 50 percent of the holding company's stock to the public, thus retaining control of the association and the holding companies." (The Savings and Loan Industry in California (1960) pp. VI–6–VI–7.) Although defendants suggest that their transfer of the insurance businesses and the later acquisition of another savings and loan association by United Financial were necessary to the creation of a market for United Financial shares and that no market could be created for the shares of a single savings and loan association, the study does not support their claim. Whether defendants could have created a market for a holding company that controlled a single association or reasonably believed that they could not, goes to their good faith and to the existence of a proper business purpose for electing the course that they chose to follow. At the trial of the cause defendants can introduce evidence relevant to the necessity for inclusion of other businesses.

controlling stockholder and neither it nor the other defendants would benefit from public trading in Association stock in competition with United Financial shares. Investors afforded an opportunity to acquire United Financial shares would not be likely to choose the less marketable and expensive Association stock in preference. Thus defendants chose a course of action in which they used their control of the Association to obtain an advantage not made available to all stockholders. They did so without regard to the resulting detriment to the minority stockholders and in the absence of any compelling business purpose. Such conduct is not consistent with their duty of good faith and inherent fairness to the minority stockholders. Had defendants afforded the minority an opportunity to exchange their stock on the same basis or offered to purchase them at a price arrived at by independent appraisal, their burden of establishing good faith and inherent fairness would have been much less. At the trial they may present evidence tending to show such good faith or compelling business purpose that would render their action fair under the circumstances. On appeal from the judgment of dismissal after the defendants' demurrer was sustained we decide only that the complaint states a cause of action entitling plaintiff to relief.

Defendants gained an additional advantage for themselves through their use of control of the Association when they pledged that control over the Association's assets and earnings to secure the holding company's debt, a debt that had been incurred for their own benefit. In so doing the defendants breached their fiduciary obligation to the minority once again and caused United Financial and its controlling shareholders to become inextricably wedded to a conflict of interest between the minority stockholders of each corporation. Alternatives were available to them that would have benefited all stockholders proportionately....

In so holding we do not suggest that the duties of corporate fiduciaries include in all cases an obligation to make a market for and to facilitate public trading in the stock of the corporation. But when, as here, no market exists, the controlling shareholders may not use their power to control the corporation for the purpose of promoting a marketing scheme that benefits themselves alone to the detriment of the minority. Nor do we suggest that a control block of shares may not be sold or transferred to a holding company. We decide only that the circumstances of any transfer of controlling shares will be subject to judicial scrutiny when it appears that the controlling shareholders may have breached their fiduciary obligation to the corporation or the remaining shareholders.

IV

Damages ...

If, after the trial of the cause, plaintiff has established facts in conformity with the allegations of the complaint and stipulation, then upon tender of her Association stock to defendants she will be entitled to receive at her election either the appraised value of her shares on the date of the exchange, May 14, 1959, with interest at 7 percent a year from the date of this action, or a sum equivalent to the fair market value of a "derived block" of United Financial stock on the date of this action with interest thereon from that date, and the sum of $927.50 (the return of capital paid to the original United Financial shareholders) with interest thereon from the date United Financial first made such payments to its original shareholders, for each share tendered. The appraised or fair market value shall be reduced, however, by the amount by which dividends paid on Association shares during the period from May 14, 1959, to the present exceeds the dividends paid on a corresponding block of United Financial shares during the same period. . . .

The judgment appealed from by plaintiff is reversed. The trial court is directed to overrule the demurrer in conformity with this opinion. Defendants' appeal is dismissed.

Peters, J., Tobriner, J., Burke, J., Sullivan, J., and Coughlin, J. pro tem., concurred.

. . . McComb, J., was of the opinion that the petition should be granted.

————

SECTION 6. SALE OF CONTROL

————

ZETLIN v. HANSON HOLDINGS, INC.

New York Court of Appeals, 1979.
48 N.Y.2d 684, 421 N.Y.S.2d 877, 397 N.E.2d 387.

MEMORANDUM.

The order of the Appellate Division should be affirmed, with costs.

Plaintiff Zetlin owned approximately 2% of the outstanding shares of Gable Industries, Inc., with defendants Hanson Holdings, Inc., and Sylvestri, together with members of the Sylvestri family, owning 44.4% of Gable's shares. The defendants sold their interests to Flintkote Co. for a premium price of $15 per share, at a time when Gable stock was selling on the open market for $7.38 per share. It is undisputed that the 44.4% acquired by Flintkote represented effective control of Gable.

Recognizing that those who invest the capital necessary to acquire a dominant position in the ownership of a corporation have the right of controlling that corporation, it has long been settled law that, absent looting of corporate assets, conversion of a corporate opportunity, fraud or other acts of bad faith, a controlling stockholder is free to sell, and a purchaser is free to buy, that controlling interest at a premium price (see *Barnes v. Brown*, 80 N.Y. 527; *Levy v. American Beverage Corp.*, 265 App.Div. 208; *Essex Universal Corp. v. Yates*, 305 F.2d 572).

Certainly, minority shareholders are entitled to protection against such abuse by controlling shareholders. They are not entitled, however, to inhibit the legitimate interests of the other stockholders. It is for this reason that control shares usually command a premium price. The premium is the added amount an investor is willing to pay for the privilege of directly influencing the corporation's affairs.

In this action plaintiff Zetlin contends that minority stockholders are entitled to an opportunity to share equally in any premium paid for a controlling interest in the corporation. This rule would profoundly affect the manner in which controlling stock interests are now transferred. It would require, essentially, that a controlling interest be transferred only by means of an offer to all stockholders, i.e., a tender offer. This would be contrary to existing law and if so radical a change is to be effected it would best be done by the Legislature.

Chief Judge COOKE and Judges JASEN, GABRIELLI, JONES, WACHTLER, FUCHSBERG and MEYER concur in memorandum.

Order affirmed.

ANDREWS, THE STOCKHOLDER'S RIGHT TO EQUAL OPPORTUNITY IN THE SALE OF SHARES

78 Harv.L.Rev. 505, 515–22 (1965).

The rule to be considered can be stated thus: whenever a controlling stockholder sells his shares, every other holder of shares (of the same class) is entitled to have an equal opportunity to sell his shares, or a prorata part of them, on substantially the same terms. Or in terms of the correlative duty: before a controlling stockholder may sell his shares to an outsider he must assure his fellow stockholders an equal opportunity to sell their shares, or as high a proportion of theirs as he ultimately sells of his own. There are qualifications in the application of the rule, to which I will return; but for purposes of argument we can begin with this broad statement of it. . . .

[*Practical reasons for the proposed rule*] (*a*).—There is a substantial danger that following a transfer of controlling shares corporate affairs may be conducted in a manner detrimental to the interests of the stockholders who have not had an opportunity to sell their shares. The corporation may be looted; it may just be badly run. Or the sale of controlling shares may operate to destroy a favorable opportunity for corporate action. . . .

The equal opportunity rule does not deal directly with the problem of mismanagement, which may occur even after a transfer of control complying with the rule; but enforcement of the rule will remove much of the incentive a purchaser can offer a controlling stockholder to sell on profitable terms. Indeed, in the case of a purchasing looter there is nothing in it for the purchaser unless he can buy less than all the shares; there is no profit in stealing from a solvent corporation if the thief owns all the stock. But the controlling stockholder will be loath to sell only part of his shares (except at a price that compensates him for all of his shares) if he expects the purchaser to destroy the value of what he keeps. The rule forces the controlling stockholder to share equally with his fellow stockholders both the benefits of the price he receives for the shares he sells and the business risks incident to the shares he retains. This will tend strongly to discourage a sale of controlling shares when the risk of looting, or other harm to the corporation, is apparent; and it will provide the seller with a direct incentive to investigate and evaluate with care when the risks are not apparent, since his own financial interest continues to be at stake. . . .

Of course a transfer of control may have advantageous effects for a corporation and its stockholders—and these may be just as subtle as any adverse effects. Many sales of controlling shares come about because the selling stockholders are not doing as well with a business as a purchaser believes he can do; and the belief is often right. Often the sellers are members of a family that has simply run out of managerial talent or interest.

If the rule of equal opportunity would prevent sales in this sort of situation, that would be a high price to pay for the prevention of harm in other cases. . . . For my own part I do not believe the rule of equal opportunity would have much tendency to discourage beneficial transactions. After all, if the purchaser is optimistic—and can convince his bankers to share his optimism—he should be willing to buy out everyone. If the seller is optimistic about the consequences of the transfer, he should be willing to retain some of his shares. If minority stockholders are optimistic, they should be willing to hold their shares. If the financial community is optimistic (in the case of a publicly held corporation), the market itself should offer the minority stockholders a chance to sell at a price that satisfies the rule. Thus, on the face of it the rule would only operate to prevent a sale when all four of these—the seller, the purchaser, the minority stockholders, and the financial community—take a pessimistic view of the transfer. . . .

(*b*). . . . [A] purchaser attains control of the corporation's business and assets equally whether he purchases all the shares or a smaller controlling block. When a purchaser buys less than all the shares, he is acquiring a business worth more than what he pays in cash, and is financing the difference by leaving the minority shares outstanding. We think of mortgage debts that way; if a person buys property subject to a mortgage and leaves the mortgage outstanding, we recognize that the mortgage provides financing for the purchaser because it has the same effect, substantially, as a new loan with the proceeds of which the purchaser might have paid full value for the property. But stock provides financing just as much as a mortgage does. A purchaser who buys only part of the stock of an enterprise might have accomplished much the same net result by purchasing all the assets in the name of a newly organized corporation in which he takes only a part of the stock. The other stockholders in the new corporation would then be viewed as providing equity financing for the acquisition. The chief difference then between a sale of assets, or of all the stock, and a sale of a controlling block of shares only, is that in the latter case the purchaser has had his acquisition partially financed, perhaps unwillingly, by the stockholders from whom he does not buy. That is no reason to give the minority stockholders less protection than if the purchaser gave them an opportunity to sell, even at a lower price. . . .

(c).—A somewhat broader way of putting the argument is even simpler: each stockholder is entitled to share proportionately in the profits of the enterprise; from the stockholder's point of view a sale of stock is one very important way of realizing a profit on his investment; profits from stock sales ought to be regarded as profits of the enterprise subject to equal sharing among stockholders just as much as profits realized through corporate action.

A minority stockholder must invest largely on the strength of the expectation that decisions will tend to be made for his benefit because of the general identity of interest between him and those in control. This identity of interest is qualified when controlling stockholders have an opportunity to profit by entering into dealings with their corporation; this is permitted because such transactions may be mutually profitable, and there is no way to enforce equality of interest beyond allowing judicial scrutiny of such transactions for fairness. It would be impossible to insist, for example, that a publicly held corporation offer all its stockholders a proportionate opportunity to serve in an executive capacity. But when an opportunity arises for profit by selling shares, there is no such simple practical reason why it cannot be made equally available to all stockholders. . . .

JAVARAS, EQUAL OPPORTUNITY IN THE SALE OF CONTROLLING SHARES: A REPLY TO PROFESSOR ANDREWS

32 U.Chi.L.Rev. 420, 425–27 (1965).

I believe that the gravest defect in Professor Andrews' theory is a grievous underassessment of the costs of a preventive rule in restraining beneficial transactions. Such restraint would operate on the purchaser by imposing higher required investment—the price of all the shares of the corporation rather than only those owned by the controlling shareholder. Professor Andrews minimizes the effects of this factor on two grounds. First, the controlling shareholder under the rule of equal opportunity, when confronted with a purchaser who wants the controlling shares and no more, may be induced to retain some of his shares and share the sale ratably with the non-controlling shareholders. Admittedly, this requires faith in the management of the purchaser. Second, a beneficial purchaser should be willing to buy all the shares because, after all, the non-controlling shares have the same investment value as the controlling shares. All the purchaser would have to do, therefore, if he did not have the capital is to borrow it. If he could not, that would be a reflection either of superior knowledge in the financial community or dislocations in the capital market.

It is doubtful whether sufficient controlling sellers can be induced to retain their shares so as to eliminate the higher capital requirement. First, . . . sales of securities are not dictated merely by an appraisal of investment value. Many sellers simply want immediate cash. Second, a controlling seller may not wish to hold, say twenty-five per cent as compared to his prior fifty per cent, because of the possibility of his views differing from those of the controlling purchaser in the future. This reticence would partly stem from . . . the controlling sellers assessment of the change in risks when he is deprived of control. The loss of control would subject him to the risk of poor management, which might dictate a lesser investment in this corporation on the principle of risk diversification.

Likewise the purchaser himself might be unwilling that the seller retain some of his shares, particularly where working control (less than fifty per cent) is the subject of the offer. He might well be reluctant to have a large block of stock outstanding whose owners, under conditions of dissension, could mobilize the other shareholders and displace his control of the board of directors.

In effect then, the rule of equal treatment would impose higher capital requirements on beneficial purchasers in a substantial number of transactions. Professor Andrews inappropriately assumes, however, that the purchasers should be willing to meet these higher costs because the investment value of the additional shares is the same. He errs in that his reasoning is incomplete. It is true that the investment value is the same. But even if the capital market did function perfectly and the purchaser could arrange the financing, a rational businessman might not want to buy all the shares at a premium price justified by the investment potential. It might be sensible to decline to buy more than the bare amount necessary for control on the principles of diversification of risk and of opportunity. This might render the equal treatment rule ineffectual as a means of automatically distinguishing "good" and "bad" purchasers. I would think that the number of prospective beneficial purchasers prevented because of a desire to diversify will be much larger than those simply unable to raise the capital. Until empirical evidence is adduced to the contrary, I am predisposed to consider this cost of restraining beneficial transactions substantial when compared with the cases of detriment with which the present law is incompetent to deal. . . .

———

PERLMAN v. FELDMANN

United States Court of Appeals, Second Circuit, 1955.
219 F.2d 173, cert. denied 349 U.S. 952, 75 S.Ct. 880, 99 L.Ed. 1277 (1955).

CLARK, Chief Judge.   This is a derivative action brought by minority stockholders of Newport Steel Corporation to compel accounting for, and restitution of, allegedly illegal gains which accrued to defendants as a result of the sale in August, 1950, of their controlling interest in the corporation.   The principal defendant, C. Russell Feldmann, who represented and acted for the others, members of his family,[1] was at that time not only the dominant stockholder, but also the chairman of the board of directors and the president of the corporation.   Newport, an Indiana corporation, operated mills for the production of steel sheets for sale to manufacturers of steel products, first at Newport, Kentucky, and later also at other places in Kentucky and Ohio.   The buyers, a syndicate organized as Wilport Company, a Delaware corporation, consisted of end-users of steel who were interested in securing a source of supply in a market becoming ever tighter in the Korean War.   Plaintiffs contend that the consideration paid for the stock included compensation for the sale of a corporate asset, a power held in trust for the corporation by Feldmann as its fiduciary. This power was the ability to control the allocation of the corporate product in a time of short supply, through control of the board of directors;   and it was effectively transferred in this sale by having Feldmann procure the resignation of his own board and the election of Wilport's nominees immediately upon consummation of the sale.

The present action represents the consolidation of three pending stockholders' actions in which yet another stockholder has been permitted to intervene.   Jurisdiction below was based upon the diverse citizenship of the parties.   Plaintiffs argue here, as they did in the court below, that in the situation here disclosed the vendors must account to the nonparticipating minority stockholders for that share of their profit which is attributable to the sale of the corporate power.   Judge Hincks denied the validity of the premise, holding that the rights involved in the sale were only those normally incident to the possession of a controlling block of shares, with which a dominant stockholder, in the absence of fraud or foreseeable looting, was entitled to deal according to his own best interests.   Furthermore, he held that plaintiffs had failed to satisfy their

---

1. The stock was not held personally by Feldmann in his own name, but was held by the members of his family and by personal corporations.   The aggregate of stock thus [held] amounted to 33% of the outstanding Newport stock and gave working control to the holder.   The actual sale included 55,552 additional shares held by friends and associates of Feldmann, so that a total of 37% of the Newport stock was transferred.

burden of proving that the sales price was not a fair price for the stock per se. Plaintiffs appeal from these rulings of law which resulted in the dismissal of their complaint.

The essential facts found by the trial judge are not in dispute. Newport was a relative newcomer in the steel industry with predominantly old installations which were in the process of being supplemented by more modern facilities. Except in times of extreme shortage Newport was not in a position to compete profitably with other steel mills for customers not in its immediate geographical area. Wilport, the purchasing syndicate, consisted of geographically remote end-users of steel who were interested in buying more steel from Newport than they had been able to obtain during recent periods of tight supply. The price of $20 per share was found by Judge Hincks to be a fair one for a control block of stock, although the over-the-counter market price had not exceeded $12 and the book value per share was $17.03. But this finding was limited by Judge Hincks' statement that "[w]hat value the block would have had if shorn of its appurtenant power to control distribution of the corporate product, the evidence does not show." It was also conditioned by his earlier ruling that the burden was on plaintiffs to prove a lesser value for the stock.

Both as director and as dominant stockholder, Feldmann stood in a fiduciary relationship to the corporation and to the minority stockholders as beneficiaries thereof. Pepper v. Litton, 308 U.S. 295, 60 S.Ct. 238, 84 L.Ed. 281; Southern Pac. Co. v. Bogert, 250 U.S. 483, 39 S.Ct. 533, 63 L.Ed. 1099. His fiduciary obligation must in the first instance be measured by the law of Indiana, the state of incorporation of Newport. Rogers v. Guaranty Trust Co. of New York, 288 U.S. 123, 136, 53 S.Ct. 295, 77 L.Ed. 652; Mayflower Hotel Stockholders Protective Committee v. Mayflower Hotel Corp., 89 U.S.App.D.C. 171, 193 F.2d 666, 668. Although there is no Indiana case directly in point, the most closely analogous one emphasizes the close scrutiny to which Indiana subjects the conduct of fiduciaries when personal benefit may stand in the way of fulfillment of trust obligations. In Schemmel v. Hill, 91 Ind.App. 373, 169 N.E. 678, 682, 683, McMahan, J., said: "Directors of a business corporation act in a strictly fiduciary capacity. Their office is a trust. Stratis v. Andreson, 1926, 254 Mass. 536, 150 N.E. 832, 44 A.L.R. 567; Hill v. Nisbet, 1885, 100 Ind. 341, 353. When a director deals with his corporation, his acts will be closely scrutinized. Bossert v. Geis, 1914, 57 Ind.App. 384, 107 N.E. 95. Directors of a corporation are its agents, and they are governed by the rules of law applicable to other agents, and, as between themselves and their principal, the rules relating to honesty and fair dealing in the management of the affairs of their principal are applicable. They must not, in any degree, allow their official conduct to be swayed by their private interest, which must yield to official duty. Leader Publishing Co. v. Grant Trust Co., 1915, 182 Ind. 651, 108 N.E. 121. In a transaction between a director and his corporation, where he acts for himself and his principal at the same time in a matter connected with the relation between them, it is presumed, where he is thus potentially on both sides of the contract, that self-interest will overcome his fidelity to his principal, to his own benefit and to his principal's hurt." And the judge added: "Absolute and most scrupulous good faith is the very essence of a director's obligation to his corporation. The first principal duty arising from his official relation is to act in all things of trust wholly for the benefit of his corporation."

In Indiana, then, as elsewhere, the responsibility of the fiduciary is not limited to a proper regard for the tangible balance sheet assets of the corporation, but includes the dedication of his uncorrupted business judgment for the sole benefit of the corporation, in any dealings which may adversely affect it.... Although the Indiana case is particularly relevant to Feldmann as a director, the same rule should apply to his fiduciary duties as majority stockholder, for in that capacity he chooses and controls the directors, and thus is held to have assumed their liability. Pepper v. Litton, supra, 308 U.S. 295, 60 S.Ct. 238. This, therefore, is the standard to which Feldmann was by law required to conform in his activities here under scrutiny.

It is true, as defendants have been at pains to point out, that this is not the ordinary case of breach of fiduciary duty. We have here no fraud, no misuse of confidential information, no outright looting of a helpless corporation. But on the other hand, we do not find compliance with that high standard which we have just stated and which we and other courts have come to expect and demand of corporate fiduciaries. In the often-quoted words of Judge Cardozo: "Many forms of conduct permissible in a workaday world for those acting at arm's length, are forbidden to those bound by fiduciary ties. A trustee is held to something stricter than the morals of the market place. Not honesty alone, but the punctilio of an honor the most sensitive, is then the standard of behavior. As to this there has developed a tradition that is unbending and inveterate. Uncompromising rigidity has been the attitude of courts of equity when petitioned to undermine the rule of undivided loyalty by the 'disintegrating erosion' of particular exceptions." Meinhard v. Salmon, supra, 249 N.Y. 458, 464, 164 N.E. 545, 546, 62 A.L.R. 1. The actions of defendants in siphoning off for personal gain corporate advantages to be derived from a favorable market situation do not betoken the necessary undivided loyalty owed by the fiduciary to his principal.

The corporate opportunities of whose misappropriation the minority stockholders complain need not have been an absolute certainty in order to support this action against Feldmann. If there was possibility of corporate gain, they are entitled to recover. In Young v. Higbee Co., supra, 324 U.S. 204, 65 S.Ct. 594, two stockholders appealing the confirmation of a plan of bankruptcy reorganization were held liable for profits received for the sale of their stock pending determination of the validity of the appeal. They were held accountable for the excess of the price of their stock over its normal price, even though there was no indication that the appeal could have succeeded on substantive grounds. And in Irving Trust Co. v. Deutsch, supra, 2 Cir., 73 F.2d 121, 124, an accounting was required of corporate directors who bought stock for themselves for corporate use, even though there was an affirmative showing that the corporation did not have the finances itself to acquire the stock. Judge Swan speaking for the court pointed out that "The defendants' argument, contrary to Wing v. Dillingham [5 Cir., 239 F. 54], that the equitable rule that fiduciaries should not be permitted to assume a position in which their individual interests might be in conflict with those of the corporation can have no application where the corporation is unable to undertake the venture, is not convincing. If directors are permitted to justify their conduct on such a theory, there will be a temptation to refrain from exerting their strongest efforts on behalf of the corporation since, if it does not meet the obligations, an opportunity of profit will be open to them personally."

This rationale is equally appropriate to a consideration of the benefits which Newport might have derived from the steel shortage. In the past Newport had used and profited by its market leverage by operation of what the industry had come to call the "Feldmann Plan." This consisted of securing interest-free advances from prospective purchasers of steel in return for firm commitments to them from future production. The funds thus acquired were used to finance improvements in existing plants and to acquire new installations. In the summer of 1950 Newport had been negotiating for cold-rolling facilities which it needed for a more fully integrated operation and a more marketable product, and Feldmann plan funds might well have been used toward this end.

Further, as plaintiffs alternatively suggest, Newport might have used the period of short supply to build up patronage in the geographical area in which it could compete profitably even when steel was more abundant. Either of these opportunities was Newport's, to be used to its advantage only. Only if defendants had been able to negate completely any possibility of gain by Newport could they have prevailed. It is true that a trial court finding states: "Whether or not, in August, 1950, Newport's position was such that it could have entered into 'Feldmann Plan' type transactions to procure funds and financing for the further expansion and integration of its steel facilities and whether such expansion would have been desirable for Newport, the evidence does not show." This, however, cannot avail the defendants, who—contrary to the ruling below—had the burden of proof on this issue, since fiduciaries always have the burden of proof in establishing the fairness of their dealings with trust property. . . .

Defendants seek to categorize the corporate opportunities which might have accrued to Newport as too unethical to warrant further consideration. It is true that reputable steel producers were not participating in the gray market brought about by the Korean War and were refraining from advancing their prices, although to do so would not have been illegal. But Feldmann plan transactions were not considered within this self-imposed interdiction; the trial court found that around the time of the Feldmann sale Jones & Laughlin Steel Corporation, Republic Steel Company, and Pittsburgh Steel Corporation were all participating in such arrangements. In any event, it ill becomes the defendants to disparage as unethical the market advantages from which they themselves reaped rich benefits.

We do not mean to suggest that a majority stockholder cannot dispose of his controlling block of stock to outsiders without having to account to his corporation for profits or even never do this with impunity when the buyer is an interested customer, actual or potential, for the corporation's product. But when the sale necessarily results in a sacrifice of this element of corporate good will and consequent unusual profit to the fiduciary who has caused the sacrifice, he should account for his gains. So in a time of market shortage, where a call on a corporation's product commands an unusually large premium, in one form or another, we think it sound law that a fiduciary may not appropriate to himself the value of this premium. Such personal gain at the expense of his coventurers seems particularly reprehensible when made by the trusted president and director of his company. In this case the violation of duty seems to be all the clearer because of this triple role in which Feldmann appears, though we are unwilling to say, and are not to be understood as saying, that we should accept a lesser obligation for any one of his roles alone.

Hence to the extent that the price received by Feldmann and his codefendants included such a bonus, he is accountable to the minority stockholders who sue here. Restatement, Restitution §§ 190, 197 (1937); Seagrave Corp. v. Mount, supra, 6 Cir., 212 F.2d 389. And plaintiffs, as they contend, are entitled to a recovery in their own right, instead of in right of the corporation (as in the usual derivative actions), since neither Wilport nor their successors in interest should share in any judgment which may be rendered. See Southern Pacific Co. v. Bogert, 250 U.S. 483, 39 S.Ct. 533, 63 L.Ed. 1099. Defendants cannot well object to this form of recovery, since the only alternative, recovery for the corporation as a whole, would subject them to a greater total liability.

The case will therefore be remanded to the district court for a determination of the question expressly left open below, namely, the value of defendants' stock without the appurtenant control over the corporation's output of steel. We reiterate that on this issue, as on all others relating to a breach of fiduciary duty, the burden of proof must rest on the defendants. Bigelow v. RKO Radio Pictures, 327 U.S. 251, 265–266, 66 S.Ct. 574, 90 L.Ed. 652; Package Closure Corp. v. Sealright Co., 2 Cir., 141 F.2d 972, 979. Judgment should go to these plaintiffs and those whom they represent for any premium value so shown to the extent of their respective stock interests.

The judgment is therefore reversed and the action remanded for further proceedings pursuant to this opinion.

SWAN, Circuit Judge (dissenting). With the general principles enunciated in the majority opinion as to the duties of fiduciaries I am, of course, in thorough accord. But, as Mr. Justice Frankfurter stated in Securities and Exchange Comm. v. Chenery Corp., 318 U.S. 80, 85, 63 S.Ct. 454, 458, 87 L.Ed. 626, "to say that a man is a fiduciary only begins analysis; it gives direction to further inquiry. To whom is he a fiduciary? What obligations does he owe as a fiduciary? In what respect has he failed to discharge these obligations?" My brothers' opinion does not specify precisely what fiduciary duty Feldmann is held to have violated or whether it was a duty imposed upon him as the dominant stockholder or as a director of Newport. Without such specification I think that both the legal profession and the business world will find the decision confusing and will be unable to foretell the extent of its impact upon customary practices in the sale of stock.

The power to control the management of a corporation, that is, to elect directors to manage its affairs, is an inseparable incident to the ownership of a majority of its stock, or sometimes, as in the present instance, to the ownership of enough shares, less than a majority, to control an election. Concededly a majority or dominant shareholder is ordinarily privileged to sell his stock at the best price obtainable from the purchaser. In so doing he acts on his own behalf, not as an agent of the corporation. If he knows or has reason to believe that the purchaser intends to exercise to the detriment of the corporation the power of management acquired by the purchase, such knowledge or reasonable suspicion will terminate the dominant shareholder's privilege to sell and will create a duty not to transfer the power of management to such purchaser. The duty seems to me to resemble the obligation which everyone is under not to assist another to commit a tort rather than the obligation of a fiduciary. But whatever the nature of the duty, a violation of it will subject the violator to liability for damages sustained by the corporation. Judge Hincks found that Feldmann had no reason to think that Wilport would use the power of management it would acquire by the purchase to injure Newport, and that there was no proof that it ever was so used. Feldmann did know, it is true, that the reason Wilport wanted the stock was to put in a board of directors who would be likely to permit Wilport's members to purchase more of Newport's steel than they might otherwise be able to get. But there is nothing illegal in a dominant shareholder purchasing from his own corporation at the same prices it offers to other customers. That is what the members of Wilport did, and there is no proof that Newport suffered any detriment therefrom.

My brothers say that "the consideration paid for the stock included compensation for the sale of a corporate asset", which they describe as "the ability to control the allocation of the corporate product in a time of short supply, through control of the board of directors; and it was effectively transferred in this sale by having Feldmann procure the resignation of his own board and the election of Wilport's nominees immediately upon consummation of the sale." The implications of this are not clear to me. If it means that when market conditions are such as to induce users of a corporation's product to wish to buy a controlling block of stock in order to be able to purchase part of the corporation's output at the same mill list prices as are offered to other customers, the dominant stockholder is under a fiduciary duty not to sell his stock, I cannot agree. For reasons already stated, in my opinion Feldmann was not proved to be under any fiduciary duty as a stockholder not to sell the stock he controlled.

Feldmann was also a director of Newport. Perhaps the quoted statement means that as a director he violated his fiduciary duty in voting to elect Wilport's nominees to fill the vacancies created by the resignations of the former directors of Newport. As a director Feldmann was under a fiduciary duty to use an honest judgment in acting on the corporation's behalf. A director is privileged to resign, but so long as he remains a director he must be faithful to his fiduciary duties and must not make a personal gain from performing them. Consequently, if the price paid for Feldmann's stock included a payment for voting to elect the new directors, he must account to the corporation for such payment, even though he honestly believed that the men he voted to elect were well qualified to serve as directors. He can not take pay for performing his fiduciary duty. There is no suggestion that he did do so, unless the price paid for his stock was more than its value. So it seems to me that decision must turn on whether finding 120 and conclusion 5 of the district judge are supportable on the evidence. They are set out in the margin.[1]

Judge Hincks went into the matter of valuation of the stock with his customary care and thoroughness. He made no error of law in applying the principles relating to valuation of stock. Concededly a controlling block of stock has greater sale value than a small lot. While the spread between $10 per share for small lots and $20 per share for the controlling block seems rather extraordinarily wide, the $20 valuation was supported by the expert testimony of Dr. Badger, whom the district judge said he could not find to be wrong. I see no justification for upsetting the valuation as clearly erroneous. Nor can I agree with my brothers that the $20 valuation "was limited" by the last sentence in finding 120. The controlling block could not by any possibility be shorn of its appurtenant power to elect directors and through them to control

---

1. "120. The 398,927 shares of Newport stock sold to Wilport as of August 31, 1950, had a fair value as a control block of $20 per share. What value the block would have had if shorn of its appurtenant power to control distribution of the corporate product, the evidence does not show."

"5. Even if Feldmann's conduct in cooperating to accomplish a transfer of control to Wilport immediately upon the sale constituted a breach of a fiduciary duty to Newport, no part of the moneys received by the defendants in connection with the sale constituted profits for which they were accountable to Newport."

distribution of the corporate product. It is this "appurtenant power" which gives a controlling block its value as such block. What evidence could be adduced to show the value of the block "if shorn" of such appurtenant power, I cannot conceive, for it cannot be shorn of it.

The opinion also asserts that the burden of proving a lesser value than $20 per share was not upon the plaintiffs but the burden was upon the defendants to prove that the stock was worth that value. Assuming that this might be true as to the defendants who were directors of Newport, they did show it, unless finding 120 be set aside. Furthermore, not all the defendants were directors; upon what theory the plaintiffs should be relieved from the burden of proof as to defendants who were not directors, the opinion does not explain.

The final conclusion of my brothers is that the plaintiffs are entitled to recover in their own right instead of in the right of the corporation. This appears to be completely inconsistent with the theory advanced at the outset of the opinion, namely, that the price of the stock "included compensation for the sale of a corporate asset." If a corporate asset was sold, surely the corporation should recover the compensation received for it by the defendants. Moreover, if the plaintiffs were suing in their own right, Newport was not a proper party. The case of Southern Pacific Co. v. Bogert, 250 U.S. 483, 39 S.Ct. 533, 63 L.Ed. 1099, relied upon as authority for the conclusion that the plaintiffs are entitled to recover in their own right, relates to a situation so different that the decision appears to me to be inapposite.

I would affirm the judgment on appeal.

NOTE ON PERLMAN v. FELDMANN

1. Upon remand, the district court determined the enterprise value of the corporation, based upon its book value and earnings potential, to be $15,825,777, or $14.67 per share. This made the premium $5.33 a share, or $2,126,280. The complaining stockholders, owning sixty-three percent of the stock, were therefore entitled to judgment of $1,339,769, with interest of 6 percent from the sale date, plus costs. Perlman v. Feldmann, 154 F.Supp. 436 (D.Conn. 1957) (see opinion for valuation methods).

2. Would the court's decision be strengthened by the additional finding with respect to the same transaction, as follows:

> "During this period [June to August, 1950] Follansbee Steel Corporation and Newport were negotiating for a merger of the two corporations, which merger, on the terms offered by Follansbee, would have been highly profitable to all the stockholders of Newport. However, in August of 1950, Feldmann, acting in his official capacity as president of Newport, rejected

the Follansbee offer, and on August 3 1950, sold his stock to the defendant Wilport Company at a price of approximately $22. per share which was twice the then market value of the stock."

This finding appears in Birnbaum v. Newport Steel Corp., 193 F.2d 461, 462 (2d Cir.1952), cert. denied 343 U.S. 956, 72 S.Ct. 1051, 96 L.Ed. 1356.

———

NOTE ON THE THEORY OF CORPORATE ACTION

If a prospective purchaser, P, wants to acquire complete control of the assets and business of a corporation, C, he has a choice of several means to do so: (1) He can try to acquire all of C's shares, and his first step would naturally be to approach those who hold the majority or at least large blocks of the shares, without which his efforts will fail. (2) He can try to induce holders of sufficient shares to make the requisite majority needed to vote for a merger with or a sale of all assets to a corporation he controls.

If P takes the first course, he deals with C's present holders individually. Each holder seems free to make his own terms of sale, and controlling shares may bring a better price than shares that do not give control. If P takes the second course, he is looking towards corporate action by C. If C's assets are sold, the consideration will pass into C's treasury. Usually the corporation will then be liquidated, and the net proceeds will be distributed pro rata to all C shares, so that each old C shareholder will receive the same amount per share. If C merges, the plan of conversion of C's shares for shares of the surviving corporation will normally provide for equal treatment of all shares of the same class. It may therefore be to the advantage of those who hold the majority, or at least large blocks, of shares of a corporation to have a purchaser like P take the first course.

If P originally proposes to take the second course, but is persuaded to take the first course, and the majority shareholders of C realize more per share for their holdings than the minority, the latter may assert that the difference in technique between the first and second courses of action is immaterial. This is the theory of "corporate action." It has been successfully employed in several cases where the buyer began on the second course and the controlling shareholders switched him to the first. See Commonwealth Title Ins. & Trust Co. v. Seltzer, 227 Pa. 410, 76 A. 77 (1910); Dunnett v. Arn, 71 F.2d 912 (10th Cir.1934); Roby v. Dunnett, 88 F.2d 68 (10th Cir.1937), cert. denied 301 U.S. 706, 57 S.Ct. 940, 81 L.Ed. 1360; American Trust Co. v. California Western States Life Ins. Co., 15 Cal.2d 42, 98 P.2d 497 (1940).

The problem with the theory of corporate action is that a controlling shareholder cannot be compelled to sell his shares at a price he does not accept. A knowledgeable seller therefore can avoid the application of the theory by simply voting down an offer to the corporation, and waiting for an offer to buy his shares.

———

ESSEX UNIVERSAL CORP. v. YATES

United States Court of Appeals, Second Circuit, 1962.
305 F.2d 572.

Before LUMBARD, Chief Judge, and CLARK and FRIENDLY, Circuit Judges.

LUMBARD, Chief Judge.

This appeal from the district court's summary judgment in favor of the defendant raises the question whether a contract for the sale of 28.3 per cent of the stock of a corporation is, under New York law, invalid as against public policy solely because it includes a clause giving the purchaser an option to require a majority of the existing directors to replace themselves, by a process of seriatim resignation, with a majority designated by the purchaser. Despite the disagreement evidenced by the diversity of our opinions, my brethren and I agree that such a provision does not on its face render the contract illegal and unenforceable, and thus that it was improper to grant summary judgment. Judge Friendly would reject the defense of illegality without further inquiry concerning the provision itself (as distinguished from any contention that control could not be safely transferred to the particular purchaser). Judge Clark and I are agreed that on remand, which must be had in any event to consider other defenses raised by the pleadings, further factual issues may be raised by the parties upon which the legality of the clause in question will depend; we disagree, however, on the nature of those factual issues, as our separate opinions reveal. Accordingly, the grant of summary judgment is reversed and the case is remanded for trial of the question of the legality of the contested provision and such further proceedings as may be proper on the other issues raised by the pleadings.

Since we are in agreement on certain preliminary questions, this opinion constitutes the opinion of the court up to the point where it is indicated that it thenceforth states only my individual views.

The defendant Herbert J. Yates, a resident of California, was president and chairman of the board of directors of Republic Pictures Corporation, a New York corporation which at the time relevant to this suit had 2,004,190 shares of common stock outstanding. Republic's stock was listed and traded on the New York Stock Exchange. In August 1957, Essex Universal Corporation, a Delaware corporation owning stock in various diversified businesses, learned of the possibility of purchasing from Yates an interest in Republic. Negotiations proceeded rapidly, and on August 28 Yates and Joseph Harris, the president of Essex, signed a contract in which Essex agreed to buy, and Yates agreed "to sell or cause to be sold" at least 500,000 and not more than 600,000 shares of Republic stock. The price was set at eight dollars a share, roughly two dollars above the then market price on the Exchange. Three dollars per share was to be paid at the closing on September 18, 1957 and the remainder in twenty-four equal monthly payments beginning January 31, 1958. The shares were to be transferred on the closing date, but Yates was to retain the certificates, endorsed in blank by Essex, as security for full payment. In addition to other provisions not relevant to the present motion, the contract contained the following paragraph:

"6. Resignations.

Upon and as a condition to the closing of this transaction if requested by Buyer at least ten (10) days prior to the date of the closing:

(a) Seller will deliver to Buyer the resignations of the majority of the directors of Republic.

(b) Seller will cause a special meeting of the board of directors of Republic to be held, legally convened pursuant to law and the by-laws of Republic, and simultaneously with the acceptance of the directors' resignations set forth in paragraph 6(a) immediately preceding will cause nominees of Buyer to be elected directors of Republic in place of the resigned directors."

Before the date of the closing, as provided in the contract, Yates notified Essex that he would deliver 566,223 shares, or 28.3 per cent of the Republic stock then outstanding, and Essex formally requested Yates to arrange for the replacement of a majority of Republic's directors with Essex nominees pursuant to paragraph 6 of the contract. This was to be accomplished by having eight of the fourteen directors resign seriatim, each in turn being replaced by an Essex nominee elected by the others; such a procedure was *in form* permissible under the charter and by-laws of Republic, which empowered the board to choose the successor of any of its members who might resign.

On September 18, the parties met as arranged for the closing at Republic's office in New York City. Essex tendered bank drafts and cashier's checks totalling $1,698,690, which was the 37½ per cent of the total price of $4,529,784 due at this time. The drafts and checks were payable to one Benjamin C. Cohen, who was Essex' banker and had arranged for the borrowing of the necessary funds. Although Cohen was prepared to endorse these to Yates, Yates upon advice of his lawyer rejected the tender as "unsatisfactory" and said, according to his deposition testimony, "Well, there can be no deal. We can't close it."

Essex began this action in the New York Supreme Court, and it was removed to the district court on account of diversity of citizenship. Essex seeks damages of $2,700,000, claiming that at the time of the aborted closing the stock was in actuality worth more than $12.75 a share.[1] Yates' answer raised a number of defenses, but the motion for summary judgment now before us was made and decided only on the theory that the provision in the contract for immediate transfer of control of the board of directors was illegal *per se* and tainted the entire contract. We have no doubt, and the parties agree, that New York law governs.

Appellant's contention that the provision for transfer of director control is separable from the rest of the contract can quickly be rejected....

... [W]e hold the provision regarding directors inseparable from the sale of shares, and proceed to a consideration of its legality.

Up to this point my brethren and I are in agreement. The following analysis is my own, except insofar as the separate opinions of Judges Clark and Friendly may indicate agreement.

It is established beyond question under New York law that it is illegal to sell corporate office or management control by itself (that is, accompanied by no stock or insufficient stock to carry voting control).... The rationale of the rule is undisputable: persons enjoying management control hold it on behalf of the corporation's stockholders, and therefore may not regard it as their own personal property to dispose of as they wish.[3] Any other rule would violate the most fundamental principle of corporate democracy, that management must represent and be chosen by, or at least with the consent of, those who own the corporation.

Essex was, however, contracting with Yates for the purchase of a very substantial percentage of Republic stock. If, by virtue of the voting power carried by this stock, it could have elected a majority of the board of directors, then the contract was not a simple agreement for the sale of office to one having no ownership interest in the corporation, and the question of its legality would require further analysis. Such stock voting control would incontestably belong to the owner of a majority of the voting stock, and it is commonly known that equivalent power usually accrues to the owner of 28.3% of the stock. For the purpose of this analysis, I shall assume that Essex was contracting to acquire a majority of the Republic stock, deferring consideration of the situation where, as here, only 28.3% is to be acquired.

Republic's board of directors at the time of the aborted closing had fourteen members divided into three classes, each class being "as nearly as may be" of the same size. Directors were elected for terms of three years, one class being elected at each annual share-

---

1. In 1959, while this action was pending, the stock was sold to another party for ten dollars a share.

3. The cases have made no distinction between contracts by directors or officers to resign and contracts by persons who in actuality control the actions of officers or directors to procure their resignations, and of course none should exist.

holder meeting on the first Tuesday in April. Thus, absent the immediate replacement of directors provided for in this contract, Essex as the hypothetical new majority shareholder of the corporation could not have obtained managing control in the form of a majority of the board in the normal course of events until April 1959, some eighteen months after the sale of the stock. The first question before us then is whether an agreement to accelerate the transfer of management control, in a manner legal in form under the corporation's charter and by-laws, violates the public policy of New York.

There is no question of the right of a controlling shareholder under New York law normally to derive a premium from the sale of a controlling block of stock. In other words, there was no impropriety *per se* in the fact that Yates was to receive more per share than the generally prevailing market price for Republic stock. Levy v. American Beverage Corp., 265 App.Div. 208, 218, 38 N.Y.S.2d 517, 526 (1st Dept.1942); Stanton v. Schenck, 140 Misc. 621, 251 N.Y.S. 221 (N.Y.County Sup.Ct.1931); see Hill, supra, 70 Harv. L.Rev. at 991–92.

The next question is whether it is legal to give and receive payment for the immediate transfer of management control to one who has achieved majority share control but would not otherwise be able to convert that share control into operating control for some time. I think that it is.

Of course under some circumstances controlling shareholders transferring immediate control may be compelled to account to the corporation for that part of the consideration received by them which exceeds the fair value of the block of stock sold, as well as for the injury which they may cause to the corporation. In Gerdes v. Reynolds, 28 N.Y.S.2d 622 (N.Y.County Sup.Ct.1941), the purchasers of control of an investment company proceeded immediately to loot the corporation of its assets, and the court required the sellers to account on the theory that the circumstances of the sale put them on notice of the buyers' evil intentions. The court found the price paid grossly in excess of the calculable fair value of a controlling interest in the corporation, and found the differential to be payment for the immediate control which, foreseeably, the buyers used to the detriment of the corporation and its other shareholders....

In Perlman v. Feldmann, 219 F.2d 173, 50 A.L.R.2d 1134 (2 Cir.), cert. denied, 349 U.S. 952, 75 S.Ct. 880, 99 L.Ed. 1277 (1955), this court, in a decision based only nominally on Indiana law, went beyond this rule to hold liable controlling shareholders who similarly sold immediate control even in the absence of illegitimate activity on the part of the purchasers. Our theory was basically that the controlling shareholders in selling control to a potential customer had appropriated to their personal benefit a corporate asset: the premium which the company's product could command in a time of market shortage. Porter v. Healy, 244 Pa. 427, 91 A. 428 (1914), may similarly be explained as "condemning ... a personal profit derived by the insiders in a liquidation situation involving in substance the sale of the corporation's assets...." Hill, supra, 70 Harv.L.Rev. at 1000–01.

A fair generalization from these cases may be that a holder of corporate control will not, as a fiduciary, be permitted to profit from facilitating actions on the part of the purchasers of control which are detrimental to the interests of the corporation or the remaining shareholders. There is, however, no suggestion that the transfer of control over Republic to Essex carried any such threat to the interests of the corporation or its other shareholders.

Our examination of the New York cases discussed thus far gives us no reason to regard as impaired the holding of the early case of Barnes v. Brown, 80 N.Y. 527 (1880), that a bargain for the sale of a majority stock interest is not made illegal by a plan for immediate transfer of management control by a program like that provided for in the Essex–Yates contract. Judge Earl wrote:

> "[The seller] had the right to sell out all his stock and interest in the corporation, ... and when he ceased to have any interest in the corporation, it was certainly legitimate and right that he should cease to control it ... It was simply the mode of transferring the control of the corporation to those who by the policy of the law ought to have it, and I am unable to see how any policy of the law was violated, or in what way, upon the evidence, any wrong was thereby done to anyone." 80 N.Y. at 537.

To be sure, in Barnes v. Brown no term of the contract of sale *required* the seller to effectuate the immediate replacement of directors, as did paragraph 6 of the Essex–Yates contract, but Judge Earl stated that "I shall assume that it was the understanding and a part of the scheme that he should do so." 80 N.Y. at 536. . . .

The easy and immediate transfer of corporate control to new interests is ordinarily beneficial to the economy and it seems inevitable that such transactions would be discouraged if the purchaser of a majority stock interest were required to wait some period before his purchase of control could become effective. Conversely it would greatly hamper the efforts of any existing majority group to dispose of its interest if it could not assure the purchaser of immediate control over corporation operations. I can see no reason why a purchaser of majority control should not ordinarily be permitted to make his control effective from the moment of the transfer of stock.

Thus if Essex had been contracting to purchase a majority of the stock of Republic, it would have been entirely proper for the contract to contain the provision for immediate replacement of directors. Although in the case at bar only 28.3 per cent of the stock was involved, it is commonly known that a person or group owning so large a percentage of the voting stock of a corporation which, like Republic, has at least the 1,500 shareholders normally requisite to listing on the New York Stock Exchange, is almost certain to have share control as a practical matter. If Essex was contracting to acquire what in reality would be equivalent to ownership of a majority of stock, i.e., if it would as a practical certainty have been guaranteed of the stock voting power to choose a majority of the directors of Republic in due course, there is no reason why the contract should not similarly be legal.[6] Whether Essex was thus to acquire the equivalent of majority stock control would, if the issue is properly raised by the defendants, be a factual issue to be determined by the district court on remand.

Because 28.3 per cent of the voting stock of a publicly owned corporation is usually tantamount to majority control, I would place the burden of proof on this issue on Yates as the party attacking the legality of the transaction. Thus, unless on remand Yates chooses to raise the question whether the block of stock in question carried the equivalent of majority control, it is my view that the trial court should regard the contract as legal and proceed to consider the other issues raised by the pleadings. If Yates chooses to raise the issue, it will, on my view, be necessary for him to prove the existence of circumstances which would have prevented Essex from electing a majority of the Republic board of directors in due course. It will not be enough for Yates to raise merely hypothetical possibilities of opposition by the other Republic shareholders to Essex' assumption of management control. Rather, it will be necessary for him to show that, assuming neutrality on the part of the retiring management, there was at the time some concretely foreseeable reason why Essex' wishes would not have prevailed in shareholder voting held in due course. In other words, I would require him to show that there was at the time of the contract some other organized block of stock of sufficient size to outvote the block Essex was buying, or else some circumstance making it likely that enough of the holders of the remaining Republic stock would band together to keep Essex from control.

Reversed and remanded for further proceedings not inconsistent with the judgment of this court.

CLARK, Circuit Judge (concurring in the result).

Since Barnes v. Brown, 80 N.Y. 527, teaches us that not all contracts like the one before us are necessarily illegal, summary judgment seems definitely improper and the action should be remanded for trial. But particularly in view of our lack of knowledge of corporate realities and the current standards of business morality, I should prefer to avoid too precise instructions to the district court in the hope that if the action again comes before us the record will be generally more instructive on this important issue than it now is. . . .

---

6. The fact that under the Essex–Yates contract only 37½% of the price of the stock was to be paid at the closing and the balance was not to be fully paid for twenty-eight months is irrelevant to this case. There is no indication that Essex did not have sound financial backing sufficient to discharge properly the obligation which had been incurred.

... I am constrained to point out that I do not believe a district court determination as to whether or not "working control" was transferred to the vendee can or should affect the outcome of this case. The contract provides for transfer of 28.3 per cent of the outstanding stock and effective control of the board of directors, and there is no evidence at this stage that the vendor's power to transfer control of the board was to be secured unlawfully, as, for example, by bribe or duress. Surely in the normal course of events a management which has behind it 28.3 per cent of the stock has working control, absent perhaps a pitched proxy battle which might unseat it. But the court cannot foresee such an unlikely event or predict its outcome; thus it is difficult to see what further evidence on the question of control could be adduced. My conclusion that there is no reason to declare this contract illegal on its face would remain unaffected by any hypothetical findings on "control." It seems that we are all agreed on the need of a remand for trial, though we disagree as to the scope of such remand. Since our decision returns the case to the jurisdiction of the trial court, with nothing settled beyond that, the trial judge will have to decide initially at least how extensive that trial is to be. For my part I believe it incumbent on the judge to explore all issues which the pleadings may eventually raise.

FRIENDLY, Circuit Judge (concurring).

Chief Judge Lumbard's thoughtful opinion illustrates a difficulty, inherent in our dual judicial system, which has led at least one state to authorize its courts to answer questions about its law that a Federal court may ask. Here we are forced to decide a question of New York law, of enormous importance to all New York corporations and their stockholders, on which there is hardly enough New York authority for a really informed prediction what the New York Court of Appeals would decide on the facts here presented, see Cooper v. American Airlines, Inc., 149 F.2d 355, 359, 162 A.L.R. 318 (2 Cir., 1945); Pomerantz v. Clark, 101 F.Supp. 341 (D.Mass.1951); Corbin, The Laws of the Several States, 50 Yale L.J. 762, 775–776 (1941), yet too much for us to have the freedom used to good effect in Perlman v. Feldmann, 219 F.2d 173 (2 Cir.), cert. denied, 349 U.S. 952, 75 S.Ct. 880, 99 L.Ed. 1277 (1955).

I have no doubt that many contracts, drawn by competent and responsible counsel, for the purchase of blocks of stock from interests thought to "control" a corporation although owning less than a majority, have contained provisions like paragraph 6 of the contract *sub judice*. However, developments over the past decades seem to me to show that such a clause violates basic principles of corporate democracy. To be sure, stockholders who have allowed a set of directors to be placed in office, whether by their vote or their failure to vote, must recognize that death, incapacity or other hazard may prevent a director from serving a full term, and that they will have no voice as to his immediate successor. But the stockholders are entitled to expect that, in that event, the remaining directors will fill the vacancy in the exercise of their fiduciary responsibility. A mass seriatim resignation directed by a selling stockholder, and the filling of vacancies by his henchmen at the dictation of a purchaser and without any consideration of the character of the latter's nominees, are beyond what the stockholders contemplated or should have been expected to contemplate. This seems to me a wrong to the corporation and the other stockholders which the law ought not countenance, whether the selling stockholder has received a premium or not. Right in this Court we have seen many cases where sudden shifts of corporate control have caused serious injury; Pettit v. Doeskin Products, Inc., 270 F.2d 95 (2 Cir., 1959), cert. denied, 362 U.S. 910, 80 S.Ct. 660, 4 L.Ed.2d 618 (1960); United States v. Crosby, 294 F.2d 928 (2 Cir., 1961), cert. denied Mittelman v. United States, 368 U.S. 984, 82 S.Ct. 599, 7 L.Ed.2d 523 (1962); and Kirtley v. Abrams, 299 F.2d 341 (2 Cir., 1962), are a few recent examples. To hold the seller for delinquencies of the new directors only if he knew the purchaser was an intending looter is not a sufficient sanction. The difficulties of proof are formidable even if receipt of too high a premium creates a presumption of such knowledge, and, all too often, the doors are locked only after the horses have been stolen. Stronger medicines are needed—refusal to enforce a contract with such a clause, even though this confers an unwarranted benefit on a defaulter, and continuing responsibility of the former directors for negligence of the new ones until an election has been held. Such prophylactics are not contraindicated, as Judge Lumbard suggests, by the conceded desirability of preventing the dead hand of a former "controlling" group from continuing to dominate the board after a sale, or of protecting a would-be purchaser from finding himself without a majority of the board after he has spent his money. A special meeting of stockholders to replace a board may always be called, and there could be no objection to making the closing of a purchase contingent on the results of such an election. I perceive some of the difficulties of mechanics such a procedure presents, but I have enough confidence in the ingenuity of the corporate bar to believe these would be surmounted.

Hence, I am inclined to think that if I were sitting on the New York Court of Appeals, I would hold a provision like [paragraph] 6 violative of public policy save when it was entirely plain that a new election would be a mere formality—i.e., when the seller owned more than 50% of the stock. I put it thus tentatively because, before making such a decision, I would want the help of briefs, including those of *amici curiae,* dealing with the serious problems of corporate policy and practice more fully than did those here, which were primarily devoted to argument as to what the New York law has been rather than what it ought to be. Moreover, in view of the perhaps unexpected character of such a holding, I doubt that I would give it retrospective effect.[2]

2. See Mr. Justice Black dissenting in Mosser v. Darrow, 341 U.S. 267, 276, 71 S.Ct. 680, 95 L.Ed. 927 (1951); Levy, Realist Jurisprudence and Prospective Overruling, 109 U.Pa.L.Rev. 1 (1960).

As a judge of this Court, my task is the more modest one of predicting how the judges of the New York Court of Appeals would rule, and I must make this prediction on the basis of legal materials rather than of personal acquaintance or hunch. Also, for obvious reasons, the prospective technique is unavailable when a Federal court is deciding an issue of state law. Although Barnes v. Brown, 80 N.Y. 527 (1880), dealt with the sale of a majority interest, I am unable to find any real indication that the doctrine there announced has been thus limited. True, there are New York cases saying that the sale of corporate offices is forbidden; but the New York decisions do not tell us what this means and I can find nothing, save perhaps one unexplained sentence in the opinion of a trial court in Ballantine v. Ferretti, 28 N.Y.S.2d 668, 682 (Sup.Ct.N.Y.Co.1941), to indicate that New York would not apply Barnes v. Brown to a case where a stockholder with much less than a majority conditioned a sale on his causing the resignation of a majority of the directors and the election of the purchaser's nominees.

Chief Judge Lumbard's proposal goes part of the way toward meeting the policy problem I have suggested. Doubtless proceeding from what, as it seems to me, is the only justification in principle for permitting even a majority stockholder to condition a sale on delivery of control of the board—namely that in such a case a vote of the stockholders would be a useless formality, he sets the allowable bounds at the line where there is "a practical certainty" that the buyer would be able to elect his nominees and, in this case, puts the burden of disproving that on the person claiming illegality.

Attractive as the proposal is in some respects, I find difficulties with it. One is that I discern no sufficient intimation of the distinction in the New York cases, or even in the writers, who either would go further in voiding such a clause, see Berle, "Control" in Corporate Law, 58 Colum.L.Rev. 1212, 1224 (1958); Leech, Transactions in Corporate Control, 104 U.Pa.L.Rev. 725, 809 (1956) [proposing legislation], or believe the courts have not yet gone that far, see Baker & Cary, Corporations: Cases and Materials (3d ed. unabr. 1959) 590. To strike down such a condition only in cases falling short of the suggested line accomplishes little to prevent what I consider the evil; in most instances a seller will not enter into a contract conditioned on his "delivering" a majority of the directors unless he has good reason to think he can do that. When an issue does arise, the "practical certainty" test is difficult to apply. The existence of such certainty will depend not merely on the proportion of the stock held by the seller but on many other factors—whether the other stock is widely or closely held, how much of it is in "street names," what success the corporation has experienced, how far its dividend policies have satisfied its stockholders, the identity of the purchasers, the presence or absence of cumulative voting, and many others. Often, unless the seller has nearly 50% of the stock, whether he has "working control" can be determined only by an election; groups who thought they had such control have experienced unpleasant surprises in recent years.

Judge Lumbard correctly recognizes that, from a policy standpoint, the pertinent question must be the buyer's prospects of election, not the seller's—yet this inevitably requires the court to canvass the likely reaction of stockholders to a group of whom they know nothing and seems rather hard to reconcile with a position that it is "right" to insert such a condition if a seller has a larger proportion of the stock and "wrong" if he has a smaller. At the very least the problems and uncertainties arising from the proposed line of demarcation are great enough, and its advantages small enough, that in my view a Federal court would do better simply to overrule the defense here, thereby accomplishing what is obviously the "just" result in this particular case, and leave the development of doctrine in this area to the State, which has primary concern for it.

I would reverse the grant of summary judgment and remand for consideration of defenses other than a claim that the inclusion of paragraph 6 *ex mero motu* renders the contract void.

NOTE ON ESSEX UNIVERSAL CORP. v. YATES

It is not at all clear that 28.3% will necessarily carry control of a publicly held corporation in and of itself, that is, unless coupled with control of the board. Consider Brannigan, Florida Businessman Seeks to Steer Bank Toward Sale, Wall Street Journal, Sept. 2, 1987, at 27, col. 1: "[Hugh F. Culverhouse] has launched a tender offer for 10% of Florida Commercial Banks Inc's shares, ... He already holds ... 39.9% of the bank's shares. Since 1984, Mr. Culverhouse has struggled unsuccessfully to win a seat on the company's board or to acquire control of the concern. As of earlier this year, 28.4% of the company's shares were controlled by a well-entrenched group of officers and directors that has opposed him...."

SECURITIES EXCHANGE ACT RULE 14f–1

[See Statutory Supplement]

ALI, PRINCIPLES OF CORPORATE GOVERNANCE § 5.16

[See Statutory Supplement]

Chapter IX

INSIDER TRADING

SECTION 1. THE COMMON LAW

GOODWIN v. AGASSIZ

Massachusetts Supreme Judicial Court, 1933.
283 Mass. 358, 186 N.E. 659.

BILL IN EQUITY, filed in the Supreme Judicial Court for the county of Suffolk on September 17, 1928, described in the opinion....

RUGG, C.J. A stockholder in a corporation seeks in this suit relief for losses suffered by him in selling shares of stock in Cliff Mining Company by way of accounting, rescission of sales, or redelivery of shares. The named defendants are MacNaughton, a resident of Michigan not served or appearing, and Agassiz, a resident of this Commonwealth, the active party defendant.

The trial judge made findings of fact, rulings, and an order dismissing the bill. There is no report of the evidence. The case must be considered on the footing that the findings are true. The facts thus displayed are these: The defendants, in May, 1926, purchased through brokers on the Boston stock exchange seven hundred shares of stock of the Cliff Mining Company which up to that time the plaintiff had owned. Agassiz was president and director and MacNaughton a director and general manager of the company. They had certain knowledge, material as to the value of the stock, which the plaintiff did not have. The plaintiff contends that such purchase in all the circumstances without disclosure to him of that knowledge was a wrong against him. That knowledge was that an experienced geologist had formulated in writing in March, 1926, a theory as to the possible existence of copper deposits under conditions prevailing in the region where the property of the company was located. That region was known as the mineral belt in northern Michigan, where are located mines of several copper mining companies. Another such company, of which the defendants were officers, had made extensive geological surveys of its lands. In consequence of recommendations resulting from that survey, exploration was started on property of the Cliff Mining Company in 1925. That exploration was ended in May, 1926, because completed unsuccessfully, and the equipment was removed. The defendants discussed the geologist's theory shortly after it was formulated. Both felt that the theory had value and should be tested, but they agreed that, before starting to test it, options should be obtained by another copper company of which they were officers on land adjacent to or nearby in the copper belt, that if the geologist's theory were known to the owners of such other land there might be difficulty in securing options, and that that theory should not be communicated to any one unless it became absolutely necessary. Thereafter, options were secured which, if taken up, would involve a large expenditure by the other company. The defendants both thought, also, that, if there was any merit in the geologist's theory, the price of Cliff Mining Company stock in the market would go up. Its stock was quoted and bought and sold on the Boston stock exchange. Pursuant to agreement, they bought many shares of that stock through agents on joint account. The plaintiff first learned of the closing of exploratory operations on property of the Cliff Mining Company from an article in a paper on May 15, 1926, and immediately sold his shares of stock through brokers. It does not appear that the defendants were in any way responsible for the publication of that article. The plaintiff did not know that the purchase was made for the defendants and they did not know that his stock was being bought for them. There was no communication between them touching the subject. The plaintiff would not have sold his stock if he had known of the geologist's theory. The finding is express that the defendants were not guilty of fraud, that they committed no breach of duty owed by them to the Cliff Mining Company, and that that company was not harmed by the nondisclosure of the geologist's theory, or by their purchases of its stock, or by shutting down the exploratory operations.

The contention of the plaintiff is that the purchase of his stock in the company by the defendants without disclosing to him as a stockholder their knowledge of the geologist's theory, their belief that the theory had value, the keeping secret the existence of the theory, discontinuance by the defendants of exploratory operations begun in 1925 on property of the Cliff Mining Company and their plan ultimately to test the value of the theory, constitute actionable wrong for which he as stockholder can recover.

The trial judge ruled that conditions may exist which would make it the duty of an officer of a corporation purchasing its stock from a stockholder to inform him as to knowledge possessed by the buyer and not by the seller, but found, on all the circumstances developed by the trial and set out at some length by him in his decision, that there was no fiduciary relation requiring such disclosure by the defendants to the plaintiff before buying his stock in the manner in which they did.

The question presented is whether the decree dismissing the bill rightly was entered on the facts found.

The directors of a commercial corporation stand in a relation of trust to the corporation and are bound to exercise the strictest good faith in respect to its property and business. *Elliott v. Baker,* 194

Mass. 518, 523. *Beaudette v. Graham*, 267 Mass. 7. *L.E. Fosgate Co. v. Boston Market Terminal Co.*, 275 Mass. 99, 107. The contention that directors also occupy the position of trustee toward individual stockholders in the corporation is plainly contrary to repeated decisions of this court and cannot be supported. In *Smith v. Hurd*, 12 Met. 371, 384, it was said by Chief Justice Shaw: "There is no legal privity, relation, or immediate connexion, between the holders of shares in a bank, in their individual capacity, on the one side, and the directors of the bank on the other. The directors are not the bailees, the factors, agents or trustees of such individual stockholders." In *Stewart v. Joyce*, 201 Mass. 301, 311, 312, and *Lee v. Fisk*, 222 Mass. 424, 426, the same principle was reiterated. In *Blabon v. Hay*, 269 Mass. 401, 407, occurs this language with reference to sale of stock in a corporation by a stockholder to two of its directors: "The fact that the defendants were directors created no fiduciary relation between them and the plaintiff in the matter of the sale of his stock."

The principle thus established is supported by an imposing weight of authority in other jurisdictions. *Steinfeld v. Nielsen*, 15 Ariz. 424. *Bawden v. Taylor*, 254 Ill. 464. *Tippecanoe County Commissioners v. Reynolds*, 44 Ind. 509. *Waller v. Hodge*, 214 Ky. 705. *Buckley v. Buckley*, 230 Mich. 504. *Dutton v. Barnes*, 162 Minn. 430. *Crowell v. Jackson*, 24 Vroom, 656. *Carpenter v. Danforth*, 52 Barb.S.C. 581. *Shaw v. Cole Manuf. Co.*, 132 Tenn. 210. *White v. Texas Co.*, 59 Utah, 180, 188. *Percival v. Wright*, [1902] 2 Ch.D. 421. *Tackey v. McBain*, [1912] A.C. 186. A rule holding that directors are trustees for individual stockholders with respect to their stock prevails in comparatively few States; but in view of our own adjudications it is not necessary to review decisions to that effect. See, for example, *Oliver v. Oliver*, 118 Ga. 362; *Dawson v. National Life Ins. Co. of America*, 176 Iowa, 362; *Stewart v. Harris*, 69 Kans. 498. See, also, for collection of authorities, 14A C.J. § 1896; 27 Yale L.J. 731; 32 Yale L.J. 637.

While the general principle is as stated, circumstances may exist requiring that transactions between a director and a stockholder as to stock in the corporation be set aside. The knowledge naturally in the possession of a director as to the condition of a corporation places upon him a peculiar obligation to observe every requirement of fair dealing when directly buying or selling its stock. Mere silence does not usually amount to a breach of duty, but parties may stand in such relation to each other that an equitable responsibility arises to communicate facts. *Wellington v. Rugg*, 243 Mass. 30, 35. Purchases and sales of stock dealt in on the stock exchange are commonly impersonal affairs. An honest director would be in a difficult situation if he could neither buy nor sell on the stock exchange shares of stock in his corporation without first seeking out the other actual ultimate party to the transaction and disclosing to him everything which a court or jury might later find that he then knew affecting the real or speculative value of such shares. Business of that nature is a matter to be governed by practical rules.

Fiduciary obligations of directors ought not to be made so onerous that men of experience and ability will be deterred from accepting such office. Law in its sanctions is not coextensive with morality. It cannot undertake to put all parties to every contract on an equality as to knowledge, experience, skill and shrewdness. It cannot undertake to relieve against hard bargains made between competent parties without fraud. On the other hand, directors cannot rightly be allowed to indulge with impunity in practices which do violence to prevailing standards of upright business men. Therefore, where a director personally seeks a stockholder for the purpose of buying his shares without making disclosure of material facts within his peculiar knowledge and not within reach of the stockholder, the transaction will be closely scrutinized and relief may be granted in appropriate instances. *Strong v. Repide,* 213 U.S. 419. *Allen v. Hyatt,* 30 T.L.R. 444. *Gammon v. Dain,* 238 Mich. 30. *George v. Ford,* 36 App.D.C. 315. See, also, *Old Dominion Copper Mining & Smelting Co. v. Bigelow,* 203 Mass. 159, 194–195. The applicable legal principles "have almost always been the fundamental ethical rules of right and wrong." *Robinson v. Mollett,* L.R. 7 H.L. 802, 817.

The precise question to be decided in the case at bar is whether on the facts found the defendants as directors had a right to buy stock of the plaintiff, a stockholder. Every element of actual fraud or misdoing by the defendants is negatived by the findings. Fraud cannot be presumed; it must be proved. *Brown v. Little, Brown & Co. (Inc.),* 269 Mass. 102, 117. The facts found afford no ground for inferring fraud or conspiracy. The only knowledge possessed by the defendants not open to the plaintiff was the existence of a theory formulated in a thesis by a geologist as to the possible existence of copper deposits where certain geological conditions existed common to the property of the Cliff Mining Company and that of other mining companies in its neighborhood. This thesis did not express an opinion that copper deposits would be found at any particular spot or on property of any specified owner. Whether that theory was sound or fallacious, no one knew, and so far as appears has never been demonstrated. The defendants made no representations to anybody about the theory. No facts found placed upon them any obligation to disclose the theory. A few days after the thesis expounding the theory was brought to the attention of the defendants, the annual report by the directors of the Cliff Mining Company for the calendar year 1925, signed by Agassiz for the directors, was issued. It did not cover the time when the theory was formulated. The report described the status of the operations under the exploration which had been begun in 1925. At the annual meeting of the stockholders of the company held early in April, 1926, no reference was made to the theory. It was then at most a hope, possibly an expectation. It had not passed the nebulous stage. No disclosure was made of it. The Cliff Mining Company was not harmed by the nondisclosure. There would have been no advantage to it, so far as appears, from a disclosure. The disclosure would have been detrimental to the interests of another mining corporation in which the defendants were directors. In the circumstances there was no duty on the part of the defendants to set forth to the stockholders at the annual meeting their faith, aspirations and plans for the future. Events as they developed might render advisable radical changes in such views. Disclosure of the theory, if it ultimately was proved to be erroneous or without foundation in fact, might involve the defendants in litigation with those who might act on the hypothesis that it was correct. The stock of the Cliff Mining Company was bought and sold on the stock exchange. The identity of buyers and seller of the stock in question in fact was not known to the parties and perhaps could not readily have been ascertained. The defendants caused the shares to be bought through brokers on the stock exchange. They said nothing to anybody as to the reasons actuating them. The plaintiff was no novice. He was a member of the Boston stock exchange and had kept a record of sales of Cliff Mining Company stock. He acted upon his own judgment in selling his stock. He made no inquiries of the defendants or of other officers of the company. The result is that the plaintiff cannot prevail.

Decree dismissing bill affirmed with costs.

————

NOTE ON THE DUTIES OF DIRECTORS AND OFFICERS UNDER THE COMMON LAW WHEN TRADING IN THEIR CORPORATION'S STOCK

1. The rule adopted in *Goodwin v. Agassiz* was the majority rule under the common law. Although the transactions in *Goodwin v. Agassiz* occurred in an impersonal market, there are cases in which the rule was applied to face-to-face transactions. See, e.g., Lank v. Steiner, 43 Del.Ch. 262, 224 A.2d 242 (1966); Gladstone v. Murray Co., 314 Mass. 584, 50 N.E.2d 958 (1943). However, there was a minority rule, sometimes known as the Kansas rule, which required full disclosure by a director or officer, at least in face-to-face transactions.

2. Perhaps the most important exception to the majority rule was the "special facts" exception, adopted in Strong v. Repide, 213 U.S. 419, 29 S.Ct. 521, 53 L.Ed. 853 (1909) and later in many other cases. Repide was a director, the administrator general, and owner of nearly three-fourths of the shares of Philippine Sugar. Philippine Sugar owned certain lands in the Philippines that the United States government wished to buy. The corporation was without funds, and the value of its shares was wholly dependent on making an advantageous sale of its properties to the government. Repide was in charge of the negotiations with the government, which dragged on for months, primarily because Repide was holding out for a higher price. Strong, who owned shares in Philippine Sugar, had given a power of attorney to sell her shares to Jones, who had an

office next door to that of Repide. While negotiations with the government were pending, Repide, knowing that a sale to the government was probable, used an intermediary to employ a broker to purchase Strong's shares from Jones. Jones was given no information as to the state of the negotiations with the government, and neither Strong nor Jones knew that Repide was the purchaser. The price paid to Strong was about one-tenth what the shares became worth less than three months later, when the sale of the corporation's property to the government was consummated.

The Supreme Court affirmed an award of damages to Strong, on the ground that even if a director has no general duty to disclose facts known to him before he purchases shares, "there are cases where, by reason of the special facts, such duty exists." Id. at 431, 29 S.Ct. at 525. Jones sold Strong's shares because the corporation was paying no dividends and the negotiations with the government had gone on for so long that he thought that there was no prospect that a sale of the corporation's property would be made in the near term. Repide was not only a director but, by reason of his ownership of three-fourths of the shares, his position as administrator general, and the acquiescence of the other shareholders, was in full charge of the negotiations and was able to come to an agreement with the government if and when he chose to do so. He concealed his identity as a purchaser and dealt in a roundabout fashion with Jones. In view of all these facts, "the law would indeed be impotent if the sale could not be set aside or [Repide] cast in damages for his fraud." Id. at 433, 29 S.Ct. at 526.

3. Since there was no meaningful way to differentiate those cases that involved "special facts" from those that didn't, the special-facts exception either ate up the majority rule or made the rule impossible to administer in a consistent fashion. At bottom, the exception was inconsistent with the majority rule, and was employed by the courts as a mechanism to escape from that rule while purporting to follow it.

———

SECTION 2. SECURITIES EXCHANGE ACT § 10(b) and RULE 10b–5

———

SECURITIES EXCHANGE ACT § 10(b)

[See Statutory Supplement]

———

SECURITIES EXCHANGE ACT RULE 10b–5

[See Statutory Supplement]

IN THE MATTER OF CADY, ROBERTS & CO., 40 S.E.C. 907, 911–12 (1961). "[Rule 10b–5 applies] to securities transactions by 'any person.' Misrepresentations will lie within [its] ambit, no matter who the speaker may be. An affirmative duty to disclose material information has been traditionally imposed on corporate 'insiders,' particularly officers, directors, or controlling stockholders. We, and the courts have consistently held that insiders must disclose material facts which are known to them by virtue of their position but which are not known to persons with whom they deal and which, if known, would affect their investment judgment. Failure to make disclosure in these circumstances constitutes a violation of the anti-fraud provisions. If, on the other hand, disclosure prior to effecting a purchase or sale would be improper or unrealistic under the circumstances, we believe the alternative is to forego the transaction. . . .

We have already noted that the anti-fraud provisions are phrased in terms of 'any person' and that a special obligation has been traditionally required of corporate insiders, e.g., officers, directors and controlling stockholders. These three groups, however, do not exhaust the classes of persons upon whom there is such an obligation. Analytically, the obligation rests on two principal elements; first, the existence of a relationship giving access, directly or indirectly, to information intended to be available only for a corporate purpose and not for the personal benefit of anyone, and second, the inherent unfairness involved where a party takes advantage of such information knowing it is unavailable to those with whom he is dealing. In considering these elements under the broad language of the anti-fraud provisions we are not to be circumscribed by fine distinctions and rigid classifications. Thus our task here is to identify those persons who are in a special relationship with a company and privy to its internal affairs, and thereby suffer correlative duties in trading in its securities. Intimacy demands restraint lest the uninformed be exploited."

SECURITIES AND EXCHANGE COMMISSION
v. TEXAS GULF SULPHUR CO.

United States Court of Appeals, Second Circuit, 1968.
401 F.2d 833 (in banc), cert. denied 394 U.S. 976, 89 S.Ct. 1454, 22 L.Ed.2d 756 (1969).

[This was an action brought by the S.E.C. against Texas Gulf Sulphur, (TGS), based on the issuance of a misleading press release, and against certain officers and employees of TGS based on their trading and tipping. The case grew out of an important mineral discovery by TGS. Four of the individual defendants were members of the geological exploration group that made the discovery: Mollison, a vice-president and mining engineer who headed the exploration group; Holyk, TGS' chief geologist; Clayton, an electrical engineer and geophysicist, and Darke, a geologist. The other individual defendants included Stephens, who was TGS's President; Fogarty, its Executive Vice–President; Kline, its Vice–President and General Counsel; and Coates, a director.

[Those portions of the opinion dealing with the liability of TGS for the misleading press release, and the liability of individual defendants for tipping, have been omitted, because the discussion of those issues has been largely superseded by later Supreme Court cases, set out below.]

This action derives from the exploratory activities of TGS begun in 1957 on the Canadian Shield in eastern Canada. In March of 1959, aerial geophysical surveys were conducted over more than 15,000 square miles of this area by a group led by defendant Mollison, a mining engineer and a Vice President of TGS. The group included defendant Holyk, TGS's chief geologist, defendant Clayton, an electrical engineer and geophysicist, and defendant Darke, a geologist. These operations resulted in the detection of numerous anomalies, i.e., extraordinary variations in the conductivity of rocks, one of which was on the Kidd 55 segment of land located near Timmins, Ontario.

On October 29 and 30, 1963, Clayton conducted a ground geophysical survey on the northeast portion of the Kidd 55 segment which confirmed the presence of an anomaly and indicated the necessity of diamond core drilling for further evaluation. Drilling of the initial hole, K–55–1, at the strongest part of the anomaly was commenced on November 8 and terminated on November 12 at a depth of 655 feet. Visual estimates by Holyk of the core of K–55–1 indicated an average copper content of 1.15% and an average zinc content of 8.64% over a length of 599 feet. This visual estimate convinced TGS that it was desirable to acquire the remainder of the Kidd 55 segment, and in order to facilitate this acquisition TGS President Stephens instructed the exploration group to keep the results of K–55–1 confidential and undisclosed even as to other officers, directors, and employees of TGS. The hole was concealed and a barren core was intentionally drilled off the anomaly. Meanwhile, the core of K–55–1 had been shipped to Utah for chemical assay which, when received in early December, revealed an average mineral content of 1.18% copper, 8.26% zinc, and 3.94% ounces of silver per ton over a length of 602 feet. These results were so remarkable that neither Clayton, an experienced geophysicist, nor four other TGS expert witnesses, had ever seen or heard of a comparable initial exploratory drill hole in a base metal deposit. So, the trial court concluded, "There is no doubt that the drill core of K–55–1 was unusually good and that it excited the interest and speculation of those who knew about it." Id. at 282. By March 27,

1964, TGS decided that the land acquisition program had advanced to such a point that the company might well resume drilling, and drilling was resumed on March 31.

During this period, from November 12, 1963 when K–55–1 was completed, to March 31, 1964 when drilling was resumed certain of the individual defendants . . . and persons . . . said to have received "tips" from them, purchased TGS stock or calls thereon. Prior to these transactions these persons had owned 1135 shares of TGS stock and possessed no calls; thereafter they owned a total of 8235 shares and possessed 12,300 calls.

On February 20, 1964, also during this period, TGS issued stock options to 26 of its officers and employees whose salaries exceeded a specified amount, five of whom were the individual defendants Stephens, Fogarty, Mollison, Holyk, and Kline. Of these, only Kline was unaware of the detailed results of K–55–1, but he, too, knew that a hole containing favorable bodies of copper and zinc ore had been drilled in Timmins. At this time, neither the TGS Stock Option Committee nor its Board of Directors had been informed of the results of K–55–1, presumably because of the pending land acquisition program which required confidentiality. All of the foregoing defendants accepted the options granted them.

When drilling was resumed on March 31, hold K–55–3 was commenced 510 feet west of K–55–1 and was drilled easterly at a 45° angle so as to cross K–55–1 in a vertical plane. Daily progress reports of the drilling of this hole K–55–3 and of all subsequently drilled holes were sent to defendants Stephens and Fogarty (President and Executive Vice President of TGS) by Holyk and Mollison. Visual estimates of K–55–3 revealed an average mineral content of 1.12% copper and 7.93% zinc over 641 of the hole's 876–foot length. On April 7, drilling of a third hole, K–55–4, 200 feet south of and parallel to K–55–1 and westerly at a 45° angle, was commenced and mineralization was encountered over 366 of its 579–foot length. Visual estimates indicated an average content of 1.14% copper and 8.24% zinc. Like K–55–1, both K–55–3 and K–55–4 established substantial copper mineralization on the eastern edge of the anomaly. On the basis of these findings relative to the foregoing drilling results, the trial court concluded that the vertical plane created by the intersection of K–55–1 and K–55–3, which measured at least 350 feet wide by 500 feet deep extended southward 200 feet to its intersection with K–55–4, and that "There was real evidence that a body of commercially mineable ore might exist." Id. at 281–82.

On April 8 TGS began with a second drill rig to drill another hole, K–55–6, 300 feet easterly of K–55–1. This hole was drilled westerly at an angle of 60° and was intended to explore mineralization beneath K–55–1. While no visual estimates of its core were immediately available, it was readily apparent by the evening of April 10 that substantial copper mineralization had been encountered over the last 127 feet of the hole's 569–foot length. On April

10, a third drill rig commenced drilling yet another hole, K–55–5, 200 feet north of K–55–1, parallel to the prior holes, and slanted westerly at a 45° angle. By the evening of April 10 in this hole, too, substantial copper mineralization had been encountered over the last 42 feet of its 97–foot length.

Meanwhile, rumors that a major ore strike was in the making had been circulating throughout Canada. On the morning of Saturday, April 11, Stephens at his home in Greenwich, Conn. read in the New York Herald Tribune and in the New York Times unauthorized reports of the TGS drilling which seemed to infer a rich strike from the fact that the drill cores had been flown to the United States for chemical assay. Stephens immediately contacted Fogarty at his home in Rye, N.Y., who in turn telephoned and later that day visited Mollison at Mollison's home in Greenwich to obtain a current report and evaluation of the drilling progress.[7] The following morning, Sunday, Fogarty again telephoned Mollison, inquiring whether Mollison had any further information and told him to return to Timmins with Holyk, the TGS Chief Geologist, as soon as possible "to move things along." With the aid of one Carroll, a public relations consultant, Fogarty drafted a press release designed to quell the rumors, which release, after having been channeled through Stephens and Huntington, a TGS attorney, was issued at 3:00 P.M. on Sunday, April 12, and which appeared in the morning newspapers of general circulation on Monday, April 13. It read in pertinent part as follows:

Press Release

> New York, April 12—The following statement was made today by Dr. Charles F. Fogarty, executive vice president of Texas Gulf Sulphur Company, in regard to the company's drilling operations near Timmins, Ontario, Canada. Dr. Fogarty said:
>
> "During the past few days, the exploration activities of Texas Gulf Sulphur in the area of Timmins, Ontario, have been widely reported in the press, coupled with rumors of a substantial copper discovery there. These reports exaggerate the scale of operations, and mention plans and statistics of size and grade of ore that are without factual basis and have evidently originated by speculation of people not connected with TGS.
>
> "The facts are as follows. TGS has been exploring in the Timmins area for six years as part of its overall search in Canada and elsewhere for various minerals—lead, copper, zinc, etc. During the course of this work, in Timmins as well as in Eastern Canada, TGS has conducted exploration entirely on its own, without the participation by others. Numerous prospects have been investigated by geophysical means and a large num-

---

7. Mollison had returned to the United States for the weekend. Friday morning April 10, he had been on the Kidd tract "and had been advised by defendant Holyk as to the drilling results to 7:00 p.m. on April 10. At that time drill holes K–55–1, K–55–3 and K–55–4 had been completed; drilling of K–55–5 had started on Section 2200 S and had been drilled to 97 feet, encountering mineralization on the last 42 feet; and drilling of K–55–6 had been started on Section 2400 S and had been drilled to 569 feet, encountering mineralization over the last 127 feet." Id. at 294.

ber of selected ones have been core-drilled. These cores are sent to the United States for assay and detailed examination as a matter of routine and on advice of expert Canadian legal counsel. No inferences as to grade can be drawn from this procedure.

"Most of the areas drilled in Eastern Canada have revealed either barren pyrite or graphite without value; a few have resulted in discoveries of small or marginal sulphide ore bodies.

"Recent drilling on one property near Timmins has led to preliminary indications that more drilling would be required for proper evaluation of this prospect. The drilling done to date has not been conclusive, but the statements made by many outside quarters are unreliable and include information and figures that are not available to TGS.

"The work done to date has not been sufficient to reach definite conclusions and any statement as to size and grade of ore would be premature and possibly misleading. When we have progressed to the point where reasonable and logical conclusions can be made, TGS will issue a definite statement to its stockholders and to the public in order to clarify the Timmins project."

* * *

The release purported to give the Timmins drilling results as of the release date, April 12. From Mollison Fogarty had been told of the developments through 7:00 P.M. on April 10, and of the remarkable discoveries made up to that time, detailed supra, which discoveries, according to the calculations of the experts who testified for the SEC at the hearing, demonstrated that TGS had already discovered 6.2 to 8.3 million tons of proven ore having gross assay values from $26 to $29 per ton. TGS experts, on the other hand, denied at the hearing that proven or probable ore could have been calculated on April 11 or 12 because there was then no assurance of continuity in the mineralized zone.

The evidence as to the effect of this release on the investing public was equivocal and less than abundant. On April 13 the New York Herald Tribune in an article head-noted "Copper Rumor Deflated" quoted from the TGS release of April 12 and backtracked from its original April 11 report of a major strike but nevertheless inferred from the TGS release that "recent mineral exploratory activity near Timmins, Ontario, has provided preliminary favorable results, sufficient at least to require a step-up in drilling operations." Some witnesses who testified at the hearing stated that they found the release encouraging. On the other hand, a Canadian mining security specialist, Roche, stated that "earlier in the week [before April 16] we had a Dow Jones saying that they [TGS] didn't have anything basically" and a TGS stock specialist for the Midwest Stock Exchange became concerned about his long position in the stock after reading the release. The trial court stated only that "While, in retrospect, the press release may appear gloomy or incomplete, this does not make it misleading or deceptive on the basis of the facts then known." Id. at 296.

Meanwhile, drilling operations continued. . . .

While drilling activity ensued to completion, TGS officials were taking steps toward ultimate disclosure of the discovery. On April 13, a previously-invited reporter for The Northern Miner, a Canadian mining industry journal, visited the drillsite, interviewed Mollison, Holyk and Darke, and prepared an article which confirmed a 10 million ton ore strike. This report, after having been submitted to Mollison and returned to the reported unamended on April 15, was published in the April 16 issue. A statement relative to the extent of the discovery, in substantial part drafted by Mollison, was given to the Ontario Minister of Mines for release to the Canadian media. Mollison and Holyk expected it to be released over the airways at 11 P.M. on April 15th, but, for undisclosed reasons, it was not released until 9:40 A.M. on the 16th. An official detailed statement, announcing a strike of at least 25 million tons of ore, based on the drilling data set forth above, was read to representatives of American financial media from 10:00 A.M. to 10:10 or 10:15 A.M. on April 16, and appeared over Merrill Lynch's private wire at 10:29 A.M. and, somewhat later than expected, over the Dow Jones ticker tape at 10:54 A.M.

Between the time the first press release was issued on April 12 and the dissemination of the TGS official announcement on the morning of April 16, the only defendants before us on appeal who engaged in market activity were Clayton and Crawford and TGS director Coates. Clayton ordered 200 shares of TGS stock through his Canadian broker on April 15 and another 300 shares at 8:30 A.M. the next day, and these orders were executed over the Midwest Exchange in Chicago at its opening on April 16. Coates left the TGS press conference and called his broker son-in-law Haemisegger shortly before 10:20 A.M. on the 16th and ordered 2,000 shares of TGS for family trust accounts of which Coates was a trustee but not a beneficiary; Haemisegger executed this order over the New York and Midwest Exchanges, and he and his customers purchased 1500 additional shares.

During the period of drilling in Timmins, the market price of TGS stock fluctuated but steadily gained overall. On Friday, November 8, when the drilling began, the stock closed at $17\frac{3}{8}$; on Friday, November 15, after K–55–1 had been completed, it closed at 18. After a slight decline to $16\frac{3}{8}$ by Friday, November 22, the price rose to $20\frac{7}{8}$ by December 13, when the chemical assay results of K–55–1 were received, and closed at a high of $24\frac{1}{8}$ on February 21, the day after the stock options had been issued. It had reached a price of 26 by March 31, after the land acquisition program had been completed and drilling had been resumed, and continued to ascend to $30\frac{1}{8}$ by the close of trading on April 10, at which time the drilling progress up to then was evaluated for the April 12th press release. On April 13, the day on which the April 12 release was disseminated, TGS opened at 30⅛, rose immediately to a high of 32 and gradually tapered off to close at 30⅞. It closed at 30¼ the next day, and at 29⅜ on April 15. On April 16, the day of the official announcement of the Timmins discovery, the price climbed to a high of 37 and closed at 36⅜. By May 15, TGS stock was selling at 58¼....*

* The purchases by the parties during this period were:

Purchase Date	Purchaser	Shares Number	Price	Calls Number	Price
Hole K–55–1 Completed November 12, 1963					
1963					
Nov. 12	Fogarty	300	17¾–18		
15	Clayton	200	17¾		
15	Fogarty	700	17⅝–17⅞		
15	Mollison	100	17⅞		
19	Fogarty	500	18⅛		
26	Fogarty	200	17¾		
29	Holyk (Mrs.)	50	18		
Chemical Assays of Drill Core of K–55–1 Received December 9–13, 1963					
Dec. 10	Holyk (Mrs.)	100	20⅜		
12	Holyk (or wife)			200	21
13	Mollison	100	21⅛		
30	Fogarty	200	22		
31	Fogarty	100	23¼		
1964					
Jan. 6	Holyk (or wife)			100	23⅝
8	Murray			400	23¼
24	Holyk (or wife)			200	22¼–22⅜
Feb. 10	Fogarty	300	22⅛–22¼		
20	Darke	300	24⅛		
24	Clayton	400	23⅞		
24	Holyk (or wife)			200	24⅛
26	Holyk (or wife)			200	23⅜
26	Huntington	50	23¼		
27	Darke (Moran as nominee)			1000	22⅝–22¾
Mar. 2	Holyk (Mrs.)	200	22⅜		
3	Clayton	100	22¼		
16	Huntington			100	22⅜
16	Holyk (or wife)			300	23¼
17	Holyk (Mrs.)	100	23⅞		
23	Darke			1000	24¾
26	Clayton	200	25		
Land Acquisition Completed March 27, 1964					
Mar. 30	Darke			100	25½
30	Holyk (Mrs.)	100	25⅞		
Core Drilling of Kidd Segment Resumed March 31, 1964					
April 1	Clayton	60	26½		
1	Fogarty	400	26½		

I. THE INDIVIDUAL DEFENDANTS

A. *Introductory*

... Whether predicated on traditional fiduciary concepts, see, e.g., Hotchkiss v. Fisher, 136 Kan. 530, 16 P.2d 531 (Kan.1932), or on the "special facts" doctrine, see, e.g., Strong v. Repide, 213 U.S. 419, 29 S.Ct. 521, 53 L.Ed. 853 (1909), ... Rule [10b–5] is based in policy on the justifiable expectation of the securities marketplace that all investors trading on impersonal exchanges have relatively equal access to material information, see Cary, Insider Trading in Stocks, 21 Bus.Law. 1009, 1010 (1966), Fleischer, Securities Trading and Corporation Information Practices: The Implications of the Texas Gulf Sulphur Proceeding, 51 Va.L.Rev. 1271, 1278–80 (1965). The essence of the Rule is that anyone who, trading for his own account in the securities of a corporation has "access, directly or indirectly, to information intended to be available only for a corporate purpose and not for the personal benefit of anyone" may not take "advantage of such information knowing it is unavailable to those with whom he is dealing," i.e., the investing public. Matter of Cady, Roberts & Co., 40 SEC 907, 912 (1961). Insiders, as directors or management officers are, of course, by this Rule, precluded from so unfairly dealing, but the Rule is also applicable to one possessing the information who may not be strictly termed an "insider" within the meaning of Sec. 16(b) of the Act. Cady, Roberts, supra. Thus, anyone in possession of material inside information must either disclose it to the investing public, or, if he is disabled from disclosing it in order to protect a corporate confidence, or he chooses not to do so, must abstain from trading in or recommending the securities concerned while such inside information remains undisclosed. So, it is here no justification for insider activity that disclosure was forbidden by the legitimate corporate objective of acquiring options to purchase the land surrounding the exploration site; if the information was, as the SEC contends, material,[9] its possessors should have kept out of the market until disclosure was accomplished. Cady, Roberts, supra at 911.

2	Clayton	100	26⅞
6	Fogarty	400	28⅛–28⅞
8	Mollison (Mrs.)	100	28⅛

First Press Release Issued April 12, 1964

April	15	Clayton	200	29⅜
	16	Crawford (and wife)	600	30⅛–30¼

Second Press Release Issued 10:00–10:10 or 10:15 A.M., April 16, 1964 ...

1963

April	16	(app. 10:20 A.M.)		
		Coates (for family trusts)	2000	31–31⅝

[Footnote by the court; relocated by the editor.]

9. Congress intended by the Exchange Act to eliminate the idea that the use of inside information for personal advantage was a normal emolument of corporate office. See Sections 2 and 16 of the Act; H.R.Rep. No. 1383, 73rd Cong., 2d Sess. 13 (1934); S.Rep. No. 792, 73rd Cong., 2d Sess. 9 (1934); S.E.C., Tenth Annual Report 50 (1944). See Cady, Roberts, supra at 912.

B. *Material Inside Information*

An insider is not, of course, always foreclosed from investing in his own company merely because he may be more familiar with company operations than are outside investors. An insider's duty to disclose information or his duty to abstain from dealing in his company's securities arises only in "those situations which are essentially extraordinary in nature and which are reasonably certain to have a substantial effect on the market price of the security if [the extraordinary situation is] disclosed." Fleischer, Securities Trading and Corporate Information Practices: The Implications of the Texas Gulf Sulphur Proceeding, 51 Va.L.Rev. 1271, 1289.

Nor is an insider obligated to confer upon outside investors the benefit of his superior financial or other expert analysis by disclosing his educated guesses or predictions. 3 Loss, op. cit. supra at 1463. The only regulatory objective is that access to material information be enjoyed equally, but this objective requires nothing more than the disclosure of basic facts so that outsiders may draw upon their own evaluative expertise in reaching their own investment decisions with knowledge equal to that of the insiders.

This is not to suggest, however, as did the trial court, that "the test of materiality must necessarily be a conservative one, particularly since many actions under Section 10(b) are brought on the basis of hindsight," 258 F.Supp. 262 at 280, in the sense that the materiality of facts is to be assessed solely by measuring the effect the knowledge of the facts would have upon prudent or conservative investors. As we stated in List v. Fashion Park, Inc., 340 F.2d 457, 462, "The basic test of materiality ... is whether a *reasonable* man would attach importance ... in determining his choice of action in the transaction in question. Restatement, Torts § 538(2)(a); accord Prosser, Torts 554–55; I Harper & James, Torts 565–66." (Emphasis supplied.) ... [M]aterial facts include not only information disclosing the earnings and distributions of a company but also those facts which affect the probable future of the company and those which may affect the desire of investors to buy, sell, or hold the company's securities.

In each case, then, whether facts are material within Rule 10b–5 when the facts relate to a particular event and are undisclosed by those persons who are knowledgeable thereof will depend at any given time upon a balancing of both the indicated probability that the event will occur and the anticipated magnitude of the event in light of the totality of the company activity. Here, notwithstanding the trial court's conclusion that the results of the first drill core, K–55–1, were "too 'remote' ... to have had any significant impact on the market, i.e., to be deemed material," [11] 258 F.Supp. at 283,

---

11. We are not, of course, bound by the trial court's determination as to materiality unless we find it "clearly erroneous" for that standard of appellate review is applicable only to issues of basic fact and not to issues of ultimate fact. See Baranow v. Gibraltar Factors Corp., 366 F.2d 584, 587 (2 Cir.1966); Mamiye Bros. v. Barber S.S. Lines, Inc., 360 F.2d 774, 776–778 (2 Cir.), cert. denied, 385 U.S. 835, 87 S.Ct. 80, 17

knowledge of the possibility, which surely was more than marginal, of the existence of a mine of the vast magnitude indicated by the remarkably rich drill core located rather close to the surface (suggesting mineability by the less expensive openpit method) within the confines of a large anomaly (suggesting an extensive region of mineralization) might well have affected the price of TGS stock and would certainly have been an important fact to a reasonable, if speculative, investor in deciding whether he should buy, sell, or hold. After all, this first drill core was "unusually good and ... excited the interest and speculation of those who knew about it." 258 F.Supp. at 282.

... Our survey of the facts found below conclusively establishes that knowledge of the results of the discovery hole, K–55–1, would have been important to a reasonable investor and might have affected the price of the stock.[12] On April 16, The Northern Miner, a trade publication in wide circulation among mining stock specialists, called K–55–1, the discovery hole, "one of the most impressive drill holes completed in modern times." Roche, a Canadian broker whose firm specialized in mining securities, characterized the importance to investors of the results of K–55–1. He stated that the completion of "the first drill hole" with "a 600 foot drill core is very very significant ... anything over 200 feet is considered very significant and 600 feet is just beyond your wildest imagination." He added, however, that it "is a natural thing to buy more stock once they give you the first drill hole." Additional testimony revealed that the prices of stocks of other companies, albeit less diversified, smaller firms, had increased substantially solely on the basis of the discovery of good anomalies or even because of the proximity of their lands to the situs of a potentially major strike.

Finally, a major factor in determining whether the K–55–1 discovery was a material fact is the importance attached to the drilling results by those who knew about it. In view of other unrelated recent developments favorably affecting TGS, participation by an informed person in a regular stock-purchase program, or even sporadic trading by an informed person, might lend only nominal support to the inference of the materiality of the K–55–1 discovery; nevertheless, the timing by those who knew of it of their stock purchases and their purchases of *short-term* calls—purchases in some cases by individuals who had never before purchased calls or even TGS stock—virtually compels the inference that the insiders

L.Ed.2d 70 (1966); see also SEC v. R.A. Holman & Co., 366 F.2d 456, 457–458 (2 Cir.1966) (by implication).

12. We do not suggest that material facts must be disclosed immediately; the timing of disclosure is a matter for the business judgment of the corporate officers entrusted with the management of the corporation within the affirmative disclosure requirements promulgated by the exchanges and by the SEC. Here, a valuable corporate purpose was served by delaying the publication of the K–55–1 discovery.

We do intend to convey, however, that where a corporate purpose is thus served by withholding the news of a material fact, those persons who are thus quite properly true to their corporate trust must not during the period of non-disclosure deal personally in the corporation's securities or give to outsiders confidential information not generally available to all the corporations' stockholders and to the public at large.

were influenced by the drilling results. This insider trading activity, which surely constitutes highly pertinent evidence and the only truly objective evidence of the materiality of the K–55–1 discovery, was apparently disregarded by the court below in favor of the testimony of defendants' expert witnesses, all of whom "agreed that one drill core does not establish an ore body, much less a mine," 258 F.Supp. at 282–283. Significantly, however, the court below, while relying upon what these defense experts said the defendant insiders *ought* to have thought about the worth to TGS of the K–55–1 discovery, and finding that from November 12, 1963 to April 6, 1964 Fogarty, Murray, Holyk and Darke spent more than $100,000 in purchasing TGS stock and calls on that stock, made no finding that the insiders were motivated by any factor other than the extraordinary K–55–1 discovery when they bought their stock and their calls. No reason appears why outside investors, perhaps better acquainted with speculative modes of investment and with, in many cases, perhaps more capital at their disposal for intelligent speculation, would have been less influenced, and would not have been similarly motivated to invest if they had known what the insider investors knew about the K–55–1 discovery.

Our decision to expand the limited protection afforded outside investors by the trial court's narrow definition of materiality is not at all shaken by fears that the elimination of insider trading benefits will deplete the ranks of capable corporate managers by taking away an incentive to accept such employment. Such benefits, in essence, are forms of secret corporate compensation, see Cary, Corporate Standards and Legal Rules, 50 Calif.L.Rev. 408, 409–10 (1962), derived at the expense of the uninformed investing public and not at the expense of the corporation which receives the sole benefit from insider incentives. Moreover, adequate incentives for corporate officers may be provided by properly administered stock options and employee purchase plans of which there are many in existence. In any event, the normal motivation induced by stock ownership, i.e., the identification of an individual with corporate progress, is ill-promoted by condoning the sort of speculative insider activity which occurred here; for example, some of the corporation's stock was sold at market in order to purchase short-term calls upon that stock, calls which would never be exercised to increase a stockholder equity in TGS unless the market price of that stock rose sharply.

The core of Rule 10b–5 is the implementation of the Congressional purpose that all investors should have equal access to the rewards of participation in securities transactions. It was the intent of Congress that all members of the investing public should be subject to identical market risks,—which market risks include, of course the risk that one's evaluative capacity or one's capital available to put at risk may exceed another's capacity or capital. The insiders here were not trading on an equal footing with the outside investors. They alone were in a position to evaluate the probability and magnitude of what seemed from the outset to be a major ore strike; they alone could invest safely, secure in the expectation that the price of TGS stock would rise substantially in the event such a major strike should materialize, but would decline little, if at all, in the event of failure, for the public, ignorant at the outset of the favorable probabilities would likewise be unaware of the unproductive exploration, and the additional exploration costs would not significantly affect TGS market prices. Such inequities based upon unequal access to knowledge should not be shrugged off as inevitable in our way of life, or, in view of the congressional concern in the area, remain uncorrected.

We hold, therefore, that all transactions in TGS stock or calls by individuals apprised of the drilling results [14] of K–55–1 were made in violation of Rule 10b–5.[15] Inasmuch as the visual evaluation of that drill core (a generally reliable estimate though less accurate than a chemical assay) constituted material information, those advised of the results of the visual evaluation as well as those informed of the chemical assay traded in violation of law. The geologist Darke possessed undisclosed material information and traded in TGS securities. Therefore we reverse the dismissal of the action as to him and his personal transactions. . . .

With reference to Huntington, the trial court found that he "had no detailed knowledge as to the work" on the Kidd–55 segment, 258 F.Supp. 281. Nevertheless, the evidence shows that he knew about and participated in TGS's land acquisition program which followed the receipt of the K–55–1 drilling results, and that on February 26, 1964 he purchased 50 shares of TGS stock. Later, on March 16, he helped prepare a letter for Dr. Holyk's signature in which TGS made a substantial offer for lands near K–55–1, and on the same day he, who had never before purchased calls on any stock, purchased a call on 100 shares of TGS stock. We are satisfied that these purchases in February and March, coupled with his readily inferable and probably reliable, understanding of the highly favorable nature of preliminary operations on the Kidd segment, demonstrate that Huntington possessed material inside information such as to make his purchase violative of the Rule and the Act.

C. *When May Insiders Act?*

Appellant Crawford, who ordered [17] the purchase of TGS stock shortly before the TGS April 16 official announcement, and defen-

---

14. The trial court found that defendant Murray "had no detailed knowledge as to the work" on the Kidd–55 segment. There is no evidence in the record suggesting that Murray purchased his stock on January 8, 1964, on the basis of material undisclosed information, and the disposition below is undisturbed as to him.

15. Even if insiders were in fact ignorant of the broad scope of the Rule and acted pursuant to a mistaken belief as to the applicable law such an ignorance does not insulate them from the consequences of their acts. Tager v. SEC, 344 F.2d 5, 8 (2 Cir.1965).

17. The effective protection of the public from insider exploitation of advance notice of material information requires that the time that an insider places an order, rather than the time of its ultimate execution, be determinative for Rule 10b–5 purposes. Otherwise, insiders would be able to "beat the news," cf. Fleischer, supra, 51 Va.L.Rev. at 1291, by requesting in advance that their orders be executed immediately after the dissemination of a major news

dant Coates, who placed orders with and communicated the news to his broker immediately after the official announcement was read at the TGS-called press conference, concede that they were in possession of material information. They contend, however, that their purchases were not proscribed purchases for the news had already been effectively disclosed. We disagree.

Crawford telephoned his orders to his Chicago broker about midnight on April 15 and again at 8:30 in the morning of the 16th, with instructions to buy at the opening of the Midwest Stock Exchange that morning. The trial court's finding that "he sought to, and did, 'beat the news,'" 258 F.Supp. at 287, is well documented by the record. The rumors of a major ore strike which had been circulated in Canada and, to a lesser extent, in New York, had been disclaimed by the TGS press release of April 12, which significantly promised the public an official detailed announcement when possibilities had ripened into actualities. The abbreviated announcement to the Canadian press at 9:40 A.M. on the 16th by the Ontario Minister of Mines and the report carried by The Northern Miner, parts of which had sporadically reached New York on the morning of the 16th through reports from Canadian affiliates to a few New York investment firms, are assuredly not the equivalent of the official 10–15 minute announcement which was not released to the American financial press until after 10:00 A.M. Crawford's orders had been placed before that. Before insiders may act upon material information, such information must have been effectively disclosed in a manner sufficient to insure its availability to the investing public. Particularly here, where a formal announcement to the entire financial news media had been promised in a prior official release known to the media, all insider activity must await dissemination of the promised official announcement.

Coates was absolved by the court below because his telephone order was placed shortly before 10:20 A.M. on April 16, which was after the announcement had been made even though the news could not be considered already a matter of public information. 258 F.Supp. at 288. This result seems to have been predicated upon a misinterpretation of dicta in *Cady, Roberts,* where the SEC instructed insiders to "keep out of the market until the established procedures for public release of the information are *carried out* instead of hastening to execute transactions in advance of, and in frustration of, the objectives of the release," 40 SEC at 915 (emphasis supplied). The reading of a news release, which prompted Coates into action, is merely the first step in the process of dissemination required for compliance with the regulatory objective of providing all investors with an equal opportunity to make informed investment judgments. Assuming that the contents of the

release but before outsiders could act on the release. Thus it is immaterial whether Crawford's orders were executed before or after the announcement was made in Canada (9:40 A.M., April 16) or in the United States (10:00 A.M.) or whether Coates's order was executed before or after the news appeared over the Merrill Lynch (10:29 A.M.) or Dow Jones (10:54 A.M.) wires.

official release could instantaneously be acted upon,[18] at the minimum Coates should have waited until the news could reasonably have been expected to appear over the media of widest circulation, the Dow Jones broad tape, rather than hastening to insure an advantage to himself and his broker son-in-law.[19] . . .

E. *May Insiders Accept Stock Options Without Disclosing Material Information to the Issuer?*

On February 20, 1964, defendants Stephens, Fogarty, Mollison, Holyk and Kline accepted stock options issued to them and a number of other top officers of TGS, although not one of them had informed the Stock Option Committee of the Board of Directors or the Board of the results of K–55–1, which information we have held was then material. The SEC sought rescission of these options. The trial court, in addition to finding the knowledge of the results of the K–55 discovery to be immaterial, held that Kline had no detailed knowledge of the drilling progress and that Holyk and Mollison could reasonably assume that their superiors, Stephens and Fogarty, who were directors of the corporation, would report the results if that was advisable; indeed all employees had been instructed not to divulge this information pending completion of the land acquisition program, 258 F.Supp. at 291. Therefore, the court below concluded that only directors Stephens and Fogarty, of the top management, would have violated the Rule by accepting stock options without disclosure, but it also found that they had not acted improperly as the information in their possession was not material. 258 F.Supp. at 292. In view of our conclusion as to materiality we hold that Stephens and Fogarty violated the Rule by accepting them. However, as they have surrendered the options and the corporation has canceled them, supra at 292, n. 17, we find it unnecessary to order that the injunctions prayed for be actually issued. We point out, nevertheless, that the surrender of these options after the SEC commenced the case is not a satisfaction of the SEC claim, and a determination as to whether the issuance of injunctions against Stephens and Fogarty is advisable in order to

18. Although the only insider who acted after the news appeared over the Dow Jones broad tape is not an appellant and therefore we need not discuss the necessity of considering the advisability of a "reasonable waiting period" during which outsiders may absorb and evaluate disclosures, we note in passing that, where the news is of a sort which is not readily translatable into investment action, insiders may not take advantage of their advance opportunity to evaluate the information by acting immediately upon dissemination. In any event, the permissible timing of insider transactions after disclosures of various sorts is one of the many areas of expertise for appropriate exercise of the SEC's rule-making power, which we hope will be utilized in the future to provide some predictability of certainty for the business community.

19. The record reveals that news usually appears on the Dow Jones broad tape 2–3 minutes after the reporter completes dictation. Here, assuming that the Dow Jones reporter left the press conference as early as possible, 10:10 A.M., the 10–15 minute release (which took at least that long to dictate) could not have appeared on the wire before 10:22, and for other reasons unknown to us did not appear until 10:54. Indeed, even the abbreviated version of the release reported by Merrill Lynch over its private wire did not appear until 10:29. Coates, however, placed his call no later than 10:20.

prevent or deter future violations of regulatory provisions is remanded for the exercise of discretion by the trial court.

Contrary to the belief of the trial court that Kline had no duty to disclose his knowledge of the Kidd project before accepting the stock option offered him, we believe that he, a vice president, who had become the general counsel of TGS in January 1964, but who had been secretary of the corporation since January 1961, and was present in that capacity when the options were granted, and who was in charge of the mechanics of issuance and acceptance of the options, was a member of top management and under a duty before accepting his option to disclose any material information he may have possessed, and, as he did not disclose such information to the Option Committee we direct rescission of the option he received.[24] As to Holyk and Mollison, the SEC has not appealed the holding below that they, not being then members of top management (although Mollison was a vice president) had no duty to disclose their knowledge of the drilling before accepting their options. Therefore, the issue of whether, by accepting, they violated the Act, is not before us, and the holding below is undisturbed....

FRIENDLY, Circuit Judge (concurring):

Agreeing with the result reached by the majority and with most of Judge Waterman's searching opinion, I take a rather different approach to two facets of the case.

I.

The first is a situation that will not often arise, involving as it does the acceptance of stock options during a period when inside information likely to produce a rapid and substantial increase in the price of the stock was known to some of the grantees but unknown to those in charge of the granting. I suppose it would be clear, under Ruckle v. Roto American Corp., 339 F.2d 24 (2 Cir.1964), that if a corporate officer having such knowledge persuaded an unknow-

---

24. The options granted on February 20, 1964 to Mollison, Holyk, and Kline were ratified by the Texas Gulf directors on July 15, 1965 after there had been, of course, a full disclosure and after this action had been commenced. However, the ratification is irrelevant here, for we would hold with the district court that a member of top management, as was Kline, is required, before accepting a stock option, to disclose material inside information which, if disclosed, might affect the price of the stock during the period when the accepted option could be exercised. Kline had known since November 1962 that K–55–1 had been drilled, that the drilling had intersected a sulphide body containing copper and zinc, and that TGS desired to acquire adjacent property.

Of course, if any of the five knowledgeable defendants had rejected his option there might well have been speculation as to the reason for the rejection. Therefore, in a case where disclosure to the grantors of an option would seriously jeopardize corporate security, it could well be desirable, in order to protect a corporation from selling securities to insiders who are in a position to appreciate their true worth at a price which may not accurately reflect the true value of the securities and at the same time to preserve when necessary the secrecy of corporate activity, not to require that an insider possessed of undisclosed material information reject the offer of a stock option, but only to require that he abstain from exercising it until such time as there shall have been a full disclosure and, after the full disclosure, a ratification such as was voted here. However, as this suggestion was not presented to us, we do not consider it or make any determination with reference to it.

ing board of directors to grant him an option at a price approximating the current market, the option would be rescindable in an action under Rule 10b–5. It would seem, by the same token, that if, to make the pill easier to swallow, he urged the directors to include others lacking the knowledge he possessed, he would be liable for all the resulting damage. The novel problem in the instant case is to define the responsibility of officers when a directors' committee administering a stock option plan proposes of its own initiative to make options available to them and others at a time when they know that the option price, geared to the market value of the stock, did not reflect a substantial increment likely to be realized in short order and was therefore unfair to the corporation.

A rule requiring a minor officer to reject an option so tendered would not comport with the realities either of human nature or of corporate life. If the SEC had appealed the ruling dismissing this portion of the complaint as to Holyk and Mollison, I would have upheld the dismissal quite apart from the special circumstance that a refusal on their part could well have broken the wall of secrecy it was important for TGS to preserve. Whatever they knew or didn't know about Timmins, they were entitled to believe their superiors had reported the facts to the Option Committee unless they had information to the contrary. Stephens, Fogarty and Kline stand on an altogether different basis; as senior officers they had an obligation to inform the Committee that this was not the right time to grant options at 95% of the current price. Silence, when there is a duty to speak, can itself be a fraud. I am unimpressed with the argument that Stephens, Fogarty and Kline could not perform this duty on the peculiar facts of this case, because of the corporate need for secrecy during the land acquisition program. Non-management directors would not normally challenge a recommendation for postponement of an option plan from the President, the Executive Vice President, and the Vice President and General Counsel. Moreover, it should be possible for officers to communicate with directors, of all people, without fearing a breach of confidence. Hence, as one of the foregoing hypotheticals suggests, I am not at all sure that a company in the position of TGS might not have a claim against top officers who breached their duty of disclosure for the entire damage suffered as a result of the untimely issuance of options, rather than merely one for rescission of the options issued to them.[2] Since that issue is not before us, I merely make the reservation of my position clear. . . .

2. Though the Board of Directors of TGS ratified the issuance of the options after the Timmins discovery had been fully publicized, it obviously was of the belief that Kline had committed no serious wrong in remaining silent. Throughout this litigation TGS has supported the legality of the actions of all the defendants—the company's counsel having represented, among others, Stephens, Fogarty and Kline. Consequently, I agree with the majority in giving the Board's action no weight here. If a fraud of this kind may ever be cured by ratification, compare Continental Securities Co. v. Belmont, 206 N.Y. 7, 99 N.E. 138, 51 L.R.A., N.S., 112 (1912), with Claman v. Robertson, 164 Ohio St. 61, 128 N.E.2d 429 (1955); cf. Wilko v. Swan, 346 U.S. 427, 74 S.Ct. 182, 98 L.Ed. 168 (1953), that cannot be done without an appreciation of the illegality of the conduct proposed to be excused, cf. United Hotels Co. v. Mealey, 147 F.2d 816, 819 (2 Cir.1945).

[The opinions of Judges Kaufman and Anderson (concurring), Judge Hays (concurring in part and dissenting in part), and Judges Moore and Lumbard (dissenting) are omitted.]

REYNOLDS v. TEXAS GULF SULPHUR CO., 309 F.Supp. 548, 559–60 (D.Utah 1970), aff'd in part, rev'd in part sub nom. Mitchell v. Texas Gulf Sulphur Co., 446 F.2d 90 (10th Cir.1971). "From the record the court concludes that the press release dated April 12, 1964, was inaccurate, misleading and deceptive with respect to material matters disclosed by the company's drilling near Timmins. The authors of the release knew from visual and chemical analyses that the first core disclosed the presence of copper and zinc mineralization of ore-grade; that the second test hole (K–55–3) virtually eliminated any chance that the initial test hole had been drilled 'down-dip'; that cores from drill holes located 200 feet south and 200 feet north of the initial test hole contained similar mineralization; and that still another drill hole core had disclosed similar mineralization at greater depths than were reached by the other drill holes.

"The release painted a bleak and gloomy picture—most of the areas drilled in Eastern Canada revealed either barren pyrite or graphite without value; a few resulted in discoveries of small or marginal sulphide ore bodies, etc. Not a word, however, about the results of any of the drilling near Timmins, except that it had led to 'preliminary indications' that more drilling would be necessary for a proper evaluation. The drilling 'to date had not been conclusive' and has not been 'sufficient to reach definite conclusions' and 'any' statement 'as to size and grade or ore would be premature and possibly misleading.' But a newspaper reporter's finding, made on the same day the press release was printed, that the drillings indicated more than 10,000,000 tons of ore, and the same reporter's statement that one hole averaged in excess of 1% copper and 8% zinc, went unchallenged when submitted to vice president Richard D. Mollison who released the article on April 15th for publication. Obviously, the reporter was quoting figures given to him by officials of the company, and given to him on April 13th. It may very well have been that the company officials when they prepared the release dated April 12, were trying to hold the big news until just before, or on the day of, the stockholders annual meeting which was held on April 23rd."

SEC v. TEXAS GULF SULPHUR CO., 446 F.2d 1301, 1307–08 (2d Cir.1971). [On remand, the] district court required Holyk, Huntington, Clayton, and Darke to pay to TGS the profits they had derived (and, in Darke's case, also the profits which his tippees had derived) from their TGS stock between their respective purchase dates and April 17, 1964, when the ore strike was fully known to the public. The payments are to be held in escrow in an interest-bearing account for a period of five years, subject to disposition in such manner as the court might direct upon application by the SEC or other interested person, or on the court's own motion. At the end of five years any money remaining undisposed of would become the property of TGS. To protect the appellants against double liability, any private judgments against these appellants arising out of the events of this case are to be paid from this fund. . . .

"Appellants, of course, contend that the required restitution is . . . a penalty assessment. . . . [However, restitution] of the profits on these transactions merely deprives the appellants of the gains of their wrongful conduct. . . .

"Finally, appellants contend that the order is punitive because it contains no element of compensation to those who have been damaged. However, as the New York Court of Appeals in Diamond v. Oreamuno, 24 N.Y.2d 494, 499, 301 N.Y.S.2d 78, 81–82, 248 N.E.2d 910, 912–913 (1969), recognized, a corporate enterprise may well suffer harm 'when officers and directors abuse their position to obtain personal profits' since 'the effect may be to cast a cloud on the corporation's name, injure stockholder relations and undermine public regard for the corporation's securities.' Although the sellers of TGS stock who sold before April 17, 1964, may have a higher equity than TGS to recover from appellants the wrongful profits appellants obtained, this fact does not preclude conditional compensation to TGS."

AMERICAN BAR ASSOCIATION, COMMITTEE ON FEDERAL REGULATION OF SECURITIES, REPORT OF THE TASK FORCE ON REGULATION OF INSIDER TRADING, PART I: REGULATION UNDER THE ANTIFRAUD PROVISIONS OF THE SECURITIES EXCHANGE ACT OF 1934

41 Bus.Law. 223 (1985).

THE POLICY BASIS FOR INSIDER TRADING REGULATION

The task force first considered whether, in today's market and legal environment, a sound policy basis remains for prohibiting the use of nonpublic information by one trader to gain advantage over others. . . .

In today's securities markets, where vast amounts of information are quickly available about corporate issuers (at least widely followed ones) and electronic communication is instantaneous, some respected scholars have argued that the markets themselves provide an adequate corrective for temporary informational advantage by promptly reporting the trading that occurs. They argue that the economic incentive of allowing a trader to use nonpublic information is of social value because it encourages and rewards analytic research and initiative. But other scholars see valid policy bases for continued regulation of unfair informational advantage even in today's impersonal, high-speed securities markets. The task force has considered these policy arguments and is persuaded that there are still valid and persuasive reasons for continuing insider trading regulation.

In our society, we traditionally abhor those who refuse to play by the rules, that is, the cheaters and the sneaks. A spitball pitcher, or a card shark with an ace up his sleeve, may win the game but not our respect. And if we know such a person is in the game, chances are we won't play. These commonsense observations suggest that two of the traditional bases for prohibitions against insider trading are still sound: the "fair play" and "integrity of the markets" arguments. The first relies on the basic policy that cheating is wrong and on the traditional sympathy for the victim of the cheat. The second rests on the oft-repeated argument that people will not entrust their resources to a marketplace they don't believe is fair, any more than a card player will put his chips on the table in a poker game that may be fixed. Although the task force knows of no empirical research that directly demonstrates that concerns about integrity affect market activity, both authoritative commentators[8] and common sense tell us that if investors do not anticipate fair treatment, they will avoid investing in securities. As a result, capital formation through securities offerings will become less attractive and more difficult. . . .

Several other forceful policy arguments favor insider trading prohibitions. When the nonpublic information originates within the corporation—as in the case of a new product discovery or an unannounced earnings increase or decrease—the information itself is corporate property until publicly released. Those who "take" it for their own advantage rather than the corporate good may be sued for their "misappropriation" of it.

If there were no penalty for personal use of such nonpublic information to gain a market profit, then officers, employees, and even directors of a corporation might keep such information to themselves for a time and trade upon it, rather than act in the corporate interest by promptly communicating the information through appropriate corporate channels. The flow of information from its corporate source to officers, directors, and other decision makers and to the investing public could thus be impeded by the incentive to delay long enough to speculate on a stock market profit. Some have argued that such profits are an appropriate

---

8. *See, e.g.,* comments of Arthur Levitt, Jr., Chairman of the American Stock Exchange, *quoted in* Business Week, April 29, 1985, at 79 ("If the investor thinks he's not getting a fair share, he's not going to invest and that is going to hurt capital formation in the long run").

reward for corporate entrepreneurs. The task force disagrees. Unbridled insider trading would distort the intended impact of corporate compensation programs approved by directors and shareholders and based on business performance. Both the beneficiaries and the amount of benefit would be unpredictable and not subject to corporate control; the random rewards would be unrelated to overall corporate performance or to specific compensation objectives.

These corporate structure arguments certainly provide support for prohibiting trading on nonpublic, *inside* information, that is, information originating from within the corporation. But these arguments provide less support for prohibiting trading on *market* information, that is, information that comes from outside the issuer but may affect the value of its securities, such as advance news of an impending tender offer, a favorable newspaper article, or an announcement of a major governmental decision.

We continue to believe, however, that a "disclose or abstain" rule should be applied even when only *market* information is involved. The traditional fairness and market integrity bases for regulating insider trading are still important to uphold when market information is involved. Moreover, one can posit that, if those having material, nonpublic market information could trade on it without fear of liability, the incentive to promptly move such information into the marketplace would be greatly reduced. Rather, those "in the know" would keep secret, and accumulate or liquidate a position on the basis of, the information for as long as possible to maximize their gain or minimize their loss. The task force believes the result of such behavior would be a less informed (not to mention less attractive) marketplace. The task force believes that fairness, information efficiency, and market integrity are served by laws that discourage retaining material market information for personal advantage.

Although it has been argued that insider trading activity affects the market quickly, so that the economic value of the undisclosed information is reflected in market prices even before the information is announced, at a minimum this involves some fundamental, and potentially costly, unfairness to the uninformed traders on the other side of the initial trades by the insiders and their tippees.

In the judgment of the task force, these policy bases provide persuasive support for prohibitions against trading on the basis of material, nonpublic "inside information." They also support extending the prohibitions beyond corporate insiders to others who may, through improper means, obtain or abuse selective access to either material "inside information" or material "market information."

In a federal system like ours, another question should be considered: to what extent are the above policies the concern of federal as opposed to state law? If insider trading prohibitions are to be imposed because of a concern for market integrity and market information efficiency, the interests would clearly be federal since the securities markets are an integral part of interstate commerce. Although the corporate structure and the misappropriation of business property are not traditional areas of federal interest, because the securities markets are national—even international—in scope, the task force believes that exclusive reliance on state regulation would be both impractical and unwise. Federal standards are required.

UNITED STATES v. CHESTMAN, 947 F.2d 551 (2d Cir.1991), cert. denied 503 U.S. 1004, 112 S.Ct. 1759, 118 L.Ed.2d 422 (1992). (Winter, J., dissenting). "One commentator has attempted to explain the Supreme Court [insider-trading] decisions in terms of [a] business-property rationale.... See Easterbrook, [Insider Trading, Secret Agents, Evidentiary Privileges, and the Production of Information, 1981 Sup.Ct.Rev. 309,] at 309–39. That rationale may be summarized as follows. Information is perhaps the most precious commodity in commercial markets. It is expensive to produce, and, because it involves facts and ideas that can be easily photocopied or carried in one's head, there is a ubiquitous risk that those who pay to produce information will see others reap the profit from it. Where the profit from an activity is likely to be diverted, investment in that activity will decline. If the law fails to protect property rights in commercial information, therefore, less will be invested in generating such information. Id. at 313.

"For example, mining companies whose investments in geological surveys have revealed valuable deposits do not want word of the strike to get out until they have secured rights to the land.[3] If word does get out, the price of the land not only will go up, but other mining companies may also secure the rights. In either case, the mining company that invested in geological surveys (including the inevitably sizeable number of unsuccessful drillings) will see profits from that investment enjoyed by others. If mining companies are unable to keep the results of such surveys confidential, less will be invested in them.

"Similarly, firms that invest money in generating information about other companies with a view to some form of combination will maintain secrecy about their efforts, and if secrecy cannot be maintained, less will be invested in acquiring such information. Hostile acquirers will want to keep such information secret lest the target mount defensive actions or speculators purchase the target's stock. Even when friendly negotiations with the other company are undertaken, the acquirer will often require the target corporation to maintain secrecy about negotiations, lest the very fact of negotiation tip off others on the important fact that the two firms think a

---

3. Although [*Texas Gulf Sulphur*] stressed the unfairness of insider trading to those who deal with the trader, the reason for the nondisclosure that allowed insider trading in TGS stock was the company's insider trading in real estate.

combination might be valuable. . . .   In the instant matter, A & P made secrecy a condition of its acquisition of Waldbaum's.

"Insider trading may reduce the return on information in two ways.   First, it creates incentives for insiders to generate or disclose information that may disregard the welfare of the corporation. Easterbrook, supra, at 332–33.   That risk is not implicated by the facts in the present case, and no further discussion is presently required.

"Second, insider trading creates a risk that information will be prematurely disclosed by such trading, and the corporation will lose part or all of its property in that information.   Id. at 331.   Although trades by an insider may rarely affect market price, others who know of the insider's trading may notice that a trader is unusually successful, or simply perceive unusual activity in a stock and guess the information and/or make piggyback trades.   Id. at 336.   A broker who executes a trade for a geologist or for a financial printer may well draw relevant conclusions.   Or, as in the instant matter, the trader . . . may tell his or her broker about the inside information, who may then trade on his or her account, on clients' accounts, or may tell friends and relatives.   One inside trader has publicly attributed his exposure in part to the fact that the bank through which he made trades piggybacked on the trades, as did the broker who made the trades for the bank.   See Levine, The Inside Story of An Inside Trader, Fortune, May 21, 1990, at 80.   Once activity in a stock reaches an unusual stage, others may guess the reason for the trading—the corporate secret.   Insider trading thus increases the risk that confidential information acquired at a cost may be disclosed.   If so, the owner of the information may lose its investment."

———————

NOTE ON BLUE CHIP STAMPS v. MANOR DRUG STORES, ERNST & ERNST v. HOCHFELDER, AND SANTA FE INDUSTRIES, INC. v. GREEN

It was early established that private actions could be brought under Rule 10b–5.   Although *Texas Gulf Sulphur* was a government action, it helped give impetus to an explosion of private actions. Three important Supreme Court cases decided between 1975 and 1977 placed important limits on actions under Rule 10b–5, but by and large the law that emerged from these cases was more important in setting outer boundaries on Rule 10b–5 than in curbing the Rule's central vitality.

In the first of these cases, Blue Chip Stamps v. Manor Drug Stores, 421 U.S. 723, 95 S.Ct. 1917, 44 L.Ed.2d 539 (1975), the plaintiff alleged that defendants' misrepresentations had caused him to refrain from purchasing stock, to his loss.   The Court rejected this claim, approving a rule (previously adopted by several Court of

Appeal cases) that only a person who had actually bought or sold securities—only a buyer or a seller—could bring a private action under Rule 10b–5.

In the second case, Ernst & Ernst v. Hochfelder, 425 U.S. 185, 96 S.Ct. 1375, 47 L.Ed.2d 668 (1976), the Court held that scienter was a necessary element of a Rule 10b–5 damage action, so that conduct by a defendant that was deceptive merely as a result of the defendant's negligence did not give rise to damages liability under the Rule. (The opinion in *Ernst & Ernst* left open whether scienter also had to be established in an injunctive action under Rule 10b–5. The Court resolved that point four years later by holding that scienter was a necessary element of an injunctive action as well. Aaron v. SEC, 446 U.S. 680, 100 S.Ct. 1945, 64 L.Ed.2d 611 (1980). *Ernst & Ernst* also left open whether recklessness was sufficient to satisfy the scienter requirement. Subsequent decisions by the Courts of Appeals have unanimously held that recklessness satisfies the scienter requirement. See, e.g., Rolf v. Blyth, Eastman Dillon & Co., Inc., 570 F.2d 38, 44–47 (2d Cir.1978), cert. denied 439 U.S. 1039, 99 S.Ct. 642, 58 L.Ed.2d 698.)

In the third case, Santa Fe Industries, Inc. v. Green, 430 U.S. 462, 97 S.Ct. 1292, 51 L.Ed.2d 480 (1977), minority shareholders who were being involuntarily cashed out through a short-form merger alleged that the price to be paid for their shares was unfairly low. However, the underlying facts concerning the value of the minority's shares had been disclosed to the minority shareholders, and under state law any minority shareholder could have turned down the merger price, and chosen instead to be paid the fair value of his shares as determined by a court. The Supreme Court rejected the plaintiffs' claim, adopting the rule that Rule 10b–5 requires deception or manipulation, so that conduct that is fully disclosed at the time it occurs will not give rise to a Rule 10b–5 action.

Although the language of the majority opinion in *Santa Fe* indicated a reluctance to extend Rule 10b–5 into the province of state law regarding corporate mismanagement, the full import of the language is not clear. It seems clear that if D, a director of Corporation C, persuades C's board, by fraud, to sell him stock, C can sue D under Rule 10b–5 even though it can also sue D for breach of fiduciary duty. Similarly, if C's board doesn't sue D, a shareholder could sue D under Rule 10b–5 in a derivative action. Suppose that a controlling shareholder causes a corporation to issue stock to him at an unfair price with the approval of a majority of the directors, when material facts are not disclosed to the minority shareholders. In Schoenbaum v. Firstbrook, 405 F.2d 215 (2d Cir.1968) (en banc), cert. denied 395 U.S. 906, 89 S.Ct. 1747, 23 L.Ed.2d 219 (1969), decided before *Santa Fe*, Aquitaine was a majority shareholder of Banff Oil Ltd. and had appointed three of its eight directors. It was alleged that Aquitaine used its controlling influence to cause Banff to sell Banff shares to Aquitaine for wholly inadequate consideration. The Second Circuit held that a minority shareholder in Banff could bring a derivative action on Banff's behalf under Rule 10b–5:

> ... [I]t is alleged that Aquitaine exercised a controlling influence over the issuance to it of treasury stock of Banff for a wholly inadequate consideration. If it is established that the transaction took place as alleged, it constituted a violation of Rule 10b–5, subdivision (3), because Aquitaine engaged in an "act, practice or course of business which operates or would operate as a fraud or deceit upon any person, in connection with the purchase or sale of any security." Moreover, Aquitaine and the directors of Banff were guilty of deceiving the stockholders of Banff (other than Aquitaine).

Id. at 219–20.

Skipped

In Goldberg v. Meridor, 567 F.2d 209 (2d Cir.1977), cert. denied 434 U.S. 1069, 98 S.Ct. 1249, 55 L.Ed.2d 771 (1978), decided shortly after *Santa Fe,* UGO Corporation was controlled by Maritimecor, which in turn was controlled by Maritime Fruit. A UGO shareholder alleged that Maritimecor, Maritime Fruit, and directors of the various companies, had caused UGO to acquire Maritimecor's assets in exchange for UGO stock, and that the agreement "was fraudulent and unfair in that the assets of Maritimecor were overpriced." Id. at 211. Press releases that described the agreement failed to disclose certain material facts concerning the value of Maritimecor's assets. The Second Circuit, in an opinion by Judge Friendly, held that *Schoenbaum* had survived *Santa Fe.* A derivative action could be brought under Rule 10b–5 on the basis of an unfair transaction between a corporation and a fiduciary or a controlling shareholder if the transaction involved stock, and material facts concerning the transaction had not been disclosed to all shareholders:

> *Schoenbaum* ... can rest solidly on the now widely recognized ground that there is deception of the corporation (in effect, of its minority shareholders) when the corporation is influenced by its controlling shareholder to engage in a transaction adverse to the corporation's interests (in effect, the minority shareholders' interests) and there is nondisclosure or misleading disclosures as to the material facts of the transaction.... The Supreme Court noted in [Green v. Santa Fe Industries, Inc.] that the court of appeals "did not disturb the District Court's conclusion that the complaint did not allege a material misrepresentation or nondisclosure with respect to the value of the stock" of Kirby; the Court's quarrel was with this court's holding that "neither misrepresentation nor nondisclosure was a necessary element of a Rule 10b–5 action," ... and that a breach of fiduciary duty would alone suffice.... It was because "the complaint failed to allege a material misrepresentation or material failure to disclose" that the Court found "inapposite the cases [including *Schoenbaum*] relied upon by respondents and the court below, in which the breaches of

fiduciary duty held violative of Rule 10b–5 included some element of deception".....

Here the complaint alleged "deceit ... upon UGO's minority shareholders".... The nub of the matter is that the conduct attacked in *Green* did not violate the " 'fundamental purpose' of the Act as implementing a 'philosophy of full disclosure' ", ... [T]he conduct here attacked does....

Id. at 217–18.

Goldberg v. Meridor has been widely followed. See Kas v. Financial General Bankshares, Inc., 796 F.2d 508, 512 (D.C.Cir. 1986); Madison Consultants v. FDIC, 710 F.2d 57, 63 (2d Cir.1983); IIT v. Cornfeld, 619 F.2d 909, 922–23 (2d Cir.1980); Healey v. Catalyst Recovery, 616 F.2d 641, 645–47 (3d Cir.1980); Alabama Farm Bureau Mutual Casualty Co. v. American Fidelity Life Insurance Co., 606 F.2d 602, 613–14 (5th Cir.1979), cert. denied 449 U.S. 820, 101 S.Ct. 77, 66 L.Ed.2d 22 (1980); Kidwell ex rel. Penfold v. Meikle, 597 F.2d 1273, 1291–92 (9th Cir.1979); see also Wright v. Heizer Corp., 560 F.2d 236, 249–51 (7th Cir.1977), cert. denied 434 U.S. 1066, 98 S.Ct. 1243, 55 L.Ed.2d 767 (1978).

BASIC INC. v. LEVINSON

Supreme Court of the United States, 1988.
485 U.S. 224, 108 S.Ct. 978, 99 L.Ed.2d 194.

Justice BLACKMUN delivered the opinion of the Court.

This case requires us to apply the materiality requirement of § 10(b) of the Securities Exchange Act of 1934, 48 Stat. 881, as amended, 15 U.S.C. § 78a *et seq.* (1934 Act), and the Securities and Exchange Commission's Rule 10b–5, promulgated thereunder, see 17 CFR § 240.10b–5 (1987), in the context of preliminary corporate merger discussions. We must also determine whether a person who traded a corporation's shares on a securities exchange after the issuance of a materially misleading statement by the corporation may invoke a rebuttable presumption that, in trading, he relied on the integrity of the price set by the market.

I

Prior to December 20, 1978, Basic Incorporated was a publicly traded company primarily engaged in the business of manufacturing chemical refractories for the steel industry. As early as 1965 or 1966, Combustion Engineering, Inc., a company producing mostly alumina-based refractories, expressed some interest in acquiring Basic, but was deterred from pursuing this inclination seriously because of antitrust concerns it then entertained. See App. 81–83. In 1976, however, regulatory action opened the way to a renewal of

Combustion's interest.[1] The "Strategic Plan," dated October 25, 1976, for Combustion's Industrial Products Group included the objective: "Acquire Basic Inc. $30 million." App. 337.

Beginning in September 1976, Combustion representatives had meetings and telephone conversations with Basic officers and directors, including petitioners here,[2] concerning the possibility of a merger.[3] During 1977 and 1978, Basic made three public statements denying that it was engaged in merger negotiations.[4] On December 18, 1978, Basic asked the New York Stock Exchange to suspend trading in its shares and issued a release stating that it had been "approached" by another company concerning a merger. *Id.,* at 413. On December 19, Basic's board endorsed Combustion's offer of $46 per share for its common stock, *id.,* at 335, 414–416, and on the following day publicly announced its approval of Combustion's tender offer for all outstanding shares.

Respondents are former Basic shareholders who sold their stock after Basic's first public statement of October 21, 1977, and before the suspension of trading in December 1978. Respondents brought a class action against Basic and its directors, asserting that the defendants issued three false or misleading public statements and thereby were in violation of § 10(b) of the 1934 Act and of Rule 10b–5. Respondents alleged that they were injured by selling Basic shares at artificially depressed prices in a market affected by petitioners' misleading statements and in reliance thereon.

1. In what are known as the *Kaiser–Lavino* proceedings, the Federal Trade Commission took the position in 1976 that basic or chemical refractories were in a market separate from nonbasic or acidic or alumina refractories; this would remove the antitrust barrier to a merger between Basic and Combustion's refractories subsidiary. On October 12, 1978, the Initial Decision of the Administrative Law Judge confirmed that position. See In re Kaiser Aluminum & Chemical Corp., 93 F.T.C. 764, 771, 809–810 (1979). See also the opinion of the Court of Appeals in this case, 786 F.2d 741, 745 (CA6 1986).

2. In addition to Basic itself, petitioners are individuals who had been members of its board of directors prior to 1979; Anthony M. Caito, Samuel Eells, Jr., John A. Gelbach, Harley C. Lee, Max Muller, H. Chapman Rose, Edmund Q. Sylvester, and John C. Wilson, Jr. Another former director, Mathew J. Ludwig, was a party to the proceedings below but died on July 17, 1986, and is not a petitioner here. See Brief for Petitioners ii.

3. In light of our disposition of this case, any further characterization of these discussions must await application, on remand, of the materiality standard adopted today.

4. On October 21, 1977, after heavy trading and a new high in Basic stock, the following news item appeared in the Cleveland Plain Dealer:

"[Basic] President Max Muller said the company knew no reason for the stock's activity and that no negotiations were under way with any company for a merger. He said Flintkote recently denied Wall Street rumors that it would make a tender offer of $25 a share for control of the Cleveland-based maker of refractories for the steel industry." App. 363.

On September 25, 1978, in reply to an inquiry from the New York Stock Exchange, Basic issued a release concerning increased activity in its stock and stated that

"management is unaware of any present or pending company development that would result in the abnormally heavy trading activity and price fluctuation in company shares that have been experienced in the past few days." *Id.,* at 401.

On November 6, 1978, Basic issued to its shareholders a "Nine Months Report 1978." This Report stated:

"With regard to the stock market activity in the Company's shares we remain unaware of any present or pending developments which would account for the high volume of trading and price fluctuations in recent months." *Id.,* at 403.

The District Court adopted a presumption of reliance by members of the plaintiff class upon petitioners' public statements that enabled the court to conclude that common questions of fact or law predominated over particular questions pertaining to individual plaintiffs. See Fed.Rule Civ.Proc. 23(b)(3). The District Court therefore certified respondents' class.[5] On the merits, however, the District Court granted summary judgment for the defendants. It held that, as a matter of law, any misstatements were immaterial: there were no negotiations ongoing at the time of the first statement, and although negotiations were taking place when the second and third statements were issued, those negotiations were not "destined, with reasonable certainty, to become a merger agreement in principle." App. to Pet. for Cert. 103a.

The United States Court of Appeals for the Sixth Circuit affirmed the class certification, but reversed the District Court's summary judgment, and remanded the case. 786 F.2d 741 (1986). The court reasoned that while petitioners were under no general duty to disclose their discussions with Combustion, any statement the company voluntarily released could not be " 'so incomplete as to mislead.' " *Id.,* at 746, quoting SEC v. Texas Gulf Sulphur Co., 401 F.2d 833, 862 (CA2 1968) (en banc), cert. denied *sub nom.* Coates v. SEC, 394 U.S. 976 (1969). In the Court of Appeals' view, Basic's statements that no negotiations were taking place, and that it knew of no corporate developments to account for the heavy trading activity, were misleading. With respect to materiality, the court rejected the argument that preliminary merger discussions are immaterial as a matter of law, and held that "once a statement is made denying the existence of any discussions, even discussions that might not have been material in absence of the denial are material because they make the statement made untrue." 786 F.2d, at 749.

The Court of Appeals joined a number of other circuits in accepting the "fraud-on-the-market theory" to create a rebuttable presumption that respondents relied on petitioners' material misrepresentations, noting that without the presumption it would be impractical to certify a class under Fed.Rule Civ.Proc. 23(b)(3). See 786 F.2d, at 750–751.

We granted certiorari, 479 U.S. 1083 (1987), to resolve the split, see Part III, *infra,* among the Courts of Appeals as to the standard of materiality applicable to preliminary merger discussions, and to determine whether the courts below properly applied a

---

5. Respondents initially sought to represent all those who sold Basic shares between October 1, 1976, and December 20, 1978. See Amended Complaint in No. C79–1220 (ND Ohio) ¶ 5. The District Court, however, recognized a class period extending only from October 21, 1977, the date of the first public statement, rather than from the date negotiations allegedly commenced.

In its certification decision, as subsequently amended, the District Court also excluded from the class those who had purchased Basic shares after the October 1977 statement but sold them before the September 1978 statement, App. to Pet. for Cert. 123a–124a, and those who sold their shares after the close of the market on Friday, December 15, 1978. *Id.,* at 137a.

presumption of reliance in certifying the class, rather than requiring each class member to show direct reliance on Basic's statements.

II

The 1934 Act was designed to protect investors against manipulation of stock prices. See S.Rep. No. 792, 73d Cong., 2d Sess., 1–5 (1934). Underlying the adoption of extensive disclosure requirements was a legislative philosophy: "There cannot be honest markets without honest publicity. Manipulation and dishonest practices of the market place thrive upon mystery and secrecy." H.R.Rep. No. 1383, 73d Cong., 2d Sess., 11 (1934). This Court "repeatedly has described the 'fundamental purpose' of the Act as implementing a 'philosophy of full disclosure.'" *Santa Fe Industries, Inc. v. Green,* 430 U.S. 462, 477–478 (1977), quoting *SEC v. Capital Gains Research Bureau, Inc.,* 375 U.S. 180, 186 (1963).

Pursuant to its authority under § 10(b) of the 1934 Act, 15 U.S.C. § 78j, the Securities and Exchange Commission promulgated Rule 10b–5.[6] Judicial interpretation and application, legislative acquiescence, and the passage of time have removed any doubt that a private cause of action exists for a violation of § 10(b) and Rule 10b–5, and constitutes an essential tool for enforcement of the 1934 Act's requirements. See, *e.g., Ernst & Ernst v. Hochfelder,* 425 U.S. 185, 196 (1976); *Blue Chip Stamps v. Manor Drug Stores,* 421 U.S. 723, 730 (1975).

The Court previously has addressed various positive and common-law requirements for a violation of § 10(b) or of Rule 10b–5. See, *e.g., Santa Fe Industries, Inc. v. Green, supra* ("manipulative or deceptive" requirement of the statute); *Blue Chip Stamps v. Manor Drug Stores, supra* ("in connection with the purchase or sale" requirement of the Rule); *Dirks v. SEC,* 463 U.S. 646 (1983) (duty to disclose); *Chiarella v. United States,* 445 U.S. 222 (1980) (same); *Ernst & Ernst v. Hochfelder, supra* (scienter). See also *Carpenter v. United States,* 484 U.S. 19 (1987) (confidentiality). The Court also explicitly has defined a standard of materiality under the securities laws, see *TSC Industries, Inc. v. Northway, Inc.,* 426 U.S. 438 (1976), concluding in the proxy-solicitation context that "[a]n omitted fact is material if there is a substantial likelihood that a reasonable shareholder would consider it important in deciding how to vote." *Id.,* at 449.[7] Acknowledging that certain information concerning corporate developments could well be of "dubious signifi-

---

6. In relevant part, Rule 10b–5 provides:

"It shall be unlawful for any person, directly or indirectly, by the use of any means or instrumentality of interstate commerce, or of the mails or of any facility of any national securities exchange,

. . .

"(b) To make any untrue statement of a material fact or to omit to state a material fact necessary in order to make the statements made, in the light of the circumstances under which they were made, not misleading. . . .

* * *

in connection with the purchase or sale of any security."

7. *TSC Industries* arose under § 14(a), as amended, of the 1934 Act, 15 U.S.C. § 78n(a), and Rule 14a–9, 17 CFR § 240.14a–9 (1975).

cance," *id.*, at 448, the Court was careful not to set too low a standard of materiality; it was concerned that a minimal standard might bring an overabundance of information within its reach, and lead management "simply to bury the shareholders in an avalanche of trivial information—a result that is hardly conducive to informed decisionmaking." *Id.*, at 448–449. It further explained that to fulfill the materiality requirement "there must be a substantial likelihood that the disclosure of the omitted fact would have been viewed by the reasonable investor as having significantly altered the 'total mix' of information made available." *Id.*, at 449. We now expressly adopt the *TSC Industries* standard of materiality for the § 10(b) and Rule 10b–5 context.[8]

III

The application of this materiality standard to preliminary merger discussions is not self-evident. Where the impact of the corporate development on the target's fortune is certain and clear, the *TSC Industries* materiality definition admits straightforward application. Where, on the other hand, the event is contingent or speculative in nature, it is difficult to ascertain whether the "reasonable investor" would have considered the omitted information significant at the time. Merger negotiations, because of the ever-present possibility that the contemplated transaction will not be effectuated, fall into the latter category.[9]

A

Petitioners urge upon us a Third Circuit test for resolving this difficulty.[10] See Brief for Petitioners 20–22. Under this approach, preliminary merger discussions do not become material until "agreement-in-principle" as to the price and structure of the transaction has been reached between the would-be merger partners. See *Greenfield v. Heublein, Inc.*, 742 F.2d 751, 757 (CA3 1984),

8. This application of the § 14(a) definition of materiality to § 10(b) and Rule 10b–5 is not disputed. See Brief for Petitioners 17, n. 12; Brief for Respondents 30, n. 10; Brief for SEC as *Amicus Curiae* 8, n. 4. See also *McGrath v. Zenith Radio Corp.*, 651 F.2d 458, 466, n. 4 (CA7), cert. denied, 454 U.S. 835 (1981), and *Goldberg v. Meridor*, 567 F.2d 209, 218–219 (CA2 1977), cert. denied, 434 U.S. 1069 (1978).

9. We do not address here any other kinds of contingent or speculative information, such as earnings forecasts or projections. See generally Hiler, The SEC and the Courts' Approach to Disclosure of Earnings Projections, Asset Appraisals, and Other Soft Information: Old Problems, Changing Views, 46 Md.L.Rev. 1114 (1987).

10. See *Staffin v. Greenberg*, 672 F.2d 1196, 1207 (CA3 1982) (defining duty to disclose existence of ongoing merger negotiations as triggered when agreement-in-principle is reached); *Greenfield v. Heublein,*

Inc., 742 F.2d 751 (CA3 1984) (applying agreement-in-principle test to materiality inquiry), cert. denied, 469 U.S. 1215 (1985). Citing *Staffin,* the United States Court of Appeals for the Second Circuit has rejected a claim that defendant was under an obligation to disclose various events related to merger negotiations. *Reiss v. Pan American World Airways, Inc.*, 711 F.2d 11, 13–14 (CA2 1983). The Seventh Circuit recently endorsed the agreement-in-principle test of materiality. See *Flamm v. Eberstadt*, 814 F.2d 1169, 1174–1179 (CA7) (describing agreement-in-principle as an agreement on price and structure), cert. denied, 484 U.S. 853 (1987). In some of these cases it is unclear whether the court based its decision on a finding that no duty arose to reveal the existence of negotiations, or whether it concluded that the negotiations were immaterial under an interpretation of the opinion in *TSC Industries, Inc. v. Northway, Inc.*, supra.

cert. denied, 469 U.S. 1215 (1985). By definition, then, information concerning any negotiations not yet at the agreement-in-principle stage could be withheld or even misrepresented without a violation of Rule 10b–5.

Three rationales have been offered in support of the "agreement-in-principle" test. The first derives from the concern expressed in *TSC Industries* that an investor not be overwhelmed by excessively detailed and trivial information, and focuses on the substantial risk that preliminary merger discussions may collapse; because such discussions are inherently tentative, disclosure of their existence itself could mislead investors and foster false optimism. See *Greenfield v. Heublein, Inc.,* 742 F.2d at 756; *Reiss v. Pan American World Airways, Inc.,* 711 F.2d 11, 14 (CA2 1983). The other two justifications for the agreement-in-principle standard are based on management concerns: because the requirement of "agreement-in-principle" limits the scope of disclosure obligations, it helps preserve the confidentiality of merger discussions where earlier disclosure might prejudice the negotiations; and the test also provides a usable, bright-line rule for determining when disclosure must be made. See *Greenfield v. Heublein, Inc.,* 742 F.2d, at 757; *Flamm v. Eberstadt,* 814 F.2d 1169, 1176–1178 (CA7), cert. denied, 484 U.S. 853 (1987).

None of these policy-based rationales, however, purports to explain why drawing the line at agreement-in-principle reflects the significance of the information upon the investor's decision. The first rationale, and the only one connected to the concerns expressed in *TSC Industries,* stands soundly rejected, even by a Court of Appeals that otherwise has accepted the wisdom of the agreement-in-principle test. "It assumes that investors are nitwits, unable to appreciate—even when told—that mergers are risky propositions up until the closing." *Flamm v. Eberstadt,* 814 F.2d, at 1175. Disclosure, and not paternalistic withholding of accurate information, is the policy chosen and expressed by Congress. We have recognized time and again, a "fundamental purpose" of the various securities acts, "was to substitute a philosophy of full disclosure for the philosophy of *caveat emptor* and thus to achieve a high standard of business ethics in the securities industry." *SEC v. Capital Gains Research Bureau, Inc.,* 375 U.S. 180, 186 (1963). Accord, *Affiliated Ute Citizens v. United States,* 406 U.S. 128, 151 (1972); *Santa Fe Industries, Inc. v. Green,* 430 U.S. 462, 477 (1977). The role of the materiality requirement is not to "attribute to investors a child-like simplicity, an inability to grasp the probabilistic significance of negotiations," *Flamm v. Eberstadt,* 814 F.2d, at 1175, but to filter out essentially useless information that a reasonable investor would not consider significant, even as part of a larger "mix" of factors to consider in making his investment decision. *TSC Industries, Inc. v. Northway, Inc.,* 426 U.S., at 448–449.

The second rationale, the importance of secrecy during the early stages of merger discussions, also seems irrelevant to an assessment whether their existence is significant to the trading decision of a reasonable investor. To avoid a "bidding war" over its target, an acquiring firm often will insist that negotiations remain confidential, see, *e.g., In re Carnation Co.,* Exchange Act Release No. 22214, 33 SEC Docket 1025 (1985), and at least one Court of Appeals has stated that "silence pending settlement of the price and structure of a deal is beneficial to most investors, most of the time." *Flamm v. Eberstadt,* 814 F.2d, at 1177.[11]

We need not ascertain, however, whether secrecy necessarily maximizes shareholder wealth—although we note that the proposition is at least disputed as a matter of theory and empirical research [12]—for this case does not concern the *timing* of a disclosure; it concerns only its accuracy and completeness.[13] We face here the narrow question whether information concerning the existence and status of preliminary merger discussions is significant to the reasonable investor's trading decision. Arguments based on the premise that some disclosure would be "premature" in a sense are more properly considered under the rubric of an issuer's duty to disclose. The "secrecy" rationale is simply inapposite to the definition of materiality.

The final justification offered in support of the agreement-in-principle test seems to be directed solely at the comfort of corporate managers. A bright-line rule indeed is easier to follow than a standard that requires the exercise of judgment in the light of all the circumstances. But ease of application alone is not an excuse for ignoring the purposes of the securities acts and Congress' policy decisions. Any approach that designates a single fact or occurrence as always determinative of an inherently fact-specific finding such as materiality, must necessarily be over- or underinclusive. In *TSC Industries* this Court explained: "The determination [of materiality] requires delicate assessments of the inferences a 'reasonable shareholder' would draw from a given set of facts and the significance of those inferences to him...." 426 U.S., at 450. After much study, the Advisory Committee on Corporate Disclosure cautioned the SEC

---

11. Reasoning backwards from a goal of economic efficiency, that Court of Appeals stated: "Rule 10b–5 is about *fraud,* after all, and it is not fraudulent to conduct business in a way that makes investors better off...." *Flamm v. Eberstadt,* 814 F.2d, at 1177.

12. See, *e.g.,* Brown, Corporate Secrecy, the Federal Securities Laws, and the Disclosure of Ongoing Negotiations, 36 Cath. U.L.Rev. 93, 145–155 (1986); Bebchuk, The Case for Facilitating Competing Tender Offers, 95 Harv.L.Rev. 1028 (1982); *Flamm v. Eberstadt,* 814 F.2d, at 1177, n. 2 (citing scholarly debate). See also *In re Carnation Co.,* Exchange Act Release No. 22214, 33 SEC Docket 1025, 1030 (1985) ("The importance of accurate and complete issuer

disclosure to the integrity of the securities markets cannot be overemphasized. To the extent that investors cannot rely upon the accuracy and completeness of issuer statements, they will be less likely to invest, thereby reducing the liquidity of the securities markets to the detriment of investors and issuers alike").

13. See *SEC v. Texas Gulf Sulphur Co.,* 401 F.2d 833, 862 (CA2 1968) (en banc) ("Rule 10b–5 is violated whenever assertions are made, as here, in a manner reasonably calculated to influence the investing public ... if such assertions are false or misleading or are so incomplete as to mislead...."), cert. denied *sub nom. Coates v. SEC,* 394 U.S. 976 (1969).

against administratively confining materiality to a rigid formula.[14] Courts also would do well to heed this advice.

We therefore find no valid justification for artificially excluding from the definition of materiality information concerning merger discussions, which would otherwise be considered significant to the trading decision of a reasonable investor, merely because agreement-in-principle as to price and structure has not yet been reached by the parties or their representatives.

B

The Sixth Circuit explicitly rejected the agreement-in-principle test, as we do today, but in its place adopted a rule that, if taken literally, would be equally insensitive, in our view, to the distinction between materiality and the other elements of an action under Rule 10b–5:

> "When a company whose stock is publicly traded makes a statement, as Basic did, that 'no negotiations' are underway, and that the corporation knows of 'no reason for the stock's activity,' and that 'management is unaware of any present or pending corporate development that would result in the abnormally heavy trading activity,' information concerning ongoing acquisition discussions becomes material *by virtue of the statement denying their existence.*

> * * *

> In analyzing whether information regarding merger discussions is material such that it must be affirmatively disclosed to avoid a violation of Rule 10b–5, the discussions and their progress are the primary considerations. However, once a statement is made denying the existence of any discussions, even discussions that might not have been material in absence of the denial are material because they make the statement made untrue." 786 F.2d, at 748–749 (emphasis in original).[15]

This approach, however, fails to recognize that, in order to prevail on a Rule 10b–5 claim, a plaintiff must show that the statements were *misleading* as to a *material* fact. It is not enough that a

---

14. "Although the Committee believes that ideally it would be desirable to have absolute certainty in the application of the materiality concept, it is its view that such a goal is illusory and unrealistic. The materiality concept is judgmental in nature and it is not possible to translate this into a numerical formula. The Committee's advice to the [SEC] is to avoid this quest for certainty and to continue consideration of materiality on a case-by-case basis as problems are identified."

Report of the Advisory Committee on Corporate Disclosure to the Securities and Exchange Commission 327 (House Committee on Interstate and Foreign Commerce, 95th Cong., 1st Sess.) (Comm. Print) (1977).

15. Subsequently, the Sixth Circuit denied a petition for rehearing en banc in this case. App. to Pet. for Cert. 144a. Concurring separately, Judge Wellford, one of the original panel members, then explained that he did not read the panel's opinion to create a "conclusive presumption of materiality for any undisclosed information claimed to render inaccurate statements denying the existence of alleged preliminary merger discussions." *Id.*, at 145a. In his view, the decision merely reversed the District Court's judgment, which had been based on the agreement-in-principle standard. *Ibid.*

statement is false or incomplete, if the misrepresented fact is otherwise insignificant.

C

Even before this Court's decision in *TSC Industries,* the Second Circuit had explained the role of the materiality requirement of Rule 10b–5, with respect to contingent or speculative information or events, in a manner that gave that term meaning that is independent of the other provisions of the Rule. Under such circumstances, materiality "will depend at any given time upon a balancing of both the indicated probability that the event will occur and the anticipated magnitude of the event in light of the totality of the company activity." *SEC v. Texas Gulf Sulphur Co.,* 401 F.2d, at 849. Interestingly, neither the Third Circuit decision adopting the agreement-in-principle test nor petitioners here take issue with this general standard. Rather, they suggest that with respect to preliminary merger discussions, there are good reasons to draw a line at agreement on price and structure.

In a subsequent decision, the late Judge Friendly, writing for a Second Circuit panel, applied the *Texas Gulf Sulphur* probability/magnitude approach in the specific context of preliminary merger negotiations. After acknowledging that materiality is something to be determined on the basis of the particular facts of each case, he stated:

> "Since a merger in which it is bought out is the most important event that can occur in a small corporation's life, to wit, its death, we think that inside information, as regards a merger of this sort, can become material at an earlier stage than would be the case as regards lesser transactions—and this even though the mortality rate of mergers in such formative stages is doubtless high."

SEC v. Geon Industries, Inc., 531 F.2d 39, 47–48 (CA2 1976). We agree with that analysis.

Whether merger discussions in any particular case are material therefore depends on the facts. Generally, in order to assess the probability that the event will occur, a factfinder will need to look to indicia of interest in the transaction at the highest corporate levels. Without attempting to catalog all such possible factors, we note by way of example that board resolutions, instructions to investment bankers, and actual negotiations between principals or their intermediaries may serve as indicia of interest. To assess the magnitude of the transaction to the issuer of the securities allegedly manipulated, a factfinder will need to consider such facts as the size of the two corporate entities and of the potential premiums over market value. No particular event or factor short of closing the transaction need be either necessary or sufficient by itself to render merger discussions material.

As we clarify today, materiality depends on the significance the reasonable investor would place on the withheld or misrepresented information. The fact-specific inquiry we endorse here is consistent with the approach a number of courts have taken in assessing the materiality of merger negotiations. Because the standard of materiality we have adopted differs from that used by both courts below, we remand the case for reconsideration of the question whether a grant of summary judgment is appropriate on this record.

IV

A

We turn to the question of reliance and the fraud-on-the-market theory. Succinctly put:

> "The fraud on the market theory is based on the hypothesis that, in an open and developed securities market, the price of a company's stock is determined by the available material information regarding the company and its business. . . . Misleading statements will therefore defraud purchasers of stock even if the purchasers do not directly rely on the misstatements. . . . The causal connection between the defendants' fraud and the plaintiffs' purchase of stock in such a case is no less significant than in a case of direct reliance on misrepresentations." *Peil v. Speiser,* 806 F.2d 1154, 1160–61 (CA3 1986).

Our task, of course, is not to assess the general validity of the theory, but to consider whether it was proper for the courts below to apply a rebuttable presumption of reliance, supported in part by the fraud-on-the-market theory.

This case required resolution of several common questions of law and fact concerning the falsity or misleading nature of the three public statements made by Basic, the presence or absence of scienter, and the materiality of the misrepresentations, if any. In their amended complaint, the named plaintiffs alleged that in reliance on Basic's statements they sold their shares of Basic stock in the depressed market created by petitioners. See Amended Complaint in No. C79–1220 (ND Ohio) ¶¶ 27, 29, 35, 40; see also *id.,* at ¶ 33 (alleging effect on market price of Basic's statements). Requiring proof of individualized reliance from each member of the proposed plaintiff class effectively would have prevented respondents from proceeding with a class action, since individual issues then would have overwhelmed the common ones. The District Court found that the presumption of reliance created by the fraud-on-the-market theory provided "a practical resolution to the problem of balancing the substantive requirement of proof of reliance in securities cases against the procedural requisites of [Fed.Rule Civ. Proc.] 23." The District Court thus concluded that with reference to each public statement and its impact upon the open market for Basic shares, common questions predominated over individual questions, as required by Fed.Rule Civ.Proc. 23(a)(2) and (b)(3).

Petitioners and their *amici* complain that the fraud-on-the-market theory effectively eliminates the requirement that a plaintiff asserting a claim under Rule 10b–5 prove reliance. They note that reliance is and long has been an element of common-law fraud, see *e.g.,* Restatement (Second) of Torts § 525 (1977); Prosser and Keeton on The Law of Torts § 108 (5th ed. 1984), and argue that because the analogous express right of action includes a reliance requirement, see, *e.g.,* § 18(a) of the 1934 Act, as amended, 15 U.S.C. § 78r(a), so too must an action implied under § 10(b).

We agree that reliance is an element of a Rule 10b–5 cause of action. See *Ernst & Ernst v. Hochfelder,* 425 U.S., at 206 (quoting Senate Report). Reliance provides the requisite causal connection between a defendant's misrepresentation and a plaintiff's injury. See, *e.g., Wilson v. Comtech Telecommunications Corp.,* 648 F.2d 88, 92 (CA2 1981); *List v. Fashion Park, Inc.,* 340 F.2d 457, 462 (CA2), cert. denied *sub nom. List v. Lerner,* 382 U.S. 811 (1965). There is, however, more than one way to demonstrate the causal connection. Indeed, we previously have dispensed with a requirement of positive proof of reliance, where a duty to disclose material information had been breached, concluding that the necessary nexus between the plaintiffs' injury and the defendant's wrongful conduct had been established. See *Affiliated Ute Citizens v. United States,* 406 U.S., at 153–154. Similarly, we did not require proof that material omissions or misstatements in a proxy statement decisively affected voting, because the proxy solicitation itself, rather than the defect in the solicitation materials, served as an essential link in the transaction. See *Mills v. Electric Auto–Lite Co.,* 396 U.S. 375, 384–385 (1970).

The modern securities markets, literally involving millions of shares changing hands daily, differ from the face-to-face transactions contemplated by early fraud cases,[21] and our understanding of Rule 10b–5's reliance requirement must encompass these differences.[22]

> "In face-to-face transactions, the inquiry into an investor's reliance upon information is into the subjective pricing of that information by that investor. With the presence of a market, the market is interposed between seller and buyer and, ideally, transmits information to the investor in the processed form of a market price. Thus the market is performing a substantial part of the valuation process performed by the investor in a face-to-face transaction. The market is acting as the unpaid agent of the investor, informing him that given all the information available to it, the value of the stock is worth the market price."

21. Prosser and Keeton on The Law of Torts 726 (5th ed. 1984) ("The reasons for the separate development of [the tort action for misrepresentation and nondisclosure], and for its peculiar limitations, are in part historical, and in part connected with the fact that in the great majority of the cases which have come before the courts the misrepresentations have been made in the course of a bargaining transaction between the parties. Consequently the action has been colored to a considerable extent by the ethics of bargaining between distrustful adversaries") (footnote omitted).

22. Actions under Rule 10b–5 are distinct from common-law deceit and misrepresentation claims, see *Blue Chip Stamps v. Manor Drug Stores,* 421 U.S. 723, 744–745 (1975), and are in part designed to add to the protections provided investors by the common law, see *Herman & MacLean v. Huddleston,* 459 U.S. 375, 388–389 (1983).

In re LTV Securities Litigation, 88 F.R.D. 134, 143 (ND Tex. 1980).

Accord, *e.g., Peil v. Speiser,* 806 F.2d, at 1161 ("In an open and developed market, the dissemination of material misrepresentations or withholding of material information typically affects the price of the stock, and purchasers generally rely on the price of the stock as a reflection of its value"); *Blackie v. Barrack,* 524 F.2d 891, 908 (CA9 1975) ("the same causal nexus can be adequately established indirectly, by proof of materiality coupled with the common sense that a stock purchaser does not ordinarily seek to purchase a loss in the form of artificially inflated stock"), cert. denied, 429 U.S. 816 (1976).

B

Presumptions typically serve to assist courts in managing circumstances in which direct proof, for one reason or another, is rendered difficult. See, *e.g.,* D. Louisell & C. Mueller, Federal Evidence 541–542 (1977). The courts below accepted a presumption, created by the fraud-on-the-market theory and subject to rebuttal by petitioners, that persons who had traded Basic shares had done so in reliance on the integrity of the price set by the market, but because of petitioners' material misrepresentations that price had been fraudulently depressed. Requiring a plaintiff to show a speculative state of facts, *i.e.,* how he would have acted if omitted material information had been disclosed, see *Affiliated Ute Citizens v. United States,* 406 U.S., at 153–154, or if the misrepresentation had not been made, see *Sharp v. Coopers & Lybrand,* 649 F.2d 175, 188 (CA3 1981), cert. denied, 455 U.S. 938 (1982), would place an unnecessarily unrealistic evidentiary burden on the Rule 10b–5 plaintiff who has traded on an impersonal market. Cf. *Mills v. Electric Auto–Lite Co.,* 396 U.S., at 385.

Arising out of considerations of fairness, public policy, and probability, as well as judicial economy, presumptions are also useful devices for allocating the burdens of proof between parties. See E. Cleary, McCormick on Evidence 968–969 (3rd ed. 1984); see also Fed.Rule Evid. 301 and notes. The presumption of reliance employed in this case is consistent with, and, by facilitating Rule 10b–5 litigation, supports, the congressional policy embodied in the 1934 Act. In drafting that Act, Congress expressly relied on the premise that securities markets are affected by information, and enacted legislation to facilitate an investor's reliance on the integrity of those markets:

> "No investor, no speculator, can safely buy and sell securities upon the exchanges without having an intelligent basis for forming his judgment as to the value of the securities he buys or sells. The idea of a free and open public market is built upon the theory that competing judgments of buyers and sellers as to the fair price of a security brings [*sic*] about a situation where the market price reflects as nearly as possible a

just price. Just as artificial manipulation tends to upset the true function of an open market, so the hiding and secreting of important information obstructs the operation of the markets as indices of real value." H.R.Rep. No. 1383, *supra,* at 11. See *Lipton v. Documation, Inc.,* 734 F.2d 740, 748 (CA11 1984), cert. denied, 469 U.S. 1132 (1985).[23]

The presumption is also supported by common sense and probability. Recent empirical studies have tended to confirm Congress' premise that the market price of shares traded on well-developed markets reflects all publicly available information, and, hence, any material misrepresentations.[24] It has been noted that "it is hard to imagine that there ever is a buyer or seller who does not rely on market integrity. Who would knowingly roll the dice in a crooked crap game?" *Schlanger v. Four–Phase Systems, Inc.,* 555 F.Supp. 535, 538 (SDNY 1982). Indeed, nearly every court that has considered the proposition has concluded that where materially misleading statements have been disseminated into an impersonal, well-developed market for securities, the reliance of individual plaintiffs on the integrity of the market price may be presumed.[25] Commentators generally have applauded the adoption of one variation or another of the fraud-on-the-market theory.[26] An investor who buys or sells stock at the price set by the market does so in reliance on the integrity of that price. Because most publicly available information is reflected in market price, an investor's reliance on any public material misrepresentations, therefore, may be presumed for purposes of a Rule 10b–5 action.

23. Contrary to the dissent's suggestion, the incentive for investors to "pay attention" to issuers' disclosures comes from their motivation to make a profit, not their attempt to preserve a cause of action under Rule 10b–5. Facilitating an investor's reliance on the market, consistently with Congress' expectations, hardly calls for "dismantling the federal scheme which mandates disclosure." ...

24. See *In re LTV Securities Litigation,* 88 F.R.D. 134, 144 (ND Tex.1980) (citing studies); Fischel, Use of Modern Finance Theory in Securities Fraud Cases Involving Actively Traded Securities, 38 Bus.Law. 1, 4, n. 9 (1982) (citing literature on efficient-capital-market theory); Dennis, Materiality and the Efficient Capital Market Model: A Recipe for the Total Mix, 25 Wm. & Mary L.Rev. 373, 374–381, and n. 1 (1984). We need not determine by adjudication what economists and social scientists have debated through the use of sophisticated statistical analysis and the application of economic theory. For purposes of accepting the presumption of reliance in this case, we need only believe that market professionals generally consider most publicly announced material statements about companies, thereby affecting stock market prices.

25. See, *e.g., Peil v. Speiser,* 806 F.2d 1154, 1161 (CA3 1986); *Harris v. Union Electric Co.,* 787 F.2d 355, 367, and n. 9 (CA8), cert. denied, ___ U.S. ___ (1986); *Lipton v. Documation, Inc.,* 734 F.2d 740 (CA11 1984), cert. denied 469 U.S. 1132 (1985); *T.J. Raney & Sons, Inc. v. Fort Cobb, Oklahoma Irrigation Fuel Authority,* 717 F.2d 1330, 1332–1333 (CA10 1983), cert. denied *sub nom. Linde, Thomson, Fairchild, Langworthy, Kohn & Van Dyke v. T.J. Raney & Sons, Inc.,* 465 U.S. 1026 (1984); *Panzirer v. Wolf,* 663 F.2d 365, 367–368 (CA2 1981), cert. granted *sub nom. Price Waterhouse v. Panzirer,* 458 U.S. 1105, judgment vacated and complaint dismissed, 459 U.S. 1027 (1982); *Ross v. A.H. Robins Co.,* 607 F.2d 545, 553 (CA2 1979), cert. denied, 446 U.S. 946 (1980); *Blackie v. Barrack,* 524 F.2d 891, 905–908 (CA9 1975), cert. denied, 429 U.S. 816 (1976).

26. See, *e.g.,* Black, Fraud on the Market: A Criticism of Dispensing with Reliance Requirements in Certain Open Market Transactions, 62 N.C.L.Rev. 435 (1984); Note, the Fraud-on-the-Market Theory, 95 Harv.L.Rev. 1143 (1982); Note, Fraud on the Market: An Emerging Theory of Recovery Under SEC Rule 10b–5, 50 Geo. Wash.L.Rev. 627 (1982).

C

The Court of Appeals found that petitioners "made public, material misrepresentations and [respondents] sold Basic stock in an impersonal, efficient market. Thus the class, as defined by the district court, has established the threshold facts for proving their loss." 786 F.2d, at 751.[27] The court acknowledged that petitioners may rebut proof of the elements giving rise to the presumption, or show that the misrepresentation in fact did not lead to a distortion of price or that an individual plaintiff traded or would have traded despite his knowing the statement was false. *Id.*, at 750, n. 6.

Any showing that severs the link between the alleged misrepresentation and either the price received (or paid) by the plaintiff, or his decision to trade at a fair market price, will be sufficient to rebut the presumption of reliance. For example, if petitioners could show that the "market makers" were privy to the truth about the merger discussions here with Combustion, and thus that the market price would not have been affected by their misrepresentations, the causal connection could be broken: the basis for finding that the fraud had been transmitted through market price would be gone.[28] Similarly, if, despite petitioners' allegedly fraudulent attempt to manipulate market price, news of the merger discussions credibly entered the market and dissipated the effects of the misstatements, those who traded Basic shares after the corrective statements would have no direct or indirect connection with the fraud.[29] Petitioners also could rebut the presumption of reliance as to plaintiffs who would have divested themselves of their Basic shares without relying on the integrity of the market. For example, a plaintiff who believed that Basic's statements were false and that Basic was indeed engaged in merger discussions, and who consequently believed that Basic stock was artificially underpriced, but sold his shares nevertheless because of other unrelated concerns, *e.g.*, po-

27. The Court of Appeals held that in order to invoke the presumption, a plaintiff must allege and prove: (1) that the defendant made public misrepresentations; (2) that the misrepresentations were material; (3) that the shares were traded on an efficient market; (4) that the misrepresentations would induce a reasonable, relying investor to misjudge the value of the shares; and (5) that the plaintiff traded the shares between the time the misrepresentations were made and the time the truth was revealed. See 786 F.2d, at 750.

Given today's decision regarding the definition of materiality as to preliminary merger discussions, elements (2) and (4) may collapse into one.

28. By accepting this rebuttable presumption, we do not intend conclusively to adopt any particular theory of how quickly and completely publicly available information is reflected in market price. Furthermore, our decision today is not to be inter-

preted as addressing the proper measure of damages in litigation of this kind.

29. We note there may be a certain incongruity between the assumption that Basic shares are traded on a well-developed, efficient, and information-hungry market, and the allegation that such a market could remain misinformed, and its valuation of Basic shares depressed, for 14 months, on the basis of the three public statements. Proof of that sort is a matter for trial, throughout which the District Court retains the authority to amend the certification order as may be appropriate. See Fed.Rule Civ.Proc. 23(c)(1) and (c)(4). See 7B C. Wright, A. Miller & M. Kane, Federal Practice and Procedure 128–132 (1986). Thus, we see no need to engage in the kind of factual analysis the dissent suggests that manifests the "oddities" of applying a rebuttable presumption of reliance in this case....

tential antitrust problems, or political pressures to divest from shares of certain businesses, could not be said to have relied on the integrity of a price he knew had been manipulated.

V

In summary:

1. We specifically adopt, for the § 10(b) and Rule 10b–5 context, the standard of materiality set forth in *TSC Industries, Inc. v. Northway, Inc.,* 426 U.S., at 449.

2. We reject "agreement-in-principle as to price and structure" as the bright-line rule for materiality.

3. We also reject the proposition that "information becomes material by virtue of a public statement denying it."

4. Materiality in the merger context depends on the probability that the transaction will be consummated, and its significance to the issuer of the securities. Materiality depends on the facts and thus is to be determined on a case-by-case basis.

5. It is not inappropriate to apply a presumption of reliance supported by the fraud-on-the-market theory.

6. That presumption, however, is rebuttable.

7. The District Court's certification of the class here was appropriate when made but is subject on remand to such adjustment, if any, as developing circumstances demand.

The judgment of the Court of Appeals is vacated and the case is remanded to that court for further proceedings consistent with this opinion.

It is so ordered.

The Chief Justice, Justice SCALIA, and Justice KENNEDY took no part in the consideration or decision of this case.

———

Justice WHITE, with whom Justice O'CONNOR joins, concurring in part and dissenting in part.

I join Parts I–III of the Court's opinion, as I agree that the standard of materiality we set forth in *TSC Industries, Inc. v. Northway, Inc.,* 426 U.S. 438, 449 (1976), should be applied to actions under § 10(b) and Rule 10b–5. But I dissent from the remainder of the Court's holding because I do not agree that the "fraud-on-the-market" theory should be applied in this case. . . .

At the bottom of the Court's conclusion that the fraud-on-the-market theory sustains a presumption of reliance is the assumption that individuals rely "on the integrity of the market price" when buying or selling stock in "impersonal, well-developed market[s] for securities." *Ante,* at 21–22. Even if I was prepared to accept (as a matter of common sense or general understanding) the assumption that most persons buying or selling stock do so in response to the market price, the fraud-on-the-market theory goes further. For in adopting a "presumption of reliance," the Court *also* assumes that buyers and sellers rely—not just on the market price—but on the "*integrity*" of that price. It is this aspect of the fraud-on-the-market hypothesis which most mystifies me.

To define the term "integrity of the market price," the majority quotes approvingly from cases which suggest that investors are entitled to " 'rely on the price of a stock as a reflection of its value.' " But the meaning of this phrase eludes me, for it implicitly suggests that stocks have some "true value" that is measurable by a standard other than their market price. While the Scholastics of Medieval times professed a means to make such a valuation of a commodity's "worth," I doubt that the federal courts of our day are similarly equipped.

Even if securities had some "value"—knowable and distinct from the market price of a stock—investors do not always share the Court's presumption that a stock's price is a "reflection of [this] value." Indeed, "many investors purchase or sell stock because they believe the price *inaccurately* reflects the corporation's worth." See Black, Fraud on the Market: A Criticism of Dispensing with Reliance Requirements in Certain Open Market Transactions, 62 N.C.L.Rev. 435, 455 (1984) (emphasis added). If investors really believed that stock prices reflected a stock's "value," many sellers would never sell, and many buyers never buy (given the time and cost associated with executing a stock transaction). As we recognized just a few years ago: "[I]nvestors act on inevitably incomplete or inaccurate information, [consequently] there are always winners and losers; but those who have 'lost' have not necessarily been defrauded." *Dirks v. SEC,* 463 U.S. 646, 667, n. 27 (1983). Yet today, the Court allows investors to recover who can show little more than that they sold stock at a lower price than what might have been....

In sum, I think the Court's embracement of the fraud-on-the-market theory represents a departure in securities law that we are ill-suited to commence—and even less equipped to control as it proceeds. As a result, I must respectfully dissent.

———

SECURITIES ACT RULE 175

SECURITIES EXCHANGE ACT RULE 3B–6

[See Statutory Supplement]

———

NOTE ON FORWARD–LOOKING STATEMENTS AND THE "BESPEAKS CAUTION" DOCTRINE

Virginia Bankshares, p. 236, supra, held that statements of belief or opinion were actionable when made with the knowledge that the belief or opinion was not held, and that not every mixture of true statements with deceptive statements will neutralize the deceptive statements. The circuit courts, however, have displayed a reluctance to hold that forward-looking statements will give rise to liability under Rule 10b–5.

In some cases, the courts rest their decisions on the ground that "forward-looking statements" are a special category under Rule 10b–5. See, e.g., Raab v. General Physics Corporation, 4 F.3d 286 (4th Cir.1993).

Other courts have applied a doctrine known as "bespeaks caution" to hold that as a matter of law a forward-looking statement may not give rise to liability, even though it is misleading, if the document in which the statement is contained includes sufficient cautionary language. See, e.g., In re Donald J. Trump Casino Securities Litigation—Taj Mahal Litigation (Kaufman v. Trump's Castle Funding), 7 F.3d 357 (3d Cir.1993), *cert. denied* Gollomp v. Trump, ___ U.S. ___, 114 S.Ct. 1219, 127 L.Ed.2d 565 (1994); Saltzberg v. TM Sterling/Austin Associates, Ltd., 45 F.3d 399 (11th Cir.1995).

R. BREALEY & S. MYERS, PRINCIPLES OF CORPORATE FINANCE

290–310 (4th ed. 1993).

Three Forms of the Efficient–Market Theory

Harry Roberts has defined three levels of market efficiency. The first is the case in which prices reflect all the information contained in the record of past prices. Roberts called this a *weak* form of efficiency. The random-walk research shows that the market is at *least* efficient in this weak sense.

The second level of efficiency is the case in which prices reflect not only past prices but all other published information. Roberts called this a *semistrong* form of efficiency. Researchers have tested this by looking at specific items of news such as announcements of earnings and dividends, forecasts of company earnings, changes in accounting practices, and mergers. Most of this information was rapidly and accurately impounded in the price of the stock.

Finally, Harry Roberts envisaged a *strong* form of efficiency in which prices reflect not just public information but *all* the information that can be acquired by painstaking fundamental analysis of the company and the economy. In such a case, the stock market would be like our ideal auction house: prices would *always* be fair and *no* investor would be able to make consistently superior forecasts of stock prices. Most tests of this view have involved an analysis of the performance of professionally managed portfolios. These studies have concluded that, after taking account of differences in risk, no group of institutions has been able to outperform the market consistently and that even the differences between the performance of individual funds are no greater than you would expect from chance.

Although few simple economic ideas are as well supported by the evidence as the efficient-market theory, it would be wrong to pretend that there are no puzzles or apparent exceptions. For instance, company managers have made consistently superior profits when they deal in their own company's stock. This does not seem to square well with the strong form of the efficient-market theory....

On Monday, October 19, 1987, the Dow Jones Industrial Average fell 23 percent in one day....

So why did prices fall so sharply? There was no obvious, new fundamental information to justify such a sharp decline in share values. For this reason, the idea that market price is the best estimate of intrinsic value seems less compelling than before. It appears that either prices were irrationally high before Black Monday or irrationally low afterward. Could the theory of efficient markets be another casualty of the crash?

... [T]he hypothesis that stock price *always* equals intrinsic value is nearly impossible to test, precisely because it's so difficult to calculate intrinsic value without referring to prices. Thus the crash didn't conclusively disprove the hypothesis. But many people now find it less *plausible.*

However, the crash does not undermine the evidence for market efficiency with respect to *relative* prices....

The First Lesson of Market Efficiency: Markets Have No Memory

The weak form of the efficient-market hypothesis states that the sequence of past price changes contains no information about future changes. Economists express the same idea more concisely when they say that the market has no memory....

The Second Lesson of Market Efficiency: Trust Market Prices

In an efficient market you can trust prices. They impound all available information about the value of each security.

This means that in an efficient market there is no way for most investors to achieve consistently superior rates of return. To do so, you not only need to know more than *anyone* else; you need to know more than *everyone* else....

The Third Lesson of Market Efficiency:

There Are No Financial Illusions

In an efficient market there are no financial illusions. Investors are unromantically concerned with the firm's cash flows and the portion of those cash flows to which they are entitled....

The Fourth Lesson of Market Efficiency:

The Do–It–Yourself Alternative

In an efficient market investors will not pay others for what they can do equally well themselves....   [M]any of the controversies in corporate financing center on how well individuals can replicate corporate financial decisions. For example, companies often justify mergers on the grounds that they produce a more diversified and hence more stable firm. But if investors can hold the stocks of both companies, why should they thank the companies for diversifying? It is much easier and cheaper for them to diversify than it is for the firm....

The Fifth Lesson of Market Efficiency:

Seen One Stock, Seen Them All

The elasticity of demand for any article measures the percentage change in the quantity demanded for each percentage addition to the price. If the article has close substitutes, the elasticity will be strongly negative; if not, it will be near zero. For example, coffee, which is a staple commodity, has a demand elasticity of about $-$ .2. This means that a 5 percent increase in the price of coffee changes sales by $-$ .2 $\times$ .05 $=$ $-$ .01; in other words it reduces demand by only 1 percent. Consumers are likely to regard different *brands* of coffee as much closer substitutes for each other. Therefore the demand elasticity for a particular brand could be in the region of, say, $-$ 2.0. A 5 percent increase in the price of Maxwell House relative to that of Nescafe would in this case reduce demand by 10 percent.

Investors don't buy a stock for its unique qualities; they buy it because it offers the prospect of a fair return for its risk. This means that stocks should be like *very* similar brands of coffee, almost perfect substitutes for each other. Therefore, the demand for the company's stock should be very elastic. If its prospective risk premium is lower relative to its risk than other stocks, *nobody* will want to hold that stock. If it is higher, *everybody* will want to hold it.

Suppose that you want to sell a large block of stock. Since demand is elastic, you naturally conclude that you need only cut the offering price very slightly to sell your stock. Unfortunately that doesn't necessarily follow. When you come to sell your stock, other investors may suspect that you want to get rid of it because you know something they don't. Therefore they will revise their assessment of the stock's value downward. Demand is still elastic but the whole demand curve moves down. Elastic demand does not imply that stock prices never change; it *does* imply that you can sell large blocks of stock at close to the market price *as long as you can convince other investors that you have no private information* . . . .

SUMMARY . . .

The efficient-market hypothesis comes in three different flavors. The weak form of the hypothesis states that prices efficiently reflect all the information contained in the past series of stock prices. In this case it is impossible to earn superior returns simply by looking for patterns in stock prices—in other words, price changes are random. The semistrong form of the hypothesis states that prices reflect all published information. That means it is impossible to make consistently superior returns just by reading the newspaper, looking at the company's annual accounts, and so on. The strong form of the hypothesis states that stock prices effectively impound all available information. It tells us that inside information is hard to find because in pursuing it you are in competition with thousands, perhaps millions, of active, intelligent, and greedy investors. The best you can do in this case is to assume that securities are fairly priced and to hope that one day . . . your humility [will be rewarded].

The concept of an efficient market is astonishingly simple and remarkably well-supported by the facts. Less than 20 years ago any suggestion that security investment is a fair game was generally regarded as bizarre. Today it is not only widely accepted in business schools, but it also permeates investment practice and government policy toward the security markets. . . .

———

IN RE VERIFONE SECURITIES LITIGATION, 784 F.Supp. 1471, 1479 (N.D.Cal.1992), aff'd sub nom. Halkin v. VeriFone, Inc., 11 F.3d 865 (9th Cir.1993). "[The] fraud-on-the-market theory recognizes that average investors in a developed securities market do not personally need access to the elaborate disclosure of documents and accounting data required by our securities laws. Market professionals obtain information from myriad sources, including the issuer, market analysts, and the financial and trade press. The professional traders analyze information about securities, and the trading activity of these knowledgeable investors pushes the price of the security toward a value which reflects all publicly available information. In this way, securities prices on the national exchanges reflect (albeit not perfectly) the expected future cash flows from the security. An investor making trades who has not relied on particular disclosures is presumed under the fraud-on-the-market theory to rely on the integrity of information reflected in the market price of the security. *Basic Inc.,* 485 U.S. at 247, 108 S.Ct. at 991.

In this way, an investor who has never seen or heard of a fraudulent disclosure is no less a victim than one who pored over its details.

"The fraud-on-the-market theory thus shifts the inquiry from whether an individual investor was fooled to whether the market as a whole was fooled. Hence, the theory not so much eliminates the reliance requirement as subsumes it in the fraud-on-the-market analysis. In the same way, the theory also subsumes the inquiry into materiality, causation and damages. For if a misleading or fraudulent disclosure or omission could have had no effect on the security's market price, the information cannot have been material. Similarly, if a misstatement or omission had no effect on the market price (because, for example, the market already had the correct information from other sources) then there could be no causation and no damages."

DAINES & HANSON, THE CORPORATE LAW PARADOX: THE CASE FOR RESTRUCTURING CORPORATE LAW, 103 Yale L.J. 577, 614–15 (1992). "Beginning in the mid–1980's, doubts regarding the ECMH emerged first in the financial economics literature, and then began to trickle into the legal literature. But what began as a trickle has more recently become a deluge. Legal scholars familiar with current financial economics literature agree that there is now reason to doubt the efficiency of markets. Professors Macey, Miller, Mitchell and Netter summarize the current research as follows: '[W]e can at a minimum conclude that substantial disagreement exists among financial economists about what conclusions empirical tests of market efficiency support.' Indeed, 'substantial disagreement exists about to what degree markets are efficient, how to test for efficiency, and even the definition of efficiency.' Similarly, Professor Langevoort concludes from his review of the current financial economics literature that 'what is important for present purposes seems beyond debate: strong claims of efficiency are debatable.'

"To understand the source of the new doubts, it is helpful to recognize that the ECMH makes *two* general efficiency claims— namely, that the stock market is both informationally efficient and fundamentally efficient: The market is 'informationally efficient' if all public information is immediately incorporated into the stock price; it is 'fundamentally efficient' if stock prices accurately reflect only information relating to the net present value of the corporation's future profits. A growing body of work in financial economics now suggests, first, that informational efficiency—for which there *is* substantial empirical support—does not imply fundamental efficiency, and, second, that both the empirical and theoretical bases for the belief that markets are fundamentally efficient are suspect."

NOTE ON CAUSATION AND RELIANCE

In principle, it is well-established that causation and reliance are required elements of a private action under Rule 10b–5. In practice, however, those requirements have sometimes proved to be elusive or even illusory.

1. *Causation.* In the area of causation, the case-law under Rule 10b–5 has distinguished between "transaction causation" and "loss causation." *Transaction causation* means that there must be a causal nexus between the defendant's violation of Rule 10b–5 and the plaintiff's purchase or sale. Thus in *Basic,* the court said that to show a Rule 10b–5 violation a private plaintiff must prove a "causal connection between a defendant's misrepresentation and [the] plaintiff's injury." This nexus or connection may be simply a requirement that but for the violation the plaintiff's purchase or sale would not have occurred, or it may be a requirement that the violation was a proximate cause, even if not the only cause, of the purchase or sale. Of course, what constitutes proximate cause is itself a notoriously slippery question. Loss & Seligman state:

> At most a plaintiff is required to prove that defendant's misstatement or misconduct was a "substantial factor" in causing a loss. "In other words a plaintiff must demonstrate that the defendant's fraudulent conduct 'touches upon the reasons for the investment's decline in value.' " Alternatively the element has been framed in terms of whether a misstatement *affected* an investment decision.

9 L. Loss & J. Seligman 4407 (3d ed. 1992).

The *Basic* case may be seen as partly turning on the meaning of the requirement of transaction causation under Rule 10b–5. As *Basic* shows, the elusive meaning of this requirement is further compounded because transaction causation can often be subsumed in the related issue of reliance, and reliance may be presumed in many Rule 10b–5 cases.

The meaning of *loss causation* is even harder to pin down. The best interpretation of this doctrine is that the defendant's wrongful act not only must have caused the plaintiff to *buy or sell* a security (transaction causation); it must also have been the cause of the plaintiff's *loss* on the security. Essentially, "loss causation" is simply a fancy and confusing name for the concept that even if an investment is induced by a violation of Rule 10b–5, a loss may have been the result, not of the violation, but of an investment risk that was independent of the violation. "[W]hen an investor makes any investment he or she assumes certain investment risks. It may be too harsh a rule under rule 10b–5 that would place the wrongdoer in the position of insurer against those market risks. Otherwise, for example, a seller who fraudulently induced a purchase of securities in early October, 1987 would be an insurer against the precipitous price decline caused in large part by the market crash on October 19." 2 T. Hazen, *Securities Regulation 104* (2d ed. 1990).

2. *Reliance.* Initially, the rule that reliance is an element of a private action seemed to require the plaintiff to prove that he relied on the defendant's wrongful statement or omission. Later, however, the requirement of reliance broke down, or at least became transformed. The reasons for the transformation differed somewhat as to (i) omissions and (ii) affirmative misstatements.

(a) The problem as to omissions is that reliance on an omission is an illogical concept. We can say that *A* acted—bought or sold—at a given price in reliance on what *B* told him, but we can't say *A* acted—bought or sold at a given price—in reliance on what *B* didn't tell him. What we can say in the latter case is that a *reasonable investor* who knew the omitted fact *probably* would or would not have bought or sold at the given price. In TSC Industries v. Northway, Inc., a major foundation for *Basic, Inc.*, the Supreme Court held that the standard of *materiality* is satisfied by "a showing of a substantial likelihood that, under all the circumstances, the omitted fact would have assumed actual significance in the deliberations of the reasonable shareholder." 426 U.S. 438, 449, 96 S.Ct. 2126, 2132, 48 L.Ed.2d 757 (1976). This standard is so close to what must be shown to prove causation in an omissions case that for all intents and purposes, causation in such a case collapses into materiality. In Affiliated Ute Citizens of Utah v. United States, 406 U.S. 128, 92 S.Ct. 1456, 31 L.Ed.2d 741 (1972), a bank purchased stock from a group of unsophisticated investors without disclosing that the stock was selling at a higher price on a secondary market made by the bank. The Tenth Circuit denied recovery because the record failed to show that the plaintiffs relied on any misstatements made by the bank. The Supreme Court reversed:

> Under the circumstances of this case, involving primarily a failure to disclose, positive proof of reliance is not a prerequisite to recovery. All that is necessary is that the facts withheld be material in the sense that a reasonable investor might have considered them important in the making of this decision.

406 U.S. at 153–54, 92 S.Ct. at 1472.

(b) On its face, *Ute* seemed to eliminate any requirement of reliance in a case of nondisclosure. In general, however, the cases have held that *Ute* "merely established a presumption that made it possible for the plaintiffs to meet their burden." Shores v. Sklar, 647 F.2d 462, 468 (5th Cir.1981) (en banc), cert. denied 459 U.S. 1102, 63 S.Ct. 722, 74 L.Ed.2d 949 (1983). The defendant can rebut this presumption "by showing that the . . . plaintiff would have have followed the same course of conduct even with full and honest disclosure, [so that] the defendant's action (or lack thereof) cannot be said to have caused plaintiff's loss." Id. The defendant might carry this burden by showing, for example, that the plaintiff learned the omitted fact from an independent source before making his investment decision, so that the decision could not have been caused by the defendant's nondisclosure. Although the cases continue to use the language of "reliance" in the omissions context, the real question is causation. When the question is properly framed, in causation terms, once the plaintiff has shown that defendant omitted to disclose a material fact he was obliged to disclose, the burden is on the defendant to prove that the plaintiff would have made the same investment decision even if disclosure had been made.

(c) Unlike the case of an omission, in the case of a face-to-face misrepresentation, reliance is a meaningful concept. For example, the defendant might be able to show that the plaintiff did not rely on a representation because he knew from other sources that the misrepresentation was false. In face-to-face misrepresentation cases, therefore, reliance continues to be an element of plaintiff's case. However, although a lack of reliance in such cases is possible, it is extremely unlikely. People who trade soon after material misrepresentations have been made to them will have almost always have relied on the misrepresentations. Accordingly, once the plaintiff shows that a material misrepresentation was made to him, and that he traded soon thereafter, as a practical matter reliance will normally be presumed, and the burden will shift to the defendant to show that the plaintiff did not rely on the misrepresentation. In the end, therefore, the misrepresentation case is similar to the omission case—that is, once the plaintiff makes a showing of materiality, the burden shifts to the defendant to show that reliance did not occur.

CHIARELLA v. UNITED STATES

United States Supreme Court, 1980.
445 U.S. 222, 100 S.Ct. 1108, 63 L.Ed.2d 348.

Mr. Justice POWELL, delivered the opinion of the Court.

The question in this case is whether a person who learns from the confidential documents of one corporation that it is planning an attempt to secure control of a second corporation violates § 10(b) of the Securities Exchange Act of 1934 if he fails to disclose the impending takeover before trading in the target company's securities.

I

Petitioner is a printer by trade. In 1975 and 1976, he worked as a "markup man" in the New York composing room of Pandick Press, a financial printer. Among documents that petitioner handled were five announcements of corporate takeover bids. When these documents were delivered to the printer, the identities of the acquiring and target corporations were concealed by blank spaces or false names. The true names were sent to the printer on the night of the final printing.

The petitioner, however, was able to deduce the names of the target companies before the final printing from other information contained in the documents. Without disclosing his knowledge, petitioner purchased stock in the target companies and sold the shares immediately after the takeover attempts were made public. By this method, petitioner realized a gain of slightly more than $30,000 in the course of 14 months. Subsequently, the Securities and Exchange Commission (Commission or SEC) began an investigation of his trading activities. In May 1977, petitioner entered into a consent decree with the Commission in which he agreed to return his profits to the sellers of the shares. On the same day, he was discharged by Pandick Press.

In January 1978, petitioner was indicted on 17 counts of violating § 10(b) of the Securities Exchange Act of 1934 (1934 Act) and SEC Rule 10b–5. After petitioner unsuccessfully moved to dismiss the indictment, he was brought to trial and convicted on all counts.

The Court of Appeals for the Second Circuit affirmed petitioner's conviction. 588 F.2d 1358 (1978). We granted certiorari, 441 U.S. 942 (1979), and we now reverse.

II . . .

This case concerns the legal effect of the petitioner's silence. The District Court's charge permitted the jury to convict the petitioner if it found that he willfully failed to inform sellers of target company securities that he knew of a forthcoming takeover bid that would make their shares more valuable. In order to decide whether silence in such circumstances violates § 10(b), it is necessary to review the language and legislative history of that statute as well as its interpretation by the Commission and the federal courts.

Although the starting point of our inquiry is the language of the statute, *Ernst & Ernst v. Hochfelder*, 425 U.S. 185, 197 (1976), § 10(b) does not state whether silence may constitute a manipulative or deceptive device. Section 10(b) was designed as a catchall clause to prevent fraudulent practices. 425 U.S., at 202, 206. But neither the legislative history nor the statute itself affords specific guidance for the resolution of this case. When Rule 10b–5 was promulgated in 1942, the SEC did not discuss the possibility that failure to provide information might run afoul of § 10(b).

The SEC took an important step in the development of § 10(b) when it held that a broker-dealer and his firm violated that section by selling securities on the basis of undisclosed information obtained from a director of the issuer corporation who was also a registered representative of the brokerage firm. In *Cady, Roberts & Co.*, 40 S.E.C. 907 (1961), the Commission decided that a corporate insider must abstain from trading in the shares of his corporation unless he has first disclosed all material inside information known to him. The obligation to disclose or abstain derives from "[a]n affirmative duty to disclose material information[, which] has been traditionally imposed on corporate 'insiders,' particularly officers, directors, or controlling stockholders. We, and the courts have consistently held that insiders must disclose material facts which are known to them by virtue of their position but which are not known to persons with whom they deal and which, if known, would affect their investment judgment." *Id.,* at 911.

The Commission emphasized that the duty arose from (i) the existence of a relationship affording access to inside information intended to be available only for a corporate purpose, and (ii) the unfairness of allowing a corporate insider to take advantage of that information by trading without disclosure. *Id.,* at 912, and n. 15.[8]

That the relationship between a corporate insider and the stockholders of his corporation gives rise to a disclosure obligation is not a novel twist of the law. At common law, misrepresentation made for the purpose of inducing reliance upon the false statement is fraudulent. But one who fails to disclose material information prior to the consummation of a transaction commits fraud only when he is under a duty to do so. And the duty to disclose arises when one party has information "that the other [party] is entitled to know because of a fiduciary or other similar relation of trust and confidence between them."[9] In its *Cady, Roberts* decision, the Commission recognized a relationship of trust and confidence between the shareholders of a corporation and those insiders who have obtained confidential information by reason of their position with that corporation.[10] This relationship gives rise to a duty to disclose because of the "necessity of preventing a corporate insider from ... tak[ing] unfair advantage of the uninformed minority stockholders." *Speed v. Transamerica Corp.,* 99 F.Supp. 808, 829 (Del.1951).

The federal courts have found violations of § 10(b) where corporate insiders used undisclosed information for their own benefit. *E.g., SEC v. Texas Gulf Sulphur Co.,* 401 F.2d 833 (CA2

---

8. In *Cady, Roberts,* the broker-dealer was liable under § 10(b) because it received nonpublic information from a corporate insider of the issuer. Since the insider could not use the information, neither could the partners in the brokerage firm with which he was associated. The transaction in *Cady, Roberts* involved sale of stock to persons who previously may not have been shareholders in the corporation. 40 S.E.C., at 913, and n. 21. The Commission embraced the reasoning of Judge Learned Hand that "the director or officer assumed a fiduciary relation to the buyer by the very sale; for it would be a sorry distinction to allow him to use the advantage of his position to induce the buyer into the position of a beneficiary although he was forbidden to do so once the buyer had become one." *Id.,* at 914, n. 23, quoting *Gratz v. Claughton,*

187 F.2d 46, 49 (CA2), cert. denied, 341 U.S. 920 (1951).

9. Restatement (Second) of Torts § 551(2)(a) (1976). See James & Gray, Misrepresentation—Part II, 37 Md.L.Rev. 488, 523–527 (1978). As regards securities transactions, the American Law Institute recognizes that "silence when there is a duty to ... speak may be a fraudulent act." ALI, Federal Securities Code § 262(b) (Prop.Off.Draft 1978).

10. See 3 W. Fletcher, Cyclopedia of the Law of Private Corporations § 838 (rev. 1975); 3A *id.,* §§ 1168.2, 1171, 1174; 3 L. Loss, Securities Regulation 1446–1448 (2d ed. 1961); 6 *id.,* at 3557–3558 (1969 Supp.). See also *Brophy v. Cities Service Co.,* 31 Del.Ch. 241, 70 A.2d 5 (1949)....

1968), cert. denied, 404 U.S. 1005 (1971). The cases also have emphasized, in accordance with the common-law rule, that "[t]he party charged with failing to disclose market information must be under a duty to disclose it." *Frigitemp Corp. v. Financial Dynamics Fund, Inc.,* 524 F.2d 275, 282 (CA2 1975). Accordingly, a purchaser of stock who has no duty to a prospective seller because he is neither an insider nor a fiduciary has been held to have no obligation to reveal material facts. See *General Time Corp. v. Talley Industries, Inc.,* 403 F.2d 159, 164 (CA2 1968), cert. denied, 393 U.S. 1026 (1969). . . .

Thus, administrative and judicial interpretations have established that silence in connection with the purchase or sale of securities may operate as a fraud actionable under § 10(b) despite the absence of statutory language or legislative history specifically addressing the legality of nondisclosure. But such liability is premised upon a duty to disclose arising from a relationship of trust and confidence between parties to a transaction. Application of a duty to disclose prior to trading guarantees that corporate insiders, who have an obligation to place the shareholder's welfare before their own, will not benefit personally through fraudulent use of material, nonpublic information.[12]

III

In this case, the petitioner was convicted of violating § 10(b) although he was not a corporate insider and he received no confidential information from the target company. Moreover, the "market information" upon which he relied did not concern the earning power or operations of the target company, but only the plans of the acquiring company. Petitioner's use of that information was not a fraud under § 10(b) unless he was subject to an affirmative duty to disclose it before trading. In this case, the jury instructions failed to specify any such duty. In effect, the trial court instructed the jury that petitioner owed a duty to everyone; to all sellers, indeed, to the market as a whole. The jury simply was told to decide whether petitioner used material, nonpublic information at a time when "he knew other people trading in the securities market did not have access to the same information." Record 677.

The Court of Appeals affirmed the conviction by holding that "[*a*]*nyone*—corporate insider or not—who regularly receives material nonpublic information may not use that information to trade in securities without incurring an affirmative duty to disclose." 588 F.2d, at 1365 (emphasis in original). Although the court said that its test would include only persons who regularly receive material, nonpublic information, *id.,* at 1366, its rationale for that limitation

---

12. "Tippees" of corporate insiders have been held liable under § 10(b) because they have a duty not to profit from the use of inside information that they know is confidential and know or should know came from a corporate insider, *Shapiro v. Merrill* *Lynch, Pierce, Fenner & Smith, Inc.,* 495 F.2d 228, 237–238 (CA2 1974). The tippee's obligation has been viewed as arising from his role as a participant after the fact in the insider's breach of a fiduciary duty. . . .

is unrelated to the existence of a duty to disclose.[14] The Court of Appeals, like the trial court, failed to identify a relationship between petitioner and the sellers that could give rise to a duty. Its decision thus rested solely upon its belief that the federal securities laws have "created a system providing equal access to information necessary for reasoned and intelligent investment decisions." *Id.,* at 1362. The use by anyone of material information not generally available is fraudulent, this theory suggests, because such information gives certain buyers or sellers an unfair advantage over less informed buyers and sellers.

This reasoning suffers from two defects. First, not every instance of financial unfairness constitutes fraudulent activity under § 10(b). See *Santa Fe Industries, Inc. v. Green,* 430 U.S. 462, 474–477 (1977). Second, the element required to make silence fraudulent—a duty to disclose—is absent in this case. No duty could arise from petitioner's relationship with the sellers of the target company's securities, for petitioner had no prior dealings with them. He was not their agent, he was not a fiduciary, he was not a person in whom the sellers had placed their trust and confidence. He was, in fact, a complete stranger who dealt with the sellers only through impersonal market transactions.

We cannot affirm petitioner's conviction without recognizing a general duty between all participants in market transactions to forgo actions based on material, nonpublic information. Formulation of such a broad duty, which departs radically from the established doctrine that duty arises from a specific relationship between two parties, see n. 9, *supra,* should not be undertaken absent some explicit evidence of congressional intent.

As we have seen, no such evidence emerges from the language or legislative history of § 10(b). Moreover, neither the Congress nor the Commission ever has adopted a parity-of-information rule. Instead the problems caused by misuse of market information have been addressed by detailed and sophisticated regulation that recognizes when use of market information may not harm operation of

---

14. The Court of Appeals said that its "regular access to market information" test would create a workable rule embracing "those who occupy ... strategic places in the market mechanism." 588 F.2d, at 1365. These considerations are insufficient to support a duty to disclose. A duty arises from the relationship between parties, see nn. 9 and 10, *supra,* and accompanying text, and not merely from one's ability to acquire information because of his position in the market.

The Court of Appeals also suggested that the acquiring corporation itself would not be a "market insider" because a tender offeror creates, rather than receives, information and takes a substantial economic risk that its offer will be unsuccessful. 588 F.2d at 1366–1367. Again, the Court of

Appeals departed from the analysis appropriate to recognition of a duty. The Court of Appeals for the Second Circuit previously held, in a manner consistent with our analysis here, that a tender offeror does not violate § 10(b) when it makes preannouncement purchases precisely because there is no relationship between the offeror and the seller:

"We know of no rule of law ... that a purchaser of stock, who was not an 'insider' and had no fiduciary relation to a prospective seller, had any obligation to reveal circumstances that might raise a seller's demands and thus abort the sale." *General Time Corp. v. Talley Industries, Inc.,* 403 F.2d 159, 164 (1968), cert. denied, 393 U.S. 1026 (1969).

the securities markets. For example, the Williams Act [15] limits but does not completely prohibit a tender offeror's purchases of target corporation stock before public announcement of the offer. Congress' careful action in this and other areas contrasts, and is in some tension, with the broad rule of liability we are asked to adopt in this case.

Indeed, the theory upon which the petitioner was convicted is at odds with the Commission's view of § 10(b) as applied to activity that has the same effect on sellers as the petitioner's purchases. "Warehousing" takes place when a corporation gives advance notice of its intention to launch a tender offer to institutional investors who then are able to purchase stock in the target company before the tender offer is made public and the price of shares rises. In this case, as in warehousing, a buyer of securities purchases stock in a target corporation on the basis of market information which is unknown to the seller. In both of these situations, the seller's behavior presumably would be altered if he had the nonpublic information. Significantly, however, the Commission has acted to bar warehousing under its authority to regulate tender offers after recognizing that action under § 10(b) would rest on a "somewhat different theory" than that previously used to regulate insider trading as fraudulent activity.

We see no basis for applying such a new and different theory of liability in this case. As we have emphasized before, the 1934 Act cannot be read " 'more broadly than its language and the statutory scheme reasonably permit.' " *Touche Ross & Co. v. Redington,* 442 U.S. 560, 578 (1979), quoting *SEC v. Sloan,* 436 U.S. 103, 116 (1978). Section 10(b) is aptly described as a catchall provision, but what it catches must be fraud. When an allegation of fraud is based upon nondisclosure, there can be no fraud absent a duty to speak. We hold that a duty to disclose under § 10(b) does not arise from the mere possession of nonpublic market information. The contrary result is without support in the legislative history of § 10(b) and would be inconsistent with the careful plan that Congress has enacted for regulation of the securities markets. Cf. *Santa Fe Industries, Inc. v. Green,* 430 U.S., at 479.[20]

IV

In its brief to this Court, the United States offers an alternative theory to support petitioner's conviction. It argues that petitioner breached a duty to the acquiring corporation when he acted upon information that he obtained by virtue of his position as an employee of a printer employed by the corporation. The breach of this

15. Title 15 U.S.C. § 78m(d)(1) (1976 ed., Supp. II) permits a tender offeror to purchase 5% of the target company's stock prior to disclosure of its plan for acquisition.

20. . . . It is worth noting that this is apparently the first case in which criminal liability has been imposed upon a purchaser for § 10(b) nondisclosure. Petitioner was sentenced to a year in prison, suspended except for one month, and a 5-year term of probation. 588 F.2d, at 1373, 1378 (Meskill, J., dissenting).

duty is said to support a conviction under § 10(b) for fraud perpetrated upon both the acquiring corporation and the sellers.

We need not decide whether this theory has merit for it was not submitted to the jury. . . .

The jury instructions demonstrate that petitioner was convicted merely because of his failure to disclose material, nonpublic information to sellers from whom he bought the stock of target corporations. The jury was not instructed on the nature or elements of a duty owed by petitioner to anyone other than the sellers. Because we cannot affirm a criminal conviction on the basis of a theory not presented to the jury, *Rewis v. United States,* 401 U.S. 808, 814 (1971), see *Dunn v. United States,* 442 U.S. 100, 106 (1979), we will not speculate upon whether such a duty exists, whether it has been breached, or whether such a breach constitutes a violation of § 10(b).

The judgment of the Court of Appeals is

Reversed. . .

Mr. Chief Justice BURGER, dissenting.

I believe that the jury instructions in this case properly charged a violation of § 10(b) and Rule 10b–5, and I would affirm the conviction.

I

As a general rule, neither party to an arm's-length business transaction has an obligation to disclose information to the other unless the parties stand in some confidential or fiduciary relation. See W. Prosser, Law of Torts § 106 (2d ed. 1955). This rule permits a businessman to capitalize on his experience and skill in securing and evaluating relevant information; it provides incentive for hard work, careful analysis, and astute forecasting. But the policies that underlie the rule also should limit its scope. In particular, the rule should give way when an informational advantage is obtained, not by superior experience, foresight, or industry, but by some unlawful means. One commentator has written:

> "[T]he way in which the buyer acquires the information which he conceals from the vendor should be a material circumstance. The information might have been acquired as the result of his bringing to bear a superior knowledge, intelligence, skill or technical judgment; it might have been acquired by mere chance; or it might have been acquired by means of some tortious action on his part. . . . *Any time information is acquired by an illegal act it would seem that there should be a duty to disclose that information.*" Keeton, Fraud—Concealment and Non–Disclosure, 15 Texas L.Rev. 1, 25–26 (1936) (emphasis added).

I would read § 10(b) and Rule 10b–5 to encompass and build on this principle: to mean that a person who has misappropriated nonpublic information has an absolute duty to disclose that information or to refrain from trading.

The language of § 10(b) and of Rule 10b–5 plainly supports such a reading. By their terms, these provisions reach *any* person engaged in *any* fraudulent scheme. This broad language negates the suggestion that congressional concern was limited to trading by "corporate insiders" or to deceptive practices related to "corporate information." [1] Just as surely Congress cannot have intended one standard of fair dealing for "white collar" insiders and another for the "blue collar" level. The very language of § 10(b) and Rule 10b–5 "by repeated use of the word 'any' [was] obviously meant to be inclusive." *Affiliated Ute Citizens v. United States,* 406 U.S. 128, 151 (1972).

The history of the statute and of the Rule also supports this reading. The antifraud provisions were designed in large measure "to assure that dealing in securities is fair and without undue preferences or advantages among investors." H.R.Conf.Rep. No. 94–229, p. 91 (1975). These provisions prohibit "those manipulative and deceptive practices which have been demonstrated to fulfill no useful function." S.Rep. No. 792, 73d Cong., 2d Sess., 6 (1934). An investor who purchases securities on the basis of misappropriated nonpublic information possesses just such an "undue" trading advantage; his conduct quite clearly serves no useful function except his own enrichment at the expense of others.

This interpretation of § 10(b) and Rule 10b–5 is in no sense novel. It follows naturally from legal principles enunciated by the Securities and Exchange Commission in its seminal *Cady, Roberts* decision. 40 S.E.C. 907 (1961). There, the Commission relied upon two factors to impose a duty to disclose on corporate insiders: (1) ". . . access . . . to information intended to be available only for a corporate purpose *and not for the personal benefit of anyone* " (emphasis added); and (2) the unfairness inherent in trading on such information when it is inaccessible to those with whom one is dealing. Both of these factors are present whenever a party gains an informational advantage by unlawful means. Indeed, in *In re Blyth & Co.,* 43 S.E.C. 1037 (1969), the Commission applied its *Cady, Roberts* decision in just such a context. In that case a broker-dealer had traded in Government securities on the basis of confidential Treasury Department information which it received from a Federal Reserve Bank employee. The Commission ruled that the trading was "improper use of inside information" in violation of § 10(b) and Rule 10b–5. 43 S.E.C., at 1040. It did not hesitate to extend *Cady, Roberts* to reach a "tippee" of a Government insider.

---

1. Academic writing in recent years has distinguished between "corporate information"—information which comes from within the corporation and reflects on expected earnings or assets—and "market information." See, *e.g.,* Fleischer, Mundheim, & Murphy, An Initial Inquiry into the Responsibility to Disclose Market Information, 121 U.Pa.L.Rev. 798, 799 (1973). It is clear that § 10(b) and Rule 10b–5 by their terms and by their history make no such distinction. See Brudney, Insiders, Outsiders, and Informational Advantages Under the Federal Securities Laws, 93 Harv.L.Rev. 322, 329–333 (1979).

Finally, it bears emphasis that this reading of § 10b and Rule 10b–5 would not threaten legitimate business practices. So read, the antifraud provisions would not impose a duty on a tender offeror to disclose its acquisition plans during the period in which it "tests the water" prior to purchasing a full 5% of the target company's stock. Nor would it proscribe "warehousing." See generally SEC, Institutional Investor Study Report, H.R.Doc. No. 92–64, pt. 4, p. 2273 (1971). Likewise, market specialists would not be subject to a disclose-or-refrain requirement in the performance of their everyday market functions. In each of these instances, trading is accomplished on the basis of material, nonpublic information, but the information has not been unlawfully converted for personal gain.

II

The Court's opinion, as I read it, leaves open the question whether § 10(b) and Rule 10b–5 prohibit trading on misappropriated nonpublic information.[4] Instead, the Court apparently concludes that this theory of the case was not submitted to the jury. In the Court's view, the instructions given the jury were premised on the erroneous notion that the mere failure to disclose nonpublic information, however acquired, is a deceptive practice. . . .

The Court's reading of the District Court's charge is unduly restrictive. Fairly read as a whole and in the context of the trial, the instructions required the jury to find that Chiarella obtained his trading advantage by misappropriating the property of his employer's customers. . . .

In sum, the evidence shows beyond all doubt that Chiarella, working literally in the shadows of the warning signs in the printshop, misappropriated—stole to put it bluntly—valuable nonpublic information entrusted to him in the utmost confidence. He then exploited his ill-gotten informational advantage by purchasing securities in the market. In my view, such conduct plainly violates § 10(b) and Rule 10b–5. Accordingly, I would affirm the judgment of the Court of Appeals.

[The concurring opinions of Justice Stevens and Justice Brennan, and the dissenting opinion of Justice Blackmun, in which Justice Marshall joined, are omitted.]

---

4. There is some language in the Court's opinion to suggest that only "a relationship between petitioner and the sellers ... could give rise to a duty [to disclose]." ... The Court's holding, however, is much more limited, namely, that mere possession of material, nonpublic information is insufficient to create a duty to disclose or to refrain from trading. . . . Accordingly, it is my understanding that the Court has not rejected the view, advanced above, that an absolute duty to disclose or refrain arises from the very act of misappropriating nonpublic information.

SECURITIES EXCHANGE ACT § 14(e) and RULE 14(e)(3)

[See Statutory Supplement]

NOTE ON RULE 14e–3

In effect, Rule 14e–3 reverses the rule in *Chiarella* insofar as the relevant information concerns a tender offer. In United States v. Chestman, 947 F.2d 551 (2d Cir.1991), cert. denied 503 U.S. 1004, 112 S.Ct. 1759, 118 L.Ed.2d 422 (1992), the Second Circuit held en banc, by a 10–1 vote, that Rule 14e–3 was authorized by Section 14(e). The court therefore upheld the conviction of a defendant who had traded on the basis of material information relating to a tender offer even though, in the court's view, under *Chiarella* and *Dirks* (infra) the defendant had not violated Rule 10b–5. Accord: SEC v. Peters, 978 F.2d 1162 (10th Cir.1992).

DIRKS v. SECURITIES AND EXCHANGE COMMISSION

Supreme Court of the United States, 1983.
463 U.S. 646, 103 S.Ct. 3255, 77 L.Ed.2d 911.

Justice POWELL delivered the opinion of the Court.

Petitioner Raymond Dirks received material nonpublic information from "insiders" of a corporation with which he had no connection. He disclosed this information to investors who relied on it in trading in the shares of the corporation. The question is whether Dirks violated the antifraud provisions of the federal securities laws by this disclosure.

I

In 1973, Dirks was an officer of a New York broker-dealer firm who specialized in providing investment analysis of insurance company securities to institutional investors. On March 6, Dirks received information from Ronald Secrist, a former officer of Equity Funding of America. Secrist alleged that the assets of Equity Funding, a diversified corporation primarily engaged in selling life insurance and mutual funds, were vastly overstated as the result of fraudulent corporate practices. Secrist also stated that various regulatory agencies had failed to act on similar charges made by Equity Funding employees. He urged Dirks to verify the fraud and disclose it publicly.

Dirks decided to investigate the allegations. He visited Equity Funding's headquarters in Los Angeles and interviewed several officers and employees of the corporation. The senior management denied any wrongdoing, but certain corporation employees corroborated the charges of fraud. Neither Dirks nor his firm owned or traded any Equity Funding stock, but throughout his investigation he openly discussed the information he had obtained with a number of clients and investors. Some of these persons sold their holdings of Equity Funding securities, including five investment advisers who liquidated holdings of more than $16 million.[2]

While Dirks was in Los Angeles, he was in touch regularly with William Blundell, the Wall Street Journal's Los Angeles bureau chief. Dirks urged Blundell to write a story on the fraud allegations. Blundell did not believe, however, that such a massive fraud could go undetected and declined to write the story. He feared that publishing such damaging hearsay might be libelous.

During the two-week period in which Dirks pursued his investigation and spread word of Secrist's charges, the price of Equity Funding stock fell from $26 per share to less than $15 per share. This led the New York Stock Exchange to halt trading on March 27. Shortly thereafter California insurance authorities impounded Equity Funding's records and uncovered evidence of the fraud. Only then did the Securities and Exchange Commission (SEC) file a complaint against Equity Funding[3] and only then, on April 2, did the Wall Street Journal publish a front-page story based largely on information assembled by Dirks. Equity Funding immediately went into receivership.[4]

The SEC began an investigation into Dirks' role in the exposure of the fraud. After a hearing by an administrative law judge, the SEC found that Dirks had aided and abetted violations of § 17(a) of the Securities Act of 1933, 15 U.S.C. § 77q(a), § 10(b) of the Securities Exchange Act of 1934, 15 U.S.C. § 78j(b), and SEC Rule 10b–5, 17 CFR § 240.10b–5 (1982), by repeating the allegations of fraud to members of the investment community who later sold their Equity Funding stock. The SEC concluded: "Where 'tippees'— regardless of their motivation or occupation—come into possession of material 'information that they know is confidential and know or should know came from a corporate insider,' they must either publicly disclose that information or refrain from trading." 21

---

2. Dirks received from his firm a salary plus a commission for securities transactions above a certain amount that his clients directed through his firm. See 21 S.E.C. Docket, at 1402, n. 3. But "[i]t is not clear how many of those with whom Dirks spoke promised to direct some brokerage business through [Dirks' firm] to compensate Dirks, or how many actually did so." 220 U.S.App.D.C., at 316, 681 F.2d, at 831. The Boston Company Institutional Investors, Inc., promised Dirks about $25,000 in commissions, but it is unclear whether Boston actually generated any brokerage business for his firm. See App. 199, 204–205; 21 S.E.C. Docket, at 1404, n. 10; 220 U.S.App.D.C., at 316, n. 5, 681 F.2d, at 831, n. 5.

3. As early as 1971, the SEC had received allegations of fraudulent accounting practices at Equity Funding. Moreover, on March 9, 1973, an official of the California Insurance Department informed the SEC's regional office in Los Angeles of Secrist's charges of fraud. Dirks himself voluntarily presented his information at the SEC's regional office beginning on March 27.

4. A federal grand jury in Los Angeles subsequently returned a 105–count indictment against 22 persons, including many of Equity Funding's officers and directors. All defendants were found guilty of one or more counts, either by a plea of guilty or a conviction after trial. See Brief for Petitioner 15; App. 149–153.

S.E.C. Docket 1401, 1407 (1981) (footnote omitted) (quoting Chiarella v. United States, 445 U.S. 222, 230 n. 12, 100 S.Ct. 1108, 1115 n. 12, 63 L.Ed.2d 348 (1980)). Recognizing, however, that Dirks "played an important role in bringing [Equity Funding's] massive fraud to light," 21 S.E.C. Docket, at 1412,[8] the SEC only censured him.

Dirks sought review in the Court of Appeals for the District of Columbia Circuit. The court entered judgment against Dirks "for the reasons stated by the Commission in its opinion." App. to Pet. for Cert. C–2. Judge Wright, a member of the panel, subsequently issued an opinion. Judge Robb concurred in the result and Judge Tamm dissented; neither filed a separate opinion. Judge Wright believed that "the obligations of corporate fiduciaries pass to all those to whom they disclose their information before it has been disseminated to the public at large." 220 U.S.App.D.C. 309, 324, 681 F.2d 824, 839 (1982). Alternatively, Judge Wright concluded that, as an employee of a broker-dealer, Dirks had violated "obligations to the SEC and to the public completely independent of any obligations he acquired" as a result of receiving the information. Id., at 325, 681 F.2d, at 840.

In view of the importance to the SEC and to the securities industry of the question presented by this case, we granted a writ of certiorari. 459 U.S. 1014, 103 S.Ct. 371, 74 L.Ed.2d 506 (1982). We now reverse.

II

In the seminal case of In re Cady, Roberts & Co., 40 S.E.C. 907 (1961), the SEC recognized that the common law in some jurisdictions imposes on "corporate 'insiders,' particularly officers, directors, or controlling stockholders" an "affirmative duty of disclosure ... when dealing in securities." Id., at 911, and n. 13.[10] The SEC found that not only did breach of this common-law duty also establish the elements of a Rule 10b–5 violation, but that individuals other than corporate insiders could be obligated either to disclose material non-public information before trading or to abstain from

---

8. Justice Blackmun's dissenting opinion minimizes the role Dirks played in making public the Equity Funding fraud.... The dissent would rewrite the history of Dirks' extensive investigative efforts. See, e.g., 21 S.E.C., at 1412 ("It is clear that Dirks played an important role in bringing [Equity Funding's] massive fraud to light, and it is also true that he reported the fraud allegation to [Equity Funding's] auditors and sought to have the information published in the Wall Street Journal."); 681 F.2d, at 829 (Wright, J.) ("Largely thanks to Dirks one of the most infamous frauds in recent memory was uncovered and exposed, while the record shows that the SEC repeatedly missed opportunities to investigate Equity Funding.").

10. The duty that insiders owe to the corporation's shareholders not to trade on inside information differs from the common-law duty that officers and directors also have to the corporation itself not to mismanage corporate assets, of which confidential information is one. See 3 Fletcher Cyclopedia of the Laws of Private Corporations §§ 848, 900 (1975 ed. and Supp.1982); 3A Fletcher §§ 1168.1, 1168.2. In holding that breaches of this duty to shareholders violated the Securities Exchange Act, the Cady, Roberts Commission recognized, and we agree, that "[a] significant purpose of the Exchange Act was to eliminate the idea that use of inside information for personal advantage was a normal emolument of corporate office." See 40 S.E.C., at 912, n. 15.

trading altogether. Id., at 912. In *Chiarella*, we accepted the two elements set out in *Cady, Roberts* for establishing a Rule 10b–5 violation: "(i) the existence of a relationship affording access to inside information intended to be available only for a corporate purpose, and (ii) the unfairness of allowing a corporate insider to take advantage of that information by trading without disclosure." 445 U.S., at 227, 100 S.Ct. at 1114. In examining whether Chiarella had an obligation to disclose or abstain, the Court found that there is no general duty to disclose before trading on material nonpublic information, and held that "a duty to disclose under § 10(b) does not arise from the mere possession of nonpublic market information." Id., at 235, 100 S.Ct., at 1118. Such a duty arises rather from the existence of a fiduciary relationship. See id., at 227–235, 100 S.Ct., at 1114–1118.

Not "all breaches of fiduciary duty in connection with a securities transaction," however, come within the ambit of Rule 10b–5. Santa Fe Industries, Inc. v. Green, 430 U.S. 462, 472, 97 S.Ct. 1292, 1300, 51 L.Ed.2d 480 (1977). There must also be "manipulation or deception." Id., at 473, 97 S.Ct., at 1300. In an inside-trading case this fraud derives from the "inherent unfairness involved where one takes advantage" of "information intended to be available only for a corporate purpose and not for the personal benefit of anyone." In re Merrill Lynch, Pierce, Fenner & Smith, Inc., 43 S.E.C. 933, 936 (1968). Thus, an insider will be liable under Rule 10b–5 for inside trading only where he fails to disclose material nonpublic information before trading on it and thus makes "secret profits." *Cady, Roberts*, 40 S.E.C., at 916, n. 31.

III

We were explicit in *Chiarella* in saying that there can be no duty to disclose where the person who has traded on inside information "was not [the corporation's] agent, ... was not a fiduciary, [or] was not a person in whom the sellers [of the securities] had placed their trust and confidence." 445 U.S., at 232, 100 S.Ct., at 1116. Not to require such a fiduciary relationship, we recognized, would "depar[t] radically from the established doctrine that duty arises from a specific relationship between two parties" and would amount to "recognizing a general duty between all participants in market transactions to forgo actions based on material, nonpublic information." Id., at 232, 233, 100 S.Ct., at 1116, 1117. This requirement of a specific relationship between the shareholders and the individual trading on inside information has created analytical difficulties for the SEC and courts in policing tippees who trade on inside information. Unlike insiders who have independent fiduciary duties to both the corporation and its shareholders, the typical tippee has no such relationships.[14] In view of

---

14. Under certain circumstances, such as where corporate information is revealed legitimately to an underwriter, accountant, lawyer, or consultant working for the corporation, these outsiders may become fiduciaries of the shareholders. The basis for recognizing this fiduciary duty is not simply that such persons acquired nonpublic corpo-

this absence, it has been unclear how a tippee acquires the *Cady, Roberts* duty to refrain from trading on inside information.

A

The SEC's position, as stated in its opinion in this case, is that a tippee "inherits" the *Cady, Roberts* obligation to shareholders whenever he receives inside information from an insider:

> "In tipping potential traders, Dirks breached a duty which he had assumed as a result of knowingly receiving confidential information from [Equity Funding] insiders. Tippees such as Dirks who receive non-public material information from insiders become 'subject to the same duty as [the] insiders.' Shapiro v. Merrill Lynch, Pierce, Fenner & Smith, Inc. [495 F.2d 228, 237 (CA2 1974) (quoting Ross v. Licht, 263 F.Supp. 395, 410 (SDNY 1967))]. Such a tippee breaches the fiduciary duty which he assumes from the insider when the tippee knowingly transmits the information to someone who will probably trade on the basis thereof.... Presumably, Dirks' informants were entitled to disclose the [Equity Funding] fraud in order to bring it to light and its perpetrators to justice. However, Dirks—standing in their shoes—committed a breach of the fiduciary duty which he had assumed in dealing with them, when he passed the information on to traders." 21 S.E.C. Docket, at 1410, n. 42.

This view differs little from the view that we rejected as inconsistent with congressional intent in *Chiarella*. In that case, the Court of Appeals agreed with the SEC and affirmed Chiarella's conviction, holding that " '[*a*]*nyone*—corporate insider or not— who regularly receives material nonpublic information may not use that information to trade in securities without incurring an affirmative duty to disclose.' " United States v. Chiarella, 588 F.2d 1358, 1365 (CA2 1978) (emphasis in original). Here, the SEC maintains that anyone who knowingly receives nonpublic material information from an insider has a fiduciary duty to disclose before trading.[15]

rate information, but rather that they have entered into a special confidential relationship in the conduct of the business of the enterprise and are given access to information solely for corporate purposes. See SEC v. Monarch Fund, 608 F.2d 938, 942 (CA2 1979); In re Investors Management Co., 44 S.E.C. 633, 645 (1971); In re Van Alystne, Noel & Co., 43 S.E.C. 1080, 1084–1085 (1969); In re Merrill Lynch, Pierce, Fenner & Smith, Inc., 43 S.E.C. 933, 937 (1968); *Cady, Roberts*, 40 S.E.C., at 912. When such a person breaches his fiduciary relationship, he may be treated more properly as a tipper than a tippee. See Shapiro v. Merrill Lynch, Pierce, Fenner & Smith, Inc., 495 F.2d 228, 237 (CA2 1974) (investment banker had access to material information when working on a proposed public offering for the corporation). For such a

duty to be imposed, however, the corporation must expect the outsider to keep the disclosed nonpublic information confidential, and the relationship at least must imply such a duty.

15. Apparently, the SEC believes this case differs from *Chiarella* in that Dirks' receipt of inside information from Secrist, an insider, carried Secrist's duties with it, while Chiarella received the information without the direct involvement of an insider and thus inherited no duty to disclose or abstain. The SEC fails to explain, however, why the receipt of nonpublic information from an insider automatically carries with it the fiduciary duty of the insider. As we emphasized in *Chiarella*, mere possession of nonpublic information does not give rise to a duty to disclose or abstain; only a specific

In effect, the SEC's theory of tippee liability in both cases appears rooted in the idea that the antifraud provisions required equal information among all traders. This conflicts with the principle set forth in *Chiarella* that only some persons, under some circumstances, will be barred from trading while in possession of material nonpublic information. Judge Wright correctly read our opinion in *Chiarella* as repudiating any notion that all traders must enjoy equal information before trading: "[T]he 'information' theory is rejected. Because the disclose-or-refrain duty is extraordinary, it attaches only when a party has legal obligations other than a mere duty to comply with the general antifraud proscriptions in the federal securities laws." 220 U.S.App.D.C., at 322, 681 F.2d at 837. See *Chiarella*, 445 U.S., at 235, n. 20, 100 S.Ct., at 1118, n. 20. We reaffirm today that "[a] duty [to disclose] arises from the relationship between parties ... and not merely from one's ability to acquire information because of his position in the market." 445 U.S., at 232–233, n. 14, 100 S.Ct., at 1116–1117, n. 14.

Imposing a duty to disclose or abstain solely because a person knowingly receives material nonpublic information from an insider and trades on it could have an inhibiting influence on the role of market analysts, which the SEC itself recognizes is necessary to the preservation of a healthy market.[17] It is commonplace for analysts to "ferret out and analyze information," 21 S.E.C., at 1406,[18] and

relationship does that. And we do not believe that the mere receipt of information from an insider creates such a special relationship between the tippee and the corporation's shareholders.

Apparently recognizing the weakness of its argument in light of *Chiarella,* the SEC attempts to distinguish that case factually as involving not "inside" information, but rather "market" information, i.e., "information generated within the company relating to its assets or earnings." Brief for Respondent 23. This Court drew no such distinction in *Chiarella* and, as The Chief Justice noted, "[i]t is clear that § 10(b) and Rule 10b–5 by their terms and by their history make no such distinction." 445 U.S., at 241, n. 1 (dissenting opinion). See ALI Fed.Sec.Code § 1603, Comment (2)(j) (Proposed Official Draft 1978).

17. The SEC expressly recognized that "[t]he value to the entire market of [analysts'] efforts cannot be gainsaid; market efficiency in pricing is significantly enhanced by [their] initiatives to ferret out and analyze information, and thus the analyst's work redounds to the benefit of all investors." 21 S.E.C., at 1406. The SEC asserts that analysts remain free to obtain from management corporate information for purposes of "filling in the 'interstices in analysis'...." Brief for Respondent 42 (quoting *Investors Management Co.,* 44 S.E.C., at 646). But this rule is inherently imprecise, and imprecision prevents parties

from ordering their actions in accord with legal requirements. Unless the parties have some guidance as to where the line is between permissible and impermissible disclosures and uses, neither corporate insiders nor analysts can be sure when the line is crossed. Cf. *Adler v. Klawans,* 267 F.2d 840, 845 (CA2 1959) (Burger, J., sitting by designation.)

18. On its facts, this case is the unusual one. Dirks is an analyst in a broker-dealer firm, and he did interview management in the course of his investigation. He uncovered, however, startling information that required no analysis or exercise of judgment as to its market relevance. Nonetheless, the principle at issue here extends beyond these facts. The SEC's rule—applicable without regard to any breach by an insider—could have serious ramifications on reporting by analysts of investment views.

Despite the unusualness of Dirks' "find," the central role that he played in uncovering the fraud at Equity Funding, and that analysts in general can play in revealing information that corporations may have reason to withhold from the public, is an important one. Dirks' careful investigation brought to light a massive fraud at the corporation. And until the Equity Funding fraud was exposed, the information in the trading market was grossly inaccurate. But for Dirks' efforts, the fraud might well have gone undetected longer. See n. 8, supra.

this often is done by meeting with and questioning corporate officers and others who are insiders. And information that the analysts obtain normally may be the basis for judgments as to the market worth of a corporation's securities. The analyst's judgment in this respect is made available in market letters or otherwise to clients of the firm. It is the nature of this type of information, and indeed of the markets themselves, that such information cannot be made simultaneously available to all of the corporation's stockholders or the public generally.

B

The conclusion that recipients of inside information do not invariably acquire a duty to disclose or abstain does not mean that such tippees always are free to trade on the information. The need for a ban on some tippee trading is clear. Not only are insiders forbidden by their fiduciary relationship from personally using undisclosed corporate information to their advantage, but they may not give such information to an outsider for the same improper purpose of exploiting the information for their personal gain. See 15 U.S.C. § 78t(b) (making it unlawful to do indirectly "by means of any other person" any act made unlawful by the federal securities laws). Similarly, the transactions of those who knowingly participate with the fiduciary in such a breach are "as forbidden" as transactions "on behalf of the trustee himself." Mosser v. Darrow, 341 U.S. 267, 272, 71 S.Ct. 680, 683, 95 L.Ed. 927 (1951). See Jackson v. Smith, 254 U.S. 586, 589, 41 S.Ct. 200, 202, 65 L.Ed. 418 (1921); Jackson v. Ludeling, 88 U.S. 616, 631–632, 22 L.Ed. 492 (1874). As the Court explained in *Mosser,* a contrary rule "would open up opportunities for devious dealings in the name of the others that the trustee could not conduct in his own." 341 U.S., at 271, 71 S.Ct., at 682. See SEC v. Texas Gulf Sulphur Co., 446 F.2d 1301, 1308 (CA2), cert. denied, 404 U.S. 1005, 92 S.Ct. 561, 30 L.Ed.2d 558 (1971). Thus, the tippee's duty to disclose or abstain is derivative from that of the insider's duty. See Tr. of Oral Arg. 38. Cf. *Chiarella,* 445 U.S., at 246, n. 1, 100 S.Ct., at 1122, n. 1 (Blackmun, J., dissenting). As we noted in *Chiarella,* "[t]he tippee's obligation has been viewed as arising from his role as a participant after the fact in the insider's breach of a fiduciary duty." 445 U.S., at 230, n. 12, 100 S.Ct., at 1115, n. 12.

Thus, some tippees must assume an insider's duty to the shareholders not because they receive inside information, but rather because it has been made available to them *improperly*. And for Rule 10b–5 purposes, the insider's disclosure is improper only where it would violate his *Cady, Roberts* duty. Thus, a tippee assumes a fiduciary duty to the shareholders of a corporation not to trade on material nonpublic information only when the insider has breached his fiduciary duty to the shareholders by disclosing the information to the tippee and the tippee knows or should know that there has been a breach. As Commissioner Smith perceptively observed in *Investors Management Co.:* "[T]ippee responsibility must be related back to insider responsibility by a necessary finding that the tippee knew the information was given to him in breach of a duty by a person having a special relationship to the issuer not to disclose the information. . . ." 44 S.E.C., at 651 (concurring in the result). Tipping thus properly is viewed only as a means of indirectly violating the *Cady, Roberts* disclose-or-abstain rule.

C

In determining whether a tippee is under an obligation to disclose or abstain, it thus is necessary to determine whether the insider's "tip" constituted a breach of the insider's fiduciary duty. All disclosures of confidential corporate information are not inconsistent with the duty insiders owe to shareholders. In contrast to the extraordinary facts of this case, the more typical situation in which there will be a question whether disclosure violates the insider's *Cady, Roberts* duty is when insiders disclose information to analysts. See n. 16, supra. In some situations, the insider will act consistently with his fiduciary duty to shareholders, and yet release of the information may affect the market. For example, it may not be clear—either to the corporate insider or to the recipient analyst—whether the information will be viewed as material nonpublic information. Corporate officials may mistakenly think the information already has been disclosed or that it is not material enough to affect the market. Whether disclosure is a breach of duty therefore depends in large part on the purpose of the disclosure. This standard was identified by the SEC itself in *Cady, Roberts:* a purpose of the securities laws was to eliminate "use of inside information for personal advantage." 40 S.E.C., at 912, n. 15. See n. 10, supra. Thus, the test is whether the insider personally will benefit, directly or indirectly, from his disclosure. Absent some personal gain, there has been no breach of duty to stockholders. And absent a breach by the insider, there is no derivative breach. As Commissioner Smith stated in *Investors Management Co.* "It is important in this type of case to focus on policing insiders and what they do . . . rather than on policing information *per se* and its possession. . . ." 44 S.E.C., at 648 (concurring in the result).

The SEC argues that, if inside-trading liability does not exist when the information is transmitted for a proper purpose but is used for trading, it would be a rare situation when the parties could not fabricate some ostensibly legitimate business justification for transmitting the information. We think the SEC is unduly concerned. In determining whether the insider's purpose in making a particular disclosure is fraudulent, the SEC and the courts are not required to read the parties' minds. Scienter in some cases is relevant in determining whether the tipper has violated his *Cady, Roberts* duty. But to determine whether the disclosure itself "deceive[s], manipulate[s], or defraud[s]" shareholders, Aaron v. SEC, 446 U.S. 680, 686, 100 S.Ct. 1945, 1950, 64 L.Ed.2d 611 (1980), the initial inquiry is whether there has been a breach of duty by the insider. This requires courts to focus on objective criteria, i.e., whether the insider receives a direct or indirect personal benefit from the disclosure, such as a pecuniary gain or a reputational benefit that will translate into future earnings. Cf. 40 S.E.C., at 912, n. 15; Brudney, Insiders, Outsiders, and Informational Advantages Under the Federal Securities Laws, 93 Harv.L.Rev. 324, 348 (1979) ("The theory ... is that the insider, by giving the information out selectively, is in effect selling the information to its recipient for cash, reciprocal information, or other things of value for himself ..."). There are objective facts and circumstances that often justify such an inference. For example, there may be a relationship between the insider and the recipient that suggests a *quid pro quo* from the latter, or an intention to benefit the particular recipient. The elements of fiduciary duty and exploitation of nonpublic information also exist when an insider makes a gift of confidential information to a trading relative or friend. The tip and trade resemble trading by the insider himself followed by a gift of the profits to the recipient.

Determining whether an insider personally benefits from a particular disclosure, a question of fact, will not always be easy for courts. But it is essential, we think, to have a guiding principle for those whose daily activities must be limited and instructed by the SEC's inside-trading rules, and we believe that there must be a breach of the insider's fiduciary duty before the tippee inherits the duty to disclose or abstain. In contrast, the rule adopted by the SEC in this case would have no limiting principle.

IV

Under the inside-trading and tipping rules set forth above, we find that there was no actionable violation by Dirks. It is undisputed that Dirks himself was a stranger to Equity Funding, with no pre-existing fiduciary duty to its shareholders. He took no action, directly or indirectly, that induced the shareholders or officers of Equity Funding to repose trust or confidence in him. There was no expectation by Dirks' sources that he would keep their information in confidence. Nor did Dirks misappropriate or illegally obtain the information about Equity Funding. Unless the insiders breached their *Cady, Roberts* duty to shareholders in disclosing the nonpublic information to Dirks, he breached no duty when he passed it on to investors as well as to the Wall Street Journal.

It is clear that neither Secrist nor the other Equity Funding employees violated their *Cady, Roberts* duty to the corporation's shareholders by providing information to Dirks. The tippers received no monetary or personal benefit for revealing Equity Funding's secrets, nor was their purpose to make a gift of valuable information to Dirks. As the facts of this case clearly indicate, the tippers were motivated by a desire to expose the fraud.... In the absence of a breach of duty to shareholders by the insiders, there was no derivative breach by Dirks. See n. 20, supra. Dirks therefore could not have been "a participant after the fact in [an] insider's breach of a fiduciary duty." *Chiarella*, 445 U.S., at 230, n. 12, 100 S.Ct., at 1115, n. 12.

V

We conclude that Dirks, in the circumstances of this case, had no duty to abstain from use of the inside information that he obtained. The judgment of the Court of Appeals therefore is reversed.

[The dissenting opinion of Justice Blackmun, in which Justice Brennan and Justice Marshall joined, is omitted.]

NOTE ON UNITED STATES v. NEWMAN AND SEC v. MATERIA

In United States v. Newman, 664 F.2d 12 (2d Cir.1981), aff'd after remand 722 F.2d 729 (2d Cir.1983) (unpublished order), cert. denied 464 U.S. 863, 104 S.Ct. 193, 78 L.Ed.2d 170, Warner–Lambert Co. retained Morgan Stanley, an investment-banking firm, to assess the desirability of making a tender offer for Deseret Pharmaceutical Co. Courtois, who was then employed in Morgan Stanley's mergers-and-acquisitions department, learned of Warner's plan, passed along the information to Adrian Antoniu, an employee of another investment banker, and urged Antoniu to purchase Deseret stock. Antoniu in turn informed Newman, a stockbroker. Newman, acting pursuant to an agreement with Courtois and Antoniu, purchased 11,700 shares of Deseret stock at approximately $28.

On December 1, 1976, the New York Stock Exchange halted trading in Deseret stock pending announcement of the tender offer. Trading remained suspended until December 7, when Warner publicly announced a tender offer for Deseret stock at $38. Newman, Courtois, and Antoniu tendered their shares and reaped a substantial profit. The Second Circuit applied the misappropriation theory and held that Newman (the only one of the three who was then within the jurisdiction of the district court) had criminally violated Rule 10b–5, if the Government's allegations were true.[1]

In SEC v. Materia, 745 F.2d 197 (2d Cir.1984), cert. denied 471 U.S. 1053, 105 S.Ct. 2112, 85 L.Ed.2d 477 (1985), Materia, like Chiarella, was employed by a financial printer and utilized confidential information obtained in that capacity to trade in the stock of target corporations. The Second Circuit upheld a conviction and fine. "[The Supreme Court in *Chiarella*] did not ... disavow the misappropriation theory.... We announced [in *Newman*], and reiterate now, that one who misappropriates nonpublic information in breach of a fiduciary duty and trades on that information to his

---

1. Courtois and Antoniu were eventually sentenced. What Happened to 50 People Involved in Insider–Trading Cases, Wall St. J., November 18, 1987, p. 27, col. 3.

own advantage violates section 10(b) and Rule 10b–5." 745 F.2d at 203.

FEDERAL MAIL FRAUD ACT

[See Statutory Supplement]

CARPENTER v. UNITED STATES

Supreme Court of the United States, 1987.
484 U.S. 19, 108 S.Ct. 316, 98 L.Ed.2d 275.

Justice WHITE delivered the opinion of the Court.

Petitioners Kenneth Felis and R. Foster Winans were convicted of violating § 10(b) of the Securities Exchange Act of 1934, 48 Stat. 891, 15 U.S.C. § 78j(b), and Rule 10b–5, 17 CFR § 240.10b–5 (1987). *United States v. Winans,* 612 F.Supp. 827 (SDNY 1985). They were also found guilty of violating the federal mail and wire fraud statutes, 18 U.S.C. §§ 1341, 1343, and were convicted for conspiracy under 18 U.S.C. § 371. Petitioner David Carpenter, Winans' roommate, was convicted for aiding and abetting. With a minor exception, the Court of Appeals for the Second Circuit affirmed, 791 F.2d 1024 (1986); we granted certiorari, 479 U.S. ____ (1986).

I

In 1981, Winans became a reporter for the Wall Street Journal (the Journal) and in the summer of 1982 became one of the two writers of a daily column, "Heard on the Street." That column discussed selected stocks or groups of stocks, giving positive and negative information about those stocks and taking "a point of view with respect to investment in the stocks that it reviews." 612 F.Supp., at 830. Winans regularly interviewed corporate executives to put together interesting perspectives on the stocks that would be highlighted in upcoming columns, but, at least for the columns at issue here, none contained corporate inside information or any "hold for release" information. *Id.,* at 830, n. 2. Because of the "Heard" column's perceived quality and integrity, it had the potential of affecting the price of the stocks which it examined. The District Court concluded on the basis of testimony presented at trial that the "Heard" column "does have an impact on the market, difficult though it may be to quantify in any particular case." *Id.,* at 830.

The official policy and practice at the Journal was that prior to publication, the contents of the column were the Journal's confidential information. Despite the rule, with which Winans was familiar, he entered into a scheme in October 1983 with Peter Brant and petitioner Felis, both connected with the Kidder Peabody brokerage firm in New York City, to give them advance information as to the timing and contents of the "Heard" column. This permitted Brant and Felis and another conspirator, David Clark, a client of Brant, to buy or sell based on the probable impact of the column on the market. Profits were to be shared. The conspirators agreed that the scheme would not affect the journalistic purity of the "Heard" column, and the District Court did not find that the contents of any of the articles were altered to further the profit potential of petitioners' stock-trading scheme. *Id.,* at 832, 834–835. Over a 4–month period, the brokers made prepublication trades on the basis of information given them by Winans about the contents of some 27 "Heard" columns. The net profits from these trades were about $690,000.

In November 1983, correlations between the "Heard" articles and trading in the Clark and Felis accounts were noted at Kidder Peabody and inquiries began. Brant and Felis denied knowing anyone at the Journal and took steps to conceal the trades. Later, the Securities and Exchange Commission began an investigation. Questions were met by denials both by the brokers at Kidder Peabody and by Winans at the Journal. As the investigation progressed, the conspirators quarreled, and on March 29, 1984, Winans and Carpenter went to the SEC and revealed the entire scheme. This indictment and a bench trial followed. Brant, who had pleaded guilty under a plea agreement, was a witness for the Government.

The District Court found, and the Court of Appeals agreed, that Winans had knowingly breached a duty of confidentiality by misappropriating prepublication information regarding the timing and contents of the "Heard" columns, information that had been gained in the course of his employment under the understanding that it would not be revealed in advance of publication and that if it were, he would report it to his employer. It was this appropriation of confidential information that underlay both the securities laws and mail and wire fraud counts. With respect to the § 10(b) charges, the courts below held that the deliberate breach of Winans' duty of confidentiality and concealment of the scheme was a fraud and deceit on the Journal. Although the victim of the fraud, the Journal, was not a buyer or seller of the stocks traded in or otherwise a market participant, the fraud was nevertheless considered to be "in connection with" a purchase or sale of securities within the meaning of the statute and the rule. The courts reasoned that the scheme's sole purpose was to buy and sell securities at a profit based on advance information of the column's contents. The courts below rejected petitioners' submission, which is one of the two questions presented here, that criminal liability could not be imposed on petitioners under Rule 10b–5 because "the newspaper is the only alleged victim of fraud and has no interest in the securities traded."

In affirming the mail and wire fraud convictions, the Court of Appeals ruled that Winans had fraudulently misappropriated "property" within the meaning of the mail and wire fraud statutes and that its revelation had harmed the Journal. It was held as well that the use of the mail and wire services had a sufficient nexus with the scheme to satisfy §§ 1341 and 1343. The petition for certiorari challenged these conclusions.

The Court is evenly divided with respect to the convictions under the securities laws and for that reason affirms the judgment below on those counts. For the reasons that follow, we also affirm the judgment with respect to the mail and wire fraud convictions.

II

Petitioners assert that their activities were not a scheme to defraud the Journal within the meaning of the mail and wire fraud statutes;[6] and that in any event, they did not obtain any "money or property" from the Journal, which is a necessary element of the crime under our decision last Term in *McNally v. United States,* 483 U.S. 350 (1987). We are unpersuaded by either submission and address the latter first.

We held in *McNally* that the mail fraud statute does not reach "schemes to defraud citizens of their intangible rights to honest and impartial government," . . . and that the statute is "limited in scope to the protection of property rights." . . . Petitioners argue that the Journal's interest in prepublication confidentiality for the "Heard" columns is no more than an intangible consideration outside the reach of § 1341; nor does that law, it is urged, protect against mere injury to reputation. This is not a case like *McNally,* however. The Journal, as Winans' employer, was defrauded of much more than its contractual right to his honest and faithful service, an interest too ethereal in itself to fall within the protection of the mail fraud statute, which "had its origin in the desire to protect individual property rights." *McNally, supra,* . . . . Here, the object of the scheme was to take the Journal's confidential business information—the publication schedule and contents of the "Heard" column—and its intangible nature does not make it any less "property" protected by the mail and wire fraud statutes. *McNally* did not limit the scope of § 1341 to tangible as distinguished from intangible property rights.

Both courts below expressly referred to the Journal's interest in the confidentiality of the contents and timing of the "Heard" column as a property right, 791 F.2d, at 1034–1035; 612 F.Supp., at 846, and we agree with that conclusion. Confidential business information has long been recognized as property. See *Ruckelhaus v. Monsanto Co.,* 467 U.S. 986, 1001–1004 (1984); *Dirks v. SEC,* 463 U.S. 646, 653, n. 10 (1983); *Board of Trade of Chicago v. Christie Grain & Stock Co.,* 198 U.S. 236, 250–251 (1905); cf. 5

---

6. The mail and wire fraud statutes share the same language in relevant part, and accordingly we apply the same analysis to both sets of offenses here.

U.S.C. § 552(b)(4). "Confidential information acquired or compiled by a corporation in the course and conduct of its business is a species of property to which the corporation has the exclusive right and benefit, and which a court of equity will protect through the injunctive process or other appropriate remedy." 3 W. Fletcher, Cyclopedia of Law of Private Corporations § 857.1, p. 260 (rev. ed. 1986) (footnote omitted). The Journal had a property right in keeping confidential and making exclusive use, prior to publication, of the schedule and contents of the "Heard" columns. *Christie Grain, supra.* As the Court has observed before:

> "[N]ews matter, however little susceptible of ownership or dominion in the absolute sense, is stock in trade, to be gathered at the cost of enterprise, organization, skill, labor, and money, and to be distributed and sold to those who will pay money for it, as for any other merchandise." *International News Service v. Associated Press,* 248 U.S. 215, 236 (1918).

Petitioners' arguments that they did not interfere with the Journal's use of the information or did not publicize it and deprive the Journal of the first public use of it, see Reply Brief for Petitioners 6, miss the point. The confidential information was generated from the business and the business had a right to decide how to use it prior to disclosing it to the public. Petitioners cannot successfully contend based on *Associated Press* that a scheme to defraud requires a monetary loss, such as giving the information to a competitor; it is sufficient that the Journal has been deprived of its right to exclusive use of the information, for exclusivity is an important aspect of confidential business information and most private property for that matter.

We cannot accept petitioners' further argument that Winans' conduct in revealing prepublication information was no more than a violation of workplace rules and did not amount to fraudulent activity that is proscribed by the mail fraud statute. Sections 1341 and 1343 reach any scheme to deprive another of money or property by means of false or fraudulent pretenses, representations, or promises. As we observed last Term in *McNally,* the words "to defraud" in the mail fraud statute have the "common understanding" of " 'wronging one in his property rights by dishonest methods or schemes,' and 'usually signify the deprivation of something of value by trick, deceit, chicane or overreaching.' " 483 U.S., at 358 (quoting *Hammerschmidt v. United States,* 265 U.S. 182, 188 (1924)). The concept of "fraud" includes the act of embezzlement, which is " 'the fraudulent appropriation to one's own use of the money or goods entrusted to one's care by another.' " *Grin v. Shine,* 187 U.S. 181, 189 (1902).

The District Court found that Winans' undertaking at the Journal was not to reveal prepublication information about his column, a promise that became a sham when in violation of his duty he passed along to his co-conspirators confidential information belonging to the Journal, pursuant to an ongoing scheme to share profits from trading in anticipation of the "Heard" column's impact on the stock market. In *Snepp v. United States,* 444 U.S. 507, 515, n. 11 (1980) (*per curiam*), although a decision grounded in the provisions of a written trust agreement prohibiting the unapproved use of confidential government information, we noted the similar prohibitions of the common law, that "even in the absence of a written contract, an employee has a fiduciary obligation to protect confidential information obtained during the course of his employment." As the New York courts have recognized, "It is well established, as a general proposition, that a person who acquires special knowledge or information by virtue of a confidential or fiduciary relationship with another is not free to exploit that knowledge or information for his own personal benefit but must account to his principal for any profits derived therefrom." *Diamond v. Oreamuno,* 24 N.Y.2d 494, 497, 248 N.E.2d 910, 912 (1969); see also Restatement (Second) of Agency §§ 388, Comment *c,* 396(c) (1958).

We have little trouble in holding that the conspiracy here to trade on the Journal's confidential information is not outside the reach of the mail and wire fraud statutes, provided the other elements of the offenses are satisfied. The Journal's business information that it intended to be kept confidential was its property; the declaration to that effect in the employee manual merely removed any doubts on that score and made the finding of specific intent to defraud that much easier. Winans continued in the employ of the Journal, appropriating its confidential business information for his own use, all the while pretending to perform his duty of safeguarding it. In fact, he told his editors twice about leaks of confidential information not related to the stock-trading scheme, 612 F.Supp., at 831, demonstrating both his knowledge that the Journal viewed information concerning the "Heard" column as confidential and his deceit as he played the role of a loyal employee. Furthermore, the District Court's conclusion that each of the petitioners acted with the required specific intent to defraud is strongly supported by the evidence. *Id.,* at 847–850.

Lastly, we reject the submission that using the wires and the mail to print and send the Journal to its customers did not satisfy the requirement that those mediums be used to execute the scheme at issue. The courts below were quite right in observing that circulation of the "Heard" column was not only anticipated but an essential part of the scheme. Had the column not been made available to Journal customers, there would have been no effect on stock prices and no likelihood of profiting from the information leaked by Winans.

The judgment below is

Affirmed.

———

In SEC v. Clark, 915 F.2d 439 (9th Cir.1990), the Ninth Circuit joined the Second Circuit in squarely adopting the misappropriation theory. For other cases adopting the misappropriation theory, see SEC v. Cherif, 933 F.2d 403 (7th Cir.1991), modified and rehearing en banc denied (7th Cir.1991), cert. denied 502 U.S. 1071, 112 S.Ct. 966, 117 L.Ed.2d 131 (1992); Rothberg v. Rosenbloom, 771 F.2d 818 (3d Cir.1985), cert. denied 481 U.S. 1017, 107 S.Ct. 1895, 95 L.Ed.2d 501 (1987).

———

UNITED STATES v. CHESTMAN, 947 F.2d 551 (2d Cir.1991), cert. denied 503 U.S. 1004, 112 S.Ct. 1759, 118 L.Ed.2d 422 (1992) (Winter, J., dissenting). "Efficient capital markets depend on the protection of property rights in information. However, they also require that persons who acquire and act on information about companies be able to profit from the information they generate so long as the method by which the information is acquired does not amount to a form of theft. A rule commanding equal access would result in a securities market governed by relative degrees of ignorance because the profit motive for independently generating information about companies would be substantially diminished.... Under such circumstances, the pricing of securities would be less accurate than in circumstances in which the production of information is encouraged by legal protection.

"One may speculate that it was for these reasons that the Supreme Court declined in *Chiarella* to adopt a broad ban on trading on material nonpublic information and then imposed in *Dirks* a breach of fiduciary duty requirement—not running to those with whom the trader buys or sells. Under the *Dirks* rule, insider trading is illegal only where the trader has received the information as a result of the trader's or tipper's breach of a duty to keep information confidential.

"The misappropriation theory adopted by several circuits fits within this rationale. Misappropriation also involves the misuse of confidential information in a way that risks making information public in a fashion similar to trading by corporate insiders. In U.S. v. Carpenter, 791 F.2d 1024 (2d Cir.1986), aff'd, 484 U.S. 19, 108 S.Ct. 316, 98 L.Ed.2d 275 (1987), for example, where the information belonged to the *Wall Street Journal* rather than to the corporations whose shares were traded, the misuse of information created an incentive on the part of the traders to create false information that might affect the efficiency of the market's pricing of the corporations' stock. Moreover, the potential for piggybacking would add to that inefficiency.

"It must be noted, however, that, although the rationale set out above provides a policy for prohibiting a specific kind of insider trading, any obvious relationship to Section 10(b) is presently missing because theft rather than fraud or deceit, seems the gravamen of the prohibition. Indeed, *Carpenter* analogized the conduct there to embezzlement. 791 F.2d at 1033 n. 11. Nevertheless, the law is far enough down this road—indeed, the Insider Trading Sanctions Act seems premised on Section 10(b)'s applicability—that a court of appeals has no option but to continue the route."

SECURITIES EXCHANGE ACT §§ 20A, 21, 21A

[See Statutory Supplement]

NOTE ON SECURITIES EXCHANGE ACT § 20A

In Moss v. Morgan Stanley, Inc., 719 F.2d 5 (2d Cir.1983), cert. denied sub nom. Moss v. Newman, 465 U.S. 1025, 104 S.Ct. 1280, 79 L.Ed.2d 684 (1984), the Second Circuit held that although trading on the basis of misappropriated information violated Rule 10b–5, and therefore subjected the trader to criminal penalties, a private action could not be brought under Rule 10b–5 on the basis of such trading.

In 1988, Congress adopted the Insider Trading and Securities Fraud Enforcement Act (ITSFEA), which added § 20A to the Securities Exchange Act. It is clear that § 20A reverses the doctrine of Moss v. Morgan Stanley, because *if* trading on the basis of misappropriated information violates Rule 10b–5, then under § 20A a private action can be brought on the basis of such trading. It has been argued that § 20A is not conclusive on the issue *whether* trading on the basis of misappropriated information violates Rule 10b–5. However, in SEC v. Clark, 915 F.2d 439 (9th Cir.1990), the Ninth Circuit rejected that argument:

> . . . The Insider Trading and Securities Fraud Enforcement Act of 1988 . . . was Congress' reaction to the stock market crash of October 19, 1987, viewed by many of its members as linked to continued insider and outsider trading despite stiff [Insider Trading Sanctions Act] penalties. . . . The House Committee reporting on the bill acknowledged that the misappropriation theory had split the Supreme Court in *Carpenter*, yet nonetheless endorsed the theory as consistent with the broad objectives of § 10(b) and Rule 10b–5. *Id.* at 6047. Furthermore, in discussing an amendment to the 1934 Exchange Act expressly creating a private right of action for various securities violations, the Committee noted:

> > [T]he codification of a right of action for contemporaneous traders is specifically intended to *overturn court cases which have precluded recovery for plaintiffs where the defendant's violation is premised upon the misappropriation theory.* See, e.g., *Moss v. Morgan Stanley,* 719 F.2d 5

(2d Cir.1983). The Committee believes that this result is *inconsistent with the remedial purposes of the Exchange Act, and that the misappropriation theory fulfills appropriate regulatory objectives in determining when communicating or trading while in possession of material nonpublic information is unlawful.*

Id. at 6063–64. . . . [Emphasis added by the court.]

NOTE ON AIDING AND ABETTING LIABILITY
UNDER RULE 10b–5

In Central Bank of Denver v. First Interstate Bank of Denver, ___ U.S. ___, 114 S.Ct. 1439, 128 L.Ed.2d 119 (1994), the Supreme Court held that liability cannot be imposed on a person under Rule 10b–5 solely because that person aided and abetted a violation of the Rule:

> As in earlier cases considering conduct prohibited by § 10(b), we again conclude that the statute prohibits only the making of a material misstatement (or omission) or the commission of a manipulative act. . . . The proscription does not include giving aid to a person who commits a manipulative or deceptive act.

Prior to *Central Bank,* issues concerning aiding-and-abetting liability under Rule 10b–5 usually arose in the context of a suit against a primary violator in which the plaintiff joined as defendants such secondary actors as lawyers, accountants, or banks who had somehow furthered the primary violator's course of conduct. The *Central Bank* opinion held that such secondary actors could not be sued on an aiding-and-abetting theory, but left open the possibility of suing such actors as primary violators:

> . . . The absence of § 10(b) aiding and abetting liability does not mean that secondary actors in the securities markets are always free from liability under the securities Acts. Any person or entity, including a lawyer, accountant, or bank, who employs a manipulative device or makes a material misstatement (or omission) on which a purchaser or seller of securities relies may be liable as a primary violator under 10b–5, assuming *all* of the requirements for primary liability under Rule 10b–5 are met. . . . In any complex securities fraud, moreover, there are likely to be multiple violators; in this case, for example, respondents named four defendants as primary violators. (Emphasis by the Court.)

NOTE ON THE OBLIGATIONS OF A NONTRADING CORPORATION UNDER RULE 10b–5

Most private actions under Rule 10b–5 are brought against persons who have traded or tipped. As *Basic* shows, an action can also be brought on the basis of a statement or omission that influences trading but is made by a person who did not himself trade or tip:

> [I]t seems clear ... that Congress when it used the phrase "in connection with the purchase or sale of any security" intended only that the device employed, whatever it might be, be of a sort that would cause reasonable investors to rely thereon, and, in connection therewith, so relying, cause them to purchase or sell a corporation's securities. There is no indication that Congress intended that the corporations or persons responsible for the issuance of a misleading statement would not violate the section unless they engaged in related securities transactions or otherwise acted with wrongful motives; indeed, the obvious purposes of the Act to protect the investing public and to secure fair dealing in the securities markets would be seriously undermined by applying such a gloss onto the legislative language.... The mere fact that an insider did not engage in securities transactions does not negate the possibility of wrongful purpose; perhaps the market did not react to the misleading statement as much as was anticipated or perhaps the wrongful purpose was something other than the desire to buy at a low price or sell at a high price.

SEC v. Texas Gulf Sulphur Co., 401 F.2d 833, 860 (2d Cir.1968), cert. denied 394 U.S. 976, 89 S.Ct. 1454, 22 L.Ed.2d 756 (1969).

Accordingly, a corporation that makes *misstatements* may be liable under Rule 10b–5 even if it does not trade.

The imposition of Rule 10b–5 liability on a nontrading corporation for *nondisclosure* is much less usual. In *Texas Gulf Sulphur Co., supra,* the court stated that "the timing of the disclosure [of material facts] is a matter for the business judgment of the corporate officers entrusted with the management of the corporation within the affirmative disclosure requirements promulgated by the exchanges and by the SEC." Id. at 850 n. 12. This is still the general rule. See Staffin v. Greenberg, 672 F.2d 1196, 1204 (3d Cir.1982); Financial Industrial Fund, Inc. v. McDonnell Douglass Corp., 474 F.2d 514, 518 (10th Cir.1973), cert. denied 414 U.S. 874, 94 S.Ct. 155, 38 L.Ed.2d 114; Electronic Specialty Co. v. International Controls Corp., 409 F.2d 937, 949 (2d Cir.1969). There are, however, several exceptions to this rule.

(i) If the corporation makes a statement that is misleading (inaccurate) when made, even though not intentionally so, and the corporation later learns that the statement was misleading, it is under a duty to *correct* the statement if the statement is still "alive," rather than "stale"—that is, if the statement would still be likely to be material to investors. See, e.g., Backman v. Polaroid Corp., 910 F.2d 10 (1st Cir.1990) (en banc); Ross v. A.H. Robins Co., Inc., 465 F.Supp. 904 (S.D.N.Y.1979), rev'd on other grounds 607 F.2d 545 (2d Cir.), cert. denied 446 U.S. 946, 100 S.Ct. 2175, 64 L.Ed.2d 802 (1980).

(ii) Several courts have held that if a corporation makes a public statement that is correct when made, but that has become materially misleading in light of subsequent events, the corporation may have a duty to *update* the statement. In the leading case, Greenfield v. Heublein, Inc., 742 F.2d 751, 758 (3d Cir.1984), cert. denied 469 U.S. 1215, 105 S.Ct. 1189, 84 L.Ed.2d 336 (1985), the court said, "[a]lthough a corporation may be under no duty to disclose . . ., if a corporation voluntarily makes a public statement that is correct when issued, [the corporation] has a duty to update the statement if it becomes materially misleading in light of subsequent events."[1]

In Backman v. Polaroid Corp., supra, the First Circuit qualified this position by taking the view that the duty to update applies only to forward-looking statements:

> Obviously, if a disclosure is in fact misleading when made, and the speaker thereafter learns of this, there is a duty correct it. . . . In Greenfield v. Heublien, Inc. . . . the court called for disclosure if a prior disclosure "becomes materially misleading in light of subsequent events". . . . We may agree that, in special circumstances, a statement, correct at the time, may have a forward intent and connotation upon which parties may be expected to rely. If this is a clear meaning, and there is a change, correction, more exactly, further disclosure may be called for. . . .

(iii) A corporation may so involve itself in the preparation of statements about the corporation by outsiders—such as analysts' reports or earnings projections—that it assumes a duty to correct material errors in those statements. Such a duty "may occur when officials of the company have, by their activity, made an implied representation that the information they have reviewed is true or at least in accordance with the company's views." Elkind v. Liggett & Myers, Inc., 635 F.2d 156, 163 (2d Cir.1980).

---

1. See also In re Time Warner Inc. Securities Litigation, 9 F.3d 259, 167 (2d Cir. 1993), cert. denied ___ U.S. ___, 114 S.Ct. 1397, 128 L.Ed.2d 70 (1994) ("a duty to update opinions and projections may arise if the original opinions or projections have become misleading as the result of intervening events."); In re Phillips Petroleum Sec. Litig., 881 F.2d 1236, 1245 (3d Cir.1989); *In re* Warner Communications Sec. Litig., 618 F.Supp. 735, 752 (S.D.N.Y.1985), aff'd 798 F.2d 35 (2d Cir.1986); Kamerman v. Steinberg, 681 F.Supp. 206 (S.D.N.Y.1988), aff'd 891 F.2d 424 (2d Cir.1989); Good v. Zenith Electronics Corp., 751 F.Supp. 1320, 1322 (N.D.Ill.1990); Ross v. A.H. Robins Co., 465 F.Supp. 904 (S.D.N.Y.1979), rev'd on other grounds 607 F.2d 545 (2d Cir.), cert. denied 446 U.S. 946, 100 S.Ct. 2175, 64 L.Ed.2d 802 (1980), reh. denied 448 U.S. 911, 100 S.Ct. 3057, 65 L.Ed.2d 1140. The SEC also takes this position. See Securities Exchange Act Release No. 6084, 17 SEC Docket 1048, 1054 (1979).

(iv) A corporation may be under a duty to correct erroneous rumors resulting from leaks by the corporation or its agents. See State Teachers Retirement Board v. Fluor Corp., 654 F.2d 843, 850 (2d Cir.1981) (dictum); In re General Motors Class E Stock Buyout Securities Litigation, 694 F.Supp. 1119, 1129 (D.Del.1988), reargument granted and case dismissed on different grounds, 790 F.Supp. 77 (D.Del.1992).

(v) It is sometimes suggested, in dictum or by inference, that nondisclosure by a corporation may violate Rule 10b–5 if no valid corporate purpose requires nondisclosure. It is not easy to see why this should be so, and no corporation seems to have been held liable under this theory.

NOTE ON THE STATUTE OF LIMITATIONS APPLICABLE TO PRIVATE ACTIONS UNDER RULE 10b–5

In Lampf, Pleva, Lipkind, Prupis & Petigrow v. Gilbertson, 501 U.S. 350, 111 S.Ct. 2773, 115 L.Ed.2d 321 (1991), the Supreme Court held that private actions under Rule 10b–5 were subject to a 1–and–3–year statute of limitations structure that is made expressly applicable to certain express causes of action under the Securities Act and the Securities Exchange Act. Under this structure, a private action cannot be brought more than one year after discovery of the facts constituting the cause of action or more than three years following accrual of the cause of action.

The Court also held that the doctrine of tolling—a well-established legal doctrine under which the Statute of Limitations stops running during the continuation of certain circumstances, such as efforts on the part of the defendant to conceal knowledge of his wrong from discovery—is inapplicable under the 1–and–3–year structure.

Finally, the Court retroactively applied the rule it adopted to all cases brought before *Lampf, Pleva* that were still pending, even though the *Lampf, Pleva* rule was new and many litigants had relied on the Circuit court opinions that had adopted different statute of limitations periods under Rule 10b–5.

In response to this retroactivity, Congress amended the Securities Exchange Act by adding § 27A, which made *Lampf, Pleva* nonretroactive.

The constitutionality of section 27A has been challenged in a number of cases. Various circuit courts have upheld the constitutionality of section 27A(a) as applied to cases that were pending when section 27A was enacted. See, e.g., Gray v. First Winthrop Corp., 989 F.2d 1564 (9th Cir.1993). However, in Plaut v. Spendthrift Farms, (1995), the Supreme Court held that Section 27A(b) contravened the Constitution's separation of powers as applied to cases that had been dismissed prior to the enactment of that section.

The one-and-three-year structure adopted in *Lampf, Pleva* does not apply to all actions under Rule 10b–5. See section 20A of the Securities Exchange Act. In addition, the SEC is not subject to any statute of limitations in civil enforcement actions. See SEC v. Maurice Rind, 991 F.2d 1486 (9th Cir.1993), cert. denied ___ U.S. ___, 114 S.Ct. 439, 126 L.Ed.2d 372 (1993).

SECTION 3.   LIABILITY FOR SHORT–SWING TRADING UNDER § 16(b) OF THE SECURITIES EXCHANGE ACT

SECURITIES EXCHANGE ACT § 16

[See Statutory Supplement]

SECURITIES EXCHANGE ACT RULES 3a–11–1, 3b–2, 16a–1, 16a–2, 16a–3, 16a–8, 16a–10, 16b–3, 16b–5, 16b–6, 16b–7, 16b–9; FORM 3; FORM 4

[See Statutory Supplement]

FELDMAN & TEBERG, BENEFICIAL OWNERSHIP UNDER SECTION 16 OF THE SECURITIES EXCHANGE ACT OF 1934, 17 Western Res.L.Rev. 1054, 1063–65 (1966). "The juxtaposition of section 16(a) and 16(b), plus the fact that both operate with respect to the same persons, has led many to erroneously conclude that section 16(a) was enacted only to reveal transactions within the scope of section 16(b). That section 16(a) is not confined to transactions within the scope of section 16(b) is clear not only from the fact that section 16(a) pre-existed section 16(b) [as a matter of legislative history], but also from the different language of the two subsections. For while section 16(b) speaks of purchases and sales within six months of each other, section 16(a) speaks of changes in beneficial ownership, a much broader concept....

"Since the terms of section 16(a) require insiders to disclose any changes in their beneficial ownership of securities, it provides a means for bringing to light possible violations of ... Rule 10b–5, as well as a 'purchase and sale' within the scope of section 16(b). However, two other functions of the section 16(a) reports are equally important to the efficacious operations of the Exchange Act's scheme to banish investors' ignorance and upgrade the ethics of corporate managers. Its second function is to reveal information which may be used in evaluating the securities of the issuer. This is a pure disclosure device in which the conclusions to be drawn from the reports and the weight to be attached thereto are left to the judgment of the individual investor. The information contained in the reports may be used (1) as a guide to the insiders' current confidence or lack thereof in the company's fortunes or (2) to detect an evolving change in control in the company. Undoubtedly this investment information function of the section largely explains why the Commission's monthly summary of transactions reported under section 16(a) has become a perennial best seller. Finally, section 16(a) is itself a deterrent to the misuse of inside information through the publicity which attaches to the reports, apart from any other statutory prohibition or liability. This is a standard by-product or goal of any disclosure provision, since presumably people are likely to refrain from improper acts, or acts which may appear improper, if they know such acts will be exposed to public scrutiny."

NOTE ON GOLLUST v. MENDELL

In Gollust v. Mendell, 501 U.S. 115, 111 S.Ct. 2173, 115 L.Ed.2d 109 (1991), the Supreme Court made the following observations about § 16(b) generally, and the procedural aspects of § 16(b) in particular:

> The statute imposes a form of strict liability on "beneficial owner[s]," as well as on the issuer's officers and directors, rendering them liable to suits requiring them to disgorge their profits even if they did not trade on inside information or intend to profit on the basis of such information.... Because the statute imposes "liability without fault within its narrowly drawn limits" ... we have been reluctant to exceed a literal, "mechanical" application of the statutory text in determining who may be subject to liability, even though in some cases a broader view of statutory liability could work to eliminate an "evil that Congress sought to correct through § 16(b)." Reliance Electric Co. v. Emerson Electric Co., [404 U.S., at 425 (1972)].

> To enforce this strict liability rule on insider trading, Congress chose to rely solely on the issuers of stock and their security holders. Unlike most of the federal securities laws, § 16(b) does not confer enforcement authority on the Securities and Exchange Commission. It is, rather, the security holders of an issuer who have the ultimate authority to sue for enforcement of § 16(b). If the issuer declines to bring a § 16(b) action within 60 days of a demand by a security holder, or fails to prosecute the action "diligently" ... then the security holder may "institut[e]" an action to recover insider short-swing profits for the issuer....

Although plaintiffs seeking to sue under the statute must own a "security," § 16(b) places no significant restriction on the type of security adequate to confer standing. "[A]ny security" will suffice, ... the statutory definition being broad enough to include stock, notes, warrants, bonds, debentures, puts, calls, and a variety of other financial instruments; it expressly excludes only "currency or any note, draft, bill of exchange, or banker's acceptance which has a maturity at the time of issuance of not exceeding nine months. . . ."

REPORT OF THE TASK FORCE ON REGULATION OF INSIDER TRADING, PART II: REFORM OF SECTION 16

42 Bus.Law. 1087, 1091–92 (1987).

In recent years, a number of commentators have suggested that section 16(b) causes more harm than good and that it should be repealed. It has been argued that section 16(b) is ineffectual in preventing insider trading and does not even address all of the ways in which insider trades can be perpetrated, while it imposes punitive liability on the innocent, the naive, and the unaware corporate officers who unwittingly sell in violation of, for example, the labyrinthine restrictions of rule 16b–3. These commentators raise the question: Given the development of the insider trading doctrine under rule 10b–5, the substantial limitations of section 16(b) in preventing insider trading, and the hardships that it imposes, is the statute needed?

The task force believes that it is. Section 16(b) has a different legislative focus than the prohibition of trading on inside information. Indeed, it is the only provision of the 1934 Act that specifically regulates insider trading. It is aimed at three specific types of insider trading abuses, only one of which involves abuse of inside information.

First, section 16(b) was intended to remove the temptation for corporation executives to profit from short-term stock price fluctuations at the expense of the long-term financial health of their companies. It prevents insiders from being obsessed with trading in their companies' securities to the detriment of their managerial and fiduciary responsibilities. In this regard, based on the testimony of insider abuses presented at the hearings, it was Congress's judgment that short-swing trading by corporate executives is not good for their companies or the American capital markets.

Second, the section was intended to penalize the unfair use of inside information by insiders. This includes both trading on inside information in violation of rule 10b–5 and the use of "softer" information of the type that insiders often have but that members of the investing public do not: the ability to make better informed guesses as to the success of new products, the likely results of negotiations, and the real risks of contingencies and other uncertainties, the underlying facts of which have been publicly disclosed.

Third, section 16(b) was designed to eliminate the temptation for insiders to manipulate corporate events so as to maximize their own short-term trading profits. Before the enactment of section 16(b), insiders had been able to make quick profits from short-term price swings by such practices as the announcement of generous (but imprudent) dividend programs followed by postinsider trading dividend reductions. Thus, the section provides a minimum standard of fiduciary conduct for corporate insiders.

The task force thus concludes that section 16 remains a useful tool for preventing speculative abuses by insiders and for focusing their attention on their fiduciary duty and on long-term corporate health, rather than on short-term trading profits.

GRATZ v. CLAUGHTON

United States Court of Appeals, Second Circuit, 1951.
187 F.2d 46, cert. denied 341 U.S. 920, 71 S.Ct. 741, 95 L.Ed. 1353 (1951).

Before L. HAND, Chief Judge, and SWAN and AUGUSTUS N. HAND, Circuit Judges.

L. HAND, Chief Judge.

This is an appeal by the defendant, Claughton, from a judgment against him, entered upon the report of a master, in an action by a shareholder of the Missouri–Kansas–Texas Railroad Company under § 16(b) of the Securities Exchange Act of 1934.... The court first granted a summary judgment as to all the issues except the amount of the profits made by the defendant, which it referred to a master, on whose report it entered final judgment. The defendant does not dispute the propriety of a summary disposition of all the issues except that referred, but he does dispute the propriety of the judgment in law. First, he argues that the venue was wrong because he was domiciled in Florida, and the summons was served upon him in that state. Second, he disputes the rule adopted by the master in computing his profits. Third, he challenges the constitutionality of the statute which imposes the liability, and of the provisions for venue. We shall take up the first and third in sequence, reserving the second for the last.

[The court held that venue was proper.] ...

The challenge to the constitutionality of § 16(b) we have answered twice before. For many years a grave omission in our corporation law had been its indifference to dealings of directors or other corporate officers in the shares of their companies. When they bought shares, they came literally within the conventional prohibitions of the law of trusts; yet the decisions were strangely slack in so deciding. When they sold shares, it could indeed be argued that they were not dealing with a beneficiary, but with one whom his purchase made a beneficiary. That should not, however, have obscured the fact that the director or officer assumed a fiduciary relation to the buyer by the very sale; for it would be a sorry distinction to allow him to use the advantage of his position to induce the buyer into the position of a beneficiary, although he was forbidden to do so, once the buyer had become one. Certainly this is true, when the buyer knows he is buying of a director or officer, for he expects to become the seller's *cestui que* trust. If the buyer does not know, he is entitled to assume that if his seller in fact is already a director or officer, he will remain so after the sale. Nor was it necessary to confine this disability to directors or other officers of the corporation. The reason for the doctrine was that a director or officer may have information not accessible to a shareholder, actual or prospective, and that advantage is not confined to them. We take judicial notice that an effective control over the affairs of a corporation often does not require anything approaching a majority of the shares; and this is particularly true in the case of those corporations whose shares are dealt in upon national exchanges. Nor is it common for the control so obtained to be in the hands of one individual; more often a number share it, who are all in a position to gain a more intimate acquaintance with the enterprise and its prospects than the shareholders at large. It is of course true that the ownership of ten per cent of the shares does not always put the owner among those who do control; but neither Congress, nor any other legislature, is obliged to limit the means which it chooses so exactly to its ends that the correspondence is exact. If only those persons were liable, who could be proved to have a bargaining advantage, the execution of the statute would be so encumbered as to defeat its whole purpose. We do not mean that the interest, of which a statute deprives an individual, may never be so vital that he must not be given a trial of his personal guilt; but that is not so when all that is at stake is a director's, officer's or "beneficial owner's" privilege to add to, or subtract from, his holdings for a period of six months. In such situations it is well settled that a statute may provide any means which can reasonably be thought necessary to deal with the evil, even though they may cover instances where it is not present. . . .

There remains the question of the computation of profits, which we dealt with in Smolowe v. Delendo Corporation. . . . [8] Section 16(b) declares that "any profit realized . . . from any purchase and sale, or any sale and purchase . . . within any period of less than six months . . . shall inure to and be recoverable by the issuer": the corporation. It is plain that this presupposes some matching of (1) purchases against sales, or of (2) sales against purchases, and that there must therefore be some principle upon which both the minuend—the sale price—and the subtrahend—the purchase price—can be determined. At first blush it might seem that the statute limited the recovery to profits derived from transac-

---

8. 2 Cir., 136 F.2d 231, 148 A.L.R. 300.

tions in the same shares; as, for example, that a dealer's profit upon the sale of any given number of shares was to be measured by subtracting what he paid for those shares from what he got upon a sale of the same certificate. However, as we observed in Smolowe v. Delendo Corporation, supra, that would allow an easy avoidance of the statute; in order to speculate freely an officer, director, or "beneficial owner" need only hold a substantial block of shares for more than six months. If, for example, on January 1st, he had 10,000 shares which he had bought before October 1st, he could buy 1,000 shares on February 1st and sell 1,000 shares at a profit on April 1st, making delivery out of certificates from the 10,000 shares purchased before October 1st. After the two transactions his position would be what it had been on January 1st save that in two months he had made a profitable turn in 1,000 shares—exactly the evil against which the statute is directed. Moreover, there is an added reason for this interpretation, if one be needed. In the case of a sale followed by a purchase it is impossible to identify any purchase with any previous sale; one would have to confine such transactions to the practically non-existent occasions when the proceeds of the sale were used to purchase. Thus it appears, regardless of anything said during the passage of the bill through Congress and of the different forms it took, that the Act does not demand—that the same shares should be sold which were bought. This accords with the fungible nature of shares of stock. Indeed, if we translate the transaction into sales and purchases, or purchases and sales, of gallons of oil in a single tank, or of bushels of wheat in a single bin, it at once appears that the ascertainment of the particular shares bought or sold must be wholly irrelevant.

Although for these reasons it appears that the transactions— sales and purchases, or purchases and sales—are not to be matched by identifying the shares dealt in, we are no nearer than before to finding an answer as to how transactions shall be matched; all that so far appeared, is that the matching is to be between contracts of sale and contracts of purchase, or vice versa. On the other hand it is manifest that the intent of the fiduciary cannot be the test; first, because he generally has no ascertainable intent; and second, because that would open the door even more widely to the evil in question. The statute does not allow the fiduciary to minimize his profits, any more than to set off his losses against them. We can therefore find no principle by which to select any two transactions which are to be matched; and, so far as we can see, we are forced to one of two alternatives: to match any given sale taken as minuend, against any given purchase, taken as subtrahend, in such a way as to reduce profits to their lowest possible amount, or in such a way as to increase them to the greatest possible amount. The master adopted the second course, following what he supposed to be the doctrine of Smolowe v. Delendo Corporation, supra. We think that he was right for the following reasons.

The question is in substance the same as when a trustee's account is to be surcharged, for, as we have said, the statute makes the fiduciary a constructive trustee for any profits he may make. It is true that on the beneficiary in an accounting rests the burden of proof of a surcharge,[9] although the fiduciary has the burden of establishing any credits.[10] Since the plaintiff was seeking to surcharge the defendant we will therefore assume that it rested upon her to show how the transactions are to be matched; and, that, if there were nothing more, since she cannot do so, she must be content to have them matched in the way that shows the least profit. Obviously that cannot be the right answer, for the reasons we have given; and perhaps the fact that it cannot be, is reason enough for adopting the alternative. But there is another ground for reaching the same result. As we have said, the statute makes all such dealings unlawful, and makes the fiduciary accountable to the corporation. Although it is impossible in the case at bar to compute the defendant's profits, except that they must fall between two limits—the minimum and the maximum—the cause of this uncertainty is the number of transactions within six months: that is, the number of defendant's derelictions. The situation falls within the doctrine which has been law since the days of the "Chimney Sweeper's Jewel Case," [11] that when damages are at some unascertainable amount below an upper limit and when the uncertainty arises from the defendant's wrong, the upper limit will be taken as the proper amount.[12]

This results in looking for six months both before and after any sale, and not for three months only, as the defendant insists. If one is seeking an equation of purchase and sale, one may take any sale as the minuend and look back for six months for a purchase at less price to match against it. On the other hand, if one is looking for an equation of sale and purchase, one may take the same sale and look forward for six months for any purchase at a lower price. Although obviously no transaction can figure in more than one equation, with that exception we can see no escape from what we have just said. It is true that this means that no director, officer, or "beneficial owner" may safely buy and sell, or sell and buy, shares of stock in the company except at intervals of six months. Whether that is too drastic a means of meeting the evil, we have not to decide; it is enough that we can find no other way to administer the statute. Therefore, not only will we follow Smolowe v. Delendo Corporation, supra, as a precedent; but as *res integra* and after independent analysis we reassert its doctrine. The defendant concedes that, except for carrying the transactions backward and for-

9. Ewen v. Peoria & Eastern Ry., D.C., 78 F.Supp. 312, 334.

10. Wootton Land and Fuel Co. v. Ownbey, 8 Cir., 265 F. 91.

11. Armory v. Delamirie, 1722, 1 Strange 505.

12. Eastman Kodak Co. v. Southern Photo Co., 273 U.S. 359, 379, 47 S.Ct. 400, 71 L.Ed. 684; Schnell v. The Vallescura, 293 U.S. 296, 307, 55 S.Ct. 194, 79 L.Ed. 373; Story Parchment Co. v. Paterson Parchment Paper Co., 282 U.S. 565, 563–565, 51 S.Ct. 248, 75 L.Ed. 544; Bigelow v. R.K.O. Radio Pictures, Inc., 327 U.S. 251, 264, 265, 66 S.Ct. 574, 90 L.Ed. 652; Great Southern Gas & Oil Co. v. Logan Natural Gas & Fuel Co., 6 Cir., 155 F. 114; Package Closure Corp. v. Seal–Right Co., Inc., 2 Cir., 141 F.2d 972, 979; President & Directors of Manhattan Co. v. Kelby, 2 Cir., 147 F.2d 465, 476.

ward for six months, instead of for three, the master followed the rule laid down in that decision; and the plaintiff has not appealed, so that she is not entitled to any more than she has recovered. On this account we have not examined the master's computations in detail and are not to be understood to have passed upon them. The crushing liabilities which § 16(b) may impose are apparent from this action in which the judgment was for over $300,000; it should certainly serve as a warning, and may prove a deterrent.*

Judgment affirmed.

———

NOTE ON THE COMPUTATION OF PROFITS UNDER § 16(b)

1. In Smolowe v. Delendo Corporation, 136 F.2d 231 (2d Cir.1943), cert. denied 320 U.S. 751, 64 S.Ct. 56, 88 L.Ed. 446, which was cited and relied upon in Gratz v. Claughton, the court considered and rejected several formulas for computing profits under § 16(b) other than those analyzed in *Gratz:*

> Once the principle of [measuring damages based on the identification of the stock certificates involved] is rejected, its corollary, the first-in, first-out rule, is left at loose ends.... Its rationalization is the same as that for the identification rule, for which it operates as a presumptive principle; and it has no other support. If we reject one, we reject the other and for like reasons. Its application would render the large stockholder with a backlog of stock not immediately devoted to trading immune from the Act. Further, we should note that it does not fit the broad statutory language; a purchase followed immediately by a sale, albeit a transaction within the exact statutory language, would often be held immune from the statutory penalty because the purchase would be deemed by arbitrary rule to have been made at an earlier date; while a sale followed by purchase would never even be within the terms of the rule....

> Another possibility might be the striking of an average purchase price and an average sale price during the period, and using these as bases of computation. What this rule would do in concrete effect is to allow as offsets all losses made by such trading. This in effect the district court first planned to do.... But it corrected this in its supplemental opinion, properly pointing out that the statute provided for the recovery of "any" profit realized and obviously precluded a setting off of losses. Even had the statutory language been more uncertain, this rule seems one not to be favored in the light of the statutory purpose. Compared to other possible rules, it tends to stimu-

---

* In Adler v. Klawans, 267 F.2d 840, 848 (2d Cir.1959), it is reported that "during the pertinent periods, [Gratz] suffered a net loss of $400,000 on trading in the stock for which he was charged under section 16(b)." (Footnote by ed.)

late more active trading by reducing the chance of penalty.... Its application to a case where trading continued more than six months might be most uncertain, depending upon how the beginning of each six months' period was ascertained. It is not a clear-cut taking of "any profit" for the corporation, and we agree with the district court in rejecting it.

Id. at 238–39.

2. The formula adopted in *Smolowe* and *Gratz* has been generally approved by the courts. It is often referred to the "lowest purchase price, highest sale price" method. See, e.g., Whittaker v. Whittaker Corp., 639 F.2d 516, 530 (9th Cir.1981). Here are three illustrations of this method:

(i) D is a director of C Corporation, whose stock is traded on a national securities exchange. On January 2, D purchases 1,000 shares of C at $10. On April 1, D sells 1,000 shares at $15. This is a short-swing "purchase and sale," and D is liable under § 16(b) for his profit of $5,000.

(ii) On January 2, D purchases 1,000 shares of C at $10. On August 1, D sells 1,000 shares at $15. On November 1, D purchases 1,000 shares at $10. D has no liability on the basis of the January–August swing, because the two ends of the swing did not occur within six months. However, the August and November transactions constitute a short-swing "sale and purchase," and D would be liable under § 16(b) for a profit of $5,000 on these two transactions. Why has D made a $5,000 "profit"? Because after D's November 1 purchase, his position in C Corporation's stock is exactly as it was just before August 1 (that is, he owns 1,000 C shares) but he has also added $5,000 cash to his bank account. D may have accomplished this result by using inside information. The sale at $15 may have been made on the basis of undisclosed bad news. The purchase at $10 may have been made on the basis of undisclosed good news.

(iii) D engages in the following pattern of activity:

Date	Action	Amount	Price
2/1	Purchase	1,000	$30
3/1	Sale	1,000	$25
4/1	Purchase	1,000	$20
5/1	Sale	1,000	$15

Under the *Smolowe/Gratz* formula, D has a profit of $5,000, because the purchase at $20 on 4/1 can be matched with the sale at $25 on 3/1. At first glance, this looks counterintuitive: it seems that D has a $10,000 loss in his total trading, not a $5,000 profit. But it may be that except for inside information, D would not have sold on 3/1, and instead would have ridden the C stock all the way down from $30 to $15, for a loss of $15,000. Accordingly, there is a possibility (which is all that § 16(b) requires) that D has profited by $5,000 by holding his loss to $10,000 through the use of inside information.[1]

————

NOTE ON SECTION 16(b)

Section 16(b) is often criticized on the ground that it can result in liability in cases where there has been no insider trading, and in cases where there has been no real profit. As the Report of the ABA Task Force makes clear, however, this criticism has failed to strike a responsive chord among most members of the corporate bar. The ABA Task Force Report addresses these kinds of criticisms by giving affirmative justifications for the operation of § 16(b). See also Fox, Insider Trading Deterrence versus Managerial Incentives: A Unified Theory of Section 16(b), 92 Mich.L.Rev. 2088.

Furthermore, it's hard to see that § 16(b) has any significant capacity for harm. It's often thought to be desirable to encourage directors and executives to become shareholders, so as to tie their fortunes more closely to those of the corporation's owners. However, it is seldom thought to be desirable to encourage, or undesirable to discourage, directors and executives from short-term, in-and-out-trading. In the overwhelming majority of cases, that's all that § 16(b) does. Moreover, if we put aside exotic scenarios that could occur in theory, but almost never occur in practice, the sanction of § 16(b) is exceptionally mild, because normally all § 16(b) does is put the director or executive back where she was before she engaged in the relevant transactions.

————

NOTE ON INSIDER STATUS AT ONLY ONE END OF A SWING

The last sentence of § 16(b) sets out an exemptive provision under which "[T]his subsection shall not be construed to cover any transaction where [a more-than-10%] beneficial owner was not such both at the time of the purchase and sale, or the sale and purchase, of the security involved." Suppose a person who owns a more-than-10% block, but is not a director or officer, makes a sale that reduces his block to less than 10 percent, but leaves him with the remainder. Are later sales by that person, of some or all of the remainder of his block, covered by § 16? The Supreme Court has held that the later sales are not covered, because the person is not a 10 percent owner at the time of those sales. Reliance Electric Co. v. Emerson Electric Co., 404 U.S. 418, 92 S.Ct. 596, 30 L.Ed.2d 575 (1972). This result is codified in Rule 16a–2(c).

What about the very purchase that makes a person a more-than-10% beneficial owner? Can that purchase be matched with a

————

1. For a hypothetical in which a finding of profits under the *Smolowe/Gratz* formula does seem counterintuitive, see Lowenfels, Section 16(b): A New Trend in Regulating Insider Trading, 54 Cornell L.Rev. 45, 46–47 n. 6 (1968).

subsequent sale within six months? In Foremost–McKesson, Inc. v. Provident Securities Co., 423 U.S. 232, 96 S.Ct. 508, 46 L.Ed.2d 464 (1976) the Supreme Court held, largely on the basis of the exemptive provision and legislative history, that in the case of a purchase-sale sequence, a more-than-10% beneficial owner is not liable unless he was such *before* he made the purchase in question. To put this differently, the purchase that first lifts a beneficial owner above 10% cannot be matched with a subsequent sale under § 16(b).

Suppose a person is a more-than-10% owner, sells enough stock to get below the 10 percent line, and then buys stock within six months after that sale? This kind of case is called a sale-repurchase sequence. The *Foremost* opinion did not cover this case, and left considerable room for arguing that this sequence should result in liability under § 16(b).

Since the exemptive clause provides that "this subsection shall not be construed to cover any transaction where [*a more-than-10%*] *beneficial owner* was not such both at the time of the purchase and sale, or the sale and purchase" (emphasis added), the clear implication is that § 16(b) does apply to a short-swing transaction by a director or officer even where the director or officer "was not such both at the time of purchase and sale, or the sale and purchase." In Feder v. Martin Marietta Corp., 406 F.2d 260 (2d Cir.1969), cert. denied 396 U.S. 1036, 90 S.Ct. 678, 24 L.Ed.2d 681 (1970), the court held that a director or officer who purchases, resigns, and then sells within six months of the purchase, is liable under § 16(b). However, no liability will be imposed if both ends of a swing occur after the director or officer resigns. Lewis v. Mellon Bank, N.A., 513 F.2d 921 (3d Cir.1975); Lewis v. Varnes, 505 F.2d 785 (2d Cir.1974). Prior to 1991, it had been held that § 16(b) applies to a transaction in shares by a person who becomes a director or officer after the transaction, and engages in a matching transaction within six months of the original transaction. In such a case, the director or officer will have had an opportunity to utilize inside information at the second end of the swing, but not at the first. This issue is now governed by Rule 16a–2(a), adopted by the SEC in 1991, which provides that transactions by a director or officer before she became a director or officer are not subject to § 16.

NOTE ON THE INTERPRETATION OF § 16(b)

The courts have tended to use two somewhat different approaches in cases in which the applicability of § 16(b) is contestable. Until the early 1960s, the predominant theory of interpreting § 16(b) was that the section should be construed to cover all transactions within its literal reach. "[T]he statute was intended to be thoroughgoing, to squeeze all possible profits out of stock transactions, and thus to establish a standard so high as to prevent any conflict between the selfish interest of [an insider] and the faithful performance of his duty." Smolowe v. Delendo Corp., 136 F.2d 231, 239 (2d Cir.1943), cert. denied 320 U.S. 751, 64 S.Ct. 56, 88 L.Ed. 446. This theory of interpreting § 16(b) was known as the "objective" approach, although it has been aptly suggested that "automatic" would be more descriptive. Blau v. Lamb, 363 F.2d 507, 520 (2d Cir.1966), cert. denied 385 U.S. 1002, 87 S.Ct. 707, 17 L.Ed.2d 542 (1967).

Beginning in the mid–1960s, § 16(b) came to be perceived by some as overly harsh, because it operates without regard to fault. A different theory of interpretation, known as the "subjective" or "pragmatic" approach, then set in. Under this approach, in borderline cases—particularly cases involving an "unorthodox" transaction, rather than a garden-variety purchase or sale—the statute would be interpreted to impose liability only if the insider actually had access to inside information, or the transaction was of a type that carries a potential for insider abuse. See Whittaker v. Whittaker Corp., 639 F.2d 516, 522 (9th Cir.1981), cert. denied, 454 U.S. 1031, 102 S.Ct. 566, 70 L.Ed.2d 473; Lowenfels, Section 16(b): A New Trend in Regulating Insider Trading, 54 Cornell L.Rev. 45 (1968).

The names given to these two approaches are misleading. The "subjective" approach does not turn, as its name suggests, on the defendant's subjective intent to use inside information. Conversely, the "objective" approach can be just as pragmatic as the "pragmatic" approach. If the names of the two approaches are put aside, the conflict is between an approach that treats § 16(b) as a prophylactic rule of thumb, whose purpose would be defeated if defendants could escape liability on the ground that in their particular case no abuse could have occurred, and an approach that treats § 16(b) as inviting an inquiry into the possibility of abuse, at least in borderline cases. To a certain extent, which approach is adopted in a given case may depend on whether the court perceives § 16(b) as a good idea or a bad idea.

Still another approach to interpreting § 16(b), or at least its exemptive provisions, was set forth in Foremost–McKesson, Inc. v. Provident Securities Co., 423 U.S. 232, 251–52, 96 S.Ct. 508, 519–20, 46 L.Ed.2d 464 (1976);

> ... It is inappropriate to reach the harsh result of imposing § 16(b)'s liability without fault on the basis of unclear language. If Congress wishes to impose such liability, we must assume it will do so expressly or by unmistakable inference.

It should be emphasized that although the tension between the approaches to the interpretation of § 16(b) is real and important, it is a tension only at the margins. In the great bulk of potential cases, the application of § 16(b) is relatively straightforward. As pointed out in *Whittaker,* supra:

> [T]he pragmatic approach has not ousted the objective view. Rather, the pragmatic approach is used to determine the

boundaries of the statute's definitional scope in borderline situations, especially unorthodox transactions.... For a garden-variety transaction which cannot be regarded as unorthodox, the pragmatic approach is not applicable.... In such cases, if the situation is within the requirements established by Congress for § 16, then the mechanical, "objective," operation of the statute imposes liability.

NOTE ON "UNORTHODOX" TRANSACTIONS

One of the major interpretive problems under Section 16(b) is the application of that Section to a transaction that is not a "garden-variety" sale, but is instead an "exotic" or "unorthodox" transaction that seems to offer no possibility for speculative abuse because the disposition of shares by the defendant is involuntary and the defendant apparently had no access to inside information. One such case is a disposition of shares by a more-than-10%-shareholder as part of a merger over which the shareholder had no control and as to which she had no special information.

In Kern County Land Co. v. Occidental Petroleum Corp., 411 U.S. 582, 93 S.Ct. 1736, 36 L.Ed.2d 503 (1973), the Supreme Court held that Section 16(b) was inapplicable to an unorthodox transaction by Occidental, a more-than-10%-shareholder. Occidental was an unsuccessful tender offeror who had no access to inside information, and disposed of its shares in connection with a defensive merger undertaken by the target company for the very purpose of defeating Occidental's tender offer. The result reached in *Kern County* may seem appealing. However, the premise of Section 16(b) is that every more-than-10%-shareholder should be deemed an insider. *Kern County* rests in part on the assumption that this premise is incorrect. That assumption may well be true as a matter of fact, but it seems inconsistent with the statute.

NOTE, SHORT–SWING PROFITS IN FAILED TAKEOVER BIDS—THE ROLE OF SECTION 16(b), 59 Wash.L.Rev. 895 (1984). "Although the *Kern* decision did not state the threshold requirement for application of the pragmatic approach, subsequent courts have generally held that an involuntary transaction is necessary. To prove that a particular transaction is involuntary, the insider must apparently show that it had no control over the timing of the transaction. If the insider fails to make this showing, liability attaches automatically. If the insider does make this showing, however, courts will regard the transaction as unorthodox and will then ask whether the defendant had access to inside information. This inquiry, though secondary, is critical. One with access to inside information can speculate profitably by relying on an imminent 'involuntary' transaction. A finding of involuntariness, therefore, does not guarantee exoneration...."

NOTE ON ATTRIBUTION OF OWNERSHIP
UNDER SECTIONS 16(a) AND (b)

Sections 16(a) and (b) use the term or the concept of "beneficial ownership" for several different purposes.

Under § 16(a), a person who is either "a beneficial owner of more than 10 per centum of any class of equity security" (hereafter, a "10 percent owner"), or an officer or director, must report the amount of all equity securities of the issuer "of which he is the beneficial owner."

Under § 16(b), a director, officer, or 10 percent owner is liable for short-swing profits "realized by him from any purchase and sale, or any sale and purchase, of any equity security" of the issuer. Given both the purpose of the statute and the context, § 16(b) seems generally intended to cover the purchase or sale of those equity securities of which a person is a beneficial owner for purposes of § 16(a).

If a person is the record owner of an equity security and also has a pecuniary interest in the security, he is undoubtedly a beneficial owner for all purposes under § 16. Problems of interpretation arise, however, if a person is a record owner of shares but has no pecuniary interest; or if a person has a pecuniary interest but is not the record owner; or if a person is neither the record owner nor has a pecuniary interest, but there is nevertheless an important relationship between the person and the security, like the right to control the security. For most although not all practical purposes, the problem can be stated as follows: when should an equity security that is not legally owned by a person in the conventional sense nevertheless be *attributed* to the person under § 16, so that either (i) the security counts toward determining whether the person's ownership crosses the 10-percent-beneficial-ownership line, (ii) the person's transactions in the security must be reported under § 16(a), or (iii) the person's transactions in the security may subject him to liability under § 16(b)?

These problems are addressed in detail by the rules under § 16. Those rules draw a distinction between what constitutes beneficial ownership for purposes of determining whether a person is a 10 percent owner, and what constitutes beneficial ownership for purposes of determining whether a person who *is* a 10 percent owner, or a director or officer, must report under § 16(a) and may be liable for short-swing profits under § 16(b).

As to the first problem (whether a person is a 10 percent owner), Rule 16a–1(a)(1) provides that, with certain exceptions, "*solely for purposes of determining whether a person is a benefi-*

cial owner of more than ten percent of any class of equity securities registered pursuant to § 12 of the Act, the term 'beneficial owner' shall mean any person who is deemed a beneficial owner pursuant to § 13(d) of the Act and the rules thereunder...." (emphasis added). Rule 13d–3, in turn, provides that a beneficial owner of a security includes "any person who, directly or indirectly, through any contract, arrangement, understanding, relationship, or otherwise has or shares: (1) Voting power which includes the power to vote, or to direct the voting of, such security; and/or, (2) Investment power which includes the power to dispose, or to direct the disposition of, such security." In short, in determining whether a person is a 10 percent owner of stock, the emphasis under Rule 16a–1 is on the person's *control* over the stock.

As to the second issue (what constitutes beneficial ownership for reporting and liability purposes) Rule 16a–1(a)(2) provides that as a general principle, with certain exceptions and elaborations, *"other than for purposes of determining whether a person is a beneficial owner of more than ten percent of any class of equity securities* registered under § 12 of the Act, the term 'beneficial owner' shall mean any person who, directly or indirectly, through any contract, arrangement, understanding, relationship or otherwise, has or shares a direct or indirect pecuniary interest in the equity securities...."; and that "[t]he term 'pecuniary interest' in any class of equity securities shall mean the opportunity, directly or indirectly, to profit or share in any profit derived from a transaction in the subject securities." (emphasis added) In short, unlike Rule 16a–1(a)(1), which emphasizes *control* for purposes of determining who is a 10 percent owner, Rule 16a–1(a)(2) emphasizes *pecuniary interest* for purposes of determining what transactions in equity securities must be reported and may give rise to liability.

After stating the pecuniary-interest test as a general principle to govern the determination of beneficial ownership for reporting and liability purposes, Rule 16a–1(a)(2) then goes on to deal with certain recurring cases in which problems of attribution based on a pecuniary interest may arise.

Family members. Rule 16a–1(a)(2)(ii)(A) provides that "[t]he term 'indirect pecuniary interest' [under Rule 16a–2] in any class of equity securities shall include, but not be limited to ... securities held by members of a person's immediate family sharing the same household; *provided, however,* that the presumption of such beneficial ownership may be rebutted...." Rule 16a–1(e) then provides that "[t]he term 'immediate family', shall mean any child, stepchild, grandchild, parent, stepparent, grandparent, spouse, sibling, mother-in-law, father-in-law, son-in-law, daughter-in-law, brother-in-law, or sister-in-law, and shall include adoptive relationships."

Partnerships. Rule 16a–1(a)(2)(ii)(B) provides that the term "indirect pecuniary interest" [under Rule 16a–1(a)(2)] includes "a general partner's proportionate interest in the portfolio securities held by a general or limited partnership."

Corporations. Rule 16a–1(a)(2)(iii) provides that "[a] shareholder shall not be deemed to have a pecuniary interest in the portfolio securities held by a corporation or similar entity in which the person owns securities if the shareholder is not a controlling shareholder of the entity and does not have or share investment control over the entity's portfolio...." Note that this Rule does not specify a general principle for determining when a corporation's portfolio securities will be attributed to shareholders in the corporation, but only provides a safe harbor in the cases that the rule specified.

The Rules under § 16 also contain elaborate provisions dealing with such matters as when a trustee is a beneficial owner for reporting and liability purposes, and when the ownership of a derivative security makes a person the beneficial owner of the derivative security.

NOTE ON DEPUTIZATION

Closely related to the theory of attribution under § 16(b) is the theory of deputization. In Blau v. Lehman, 368 U.S. 403, 82 S.Ct. 451, 7 L.Ed.2d 403 (1962), the Supreme Court held that one enterprise, A, could be a "director" of second enterprise, B, within the meaning of § 16(b), if one of B's directors had been deputized by A to act on its behalf. In *Blau*, Thomas, a partner in Lehman Brothers (Enterprise A) sat on the board of Tide Water (Enterprise B), and Lehman profited from short-swing trading in Tide Water stock. The Court said:

> No doubt Lehman Brothers, though a partnership, could for purposes of § 16 be a "director" of Tide Water and function through a deputy, since § 3(a)(9) of the Act provides that " 'person' means ... partnership" and § 3(a)(7) that " 'director' means any director of a corporation or any person performing similar functions with respect to any organization, whether incorporated or unincorporated." Consequently, Lehman Brothers would be a "director" of Tide Water, if as petitioner's complaint charged Lehman actually functioned as a director through Thomas, who had been deputized by Lehman to perform a director's duties not for himself but for Lehman.

Id. at 409. However, the courts below had made findings that the Supreme Court believed precluded the conclusion that deputization had actually occurred, and Lehman Brothers was therefore not held liable. (Thomas himself was held liable below for his pro rata share of the short-swing profits made by Lehman, and this aspect of the case was not appealed.)

Deputization was found to be present in Feder v. Martin Marietta Corp., 406 F.2d 260 (2d Cir.1969), cert. denied 396 U.S. 1036, 90 S.Ct. 678, 24 L.Ed.2d 681 (1970). Bunker, the president of Martin Marietta (Enterprise A), had become a director of Sperry (Enterprise B), in which Martin Marietta held substantial stock. Bunker was ultimately responsible for the total operation of Martin Marietta, and personally approved all of the firm's financial investments—in particular, its purchase of the Sperry stock. Bunker's control over Martin Marietta, coupled with his membership on Sperry's Board, placed him in a position in which he could acquire inside information concerning Sperry and could utilize such information for Martin. Further, Bunker admitted discussing Sperry's affairs with two officials at Martin Marietta and participating in sessions when Martin Marietta's investment in Sperry was reviewed, and Bunker's ultimate letter of resignation to Martin Marietta's president stated that "When I became a member of the [Sperry] board ... it appeared to your associates that the Martin Marietta ownership of a substantial number of shares of Sperry Rand should have representation on your Board." On these facts, the Second Circuit concluded that "The control possessed by Bunker, his letter of resignation, the approval by the Martin Board of Bunker's directorship with Sperry and the functional similarity between Bunker's acts as a Sperry director and the acts of Martin's representatives on other boards ... are all definite and concrete indicatives that Bunker, in fact, was a Martin deputy." Martin Marietta was therefore held liable, as a director, for its short-swing profits in Sperry stock.

SECTION 4. THE COMMON LAW REVISITED

DIAMOND v. OREAMUNO
New York Court of Appeals, 1969.
24 N.Y.2d 494, 301 N.Y.S.2d 78, 248 N.E.2d 910.

Chief Judge FULD. Upon this appeal from an order denying a motion to dismiss the complaint as insufficient on its face, the question presented—one of first impression in this court—is whether officers and directors may be held accountable to their corporation for gains realized by them from transactions in the company's stock as a result of their use of material inside information.

The complaint was filed by a shareholder of Management Assistance, Inc. (MAI) asserting a derivative action against a number of its officers and directors to compel an accounting for profits allegedly acquired as a result of a breach of fiduciary duty. It charges that two of the defendants—Oreamuno, chairman of the board of directors, and Gonzalez, its president—had used inside information, acquired by them solely by virtue of their positions, in order to reap large personal profits from the sale of MAI shares and that these profits rightfully belong to the corporation. Other officers and directors were joined as defendants on the ground that they acquiesced in or ratified the assertedly wrongful transactions.

MAI is in the business of financing computer installations through sale and lease back arrangements with various commercial and industrial users. Under its lease provisions, MAI was required to maintain and repair the computers but, at the time of this suit, it lacked the capacity to perform this function itself and was forced to engage the manufacturer of the computers, International Business Machines (IBM), to service the machines. As a result of a sharp increase by IBM of its charges for such service, MAI's expenses for August of 1966 rose considerably and its net earnings declined from $262,253 in July to $66,233 in August, a decrease of about 75%. This information, although earlier known to the defendants, was not made public until October of 1966. Prior to the release of the information, however, Oreamuno and Gonzalez sold off a total of 56,500 shares of their MAI stock at the then current market price of $28 a share.

After the information concerning the drop in earnings was made available to the public, the value of a share of MAI stock immediately fell from the $28 realized by the defendants to $11. Thus, the plaintiff alleges, by taking advantage of their privileged position and their access to confidential information, Oreamuno and Gonzalez were able to realize $800,000 more for their securities than they would have had this inside information not been available to them. Stating that the defendants were "forbidden to use [such] information . . . for their own personal profit or gain", the plaintiff brought this derivative action seeking to have the defendants account to the corporation for this difference. A motion by the defendants to dismiss the complaint—pursuant to CPLR 3211 (subd. [a], par. 7)—for failure to state a cause of action was granted by the court at Special Term. The Appellate Division, with one dissent, modified Special Term's order by reinstating the complaint as to the defendants Oreamuno and Gonzalez. The appeal is before us on a certified question.

In reaching a decision in this case, we are, of course, passing only upon the sufficiency of the complaint and we necessarily accept the charges contained in that pleading as true.

It is well established, as a general proposition, that a person who acquires special knowledge or information by virtue of a confidential or fiduciary relationship with another is not free to exploit that knowledge or information for his own personal benefit but must account to his principal for any profits derived therefrom. (See, e.g., *Byrne v. Barrett,* 268 N.Y. 199.) This, in turn, is merely a corollary of the broader principle, inherent in the nature of the fiduciary relationship, that prohibits a trustee or agent from extracting secret profits from his position of trust.

In support of their claim that the complaint fails to state a cause of action, the defendants take the position that, although it is admittedly wrong for an officer or director to use his position to obtain trading profits for himself in the stock of his corporation, the action ascribed to them did not injure or damage MAI in any way. Accordingly, the defendants continue, the corporation should not be permitted to recover the proceeds. They acknowledge that, by virtue of the exclusive access which officers and directors have to inside information, they possess an unfair advantage over other shareholders and, particularly, the persons who had purchased the stock from them but, they contend, the corporation itself was unaffected and, for that reason, a derivative action is an inappropriate remedy.

It is true that the complaint before us does not contain any allegation of damages to the corporation but this has never been considered to be an essential requirement for a cause of action founded on a breach of fiduciary duty. (See, e.g., *Matter of People* [*Bond & Mtge. Guar. Co.*], 303 N.Y. 423, 431; *Wendt v. Fischer,* 243 N.Y. 439, 443; *Dutton v. Willner,* 52 N.Y. 312, 319.) This is because the function of such an action, unlike an ordinary tort or contract case, is not merely to *compensate* the plaintiff for wrongs committed by the defendant but, as this court declared many years ago (*Dutton v. Willner,* 52 N.Y. 312, 319, *supra*), "to *prevent* them, by removing from agents and trustees all inducement to attempt dealing for their own benefit in matters which they have undertaken for others, or to which their agency or trust relates." (Emphasis supplied.)

Just as a trustee has no right to retain for himself the profits yielded by property placed in his possession but must account to his beneficiaries, a corporate fiduciary, who is entrusted with potentially valuable information, may not appropriate that asset for his own use even though, in so doing, he causes no injury to the corporation. The primary concern, in a case such as this, is not to determine whether the corporation has been damaged but to decide, as between the corporation and the defendants, who has a higher claim to the proceeds derived from the exploitation of the information. In our opinion, there can be no justification for permitting officers and directors, such as the defendants, to retain for themselves profits which, it is alleged, they derived solely from exploiting information gained by virtue of their inside position as corporate officials.

In addition, it is pertinent to observe that, despite the lack of any specific allegation of damage, it may well be inferred that the defendants' actions might have caused some harm to the enterprise. Although the corporation may have little concern with the day-to-day transactions in its shares, it has a great interest in maintaining a reputation of integrity, an image of probity, for its management and in insuring the continued public acceptance and marketability of its stock. When officers and directors abuse their position in order to gain personal profits, the effect may be to cast a cloud on the corporation's name, injure stockholder relations and undermine public regard for the corporation's securities. As Presiding Justice BOTEIN aptly put it, in the course of his opinion for the Appellate

Division, "[t]he prestige and good will of a corporation, so vital to its prosperity, may be undermined by the revelation that its chief officers had been making personal profits out of corporate events which they had not disclosed to the community of stockholders." (29 A.D.2d, at p. 287.)

The defendants maintain that extending the prohibition against personal exploitation of a fiduciary relationship to officers and directors of a corporation will discourage such officials from maintaining a stake in the success of the corporate venture through share ownership, which, they urge, is an important incentive to proper performance of their duties. There is, however, a considerable difference between corporate officers who assume the same risks and obtain the same benefits as other shareholders and those who use their privileged position to gain special advantages not available to others. The sale of shares by the defendants for the reasons charged was not merely a wise investment decision which any prudent investor might have made. Rather, they were assertedly able in this case to profit solely because they had information which was not available to any one else—including the other shareholders whose interests they, as corporate fiduciaries, were bound to protect.

Although no appellate court in this State has had occasion to pass upon the precise question before us, the concept underlying the present cause of action is hardly a new one. (See, e.g., Securities Exchange Act of 1934 [48 U.S.Stat. 881], § 16[b]; U.S.Code, tit. 15, § 78p, subd. [b]; *Brophy v. Cities Serv. Co.*, 31 Del.Ch. 241; Restatement, 2d, Agency, § 388, comment *c*; Israels, A New Look at Corporate Directorship, 24 Business Lawyer 727, 732 *et seq.;* Note, 54 Cornell L.Rev. 306, 309–312.) Under Federal law (Securities Exchange Act of 1934, § 16[b]), for example, it is conclusively presumed that, when a director, officer or 10% shareholder buys and sells securities of his corporation within a six-month period, he is trading on inside information. The remedy which the Federal statute provides in that situation is precisely the same as that sought in the present case under State law, namely, an action brought by the corporation or on its behalf to recover all profits derived from the transactions.

In providing this remedy, Congress accomplished a dual purpose. It not only provided for an efficient and effective method of accomplishing its primary goal—the protection of the investing public from unfair treatment at the hands of corporate insiders—but extended to the corporation the right to secure for itself benefits derived by those insiders from their exploitation of their privileged position. The United States Court of Appeals for the Second Circuit has stated the policy behind section 16(b) in the following terms (*Adler v. Klawans*, 267 F.2d 840, 844):

"The undoubted congressional intent in the enactment of § 16(b) was to discourage what was reasonably thought to be a widespread abuse of a fiduciary relationship—specifically to discourage if not prevent three classes of persons from making private and gainful use of information acquired by them by virtue of their official relationship to a corporation."

Although the provisions of section 16(b) may not apply to all cases of trading on inside information, it demonstrates that a derivative action can be an effective method for dealing with such abuses which may be used to accomplish a similar purpose in cases not specifically covered by the statute.   In *Brophy v. Cities Serv. Co.* (31 Del.Ch. 241, *supra*), for example, the Chancery Court of Delaware allowed a similar remedy in a situation not covered by the Federal legislation.   One of the defendants in that case was an employee who had acquired inside information that the corporate plaintiff was about to enter the market and purchase its own shares. On the basis of this confidential information, the employee, who was not an officer and, hence, not liable under Federal law, bought a large block of shares and, after the corporation's purchases had caused the price to rise, resold them at a profit.   The court sustained the complaint in a derivative action brought for an accounting, stating that "[p]ublic policy will not permit an employee occupying a position of trust and confidence toward his employer to abuse that relation to his own profit, regardless of whether his employer suffers a loss" (31 Del.Ch., at p. 246).   And a similar view has been expressed in the Restatement, 2d, Agency (§ 388, comment *c*):

> "*c.   Use of confidential information.*   An agent who acquires confidential information in the course of his employment or in violation of his duties has a duty . . . to account for any profits made by the use of such information, although this does not harm the principal. . . .   So, if [a corporate officer] has 'inside' information that the corporation is about to purchase or sell securities, or to declare or to pass a dividend, profits made by him in stock transactions undertaken because of his knowledge are held in constructive trust for the principal."

In the present case, the defendants may be able to avoid liability to the corporation under section 16(b) of the Federal law since they had held the MAI shares for more than six months prior to the sales.   Nevertheless, the alleged use of the inside information to dispose of their stock at a price considerably higher than its known value constituted the same sort of "abuse of a fiduciary relationship" as is condemned by the Federal law.   Sitting as we are in this case as a court of equity, we should not hesitate to permit an action to prevent any unjust enrichment realized by the defendants from their allegedly wrongful act.

The defendants recognize that the conduct charged against them directly contravened the policy embodied in the Securities Exchange Act but, they maintain, the Federal legislation constitutes a comprehensive and carefully wrought plan for dealing with the abuse of inside information and that allowing a derivative action to be maintained under State law would interfere with the Federal scheme. Moreover, they urge, the existence of dual Federal and State remedies for the same act would create the possibility of double liability.

An examination of the Federal regulatory scheme refutes the contention that it was designed to establish any particular remedy as exclusive. In addition to the specific provisions of section 16(b), the Securities and Exchange Act contains a general anti-fraud provision in section 10(b), (U.S.Code, tit. 15, § 78j, subd. [b]) which, as implemented by rule 10b–5 (Code of Fed.Reg., tit. 17, § 240.10b–5) under that section, renders it unlawful to engage in a variety of acts considered to be fraudulent. In interpreting this rule, the Securities and Exchange Commission and the Federal courts have extended the common-law definition of fraud to include not only affirmative misrepresentations, relied upon by the purchaser or seller, but also a failure to disclose material information which might have affected the transaction. (See, e.g., *Securities & Exch. Comm. v. Texas Gulf Sulphur Co.,* 401 F.2d 833, 847–848; *Myzel v. Fields,* 386 F.2d 718, 733–735.)

Accepting the truth of the complaint's allegations, there is no question but that the defendants were guilty of withholding material information from the purchasers of the shares and, indeed, the defendants acknowledge that the facts asserted constitute a violation of rule 10b–5. The remedies which the Federal law provides for such violation, however, are rather limited. An action could be brought, in an exceptional case, by the SEC for injunctive relief. This, in fact, is what happened in the *Texas Gulf Sulphur* case (401 F.2d 833, *supra*). The purpose of such an action, however, would appear to be more to establish a principle than to provide a regular method of enforcement. A class action under the Federal rule might be a more effective remedy but the mechanics of such an action have, as far as we have been able to ascertain, not yet been worked out by the Federal courts and several questions relating thereto have never been resolved. These include the definition of the class entitled to bring such an action, the measure of damages, the administration of the fund which would be recovered and its distribution to the members of the class. (See Note, 54 Cornell L.Rev. 306, 309, *supra.*) Of course, any individual purchaser, who could prove his own injury as a result of a rule 10b–5 violation can bring an action for rescission but we have not been referred to a single case in which such an action has been successfully prosecuted where the public sale of securities is involved. The reason for this is that sales of securities, whether through a stock exchange or over-the-counter, are characteristically anonymous transactions, usually handled through brokers, and the matching of the ultimate buyer with the ultimate seller presents virtually insurmountable obstacles. Thus, unless a section 16(b) violation is also present, the Federal law does not yet provide a really effective remedy.

In view of the practical difficulties inherent in an action under the Federal law, the desirability of creating an effective common-law remedy is manifest. "Dishonest directors should not find absolution from retributive justice", Ballantine observed in his work on Corporations ([rev. ed., 1946], p. 216), "by concealing their identity from their victims under the mask of the stock exchange." There is ample room in a situation such as is here presented for a "private Attorney General" to come forward and enforce proper behavior on the part of corporate officials through the medium of the derivative action brought in the name of the corporation. (See, e.g., *Associated Ind. v. Ickes,* 134 F.2d 694, 704; *Cherner v. Transitron Electronic Corp.,* 201 F.Supp. 934, 936.) Only by sanctioning such a cause of action will there be any effective method to prevent the type of abuse of corporate office complained of in this case.

There is nothing in the Federal law which indicates that it was intended to limit the power of the States to fashion additional remedies to effectuate similar purposes. Although the impact of Federal securities regulation has on occasion been said to have created a "Federal corporation law," in fact, its effect on the duties and obligations of directors and officers and their relation to the corporation and its shareholders is only occasional and peripheral. The primary source of the law in this area ever remains that of the State which created the corporation. Indeed, Congress expressly provided against any implication that it intended to pre-empt the field by declaring, in section 28(a) of the Securities Exchange Act of 1934 (48 U.S.Code 903), that "[t]he rights and remedies provided by this title shall be in addition to any and all other rights and remedies that may exist at law or in equity".

Nor should we be deterred, in formulating a State remedy, by the defendants' claim of possible double liability. Certainly, as already indicated, if the sales in question were publicly made, the likelihood that a suit will be brought by purchasers of the shares is quite remote. But, even if it were not, the mere possibility of such a suit is not a defense nor does it render the complaint insufficient. It is not unusual for an action to be brought to recover a fund which may be subject to a superior claim by a third party. If that be the situation, a defendant should not be permitted to retain the fund for his own use on the chance that such a party may eventually appear. A defendant's course, if he wishes to protect himself against double liability, is to interplead any and all possible claimants and bind them to the judgment (CPLR 1006, subd. [b]).

In any event, though, no suggestion has been made either in brief or on oral argument that any purchaser has come forward with a claim against the defendants or even that anyone is in a position to advance such a claim.[1] As we have stated, the defendants' assertion that such a party may come forward at some future date is not a basis for permitting them to retain for their own benefit the fruits of their allegedly wrongful acts. For all that appears, the present derivative action is the only effective remedy now available against the abuse by these defendants of their privileged position.

---

1. In the absence of any such appearance by adverse claimants, we need not now decide whether the corporation's recovery would be affected by any amounts which might have to be refunded by the defendant to the injured purchasers.

As we have previously indicated, what we have written must be read in the light of the charges contained in the complaint, and it must be borne in mind that "it will be incumbent upon the plaintiff, if he is to succeed, to prove upon the trial the truth and correctness of his allegations." (*Walkovszky v. Carlton,* 23 N.Y.2d 714, 715.)

The order appealed from should be affirmed, with costs, and the question certified answered in the affirmative.

Judges BURKE, SCILEPPI, BERGAN, KEATING, BREITEL and JASEN concur.

Order affirmed, etc.

————

Accord: Brophy v. Cities Service Co., 31 Del.Ch. 241, 70 A.2d 5 (1949). See also Carpenter v. United States, 484 U.S. 19, 108 S.Ct. 316, 98 L.Ed.2d 275 (1987), supra, p. 618; Thomas v. Roblin Indus., Inc., 520 F.2d 1393, 1397 (3d Cir.1975); In re ORFA Securities Litigation, 654 F.Supp. 1449 (D.N.J.1987). Contra: Freeman v. Decio, 584 F.2d 186 (7th Cir.1978); Schein v. Chasen, 313 So.2d 739 (Fla.1975).

Chapter X

SHAREHOLDER SUITS

SECTION 1. INTRODUCTION

BACKGROUND NOTE

If the duties of care and loyalty that managers owe to their corporations could be enforced only in suits by the corporation, many wrongs done by managers would never be remedied. Where a majority of the corporation's shareholders benefit by the managers' breach of duty, they will normally continue to elect either the same managers or others who can be relied on not to institute litigation designed to remedy the wrong. Even where a majority of the shareholders do not benefit by the managers' wrongdoing, in publicly held corporations the difficulty of organizing the shareholders to oust the wrongdoers from office, and elect new directors who will bring suit against their predecessors, is often insuperable. To overcome these obstacles and hold wrongdoing managers and controlling shareholders to account, the law permits shareholders to bring suit on the corporation's behalf.

In Ross v. Bernhard, 396 U.S. 531, 534–35, 90 S.Ct. 733, 735–6, 24 L.Ed.2d 729 (1970), the Supreme Court sketched the background and nature of such suits in the following terms:

The common law refused . . . to permit stockholders to call corporate managers to account in actions at law. The possibilities for abuse, thus presented, were not ignored by corporate officers and directors. Early in the 19th century, equity provided relief both in this country and in England. Without detailing these developments, it suffices to say that the remedy in this country, first dealt with by this Court in Dodge v. Woolsey, 18 How. 331 (1856), provided redress not only against faithless officers and directors but also against third parties who had damaged or threatened the corporate properties and whom the corporation through its managers refused to pursue. The remedy made available in equity was the derivative suit, viewed in this country as a suit to enforce a *corporate* cause of action against officers, directors, and third parties. As elaborated in the cases, one precondition for the suit was a valid claim on which the corporation could have sued; another was that the corporation itself had refused to proceed after suitable demand, unless excused by extraordinary conditions. Thus the dual

653

nature of the stockholder's action: first, the plaintiff's right to sue on behalf of the corporation and, second, the merits of the corporation's claim itself.

This type of suit is commonly known as a derivative action, since the shareholder's right to bring the suit derives from the corporation.

Two features of the derivative action warrant highlighting at the outset. First is the extraordinary procedural complexity inherent in such actions—complexity involving, for example, proper parties and their alignment, jurisdiction, demand on the board, demand on the shareholders, right to sue, intervention, settlement, and dismissal. Second is the difficult problem of social policy raised by such actions, particularly in the publicly held corporation. Through the derivative action, a shareholder with a tiny investment can force an expenditure by the corporation of a large amount of funds and executive time. The question is whether the overall benefits of such actions justify their overall costs, which are, in effect, borne involuntarily by the noncomplaining shareholders.

Many or most of the issues to be considered in this chapter, although couched in technical terms, reflect an underlying tension between a concern that managers be held accountable for their wrongdoing, on the one hand, and a concern with the strike-suit potential of derivative actions, on the other. Emphasis on the former element leads to liberality in permitting derivative actions; emphasis on the latter leads to rules that restrict their maintenance. In weighing these concerns, it should be borne in mind that the derivative action and the disclosure requirements of the securities acts constitute the two major legal bulwarks against managerial self-dealing. In considering the various rules taken up in this chapter, it is therefore critical to evaluate the extent to which each rule cuts into the effectiveness of the derivative action, and whether the benefits of the rule justify that cost.

It should also be kept in mind, while considering the problems raised in this chapter, that significant substantive consequences often turn on the success of a motion to dismiss a derivative action on procedural grounds. If the plaintiff can survive such a motion, the facts that he already knows together with the material that he can develop through discovery will often lead to a quick and substantial settlement. If the defendant can get the case dismissed on procedural grounds, however, no other plaintiff may come forward—either because no other shareholder who would bring suit knows all the relevant facts, or because the statute of limitations has run. For practical purposes, then, many derivative actions will be won or lost on the basis of procedural motions that do not go to the merits of the case.

———

FEDERAL RULES OF CIVIL PROCEDURE, RULE 11

[See Statutory Supplement]

———

**AMERICAN LAW INSTITUTE, PRINCIPLES
OF CORPORATE GOVERNANCE
§§ 7.04(a)(1), (b), (d)**

[See Statutory Supplement]

———

NOTE ON WHO CAN BRING A DERIVATIVE ACTION

1.   It is generally agreed that the plaintiff in a derivative action must be a shareholder at the time the action is begun,[1] and must remain a shareholder during the pendency of the action.[2]   What constitutes shareholdership for derivative-action purposes?   In a few states, a statute or rule speaks to the issue directly.   For example, N.Y.Bus.Corp.Law § 626(a) provides that the plaintiff in a derivative suit must be "a holder of shares or of voting trust certificates . . . or of a beneficial interest in such shares or certificates."

Where the statute is silent, courts normally define shareholdership in a very expansive manner.   First, record ownership is generally not required; an unregistered shareholder will qualify.   Rosenthal v. Burry Biscuit Corp., 30 Del.Ch. 299, 60 A.2d 106 (Ch.1948), noted in 17 U.Chi.L.Rev. 194 (1949); H.F.G. Co. v. Pioneer Pub. Co., 162 F.2d 536 (7th Cir.1947); Gallup v. Caldwell, 120 F.2d 90 (3d Cir.1941).   Second, legal ownership is not required—equitable ownership suffices.   The latter category has been held to include, among others, an owner of stock held by a broker in a margin account in the broker's street name, a pledgee, the beneficiary of a trust, a legatee, a surviving widow with a community interest in stock held in her husband's name, and a person who has contracted to purchase stock.

It is also established that in an appropriate case a shareholder in a parent corporation can bring a derivative action on behalf of a subsidiary, despite the fact that he is not a shareholder in the subsidiary.   See Painter, Double Derivative Suits and Other Remedies With Regard to Damaged Subsidiaries, 36 Ind.L.J. 143, 147–49 (1961); Note, Suits by a Shareholder in a Parent Corporation to Redress Injuries to the Subsidiary, 64 Harv.L.Rev. 1313 (1951).

---

1. See deHaas v. Empire Petroleum Co., 435 F.2d 1223 (10th Cir.1970); Werfel v. Kramarsky, 61 F.R.D. 674 (S.D.N.Y.1974); Vista Fund v. Garis, 277 N.W.2d 19 (Minn. 1979).

2. See Schilling v. Belcher, 582 F.2d 995 (5th Cir.1978); Tryforos v. Icarian Develop. Co., 518 F.2d 1258 (7th Cir.1975), cert. denied 423 U.S. 1091, 96 S.Ct. 887, 47 L.Ed.2d 103 (1976).

2.   An implication from the rule that the plaintiff in a derivative action must be a shareholder at the time he brings suit is that a creditor (including a bondholder) ordinarily has no right to bring a derivative action.   Dodge v. First Wisconsin Trust Co., 394 F.Supp. 1124 (E.D.Wis.1975);   Brooks v. Weiser, 57 F.R.D. 491 (S.D.N.Y. 1972);   Dorfman v. Chemical Bank, 56 F.R.D. 363 (S.D.N.Y.1972).[3] Compare Hoff v. Sprayregan, 52 F.R.D. 243 (S.D.N.Y.1971) (holder of a convertible bond is a shareholder for derivative-action purposes) with Harff v. Kerkorian, 324 A.2d 215 (Del.Ch.1974), aff'd in pertinent part 347 A.2d 133 (Del.1975) (contra).   However, if a corporation is insolvent in fact, the directors owe fiduciary duties to the creditors, whether or not there has been a statutory filing under bankruptcy law.   See Geyer v. Ingersoll Publications Co., 621 A.2d 784 (Del.Ch.1992).   Presumably, therefore, creditors could bring an action against directors for violation of those duties.   Moreover, in Credit Lyonnais Bank Nederland, N.V. v. Pathe Communications Corp., 1991 WL 277613 (Del.Ch.1991), Chancellor Allen stated that "At least where a corporation is operating *in the vicinity* of bankruptcy, a board of directors is not merely the agent of the [shareholders], but owes its duty to the corporate enterprise."   (Emphasis added.)   And in Francis v. United Jersey Bank, p. 379, supra, the court stated that in the case of certain corporations and certain kinds of creditors, directors owed a duty to creditors even while the corporation was solvent.   The court singled out bank depositors and persons for whom a corporation holds money in trust.

3.   Occasionally a statute gives an officer or director the right to bring a derivative action.   See N.Y.Bus.Corp.Law § 720(b).

NOTE ON THE CORPORATION AS AN INDISPENSABLE PARTY

It is well established that the corporation is an indispensable party to a derivative action:

> If the defendants account, it must be to the corporation and not to the shareholders.   As to the defendants charged with

---

3.   Furthermore, some modern cases have either allowed a derivative action by a creditor without discussion, see Devereux v. Berger, 264 Md. 20, 284 A.2d 605 (1971), or have indicated in dicta that such an action would be allowed, see Capitol Wine & Spirit v. Pokrass, 277 App.Div. 184, 98 N.Y.S.2d 291 (1950), aff'd 302 N.Y. 734, 98 N.E.2d 704 (1951).

Also, a creditor who cannot bring a derivative action may nevertheless be able to bring a direct suit against an officer or director through some other mechanism. For example, a statute may permit direct suit by a creditor against an officer or director in certain defined cases, such as misappropriation of corporate assets. If a corporation is insolvent, its receiver or trustee-

in-bankruptcy can pursue a corporate cause of action against officers or directors on the creditors' behalf. (Such a suit is not derivative, since the receiver or trustee is vested with power to manage the corporation's affairs. However, where the receiver or trustee fails to bring such a suit a creditor may be able to bring it on the corporation's behalf if he is given permission to do so by a court with jurisdiction over the insolvent corporation's affairs.) See generally Note, Creditors' Derivative Suits on Behalf of Solvent Corporations, 88 Yale L.J. 1299 (1979).

If the corporation is in receivership, a shareholder may also need permission of the supervising court to bring suit. See Fields v. Fidelity General Ins. Co., 454 F.2d 682, 685 (7th Cir.1971).

defrauding it, the corporation is an indispensable party.... Furthermore, the decree must protect the defendants against any further suit by the corporation, and this will not be true unless it properly be made a party to the action.... The usual American practice is to name the beneficiary corporation as a party defendant, although in substance it is a party plaintiff; the flexibility of equity procedure permits an affirmative judgment to be entered in favor of one defendant against other defendants.

Dean v. Kellogg, 294 Mich. 200, 207–08, 292 N.W. 704, 707–08 (1940).

SECTION 2.   THE NATURE OF THE DERIVATIVE ACTION

SAX v. WORLD WIDE PRESS, INC.

United States Court of Appeals, Ninth Circuit, 1987.
809 F.2d 610.

Before NELSON, HALL and KOZINSKI, Circuit Judges.

NELSON, Circuit Judge:

Arnold J. Sax appeals the district court's dismissal of his amended complaint in a diversity action. The district court concluded that Sax's claims for damages stated a derivative cause of action under Montana law and that he had failed to comply with Fed.R.Civ.P. 23.1.... Sax contends that the counts seeking damages state grounds for a direct shareholder action because they allege conduct by the defendants that injured Sax personally.... We disagree. Accordingly, we affirm the district court's dismissal of Sax's amended complaint.

FACTS

World Wide, a Montana corporation, manufactures and markets punchboards and other gambling supplies and equipment. The individual defendants own more than half of the stock of World Wide. In 1972, World Wide hired Sax as its general manager for the purpose of creating a plant at Great Falls, Montana. The oral employment agreement gave Sax an option to purchase up to 75,000 shares of stock in World Wide. After Sax successfully started the business and had acquired approximately 5% of World Wide's outstanding stock, World Wide allegedly breached the option agreement by refusing to sell him further stock. Sax terminated his employment on June 30, 1976.

After he terminated his employment, Sax alleges that the individual defendants conspired to deplete World Wide's assets and depreciate the value of his stock, which "deprived [him] of income consisting of the going rate of interest of the value of his stock." He claims that the members of the conspiracy illegally sold punchboards and kept inadequate records of inventory. He also alleges that the conspirators diverted World Wide's assets to their own use by selling punchboards to their corporation, Instant Ticket Factory, Inc., at less than fair market value, by causing World Wide to make unsecured loans to themselves, and by using World Wide assets to secure personal investments. Furthermore, Sax claims that the conspirators published false and fraudulent annual statements concealing their personal interests and conflicts of interest.

On December 3, 1983, Sax filed a complaint as an individual shareholder seeking compensation for actual and punitive damages caused by the alleged wrongful conduct of the conspiracy. . . . In response to the defendants' motions, the district court struck Sax's claims for actual and punitive damages under Fed.R.Civ.P. 12(f) . . . .

Sax filed an amended complaint in an attempt to comply with the district court's opinion and order. On July 19, 1985, the district court withdrew its earlier opinion and dismissed the counts seeking damages in the amended complaint on the ground that the claims stated a derivative cause of action and that Sax had failed to comply with Fed.R.Civ.P. 23.1. It reasoned that the alleged wrongful acts of the defendants did not injure Sax personally but rather damaged World Wide and that therefore the action must be brought derivatively. . . . Accordingly, the district court dismissed Sax's complaint.

DISCUSSION

I. *Standard of Review*

We review de novo a dismissal for failure to state a claim pursuant to Fed.R.Civ.P. 12(b)(6).[1] . . .

II. *The Claims for Damages*

In diversity actions, the characterization of an action as derivative or direct is a question of state law. C. Wright, A. Miller & M. Kane, *Federal Practice and Procedure* § 1821 (2d ed. 1986); *see Lewis v. Chiles,* 719 F.2d 1044, 1048–49 (9th Cir.1983) (citing state law in diversity action to determine the nature of the appropriate cause of action). Once state law characterizes the action as either derivative or direct, the applicable procedural rules are determined by federal law. *Gadd v. Pearson,* 351 F.Supp. 895, 900 (M.D.Fla. 1972); *see Hanna v. Plumer,* 380 U.S. 460, 464–74, 85 S.Ct. 1136, 1140–45, 14 L.Ed.2d 8 (1965) . . . . In federal courts, derivative suits are subject to the procedural requirements of Fed.R.Civ.P. 23.1. . . . Rule 23.1 governs derivative actions " 'to enforce a right of a corporation' when the corporation itself 'failed to enforce a right which may properly be asserted by it' in court." *Daily Income*

---

1. The district court dismissed Sax's complaint for failure to comply with Fed. R.Civ.P. 23.1. We interpret this decision as a dismissal for failure to state a claim under Fed.R.Civ.P. 12(b)(6).

Fund, Inc. v. Fox, 464 U.S. 523, 533–34, 104 S.Ct. 831, 836–37, 78 L.Ed.2d 645 (1984) (quoting Fed.R.Civ.P. 23.1).

Under Montana law, a shareholder can enforce a corporate right in a derivative action if certain conditions are met. Mont. R.Civ.P. 23.1; *see S–W Co. v. John Wight, Inc.,* 179 Mont. 392, 402–03, 587 P.2d 348, 354 (1978). As a general rule, an action enforces a corporate right "if the gravamen of the complaint is injury to the corporation, or to the whole body of its stock or property without any severance or distribution among individual holders." 12B W. Fletcher, *Cyclopedia of the Law of Private Corporations,* § 5911 (rev. perm. ed. 1984).... Therefore, if the corporate wrong decreases the value of the corporation's stock, it does not necessarily create a direct cause of action for shareholders. *Lewis,* 719 F.2d at 1049 (applying Oregon law); W. Fletcher, *supra,* § 5913; Annot., 167 A.L.R. 279, 280 (1947). The general rule that a shareholder cannot enforce corporate rights in a direct action applies to actions arising out of either contract or tort law. *Schaffer v. Universal Rundle Corp.,* 397 F.2d 893, 896 (5th Cir.1968) (applying Texas law). A direct action can be brought either when there is a special duty, such as a contractual duty, between the wrongdoer and the shareholder, or when the shareholder suffers injury separate and distinct from that suffered by other shareholders. W. Fletcher, *supra,* § 5911; *see Schaffer,* 397 F.2d at 896.

Sax argues that the district court improperly dismissed the damage counts of his amended complaint. He contends that he has an individual cause of action to which Rule 23.1 does not apply because he "gave up his prior job in Indiana, moved to Montana, successfully started World Wide, was refused his contractual right to purchase additional stock and therefore resigned," and because he was unable to sell his stock as a result of the defendants' actions. He cites *Jones v. H.F. Ahmanson & Co.,* 1 Cal.3d 93, 460 P.2d 464, 81 Cal.Rptr. 592 (1969) and *Davis v. Ben O'Callaghan Co.,* 238 Ga. 218, 232 S.E.2d 53 (1977), as support for the argument that he has stated grounds for a direct action. We disagree. The damages sought by Sax for the loss of interest income on his stock investment are incidental to injuries to World Wide and, therefore, are not injuries to Sax personally. *See* W. Fletcher, *supra* p. 6, at § 5913; Annot., 167 A.L.R. 279, 280 (1947).

Sax alleges that the conspiracy depleted World Wide's assets through corporate mismanagement and diversion of corporate assets. These actions are injuries to the corporation. *See* W. Fletcher, *supra* p. 6, at § 5913. Even if the defendants depleted World Wide's assets with the sole purpose of decreasing the value of Sax's stock and destroying his return on his investment, the action would nonetheless be derivative. *See id.*

Sax attempts to invoke the exception to the general rule that actions to redress corporate injuries must be brought derivatively by establishing that his employment contract with World Wide created a special duty between himself and the defendants. However, the employment relationship is irrelevant to the gravamen of Sax's complaint. The acts that allegedly caused Sax's damages occurred after Sax terminated his employment with World Wide and are unrelated to the defendants' breach of the employment agreement. Indeed, Sax does not request damages for World Wide's refusal to sell him the promised stock; rather, the alleged damages are based on the unmarketability of his stock as a result of the defendants' actions. This is an injury suffered by all of World Wide's shareholders and not by Sax alone. Therefore, the injury is incidental to injuries to World Wide and is not an injury to Sax personally. . . .

Sax cites *Jones v. H.F. Ahmanson & Co.* as support for his contention that he can bring a direct action under Montana law. This case is distinguishable. In *Jones,* the majority shareholders of a closely held corporation contributed their shares to a new corporation in exchange for stock. They sold a portion of their shares in the new corporation for a considerable profit. As a result, the value of the minority shareholders' stock in the close corporation fell. The California Supreme Court permitted the class of minority shareholders to bring a direct action. Unlike the present case, however, the minority shareholders in *Jones* were excluded from participating in the new corporation and, therefore, were uniquely injured by the acts of the majority shareholders. Moreover, because the majority shareholders were merely selling their stock at a profit, they probably breached no fiduciary duty to the corporation. Therefore, unlike the present case, it is questionable whether the corporation could have collected damages in a derivative suit.

Sax also argues that he should be permitted to bring a direct action on the grounds that the defendants control the corporation and that a derivative action would place any judgment into the corporate treasury and therefore under the defendants' control. *See Davis,* 238 Ga. at 222, 232 S.E.2d at 56; *Thomas v. Dickson,* 162 Ga.App. 569, 571, 291 S.E.2d 747, 749 (1982), *aff'd,* 250 Ga. 772, 301 S.E.2d 49 (1983); W. Fletcher, *supra* p. 6, at § 5911. Although some jurisdictions recognize this exception, it is an undecided question in Montana courts. However, the official comment in the annotations to Mont.Code Ann. § 35-1-514 states that "[t]he need for the derivative remedy is *best* illustrated when those in control of the corporation are the alleged wrongdoers." (emphasis added). Moreover, we believe that the strong policy in favor of preventing unnecessary litigation countenances against recognizing such an exception in the case of suits brought individually by shareholders.[2] Otherwise, there would be as many suits as there were shareholders in the corporation. *See* 4 D. Dowling, Mont. Code Annotated (Annotations) 66–67 (1986) ("Redress in the form of a separate suit by each individual shareholder whenever the value of his shares is impaired by a wrong to the corporation would result

---

2. In a direct action brought by injured shareholders as a class, there would be no unnecessary litigation and this policy concern would not arise. However, we need not decide whether this exception would have applied had Sax brought the suit as a class action.

in unnecessary ·multiplicity of actions.''). Therefore, we refrain from recognizing this exception under the facts of this case. Accordingly, we affirm the district court's dismissal of the damage counts of Sax's complaint because they state a derivative cause of action and Sax failed to comply with the requirements of Fed. R.Civ.P. 23.1. . . .

For the reasons above, the district court's dismissal of Sax's complaint is AFFIRMED.

––––––––

EISENBERG v. FLYING TIGER LINE, INC., 451 F.2d 267 (2d Cir.1971). "In this action, Eisenberg is seeking to overturn a reorganization and merger which Flying Tiger effected in 1969. He charges that a series of corporate maneuvers were intended to dilute his voting rights. In order to achieve this end, he alleges, Flying Tiger in July 1969 organized a wholly owned Delaware subsidiary, the Flying Tiger Corporation ('FTC'). In August, FTC in turn organized a wholly owned subsidiary, FTL Air Freight Corporation ('FTL'). The three Delaware corporations then entered into a plan of reorganization, subject to stockholder approval, by which Flying Tiger merged into FTL and only FTL survived. . . .

["Flying Tiger pleaded several affirmative defenses and moved for an order to require Eisenberg to comply with New York Business Corporation Law § 627 (McKinney's Consol. Laws, c. 4, 1963), which requires a plaintiff suing derivatively on behalf of a corporation to post security for the corporation's costs. Judge Travia granted the motion without opinion and afforded Eisenberg thirty days to post security in the sum of $35,000. Eisenberg did not comply, his action was dismissed and he appeals. We find Eisenberg's cause of action to be personal and not derivative within the meaning of § 627. We therefore reverse the dismissal."] *

". . . [A]ctions to compel the dissolution of a corporation have been held representative, since the corporation could not possibly benefit therefrom. Fontheim v. Walker, 141 N.Y.S.2d 62 (Sup.Ct. 1955); Davidson v. Rabinowitz, supra. . . . And . . . an action by a stockholder complaining that a proposed recapitalization would unfairly benefit holders of another class of stock was representative. . . . Professor Moore instructs that 'where a shareholder sues on behalf of himself and all others similarly situated to * * * enjoin a proposed merger or consolidation * * * he is not enforcing a derivative right; he is, by an appropriate type of class suit enforcing a right common to all the shareholders which runs against the corporation.'

"Eisenberg's position is even stronger than it would be in the ordinary merger case. In routine merger circumstances the stockholders retain a voice in the operation of the company, albeit a corporation other than their original choice. Here, however, the

* This paragraph is transposed. (Footnote by ed.)

reorganization deprived him and other minority stockholders of any voice in the affairs of their previously existing operating company. . . .

"Reversed."

———

NOTE ON THE DISTINCTION BETWEEN DERIVATIVE AND DIRECT ACTIONS

1. Two kinds of reasons are commonly advanced for distinguishing between a *derivative* action, which is brought on the corporation's behalf against either corporate fiduciaries or third persons, and a *direct* action, which is brought on a shareholder's own behalf against either corporate fiduciaries or the corporation itself. The first kind of reason is theoretical: Since a corporation is a legal person separate from its shareholders, an injury to the corporation is not an injury to its shareholders. This proposition is somewhat dubious, since every injury to a corporation must also have an impact, however slight, on the shareholders as well. The second kind of reason is pragmatic: "(1) To avoid a multiplicity of suits by each injured shareholder, (2) to protect the corporate creditors, and (3) to protect all the stockholders since a corporate recovery benefits all equally." Watson v. Button, 235 F.2d 235 (9th Cir. 1965).

2. Some principles concerning the distinction between derivative and direct actions are relatively well-established. At one end of the spectrum, a wrongful act that depletes or destroys corporate assets, and affects the shareholder only by reducing the value of his stock, gives rise only to an action on the corporation's behalf. At the other end, a wrongful act that does not deplete or divert corporate assets, and interferes with rights that are traditionally viewed as either incident to the ownership of stock or inhering in the shares themselves (such as voting or pre-emptive rights), gives rise only to a direct action by the injured shareholders. Thus in Reifsnyder v. Pittsburgh Outdoor Advertising Co., 405 Pa. 142, 173 A.2d 319 (1961), Reifsnyder had brought suit attacking a transaction in which Pittsburgh Outdoor Advertising, acting pursuant to a shareholder resolution, had purchased all the Pittsburgh stock owned by General (Pittsburgh's largest shareholder), and had increased its indebtedness to finance the purchase. Reifsnyder's theories were that (i) the transaction was accomplished only by the vote of General, acting in its shareholder capacity, and General's shares were not entitled to vote on the resolution because of its self-interest; and (ii) the price paid by Pittsburgh for General's shares was excessive. The court held the suit was direct, not derivative. If the complaint had been limited to the excessive-price theory, the court said, the action may have been deemed derivative. However, the gravamen of the complaint concerned the right of a majority shareholder to vote on a resolution in which it had a personal

pecuniary interest, and this theory gave rise to a direct action. "If it should become a rule of law that a shareholder cannot vote on matters in which he has an interest, an aggrieved shareholder would necessarily be permitted to bring an action to enjoin the voting of 'interested' shares or to require the corporate officers to rescind action taken in reliance upon the votes of such shares. The aggrieved shareholder in those instances would, in essence, be preventing the dilution of his own votes by challenging and disqualifying improper votes. The right to vote is basic and fundamental to most shares of stock and is independent of any right that the corporate entity possesses and the shareholder could enforce and protect such rights by bringing a direct action." [1]

3. Many kinds of cases fall between the two ends of the spectrum described in the preceding paragraph. In some of these cases, the rules are relatively clear; in others, rules are just beginning to emerge. For example, it is relatively clear that a direct action will lie based on the issuance of stock for the wrongful purpose of perpetuating or shifting control (e.g., Sheppard v. Wilcox, 210 Cal.App.2d 53, 26 Cal.Rptr. 412 (1962)), or to enjoin a threatened ultra vires act (e.g., Alexander v. Atlanta & West Point R.R., 113 Ga. 193, 38 S.E. 772 (1901)). A rule permitting a direct action seems to be emerging in suits based on wrongs by controlling against noncontrolling shareholders (e.g., Jones v. H.F. Ahmanson & Co., p. 766, supra. Suits to enjoin improperly authorized corporate actions are also commonly treated as direct actions, either implicitly (that is, without discussion of the issue), or explicitly, but the authorities are in conflict on this type of case. See G. Hornstein, 2 Corporation Law and Practice § 627 (1959).

4. In many cases a wrongful act both depletes corporate assets *and* interferes with rights traditionally viewed as inhering in shares. The general principle governing such cases is that a direct action is not precluded simply because the same facts could also give rise to a derivative action. A recent illustration is Snyder v. Epstein, 290 F.Supp. 652, 655 (E.D.Wis.1968), where the court held that "[t]he sale of a corporate office gives rise to a cause of action for breach . . . of the fiduciary duties owed to both the corporation and the stockholders." Similarly, in Bennett v. Breuil Petroleum Corp., 34 Del.Ch. 6, 99 A.2d 236 (1953), the plaintiff claimed that the controlling shareholders had caused the corporation to issue stock for an improper purpose (impairing his interest and forcing him out on management's terms), and at a grossly inadequate consideration.

---

1. In Knapp v. Bankers Securities Corp., 230 F.2d 717, 721 (3d Cir.1956), the Third Circuit held that as a matter of Pennsylvania law "[t]he right to dividends is an incident of the ownership of stock," so that a suit to compel the declaration of dividends lies as a direct action. The New York Court of Appeals had earlier reached a different result in Gordon v. Elliman, 306 N.Y. 456, 119 N.E.2d 331 (1954), but as the opinion in *Flying Tiger* points out, that decision was widely criticized and the rule it handed down was eventually reversed by the New York legislature. See also Bokat v. Getty Oil Co., 262 A.2d 246 (Del.1970).

The court held that the first claim stated a direct and the second a derivative cause of action.[2]

Another important kind of case in which suit may be either direct or derivative is that involving proxy-rule violations. Insofar as such a violation interferes with the individual shareholder's voting right, suit can be regarded as direct; insofar as it involves a breach of management's fiduciary obligations, suit can be regarded as derivative.

AMERICAN LAW INSTITUTE, PRINCIPLES OF CORPORATE GOVERNANCE § 7.01

[See Statutory Supplement]

SECTION 3.   INDIVIDUAL RECOVERY IN DERIVATIVE ACTIONS

GLENN v. HOTELTRON SYSTEMS, INC.

Court of Appeals of New York, 1989.
74 N.Y.2d 386, 547 N.Y.S.2d 816, 547 N.E.2d 71.

WACHTLER, Chief Judge. . . .

The dispute here is between Jacob Schachter and Herbert Kulik, the founders of Ketek Electric Corporation. Schachter and Kulik each own 50% of the corporation's shares and serve as the corporation's only officers. . . . [T]he Appellate Division, on [a] prior appeal, found Schachter liable for diverting Ketek assets and opportunities to Hoteltron Systems, Inc., a corporation wholly owned by Schachter.

Following the trial on damages, Supreme Court concluded that Hoteltron had earned profits of $362,242.84 from Schachter's usurpation of Ketek assets and opportunities. . . .

On Schachter's appeal, the Appellate Division . . . concluded that the Hoteltron profits should be awarded to the injured corporation, Ketek, rather than the innocent shareholder Kulik. . . .

----

2. See also, e.g., Buschmann v. Professional Men's Ass'n, 405 F.2d 659 (7th Cir. 1969). In General Rubber Co. v. Benedict, 215 N.Y. 18, 109 N.E. 96 (1915), a parent corporation sued one of its directors for acquiescing in the looting of a subsidiary, thereby injuring the parent by reducing the value of its shares in the subsidiary. The court held that the complaint stated a good cause of action. In answer to the argument that recovery would subject the defendant to double liability, the court said: (1) the subsidiary might not have a cause of action, since the defendant was not its director and would be liable to it only if he participated in—rather than merely failed to prevent—the wrong; and (2) the possibility that the subsidiary had an enforceable cause of action should be taken into consideration in determining the extent to which the value of the parent's shares had been depreciated. Cf. In re Auditore's Will, 249 N.Y. 335, 164 N.E. 242 (1928).

It is the general rule that, because a shareholders' derivative suit seeks to vindicate a wrong done to the corporation through enforcement of a corporate cause of action, any recovery obtained is for the benefit of the injured corporation. . . .

Kulik argues that this result is inequitable because Schachter, as a shareholder of Ketek, will ultimately share in the proceeds of the damage award. But that prospect exists in any successful derivative action in which the wrongdoer is a shareholder of the injured corporation. An exception based on that fact alone would effectively nullify the general rule that damages for a corporate injury should be awarded to the corporation.

It is true that this anomaly is magnified in cases involving closely held corporations, because the errant fiduciary is likely to own a large share of the corporation—as Schachter owns 50% of Ketek—and will share proportionately in the restitution to the corporation generated by a successful suit against him. Thus, it may be argued that in such circumstances an award of damages to the corporation does not provide a sufficient deterrent to the potential wrongdoer. We conclude, however, that this consideration does not require a different damage rule for close corporations.

While awarding damages directly to the innocent shareholder may seem equitable with respect to the parties before the court, other interests, particularly those of the corporation's creditors, should not be overlooked. The fruits of a diverted corporate opportunity are properly a corporate asset. Awarding that asset directly to a shareholder could impair the rights of creditors whose claims may be superior to that of the innocent shareholder. . . .

Thus, while we do not rule out the possibility that an award to innocent shareholders rather than to the corporation would be appropriate in some circumstances, we find no need to invoke such an exception here.

Accordingly, the order of the Appellate Division should be affirmed, without costs.

SIMONS, KAYE, ALEXANDER, TITONE, HANCOCK and BELLACOSA, JJ., concur.

Order affirmed, without costs.

———

PERLMAN v. FELDMANN

United States Court of Appeals, Second Circuit, 1955.
219 F.2d 173.

Page 527, supra.

———

NOTE ON INDIVIDUAL RECOVERY IN DERIVATIVE ACTIONS

1. It is frequently said that pro rata recovery may be decreed to prevent the wrongdoers from sharing in the recovery. See, e.g., Atkinson v. Marquart, 112 Ariz. 304, 541 P.2d 556 (1975). However, in most derivative actions the defendants own stock in the corporation, and this in itself seldom leads to pro rata recovery. Nor should it, in the typical case. For example, suppose D, the owner of forty percent of Blue Corporation, is found liable in a derivative suit in the amount of $1 million. If corporate recovery is decreed, D must pay Blue $1 million. Since D "shares" in the recovery, his net output is only $600,000 (assuming that he can recover the balance through a dividend or appreciation in the value of his stock). But if pro rata recovery is decreed, D's output will also be $600,000. Indeed, for reasons of liquidity D may very well prefer the pro rata alternative. The fact that D "shares" in a corporate recovery is therefore not sufficient in itself to justify pro rata relief.

2. Similarly, it is sometimes said that pro rata recovery is appropriate where the wrongdoers are still in control of the corporation, and therefore would control any corporate recovery. See Backus v. Finkelstein, 23 F.2d 357, 366 (D.C.Minn.1927); Note, 69 Harv.L.Rev. 1314, at 1314–16 (1956). However, derivative actions in situations where the wrongdoers still control the corporation are legion, and pro rata recovery will normally not be decreed on this ground alone.

3. The cases suggest that pro rata relief will be decreed where the great bulk of the corporation's shares are held by persons who could not themselves have brought suit because they are subject to a personal defense. For example, in Young v. Columbia Oil Co., 110 W.Va. 364, 158 S.E. 678 (1931), pro rata recovery was decreed where thirteen of sixteen shareholders were barred by laches or acquiescence, and the remaining three shareholders owned only 145 of the corporation's 5000 outstanding shares. In Joyce v. Congdon, 114 Wash. 239, 195 P. 29 (1921), pro rata recovery was decreed where 423 out of the corporation's 429 shares were owned by either the wrongdoers, persons alleged by the plaintiff to be in collusion with the wrongdoers, or persons who had acquired their stock from the wrongdoers. In Chounis v. Laing, 125 W.Va. 275, 23 S.E.2d 628 (1942), more than ninety-five percent of the shareholders had either ratified or participated in the defendant's wrongful actions. The court held that the ratification was not effective as against innocent minority shareholders, but decreed pro rata relief, excluding all those shareholders who had either participated or ratified. See also, e.g., May v. Midwest Refining Co., 121 F.2d 431 (1st Cir.1941), cert. denied 314 U.S. 668, 62 S.Ct. 129, 86 L.Ed. 534, noted, 30 Calif.L.Rev. 338 (1942).

4. Still another type of case in which pro rata recovery may be decreed is that in which Corporation A, against whom a wrong was

committed, is merged into Corporation B, and some or all of B's shareholders are barred from bringing a derivative suit—for example, because they had all participated in the wrong. In Gabhart v. Gabhart, 267 Ind. 370, 370 N.E.2d 345 (1977) the court said that in such cases, "[s]ince no wrong should be without a remedy a Court of Equity may grant relief, pro-rata, to a former shareholder of a merged corporation, whose equity was adversely affected by the fraudulent act of an officer or director and whose means of redress otherwise would be cut off by the merger, if there is no shareholder of the surviving corporation eligible to maintain a derivative action for such wrong and said shareholder had no prior opportunity for redress by derivative action against either the merged or the surviving corporation." Cf. Bokat v. Getty Oil Co., 262 A.2d 246 (Del. 1970).

_____

SECTION 4. THE CONTEMPORANEOUS–OWNERSHIP RULE

_____

FEDERAL RULES OF CIVIL PROCEDURE, RULE 23.1

[See Statutory Supplement]

_____

DELAWARE GEN. CORP. LAW § 327

[See Statutory Supplement]

_____

REV. MODEL BUS. CORP. ACT § 7.41

[See Statutory Supplement]

_____

N.Y. BUS. CORP. LAW § 626

[See Statutory Supplement]

_____

CAL. CORP. CODE § 800(b)(1)

[See Statutory Supplement]

_____

ALI, PRINCIPLES OF CORPORATE GOVERNANCE § 7.03(a)

[See Statutory Supplement]

BANGOR PUNTA OPERATIONS, INC. v. BANGOR & AROOSTOOK R.R.

Supreme Court of the United States, 1974.
417 U.S. 703, 94 S.Ct. 2578, 41 L.Ed.2d 418.

Mr. Justice POWELL delivered the opinion of the Court....

I

[Prior to October 1964, Bangor & Aroostook Corporation ("B & A") held 98.3% of the stock of the Bangor & Aroostook Railroad Company ("BAR"), a Maine corporation. In October 1964, B & A sold its BAR stock to Bangor Punta, a Delaware corporation. Bangor Punta held the stock for five years, and then sold it in October 1969 to Amoskeag Co. for $5 million. Amoskeag later acquired additional shares which gave it ownership of more than 99% (but less than 100%) of BAR.] *

In 1971, BAR ... filed the present action against Bangor Punta ... in the United States District Court for the District of Maine. The complaint specified 13 counts of alleged mismanagement, misappropriation, and waste of BAR's corporate assets occurring during the period from 1960 through 1967 when B & A and then Bangor Punta controlled BAR.[1] Damages were sought in the amount of $7,000,000 for violations of both federal and state laws. The federal statutes and regulations alleged to have been violated included § 10 of the Clayton Act, 15 U.S.C.A. § 20; § 10(b) of the Securities Exchange Act of 1934, 15 U.S.C.A. § 78j(b); and Rule 10b–5.... The state claims were grounded on § 104 of the Maine Public Utilities Act, Maine Rev.Stat.Ann., Tit. 35, § 104 (1965), and the common law of Maine.

The complaint focused on four intercompany transactions which allegedly resulted in injury to BAR. Counts I and II averred that B & A, and later Bangor Punta, overcharged BAR for various legal, accounting, printing, and other services. Counts III, IV, V, and VI averred that B & A improperly acquired the stock of the St.

---

* In the interests of clarity, the statement of facts eliminates subsidiaries that do not figure in the opinion. (Footnote by ed.)

1. Several of the alleged acts of corporate mismanagement occurred between 1960 and 1964 when B & A ... was in control of the railroad. Liability for these acts was nevertheless sought to be imposed on Bangor Punta, even though it had no

interest in either BAR or B & A during this period. The apparent basis for liability was the 1964 purchase agreement between B & A and Bangor Punta. The complaint in the instant case alleged that under the agreement Bangor Punta, through its subsidiary, assumed "all ... debts, obligations, contracts and liabilities" of B & A.

Croix Paper Co. which BAR owned through its subsidiary. Counts VII, VIII, IX, and X charged that B & A and Bangor Punta improperly caused BAR to declare special dividends to its stockholders, including B & A and Bangor Punta, and also caused BAR's subsidiary to borrow in order to pay regular dividends. Counts XI, XII, and XIII charged that B & A improperly caused BAR to excuse payment by B & A and Bangor Punta of the interest due on a loan made by BAR to B & A. In sum, the complaint alleged that during the period of their control of BAR, Bangor Punta, and its predecessor in interest B & A, "exploited it solely for their own purposes" and "calculatedly drained the resources of BAR in violation of law for their own benefit."

The District Court granted petitioners' motion for summary judgment and dismissed the action. 353 F.Supp. 724 (1972). The court first observed that although the suit purported to be a primary action brought in the name of the corporation, the real party in interest and hence the actual beneficiary of any recovery, was Amoskeag, the present owner of more than 99% of the outstanding stock of BAR. The court then noted that Amoskeag had acquired all of its BAR stock long after the alleged wrongs occurred and that Amoskeag did not contend that it had not received full value for its purchase price, or that the purchase transaction was tainted by fraud or deceit. Thus, any recovery on Amoskeag's part would constitute a windfall because it had sustained no injury. With this in mind, the court then addressed the claims based on federal law and determined that Amoskeag would have been barred from maintaining a shareholder derivative action because of its failure to satisfy the "contemporaneous ownership" requirement of Fed.Rule Civ.Proc. 23.1(1).[3] Finding that equitable principles prevented the use of the corporate fiction to evade the proscription of Rule 23.1, the court concluded that Amoskeag's efforts to recover under the Securities Exchange Act and the Clayton Act must fail. Turning to the claims based on state law, the court recognized that the applicability of Rule 23.1(1) has been questioned where federal jurisdiction is based on diversity of citizenship.[4] The court found it unnecessary to resolve this issue, however, since its examination of state law indicated that Maine probably followed the "prevailing rule" requir-

---

3. Rule 23.1(1), which specifies the requirements applicable to shareholder derivative actions, states that the complaint shall aver that "the plaintiff was a shareholder or member at the time of the transaction of which he complains...." This provision is known as the "contemporaneous ownership" requirement. See 3B J. Moore, Federal Practice ¶ 23.1 et seq. (2d ed. 1974).

4. The "contemporaneous ownership" requirement in shareholder derivative actions was first announced in Hawes v. Oakland, 104 U.S. 450 (1882), and soon thereafter adopted as Equity Rule 97. This provision was later incorporated in Equity Rule

27 and finally in the present Rule 23.1. After the decision in Erie R. Co. v. Tompkins, 304 U.S. 64 (1938), the question arose whether the contemporaneous-ownership requirement was one of procedure or substantive law. If the requirement were substantive, then under the regime of *Erie* it could not be validly applied in federal diversity cases where state law permitted a non-contemporaneous shareholder to maintain a derivative action. See 3B J. Moore, Federal Practice ¶¶ 23.1.01–23.1.15[2] (2d ed. 1974). Although most cases treat the requirement as one of procedure, this Court has never resolved the issue. Ibid.

ing contemporaneous ownership in order to maintain a shareholder derivative action. Thus, whether the federal rule or state substantive law applied, the present action could not be maintained.

The United States Court of Appeals for the First Circuit reversed. . . .

We granted petitioners' application for certiorari. 414 U.S. 1127 (1974). We now reverse.

II

A

We first turn to the question whether respondent corporations * may maintain the present action under § 10 of the Clayton Act, 15 U.S.C.A. § 20, and § 10(b) of the Securities Exchange Act of 1934, 15 U.S.C.A. § 78j(b), and Rule 10b–5, 17 CFR § 240.10b–5. The resolution of this issue depends upon the applicability of the settled principle of equity that a shareholder may not complain of acts of corporate mismanagement if he acquired his shares from those who participated or acquiesced in the allegedly wrongful transactions. See, e.g., Bloodworth v. Bloodworth, 225 Ga. 379, 387, 169 S.E.2d 150, 156–157 (1969). . . .[5] This principle has been invoked with special force where a shareholder purchases all or substantially all the shares of a corporation from a vendor at a fair price, and then seeks to have the corporation recover against that vendor for prior corporate mismanagement. See, e.g., Matthews v. Headley Chocolate Co., 130 Md. 523, 532–535, 100 A. 645, 650–651 (1917); Home Fire Insurance Co. v. Barber, 67 Neb. 644, 661–662, 93 N.W. 1024, 1030–1031 (1903). See also Amen v. Black, 234 F.2d 12, 23 (CA10 1956). The equitable considerations precluding recovery in such cases were explicated long ago by Dean (then Commissioner) Roscoe Pound in Home Fire Insurance Co. v. Barber, supra. Dean Pound, writing for the Supreme Court of Nebraska, observed that the shareholders of the plaintiff corporation in that case had sustained no injury since they had acquired their shares from the alleged wrongdoers after the disputed transactions occurred and had received full value for their purchase price. Thus, any recovery on their part would constitute a windfall, for it would enable them to obtain funds to which they had no just title or claim. Moreover, it would in effect allow the shareholders to recoup a large part of the price they agreed to pay for their shares, notwithstanding the fact that they received all they had bargained for. Finally, it would permit the shareholders to reap a profit from wrongs done to others, thus encouraging further such speculation. Dean Pound stated that these consequences rendered any recovery highly inequitable and mandated dismissal of the suit.

---

* The respondents were BAR and a wholly owned subsidiary. (Footnote by ed.)

5. This principle obtains in the great majority of jurisdictions. See, e.g., Russell v. Louis Melind Co., 331 Ill.App. 182, 72 N.E.2d 869 (1947).

The considerations supporting the *Home Fire* principle are especially pertinent in the present case. As the District Court pointed out, Amoskeag, the present owner of more than 99% of the BAR shares, would be the principal beneficiary of any recovery obtained by BAR. Amoskeag, however, acquired 98.3% of the outstanding shares of BAR from petitioner Bangor Punta in 1969, well after the alleged wrongs were said to have occurred. Amoskeag does not contend that the purchase transaction was tainted by fraud or deceit, or that it received less than full value for its money. Indeed, it does not assert that it has sustained any injury at all. Nor does it appear that the alleged acts of prior mismanagement have had any continuing effect on the corporations involved or the value of their shares.[6] Nevertheless, by causing the present action to be brought in the name of respondent corporations, Amoskeag seeks to recover indirectly an amount equal to the $5,000,000 it paid for its stock, plus an additional $2,000,000. All this would be in the form of damages for wrongs petitioner Bangor Punta is said to have inflicted, not upon Amoskeag, but upon respondent corporations during the period in which Bangor Punta owned 98.3% of the BAR shares. In other words, Amoskeag seeks to recover for wrongs Bangor Punta did to *itself* as owner of the railroad.[7] At the same time it reaps this windfall, Amoskeag desires to retain all its BAR stock. Under *Home Fire,* it is evident that Amoskeag would have no standing in equity to maintain the present action.[8]

We are met with the argument, however, that since the present action is brought in the name of respondent corporations, we may not look behind the corporate entity to the true substance of the claims and the actual beneficiaries. The established law is to the contrary. Although a corporation and its shareholders are deemed separate entities for most purposes, the corporate form may be

---

6. In *Home Fire,* Dean Pound suggested that equitable principles might not prevent recovery where the effects of the wrongful acts continued and resulted in injury to present shareholders. 67 Neb. 644, 662, 93 N.W. 1024, 1031. In their complaint in the instant case, respondents alleged that "[t]he injury to BAR is a continuing one surviving the aforesaid sale [from petitioner BPO] to Amoskeag." The District Court noted that respondents alleged no facts to support this contention and therefore found any such exception inapplicable. 353 F.Supp. 724, 727 n. 1 (1972). Respondents apparently did not renew this contention on appeal.

7. Similarly, as to the period before October 1964, Amoskeag seeks to recover for wrongs B & A and its shareholders did to *themselves* as owners of the railroad.

8. Conceding the lack of equity in any recovery by Amoskeag, the dissent argues that the present action can nevertheless be maintained because there are 20 minority

shareholders, holding less than 1% of the BAR stock, who owned their shares "during the period from 1960 through 1967 when the transactions underlying the railroad's complaint took place, and who still owned that stock in 1971 when the complaint was filed." ... The dissent would conclude that the existence of these innocent minority shareholders entitled BAR, and hence Amoskeag, to recover the entire $7,000,000 amount of alleged damages.

Aside from the illogic of such an approach, the dissent's position is at war with the precedents, for the *Home Fire* principle has long been applied to preclude full recovery by a corporation even where there are innocent minority shareholders who acquired their shares prior to the alleged wrongs. See cases cited at n. 5, supra, and accompanying text. The dissent also mistakes the factual posture of this case, since the respondent corporations did not institute this action for the benefit of the minority shareholders. See discussion at n. 15, infra.

disregarded in the interests of justice where it is used to defeat an overriding public policy. New Colonial Ice Co. v. Helvering, 292 U.S. 435, 442 (1934); Chicago, M. & St. P.R. Co. v. Minneapolis Civic Assn., 247 U.S. 490, 501 (1918). In such cases, courts of equity, piercing all fictions and disguises, will deal with the substance of the action and not blindly adhere to the corporate form. Thus, where equity would preclude the shareholders from maintaining an action in their own right, the corporation would also be precluded. Amen v. Black, supra; Capitol Wine & Spirit Corp. v. Pokrass, 277 App.Div. 184, 98 N.Y.S.2d 291 (1950), aff'd, 302 N.Y. 734, 98 N.E.2d 704 (1951); Matthews v. Headley Chocolate Co., supra; Home Fire Insurance Co. v. Barber, supra. It follows that Amoskeag, the principal beneficiary of any recovery and itself estopped from complaining of petitioners' alleged wrongs, cannot avoid the command of equity through the guise of proceeding in the name of respondent corporations which it owns and controls.

B

Respondents fare no better in their efforts to maintain the present actions under state law, specifically § 104 of the Maine Public Utilities Act, Maine Rev.Stat.Ann., Tit. 35, § 104 (1965), and the common law of Maine. In Forbes v. Wells Beach Casino, Inc., 307 A.2d 210, 223 n. 10 (1973), the Maine Supreme Judicial Court recently declared that it had long accepted the equitable principle that a "stockholder has no standing if either he or his vendor participated or acquiesced in the wrong. . . ." See Hyams v. Old Dominion Co., 113 Me. 294, 302, 93 A. 747, 750 (1959).[9] . . .

III

In reaching the contrary conclusion, the Court of Appeals stated that it could not accept the proposition that Amoskeag would be the "sole beneficiary" of any recovery by BAR. 482 F.2d, at 868. The court noted that in view of the railroad's status as a "quasi-public" corporation and the essential nature of the services it provides, the public had an identifiable interest in BAR's financial health. Thus, any recovery by BAR would accrue to the benefit of the public through the improvement in BAR's economic position and the quality of its services. The court thought that this factor rendered any windfall to Amoskeag irrelevant.

At the outset, we note that the Court of Appeals' assumption that any recovery would necessarily benefit the public is unwarranted. As that court explicitly recognized, any recovery by BAR could

9. In addition, the new Maine Business Corporation Act adopts the contemporaneous-ownership requirement for shareholder derivative actions. See Maine Rev.Stat. Ann., Tit. 13–A, § 627.1.A (1974). This provision apparently became effective two days after the present action was filed. As the District Court noted, it is an open question whether Maine in fact had a contempo-raneous-ownership requirement prior to that time. 353 F.Supp., at 727. See R. Field, V. McKusick & L. Wroth, Maine Civil Practice § 23.2, p. 393 (2d ed. 1970). In the absence of any indication that Maine would not have followed the "prevailing view," the District Court determined that the contemporaneous-ownership requirement of Fed.Rule Civ.Proc. 23.1 applied.

be diverted to its shareholders, namely Amoskeag, rather than re-invested in the railroad for the benefit of the public. . . .

The Court of Appeals' position also appears to overlook the fact that Amoskeag, the actual beneficiary of any recovery through its ownership of more than 99% of the BAR shares, would be unjustly enriched since it has sustained no injury. . . .

The Court of Appeals further stated that it was important to insure that petitioners would not be immune from liability for their wrongful conduct and noted that BAR's recovery would provide a needed deterrent to mismanagement of railroads.   Our difficulty with this argument is that it proves too much.   If deterrence were the only objective, then in logic any plaintiff willing to file a complaint would suffice.   No injury or violation of a legal duty to the particular plaintiff would have to be alleged.   The only prerequisite would be that the plaintiff agree to accept the recovery, lest the supposed wrongdoer be allowed to escape a reckoning.   Suffice it to say that we have been referred to no authority which would support so novel a result, and we decline to adopt it.

We therefore conclude that respondent corporations may not maintain the present action.[15]   The judgment of the Court of Appeals is reversed.

Mr. Justice MARSHALL, with whom Mr. Justice DOUGLAS, Mr. Justice BRENNAN, and Mr. Justice WHITE join, dissenting. . . .

The majority places primary reliance on Dean Pound's decision in Home Fire Insurance Co. v. Barber, supra.   In that case, *all* of the shares of the plaintiff corporation had been acquired from the alleged wrongdoers after the transactions giving rise to the causes of action stated in the complaint.   Since none of the corporation's shareholders held stock at the time of the alleged wrongful transactions, none had been injured thereby.   Dean Pound therefore held that equity barred the corporation from pursuing a claim where none of its shareholders could complain of injury.

---

15. Our decision rests on the conclusion that equitable principles preclude recovery by Amoskeag, the present owner of more than 99% of the BAR shares.   The record does not reveal whether the minority shareholders who hold the remaining fraction of 1% of the BAR shares stand in the same position as Amoskeag.   Some courts have adopted the concept of a pro-rata recovery where there are innocent minority shareholders.   Under this procedure, damages are distributed to the minority shareholders individually on a proportional basis, even though the action is brought in the name of the corporation to enforce primary rights.   See, e.g., Matthews v. Headley Chocolate Co., 130 Md. 523, 536–540, 100 A. 645, 650–652 (1917).   In the present case, respondents have expressly disavowed any intent to obtain a pro-rata recovery on behalf of the 1% minority shareholders of BAR.   We therefore do not reach the question whether such recovery would be appropriate.

The dissent asserts that the alleged acts of corporate mismanagement have placed BAR "close to the brink of bankruptcy" and that the present action is maintained for the benefit of BAR's creditors. . . .   With all respect, it appears that the dissent has sought to redraft respondents' complaint.   As the District Court noted, respondents have not brought this action on behalf of any creditors.   353 F.Supp., at 726.   Indeed, they have never so contended.   Moreover, respondents have conceded that the financial health of the railroad is excellent.   Tr. of Oral Arg. 18.

Dean Pound thought it clear, however, that the opposite result would obtain if *any* of the present shareholders

"are entitled to complain of the acts of the defendant and of his past management of the company; for if any of them are so entitled, there can be no doubt of the right and duty of the corporation to maintain this suit. It would be maintainable in such a case even though the wrongdoers continued to be stockholders and would share in the proceeds." 67 Neb., at 655, 93 N.W., at 1028.

Cf. Capitol Wine & Spirit Corp. v. Pokrass, 277 App.Div. 184, 186, 98 N.Y.S.2d 291, 293 (1950), aff'd, 302 N.Y. 734, 98 N.E.2d 704 (1951).

The rationale for the distinction drawn by Dean Pound is simple enough. The sole shareholder who defrauds or mismanages his own corporation hurts only himself. For the corporation to sue him for his wrongs is simply to take money out of his right pocket and put it in his left. It is therefore appropriate for equity to intervene to pierce the corporate veil. But where there are minority shareholders, misappropriation and conversion of corporate assets injure their interests as well as the interest of the majority shareholder. The law imposes upon the directors of a corporation a fiduciary obligation to all of the corporation's shareholders, and part of that obligation is to use due care to ensure that the corporation seek redress where a majority shareholder has drained the corporation's resources for his own benefit and to the detriment of minority shareholders.[1] ...

See also Courtland Manor, Inc. v. Leeds, 347 A.2d 144 (Del.Ch. 1975); cf. American Timber & Trading Co. v. Niedermeyer, 276 Or. 1135, 558 P.2d 1211 (1976).

RIFKIN v. STEELE PLATT

Colorado Court of Appeals, 1991.
824 P.2d 32.

Opinion by Judge PLANK.

Defendants, Steele Platt and Fas–Wok, Inc. (sellers), appeal the judgment of the trial court in favor of the corporate plaintiff, The Boiler Room, Inc. (the corporation). Plaintiffs cross-appeal the award of damages. We affirm in part and remand for further proceedings consistent with this opinion.

1. Under a separate rule, the plaintiff must be a shareholder at the time the action is brought. See Note on Who Can Bring a Derivative Action, Section 1, supra. The two rules are bridged by a third rule requiring that the plaintiff's ownership between the time of the wrong and the time of the suit must be uninterrupted. Vista Fund v. Garis, 277 N.W.2d 19 (Minn.1979); Gresov v. Shattuck Denn Mining Corp., 40 Misc.2d 569, 243 N.Y.S.2d 760 (1963).

This matter involves the sale of the controlling shares of the corporation, which owns a restaurant of the same name located in the Tivoli Shopping Center in Denver, Colorado. Plaintiffs include the corporation and its present principal shareholders, Robert C. Rifkin, Gerald N. Kernis, and Gary G. Kortz (buyers). Sellers are the former controlling shareholders.

Buyers and sellers executed a Stock Purchase Agreement to effectuate the sale of the corporation. After the closing, the buyers discovered inaccuracies in financial representations made in the agreement. Consequently, they filed suit against the sellers asserting claims of breach of contract, breach of good faith, breach of fiduciary duty, and unjust enrichment.

The complaint alleged, in part, that Platt, as officer and director of the corporation, had misappropriated funds from it and that certain assets on the balance sheet were actually owned by Platt or other entities that he controlled. Sellers counterclaimed seeking rescission of the agreement.

After a trial to the court, judgment was entered in favor of the buyers on the breach of contract claim and the corporation on the breach of fiduciary duty claim. The court also awarded attorney fees pursuant to the agreement. Sellers do not appeal that part of the judgment concerning the breach of contract claim. . . .

Sellers . . . contend that the trial court erred in awarding the corporation damages for breach of fiduciary duty for conduct which occurred prior to buyers' acquisition of stock. They cite *Bangor Punta Operations, Inc. v. Bangor & Aroostook R. Co.,* 417 U.S. 703, 94 S.Ct. 2578, 41 L.Ed.2d 418 (1974) in support of this argument. We agree that *Bangor Punta* raises issues which must be resolved in this matter.

In *Bangor Punta,* the new shareholders of the corporation, in the name of the corporation, sought damages from the former shareholders for violations of state and federal law which occurred before the sale. The United States Supreme Court held that the corporation could not maintain the action for wrongs that occurred before the new shareholders' acquisition of the shares. The court reasoned that the real parties that would gain from a successful lawsuit would be the new shareholders. It presumed that the purchase price that they paid reflected the prior wrongdoings. Thus, the shareholders would improperly receive a windfall if allowed to recover damages.

Here, it is undisputed that the acts which constituted Platt's breach of fiduciary duty occurred prior to the buyers' acquisition of stock in The Boiler Room. However, the parties dispute whether the purchase price reflected the prior wrongdoings. The trial court did not make a finding on this issue. Therefore, we remand it to the trial court for further findings. *See El Dorado Bancshares v. Martin,* 701 F.Supp. 1515 (D.Kan.1988).

If on review the court finds that the price, in fact, reflected Platt's wrongdoings, it must dismiss the breach of fiduciary duty claim. If, on the other hand, it finds that the purchase price of the shares did not reflect the wrongdoings, then the corporation's previous damage award may stand.....

HUME and NEY, JJ., concur.

NOTE ON THE CONTEMPORANEOUS–OWNERSHIP RULE

1. At common law, the cases were divided on whether a shareholder was barred from bringing a derivative action if he was not a "contemporaneous shareholder"—that is, if he did not hold his shares when the wrong occurred. 2 Model Bus.Corp.Act Ann. § 49, ¶ 4.11 (1971). Today, however, most jurisdictions have adopted some version of the contemporaneous-ownership rule by either case-law, statute, or court rule. 13 W. Fletcher, Cyclopedia of the Law of Private Corporations § 5981 (1991 rev. vol.). The rule is subject to several important exceptions:

(a) Devolution by Operation of Law. A non-contemporaneous shareholder is normally allowed to bring a derivative action if his shares devolved upon him "by operation of law"—for example, by inheritance. (This exception is sometimes made applicable only where the shares have devolved from a person who was a shareholder at the time of the wrong.) See Note, 54 B.U.L.Rev. 355 (1974).

(b) Continuing–Wrong Theory. Under the continuing-wrong theory, a plaintiff can bring an action to challenge a wrong that began before he acquired his shares, but continued thereafter. In principle this may not seem to be an exception at all, since the plaintiff is only complaining about what happened after he became a shareholder. In practice, however, it is often difficult to distinguish between a wrongful continuing course of conduct, on the one hand, and the continued effect of a completed wrongful transaction, on the other. Therefore, while the continuing-wrong exception is widely accepted in principle, in practice there is considerable divergence in the way it is applied, and different cases often seem to come out differently on virtually the same facts. For example, in Maclary v. Pleasant Hills, Inc., 35 Del.Ch. 39, 109 A.2d 830 (1954), the plaintiff was allowed to sue under the continuing-wrong theory where he had purchased his stock after an allegedly wrongful resolution authorizing the issuance of stock certificates, but before the certificates were actually issued. In contrast, in Elster v. American Airlines, Inc., 34 Del.Ch. 94, 100 A.2d 219 (1953), the continuing-wrong theory was deemed inapplicable where the plaintiff had purchased after the corporation had allegedly issued stock options for no consideration, but before the options were exercised. Similarly, in Forbes v. Wells Beach Casino, Inc., 307 A.2d 210 (Me.1973), the plaintiff was allowed to sue under the continuing-wrong theory

where he had purchased his stock after a fiduciary had wrongfully taken possession of corporate property, but while the fiduciary continued to hold it. In contrast, in Weinhaus v. Gale, 237 F.2d 197 (7th Cir.1956), the continuing-wrong theory was deemed inapplicable where plaintiff had purchased after stock had been sold by a subsidiary to its parent at a price alleged to be unfairly low, but before the parent had resold the stock. In Palmer v. Morris, 316 F.2d 649 (5th Cir.1963), the plaintiff was allowed to sue under the continuing-wrong theory where he had purchased his stock after an allegedly wrongful deal was made, but while payments under the deal continued. In contrast, in Chaft v. Kass, 19 A.D.2d 610, 241 N.Y.S.2d 284 (1963), the theory was deemed inapplicable where plaintiff purchased his stock after the corporation had entered into an allegedly invalid contract, but while payments under the contract were still being made.

Several statutes provide that the plaintiff must allege that he was a shareholder at the time of the transaction "or any part thereof." E.g., Cal. § 800(b)(1); Wis. § 180.405. Where there is a close question whether the continuing-wrong theory applies to a given case, such a statute might tip the scale in the plaintiff's favor.

SECTION 5.　THE RIGHT TO TRIAL BY JURY IN DERIVATIVE ACTIONS

NOTE ON THE RIGHT TO TRIAL BY JURY IN DERIVATIVE ACTIONS

Since a derivative action has traditionally been conceived of as an equitable remedy, until recently it did not carry the right to a trial by jury. In 1970, however, the Supreme Court held in Ross v. Bernhard, 396 U.S. 531, 90 S.Ct. 733, 24 L.Ed.2d 729 that in a derivative action brought in federal court the parties have a right to a jury where the action would be triable to a jury if it had been brought by the corporation itself rather than by a shareholder.

The Seventh Amendment applies only to federal proceedings, and the extent to which state courts will follow Ross v. Bernhard remains to be seen. Compare Rankin v. Frebank Co., 47 Cal.App.3d 75, 121 Cal.Rptr. 348 (1975) (under the California Constitution there is no right to a jury in derivative actions), and Pelfrey v. Bank of Greer, 270 S.C. 691, 244 S.E.2d 315 (1978) (same result under South Carolina statute) with Finance, Investment & Rediscount Co. v. Wells, 409 So.2d 1341 (Ala.1981) (there is a right to a jury trial under Alabama law), and Fedoryszyn v. Weiss, 62 Misc.2d 889, 310 N.Y.S.2d 55 (1970) (same under New York law). See generally D. DeMott, Shareholder Derivative Actions § 4.18 (1987).

SECTION 6. DEMAND ON THE BOARD AND TERMINATION OF DERIVATIVE ACTIONS ON THE RECOMMENDATION OF THE BOARD OR A COMMITTEE

———

CAL. CORP. CODE § 800(b)(2)

[See Statutory Supplement]

———

FEDERAL RULES OF CIVIL PROCEDURE RULE 23.1

[See Statutory Supplement]

———

INTRODUCTORY NOTE

Until about the 1970s, it was well settled that before bringing a derivative action a shareholder was required to make a demand on the board, unless demand was excused. Two related issues, however, were much less well settled. The first issue was, when was demand excused? The general rule was that demand was excused if it was futile. The scope of that exception, however, was unclear. The most important application of the exception was that demand was excused if a majority of the directors were interested. It was not clear, however, what constituted interest for these matters. For example, it was not clear whether a director was interested merely because he or she was named as a defendant, and if not, how much more had to be shown.

The second unsettled issue was the consequence of *not* making demand. In most of the reported cases, demand had not been made and the corporation moved to dismiss the action on the ground that demand was required. The courts in such cases often simply held that demand was or was not required, without getting into what consequences would follow if a required demand was made and rejected—although some courts did say or hold that if demand was required and rejected, and the rejection was by disinterested directors who constituted a majority of the board, a derivative action could not proceed unless in rejecting demand the board violated the business judgment rule.

The picture was complicated further in the 1970s, when a series of cases held that even when a majority of directors were interested, so that demand was not required, the board could appoint a committee to consider whether the derivative action was in the best interests of the corporation.   If the committee concluded that the action was not in the corporation's best interests, and the committee had engaged in an adequate investigation, the court could dismiss the action on the committee's motion, subject to a designated standard of review.   (If the board was disinterested, the board itself could conduct the investigation and make the motion.)

In short, as of the 1970s a cluster of related issues were raised concerning the role and power of the board in derivative actions. When was demand on the board excused?   What were the consequences if demand was required, made, and denied?   What, if anything, could a board do if demand was excused?

It was against this background that the cases in this Section were decided.

BARR v. WACKMAN

Court of Appeals of New York, 1975.
36 N.Y.2d 371, 368 N.Y.S.2d 497, 329 N.E.2d 180.

FUCHSBERG, Judge.

Plaintiff brought this shareholder's derivative action without first making a demand upon the corporation's board of directors to secure initiation of an action in favor of the corporation or otherwise to remedy the acts of which he complains.   He alleges that a demand would have been futile because the board of directors participated in, authorized and approved the challenged acts and its members are themselves subject to liability and, therefore, cannot be expected to vote to sue themselves.

Three of the defendants moved to dismiss the complaint on the ground that the reasons offered in justification of the failure to make a demand are insufficient under subdivision (c) of section 626 of the Business Corporation Law, Consol.Laws, c. 4.   The issue is whether allegations of board participation in and approval of acts involving bias and self-dealing by minority "affiliated" directors and breach of fiduciary duties of due care and diligence by the remaining majority "unaffiliated" directors through their participation and approval, though there is no claim of self-dealing as to them, are sufficient to withstand a motion to dismiss for failure to make a demand.

Subdivision (c) of section 626 of the Business Corporation Law provides that, in any shareholder's derivative action brought in the right of the corporation to procure judgment in its favor, "the complaint shall set forth with particularity the efforts of the plaintiff to secure the initiation of such action by the board or the reasons for not making such effort."   ...

Plaintiff, a shareholder of Talcott National Corporation ("Talcott"), brought this shareholder's derivative action against defendants Gulf & Western Industries ("Gulf & Western"), Associates First Capital Corporation ("First Capital"), a subsidiary of Gulf & Western, and 16 Talcott directors.   Five of those 16 are affiliated with Talcott in official capacities in addition to their positions as directors. Defendant Silverman is chief executive officer as well as chairman of the board of directors. Defendant Wackman is Talcott's president, defendant Campbell the senior executive vice-president, and defendant Remis the president and chief executive officer of Beggs & Cobb, Inc. ("Beggs"), a wholly-owned subsidiary of Talcott. These affiliated directors, characterized as the "controlling defendants" in the complaint, are alleged to have dominated and controlled Talcott and its board of directors.

The remaining 11 defendants are not alleged to be affiliated with Talcott otherwise than in their capacity as directors. In the complaint they are characterized as "men of affairs actively engaged in the pursuit of their own substantial business interests", and hereinafter will be referred to as the unaffiliated directors. They are alleged to have failed to exercise their independent judgment as directors. The complaint also alleges that the individual defendants constitute the present members of Talcott's board of directors, and were directors at the time of the contested acts....

According to the complaint, Talcott is engaged through its various subdivisions in the fields of commercial, industrial and real estate financing, product and equipment manufacturing, insurance, and leather processing. It is alleged that in late 1972 defendant Gulf & Western determined to acquire control of Talcott because Talcott's finance-related business (principally operated by its 93% owned subsidiary, James F. Talcott, Inc.) represented a potential valuable expansion of the finance business conducted by Gulf & Western's wholly-owned subsidiary, defendant First Capital. This led to an "agreement in principle" for the merger of Talcott into Gulf & Western at a value of $24 per Talcott share. The agreement was approved by the board of directors of each corporation. Thereafter, plaintiff asserts, the affiliated directors, in return for certain pecuniary and other personal benefits, entered into a "plan and scheme" with Gulf & Western to help it obtain control over Talcott on an altered basis substantially less favorable to Talcott and its shareholders than the previously approved merger proposal.

Various actions are claimed to have been taken pursuant to this scheme, not only by the individual affiliated directors and the corporate defendants but also by Talcott's board itself. (1) The Talcott–Gulf & Western merger was abandoned by Talcott's board of directors and in its place was substituted a tender offer by First Capital of $20 per Talcott share. Talcott's board of directors is claimed to have approved this tender offer as "fair and reasonable" and recommended it to Talcott's common shareholders. The complaint alleges that "[s]uch approval and recommendation were not in the exercise of an honest business appraisal of the tender offer but was [sic] made for the benefit of G & W and the controlling defendants." (2) Nine Talcott officers, three of whom are presently directors, entered into favorable new employment contracts with James F. Talcott, Inc., Talcott's coveted finance-related subsidiary and the principal object of the proposed acquisition of Talcott.

These contracts were authorized by Talcott's board of directors. (3) If the tender offer proved successful and First Capital acquired control of Talcott, defendant Silverman (Talcott's board chairman and chief executive), in addition to his $125,000 approved annual salary with Talcott, was to become vice chairman of First Capital under a five-year employment contract providing an annual salary of $60,000; for the following five years he was to be denominated a consultant under an arrangement with First Capital, providing for an aggregate compensation of $275,000. (4) Gulf & Western and First Capital agreed to pay an allegedly excessive finder's fee of $340,000 in connection with the tender offer to a corporation whose executive vice-president was defendant Silverman's son. (5) Talcott's board of directors decided to sell Talcott's non-finance-related subsidiary, Beggs. The complaint alleges that "[s]aid decision was in disregard of the interests of Talcott and its shareholders, who would be greatly harmed thereby, and was taken solely to accommodate G & W, which was interested in acquiring only the finance related business of Talcott." Pursuant to this board decision, the affiliated directors allegedly caused Talcott to sell Beggs for $7,000,000 cash and to repurchase for $13,100,000 Series D Preferred Shares which Talcott had originally issued when it acquired Beggs. These related transactions to accomplish the sale of Beggs are said to have resulted in a $6,100,000 net loss to Talcott.

The complaint goes on to assert that the "controlling defendants", the six affiliated directors, including the three appellants, have breached their fiduciary obligations to Talcott in return for personal benefits, have failed to exercise due care, skill and diligence in the conduct of Talcott's affairs and have wasted its assets. The complaint then alleges that "the other defendants, as directors of Talcott, by participating in, authorizing or approving the acts and transactions complained of, have breached their fiduciary duties to Talcott and its shareholders, have failed to exercise due care and diligence in discharging their duties, and have wasted Talcott's assets." . . .

On behalf of Talcott . . . the complaint seeks judgment directing defendants to account to Talcott for profits they gained by reason of the acts alleged and for damages sustained by Talcott. It also seeks to enjoin the defendants from effectuating the employment and consulting agreements already described as well as to enjoin Gulf & Western and First Capital from voting any shares acquired in the tender offer and exercising any control over Talcott.

Appellants claim that the challenged acts are "plainly corporate" and at most indicate erroneous business judgments which as a matter of law are not wrongful.

In affirming the Supreme Court's denial of appellants' motion to dismiss, the Appellate Division stated that a demand is excused "where the board itself is accused of patent breach of its fiduciary duties and its members are named as parties defendant". We agree. Liberally construed, the complaint alleges acts for which a majority of the directors may be liable and plaintiff reasonably concluded that the board would not be responsive to a demand. In our view, this conclusion finds support in the history and purposes of the demand rule in shareholder derivative suits, in the liberal rules of pleading and in the law of corporate directors' liability for breach of duty.

Though the demand requirements stated in subdivision (c) of section 626 of the Business Corporation Law were enacted on the basis of part of former rule 23 (subd. [b]) (now rule 23.1) of the Federal Rules of Civil Procedure ... the statute actually codifies an early rule of equity in shareholder derivative actions.... The rule was sometimes stated as a strict pleading requirement (see, e.g., Greaves v. Gouge, 69 N.Y. 154, 157; Hawes v. Oakland, 104 U.S. 450, 461, 26 L.Ed. 827), and has been codified as such in New York ("the complaint *shall* set forth *with particularity* " [Business Corporation Law, § 626, subd. (c); italics supplied]).

The requirement of demand, or of sufficient explanation for failure to make one, derives from one of the basic principles of corporate control—that the management of the corporation is entrusted to its board of directors (Business Corporation Law, § 701), who have primary responsibility for acting in the name of the corporation and who are often in a position to correct alleged abuses without resort to the courts. Their authorization of a particular corporate act, if made in their *considered* opinion that it is in the best interests of the corporation, and fair to the corporation, will not be interfered with by the courts (Chelrob, Inc. v. Barrett, 293 N.Y. 442, 449, 460, 57 N.E.2d 825, 828, 834). A corollary foundation for the requirement is that it serves the interests of judicial economy since a demand may often result in corrective action short of suit and, thereby, not only relieve the courts from entanglement in the management of internal corporate affairs, but also protect them from vain rulings on challenged acts which are later ratified by the board. (See, generally, Foss v. Harbottle, 2 Hare. 461, 492–494, 67 Eng.Rep. 189, 203–204; Hawes v. Oakland, 104 U.S. 450, 26 L.Ed. 827 supra.) The demand requirement also affords corporate directors reasonable protection from the harassment of litigious, dissident shareholders who might otherwise contest decisions on matters clearly within the directors' discretion. Finally, the requirement is additionally designed to discourage "strike suits" by shareholders making reckless charges for personal gain rather than corporate benefit....

It is clear then that the demand is generally designed to weed out unnecessary or illegitimate shareholder derivative suits. This prophylactic device assuredly should not be allowed to frustrate the true derivative suit, the very thing it was designed to protect....

Accordingly, a futile demand need not be made....

The basic question is whether from the particular circumstances of the liability charged it may be inferred that the making of such a demand would indeed be futile. Thus, it is well established that a demand will be excused where the alleged wrongdoers control or comprise a majority of the directors.... And, while justification for failure to give directors notice prior to the institution of a derivative action is not automatically to be found in bare allegations which merely set forth prima facie personal liability of directors without spelling out some detail, such justification may be found when the claim of liability is based on formal action of the board in which the individual directors were participants.

It is not sufficient, however, merely to name a majority of the directors as parties defendant with conclusory allegations of wrong-doing or control by wrongdoers. This pleading tactic would only beg the question of actual futility and ignore the particularity requirement of the statute. The complaint here does much more than simply name the individual board members as defendants. It sets out, with particularity, a series of transactions allegedly for the benefit of Gulf & Western and the affiliated directors. Though there are no allegations that the unaffiliated directors personally benefited from the transactions, they are claimed to have disregard-ed Talcott's interests for the sole purpose of accommodating Gulf & Western, which, in turn, would allegedly reciprocate by promoting the self-interest of the affiliated directors. Acting officially, the board, qua board, is claimed to have participated or acquiesced in assertedly wrongful transactions.

Considered most favorably to the plaintiff the board's acts, as a necessary part of a series of intertwined events and agreements which benefited the affiliated directors rather than Talcott, cannot be regarded as immune from question in a shareholder's derivative action as a matter of law. If true, the allegations of the complaint— the circumstances surrounding the board's approval of the tender offer for First Capital's acquisition of control over Talcott, including the employment and finders fee agreements and the substantial financial emoluments which were to accrue to defendant board chairman and chief executive Silverman, and the sale of Beggs, the allegedly profitable nonfinance subsidiary at a six million dollar loss to Talcott—state a cause of action against the defendants, including the unaffiliated directors, for breach of their duties of due care and diligence to the corporation. Plaintiff may prove that the exercise of reasonable diligence and independent judgment under all the circumstances by the unaffiliated directors, at least to meaningfully check the decisions of the active corporate managers, would have put them on notice of the claimed self-dealing of the affiliated directors and avoided the alleged damage to Talcott. If the unaffili-ated directors abdicated their responsibility, they may be liable for their omissions. Taking their potential liability from the face of the complaint, plaintiff's failure to make a demand on the board was warranted.

We reject appellants' proposition that allegations of directorial fraud or self-interest is, in every case, a prerequisite to excusing a derivative shareholder from making a demand upon the board. (Compare, e.g., Matter of Kauffman Mut. Fund Actions, 1 Cir., 479

F.2d 257, 265, cert. den. 414 U.S. 857, 94 S.Ct. 161, 38 L.Ed.2d 107; but see concurring opn. of Chief Judge Coffin; see, also, 8 Suffolk U.L.Rev. 287.) Directors undertake affirmative duties of due care and diligence to a corporation and its shareholders in addition to their obligation merely to avoid self-dealing. That unaffiliated directors may not have personally profited from challenged actions does not necessarily end the question of their potential liability to the corporation and the consequent unlikelihood that they would prosecute the action. "No custom or practice can make a directorship a mere position of honor void of responsibility, or cause a name to become a substitute for care and attention. The personnel of a directorate may give confidence and attract custom; it must also afford protection." (Kavanaugh v. Commonwealth Trust Co., 223 N.Y. 103, 106, 119 N.E. 237, 238.) Of course, the degree of care and diligence to be exercised (see Business Corporation Law, § 717) will depend upon the subjects to which it is to be applied and the particular facts of each case. But the so-called "business judgment" rule (cf. Pollitz v. Wabash R.R. Co., 207 N.Y. 113, 124, 100 N.E. 721, 724) urged by appellants has not drained the traditional duties of prudence and diligence of all their contemporary validity and force. . . .

This case does not require us to delimit the boundaries of a director's affirmative duties to the corporation which he undertakes to serve. We regard it as sufficient to reiterate the long-standing rule that he does not exempt himself from liability by failing to do more than passively rubber-stamp the decisions of the active managers. . . . As a consequence, a derivative shareholder's complaint may, in a particular case, withstand a motion to dismiss for failure to make a demand upon the board, even though a majority of the board are not individually charged with fraud or self-dealing. Particular allegations of formal board participation in and approval of active wrongdoing may, as here, suffice to defeat a motion to dismiss. We believe the better approach in these cases is to rest the determination of the necessity for a demand in the sound discretion of the court to which the issue is first presented,[4] to be determined from the sufficiency of the complaint, liberally construed.

We hold, therefore that, in light of the allegations of the complaint, the Supreme Court did not abuse its discretion in finding substantial compliance with subdivision (c) of section 626 of the Business Corporation Law and in denying appellants' motion to dismiss for failure to make a demand on the board of directors. The certified question should be answered in the affirmative.

JASEN, GABRIELLI, JONES, WACHTLER and COOKE, JJ., concur.

BREITEL, C.J., taking no part.

---

4. This seems to be the preferred approach in the Federal courts (see 3B Moore, Federal Practice [2d ed.], par. 23.1.19; see, e.g., Herpich v. Wallace, 5 Cir., 430 F.2d 792, 802; Fields v. Fidelity Gen. Ins. Co., 7 Cir., 454 F.2d 682, 685).

Order affirmed, with costs.　Question certified answered in the affirmative.

Affirmed.

———

BACKGROUND NOTE ON DEMAND ON THE BOARD

It is well-established that demand need not be made on the board if a majority of the directors are interested; and this rule is normally extended to cases where nominally disinterested directors are under the "domination and control"—or not independent—of interested directors.　See, e.g., Papilsky v. Berndt, 59 F.R.D. 95 (S.D.N.Y.1973), appeal dism'd 503 F.2d 554 (2d Cir.1974), cert. denied 419 U.S. 1048, 95 S.Ct. 624, 42 L.Ed.2d 643.　The more difficult issue is what constitutes a lack of independence for these purposes.　Since the chief executive normally has ultimate power over employment, promotion, and contracts, certainly any director who is in the corporation's employ, or who supplies it with goods or services, should not be deemed independent of the chief executive.　Frequently, however, the problem is more subtle, for it involves the extent to which nominally independent directors are independent in fact.　In the modern publicly held corporation the reality is that outside directors are typically selected not by the board but by the chief executive, and in making these selections most chief executives will take into consideration whether the candidate can be counted on not to rock the boat.　In a noted study, the retired chairman of a medium-sized midwestern company reported, " 'In the companies I know, the outside directors always agree with management.　That's why they are there.　I have one friend that's just the greatest agreer that ever was, and he is on a dozen boards....' "　M. Mace, Directors: Myth and Reality 99 (1971).[1]　Or, as a noted plaintiff's lawyer has put it, "[O]bviously, you know and I know that if you are choosing ... an independent director you are not going to choose anybody who is going to be

1. Cf. deHaas v. Empire Petroleum Co., 286 F.Supp. 809 (D.Colo.1968), modified and aff'd 435 F.2d 1223, 1228 (10th Cir. 1970). The corporation, American Industries, had five directors, including three outside directors. In excusing demand on the board, the court stated:

The three outside directors were elected by the defendants, and they had taken only a limited interest in the corporation's affairs.　None of them had ever seen a statement of American's financial position, and they had little knowledge of the value or nature of its assets, the extent of its earnings and liabilities, or the general nature of its business.　One of the directors was unaware that the corporation had public shareholders, and the other two were only vaguely aware of this fact.　Furthermore, in at least one instance, two of the outside directors acceded to [the wishes of the chief executive, Stone] by voting for an acquisition which they were convinced was doomed to failure.　In short while it cannot be said that the three outside directors were wholly dominated by Stone, they were dependent on Stone for information and did not evidence that they were the kind of active and aggressive majority that would be likely to undertake the difficult and demanding task of prosecuting a lawsuit for fraud against those who elected them.

286 F.Supp. at 814.

too hard on you."[2]

Apart from the fact that most outside directors are selected in part on the basis of their probable deference to management, a director—even a nominally independent director—who has been brought on the board by a chief executive is likely to regard himself as serving at the latter's sufferance. "Also communicated to, and generally accepted by, directors was the fact that the president possessed the complete powers of control. Those members of the board who elected to challenge the president's powers of control were advised, usually outside the board meetings, that such conduct was inappropriate or they were asked to resign." M. Mace, supra, at 80. Nor is this power exercised infrequently: Almost 37 percent of the industrial respondents in a survey reported that they had fired directors. Heidrick & Struggles, Profile of the Board of Directors 11 (1971).

AUERBACH v. BENNETT

Court of Appeals of New York, 1979.
47 N.Y.2d 619, 419 N.Y.S.2d 920, 393 N.E.2d 994.

JONES, Judge.

While the substantive aspects of a decision to terminate a shareholders' derivative action against defendant corporate directors made by a committee of disinterested directors appointed by the corporation's board of directors are beyond judicial inquiry under the business judgment doctrine, the court may inquire as to the disinterested independence of the members of that committee and as to the appropriateness and sufficiency of the investigative procedures chosen and pursued by the committee. In this instance, however, no basis is shown to warrant either inquiry by the court. Accordingly we hold that it was error to reverse the lower court's dismissal of the shareholders' derivative action.

In the summer of 1975 the management of General Telephone & Electronics Corporation, in response to reports that numerous other multinational companies had made questionable payments to public officials or political parties in foreign countries, directed that an internal preliminary investigation be made to ascertain whether that corporation had engaged in similar transactions. On the basis of the report of this survey, received in October, 1975, management brought the issue to the attention of the corporation's board of directors. At a meeting held on November 6 of that year the board referred the matter to the board's audit committee. The audit committee retained as its special counsel the Washington, D.C., law firm of Wilmer, Cutler & Pickering which had not previously acted

---

2. Mutual Funds as Investors of Large Pools of Money, 115 U.Pa.L.Rev. 669, 739   (1967) (remarks of Abraham Pomerantz).

as counsel to the corporation. With the assistance of such special counsel and Arthur Andersen & Co., the corporation's outside auditors, the audit committee engaged in an investigation into the corporation's worldwide operations, focusing on whether, in the period January 1, 1971 to December 31, 1975, corporate funds had been (1) paid directly or indirectly to any political party or person or to any officer, employee, shareholder or director of any governmental or private customer, or (2) used to reimburse any officer of the corporation or other person for such payments.

On March 4, 1976 the audit committee released its report which was filed with the Securities and Exchange Commission and disclosed to the corporation's shareholders in a proxy statement prior to the annual meeting of shareholders held in April, 1976. The audit committee reported that it had found evidence that in the period from 1971 to 1975 the corporation or its subsidiaries had made payments abroad and in the United States constituting bribes and kickbacks in amounts perhaps totaling more than 11 million dollars and that some of the individual defendant directors had been personally involved in certain of the transactions.

Almost immediately Auerbach, a shareholder in the corporation, instituted the present shareholders' derivative action on behalf of the corporation against the corporation's directors, Arthur Andersen & Co. and the corporation. The complaint alleged that in connection with the transactions reported by the audit committee defendants, present and former members of the corporation's board of directors and Arthur Andersen & Co., are liable to the corporation for breach of their duties to the corporation and should be made to account for payments made in those transactions.

On April 21, 1976 the board of directors of the corporation adopted a resolution creating a special litigation committee "for the purpose of establishing a point of contact between the Board of Directors and the Corporation's General Counsel concerning the position to be taken by the Corporation in certain litigation involving shareholder derivative claims on behalf of the Corporation against certain of its directors and officers" and authorizing that committee "to take such steps from time to time as it deems necessary to pursue its objectives including the retention of special outside counsel." The special committee comprised three disinterested directors who had joined the board after the challenged transactions had occurred. The board subsequently additionally vested in the committee "all of the authority of the Board of Directors to determine, on behalf of the Board, the position that the Corporation shall take with respect to the derivative claims alleged on its behalf' in the present and similar shareholder derivative actions.

The special litigation committee reported under date of November 22, 1976. It found that defendant Arthur Andersen & Co. had conducted its examination of the corporation's affairs in accordance with generally accepted auditing standards and in good faith and concluded that no proper interest of the corporation or its share-holders would be served by the continued assertion of a claim against it. The committee also concluded that none of the individu-al defendants had violated the New York State statutory standard of care, that none had profited personally or gained in any way, that the claims asserted in the present action are without merit, that if the action were allowed to proceed the time and talents of the corporation's senior management would be wasted on lengthy pretrial and trial proceedings, that litigation costs would be inordi-nately high in view of the unlikelihood of success, and that the continuing publicity could be damaging to the corporation's busi-ness. The committee determined that it would not be in the best interests of the corporation for the present derivative action to proceed, and, exercising the authority delegated to it, directed the corporation's general counsel to take that position in the present litigation as well as in pending comparable shareholders' derivative actions.

On December 17, 1976 the corporation and the four individual defendants who had been served moved for an order pursuant to CPLR 3211 (subd. [a], pars. [3], [7]) dismissing the complaint or in the alternative for an order pursuant to CPLR 3211 (subd. [c]) for summary judgment. On January 7, 1977 Arthur Andersen & Co. made a similar motion. On May 13, 1977 Supreme Court, Special Term, granted the motions of all defendants and dismissed the complaint on the merits. . . .

As all parties and both courts below recognize, the disposition of this case on the merits turns on the proper application of the business judgment doctrine, in particular to the decision of a specially appointed committee of disinterested directors acting on behalf of the board to terminate a shareholders' derivative action. That doctrine bars judicial inquiry into actions of corporate di-rectors taken in good faith and in the exercise of honest judgment in the lawful and legitimate furtherance of corporate purposes. "Questions of policy of management, expediency of contracts or action, adequacy of consideration, lawful appropriation of corporate funds to advance corporate interests, are left solely to their honest and unselfish decision, for their powers therein are without limita-tion and free from restraint, and the exercise of them for the common and general interests of the corporation may not be questioned, although the results show that what they did was unwise or inexpedient." (Pollitz v. Wabash, R.R. Co., 207 N.Y. 113, 124, 100 N.E. 721, 724.)

In this instance our inquiry, to the limited extent to which it may be pursued, has a two-tiered aspect. The complaint initially asserted liability on the part of defendants based on the payments made to foreign governmental customers and privately owned cus-tomers, some unspecified portions of which were allegedly passed on to officials of the customers, i.e., the focus was on first-tier bribes and kickbacks. Then subsequent to the service of the complaint there came the report of a special litigation committee, particularly appointed by the corporation's board of directors to consider the merits of the present and similar shareholders' derivative actions, and its determination that it would not be in the best interests of the corporation to press claims against defendants based on their possible first-tier liability. The motions for summary judgment were predicated principally on the report and determination of the special litigation committee and on the contention that this second-tier corporate action insulated the first-tier transactions from judicial inquiry and was itself subject to the shelter of the business judgment doctrine. The disposition at Special Term was predicated on this analysis; its decision focused on the actions of the special litigation committee, and the motions for summary judgment were granted on the ground that the business judgment doctrine precluded the courts from going back of the decision of the special litigation committee on behalf of the corporation not to pursue the claims alleged in the complaint. Similarly the reversal at the Appellate Division was based on that court's perception of the proper application of the business judgment rule to the actions and determination of the special litigation committee. We proceed on the same analysis, concluding, however, on the record before us, at variance with the Appellate Division, that the determination of the special litigation committee forecloses further judicial inquiry in this case.

It appears to us that the business judgment doctrine, at least in part, is grounded in the prudent recognition that courts are ill equipped and infrequently called on to evaluate what are and must be essentially business judgments. The authority and responsibilities vested in corporate directors both by statute and decisional law proceed on the assumption that inescapably there can be no available objective standard by which the correctness of every corporate decision may be measured, by the courts or otherwise. Even if that were not the case, by definition the responsibility for business judgments must rest with the corporate directors; their individual capabilities and experience peculiarly qualify them for the discharge of that responsibility. Thus, absent evidence of bad faith or fraud (of which there is none here) the courts must and properly should respect their determinations.

Derivative claims against corporate directors belong to the corporation itself. As with other questions of corporate policy and management, the decision whether and to what extent to explore and prosecute such claims lies within the judgment and control of the corporation's board of directors. Necessarily such decision must be predicated on the weighing and balancing of a variety of disparate considerations to reach a considered conclusion as to what course of action or inaction is best calculated to protect and advance the interests of the corporation. This is the essence of the responsibility and role of the board of directors, and courts may not intrude to interfere.

In the present case we confront a special instance of the application of the business judgment rule and inquire whether it applies in its full vigor to shield from judicial scrutiny the decision of a three-person minority committee of the board acting on behalf of the full board not to prosecute a shareholder's derivative action. The record in this case reveals that the board is a 15–member board, and that the derivative suit was brought against four of the directors. Nothing suggests that any of the other directors participated in any of the challenged first-tier transactions. Indeed the report of the audit committee on which the complaint is based specifically found that no other directors had any prior knowledge of or were in any way involved in any of these transactions. Other directors had, however, been members of the board in the period during which the transactions occurred. Each of the three director members of the special litigation committee joined the board thereafter.

The business judgment rule does not foreclose inquiry by the courts into the disinterested independence of those members of the board chosen by it to make the corporate decision on its behalf— here the members of the special litigation committee. Indeed the rule shields the deliberations and conclusions of the chosen representatives of the board only if they possess a disinterested independence and do not stand in a dual relation which prevents an unprejudicial exercise of judgment. (Cf. Koral v. Savory, Inc., 276 N.Y. 215, 11 N.E.2d 883.)

We examine then the proof submitted by defendants. It is not disputed that the members of the special litigation committee were not members of the corporation's board of directors at the time of the first-tier transactions in question. Howard Blauvelt, chairman of the board of Continental Oil Company, had been elected to the corporation's board of directors on October 9, 1975. Dr. John T. Dunlop, Lamont University professor at the Graduate School of Business Administration of Harvard University had been elected to the board on April 21, 1976. James R. Barker, chairman of the board and chief executive officer of Moore McCormack Resources, Inc., was added as the third member of the committee when he was elected to the board on July 19, 1976. None of the three had had any prior affiliation with the corporation. Notwithstanding the vigorous and imaginative hypothesizing and innuendo of counsel there is nothing in this record to raise a triable issue of fact as to the independence and disinterested status of these three directors.

The contention of Wallenstein that any committee authorized by the board of which defendant directors were members must be held to be legally infirm and may not be delegated power to terminate a derivative action must be rejected. In the very nature of the corporate organization it was only the existing board of directors which had authority on behalf of the corporation to direct the investigation and to assure the cooperation of corporate employees, and it is only that same board by its own action—or as here pursuant to authority duly delegated by it—which had authority to decide whether to prosecute the claims against defendant directors. The board in this instance, with slight adaptation, followed prudent practice in observing the general policy that when individual members of a board of directors prove to have personal interests which may conflict with the interests of the corporation, such interested directors must be excluded while the remaining members of the board proceed to consideration and action. (Cf. Business Corporation Law, § 713, which contemplates such situations and provides that the interested directors may nonetheless be included in the quorum count.) Courts have consistently held that the business judgment rule applies where some directors are charged with wrongdoing, so long as the remaining directors making the decision are disinterested and independent. (Swanson v. Traer, 249 F.2d 854, 858–859; Gall v. Exxon Corp., 418 F.Supp. 508, supplemented 75 Civ. 3582 [U.S.Dist.Ct., S.D.N.Y., Jan. 17, 1977]; Issner v. Aldrich, 254 F.Supp. 696, 701–702; Republic Nat. Life Ins. Co. v. Beasley, 73 F.R.D. 658, 668–669; Gilbert v. Curtiss–Wright Corp., 179 Misc. 641, 645, 38 N.Y.S.2d 548, 552.)

To accept the assertions of the intervenor and to disqualify the entire board would be to render the corporation powerless to make an effective business judgment with respect to prosecution of the derivative action. The possible risk of hesitancy on the part of the members of any committee, even if composed of outside, independent, disinterested directors, to investigate the activities of fellow members of the board where personal liability is at stake is an inherent, inescapable, given aspect of the corporation's predicament. To assign responsibility of the dimension here involved to individuals wholly separate and apart from the board of directors would, except in the most extraordinary circumstances, itself be an act of default and breach of the nondelegable fiduciary duty owed by the members of the board to the corporation and to its shareholders, employees and creditors. For the courts to preside over such determinations would similarly work an ouster of the board's fundamental responsibility and authority for corporate management.

We turn then to the action of the special litigation committee itself which comprised two components. First, there was the selection of procedures appropriate to the pursuit of its charge, and second, there was the ultimate substantive decision; predicated on the procedures chosen and the data produced thereby, not to pursue the claims advanced in the shareholders' derivative actions. The latter, substantive decision falls squarely within the embrace of the business judgment doctrine, involving as it did the weighing and balancing of legal, ethical, commercial, promotional, public relations, fiscal and other factors familiar to the resolution of many if not most corporate problems. To this extent the conclusion reached by the special litigation committee is outside the scope of our review. Thus, the courts cannot inquire as to which factors were considered by that committee or the relative weight accorded them in reaching that substantive decision—"the reasons for the payments, the advantages or disadvantages accruing to the corporation by reason of the transactions, the extent of the participation or profit by the respondent directors and the loss, if any, of public confidence in the corporation which might be incurred" (64 A.D.2d, at p. 107, 408 N.Y.S.2d at pp. 87–88). Inquiry into such matters would go to the very core of the business judgment made by the committee. To permit judicial probing of such issues would be to emasculate the business judgment doctrine as applied to the actions and determinations of the special litigation committee. Its substantive evaluation of the problems posed and its judgment in their resolution are beyond our reach.

As to the other component of the committee's activities, however, the situation is different, and here we agree with the Appellate Division. As to the methodologies and procedures best suited to the conduct of an investigation of facts and the determination of legal liability, the courts are well equipped by long and continuing experience and practice to make determinations. In fact they are better qualified in this regard than are corporate directors in general. Nor do the determinations to be made in the adoption of procedures partake of the nuances or special perceptions or comprehensions of business judgment or corporate activities or interests. The question is solely how appropriately to set about to gather the pertinent data.

While the court may properly inquire as to the adequacy and appropriateness of the committee's investigative procedures and methodologies, it may not under the guise of consideration of such factors trespass in the domain of business judgment. At the same time those responsible for the procedures by which the business judgment is reached may reasonably be required to show that they have pursued their chosen investigative methods in good faith. What evidentiary proof may be required to this end will, of course, depend on the nature of the particular investigation, and the proper reach of disclosure at the instance of the shareholders will in turn relate inversely to the showing made by the corporate representatives themselves. The latter may be expected to show that the areas and subjects to be examined are reasonably complete and that there has been a good-faith pursuit of inquiry into such areas and subjects. What has been uncovered and the relative weight accorded in evaluating and balancing the several factors and considerations are beyond the scope of judicial concern. Proof, however, that the investigation has been so restricted in scope, so shallow in execution, or otherwise so *pro forma* or halfhearted as to constitute a pretext or sham, consistent with the principles underlying the application of the business judgment doctrine, would raise questions of good faith or conceivably fraud which would never be shielded by that doctrine.

In addition to the issue of the disinterested independence of the special litigation committee, addressed above, the disposition of the present appeal turns, then, on whether on defendants' motions for summary judgment predicated on the investigation and determination of the special litigation committee, Wallenstein by tender of evidentiary proof in admissible form has shown facts sufficient to require a trial of any material issue of fact as to the adequacy or appropriateness of the *modus operandi* of that committee or has demonstrated acceptable excuse for failure to make such tender. (Friends of Animals v. Associated Fur Mfrs., 46 N.Y.2d 1065, 416 N.Y.S.2d 790, 390 N.E.2d 298; CPLR 3212, subd. [b].) We conclude that the requisite showing has not been made on this record.

At the outset we observe that Wallenstein, the intervenor, must accept the record in the state in which he finds it at the time he was granted leave to intervene in the Appellate Division. No application for intervention was made prior thereto, nor did the application when made seek any relief other than the right to appeal from the order of Special Term. (Cf. Matter of Martin v. Ronan, 47 N.Y.2d 486, 419 N.Y.S.2d 42, 392 N.E.2d 1226). Thus, because plaintiff Auerbach had submitted none, the record in this case is devoid of any affidavits or documentary evidence in opposition to the motions for summary judgment.

On the submissions made by defendants in support of their motions, we do not find either insufficiency or infirmity as to the procedures and methodologies chosen and pursued by the special litigation committee. That committee promptly engaged eminent special counsel to guide its deliberations and to advise it. The committee reviewed the prior work of the audit committee, testing its completeness, accuracy and thoroughness by interviewing representatives of Wilmer, Cutler & Pickering, reviewing transcripts of the testimony of 10 corporate officers and employees before the Securities and Exchange Commission, and studying documents collected by and work papers of the Washington law firm. Individual interviews were conducted with the directors found to have participated in any way in the questioned payments, and with representatives of Arthur Andersen & Co. Questionnaires were sent to and answered by each of the corporation's nonmanagement directors. At the conclusion of its investigation the special litigation committee sought and obtained pertinent legal advice from its special counsel. The selection of appropriate investigative methods must always turn on the nature and characteristics of the particular subject being investigated, but we find nothing in this record that requires a trial of any material issue of fact concerning the sufficiency or appropriateness of the procedures chosen by this special litigation committee. Nor is there anything in this record to raise a triable issue of fact as to the good-faith pursuit of its examination by that committee.

Finally, there should be a word as to the contention advanced by the intervenor that summary judgment should at least be withheld until there has been opportunity for disclosure. We note preliminarily as a matter of procedure that there was no application at Special Term for any such relief nor is there in the record any opposing affidavit from which it appears that essential facts may exist which could be obtained by disclosure (CPLR 3212, subd. [f]). It is also significant that neither in his brief nor on oral argument did Wallenstein identify any particulars as to which he desires discovery relating to the disinterestedness of the members of the special litigation committee or to the procedures followed by that committee. To speculate that something might be caught on a fishing expedition provides no basis to postpone decision on the summary judgment motions under the authority of CPLR 3212 (subd. [f]). The disclosure proposed and described by Wallenstein on oral argument would go only to particulars as to the results of the committee's investigation and work, the factors bearing on its substantive decision not to prosecute the derivative actions and the factual aspects of the underlying first-tier activities of defendants— all matters falling within the ambit of the business judgment doctrine and thus excluded from judicial scrutiny.

For the reasons stated the order of the Appellate Division should be modified, with costs to defendants, by reversing so much thereof as reversed the order of Supreme Court, and, as so modified, affirmed.

COOKE, Chief Judge (dissenting).

There should be an affirmance for the reasons set forth in the excellent analysis of Mr. Justice James D. Hopkins who wrote for a unanimous Appellate Division. In response to the majority opinion, a few remarks are added.

True, the "business judgment rule" is potentially applicable in these circumstances. But this case differs markedly from the typical situation in which that rule would be invoked. Here, the alleged wrongdoers are directors of the corporation. Of course, it would be most inappropriate to allow these interested directors to vote to preclude a shareholder's suit and thereby insulate themselves from liability (see Koral v. Savory, Inc., 276 N.Y. 215, 217–218, 11 N.E.2d 883, 885; see, also, United Copper Co. v. Amalgamated Copper Co., 244 U.S. 261, 263, 37 S.Ct. 509, 61 L.Ed. 1119). Hence, the lawsuit should be terminated only if a sufficient number of disinterested directors (cf. Business Corporation Law, § 713; Rapoport v. Schneider, 29 N.Y.2d 396, 402, 328 N.Y.S.2d 431, 436, 278 N.E.2d 642, 645), in this case the special litigation committee, rendered a good faith, " 'unprejudiced exercise of judgment' ", determining that maintenance of the action would not be in the best interests of the corporation (see Koral v. Savory, Inc., supra, 276 N.Y. at p. 217, 11 N.E.2d at p. 885).

Since the continuation of the suit is dependent, in large measure, upon the motives and actions of the defendants and the special litigation committee, and since knowledge of these matters "is peculiarly in the possession of the defendants themselves", summary judgment should not be granted prior to disclosure proceedings (Terranova v. Emil, 20 N.Y.2d 493, 496–497, 285 N.Y.S.2d 51, 54, 231 N.E.2d 753, 755). That the intervenor has not proposed potentially fruitful areas for disclosure should not, contrary to the majority holding, be determinative (see Udoff v. Zipf, 44 N.Y.2d 117, 122, 404 N.Y.S.2d 332, 334, 375 N.E.2d 392, 394). It is precisely because certain defendants and the members of the committee are possessed of exclusive knowledge of the facts that the intervenor is now unable to suggest the possible avenues which might successfully be pursued upon pretrial disclosure. And it is for this reason that we have formulated a rule precluding a grant of summary judgment where the case is likely to turn on "knowledge in the possession of the" moving party (e.g., Udoff v. Zipf, 44 N.Y.2d 117, 122, 404 N.Y.S.2d 332, 334, 375 N.E.2d 392, 394, supra; Terranova v. Emil, supra, 20 N.Y.2d at p. 497, 285 N.Y.S.2d at p. 53, 231 N.E.2d 753, 755; 4 Weinstein–Korn–Miller, N.Y.Civ.Prac., par. 3212.18). No reason can be discerned for denying application of that rule at this early stage in these obvious circumstances. The result of the majority ruling is to place the intervenor in a classic "Catch–22" situation, denying him disclosure because he has not come forward with facts—facts which by their very nature are discernible only after disclosure.

In sum, to deny the intervenor an opportunity for pretrial disclosure is to mistakenly group this case with the typical case involving the business judgment rule. Since the business judgment rule is only conditionally applicable here, and since certain defendants as well as the members of the special litigation committee have the sole knowledge of the facts upon which its applicability turns, summary judgment should be withheld pending disclosure proceedings. The result reached by the majority not only effectively dilutes the substantive rule of law at issue, but may also render corporate directors largely unaccountable to the shareholders whose business they are elected to govern.

JASEN, WACHTLER, FUCHSBERG and MEYER, JJ., concur with JONES, J.

COOKE, C.J., dissents and votes to affirm in a separate opinion.

GABRIELLI, J., taking no part.

Order modified, with costs to defendants, in accordance with the opinion herein and, as so modified, affirmed. Question certified answered in the negative.

ZAPATA CORP. v. MALDONADO

Supreme Court of Delaware, 1981.
430 A.2d 779.

Before DUFFY, QUILLEN and HORSEY, JJ.

[The claims on which this case was apparently based are stated as follows in Maldonado v. Flynn, 597 F.2d 789 (2d Cir.1979): A stock-option plan had been adopted by the board of Zapata Corporation in 1970 and approved by Zapata's shareholders in 1971. The board was authorized to amend the plan freely. The options were exercisable in five equal installments; the last exercise date was July 14, 1970. Flynn, the chief executive officer and a director of

Zapata, as well as other senior officers of Zapata, were granted options under the plan to purchase Zapata stock at $12.15 per share.

[In 1974, Flynn and the board had decided Zapata should make a cash tender offer for its own stock at $25–$30 per share. Since Zapata stock was then trading at only $19 per share, the announcement of the tender offer would trigger a sharp rise in the price of Zapata stock. The tender offer was to be publicly announced on July 2, 1974. Early that day, trading in Zapata stock on the New York Stock Exchange was suspended at the request of Zapata's management, pending the announcement. Before trading resumed, the board accelerated the final exercise date for the options held by Flynn and the other senior officers from July 14, 1974 to July 2, 1974. The board also modified the plan to authorize Zapata to make interest-free loans to Flynn and the other senior officers in the amount of (i) the purchase price of the options they exercised and (ii) the tax liability they would incur by exercising the options. The purpose and effect of these amendments were to permit Flynn and the other senior officers to benefit at Zapata's expense. Under applicable federal tax laws, on the exercise of the option Flynn and the other senior officers would realize ordinary income in the amount of the spread between the option price and the fair market price of the stock at the time the option was exercised. Correspondingly, Zapata could deduct the amount of that spread as a business expense. By accelerating the last exercise date, and allowing Flynn and the other senior officers to exercise their options before the market price of the stock rose as a result of the tender offer, the board permitted the optionees to save a considerable amount of taxes but prevented Zapata from enjoying a correspondingly higher tax deduction.]

QUILLEN, Justice. This is an interlocutory appeal from an order entered on April 9, 1980, by the Court of Chancery denying appellant-defendant Zapata Corporation's (Zapata) alternative motions to dismiss the complaint or for summary judgment. The issue to be addressed has reached this Court by way of a rather convoluted path.

In June, 1975, William Maldonado, a stockholder of Zapata, instituted a derivative action in the Court of Chancery on behalf of Zapata against ten officers and/or directors of Zapata, alleging, essentially, breaches of fiduciary duty. Maldonado did not first demand that the board bring this action, stating instead such demand's futility because all directors were named as defendants and allegedly participated in the acts specified.[1] In June, 1977, Maldonado commenced an action in the United States District Court for the Southern District of New York against the same defendants,

1. Court of Chancery Rule 23.1 states in part: "The complaint shall also allege with particularity the efforts, if any, made by the plaintiff to obtain the action he desires from the directors or comparable authority and the reasons for his failure to obtain the action or for not making the effort."

save one, alleging federal security law violations as well as the same common law claims made previously in the Court of Chancery.

By June, 1979, four of the defendant-directors were no longer on the board, and the remaining directors appointed two new outside directors to the board. The board then created an "Independent Investigation Committee" (Committee), composed solely of the two new directors, to investigate Maldonado's actions . . . and to determine whether the corporation should continue any or all of the litigation. The Committee's determination was stated to be "final, . . . not . . . subject to review by the Board of Directors and . . . in all respects . . . binding upon the Corporation."

Following an investigation, the Committee concluded, in September, 1979, that each action should "be dismissed forthwith as their continued maintenance is inimical to the Company's best interests. . . ." Consequently, Zapata moved for dismissal or summary judgment. . . .

On March 18, 1980, the Court of Chancery, in a reported opinion, the basis for the order of April 9, 1980, denied Zapata's motions, holding that Delaware law does not sanction this means of dismissal. More specifically, it held that the "business judgment" rule is not a grant of authority to dismiss derivative actions and that a stockholder has an individual right to maintain derivative actions in certain instances. Maldonado v. Flynn, Del.Ch., 413 A.2d 1251 (1980) (herein *Maldonado*). Pursuant to the provisions of Supreme Court Rule 42, Zapata filed an interlocutory appeal with this Court shortly thereafter. . . .

. . . As the Vice Chancellor noted, 413 A.2d at 1257, "it is the law of the State of incorporation which determines whether the directors have this power of dismissal, Burks v. Lasker, 441 U.S. 471, 99 S.Ct. 1831, 60 L.Ed.2d 404 (1979)". We limit our review in this interlocutory appeal to whether the Committee has the power to cause the present action to be dismissed.

We begin with an examination of the carefully considered opinion of the Vice Chancellor which states, in part, that the "business judgment" rule does not confer power "to a corporate board of directors to terminate a derivative suit", 413 A.2d at 1257. His conclusion is particularly pertinent because several federal courts, applying Delaware law, have held that the business judgment rule enables boards (or their committees) to terminate derivative suits, decisions now in conflict with the holding below.

As the term is most commonly used, and given the disposition below, we can understand the Vice Chancellor's comment that "the business judgment rule is irrelevant to the question of whether the Committee has the authority to compel the dismissal of this suit." 413 A.2d at 1257. Corporations, existing because of legislative grace, possess authority as granted by the legislature. Directors of Delaware corporations derive their managerial decision making power, which encompasses decisions whether to initiate, or refrain from entering, litigation, from 8 Del.C. § 141(a). This statute is the fount of directorial powers. The "business judgment" rule is a judicial creation that presumes propriety, under certain circumstances, in a board's decision. Viewed defensively, it does not create authority. In this sense the "business judgment" rule is not relevant in corporate decision making until after a decision is made. It is generally used as a defense to an attack on the decision's soundness. The board's managerial decision making power, however, comes from § 141(a). The judicial creation and legislative grant are related because the "business judgment" rule evolved to give recognition and deference to directors' business expertise when exercising their managerial power under § 141(a).

In the case before us, although the corporation's decision to move to dismiss or for summary judgment was, literally, a decision resulting from an exercise of the directors' (as delegated to the Committee) business judgment, the question of "business judgment", in a defensive sense, would not become relevant until and unless the decision to seek termination of the derivative lawsuit was attacked as improper.... This question was not reached by the Vice Chancellor because he determined that the stockholder had an individual right to maintain this derivative action....

Thus, the focus in this case is on the power to speak for the corporation as to whether the lawsuit should be continued or terminated. As we see it, this issue in the current appellate posture of this case has three aspects: the conclusions of the Court below concerning the continuing right of a stockholder to maintain a derivative action; the corporate power under Delaware law of an authorized board committee to cause dismissal of litigation instituted for the benefit of the corporation; and the role of the Court of Chancery in resolving conflicts between the stockholder and the committee.

Accordingly, we turn first to the Court of Chancery's conclusions concerning the right of a plaintiff stockholder in a derivative action. We find that its determination that a stockholder, once demand is made and refused, possesses an independent, individual right to continue a derivative suit for breaches of fiduciary duty over objection by the corporation, *Maldonado,* 413 A.2d at 1262–63, as an absolute rule, is erroneous....

... McKee v. Rogers, Del.Ch., 156 A. 191 (1931), stated "as a general rule" that "a stockholder cannot be permitted ... to invade the discretionary field committed to the judgment of the directors and sue in the corporation's behalf when the managing body refuses. This rule is a well settled one." 156 A. at 193.

The *McKee* rule, of course, should not be read so broadly that the board's refusal will be determinative in every instance. Board members, owing a well-established fiduciary duty to the corporation, will not be allowed to cause a derivative suit to be dismissed when it would be a breach of their fiduciary duty. Generally disputes pertaining to control of the suit arise in two contexts.

Consistent with the purpose of requiring a demand, a board decision to cause a derivative suit to be dismissed as detrimental to the company, after demand has been made and refused, will be respected unless it was wrongful.[10]   ... A claim of a wrongful decision not to sue is thus the first exception and the first context of dispute.   Absent a wrongful refusal, the stockholder in such a situation simply lacks legal managerial power. . . .

But it cannot be implied that, absent a wrongful board refusal, a stockholder can never have an individual right to initiate an action.   For, as is stated in *McKee*, a "well settled" exception exists to the general rule.

> "[A] stockholder may sue in equity in his derivative right to assert a cause of action in behalf of the corporation, *without prior demand* upon the directors to sue, when it is apparent that a demand would be futile, that the officers are under an influence that sterilizes discretion and could not be proper persons to conduct the litigation."

156 A. at 193 (emphasis added).   This exception, the second context for dispute, is consistent with the Court of Chancery's statement below, that "[t]he stockholders' individual right to bring the action does not ripen, however, ... unless he can show a demand to be futile." *Maldonado*, 413 A.2d at 1262.[11]

These comments in *McKee* and in the opinion below make obvious sense.   A demand, when required and refused (if not wrongful), terminates a stockholder's legal ability to initiate a derivative action.   But where demand is properly excused, the stockholder does possess the ability to initiate the action on his corporation's behalf.

These conclusions, however, do not determine the question before us.   Rather, they merely bring us to the question to be decided.   It is here that we part company with the Court below. Derivative suits enforce corporate rights and any recovery obtained goes to the corporation. . . .   We see no inherent reason why the "two phases" of a derivative suit, the stockholder's suit to compel the corporation to sue and the corporation's suit, ... should automatically result in the placement in the hands of the litigating stockholder [of] sole control of the corporate right throughout the litigation.   To the contrary, it seems to us that such an inflexible rule would recognize the interest of one person or group to the exclusion of all others within the corporate entity.   Thus, we reject the view of the Vice Chancellor as to the first aspect of the issue on appeal.

10. In other words, when stockholders, after making demand and having their suit rejected, attack the board's decision as improper, the board's decision falls under the "business judgment" rule and will be respected if the requirements of the rule are met. . . .   That situation should be distinguished from the instant case, where demand was not made, and the *power* of the board to seek a dismissal, due to disqualification, presents a threshold issue. . . .

11. These statements are consistent with Rule 23.1's "reasons for ... failure" to make demand. . . .

The question to be decided becomes: When, if at all, should an authorized board committee be permitted to cause litigation, properly initiated by a derivative stockholder in his own right, to be dismissed? As noted above, a board has the power to choose not to pursue litigation when demand is made upon it, so long as the decision is not wrongful. If the board determines that a suit would be detrimental to the company, the board's determination prevails. Even when demand is excusable, circumstances may arise when continuation of the litigation would not be in the corporation's best interests. Our inquiry is whether, under such circumstances, there is a permissible procedure under § 141(a) by which a corporation can rid itself of detrimental litigation. If there is not, a single stockholder in an extreme case might control the destiny of the entire corporation. This concern was bluntly expressed by the Ninth Circuit in Lewis v. Anderson, 9th Cir., 615 F.2d 778, 783 (1979), cert. denied, 449 U.S. 869, 101 S.Ct. 206, 66 L.Ed.2d 89 (1980): "To allow one shareholder to incapacitate an entire board of directors merely by leveling charges against them gives too much leverage to dissident shareholders." But, when examining the means, including the committee mechanism examined in this case, potentials for abuse must be recognized. This takes us to the second and third aspects of the issue on appeal.

Before we pass to equitable considerations as to the mechanism at issue here, it must be clear that an independent committee possesses the corporate power to seek the termination of a derivative suit. Section 141(c) allows a board to delegate all of its authority to a committee. Accordingly, a committee with properly delegated authority would have the power to move for dismissal or summary judgment if the entire board did.

Even though demand was not made in this case and the initial decision of whether to litigate was not placed before the board, Zapata's board, it seems to us, retained all of its corporate power concerning litigation decisions. If Maldonado had made demand on the board in this case, it could have refused to bring suit. Maldonado could then have asserted that the decision not to sue was wrongful and, if correct, would have been allowed to maintain the suit. The board, however, never would have lost its statutory managerial authority. The demand requirement itself evidences that the managerial power is retained by the board. When a derivative plaintiff is allowed to bring suit after a wrongful refusal, the board's authority to choose whether to pursue the litigation is not challenged although its conclusion—reached through the exercise of that authority—is not respected since it is wrongful. Similarly, Rule 23.1, by excusing demand in certain instances, does not strip the board of its corporate power. It merely saves the plaintiff the expense and delay of making a futile demand resulting in a probable tainted exercise of that authority in a refusal by the board or in giving control of litigation to the opposing side. But the board entity remains empowered under § 141(a) to make decisions regarding corporate litigation. The problem is one of member disqualification, not the absence of power in the board.

The corporate power inquiry then focuses on whether the board, tainted by the self-interest of a majority of its members, can legally delegate its authority to a committee of two disinterested directors. We find our statute clearly requires an affirmative answer to this question. As has been noted, under an express provision of the statute, § 141(c), a committee can exercise all of the authority of the board to the extent provided in the resolution of the board. Moreover, at least by analogy to our statutory section on interested directors, 8 Del.C. § 141, it seems clear that the Delaware statute is designed to permit disinterested directors to act for the board.[14] Compare Puma v. Marriott, Del.Ch., 283 A.2d 693, 695–96 (1971).

We do not think that the interest taint of the board majority is per se a legal bar to the delegation of the board's power to an independent committee composed of disinterested board members. The committee can properly act for the corporation to move to dismiss derivative litigation that is believed to be detrimental to the corporation's best interest.

Our focus now switches to the Court of Chancery which is faced with a stockholder assertion that a derivative suit, properly instituted, should continue for the benefit of the corporation and a corporate assertion, properly made by a board committee acting with board authority, that the same derivative suit should be dismissed as inimical to the best interests of the corporation.

At the risk of stating the obvious, the problem is relatively simple. If, on the one hand, corporations can consistently wrest bona fide derivative actions away from well-meaning derivative plaintiffs through the use of the committee mechanism, the derivative suit will lose much, if not all, of its generally-recognized effectiveness as an intra-corporate means of policing boards of directors. See Dent, supra note 5, 75 Nw.U.L.Rev. at 96 & n. 3, 144 & n. 241. If, on the other hand, corporations are unable to rid themselves of meritless or harmful litigation and strike suits, the derivative action, created to benefit the corporation, will produce the opposite, unintended result. For a discussion of strike suits, see Dent, supra, 75 Nw.U.L.Rev. at 137. See also Cramer v. General Telephone & Electronics Corp., 3d Cir., 582 F.2d 259, 275 (1978), cert. denied, 439 U.S. 1129, 99 S.Ct. 1048, 59 L.Ed.2d 90 (1979). It thus appears desirable to us to find a balancing point where bona fide stockholder power to bring corporation causes of action cannot be unfairly trampled on by the board of directors, but the corporation can rid itself of detrimental litigation.

As we noted, the question has been treated by other courts as one of the "business judgment" of the board committee. If a "committee, composed of independent and disinterested directors, conducted a proper review of the matters before it, considered a

---

14. [The court quoted Del. § 144.]

variety of factors and reached, in good faith, a business judgment that [the] action was not in the best interest of [the corporation]", the action must be dismissed. See, e.g., Maldonado v. Flynn, ... 485 F.Supp. at 282, 286. The issues become solely independence, good faith, and reasonable investigation. The ultimate conclusion of the committee, under that view, is not subject to judicial review.

We are not satisfied, however, that acceptance of the "business judgment" rationale at this stage of derivative litigation is a proper balancing point. While we admit an analogy with a normal case respecting board judgment, it seems to us that there is sufficient risk in the realities of a situation like the one presented in this case to justify caution beyond adherence to the theory of business judgment.

The context here is a suit against directors where demand on the board is excused. We think some tribute must be paid to the fact that the lawsuit was properly initiated. It is not a board refusal case. Moreover, this complaint was filed in June of 1975 and, while the parties undoubtedly would take differing views on the degree of litigation activity, we have to be concerned about the creation of an "Independent Investigation Committee" four years later, after the election of two new outside directors. Situations could develop where such motions could be filed after years of vigorous litigation for reasons unconnected with the merits of the lawsuit.

Moreover, notwithstanding our conviction that Delaware law entrusts the corporate power to a properly authorized committee, we must be mindful that directors are passing judgment on fellow directors in the same corporation and fellow directors, in this instance, who designated them to serve both as directors and committee members. The question naturally arises whether a "there but for the grace of God go I" empathy might not play a role. And the further question arises whether inquiry as to independence, good faith and reasonable investigation is sufficient safeguard against abuse, perhaps subconscious abuse.

There is another line of exploration besides the factual context of this litigation which we find helpful. The nature of this motion finds no ready pigeonhole, as perhaps illustrated by its being set forth in the alternative. It is perhaps best considered as a hybrid summary judgment motion for dismissal because the stockholder plaintiff's standing to maintain the suit has been lost. But it does not fit neatly into a category described in Rule 12(b) of the Court of Chancery Rules nor does it correspond directly with Rule 56 since the question of genuine issues of fact on the merits of the stockholder's claim are not reached.

It seems to us that there are two other procedural analogies that are helpful in addition to reference to Rules 12 and 56. There is some analogy to a settlement in that there is a request to terminate litigation without a judicial determination of the merits. See Perrine v. Pennroad Corp., Del.Super., 47 A.2d 479, 487 (1946). "In determining whether or not to approve a proposed settlement of a derivative stockholders' action [when directors are on both sides of the transaction], the Court of Chancery is called upon to exercise its own business judgment." Neponsit Investment Co. v. Abramson, Del.Super., 405 A.2d 97, 100 (1979) and cases therein cited. In this case, the litigating stockholder plaintiff facing dismissal of a lawsuit properly commenced ought, in our judgment, to have sufficient status for strict Court review.

Finally, if the committee is in effect given status to speak for the corporation as the plaintiff in interest, then it seems to us there is an analogy to Court of Chancery Rule 41(a)(2) where the plaintiff seeks a dismissal after an answer. Certainly, the position of record of the litigating stockholder is adverse to the position advocated by the corporation in the motion to dismiss. Accordingly, there is perhaps some wisdom to be gained by the direction in Rule 41(a)(2) that "an action shall not be dismissed at the plaintiff's instance save upon order of the Court and upon such terms and conditions as the Court deems proper."

Whether the Court of Chancery will be persuaded by the exercise of a committee power resulting in a summary motion for dismissal of a derivative action, where a demand has not been initially made, should rest, in our judgment, in the independent discretion of the Court of Chancery. We thus steer a middle course between those cases which yield to the independent business judgment of a board committee and this case as determined below which would yield to unbridled plaintiff stockholder control. In pursuit of the course, we recognize that "[t]he final substantive judgment whether a particular lawsuit should be maintained requires a balance of many factors—ethical, commercial, promotional, public relations, employee relations, fiscal as well as legal." Maldonado v. Flynn, supra, 485 F.Supp. at 285. But we are content that such factors are not "beyond the judicial reach" of the Court of Chancery which regularly and competently deals with fiduciary relationships, disposition of trust property, approval of settlements and scores of similar problems. We recognize the danger of judicial overreaching but the alternatives seem to us to be outweighed by the fresh view of a judicial outsider. Moreover, if we failed to balance all the interests involved, we would in the name of practicality and judicial economy foreclose a judicial decision on the merits. At this point, we are not convinced that is necessary or desirable.

After an objective and thorough investigation of a derivative suit, an independent committee may cause its corporation to file a pretrial motion to dismiss in the Court of Chancery. The basis of the motion is the best interests of the corporation, as determined by the committee. The motion should include a thorough written record of the investigation and its findings and recommendations. Under appropriate court supervision, akin to proceedings on summary judgment, each side should have an opportunity to make a record on the motion. As to the limited issues presented by the motion noted below, the moving party should be prepared to meet the normal burden under Rule 56 that there is no genuine issue as to any material fact and that the moving party is entitled to dismiss as a matter of law.[15] The Court should apply a two-step test to the motion.

First, the Court should inquire into the independence and good faith of the committee and the bases supporting its conclusions. Limited discovery may be ordered to facilitate such inquiries. The corporation should have the burden of proving independence, good faith and a reasonable investigation, rather than presuming independence, good faith and reasonableness.[17] If the Court determines that the committee is not independent or has not shown reasonable bases for its conclusions, or, if the Court is not satisfied for other reasons relating to the process, including but not limited to the good faith of the committee, the Court shall deny the corporation's motion. If, however, the Court is satisfied under Rule 56 standards that the committee was independent and showed reasonable bases for good faith findings and recommendations, the Court may proceed, in its discretion, to the next step.

The second step provides, we believe, the essential key in striking the balance between legitimate corporate claims as expressed in a derivative stockholder suit and a corporation's best interests as expressed by an independent investigating committee. The Court should determine, applying its own independent business judgment, whether the motion should be granted.[18] This means, of course, that instances could arise where a committee can establish its independence and sound bases for its good faith decisions and still have the corporation's motion denied. The second step is intended to thwart instances where corporate actions meet the criteria of step one, but the result does not appear to satisfy its spirit, or where corporate actions would simply prematurely terminate a stockholder grievance deserving of further consideration in the corporation's interest. The Court of Chancery of course must carefully consider and weigh how compelling the corporate interest in dismissal is when faced with a nonfrivolous lawsuit. The Court of Chancery should, when appropriate, give special consideration to matters of law and public policy in addition to the corporation's best interests.

---

15. We do not foreclose a discretionary trial of factual issues but that issue is not presented in this appeal. See Lewis v. Anderson, supra, 615 F.2d at 780. Nor do we foreclose the possibility that other motions may proceed or be joined with such a pretrial summary judgment motion to dismiss, e.g., a partial motion for summary judgment on the merits.

17. Compare Auerbach v. Bennett, 47 N.Y.2d 619, 419 N.Y.S.2d 920, 928–29, 393 N.E.2d 994 (1979). Our approach here is analogous to and consistent with the Dela-

ware approach to "interested director" transactions, where the directors, once the transaction is attacked, have the burden of establishing its "intrinsic fairness" to a court's careful scrutiny. See, e.g., Sterling v. Mayflower Hotel Corp., Del.Supr., 93 A.2d 107 (1952).

18. This step shares some of the same spirit and philosophy of the statement by the Vice Chancellor: "Under our system of law, courts and not litigants should decide the merits of litigation." 413 A.2d at 1263.

If the Court's independent business judgment is satisfied, the Court may proceed to grant the motion, subject, of course, to any equitable terms or conditions the Court finds necessary or desirable.

The interlocutory order of the Court of Chancery is reversed and the cause is remanded for further proceedings consistent with this opinion.

———

ARONSON v. LEWIS, 473 A.2d 805 (Del.1984). "The gap in our law, which we address today, arises from this Court's decision in Zapata Corp. v. Maldonado. There, the Court defined the limits of a board's managerial power granted by Section 141(a) and restricted application of the business judgment rule in a factual context similar to this action. . . .

"After *Zapata* numerous derivative suits were filed without prior demand upon boards of directors. The complaints in such actions all alleged that demand was excused because of board interest, approval or acquiescence in the wrongdoing. In any event, the *Zapata* demand-excused/demand-refused bifurcation, has left a crucial issue unanswered: when is demand futile and, therefore, excused?

"Delaware courts have addressed the issue of demand futility on several earlier occasions. . . . The rule emerging from these decisions is that where officers and directors are under an influence which sterilizes their discretion, they cannot be considered proper persons to conduct litigation on behalf of the corporation. Thus, demand would be futile. See e.g., McKee v. Rogers, Del.Ch., 156 A. 191, 192 (1931) (holding that where a defendant controlled the board of directors, '[i]t is manifest then that there can be no expectation that the corporation would sue him, and if it did, it can hardly be said that the prosecution of the suit would be entrusted to proper hands'). . . .

"However, those cases cannot be taken to mean that any board approval of a challenged transaction automatically connotes 'hostile interest' and 'guilty participation' by directors, or some other form of sterilizing influence upon them. Were that so, the demand requirements of our law would be meaningless, leaving the clear mandate of Chancery Rule 23.1 devoid of its purpose and substance. . . .

"Our view is that in determining demand futility the Court of Chancery in the proper exercise of its discretion must decide whether, under the particularized facts alleged, a reasonable doubt is created that: (1) the directors are disinterested and independent and (2) the challenged transaction was otherwise the product of a valid exercise of business judgment. Hence, the Court of Chancery must make two inquiries, one into the independence and disinterestedness of the directors and the other into the substantive nature of the challenged transaction and the board's approval thereof. As to the latter inquiry the court does not assume that the transaction is a wrong to the corporation requiring corrective steps by the board. Rather, the alleged wrong is substantively reviewed against the factual background alleged in the complaint. As to the former inquiry, directorial independence and disinterestedness, the court reviews the factual allegations to decide whether they raise a reasonable doubt, as a threshold matter, that the protections of the business judgment rule are available to the board. Certainly, if this is an 'interested' director transaction, such that the business judgment rule is inapplicable to the board majority approving the transaction, then the inquiry ceases. In that event futility of demand has been established by any objective or subjective standard.[8] See, e.g., Bergstein v. Texas Internat'l Co., Del.Ch., 453 A.2d 467, 471 (1982) (because five of nine directors approved stock appreciation rights plan likely to benefit them, board was interested for demand purposes and demand held futile). This includes situations involving self-dealing directors....

"However, the mere threat of personal liability for approving a questioned transaction, standing alone, is insufficient to challenge either the independence or disinterestedness of directors, although in rare cases a transaction may be so egregious on its face that board approval cannot meet the test of business judgment, and a substantial likelihood of director liability therefore exists.... In sum the entire review is factual in nature. The Court of Chancery in the exercise of its sound discretion must be satisfied that a plaintiff has alleged facts with particularity which, taken as true, support a reasonable doubt that the challenged transaction was the product of a valid exercise of business judgment. Only in that context is demand excused."

    KAPLAN v. WYATT, 499 A.2d 1184 (Del.1985). In this case, the Delaware Supreme Court put still another gloss on *Zapata.* There the trial court had dismissed a derivative action on the basis of a litigation committee report. The trial court reviewed the independence of the committee and the conduct of the investigation, but did not formally proceed to the "second step" of *Zapata,* as set out at the end of that opinion. In *Zapata,* the Delaware court had said that the second step was discretionary. In *Kaplan,* the court held that it meant what it had said:

    Kaplan contends that even if the Court of Chancery found that Coastal's Committee satisfied the first step of *Zapata,* the

---

8. We recognize that drawing the line at a majority of the board may be an arguably arbitrary dividing point. Critics will charge that we are ignoring the structural bias common to corporate boards throughout America, as well as the other unseen socialization processes cutting against independent discussion and decisionmaking in the boardroom. The difficulty with structural bias in a demand futile case is simply one of establishing it in the complaint for purposes of Rule 23.1. We are satisfied that discretionary review by the Court of Chancery of complaints alleging specific facts pointing to bias on a particular board will be sufficient for determining demand futility.

Court erred in not proceeding to the discretionary second step of the analysis. This step "is intended to thwart instances where corporate actions meet the criterion of step one, but the result does not appear to satisfy its spirit, or where the corporate actions would simply prematurely terminate a stockholder grievance deserving of further consideration in the corporation's interest." 430 A.2d at 789. Kaplan contends that his suit is one that this step is meant to preserve.

Proceeding to the second step of the *Zapata* analysis is wholly within the discretion of the court, and the Court of Chancery did not abuse its discretion when it declined to proceed to this step. Dismissing Kaplan's suit does not disturb the spirit of *Zapata*. The Committee's report supports the finding that further litigation would not be in the best interest of Coastal. The corporation's resources would be misspent in litigation based on the allegations in Kaplan's complaint. Therefore, the Court of Chancery properly applied the *Zapata* guidelines, and its decision to dismiss the suit was correct.

It is difficult to fit *Kaplan* together with *Zapata*. Although the court in *Zapata* said that the second step was discretionary, it also said that the second step "provides ... the *essential* key in striking the balance between legitimate corporate claims as expressed in a derivative stockholder suit and a corporation's best interests as expressed by an independent investigating committee." (Emphasis added.)

It is also difficult to assess the significance of *Kaplan*. Even under the first step, as formulated in *Zapata*, the court must inquire into the bases supporting the committee's conclusions. If, as a result of that inquiry, "the Court determines either that the committee ... has not shown reasonable bases for its conclusions, or ... the Court is not satisfied for other reasons relating to the process, including but not limited to the good faith of the committee, the Court shall deny the corporation's motion." Thus the distinction between the first and second steps is not entirely clear. While the trial court in *Kaplan* did not proceed to the second step as a formal matter, it nevertheless considered with care the report of the litigation committee and the justifications advanced in that report, as did the Supreme Court. Furthermore, the committee had caused the defendant to return $195,000 to the corporation, based on overpayments and billing errors the committee unearthed, and the plaintiff apparently could come up with no information in support of the charges in its complaint.

———

GROBOW v. PEROT, 539 A.2d 180 (Del.1988). "[G]iven the highly factual nature of the inquiry presented to the Trial Court by a Rule 23.1 defense, we conclude that it would be neither practicable nor wise to attempt to formulate a criterion of general application for determining reasonable doubt [under *Aronson v. Lewis*]. The facts necessary to support a finding of reasonable doubt either of director disinterest or independence, or whether proper business judgment was exercised in the transaction will vary with each case. Reasonable doubt must be decided by the trial court on a case-by-case basis employing an objective analysis. Were we to adopt a standard criterion for resolving a motion to dismiss based on Rule 23.1, the test for demand excusal would, in all likelihood, become rote and inelastic. . . .

"We think it sufficient simply to say that the Court of Chancery must weigh the presumption of the business judgment rule that attaches to a board of directors' decision against the well-pleaded facts alleged in a plaintiff's demand-futility complaint."

See also Levine v. Smith, 591 A.2d 194 (Del.Supr.1991).

SPARKS & MIRVIS, RECENT DEVELOPMENTS WITH RESPECT TO THE DEMAND REQUIREMENT IN DERIVATIVE SUITS

ABA, The New Dynamics of Corporate Governance (1993).

A strict reading of *Aronson* and its progeny . . . might suggest that it has become difficult, if not impossible, to successfully allege demand futility. The reality is to the contrary. Since the decision of the Delaware Supreme Court in *Levine v. Smith* in 1991, there have been a number of decisions where the Delaware Court of Chancery has excused stockholders from making a demand. . . .

For example, in *Abajian v. Kennedy,* C.A. No. 11425 (Del.Ch. Jan. 17, 1992), Chancellor Allen, emphasizing the highly discretionary nature of the "reasonable doubt" determination set forth in *Aronson* and its progeny, denied defendants' motion to dismiss entrenchment claims arising as the result of an issuance of preferred stock and a loan to an ESOP for failure to make demand, concluding that the facts alleged in the amended complaint were "sufficient to create a reasonable doubt concerning the availability of the business judgment protections." *Abajian, supra,* slip op. at 2.

Similarly, in *In re Chrysler Corp. Shareholders Litig.,* C.A. No. 11873 (Del.Ch. July 27, 1992), Vice Chancellor Jacobs found that the entrenchment claims in the complaint contained particularized facts sufficient to create a reasonable doubt that the directors were motivated solely or primarily by entrenchment concerns and that they were disinterested when they adopted the amendments which lowered the trigger on the corporation's rights plan. *Chrysler, supra,* slip op. at 9.

Continuing the spate of recent cases excusing demand, the most recent pronouncement from the Delaware Supreme Court on the demand requirement came in *Heineman v. Datapoint Corp.,* 611 A.2d 950 (Del.1992). In *Heineman,* the Court reversed, as an abuse of discretion, the decision of the Court of Chancery dismissing the plaintiff's amended complaint for failure to allege with particularity facts sufficient to excuse demand. While the Supreme Court reaffirmed the principles in *Aronson* and *Levine* with respect to the pertinent legal standards, the Court emphasized that the Court of Chancery's decision under those principles "involves essentially a discretionary ruling on a predominantly factual issue." *Id.* at 952. In reviewing the Court of Chancery's decision, the Supreme Court separately analyzed all four of the transactions challenged in the complaint under the abuse of discretion standard, and rebuked the lower court for giving "conclusory treatment" to the claims in the complaint and for not analyzing the claims separately. The Court went on to find that, with respect to two of the transactions at issue, the plaintiff had "alleged sufficient facts of apparent self-dealing to raise a reasonable doubt concerning director disinterest." With respect to the other two transactions, the Court gave the benefit of the doubt to plaintiff and refused to affirm the dismissal of the claims even though the Court stated that it was "at least arguable" that the factual allegations underlying the claims were inadequate. Instead, the Court gave the plaintiff leave to amend his complaint with respect to those claims. . . .

These recent Delaware cases suggest that the demand pendulum may have reached its furthest point in *Levine,* and are illustrative of the fact that the demand requirement has not led to a wholesale dismissal of meritorious derivative actions. Instead, the demand requirement, with thoughtful application, appears to be evolving into a sensitive device for sorting out frivolous claims at an early stage in litigation. . . .

———

ALFORD v. SHAW, 320 N.C. 465, 358 S.E.2d 323 (1987). "The recent trend among courts which have been faced with the choice of applying an *Auerbach*-type rule of judicial deference or a *Zapata*-type rule of judicial scrutiny has been to require judicial inquiry on the merits of the special litigation committee's report. . . .

" . . . We interpret the trend away from *Auerbach* among other jurisdictions as an indication of growing concern about the deficiencies inherent in a rule giving great deference to the decisions of a corporate committee whose institutional symbiosis with the corporation necessarily affects its ability to render a decision that fairly considers the interest of plaintiffs forced to bring suit on behalf of the corporation. *See generally* Cox & Munsinger, *Bias in the Boardroom: Psychological Foundations and Legal Implications of Corporate Cohesion,* 48 Law and Contemporary Problems, Summer 1985 at 83 (1985). Such concerns are legitimate ones and, upon further reflection, we find that they must be resolved not by slavish adherence to the business judgment rule, but by careful interpretation of the provisions of our own Business Corporation Act. . . .

"[A] policy of protecting minority shareholders is manifested by section 55–55(c), which states that a shareholder's derivative action shall not be discontinued, dismissed, compromised or settled without the approval of the court. If the court shall determine that the interest of the shareholders or any class or classes thereof, or of the creditors of the corporation, will be substantially affected by such discontinuance, dismissal, compromise or settlement, the court, in its discretion, may direct that notice, by publication or otherwise, shall be given to such shareholders or creditors whose interests it determines will be so affected. . . .

"Although the recommendation of the special litigation committee is not binding on the court, in making this determination the court may choose to rely on such recommendation. To rely blindly on the report of a corporation-appointed committee which assembled such materials on behalf of the corporation is to abdicate the judicial duty to consider the interests of shareholders imposed by the statute. . . .

"The *Zapata* Court limited its two-step judicial inquiry to cases in which demand upon the corporation was futile and therefore excused. However, we find no justification for such limitation in our statutes. The language of section 55–55(c) is inclusive and draws no distinctions between demand-excused and other types of cases. *Cf.* ALI Principles of Corporate Governance: Analysis and Recommendations § 7.08 & Reporter's Notes 2 & 4 at 135–139 (Council Draft No. 6, Oct. 10, 1986) (issue of demand of minimal importance in determining scope of review; demand-excused/demand-required distinction not determinative). Thus, court approval is required for disposition of *all* derivative suits, even where the directors are not charged with fraud or self-dealing, or where the plaintiff and the board agree to discontinue, dismiss, compromise, or settle the lawsuit."

———

REVISED MODEL BUSINESS CORPORATION ACT §§ 7.42–7.44

[See Statutory Supplement]

———

AMERICAN LAW INSTITUTE, PRINCIPLES OF CORPORATE GOVERNANCE §§ 7.03, 7.04, 7.08–7.13

[See Statutory Supplement]

———

SECTION 7. DEMAND ON THE SHAREHOLDERS

NOTE ON DEMAND ON SHAREHOLDERS

1. The rules governing demand on the shareholders vary widely, both from state to state and among federal courts. Under the law of many jurisdictions, demand on shareholders is not required at all. For example, the California and New York statutory counterparts to FRCP 23.1—Cal. § 800(b) and N.Y. § 626—omit any reference to demand on the shareholders, and it is clear that this omission was deliberate. See Syracuse Television, Inc. v. Channel 9, Syracuse, Inc., 51 Misc.2d 188, 273 N.Y.S.2d 16 (1966). In a number of jurisdictions, demand on the shareholders is required unless excused, but, there is considerable divergence concerning what constitutes an acceptable excuse.

2. Of those jurisdictions that normally require demand:

(a) All agree that demand is excused when the alleged wrongdoers hold a majority of the stock. See, e.g., Heilbrunn v. Hanover Equities Corp., 259 F.Supp. 936 (S.D.N.Y.1966). Most would probably come to the same result where the wrongdoers hold a controlling but less-than-majority interest. See Gottesman v. General Motors Corp., 268 F.2d 194 (2d Cir.1959). But see Levitan v. Stout, 97 F.Supp. 105 (W.D.Ky.1951).

(b) All would probably agree that demand is also excused when it is futile for other reasons (although there might be considerable divergence as to whether a given state of facts constitutes futility). See, e.g., Pioche Mines Consolidated, Inc. v. Dolman, 333 F.2d 257, 264–65 (9th Cir.1964), cert. denied 380 U.S. 956, 85 S.Ct. 1081, 13 L.Ed.2d 972 (1965) (demand excused where only one shareholders' meeting had been held for many years, and management had ignored earlier demands that such meetings be held).

(c) The cases are split on whether demand is excused because the corporation has a large number of shareholders, compare Weiss v. Sunasco Inc., 316 F.Supp. 1197 (E.D.Pa.1970) (demand excused), with Quirke v. St. Louis–San Francisco Ry., 277 F.2d 705 (8th Cir.1960), cert. denied 363 U.S. 845, 80 S.Ct. 1615, 4 L.Ed.2d 1728 (contra); or because management has refused to supply plaintiff with a shareholders' list, compare Escoett v. Aldecress Country Club, 16 N.J. 438, 109 A.2d 277 (1954) (demand excused), with Bell v. Arnold, 175 Colo. 277, 487 P.2d 545 (1971) (plaintiffs alleged that the corporation had 26,000 shareholders, but this allegation was apparently made as part of the argument that access to the shareholder list had been unreasonably restricted. The court stated, "[s]ince the number of shareholders . . . was not pled as an excuse, nor was it accompanied by any allegation regarding unreasonable costs of making the demand, we do not, on this writ of error, determine whether 26,000 shareholders did, or did not, formulate a valid basis for an excuse in making demand on them").

(d) The cases are also split on whether demand is excused where the alleged wrong could not be ratified. The majority rule, reflected in Mayer v. Adams, 37 Del.Ch. 298, 141 A.2d 458 (1958) is that nonratifiability excuses demand. However, there is a very strong minority view. For example, in Bell v. Arnold, supra, the court stated:

> One reason set forth in the complaint for not making a demand on the shareholders is that they could not ratify the alleged wrongs because of the illegal nature of the wrongs. We hold this is not an acceptable reason or a valid excuse for not making a demand on the shareholders here. The purpose of making demand on the shareholders is to inform them of the alleged nonratifiable wrongs; to seek their participation in available courses of action, such as, the removal of the involved directors and the election of new directors who will seek the redress required in the circumstances; or to secure shareholder approval of an action for damages to the corporation caused by the alleged wrongdoing directors.

See also Claman v. Robertson, 164 Ohio St. 61, 128 N.E.2d 429 (1955).

As a practical matter, precisely how does a shareholder in a publicly held corporation go about making a demand on the shareholders where such a demand is required? By a shareholder proposal under the Proxy Rules? If so, must the shareholder wait until the next annual meeting? What if the corporation is publicly held, but not registered under the 1934 Act?

3. Cases like Bell v. Arnold and Claman v. Robertson point up the difference between the question whether a plaintiff must make a demand on shareholders and the question whether shareholder ratification has a substantive effect. A further distinction is drawn by some courts (most notably Massachusetts) which hold that the shareholders have power to preclude suit even where they do not have power to ratify. The leading case is S. Solomont & Sons Trust v. New England Theatres Operating Corp., 326 Mass. 99, 111–12, 93 N.E.2d 241, 247–48 (1950).

SECTION 8.　PLAINTIFF'S COUNSEL FEES

SUGARLAND INDUSTRIES, INC. v. THOMAS

Supreme Court of Delaware, 1980.
420 A.2d 142.*

Before DUFFY, QUILLEN and HORSEY, JJ.

DUFFY, Justice:

This is an appeal from an order of the Court of Chancery awarding $3.5 million in attorney fees. Counsel's efforts in the case

---

* On appeal after remand, 431 A.2d 1271 (Del. 1981) (footnote by ed.)

are separable into two phases, and the appeal places both of them in issue, that is, a Phase I award of $3 million and a Phase II award of $500,000. Plaintiffs have cross-appealed as to the orders governing interest on the awards.

I

The relevant facts are as follows:

In January 1973, Sugarland Industries, Inc., a Delaware corporation (defendant) controlled by the Kempner family,[1] owned 7,500 acres of land in Texas south of Houston which it was attempting to sell. Lyda Ann Q. Thomas and her husband, J. Redmond Thomas (plaintiffs), who are members of the Kempner family and shareholders in Sugarland, were concerned about a proposed sale of the so-called South Tract (which is the major part of the property and includes some 5,900 acres) to White and Hill, a Texas partnership involved in real estate development, for $23,800,000. Plaintiffs considered the price to be inadequate and retained Brantly Harris, a Houston lawyer and a partner in the firm of Prappas, Caldwell & Moncure (now, Prappas, Moncure, Harris & Termini) to represent their interest in the proposed sale. Shortly thereafter, and at least partially as a result of Mr. Harris' efforts, a syndicate known as R–S–C was formed and it offered to buy the South Tract for $27,000,000, or $3.2 million more than White and Hill had offered.

Ignoring the higher bid by R–S–C, Sugarland's directors continued to favor White and Hill and gave notice that a special meeting of stockholders would be held on March 7, 1973, to consider and accept the $23.8 million proposal. After being informed of such a meeting, the Prappas firm, concerned that the Sugarland directors had excluded the possibility of selling the property to anyone other than White and Hill, consulted counsel in Delaware about litigation to block the sale. Prappas had suggested to R–S–C that it would be helpful if R–S–C, which would benefit if plaintiffs prevailed in such litigation, advanced $10,000 as a retainer for Delaware counsel; under this plan, plaintiffs would pay any fees in excess of the $10,000. Both R–S–C and plaintiffs agreed to that arrangement.

Shortly thereafter, on March 6, plaintiffs filed a stockholders' derivative action in the Court of Chancery to enjoin the proposed sale of the South Tract to White and Hill. On March 9, Mr. Prappas wrote a letter to the Thomases confirming their fee arrangement with his firm. . . .

[The court held that the fee agreement entered into by the plaintiffs' lawyers did not preclude their application to the court for attorneys' fees on a basis other than hourly rates.]

On March 22, the Chancellor filed an opinion in which he ruled that Sugarland would be enjoined from accepting the White and Hill proposal and ordered competitive bidding for the Sugarland proper-

---

1. All members of the Board of Directors of Sugarland are members of the Kempner family, with one exception.

ties. The opinion was implemented by order dated April 10. Because this created a conflict between the Thomases who, as Sugarland shareholders, wanted the sale to bring top dollar, and R–S–C, which wanted the property at the lowest possible price, the Prappas firm (by letter dated April 6, 1973) withdrew from its representation of R–S–C.

Thereafter, Sugarland conducted a sale by sealed bids, and on April 30, the Gerald D. Hines Interests submitted the highest bid, an offer of $37,229,069 for the South Tract. Hines later negotiated for Sugarland's North Tract and on July 3 entered into a contract for both the North and South Tracts. Hines' bid on the North Tract similarly exceeded the next highest bid on that tract by about $1,243,139. The total price for both properties was about $44,000,-000. (The closing was held on December 14, 1973.)

On July 25, after Hines had contracted to buy both Tracts, the Prappas firm wrote to the Thomases "releasing" them from the fee agreement....

Meanwhile, on April 30, a second action on behalf of the same plaintiffs by the same attorneys against the same defendants had been filed in the Court of Chancery; on November 12, a supplemental complaint was filed, thereby beginning the "damage" or Phase II of this controversy. That action was essentially a claim for damages against the Sugarland directors. Unlike the first or injunctive phase which was swiftly concluded, the second phase remained unresolved over the next three years and consumed some 13,000 hours on the part of lawyers (and their respective staffs) representing plaintiffs.

On November 10, 1977, a settlement of the Phase II litigation was finally made and approved by the Court of Chancery. While the complaint addressed to the second phase had alleged wrongdoing involving Sugarland, the terms of settlement did not directly affect the corporation; they centered, rather, on a reorganization of the management of various other business entities owned by the Kempner family.

After the settlement had been approved, plaintiffs' attorneys filed an application in the Court of Chancery seeking a combined fee of approximately $6 million for their services as to Phases I and II of the litigation.

The United States National Bank of Galveston, Trustee (intervenor) owns some 47,500 shares (about 23%) of Sugarland stock. It entered the litigation as an objector to the fee application.

On January 26, 1979, the Chancellor awarded plaintiffs' counsel[2] a fee of $3,500,000 computed as follows: (a) as to Phase I, a fee equal to 20% of the benefit created by their efforts, with a cap of

---

2. For convenience, we will hereafter refer to the attorneys whose compensation is in issue as "petitioners." They include, of course, both the Delaware and Texas firms.

All parties tacitly concede that whatever fee arrangements plaintiffs made with Prappas are equally applicable to Delaware counsel.

$3 million, and (b) as to Phase II, the sum of $500,000 for time expended in achieving the settlement. An order implementing the opinion was entered on May 11, 1979. It directed that $1,376,130 be paid within the month, and required that the remainder be paid "if, as, and when" Sugarland received additional monies in the future from Hines. It also provided that petitioners would be entitled to 6% interest on any late payments made by Sugarland.

Defendant and the intervenor have docketed this appeal....

II

We consider, first, the arguments made by the United States National Bank of Galveston, Trustee.... [The Bank contends that] Sugarland did not benefit from the Phase II efforts of counsel and, therefore, should not be obliged to pay for them....

The Phase II settlement did not result in the creation of a fund or transfer of a tangible benefit to Sugarland. The Bank concedes, tacitly at least, that the case was settled in the interest of "family harmony" by effecting a reorganization of the personnel of the boards or management of the various Kempner entities.

In his opinion, the Chancellor described in some detail the changes in management effected by the settlement agreement, and it is unnecessary to repeat them here. It is enough to say that they were numerous and relatively complex; they involved some eight or nine separate entities and a seemingly endless series of personnel changes and power balancing. As we see it, the result was accurately summarized in the Chancellor's opinion, thus:

> "... As to the second phase application, I am satisfied that petitioners are entitled to be compensated on the non-pecuniary results of their effort to bring harmony to the Kempner family although such benefit does not inure directly to the benefit of Sugarland Industries and its stockholders....

> Petitioners will be allowed the amount of $500,000 for the time expended and effort exerted by them during the second phase of this case, which resulted in a settlement which promises to terminate the feud which has split the Kempner family in recent years, thus indirectly benefiting Sugarland Industries and its stockholders...."

It is undisputed that the settlement agreement was the culmination of long and intensive efforts by counsel over many years. Sugarland was not a direct beneficiary of the "family harmony" which, legally speaking at least, resulted from the settlement. But it was very much involved in both lawsuits and it was a party to the settlement of both of them. Indeed, the purpose of the settlement agreement was to "settle all claims" in both actions [5] and thus to

---

5. The agreement provides in part, as follows:

"I. 1. The purpose of this agreement is to settle all claims remaining in the above litigation, and the agreement and actions contemplated in Section II hereof are the direct result of the assertion and prosecution of such claims, derivatively

put an end to the controversy and the issues in litigation. A hearing was held and the settlement was approved on the basis of Sugarland participation in it. Prior thereto, notice as to the agreement, the stipulation of settlement, the other pertinent documents and the date of hearing was sent to all Sugarland stockholders, including the Bank. The Bank elected not to appear nor to challenge the settlement. It arrived only after the *fait accompli* to challenge the right of the settling corporation to pay counsel fees.

In the stipulation of settlement, Sugarland reserved the right "to object to any application for allowance of fees and expenses of plaintiffs and their attorneys," but the stipulation also provides that "Sugarland has determined that this settlement is beneficial to it and in the best interests of Sugarland and its stockholders." Given that representation by Sugarland to the Court before the settlement was approved, Sugarland's reservations as to fees might well be construed as going to the amount of any allowance, not to whether it had, in principle, any duty to pay an allowance.

In any event, we are satisfied that the Chancellor properly invoked his power to order Sugarland to pay fees to petitioners for Phase II services. In saying this, we note that most of the stockholders of Sugarland are also (in the same proportion) stockholders in or beneficial owners of other Kempner enterprises, and that Sugarland was in liquidation. Compare *Mills v. Electric Auto Lite Co.,* 396 U.S. 375, 90 S.Ct. 616, 24 L.Ed.2d 593 (1970); *Richman v. DeVal Aerodynamics, Inc.,* Del.Ch., 185 A.2d 884 (1962).

III

We now consider Sugarland's argument that the fee awarded for Phase I is grossly excessive under any standard. The thrust of the argument is that petitioners had expended only $122,881 worth of time, at their regular hourly rates, and that the percentage approach adopted by the Chancellor was arbitrary under the circumstances.

The standard of review of an award of attorney fees in Chancery is well settled under Delaware case law: the test is abuse of discretion. *Chrysler Corporation v. Dann,* Del.Supr., 223 A.2d 384 (1966); *Krinsky v. Helfand,* Del.Supr., 156 A.2d 90 (1959); *Treves v. Servel, Inc.,* Del.Supr., 154 A.2d 188 (1959); cf. *Allied Artists Pictures Corporation v. Baron,* Del.Supr., 413 A.2d 876 (1980). The Third Circuit applies the same standard, *Lindy I.*

As to the amount of the fee, Sugarland observes that there is no real dispute between the parties as to the "elements of the Delaware standard" governing fees. It argues that the "results

---

by plaintiffs for the benefit of defendant Sugarland Industries, Inc. ("Sugarland").

2. Section II of this agreement and the actions that it contemplates provide a substantial, real benefit to the body of stockholders of Sugarland, constituting a proper basis and appropriate, commensu-

rate consideration for the settlement of the remaining claims of Sugarland, which is itself in the course of liquidation.

3. The parties will each support the settlement and will each promptly seek the required judicial approval for it."

achieved" by counsel plus the following factors stated by the Chancellor are pertinent:

> ". . . the amount of time and effort applied to a case by counsel for plaintiff, the relative complexities of the litigation, the skills applied to their resolution by counsel, as well as any contingency factor and the standing and ability of petitioning counsel are, of course, considered in the award of fees in an appropriate case. . . ."

Sugarland invites our attention to *Lindy I,* an opinion authored by Chief Judge Seitz, who served as Chancellor of Delaware (and before then as Vice Chancellor) for some twenty years during which he ruled on many applications for counsel fees. Sugarland argues that Delaware should adopt the *Lindy I* guidelines as other jurisdictions have done.[8]

The evolution of *Lindy I* has not been limited to jurisdictions other than the Third Circuit. Indeed, the case has its own progeny in *Lindy II,* an *en banc* ruling by the Third Circuit; see also *Baughman v. Wilson Freight Forwarding Co.,* 3 Cir., 583 F.2d 1208 (1978).

As we understand Sugarland's contention, *Lindy I's* principal significance for Phase I purposes is its emphasis on the "time factor" and because petitioners' entire fee was not "at risk."

Under *Lindy I,* the Court's analysis must begin with a calculation of the number of hours to be credited to the attorney seeking compensation. The total hours multiplied by the approved hourly rate is the "lodestar" in the Third Circuit's formulation. It has, indeed, been said that the time approach is virtually the sole consideration in making a fee ruling under *Lindy I.* Be that as it may, we conclude that our Chancery Judges should not be obliged to make the kind of elaborate analyses called for by the several opinions in *Lindy I* and *Lindy II.* To put it another way, while *Lindy's* careful craftsmanship has much to commend it, we are not persuaded that our case law governing fee applications is an inadequate criterion for a fair judgment in this case, nor that new guidelines are needed for the Court of Chancery.

It is undisputed that the White and Hill offer was $23,800,000, so, in one sense, petitioners are entitled to "some" credit for any amount received by Sugarland in excess of that sum.

The Chancellor determined that petitioners are entitled to a fair percentage of the benefit inuring to Sugarland and its stockholders from the sale of both Tracts to the Hines group; he computed the monetary benefit to Sugarland, as a result of petitioners' efforts, to be about $21,812,000. That figure gives petitioners full credit for all of the additional cash received or to be received, including

---

8. See, for example, *City of Detroit v. Grinnell Corporation,* 2 Cir., 495 F.2d 448 (1974); *Grunin v. International House of Pancakes,* 8 Cir., 513 F.2d 114 (1975), *cert.* denied 423 U.S. 864, 96 S.Ct. 124, 46 L.Ed.2d 93 (1975); *National Treasury Employees Union v. Nixon,* D.C.Cir., 521 F.2d 317 (1975).

principal and interest, from the sale of both tracts. The Chancellor held that petitioners are entitled to 20% of the fund thus created through their efforts, but subject to a $3,000,000 cap. Petitioners say that with that limitation, the award computes to about 14% of the benefit conferred.

We agree with substantially all of the Chancellor's findings and most of his conclusions, but we are unable to agree with him on one significant element in his formulations: in measuring benefit, he credited petitioners with all amounts received or to be received by Sugarland in excess of the White and Hill offer of $23,800,000. In our view of the case, petitioners' services and the nature of the benefits separate into two distinct parts and the R–S–C offer is at the dividing line between them.

It is crystal clear from the record that the services of petitioners benefited Sugarland to the extent of the difference between the White and Hill offer of $23,800,000 and the $27,000,000 which was submitted by R–S–C. But how one should view the amount received by Sugarland in excess of the $27,000,000 is not so clear. Petitioners had sought the best price obtainable and but for their initiative (and success) at the injunctive stage, Sugarland might not have received anything over the White and Hill offer. Thus, there is, as we have noted, "some" cause and effect between what petitioners did and the ultimate price received. But petitioners are attorneys seeking compensation for services rendered in litigation. They are not brokers or real estate agents seeking a commission or a percentage of sale price for having produced a buyer. And how much anyone would pay, at least in excess of the $27,000,000 offered by R–S–C, was a circumstance neither caused nor influenced by petitioners. The highest offer eventually made has in it something in the nature of the "windfall" to which Chancellor Seitz referred in the *Chrysler* case, where "benefit" for fee purposes was also in issue; he wrote:

> "... Certainly plaintiffs cannot take credit for the benefit flowing from the great increase in profits to the extent they resulted from the general resurgence of the automobile industry."

215 A.2d at 716. While the cases certainly are not parallel, petitioners here cannot take full credit for the price which Hines was willing to pay for both tracts.

There is also another factor which relates to the amount of compensation.... [The Prappas firm's contract] did assure *some* compensation for services, at least through the restraining order phrase, and thus petitioners were not providing services entirely on a contingent basis.

Sugarland has taken the position that if the Court reduces the fee award, we should, in the interest of justice and judicial economy, determine the appropriate fee. We conclude that it is appropriate for us to do so in this case.

In making the award, the Chancellor used a 20%–of–benefit factor and that seems reasonable to us when applied to the difference between the respective offers. But for the reasons we have discussed, it is unreasonable when applied to the amounts paid by the buyer in excess of the $27,000,000. We have held that petitioners are entitled to some credit for the benefit received in excess of that sum and, in view of the circumstances, any percentage is arguably fair or not, depending on one's point of view. In our judgment, based on the various factors we have noted, compensation at the rate of 5% of the benefit achieved is fair and should be applied to the additional benefits Sugarland received from the sale of both the North and South Tracts. Given the fee which that percentage generates (about $573,609 in all), we conclude that it is reasonable (and perhaps generous) compensation for the significant skills and expertise which petitioners demonstrated in identifying an inadequate price for the Tracts, in stimulating the competitive offer from R–S–C, in quickly initiating the litigation, in successfully carrying it to a conclusion against highly competent counsel and thus opening the door for entry by the Hines Interests with their offers.

The total amount to be allowed to petitioners as compensation for Phase I services (on an "if, as and when" received basis) is computed as follows:

South Tract	
R–S–C Offer	$27,000,000
White and Hill Offer	23,800,000
	$ 3,200,000
Hines Purchase Price	$37,229,069
R–S–C Offer	27,000,000
	$10,229,069
North Tract	
Additional Benefit (Cash)	$ 1,243,139
Computation of the Fee	
20% × $ 3,200,000	$ 640,000
5% × 10,229,069	511,453
5% × 1,243,139	62,156
Total	$ 1,213,609

It is difficult to test this allowance on an hourly rate basis because that was not determined by the Chancellor and, indeed, was not crucial to the awards he made. And the allocation of hours is a matter of dispute in this Court. For present purposes, we note only that Sugarland agreed that the total time given to both phases of the litigation by petitioners and their staffs totals 15,110.8 hours. Petitioners say that it amounts to more than that, including about 2,800[10] hours in 1973 for the Phase I representation. In our view of the appeal, we need not resolve the time controversy.

10. All of Phase I was completed in 1973. Accepting petitioners' representations that they gave 2,800 hours to that Phase, then the allowance made herein computes to about $433 per hour.

IV

Turning now to Phase II, Sugarland also argues that the $500,-000 allowed by the Chancellor is grossly excessive, under any standard.

It is apparent that the Chancellor based the award for this phase largely on a "time and effort" basis. Specifically, he said:

> "As to the second phase application, I am satisfied that petitioners are entitled to be compensated on the nonpecuniary results of their efforts to bring harmony to the Kempner family although such benefit does not inure directly to the benefit of Sugarland Industries and its stockholders.
>
>   * * *
>
> Petitioners will be allowed the amount of $500,000 for the time expended and effort exerted by them during the second phase of this case. . . ."

Given the extraordinary difficulties involved in this phase and the central purpose accomplished (family peace by litigation settlement), we conclude that the Chancellor did not abuse his discretion in making the award. Tested on an hourly rate basis, the $500,000 computes to $50 per hour, if only 10,000 of the agreed 15,110.8 hours were assigned to this phase. And that is a modest rate. . . .

Affirmed in part and reversed in part with directions to enter judgment in accordance herewith.

[A motion by the petitioners for reargument was denied. 420 A.2d 142, 146.]

———

ALI, PRINCIPLES OF CORPORATE GOVERNANCE
§ 7.17, COMMENTS c, d

[See Statutory Supplement]

———

BACKGROUND NOTE ON THE AWARD OF COUNSEL FEES TO SUCCESSFUL DERIVATIVE–ACTION PLAINTIFFS

1. As indicated in the Introduction to this chapter, the derivative action constitutes a major legal bulwark against managerial self-dealing. As a practical matter this means that the rules governing plaintiffs' legal fees are critical to the operation of the corporate system: Since very few shareholders would pay an attorney's fee out of their own pocket to finance a suit that is brought on the

corporation's behalf and normally holds only a slight and indirect benefit for the plaintiff, very few derivative actions would be brought if the law did not allow the plaintiff's attorney to be compensated by a contingent fee payable out of the corporate recovery.

2. As a conceptual matter, the award of counsel fees to successful plaintiffs in derivative actions has been justified by several overlapping theories, none of which is unique to derivative actions. The most important of these is the "common fund" theory, under which a plaintiff who has successfully established a fund under the control of the court, from which many besides himself will benefit, may recover his counsel fees out of that fund. As stated in the seminal case of Trustees v. Greenough, 105 U.S. (15 Otto) 527, 532, 26 L.Ed. 1157 (1882), to deny an allowance for fees in such circumstances "would not only be unjust to [plaintiff], but ... would give to the other parties entitled to participate in the benefits of the fund an unfair advantage." This theory was later elaborated, under the heading of the "substantial benefit" (or common-benefit) theory, to cover cases where the plaintiff had not brought a fund into the court's control but had established a right to a fund from which others would benefit. See Sprague v. Ticonic Nat. Bank, 307 U.S. 161, 59 S.Ct. 777, 83 L.Ed. 1184 (1939). Eventually the substantial benefit theory was extended to cover cases involving the establishment of nonpecuniary benefits.

Another basic theory is the "private attorney-general" doctrine—that plaintiff's counsel fees should be awarded in appropriate cases to encourage the initiation of private actions that vindicate important legal policies.[1] In the corporate area this doctrine is important chiefly as a reinforcement to the common-fund or common-benefit theory, particularly where the benefit is not pecuniary. For example, in Mills v. Electric Auto–Lite Co., 396 U.S. 375, 90 S.Ct. 616, 24 L.Ed.2d 593 (1970), plaintiffs, who were former Auto–Lite shareholders, alleged that defendants had violated the Proxy Rules in connection with a merger of Auto–Lite into Mergenthaler. The Court held that plaintiffs were entitled to summary judgment on the merits. It then went on to award interim counsel fees, although it recognized that if on remand the merger were found to be fair, there might be no feasible way to remedy the violation, and therefore no economically measurable benefit to either Auto–Lite or its shareholders. The opinion began by attempting to bring the case within the common benefit rule: "In many suits under § 14(a) ... it may be impossible to assign monetary value to the benefit. Nevertheless, the stress placed by Congress on the importance of fair and informed corporate suffrage leads to the conclusion that, in vindicating the statutory policy, petitioners have rendered a substantial service to the corporation and its shareholders." However, the Court then seemed to shift rationales by stressing that the action

---

1. See Newman v. Piggie Park Enterprises, Inc., 390 U.S. 400, 402, 88 S.Ct. 964, 966, 19 L.Ed.2d 1263 (1968).

conferred a benefit on a subsector of the public, that is, shareholders as a class.

In Alyeska Pipeline Service Co. v. Wilderness Society, 421 U.S. 240, 95 S.Ct. 1612, 44 L.Ed.2d 141 (1975), the Supreme Court held that in the absence of statutory authorization, attorney's fees may not be awarded on the private-attorney-general theory in suits brought under federal statutes. While the opinion left the common-fund theory (and its derivative, the common-benefit theory) undisturbed, and cited *Sprague* and *Mills* with approval, it is open to question whether the Court would again go as far as it did in *Mills* in determining what constitutes a benefit for these purposes.

3. A widely accepted list of the criteria to be considered in setting counsel fees is set out in Angoff v. Goldfine, 270 F.2d 185, 189 (1st Cir.1959):

> [T]he amount recovered for the corporation; the time fairly required to be spent on the case; the skill required and employed on the case with reference to the intricacy, novelty and complexity of issues; the difficulty encountered in unearthing the facts and the skill and resourcefulness of opposing counsel; the prevailing rate of compensation for those with the skill, experience and standing of the attorneys, accountants or others involved; the contingent nature of the fees, with the accompanying risk of wasting hours of work, overhead and expenses (for it is clearly established that compensation is awarded only in the event of success); and the benefits accruing to the public from such suits as this.

Traditionally, the most important of these elements was the first—the amount recovered by the corporation—and as a practical matter the courts tended to calculate counsel fees in derivative actions as a percentage of that amount.[2] Although the percentage varied from case to case, awards calculated on this basis tended to run around 20–35% of the recovery when the recovery was less than $1 million, and 15–25% when it was more....

4. The 1973 revision of the Federal Judicial Manual for Complex Litigation stated that "the reasonableness of the fee arrived at [in class actions] should not rest primarily on the selection of a percentage of the total recovery," and suggested instead emphasizing "the time and labor required and the effect of the allowance on the public interest and the reputation of the courts." Id. at § 1.47. This approach was adopted by the Third Circuit in the leading case of Lindy Bros. Builders, Inc. v. American Radiator & Standard Sanitary Corp., 487 F.2d 161 (3d Cir.1973), a class action under the antitrust laws. Under *Lindy,* the value of the lawyer's time is made the dominant factor:

2. "[These cases] find their true analogue in salvage causes on a pure salvage basis of no cure no pay.... [B]enefits conferred in the light of the efforts required are the real basis of the salvage awards, as they should be in causes like these." Murphy v. North American Light & Power Co., 33 F.Supp. 567, 570–571 (S.D.N.Y.1940).

... [T]he first inquiry of the court should be into the hours spent by the attorneys....

After determining ... the services performed by the attorneys, the district court must attempt to value those services....

The value of an attorney's time generally is reflected in his normal billing rate. A logical beginning in valuing an attorney's services is to fix a reasonable hourly rate for his time—taking account of the attorney's legal reputation and status (partner, associate)....

While the amount thus found to constitute reasonable compensation should be the lodestar of the court's fee determination, there are at least two other factors that must be taken into account in computing the value of attorneys' services. The first of these is the contingent nature of success....

The second additional factor the district court must consider is the extent, if any, to which the quality of an attorney's work mandates increasing or decreasing the amount to which the court has found the attorney reasonably entitled.[3]

Under this approach, which is known as the "lodestar" approach (because hourly time is used as a lodestar), the benefit produced is important chiefly insofar as it bears on the quality of the lawyer's work, as where "a particularly resourceful attorney ... secures a substantial benefit for his clients with a minimum of time invested...."

In 1974 the Second Circuit fell into line with *Lindy* in Detroit v. Grinnell Corp., 495 F.2d 448 (2d Cir.1974). Since a derivative action is in effect a special type of class action, the emphasis placed on lawyer's time by cases like *Lindy* and *Grinnell* came to figure prominently in derivative actions.

There is considerable variation in the percentages applied to basic hourly rates, under the lodestar approach, to adjust for contingency and quality factors. Increases of 50 or 100% are common, but much higher and much lower increases can also be found.

5. Even at the height of the lodestar approach, the data suggested that courts managed to apply the lodestar formula in such a way as to produce results comparable to those obtained under the percentage-of-the-benefit formula. See Mowrey, Attorney Fees in Securities Class Actions and Derivative Suits, 3 J.Corp.Law 267 (1978). In 1984, the Supreme Court explicitly stated—albeit in a footnote—that in a common-fund case, a reasonable fee "is based on the percentage of the fund bestowed on the class." Blum v. Stenson, 465 U.S. 886, 900 n. 16, 104 S.Ct. 1541, 1550 n. 16, 79 L.Ed.2d 891 (1984). (The Court contrasted this approach to that under the Civil Rights Attorney's Fee Awards Act, where, the Court said, a reasonable fee was based on the attorney's time.) The

---

3. 487 F.2d at 167–69.

following year, the Third Circuit, which had begun the movement to the lodestar approach with its decision in *Lindy,* issued a Task Force Report on Court Awarded Attorney Fees, 109 F.R.D. 257 (1985), that advocated a return to the percentage-of-recovery approach in common-fund cases.

6.   The Third Circuit Task Force Report was extremely influential.   Since 1985, a number of other Circuits have held that the percentage-of-recovery method is mandatory or permissible in common-fund cases.   See Swedish Hospital Corp. v. Shalala, 1 F.3d 1261 (D.C.Cir.1993); In re Continental Illinois Securities Litigation, 962 F.2d 566 (7th Cir.1992); Camden I Condominium Association v. Dunkle, 946 F.2d 768 (11th Cir.1991); Weinberger v. Great Northern Nekoosa Corp., 925 F.2d 518 (1st Cir.1991); Paul, Johnson, Alston & Hunt v. Graulty, 886 F.2d 268 (9th Cir.1989); Brown v. Phillips Petroleum Co., 838 F.2d 451 (10th Cir.1988), cert. denied 488 U.S. 822, 109 S.Ct. 66, 102 L.Ed.2d 43.   In a striking and widely remarked-upon opinion in In re Oracle Securities Litigation, 131 F.R.D. 688 (N.D.Cal.1990) (a class-action securities case), Judge Vaughan Walker said, "the lodestar approach . . . is now thoroughly discredited by experience.   The lodestar approach is unworkable because, among other things, it abandons the adversary process upon which our judicial system is based. . . ."

7.   In a widely cited decision, In re Activision Securities Litigation, 723 F.Supp. 1373 (N.D.Cal.1989), the court determined, on the basis of a review of recent reported cases, that in nearly all common fund cases the attorney's fee award ranges around 30% of the fund, even if the fee is purportedly calculated under the lodestar or related methods.   The court observed that "[m]ost of these cases achieve this result after lengthy motion practice, volumes of discovery, and hence, the accumulation of extensive attorney time on behalf of all parties."   Id. at 1377.   Accordingly, the court concluded that the better practice in common fund cases is to set a percentage fee, and that the percentage should be 30%, absent extraordinary circumstances.   Other courts have mentioned other benchmark percentages.   For example, in Paul, Johnson, Alston & Hunt v. Graulty, 886 F.2d 268 (9th Cir.1989), the court noted with approval a benchmark fee of 25%.   In In re Warner Communications Securities Litigation, 618 F.Supp. 735, 750 (S.D.N.Y.1985), aff'd 798 F.2d 35 (2d Cir.1986), the court concluded that fee awards had averaged 20%–30% in the Second Circuit.

8.   While *success* is a prerequisite to an award of counsel fees, a *judgment* is not.   Counsel fees may be awarded even if a case is settled or a unilateral act by the defendant renders moot the plaintiff's demand or complaint.   In the latter case, the plaintiff must show that his course of action was a significant cause of the defendant's act.   Normally, however, the plaintiff is allowed to prove causation indirectly, by showing that his claim or demand was meritorious and that corrective action followed.   It has been said

that "[a] claim is meritorious within the meaning of the rule if it can withstand a motion to dismiss on the pleadings [and] if, at the same time, the plaintiff possesses knowledge of provable facts which hold out some reasonable likelihood of ultimate success. It is not necessary that factually there be absolute assurance of ultimate success, but only that there be some reasonable hope." Chrysler Corp. v. Dann, 43 Del.Ch. 252, 256–57, 223 A.2d 384, 387 (1966). Although a few cases suggest that meritoriousness is the only relevant issue in such cases, the rule seems to be that the plaintiff has the burden of showing meritoriousness, and once that showing is made the burden shifts to defendants to show that their actions did not result from plaintiff's course of action.[1]

9. The rule that attorneys' fees can be awarded to a plaintiff on the basis of a common (but nonmonetary) benefit, as opposed to a common fund, has two important implications in derivative actions.

First, it is often very difficult to attribute any realistic value to nonmonetary common benefits. As a result, in such cases attorney's fees usually must be, and are, measured under the lodestar method, even by courts that employ the percentage-of-the-benefit test in common-fund cases.

Second, the rule that a plaintiff's attorney is entitled to a fee based for producing a nonmonetary common benefit opens the door to the possibility of collusive settlements in which the real defendants in a derivative action (the directors or officers) pay little or nothing; the corporation agrees to a change that is largely cosmetic; plaintiff's attorney and the corporation join hands to inflate the importance of the change; and plaintiff's attorney is then paid a fee that is supposed to be justified by that importance, but is really a bribe to drop the case. The real defendants are happy, because they get a release although they have paid little or nothing. Plaintiff's counsel is happy, because she gets a very nice fee. The shareholders aren't unhappy, because they don't realize what happened, but if they did realize what happened they would be very unhappy.

This doesn't mean that every settlement involving a nonmonetary common benefit is collusive. It takes two villains to make a collusive settlement, and villains may not be thick on the ground. Furthermore, nonmonetary benefits that result from derivative actions often have very substantial value. Nevertheless, the possibility that settlements involving only nonmonetary benefits may be collusive suggests that the courts should be especially cautious in reviewing such settlements. See section 11, infra.

---

1. See Wechsler v. Southeastern Properties, Inc., 506 F.2d 631 (2d Cir.1974); McDonnell Douglas Corp. v. Palley, 310 A.2d 635 (Del.1973); Baron v. Allied Artists Pictures Corp., 395 A.2d 375 (Del.Ch.1978); cf. Kahan v. Rosenstiel, 424 F.2d 161 (3d Cir.1970), cert. denied 398 U.S. 950, 90 S.Ct. 1870, 26 L.Ed.2d 290; Academic Computer Systems, Inc. v. Yarmuth, 71 F.R.D. 198 (S.D.N.Y.1976).

SECTION 9.   SECURITY FOR EXPENSES

N.Y. BUS. CORP. LAW § 627

[See Statutory Supplement]

CAL. CORP. CODE § 800(c)–(f)

[See Statutory Supplement]

SECURITIES ACT § 11(e)

[See Statutory Supplement]

BACKGROUND NOTE ON SECURITY–FOR–EXPENSES STATUTES

1.   Security-for-expenses statutes must be considered against the background of the general American rule that the losing party in a lawsuit does not have to pay the winner's expenses, except for "taxable costs," such as clerk's, witness, docket, and transcript fees. (Local Rule 2 in Haberman v. Tobin, supra, presumably covered only taxable costs, not attorneys' fees.) Security-for-expenses statutes are normally not interpreted to impose *individual* liability on the plaintiff for expenses—that is, liability beyond the amount of his bond.

2.   A shareholder who wants to bring a derivative action in a state that has a security-for-expenses statute is under heavy pressure to find some way to bring suit without posting security. Since the statutes are normally interpreted to be inapplicable to direct (as opposed to derivative) actions, one alternative is to frame the suit as a direct action. A second alternative is to bring the action under some provision of federal law, such as the Proxy Rules or Rule 10b–5.[1]

Even where these alternatives are infeasible, two judicial practices tend to soften the impact of the security-for-expenses statutes. The first practice is to stay the effectiveness of an order to post

---

1. The security-for-expenses requirement may also be avoided in certain types of cases by petitioning for dissolution or the appointment of a receiver. See Leibert v. Clapp, 13 N.Y.2d 313, 247 N.Y.S.2d 102, 196 N.E.2d 540 (1963); Chapter V, Section 7, supra.

security so that the plaintiff can find intervenors to help qualify under an exemption based on the percentage or dollar value of complaining shares. See Baker v. MacFadden Publications, 300 N.Y. 325, 90 N.E.2d 876 (1950).

A second judicial practice, which builds on the first, is to order a corporation that moves for the posting of security to produce a shareholders' list, so that during the period of the stay the plaintiff can solicit other shareholders to join the action. A study based on interviews with knowledgeable plaintiffs' and defense attorneys in New York concluded that the courts have been extremely permissive in granting these motions. The study continues:

> [Thus if] the motion for security for expenses were to be made, it is likely that the plaintiff would request and obtain a 60–day stay and access to the corporate stocklist. By granting the plaintiff access to the list, defendants have hurt themselves in several ways. The motion involves additional expense in corporate time and effort in furnishing a stockholders' list to the plaintiff. Moreover, circularization by the plaintiff apprises stockholders and the press that a lawsuit involving management is pending. "Most if not all directors don't like to have their deeds or misdeeds advertised. They are sensitive to public opinion, particularly when a proxy fight is involved or imminent." Further, the plaintiffs' counsel now has a list of potential plaintiffs which may be used against the corporation in future litigation. Finally, there is a risk that a motion for security may cause the plaintiff to discontinue the original action and start another in a sister-state having no security-for-expenses statute. . . .

As a result, it is not uncommon for defendants in New York cases to refrain from moving for security. Note, Security for Expenses in Shareholders' Derivative Suits: 23 Years' Experience, 4 Colum.J.L. & Soc.Prob. 50, 62–65 (1968).

———

SECTION 10.   INDEMNIFICATION AND INSURANCE

———

(a) INDEMNIFICATION

———

DEL. GEN. CORP. LAW § 145

[See Statutory Supplement]

———

REV. MODEL BUS. CORP. ACT §§ 8.50–8.59

[See Statutory Supplement]

N.Y. BUS. CORP. LAW §§ 721–726

[See Statutory Supplement]

CAL. CORP. CODE § 317

[See Statutory Supplement]

ALI, PRINCIPLES OF CORPORATE GOVERNANCE § 7.20

[See Statutory Supplement]

HEFFERNAN v. PACIFIC DUNLOP GNB CORP.

United States Court of Appeals, Seventh Circuit, 1992.
965 F.2d 369.

Before FLAUM and RIPPLE, Circuit Judges, and ESCHBACH, Senior Circuit Judge.

ESCHBACH, Senior Circuit Judge.

Litigation is an occupational hazard for corporate directors, albeit one that may often be shifted to the corporation through indemnification. In this diversity case, we consider whether Delaware law precludes a former director from obtaining indemnification from the corporations he served. For the reasons that follow, we hold that the district court prematurely dismissed this case under Rule 12(b)(6) by concluding that it was one in which the director could prove no set of facts entitling him to indemnification. Accordingly, we reverse and remand for further proceedings.

I.

Daniel E. Heffernan is a former director and 6.7% shareholder of GNB Holdings, Inc. (Holdings) and its wholly-owned subsidiary, GNB Inc. (GNB). In October 1987, a third firm, Pacific Dunlop Holdings, Inc. (Pacific) acquired control of Holdings (and in turn, GNB) pursuant to a stock purchase transaction whereby Pacific acquired approximately 60% of Holdings' stock, boosting its total ownership to 92%.   Prior to Pacific's stock purchase, Holdings had filed a registration statement with the Securities and Exchange Commission (SEC) in contemplation of an initial public offering of its stock.   Holdings later abandoned the public offering, opting instead to structure a private transaction with Pacific.   The transaction was pursuant to an agreement (the Stock Purchase Agreement) by and among Pacific, Holdings, certain management shareholders, Heffernan and Allen & Co. (an investment company that owned approximately 20% of Holdings' stock and for which Heffernan was a vice president).   Pursuant to the Stock Purchase Agreement, which apparently incorporated the material that Holdings previously had prepared for the SEC, Heffernan sold Pacific his 6.7% interest in Holdings and ceased to be a director.

Litigation subsequently arose out of the Stock Purchase Agreement.   In September 1990, Pacific sued Heffernan and Allen & Co. under section 12(2) of the Securities Act of 1933, 15 U.S.C. § 77*l* (2), and under Illinois securities law.   *See Pacific Dunlop Holdings, Inc. v. Allen & Co.,* No. 90–C–5678 slip op., 1991 U.S.Dist. Lexis 6748 (N.D.Ill. May 15, 1991).   Pacific sought to rescind its purchase of Heffernan's and Allen & Co.'s shares in Holdings on the ground that the Stock Purchase Agreement was materially misleading in regard to its disclosure of certain liabilities facing Holdings and GNB.   At oral argument, the parties indicated that Pacific has sued some of the other parties to the Stock Purchase Agreement as well, although the record leaves unclear specifically whom it sued.   Heffernan requested indemnification and an advance on his litigation expenses from Holdings and GNB pursuant to section 145 of the Delaware General Corporation Law and the companies' corporate bylaws.   *See* Del.Code Ann. tit. 8, § 145; R. 1–1 Exhibits A, B. When Holdings refused (and GNB failed to respond to) Heffernan's request, he initiated this action against the two companies seeking to establish his rights to indemnification and advances.

Under Delaware law, "a corporation may indemnify any person who was or is a party to any [suit] by reason of the fact that he is or was a director...." § 145(a).   Holdings' and GNB's bylaws make mandatory the provision for permissive indemnification in section 145(a).   *See* R. 1–1 Exhibit A § 6.01;   Exhibit B § 7.   Holdings' bylaws state that "the Corporation shall, to the fullest extent permitted by the Delaware General Corporation law ... indemnify and hold harmless any person who is or was a party [to] any [suit] by reason of his status as, or the fact that he is or was or has agreed to become, a director [of] the Corporation or of an affiliate, and as to acts performed in the course of the [director's] duty to the Corporation...."   R. 1–1 Exhibit A § 6.01(a).   GNB's bylaws simply state that "[t]he corporation shall indemnify its officers, directors, employees and agents to the extent permitted by the law of Delaware." *Id.* at Exhibit B § 7.

Heffernan does not argue that there is a material difference between the statutory requirement that a director be sued "by reason of the fact that" he was a director and Holdings' bylaw requirement that a director be sued "by reason of his status as, or the fact that" he was a director. And Holdings' brief footnote argument that its bylaw standard is narrower in scope than the statutory one fails in light of its bylaws' stated objective to indemnify directors "to the fullest extent permitted" by Delaware law. Thus, we focus our inquiry on whether Pacific may have sued Heffernan "by reason of the fact that" he was a director of Holdings and GNB.

II.

The district court dismissed Heffernan's complaint, holding that he was not entitled to indemnification under the terms of the statute and bylaws because he had been sued for "wrongs he committed as an individual, not as a director." *Heffernan v. Pacific Dunlop GNB Corp.*, 767 F.Supp. 913, 916 (N.D.Ill.1991). Furthermore, the district court reasoned that because "Heffernan's status as a director is not a necessary element of the section 12(2) claim" he was not sued by reason of the fact that he was a director. *Id.* On appeal, Heffernan argues that although he was sued over a transaction in which he sold his own stock in Holdings, it does not necessarily follow as a matter of law that he was not sued "by reason of the fact that" he was a director of Holdings and GNB. He asserts that Delaware's "by reason of the fact that" phrase reaches Pacific's suit against him because the suit involves his status as a director. Conversely, appellees Holdings and GNB contend that Pacific's complaint against Heffernan has nothing whatsoever to do with Heffernan's former status as a director for Holdings and GNB. They argue that Delaware's "by reason of the fact that" requirement means that a director must be sued for a breach of duty to the corporation or for a wrong committed on behalf of the corporation to be entitled to indemnification. Accordingly, Holdings and GNB assert that Heffernan is not entitled to indemnification because the "sale of his stock was a personal transaction which did not involve his duties or status as a director." Brief of Appellees at 3.

Despite a surprising dearth of case law addressing the reach of Delaware's "by reason of the fact that" language, our review of the substance of Pacific's complaint against Heffernan in light of the language and purpose of [Delaware's] indemnification law convinces us that the district court's view of Pacific's complaint and Delaware's indemnification law is too restrictive. Standing alone, neither the fact that Heffernan sold his own shares in Holdings during the transaction nor the particular statutory provision on which Pacific's suit is based thwarts Heffernan's right to indemnification as a matter of law. Rather, the substance of Pacific's allegations and the nature and context of the transaction giving rise to the complaint indicate that Heffernan may have been sued, at least in part, because he was a director of Holdings and GNB. Furthermore, we find no support in the language and purpose of Delaware's indemnification statute for the defendants' argument that it limits indemnification to suits asserted against a director for breaching a duty of his directorship or for acting wrongfully on behalf of the corporation he serves.   Thus, we conclude that Heffernan's complaint was improperly dismissed; it does not appear beyond doubt that Heffernan can prove no set of facts in support of his claim that would entitle him to the advances or indemnification he requests.   *See Illinois Health Care Ass'n. v. Illinois Dept. of Public Health,* 879 F.2d 286, 288 (7th Cir.1989), citing *Conley v. Gibson,* 355 U.S. 41, 45–46, 78 S.Ct. 99, 102, 2 L.Ed.2d 80 (1957).

III.

To determine whether Heffernan was sued "by reason of the fact" that he was a director of Holdings and GNB, we begin by reviewing the allegations in the underlying action's complaint. *Mooney v. Willys–Overland Motors, Inc.,* 204 F.2d 888, 896 (3d Cir.1953).   Here, the underlying complaint is based on Heffernan's sale of his shares in Holdings to Pacific pursuant to the Stock Purchase Agreement.   More specifically, Pacific contends that Heffernan violated section 12(2) of the Securities Act by selling those securities pursuant to a misleading prospectus—that is, the Stock Purchase Agreement.[4]   Under section 12(2), a person who offers or sells a security through a prospectus or oral communication containing a material misrepresentation or omission may be liable to the purchaser.[5]   *See Ballay v. Legg Mason Wood Walker, Inc.,* 925 F.2d 682, 687–88 (3d Cir.1991), *cert. denied,* ___ U.S. ___, 112 S.Ct. 79, 116 L.Ed.2d 52 (1991);   *see also Sanders v. John Nuveen & Co.,* 619 F.2d 1222 (7th Cir.1980), *cert. denied,* 450 U.S. 1005, 101 S.Ct. 1719, 68 L.Ed.2d 210 (1981).   To avoid liability, the seller must prove that he did not know, and in the exercise of reasonable care could not have known, of the misrepresentation or omission.   *Id.*

In complaining of Heffernan's alleged failure to disclose environmental and other liabilities of Holdings and GNB in the Stock Purchase Agreement, Pacific's complaint repeatedly states that Heffernan's status as a director put him in a position where, in the performance of his duties as a director, he either learned or should have learned of those liabilities.   *See* R. 1–1, Exhibit C ¶¶ 5, 16, 19, 21.   Because Pacific realleges these provisions under both counts of its complaint, *see id.* ¶¶ 42, 47, its argument that Heffernan's status as a director was not specifically alleged in the complaint is without merit.   Moreover, assuming for the moment that Pacific's section

---

4. A "prospectus" is defined broadly in section 2(10) of the Securities Act of 1933. In short, the term refers to any notice, circular, advertisement, letter or communication, written or by radio or television, which offers any security for sale or confirms the sale of any security.   *See* 15 U.S.C. § 77b(10).

5. Some lower federal courts have limited section 12(2)'s reach to primary offerings, finding it inapplicable to secondary market transactions.   *See* J. William Hicks, *Civil Liabilities: Enforcement and Litigation Under the 1933 Act* § 6.01 at 6–13 n. 8 (1991).   *Ballay v. Legg Mason Wood Walk-*

er, Inc., 925 F.2d 682 (3d Cir.1991), *cert. denied,* ___ U.S. ___, 112 S.Ct. 79, 116 L.Ed.2d 52 (1991), is the first federal court of appeals to reach this result.   *See id.* at 687–693.   Although we do not reach this issue here, we note that Pacific's complaint against Heffernan was dismissed for this reason.   *Pacific Dunlop Holdings, Inc. v. Allen & Co.,* slip op. No. 90–C–5678, 1991 WL 348493, 1991 U.S. Dist. Lexis 6748 (E.D.Ill. May 15, 1991)....

[In 1995, the Supreme Court took the position, adopted in *Ballay,* that section 12(2) is limited to primary offerings. See p. 960, infra.]   (Bracketed material by ed.).

12(2) claim against Heffernan is viable, his status as a director is directly relevant to his defense. As noted earlier, to avoid liability under section 12(2), a defendant must prove that he did not know, and in the exercise of reasonable care could not have known, of the misrepresentation or omission. The defendant's position gives content to the term "reasonable care." For instance, reasonable care for a director requires more than does reasonable care for an individual owning a few shares of stock with no other connection to the corporation. *See Sanders*, 619 F.2d at 1228 n. 12; J. William Hicks, *Civil Liabilities: Enforcement and Litigation Under the 1933 Act* § 6.12[2][a][ii], at 6–297 n. 2 (1991). It is accordingly no answer to our inquiry as to whether Heffernan was sued "by reason of the fact that" he was a director to label his participation in Pacific's acquisition of Holdings a "personal" transaction. Despite the fact that Heffernan sold his own shares to Pacific, a nexus exists between Heffernan's status as a director and Pacific's suit.

Moreover, the transaction at the heart of Pacific's complaint is not a purely personal transaction of Heffernan's. Despite Holdings' and GNB's arguments to the contrary, Heffernan was not "trading securities for his own account" in the usual meaning of that phrase. That is, this is not a situation in which Heffernan maintained a personal trading portfolio and encountered litigation over his individual sale of a security in an unrelated company. In such a scenario, "there is no reason why the corporation should be obligated or permitted to bear the executives' [litigation] expenses." Joseph W. Bishop, Jr., *The Law of Corporate Officers and Directors: Indemnification and Insurance* § 2.03 at 4 (1988). Rather, this was a structured sale of control transaction pursuant to one agreement—all of the stock that Pacific acquired in this transaction was pursuant to the Stock Purchase Agreement.[6] We decline to distort the context in which Pacific's complaint arose by accepting Holdings' and GNB's unsupported invitation to carve Pacific's acquisition of Holdings' into various component parts.

Furthermore, neither the specific statutory provision under which a director is sued nor the mere form of the underlying complaint is dispositive of his right to indemnification. The logical extension of the district court's reliance on the "necessary elements" of section 12(2) in denying Heffernan indemnification as a matter of law is that Delaware did not intend for any suit under section 12(2) to fall within its indemnification provisions. Delaware's case-by-case approach to indemnification counsels against such a formalistic gloss. *See, e.g., MCI Telecommunications Corp. v.*

---

6. Because Pacific's suit arises from Heffernan's participation with Holdings in a structured sale of control transaction, we find the district court's exclusive reliance on *Spring v. Moncrieff,* 10 Misc.2d 731, 173 N.Y.S.2d 86 (N.Y.Sup.Ct.1958) unpersuasive. Unlike Heffernan, Moncrieff subverted his company's planned sale by selling his stock to a third party rather than the would-be acquirer. Thus, Moncrieff was acting in opposition to his company, unlike Heffernan who was acting in concert with Holdings. When Moncrieff was later sued by a broker for commissions the broker lost when Moncrieff wrecked his company's deal, the court had little trouble finding that an individual who had caused litigation by acting in his own interest rather than in the corporation's should not be entitled to indemnification from that corporation....

Wanzer, 1990 WL 91100, 1990 Del.Super. Lexis 222; *Green v. Westcap Corp.,* 492 A.2d 260 (Del.Super.Ct.1985); *Essential Enterprises Corp. v. Automatic Steel Products, Inc.,* 164 A.2d 437 (Del. Ch.1960). Otherwise, a director could be forced to bear the costs of unfounded, harassing litigation just because the particular cause of action does not specify a breach of a duty to the corporation, regardless of the connection between the suit and the individual's service as a director.[7] As a practical matter, it is unsurprising that Pacific's complaint is not more explicit in its reliance on Heffernan's role as a director of Holdings and GNB. Because Pacific now controls Holdings and GNB, those three corporations' interests are aligned; thus Pacific has the incentive and opportunity to structure its complaint so as to avoid triggering its subsidiaries' duty of indemnification.[8] Nevertheless, artful drafting cannot disguise the fact that the gravamen of Pacific's complaint is that Heffernan, at least in part because he was a director of Holdings and GNB, either knew or should have known that Holdings and GNB may be subject to environmental and other liabilities inadequately reflected in the Stock Purchase Agreement. We recognize that because Heffernan wore three hats—director, shareholder and investment banker—his director status may not be the *only* reason that he was sued by Pacific. But at this stage of this litigation, we cannot, as a matter of law, rule out the fact that it may have been *one* reason.

IV.

Having established that Pacific's complaint is connected to Heffernan's status as a director, we now turn to whether Delaware's "by reason of" requirement necessarily requires more than the nexus present here. Without delineating the precise contours of the "by reason of" phrase, we conclude that it may be broad enough to encompass the litigation that Heffernan has incurred, at least in part, because of his status as a director of Holdings and GNB. Both the language and the purpose of Delaware's indemnification statute support interpreting its scope expansively.

---

7. One commentator has noted that the language of the Delaware statute is

    intended to cover the cost of at least the successful defense of suits based on executives' trading in the corporation's securities for their own account, particularly suits under Sections 10(b) and 16(b) of the Securities Exchange Act of 1934. [T]he policies behind the securities laws do not preclude indemnification of legal expenses incurred in the successful defense of security laws claims.

Joseph W. Bishop, Jr., *The Law of Corporate Officers and Directors: Indemnification and Insurance* § 2.03 at 5–6 (citations omitted).

8. Put differently, in seeking funds from Pacific's subsidiaries, Heffernan is effectively assailing Pacific's coffers. Moreover, the same law firm that is defending Holdings and GNB in this action drafted Pacific's complaint against Heffernan. In arguing that Heffernan is not entitled to indemnification for his costs in defending Pacific's suit, Holdings and GNB make much of the fact that Pacific sued Heffernan under section 12(2) rather [than] for "insider trading" (presumably under section 10(b) and Rule 10b–5 of the Securities Act of 1934). We note, however, that when Pacific sued other parties to the same transaction (the principal operating personnel of GNB), for the same disclosure problems, it employed section 10(b) and Rule 10(b)5 rather than section 12(2). *See Pacific Dunlop Holdings, Inc. v. Barosh,* No. 91–C–0002 slip op., 1991 WL 348494, 1991 U.S. Dist. Lexis 6662 (N.D.Ill. May 15, 1991).

First, Delaware is no neophyte in corporate law matters. Had it desired to limit permissible indemnification solely to those suits in which a director is sued for breaching a duty of his directorship or for certain enumerated causes of action, it would have jettisoned the supple "by reason of the fact that" phrase in favor of more specific language. Had Delaware desired to so limit its indemnification statute, we are confident that it could have found the words. Holdings and GNB have given us no reason to doubt that Delaware's choice of language was anything but purposeful and strategic. We believe that Delaware's "by reason of the fact that" phrase is broad enough to encompass suits against a director in his official capacity as well as suits against a director that arise more tangentially from his role, position or status as a director. Flexibility of language is vexing as well as liberating. In employing its "by reason of" phrase, Delaware is able to cover a myriad of potential factual scenarios that cannot be anticipated *ex ante* by the legislature or by corporate officials in drafting their articles and bylaws. The task of giving content to that flexible phrase, however, falls on the courts when the parties encounter interpretive differences.

Finally, we think that the policy of Delaware's indemnification statute supports permitting Heffernan to proceed to establish his right to advances and indemnification from Holdings and GNB. One of the primary purposes of Delaware's indemnification statute is to encourage capable individuals "to serve as corporate directors, secure in the knowledge that expenses incurred by them in upholding their honesty and integrity as directors will be borne by the corporation they serve." *MCI Telecommunications Corp. v. Wanzer,* 1990 Del.Super. Lexis 222 (citations omitted). Additionally, the statute ought to promote the "desirable end that corporate officials will resist what they consider unjustified suits and claims, secure in the knowledge that their reasonable expenses will be borne by the corporation they have served if they are vindicated." *Id.* Delaware has effectuated these policies by gradually expanding its indemnification provisions to cover the everchanging contexts in which a director may encounter litigation. *See Hibbert v. Hollywood Park, Inc.,* 457 A.2d 339 (Del.1983) (indemnification provided to directors acting as plaintiffs). *See generally* Veasey, Finkelstein & Bigler, *Delaware Supports Directors with a Three–Legged Stool of Limited Liability, Indemnification and Insurance,* 42 Bus.Law. 401 (1987). The district court's restrictive interpretation of Heffernan's claim diminishes the broad and expansive flavor of Delaware's indemnification provisions.

V.

In sum, while a fine line often separates those suits emanating purely from a director's personal transactions and those suits emanating from a director's duties, role or status, we think the district court erred in prematurely concluding that Pacific's suit against Heffernan fell squarely on the personal side. We emphasize that our inquiry in this case has been a narrow one, confined to whether

Heffernan's indemnification and advances claim against Holdings and GNB should be allowed to proceed. We express no opinion on the merits of Heffernan's right to advances, *see Citadel Holding Corp. v. Roven,* 603 A.2d 818 (Del.Supr.1992), or on his ultimate right to indemnification. We hold only that his suit was prematurely dismissed under an unduly restrictive reading of Delaware's indemnification law. Holdings' bylaws have numerous prerequisites that a director must meet before being entitled to indemnification. Those remain to be explored in the district court. In addition, on remand the district court should first consider Heffernan's right to advances, which the Delaware Supreme Court has recently indicated may present a prior and distinct inquiry from a director's ultimate right to indemnification. *Citadel Holding Corp.,* 603 A.2d 818; *see also id.* (resolving entitlement to interest in indemnification claims).

REVERSED AND REMANDED.

[The concurring opinion of Judge Ripple is omitted.]

––––––––

On remand, Heffernan v. Pacific Dunlop GNB Corp., 1992 WL 275573 (N.D.Ill.1992), the District Court distinguished Heffernan's claims to indemnification from his claims for advancement. Under Delaware law, the court concluded, a bylaw requiring mandatory indemnification did not, without more, require mandatory advances as well:

> The advance payment claim asserted in Count IV is sufficient legally if, under Delaware law, the right to advance payments exists as an inseparable subset of a director's indemnification rights. If that is so, then GNB's bylaw provision that states GNB "shall indemnify" means, by definition, that GNB shall provide advances. Alternatively, this claim is legally sufficient if, under Delaware law, advance payments exist as a permissible part of a director's indemnification rights and GNB's "shall indemnify" provision included advances as part of the right to indemnification.

> A recent decision of the Delaware Chancery Court addressed both alternative theories. Advanced Mining Systems, Inc. v. Fricke, [623 A.2d 82 (Del.Ch.1982)]. In *Advanced Mining,* the Delaware court decided an issue strikingly similar to the one presented here. Fricke argued that he was entitled to advance payments based upon a bylaw provision worded almost identically to GNB's indemnification provision. The Delaware court held that no entitlement to advance payments existed. The court concluded that indemnification rights and advancement rights stand apart as two "distinct types of legal rights." ... More importantly, the Delaware court concluded, as a matter of law, that a bylaw provision that required Advanced Mining to "indemnify ... to the extent permitted"

under Delaware law did not wrest from a corporation the ability, granted by § 145(e), to refuse advance payments....

In Barry v. Barry, 28 F.3d 848, 851 (8th Cir.1994), decided under Minnesota law, the court distinguished *Advanced Mining* on the ground that under the Minnesota statute, unlike the Delaware statute, indemnification and advances are both mandatory unless the corporation provides otherwise. See also Rev. Model Bus. Corp. Act § 8.58(a) and Official Comment.

BACKGROUND NOTE ON INDEMNIFICATION

1.   The right of a director or officer to indemnification under the common law was not completely clear. New York Dock Co. v. McCollom, 173 Misc. 106, 16 N.Y.S.2d 844 (1939), decided prior to the enactment of the New York indemnification statute, held that directors who had successfully defended themselves in a derivative suit were not entitled to reimbursement of their counsel fees, absent a showing that the corporation had benefited. Later decisions in other jurisdictions, however, upheld the common law right of a vindicated director to recover the expenses of his defense without any showing of a specific benefit. In re E.C. Warner Co., 232 Minn. 207, 45 N.W.2d 388 (1950); Solimine v. Hollander, 129 N.J.Eq. 264, 19 A.2d 344 (Ch.1941). The policy reasons why the corporation should indemnify a director, as set forth in *Solimine,* are (1) to encourage innocent directors to resist unjust charges and provide them an opportunity to hire competent counsel; (2) to induce "responsible business men to accept the post of directors": and (3) "to discourage in large measure stockholders' litigation of the strike variety." Id. at 272, 19 A.2d at 348.

2.   Today virtually every state has an indemnification statute, but the statutes vary widely in detail.[1] Some apply only to the indemnification of officers and directors, while others also apply to the indemnification of employees and agents. Some are exclusive— that is, they prohibit any provision for indemnification that is not consistent with the statute—while others are non-exclusive. In corporations governed by a nonexclusive statute, charter and by-law provisions affording indemnification in situations well beyond the boundaries explicitly authorized by statute are not uncommon. See Citadel Holding Corp. v. Roven, 603 A.2d 818 (Del.1992).

3.   Most modern indemnification statutes provide for indemnification as of right when the director or officer has been successful. However, what constitutes "success" for these purposes varies widely. Under Rev.Model Bus.Corp. Act § 8.52, the director must be "wholly successful, on the merits or otherwise." Under Del.

---

1. In Gross v. Texas Plastics, Inc., 344 F.Supp. 564 (D.N.J.1972), the court held that under accepted conflicts principles indemnification is governed by the law of the state of incorporation, not the law of the forum state. For a statutory treatment of this issue, see N.Y.Law § 726(d).

Gen.Corp.Law § 145(c) and N.Y.Bus.Corp.Law § 722(a), the officer or director must be "successful, on the merits or otherwise." Under Cal.Corp.Code § 317(d), the officer or director must be "successful on the merits." Each of these phrases is subject to considerable interpretation. See, e.g., Wisener v. Air Express Int'l Corp., 583 F.2d 579 (2d Cir.1978) (where a third-party claim against an officer is terminated without any payment, the officer is "successful, on the merits or otherwise" under the Illinois statute); Dornan v. Humphrey, 278 App.Div. 1010, 1011, 106 N.Y.S.2d 142, 144 (1951), modified 279 App.Div. 1040, 112 N.Y.S.2d 585 (1952) (where a complaint is dismissed under the statute of limitations, the defendants are "successful" under the predecessor of N.Y. § 724); American Nat. Bank & Trust Co. v. Schigur, 83 Cal.App.3d 790, 148 Cal.Rptr. 116 (1978). Suppose that a four-count indictment is issued against a director, one count is dismissed by the court, the jury is unable to reach a verdict, the director enters a plea on count 2, and in exchange counts 3 and 4 are dropped. In Merritt–Chapman & Scott v. Wolfson, 321 A.2d 138 (Del.Super.1974), it was held in such a case that the director was "successful" on counts 3 and 4 within the meaning of the Delaware statute. According to the Official Comment to section 8.52 of the Model Act, which adopts the "wholly successful, on the merits or otherwise" standard, "[t]he word 'wholly' is added to avoid the argument accepted in Merritt–Chapman & Scott Corp. v. Wolfson, 321 A.2d 138 (Del.1974), that a defendant may be entitled to partial mandatory indemnification if he succeeded by plea bargaining or otherwise to obtain the dismissal of some but not all counts of an indictment. A defendant is 'wholly successful' only if the entire proceeding is disposed of on a basis which involves a finding of nonliability."

4. Many of the modern indemnification statutes permit a corporation to indemnify an officer or director for fines and judgments levied against him because he has violated some rule of civil or criminal law other than the rules governing his obligations to the corporation itself. The theory of these provisions is that indemnification may be appropriate where the officer or director incurred the liability in a good faith attempt to further the corporation's interests. These provisions raise an obvious issue of policy, however, since the prospect of indemnification may diminish the fear of liability that normally provides one of the major incentives for obedience to law. As a result, corporate interests and social interests may cut in two very different directions. Koster v. Warren, 297 F.2d 418 (9th Cir.1961), the court said, "It may well be that public policy would strike down, as lacking in quid pro quo, any arrangement whereby a corporate officer could with immunity from personal liability involve his company in antitrust violations." The court went on to hold, however, that an after-the-fact agreement to indemnify two executives for fines they had paid was valid under the circumstances of

the case. See also Witco Corp. v. Beekhuis, 38 F.3d 682 (3d Cir.1994).

———

(b) INSURANCE

———

[See Chapter 7, Section 4 (D & O Insurance)]

———

SECTION 11. SETTLEMENT OF DERIVATIVE ACTIONS

———

CLARKE v. GREENBERG

Court of Appeals of New York, 1947.
296 N.Y. 146, 71 N.E.2d 443.

DYE, Judge. The challenge to the within complaint, for failure to state a cause of action, raises the question of whether a plaintiff in a stockholder's derivative action may be required to account to the corporation for moneys received in private settlement for discontinuance of the action.

The complaint alleges that the defendants commenced a stockholder's derivative action in behalf of the Associated Gas & Electric Company (called AGECO) entitled "Greenberg v. Mange et al." in which it was alleged that the defendants, as officers and directors, had so mismanaged its affairs that the company and its stockholders were damaged and prayed that an accounting be had, and that the court "impress a trust in favor of the Company (AGECO) upon all secret profits and gains obtained by any of the defendant directors," etc. No individual relief was asked except reimbursement for expenses. Later and before trial, a stipulation was made settling and discontinuing the action without notice to other stockholders and without approval of the court, by the terms of which Greenberg executed releases in his individual and representative capacity and transferred and delivered his stock, having a market value of $51.88, to the defendant directors and defendants herein received from them the sum of $9,000.

The complaint in this action alleges that the defendants received the money "to the use of, and in trust for AGECO"; that they had failed to account to it or its trustee, the plaintiff herein, and had accordingly unjustly enriched themselves in the sum of $8,948.12 which, in equity, should be paid over to the plaintiff, and prayed judgment accordingly.

The Appellate Division unanimously affirmed the dismissal of the complaint by the Special Term which relied upon Manufacturers Mutual Fire Ins. Co. of Rhode Island v. Hopson, 176 Misc. 220, 25 N.Y.S.2d 502, affirmed 262 App.Div. 731, 29 N.Y.S.2d 139, affirmed 288 N.Y. 668, 43 N.E.2d 71 in which we refused to set aside a stipulation settling a stockholder's derivative suit and revive the action. That case was limited to the right to discontinue and it did not consider whether the moneys received in settlement were impressed with a trust in favor of the corporation for which an accounting should be made.

The very nature of the derivative suit by a stockholder-plaintiff suing in the corporation's behalf suggests the application of the fiduciary principle to the proceeds realized from such litigation whether received by way of judgment, by settlement with approval of the court, which presupposes stockholders' approval, or by private settlement and discontinuance of the action at any stage of the proceeding. Such action, we have held, belongs primarily to the corporation, the real party in interest ... and a judgment so obtained, as well as the proceeds of a settlement with court approval belongs to it and not the individual stockholder plaintiffs.... While the stockholder-plaintiff, with such others as join with him, controls the course of the litigation at all stages of the proceeding before final judgment, he does not bind the nonparticipating stockholders by his action, or deprive them of their own right of action against the unfaithful directors, nor is he subject to their interference.... When, however, success crowns his effort, the amount received is in behalf and for the account of the corporation. This is so because the action belongs primarily to it. The manner and method by which such success is accomplished whether by way of judgment, settlement with court approval or by stipulation of the parties, makes no substantial difference in the interest of the corporation upon distribution of the proceeds. Requiring an accounting for moneys received in a private settlement introduces no new element. It simply amounts to a logical application of a fundamental principle inherent in the representative relation. When one assumes to act for another, regardless of the manner or method used in accomplishing a successful termination, he should willingly account for his stewardship. The plaintiff-stockholder, in good conscience, should not be allowed to retain the proceeds of a derivative suit discontinued by stipulation, to his individual use, in opposition to the corporation, any more than the proceeds of a judgment or a settlement with court approval.

The complaint, we believe, states a cause of action.

The judgments should be reversed and the motion to dismiss the complaint denied, with costs in all courts.

LOUGHRAN, C.J., and LEWIS, CONWAY, DESMOND, THACHER, and FULD, JJ., concur.

Judgments reversed, etc.*

—————

FEDERAL RULES OF CIVIL PROCEDURE, RULE 23.1

[See Statutory Supplement]

—————

REVISED MODEL BUSINESS CORPORATION ACT § 7.45

[See Statutory Supplement]

—————

NEW YORK BUS. CORP. LAW § 626(d), (e)

[See Statutory Supplement]

—————

LEWIS v. HIRSCH

Delaware Court of Chancery, 1994.
CCH Federal Securities Law Reports ¶ 98,382, 1994 WL 263551.

Opinion of HARTNETT, Justice, sitting as Vice Chancellor.

Plaintiff, Harry Lewis ("Lewis"), and the defendants seek approval of a proposed settlement of this stockholder derivative action that asserts various claims against defendant, United States Surgical Corporation ("U.S. Surgical" or "Corporation") and its directors. Because this Court is not satisfied that Lewis has adequately investigated the insider trading claims alleged against the individual defendants, approval of the proposed settlement cannot be given without further development of the record.

I

According to the Amended Complaint, plaintiff Lewis is and has been a stockholder of the Corporation at all times relevant to this lawsuit. The individual defendants, with the exception of Messrs. Korthoff and Fisher, are current directors of U.S. Surgical. Defendants Korthoff and Fisher are former officers and directors....

The Amended Complaint ... alleges that between May 1991 and April 1993, the individual defendants, with the exception of

—————

* Cf. Young v. Higbee Co., 324 U.S. 204, 65 S.Ct. 594, 89 L.Ed. 890 (1945). In Certain–Teed Products Corporation v. Topping, 171 F.2d 241 (2d Cir.1948) a shareholder-plaintiff in a derivative suit consented to the entry of a summary judgment in favor of the individual defendant on payment of $5,000 to the plaintiff's attorney. Plaintiff was held liable to the corporation for the $5,000 less such amount as the district court might allow as a reasonable attorney's fee. (Footnote by eds.)

defendant Fisher, breached the fiduciary duties they owed to the Corporation by using U.S. Surgical's material non-public information when deciding to sell large quantities of their U.S. Surgical stock, thereby making huge profits for themselves before the value of the stock plummeted (collectively, the "insider trading claims")....*

In the Amended Complaint ... it is alleged that defendants knew about the adverse effects that increased competitive pressures and new developments would have on the Corporation's growth and sales and sold their stock at high prices before those adverse effects were disclosed to the other stockholders and the general public and before the price of U.S. Surgical stock began to plummet in 1993.

One of the new developments that allegedly led to a significant decline in the price of U.S. Surgical stock was its implementation of a domestic Just In Time Program ("JIT"), thereby changing the way U.S. Surgical did business. Before the JIT program, U.S. Surgical sold its surgical products directly to hospitals and the hospitals would maintain an inventory of those products. With the implementation of the JIT program, U.S. Surgical began selling its products to distributors at a reduced price. The distributors, in turn, maintained an inventory of the products and then sold them to hospitals on an "as needed" basis. A significant 1993 decline in U.S. Surgical sales and the corresponding fall of the price of U.S. Surgical stock has been largely attributed to the implementation and growth of the JIT program....

II

The law of Delaware favors the voluntary settlement of class actions and shareholder derivative suits. *Polk v. Good*, Del.Supr., 507 A.2d 531, 535 (1986); *In re MCA, Inc.*, Del.Ch., 598 A.2d 687 (1991). This preference for settlement of contested matters, however, must be balanced "against the need to insure that the interests of the class have been fairly represented." *Barkan v. Amsted Industries, Inc.*, Del.Supr., 567 A.2d 1279, 1283 (1989). While this Court should not try the factual issues that are part of a proposed settlement proceeding, it "must engage in more than a cursory examination of the facts underlying each settlement." *In re Resorts Intern. Shareholders Lit.*, Del.Supr., 570 A.2d 259, 265–66 (1990).

In reviewing a proposed settlement of a stockholder derivative action, this Court must exercise its business judgment to determine whether the proposed settlement is reasonable and fair in light of all of the factual and legal circumstances of the case. *In re Resorts*, 570 A.2d at 266. As part of this determination, this Court must weigh the likelihood that Lewis would be successful as to the asserted claims against the value of the benefits conferred upon the

* The court's discussion of the settlement   note by ed.)
of certain other claims is omitted. (Foot-

Corporation and its shareholders by the settlement. *In re MCA,* 598 A.2d at 691; *In re Amsted Industries, Inc. Litigation,* Del.Ch., 521 A.2d 1104, 1107 (1986). Other factors to be considered in this weighing analysis include: (1) the risks, expenses, and delays of litigation; (2) the collectibility of any judgment that might be recovered; and (3) the value of the compromise as compared with the value and collectibility of a possible judgment. *Polk,* 507 A.2d at 536.

This Court, in reviewing a proposed settlement, necessarily does not make a finding as to a disputed fact because the review of a proposed settlement does not involve a trial of the issues on the merits. *In re Amsted Industries,* 521 A.2d at 1107; see *In re Resorts,* 570 A.2d at 266. The record, however, must be adequate as to the strengths and weaknesses of the claims as compared to any defenses to those claims in order for the Court to "sensibly and competently evaluate the value of the claims" *In re Amsted Industries,* 521 A.2d at 1107.

The proponents of a proposed settlement bear the burden of proving its fairness. *Barkan,* 567 A.2d at 1286; *Manacher v. Reynolds,* Del.Ch., 165 A.2d 741, 748 (1960).

III

Two groups of Objectors, "the Chanoff Objectors" and "the DiCicco Objectors", object to the proposed settlement of this action.

William Chanoff is the beneficial owner of over 170,000 shares of U.S. Surgical stock. His son, David Chanoff, is the beneficial owner of over 5,500 shares of U.S. Surgical stock. William Chanoff is a former director of U.S. Surgical. . . .

VIII

The objection that has the most merit is that Lewis failed to adequately investigate the insider trading claims before agreeing to settle them. This objection focuses upon the Corporation's "Just In Time" (JIT) program and it is alleged that Lewis made no effort to obtain documents concerning the development of the program, the timing of its implementation, or its anticipated effects upon the price of the Corporation's stock. . . .

[The Chanoff Objectors argue] that although Lewis took the depositions of two defendants, Mr. Lustman (executive vice-president and chief operating officer) and Mr. King (a non-officer director), he failed to adequately investigate the insider trading claims. The Chanoff Objectors point out that Lewis did not depose defendant Hirsch (the president and chief executive officer of U.S. Surgical). Hirsch apparently received over $78 million by exercising U.S. Surgical stock options during 1991 and 1992. And, Hirsch publicly stated on April 7, 1993, that

> For approximately one year, the company has been experimenting with a Just–In–Time (JIT) distributor program. As a result

of the positive reaction of its test hospitals, the company accelerated significantly its JIT program *during the later part of the first quarter* ... (Emphasis added).

Finally, the Chanoff Objectors argue that Lewis failed to follow up on the deposition testimony of defendant Lustman. Lustman's testimony is characterized by the Chanoff Objectors as being to the effect that the JIT program was introduced all at once and almost as a surprise in the first quarter of 1993. According to the Objectors, Lewis also failed to request documents, such as sales projections, that Lustman referred to during his deposition. These documents allegedly would have provided evidence of the Corporation's internal timetable for introduction of the JIT program.

IX

In response, Lewis alleges that he has conducted a thorough investigation of the insider trading claims and found them to be unsupported by the evidence.

Lewis asserts that soon after [a complaint in a related action] was filed, he began an investigation into the insider trading claims. He asserts that he obtained copies of every press release the company had made over a period of time and he reviewed internal documents. He further asserts that President Clinton's election in November 1992 caused a decline in the price of U.S. Surgical stock, as well as the stock of other health care companies. (This assertion, however, does not shed light on whether the individual defendants traded on any inside information).

Lewis further explains that the "same day sale rule", established by the Securities Exchange Commission in 1991, provides a perfectly logical and legal explanation for the individual defendants' stock sales. The same day sale rule permits immediate disposition of option stock on the day of the exercise of the option. Lewis maintains that the record of all of the stock sales by defendants from January 1, 1991, through April, 1993, demonstrates that most of the stock sales by the individual defendants occurred pursuant to the same day sale rule.

Lewis alleges that the record reveals that two of the "principal sellers", defendants Hirsch and Josefsen, engaged in a systematic program of selling U.S. Surgical stock. These defendants sold stock on a regular, monthly basis. Lewis, therefore, argues that evidence of such a selling pattern would be difficult to overcome in an attempt to prove claims of insider trading.

Lewis claims that it is clear that the defendants did not trade on inside information because: (1) defendant Lustman apparently was motivated by the same day sale rule and income tax considerations in his sales of stock; (2) defendant Korthoff resigned as an officer at the end of 1991 and would not have been privy to any U.S. Surgical secrets (Korthoff, however, remained a director until May 1992); (3) the defendants' sales of stock were matters of public knowledge; (4) according to the deposition of defendant King, JIT sales accounted for only two to three percent of overall sales in 1992 and direct sales accounted for most of the projected sales in the Corporation's 1993 budget; thus, Lewis argues that "it can hardly be said that the directors' internal planning exhibited knowledge or anticipation of a large-scale shift from direct sales to JIT when they planned ahead" for 1993; and (5) as detailed in an April 16, 1993, research report by Paine Webber, the widespread implementation of JIT programs by hospitals was public knowledge, being "an outgrowth of the widely publicized and politically popular outcry about escalating health care costs."

X

Upon review of all the factual and legal circumstances of this case, the Court concludes that it is unable to evaluate the overall reasonableness of the proposed settlement at the present time because Lewis has not shown that he adequately investigated the insider trading claims. The proposed settlement, therefore, cannot be approved on the present record.

Notwithstanding the assertions made by Lewis in support of his belief that the insider trading claims could not be proven at trial, the record does not presently adequately support that contention. Lewis cites many public occurrences and events such as the 1992 Presidential election, the 1993 Paine Webber report, the public knowledge of defendants' stock sales, and the public outcry for health care reform as evidence that the individual defendants did not profit by trading on inside information.

Lewis, however, misses the point by focusing on those events. He has failed to address the key issues involved in the insider trading claims, namely: (1) at what point did the individual defendants know that increased competitive pressures and implementation and increased use of the JIT program would have adverse effects on Company sales and the price of U.S. Surgical stock; (2) whether the individual defendants delayed advising the other stockholders of this adverse information; and (3) whether the defendants sold their stock based on this inside knowledge before the public was informed of these developments and adverse effects, thereby making huge profits for themselves before the price of U.S. Surgical stock plummeted.

Lewis should have deposed defendants Hirsch, Josefsen, and Korthoff, the primary sellers of stock along with defendant Lustman. And he should have deposed defendant Scipione, who allegedly told William Chanoff that JIT sales became heavy in the last quarter of 1992. Such an allegation, if true, may be inconsistent with the April 7, 1993, release made by Hirsch in which he states that the JIT program was not accelerated significantly until the first quarter of 1993. That allegation should at least be investigated to determine its merit. Lewis has not shown how he investigated this purported discrepancy. He also has not specified what types of documents were examined and what those documents revealed concerning the known effects of the implementation and subsequent increased use of the JIT program.

The Court is cognizant of the defenses that could be raised at a trial in response to the insider trading claims, such as, the same day sale rule and the systematic, monthly trading by defendants Hirsch and Josefsen. Those defenses, however, are not absolute bars to recovery and might be overcome by evidence showing that defendants withheld or took advantage of material inside information and exercised their stock options to make huge profits for themselves before the information was disclosed and the price of the stock fell.

In sum, the Court, upon the record before it at this time, is unable to adequately evaluate the value of the insider trading claims as compared to the value of the somewhat speculative benefits conferred by the settlement because Lewis has so far failed to adequately investigate those claims. The Court, therefore, is unable to presently conclude, in the exercise of its business judgment, and in its discretion, that the settlement is reasonable and fair in light of all of the factual and legal circumstances.

While Lewis, after further discovery, may well be able to show that the insider claims have little value, he has not yet done so. Approval of the proposed settlement therefore must be withheld at this time pending further development of the record.

It is so ordered.

ALI, PRINCIPLES OF CORPORATE GOVERNANCE §§ 7.14, 7.16

[See Statutory Supplement]

DESIMONE v. INDUSTRIAL BIO–TEST LABORATORIES, INC., 83 F.R.D. 615 (S.D.N.Y.1979). "The court will approve a proposed settlement of a class action if the proposal is fair, reasonable and adequate. This determination requires three levels of analysis. First, the proponents have the burden of proving that (1) the settlement is not collusive but was reached after arm's length negotiation; (2) the proponents are counsel experienced in similar cases; (3) there has been sufficient discovery to enable counsel to act intelligently and (4) the number of objectants or their relative interest is small. If the proponents establish these propositions, the burden of attacking the settlement then shifts to the objectants, if any. Finally, the court must approve the settlement only after finding it to be reasonable in light of the plaintiffs' ultimate probability of success in the lawsuit....

"In determining reasonableness, the courts in this circuit have not applied any single, inflexible test. Instead, they have considered the amount of the settlement in light of all the circumstances, including such factors as: (1) the best possible recovery; (2) the likely recovery if the claims were fully litigated; (3) the complexity, expense and probable duration of continued litigation; (4) the risk of establishing liability; (5) the risk of establishing damages; (6) the risk of maintaining the class action throughout trial; (7) the reaction of the class to the settlement; (8) the stage of the proceedings and (9) the ability of the defendants to withstand a greater judgment." ...

BACKGROUND NOTE ON JUDICIAL APPROVAL OF SETTLEMENTS

1. The mechanics of obtaining judicial approval of a settlement agreement are described in Haudek, The Settlement and Dismissal of Stockholders' Action—Part II: The Settlement, 23 Sw. L.J. 765 (1969). Generally speaking, the courts tend to rely heavily on affidavits, documents, depositions, and answers to interrogatories.

2. Once notice of settlement has been given, shareholders who object to the proposed settlement can enter the case. The objector becomes, in effect, a party to the settlement proceedings (although not to the underlying action). He therefore has a right to cross-examine the proponent's witnesses, to obtain a reasonable adjournment of the settlement hearing, and to appeal approval of the settlement, and he may also be given discovery rights. See Wolf v. Nazareth Enterprises, 303 F.2d 152, 154–55 (2d Cir.1962); Haudek, 23 Sw.L.J., supra, at 803–06. Moreover, if he succeeds in improving the settlement, he—or more accurately his lawyer—is entitled to counsel fees. White v. Auerbach, 500 F.2d 822 (2d Cir.1974), noted, 1 J.Corp.Law 194 (1975). Not infrequently the efforts of objectors result in a significant improvement of the settlement. In a well-known episode involving the Alleghany Corporation, a settlement involving a cash payment of $700,000 was increased under objection to $1,000,000, and under continued objection was further increased to $3 million. See Alleghany Corp. v. Kirby, 333 F.2d 327 (2d Cir.1964), aff'd in banc by an equally divided court 340 F.2d 311 (2d Cir.1965), cert. dismissed 384 U.S. 28, 86 S.Ct. 1250, 16 L.Ed.2d 335 (1966).[1]

---

1. The history of this case is both interesting and instructive. Originally, proceedings were begun by a number of different lawyers in both state and federal courts. The state court actions were consolidated under a lead counsel who negotiated the original settlement. However, counsel in an action brought in federal district court had not been allowed to participate in the settlement negotiation, and that court enjoined the defendants from setting up, as res judicata in the federal action, any judgment resulting from the settlement. The practical effect of this injunction was to preclude consummation of any settlement that did not have the federal court's approval, and new negotiations, leading to the revised settlement, were therefore undertaken. See Breswick & Co. v. Briggs, 135 F.Supp. 397 (S.D.N.Y.1955); Zenn v. Anzalone, 17 Misc.2d 897, 191 N.Y.S.2d 840

3.   As a practical matter, the engine that normally drives a derivative action involving a publicly held corporation is not the plaintiff, but the plaintiff's attorney.   The plaintiff typically makes little or no investment in the action and stands to gain very little benefit.   His attorney, on the other hand, makes a very substantial investment (in the form of his time and disbursements) and stands to reap a very substantial benefit (in the form of a fee).   This raises the unwholesome possibility that the defendants may be able to make an improper settlement by giving their acquiescence to an inflated fee in exchange for acquiescence by plaintiff's counsel to an inadequate corporate recovery.[2]   In Alleghany Corp. v. Kirby, supra, Judge Friendly remarked on the manner in which the interests of a plaintiff's attorney may conflict with the interests of the shareholders in settling cases where very large amounts are at stake:

> I cannot at all agree . . . that standard procedures for the approval of settlements afford sufficient safeguards in the "big" case. . . .   The plaintiff stockholders or, more realistically, their attorneys have every incentive to accept a settlement that runs into high six figures or more regardless of how strong the claims for much larger amounts may be.   The percentage allowance in stockholders' actions is "reduced as the amount of recovery passes the million dollar mark," 2 Hornstein, Corporation Law and Practice 253 (1959) . . . the income tax also plays a role; and a juicy bird in the hand is worth more than the vision of a much larger one in the bush, attainable only after years of effort not currently compensated and possibly a mirage.   Once a settlement is agreed, the attorneys for the plaintiff stockholders link arms with their former adversaries to defend the joint handiwork—as is vividly shown here where the stockholders' general counsel sometimes opposed [the objector's] efforts to gain information, although the settlement so vigorously defended before the Referee would have produced less than a quarter as much cash for Alleghany, $700,000, as the $3,000,000 ultimately secured. . . .

ALI, PRINCIPLES OF CORPORATE GOVERNANCE § 7.15

[See Statutory Supplement]

(1959), appeal dism'd 11 A.D.2d 938, 210 N.Y.S.2d 748 (1960); noted, 69 Harv.L.Rev. 1501 (1956); 65 Yale L.J. 543 (1956).

2.   Cf. Fistel v. Christman, 133 F.Supp. 300 (S.D.N.Y.1955) (plaintiff's attorney agreed to dismiss a § 16(b) action on condition that the defendant pay him $2,500 for legal services); Jamison v. Butcher & Sherrerd, 68 F.R.D. 479 (E.D.Pa.1975) (proposed settlement of class action involved no benefit to the class but called for payment by defendants of a $50,000 attorneys' fee); Norman v. McKee, 290 F.Supp. 29 (N.D.Cal.1968), aff'd 431 F.2d 769 (9th Cir. 1970) (similar to Jamison); Rosenfeld, An Empirical Test of Class–Action Settlement, 5 J.Leg.Studies 113 (1976).

Chapter XI

STRUCTURAL CHANGES: COMBINATIONS, TENDER OFFERS, RECAPITALIZATIONS, AND CHARTER AMENDMENTS

SECTION 1. CORPORATE COMBINATIONS

(a) INTRODUCTION; MOTIVES FOR BUSINESS COMBINATIONS

The combination of two corporations presents in a single transaction basic questions of business policy, finance, accounting, corporate law, taxation, and, at times, antitrust law. The prototypical corporate combination is a transaction that may be referred to as a "classical merger." Although "merger" is often used by nonlawyers to describe any form of combination, to a lawyer it normally means a combination involving the fusion of two constituent corporations, pursuant to a formal agreement executed with reference to specific statutory merger provisions, under which the stock of one corporation (the transferor) is converted into stock of the other (the survivor). The survivor then succeeds to the transferor's assets and liabilities by operation of law. At one time the classical merger probably was the dominant mode of corporate combination, but in present times its scope has been significantly reduced. Broadly speaking, the upstart modes of combination that have shouldered this form aside fall into four categories: cash-for-assets, cash-for-stock, stock-for-assets, and stock-for-stock.

In a *cash-for-assets* combination, Corporation A purchases substantially all of the assets of Corporation B for cash or equivalent.

In a *cash-for-stock* combination, Corporation A purchases (at least) a majority of the stock of Corporation B for cash or equivalent.

In a *stock-for-assets* combination, Corporation A issues shares of its own stock to Corporation B in exchange for substantially all of B's assets. Often, in such a combination, A agrees to assume B's liabilities. In some cases, however, A may assume B's liabilities on only a selective basis. (Indeed, one reason for using this mode in preference to a classical merger may be A's desire to avoid assuming all of B's liabilities.) Usually, B agrees that it will dissolve and distribute its stock in A to its own shareholders. (The major reason for this is that A does not want a large block of its stock concentrated in a single holder.) Frequently it is also agreed or understood that some or all of B's officers and directors will join A's management.

In a *stock-for-stock* combination, Corporation A issues shares of its own stock directly to the shareholders of Corporation B in exchange for an amount of B stock—normally at least a majority—sufficient to carry control. By virtue of such a combination the shareholder groups of the two corporations are combined to a substantial extent, and B becomes a subsidiary of A. Frequently B is then liquidated or merged into A, but whether or not this occurs, B's assets will be under A's control. Such a combination does not require approval by B's management (since corporate action by B is not required). Often, however, the terms of the exchange of stock are worked out beforehand by the managements of both corporations, and often too it is agreed or understood that some or all of B's management will stay on with B in its new role as a subsidiary, or will join Corporation A itself.

(b) SALE OF SUBSTANTIALLY ALL ASSETS

DEL. GEN. CORP. LAW § 271

[See Statutory Supplement]

REV. MODEL BUS. CORP. ACT §§ 12.01, 12.02, 13.02

[See Statutory Supplement]

KATZ v. BREGMAN

Court of Chancery of Delaware, 1981.
431 A.2d 1274, appeal ref'd sub nom. Plant Indus., Inc. v. Katz, 435 A.2d 1044 (Del.1981).

MARVEL, Chancellor:

The complaint herein seeks the entry of an order preliminarily enjoining the proposed sale of the Canadian assets of Plant Industries, Inc. to Vulcan Industrial Packaging, Ltd., the plaintiff Hyman Katz allegedly being the owner of approximately 170,000 shares of common stock of the defendant Plant Industries, Inc., on whose behalf he has brought this action, suing not only for his own benefit as a stockholder but for the alleged benefit of all other record owners of common stock of the defendant Plant Industries, Inc.... Significantly, at common law, a sale of all or substantially all of the assets of a corporation required the unanimous vote of the stockholders, Folk, The Delaware General Corporation Law, p. 400.

The complaint alleges that during the last six months of 1980 the board of directors of Plant Industries, Inc., under the guidance of the individual defendant Robert B. Bregman, the present chief executive officer of such corporation, embarked on a course of action which resulted in the disposal of several unprofitable subsidiaries of the corporate defendant located in the United States, namely Louisiana Foliage Inc., a horticultural business, Sunaid Food Products, Inc., a Florida packaging business, and Plant Industries (Texas), Inc., a business concerned with the manufacture of woven synthetic cloth. As a result of these sales Plant Industries, Inc. by the end of 1980 had disposed of a significant part of its unprofitable assets.

According to the complaint, Mr. Bregman thereupon proceeded on a course of action designed to dispose of a subsidiary of the corporate defendant known as Plant National (Quebec) Ltd., a business which constitutes Plant Industries, Inc.'s entire business operation in Canada and has allegedly constituted Plant's only income producing facility during the past four years. The professed principal purpose of such proposed sale is to raise needed cash and thus improve Plant's balance sheets. And while interest in purchasing the corporate defendant's Canadian plant was thereafter evinced not only by Vulcan Industrial Packaging, Ltd. but also by Universal Drum Reconditioning Co., which latter corporation originally undertook to match or approximate and recently to top Vulcan's bid, a formal contract was entered into between Plant Industries, Inc. and Vulcan on April 2, 1981 for the purchase and sale of Plant National (Quebec) despite the constantly increasing bids for the same property being made by Universal. One reason advanced by Plant's management for declining to negotiate with Universal is that a firm undertaking having been entered into with Vulcan that the board of directors of Plant may not legally or ethically negotiate with Universal. But see *Thomas v. Kempner*, C.A. 4138, March 22, 1973.

In seeking injunctive relief, as prayed for, plaintiff relies on two principles, one that found in 8 Del.C. § 271 to the effect that a decision of a Delaware corporation to sell "... all or substantially all of its property and assets ..." requires not only the approval of such corporation's board of directors but also a resolution adopted by a majority of the outstanding stockholders of the corporation entitled to vote thereon at a meeting duly called upon at least twenty days' notice.

Support for the other principle relied on by plaintiff for the relief sought, namely an alleged breach of fiduciary duty on the part of the board of directors of Plant Industries, Inc. is allegedly found in such board's studied refusal to consider a potentially higher bid for the assets in question which is being advanced by Universal, *Thomas v. Kempner*, supra.

Turning to the possible application of 8 Del.C. § 271 to the proposed sale of substantial corporate assets of National to Vulcan, it is stated in *Gimbel v. Signal Companies, Inc.,* Del.Ch., 316 A.2d 599 (1974) as follows:

> "If the sale is of assets quantitatively vital to the operation of the corporation and is out of the ordinary [course] and substantially affects the existence and purpose of the corporation then it is beyond the power of the Board of Directors."

According to Plant's 1980 10K form, it appears that at the end of 1980, Plant's Canadian operations represented 51% of Plant's remaining assets. Defendants also concede that National represents 44.9% of Plant's sales' revenues and 52.4% of its pretax net operating income. Furthermore, such report by Plant discloses, in rough figures, that while National made a profit in 1978 of $2,900,000, the profit from the United States businesses in that year was only $770,000. In 1979, the Canadian business profit was $3,500,000 while the loss of the United States businesses was $344,000. Furthermore, in 1980, while the Canadian business profit was $5,300,-000, the corporate loss in the United States was $4,500,000. And while these figures may be somewhat distorted by the allocation of overhead expenses and taxes, they are significant. In any event, defendants concede that ". . . National accounted for 34.9% of Plant's pretax income in 1976, 36.9% in 1977, 42% in 1978, 51% in 1979 and 52.4% in 1980."

While in the case of *Philadelphia National Bank v. B.S.F. Co.,* Del.Ch., 199 A.2d 557 (1969), rev'd on other grounds, Del.Supr., 204 A.2d 746 (1964), the question of whether or not there had been a proposed sale of substantially all corporate assets was tested by provisions of an indenture agreement covering subordinated debentures, the result was the same as if the provisions of 8 Del.C. § 271 had been applicable, the trial Court stating:

> "While no pertinent Pennsylvania case is cited, the critical factor in determining the character of a sale of assets is generally considered not the amount of property sold but whether the sale is in fact an unusual transaction or one made in the regular course of business of the seller * * *".

Furthermore, in the case of *Wingate v. Bercut* (C.A.9) 146 F.2d 725 (1945), in which the Court declined to apply the provisions of 8 Del.C. § 271, it was noted that the transfer of shares of stock there involved, being a dealing in securities, constituted an ordinary business transaction.

In the case at bar, I am first of all satisfied that historically the principal business of Plant Industries, Inc. has not been to buy and sell industrial facilities but rather to manufacture steel drums for use in bulk shipping as well as for the storage of petroleum products, chemicals, food, paint, adhesives and cleaning agents, a business which has been profitably performed by National of Quebec. Furthermore, the proposal, after the sale of National, to embark on the manufacture of plastic drums represents a radical departure from

Plant's historically successful line of business, namely steel drums. I therefore conclude that the proposed sale of Plant's Canadian operations, which constitute over 51% of Plant's total assets and in which are generated approximately 45% of Plant's 1980 net sales, would, if consummated, constitute a sale of substantially all of Plant's assets. By way of contrast, the proposed sale of Signal Oil in *Gimbel v. Signal Companies, Inc.,* supra, represented only about 26% of the total assets of Signal Companies, Inc. And while Signal Oil represented 41% of Signal Companies, Inc. total net worth, it generated only about 15% of Signal Companies, Inc. revenue and earnings.

I conclude that because the proposed sale of Plant National (Quebec) Ltd. would, if consummated, constitute a sale of substantially all of the assets of Plant Industries, Inc., as presently constituted, that an injunction should issue preventing the consummation of such sale at least until it has been approved by a majority of the outstanding stockholders of Plant Industries, Inc., entitled to vote at a meeting duly called on at least twenty days' notice. Compare *Robinson v. Pittsburg Oil Refining Company,* Del.Ch., 126 A. 46 (1933).

In light of this conclusion it will be unnecessary to consider whether or not the sale here under attack, as proposed to be made, is for such an inadequate consideration, viewed in light of the competing bid of Universal, as to constitute a breach of trust on the part of the directors of Plant Industries, Inc., *Robinson v. Pittsburg Oil Refining Company,* supra.

Being persuaded for the reasons stated that plaintiff has demonstrated a reasonable probability of ultimate success on final hearing in the absence of stockholder approval of the proposed sale of the corporate assets here in issue to Vulcan, a preliminary injunction against the consummation of such transaction, at least until stockholder approval is obtained, will be granted.

On notice, an appropriate form of order in conformity with the above may be submitted.

NOTE

It is generally accepted that at common law a sale of substantially all assets required unanimous shareholder approval, on the theory that it breached an implied contract among the shareholders to further the corporate enterprise. See, e.g., Note, Interplay of Rights of Stockholders Dissenting from Sale of Corporate Assets, 58 Colum.L.Rev. 251, 251–252 (1958); Comment, Disposition of Corporate Assets, 43 N.C.L.Rev. 957, 958–59 (1965); Fontaine v. Brown County Motors Co., 251 Wis. 433, 437, 29 N.W.2d 744, 746–47 (1947). The sale-of-substantially-all assets provisions were enacted against this backdrop. It has been held that a sale of substantially all assets in the ordinary course of business does not require shareholder approval. See Jeppi v. Brockman Holding Co., 34 Cal.2d 11, 206 P.2d 847 (1949); Comment, Disposition of Corporate Assets, supra, at 960. The theory is that since such a sale does not prevent furtherance of the corporate enterprise it would not have required unanimous shareholder approval at common law, and the sale-of-substantially-all-assets statutes were not intended to change that result.

(c) THE APPRAISAL REMEDY

DEL. GEN. CORP. LAW § 262

[See Statutory Supplement]

REV. MODEL BUS. CORP. ACT §§ 13.01–13.03, 13.20–13.28, 13.30–13.31

[See Statutory Supplement]

ALI, PRINCIPLES OF CORPORATE GOVERNANCE §§ 7.21–7.23

[See Statutory Supplement]

CAL. CORP. CODE § 1300

[See Statutory Supplement]

NOTE ON WEINBERGER v. UOP

In Weinberger v. UOP, 457 A.2d 701 (1983), the Delaware Supreme Court overturned the traditional Delaware block method of valuation (See *Piemonte*, p. 327, supra):

> Turning to the matter of price, plaintiff also challenges its fairness. His evidence was that on the date the merger was approved the stock was worth at least $26 per share. In support, he offered the testimony of a chartered investment

analyst who used two basic approaches to valuation: a comparative analysis of the premium paid over market in ten other tender offer-merger combinations, and a discounted cash flow analysis.

In this breach of fiduciary duty case, the Chancellor perceived that the approach to valuation was the same as that in an appraisal proceeding. Consistent with precedent, he rejected plaintiff's method of proof and accepted defendants' evidence of value as being in accord with practice under prior case law. This means that the so-called "Delaware block" or weighted average method was employed wherein the elements of value, i.e., assets, market price, earnings, etc., were assigned a particular weight and the resulting amounts added to determine the value per share. This procedure has been in use for decades. See In re General Realty & Utilities Corp., Del.Ch., 52 A.2d 6, 14–15 (1947). However, to the extent it excludes other generally accepted techniques used in the financial community and the courts, it is now clearly outmoded. It is time we recognize this in appraisal and other stock valuation proceedings and bring our law current on the subject.

While the Chancellor rejected plaintiff's discounted cash flow method of valuing UOP's stock, as not corresponding with "either logic or the existing law" (426 A.2d at 1360), it is significant that this was essentially the focus, i.e., earnings potential of UOP, of Messrs. Arledge and Chitiea in their evaluation of the merger. Accordingly, the standard "Delaware block" or weighted average method of valuation, formerly employed in appraisal and other stock valuation cases, shall no longer exclusively control such proceedings. We believe that a more liberal approach must include proof of value by any techniques or methods which are generally considered acceptable in the financial community and otherwise admissible in court, subject only to our interpretation of 8 Del.C. § 262(h), infra. . . . . This will obviate the very structured and mechanistic procedure that has heretofore governed such matters. See Jacques Coe & Co. v. Minneapolis–Moline Co., Del.Ch., 75 A.2d 244, 247 (1950); Tri–Continental Corp. v. Battye, Del.Ch., 66 A.2d 910, 917–18 (1949); In re General Realty and Utilities Corp., supra.

> . . . This [approach] is not only in accord with the realities of present day affairs, but it is thoroughly consonant with the purpose and intent of our statutory law. Under 8 Del.C. § 262(h), the Court of Chancery:
>
>> shall appraise the shares, determining their *fair* value exclusive of any element of value arising from the accomplishment or expectation of the merger, together with a fair rate of interest, if any, to be paid upon the amount determined to be the *fair* value. In

determining such *fair* value, the Court shall take into account *all relevant factors* ... (Emphasis added)

See also Bell v. Kirby Lumber Corp., Del.Supr., 413 A.2d 137, 150–51 (1980) (Quillen, J., concurring).

It is significant that section 262 now mandates the determination of "fair" value based upon "all relevant factors". Only the speculative elements of value that may arise from the "accomplishment or expectation" of the merger are excluded. We take this to be a very narrow exception to the appraisal process, designed to eliminate use of *pro forma* data and projections of a speculative variety relating to the completion of a merger. But elements of future value, including the nature of the enterprise, which are known or susceptible of proof as of the date of the merger and not the product of speculation, may be considered. When the trial court deems it appropriate, fair value also includes any damages, resulting from the taking, which the stockholders sustain as a class. If that was not the case, then the obligation to consider "all relevant factors" in the valuation process would be eroded.

———

CALIO, NEW APPRAISALS OF OLD PROBLEMS: REFLECTIONS ON THE DELAWARE APPRAISAL PROCEEDING, 32 Am. Bus.J. 1, 48–49 (1994). "Since *Weinberger,* the viability of the Block Method as a valuation method is questionable. Consistent with its general acceptance and vast application in the financial community, the "discounted cash flow" method has become the valuation "methodology of choice" in Delaware appraisal proceedings. While this is currently the favored method of valuation, it is not exclusive; other models are employed when the circumstances dictate."

———

NEW YORK BUS. CORP. LAW § 623(h)(4)

[See Statutory Supplement]

———

LEADER v. HYCOR, INC., 395 Mass. 215, 479 N.E.2d 173 (1985). "Because the issue of the continuing validity of the 'Delaware block method' of stock valuation is likely to arise on remand, we express our opinion on this matter. We do not agree that the 'Delaware block method' for valuing closely held stock, as set forth in our decision in *Piemonte v. New Boston Garden Corp.,* 377 Mass. 719, 387 N.E.2d 1145 (1979), is outmoded. Citing *Weinberger v.*

UOP, Inc., 457 A.2d 701 (Del.1983), the plaintiffs contend that the Delaware Supreme Court has rejected this valuation method. The *Weinberger* court stated that this method is outmoded 'to the extent it excludes other generally accepted techniques used in the financial community and the courts' and that it would no longer '*exclusively* control such proceedings' (emphasis added). *Weinberger, supra* at 712–713. We need not accept judicial interpretations of Delaware law made subsequent to our Legislature's adoption of c. 156B. *Id.* at 723. In any event, we have never held that the Delaware block method is the only approach that a judge may employ in valuing stock. In *Piemonte,* we stated that a judge 'might appropriately follow' this general approach. *Id.* at 723–724.''

(d) STATUTORY MERGERS

----

(1) Classical Mergers

DEL. GEN. CORP. LAW §§ 251(a)–(e), 259–261

[See Statutory Supplement]

REV. MODEL BUS. CORP. ACT §§ 11.01, 11.03, 11.05, 11.06

[See Statutory Supplement]

NOTE ON STATUTORY MERGERS

1. Del.Gen.Corp.Law §§ 251(a)–(e), 259–61 and Rev.Model Bus.Corp.Act §§ 11.01, 11.03, 11.05, 11.06 authorize a type of transaction commonly referred to as a statutory merger. While details vary from state to state, generally the first formal step in such a merger, after negotiations have been completed, is a preliminary agreement (often embodied in a "letter of intent") signed by representatives of the constituent companies. If the merger is approved by the board and shareholders of each constituent, articles of merger are then filed with the secretary of state, and securities of the surviving corporation are exchanged for those of the disappearing or transferor corporation, which is fused into the transferee, and loses its identity. In general, no instruments of conveyance, such as deeds or bills of sale, are necessary to pass title from the transferor to the survivor: by operation of law the survivor

has all the rights, privileges, franchises, and assets of the constituents, and assumes all of their liabilities.

2.   A statutory consolidation is identical to a statutory merger except for the fact that in a merger one constituent fuses into another, while in a consolidation the constituents fuse to form a new corporation.   Because the consolidation technique is seldom employed, and when employed is treated almost identically to a merger, no separate consideration will be given in this Chapter to statutory consolidations.

3.   At one time, virtually all statutory mergers required approval by a majority or two-thirds vote of the outstanding shares of each constituent and also triggered appraisal rights for the shareholders of each constituent.   Many statutes now carve out exceptions to these requirements in the case of "short-form" and "small-scale" mergers.   These types of merger will be considered in the next two sections.

(2) Small–Scale Mergers

DEL. GEN. CORP. LAW § 251(f)

[See Statutory Supplement]

REV. MODEL BUS. CORP. ACT § 11.03(g)

[See Statutory Supplement]

---

2 E. FOLK, R. WARD & E. WELCH, FOLK ON THE DELAWARE GENERAL CORPORATION LAW § 251.2.1.1

3d ed. 1994.

(1) [The requirement of Del. § 251(f) that the survivor's certificate of incorporation not be amended] is designed to assure that the merger technique cannot be used to deprive stockholders of the voting rights that they would enjoy if the certificate were being amended under section 242. . . .

(2) The theory underlying the second condition—the 20 percent limitation on increasing the number of common shares—is that a merger which involves less than 20 percent of the survivor's shares is not such a major change as to require a stockholder vote, and is really no more than an enlargement of the business that could be achieved by other means without triggering voting rights.   For

instance, a corporation purchasing assets need not secure approval of its stockholders to issue already authorized shares to the seller. Nor would voting rights exist if a corporation offered its own authorized shares in exchange for the shares of another corporation and thereby gained control, or if the corporation were to sell its authorized shares for cash and then use the proceeds of the sale to purchase assets. When business needs demand that the acquisition take the form of a merger rather than a purchase of assets or shares, the premise of the statute is that the merger should not require a stockholder vote when other procedures with nearly identical economic consequences do not require a stockholder vote. Stated otherwise, [§ 251(f)] puts mergers more on a parity with acquisition of assets or shares so far as the legal requirements are concerned.

———

(3) Short–Form Mergers

———

DEL. GEN. CORP. LAW § 253

[See Statutory Supplement]

———

REV. MODEL BUS. CORP. ACT § 11.04

[See Statutory Supplement]

———

NOTE ON SHORT–FORM MERGERS

Most of the major corporate statutes now include provisions authorizing the so-called short-form merger, under which certain parent-subsidiary mergers can be effected simply by vote of the parent's board—that is, without a vote of the parent's or the subsidiary's shareholders, without appraisal rights in the parent's shareholders, and frequently without a vote of the subsidiary's board. Most of the early short-form statutes were applicable only to mergers involving a parent and its 100–percent–owned subsidiary, and were probably conceived as procedural in nature, designed to simplify the mechanics of mergers. Today, however, the reach of short-form merger provisions has been substantively extended in two important ways. First, many such provisions are now applicable to mergers between parents and less–than–100–percent–owned subsidiaries—typically, although not invariably, the floor is set at 90 percent. Second, it has been held that the purpose of these statutes is to provide the parent corporation with a means of eliminating the minority shareholder's interest in the enterprise by issuing cash rather than stock to the minority.[1] To the extent this view is followed, these statutory provisions operate as *cash-out* rather than *merger* statutes. Furthermore, they are cash-out statutes that run in one direction only: the parent can force the minority to sell at any time, but the minority cannot force the parent to buy.

(e) TAX AND ACCOUNTING ASPECTS OF CORPORATE COMBINATIONS

NOTE ON TAX AND ACCOUNTING TREATMENTS

1. *Tax Treatment.* Much is made of taxation as a principal motive for corporate combinations, but this factor, while significant, can be exaggerated. Whatever its role as a motive, taxation is often critical in determining *how* a combination will be effected. The principal issue is whether the combination will be tax-free—which means, essentially, that taxes on the transferor's gain will be postponed, that the basis in the stock or property received will remain the same, and that past operating losses of both companies can generally be carried over to apply against future earnings. See IRC §§ 354(a)(1), 358, 361(a), 381, 382.

In general, the Code provides three basic routes by which a tax-free combination—or, in tax parlance, a "reorganization"—can be achieved. These routes are popularly known as Type A, B, and C reorganizations, and are the tax counterparts of statutory mergers, stock-for-stock combinations, and stock-for-assets combinations, respectively.

(a) A "Type A" reorganization—covered by IRC § 368(a)(1)(A)—is defined as a statutory merger or consolidation.

(b) A "Type B" reorganization—covered by § 368(a)(1)(B)—is defined as the acquisition by one corporation, in exchange solely for all or part of its voting stock (or the voting stock of a parent corporation) of stock of another corporation, if the acquiring corporation has control of the acquired corporation immediately after the acquisition. Control is defined by § 368(c) as the ownership of stock possessing at least 80 percent of total combined voting power, plus at least 80 percent of the total number of shares of all other classes of stock.

(c) A "Type C" reorganization—covered by § 368(a)(1)(C)—is defined as the acquisition by one corporation, in exchange for all or part of its voting stock (or the voting stock of a parent corporation), of substantially all the properties of another corporation.

---

1. See Joseph v. Wallace–Murray Corp., 354 Mass. 477, 238 N.E.2d 360 (1968); Willcox v. Stern, 18 N.Y.2d 195, 273 N.Y.S.2d 38, 219 N.E.2d 401 (1966); Beloff v. Consolidated Edison Co., 300 N.Y. 11, 87 N.E.2d 561 (1949).

In a Type B reorganization the consideration given by the acquiring corporation must consist solely of voting stock. In a Type C reorganization the consideration must consist primarily of voting stock, but the use of money or other property is permitted if at least 80 percent of the fair market value of all the property of the transferor corporation is acquired for voting stock.[1] Section 368(a)(1)(A), which covers Type A reorganizations, does not explicitly restrict the consideration issued by the survivor to voting stock, or indeed to stock. Thus the survivor in a statutory merger can use consideration other than voting stock—including bonds, nonvoting stock, short-term notes, and cash. However, if property other than "stock or securities" is permissibly issued to the transferor or its shareholders under a Type A or Type C reorganization, gain will be recognized in an amount not exceeding the value of this property or "boot." IRC § 356. Furthermore, under the "continuity of interest" doctrine, in a statutory merger the transferor's shareholders must receive a significant equity interest in the survivor if the merger is to qualify as a tax-free reorganization. See Treas.Reg. § 1.368–1(b), (c). In Helvering v. Minnesota Tea Co., 296 U.S. 378, 56 S.Ct. 269, 80 L.Ed. 284 (1935), the Supreme Court held that under this doctrine the equity issued to the transferor must represent a "substantial part of the value of the [transferred assets]" and that 56 percent was sufficient under this standard. See also May B. Kass, 60 T.C. 218 (1973) (16 percent insufficient); Yoc Heating Corp., 61 T.C. 168 (1973) (15 percent insufficient).

2. *Accounting Aspects.* Although in theory accounting statements should simply report the results of business decisions, in practice business decisions are frequently controlled by the manner in which they will be accounted for. This is nowhere more true than in the area of business combinations.

There are two basic methods of accounting for business combinations—purchase, and pooling of interests. Under the *purchase* method, a combination is accounted for as an acquisition by one corporation (herein called A) of another (herein called B). Accordingly, A records B's assets and liabilities at A's cost—i.e., the price A paid to effect the combination. If that price differs from the fair value of B's tangible assets minus B's liabilities, the difference is recorded as "goodwill." Under the *pooling of interests* method, a combination is accounted for as a uniting of ownership interests. Accordingly, A records B's assets at B's costs, and the assets, liabilities, and equity accounts of A and B are then carried forward at their combined historical or book values.

The two methods can be illustrated by the following example. Suppose A engages in a combination with B involving the issuance by A of $4000 in A common stock (with a par value of $400), in exchange for all of B's assets and the assumption by A of B's

---

1. IRC § 368(a)(2)(B). The survivor's assumption of the transferor's liabilities is not treated as money paid for the transfer-or's property unless the survivor uses consideration other than voting stock. Id.

liabilities of $1000, i.e., a total price of $5000. A's business has a fair market value of $7000. B's business, if sold as a going concern, has a fair market value of $5000, and its physical assets have a fair market value of $3800 ($3300 plant and $500 inventory). The results under the pooling and purchase methods are as follows:

	A's Pre–Combination Balance Sheet	B's Pre–Combination Balance Sheet	A's Post–Combination Balance Sheet Under Pooling Accounting	A's Post–Combination Balance Sheet Under Purchase Accounting
Plant	$800	$2,000	$2,800	$4,100
Inventory	$200	$ 500	$ 700	$ 700
Goodwill	—	—	—	$1,200
Liabilities	$ 0	$1,000	$1,000	$1,000
Stated Capital	$500	$ 700	$ 900 (1)	$ 900 (1)
Capital Surplus	$300	$ 0	$ 600 (2)	$3,900 (4)
Earned Surplus	$200	$ 800	$1,000 (3)	$ 200 (5)

Notes: (1) Under either purchase or pooling accounting, A adds to its stated capital the par value of the shares it issues to effect the combination.

(2) Under pooling accounting, A adds to its capital surplus the amount of B's equity ($1500), minus the increases in A's stated capital ($400) and earned surplus ($800).

(3) Under pooling accounting, A adds to its earned surplus the amount of B's earned surplus.

(4) Under purchase accounting, A adds to its capital surplus the value of the consideration received for its stock ($4000), minus the amount of that consideration allocated to stated capital ($400).

(5) Under purchase accounting, A's earned surplus is not increased by B's, since the transaction is treated as if A was acquiring assets, rather than combining.

(f) THE STOCK MODES AND THE DE FACTO MERGER THEORY

We now pass to a consideration of two newer modes of corporate combination—stock-for-assets and stock-for-stock. (For a description of these modes, see Section 1(a).) Several statutes have come directly to grips with these modes (see Section (f)(3), infra), but traditional corporate statutes still fail to deal with them explicitly. In cases decided under the traditional statutes, there has been a sharp division as to exactly which statutory provisions are applicable. A stock-for-assets combination, for example, might be viewed as either (1) a merger, or (2) a purchase and sale of the transferor's assets, effected through the issuance of stock by the survivor. The rights of shareholders will often differ sharply according to which view is taken. For a *merger*, the traditional statutes usually require approval by a majority or two-thirds of the outstanding voting shares of each constituent, and normally give appraisal rights to shareholders of both constituents. For a *sale of substantially all assets*, the traditional statutes speak only to the rights of the transferor's shareholders (except insofar as they confer on the board the power to issue authorized but unissued stock, or the power to determine the consideration for which stock can be issued). While the traditional statutes normally do require approval by the transferor's shareholders, they do not invariably confer appraisal rights even on those shareholders. Critical shareholder rights may therefore depend on precisely how a corporate combination is viewed. In fact, the desire to accomplish a corporate combination without giving shareholders voting or appraisal rights, or at least holding such rights to a minimum, has probably been a major impetus behind the rise of the stock modes.

HARITON v. ARCO ELECTRONICS, INC.

Supreme Court of Delaware, 1963.
41 Del.Ch. 74, 188 A.2d 123.

SOUTHERLAND, Chief Justice: This case involves a sale of assets under § 271 of the corporation law, 8 Del.C. It presents for decision the question presented, but not decided, in Heilbrunn v. Sun Chemical Corporation, 38 Del.Ch. 321, 150 A.2d 755. It may be stated as follows:

A sale of assets is effected under § 271 in consideration of shares of stock of the purchasing corporation. The agreement of sale embodies also a plan to dissolve the selling corporation and distribute the shares so received to the stockholders of the seller, so as to accomplish the same result as would be accomplished by a merger of the seller into the purchaser. Is the sale legal?

The facts are these:

The defendant Arco and Loral Electronics Corporation, a New York corporation, are both engaged, in somewhat different forms, in the electronic equipment business. In the summer of 1961 they negotiated for an amalgamation of the companies. As of October 27, 1961, they entered into a "Reorganization Agreement and Plan." The provisions of this Plan pertinent here are in substance as follows:

1. Arco agrees to sell all its assets to Loral in consideration (*inter alia*) of the issuance to it of 283,000 shares of Loral.

2. Arco agrees to call a stockholders meeting for the purpose of approving the Plan and the voluntary dissolution.

3. Arco agrees to distribute to its stockholders all the Loral

shares received by it as a part of the complete liquidation of Arco.*

At the Arco meeting all the stockholders voting (about 80%) approved the Plan. It was thereafter consummated.

Plaintiff, a stockholder who did not vote at the meeting, sued to enjoin the consummation of the Plan on the grounds (1) that it was illegal, and (2) that it was unfair. The second ground was abandoned. Affidavits and documentary evidence were filed, and defendant moved for summary judgment and dismissal of the complaint. The Vice Chancellor granted the motion and plaintiff appeals.

The question before us we have stated above. Plaintiff's argument that the sale is illegal runs as follows:

The several steps taken here accomplish the same result as a merger of Arco into Loral. In a "true" sale of assets, the stockholder of the seller retains the right to elect whether the selling company shall continue as a holding company. Moreover, the stockholder of the selling company is forced to accept an investment in a new enterprise without the right of appraisal granted under the merger statute. § 271 cannot therefore be legally combined with a dissolution proceeding under § 275 and a consequent distribution of the purchaser's stock. Such a proceeding is a misuse of the power granted under § 271, and a *de facto* merger results.

The foregoing is a brief summary of plaintiff's contention.

Plaintiff's contention that this sale has achieved the same result as a merger is plainly correct. The same contention was made to us in Heilbrunn v. Sun Chemical Corporation, 38 Del.Ch. 321, 150 A.2d 755. Accepting it as correct, we noted that this result is made possible by the overlapping scope of the merger statute and section 271, mentioned in Sterling v. Mayflower Hotel Corporation, 33 Del.Ch. 293, 93 A.2d 107, 38 A.L.R.2d 425. We also adverted to the increased use, in connection with corporate reorganization plans, of § 271 instead of the merger statute. Further, we observed that no Delaware case has held such procedure to be improper, and that two cases appear to assume its legality. Finch v. Warrior Cement Corporation, 16 Del.Ch. 44, 141 A. 54, and Argenbright v. Phoenix Finance Co., 21 Del.Ch. 288, 187 A. 124. But we were not required in the *Heilbrunn* case to decide the point.

We now hold that the reorganization here accomplished through § 271 and a mandatory plan of dissolution and distribution is legal. This is so because the sale-of-assets statute and the merger statute are independent of each other. They are, so to speak, of equal dignity, and the framers of a reorganization plan may resort to either type of corporate mechanics to achieve the desired end. This is not an anomalous result in our corporation law. As the Vice Chancellor pointed out, the elimination of accrued dividends,

---

* According to the Vice Chancellor's opinion below, 40 Del.Ch. 326, 182 A.2d 22 (1962), the agreement also provided that Loral would assume and pay all of Arco's debts and liabilities, and that after the closing date Arco would not engage in any business or activity except as might be required to complete the liquidation and dissolution of Arco. (Footnote by ed.)

though forbidden under a charter amendment (Keller v. Wilson & Co., 21 Del.Ch. 391, 190 A. 115) may be accomplished by a merger. Federal United Corporation v. Havender, 24 Del.Ch. 318, 11 A.2d 331.

In Langfelder v. Universal Laboratories, D.C., 68 F.Supp. 209, Judge Leahy commented upon "the general theory of the Delaware Corporation Law that action taken pursuant to the authority of the various sections of that law constitute acts of independent legal significance and their validity is not dependent on other sections of the Act." 68 F.Supp. 211, footnote.

In support of his contentions of a *de facto* merger plaintiff cites Finch v. Warrior Cement Corporation, 16 Del.Ch. 44, 141 A. 54, and Drug Inc. v. Hunt, 5 W.W.Harr. 339, 35 Del. 339, 168 A. 87. They are patently inapplicable. Each involved a disregard of the statutory provisions governing sales of assets. Here it is admitted that the provisions of the statute were fully complied with.

Plaintiff concedes, as we read his brief, that if the several steps taken in this case had been taken separately they would have been legal. That is, he concedes that a sale of assets, followed by a separate proceeding to dissolve and distribute, would be legal, even though the same result would follow. This concession exposes the weakness of his contention. To attempt to make any such distinction between sales under § 271 would be to create uncertainty in the law and invite litigation.

We are in accord with the Vice Chancellor's ruling, and the judgment below is affirmed.

NOTE ON HEILBRUNN v. SUN CHEMICAL CORPORATION

In *Hariton,* suit was brought by a shareholder of the *transferor* in a stock-for-assets combination. In the earlier case of Heilbrunn v. Sun Chemical Corporation, 38 Del.Ch. 321, 150 A.2d 755 (1959), referred to in the *Hariton* opinion, suit was brought by the shareholders of Sun, the *survivor* in a stock-for-assets combination between Sun and Ansbacher. Plaintiff claimed that the transaction was a merger, and therefore gave rise to appraisal rights. The court rejected this claim:

> The argument that the result of this transaction is substantially the same as the result that would have followed a merger may be readily accepted. As plaintiffs correctly say, the Ansbacher enterprise is continued in altered form as a part of Sun. This is ordinarily a typical characteristic of a merger.... Moreover the plan of reorganization *requires* the dissolution of Ansbacher and the distribution to its stockholders of the Sun stock received by it for the assets. As a part of the plan, the Ansbacher stockholders are compelled to receive Sun stock.

From the viewpoint of Ansbacher, the result is the same as if Ansbacher had formally merged into Sun.

This result is made possible, of course, by the overlapping scope of the merger statute and the statute authorizing the sale of all the corporate assets. . . .

Our Court of Chancery has said that the appraisal right is given to the stockholder in compensation for his former right at common law to prevent a merger. . . . By the use of the sale-of-assets method of reorganization, it is contended, he has been unjustly deprived of this right.

. . . [W]e do not reach this question, because we fail to see how any injury has been inflicted upon the Sun stockholders. Their corporation has simply acquired property and paid for it in shares of stock. The business of Sun will go on as before, with additional assets. The Sun stockholder is not forced to accept stock in another corporation. Nor has the reorganization changed the essential nature of the enterprise of the purchasing corporation. . . .

FARRIS v. GLEN ALDEN CORP.

Supreme Court of Pennsylvania, 1958.
393 Pa. 427, 143 A.2d 25.

COHEN, Justice. We are required to determine on this appeal whether, as a result of a "Reorganization Agreement" executed by the officers of Glen Alden Corporation and List Industries Corporation, and approved by the shareholders of the former company, the rights and remedies of a dissenting shareholder accrue to the plaintiff.

Glen Alden is a Pennsylvania corporation engaged principally in the mining of anthracite coal and lately in the manufacture of air conditioning units and fire-fighting equipment. In recent years the company's operating revenue has declined substantially, and in fact, its coal operations have resulted in tax loss carryovers of approximately $14,000,000. In October 1957, List, a Delaware holding company owning interests in motion picture theaters, textile companies and real estate, and to a lesser extent, in oil and gas operations, warehouses and aluminum piston manufacturing, purchased through a wholly owned subsidiary 38.5% of Glen Alden's outstanding stock.[1] This acquisition enabled List to place three of its directors on the Glen Alden board.

On March 20, 1958, the two corporations entered into a "reorganization agreement," subject to stockholder approval, which contemplated the following actions:

---

1. Of the purchase price of $8,719,109, $5,000,000 was borrowed.

1.   Glen Alden is to acquire all of the assets of List, excepting a small amount of cash reserved for the payment of List's expenses in connection with the transaction.   These assets include over $8,000,-000 in cash held chiefly in the treasuries of List's wholly owned subsidiaries.

2.   In consideration of the transfer, Glen Alden is to issue 3,621,703 shares of stock to List.   List in turn is to distribute the stock to its shareholders at a ratio of five shares of Glen Alden stock for each six shares of List stock.   In order to accomplish the necessary distribution, Glen Alden is to increase the authorized number of its shares of capital stock from 2,500,000 shares to 7,500,000 shares without according preemptive rights to the present shareholders upon the issuance of any such shares.

3.   Further, Glen Alden is to assume all of List's liabilities including a $5,000,000 note incurred by List in order to purchase Glen Alden stock in 1957, outstanding stock options, incentive stock options plans, and pension obligations.

4.   Glen Alden is to change its corporate name from Glen Alden Corporation to List Alden Corporation.

5.   The present directors of both corporations are to become directors of List Alden.

6.   List is to be dissolved and List Alden is to then carry on the operations of both former corporations.

Two days after the agreement was executed notice of the annual meeting of Glen Alden to be held on April 11, 1958, was mailed to the shareholders together with a proxy statement analyzing the reorganization agreement and recommending its approval as well as approval of certain amendments to Glen Alden's articles of incorporation and bylaws necessary to implement the agreement. At this meeting the holders of a majority of the outstanding shares, (not including those owned by List), voted in favor of a resolution approving the reorganization agreement.

On the day of the shareholders' meeting, plaintiff, a shareholder of Glen Alden, filed a complaint in equity against the corporation and its officers seeking to enjoin them temporarily until final hearing, and perpetually thereafter, from executing and carrying out the agreement.[2]

The gravamen of the complaint was that the notice of the annual shareholders' meeting did not conform to the requirements of the Business Corporation Law, 15 P.S. § 2852–1 et seq., in three respects: (1) It did not give notice to the shareholders that the true intent and purpose of the meeting was to effect a merger or consolidation of Glen Alden and List; (2) It failed to give notice to

---

2.   The plaintiff also sought to enjoin the shareholders of Glen Alden from approving the reorganization agreement and from adopting amendments to Glen Alden's articles of incorporation, certificate of incorpo-ration and bylaws in implementation of the agreement.   However, apparently because of the shortness of time, this prayer was refused by the court.

the shareholders of their right to dissent to the plan of merger or consolidation and claim fair value for their shares, and (3) It did not contain copies of the text of certain sections of the Business Corporation Law as required.[3]

By reason of these omissions, plaintiff contended that the approval of the reorganization agreement by the shareholders at the annual meeting was invalid and unless the carrying out of the plan were enjoined, he would suffer irreparable loss by being deprived of substantial property rights.[4]

The defendants answered admitting the material allegations of fact in the complaint but denying that they gave rise to a cause of action because the transaction complained of was a purchase of corporate assets as to which shareholders had no rights of dissent or appraisal.   For these reasons the defendants then moved for judgment on the pleadings.[5]

The court below concluded that the reorganization agreement entered into between the two corporations was a plan for a *de facto* merger, and that therefore the failure of the notice of the annual meeting to conform to the pertinent requirements of the merger provisions of the Business Corporation Law rendered the notice defective and all proceedings in furtherance of the agreement void. Wherefore, the court entered a final decree denying defendants' motion for judgment on the pleadings, entering judgment upon plaintiff's complaint and granting the injunctive relief therein sought.   This appeal followed.

When use of the corporate form of business organization first became widespread, it was relatively easy for courts to define a "merger" or a "sale of assets" and to label a particular transaction as one or the other.   See, e.g., 15 Fletcher, Corporations §§ 7040–7045 (rev. vol. 1938); In re Buist's Estate, 1929, 297 Pa. 537, 541, 147 A. 606; Koehler v. St. Mary's Brewing Co., 1910, 228 Pa. 648, 653–654, 77 A. 1016.   But prompted by the desire to avoid the impact of adverse, and to obtain the benefits of favorable, government regulations, particularly federal tax laws, new accounting and legal techniques were developed by lawyers and accountants which interwove the elements characteristic of each, thereby creating

3.   The proxy statement included the following declaration: "Appraisal Rights.

"In the opinion of counsel, the shareholders of neither Glen Alden nor List Industries will have any rights of appraisal or similar rights of dissenters with respect to any matter to be acted upon at their respective meetings."

4.   The complaint also set forth that the exchange of shares of Glen Alden's stock for those of List would constitute a violation of the pre-emptive rights of Glen Alden shareholders as established by the law of Pennsylvania at the time of Glen Alden's incorporation in 1917.   The defendants answered that under both statute and prior

common law no pre-emptive rights existed with respect to stock issued in exchange for property.

5.   Counsel for the defendants concedes that if the corporation is required to pay the dissenting shareholders the appraised fair value of their shares, the resultant drain of cash would prevent Glen Alden from carrying out the agreement.   On the other hand, plaintiff contends that if the shareholders had been told of their rights as dissenters, rather than specifically advised that they had no such rights, the resolution approving the reorganization agreement would have been defeated.

hybrid forms of corporate amalgamation. Thus, it is no longer helpful to consider an individual transaction in the abstract and solely by reference to the various elements therein determine whether it is a "merger" or a "sale". Instead, to determine properly the nature of a corporate transaction, we must refer not only to all the provisions of the agreement, but also to the consequences of the transaction and to the purposes of the provisions of the corporation law said to be applicable. We shall apply this principle to the instant case.

Section 908, subd. A of the Pennsylvania Business Corporation Law provides: "If any shareholder of a domestic corporation which becomes a party to a plan of merger or consolidation shall object to such plan of merger or consolidation ... such shareholder shall be entitled to ... [the fair value of his shares upon surrender of the share certificate or certificates representing his shares]." Act of May 5, 1933, P.L. 364, as amended, 15 P.S. § 2852–908, subd. A.[6]

This provision had its origin in the early decision of this Court in Lauman v. Lebanon Valley R.R. Co., 1858, 30 Pa. 42. There a shareholder who objected to the consolidation of his company with another was held to have a right in the absence of statute to treat the consolidation as a dissolution of his company and to receive the value of his shares upon their surrender.

The rationale of the Lauman case, and of the present section of the Business Corporation Law based thereon, is that when a corporation combines with another so as to lose its essential nature and alter the original fundamental relationships of the shareholders among themselves and to the corporation, a shareholder who does not wish to continue his membership therein may treat his membership in the original corporation as terminated and have the value of his shares paid to him. See Lauman v. Lebanon Vally R.R. Co., supra, 30 Pa. at pages 46–47. See also Bloch v. Baldwin Locomotive Works, C.P., Del.1950, 75 Pa.Dist. & Co.R. 24, 35–38.

Does the combination outlined in the present "reorganization" agreement so fundamentally change the corporate character of Glen Alden and the interest of the plaintiff as a shareholder therein, that to refuse him the rights and remedies of a dissenting shareholder would in reality force him to give up his stock in one corporation and against his will accept shares in another? If so, the combination is a merger within the meaning of section 908, subd. A of the corporation law. See Bloch v. Baldwin Locomotive Works, supra. Cf. Marks v. Autocar Co., D.C.E.D.Pa.1954, 153 F.Supp. 768. See also Troupiansky v. Henry Disston & Sons, D.C.E.D.Pa.1957, 151 F.Supp. 609.

---

6. Furthermore, section 902, subd. B provides that notice of the proposed merger and of the right to dissent thereto must be given the shareholders. "There shall be included in, or enclosed with ... notice [of meeting of shareholders to vote on plan of merger] a copy or a summary of the plan of merger or plan of consolidation, as the case may be, and ... a copy of subsection A of section 908 and of subsections B, C and D of section 515 of this act." Act of May 5, 1933, P.L. 364, § 902, subd. B, as amended, 15 P.S. § 2852–902, subd. B.

If the reorganization agreement were consummated plaintiff would find that the "List Alden" resulting from the amalgamation would be quite a different corporation than the "Glen Alden" in which he is now a shareholder. Instead of continuing primarily as a coal mining company, Glen Alden would be transformed, after amendment of its articles of incorporation, into a diversified holding company whose interests would range from motion picture theaters to textile companies. Plaintiff would find himself a member of a company with assets of $169,000,000 and a long-term debt of $38,000,000 in lieu of a company one-half that size and with but one-seventh the long-term debt.

While the administration of the operations, and properties of Glen Alden as well as List would be in the hands of management common to both companies, since all executives of List would be retained in List Alden, the control of Glen Alden would pass to the directors of List; for List would hold eleven of the seventeen directorships on the new board of directors.

As an aftermath of the transaction plaintiff's proportionate interest in Glen Alden would have been reduced to only two-fifths of what it presently is because of the issuance of an additional 3,621,703 shares to List which would not be subject to pre-emptive rights. In fact, ownership of Glen Alden would pass to the stockholders of List who would hold 76.5% of the outstanding shares as compared with but 23.5% retained by the present Glen Alden shareholders.

Perhaps the most important consequence to the plaintiff, if he were denied the right to have his shares redeemed at their fair value, would be the serious financial loss suffered upon consummation of the agreement. While the present book value of his stock is $38 a share after combination it would be worth only $21 a share. In contrast, the shareholders of List who presently hold stock with a total book value of $33,000,000 or $7.50 a share, would receive stock with a book value of $76,000,000 or $21 a share.

Under these circumstances it may well be said that if the proposed combination is allowed to take place without right of dissent, plaintiff would have his stock in Glen Alden taken away from him and the stock of a new company thrust upon him in its place. He would be projected against his will into a new enterprise under terms not of his own choosing. It was to protect dissident shareholders against just such a result that this Court one hundred years ago in the Lauman case, and the legislature thereafter in section 908, subd. A, granted the right of dissent. And it is to accord that protection to the plaintiff that we conclude that the combination proposed in the case at hand is a merger within the intendment of section 908, subd. A.

Nevertheless, defendants contend that the 1957 amendments to sections 311 and 908 of the corporation law preclude us from reaching this result and require the entry of judgment in their favor.

Subsection F of section 311 dealing with the voluntary transfer of corporate assets provides: "The shareholders of a business corporation which acquires by sale, lease or exchange all or substantially all of the property of another corporation by the issuance of stock, securities or otherwise shall not be entitled to the rights and remedies of dissenting shareholders...." Act of July 11, 1957, P.L. 711, § 1, 15 P.S. § 2852–311, subd. F.

And the amendment to section 908 reads as follows: "The right of dissenting shareholders ... shall not apply to the purchase by a corporation of assets whether or not the consideration therefor be money or property, real or personal, including shares of bonds or other evidences of indebtedness of such corporation. The shareholders of such corporation shall have no right to dissent from any such purchase." Act of July 11, 1957, P.L. 711, § 1, 15 P.S. § 2852–908, subd. C.

Defendants view these amendments as abridging the right of shareholders to dissent to a transaction between two corporations which involves a transfer of assets for a consideration even though the transfer has all the legal incidents of a merger. They claim that only if the merger is accomplished in accordance with the prescribed statutory procedure does the right of dissent accrue. In support of this position they cite to us the comment on the amendments by the Committee on Corporation Law of the Pennsylvania Bar Association, the committee which originally drafted these provisions. The comment states that the provisions were intended to overrule cases which granted shareholders the right to dissent to a sale of assets when accompanied by the legal incidents of a merger. See 61 Ann.Rep.Pa.Bar Ass'n. 277, 284 (1957).[7] Whatever may have been the intent of the *committee,* there is no evidence to indicate that the *legislature* intended the 1957 amendments to have the effect contended for. But furthermore, the language of these two provisions does not support the opinion of the committee and is inept to achieve any such purpose. The amendments of 1957 do not provide that a transaction between two corporations which has the effect of a merger but which includes a transfer of assets for

---

7. "The amendment to Section 311 expressly provides that a sale, lease or exchange of substantially all corporate assets in connection with its liquidation or dissolution is subject to the provisions of Article XI of the Act, and that no consent or authorization of shareholders other than what is required by Article XI is necessary. The recent decision in Marks v. Autocar Co., D.C.E.D.Pa., Civil Action No. 16075 [153 F.Supp. 768] is to the contrary. This amendment, together with the proposed amendment to Section 1104 expressly permitting the directors in liquidating the corporation to sell only such assets as may be required to pay its debts and distribute any assets remaining among shareholders (Sec-tion 1108, [subd.] B now so provides in the case of receivers) have the effect of overruling Marks v. Autocar Co. case which permits a shareholder dissenting from such a sale to obtain the fair value of his shares. The Marks case relies substantially on Bloch v. Baldwin Locomotive Works, 75 [Pa.] Dist. & Co. R. 24, also believed to be an undesirable decision. That case permitted a holder of stock in a corporation which *purchased* for stock all the assets of another corporation to obtain the fair value of his shares. That case is also in effect overruled by the new Sections 311 [subd.] F and 908 [subd.] C." 61 Ann.Rep.Pa.Bar Ass'n. 277, 284 (1957).

consideration is to be exempt from the protective provisions of sections 908, subd. A and 515. They provide only that the shareholders of a corporation which acquires the property or purchases the assets of another corporation, *without more,* are not entitled to the right to dissent from the transaction. So, as in the present case, when as part of a transaction between two corporations, one corporation dissolves, its liabilities are assumed by the survivor, its executives and directors take over the management and control of the survivor, and, as consideration for the transfer, its stockholders acquire a majority of the shares of stock of the survivor, then the transaction is no longer simply a purchase of assets or acquisition of property to which sections 311, subd. F and 908, subd. C apply, but a merger governed by section 908, subd. A of the corporation law. To divest shareholders of their right of dissent under such circumstances would require express language which is absent from the 1957 amendments.

Even were we to assume that the combination provided for in the reorganization agreement is a "sale of assets" to which section 908, subd. A does not apply, it would avail the defendants nothing; we will not blind our eyes to the realities of the transaction. Despite the designation of the parties and the form employed, Glen Alden does not in fact acquire List, rather, List acquires Glen Alden, cf. Metropolitan Edison Co. v. Commissioner, 3 Cir., 1938, 98 F.2d 807, affirmed sub nom., Helvering v. Metropolitan Edison Co., 1939, 306 U.S. 522, 59 S.Ct. 634, 83 L.Ed. 957, and under section 311, subd. D [8] the right of dissent would remain with the shareholders of Glen Alden.

We hold that the combination contemplated by the reorganization agreement, although consummated by contract rather than in accordance with the statutory procedure, is a merger within the protective purview of sections 908, subd. A and 515 of the corporation law. The shareholders of Glen Alden should have been notified accordingly and advised of their statutory rights of dissent and appraisal. The failure of the corporate officers to take these steps renders the stockholder approval of the agreement at the 1958 shareholders' meeting invalid. The lower court did not err in enjoining the officers and directors of Glen Alden from carrying out this agreement.[9]

8. "If any shareholder of a business corporation which sells, leases or exchanges all or substantially all of its property and assets otherwise than in (1) in the usual and regular course of its business, (2) for the purpose of relocating its business, or (3) in connection with its dissolution and liquidation, shall object to such sale, lease or exchange and comply with the provisions of section 515 of this act, such shareholder shall be entitled to the rights and remedies of dissenting shareholders as therein provided." Act of July 11, 1957, P.L. 711, 15 P.S. § 2852–311, subd. D.

9. Because of our disposition of this appeal, it is unnecessary for us to consider whether the plaintiff had any pre-emptive rights in the proposed issuance of newly authorized shares as payment for the transfer of assets from List, or whether amended sections 908, subd. C and 311, subd. F of the corporation law may constitutionally be applied to the present transaction to divest the plaintiff of his dissenter's rights.

Decree affirmed at appellants' costs.**

NOTE ON FARRIS

It is clear that a major reason for structuring the transaction in *Farris* as a stock-for-assets combination, rather than as a classical merger, was to avoid conferring appraisal rights on the Glen Alden shareholders. (In many cases, the stock-for-assets form is used to deny voting rights to the survivor's shareholders, but this may not have been significant in *Farris* itself.) Given the stock-for-assets mode, why did the parties use the upside-down format, in which the smaller corporation "purchased" the larger corporation's assets? Again, one reason had to do with appraisal rights. List was a Delaware corporation, and under Delaware law in a purchase and sale of assets neither the purchaser's nor the seller's shareholders had appraisal rights. Under Pennsylvania law, however, the seller's shareholders clearly had appraisal rights, while the purchaser's did not—or so counsel thought. Therefore, by making List the seller and Glen Alden the purchaser, the parties hoped to avoid appraisal rights for the shareholders of either corporation. A second reason for the upside-down format may have been a desire to keep alive Glen Alden's tax loss carryover. While the rules governing the survival of such carryovers were complex, in general survival was more likely if the entity of the carryover corporation was left intact. A third reason is given in the Supplemental Brief for Appellee: "In answer to the question of Mr. Justice Bell as to why List did not purchase the assets of Glen Alden, Mr. Littleton answered that the one percent Pennsylvania realty tax on the transfer of [the huge coal-mining] holdings of Glen Alden would make such a sale prohibitive." Following the decision in Farris v. Glen Alden, the two corporations were combined pursuant to a statutory merger. Probably for the reasons just given, Glen Alden was the surviving

---

** Pa. §§ 311(F) and 908(B)—numbered §§ 1311(F) and 1908(B) in the annotated statutes—were subsequently amended, and now read as follows:

§ 1311. Voluntary Transfer of Corporate Assets

* * *

F. The shareholders of a business corporation which acquires by purchase, lease or exchange all or substantially all of the property of another corporation by the issuance of shares, evidences of indebtedness or otherwise, with or without assuming the liabilities of such other corporation, shall be entitled to the rights and remedies of dissenting shareholders provided in ... this act, if any, if, but only if, such acquisition shall have been accomplished by the issuance of voting shares of such corporation to be out-

standing immediately after the acquisition sufficient to elect a majority of the directors of the corporation.

§ 1908. Rights of Dissenting Shareholders

* * *

B. Where a corporation acquires assets by purchase, lease or exchange, by the issuance of shares, evidences of indebtedness or otherwise, with or without assuming liabilities other than by the procedure for merger or consolidation prescribed in this Article IX, the rights, if any, of dissenting shareholders shall be governed by section [1311] and not by this section.

(Footnote by ed.)

corporation. The List shareholders received one Glen Alden share for each List share, and the Glen Alden shareholders ended up with five Glen Alden shares for each four they had previously held. New York Times, March 7, 1959; Moody's Industrial Manual 954 (1972).

NEW YORK STOCK EXCHANGE, LISTED COMPANY MANUAL § 312.00

[See Statutory Supplement]

CAL. CORP. CODE §§ 152, 160, 168, 181, 187, 194.5, 1001, 1101, 1200, 1201, 1300

[See Statutory Supplement]

(g) TRIANGULAR MERGERS AND SHARE EXCHANGES

TERRY v. PENN CENTRAL CORP.

United States Court of Appeals, Third Circuit, 1981.
668 F.2d 188.

Before ADAMS, MARIS and HIGGINBOTHAM, Circuit Judges....

ADAMS, Circuit Judge.

The Penn Central Corporation ("Penn Central"), an appellee in this case, has sought to acquire Colt Industries Inc. ("Colt"), also an appellee, by merging Colt with PCC Holdings, Inc. ("Holdings"), a wholly-owned subsidiary of Penn Central. Howard L. Terry and W.H. Hunt, the appellants, are shareholders of Penn Central who objected to the transaction. In a diversity action before the United States District Court for the Eastern District of Pennsylvania, appellants sought injunctive and declaratory relief to enforce voting and dissenters' rights to which appellants asserted they were entitled. Appellants further sought to enjoin Holdings from proceeding with the proposed merger, and in particular moved to enjoin a vote on the transaction, scheduled for October 29, 1981, by the shareholders of Penn Central. In an opinion issued on October 22, 1981, Judge Pollak denied appellants' requests. Appellants thereupon filed an appeal in this Court, and then petitioned for a temporary injunction against the proposed shareholder vote until the appeal on the merits of the district court order could be heard. On

October 27, following oral argument, we entered an order denying the petition for temporary injunction, stating that appellants had failed to demonstrate a sufficient likelihood of prevailing on the merits. C.A. No. 81–3955. The shareholders of Penn Central voted, as scheduled, on October 29. Pursuant to an expedited hearing schedule, the appeal from the district court's denial of injunctive and declaratory relief was submitted to this Court following oral argument on November 5.

After argument on appeal, the shareholders disapproved of the merger, and the corporations thereafter publicly announced their abandonment of this particular merger. Penn Central, however, has not abandoned its proposed series of acquisitions, of which the Colt acquisition was merely one instance.

I.

Penn Central is the successor to the Penn Central Transportation Corporation, which underwent a reorganization under the bankruptcy laws that was completed in 1978. No longer involved in the railroading business, Penn Central, since 1978, has had the advantage, for tax purposes, of a large loss carry-forward. In order to put that loss carry-forward to its best use, Penn Central has embarked on a program of acquiring corporations whose profits could be sheltered. To this end Penn Central created Holdings, a wholly-owned subsidiary which was to acquire the businesses that Penn Central desired. The first acquisition under the plan was Marathon Manufacturing Company ("Marathon"), in 1979. In the Marathon acquisition, a class of preferred Penn Central stock was created, and 30 million shares of "First Series Preference Stock" was issued to the owners of Marathon stock. Appellants were shareholders of Marathon who thereby obtained shares of this First Series Preference Stock. Terry was promptly elected to the Penn Central board of directors.

In 1981, Penn Central decided upon another acquisition: Colt. The management and directors of Colt and Penn Central agreed upon a merger of Colt into Holdings, compensated for by issuance of a second series of Penn Central preference stock to Colt shareholders. Terry opposed the merger at the directors' meeting, and sought to preclude the consummation of the transaction.

. . . [A]ppellants argue that under Pennsylvania's corporate law, they are entitled to dissent and appraisal rights if the merger is adopted over their opposition.[2] . . .

---

2. In addition, appellants claim a right under Pennsylvania law to require approval of an absolute majority vote of the shares outstanding on the proposed merger, relying on § 902(B) of the Pennsylvania Business Corporation Law (PBCL), 15 P.S. § 1902(B) (Purdon Supp.1981–82). For the reasons discussed in Part III of this opinion, we conclude that Penn Central is not a "party" to the merger, within the technical meaning of the term under that section and the related Section 908 of the PBCL, 15 P.S. § 1908 (Purdon Supp.1981–82). Accordingly, section 902 does not apply to the Penn Central vote on the merger.

Because Colt and Penn Central have now announced their abandonment of the proposed merger, the request for injunctive relief considered by the district court is now conceded by all parties to be moot. However, the appellants' request for declaratory relief, which the appellants now contend is moot as well, involves legal questions that go to Penn Central's plan of acquisitions, rather than to the Colt transaction alone, and these questions appear likely to recur in future disputes between the parties here.... In a case such as this, a voluntary termination by the parties of the specific activity challenged in the lawsuit—here, the proposed treatment of the dissenting preferred shareholders in the Colt–Holdings plan—does not render the action moot because there is "a reasonable likelihood that the parties or those in privity with them will be involved in a suit on the same issues in the future." American Bible Society v. Blount, 446 F.2d 588, 595 (3d Cir.1971)....

III.

Terry and Hunt contend that under Pennsylvania law they are entitled to dissent and appraisal rights if a merger is approved by the Penn Central shareholders. As the district court concluded, this assertion is unsupported by Pennsylvania statute or caselaw. Sitting as a court in diversity, we are not at liberty to diverge from the outcome that the Pennsylvania legislature and the Pennsylvania courts prescribe. Briefly, appellants' argument is that the proposed merger between Holdings and Colt constitutes a *de facto* merger between Colt and Penn Central, and that the Penn Central shareholders are therefore entitled to the protections for dissenting shareholders that Pennsylvania corporate law provides for shareholders of parties to a merger. Although this reasoning, with its emphasis on the substance of the transaction rather than its formal trappings, may be attractive as a matter of policy, see, e.g., Note, Three–Party Mergers: The Fourth Form of Corporate Acquisition, 57 Va.L.Rev. 1242 (1971), it contravenes the language employed by the Pennsylvania legislature in setting out the rights of shareholders.

Section 908 of the Pennsylvania Business Corporation Law (PBCL), 15 P.S. § 1908, provides that shareholders of corporations that are parties to a plan of merger are entitled to dissent and appraisal rights, but adds that for an acquisition other than such a merger, the only rights are those provided for in Section 311 of the PBCL, 15 P.S. § 1311 (Purdon 1967 & Supp.1981–82). Section 311, in turn, provides for dissent and appraisal rights only when an acquisition has been accomplished by "the issuance of voting shares of such corporation to be outstanding immediately after the acquisition sufficient to elect a majority of the directors of the corporation." In this case the shares of Penn Central stock to be issued in the Colt transaction do not exceed the number of shares already existing, and thus the transaction is not covered by Section 311. Any statutory dissent and appraisal rights for Penn Central shareholders are therefore contingent upon Penn Central's status as a party to the merger within the meaning of Section 908. And as the district court points out, the PBCL describes the parties to a merger as those entities that are *actually* combined into a single corporation. Section 907, 15 P.S. § 1907 (Purdon Supp.1981–82), states that:

> Upon the merger or consolidation becoming effective, the several corporations parties to the plan of merger or consolidation shall be a single corporation which, in the case of a merger, shall be that corporation designated in the plan of merger as the surviving corporation. . . .

At the consummation of the proposed merger plan here, both Holdings and Penn Central would survive as separate entities, and it would therefore appear that Penn Central is not a party within the meaning of . . . Section 907. We can discern no reason to infer that the legislature intended the word "party" to have different meanings in Sections 907 and 908, and accordingly conclude that Penn Central is not a party to the merger.

Appellants argue that Penn Central is nevertheless brought into the amalgamation by the *de facto* merger doctrine as set out in Pennsylvania law in Farris v. Glen Alden Corp., 393 Pa. 427, 143 A.2d 25 (1958). *Farris* was the penultimate step in a *pas de deux* involving the Pennsylvania courts and the Pennsylvania legislature regarding the proper treatment for transactions that reached the same practical result as a merger but avoided the legal form of merger and the concomitant legal obligations. In the 1950s the Pennsylvania courts advanced the doctrine that a transaction having the effect of an amalgamation would be treated as a *de facto* merger. See, e.g., Bloch v. The Baldwin Locomotive Works, 75 Pa.D. & C. 24 (1950). The legislature responded with efforts to constrict the *de facto* merger doctrine. *Farris,* addressing those efforts, held that the doctrine still covered a reorganization agreement that had the effect of merging a large corporation into a smaller corporation. In a 1959 response to *Farris,* the legislature made explicit its objection to earlier cases that found certain transactions to be *de facto* mergers. The legislature enacted a law, modifying *inter alia* Sections 311 and 908, entitled in part:

> An Act . . . changing the law as to . . . the acquisition or transfer of corporate assets, the rights of dissenting shareholders, . . . abolishing the doctrine of de facto mergers or consolidation and reversing the rules laid down in *Bloch v. Baldwin Locomotive Works,* 75 D. & C. 24, and *Marks v. The Autocar Co.,* 153 F.Supp. 768, ...

Act of November 10, 1959 (P.L. 1406, No. 502).

Following this explicit statement, the *de facto* merger doctrine has rarely been invoked by the Pennsylvania courts. Only once has the Pennsylvania Supreme Court made reference to it, in In re Jones & Laughlin Steel Corp., 488 Pa. 524, 412 A.2d 1099 (1980). Even there, the Court's reference was oblique. It merely cited *Farris* for the proposition that shareholders have the right to enjoin "proposed unfair or fraudulent corporate actions." 488 Pa. at 533, 412

A.2d at 1104.　This Court, sitting in diversity in Knapp v. North American Rockwell Corp., 506 F.2d 361 (3d Cir.1974), cert. denied, 421 U.S. 965, 95 S.Ct. 1955, 44 L.Ed.2d 452 (1975), made reference to the *de facto* merger doctrine to hold that a transaction structured as a sale of assets could nevertheless be deemed a merger for purposes of requiring the merging corporation to assume the acquired corporation's liability for damages to a worker who was injured by a faulty piece of equipment manufactured by the acquired company.　Perhaps the broadest application of the doctrine was made in In re Penn Central Securities Litigation, 367 F.Supp. 1158 (E.D.Pa.1973), in which the district court held that the doctrine provided the plaintiffs in that case with standing for a 10b–5 lawsuit alleging *fraud* and also gave rise to dissent and appraisal rights in a triangular merger situation.[6]

None of these cases persuades us that a Pennsylvania court would apply the *de facto* merger doctrine to the situation before us. Although *Jones & Laughlin Steel* suggests that dissent and appraisal rights might be available if fraud or fundamental unfairness were shown, we are not faced with such a situation.　No allegation of fraud has been advanced, and the only allegation of fundamental unfairness is that the appellants will, if the merger is consummated, be forced into what they consider a poor investment on the part of Penn Central without the opportunity to receive an appraised value for their stock.　Even if appellants' evaluation of the merits of the proposed merger is accurate, poor business judgment on the part of management would not be enough to constitute unfairness cognizable by a court.　And the denial of appraisal rights to dissenters cannot constitute fundamental unfairness, or the *de facto* merger doctrine would apply in every instance in which dissenters' rights were sought and the 1959 amendments by the legislature would be rendered nugatory.[7]

The two federal cases invoking the doctrine, *Knapp* and *Penn Central Securities,* are not persuasive as to the applicability of the *de facto* merger to the present situation.　*Knapp* was not concerned with the rights of shareholders as the Pennsylvania legislature was in 1959.　Although *Penn Central Securities* did hold, in part, that the triangular merger there constituted a *de facto* merger, it is clear from the briefs submitted to the district court in that case that the

---

6.　Two other cases in the Eastern District of Pennsylvania have also discussed *Farris* and *de facto* mergers, each case holding that the transaction before the court did not constitute a *de facto* merger.　In Dower v. Mosser Industries, Inc., 488 F.Supp. 1328, 1341 (E.D.Pa.1980), aff'd, 648 F.2d 183 (1981), the district court distinguished *Farris* because the transaction in *Dower,* unlike that in *Farris,* was not fraudulent in any way.　In Lopata v. Bemis Co., 383 F.Supp. 342 (E.D.Pa.1974), vacated on other grounds, 517 F.2d 1398 (1975), the district court found *Farris* inapplicable because in *Lopata,* unlike *Farris,* there was no

"basic fundamental change in the relationship of the stockholders to their respective corporations."　383 F.Supp. at 345.

7.　A different result might be reached if here, as in *Farris,* the acquiring corporation were significantly smaller than the acquired corporation such that the acquisition greatly transformed the nature of the successor corporation.　But in this situation we do not have such a case; after the merger Penn Central would remain a major, diversified corporation, and would continue on the course of acquiring other corporations.

court was not made aware of the post-*Farris* 1959 amendments or the legislative statement of intent to limit the *de facto* merger doctrine.

In the absence of any explicit guidance to the contrary by the Pennsylvania courts, we conclude that the language of the legislature in 1959 precludes a decision that the transaction in this case constitutes a *de facto* merger sufficient to entitle Penn Central shareholders to dissent and appraisal rights. We therefore hold that appellants do not possess such rights if a transaction such as the one involved here is consummated. . . .

———

REV. MODEL BUS. CORP. ACT §§ 11.02, 11.03, 11.05, 11.06

[See Statutory Supplement]

———

NOTE ON TRIANGULAR MERGERS AND SHARE EXCHANGES

1. *Triangular Mergers.* As the previous section suggests, in many cases a statutory merger would be the preferred form of combination except for a particular disadvantage of that mode which looms large in a given transaction. A number of states have therefore amended their statutory merger provisions to allow new forms of combination, known as "triangular mergers" and "reverse triangular mergers," which carry the advantages of a statutory merger without some of the disadvantages.

A conventional or foreward triangular merger works this way: Assume that Corporations S and T want to engage in a merger in which S will be the survivor and T's shareholders will end up with 100,000 shares of S. In a normal merger this would be accomplished by having S issue 100,000 shares to T's shareholders. In a conventional triangular merger, however, S instead begins by creating a new subsidiary, S/Sub, and then transfers 100,000 shares of its own stock to S/Sub in exchange for all of S/Sub's stock. S/Sub and T then engage in a statutory merger, but instead of issuing its *own* stock to T's shareholders, S/Sub issues its 100,000 shares of S stock. The net result is that T's business is owned by S's wholly owned subsidiary (rather than by S itself, as in a normal merger), and T's shareholders own 100,000 shares of S stock. By use of this technique, S may therefore achieve the advantages of a statutory merger while insulating itself from direct responsibility for T's liabilities.[1]

Such a transaction would probably not have been permissible under the traditional statutory merger provisions, because those provisions usually contemplated that the surviving corporation

---

1. However, a court might impose these liabilities on S under the de facto merger doctrine, on the theory that in effect S itself is a constituent to the merger.

would issue its *own* shares or securities. In the last 10 or 15 years, however, the merger statutes of most leading corporate jurisdictions have been amended to permit the survivor to issue shares or securities of *any* corporation. (See, e.g., Del. § 251(b)(4).) In tandem with this development, the Internal Revenue Code was amended by adding § 368(a)(2)(D), which permits a conventional triangular merger to qualify as a tax-free A reorganization, if (i) substantially all of T's properties are acquired by S/Sub; (ii) the merger would have qualified as an A reorganization if T had merged directly into S; and (iii) no stock of S/Sub is used in the transaction.

A *reverse* triangular merger proceeds like a conventional triangular merger, except that instead of merging T into S/Sub, S/Sub is merged into T. The merger agreement provides that all previously outstanding T shares are automatically converted into the 100,000 shares of S held by S/Sub, and that all shares in S/Sub (which are held by S) are automatically converted into shares in T. When all the shooting is over, therefore, S/Sub will have disappeared, T will be a wholly owned subsidiary of S, and T's shareholders will own 100,000 shares of S stock. By use of this technique S may therefore achieve the advantages of a statutory merger while preserving T's legal status, which could be important where T has valuable rights under contracts, leases, licenses, or franchises. Under IRC § 368(a)(2)(E), a reverse triangular merger will qualify as a tax-free A reorganization, if (i) T ends up with substantially all of the properties of both S/Sub and T, and (ii) S voting stock is exchanged for at least 80% of T's voting and nonvoting stock. (The balance of T's stock can be acquired for other types of consideration.)

An important problem raised by triangular mergers is that they may allow subversion of shareholder voting and appraisal rights, since it can be argued that voting and appraisal rights on the survivor's side are vested in S (as the sole shareholder of S/Sub) rather than in S's shareholders. Ideally this problem should be dealt with by statute. For example, under Cal. §§ 1200(d), 1201, a merger reorganization must be approved by the shareholders of a corporation which is "in control of any constituent . . . corporation . . . and whose equity securities are issued or transferred in the reorganization." Even where a statute does not deal with the problem explicitly, it can be argued that a triangular merger triggers voting and appraisal rights in S's shareholders on the theory that S should be deemed a constituent to the merger, or alternatively that such a result is necessary to prevent subversion of the merger statutes. See generally M. Eisenberg, The Structure of the Corporation 275–315 (1976). This argument was rejected in Terry v. Penn Central Corp., supra, but that case was at least partly controlled by the unusual Pennsylvania legislative history.

2. *Share Exchanges.* The newest mode of combination, inspired by the triangular merger, is known as the share exchange. This mode is similar to a stock-for-stock combination, in that the survivor issues stock in exchange for stock of the acquired corporation. However, in a stock-for-stock combination each shareholder

of the acquired corporation makes an individual decision whether or not to sell his stock, and there is no formal action by the acquired corporation itself. In contrast, in a share exchange the shareholders of the acquired corporation vote on whether to engage in the exchange. If the proposed transaction is approved by a majority of that corporation's outstanding shares, *all of the shares* must be surrendered—including those of nonconsenting sharehold-ers (unless they exercise appraisal rights). So far, only a few statutes have authorized share exchanges for ordinary business corporations.

(h) EXCLUSIVITY OF THE APPRAISAL REMEDY

REV. MODEL BUS. CORP. ACT § 13.02(b)

[See Statutory Supplement]

ALI, PRINCIPLES OF CORPORATE GOVERNANCE §§ 7.24, 7.25

[See Statutory Supplement]

NOTE ON EXCLUSIVITY OF THE APPRAISAL REMEDY

The question frequently arises whether the appraisal right is intended by the legislature as an exclusive remedy, so that the availability of appraisal precludes shareholders from seeking equita-ble relief such as injunction or rescission. This question does not always admit of a hard-and-fast answer.

1. In some cases the issue is specifically addressed by lan-guage in the appraisal statute itself. However, such language is not always read literally. For example, an exclusivity provision in former Mich. § 450.44(2) was interpreted as applicable only to transactions undertaken in good faith. Weckler v. Valley City Mill. Co., 93 F.Supp. 444 (W.D.Mich.1950), aff'd per curiam 188 F.2d 367 (6th Cir.1951). See also Miller v. Steinbach, 268 F.Supp. 255 (S.D.N.Y.1967). But see In re Jones & Laughlin Steel Corp., 263 Pa.Super. 378, 398 A.2d 186 (1979).

2. At least in the absence of explicit statutory language, it is clear that the availability of appraisal rights normally does not preclude an attack based on any of the following grounds:

(a) That the transaction is illegal under corporation law in that it is not authorized by the statute. See, e.g., Eisenberg v. Central Zone Property Corp., 306 N.Y. 58, 115 N.E.2d 652 (1953).

(b) That the transaction is illegal under corporation law in that the procedural steps required to authorize the transaction were not properly taken. See, e.g., Starrett Corp. v. Fifth Ave. & Twenty–Ninth St. Corp., 1 F.Supp. 868, 878 (S.D.N.Y.1932) (lack of adequate notice to shareholders); Johnson v. Spartanburg County Fair Ass'n, 210 S.C. 56, 41 S.E.2d 599 (1947) (required number of votes not validly cast).

(c) That shareholder approval of the transaction was improperly obtained, as through fraudulent misrepresentation or violation of the Proxy Rules. See Victor Broadcasting Co. v. Mahurin, 236 Ark. 196, 365 S.W.2d 265 (1963).

At least in the past, it has also been clear that the availability of appraisal rights normally *does* preclude a shareholder from seeking to recover the money value of his shares under a nonstatutory remedy in connection with transactions for which appraisal rights are given. See, e.g., Walter J. Schloss Associates v. Arkwin Industries, Inc., 61 N.Y.2d 700, 472 N.Y.S.2d 605, 460 N.E.2d 1090 (1984), rev'g 90 A.D.2d 149, 455 N.Y.S.2d 844 (1982); Adams v. United States Distributing Corp., 184 Va. 134, 34 S.E.2d 244 (1945).

Beyond this, the matter is less clear. A few cases have suggested or implied that even in the absence of explicit statutory language, the availability of appraisal rights precludes an attack based on any ground other than illegality or fraudulent misrepresentation. See, e.g., Blumenthal v. Roosevelt Hotel, Inc., 202 Misc. 988, 115 N.Y.S.2d 52 (1952); Blumner v. Federated Department Stores, 99 N.Y.S.2d 691 (1950). The general rule, however, is that the mere availability of appraisal rights does not preclude shareholders from seeking injunctive relief or rescission for fraud, using that term in the broad sense to include unfair self-dealing by fiduciaries. The net result is that, in the absence of explicit statutory language, the availability of appraisal rights may preclude a shareholder from attacking an *arm's-length* transaction on the ground of unfairness, but will usually not insulate *self-interested* transactions from an attack on that ground—although in the latter case it may lead the court to impose a somewhat less rigorous standard of fairness than would otherwise prevail. See Vorenberg, Exclusiveness of the Dissenting Stockholder's Appraisal Right, 77 Harv.L.Rev. 1189, 1214–15 (1964).

———

CAL. CORP. CODE § 1312

[See Statutory Supplement]

———

(i) FREEZEOUTS

NOTE ON FREEZEOUT TECHNIQUES

A freezeout is a corporate transaction whose principal purpose is to reconstitute the corporation's ownership by involuntarily eliminating the equity interest of minority shareholders.[1] Until twenty or twenty-five years ago, freezeouts tended to take one of three forms, all of which met with only indifferent success at the hands of the courts.

1. *Dissolution Freezeouts.* Assume that S (who may be an individual, a group, or a corporation) owns 70% of C Corporation, and wishes to eliminate C's minority shareholders. In a dissolution freezeout, S causes C to dissolve under a plan of dissolution which provides that C's productive assets will be distributed to S (or to an entity S controls), while cash or notes will be distributed to C's minority shareholders. This technique has been held illegal in a number of cases, most of which stress that such a plan of dissolution violates a corporate norm of equal treatment among all shareholders of the same class. See Mason v. Pewabic Mining Co., 133 U.S. 50, 10 S.Ct. 224, 33 L.Ed. 524 (1890); Kellogg v. Georgia–Pacific Paper Corp., 227 F.Supp. 719 (W.D.Ark.1964); Zimmermann v. Tide Water Associated Oil Co., 61 Cal.App.2d 585, 143 P.2d 409 (1943); In re San Joaquin Light & Power Corp., 52 Cal.App.2d 814, 127 P.2d 29 (1942); In re Paine, 200 Mich. 58, 166 N.W. 1036 (1918).

2. *Sale-of-Assets Freezeouts.* In a sale-of-assets freezeout, C's controlling shareholder, S, organizes a new corporation, T, all of whose stock S owns. S then causes C to sell its assets to T for cash or notes. Result: S owns C's business through T, while the equity interest of C's minority shareholders in C's business is involuntarily terminated. (C is then normally dissolved, although a freezeout will be effected even without dissolution.) Such a procedure was disapproved in Cathedral Estates, Inc. v. Taft Realty Corp., 157 F.Supp. 895, 897 (D.Conn.1954), aff'd 251 F.2d 340 (2d Cir.1957); Cardiff v. Johnson, 126 Wash. 454, 218 P. 269 (1923); and Theis v. Spokane Falls Gaslight Co., 34 Wash. 23, 74 P. 1004 (1904).

3. *Debt or redeemable-preferred mergers.* A debt or redeemable-preferred merger begins, like a sale-of-assets freezeout, with the organization by S of a new corporation, T. S then causes C to merge with T, but instead of issuing common stock, T issues either short-term debentures or redeemable preferred stock. Accordingly, the interest of C's minority shareholders in T either terminates

---

1. In some cases controlling shareholders have adopted a corporate policy (such as cutting dividends) which puts pressure on minority shareholders to sell their shares, but does not in itself terminate the minority's interest. Such a technique is sometimes referred to as a "squeezeout."

automatically after a period of years (in the case of debentures) or is terminable at T's election (in the case of redeemable preferred).

Modern freezeouts commonly employ still a fourth technique. Many states have amended their regular merger statutes to allow the survivor in a regular merger to issue cash as well as stock or securities. This opened the door to the possibility of cash mergers, which resemble debt or redeemable stock mergers except that the survivor issues cash rather than stock or securities. Under this technique, the freezeout possibilities of the short-form merger are extended to cases where the parent does not own the percentage of stock requisite for a short-form merger.

A recurrent issue in the freezeout area is whether such transactions are permissible if effected with no business purpose other than to increase the controlling shareholders' portion of the pie.

WEINBERGER v. UOP, INC.

Supreme Court of Delaware, 1983.
457 A.2d 701.

Before HERRMANN, C.J., McNEILLY, QUILLEN, HORSEY and MOORE, JJ., constituting the Court en Banc.

MOORE, Justice:

This post-trial appeal was reheard en banc from a decision of the Court of Chancery. It was brought by the class action plaintiff below, a former shareholder of UOP, Inc., who challenged the elimination of UOP's minority shareholders by a cash-out merger between UOP and its majority owner, The Signal Companies, Inc.[2] Originally, the defendants in this action were Signal, UOP, certain officers and directors of those companies, and UOP's investment banker, Lehman Brothers Kuhn Loeb, Inc.[3] The present Chancellor held that the terms of the merger were fair to the plaintiff and the other minority shareholders of UOP. Accordingly, he entered judgment in favor of the defendants.

Numerous points were raised by the parties, but we address only the following questions presented by the trial court's opinion:

(1) The plaintiff's duty to plead sufficient facts demonstrating the unfairness of the challenged merger;

(2) The burden of proof upon the parties where the merger has been approved by the purportedly informed vote of a majority of the minority shareholders;

2. For the opinion of the trial court see Weinberger v. UOP, Inc., Del.Ch., 426 A.2d 1333 (1981).

3. Shortly before the last oral argument, the plaintiff dismissed Lehman Brothers from the action. Thus, we do not deal with the issues raised by the plaintiff's claims against this defendant.

(3) The fairness of the merger in terms of adequacy of the defendants' disclosures to the minority shareholders;

(4) The fairness of the merger in terms of adequacy of the price paid for the minority shares and the remedy appropriate to that issue; and

(5) The continued force and effect of Singer v. Magnavox Co., Del.Supr., 380 A.2d 969, 980 (1977), and its progeny.

In ruling for the defendants, the Chancellor re-stated his earlier conclusion that the plaintiff in a suit challenging a cash-out merger must allege specific acts of fraud, misrepresentation, or other items of misconduct to demonstrate the unfairness of the merger terms to the minority.[4] We approve this rule and affirm it.

The Chancellor also held that even though the ultimate burden of proof is on the majority shareholder to show by a preponderance of the evidence that the transaction is fair, it is first the burden of the plaintiff attacking the merger to demonstrate some basis for invoking the fairness obligation. We agree with that principle. However, where corporate action has been approved by an informed vote of a majority of the minority shareholders, we conclude that the burden entirely shifts to the plaintiff to show that the transaction was unfair to the minority. See, e.g., Michelson v. Duncan, Del.Supr., 407 A.2d 211, 224 (1979). But in all this, the burden clearly remains on those relying on the vote to show that they completely disclosed all material facts relevant to the transaction.

Here, the record does not support a conclusion that the minority stockholder vote was an informed one. Material information, necessary to acquaint those shareholders with the bargaining positions of Signal and UOP, was withheld under circumstances amounting to a breach of fiduciary duty. We therefore conclude that this merger does not meet the test of fairness, at least as we address that concept, and no burden thus shifted to the plaintiff by reason of the minority shareholder vote. Accordingly, we reverse and remand for further proceedings consistent herewith.

In considering the nature of the remedy available under our law to minority shareholders in a cash-out merger, we believe that it is, and hereafter should be, an appraisal under 8 Del.C. § 262 as hereinafter construed. We therefore overrule Lynch v. Vickers Energy Corp., Del.Supr., 429 A.2d 497 (1981) (*Lynch II*) to the extent that it purports to limit a stockholder's monetary relief to a specific damage formula. See *Lynch II.* 429 A.2d at 507–08 (McNeilly & Quillen, JJ., dissenting). But to give full effect to section 262 within the framework of the General Corporation Law we adopt a more liberal, less rigid and stylized, approach to the valuation process than has heretofore been permitted by our courts. While the present state of these proceedings does not admit the

---

4. In a pre-trial ruling the Chancellor ordered the complaint dismissed for failure to state a cause of action. See Weinberger v. UOP, Inc., Del.Ch., 409 A.2d 1262 (1979).

plaintiff to the appraisal remedy per se, the practical effect of the remedy we do grant him will be co-extensive with the liberalized valuation and appraisal methods we herein approve for cases coming after this decision.

Our treatment of these matters has necessarily led us to a reconsideration of the business purpose rule announced in the trilogy of Singer v. Magnavox Co., supra; Tanzer v. International General Industries, Inc., Del.Supr., 379 A.2d 1121 (1977); and Roland International Corp. v. Najjar, Del.Supr., 407 A.2d 1032 (1979). For the reasons hereafter set forth we consider that the business purpose requirement of these cases is no longer the law of Delaware.

I.

The facts found by the trial court, pertinent to the issues before us, are supported by the record, and we draw from them as set out in the Chancellor's opinion.[5]

Signal is a diversified, technically based company operating through various subsidiaries. Its stock is publicly traded on the New York, Philadelphia and Pacific Stock Exchanges. UOP, formerly known as Universal Oil Products Company, was a diversified industrial company engaged in various lines of business, including petroleum and petro-chemical services and related products, construction, fabricated metal products, transportation equipment products, chemicals and plastics, and other products and services including land development, lumber products and waste disposal. Its stock was publicly held and listed on the New York Stock Exchange.

In 1974 Signal sold one of its wholly-owned subsidiaries for $420,000,000 in cash. See Gimbel v. Signal Companies, Inc., Del. Ch., 316 A.2d 599, aff'd, Del.Supr., 316 A.2d 619 (1974). While looking to invest this cash surplus, Signal became interested in UOP as a possible acquisition. Friendly negotiations ensued, and Signal proposed to acquire a controlling interest in UOP at a price of $19 per share. UOP's representatives sought $25 per share. In the arm's length bargaining that followed, an understanding was reached whereby Signal agreed to purchase from UOP 1,500,000 shares of UOP's authorized but unissued stock at $21 per share.

This purchase was contingent upon Signal making a successful cash tender offer for 4,300,000 publicly held shares of UOP, also at a price of $21 per share. This combined method of acquisition permitted Signal to acquire 5,800,000 shares of stock, representing 50.5% of UOP's outstanding shares. The UOP board of directors advised the company's shareholders that it had no objection to Signal's tender offer at that price. Immediately before the announcement of the tender offer, UOP's common stock had been trading on the New York Stock Exchange at a fraction under $14 per share.

---

5. Weinberger v. UOP, Inc., Del.Ch.,
426 A.2d 1333, 1335–40 (1981).

The negotiations between Signal and UOP occurred during April 1975, and the resulting tender offer was greatly oversubscribed. However, Signal limited its total purchase of the tendered shares so that, when coupled with the stock bought from UOP, it had achieved its goal of becoming a 50.5% shareholder of UOP.

Although UOP's board consisted of thirteen directors, Signal nominated and elected only six. Of these, five were either directors or employees of Signal. The sixth, a partner in the banking firm of Lazard Freres & Co., had been one of Signal's representatives in the negotiations and bargaining with UOP concerning the tender offer and purchase price of the UOP shares.

However, the president and chief executive officer of UOP retired during 1975, and Signal caused him to be replaced by James V. Crawford, a long-time employee and senior executive vice president of one of Signal's wholly-owned subsidiaries. Crawford succeeded his predecessor on UOP's board of directors and also was made a director of Signal.

By the end of 1977 Signal basically was unsuccessful in finding other suitable investment candidates for its excess cash, and by February 1978 considered that it had no other realistic acquisitions available to it on a friendly basis. Once again its attention turned to UOP.

The trial court found that at the instigation of certain Signal management personnel, including William W. Walkup, its board chairman, and Forrest N. Shumway, its president, a feasibility study was made concerning the possible acquisition of the balance of UOP's outstanding shares. This study was performed by two Signal officers, Charles S. Arledge, vice president (director of planning), and Andrew J. Chitiea, senior vice president (chief financial officer). Messrs. Walkup, Shumway, Arledge and Chitiea were all directors of UOP in addition to their membership on the Signal board.

Arledge and Chitiea concluded that it would be a good investment for Signal to acquire the remaining 49.5% of UOP shares at any price up to $24 each. Their report was discussed between Walkup and Shumway who, along with Arledge, Chitiea and Brewster L. Arms, internal counsel for Signal, constituted Signal's senior management. In particular, they talked about the proper price to be paid if the acquisition was pursued, purportedly keeping in mind that as UOP's majority shareholder, Signal owed a fiduciary responsibility to both its own stockholders as well as to UOP's minority. It was ultimately agreed that a meeting of Signal's Executive Committee would be called to propose that Signal acquire the remaining outstanding stock of UOP through a cash-out merger in the range of $20 to $21 per share.

The Executive Committee meeting was set for February 28, 1978. As a courtesy, UOP's President, Crawford, was invited to attend, although he was not a member of Signal's executive committee. On his arrival, and prior to the meeting, Crawford was asked to meet privately with Walkup and Shumway. He was then told of

Signal's plan to acquire full ownership of UOP and was asked for his reaction to the proposed price range of $20 to $21 per share. Crawford said he thought such a price would be "generous", and that it was certainly one which should be submitted to UOP's minority shareholders for their ultimate consideration. He stated, however, that Signal's 100% ownership could cause internal problems at UOP. He believed that employees would have to be given some assurance of their future place in a fully-owned Signal subsidiary. Otherwise, he feared the departure of essential personnel. Also, many of UOP's key employees had stock option incentive programs which would be wiped out by a merger. Crawford therefore urged that some adjustment would have to be made, such as providing a comparable incentive in Signals' shares, if after the merger he was to maintain his quality of personnel and efficiency at UOP.

Thus, Crawford voiced no objection to the $20 to $21 price range, nor did he suggest that Signal should consider paying more than $21 per share for the minority interests. Later, at the Executive Committee meeting the same factors were discussed, with Crawford repeating the position he earlier took with Walkup and Shumway. Also considered was the 1975 tender offer and the fact that it had been greatly oversubscribed at $21 per share. For many reasons, Signal's management concluded that the acquisition of UOP's minority shares provided the solution to a number of its business problems.

Thus, it was the consensus that a price of $20 to $21 per share would be fair to both Signal and the minority shareholders of UOP. Signal's executive committee authorized its management "to negotiate" with UOP "for a cash acquisition of the minority ownership in UOP, Inc., with the intention of presenting a proposal to [Signal's] board of directors ... on March 6, 1978". Immediately after this February 28, 1978 meeting, Signal issued a press release stating:

> The Signal Companies, Inc. and UOP, Inc. are conducting negotiations for the acquisition for cash by Signal of the 49.5 per cent of UOP which it does not presently own, announced Forrest N. Shumway, president and chief executive officer of Signal, and James V. Crawford, UOP president.

> Price and other terms of the proposed transaction have not yet been finalized and would be subject to approval of the boards of directors of Signal and UOP, scheduled to meet early next week, the stockholders of UOP and certain federal agencies.

The announcement also referred to the fact that the closing price of UOP's common stock on that day was $14.50 per share.

Two days later, on March 2, 1978, Signal issued a second press release stating that its management would recommend a price in the range of $20 to $21 per share for UOP's 49.5% minority interest. This announcement referred to Signal's earlier statement that "negotiations" were being conducted for the acquisition of the minority shares.

Between Tuesday, February 28, 1978 and Monday, March 6, 1978, a total of four business days, Crawford spoke by telephone with all of UOP's non-Signal, i.e., outside, directors. Also during that period, Crawford retained Lehman Brothers to render a fairness opinion as to the price offered the minority for its stock. He gave two reasons for this choice. First, the time schedule between the announcement and the board meetings was short (by then only three business days) and since Lehman Brothers had been acting as UOP's investment banker for many years, Crawford felt that it would be in the best position to respond on such brief notice. Second, James W. Glanville, a long-time director of UOP and a partner in Lehman Brothers, had acted as a financial advisor to UOP for many years. Crawford believed that Glanville's familiarity with UOP, as a member of its board, would also be of assistance in enabling Lehman Brothers to render a fairness opinion within the existing time constraints.

Crawford telephoned Glanville, who gave his assurance that Lehman Brothers had no conflicts that would prevent it from accepting the task. Glanville's immediate personal reaction was that a price of $20 to $21 would certainly be fair, since it represented almost a 50% premium over UOP's market price. Glanville sought a $250,000 fee for Lehman Brothers' services, but Crawford thought this too much. After further discussions Glanville finally agreed that Lehman Brothers would render its fairness opinion for $150,000.

During this period Crawford also had several telephone contacts with Signal officials. In only one of them, however, was the price of the shares discussed. In a conversation with Walkup, Crawford advised that as a result of his communications with UOP's non-Signal directors, it was his feeling that the price would have to be the top of the proposed range, or $21 per share, if the approval of UOP's outside directors was to be obtained. But again, he did not seek any price higher than $21.

Glanville assembled a three-man Lehman Brothers team to do the work on the fairness opinion. These persons examined relevant documents and information concerning UOP, including its annual reports and its Securities and Exchange Commission filings from 1973 through 1976, as well as its audited financial statements for 1977, its interim reports to shareholders, and its recent and historical market prices and trading volumes. In addition, on Friday, March 3, 1978, two members of the Lehman Brothers team flew to UOP's headquarters in Des Plaines, Illinois, to perform a "due diligence" visit, during the course of which they interviewed Crawford as well as UOP's general counsel, its chief financial officer, and other key executives and personnel.

As a result, the Lehman Brothers team concluded that "the price of either $20 or $21 would be a fair price for the remaining shares of UOP". They telephoned this impression to Glanville, who was spending the weekend in Vermont.

On Monday morning, March 6, 1978, Glanville and the senior member of the Lehman Brothers team flew to Des Plaines to attend the scheduled UOP directors meeting. Glanville looked over the assembled information during the flight. The two had with them the draft of a "fairness opinion letter" in which the price had been left blank. Either during or immediately prior to the directors' meeting, the two-page "fairness opinion letter" was typed in final form and the price of $21 per share was inserted.

On March 6, 1978, both the Signal and UOP boards were convened to consider the proposed merger. Telephone communications were maintained between the two meetings. Walkup, Signal's board chairman, and also a UOP director, attended UOP's meeting with Crawford in order to present Signal's position and answer any questions that UOP's non-Signal directors might have. Arledge and Chitiea, along with Signal's other designees on UOP's board, participated by conference telephone. All of UOP's outside directors attended the meeting either in person or by conference telephone.

First, Signal's board unanimously adopted a resolution authorizing Signal to proposed to UOP a cash merger of $21 per share as outlined in a certain merger agreement and other supporting documents. This proposal required that the merger be approved by a majority of UOP's outstanding minority shares voting at the stockholders meeting at which the merger would be considered, and that the minority shares voting in favor of the merger, when coupled with Signal's 50.5% interest would have to comprise at least two-thirds of all UOP shares. Otherwise the proposed merger would be deemed disapproved.

UOP's board then considered the proposal. Copies of the agreement were delivered to the directors in attendance, and other copies had been forwarded earlier to the directors participating by telephone. They also had before them UOP financial data for 1974–1977, UOP's most recent financial statements, market price information, and budget projections for 1978. In addition they had Lehman Brothers' hurriedly prepared fairness opinion letter finding the price of $21 to be fair. Glanville, the Lehman Brothers partner, and UOP director, commented on the information that had gone into preparation of the letter.

Signal also suggests that the Arledge–Chitiea feasibility study, indicating that a price of up to $24 per share would be a "good investment" for Signal, was discussed at the UOP directors' meeting. The Chancellor made no such finding, and our independent review of the record, detailed infra, satisfies us by a preponderance of the evidence that there was no discussion of this document at UOP's board meeting. Furthermore, it is clear beyond peradventure that nothing in that report was ever disclosed to UOP's minority shareholders prior to their approval of the merger.

After consideration of Signal's proposal, Walkup and Crawford left the meeting to permit a free and uninhibited exchange between UOP's non-Signal directors. Upon their return a resolution to accept Signal's offer was then proposed and adopted. While Signal's men on UOP's board participated in various aspects of the meeting they abstained from voting. However, the minutes show that each of them "if voting would have voted yes".

On March 7, 1978, UOP sent a letter to its shareholders advising them of the action taken by UOP's board with respect to Signal's offer. This document pointed out, among other things, that on February 28, 1978 "both companies had announced negotiations were being conducted."

Despite the swift board action of the two companies, the merger was not submitted to UOP's shareholders until their annual meeting on May 26, 1978. In the notice of that meeting and proxy statement sent to shareholders in May, UOP's management and board urged that the merger be approved. The proxy statement also advised:

> The price was determined after *discussions* between James V. Crawford, a director of Signal and Chief Executive Officer of UOP, and officers of Signal which took place during meetings on February 28, 1978, and in the course of several subsequent telephone conversations. (Emphasis added.)

In the original draft of the proxy statement the word "negotiations" had been used rather than "discussions". However, when the Securities and Exchange Commission sought details of the "negotiations" as part of its review of these materials, the term was deleted and the word "discussions" was substituted. The proxy statement indicated that the vote of UOP's board in approving the merger had been unanimous. It also advised the shareholders that Lehman Brothers had given its opinion that the merger price of $21 per share was fair to UOP's minority. However, it did not disclose the hurried method by which this conclusion was reached.

As of the record date for UOP's annual meeting, there were 11,488,302 shares of UOP common stock outstanding, 5,688,302 of which were owned by the minority. At the meeting only 56%, or 3,208,652, of the minority shares were voted. Of these, 2,953,812, or 51.9% of the total minority, voted for the merger, and 254,840 voted against it. When Signal's stock was added to the minority shares voting in favor, a total of 76.2% of UOP's outstanding shares approved the merger while only 2.2% opposed it.

By its terms the merger became effective on May 26, 1978, and each share of UOP's stock held by the minority was automatically converted into a right to receive $21 cash.

II.

A.

A primary issue mandating reversal is the preparation by two UOP directors, Arledge and Chitiea, of their feasibility study for the exclusive use and benefit of Signal. This document was of obvious significance to both Signal and UOP. Using UOP data, it described the advantages to Signal of ousting the minority at a price range of $21–$24 per share. Mr. Arledge, one of the authors, outlined the benefits to Signal: [6]

Purpose of the Merger

(1) Provides an outstanding investment opportunity for Signal—(Better than any recent acquisition we have seen.)

(2) Increases Signal's earnings.

(3) Facilitates the flow of resources between Signal and its subsidiaries—(Big factor—works both ways.)

(4) Provides cost savings potential for Signal and UOP.

(5) Improves the percentage of Signal's 'operating earnings' as opposed to 'holding company earnings'.

(6) Simplifies the understanding of Signal.

(7) Facilitates technological exchange among Signal's subsidiaries.

(8) Eliminates potential conflicts of interest.

Having written those words, solely for the use of Signal, it is clear from the record that neither Arledge nor Chitiea shared this report with their fellow directors of UOP. We are satisfied that no one else did either. This conduct hardly meets the fiduciary standards applicable to such a transaction. While Mr. Walkup, Signal's chairman of the board and a UOP director, attended the March 6, 1978 UOP board meeting and testified at trial that he had discussed the Arledge–Chitiea report with the UOP directors at this meeting, the record does not support this assertion. Perhaps it is the result of some confusion on Mr. Walkup's part. In any event Mr. Shumway, Signal's president, testified that he made sure the Signal outside directors had this report prior to the March 6, 1978 Signal board meeting, but he did not testify that the Arledge–Chitiea report was also sent to UOP's outside directors.

Mr. Crawford, UOP's president, could not recall that any documents, other than a draft of the merger agreement, were sent to UOP's directors before the March 6, 1978 UOP meeting. Mr. Chitiea, an author of the report, testified that it was made available to Signal's directors, but to his knowledge it was not circulated to the outside directors of UOP. He specifically testified that he "didn't share" that information with the outside directors of UOP with whom he served.

None of UOP's outside directors who testified stated that they had seen this document. The minutes of the UOP board meeting do not identify the Arledge–Chitiea report as having been delivered to UOP's outside directors. This is particularly significant since the minutes describe in considerable detail the materials that actually

---

6. The parentheses indicate certain handwritten comments of Mr. Arledge.

were distributed. While these minutes recite Mr. Walkup's presentation of the Signal offer, they do not mention the Arledge–Chitiea report or any disclosure that Signal considered a price of up to $24 to be a good investment. If Mr. Walkup had in fact provided such important information to UOP's outside directors, it is logical to assume that these carefully drafted minutes would disclose it. The post-trial briefs of Signal and UOP contain a thorough description of the documents purportedly available to their boards at the March 6, 1978, meetings. Although the Arledge–Chitiea report is specifically identified as being available to the Signal directors, there is no mention of it being among the documents submitted to the UOP board. Even when queried at a prior oral argument before this Court, counsel for Signal did not claim that the Arledge–Chitiea report had been disclosed to UOP's outside directors. Instead, he chose to belittle its contents. This was the same approach taken before us at the last oral argument.

Actually, it appears that a three-page summary of figures was given to all UOP directors. Its first page is identical to one page of the Arledge–Chitiea report, but this dealt with nothing more than a justification of the $21 price. Significantly, the contents of this three-page summary are what the minutes reflect Mr. Walkup told the UOP board. However, nothing contained in either the minutes or this three-page summary reflects Signal's study regarding the $24 price.

The Arledge–Chitiea report speaks for itself in supporting the Chancellor's finding that a price of up to $24 was a "good investment" for Signal. It shows that a return on the investment at $21 would be 15.7% versus 15.5% at $24 per share. This was a difference of only two-tenths of one percent, while it meant over $17,000,000 to the minority. Under such circumstances, paying UOP's minority shareholders $24 would have had relatively little long-term effect on Signal, and the Chancellor's findings concerning the benefit to Signal, even at a price of $24, were obviously correct. Levitt v. Bouvier, Del.Supr., 287 A.2d 671, 673 (1972).

Certainly, this was a matter of material significance to UOP and its shareholders. Since the study was prepared by two UOP directors, using UOP information for the exclusive benefit of Signal, and nothing whatever was done to disclose it to the outside UOP directors or the minority shareholders, a question of breach of fiduciary duty arises. This problem occurs because there were common Signal–UOP directors participating, at least to some extent, in the UOP board's decision-making processes without full disclosure of the conflicts they faced.[7]

---

7. Although perfection is not possible, or expected, the result here could have been entirely different if UOP had appointed an independent negotiating committee of its outside directors to deal with Signal at arm's length. See, e.g., Harriman v. E.I. duPont de Nemours & Co., 411 F.Supp. 133 (D.Del.1975). Since fairness in this context can be equated to conduct by a theoretical, wholly independent, board of directors acting upon the matter before them, it is unfortunate that this course apparently was neither considered nor pursued. Johnston v. Greene, Del.Supr., 121 A.2d 919, 925

B.

In assessing this situation, the Court of Chancery was required to:

> examine what information defendants had and to measure it against what they gave to the minority stockholders, in a context in which "complete candor" is required. In other words, the limited function of the Court was to determine whether defendants had disclosed all information in their possession germane to the transaction in issue. And by "germane" we mean, for present purposes, information such as a reasonable shareholder would consider important in deciding whether to sell or retain stock.

* * *

> ... Completeness, not adequacy, is both the norm and the mandate under present circumstances.

Lynch v. Vickers Energy Corp., Del.Supr., 383 A.2d 278, 281 (1977) (*Lynch I*). This is merely stating in another way the long-existing principle of Delaware law that these Signal designated directors on UOP's board still owed UOP and its shareholders an uncompromising duty of loyalty. The classic language of Guth v. Loft, Inc., Del.Supr., 5 A.2d 503, 510 (1939), requires no embellishment:

> A public policy, existing through the years, and derived from a profound knowledge of human characteristics and motives, has established a rule that demands of a corporate officer or director, peremptorily and inexorably, the most scrupulous observance of his duty, not only affirmatively to protect the interests of the corporation committed to his charge, but also to refrain from doing anything that would work injury to the corporation, or to deprive it of profit or advantage which his skill and ability might properly bring to it, or to enable it to make in the reasonable and lawful exercise of its powers. The rule that requires an undivided and unselfish loyalty to the corporation demands that there shall be no conflict between duty and self-interest.

Given the absence of any attempt to structure this transaction on an arm's length basis, Signal cannot escape the effects of the conflicts it faced, particularly when its designees on UOP's board did not totally abstain from participation in the matter. There is no "safe harbor" for such divided loyalties in Delaware. When directors of a Delaware corporation are on both sides of a transaction, they are required to demonstrate their utmost good faith and the most scrupulous inherent fairness of the bargain. Gottlieb v. Heyden Chemical Corp., Del.Supr., 91 A.2d 57, 57–58 (1952). The

(1956). Particularly in a parent-subsidiary context, a showing that the action taken was as though each of the contending parties had in fact exerted its bargaining power against the other at arm's length is strong evidence that the transaction meets the test of fairness. Getty Oil Co. v. Skelly Oil Co., Del.Supr., 267 A.2d 883, 886 (1970); Puma v. Marriott, Del.Ch., 283 A.2d 693, 696 (1971).

requirement of fairness is unflinching in its demand that where one stands on both sides of a transaction, he has the burden of establishing its entire fairness, sufficient to pass the test of careful scrutiny by the courts. Sterling v. Mayflower Hotel Corp., Del.Supr., 93 A.2d 107, 110 (1952); Bastian v. Bourns, Inc., Del.Ch., 256 A.2d 680, 681 (1969), aff'd, Del.Supr., 278 A.2d 467 (1970); David J. Greene & Co. v. Dunhill International Inc., Del.Ch., 249 A.2d 427, 431 (1968).

There is no dilution of this obligation where one holds dual or multiple directorships, as in a parent-subsidiary context. Levien v. Sinclair Oil Corp., Del.Ch., 261 A.2d 911, 915 (1969). Thus, individuals who act in a dual capacity as directors of two corporations, one of whom is parent and the other subsidiary, owe the same duty of good management to both corporations, and in the absence of an independent negotiating structure (see note 7, supra), or the directors' total abstention from any participation in the matter, this duty is to be exercised in light of what is best for both companies. Warshaw v. Calhoun, Del.Supr., 221 A.2d 487, 492 (1966). The record demonstrates that Signal has not met this obligation.

C.

The concept of fairness has two basic aspects: fair dealing and fair price. The former embraces questions of when the transaction was timed, how it was initiated, structured, negotiated, disclosed to the directors, and how the approvals of the directors and the stockholders were obtained. The latter aspect of fairness relates to the economic and financial considerations of the proposed merger, including all relevant factors: assets, market value, earnings, future prospects, and any other elements that affect the intrinsic or inherent value of a company's stock. Moore, The "Interested" Director or Officer Transaction, 4 Del.J.Corp.L. 674, 676 (1979); Nathan & Shapiro, Legal Standard of Fairness of Merger Terms Under Delaware Law, 2 Del.J.Corp.L. 44, 46–47 (1977). See Tri–Continental Corp. v. Battye, Del.Supr., 74 A.2d 71, 72 (1950); 8 Del.C. § 262(h). However, the test for fairness is not a bifurcated one as between fair dealing and price. All aspects of the issue must be examined as a whole since the question is one of entire fairness. However, in a non-fraudulent transaction we recognize that price may be the preponderant consideration outweighing other features of the merger. Here, we address the two basic aspects of fairness separately because we find reversible error as to both.

D.

Part of fair dealing is the obvious duty of candor required by *Lynch I,* supra. Moreover, one possessing superior knowledge may not mislead any stockholder by use of corporate information to which the latter is not privy. Lank v. Steiner, Del.Supr., 224 A.2d 242, 244 (1966). Delaware has long imposed this duty even upon persons who are not corporate officers or directors, but who nonetheless are privy to matters of interest or significance to their company. Brophy v. Cities Service Co., Del.Ch., 70 A.2d 5, 7 (1949). With the well-established Delaware law on the subject, and the Court of Chancery's findings of fact here, it is inevitable that the obvious conflicts posed by Arledge and Chitiea's preparation of their "feasibility study", derived from UOP information, for the sole use and benefit of Signal, cannot pass muster.

The Arledge–Chitiea report is but one aspect of the element of fair dealing. How did this merger evolve? It is clear that it was entirely initiated by Signal. The serious time constraints under which the principals acted were all set by Signal. It had not found a suitable outlet for its excess cash and considered UOP a desirable investment, particularly since it was now in a position to acquire the whole company for itself. For whatever reasons, and they were only Signal's, the entire transaction was presented to and approved by UOP's board within four business days. Standing alone, this is not necessarily indicative of any lack of fairness by a majority shareholder. It was what occurred, or more properly, what did not occur, during this brief period that makes the time constraints imposed by Signal relevant to the issue of fairness.

The structure of the transaction, again, was Signal's doing. So far as negotiations were concerned, it is clear that they were modest at best. Crawford, Signal's man at UOP, never really talked price with Signal, except to accede to its management's statements on the subject, and to convey to Signal the UOP outside directors' view that as between the $20–$21 range under consideration, it would have to be $21. The latter is not a surprising outcome, but hardly arm's length negotiations. Only the protection of benefits for UOP's key employees and the issue of Lehman Brothers' fee approached any concept of bargaining.

As we have noted, the matter of disclosure to the UOP directors was wholly flawed by the conflicts of interest raised by the Arledge–Chitiea report. All of those conflicts were resolved by Signal in its own favor without divulging any aspect of them to UOP.

This cannot but undermine a conclusion that this merger meets any reasonable test of fairness. The outside UOP directors lacked one material piece of information generated by two of their colleagues, but shared only with Signal. True, the UOP board had the Lehman Brothers' fairness opinion, but that firm has been blamed by the plaintiff for the hurried task it performed, when more properly the responsibility for this lies with Signal. There was no disclosure of the circumstances surrounding the rather cursory preparation of the Lehman Brothers' fairness opinion. Instead, the impression was given UOP's minority that a careful study had been made, when in fact speed was the hallmark, and Mr. Glanville, Lehman's partner in charge of the matter, and also a UOP director, having spent the weekend in Vermont, brought a draft of the "fairness opinion letter" to the UOP directors' meeting on March 6, 1978 with the price left blank. We can only conclude from the record that the rush imposed on Lehman Brothers by Signal's timetable contributed to the difficulties under which this investment banking firm attempted to perform its responsibilities. Yet, none of this was disclosed to UOP's minority.

Finally, the minority stockholders were denied the critical information that Signal considered a price of $24 to be a good investment. Since this would have meant over $17,000,000 more to the minority, we cannot conclude that the shareholder vote was an informed one. Under the circumstances, an approval by a majority of the minority was meaningless. *Lynch I,* 383 A.2d at 279, 281; Cahall v. Lofland, Del.Ch., 114 A. 224 (1921).

Given these particulars and the Delaware law on the subject, the record does not establish that this transaction satisfies any reasonable concept of fair dealing, and the Chancellor's findings in that regard must be reversed.

E.

Turning to the matter of price, plaintiff also challenges its fairness. His evidence was that on the date the merger was approved the stock was worth at least $26 per share. In support, he offered the testimony of a chartered investment analyst who used two basic approaches to valuation: a comparative analysis of the premium paid over market in ten other tender offer-merger combinations, and a discounted cash flow analysis.

In this breach of fiduciary duty case, the Chancellor perceived that the approach to valuation was the same as that in an appraisal proceeding. Consistent with precedent, he rejected plaintiff's method of proof and accepted defendants' evidence of value as being in accord with practice under prior case law. This means that the so-called "Delaware block" or weighted average method was employed wherein the elements of value, i.e., assets, market price, earnings, etc., were assigned a particular weight and the resulting amounts added to determine the value per share.

[The court held that the use of this valuation technique was in error. See pp. 753–755, supra.]

Although the Chancellor received the plaintiff's evidence, his opinion indicates that the use of it was precluded because of past Delaware practice. While we do not suggest a monetary result one way or the other, we do think the plaintiff's evidence should be part of the factual mix and weighed as such. Until the $21 price is measured on remand by the valuation standards mandated by Delaware law, there can be no finding at the present stage of these proceedings that the price is fair. Given the lack of any candid disclosure of the material facts surrounding establishment of the $21 price, the majority of the minority vote, approving the merger, is meaningless.

The plaintiff has not sought an appraisal, but rescissory damages of the type contemplated by Lynch v. Vickers Energy Corp., Del.Supr., 429 A.2d 497, 505–06 (1981) (*Lynch II*). In view of the approach to valuation that we announce today, we see no basis in our law for *Lynch II*'s exclusive monetary formula for relief. On remand the plaintiff will be permitted to test the fairness of the $21 price by the standards we herein establish, in conformity with the principle applicable to an appraisal—that fair value be determined by taking "into account all relevant factors" [see 8 Del.C. § 262(h), supra]. In our view this includes the elements of rescissory damages if the Chancellor considers them susceptible of proof and a remedy appropriate to all the issues of fairness before him. To the extent that *Lynch II*, 429 A.2d at 505–06, purports to limit the Chancellor's discretion to a single remedial formula for monetary damages in a cash-out merger, it is overruled.

While a plaintiff's monetary remedy ordinarily should be confined to the more liberalized appraisal proceeding herein established, we do not intend any limitation on the historic powers of the Chancellor to grant such other relief as the facts of a particular case may dictate. The appraisal remedy we approve may not be adequate in certain cases, particularly where fraud, misrepresentation, self-dealing, deliberate waste of corporate assets, or gross and palpable overreaching are involved. Cole v. National Cash Credit Association, Del.Ch., 156 A. 183, 187 (1931). Under such circumstances, the Chancellor's powers are complete to fashion any form of equitable and monetary relief as may be appropriate, including rescissory damages. Since it is apparent that this long completed transaction is too involved to undo, and in view of the Chancellor's discretion, the award, if any, should be in the form of monetary damages based upon entire fairness standards, i.e., fair dealing and fair price.

Obviously, there are other litigants, like the plaintiff, who abjured an appraisal and whose rights to challenge the element of fair value must be preserved.[8] Accordingly, the quasi-appraisal remedy we grant the plaintiff here will apply only to: (1) this case; (2) any case now pending on appeal to this Court; (3) any case now pending in the Court of Chancery which has not yet been appealed but which may be eligible for direct appeal to this Court; (4) any case challenging a cash-out merger, the effective date of which is on or before February 1, 1983; and (5) any proposed merger to be presented at a shareholders' meeting, the notification of which is mailed to the stockholders on or before February 23, 1983. Thereafter, the provisions of 8 Del.C. § 262, as herein construed, respecting the scope of an appraisal and the means for perfecting the same, shall govern the financial remedy available to minority shareholders in a cash-out merger. Thus, we return to the well established principles of Stauffer v. Standard Brands, Inc., Del.Supr., 187 A.2d 78 (1962) and David J. Greene & Co. v. Schenley Industries, Inc., Del.Ch., 281 A.2d 30 (1971), mandating a stockholder's recourse to the basic remedy of an appraisal.

8. Under 8 Del.C. § 262(a), (d) & (e), a stockholder is required to act within certain time periods to perfect the right to an appraisal.

III.

Finally, we address the matter of business purpose. The defendants contend that the purpose of this merger was not a proper subject of inquiry by the trial court. The plaintiff says that no valid purpose existed—the entire transaction was a mere subterfuge designed to eliminate the minority. The Chancellor ruled otherwise, but in so doing he clearly circumscribed the thrust and effect of *Singer.* Weinberger v. UOP, 426 A.2d at 1342–43, 1348–50. This has led to the thoroughly sound observation that the business purpose test "may be . . . virtually interpreted out of existence, as it was in *Weinberger* ".[9]

The requirement of a business purpose is new to our law of mergers and was a departure from prior case law. See Stauffer v. Standard Brands, Inc., supra; David J. Greene & Co. v. Schenley Industries, Inc., supra.

In view of the fairness test which has long been applicable to parent-subsidiary mergers, Sterling v. Mayflower Hotel Corp., Del. Supr., 93 A.2d 107, 109–10 (1952), the expanded appraisal remedy now available to shareholders, and the broad discretion of the Chancellor to fashion such relief as the facts of a given case may dictate we do not believe that any additional meaningful protection is afforded minority shareholders by the business purpose requirement of the trilogy of *Singer, Tanzer,*[10] *Najjar,*[11] and their progeny. Accordingly, such requirement shall no longer be of any force or effect.

The judgment of the Court of Chancery, finding both the circumstances of the merger and the price paid the minority shareholders to be fair, is reversed. The matter is remanded for further proceedings consistent herewith. Upon remand the plaintiff's post-trial motion to enlarge the class should be granted.

* * *

Reversed and Remanded.

KAHN v. LYNCH COMMUNICATION SYSTEMS

p. 501, supra

COGGINS v. NEW ENGLAND PATRIOTS FOOTBALL CLUB, INC., 397 Mass. 525, 492 N.E.2d 1112 (1986). "Unlike the Dela-

---

9. Weiss, The Law of Take Out Mergers: A Historical Perspective, 56 N.Y.U.L.Rev. 624, 671, n. 300 (1981).

10. Tanzer v. International General Industries, Inc., Del.Supr., 379 A.2d 1121, 1124–25 (1977).

11. Roland International Corp. v. Najjar, Del.Supr., 407 A.2d 1032, 1036 (1979).

ware court . . . we believe that the "business-purpose" test is an additional useful means under our statutes and case law for examining a transaction in which a controlling stockholder eliminates the minority interest in a corporation. . . . This concept of fair dealing is not limited to close corporations but applies to judicial review of cash freeze-out mergers. . . .

"The defendants argue that judicial review of a merger cannot be invoked by disgruntled stockholders, absent illegal or fraudulent conduct. They rely on G.L. c. 156B, § 98 (1984 ed.).[12] In the defendants' view, 'the Superior Court's finding of liability was premised solely on the claimed inadequacy of the offering price.' Any dispute over offering price, they urge, must be resolved solely through the statutory remedy of appraisal. . . .

"We have held in regard to so called 'close corporations' that the statute does not divest the courts of their equitable jurisdiction to assure that the conduct of controlling stockholders does not violate the fiduciary principles governing the relationship between majority and minority stockholders. *Pupecki v. James Madison Corp.*, 376 Mass. 212, 216–217, 382 N.E.2d 1030 (1978) (when controlling stockholder fails to assure that corporation receives adequate consideration for its assets, transaction is illegal or fraudulent, and G.L. c. 156B, § 98, does not foreclose review). 'Where the director's duty of loyalty to the corporation is in conflict with his self-interest the court will vigorously scrutinize the situation.' *American Discount Corp. v. Kaitz*, 348 Mass. 706, 711, 206 N.E.2d 156 (1965). The court is justified in exercising its equitable power when a violation of fiduciary duty is claimed.

"The dangers of self-dealing and abuse of fiduciary duty are greatest in freeze-out situations like the Patriots merger, where a controlling stockholder and corporate director chooses to eliminate public ownership. It is in these cases that a judge should examine with closest scrutiny the motives and the behavior of the controlling stockholder. A showing of compliance with statutory procedures is an insufficient substitute for the inquiry of the courts when a minority stockholder claims that the corporate action 'will be or is illegal or fraudulent as to him.' G.L. c. 156B, § 98. *Leader v. Hycor, Inc.*, 395 Mass. 215, 221, 479 N.E.2d 173 (1985) (judicial review may be had of claims of breach of fiduciary duty and unfairness).

"Judicial scrutiny should begin with recognition of the basic principle that the duty of a corporate director must be to further the legitimate goals of the corporation. The result of a freeze-out merger is the elimination of public ownership in the corporation. The controlling faction increases its equity from a majority to 100%, using corporate processes and corporate assets. The corporate

---

12. "The enforcement by a stockholder of his right to receive payment for his shares in the manner provided in this chapter shall be an exclusive remedy except that this chapter shall not exclude the right of such stockholder to bring or maintain an appropriate proceeding to obtain relief on the ground that such corporate action will be or is illegal or fraudulent as to him." G.L. c. 156B, § 98.

directors who benefit from this transfer of ownership must demonstrate how the legitimate goals of the corporation are furthered. A director of a corporation violates his fiduciary duty when he uses the corporation for his or his family's personal benefit in a manner detrimental to the corporation. *Widett & Widett v. Snyder,* 392 Mass. 778, 785–786, 467 N.E.2d 1312 (1984). See *Buckman v. Elm Hill Realty Co. of Peabody,* 312 Mass. 10, 15, 42 N.E.2d 814 (1942). Because the danger of abuse of fiduciary duty is especially great in a freeze-out merger, the court must be satisfied that the freeze-out was for the advancement of a legitimate corporate purpose. If satisfied that elimination of public ownership is in furtherance of a business purpose, the court should then proceed to determine if the transaction was fair by examining the totality of the circumstances. . . ."

ALPERT v. 28 WILLIAMS ST. CORP., 63 N.Y.2d 557, 483 N.Y.S.2d 667, 473 N.E.2d 19 (1984). "In the context of a freeze-out merger, variant treatment of the minority shareholders—i.e., causing their removal—will be justified when related to the advancement of a general corporate interest. The benefit need not be great, but it must be for the corporation. For example, if the sole purpose of the merger is reduction of the number of profit sharers—in contrast to increasing the corporation's capital or profits, or improving its management structure—there will exist no 'independent corporate interest' (see Schwartz v. Marien, 37 N.Y.2d 487, 492, 373 N.Y.S.2d 122, 335 N.E.2d 334, supra). All of these purposes ultimately seek to increase the individual wealth of the remaining shareholders. What distinguishes a proper corporate purpose from an improper one is that, with the former, removal of the minority shareholders furthers the objective of conferring some general gain upon the corporation. Only then will the fiduciary duty of good and prudent management of the corporation serve to override the concurrent duty to treat all shareholders fairly (see Klurfeld v. Equity Enterprises, 79 A.D.2d 124, 136, 436 N.Y.S.2d 303, supra). We further note that a finding that there was an independent corporate purpose for the action taken by the majority will not be defeated merely by the fact that the corporate objective could have been accomplished in another way, or by the fact that the action chosen was not the best way to achieve the bona fide business objective."

See also Grimes v. Donaldson, Lufkin & Jenrette, Inc., 392 F.Supp. 1393 (N.D.Fla.1974), aff'd without opinion 521 F.2d 812 (5th Cir.1975).

CAL. CORP. CODE §§ 1001, 1101, 1101.1, 1312

[See Statutory Supplement]

———

CAL. CORP. CODE § 407

[See Statutory Supplement]

———

ALI, PRINCIPLES OF CORPORATE GOVERNANCE §§ 5.15, 7.25

[See Statutory Supplement]

———

(j) Going Private

"Going private" involves the conversion of a corporation that is publicly held into one that is privately held—or, more particularly, the conversion of a corporation whose stock is registered under the 1934 Act, and listed on a Stock Exchange or actively traded over the counter, into one whose stock is unregistered, unlisted, and traded thinly if at all. While going private is often accomplished through a freezeout, the two categories are not entirely coextensive: going private, unlike freezeouts, does not necessarily involve *legal* compulsion, since it may be accomplished through purchase of the minority's shares. On the other hand, as the following material shows, such purchases, while apparently involving voluntary action on the minority's part, may in fact involve very little meaningful choice, and are often accomplished in part by the implicit or explicit threat that those who do not sell voluntarily will be made to sell involuntarily through use of a cashout merger or other freezeout device.

———

ADDRESS BY A.A. SOMMER, JR., COMMISSIONER, SECURITIES AND EXCHANGE COMMISSION, CCH, FED'L SEC.L.REP. [1974–'75 TRANSFER BINDER] ¶ 80,010

During the sixties and early seventies innumerable companies "went public," that is, publicly offered their securities. . . . All of these companies invited the public to share in their fortunes. . . .

What is happening now is this: as market prices of stock have plummeted, often to levels below book value, many companies have commenced the process of going private. . . .

The simplest way is an offer to pay the shareholders who accept a stipulated price, usually something in excess of the market price. This seems simple enough: the shareholder can take the offer or leave it, he is under no compulsion, and in fact, the offer may be a significant favor to him, since it may be the highest price he will see for some time. But even this simple approach has within it, in my estimation, troublesome elements. Usually, because of the necessities of full disclosure in our corporate life—largely policed and demanded by the SEC—the document which communicates the tender offer tells the awful truth. First, if significant numbers of shareholders respond to the tender, the shareholder who considers staying aboard faces significant losses. If the number of shareholders drops under 300 he will lose the network of federal protections built over a period of forty years for his benefit: no assurance of comprehensive disclosure, only limited protections against insider chicanery and so on. If he chooses to stay aboard he may find the liquidity of his investment—the ability to sell readily at a price reasonably proximate to the last sale—reduced, perhaps completely destroyed. Further, if management buys or otherwise acquires or has the power to bring it about, it may "merge out" the remaining minority and compel them in effect to sell their investments. Under the laws of the states in which most public corporations are incorporated, so-called cash mergers are allowed, that is, the shareholders of a company being acquired by another, instead of receiving stock of the acquiring company (the pattern of the typical merger) can be compelled to take cash in the amount determined by the merger agreement. . . .

Faced with the prospect of a force-out merger, or a market reduced to glacial activity and the liquidity of the Mojave Desert, and deprived of most of the benefits of the federal securities laws, how real is the choice of the shareholder confronting the offer of management to acquire his shares, usually not with their own resources, but with the corporation's resources that really belong to him and his fellow shareholders? In short, he usually decides he damn well better take the money and run. . . .

Is all this ethical? I would say to you there is at the minimum deep doubt of that. The spectacle of entrepreneurs inviting the public in when they can command high prices for their stock, and then squeezing them out with little or no practical choice in the matter at substantially reduced prices is hardly one to warm the soul of Thomas Aquinas or Aristotle. The corporation, and often the controlling interests, have been enriched with the proceeds of the public offerings of the past; with those proceeds the corporation grew and prospered, then, with the power deriving from their managerial positions and shareholdings, the insiders take over the whole corporation for themselves.

In one recent instance public offerings netted $696,000 for the corporation, over $12,500,000 for the offering shareholders. The corporation has now proposed to acquire all the stock held by minority shareholders for $11.00 per share. If all of the minority shareholders tender, they would receive $3.00 in cash and $8.00 in ten year subordinated debentures (which the company believes will sell at a substantial discount) for shares which were originally offered at $17.50 a share and three years ago at $21.75 a share; the dominant shareholder would go from a 7% interest to 43%, with over 3.7 million dollars (less taxes) provided by the public now safely locked up for her benefit. On a pro forma basis, had all public shares been repurchased on the basis proposed at the beginning of 1973, the corporate profits attributable to her interest would have risen from $236,000 to $1,107,000 in 1973—over 400%—and from $167,000 to $688,000 for the first ten months of 1974—again over 400%—and without a single dime of additional investment by her!

I would suggest there is something wrong with that. . . .*

SECURITIES EXCHANGE ACT RULE 13e–3 AND SCHEDULE 13e–3

[See Statutory Supplement]

SECTION 2.   TENDER OFFERS

SECURITIES EXCHANGE ACT §§ 13(d), (e), 14(d), (e)

SECURITIES EXCHANGE ACT RULES 13d–3, 13d–5, 13e–1, 13e–4, 14d–1 to 14d–4, 14d–6 to 14d–10, 14e–1 to 14e–3

SCHEDULES 13D, 13E–4, 14D–9

[See Statutory Supplement]

HART–SCOTT–RODINO ACT

[See Statutory Supplement]

---

* See also Kahn v. United States Sugar Corp., 1985 WL 4449 (Del.Ch.1985). (Footnote by ed.)

NOTE ON TERMINOLOGY

The legal profession has developed a rich terminology in connection with tender offers. The terms are too numerous and change too quickly to permit a comprehensive glossary, and some of the terms are fairly well defined in the cases that follow. This Note defines a few of the more important terms that are not defined in those cases.

Raider. The term *raider* refers to a person (normally, although not necessarily, a corporation) that makes a tender offer. The term is invidious; a more accurate term is *bidder.*

Target. The corporation whose shares the bidder seeks to acquire is referred to as the *target.*

White knight. Often the management of a target realizes that it will be taken over, but prefers a takeover by someone (sometimes, anyone) other than the original bidder. The management therefore solicits competing tender offers from other corporations. These more friendly corporations are known as *white knights.*

Lock-up. A *lock-up* is a device that is designed to protect one bidder (normally, a friendly bidder) against competition by other bidders (deemed less friendly). The favored bidder is given an option to acquire selected assets or a given amount of shares of the target at a favorable price under designated conditions. These conditions usually involve either defeat of the favored bidder's attempt to acquire the corporation, or the occurrence of events that would make that defeat likely.

Crown jewels. To defeat or discourage a takeover bid by a disfavored bidder, the target's management may sell or (more usually) give to a white knight a lock-up option that covers the target's most desirable business or, at least, the business most coveted by the disfavored bidder—its *crown jewels.*

Standstill. A target may seek an accommodation with a shareholder who has acquired a significant amount of stock, under which the shareholder agrees to limit his stock purchases—hence, *standstill.* In the typical standstill agreement, the shareholder makes one or more commitments: (i) it will not increase its shareholdings above designated limits for a specified period of time; (ii) it will not sell its shares without giving the corporation a right of first refusal; (iii) it will not engage in a proxy contest; and (iv) it will vote its stock in a designated manner in the election of directors, and perhaps on other issues. In return, the corporation typically agrees to give the shareholder board representation, to register the shareholder's stock under the Securities Act on demand, and not to oppose the shareholder's acquisition of stock up to the specified limit. See ALI, Principles of Corporate Governance, Council Draft No. 11, Section 6.01, Reporters' Note (1988).

No-shop clauses. A board of a corporation that enters into an agreement for a merger or other corporate combination (whether with a white knight or otherwise) may agree that it will recommend the combination to the shareholders, that it will not shop around for a more attractive deal, or both. The courts have divided on the question whether such provisions are unenforceable on the ground that they conflict with the director's fiduciary obligation to maximize the shareholders' best interests. Compare Jewel Companies, Inc. v. Pay Less Drug Stores Northwest, Inc., 741 F.2d 1555 (9th Cir.1984) (no-shop clause enforceable) with Great Western Producers Co–Operative v. Great Western United Corporation, 200 Colo. 180, 613 P.2d 873 (1980) (agreement to recommend transaction to the shareholders not effectively enforceable).

Fair-price provisions. A *fair-price provision* requires that a supermajority (usually eighty percent) of the voting power of a corporation must approve any merger or similar combination with an acquiror who owns a specified interest in the corporation (usually twenty percent of the voting power). The supermajority vote is not required under certain conditions—most notably, if the transaction is approved by a majority of those directors who are not affiliated with the acquiror and were directors at the time the acquiror reached the specified level of ownership of the company, or if certain minimum-price criteria and procedural requirements are satisfied. A fair-price provision discourages purchasers whose objective is to seek control of a corporation at a relatively cheap price, and discourages accumulations of large blocks, since it reduces the options an acquiror has once it reaches the specified level of shares. M. Lipton & E. Steinberger, Takeovers & Freezeouts § 6.03[2] (1987).

Leveraged buyout. A leveraged buyout is a combination of a management buyout and a high degree of leverage. A *management buyout* (MBO) is the acquisition for cash or non-convertible senior securities of the business of a public corporation, by a newly organized corporation in which members of the former management of the public corporation will have a significant equity interest, pursuant to a merger or other form of combination. See Lowenstein, Management Buyouts, 85 Colum.L.Rev. 730, 732 (1985). *Leverage* involves the use of debt to increase the return on equity. The extent of leverage is measured by the ratio of (i) debt to (ii) debt plus equity. The higher the ratio, the greater the leverage (or, to put it differently, the more highly leveraged the corporation is). A *leveraged buyout* (LBO) is an MBO that is highly leveraged—that is, in which the newly organized acquiring corporation has a very high amount of debt in relation to its equity. Characteristically, an LBO is arranged by a firm that specializes in such transactions, can find investors (or will itself invest) along with senior management in the new firm's securities, and can arrange for (or help arrange for) placement of the massive amount of debt that the new corporation must issue to finance the acquisition of the old corporation's business.

Junk bonds. A *junk bond* is a bond that has an unusually high risk of default (and is therefore below investment grade), but, correspondingly, carries an unusually high yield. (The theory is that by diversification—that is, by holding a portfolio of junk

bonds—investors in junk bonds can insulate themselves from cata-
strophic loss if any one bond issue goes under.)   Because an LBO is
so highly leveraged, much or most of the debt issued to finance an
LBO usually consists of junk bonds.

————

NOTE ON THE WILLIAMS ACT

Tender offers, and the toehold share acquisitions that often
precede them, are regulated in a great number of respects by the
Williams Act (and its amendments), which added sections 13(d),
14(d), and 14(e) to the Securities Exchange Act of 1934.

1. *Toehold acquisitions.*   Under section 13(d), of the Securities Exchange Act, a person who has acquired beneficial ownership
of more than 5% of any class of equity securities registered under
section 12 of the Act must file a Schedule 13D within 10 days of the
acquisition.   The Schedule 13D must include the purchaser's identity and background; the amount and sources of the funds for the
purchase; the purpose of the purchase; any plans with respect to
extraordinary corporate transactions involving the corporation
whose stock has been acquired; and any contracts, arrangements,
or understandings with other persons regarding the corporation's
securities.   For this purpose, the term "person" includes a group.
Merely combining existing shareholders for the purpose of control,
without more, is sufficient to constitute a "group," and trigger the
filing requirements, if the members of the newly constituted group
own more than 5% of the corporation's stock.   Rule 13–5(b); GAF
Corp. v. Milstein, 453 F.2d 709 (2d Cir.1971).

2. *What constitutes a tender offer.*   What constitutes a "tender offer" within the meaning of the Williams Act is not completely
settled.   Purchases made anonymously on the open market almost
certainly do not constitute a tender offer within the meaning of the
Act.   Kennecott Copper Corp. v. Curtiss–Wright Corp., 584 F.2d
1195 (2d Cir.1978); Calumet Industries, Inc. v. MacClure, 464
F.Supp. 19 (N.D.Ill.1978).   As a practical matter, therefore, the
problem arises when an offer is made to a limited number of
potential sellers, rather than to all the shareholders as in a conventional tender offer.   Some courts have adopted an eight-factor test
to determine whether an offer to buy stock is a tender offer under
the Act.   These factors are: (i) Whether the purchasers engage in
active and widespread solicitation of public shareholders.   (ii)
Whether the solicitation is made for a substantial percentage of the
issuer's stock.   (iii) Whether the offer to purchase is made at a
premium over the prevailing market price.   (iv) Whether the terms
of the offer are firm rather than negotiable.   (v) Whether the offer is
contingent on the tender of a fixed number of shares.   (vi) Whether
the offer is open only for a limited person of time.   (vii) Whether
the offerees are under pressure to sell their stock.   (viii) Whether
public announcements of a purchasing program preceded or accom-

panied a rapid accumulation of large amounts of the target's securities. Wellman v. Dickinson, 475 F.Supp. 783 (S.D.N.Y.1979), aff'd on other grounds 682 F.2d 355 (2d Cir.1982), cert. denied 460 U.S. 1069, 103 S.Ct. 1522, 75 L.Ed.2d 946 (1983); SEC v. Carter Hawley Hale Stores, Inc., 760 F.2d 945 (9th Cir.1985).

In Hanson Trust PLC v. SCM Corp., 774 F.2d 47 (2d Cir.1985), the Second Circuit rejected the eight-factor test, and held instead that whether an offer to buy stock constitutes a tender offer under the Williams Act turns on whether there appears to be a likelihood that unless the Act's rules are followed, there will be a substantial risk that solicited shareholders will lack information needed to make a carefully considered appraisal of the proposal put before them. Applying that standard, the Second Circuit held in *Hanson* that the transaction before it was not a tender offer. The target had 22,800 shareholders and offers were made to only six. At least five of the sellers were highly sophisticated professionals, knowledgeable in the market place and well aware of the essential facts needed to exercise their professional skills and to appraise the offer. The sellers were not pressured to sell their shares by any conduct that the Williams Act was designed to alleviate, but only by the forces of the market place. There was no active or widespread advance publicity or public solicitation. The price received by the six sellers was not at a premium over the then-market price. The purchases were not made contingent upon acquiring a fixed minimum number or percentage of the target's outstanding shares. There was no time limit within which the buyer would purchase the target's stock.

3. *Schedule 14D.* Section 14(d) of the Securities Exchange Act requires any person who makes a tender offer for a class of registered equity securities that would result in that person owning more than 5% of the class to file a Schedule 14D containing specific information. The Schedule 14D must contain extensive disclosure of such matters as the offer; the identity of the bidder; past dealings between the bidder and the corporation; the bidder's source of funds; the bidder's purposes and plans concerning the corporation; the bidder's contracts and understandings or relationships with respect to securities of the corporation; financial statements of the bidder, if they are material and the bidder is not an individual; and arrangements between the bidder and those holding important positions with the corporation.

4. *Regulation of the terms of tender offers.* Section 14(d) of the Securities Exchange Act, and rules 14d and 14e, regulate the terms of tender offers. Under these provisions: (i) A tender offer must be held open for at least 20 days. (ii) A tender offer must be open to all security holders of the class of securities subject to the tender offer (the "all holders rule"). (iii) Shareholders must be permitted to withdraw tendered shares during the first 15 days of an offer, or after 60 days if the shares have not been purchased by then. (iv) If the tender offer is oversubscribed, the offeror must purchase on a pro rata basis from among the shares deposited

during the first 10 days, or such longer period as the bidder may designate. (iv) If the tender-offer price is increased, the higher price must be paid to all tendering shareholders—even those who tendered in response to the lower price—and the offer must remain open at least 10 days after notice of the increase is first published.

5. *Obligations of the target's management.* Rule 14e–2 under the Securities Exchange Act requires the target company, no later than 10 business days from the date the tender offer is first published, to give its shareholders a statement disclosing that the target either: (i) recommends acceptance or rejection of the tender offer; (ii) expresses no opinion and is remaining neutral toward the tender offer; or (iii) is unable to take a position with respect to the tender offer. The statement must also include the reason for the position or for the inability to take a position.

6. *Tender offers by issuers.* Under section 13(e) of the Securities Exchange Act and rule 13e, corporations that tender for their own stock ("issuer" or "self" tenders) are subject to obligations similar to those imposed on outside bidders under rules 14d and 14e.

7. *Anti-fraud provision.* Section 14(e) of the Securities Exchange Act prohibits material misstatements, misleading omissions, and fraudulent or manipulative acts, in connection with a tender offer or any solicitation in favor of or in opposition to a tender offer. Section 14(e) is closely comparable to rule 10b–5, except that it does not contain the limiting language, "in connection with the purchase or sale" of securities, found in rule 10b–5.

It is not yet completely clear who may bring an action under section 14(e). A major Supreme Court decision, Piper v. Chris–Craft Industries, Inc., 430 U.S. 1, 97 S.Ct. 926, 51 L.Ed.2d 124 (1977), lays down some important rules, but leaves a number of gaps. Under *Piper,* the *bidder* does not have standing to sue for damages under section 14(e)—particularly a suit for damages against the target corporation's management for false statements made in opposition to the tender offer—on the theory that the Williams Act was designed to protect the target's shareholders. Under this theory, the target corporation itself also would not have standing to sue the bidder for damages under rule 14e. The target corporation, can, however, sue for an injunction against the bidder for violation of section 14(e), since such an injunction will protect the interests of the target's shareholders. Gearhart Industries, Inc. v. Smith International, Inc., 741 F.2d 707 (5th Cir.1984). Based on *Piper,* shareholders of the target have standing to sue for both damages and injunctive relief if they tender their shares on the basis of false and misleading information. The Court did not express a view on suits by nontendering shareholders, but since the statute does not contain the purchaser-seller limitation associated with rule 10b–5, nontendering shareholders can probably sue under section

14(e), provided they can show damage resulting from a violation of that section.

---

9 L. LOSS & J. SELIGMAN, SECURITIES REGULATION 4376–78 (3d ed. 1992). "The big question . . . is what implied liability, if any, survives *Piper,* where the Court expressly reserved its views on (A) whether either the target or its stockholders had standing, and (B) whether a *tender offeror* might obtain injunctive relief as distinct from damages.

"Several Circuits—one of them *since Piper*—have permitted *injunctive* actions by target companies. The First Circuit, in a *pre-Piper* case, recognized target actions for damages as well, as has the Second Circuit in a *post-Piper* damage action by target stockholders under § 14(d)(6), the proration provision. The Second Circuit, in the first appellate opinion under the tender offer provisions, permitted *nontendering stockholders* to join the target company as plaintiffs; stockholders who have tendered do not need § 14(e) because they are classic sellers within Rule 10b–5. On the other hand there is authority that target stockholders may not sue *their own company* for chilling the offer by misrepresenting the offeror's intentions, because the very fact that no offer was ever made precluded the required proof of reliance on misrepresentations made by target management."

UNOCAL CORP. v. MESA PETROLEUM CO.

Supreme Court of Delaware, 1985.
493 A.2d 946.

Before McNEILLY and MOORE, JJ., and TAYLOR, Judge (Sitting by designation pursuant to Del.Const. Art. 4, § 12.)

MOORE, Justice.

We confront an issue of first impression in Delaware—the validity of a corporation's self-tender for its own shares which excludes from participation a stockholder making a hostile tender offer for the company's stock.

The Court of Chancery granted a preliminary injunction to the plaintiffs, Mesa Petroleum Co., Mesa Asset Co., Mesa Partners II, and Mesa Eastern, Inc. (collectively "Mesa")[1], enjoining an exchange offer of the defendant, Unocal Corporation (Unocal) for its own stock. The trial court concluded that a selective exchange offer, excluding Mesa, was legally impermissible. We cannot agree with such a blanket rule. The factual findings of the Vice Chancellor, fully supported by the record, establish that Unocal's board, consist-

---

1. T. Boone Pickens, Jr., is President and Chairman of the Board of Mesa Petroleum and President of Mesa Asset and controls the related Mesa entities.

ing of a majority of independent directors, acted in good faith, and after reasonable investigation found that Mesa's tender offer was both inadequate and coercive. Under the circumstances the board had both the power and duty to oppose a bid it perceived to be harmful to the corporate enterprise. On this record we are satisfied that the device Unocal adopted is reasonable in relation to the threat posed, and that the board acted in the proper exercise of sound business judgment. We will not substitute our views for those of the board if the latter's decision can be "attributed to any rational business purpose." Sinclair Oil Corp. v. Levien, Del.Supr., 280 A.2d 717, 720 (1971). Accordingly, we reverse the decision of the Court of Chancery and order the preliminary injunction vacated.[2]

I.

The factual background of this matter bears a significant relationship to its ultimate outcome.

On April 8, 1985, Mesa, the owner of approximately 13% of Unocal's stock, commenced a two-tier "front loaded" cash tender offer for 64 million shares, or approximately 37%, of Unocal's outstanding stock at a price of $54 per share. The "back-end" was designed to eliminate the remaining publicly held shares by an exchange of securities purportedly worth $54 per share. However, pursuant to an order entered by the United States District Court for the Central District of California on April 26, 1985, Mesa issued a supplemental proxy statement to Unocal's stockholders disclosing that the securities offered in the second-step merger would be highly subordinated, and that Unocal's capitalization would differ significantly from its present structure. Unocal has rather aptly termed such securities "junk bonds".[3]

---

2. This appeal was heard on an expedited basis in light of the pending Mesa tender offer and Unocal exchange offer. We announced our decision to reverse in an oral ruling in open court on May 17, 1985 with the further statement that this opinion would follow shortly thereafter. See infra n. 5.

3. Mesa's May 3, 1985 supplement to its proxy statement states:

(i) following the Offer, the Purchasers would seek to effect a merger of Unocal and Mesa Eastern or an affiliate of Mesa Eastern (the "Merger") in which the remaining Shares would be acquired for a combination of subordinated debt securities and preferred stock; (ii) the securities to be received by Unocal shareholders in the Merger would be subordinated to $2,400 million of debt securities of Mesa Eastern, indebtedness incurred to refinance up to $1,000 million of bank debt which was incurred by affiliates of Mesa Partners II to purchase Shares and to pay

related interest and expenses and all then-existing debt of Unocal; (iii) the corporation surviving the Merger would be responsible for the payment of all securities of Mesa Eastern (including any such securities issued pursuant to the Merger) and the indebtedness referred to in item (ii) above, and such securities and indebtedness would be repaid out of funds generated by the operations of Unocal; (iv) the indebtedness incurred in the Offer and the Merger would result in Unocal being much more highly leveraged, and the capitalization of the corporation surviving the Merger would differ significantly from that of Unocal at present; and (v) in their analyses of cash flows provided by operations of Unocal which would be available to service and repay securities and other obligations of the corporation surviving the Merger, the Purchasers assumed that the capital expenditures and expenditures for exploration of such corporation would be significantly reduced.

Unocal's board consists of eight independent outside directors and six insiders. It met on April 13, 1985, to consider the Mesa tender offer. Thirteen directors were present, and the meeting lasted nine and one-half hours. The directors were given no agenda or written materials prior to the session. However, detailed presentations were made by legal counsel regarding the board's obligations under both Delaware corporate law and the federal securities laws. The board then received a presentation from Peter Sachs on behalf of Goldman Sachs & Co. (Goldman Sachs) and Dillon, Read & Co. (Dillon Read) discussing the bases for their opinions that the Mesa proposal was wholly inadequate. Mr. Sachs opined that the minimum cash value that could be expected from a sale or orderly liquidation for 100% of Unocal's stock was in excess of $60 per share. In making his presentation, Mr. Sachs showed slides outlining the valuation techniques used by the financial advisors, and others, depicting recent business combinations in the oil and gas industry. The Court of Chancery found that the Sachs presentation was designed to apprise the directors of the scope of the analyses performed rather than the facts and numbers used in reaching the conclusion that Mesa's tender offer price was inadequate.

Mr. Sachs also presented various defensive strategies available to the board if it concluded that Mesa's two-step tender offer was inadequate and should be opposed. One of the devices outlined was a self-tender by Unocal for its own stock with a reasonable price range of $70 to $75 per share. The cost of such a proposal would cause the company to incur $6.1–6.5 billion of additional debt, and a presentation was made informing the board of Unocal's ability to handle it. The directors were told that the primary effect of this obligation would be to reduce exploratory drilling, but that the company would nonetheless remain a viable entity.

The eight outside directors, comprising a clear majority of the thirteen members present, then met separately with Unocal's financial advisors and attorneys. Thereafter, they unanimously agreed to advise the board that it should reject Mesa's tender offer as inadequate, and that Unocal should pursue a self-tender to provide the stockholders with a fairly priced alternative to the Mesa proposal. The board then reconvened and unanimously adopted a resolution rejecting as grossly inadequate Mesa's tender offer. Despite the nine and one-half hour length of the meeting, no formal decision was made on the proposed defensive self-tender.

On April 15, the board met again with four of the directors present by telephone and one member still absent.[4] This session lasted two hours. Unocal's Vice President of Finance and its Assistant General Counsel made a detailed presentation of the proposed terms of the exchange offer. A price range between $70

4. Under Delaware law directors may participate in a board meeting by telephone. . . .

and $80 per share was considered, and ultimately the directors agreed upon $72. The board was also advised about the debt securities that would be issued, and the necessity of placing restrictive covenants upon certain corporate activities until the obligations were paid. The board's decisions were made in reliance on the advice of its investment bankers, including the terms and conditions upon which the securities were to be issued. Based upon this advice, and the board's own deliberations, the directors unanimously approved the exchange offer. Their resolution provided that if Mesa acquired 64 million shares of Unocal stock through its own offer (the Mesa Purchase Condition), Unocal would buy the remaining 49% outstanding for an exchange of debt securities having an aggregate par value of $72 per share. The board resolution also stated that the offer would be subject to other conditions that had been described to the board at the meeting, or which were deemed necessary by Unocal's officers, including the exclusion of Mesa from the proposal (the Mesa exclusion). Any such conditions were required to be in accordance with the "purport and intent" of the offer.

Unocal's exchange offer was commenced on April 17, 1985, and Mesa promptly challenged it by filing this suit in the Court of Chancery. On April 22, the Unocal board met again and was advised by Goldman Sachs and Dillon Read to waive the Mesa Purchase Condition as to 50 million shares. This recommendation was in response to a perceived concern of the shareholders that, if shares were tendered to Unocal, no shares would be purchased by either offeror. The directors were also advised that they should tender their own Unocal stock into the exchange offer as a mark of their confidence in it.

Another focus of the board was the Mesa exclusion. Legal counsel advised that under Delaware law Mesa could only be excluded for what the directors reasonably believed to be a valid corporate purpose. The directors' discussion centered on the objective of adequately compensating shareholders at the "back-end" of Mesa's proposal, which the latter would finance with "junk bonds". To include Mesa would defeat that goal, because under the proration aspect of the exchange offer (49%) every Mesa share accepted by Unocal would displace one held by another stockholder. Further, if Mesa were permitted to tender to Unocal, the latter would in effect be financing Mesa's own inadequate proposal.

On April 24, 1985 Unocal issued a supplement to the exchange offer describing the partial waiver of the Mesa Purchase Condition. On May 1, 1985, in another supplement, Unocal extended the withdrawal, proration and expiration dates of its exchange offer to May 17, 1985.

Meanwhile, on April 22, 1985, Mesa amended its complaint in this action to challenge the Mesa exclusion. A preliminary injunction hearing was scheduled for May 8, 1985. However, on April 23, 1985, Mesa moved for a temporary restraining order in response to

Unocal's announcement that it was partially waiving the Mesa Purchase Condition. After expedited briefing, the Court of Chancery heard Mesa's motion on April 26.

On April 29, 1985, the Vice Chancellor temporarily restrained Unocal from proceeding with the exchange offer unless it included Mesa. The trial court recognized that directors could oppose, and attempt to defeat, a hostile takeover which they considered adverse to the best interests of the corporation. However, the Vice Chancellor decided that in a selective purchase of the company's stock, the corporation bears the burden of showing: (1) a valid corporate purpose, and (2) that the transaction was fair to all of the stockholders, including those excluded.

Unocal immediately sought certification of an interlocutory appeal to this Court pursuant to Supreme Court Rule 42(b). On May 1, 1985, the Vice Chancellor declined to certify the appeal on the grounds that the decision granting a temporary restraining order did not decide a legal issue of first impression, and was not a matter to which the decisions of the Court of Chancery were in conflict.

However, in an Order dated May 2, 1985, this Court ruled that the Chancery decision was clearly determinative of substantive rights of the parties, and in fact decided the main question of law before the Vice Chancellor, which was indeed a question of first impression. We therefore concluded that the temporary restraining order was an appealable decision. However, because the Court of Chancery was scheduled to hold a preliminary injunction hearing on May 8 at which there would be an enlarged record on the various issues, action on the interlocutory appeal was deferred pending an outcome of those proceedings.

In deferring action on the interlocutory appeal, we noted that on the record before us we could not determine whether the parties had articulated certain issues which the Vice Chancellor should have an opportunity to consider in the first instance. These included the following:

a) Does the directors' duty of care to the corporation extend to protecting the corporate enterprise in good faith from perceived depredations of others, including persons who may own stock in the company?

b) Have one or more of the plaintiffs, their affiliates, or persons acting in concert with them, either in dealing with Unocal or others, demonstrated a pattern of conduct sufficient to justify a reasonable inference by defendants that a principle objective of the plaintiffs is to achieve selective treatment for themselves by the repurchase of their Unocal shares at a substantial premium?

c) If so, may the directors of Unocal in the proper exercise of business judgment employ the exchange offer to protect the corporation and its shareholders from such tactics? See Pogostin v. Rice, Del.Supr., 480 A.2d 619 (1984).

d) If it is determined that the purpose of the exchange offer was not illegal as a matter of law, have the directors of Unocal carried their burden of showing that they acted in good faith? See Martin v. American Potash & Chemical Corp., 33 Del.Ch. 234, 92 A.2d 295 at 302.

After the May 8 hearing the Vice Chancellor issued an unreported opinion on May 13, 1985 granting Mesa a preliminary injunction. Specifically, the trial court noted that "[t]he parties basically agree that the directors' duty of care extends to protecting the corporation from perceived harm whether it be from third parties or shareholders." The trial court also concluded in response to the second inquiry in the Supreme Court's May 2 order, that "[a]lthough the facts, ... do not appear to be sufficient to prove that Mesa's principle objective is to be bought off at a substantial premium, they do justify a reasonable inference to the same effect."

As to the third and fourth questions posed by this Court, the Vice Chancellor stated that they "appear to raise the more fundamental issue of whether directors owe fiduciary duties to shareholders who they perceive to be acting contrary to the best interests of the corporation as a whole." While determining that the directors' decision to oppose Mesa's tender offer was made in a good faith belief that the Mesa proposal was inadequate, the court stated that the business judgment rule does not apply to a selective exchange offer such as this.

On May 13, 1985 the Court of Chancery certified this interlocutory appeal to us as a question of first impression, and we accepted it on May 14. The entire matter was scheduled on an expedited basis.[5]

II.

The issues we address involve these fundamental questions: Did the Unocal board have the power and duty to oppose a takeover threat it reasonably perceived to be harmful to the corporate enterprise, and if so, is its action here entitled to the protection of the business judgment rule?

Mesa contends that the discriminatory exchange offer violates the fiduciary duties Unocal owes it. Mesa argues that because of the Mesa exclusion the business judgment rule is inapplicable, because the directors by tendering their own shares will derive a financial benefit that is not available to *all* Unocal stockholders. Thus, it is Mesa's ultimate contention that Unocal cannot establish that the exchange offer is fair to *all* shareholders, and argues that the Court of Chancery was correct in concluding that Unocal was unable to meet this burden.

---

5. Such expedition was required by the fact that if Unocal's exchange offer was permitted to proceed, the proration date for the shares entitled to be exchanged was May 17, 1985, while Mesa's tender offer expired on May 23. After acceptance of this appeal on May 14, we received excellent briefs from the parties, heard argument on May 16 and announced our oral ruling in open court at 9:00 a.m. on May 17. *See supra* n. 2.

Unocal answers that it does not owe a duty of "fairness" to Mesa, given the facts here. Specifically, Unocal contends that its board of directors reasonably and in good faith concluded that Mesa's $54 two-tier tender offer was coercive and inadequate, and that Mesa sought selective treatment for itself. Furthermore, Unocal argues that the board's approval of the exchange offer was made in good faith, on an informed basis, and in the exercise of due care. Under these circumstances, Unocal contends that its directors properly employed this device to protect the company and its stockholders from Mesa's harmful tactics.

III.

We begin with the basic issue of the power of a board of directors of a Delaware corporation to adopt a defensive measure of this type. Absent such authority, all other questions are moot. Neither issues of fairness nor business judgment are pertinent without the basic underpinning of a board's legal power to act.

The board has a large reservoir of authority upon which to draw. Its duties and responsibilities proceed from the inherent powers conferred by 8 Del.C. § 141(a), respecting management of the corporation's "business and affairs". Additionally, the powers here being exercised derive from 8 Del.C. § 160(a), conferring broad authority upon a corporation to deal in its own stock. From this it is now well established that in the acquisition of its shares a Delaware corporation may deal selectively with its stockholders, provided the directors have not acted out of a sole or primary purpose to entrench themselves in office. Cheff v. Mathes, Del. Supr., 199 A.2d 548, 554 (1964); Bennett v. Propp, Del.Supr., 187 A.2d 405, 408 (1962); Martin v. American Potash & Chemical Corporation, Del.Supr., 92 A.2d 295, 302 (1952); Kaplan v. Goldsamt, Del.Ch., 380 A.2d 556, 568–569 (1977); Kors v. Carey, Del.Ch., 158 A.2d 136, 140–141 (1960).

Finally, the board's power to act derives from its fundamental duty and obligation to protect the corporate enterprise, which includes stockholders, from harm reasonably perceived, irrespective of its source. See e.g. Panter v. Marshall Field & Co., 646 F.2d 271, 297 (7th Cir.1981); Crouse–Hinds Co. v. Internorth, Inc., 634 F.2d 690, 704 (2d Cir.1980); Heit v. Baird, 567 F.2d 1157, 1161 (1st Cir.1977); Cheff v. Mathes, 199 A.2d at 556; Martin v. American Potash & Chemical Corp., 92 A.2d at 302; Kaplan v. Goldsamt, 380 A.2d at 568–69; Kors v. Carey, 158 A.2d at 141; Northwest Industries, Inc. v. B.F. Goodrich Co., 301 F.Supp. 706, 712 (M.D.Ill.1969). Thus, we are satisfied that in the broad context of corporate governance, including issues of fundamental corporate change, a board of directors is not a passive instrumentality.[8]

---

8. Even in the traditional areas of fundamental corporate change, i.e., charter amendments [8 Del.C. § 242(b)], mergers [8 Del.C. §§ 251(b), 252(c), 253(a), and 254(d)], sale of assets [8 Del.C. § 271(a)], and dissolution [8 Del.C. § 275(a)], director action is a prerequisite to the ultimate disposition of such matters. See also, Smith v. Van Gorkom, Del.Supr., 488 A.2d 858, 888 (1985).

Given the foregoing principles, we turn to the standards by which director action is to be measured. In Pogostin v. Rice, Del.Supr., 480 A.2d 619 (1984), we held that the business judgment rule, including the standards by which director conduct is judged, is applicable in the context of a takeover. Id. at 627. The business judgment rule is a "presumption that in making a business decision the directors of a corporation acted on an informed basis, in good faith and in the honest belief that the action taken was in the best interests of the company." Aronson v. Lewis, Del.Supr., 473 A.2d 805, 812 (1984) (citations omitted). A hallmark of the business judgment rule is that a court will not substitute its judgment for that of the board if the latter's decision can be "attributed to any rational business purpose." Sinclair Oil Corp. v. Levien, Del.Supr., 280 A.2d 717, 720 (1971).

When a board addresses a pending takeover bid it has an obligation to determine whether the offer is in the best interests of the corporation and its shareholders. In that respect a board's duty is no different from any other responsibility it shoulders, and its decision should be no less entitled to the respect they otherwise would be accorded in the realm of business judgment.[9] See also Johnson v. Trueblood, 629 F.2d 287, 292–293 (3d Cir.1980). There are, however, certain caveats to a proper exercise of this function. Because of the omnipresent specter that a board may be acting primarily in its own interests, rather than those of the corporation and its shareholders, there is an enhanced duty which calls for judicial examination at the threshold before the protections of the business judgment rule may be conferred.

This Court has long recognized that:

> We must bear in mind the inherent danger in the purchase of shares with corporate funds to remove a threat to corporate policy when a threat to control is involved. The directors are of necessity confronted with a conflict of interest, and an objective decision is difficult.

Bennett v. Propp, Del.Supr., 187 A.2d 405, 409 (1962). In the face of this inherent conflict directors must show that they had reasonable grounds for believing that a danger to corporate policy and effectiveness existed because of another person's stock ownership. Cheff v. Mathes, 199 A.2d at 554–55. However, they satisfy that burden "by showing good faith and reasonable investigation...." Id. at 555. Furthermore, such proof is materially enhanced, as here, by the approval of a board comprised of a majority of outside independent directors who have acted in accordance with the

---

9. This is a subject of intense debate among practicing members of the bar and legal scholars. Excellent examples of these contending views are: Block & Miller, The Responsibilities and Obligations of Corporate Directors in Take-over Contests, 11 Sec.Reg.L.J. 44 (1983); Easterbrook & Fischel, Takeover Bids, Defensive Tactics, and Shareholders' Welfare, 36 Bus.Law. 1733 (1981); Easterbrook & Fischel, The Proper Role of a Target's Management In Responding to a Tender Offer, 94 Harv.L.Rev. 1161 (1981); Herzel, Schmidt & Davis, Why Corporate Directors Have a Right To Resist Tender Offers, 3 Corp.L.Rev. 107 (1980); Lipton, Takeover Bids in the Target's Boardroom, 35 Bus.Law. 101 (1979).

foregoing standards. See Aronson v. Lewis, 473 A.2d at 812, 815; Puma v. Marriott, Del.Ch., 283 A.2d 693, 695 (1971); Panter v. Marshall Field & Co., 646 F.2d 271, 295 (7th Cir.1981).

IV.

A.

In the board's exercise of corporate power to forestall a take-over bid our analysis begins with the basic principle that corporate directors have a fiduciary duty to act in the best interests of the corporation's stockholders. Guth v. Loft, Inc., Del.Supr., 5 A.2d 503, 510 (1939). As we have noted, their duty of care extends to protecting the corporation and its owners from perceived harm whether a threat originates from third parties or other shareholders.[10] But such powers are not absolute. A corporation does not have unbridled discretion to defeat any perceived threat by any Draconian means available.

The restriction placed upon a selective stock repurchase is that the directors may not have acted solely or primarily out of a desire to perpetuate themselves in office. See Cheff v. Mathes, 199 A.2d at 556; Kors v. Carey, 158 A.2d at 140. Of course, to this is added the further caveat that inequitable action may not be taken under the guise of law. Schnell v. Chris–Craft Industries, Inc., Del.Supr. 285 A.2d 437, 439 (1971). The standard of proof established in Cheff v. Mathes . . . is designed to ensure that a defensive measure to thwart or impede a takeover is indeed motivated by a good faith concern for the welfare of the corporation and its stockholders, which in all circumstances must be free of any fraud or other misconduct. Cheff v. Mathes, 199 A.2d at 554–55. However, this does not end the inquiry.

B.

A further aspect is the element of balance. If a defensive measure is to come within the ambit of the business judgment rule, it must be reasonable in relation to the threat posed. This entails an analysis by the directors of the nature of the takeover bid and its effect on the corporate enterprise. Examples of such concerns may include: inadequacy of the price offered, nature and timing of the offer, questions of illegality, the impact on "constituencies" other than shareholders (i.e., creditors, customers, employees, and perhaps even the community generally), the risk of nonconsummation, and the quality of securities being offered in the exchange. See Lipton and Brownstein, Takeover Responses and Directors' Responsibilities: An Update, p. 7, ABA National Institute on the Dynamics of Corporate Control (December 8, 1983). While not a controlling factor, it also seems to us that a board may reasonably consider the

---

10. It has been suggested that a board's response to a takeover threat should be a passive one. Easterbrook & Fischel, supra, 36 Bus.Law. at 1750. However, that clearly is not the law of Delaware, and as the proponents of this rule of passivity readily concede, it has not been adopted either by courts or state legislatures. Easterbrook & Fischel, supra, 94 Harv.L.Rev. at 1194.

basic stockholder interests at stake, including those of short term speculators, whose actions may have fueled the coercive aspect of the offer at the expense of the long term investor.[11]   Here, the threat posed was viewed by the Unocal board as a grossly inadequate two-tier coercive tender offer coupled with the threat of greenmail.

Specifically, the Unocal directors had concluded that the value of Unocal was substantially above the $54 per share offered in cash at the front end.   Furthermore, they determined that the subordinated securities to be exchanged in Mesa's announced squeeze out of the remaining shareholders in the "back-end" merger were "junk bonds" worth far less than $54.   It is now well recognized that such offers are a classic coercive measure designed to stampede shareholders into tendering at the first tier, even if the price is inadequate, out of fear of what they will receive at the back end of the transaction.   Wholly beyond the coercive aspect of an inadequate two-tier tender offer, the threat was posed by a corporate raider with a national reputation as a "greenmailer".[13]

In adopting the selective exchange offer, the board stated that its objective was either to defeat the inadequate Mesa offer or, should the offer still succeed, provide the 49% of its stockholders, who would otherwise be forced to accept "junk bonds", with $72 worth of senior debt.   We find that both purposes are valid.

However, such efforts would have been thwarted by Mesa's participation in the exchange offer.   First, if Mesa could tender its shares, Unocal would effectively be subsidizing the former's continuing effort to buy Unocal stock at $54 per share.   Second, Mesa could not, by definition, fit within the class of shareholders being protected from its own coercive and inadequate tender offer.

Thus, we are satisfied that the selective exchange offer is reasonably related to the threats posed.   It is consistent with the

---

11. There has been much debate respecting such stockholder interests. One rather impressive study indicates that the stock of over 50 percent of target companies, who resisted hostile takeovers, later traded at higher market prices than the rejected offer price, or were acquired after the tender offer was defeated by another company at a price higher than the offer price. See Lipton, supra 35 Bus.Law. at 106–109, 132–133. Moreover, an update by Kidder Peabody & Company of this study, involving the stock prices of target companies that have defeated hostile tender offers during the period from 1973 to 1982 demonstrates that in a majority of cases the target's shareholders benefited from the defeat. The stock of 81% of the targets studied has, since the tender offer, sold at prices higher than the tender offer price. When adjusted for the time value of money, the figure is 64%. See Lipton & Brownstein, supra ABA Institute at 10. The thesis be-

ing that this strongly supports application of the business judgment rule in response to takeover threats. There is, however, a rather vehement contrary view. See Easterbrook & Fischel, supra 36 Bus.Law. at 1739–1745.

13. The term "greenmail" refers to the practice of buying out a takeover bidder's stock at a premium that is not available to other shareholders in order to prevent the takeover. The Chancery Court noted that "Mesa has made tremendous profits from its takeover activities although in the past few years it has not been successful in acquiring any of the target companies on an unfriendly basis." Moreover, the trial court specifically found that the actions of the Unocal board were taken in good faith to eliminate both the inadequacies of the tender offer and to forestall the payment of "greenmail".

principle that "the minority stockholder shall receive the substantial equivalent in value of what he had before." Sterling v. Mayflower Hotel Corp., Del.Supr., 93 A.2d 107, 114 (1952). See also Rosenblatt v. Getty Oil Co., Del.Supr., 493 A.2d 929, 940 (1985). This concept of fairness, while stated in the merger context, is also relevant in the area of tender offer law. Thus, the board's decision to offer what it determined to be the fair value of the corporation to the 49% of its shareholders, who would otherwise be forced to accept highly subordinated "junk bonds", is reasonable and consistent with the directors' duty to ensure that the minority stockholders receive equal value for their shares.

V.

Mesa contends that it is unlawful, and the trial court agreed, for a corporation to discriminate in this fashion against one shareholder. It argues correctly that no case has ever sanctioned a device that precludes a raider from sharing in a benefit available to all other stockholders. However, as we have noted earlier, the principle of selective stock repurchases by a Delaware corporation is neither unknown nor unauthorized. Cheff v. Mathes, 199 A.2d at 554; Bennett v. Propp, 187 A.2d at 408; Martin v. American Potash & Chemical Corporation, 92 A.2d at 302; Kaplan v. Goldsamt, 380 A.2d 568–569; Kors v. Carey, 158 A.2d at 140–141; 8 Del.C. § 160. The only difference is that heretofore the approved transaction was the payment of "greenmail" to a raider or dissident posing a threat to the corporate enterprise. All other stockholders were denied such favored treatment, and given Mesa's past history of greenmail, its claims here are rather ironic.

However, our corporate law is not static. It must grow and develop in response to, indeed in anticipation of, evolving concepts and needs. Merely because the General Corporation Law is silent as to a specific matter does not mean that it is prohibited. See Providence and Worcester Co. v. Baker, Del.Supr., 378 A.2d 121, 123–124 (1977). In the days when *Cheff, Bennett, Martin* and *Kors* were decided, the tender offer, while not an unknown device, was virtually unused, and little was known of such methods as two-tier "front-end" loaded offers with their coercive effects. Then, the favored attack of a raider was stock acquisition followed by a proxy contest. Various defensive tactics, which provided no benefit whatever to the raider, evolved. Thus, the use of corporate funds by management to counter a proxy battle was approved. Hall v. Trans–Lux Daylight Picture Screen Corp., Del.Supr., 171 A. 226 (1934); Hibbert v. Hollywood Park, Inc., Del.Supr., 457 A.2d 339 (1983). Litigation, supported by corporate funds, aimed at the raider has long been a popular device.

More recently, as the sophistication of both raiders and targets has developed, a host of other defensive measures to counter such ever mounting threats has evolved and received judicial sanction. These include defensive charter amendments and other devices bearing some rather exotic, but apt, names: Crown Jewel, White

Knight, Pac Man, and Golden Parachute. Each has highly selective features, the object of which is to deter or defeat the raider.

Thus, while the exchange offer is a form of selective treatment, given the nature of the threat posed here the response is neither unlawful nor unreasonable. If the board of directors is disinterested, has acted in good faith and with due care, its decision in the absence of an abuse of discretion will be upheld as a proper exercise of business judgment.

To this Mesa responds that the board is not disinterested, because the directors are receiving a benefit from the tender of their own shares, which because of the Mesa exclusion, does not devolve upon *all* stockholders equally. See Aronson v. Lewis, Del.Supr., 473 A.2d 805, 812 (1984). However, Mesa concedes that if the exclusion is valid, then the directors and all other stockholders share the same benefit. The answer of course is that the exclusion is valid, and the directors' participation in the exchange offer does not rise to the level of a disqualifying interest. The excellent discussion in Johnson v. Trueblood, 629 F.2d at 292–293, of the use of the business judgment rule in takeover contests also seems pertinent here.

Nor does this become an "interested" director transaction merely because certain board members are large stockholders. As this Court has previously noted, that fact alone does not create a disqualifying "personal pecuniary interest" to defeat the operation of the business judgment rule. Cheff v. Mathes, 199 A.2d at 554.

Mesa also argues that the exclusion permits the directors to abdicate the fiduciary duties they owe it. However, that is not so. The board continues to owe Mesa the duties of due care and loyalty. But in the face of the destructive threat Mesa's tender offer was perceived to pose, the board had a supervening duty to protect the corporate enterprise, which includes the other shareholders, from threatened harm.

Mesa contends that the basis of this action is punitive, and solely in response to the exercise of its rights of corporate democracy.[14] Nothing precludes Mesa, as a stockholder, from acting in its own self-interest. See e.g., DuPont v. DuPont, 251 Fed. 937 (D.Del. 1918), aff'd 256 Fed. 129 (3d Cir.1918); Ringling Bros.–Barnum & Bailey Combined Shows, Inc. v. Ringling, Del.Supr., 53 A.2d 441, 447 (1947); Heil v. Standard Gas & Electric Co., Del.Ch., 151 A. 303, 304 (1930). But see, Allied Chemical & Dye Corp. v. Steel & Tube Co. of America, Del.Ch., 120 A. 486, 491 (1923) (majority shareholder owes a fiduciary duty to the minority shareholders).

---

14. This seems to be the underlying basis of the trial court's principal reliance on the unreported Chancery decision of Fisher v. Moltz, Del.Ch. No. 6068 (1979), published in 5 Del.J.Corp.L. 530 (1980). However, the facts in *Fisher* are thoroughly distinguishable. There, a corporation offered to repurchase the shares of its former employees, except those of the plaintiffs, merely because the latter were then engaged in lawful competition with the company. No threat to the enterprise was posed, and at best it can be said that the exclusion was motivated by pique instead of a rational corporate purpose.

However, Mesa, while pursuing its own interests, has acted in a manner which a board consisting of a majority of independent directors has reasonably determined to be contrary to the best interests of Unocal and its other shareholders. In this situation, there is no support in Delaware law for the proposition that, when responding to a perceived harm, a corporation must guarantee a benefit to a stockholder who is deliberately provoking the danger being addressed. There is no obligation of self-sacrifice by a corporation and its shareholders in the face of such a challenge.

Here, the Court of Chancery specifically found that the "directors' decision [to oppose the Mesa tender offer] was made in the good faith belief that the Mesa tender offer is inadequate." Given our standard of review under Levitt v. Bouvier, Del.Supr., 287 A.2d 671, 673 (1972), and Application of Delaware Racing Association, Del.Supr., 213 A.2d 203, 207 (1965), we are satisfied that Unocal's board has met its burden of proof. Cheff v. Mathes, 199 A.2d at 555.

VI.

In conclusion, there was directorial power to oppose the Mesa tender offer, and to undertake a selective stock exchange made in good faith and upon a reasonable investigation pursuant to a clear duty to protect the corporate enterprise. Further, the selective stock repurchase plan chosen by Unocal is reasonable in relation to the threat that the board rationally and reasonably believed was posed by Mesa's inadequate and coercive two-tier tender offer. Under those circumstances the board's action is entitled to be measured by the standards of the business judgment rule. Thus, unless it is shown by a preponderance of the evidence that the directors' decisions were primarily based on perpetuating themselves in office, or some other breach of fiduciary duty such as fraud, overreaching, lack of good faith, or being uninformed, a Court will not substitute its judgment for that of the board.

In this case that protection is not lost merely because Unocal's directors have tendered their shares in the exchange offer. Given the validity of the Mesa exclusion, they are receiving a benefit shared generally by all other stockholders except Mesa. In this circumstance the test of Aronson v. Lewis, 473 A.2d at 812, is satisfied. See also Cheff v. Mathes, 199 A.2d at 554. If the stockholders are displeased with the action of their elected representatives, the powers of corporate democracy are at their disposal to turn the board out. Aronson v. Lewis, Del.Supr., 473 A.2d 805, 811 (1984). See also 8 Del.C. §§ 141(k) and 211(b).

With the Court of Chancery's findings that the exchange offer was based on the board's good faith belief that the Mesa offer was inadequate, that the board's action was informed and taken with due care, that Mesa's prior activities justify a reasonable inference that its principle objective was greenmail, and implicitly, that the substance of the offer itself was reasonable and fair to the corporation and its stockholders if Mesa were included, we cannot say that the Unocal directors have acted in such a manner as to have passed an "unintelligent and unadvised judgment". Mitchell v. Highland–Western Glass Co., Del.Ch., 167 A. 831, 833 (1933). The decision of the Court of Chancery is therefore REVERSED, and the preliminary injunction is VACATED.

———

ALI, PRINCIPLES OF CORPORATE GOVERNANCE § 6.02

[See Statutory Supplement]

———

REVLON, INC. v. MacANDREWS & FORBES HOLDINGS, INC., 506 A.2d 173 (Del.1985). "[W]hen Pantry Pride increased its offer to $50 per share, and then to $53, it became apparent to all that the break-up of the company was inevitable. The Revlon board's authorization permitting management to negotiate a merger or buyout with a third party was a recognition that the company was for sale. The duty of the board had thus changed from the preservation of Revlon as a corporate entity to the maximization of the company's value at a sale for the stockholders' benefit. This significantly altered the board's responsibilities under the *Unocal* standards. It no longer faced threats to corporate policy and effectiveness, or to the stockholders' interests, from a grossly inadequate bid. The whole question of defensive measures became moot. The directors' role changed from defenders of the corporate bastion to auctioneers charged with getting the best price for the stockholders at a sale of the company."

———

CAL. CORP. CODE § 1203

[See Statutory Supplement]

———

PARAMOUNT COMMUNICATIONS, INC. v. TIME INC.

Supreme Court of Delaware, 1989.
571 A.2d 1140.

HORSEY, Justice:

Paramount Communications, Inc. ("Paramount") and two other groups of plaintiffs [1] ("Shareholder Plaintiffs"), shareholders of Time

---

1. Plaintiffs in these three consolidated appeals are: (i) Paramount Communica-   tions, Inc. and KDS Acquisition Corp. (collectively "Paramount"); (ii) Literary Part-

Incorporated ("Time"), a Delaware corporation, separately filed suits in the Delaware Court of Chancery seeking a preliminary injunction to halt Time's tender offer for 51% of Warner Communication, Inc.'s ("Warner") outstanding shares at $70 cash per share. The court below consolidated the cases and, following the development of an extensive record, after discovery and an evidentiary hearing, denied plaintiffs' motion. In a 50–page unreported opinion and order entered July 14, 1989, the Chancellor refused to enjoin Time's consummation of its tender offer, concluding that the plaintiffs were unlikely to prevail on the merits. In re Time Incorporated Shareholder Litigation, Del.Ch., C.A. No. 10670, Allen, C. (July 14, 1989).

On the same day, plaintiffs filed in this Court an interlocutory appeal, which we accepted on an expedited basis. Pending the appeal, a stay of execution of Time's tender offer was entered for ten days, or until July 24, 1989, at 5:00 p.m. Following briefing and oral argument, on July 24 we concluded that the decision below should be affirmed. We so held in a brief ruling from the bench and a separate Order entered on that date. The effect of our decision was to permit Time to proceed with its tender offer for Warner's outstanding shares. This is the written opinion articulating the reasons for our July 24 bench ruling. 565 A.2d 280.

The principal ground for reversal, asserted by all plaintiffs, is that Paramount's June 7, 1989 uninvited all-cash, all-shares, "fully negotiable" (though conditional) tender offer for Time triggered duties under Unocal Corp. v. Mesa Petroleum Co., Del.Supr., 493 A.2d 946 (1985), and that Time's board of directors, in responding to Paramount's offer, breached those duties. As a consequence, plaintiffs argue that in our review of the Time board's decision of June 16, 1989 to enter into a revised merger agreement with Warner, Time is not entitled to the benefit and protection of the business judgment rule.

Shareholder Plaintiffs also assert a claim based on Revlon v. MacAndrews & Forbes Holdings, Inc., Del.Supr., 506 A.2d 173 (1986). They argue that the original Time–Warner merger agreement of March 4, 1989 resulted in a change of control which effectively put Time up for sale, thereby triggering *Revlon* duties. Those plaintiffs argue that Time's board breached its *Revlon* duties by failing, in the face of the change of control, to maximize shareholder value in the immediate term.

Applying our standard of review, we affirm the Chancellor's ultimate finding and conclusion under *Unocal*. We find that Paramount's tender offer was reasonably perceived by Time's board to pose a threat to Time and that the Time board's "response" to that threat was, under the circumstances, reasonable and proportionate.

ners L.P., Cablevision Media Partners, L.P., and A. Jerrold Perenchio (collectively "Literary Partners"), suing individually; and (iii) certain other shareholder plaintiffs, suing individually and as an uncertified class.

Applying *Unocal,* we reject the argument that the only corporate threat posed by an all-shares, all-cash tender offer is the possibility of inadequate value.

We also find that Time's board did not by entering into its initial merger agreement with Warner come under a *Revlon* duty either to auction the company or to maximize short-term shareholder value, notwithstanding the unequal share exchange. Therefore, the Time board's original plan of merger with Warner was subject only to a business judgment rule analysis. See Smith v. Van Gorkom, Del.Supr., 488 A.2d 858, 873–74 (1985).[2]

I

Time is a Delaware corporation with its principal offices in New York City. Time's traditional business is publication of magazines and books; however, Time also provides pay television programming through its Home Box Office, Inc. and Cinemax subsidiaries. In addition, Time owns and operates cable television franchises through its subsidiary, American Television and Communication Corporation. During the relevant time period, Time's board consisted of sixteen directors. Twelve of the directors were "outside," nonemployee directors. Four of the directors were also officers of the company. The outside directors included: James F. Bere, chairman of the board and CEO of Borg–Warner Corporation (Time director since 1979); Clifford J. Grum, president and CEO of Temple–Inland, Inc. (Time director since 1980); Henry C. Goodwin, former chairman of Sonat, Inc. (Time directors since 1978); Matina S. Horner, then president of Radcliffe College (Time director since 1975); David T. Kearns, chairman and CEO of Xerox Corporation (Time director since 1978); Donald S. Perkins, former chairman and CEO of Jewel Companies, Inc. (Time director since 1979); Michael D. Dingman, chairman and CEO of The Henley Group, Inc. (Time director since 1978); Edward S. Finkelstein, chairman and CEO of Macy's Inc. (Time director since 1984); John R. Opel, former chairman and CEO of IBM Corporation (Time director since 1984); Arthur Temple, chairman of Temple–Inland, Inc. (Time director since 1983); Clifton R. Wharton, Jr., chairman and CEO of The Henley Group, Inc. (Time director since 1978); and Henry R. Luce III, president of The Henry Luce Foundation, Inc. (Time director since 1967). Mr. Luce, the son of the founder of Time, individually and in a representative capacity controlled 4.2% of the outstanding Time stock. The inside officer directors were: J.

---

2. In the specific context of a proposed merger of domestic corporations, a director has a duty under 8 Del.C. § 251(b), along with his fellow directors, to act in an informed and deliberate manner in determining whether to approve an agreement of merger before submitting the proposal to the stockholders. Certainly in the merger context, a director may not abdicate that duty by leaving to the shareholders alone the decision to approve or disapprove the agreement. See Beard v. Elster, Del.Supr., 160 A.2d 731, 737 (1960). Only an agreement of merger satisfying the requirements of 8 Del.C. § 251(b) may be submitted to the shareholders under § 251(c). See generally Aronson v. Lewis, Del.Supr., 473 A.2d 805, 811–13 (1984); see also Pogostin v. Rice, Del.Supr., 480 A.2d 619 (1984); Smith v. Van Gorkom, Del.Supr., 488 A.2d 858, 873 (footnote omitted).

Richard Munro, Time's chairman and CEO since 1980; N.J. Nicholas, Jr., president and chief operating officer of the company since 1986; Gerald M. Levin, vice chairman of the board; and Jason D. McManus, editor-in-chief of *Time* magazine and a board member since 1988.[3]

As early as 1983 and 1984, Time's executive board began considering expanding Time's operations into the entertainment industry. In 1987, Time established a special committee of executives to consider and propose corporate strategies for the 1990s. The consensus of the committee was that Time should move ahead in the area of ownership and creation of video programming. This expansion, as the Chancellor noted, was predicated upon two considerations: first, Time's desire to have greater control, in terms of quality and price, over the film products delivered by way of its cable network and franchises; and second, Time's concern over the increasing globalization of the world economy. Some of Time's outside directors, especially Luce and Temple, had opposed this move as a threat to the editorial integrity and journalistic focus of Time.[4] Despite this concern, the board saw the advantages of a vertically integrated video enterprise to complement Time's existing HBO and cable networks would enable it to compete on a global basis.

In late spring of 1987, a meeting took place between Steve Ross, CEO of Warner Brothers, and Nicholas of Time. Ross and Nicholas discussed the possibility of a joint venture between the two companies through the creation of a jointly-owned cable company. Time would contribute its cable system and HBO. Warner would contribute its cable system and provide access to Warner Brothers Studio. The resulting venture would be a larger, more efficient cable network, able to produce and distribute its own movies on a worldwide basis. Ultimately the parties abandoned this plan, determining that it was impractical for several reasons, chief among them being tax considerations.

On August 11, 1987, Gerald M. Levin, Time's vice chairman and chief strategist, wrote J. Richard Munro a confidential memorandum in which he strongly recommended a strategic consolidation with Warner. In June 1988, Nicholas and Munro sent to each outside

---

3. Four directors, Arthur Temple, Henry C. Goodrich, Clifton R. Wharton, and Clifford J. Grum, have since resigned from Time's board. The Chancellor found, with the exception of Temple, their resignations to reflect more a willingness to step down than disagreement or dissension over the Time–Warner merger. Temple did not choose to continue to be associated with a corporation that was expanding into the entertainment field. Under the board of the combined Time–Warner corporation, the number of Time directors, as well as Warner directors, was limited to twelve each.

4. The primary concern of Time's outside directors was the preservation of the "Time Culture." They believed that Time had become recognized in this country as an institution built upon a foundation of journalistic integrity. Time's management made a studious effort to refrain from involvement in Time's editorial policy. Several of Time's outside directors feared that a merger with an entertainment company would divert Time's focus from news journalism and threaten the Time Culture.

director a copy of the "comprehensive long-term planning document" prepared by the committee of Time executives that had been examining strategies for the 1990s. The memo included reference to and a description of Warner as a potential acquisition candidate.

Thereafter, Munro and Nicholas held meetings with Time's outside directors to discuss, generally, long-term strategies for Time and, specifically, a combination with Warner. Nearly a year later, Time's board reached the point of serious discussion of the "nuts and bolts" of a consolidation with an entertainment company. On July 21, 1988, Time's board met, with all outside directors present. The meeting's purpose was to consider Time's expansion into the entertainment industry on a global scale. Management presented the board with a profile of various entertainment companies in addition to Warner, including Disney, 20th Century Fox, Universal, and Paramount.

Without any definitive decision on choice of a company, the board approved in principle a strategic plan for Time's expansion. The board gave management the "go-ahead" to continue discussions with Warner concerning the possibility of a merger. With the exception of Temple and Luce, most of the outside directors agreed that a merger involving expansion into the entertainment field promised great growth opportunity for Time. Temple and Luce remained unenthusiastic about Time's entry into the entertainment field. See supra note 2.

The board's consensus was that a merger of Time and Warner was feasible, but only if Time controlled the board of the resulting corporation and thereby preserved a management committed to Time's journalistic integrity. To accomplish this goal, the board stressed the importance of carefully defining in advance the corporate governance provisions that would control the resulting entity. Some board members expressed concern over whether such a business combination would place Time "*in play.*" The board discussed the wisdom of adopting further defensive measures to lessen such a possibility.[5]

Of a wide range of companies considered by Time's board as possible merger candidates, Warner Brothers, Paramount, Columbia, M.C.A., Fox, MGM, Disney, and Orion, the board, in July 1988, concluded that Warner was the superior candidate for a consolidation. Warner stood out on a number of counts. Warner had just acquired Lorimar and its film studios. Time–Warner could make movies and television shows for use on HBO. Warner had an international distribution system, which Time could use to sell films, videos, books and magazines. Warner was a giant in the music and recording business, an area into which Time wanted to expand. None of the other companies considered had the musical clout of

---

5. Time had in place a panoply of defensive devices, including a staggered board, a "poison pill" preferred stock rights plan triggered by an acquisition of 15% of the company, a fifty-day notice period for shareholder motions, and restrictions on shareholders' ability to call a meeting or act by consent.

Warner. Time and Warner's cable systems were compatible and could be easily integrated; none of the other companies considered presented such a compatible cable partner. Together, Time and Warner would control half of New York City's cable system; Warner had cable systems in Brooklyn and Queens; and Time controlled cable systems in Manhattan and Queens. Warner's publishing company would integrate well with Time's established publishing company. Time sells hardcover books and magazines, and Warner sells softcover books and comics.[6] Time–Warner could sell all of these publications and Warner's videos by using Time's direct mailing network and Warner's international distribution system. Time's network could be used to promote and merchandise Warner's movies.

In August 1988, Levin, Nicholas, and Munro, acting on instructions from Time's board, continued to explore a business combination with Warner. By letter dated August 4, 1988, management informed the outside directors of proposed corporate governance provisions to be discussed with Warner. The provisions incorporated the recommendations of several of Time's outside directors.

From the outset, Time's board favored an all-cash or cash and securities acquisition of Warner as the basis for consolidation. Bruce Wasserstein, Time's financial advisor, also favored an outright purchase of Warner. However, Steve Ross, Warner's CEO, was adamant that a business combination was only practicable on a stock-for-stock basis. Warner insisted on a stock swap in order to preserve its shareholders' equity in the resulting corporation. Time's officers, on the other hand, made it abundantly clear that Time would be the acquiring corporation and that Time would control the resulting board. Time refused to permit itself to be cast as the "acquired" company.

Eventually Time acquiesced in Warner's insistence on a stock-for-stock deal, but talks broke down over corporate governance issues. Time wanted Ross' position as a co-CEO to be temporary and wanted Ross to retire in five years. Ross, however, refused to set a time for his retirement and viewed Time's proposal as indicating a lack of confidence in his leadership. Warner considered it vital that their executives and creative staff not perceive Warner as selling out to Time. Time's request of a guarantee that Time would dominate the CEO succession was objected to as inconsistent with the concept of a Time–Warner merger "of equals." Negotiations ended when the parties reached an impasse. Time's board refused to compromise on its position on corporate governance. Time, and particularly its outside directors, viewed the corporate governance provisions as critical for preserving the "Time Culture" through a pro-Time management at the top. See supra note 4.

---

6. In contrast, Paramount's publishing endeavors were in the areas of professional volumes and text books. Time's board did not find Paramount's publishing as compatible as Warner's publishing efforts.

Throughout the fall of 1988 Time pursued its plan of expansion into the entertainment field; Time held informal discussions with several companies, including Paramount. Capital Cities/ABC approached Time to propose a merger. Talks terminated, however, when Capital Cities/ABC suggested that it was interested in purchasing Time or in controlling the resulting board. Time steadfastly maintained it was not placing itself up for sale.

Warner and Time resumed negotiations in January 1989. The catalyst for the resumption of talks was a private dinner between Steve Ross and Time outside director, Michael Dingman. Dingman was able to convince Ross that the transitional nature of the proposed co–CEO arrangement did not reflect a lack of confidence in Ross. Ross agreed that this course was best for the company and a meeting between Ross and Munro resulted. Ross agreed to retire in five years and let Nicholas succeed him. Negotiations resumed and many of the details of the original stock-for-stock exchange agreement remained intact. In addition, Time's senior management agreed to long-term contracts.

Time insider directors Levin and Nicholas met with Warner's financial advisors to decide upon a stock exchange ratio. Time's board had recognized the potential need to pay a premium in the stock ratio in exchange for dictating the governing arrangement of the new Time–Warner. Levin and outside director Finkelstein were the primary proponents of paying a premium to protect the "Time Culture." The board discussed premium rates of 10%, 15% and 20%. Wasserstein also suggested paying a premium for Warner due to Warner's rapid growth rate. The market exchange ratio of Time stock for Warner stock was .38 in favor of Warner. Warner's financial advisors informed the board that any exchange rate over .400 was a fair deal and any exchange rate over .450 was "one hell of a deal." The parties ultimately agreed upon an exchange rate favoring Warner of .465. On that basis, Warner stockholders would own slightly over 62%[7] of the common stock of Time–Warner.

On March 3, 1989, Time's board, with all but one director in attendance, met and unanimously approved the stock-for-stock merger with Warner. Warner's board likewise approved the merger. The agreement called for Warner to be merged into a wholly-owned Time subsidiary with Warner becoming the surviving corporation. The common stock of Warner would then be converted into common stock of Time at the agreed upon ratio. Thereafter, the name of Time would be changed to Time–Warner, Inc.

The rules of the New York Stock Exchange required that Time's issuance of shares to effectuate the merger be approved by a vote of Time's stockholders. The Delaware General Corporation Law required approval of the merger by a majority of the Warner stockholders. Delaware law did not require any vote by Time stockhold-

---

7. As was noted in the briefs and at oral argument, this figure is somewhat misleading because it does not take into consideration the number of individuals who owned stock in both companies.

ers. The Chancellor concluded that the agreement was the product of "an arms-length negotiation between two parties seeking individual advantage through mutual action."

The resulting company would have a 24–member board, with 12 members representing each corporation. The company would have co–CEO's, at first Ross and Munro, then Ross and Nicholas, and finally, after Ross' retirement, ... Nicholas alone. The board would create an editorial committee with a majority of members representing Time. A similar entertainment committee would be controlled by Warner board members. A two-thirds supermajority vote was required to alter CEO successions but an earlier proposal to have supermajority protection for the editorial committee was abandoned. Warner's board suggested raising the compensation levels for Time's senior management under the new corporation. Warner's management, as with most entertainment executives, received higher salaries than comparable executives in news journalism. Time's board, however, rejected Warner's proposal to equalize the salaries of the two management teams.

At its March 3, 1989 meeting, Time's board adopted several defensive tactics. Time entered an automatic share exchange agreement with Warner. Time would receive 17,292,747 shares of Warner's outstanding common stock (9.4%) and Warner would receive 7,080,016 shares of Time's outstanding common stock (11.1%). Either party could trigger the exchange. Time sought out and paid for "confidence" letters from various banks with which they did business. In these letters, the banks promised not to finance any third-party attempt to acquire Time. Time argues these agreements served only to preserve the confidential relationship between itself and the banks. The Chancellor found these agreements to be inconsequential and futile attempts to "dry up" money for a hostile takeover. Time also agreed to a "no-shop" clause, preventing Time from considering any other consolidation proposal, thus relinquishing its power to consider other proposals, regardless of their merits. Time did so at Warner's insistence. Warner did not want to be left "on the auction block" for an unfriendly suitor, if Time were to withdraw from the deal.

Time's board simultaneously established a special committee of outside directors, Finkelstein, Kearns, and Opel, to oversee the merger. The committee's assignment was to resolve any impediments that might arise in the course of working out the details of the merger and its consummation.

Time representatives lauded the lack of debt to the United States Senate and to the President of the United States. Public reaction to the announcement of the merger was positive. Time–Warner would be a media colossus with international scope. The board scheduled the stockholder vote for June 23; and a May 1 record date was set. On May 24, 1989, Time sent out extensive proxy statements to the stockholders regarding the approval vote on the merger. In the meantime, with the merger proceeding without impediment, the special committee had concluded, shortly after its creation, that it was not necessary either to retain independent consultants, legal or financial, or even to meet. Time's board was unanimously in favor of the proposed merger with Warner; and, by the end of May, the Time–Warner merger appeared to be an accomplished fact.

On June 7, 1989, these wishful assumptions were shattered by Paramount's surprising announcement of its all-cash offer to purchase all outstanding shares of Time for $175 per share. The following day, June 8, the trading price of Time's stock rose from $126 to $170 per share. Paramount's offer was said to be "fully negotiable."[8]

Time found Paramount's "fully negotiable" offer to be in fact subject to at least three conditions. First, Time had to terminate its merger agreement and stock exchange agreement with Warner, and remove certain other of its defensive devices, including the redemption of Time's shareholder rights. Second, Paramount had to obtain the required cable franchise transfers from Time in a fashion acceptable to Paramount in its sole discretion. Finally, the offer depended upon a judicial determination that section 203 of the General Corporate Law of Delaware (The Delaware Anti–Takeover Statute) was inapplicable to any Time–Paramount merger. While Paramount's board had been privately advised that it could take months, perhaps over a year, to forge and consummate the deal, Paramount's board publicly proclaimed its ability to close the offer by July 5, 1989. Paramount executives later conceded that none of its directors believed that July 5th was a realistic date to close the transaction.

On June 8, 1989, Time formally responded to Paramount's offer. Time's chairman and CEO, J. Richard Munro, sent an aggressively worded letter to Paramount's CEO, Martin Davis. Munro's letter attacked Davis' personal integrity and called Paramount's offer "smoke and mirrors." Time's nonmanagement directors were not shown the letter before it was sent. However, at a board meeting that same day, all members endorsed management's response as well as the letter's content.

Over the following eight days, Time's board met three times to discuss Paramount's $175 offer. The board viewed Paramount's offer as inadequate and concluded that its proposed merger with Warner was the better course of action. Therefore, the board declined to open any negotiations with Paramount and held steady its course toward a merger with Warner.

In June, Time's board of directors met several times. During the course of their June meetings, Time's outside directors met frequently without management, officers or directors being present.

---

8. Subsequently, it was established that Paramount's board had decided as early as March 1989 to move to acquire Time. However, Paramount management intentionally delayed publicizing its proposal until Time had mailed to its stockholders its Time–Warner merger proposal along with the required proxy statements.

At the request of the outside directors, corporate counsel was present during the board meetings and, from time to time, the management directors were asked to leave the board sessions. During the course of these meetings, Time's financial advisors informed the board that, on an auction basis, Time's per share value was materially higher than Warner's $175 per share offer.[9] On this basis, the board concluded that Paramount's $175 offer was inadequate.

At these June meetings, certain Time directors expressed their concern that Time stockholders would not comprehend the long-term benefits of the Warner merger. Large quantities of Time shares were held by institutional investors. The board feared that even though there appeared to be wide support for the Warner transaction, Paramount's cash premium would be a tempting prospect to these investors. In mid-June, Time sought permission from the New York Stock Exchange to alter its rules and allow the Time–Warner merger to proceed without stockholder approval. Time did so at Warner's insistence. The New York Stock Exchange rejected Time's request on June 15; and on that day, the value of Time stock reached $182 per share.

The following day, June 16, Time's board met to take up Paramount's offer. The board's prevailing belief was that Paramount's bid presented a threat to Time's control of its own destiny and retention of the "Time Culture." Even after Time's financial advisors made another presentation of Paramount and its business attributes, Time's board maintained its position that a combination within Warner presented greater potential for Time. Warner presented Time with a much desired production capability and an established international marketing chain. Time's advisors presented the board with various options, including defensive measures. The board considered and rejected the idea of purchasing Paramount in a "Pac Man" defense.[10] The board considered other defenses as well, including a recapitalization, the acquisition of another company, and a material change in the present capitalization structure or dividend policy. The board determined to retain its same advisors even in light of the changed circumstances. The board rescinded its agreement to pay its advisors a bonus based on the consummation of the Time–Warner merger and agreed to pay a flat fee for any advice the advisors rendered. Finally, Time's board formally rejected Paramount's offer.[11]

At the same meeting, Time's board decided to recast its consolidation with Warner into an outright cash and securities acquisition of Warner by Time; and Time so informed Warner. Time accord-

---

9. Time's advisors estimated the value of Time in a control premium situation to be significantly higher than the value of Time in other than a sale situation.

10. In a "Pac Man" defense, Time would launch a tender offer for the stock of Paramount, thus consuming its rival. Mor-

an v. Household Intern., Inc., Del.Supr., 500 A.2d 1346, 1350 n. 6 (1985).

11. Meanwhile, Time had already begun erecting impediments to Paramount's offer. Time encouraged local cable franchises to sue Paramount to prevent it from easily obtaining the franchises.

ingly restructured its proposal to acquire Warner as follows: Time would make an immediate all-cash offer for 51% of Warner's outstanding stock at $70 per share. The remaining 49% would be purchased at some later date for a mixture of cash and securities worth $70 per share. To provide the funds required for its outright acquisition of Warner, Time would assume 7–10 billion dollars worth of debt, thus eliminating one of the principal transaction-related benefits of the original merger agreement. Nine billion dollars of the total purchase price would be allocated to the purchase of Warner's goodwill.

Warner agreed but insisted on certain terms. Warner sought a control premium and guarantees that the governance provisions found in the original merger agreement would remain intact. Warner further sought agreements that Time would not employ its poison pill against Warner and that, unless enjoined, Time would be legally bound to complete the transaction. Time's board agreed to these last measures only at the insistence of Warner. For its part, Time was assured of its ability to extend its efforts into production arenas and international markets, all the while maintaining the Time identity and culture. The Chancellor found the initial Time–Warner transaction to have been negotiated at arms length and the restructured Time–Warner transaction to have resulted from Paramount's offer and its expected effect on a Time shareholder vote.

On June 23, 1989, Paramount raised its all-cash offer to buy Time's outstanding stock to $200 per share. Paramount still professed that all aspects of the offer were negotiable. Time's board met on June 26, 1989 and formally rejected Paramount's $200 per share second offer. The board reiterated its belief that, despite the $25 increase, the offer was still inadequate. The Time board maintained that the Warner transaction offered a greater long-term value for the stockholders and, unlike Paramount, did not pose a threat to Time's survival and its "culture." Paramount then filed this action in the Court of Chancery.

II

The Shareholder Plaintiffs first assert a *Revlon* claim. They contend that the March 4 Time–Warner agreement effectively put Time up for sale, triggering *Revlon* duties, requiring Time's board to enhance short-term shareholder value and to treat all other interested acquirors on an equal basis. The Shareholder Plaintiffs base this argument on two facts: (i) the ultimate Time–Warner exchange ratio of .465 favoring Warner, resulting in Warner shareholders' receipt of 62% of the combined company; and (ii) the subjective intent of Time's directors as evidenced in their statements that the market might perceive the Time–Warner merger as putting Time up "for sale" and their adoption of various defensive measures.

The Shareholder Plaintiffs further contend that Time's directors, in structuring the original merger transaction to be "takeover-proof," triggered *Revlon* duties by foreclosing their shareholders from any prospect of obtaining a control premium. In short, plaintiffs argue that Time's board's decision to merge with Warner imposed a fiduciary duty to maximize immediate share value and not erect unreasonable barriers to further bids. Therefore, they argue, the Chancellor erred in finding: that Paramount's bid for Time did not place Time "for sale"; that Time's transaction with Warner did not result in any transfer of control; and that the combined Time–Warner was not so large as to preclude the possibility of the stockholders of Time–Warner receiving a future control premium.

Paramount asserts only a *Unocal* claim in which the shareholder plaintiffs join. Paramount contends that the Chancellor, in applying the first part of the *Unocal* test, erred in finding that Time's board had reasonable grounds to believe that Paramount posed both a legally cognizable threat to Time shareholders and a danger to Time's corporate policy and effectiveness. Paramount also contests the court's finding that Time's board made a reasonable and objective investigation of Paramount's offer so as to be informed before rejecting it. Paramount further claims that the court erred in applying *Unocal*'s second part in finding Time's response to be "reasonable." Paramount points primarily to the preclusive effect of the revised agreement which denied Time shareholders the opportunity both to vote on the agreement and to respond to Paramount's tender offer. Paramount argues that the underlying motivation of Time's board in adopting these defensive measures was management's desire to perpetuate itself in office.

The Court of Chancery posed the pivotal question presented by this case to be: Under what circumstances must a board of directors abandon an in-place plan of corporate development in order to provide its shareholders with the option to elect and realize an immediate control premium? As applied to this case, the question becomes: Did Time's board, having developed a strategic plan of global expansion to be launched through a business combination with Warner, come under a fiduciary duty to jettison its plan and put the corporation's future in the hands of its shareholders?

While we affirm the result reached by the Chancellor, we think it unwise to place undue emphasis upon long-term versus short-term corporate strategy. Two key predicates underpin our analysis. First, Delaware law imposes on a board of directors the duty to manage the business and affairs of the corporation. 8 Del.C. § 141(a). This broad mandate includes a conferred authority to set a corporate course of action, including time frame, designed to enhance corporate profitability. Thus, the question of "long-term" versus "short-term" values is largely irrelevant because directors, generally, are obliged to charter a course for a corporation which is in its best interests without regard to a fixed investment horizon. Second, absent a limited set of circumstances as defined under *Revlon,* a board of directors, while always required to act in an informed manner, is not under any *per se* duty to maximize shareholder value in the short term, even in the context of a takeover.[12] In our view, the pivotal question presented by this case is: "Did Time, by entering into the proposed merger with Warner, put itself up for sale?" A resolution of that issue through application of *Revlon* has a significant bearing upon the resolution of the derivative *Unocal* issue.

A.

We first take up plaintiffs' principal *Revlon* argument, summarized above. In rejecting this argument, the Chancellor found the original Time–Warner merger agreement not to constitute a "change of control" and concluded that the transaction did not trigger *Revlon* duties. The Chancellor's conclusion is premised on a finding that "[b]efore the merger agreement was signed, control of the corporation existed in a fluid aggregation of unaffiliated shareholders representing a voting majority—in other words, in the market." The Chancellor's findings of fact are supported by the record and his conclusion is correct as a matter of law. However, we premise our rejection of plaintiffs' *Revlon* claim on different grounds, namely, the absence of any substantial evidence to conclude that Time's board, in negotiating with Warner, made the dissolution or breakup of the corporate entity inevitable, as was the case in *Revlon.*

Under Delaware law there are, generally speaking and without excluding other possibilities, two circumstances which may implicate *Revlon* duties. The first, and clearer one, is when a corporation initiates an active bidding process seeking to sell itself or to effect a business reorganization involving a clear break-up of the company. See, e.g., Mills Acquisition Co. v. Macmillan, Inc., Del. Supr., 559 A.2d 1261 (1989). However, *Revlon* duties may also be triggered where, in response to a bidder's offer, a target abandons its long-term strategy and seeks an alternative transaction also involving the breakup of the company.[13] Thus, in *Revlon,* when the board responded to Pantry Pride's offer by contemplating a "bust-up" sale of assets in a leveraged acquisition, we imposed upon the board a duty to maximize immediate shareholder value and an obligation to auction the company fairly. If, however, the board's reaction to a hostile tender offer is found to constitute only a defensive response and not an abandonment of the corporation's continued existence, *Revlon* duties are not triggered, though *Unocal*

12. Thus, we endorse the Chancellor's conclusion that it is not a breach of faith for directors to determine that the present stock market price of shares is not representative of true value or that there may indeed be several market values for any corporation's stock. We have so held in another context. See *Van Gorkom,* 488 A.2d at 876.

13. As we stated in *Revlon,* in both such cases, "[t]he duty of the board [has] changed from the preservation of . . . [the] corporate entity to the maximization of the company's value at a sale for the stockholder's benefit. . . . [The board] no longer face[s] threats to corporate policy and effectiveness, or to the stockholders' interests, from a grossly inadequate bid." Revlon v.

duties attach.[14] See, e.g., Ivanhoe Partners v. Newmont Mining Corp., Del.Supr., 535 A.2d 1334, 1345 (1987).

The plaintiffs insist that even though the original Time–Warner agreement may not have worked "an objective change of control," the transaction made a "sale" of Time inevitable. Plaintiffs rely on the subjective intent of Time's board of directors and principally upon certain board members' expressions of concern that the Warner transaction *might* be viewed as effectively putting Time up for sale. Plaintiffs argue that the use of a lock-up agreement, a no-shop clause, and so-called "dry-up" agreements prevented shareholders from obtaining a control premium in the immediate future and thus violated *Revlon.*

We agree with the Chancellor that such evidence is entirely insufficient to invoke *Revlon* duties; and we decline to extend *Revlon's* application to corporate transactions simply because they might be construed as putting a corporation either "in play" or "up for sale." See Citron v. Fairchild Camera, Del.Supr., 569 A.2d 53 (1989); *Macmillan,* 559 A.2d at 1285 n. 35. The adoption of structural safety devices alone does not trigger *Revlon.*[15] Rather, as the Chancellor stated, such devices are properly subject to a *Unocal* analysis.

Finally, we do not find in Time's recasting of its merger agreement with Warner from a share exchange to a share purchase a basis to conclude that Time had either abandoned its strategic plan or made a sale of Time inevitable. The Chancellor found that although the merged Time–Warner company would be large (with a value approaching approximately $30 billion), recent takeover cases have proven that acquisition of the combined company might nonetheless be possible. In re Time Incorporated Shareholder Litigation, Del.Ch., C.A. No. 10670, Allen, C. (July 14, 1989), slip op. at 56. The legal consequence is that *Unocal* alone applies to determine whether the business judgment rule attaches to the revised agreement. Plaintiffs' analogy to *Macmillan* thus collapses and plaintiffs' reliance on *Macmillan* is misplaced.

MacAndrews & Forbes Holdings, Inc., Del. Supr., 506 A.2d 173, 182 (1986).

14. Within the auction process, any action taken by the board must be reasonably related to the threat posed or reasonable in relation to the advantage sought, see Mills Acquisition Co. v. Macmillan, Inc., Del. Supr., 559 A.2d 1261, 1288 (1989). Thus, a *Unocal* analysis may be appropriate when a corporation is in a *Revlon* situation and *Revlon* duties may be triggered by a defensive action taken in response to a hostile offer. Since *Revlon,* we have stated that differing treatment of various bidders is not actionable when such action reasonably relates to achieving the best price available for the stockholders. *Macmillan,* 559 A.2d at 1286–87.

15. Although the legality of the various safety devices adopted to protect the original agreement is not a central issue, there is substantial evidence to support each of the trial court's related conclusions. Thus, the court found that the concept of the Share Exchange Agreement predated any takeover threat by Paramount and had been adopted for a rational business purpose: to deter Time and Warner from being "put in play" by their March 4 Agreement. The court further found that Time had adopted the "no-shop" clause at Warner's insistence and for Warner's protection. Finally, although certain aspects of the "dry-up" agreements were suspect on their face, we concur in the Chancellor's view that in this case they were inconsequential.

B.

We turn now to plaintiffs' *Unocal* claim. We begin by noting, as did the Chancellor, that our decision does not require us to pass on the wisdom of the board's decision to enter into the original Time–Warner agreement. That is not a court's task. Our task is simply to review the record to determine whether there is sufficient evidence to support the Chancellor's conclusion that the initial Time–Warner agreement was the product of a proper exercise of business judgment. *Macmillan,* 559 A.2d at 1288.

We have purposely detailed the evidence of the Time board's deliberative approach, beginning in 1983–84, to expand itself. Time's decision in 1988 to combine with Warner was made only after what could be fairly characterized as an exhaustive appraisal of Time's future as a corporation. After concluding in 1983–84 that the corporation must expand to survive, and beyond journalism into entertainment, the board combed the field of available entertainment companies. By 1987 Time had focused upon Warner; by late July 1988 Time's board was convinced that Warner would provide the best "fit" for Time to achieve its strategic objectives. The record attests to the zealousness of Time's executives, fully supported by their directors, in seeing to the preservation of Time's "culture," i.e., its perceived editorial integrity in journalism. We find ample evidence in the record to support the Chancellor's conclusion that the Time board's decision to expand the business of the company through its March 3 merger with Warner was entitled to the protection of the business judgment rule. See Aronson v. Lewis, Del.Supr., 473 A.2d 805, 812 (1984).

The Chancellor reached a different conclusion in addressing the Time–Warner transaction as revised three months later. He found that the revised agreement was defense-motivated and designed to avoid the potentially disruptive effect that Paramount's offer would have had on consummation of the proposed merger were it put to a shareholder vote. Thus, the court declined to apply the traditional business judgment rule to the revised transaction and instead analyzed the Time board's June 16 decision under *Unocal.* The court ruled that *Unocal* applied to all director actions taken, following receipt of Paramount's hostile tender offer, that were reasonably determined to be defensive. Clearly that was a correct ruling and no party disputes that ruling.

In *Unocal,* we held that before the business judgment rule is applied to a board's adoption of a defensive measure, the burden will lie with the board to prove (a) reasonable grounds for believing that a danger to corporate policy and effectiveness existed; and (b) that the defensive measure adopted was reasonable in relation to the threat posed. *Unocal,* 493 A.2d 946. Directors satisfy the first part of the *Unocal* test by demonstrating good faith and reasonable investigation. We have repeatedly stated that the refusal to entertain an offer may comport with a valid exercise of a board's business judgment. See, e.g., *MacMillan,* 559 A.2d at 1285 n. 35; *Van*

Gorkom, 488 A.2d at 881; Pogostin v. Rice, Del.Supr., 480 A.2d 619, 627 (1984).

Unocal involved a two-tier, highly coercive tender offer. In such a case, the threat is obvious: shareholders may be compelled to tender to avoid being treated adversely in the second stage of the transaction. Accord *Ivanhoe,* 535 at 1344. In subsequent cases, the Court of Chancery has suggested that an all-cash, all-shares offer, falling within a range of values that a shareholder might reasonably prefer, cannot constitute a legally recognized "threat" to shareholder interests sufficient to withstand a *Unocal* analysis. AC Acquisitions Corp. v. Anderson, Clayton & Co., Del.Ch., 519 A.2d 103 (1986); see Grand Metropolitan, PLC v. Pillsbury Co., Del.Ch., 558 A.2d 1049 (1988); City Capital Associates v. Interco, Inc., Del.Ch., 551 A.2d 787 (1988). In those cases, the Court of Chancery determined that whatever threat existed related only to the shareholders and only to price and not to the corporation.

From those decisions by our Court of Chancery, Paramount and the individual plaintiffs extrapolate a rule of law that an all-cash, all-shares offer with values reasonably in the range of acceptable price cannot pose any objective threat to a corporation or its shareholders. Thus, Paramount would have us hold that only if the value of Paramount's offer were determined to be clearly inferior to the value created by management's plan to merge with Warner could the offer be viewed—objectively—as a threat.

Implicit in the plaintiffs' argument is the view that a hostile tender offer can pose only two types of threats: the threat of coercion that results from a two-tier offer promising unequal treatment for nontendering shareholders, and the threat of inadequate value from an all-shares, all-cash offer at a price below what a target board in good faith deems to be the present value of its shares. See, e.g., *Interco,* 551 A.2d at 797; *see also* BNS, Inc. v. Koppers, D.Del., 683 F.Supp. 458 (1988). Since Paramount's offer was all-cash, the only conceivable "threat," plaintiffs argue, was inadequate value.[17] We disapprove of such a narrow and rigid construction of *Unocal,* for the reasons which follow.

Plaintiffs' position represents a fundamental misconception of our standard of review under *Unocal* principally because it would involve the court in substituting its judgment for what is a "better" deal for that of a corporation's board of directors. To the extent

---

17. Some commentators have suggested that the threats posed by hostile offers be categorized into not two but three types: "(i) *opportunity loss* ... [where] a hostile offer might deprive target shareholders of the opportunity to select a superior alternative offered by target management [or, we would add, offered by another bidder], (ii) *structural coercion,* ... the risk that disparate treatment of non-tendering shareholders might distort shareholders' tender decisions; and ... (iii) *substantive coercion,* ... the risk that shareholders will mistakenly accept an underpriced offer because they disbelieve management's representations of intrinsic value." The recognition of substantive coercion, the authors suggest, would help guarantee that the *Unocal* standard becomes an effective intermediate standard of review. Gilson & Kraakman, *Delaware's Intermediate Standard for Defensive Tactics: Is There Substance to Proportionality Review?,* 44 The Business Lawyer, 247, 267 (1989).

that the Court of Chancery has recently done so in certain of its opinions, we hereby reject such approach as not in keeping with a proper *Unocal* analysis.   See, e.g., *Interco,* 551 A.2d 787, and its progeny;   but see TW Services, Inc. v. SWT Acquisition Corp., Del.Ch., C.A. No. 10427, Allen, C. 1989 WL 20290 (March 2, 1989).

The usefulness of *Unocal* as an analytical tool is precisely its flexibility in the face of a variety of fact scenarios.   *Unocal* is not intended as an abstract standard;   neither is it a structured and mechanistic procedure of appraisal.   Thus, we have said that directors may consider, when evaluating the threat posed by a takeover bid, the "inadequacy of the price offered, nature and timing of the offer, questions of illegality, the impact on [constituencies] other than shareholders, the risk of nonconsummation and the quality of securities being offered in the exchange."   493 A.2d at 955.   The open-ended analysis mandated by *Unocal* is not intended to lead to a simple mathematical exercise: that is, of comparing the discounted value of Time–Warner's expected trading price at some future date with Paramount's offer and determining which is the higher.   Indeed, in our view, precepts underlying the business judgment rule mitigate against a court's engaging in the process of attempting to appraise and evaluate the relative merits of a long-term versus a short-term investment goal for shareholders.   To engage in such an exercise is a distortion of the *Unocal* process and, in particular, the application of the second part of *Unocal*'s test, discussed below.

In this case, the Time board reasonably determined that inadequate value was not the only legally cognizable threat that Paramount's all-cash, all-shares offer could present.   Time's board concluded that Paramount's eleventh hour offer posed other threats. One concern was that Time shareholders might elect to tender into Paramount's cash offer in ignorance or a mistaken belief of the strategic benefit which a business combination with Warner might produce.   Moreover, Time viewed the conditions attached to Paramount's offer as introducing a degree of uncertainty that skewed a comparative analysis.   Further, the timing of Paramount's offer to follow issuance of Time's proxy notice was viewed as arguably designed to upset, if not confuse, the Time stockholders' vote. Given this record evidence, we cannot conclude that the Time board's decision of June 6 that Paramount's offer posed a threat to corporate policy and effectiveness was lacking in good faith or dominated by motives of either entrenchment or self-interest.

Paramount also contends that the Time board had not duly investigated Paramount's offer.   Therefore, Paramount argues, Time was unable to make an informed decision that the offer posed a threat to Time's corporate policy.   Although the Chancellor did not address this issue directly, his findings of fact do detail Time's exploration of the available entertainment companies, including Paramount, before determining that Warner provided the best strategic "fit."   In addition, the court found that Time's board rejected Paramount's offer because Paramount did not serve Time's objectives or meet Time's needs. Thus, the record does, in our judg-ment, demonstrate that Time's board was adequately informed of the potential benefits of a transaction with Paramount. We agree with the Chancellor that the Time board's lengthy pre-June investi-gation of potential merger candidates, including Paramount, moot-ed any obligation on Time's part to halt its merger process with Warner to reconsider Paramount. Time's board was under no obligation to negotiate with Paramount. *Unocal*, 493 A.2d at 954–55; see also *Macmillan*, 559 A.2d at 1285 n. 35. Time's failure to negotiate cannot be fairly found to have been uninformed. The evidence supporting this finding is materially enhanced by the fact that twelve of Time's sixteen board members were outside indepen-dent directors. *Unocal*, 493 A.2d at 955; Moran v. Household Intern., Inc., Del.Supr., 500 A.2d 1346, 1356 (1985).

We turn to the second part of the *Unocal* analysis. The obvious requisite to determining the reasonableness of a defensive action is a clear identification of the nature of the threat. As the Chancellor correctly noted, this "requires an evaluation of the importance of the corporate objective threatened; alternative meth-ods of protecting that objective; impacts of the 'defensive' action, and other relevant factors." In Re: Time Incorporated Shareholder Litigation, Del.Ch., 565 A.2d 281 (1989). It is not until both parts of the *Unocal* inquiry have been satisfied that the business judgment rule attaches to defensive actions of a board of directors. *Unocal*, 493 A.2d at 954.[18] As applied to the facts of this case, the question is whether the record evidence supports the Court of Chancery's conclusion that the restructuring of the Time–Warner transaction, including the adoption of several preclusive defensive measures, was a *reasonable response* in relation to a perceived threat.

Paramount argues that, assuming its tender offer posed a threat, Time's response was unreasonable in precluding Time's shareholders from accepting the tender offer or receiving a control premium in the immediately foreseeable future. Once again, the contention stems, we believe, from a fundamental misunderstand-ing of where the power of corporate governance lies. Delaware law confers the management of the corporate enterprise to the stock-holders' duly elected board representatives. 8 Del.C. § 141(a). The fiduciary duty to manage a corporate enterprise includes the selection of a time frame for achievement of corporate goals. That duty may not be delegated to the stockholders. *Van Gorkom*, 488 A.2d at 873. Directors are not obliged to abandon a deliberately conceived corporate plan for a short-term shareholder profit unless there is clearly no basis to sustain the corporate strategy. See, e.g., *Revlon*, 506 A.2d 173.

---

18. Some commentators have criticized *Unocal* by arguing that once the board's deliberative process has been analyzed and found not to be wanting in objectivity, good faith or deliberateness, the so-called "en-hanced" business judgment rule has been satisfied and no further inquiry is under-taken. See generally Johnson, Siegel, *Cor-porate Mergers: Redefining the Role of Tar-get Directors*, 136 U.Pa.L.Rev. 315 (1987). We reject such views.

Although the Chancellor blurred somewhat the discrete analyses required under *Unocal,* he did conclude that Time's board reasonably perceived Paramount's offer to be a significant threat to the planned Time–Warner merger and that Time's response was not "overly broad." We have found that even in light of a valid threat, management actions that are coercive in nature or force upon shareholders a management-sponsored alternative to a hostile offer may be struck down as unreasonable and nonproportionate responses. *Macmillan,* 559 A.2d 1261; *AC Acquisitions Corp.,* 519 A.2d 103.

Here, on the record facts, the Chancellor found that Time's responsive action to Paramount's tender offer was not aimed at "cramming down" on its shareholders a management-sponsored alternative, but rather had as its goal the carrying forward of a pre-existing transaction in an altered form.[19] Thus, the response was reasonably related to the threat. The Chancellor noted that the revised agreement and its accompanying safety devices did not preclude Paramount from making an offer for the combined Time–Warner company or from changing the conditions of its offer so as not to make the offer dependent upon the nullification of the Time–Warner agreement. Thus, the response was proportionate. We affirm the Chancellor's rulings as clearly supported by the record. Finally, we note that although Time was required, as a result of Paramount's hostile offer, to incur a heavy debt to finance its acquisition of Warner, that fact alone does not render the board's decision unreasonable so long as the directors could reasonably perceive the debt load not to be so injurious to the corporation as to jeopardize its well being.

C.

Conclusion

Applying the test for grant or denial of preliminary injunctive relief, we find plaintiffs failed to establish a reasonable likelihood of ultimate success on the merits. Therefore, we affirm.

PARAMOUNT COMMUNICATIONS INC. v. QVC NETWORK

Supreme Court of Delaware, 1994.
637 A.2d 34.

Before VEASEY, Chief Justice, MOORE and HOLLAND, Justices.

19. The Chancellor cited Shamrock Holdings, Inc. v. Polaroid Corp., Del.Ch., C.A. Nos. 10075 and 10079, Berger, V.C. (Jan. 6, 1989), as a closely analogous case. In that case, the Court of Chancery upheld, in the face of a takeover bid, the establishment of an employee stock ownership plan that had a significant antitakeover effect. The Court of Chancery upheld the board's action largely because the ESOP had been adopted *prior* to any contest for control and was reasonably determined to increase productivity and enhance profits. The ESOP did not appear to be primarily a device to affect or secure corporate control.

Upon appeal from the Court of Chancery.　AFFIRMED.

VEASEY, Chief Justice.

In this appeal we review an order of the Court of Chancery dated November 24, 1993 (the "November 24 Order"), preliminarily enjoining certain defensive measures designed to facilitate a so-called strategic alliance between Viacom Inc. ("Viacom") and Paramount Communications Inc. ("Paramount") approved by the board of directors of Paramount (the "Paramount Board" or the "Paramount directors") and to thwart an unsolicited, more valuable, tender offer by QVC Network Inc. ("QVC").　In affirming, we hold that the sale of control in this case, which is at the heart of the proposed strategic alliance, implicates enhanced judicial scrutiny of the conduct of the Paramount Board under Unocal Corp. v. Mesa Petroleum Co., Del.Supr., 493 A.2d 946 (1985), and Revlon, Inc. v. MacAndrews & Forbes Holdings, Inc., Del.Supr., 506 A.2d 173 (1986).　We further hold that the conduct of the Paramount Board was not reasonable as to process or result.

QVC and certain stockholders of Paramount commenced separate actions (later consolidated) in the Court of Chancery seeking preliminary and permanent injunctive relief against Paramount, certain members of the Paramount Board, and Viacom.　This action arises out of a proposed acquisition of Paramount by Viacom through a tender offer followed by a second-step merger (the "Paramount–Viacom transaction"), and a competing unsolicited tender offer by QVC.　The Court of Chancery granted a preliminary injunction.　QVC Network, Inc. v. Paramount Communications Inc., Del.Ch., 635 A.2d 1245, Jacobs, V.C. (1993) (the "Court of Chancery Opinion").　We affirmed by order dated December 9, 1993, Paramount Communications Inc. v. QVC Network Inc., Del.Supr., Nos. 427 and 428, 1993, 637 A.2d 828, Veasey, C.J. (Dec. 9, 1993) (the "December 9 Order").[1]

The Court of Chancery found that the Paramount directors violated their fiduciary duties by favoring the Paramount–Viacom transaction over the more valuable unsolicited offer of QVC.　The Court of Chancery preliminarily enjoined Paramount and the individual defendants (the "Paramount defendants") from amending or modifying Paramount's stockholder rights agreement (the "Rights Agreement"), including the redemption of the Rights, or taking other action to facilitate the consummation of the pending tender offer by Viacom or any proposed second-step merger, including the Merger Agreement between Paramount and Viacom dated September 12, 1993 (the "Original Merger Agreement"), as amended on

---

1.　We accepted this expedited interlocutory appeal on November 29, 1993.　After briefing and oral argument in this Court held on December 9, 1993, we issued our December 9 Order affirming the November 24 Order of the Court of Chancery.　In our December 9 Order, we stated, "It is not feasible, because of the exigencies of time, for this Court to complete an opinion setting forth more comprehensively the rationale of the Court's decision.　Unless otherwise ordered by the Court, such an opinion will follow in due course."　December 9 Order at 3.　This is the opinion referred to therein.

October 24, 1993 (the "Amended Merger Agreement"). Viacom and the Paramount defendants were enjoined from taking any action to exercise any provision of the Stock Option Agreement between Paramount and Viacom dated September 12, 1993 (the "Stock Option Agreement"), as amended on October 24, 1993. The Court of Chancery did not grant preliminary injunctive relief as to the termination fee provided for the benefit of Viacom in Section 8.05 of the Original Merger Agreement and the Amended Merger Agreement (the "Termination Fee").

Under the circumstances of this case, the pending sale of control implicated in the Paramount–Viacom transaction required the Paramount Board to act on an informed basis to secure the best value reasonably available to the stockholders. Since we agree with the Court of Chancery that the Paramount directors violated their fiduciary duties, we have AFFIRMED the entry of the order of the Vice Chancellor granting the preliminary injunction and have REMANDED these proceedings to the Court of Chancery for proceedings consistent herewith....

I.   FACTS

The Court of Chancery Opinion contains a detailed recitation of its factual findings in this matter. Court of Chancery Opinion, 635 A.2d 1245, 1246–1259. Only a brief summary of the facts is necessary for purposes of this opinion. The following summary is drawn from the findings of fact set forth in the Court of Chancery Opinion and our independent review of the record.

Paramount is a Delaware corporation with its principal offices in New York City. Approximately 118 million shares of Paramount's common stock are outstanding and traded on the New York Stock Exchange. The majority of Paramount's stock is publicly held by numerous unaffiliated investors. Paramount owns and operates a diverse group of entertainment businesses, including motion picture and television studios, book publishers, professional sports teams, and amusement parks.

There are 15 persons serving on the Paramount Board. Four directors are officer-employees of Paramount: Martin S. Davis ("Davis"), Paramount's Chairman and Chief Executive Officer since 1983; Donald Oresman ("Oresman"), Executive Vice–President, Chief Administrative Officer, and General Counsel; Stanley R. Jaffe, President and Chief Operating Officer; and Ronald L. Nelson, Executive Vice President and Chief Financial Officer. Paramount's 11 outside directors are distinguished and experienced business persons who are present or former senior executives of public corporations or financial institutions.

Viacom is a Delaware corporation with its headquarters in Massachusetts. Viacom is controlled by Sumner M. Redstone ("Redstone"), its Chairman and Chief Executive Officer, who owns indirectly approximately 85.2 percent of Viacom's voting Class A stock and approximately 69.2 percent of Viacom's nonvoting Class B stock through National Amusements, Inc. ("NAI"), an entity 91.7 percent owned by Redstone. Viacom has a wide range of entertainment operations, including a number of well-known cable television channels such as MTV, Nickelodeon, Showtime, and The Movie Channel. Viacom's equity co-investors in the Paramount–Viacom transaction include NYNEX Corporation and Blockbuster Entertainment Corporation.

QVC is a Delaware corporation with its headquarters in West Chester, Pennsylvania. QVC has several large stockholders, including Liberty Media Corporation, Comcast Corporation, Advance Publications, Inc., and Cox Enterprises Inc. Barry Diller ("Diller"), the Chairman and Chief Executive Officer of QVC, is also a substantial stockholder. QVC sells a variety of merchandise through a televised shopping channel. QVC has several equity co-investors in its proposed combination with Paramount including BellSouth Corporation and Comcast Corporation.

Beginning in the late 1980s, Paramount investigated the possibility of acquiring or merging with other companies in the entertainment, media, or communications industry. Paramount considered such transactions to be desirable, and perhaps necessary, in order to keep pace with competitors in the rapidly evolving field of entertainment and communications. Consistent with its goal of strategic expansion, Paramount made a tender offer for Time Inc. in 1989, but was ultimately unsuccessful. See Paramount Communications, Inc. v. Time Inc., Del.Supr., 571 A.2d 1140 (1990) ("*Time–Warner*").

Although Paramount had considered a possible combination of Paramount and Viacom as early as 1990, recent efforts to explore such a transaction began at a dinner meeting between Redstone and Davis on April 20, 1993. Robert Greenhill ("Greenhill"), Chairman of Smith Barney Shearson Inc. ("Smith Barney"), attended and helped facilitate this meeting. After several more meetings between Redstone and Davis, serious negotiations began taking place in early July.

It was tentatively agreed that Davis would be the chief executive officer and Redstone would be the controlling stockholder of the combined company, but the parties could not reach agreement on the merger price and the terms of a stock option to be granted to Viacom. With respect to price, Viacom offered a package of cash and stock (primarily Viacom Class B nonvoting stock) with a market value of approximately $61 per share, but Paramount wanted at least $70 per share.

Shortly after negotiations broke down in July 1993, two notable events occurred. First, Davis apparently learned of QVC's potential interest in Paramount, and told Diller over lunch on July 21, 1993, that Paramount was not for sale. Second, the market value of Viacom's Class B nonvoting stock increased from $46.875 on July 6 to $57.25 on August 20. QVC claims (and Viacom disputes) that this price increase was caused by open market purchases of such stock by Redstone or entities controlled by him.

On August 20, 1993, discussions between Paramount and Viacom resumed when Greenhill arranged another meeting between Davis and Redstone. After a short hiatus, the parties negotiated in earnest in early September, and performed due diligence with the assistance of their financial advisors, Lazard Freres & Co. ("Lazard") for Paramount and Smith Barney for Viacom. On September 9, 1993, the Paramount Board was informed about the status of the negotiations and was provided information by Lazard, including an analysis of the proposed transaction.

On September 12, 1993, the Paramount Board met again and unanimously approved the Original Merger Agreement whereby Paramount would merge with and into Viacom. The terms of the merger provided that each share of Paramount common stock would be converted into 0.10 shares of Viacom Class A voting stock, 0.90 shares of Viacom Class B nonvoting stock, and $9.10 in cash. In addition, the Paramount Board agreed to amend its "poison pill" Rights Agreement to exempt the proposed merger with Viacom. The Original Merger Agreement also contained several provisions designed to make it more difficult for a potential competing bid to succeed. We focus, as did the Court of Chancery, on three of these defensive provisions: a "no-shop" provision (the "No–Shop Provision"), the Termination Fee, and the Stock Option Agreement.

First, under the No–Shop Provision, the Paramount Board agreed that Paramount would not solicit, encourage, discuss, negotiate, or endorse any competing transaction unless: (a) a third party "makes an unsolicited written, bona fide proposal, which is not subject to any material contingencies relating to financing"; and (b) the Paramount Board determines that discussions or negotiations with the third party are necessary for the Paramount Board to comply with its fiduciary duties.

Second, under the Termination Fee provision, Viacom would receive a $100 million termination fee if: (a) Paramount terminated the Original Merger Agreement because of a competing transaction; (b) Paramount's stockholders did not approve the merger; or (c) the Paramount Board recommended a competing transaction.

The third and most significant deterrent device was the Stock Option Agreement, which granted to Viacom an option to purchase approximately 19.9 percent (23,699,000 shares) of Paramount's outstanding common stock at $69.14 per share if any of the triggering events for the Termination Fee occurred. In addition to the customary terms that are normally associated with a stock option, the Stock Option Agreement contained two provisions that were both unusual and highly beneficial to Viacom: (a) Viacom was permitted to pay for the shares with a senior subordinated note of questionable marketability instead of cash, thereby avoiding the need to raise the $1.6 billion purchase price (the "Note Feature"); and (b) Viacom could elect to require Paramount to pay Viacom in cash a sum equal to the difference between the purchase price and the market price of Paramount's stock (the "Put Feature"). Because the Stock Option Agreement was not "capped" to limit its maximum dollar value, it had the potential to reach (and in this case did reach) unreasonable levels.

After the execution of the Original Merger Agreement and the Stock Option Agreement on September 12, 1993, Paramount and Viacom announced their proposed merger. In a number of public statements, the parties indicated that the pending transaction was a virtual certainty. Redstone described it as a "marriage" that would "never be torn asunder" and stated that only a "nuclear attack" could break the deal. Redstone also called Diller and John Malone of Tele–Communications Inc., a major stockholder of QVC, to dissuade them from making a competing bid.

Despite these attempts to discourage a competing bid, Diller sent a letter to Davis on September 20, 1993, proposing a merger in which QVC would acquire Paramount for approximately $80 per share, consisting of 0.893 shares of QVC common stock and $30 in cash. QVC also expressed its eagerness to meet with Paramount to negotiate the details of a transaction. When the Paramount Board met on September 27, it was advised by Davis that the Original Merger Agreement prohibited Paramount from having discussions with QVC (or anyone else) unless certain conditions were satisfied. In particular, QVC had to supply evidence that its proposal was not subject to financing contingencies. The Paramount Board was also provided information from Lazard describing QVC and its proposal.

On October 5, 1993, QVC provided Paramount with evidence of QVC's financing. The Paramount Board then held another meeting on October 11, and decided to authorize management to meet with QVC. Davis also informed the Paramount Board that Booz–Allen & Hamilton ("Booz–Allen"), a management consulting firm, had been retained to assess, *inter alia*, the incremental earnings potential from a Paramount–Viacom merger and a Paramount–QVC merger. Discussions proceeded slowly, however, due to a delay in Paramount signing a confidentiality agreement. In response to Paramount's request for information, QVC provided two binders of documents to Paramount on October 20.

On October 21, 1993, QVC filed this action and publicly announced an $80 cash tender offer for 51 percent of Paramount's outstanding shares (the "QVC tender offer"). Each remaining share of Paramount common stock would be converted into 1.42857 shares of QVC common stock in a second-step merger. The tender offer was conditioned on, among other things, the invalidation of the Stock Option Agreement, which was worth over $200 million by that point.[5] QVC contends that it had to commence a tender offer

---

5. By November 15, 1993, the value of the Stock Option Agreement had increased to nearly $500 million based on the $90 QVC bid. See Court of Chancery Opinion, 635 A.2d 1245, 1271.

because of the slow pace of the merger discussions and the need to begin seeking clearance under federal antitrust laws.

Confronted by QVC's hostile bid, which on its face offered over $10 per share more than the consideration provided by the Original Merger Agreement, Viacom realized that it would need to raise its bid in order to remain competitive. Within hours after QVC's tender offer was announced, Viacom entered into discussions with Paramount concerning a revised transaction. These discussions led to serious negotiations concerning a comprehensive amendment to the original Paramount–Viacom transaction. In effect, the opportunity for a "new deal" with Viacom was at hand for the Paramount Board. With the QVC hostile bid offering greater value to the Paramount stockholders, the Paramount Board had considerable leverage with Viacom.

At a special meeting on October 24, 1993, the Paramount Board approved the Amended Merger Agreement and an amendment to the Stock Option Agreement. The Amended Merger Agreement was, however, essentially the same as the Original Merger Agreement, except that it included a few new provisions. One provision related to an $80 per share cash tender offer by Viacom for 51 percent of Paramount's stock, and another changed the merger consideration so that each share of Paramount would be converted into 0.20408 shares of Viacom Class A voting stock, 1.08317 shares of Viacom Class B nonvoting stock, and 0.20408 shares of a new series of Viacom convertible preferred stock. The Amended Merger Agreement also added a provision giving Paramount the right not to amend its Rights Agreement to exempt Viacom if the Paramount Board determined that such an amendment would be inconsistent with its fiduciary duties because another offer constituted a "better alternative." [6] Finally, the Paramount Board was given the power to terminate the Amended Merger Agreement if it withdrew its recommendation of the Viacom transaction or recommended a competing transaction.

Although the Amended Merger Agreement offered more consideration to the Paramount stockholders and somewhat more flexibility to the Paramount Board than did the Original Merger Agreement, the defensive measures designed to make a competing bid more difficult were not removed or modified. In particular, there is no evidence in the record that Paramount sought to use its newly-acquired leverage to eliminate or modify the No–Shop Provision, the Termination Fee, or the Stock Option Agreement when the subject of amending the Original Merger Agreement was on the table.

Viacom's tender offer commenced on October 25, 1993, and QVC's tender offer was formally launched on October 27, 1993. Diller sent a letter to the Paramount Board on October 28 request-

6. Under the Amended Merger Agreement and the Paramount Board's resolutions approving it, no further action of the Paramount Board would be required in order for Paramount's Rights Agreement to be amended. As a result, the proper officers of the company were authorized to implement the amendment unless they were instructed otherwise by the Paramount Board.

ing an opportunity to negotiate with Paramount, and Oresman responded the following day by agreeing to meet. The meeting, held on November 1, was not very fruitful, however, after QVC's proposed guidelines for a "fair bidding process" were rejected by Paramount on the ground that "auction procedures" were inappropriate and contrary to Paramount's contractual obligations to Viacom.

On November 6, 1993, Viacom unilaterally raised its tender offer price to $85 per share in cash and offered a comparable increase in the value of the securities being proposed in the second-step merger. At a telephonic meeting held later that day, the Paramount Board agreed to recommend Viacom's higher bid to Paramount's stockholders.

QVC responded to Viacom's higher bid on November 12 by increasing its tender offer to $90 per share and by increasing the securities for its second-step merger by a similar amount. In response to QVC's latest offer, the Paramount Board scheduled a meeting for November 15, 1993. Prior to the meeting, Oresman sent the members of the Paramount Board a document summarizing the "conditions and uncertainties" of QVC's offer. One director testified that this document gave him a very negative impression of the QVC bid.

At its meeting on November 15, 1993, the Paramount Board determined that the new QVC offer was not in the best interests of the stockholders. The purported basis for this conclusion was that QVC's bid was excessively conditional. The Paramount Board did not communicate with QVC regarding the status of the conditions because it believed that the No–Shop Provision prevented such communication in the absence of firm financing. Several Paramount directors also testified that they believed the Viacom transaction would be more advantageous to Paramount's future business prospects than a QVC transaction.[7] Although a number of materials were distributed to the Paramount Board describing the Viacom and QVC transactions, the only quantitative analysis of the consideration to be received by the stockholders under each proposal was based on then-current market prices of the securities involved, not on the anticipated value of such securities at the time when the stockholders would receive them.[8]

The preliminary injunction hearing in this case took place on November 16, 1993. On November 19, Diller wrote to the Paramount Board to inform it that QVC had obtained financing commitments for its tender offer and that there was no antitrust obstacle to

---

7. This belief may have been based on a report prepared by Booz–Allen and distributed to the Paramount Board at its October 24 meeting. The report, which relied on public information regarding QVC, concluded that the synergies of a Paramount–Viacom merger were significantly superior to those of a Paramount–QVC merger. QVC has labelled the Booz–Allen report as a "joke."

8. The market prices of Viacom's and QVC's stock were poor measures of their actual values because such prices constantly fluctuated depending upon which company was perceived to be the more likely to acquire Paramount.

the offer. On November 24, 1993, the Court of Chancery issued its decision granting a preliminary injunction in favor of QVC and the plaintiff stockholders. This appeal followed.

II. APPLICABLE PRINCIPLES OF ESTABLISHED DELAWARE LAW

The General Corporation Law of the State of Delaware (the "General Corporation Law") and the decisions of this Court have repeatedly recognized the fundamental principle that the management of the business and affairs of a Delaware corporation is entrusted to its directors, who are the duly elected and authorized representatives of the stockholders. 8 Del.C. § 141(a); Aronson v. Lewis, Del.Supr., 473 A.2d 805, 811–12 (1984); Pogostin v. Rice, Del.Supr., 480 A.2d 619, 624 (1984). Under normal circumstances, neither the courts nor the stockholders should interfere with the managerial decisions of the directors. The business judgment rule embodies the deference to which such decisions are entitled. *Aronson,* 473 A.2d at 812.

Nevertheless, there are rare situations which mandate that a court take a more direct and active role in overseeing the decisions made and actions taken by directors. In these situations, a court subjects the directors' conduct to enhanced scrutiny to ensure that it is reasonable.[9] The decisions of this Court have clearly established the circumstances where such enhanced scrutiny will be applied. E.g., *Unocal,* 493 A.2d 946; Moran v. Household Int'l, Inc., Del.Supr., 500 A.2d 1346 (1985); *Revlon,* 506 A.2d 173; Mills Acquisition Co. v. Macmillan, Inc., Del.Supr., 559 A.2d 1261 (1989); Gilbert v. El Paso Co., Del.Supr., 575 A.2d 1131 (1990). The case at bar implicates two such circumstances: (1) the approval of a transaction resulting in a sale of control, and (2) the adoption of defensive measures in response to a threat to corporate control.

A. The Significance of a Sale or Change [10] of Control

When a majority of a corporation's voting shares are acquired by a single person or entity, or by a cohesive group acting together, there is a significant diminution in the voting power of those who thereby become minority stockholders. Under the statutory framework of the General Corporation Law, many of the most fundamental corporate changes can be implemented only if they are approved by a majority vote of the stockholders. Such actions include elections of directors, amendments to the certificate of incorporation, mergers, consolidations, sales of all or substantially all of the assets of the corporation, and dissolution. 8 Del.C. §§ 211, 242,

---

9. Where actual self-interest is present and affects a majority of the directors approving a transaction, a court will apply even more exacting scrutiny to determine whether the transaction is entirely fair to the stockholders. E.g., Weinberger v. UOP, Inc., Del.Supr., 457 A.2d 701, 710–11 (1983); Nixon v. Blackwell, Del.Supr., 626 A.2d 1366, 1376 (1993).

10. For purposes of our December 9 Order and this Opinion, we have used the terms "sale of control" and "change of control" interchangeably without intending any doctrinal distinction.

251–258, 263, 271, 275. Because of the overriding importance of voting rights, this Court and the Court of Chancery have consistently acted to protect stockholders from unwarranted interference with such rights.[11]

In the absence of devices protecting the minority stockholders,[12] stockholder votes are likely to become mere formalities where there is a majority stockholder. For example, minority stockholders can be deprived of a continuing equity interest in their corporation by means of a cash-out merger. *Weinberger,* 457 A.2d at 703. Absent effective protective provisions, minority stockholders must rely for protection solely on the fiduciary duties owed to them by the directors and the majority stockholder, since the minority stockholders have lost the power to influence corporate direction through the ballot. The acquisition of majority status and the consequent privilege of exerting the powers of majority ownership come at a price. That price is usually a control premium which recognizes not only the value of a control block of shares, but also compensates the minority stockholders for their resulting loss of voting power.

In the case before us, the public stockholders (in the aggregate) currently own a majority of Paramount's voting stock. Control of the corporation is not vested in a single person, entity, or group, but vested in the fluid aggregation of unaffiliated stockholders. In the event the Paramount–Viacom transaction is consummated, the public stockholders will receive cash and a minority equity voting position in the surviving corporation. Following such consummation, there will be a controlling stockholder who will have the voting power to: (a) elect directors; (b) cause a break-up of the corporation; (c) merge it with another company; (d) cash-out the public stockholders; (e) amend the certificate of incorporation; (f) sell all or substantially all of the corporate assets; or (g) otherwise alter materially the nature of the corporation and the public stockholders' interests. Irrespective of the present Paramount Board's

---

11. See Schnell v. Chris–Craft Indus., Inc., Del.Supr., 285 A.2d 437, 439 (1971) (holding that actions taken by management to manipulate corporate machinery "for the purpose of obstructing the legitimate efforts of dissident stockholders in the exercise of their rights to undertake a proxy contest against management" were "contrary to established principles of corporate democracy" and therefore invalid); Giuricich v. Emtrol Corp., Del.Supr., 449 A.2d 232, 239 (1982) (holding that "careful judicial scrutiny will be given a situation in which the right to vote for the election of successor directors has been effectively frustrated"); Centaur Partners, IV v. Nat'l Intergroup, Del.Supr., 582 A.2d 923 (1990) (holding that supermajority voting provisions must be clear and unambiguous because they have the effect of disenfranchising the majority); Stroud v. Grace, Del.Supr., 606 A.2d 75, 84 (1992) (directors' duty of disclosure is premised on the importance of stockholders being fully informed when voting on a specific matter); Blasius Indus., Inc. v. Atlas Corp., Del.Ch., 564 A.2d 651, 659 n. 2 (1988) ("Delaware courts have long exercised a most sensitive and protective regard for the free and effective exercise of voting rights.").

12. Examples of such protective provisions are supermajority voting provisions, majority of the minority requirements, etc. Although we express no opinion on what effect the inclusion of any such stockholder protective devices would have had in this case, we note that this Court has upheld, under different circumstances, the reasonableness of a standstill agreement which limited a 49.9 percent stockholder to 40 percent board representation. *Ivanhoe,* 535 A.2d at 1343.

vision of a long-term strategic alliance with Viacom, the proposed sale of control would provide the new controlling stockholder with the power to alter that vision.

Because of the intended sale of control, the Paramount–Viacom transaction has economic consequences of considerable significance to the Paramount stockholders. Once control has shifted, the current Paramount stockholders will have no leverage in the future to demand another control premium. As a result, the Paramount stockholders are entitled to receive, and should receive, a control premium and/or protective devices of significant value. There being no such protective provisions in the Viacom–Paramount transaction, the Paramount directors had an obligation to take the maximum advantage of the current opportunity to realize for the stockholders the best value reasonably available.

B. The Obligations of Directors in a Sale or Change of Control Transaction

The consequences of a sale of control impose special obligations on the directors of a corporation.[13] In particular, they have the obligation of acting reasonably to seek the transaction offering the best value reasonably available to the stockholders. The courts will apply enhanced scrutiny to ensure that the directors have acted reasonably. The obligations of the directors and the enhanced scrutiny of the courts are well-established by the decisions of this Court. The directors' fiduciary duties in a sale of control context are those which generally attach. In short, "the directors must act in accordance with their fundamental duties of care and loyalty." Barkan v. Amsted Indus., Inc., Del.Supr., 567 A.2d 1279, 1286 (1989). As we held in *Macmillan:*

> It is basic to our law that the board of directors has the ultimate responsibility for managing the business and affairs of a corporation. In discharging this function, the directors owe fiduciary duties of care and loyalty to the corporation and its shareholders. **This unremitting obligation extends equally to board conduct in a sale of corporate control.**

559 A.2d at 1280 (emphasis supplied) (citations omitted).

In the sale of control context, the directors must focus on one primary objective—to secure the transaction offering the best value reasonably available for the stockholders—and they must exercise

---

13. We express no opinion on any scenario except the actual facts before the Court, and our precise holding herein. Unsolicited tender offers in other contexts may be governed by different precedent. For example, where a potential sale of control by a corporation is not the consequence of a board's action, this Court has recognized the prerogative of a board of directors to resist a third party's unsolicited acquisition proposal or offer. See *Pogostin*, 480 A.2d at 627; *Time–Warner*, 571 A.2d at 1152; Ber-

shad v. Curtiss–Wright Corp., Del.Supr., 535 A.2d 830, 845 (1987); *Macmillan*, 449 A.2d at 1285 n. 35. The decision of a board to resist such an acquisition, like all decisions of a properly-functioning board, must be informed. *Unocal*, 493 A.2d at 954–55, and the circumstances of each particular case will determine the steps that a board must take to inform itself, and what other action, if any, is required as a matter of fiduciary duty.

their fiduciary duties to further that end. The decisions of this Court have consistently emphasized this goal. *Revlon*, 506 A.2d at 182 ("The duty of the board ... [is] the maximization of the company's value at a sale for the stockholders' benefit."); *Macmillan*, 559 A.2d at 1288 ("[I]n a sale of corporate control the responsibility of the directors is to get the highest value reasonably attainable for the shareholders."); *Barkan*, 567 A.2d at 1286 ("[T]he board must act in a neutral manner to encourage the highest possible price for shareholders."). See also Wilmington Trust Co. v. Coulter, Del.Supr., 200 A.2d 441, 448 (1964) (in the context of the duty of a trustee, "[w]hen all is equal ... it is plain that the Trustee is bound to obtain the best price obtainable").

In pursuing this objective, the directors must be especially diligent. See Citron v. Fairchild Camera and Instrument Corp., Del.Supr., 569 A.2d 53, 66 (1989) (discussing "a board's active and direct role in the sale process"). In particular, this Court has stressed the importance of the board being adequately informed in negotiating a sale of control: "The need for adequate information is central to the enlightened evaluation of a transaction that a board must make." *Barkan*, 567 A.2d at 1287. This requirement is consistent with the general principle that "directors have a duty to inform themselves, prior to making a business decision, of all material information reasonably available to them." *Aronson*, 473 A.2d at 812. See also Cede & Co. v. Technicolor, Inc., Del.Supr., 634 A.2d 345, 367 (1993); Smith v. Van Gorkom, Del.Supr., 488 A.2d 858, 872 (1985). Moreover, the role of outside, independent directors becomes particularly important because of the magnitude of a sale of control transaction and the possibility, in certain cases, that management may not necessarily be impartial. See *Macmillan*, 559 A.2d at 1285 (requiring "the intense scrutiny and participation of the independent directors").

Barkan teaches some of the methods by which a board can fulfill its obligation to seek the best value reasonably available to the stockholders. 567 A.2d at 1286–87. These methods are designed to determine the existence and viability of possible alternatives. They include conducting an auction, canvassing the market, etc. Delaware law recognizes that there is "no single blueprint" that directors must follow. Id. at 1286–87; *Citron*, 569 A.2d at 68; *Macmillan*, 559 A.2d at 1287.

In determining which alternative provides the best value for the stockholders, a board of directors is not limited to considering only the amount of cash involved, and is not required to ignore totally its view of the future value of a strategic alliance. See *Macmillan*, 559 A.2d at 1282 n. 29. Instead, the directors should analyze the entire situation and evaluate in a disciplined manner the consideration being offered. Where stock or other non-cash consideration is involved, the board should try to quantify its value, if feasible, to achieve an objective comparison of the alternatives.[14] In addition,

---

14. When assessing the value of non-   cash consideration, a board should focus on

the board may assess a variety of practical considerations relating to each alternative, including:

> [an offer's] fairness and feasibility; the proposed or actual financing for the offer, and the consequences of that financing; questions of illegality; ... the risk of non-consum[m]ation; ... the bidder's identity, prior background and other business venture experiences; and the bidder's business plans for the corporation and their effects on stockholder interests.

Macmillan, 559 A.2d at 1282 n. 29. These considerations are important because the selection of one alternative may permanently foreclose other opportunities. While the assessment of these factors may be complex, the board's goal is straightforward: having informed themselves of all material information reasonably available, the directors must decide which alternative is most likely to offer the best value reasonably available to the stockholders.

C. Enhanced Judicial Scrutiny of a Sale or Change of Control Transaction

Board action in the circumstances presented here is subject to enhanced scrutiny. Such scrutiny is mandated by: (a) the threatened diminution of the current stockholders' voting power; (b) the fact that an asset belonging to public stockholders (a control premium) is being sold and may never be available again; and (c) the traditional concern of Delaware courts for actions which impair or impede stockholder voting rights (see supra note 11). In *Macmillan,* this Court held:

> When *Revlon* duties devolve upon directors, this Court will continue to exact an enhanced judicial scrutiny at the threshold, as in *Unocal,* before the normal presumptions of the business judgment rule will apply.[15]

559 A.2d at 1288. The *Macmillan* decision articulates a specific two-part test for analyzing board action where competing bidders are not treated equally: [16]

> In the face of disparate treatment, the trial court must first examine whether the directors properly perceived that shareholder interests were enhanced. In any event the board's action must be reasonable in relation to the advantage sought to be achieved, or conversely, to the threat which a particular bid allegedly poses to stockholder interests.

its value as of the date it will be received by the stockholders. Normally, such value will be determined with the assistance of experts using generally accepted methods of valuation. See In re RJR Nabisco, Inc. Shareholders Litig., Del.Ch., C.A. No. 10389, Allen, C. (Jan. 31, 1989), reprinted at 14 Del.J.Corp.L. 1132, 1161.

15. Because the Paramount Board acted unreasonably as to process and result in this sale of control situation, the business judgment rule did not become operative.

16. Before this test is invoked, "the plaintiff must show, and the trial court must find, that the directors of the target company treated one or more of the respective bidders on unequal terms." *Macmillan,* 559 A.2d at 1288.

Id. See also Roberts v. General Instrument Corp., Del.Ch., C.A. No. 11639, Allen, C. (Aug. 13, 1990), reprinted at 16 Del.J.Corp.L. 1540, 1554 ("This enhanced test requires a judicial judgment of reasonableness in the circumstances.").

The key features of an enhanced scrutiny test are: (a) a judicial determination regarding the adequacy of the decisionmaking process employed by the directors, including the information on which the directors based their decision; and (b) a judicial examination of the reasonableness of the directors' action in light of the circumstances then existing. The directors have the burden of proving that they were adequately informed and acted reasonably.

Although an enhanced scrutiny test involves a review of the reasonableness of the substantive merits of a board's actions,[17] a court should not ignore the complexity of the directors' task in a sale of control. There are many business and financial considerations implicated in investigating and selecting the best value reasonably available. The board of directors is the corporate decisionmaking body best equipped to make these judgments. Accordingly, a court applying enhanced judicial scrutiny should be deciding whether the directors made a **reasonable** decision, not a **perfect** decision. If a board selected one of several reasonable alternatives, a court should not second-guess that choice even though it might have decided otherwise or subsequent events may have cast doubt on the board's determination. Thus, courts will not substitute their business judgment for that of the directors, but will determine if the directors' decision was, on balance, within a range of reasonableness. See Unocal, 493 A.2d at 955–56; Macmillan, 559 A.2d at 1288; Nixon, 626 A.2d at 1378.

D. *Revlon* and *Time–Warner* Distinguished

The Paramount defendants and Viacom assert that the fiduciary obligations and the enhanced judicial scrutiny discussed above are not implicated in this case in the absence of a "break-up" of the corporation, and that the order granting the preliminary injunction should be reversed. This argument is based on their erroneous interpretation of our decisions in *Revlon* and *Time–Warner*.

In *Revlon*, we reviewed the actions of the board of directors of Revlon, Inc. ("Revlon"), which had rebuffed the overtures of Pantry Pride, Inc. and had instead entered into an agreement with Forstmann Little & Co. ("Forstmann") providing for the acquisition of 100 percent of Revlon's outstanding stock by Forstmann and the subsequent breakup of Revlon. Based on the facts and circumstances present in *Revlon*, we held that "[t]he directors' role

---

17. It is to be remembered that, in cases where the traditional business judgment rule is applicable and the board acted with due care, in good faith, and in the honest belief that they are acting in the best interests of the stockholders (which is not this case), the Court gives great deference to the substance of the directors' decision and will not invalidate the decision, will not examine its reasonableness, and "will not substitute our views for those of the board if the latter's decision can be 'attributed to any rational business purpose.'" *Unocal*, 493 A.2d at 949 (quoting Sinclair Oil Corp. v. Levien, Del.Supr., 280 A.2d 717, 720 (1971)). See *Aronson*, 473 A.2d at 812.

changed from defenders of the corporate bastion to auctioneers charged with getting the best price for the stockholders at a sale of the company." 506 A.2d at 182. We further held that "when a board ends an intense bidding contest on an insubstantial basis, . . . [that] action cannot withstand the enhanced scrutiny which *Unocal* requires of director conduct." Id. at 184.

It is true that one of the circumstances bearing on these holdings was the fact that "the break-up of the company . . . had become a reality which even the directors embraced." Id. at 182. It does not follow, however, that a "break-up" must be present and "inevitable" before directors are subject to enhanced judicial scrutiny and are required to pursue a transaction that is calculated to produce the best value reasonably available to the stockholders. In fact, we stated in *Revlon* that "when bidders make relatively similar offers, or dissolution of the company becomes inevitable, the directors cannot fulfill their enhanced *Unocal* duties by playing favorites with the contending factions." Id. at 184 (emphasis added). *Revlon* thus does not hold that an inevitable dissolution or "break-up" is necessary.

The decisions of this Court following *Revlon* reinforced the applicability of enhanced scrutiny and the directors' obligation to seek the best value reasonably available for the stockholders where there is a pending sale of control, regardless of whether or not there is to be a break-up of the corporation. In *Macmillan,* this Court held:

> We stated in *Revlon,* and again here, that **in a sale of corporate control** the responsibility of the directors is to get the highest value reasonably attainable for the shareholders.

559 A.2d at 1288 (emphasis added). In *Barkan,* we observed further:

> We believe that the general principles announced in *Revlon,* in Unocal Corp. v. Mesa Petroleum Co., Del.Supr., 493 A.2d 946 (1985), and in Moran v. Household International, Inc., Del. Supr., 500 A.2d 1346 (1985) govern this case and every case in which a **fundamental change of corporate control** occurs or is contemplated.

567 A.2d at 1286 (emphasis added).

Although *Macmillan* and *Barkan* are clear in holding that a change of control imposes on directors the obligation to obtain the best value reasonably available to the stockholders, the Paramount defendants have interpreted our decision in *Time–Warner* as requiring a corporate break-up in order for that obligation to apply. The facts in *Time–Warner,* however, were quite different from the facts of this case, and refute Paramount's position here. In *Time–Warner,* the Chancellor held that there was no change of control in the original stock-for-stock merger between Time and Warner because Time would be owned by a fluid aggregation of unaffiliated stockholders both before and after the merger:

If the appropriate inquiry is whether a change in control is contemplated, the answer must be sought in the specific circumstances surrounding the transaction. Surely under some circumstances a stock for stock merger could reflect a transfer of corporate control. That would, for example, plainly be the case here if Warner were a private company. But where, as here, the shares of both constituent corporations are widely held, corporate control can be expected to remain unaffected by a stock for stock merger. This in my judgment was the situation with respect to the original merger agreement. When the specifics of that situation are reviewed, it is seen that, aside from legal technicalities and aside from arrangements thought to enhance the prospect for the ultimate succession of [Nicholas J. Nicholas, Jr., president of Time], neither corporation could be said to be acquiring the other. **Control of both remained in a large, fluid, changeable and changing market.**

The existence of a control block of stock in the hands of a single shareholder or a group with loyalty to each other does have real consequences to the financial value of "minority" stock. The law offers some protection to such shares through the imposition of a fiduciary duty upon controlling shareholders. **But here, effectuation of the merger would not have subjected Time shareholders to the risks and consequences of holders of minority shares. This is a reflection of the fact that no control passed to anyone in the transaction contemplated.** The shareholders of Time would have "suffered" dilution, of course, but they would suffer the same type of dilution upon the public distribution of new stock.

Paramount Communications, Inc. v. Time Inc., Del.Ch., No. 10866, Allen, C. (July 17, 1989), reprinted at 15 Del.J.Corp.L. 700, 739 (emphasis added). Moreover, the transaction actually consummated in *Time–Warner* was not a merger, as originally planned, but a sale of Warner's stock to Time.

In our affirmance of the Court of Chancery's well-reasoned decision, this Court held that "The Chancellor's findings of fact are supported by the record and **his conclusion is correct as a matter of law.**" 571 A.2d at 1150 (emphasis added). Nevertheless, the Paramount defendants here have argued that a break-up is a requirement and have focused on the following language in our *Time–Warner* decision:

However, we premise our rejection of plaintiffs' *Revlon* claim on different grounds, namely, the absence of any substantial evidence to conclude that Time's board, in negotiating with Warner, made the dissolution or break-up of the corporate entity inevitable, as was the case in *Revlon.*

Under Delaware law there are, generally speaking and **without excluding other possibilities,** two circumstances which may implicate *Revlon* duties. The first, and clearer one, is when a corporation **initiates an active bidding process seeking to sell itself** or to effect a business reorganization involving a clear break-up of the company. However, *Revlon* duties may also be triggered where, in response to a bidder's offer, a target abandons its long-term strategy and seeks an alternative transaction involving the breakup of the company.

Id. at 1150 (emphasis added) (citation and footnote omitted).

The Paramount defendants have misread the holding of *Time–Warner.* Contrary to their argument, our decision in *Time–Warner* expressly states that the two general scenarios discussed in the above-quoted paragraph are not the only instances where "*Revlon* duties" may be implicated. The Paramount defendants' argument totally ignores the phrase "without excluding other possibilities." Moreover, the instant case is clearly within the first general scenario set forth in *Time–Warner.* The Paramount Board, albeit unintentionally, had "initiate[d] an active bidding process seeking to sell itself" by agreeing to sell control of the corporation to Viacom in circumstances where another potential acquiror (QVC) was equally interested in being a bidder.

The Paramount defendants' position that both a change of control and a break-up are required must be rejected. Such a holding would unduly restrict the application of *Revlon,* is inconsistent with this Court's decisions in *Barkan* and *Macmillan,* and has no basis in policy. There are few events that have a more significant impact on the stockholders than a sale of control or a corporate break-up. Each event represents a fundamental (and perhaps irrevocable) change in the nature of the corporate enterprise from a practical standpoint. It is the significance of **each** of these events that justifies: (a) focusing on the directors' obligation to seek the best value reasonably available to the stockholders; and (b) requiring a close scrutiny of board action which could be contrary to the stockholders' interests.

Accordingly, when a corporation undertakes a transaction which will cause: (a) a change in corporate control; or (b) a break-up of the corporate entity, the directors' obligation is to seek the best value reasonably available to the stockholders. This obligation arises because the effect of the Viacom–Paramount transaction, if consummated, is to shift control of Paramount from the public stockholders to a controlling stockholder, Viacom. Neither *Time–Warner* nor any other decision of this Court holds that a "break-up" of the company is essential to give rise to this obligation where there is a sale of control.

III. BREACH OF FIDUCIARY DUTIES BY PARAMOUNT BOARD

We now turn to duties of the Paramount Board under the facts of this case and our conclusions as to the breaches of those duties which warrant injunctive relief.

A. The Specific Obligations of the Paramount Board

Under the facts of this case, the Paramount directors had the obligation: (a) to be diligent and vigilant in examining critically the Paramount–Viacom transaction and the QVC tender offers; (b) to act in good faith; (c) to obtain, and act with due care on, all material information reasonably available, including information necessary to compare the two offers to determine which of these transactions, or an alternative course of action, would provide the best value reasonably available to the stockholders; and (d) to negotiate actively and in good faith with both Viacom and QVC to that end.

Having decided to sell control of the corporation, the Paramount directors were required to evaluate critically whether or not all material aspects of the Paramount–Viacom transaction (separately and in the aggregate) were reasonable and in the best interests of the Paramount stockholders in light of current circumstances, including: the change of control premium, the Stock Option Agreement, the Termination Fee, the coercive nature of both the Viacom and QVC tender offers,[18] the No–Shop Provision, and the proposed disparate use of the Rights Agreement as to the Viacom and QVC tender offers, respectively.

These obligations necessarily implicated various issues, including the questions of whether or not those provisions and other aspects of the Paramount–Viacom transaction (separately and in the aggregate): (a) adversely affected the value provided to the Paramount stockholders; (b) inhibited or encouraged alternative bids; (c) were enforceable contractual obligations in light of the directors' fiduciary duties; and (d) in the end would advance or retard the Paramount directors' obligation to secure for the Paramount stockholders the best value reasonably available under the circumstances.

The Paramount defendants contend that they were precluded by certain contractual provisions, including the No–Shop Provision, from negotiating with QVC or seeking alternatives. Such provisions, whether or not they are presumptively valid in the abstract, may not, validly define or limit the directors' fiduciary duties under Delaware law or prevent the Paramount directors from carrying out their fiduciary duties under Delaware law. To the extent such provisions are inconsistent with those duties, they are invalid and unenforceable. See *Revlon,* 506 A.2d at 184–85.

Since the Paramount directors had already decided to sell control, they had an obligation to continue their search for the best value reasonably available to the stockholders. This continuing obligation included the responsibility, at the October 24 board meeting and thereafter, to evaluate critically both the QVC tender

---

18. Both the Viacom and the QVC tender offers were for 51 percent cash and a "back-end" of various securities, the value of each of which depended on the fluctuating value of Viacom and QVC stock at any given time. Thus, both tender offers were two-tiered, front-end loaded, and coercive. Such coercive offers are inherently problematic and should be expected to receive particularly careful analysis by a target board. See *Unocal,* 493 A.2d at 956.

offers and the Paramount–Viacom transaction to determine if: (a) the QVC tender offer was, or would continue to be, conditional; (b) the QVC tender offer could be improved; (c) the Viacom tender offer or other aspects of the Paramount–Viacom transaction could be improved; (d) each of the respective offers would be reasonably likely to come to closure, and under what circumstances; (e) other material information was reasonably available for consideration by the Paramount directors; (f) there were viable and realistic alternative courses of action; and (g) the timing constraints could be managed so the directors could consider these matters carefully and deliberately.

B. The Breaches of Fiduciary Duty by the Paramount Board

The Paramount directors made the decision on September 12, 1993, that, in their judgment, a strategic merger with Viacom on the economic terms of the Original Merger Agreement was in the best interests of Paramount and its stockholders. Those terms provided a modest change of control premium to the stockholders. The directors also decided at that time that it was appropriate to agree to certain defensive measures (the Stock Option Agreement, the Termination Fee, and the No–Shop Provision) insisted upon by Viacom as part of that economic transaction. Those defensive measures, coupled with the sale of control and subsequent disparate treatment of competing bidders, implicated the judicial scrutiny of *Unocal, Revlon, Macmillan,* and their progeny. We conclude that the Paramount directors' process was not reasonable, and the result achieved for the stockholders was not reasonable under the circumstances.

When entering into the Original Merger Agreement, and thereafter, the Paramount Board clearly gave insufficient attention to the potential consequences of the defensive measures demanded by Viacom. The Stock Option Agreement had a number of unusual and potentially "draconian" [19] provisions, including the Note Feature and the Put Feature. Furthermore, the Termination Fee, whether or not unreasonable by itself, clearly made Paramount less attractive to other bidders, when coupled with the Stock Option Agreement. Finally, the No–Shop Provision inhibited the Paramount Board's ability to negotiate with other potential bidders, particularly QVC which had already expressed an interest in Paramount. [20]

---

19. The Vice Chancellor so characterized the Stock Option Agreement. Court of Chancery Opinion, 635 A.2d 1245, 1272. We express no opinion whether a stock option agreement of essentially this magnitude, but with a reasonable "cap" and without the Note and Put Features, would be valid or invalid under other circumstances. See Hecco Ventures v. Sea–Land Corp., Del. Ch., C.A. No. 8486, Jacobs, V.C. (May 19, 1986) (21.7 percent stock option); In re Vitalink Communications Corp. Shareholders Litig., Del.Ch., C.A. No. 12085, Chandler, V.C. (May 16, 1990) (19.9 percent stock option).

20. We express no opinion whether certain aspects of the No–Shop Provision here could be valid in another context. Whether or not it could validly have operated here at an early stage solely to prevent Paramount from actively "shopping" the company, it

Throughout the applicable time period, and especially from the first QVC merger proposal on September 20 through the Paramount Board meeting on November 15, QVC's interest in Paramount provided the **opportunity** for the Paramount Board to seek significantly higher value for the Paramount stockholders than that being offered by Viacom. QVC persistently demonstrated its intention to meet and exceed the Viacom offers, and frequently expressed its willingness to negotiate possible further increases.

The Paramount directors had the opportunity in the October 23–24 time frame, when the Original Merger Agreement was renegotiated, to take appropriate action to modify the improper defensive measures as well as to improve the economic terms of the Paramount–Viacom transaction. Under the circumstances existing at that time, it should have been clear to the Paramount Board that the Stock Option Agreement, coupled with the Termination Fee and the No–Shop Clause, were impeding the realization of the best value reasonably available to the Paramount stockholders. Nevertheless, the Paramount Board made no effort to eliminate or modify these counterproductive devices, and instead continued to cling to its vision of a strategic alliance with Viacom. Moreover, based on advice from the Paramount management, the Paramount directors considered the QVC offer to be "conditional" and asserted that they were precluded by the No–Shop Provision from seeking more information from, or negotiating with, QVC.

By November 12, 1993, the value of the revised QVC offer on its face exceeded that of the Viacom offer by over $1 billion at then current values. This significant disparity of value cannot be justified on the basis of the directors' vision of future strategy, primarily because the change of control would supplant the authority of the current Paramount Board to continue to hold and implement their strategic vision in any meaningful way. Moreover, their uninformed process had deprived their strategic vision of much of its credibility. See *Van Gorkom,* 488 A.2d at 872; Cede v. Technicolor, 634 A.2d at 367; Hanson Trust PLC v. ML SCM Acquisition Inc., 2d Cir., 781 F.2d 264, 274 (1986).

When the Paramount directors met on November 15 to consider QVC's increased tender offer, they remained prisoners of their own misconceptions and missed opportunities to eliminate the restrictions they had imposed on themselves. Yet, it was not "too late" to reconsider negotiating with QVC. The circumstances existing on November 15 made it clear that the defensive measures, taken as a whole, were problematic: (a) the No–Shop Provision

could not prevent the Paramount directors from carrying out their fiduciary duties in considering unsolicited bids or in negotiating for the best value reasonably available to the stockholders. *Macmillan,* 559 A.2d at 1287. As we said in *Barkan:* "Where a board has no reasonable basis upon which to judge the adequacy of a contemplated transaction, a no-shop restriction gives rise to the inference that the board seeks to forestall competing bids." 567 A.2d at 1288. See also *Revlon,* 506 A.2d at 184 (holding that "[t]he no-shop provision, like the lock-up option, while not *per se* illegal, is impermissible under the *Unocal* standards when a board's primary duty becomes that of an auctioneer responsible for selling the company to the highest bidder").

could not define or limit their fiduciary duties; (b) the Stock Option Agreement had become "draconian"; and (c) the Termination Fee, in context with all the circumstances, was similarly deterring the realization of possibly higher bids. Nevertheless, the Paramount directors remained paralyzed by their uninformed belief that the QVC offer was "illusory." This final opportunity to negotiate on the stockholders' behalf and to fulfill their obligation to seek the best value reasonably available was thereby squandered.[21]

IV. VIACOM'S CLAIM OF VESTED CONTRACT RIGHTS

Viacom argues that it had certain "vested" contract rights with respect to the No–Shop Provision and the Stock Option Agreement.[22] In effect, Viacom's argument is that the Paramount directors could enter into an agreement in violation of their fiduciary duties and then render Paramount, and ultimately its stockholders, liable for failing to carry out an agreement in violation of those duties. Viacom's protestations about vested rights are without merit. This Court has found that those defensive measures were improperly designed to deter potential bidders, and that such measures do not meet the reasonableness test to which they must be subjected. They are consequently invalid and unenforceable under the facts of this case.

The No–Shop Provision could not validly define or limit the fiduciary duties of the Paramount directors. To the extent that a contract, or a provision thereof, purports to require a board to act or not act in such a fashion as to limit the exercise of fiduciary duties, it is invalid and unenforceable. Cf. Wilmington Trust v. Coulter, 200 A.2d at 452–54. Despite the arguments of Paramount and Viacom to the contrary, the Paramount directors could not contract away their fiduciary obligations. Since the No–Shop Provision was invalid, Viacom never had any vested contract rights in the provision.

As discussed previously, the Stock Option Agreement contained several "draconian" aspects, including the Note Feature and the Put Feature. While we have held that lock-up options are not *per se* illegal, see *Revlon*, 506 A.2d at 183, no options with similar features have ever been upheld by this Court. Under the circumstances of

---

21. The Paramount defendants argue that the Court of Chancery erred by assuming that the Rights Agreement was "pulled" at the November 15 meeting of the Paramount Board. The problem with this argument is that, under the Amended Merger Agreement and the resolutions of the Paramount Board related thereto, Viacom would be exempted from the Rights Agreement in the absence of further action of the Paramount Board and no further meeting had been scheduled or even contemplated prior to the closing of the Viacom tender offer. This failure to schedule and hold a meeting shortly before the closing date in order to make a final decision, based on all of the information and circumstances then existing, whether to exempt Viacom from the Rights Agreement was inconsistent with the Paramount Board's responsibilities and does not provide a basis to challenge the Court of Chancery's decision.

22. Presumably this argument would have included the Termination Fee had the Vice Chancellor invalidated that provision or if appellees had cross-appealed from the Vice Chancellor's refusal to invalidate that provision.

this case, the Stock Option Agreement clearly is invalid. Accordingly, Viacom never had any vested contract rights in that Agreement.

Viacom, a sophisticated party with experienced legal and financial advisors, knew of (and in fact demanded) the unreasonable features of the Stock Option Agreement. It cannot be now heard to argue that it obtained vested contract rights by negotiating and obtaining contractual provisions from a board acting in violation of its fiduciary duties. As the Nebraska Supreme Court said in rejecting a similar argument in Con–Agra, Inc. v. Cargill, Inc., Neb.Supr., 382 N.W.2d 576, 587–88 (1986), "To so hold, it would seem, would be to get the shareholders coming and going." Likewise, we reject Viacom's arguments and hold that its fate must rise and fall, and in this instance fall, with the determination that the actions of the Paramount Board were invalid.

V. CONCLUSION

The realization of the best value reasonably available to the stockholders became the Paramount directors' primary obligation under these facts in light of the change of control. That obligation was not satisfied, and the Paramount Board's process was deficient. The directors' initial hope and expectation for a strategic alliance with Viacom was allowed to dominate their decisionmaking process to the point where the arsenal of defensive measures established at the outset was perpetuated (not modified or eliminated) when the situation was dramatically altered. QVC's unsolicited bid presented the opportunity for significantly greater value for the stockholders and enhanced negotiating leverage for the directors. Rather than seizing those opportunities, the Paramount directors chose to wall themselves off from material information which was reasonably available and to hide behind the defensive measures as a rationalization for refusing to negotiate with QVC or seeking other alternatives. Their view of the strategic alliance likewise became an empty rationalization as the opportunities for higher value for the stockholders continued to develop.

It is the nature of the judicial process that we decide only the case before us—a case which, on its facts, is clearly controlled by established Delaware law. Here, the proposed change of control and the implications thereof were crystal clear. In other cases they may be less clear. The holding of this case on its facts, coupled with the holdings of the principal cases discussed herein where the issue of sale of control is implicated, should provide a workable precedent against which to measure future cases.

For the reasons set forth herein, the November 24, 1993, Order of the Court of Chancery has been AFFIRMED, and this matter has been REMANDED for proceedings consistent herewith, as set forth in the December 9, 1993, Order of this Court.

NOTE ON STATE TENDER–OFFER LEGISLATION

One of the responses to the tender-offer phenomena was the adoption in many states of statutes regulating takeover bids. Almost invariably, these statutes are designed to favor incumbents. The so-called "first-generation" statutes imposed very stringent requirements on takeover bids. In Edgar v. MITE Corp., 457 U.S. 624, 102 S.Ct. 2629, 73 L.Ed.2d 269 (1982), the Supreme Court held one such statute, the Illinois Takeover Act, unconstitutional. Three of the six judges who passed on the merits of the case held that the Illinois statute was unconstitutional under the Supremacy Clause, on the ground that a major objective of the Williams Act was maintaining a neutral balance between management and the bidder, and the Illinois Act violated this balance. All six judges who addressed the merits held that the Illinois Act violated the Commerce Clause, by directly regulating commerce taking place across state lines, because it applied to prevent an offeror from making an offer even to non-Illinois shareholders, and by imposing an excessive burden on interstate commerce, by permitting the secretary of state to block a nationwide tender offer.

After the decision in Edgar v. MITE Corp., a number of states adopted "second-generation" takeover statutes. Most of these statutes fall into two major categories: "fair price" statutes and "control share acquisition" statutes. Under the fair-price statutes, an acquiror must pay all shareholders the "best price" paid to any one shareholder. Under control-share acquisition statutes, if a designated stock-ownership threshold is crossed by an acquiring shareholder, he cannot vote the acquired shares without the approval of a majority of the disinterested shareholders. The validity of one of these second-generation statutes was addressed by the Supreme Court in the following case, *CTS*. The case following *CTS* concerns a third-generation statute.

———

NOTE ON CTS CORPORATION v. DYNAMICS
CORPORATION OF AMERICA

A number of states have adopted statutes regulating tender offers. These statutes are of various types, but most are intended to make tender offers more difficult. In Edgar v. MITE Corp., 457 U.S. 624, 102 S.Ct. 2629, 73 L.Ed.2d 269 (1982) a plurality of the Supreme Court struck down, as unconstitutional, one type of state tender-offer statute. However, in CTS Corporation v. Dynamics Corporation of America, 481 U.S. 69, 107 S.Ct. 1637, 95 L.Ed.2d 67 (1987), the Supreme Court distinguished *MITE* and upheld another type of statute, which had been adopted by Indiana. The Court described the Indiana statute as follows:

> ... The Act applies only to "issuing public corporations." The term "corporation" includes only businesses incorporated

in Indiana. See § 23–1–20–5. An "issuing public corporation" is defined as:

"a corporation that has:

"(1) one hundred (100) or more shareholders;

"(2) its principal place of business, its principal office, or substantial assets within Indiana; and

"(3) either:

"(A) more than ten percent (10%) of its share-holders resident in Indiana;

"(B) more than ten percent (10%) of its shares owned by Indiana residents; or

"(C) ten thousand (10,000) shareholders resident in Indiana." § 23–1–42–4(a).

The Act focuses on the acquisition of "control shares" in an issuing public corporation. Under the Act, an entity acquires "control shares" whenever it acquires shares that, but for the operation of the Act, would bring its voting power in the corporation to or above any of three thresholds: 20%, 33⅓, or 50%. § 23–1–42–1. An entity that acquires control shares does not necessarily acquire voting rights. Rather, it gains those rights only "to the extent granted by resolution approved by the shareholders of the issuing public corporation." § 23–1–42–9(a). Section 9 requires a majority vote of all disinterested shareholders holding each class of stock for passage of such a resolution. § 23–1–42–9(b). The practical effect of this requirement is to condition acquisition of control of a corporation on approval of a majority of the pre-existing disinterested shareholders.

The shareholders decide whether to confer rights on the control shares at the next regularly scheduled meeting of the shareholders, or at a specially scheduled meeting. The acquiror can require management of the corporation to hold such a special meeting within 50 days if it files an "acquiring person statement," requests the meeting, and agrees to pay the expenses of the meeting. See § 23–1–42–7. If the shareholders do not vote to restore voting rights to the shares, the corporation may redeem the control shares from the acquiror at fair market value, but it is not required to do so. § 23–1–42–10(b). Similarly, if the acquiror does not file an acquiring person statement with the corporation, the corporation may, if its bylaws or articles of incorporation so provide, redeem the shares at any time after 60 days after the acquiror's last acquisition. § 23–1–42–10(a).

The Court first held that the Indiana Act was not preempted by the Williams Act:

. . . [T]he overriding concern of the MITE plurality was that the Illinois statute considered in that case operated to favor management against offerors, to the detriment of shareholders. By contrast, the statute now before the Court protects the independent shareholder against both of the contending parties. Thus, the Act furthers a basic purpose of the Williams Act, " 'plac[ing] investors on an equal footing with the takeover bidder,' " Piper v. Chris–Craft Industries, 430 U.S., at 30 (quoting the Senate Report accompanying the Williams Act, S.Rep. No. 550, 90th Cong., 1st Sess., 4 (1967)).

The Indiana Act, operates on the assumption, implicit in the Williams Act, that independent shareholders faced with tender offers often are at a disadvantage. By allowing such shareholders to vote as a group, the Act protects them from the coercive aspects of some tender offers. If, for example, shareholders believe that a successful tender offer will be followed by a purchase of nontendering shares at a depressed price, individual shareholders may tender their shares—even if they doubt the tender offer is in the corporation's best interest—to protect themselves from being forced to sell their shares at a depressed price. . . . In such a situation under the Indiana Act, the shareholders as a group, acting in the corporation's best interest, could reject the offer, although individual shareholders might be inclined to accept it. The desire of the Indiana Legislature to protect shareholders of Indiana corporations from this type of coercive offer does not conflict with the Williams Act. Rather, it furthers the federal policy of investor protection.

In implementing its goal, the Indiana Act avoids the problems the plurality discussed in MITE. Unlike the MITE statute, the Indiana Act does not give either management or the offeror an advantage in communicating with the shareholders about the impending offer. The Act also does not impose an indefinite delay on tender offers. Nothing in the Act prohibits an offeror from consummating an offer on the 20th business day, the earliest day permitted under applicable federal regulations, see 17 CFR § 240.14e–1(a) (1986). Nor does the Act allow the state government to interpose its views of fairness between willing buyers and sellers of shares of the target company. Rather, the Act allows *shareholders* to evaluate the fairness of the offer collectively. . . .

The Court of Appeals based its finding of pre-emption on its view that the practical effect of the Indiana Act is to delay consummation of tender offers until 50 days after the commencement of the offer. 794 F.2d, at 263. As did the Court of Appeals, Dynamics reasons that no rational offeror will purchase shares until it gains assurance that those shares will carry voting rights. Because it is possible that voting rights will not be conferred until a shareholder meeting 50 days after commencement of the offer, Dynamics concludes that the Act imposes a 50–day delay. This, it argues, conflicts with the shorter 20–business–day period established by the SEC as the minimum period for which a tender offer may be held open. 17 CFR § 240.14e–1 (1986). We find the alleged conflict illusory.

The Act does not impose an absolute 50–day delay on tender offers, nor does it preclude an offeror from purchasing shares as soon as federal law permits. If the offeror fears an adverse shareholder vote under the Act, it can make a conditional tender offer, offering to accept shares on the condition that the shares receive voting rights within a certain period of time. The Williams Act permits tender offers to be conditioned on the offeror's subsequently obtaining regulatory approval. . . . There is no reason to doubt that this type of conditional tender offer would be legitimate as well.

Even assuming that the Indiana Act imposes some additional delay, nothing in MITE suggested that *any* delay imposed by state regulation, however short, would create a conflict with the Williams Act. The plurality argued only that the offeror should "be free to go forward without *unreasonable* delay." 457 U.S., at 639 (emphasis added). In that case, the Court was confronted with the potential for indefinite delay and presented with no persuasive reason why some deadline could not be established. By contrast, the Indiana Act provides that full voting rights will be vested—if this eventually is to occur—within 50 days after commencement of the offer. This period is within the 60–day maximum period Congress established for tender offers in 15 U.S.C. § 78n(d)(5). We cannot say that a delay within that congressionally determined period is unreasonable.

The Court then held that the Indiana Act did not violate the Commerce Clause:

The Court of Appeals . . . [held that the Indiana Act was unconstitutional because of its] potential to hinder tender offers. We think the Court of Appeals failed to appreciate the significance for Commerce Clause analysis of the fact that state regulation of corporate governance is regulation of entities whose very existence and attributes are a product of state law. . . . Every State in this country has enacted laws regulating corporate governance. By prohibiting certain transactions, and regulating others, such laws necessarily affect certain aspects of interstate commerce. This necessarily is true with respect to corporations with shareholders in States other than the State of incorporation. . . .

It thus is an accepted part of the business landscape in this country for States to create corporations, to prescribe their powers, and to define the rights that are acquired by purchasing their shares. A State has an interest in promoting stable relationships among parties involved in the corporations it charters, as well as in ensuring that investors in such corporations have an effective voice in corporate affairs. . . .

Dynamics' argument that the Act is unconstitutional ultimately rests on its contention that the Act will limit the number of successful tender offers. There is little evidence that this will occur. But even if true, this result would not substantially affect our Commerce Clause analysis. We reiterate that this Act does not prohibit any entity—resident or nonresident—from offering to purchase, or from purchasing, shares in Indiana corporations, or from attempting thereby to gain control. It only provides regulatory procedures designed for the better protection of the corporations' shareholders. We have rejected the "notion that the Commerce Clause protects the particular structure or methods of operation in a ... market." Exxon Corp. v. Governor of Maryland, 437 U.S., at 127. The very commodity that is traded in the securities market is one whose characteristics are defined by state law. Similarly, the very commodity that is traded in the "market for corporate control"—the corporation—is one that owes its existence and attributes to state law. Indiana need not define these commodities as other States do; it need only provide that residents and nonresidents have equal access to them. This Indiana has done. Accordingly, even if the Act should decrease the number of successful tender offers for Indiana corporations, this would not offend the Commerce Clause.

———

DEL. GEN. CORP. LAW § 203

[See Statutory Supplement]

———

N.Y. BUS. CORP. LAW § 912

[See Statutory Supplement]

———

IND. CODE ANN. §§ 23–1–42–1 through 23–1–42–11

[See Statutory Supplement]

———

PENNSYLVANIA CONSOL. STATS.ANN., TIT. 15, §§ 1103, 2502, 2552, 2562, 2571–2576

[See Statutory Supplement]

———

AMANDA ACQUISITION CORP. v.
UNIVERSAL FOODS CORP.

United States Court of Appeals, Seventh Circuit, 1989.
877 F.2d 496, cert. denied 493 U.S. 955, 110 S.Ct. 367, 107 L.Ed.2d 353 (1989).

Before BAUER, Chief Judge, EASTERBROOK, Circuit Judge, and WILL, Senior District Judge.*

EASTERBROOK, Circuit Judge.

States have enacted three generations of takeover statutes in the last 20 years. Illinois enacted a first-generation statute, which forbade acquisitions of any firm with substantial assets in Illinois unless a public official approved. We concluded that such a statute injures investors, is preempted by the Williams Act, and is unconstitutional under the dormant Commerce Clause. MITE Corp. v. Dixon, 633 F.2d 486 (7th Cir.1980). The Supreme Court affirmed the judgment under the Commerce Clause, Edgar v. MITE Corp., 457 U.S. 624, 643–46, 102 S.Ct. 2629, 2641–43, 73 L.Ed.2d 269 (1982). Three Justices also agreed with our view of the Williams Act, id. at 634–40, 102 S.Ct. at 2636–39 (White, J., joined by Burger, C.J. & Blackmun, J.), while two disagreed, id., at 646–47, 102 S.Ct. at 2642–43 (Powell, J.), and 655, 102 S.Ct. at 2647 (Stevens, J.), and four did not address the subject.

Indiana enacted a second-generation statute, applicable only to firms incorporated there and eliminating governmental veto power. Indiana's law provides that the acquiring firm's shares lose their voting power unless the target's directors approve the acquisition or the shareholders not affiliated with either bidder or management authorize restoration of votes. We concluded that this statute, too, is inimical to investors' interests, preempted by the Williams Act, and unconstitutional under the Commerce Clause. Dynamics Corp. of America v. CTS Corp., 794 F.2d 250 (7th Cir.1986). This time the Supreme Court did not agree. It thought the Indiana statute consistent with both Williams Act and Commerce Clause. CTS Corp. v. Dynamics Corp. of America, 481 U.S. 69, 107 S.Ct. 1637, 95 L.Ed.2d 67 (1987). Adopting Justice White's view of preemption for the sake of argument, id. at 81, 107 S.Ct. at 1645, the Court found no inconsistency between state and federal law because Indiana allowed the bidder to *acquire* the shares without hindrance. Such a law makes the shares less attractive, but it does not regulate the process of bidding. As for the Commerce Clause, the Court took Indiana's law to be regulation of internal corporate affairs, potentially beneficial because it would allow investors to avoid the "coercion" of two-tier bids and other tactics. 481 U.S. at 83, 91–93, 107 S.Ct. at 1646, 1650–51. Justices White, Blackmun, and Stevens disagreed with the analysis under the Commerce Clause, id. at 99–101, 107 S.Ct. at 1655–56; only Justice White disagreed with the conclusion about preemption, id. at 97–99, 107 S.Ct. at 1653–55.

---

* Hon. Hubert L. Will, of the Northern District of Illinois, sitting by designation.

Wisconsin has a third-generation take-over statute. Enacted after *CTS*, it postpones the kinds of transactions that often follow tender offers (and often are the reason for making the offers in the first place). Unless the target's board agrees to the transaction in advance, the bidder must wait three years after buying the shares to merge with the target or acquire more than 5% of its assets. We must decide whether that is consistent with the Williams Act and Commerce Clause.

I

Amanda Acquisition Corporation is a shell with a single purpose: to acquire Universal Foods Corporation, a diversified firm incorporated in Wisconsin and traded on the New York Stock Exchange. Universal is covered by Wisconsin's anti-takeover law. Amanda is a subsidiary of High Voltage Engineering Corp., a small electronics firm in Massachusetts. Most of High Voltage's equity capital comes from Berisford Capital PLC, a British venture capital firm, and Hyde Park Partners L.P., a partnership affiliated with the principals of Berisford. Chase Manhattan Bank has promised to lend Amanda 50% of the cost of the acquisition, secured by the stock of Universal.

In mid-November 1988 Universal's stock was trading for about $25 per share. On December 1 Amanda commenced a tender offer at $30.50, to be effective if at least 75% of the stock should be tendered.[1] This all-cash, all-shares offer has been increased by stages to $38.00. Amanda's financing is contingent on a prompt merger with Universal if the offer succeeds, so the offer is conditional on a judicial declaration that the law is invalid. (It is also conditional on Universal's redemption of poison pill stock. For reasons that we discuss below, it is unnecessary to discuss the subject in detail.)

No firm incorporated in Wisconsin and having its headquarters, substantial operations, or 10% of its shares or shareholders there may "engage in a business combination with an interested stockholder ... for 3 years after the interested stockholder's stock acquisition date unless the board of directors of the [Wisconsin] corporation has approved, before the interested stockholder's stock acquisition date, that business combination or the purchase of stock", Wis.Stat. § 180.726(2). An "interested stockholder" is one owning 10% of the voting stock, directly or through associates (anyone acting in concert with it), § 180.726(1)(j). A "business combination" is a merger with the bidder or any of its affiliates, sale of more than 5% of the assets to bidder or affiliate, liquidation of the target, or a transaction by which the target guarantees the bidder's or [affiliate's] debts or passes tax benefits to the bidder or affiliate, § 180.726(1)(e). The law, in other words, provides for

---

1. Wisconsin has, in addition to § 180.726, a statute modeled on Indiana's, providing that an acquiring firm's shares lose their votes, which may be restored under specified circumstances. Wis.Stat. § 180.25(9). That law accounts for the 75% condition, but it is not pertinent to the questions we resolve.

almost hermetic separation of bidder and target for three years after the bidder obtains 10% of the stock—unless the target's board consented before then. No matter how popular the offer, the ban applies: obtaining 85% (even 100%) of the stock held by non-management shareholders won't allow the bidder to engage in a business combination, as it would under Delaware law. See BNS, Inc. v. Koppers Co., 683 F.Supp. 458 (D.Del.1988); RP Acquisition Corp. v. Staley Continental, Inc., 686 F.Supp. 476 (D.Del.1988); City Capital Associates L.P. v. Interco, Inc., 696 F.Supp. 1551 (D.Del.), affirmed, 860 F.2d 60 (3d Cir.1988). Wisconsin firms cannot opt out of the law, as may corporations subject to almost all other state takeover statutes. In Wisconsin it is management's approval in advance, or wait three years. Even when the time is up, the bidder needs the approval of a majority of the remaining investors, without any provision disqualifying shares still held by the managers who resisted the transaction, § 180.726(3)(b).[3] The district court found that this statute "effectively eliminates hostile leveraged buyouts". As a practical matter, Wisconsin prohibits any offer contingent on a merger between bidder and target, a condition attached to about 90% of contemporary tender offers.

Amanda filed this suit seeking a declaration that this law is preempted by the Williams Act and inconsistent with the Commerce Clause.... The district court declined to issue a preliminary injunction. 708 F.Supp. 984 (E.D.Wis.1989). It concluded that the statute is constitutional and not preempted, and that under Wisconsin law (which the court believed would follow Delaware's) directors are entitled to prevent investors from accepting tender offers of which the directors do not approve....

As a practical matter, the decision denying preliminary relief ends the case. The parties treat their appeals as if taken from the conclusive denial of relief; so shall we. The financial stakes on both sides cancel out, and the question becomes who is right on the merits. CTS, 794 F.2d at 252; see also FTC v. Elders Grain, Inc., 868 F.2d 901, 903–05 (7th Cir.1989).

II ...

A

If our views of the wisdom of state law mattered, Wisconsin's takeover statute would not survive. Like our colleagues who decided *MITE* and *CTS*, we believe that antitakeover legislation injures shareholders. *MITE*, 633 F.2d at 496–98 and 457 U.S. at 643–44, 102 S.Ct. at 2641–42; *CTS*, 794 F.2d at 253–55. Managers frequently realize gains for investors via voluntary combinations (mergers). If gaines are to be had, but managers balk, tender offers are investors' way to go over managers' heads. If managers are not maximizing the firm's value—perhaps because they have missed the possibility of a synergistic combination, perhaps because they are

---

3. Acquirors can avoid this requirement by buying out the remaining shareholders at a price defined by § 180.726(3)(c), but this is not a practical option.

clinging to divisions that could be better run in other hands, perhaps because they are just not the best persons for the job—a bidder that believes it can realize more of the firm's value will make investors a higher offer. Investors tender; the bidder gets control and changes things. Michael Bradley, Anand Desai & E. Han Kim, *Synergistic Gains from Corporate Acquisitions and Their Division Between the Stockholders of Target and Acquiring Firms,* 21 J.Fin. Econ. 3 (1988). The prospect of monitoring by would-be bidders, and an occasional bid at a premium, induces managers to run corporations more efficiently and replaces them if they will not.

Premium bids reflect the benefits for investors. The price of a firm's stock represents investors' consensus estimate of the value of the shares under current and anticipated conditions. Stock is worth the present value of anticipated future returns—dividends and other distributions. Tender offers succeed when bidders offer more. Only when the bid exceeds the value of the stock (however investors compute value) will it succeed. A statute that precludes investors from receiving or accepting a premium offer makes them worse off. It makes the economy worse off too, because the higher bid reflects the better use to which the bidder can put the target's assets. (If the bidder can't improve the use of the assets, it injures itself by paying a premium.)

Universal, making an argument common among supporters of anti-takeover laws, contends that its investors do not appreciate the worth of its business plans, that its stock is trading for too little, and that if investors tender reflexively they injure themselves. If only they would wait, Universal submits, they would do better under current management. A variant of the argument has it that although smart investors know that the stock is underpriced, many investors are passive and will tender; even the smart investors then must tender to avoid doing worse on the "back end" of the deal. State laws giving management the power to block an offer enable the managers to protect the investors from themselves.

Both versions of this price-is-wrong argument imply: (a) that the stock of firms defeating offers later appreciates in price topping the bid, thus revealing the wisdom of waiting till the market wises up; and (b) that investors in firms for which no offer is outstanding gain when they adopt devices so that managers may fend off unwanted offers (or states adopt laws with the same consequence). Efforts to verify these implications have failed. The best available data show that if a firm fends off a bid, its profits decline, and its stock price (adjusted for inflation and market-wide changes) never tops the initial bid, even if it is later acquired by another firm. Gregg A. Jarrell, James A. Brickley & Jeffrey M. Netter, *The Market for Corporate Control: The Empirical Evidence Since 1980,* 2 J.Econ.Perspectives 49, 55 (1988) (collecting studies); John Pound, *The Information Effects of Takeover Bids and Resistance,* 22 J.Fin. Econ. 207 (1988). Stock of firms adopting poison pills falls in price, as does the stock of firms that adopt most kinds of anti-takeover amendments to their articles of incorporation. Jarrell,

Brickley & Netter, 2 J.Econ.Perspectives at 58–65 (collecting studies); Michael C. Jensen, *Takeovers: Their Causes and Consequences*, 2 J.Econ.Perspectives, 21, 25–28, 41–45 (1988); Michael Ryngaert, *The Effect of Poison Pill Securities on Shareholder Wealth*, 20 J.Fin.Econ. 377 (1988); cf. John Pound, *The Effects of Antitakeover Amendments on Takeover Activity: Some Direct Evidence*, 30 J.L. & Econ. 353 (1987). Studies of laws similar to Wisconsin's produce the same conclusion: share prices of firms incorporated in the state drop when the legislation is enacted. Jonathan M. Karpoff & Paul H. Malatesta, *The Wealth Effects of Second Generation State Takeover Legislation*, University of Washington Graduate School of Business Working Paper (Dec. 22, 1988).

Although a takeover-*proof* firm leaves investors at the mercy of incumbent managers (who may be mistaken about the wisdom of their business plan even when they act in the best of faith), a takeover-*resistant* firm may be able to assist its investors. An auction may run up the price, and delay may be essential to an auction. Auctions transfer money from bidders to targets, and diversified investors would not gain from them (their left pocket loses what the right pocket gains); diversified investors would lose from auctions if the lower returns to bidders discourage future bids. But from targets' perspectives, once a bid is on the table an auction may be the best strategy. The full effects of auctions are hard to unravel, sparking scholarly debate. Devices giving managers some ability to orchestrate investors' responses, in order to avoid panic tenders in response to front-end-loaded offers, also could be beneficial, as the Supreme Court emphasized in *CTS*, 481 U.S. at 92–93, 107 S.Ct. at 1651–52. ("Could be" is an important qualifier; even from a perspective limited to targets' shareholders given a bid on the table, it is important to know whether managers use this power to augment bids or to stifle them, and whether courts can tell the two apart.)

State anti-takeover laws do not serve these ends well, however. Investors who prefer to give managers the discretion to orchestrate responses to bids may do so through "fair-price" clauses in the articles of incorporation and other consensual devices. Other firms may choose different strategies. A law such as Wisconsin's does not add options to firms that would like to give more discretion to their managers; instead it destroys the possibility of divergent choices. Wisconsin's law applies even when the investors prefer to leave their managers under the gun, to allow the market full sway. Karpoff and Malatesta found that state anti-takeover laws have little or no effect on the price of shares if the firm already has poison pills (or related devices) in place, but strongly negative effects on price when firms have no such contractual devices. To put this differently, state laws have bite only when investors, given the choice, would deny managers the power to interfere with tender offers (maybe already *have* denied managers that power). See also Roberta Romano, *The Political Economy of Takeover Statutes*, 73 Va.L.Rev. 111, 128–31 (1987).

B

Skepticism about the wisdom of a state's law does not lead to the conclusion that the law is beyond the state's power, however. We have not been elected custodians of investors' wealth. States need not treat investors' welfare as their summun bonum. Perhaps they choose to protect managers' welfare instead, or believe that the current economic literature reaches an incorrect conclusion and that despite appearances takeovers injure investors in the long run. Unless a federal statute or the Constitution bars the way, Wisconsin's choice must be respected.

Amanda relies on the Williams Act of 1968, incorporated into §§ 13(d), (e) and 14(d)–(f) of the Securities Exchange Act of 1934, 15 U.S.C. §§ 78m(d), (e), 78n(d)–(f). The Williams Act regulates the conduct of tender offers. Amanda believes that Congress created an entitlement for investors to receive the benefit of tender offers, and that because Wisconsin's law makes tender offers unattractive to many potential bidders, it is preempted. See *MITE*, 633 F.2d at 490–99, and Justice White's views, 457 U.S. at 630–40, 102 S.Ct. at 2634–40.

Preemption has not won easy acceptance among the Justices for several reasons. First there is § 28(a) of the '34 Act, 15 U.S.C. § 78bb(a), which provides that "[n]othing in this chapter shall affect the jurisdiction of the securities commission . . . of any State over any security or any person insofar as it does not conflict with the provisions of this chapter or the rules and regulations thereunder." Although some of the SEC's regulations (particularly the one defining the commencement of an offer) conflict with some state takeover laws, the SEC has not drafted regulations concerning mergers with controlling shareholders, and the Act itself does not address the subject. States have used the leeway afforded by § 28(a) to carry out "merit regulation" of securities—"blue sky" laws that allow securities commissioners to forbid sales altogether, in contrast with the federal regimen emphasizing disclosure. So § 28(a) allows states to stop some transactions federal law would permit, in pursuit of an approach at odds with a system emphasizing disclosure and investors' choice. Then there is the traditional reluctance of federal courts to infer preemption of "state law in areas traditionally regulated by the States", California v. ARC America Corp., ___ U.S. ___, 109 S.Ct. 1661, 1665, 104 L.Ed.2d 86 (1989); see also, e.g., Hillsborough County v. Automated Medical Laboratories, Inc., 471 U.S. 707, 716, 105 S.Ct. 2371, 2376, 85 L.Ed.2d 714 (1985); Air Line Pilots Ass'n v. UAL Corp., 874 F.2d 439, 447–48 (7th Cir.1989). States have regulated corporate affairs, including mergers and sales of assets, since before the beginning of the nation.

Because Justice White's views of the Williams Act did not garner the support of a majority of the Court in *MITE*, we reexamined that subject in *CTS* and observed that the best argument for preemption is the Williams Act's "neutrality" between bidder and management, a balance designed to leave investors free to choose. This is not a confident jumping-off point, though: "Of course it is a big leap from saying that the Williams Act does not itself exhibit much hostility to tender offers to saying that it implicitly forbids states to adopt more hostile regulations, but this leap was taken by the Supreme Court plurality and us in *MITE* and by every court to consider the question since.... [W]hatever doubts of the Williams' Act preemptive intent we might entertain as an original matter are stifled by the weight of precedent." 794 F.2d at 262. The rough treatment of our views received from the Court—only Justice White supported the holding on preemption—lifts the "weight of precedent".

There is a big difference between what Congress *enacts* and what it *supposes* will ensue. Expectations about the consequences of a law are not themselves law. To say that Congress wanted to be neutral between bidder and target—a conclusion reached in many of the Court's opinions, e.g., Piper v. Chris–Craft Industries, Inc., 430 U.S. 1, 97 S.Ct. 926, 51 L.Ed.2d 124 (1977)—is not to say that it also forbade the states to favor one of these sides. Every law has a stopping point, likely one selected because of a belief that it would be unwise (for now, maybe forever) to do more. Rodriguez v. United States, 480 U.S. 522, 525–26, 107 S.Ct. 1391, 1393–94, 94 L.Ed.2d 533 (1987); Covalt v. Carey Canada Inc., 860 F.2d 1434, 1439 (7th Cir.1988). Nothing in the Williams Act says that the federal compromise among bidders, targets' managers, and investors is the only permissible one. See Daniel R. Fischel, *From MITE to CTS: State Anti–Takeover Statutes, the Williams Act, the Commerce Clause, and Insider Trading,* 1987 Sup.Ct.Rev. 47, 71–74. Like the majority of the Court in *CTS,* however, we stop short of the precipice. 481 U.S. at 78–87, 107 S.Ct. at 1643–49.

The Williams Act regulates the *process* of tender offers: timing, disclosure, proration if tenders exceed what the bidder is willing to buy, best-price rules. It slows things down, allowing investors to evaluate the offer and management's response. Best-price, proration, and short-tender rules ensure that investors who decide at the end of the offer get the same treatment as those who decide immediately, reducing pressure to leap before looking.[7] After complying with the disclosure and delay requirements, the bidder is free to take the shares. *MITE* held invalid a state law that increased the delay and, by authorizing a regulator to nix the offer, created a distinct possibility that the bidder would be unable to buy the stock (and the holders to sell it) despite compliance with federal law. Illinois tried to regulate the process of tender offers, contradicting in some respects the federal rules. Indiana, by contrast, allowed the tender offer to take its course as the Williams Act specified but "sterilized" the acquired shares until the remaining investors restored their voting rights. Congress said nothing about the voting

---

7. To reduce is not to eliminate. Investors' options include selling to arbitrageurs in the market. This price fluctuates daily and may drop suddenly if the prospects of the bid's success dim.

power of shares acquired in tender offers. Indiana's law reduced the benefits the bidder anticipated from the acquisition but left the process alone. So the Court, although accepting Justice White's views for the purpose of argument, held that Indiana's rules do not conflict with the federal norms.

CTS observed that laws affecting the voting power of acquired shares do not differ in principle from many other rules governing the internal affairs of corporations. Laws requiring staggered or classified boards of directors delay the transfer of control to the bidder; laws requiring supermajority vote for a merger may make a transaction less attractive or impossible. 481 U.S. at 85–86, 107 S.Ct. at 1647–48. Yet these are not preempted by the Williams Act, any more than state laws concerning the *effect* of investors' votes are preempted by the portions of the Exchange Act, 15 U.S.C. § 78n(a)–(c), regulating the process of soliciting proxies. Federal securities laws frequently regulate process while state corporate law regulates substance. Federal proxy rules demand that firms disclose many things, in order to promote informed voting. Yet states may permit or compel a supermajority rule (even a unanimity rule) rendering it all but impossible for a particular side to prevail in the voting. See Robert Charles Clark, *Corporate Law* § 9.1.3 (1986). Are the state laws therefore preempted? How about state laws that allow many firms to organize without traded shares? Universities, hospitals, and other charities have self-perpetuating boards and cannot be acquired by tender offer. Insurance companies may be organized as mutuals, without traded shares; retailers often organize as co-operatives, without traded stock; some decently large companies (large enough to be "reporting companies" under the '34 Act) issue stock subject to buy-sell agreements under which the investors cannot sell to strangers without offering stock to the firm at a formula price; Ford Motor Co. issued non-voting stock to outside investors while reserving voting stock for the family, thus preventing outsiders from gaining control (dual-class stock is becoming more common); first issue and state law enforces poison pills. All of these devices make tender offers unattractive (even impossible) and greatly diminish the power of proxy fights, success in which often depends on buying votes by acquiring the equity to which the vote is attached. See Douglas H. Blair, Devra L. Golbe & James M. Gerard, *Unbundling the Voting Rights and Profit Claims of Common Shares*, 97 J.Pol.Econ. 420 (1989). None of these devices could be though preempted by the Williams Act or the proxy rules. If they are not preempted, neither is Wis.Stat. § 180.726.

Any bidder complying with federal law is free to acquire shares of Wisconsin firms on schedule. Delay in completing a second-stage merger may make the target less attractive, and thus depress the price offered or even lead to an absence of bids; it does not, however, alter any of the procedures governed by federal regulation. Indeed Wisconsin's law does not depend in any way on how the acquiring firm came by its stock: open-market purchases, private acquisitions of blocs, and acquisitions via tender offers are treated identically. Wisconsin's law is no different in effect from one saying that for the three years after a person acquires 10% of a firm's stock, a unanimous vote is required to merge. Corporate law once had a generally-applicable unanimity rule in major transactions, a rule discarded because giving every investor the power to block every reorganization stopped many desirable changes. (Many investors could use their "hold-up" power to try to engross a larger portion of the gains, creating a complex bargaining problem that often could not be solved.) Wisconsin's more restrained version of unanimity also may block beneficial transactions, but not by tinkering with any of the procedures established in federal law.

Only if the Williams Act gives investors a right to be the beneficiary of offers could Wisconsin's law run afoul of the federal rule. No such entitlement can be mined out of the Williams Act, however. Schreiber v. Burlington Northern, Inc., 472 U.S. 1, 105 S.Ct. 2458, 86 L.Ed.2d 1 (1985), holds that the cancellation of a pending offer because of machinations between bidder and target does not deprive investors of their due under the Williams Act. The Court treated § 14(e) as a disclosure law, so that investors could make informed decisions; it follows that events leading bidders to cease their quest do not conflict with the Williams Act any more than a state law leading a firm not to issue new securities could conflict with the Securities Act of 1933. See also Panter v. Marshall Field & Co., 646 F.2d 271, 283–85 (7th Cir.1981); Lewis v. McGraw, 619 F.2d 192 (2d Cir.1980), both holding that the evaporation of an opportunity to tender one's shares when a defensive tactic leads the bidder to withdraw the invitation does not violate the Williams Act. Investors have no right to receive tender offers. More to the point—since Amanda sues as bidder rather than as investor seeking to sell—the Williams Act does not create a right to profit from the business of making tender offers. It is not attractive to put bids on the table for Wisconsin corporations, but because Wisconsin leaves the process alone once a bidder appears, its law may co-exist with the Williams Act.

C

The Commerce Clause, Art. I, § 8 cl. 3 of the Constitution, grants Congress the power "[t]o regulate Commerce . . . among the several States". For many decades the Court took this to be what it says: a grant to Congress with no implications for the states' authority to act when Congress is silent. . . . Broad dicta in *Cooley v. Board of Wardens,* 53 U.S. (12 How.) 299, 13 L.Ed. 996 (1852), eventually led to holdings denying states the power to regulate interstate commerce directly or discriminatorily, or to take steps that had unjustified consequences in other states. . . .

When state law discriminates against interstate commerce expressly—for example, when Wisconsin closes its border to butter from Minnesota—the negative Commerce Clause steps in. The law before us is not of this type: it is neutral between inter-state and intra-state commerce. Amanda therefore presses on us the broader, all-weather, be-reasonable vision of the Constitution. Wisconsin has passed a law that unreasonably injures investors, most of whom live outside of Wisconsin, and therefore it *has* to be unconstitutional, as Amanda sees things. Although Pike v. Bruce Church, Inc., 397 U.S. 137, 90 S.Ct. 844, 25 L.Ed.2d 174 (1970), sometimes is understood to authorize such general-purpose balancing, a closer examination of the cases may support the conclusion that the Court has looked for discrimination rather than for baleful effects. See Donald H. Regan, *The Supreme Court and State Protectionism: Making Sense of the Dormant Commerce Clause,* 84 Mich.L.Rev. 1091 (1986); Julian N. Eule, Laying the Dormant Commerce Clause to Rest, 91 Yale L.J. 425 (1982). At all events, although *MITE* employed the balancing process described in *Pike* to deal with a statute that regulated all firms having "contacts" with the state, *CTS* did not even cite that case when dealing with a statute regulating only the affairs of a firm incorporated in the state, and Justice Scalia's concurring opinion questioned its application. 481 U.S. at 95–96, 107 S.Ct. at 1652–53. The Court took a decidedly confined view of the judicial role: "We are not inclined 'to second-guess the empirical judgments of lawmakers concerning the utility of legislation,' *Kassel v. Consolidated Freightways Corp.,* 450 U.S. [662] at 679 [101 S.Ct. 1309, 1320, 67 L.Ed.2d 580 (1981)] (BRENNAN, J., concurring in judgment)." 481 U.S. at 92, 107 S.Ct. at 1651. Although the scholars whose writings we cited in Part II.A conclude that laws such as Wisconsin's injure investors, Wisconsin is entitled to give a different answer to this empirical question—or to decide that investors' interests should be sacrificed to protect managers' interests or promote the stability of corporate arrangements.

Illinois's law, held invalid in *MITE,* regulated sales of stock elsewhere. Illinois tried to tell a Texas owner of stock in a Delaware corporation that he could not sell to a buyer in California. By contrast, Wisconsin's law, like the Indiana statute sustained by *CTS,* regulates the internal affairs of firms incorporated there. Investors may buy or sell stock as they please. Wisconsin's law differs in this respect not only from that of Illinois but also from that of Massachusetts, which forbade any transfer of shares for one year after the failure to disclose any material fact, a flaw that led the First Circuit to condemn it. Hyde Park Partners, L.P. v. Connolly, 839 F.2d 837, 847–48 (1st Cir.1988).

Buyers of stock in Wisconsin firms may exercise full rights as investors, taking immediate control. No interstate transaction is regulated or forbidden. True, Wisconsin's law makes a potential buyer less willing to buy (or depresses the bid), but this is equally true of Indiana's rule. Many other rules of corporate law—super majority voting requirements, staggered and classified boards, and so on—have similar or greater effects on some persons' willingness to purchase stock. *CTS,* 481 U.S. at 89–90, 107 S.Ct. at 1649–50. States could ban mergers outright, with even more powerful consequences. Louisville & Nashville R.R. v. Kentucky, 161 U.S. 677,

701–04, 16 S.Ct. 714, 723–25, 40 L.Ed. 849 (1896); see also Kansas City, Memphis & Birmingham R.R. v. Stiles, 242 U.S. 111, 117, 37 S.Ct. 58, 60, 61 L.Ed. 176 (1916); Ashley v. Ryan, 153 U.S. 436, 443, 14 S.Ct. 865, 867, 38 L.Ed. 773 (18940. Wisconsin did not allow mergers among firms chartered there until 1947. We doubt that it was violating the Commerce Clause all those years. Cf. Edmund W. Kitch, *Regulation and the American Common Market, in Regulation, Federalism, and Interstate Commerce* 7 (A. Dan Tarlock ed. 1981). Every rule of corporate law affects investors who live outside the state of incorporation, yet this has never been thought sufficient to authorize a form of cost-benefit inquiry through the medium of the Commerce Clause.

Wisconsin, like Indiana, is indifferent to the domicile of the bidder. A putative bidder located in Wisconsin enjoys no privilege over a firm located in New York. So too with investors: all are treated identically, regardless of residence. Doubtless most bidders (and investors) are located outside Wisconsin, but unless the law discriminates according to residence this alone does not matter. *CTS,* 481 U.S. at 87–88, 107 S.Ct. at 1648–49. . . . "Because nothing in the [Wisconsin] Act imposes a greater burden on out-of-state offerors than it does on similarly situated [Wisconsin] offerors, we reject the contention that the Act discriminates against interstate commerce." *CTS,* 481 U.S. at 88, 107 S.Ct. at 1649. For the same reason, the Court long ago held that state blue sky laws comport with the Commerce Clause. Hall v. Geiger–Jones Co., 242 U.S. 539, 37 S.Ct. 217, 61 L.Ed. 480 (1917); Caldwell v. Sioux Falls Stock Yards Co., 242 U.S. 559, 37 S.Ct. 224, 61 L.Ed. 493 (1917); Merrick v. N.W. Halsey & Co., 242 U.S. 568, 37 S.Ct. 227, 61 L.Ed. 498 (1917). Blue sky laws may bar Texans from selling stock in Wisconsin, but they apply equally to local residents' attempts to sell. That their application blocks a form of commerce altogether does not strip the states of power.

Wisconsin could exceed its powers by subjecting firms to inconsistent regulation. Because § 180.726 applies only to a subset of firms incorporated in Wisconsin, however, there is no possibility of inconsistent regulation. Here, too, the Wisconsin law is materially identical to Indiana's. *CTS,* 481 U.S. at 88–89, 107 S.Ct. at 1649–50. This leaves only the argument that Wisconsin's law hinders the flow of interstate trade "too much". *CTS* dispatched this concern by declaring it inapplicable to laws that apply only to the internal affairs of firms incorporated in the regulating state. 481 U.S. at 89–94, 107 S.Ct. at 1649–52. States may regulate corporate transactions as they choose without having to demonstrate under an unfocused balancing test that the benefits are "enough" to justify the consequences. . . .

The three district judges who have considered and sustained Delaware's law delaying mergers did so in large measure because they believed that the law left hostile offers "a meaningful opportunity for success". BNS, Inc. v. Koppers Co., 683 F.Supp. at 469. See also RP Acquisition Corp., 686 F.Supp. at 482–84, 488; City

Capital Associates, 696 F.Supp. at 1555. Delaware allows a merger to occur forthwith if the bidder obtains 85% of the shares other than those held by management and employee stock plans. If the bid is attractive to the bulk of the unaffiliated investors, it succeeds. Wisconsin offers no such opportunity, which Amanda believes is fatal.

Even in Wisconsin, though, options remain. Defenses impenetrable to the naked eye may have cracks. . . . [T]here are countermeasures to statutes deferring mergers. The cheapest is to lower the bid to reflect the costs of delay. Because every potential bidder labors under the same drawback, the firm placing the highest value on the target still should win. Or a bidder might take down the stock and pledge it (or its dividends) as security for any loans. That is, the bidder would operate the target as a subsidiary for three years. The corporate world is full of partially owned subsidiaries. If there is gain to be had from changing the debt-equity ratio of the target, that can be done consistent with Wisconsin law. The prospect of being locked into place as holders of illiquid minority positions would cause many persons to sell out, and the threat of being locked in would cause many managers to give assent in advance, as Wisconsin allows. (Or bidders might demand that directors waive their protections of state law. . . . Many bidders would find lock-in unattractive because of the potential for litigation by minority investors, and the need to operate the firm as a subsidiary might foreclose savings or synergies from merger. So none of these options is a perfect substitute for immediate merger, but each is a crack in the defensive wall allowing some value-increasing bids to proceed.

At the end of the day, however, it does not matter whether these countermeasures are "enough". The Commerce Clause does not demand that states leave bidders a "meaningful opportunity for success". Maryland enacted a law that absolutely banned vertical integration in the oil business. No opportunities, "meaningful" or otherwise, remained to firms wanting to own retail outlets. Exxon Corp. v. Governor of Maryland held that the law is consistent with the Commerce Clause, even on the assumption that it injures consumers and investors alike. A state with the power to forbid mergers has the power to defer them for three years. Investors can turn to firms incorporated in states committed to the dominance of market forces, or they can turn on legislators who enact unwise laws. The Constitution has room for many economic policies. "[A] law can be both economic folly and constitutional." *CTS*, 481 U.S. at 96–97, 107 S.Ct. at 1653–54 (Scalia, J., concurring). Wisconsin's law may well be folly; we are confident that it is constitutional.

AFFIRMED.

Chapter XII

LEGAL CAPITAL AND DISTRIBUTIONS

SECTION 1. LEGAL CAPITAL AND LIABILITY FOR WATERED STOCK

Most of this Chapter (Sections 2 and 3) concerns distributions to shareholders—that is, amounts paid by the corporation to shareholders, in that capacity, through dividends or repurchases of stock. The law of distributions can only be understood, however, against the background of the law concerning legal capital. That law, in turn, can only be understood against the background of a concept known as "par" or "par value," because traditionally a corporation's legal capital consisted of the aggregate par value of its issued shares.

At one time, all shares carried a par value. Normally, the par value of a share was the price at which it was expected that the share would be sold ("issued") by the corporation. Thus in the paradigm case, a share that carried a $100 par value would be issued for $100. Often, however, shares were issued at less than par. Sometimes, shares could not be issued at par because the real value of the shares was less than their par value. Sometimes, shares were sold for property that was supposed to be worth the aggregate par value of the shares but was not, because it was overvalued. These and other reasons gave rise to a large and complicated body of law, which centered on "bonus," "discount" and "watered" stock. " 'Bonus' shares are shares issued without payment or any amount, perhaps as a 'bonus' for the purchase of another class of security. . . . 'Discount' shares are shares issued for an amount less than par; e.g., $10 par stock issued for a $7 cash payment. . . . 'Watered shares' . . . are shares issued for non-liquid property which is worth less than par although asserted to be worth at least par." T. Fiflis, Accounting Issues for Lawyers 366 note h (4th ed. 1991). The term "watered" stock—which is commonly used to describe bonus and discount stock as well, "is a pun derived from the practice of certain ranchers or traders who watered their livestock before weighing at sale points." Id. at 366.

A shareholder to whom watered stock had been issued would not be liable to make any further payment solely as a matter of contract, because he would have paid all that he agreed to pay. However, a holder of watered stock was often subject to liability to the corporation, or more usually to its creditors, as a matter of corporation law, in the amount of the difference between par value and either (i) the price the shareholder paid, or (ii) the actual value of property the shareholder exchanged for the stock. This liability was grounded on various theories. Early on, the liability was grounded on the "trust fund" theory, associated with Wood v. Dummer, 30 Fed.Cas. 435, 436 (C.C.Me.1824). This case involved a suit by creditors against shareholders to whom an allegedly improper dividend had been paid. In the following, famous passage, Judge Store established the trust fund theory of capital and dividends:

> It appears to me very clear upon general principles, ... that the capital stock of banks is to be deemed a pledge or trust fund for the payment of the debts contracted by the bank. The public, as well as the legislature, have always supposed this to be a fund appropriated for such purpose. The individual stockholders are not liable for the debts of the bank in their private capacities. The charter relieves them from personal responsibility, and substitutes the capital stock in its stead. Credit is universally given to this fund by the public, as the only means of repayment. During the existence of the corporation it is the sole property of the corporation, and can be applied only according to its charter, that is, as a fund for payment of its debts, upon the security of which it may discount and circulate notes. Why, otherwise, is any capital stock required by our charters? If the stock may, the next day after it is paid in, be withdrawn by the stockholders without payment of the debts of the corporation, why is its amount so studiously provided for, and its payment by the stockholders so diligently required? To me this point appears so plain upon principles of law, as well as common sense, that I cannot be brought into any doubt, that the charters of our banks make the capital stock a trust fund for the payment of all the debts of the corporation. The billholders and other creditors have the first claims upon it; and the stockholders have no rights, until all the other creditors are satisfied. They have the full benefit of all the profits made by the establishment, and cannot take any portion of the fund, until all the other claims on it are extinguished. Their rights are not to the capital stock, but to the residuum after all demands on it are paid.

Although now outmoded and superseded in many respects, the trust-fund theory served as the conceptual backdrop not only for watered-stock liability, but for traditional dividend statutes, discussed in Section 2, which at least nominally were aimed in large part at preserving capital for the benefit of creditors. In Hospes v. Northwestern Mfg. & Car Co., 48 Minn. 174, 50 N.W. 1117 (1892), however, the Minnesota court showed that the trust fund theory for liability on watered stock didn't make sense and was riddled with exceptions. *Hospes* substituted a new theory, known as the constructive-fraud, misrepresentation, or holding-out theory. The basis of the theory was that:

The capital of a corporation is the basis of its credit. It is a substitute for the individual liability of those who own its stock. People deal with it and give it credit on the faith of it. They have a right to assume that it has paid-in capital to the amount which it represents itself as having; and if they give it credit on the faith of that representation, and if the representation is false, it is a fraud upon them; and, in case the corporation becomes insolvent, the law, upon the plainest principles of common justice, says to the delinquent stockholder, "Make that representation good by paying for your stock."

The difference between the trust-fund and constructive-fraud theories was that "the trust fund theory purported to hold the shareholder liable in all events to make up this difference for the benefit of creditors, although certain exceptions were later made by the courts following this theory; whereas, the fraud theory made certain exceptions in cases where the particular creditor plaintiff could not have relied on the full amount of the par value of the stock having been paid in, for example, if his debt arose before the transaction in which the stock was issued." 2 H. Marsh & R. Finkle, Marsh's California Corporations Law § 16.14 (3d ed. 1990).

Eventually, watered-stock liability became unimportant. A practice emerged under which the par value of stock is not the price at which the stock is to be issued, but a purely nominal amount. For example, stock that is to be issued at $50 might carry a par value of only $1, or even less. Such stock is known as "low-par" stock.

Furthermore, the statutes were universally amended to allow the issuance of "no-par" stock—stock that did not carry any par value at all. In addition, people began to care less about the whole problem, because modern legal disclosure requirements and fiduciary obligations obviated the underlying problems that gave rise to watered-stock liability. These changes in law and practice rendered the watered-stock issue almost nonexistent, because liability for watered stock is based on stock having been issued for less than par value, and with low-par or no-par stock that can seldom happen.[1]

When no-par stock is utilized, the corporation's legal or stated capital is basically that portion of the issue price of the no-par stock that the board allocates to legal capital when the stock is issued.

When low-par stock is utilized, the corporation's legal (or "stated") capital is basically determined by the same formula that applies to high-par stock—the total par value of all issued shares. However, although the formula is the same, the impact of the

---

1. Nevertheless, shareholder liability based on the purchase of stock is not completely a dead letter. Many or most statutes still make provision for par value, and in such states watered stock liability may arise where, as a result of bad planning or other factors, the corporation uses a high-par value stock. See, e.g., Hanewald v. Bryan's, Inc., 429 N.W.2d 414 (N.D.1988). Furthermore, under all statutes a shareholder is liable for the unpaid balance of the amount he agreed to pay for his stock, and this liability can often be enforced directly by creditors. See, e.g., Del.Gen.Corp.Law §§ 162, 325; RMBCA § 6.20(d).

formula is much different.   If stock is issued at a price equal to par, there is a relationship between the corporation's economic capital— what the shareholders have contributed for their shares—and the corporation's legal capital.   When stock is issued at a price far above par, there is no such relationship.

In either case, capital will also include any amounts later transferred to legal or stated capital by the board.

Many newer dividend statutes, such as the California statute and the Revised Model Business Corporation Act (discussed below in Section 2 (j)), eliminate the concept of par value for all practical purposes.   As stated in the Comment to RMBCA § 6.21, "Since shares need not have a par value, under section 6.21 there is no minimum price at which specific shares must be issued and therefore there can be no 'watered stock' liability for issuing shares below an arbitrarily fixed price."

SECTION 2.   DIVIDENDS

Conventionally, a corporation distributes funds to its shareholders in one or two ways: by paying a dividend, or by repurchasing shares of its stock.   Corporate law and (in a less elaborate way) the law of creditors' remedies have traditionally set limits on such distributions through the use of various financial tests.   Section 2 will concern financial limitations imposed on the payment of dividends.   Section 3 will concern the subject of repurchases.[1]

(a) DIVIDEND POLICY

R. BREALEY & S. MYERS PRINCIPLES OF CORPORATE FINANCE 371–388

Fourth Edition, 1991.

16–2 HOW DO COMPANIES DECIDE ON DIVIDEND PAYMENTS?

In the mid–1950s John Lintner conducted a classic series of interviews with corporate managers about their dividend policies.[6] His description of how dividends are determined can be summarized in four "stylized facts":

1. A purchase by a corporation of its own stock is conventionally referred to as a "repurchase."   The term is used in the sense "to regain by purchase," rather than in its other sense, "to buy again."

6. J. Lintner, "Distribution of Incomes of Corporations among Dividends, Retained Earnings, and Taxes," *American Economic Review,* 46: 97–113 (May 1956).

1. Firms have long-run target dividend payout ratios.

2. Managers focus more on dividend changes than on absolute levels. Thus, paying a $2.00 dividend is an important financial decision if last year's dividend was $1.00, but no big deal if last year's dividend was $2.00.

3. Dividend changes follow shifts in long-run, sustainable earnings. Managers "smooth" dividends. Transitory earnings changes are unlikely to affect dividend payouts.

4. Managers are reluctant to make dividend changes that might have to be reversed. They are particularly worried about having to rescind a dividend increase....

Lintner's simple model [of dividend decisions] suggests that the dividend depends in part on the firm's current earnings and in part on the dividend for the previous year, which in turn depends on that year's earnings and the dividend in the year before. Therefore if Lintner is correct, we should be able to describe dividends in terms of a weighted average of current and past earnings. The probability of an increase in the dividend rate should be greatest when *current* earnings have increased; it should be somewhat less when only the earnings from the previous year have increased and so on. An extensive study by Fama and Babiak confirmed this hypothesis.[9]

... This simple model seems to provide a fairly good explanation of how companies decide on the dividend rate, but it is unlikely to be the whole story. We would also expect managers to take future prospects into account when setting the payment. And that is what we find.

For example, Healy and Palepu report that between 1970 and 1979 companies that made a dividend payment for the first time experienced relatively flat earnings growth until the year before the announcement.[10] In that year earnings grew by an average 43 percent. If managers thought that this was a temporary windfall, they might have been cautious about committing themselves to paying out cash. But it looks as if they had good reason to be confident about prospects, for over the next 4 years earnings grew by a further 164 percent.

Since dividends anticipate future earnings, it is no surprise to find that announcements of dividend cuts are usually taken as bad news (stock price typically falls) and that dividend increases are good news (stock price rises). In the case of the dividend initiations studied by Healy and Palepu, the announcement of the dividend resulted in an abnormal rise of 4 percent in the stock price. It's important not to jump to the conclusion that this shows

9. E. F. Fama and H. Babiak, "Dividend Policy: An Empirical Analysis," *Journal of the American Statistical Association*, 63: 1132–1161 (December 1968), p. 1134.

10. See P. Healy and K. Palepu, "Earnings Information Conveyed by Dividend Initiations and Omissions," *Journal of Financial Economics*, 21: 149–175 (1988).

that investors like higher dividends for their own sake. The dividend may be welcomed only as a sign of higher future earnings....

Market efficiency means that all information available to investors is quickly and accurately impounded in stock prices. It does not imply that fundamental information about a company's operations or prospects is always cheaply or easily obtained. Investors therefore seize on any clue. That is why stock prices respond to stock splits, dividend changes, and other actions or announcements which reveal managements' optimism or pessimism about their firms' futures.

16–3   CONTROVERSY ABOUT DIVIDEND POLICY

Now we turn to the controversial question of how dividend policy affects value. One endearing feature of economics is that it can always accommodate not just two, but three opposing points of view. And so it is with the controversy about dividend policy. On the right there is a conservative group which believes that an increase in dividend payout increases firm value. On the left, there is a radical group which believes that an increase in payout reduces value. And in the center there is a middle-of-the-road party which claims that dividend policy makes no difference.

The middle-of-the-road party was founded in 1961 by Miller and Modigliani (always referred to as *MM* or *M* and *M*), when they published a theoretical paper showing the irrelevance of dividend policy in a world without taxes, transaction costs, or other market imperfections.[12]   ...

In their classic 1961 article MM argued as follows: Suppose your firm has settled on its investment program. You have worked out how much of this program can be financed from borrowing, and you plan to meet the remaining funds requirement from retained earnings. Any surplus money is to be paid out as dividends.

Now think what happens if you want to increase the dividend payment without changing the investment and borrowing policy. The extra money must come from somewhere. If the firm fixes its borrowing, the only way it can finance the extra dividend is to print some more shares and sell them. The new stockholders are going to part with their money only if you can offer them shares that are worth as much as they cost. But how can the firm do this when its assets, earnings, investment opportunities and, therefore, market value are all unchanged? The answer is that there must be a *transfer of value* from the old to the new stockholders. The new ones get the newly printed shares, each one worth less than before the dividend change was announced, and the old ones suffer a capital loss on their shares. The capital loss borne by the old shareholders just offsets the extra cash dividend they receive....

12. M.H. Miller and F. Modigliani: "Dividend Policy, Growth and the Valua- tion of Shares," *Journal of Business,* 34: 411–433 (October 1961).

Does it make any difference to the old stockholders that they receive an extra dividend payment plus an offsetting capital loss? It might if that were the only way they could get their hands on cash. But as long as there are efficient capital markets, they can raise the cash by selling shares. Thus the old shareholders can "cash in" either by persuading the management to pay a higher dividend or by selling some of their shares. In either case there will be a transfer of value from old to new shareholders. The only difference is that in the former case this transfer is caused by a dilution in the value of each of the firm's shares, and in the latter case it is caused by a reduction in the number of shares held by the old shareholders. . . .

Because investors do not need dividends to get their hands on cash, they will not pay higher prices for the shares of firms with high payouts. Therefore firms ought not to worry about dividend policy. They should let dividends fluctuate as a by-product of their investment and financing decisions. [This conclusion is known as the MM dividend-irrelevance proposition.] . . .

We believe—and it is widely believed—that MM's conclusions follow from their assumption of perfect and efficient capital markets. Nobody claims their model is an exact description of the so-called "real world." Thus the dividend controversy finally boils down to arguments about imperfections, inefficiencies, or whether stockholders are fully rational.

[One reason that some or many corporations may pay high dividends in the real world is that there] is a natural clientele for high-payout stocks. For example, some financial institutions are legally restricted from holding stocks lacking established dividend records. Trusts and endowment funds may prefer high-dividend stocks because dividends are regarded as spendable "income," whereas capital gains are "additions to principal," which cannot be spent.

There is also a natural clientele of investors who look to their stock portfolios for a steady source of cash to live on. In principle this cash could be easily generated from stocks paying no dividends at all; the investor could just sell off a small fraction of his or her holdings from time to time. But it is simpler and cheaper for AT & T to send a quarterly check than for its stockholders to sell, say, one share every 3 months. AT & T's regular dividends relieve many of its shareholders of transaction costs and considerable inconvenience. . . .

There is another line of argument that you can use to justify high payouts. Think of a market in which investors receive very little reliable information about a firm's earnings. Such markets exist in some European countries where a passion for secrecy and a tendency to construct many-layered corporate organizations produce asset and earnings figures that are next to meaningless. Some people say that, thanks to creative accounting, the situation is little better in the United States. How does an investor in such a world separate marginally profitable firms from the real money makers? One clue is dividends. A firm which reports good earnings and pays a generous dividend is putting its money where its mouth is. We can understand why investors would favor firms with established dividend records. We can also see how the information content of dividends would come about. Investors would refuse to believe a firm's reported earnings announcements unless they were backed up by an appropriate dividend policy.

MM regard the informational content of dividends as a temporary thing. A dividend increase signals management's optimism about future earnings, but investors will be able to *see for themselves* whether the optimism is justified. The jump in stock price that accompanies an unexpected dividend increase *would have happened anyway* as information about future earnings came out through other channels. Therefore, MM expect to find changes in dividends associated with stock price movements, but no permanent relationship between stock price and the firm's long-run target payout ratio. MM believe management should be concerned with dividend *changes*, but not with the average *level* of payout. . . .

(b) INTRODUCTION TO THE LEGAL ISSUES

INTRODUCTORY NOTE

The law of dividends is ultimately controlled by statute. Historically, dividend statutes incorporated one or more of the following four tests:

(i) An *insolvency* test, based on the corporation's actual financial condition, in terms of either its ability to pay its debts as they mature, or whether its assets exceed its liabilities.

(ii) A *balance-sheet* test, based on whether the corporation's assets exceed its liabilities plus its capital.

(iii) A *nimble-dividend* test, based on the corporation's current profits.

(iv) An *earned-surplus* test, based on the corporation's accumulated profits.

The traditional dividend statutes centered on the concepts of legal capital and surplus. Subsections (b)–(g) concern these statutes. The focus of these Subsections will be the New York and Delaware statutes. Thereafter, two leading modern statutes will be introduced in Subsection (j): California and the Revised Model Business Corporation Act.

(c) THE INSOLVENCY TEST

N.Y. BUS. CORP. LAW §§ 102(a)(8), 510(a), (b)

[See Statutory Supplement]

UNIFORM FRAUDULENT TRANSFER ACT §§ 1, 2, 4, 5

[See Statutory Supplement]

BANKRUPTCY ACT §§ 101(32), 548(a)

[See Statutory Supplement]

BACKGROUND NOTE ON THE INSOLVENCY TEST

1. There are two broad definitions of the term "insolvency." The definition embodied in N.Y.Bus.Corp.Law § 102(a)(8) is known as the "equity meaning," because it was the test generally applied by the equity courts, which had jurisdiction over insolvent estates before the enactment of the bankruptcy statute. The definition embodied in the Bankruptcy Act, 11 U.S.C.A. § 101(32), is known as the "bankruptcy meaning."[1]

The difference between these two conceptions can be very great. The equity insolvency test is concerned with current liquidity of the going enterprise; the emphasis of the bankruptcy sense of insolvency is upon liquidation of the enterprise. It is easily possible for an enterprise to be short of cash and other liquid means of payment while at the same time holding illiquid assets of great value; such an enterprise may well fail the equity insolvency test. It is also a quite possible occurrence for an enterprise to have a large current cash flow while steadily operating at a loss and suffering a continuing erosion of its asset base; in time, such an enterprise will fail to meet the bankruptcy test of insolvency.

---

1. Under the Bankruptcy Act, the test for whether a person can be put into involuntary bankruptcy turns principally on whether the debtor is insolvent in the equity sense. See 11 U.S.C.A. § 303(h). However, once a debtor has been put into bankruptcy, the trustee's right to avoid a pre-bankruptcy transfer turns in large part on whether at the time of the transfer the debtor was insolvent in the bankruptcy sense. See 11 U.S.C.A. §§ 101(32), 548.

The bankruptcy meaning of insolvency is itself susceptible to different nuances, as may be seen by comparing 11 U.S.C.A. § 101(32) with UFTA § 2(a).

Those with any familiarity with accounting will recognizes that the equity insolvency test is concerned with the income and cash flow statements of the enterprise while the bankruptcy insolvency test is focused on the balance sheet of the enterprise. For this reason, the bankruptcy insolvency test is frequently referred to as the "balance sheet" or "net worth" test.

B. Manning & J. Hanks, Legal Capital 64 (3d ed. 1990). To put this differently, insolvency in the equity sense is based on cash flow; insolvency in the bankruptcy sense is based on market value.

2. Many dividend statutes explicitly incorporate an insolvency standard. See, e.g., N.Y.Bus.Corp.Law § 510. Others, like the California statute and the RMBCA, do not. The Official Comment to RMBCA § 6.40 states that "[t]he revised Model Business Corporation Act establishes the validity of distributions from the corporate law standpoint under section 6.40 and determines the potential liability of directors for improper distributions under sections 8.30 and 8.33. The federal Bankruptcy Act and state fraudulent conveyance statutes, on the other hand, are designed to enable the trustee or other representative to recapture for the benefit of creditors funds distributed to others in some circumstances. In light of these diverse purposes, it was not thought necessary to make the tests of section 6.40 identical to the tests for insolvency under these various statutes." Cal.Corp.Code § 506(d), which governs the liability of shareholders who have received improper dividends, provides that "[n]othing contained in this section affects any liability which any shareholder may have under [the Uniform Fraudulent (Transfer) Act.]."

3. In considering the relationship among the Bankruptcy Act, the UFTA, and corporate dividend statutes, two points must be kept in mind: (i) The three kinds of statutes may impose different *substantive rules,* because they may use the term "insolvency" in different senses. (ii) Even where the statutes impose the same substantive rule, they may involve different *remedies* against different *actors*.

(d) THE BALANCE SHEET TEST

NOTE ON BALANCE SHEET ACCOUNTING
FOR CORPORATE EQUITY

Corporate accounting has traditionally differed from accounting for proprietorships and partnerships primarily in the way equity is treated. In the sole proprietorship and the partnership, equity is normally a fairly simple account. In the corporation, however, equity has traditionally been divided into Stated Capital and Surplus, and Surplus has been redivided into a number of further accounts.

Stated Capital (or Capital Stock) consists of the total par value of issued stock that has par value, or, if issued stock has no par value, the total amount allocated to capital by the board. To illustrate, if 10 shares of $100 par value common stock are issued for $1,000 in cash, the balance sheet entries would be:

Cash	$1,000	
Stated Capital		$1,000 [1]

The two most important Surplus accounts are Earned Surplus and Paid-in Surplus. Earned Surplus consists of internally generated profits that are reinvested in the business. Paid-in Surplus consists of the consideration paid to the corporation for par value stock in excess of the par value, or the consideration paid for no-par shares in excess of the amount allocated to Stated Capital. Thus if 10 shares of $100 par stock are issued for $1,500, the entries might be:

Cash	$1,500
Stated Capital	$1,000
Paid-in Surplus	500

Other Surplus accounts will be considered elsewhere in this chapter.

In recent years, accountants have tended to substitute descriptive nomenclature for the traditional Surplus terminology. Thus Earned Surplus is given a title such as Retained Income, Retained Earnings, or Accumulated Earnings, and Paid-in Surplus is given a title such as Capital Contributed for Shares in Excess of Par or Stated Value. However, the new titles do not work a difference in substance, and courts, legislators, and lawyers have continued to use the old terminology.

As will be shown later in this Chapter, Capital and Surplus accounts, and their modern counterparts like Retained Earnings, have become irrelevant under many of the newer statutes. See Subsection (j), infra. However, the terms are likely to continue in use on financial statements, both because many statutes (including those of important corporate states like Delaware and New York) still turn on capital and surplus concepts, and because accountants are unlikely to quickly drop long-established practices.

N.Y. BUS. CORP. LAW §§ 102, 506, 510, 717

[See Statutory Supplement]

---

1. When there are separate classes of stock outstanding, a separate Stated Capital account is maintained for each class.

DEL. GEN. CORP. LAW §§ 141(e), 154, 170

[See Statutory Supplement]

NOTE ON THE OPERATION OF THE BALANCE–SHEET TEST

The purpose of this Note is to illustrate the operation of the balance-sheet test as compared to the insolvency test.

Assume that Corporation C was organized at the end of 1992, at which time it issued 500 shares of $10 par value common stock for $100 per share. At that point, C's balance sheet was as follows:

ASSETS		LIABILITIES	
Cash	$50,000	Liabilities	0
		SHAREHOLDERS' EQUITY	
		Capital: $100 par common, 500 shares	$50,000
		Surplus:	0
	$50,000		$50,000

In 1993, C bought land, built up inventory, developed some accounts receivable and payable, borrowed $10,000 from a bank, and incurred an operating loss of $20,000. In 1994, C had a small profit of $5,000, all of which was reflected in further build-up of inventory. Taking account of these various transactions, C's balance sheet at the end of 1994 was as follows:

ASSETS		LIABILITIES	
Cash	$20,000	Accounts payable	$ 2,000
Accounts receivable	$11,000	Bank loan	10,000
Inventory	$16,000		$12,000
		SHAREHOLDERS' EQUITY	
		Capital: $100 par common, 500 shares	$50,000
		Earned surplus (deficit)	(15,000)
		Shareholder's equity	$35,000
	$47,000		$47,000 [1]

---

1. This hypothetical is derived from B. Manning & J. Hanks, Legal Capital (3d ed. 1990).

Assume that the market value of C's assets and liabilities was fairly reflected in their book values, and that C could pay its debts as they became due. In that case, under a pure insolvency test C could pay a dividend. Under a balance-sheet test, however, C could not pay a dividend, because it had a capital deficit.

NOTE ON RANDALL v. BAILEY

A critical issue under balance-sheet statutes is whether the amount available for the payment of dividends is limited to the difference between assets and liabilities as recorded on the corporation's balance sheet under generally accepted accounting principles, or the difference between the actual value of the corporation's assets and liabilities. In particular, the question arises whether if (as is often the case) assets such as land and buildings are worth more than the book value recorded on the balance sheet, that extra value is a legally permissible source of dividends. In the famous case, Randall v. Bailey, 288 N.Y. 280, 43 N.E.2d 43 (1942), aff'g 23 N.Y.S.2d 173 (1940) the New York court held that under the New York balance-sheet statute, dividends could be based on actual as opposed to recorded values.

Randall v. Bailey was based in part on the wording and history of the New York statute, and some of the cases that have addressed this issue under other balance-sheet jurisdictions look the other way. See, e.g., Kingston v. Home Life Ins. Co., 11 Del.Ch. 258, 101 A. 898 (1917), aff'd without discussion of the point 11 Del.Ch. 428, 104 A. 25 (1918); Vogtman v. Merchants' Mortgage & Credit Co., 20 Del.Ch. 364, 178 A. 99 (1935).

On the other hand, a number of cases provide direct or indirect support for the doctrine of Randall v. Bailey. See, e.g., Cannon v. Wiscassett Mills Co., 195 N.C. 119, 141 S.E. 344 (1928); Goldberg v. Peltier, 75 R.I. 314, 66 A.2d 107 (1949); Bishop v. Prosser–Grandview Broadcasters, Inc., 3 Wash.App. 43, 472 P.2d 560 (1970).

(e) THE CURRENT EARNINGS TEST: NIMBLE DIVIDENDS

DEL. GEN. CORP. LAW § 170

[See Statutory Supplement]

Dividends that are allowed to be paid out of current profits, although no other legal source is then available, have been termed "nimble dividends"—a phrase originated by Professor Baker. Note, 62 Harv.L.Rev. 130 (1948). Directors must be "nimble," by declaring the dividends before the close of the relevant period or within a short time thereafter. In effect, such dividends are distributions out of capital in the sense that they can be paid in the face of a capital deficit.

——

(f) THE EARNED SURPLUS TEST

——

NOTE ON THE EARNED SURPLUS TEST

1. The old version of the Model Act employed a test for dividends that centered on whether a corporation had "earned surplus." A great many states adopted some version of that Model Act test. The Revised Model Act has dropped the earned surplus test (see Section 2(j), infra), and many of the states that followed the old Model Act have now switched to the new approach. As of the time this casebook is written, a number of states have retained the earned surplus test, so the test is still important. Given the momentum of the newer test, however, most of all of these remaining states may eventually make the switch.

2. Under the old Model Act, and the statutes that continue to follow that Act, earned surplus is defined as "the portion of . . . surplus . . . equal to the balance of . . . net profits, income, gains and losses from the date of incorporation . . . after deducting subsequent distributions to shareholders and transfers to stated capital and capital surplus made out of earned surplus." William Hackney comments as follows:

> In attempting to formulate statutory language limiting dividends to income, two distinct approaches were found possible.

> One is, like the capital-impairment restriction, a balance-sheet test. The surplus of net assets in excess of capital is obtained and then analyzed and any which is not paid-in or other capital surplus is deemed accumulated income.

> The second approach . . . is to take the balance of all the corporate income statements to date and deduct dividends and other transfers therefrom, with the remainder being earned surplus.

> The Model Act definition, it seems, utilizes the aggregate-income-statement method of arriving at earned surplus. It does not use the balance sheet as a source of reference but directs one to take the balance of net profits, income, gains and losses over a period of time. The Model Act's adoption of the American Institute of Accountants' definition of earned surplus argues strongly that just as accounting today is mainly con-

cerned with the fairest possible presentation of period net income, regarding the balance sheet merely as a connecting link between successive income statements, so earned surplus as used in the act is intended to signify a composite income statement from the year of inception and not simply a balance-sheet increase in net assets.[1]

_____

(g) DIVIDENDS OUT OF CAPITAL SURPLUS

_____

N.Y. BUS. CORP. LAW §§ 102, 510, 520

[See Statutory Supplement]

_____

DEL. GEN. CORP. LAW §§ 154, 170

[See Statutory Supplement]

_____

INTRODUCTORY NOTE

Broadly speaking, capital surplus is that portion of surplus which is derived from sources other than corporate earnings, such as amounts paid for stock in excess of par value. In theory, the permissibility of dividends out of capital surplus marks the major difference between the balance sheet and earned surplus tests: Under a balance sheet test dividends can be paid out of capital surplus unless specifically prohibited. In contrast, under an earned surplus test dividends can be paid out of capital surplus only if specifically permitted. In practice, however, balance sheet statutes often contain provisions giving special treatment to dividends out of capital surplus, while earned surplus statutes often contain provisions permitting dividends out of capital surplus.

The most important types of capital surplus are paid-in, reduction, and revaluation surplus. Paid-in surplus is the amount by which the price of newly issued stock exceeds that portion of the price which is allocated to stated capital. Reduction surplus is the

_____

1. Hackney, The Financial Provisions of the Model Business Corporations Act, 70 Harv.L.Rev. 1357, 1365–66 (1957).

amount by which stated capital is reduced through corporate action pursuant to statutory authority.   Revaluation surplus is based on the unrealized appreciation in the value of fixed assets.

NOTE ON PAID-IN SURPLUS

1.   Paid-in surplus is the excess of (i) the total purchase price of newly issued stock over (ii) that portion of the price allocated to stated capital.   This type of surplus is a byproduct of the low par and no par phenomena, because it does not arise if stock is issued at par value.   In an economic sense paid-in surplus constitutes capital, since it is part of the shareholders' initial equity investment. Therefore, it is difficult to reconcile permission to pay dividends out of paid-in surplus with the creditor-protection purpose of dividend law, unless the statute limits such permission to corporations with some minimum degree of financial health.   A few states do employ this kind of limitation.   For example, R.I. § 7–1.1–41 provides that "No [distribution of capital surplus] shall be made . . . unless the fair value of the net assets of the corporation remaining after the distribution is at least equal to . . . [25%] of the total liabilities of the corporation."

2.   Under traditional dividend statutes, the possibility of declaring dividends out of paid-in capital surplus was one of the elements that led to the use of no par or low par stock, because the use of such stock would automatically create paid-in capital surplus, which provided a potential fund out of which dividends could be paid.

DEL. GEN. CORP. LAW §§ 242(a)(3), 243, 244

[See Statutory Supplement]

N.Y. BUS. CORP. LAW § 516

[See Statutory Supplement]

NOTE ON REDUCTION SURPLUS

1.   There are a number of techniques for reducing capital, of which the most significant is amendment of the certificate of incorporation to reduce the par value of the corporation's stock.   A reduction of capital by this means does not in itself impair the interests of any group protected by the dividend-regulation statutes. However, such a reduction creates a new surplus fund equal to the

amount by which stated capital has been reduced. This fund is called reduction surplus, and is a subcategory of capital surplus. Reduction surplus can be used in two ways: (i) It can be distributed to shareholders directly. (ii) It can be used to eliminate an earned surplus deficit, thereby freeing future earnings for distribution. The former alternative will be considered in this section; the latter, in the next.

2. The payment of dividends out of reduction surplus seems anomalous under either a balance sheet statute, in which the emphasis is placed on preservation of capital, or an earned surplus statute, in which the emphasis is placed on limiting dividends to earnings. Nevertheless, statutes of both types routinely permit such dividends on pretty much the same terms as dividends out of paid-in surplus, with no safeguards for creditors beyond those imposed by the insolvency test. The power to reduce capital therefore creates a gaping breach in the protective wall set up by dividend law as regards the interests of creditors.

(h) A CRITIQUE OF THE TRADITIONAL STATUTES

B. MANNING & J. HANKS, LEGAL CAPITAL

3d ed. 1990, at p. 91–92.

The legal capital schemes embedded in the nation's state corporation acts are inherently doomed to a low level of effectiveness (perhaps even zero). Some of the reasons are:

1. The system is analytically incomplete in the same sense that an encircling wall is useless for containment if not closed throughout its perimeter. A stated capital/surplus figure, and even a stated capital/earned surplus figure, is the product of dozens of judgmental accounting decisions. If one were seriously interested in using surplus accounts as an on-off switch for certain transactions, he would inevitably find himself involved in full-scale regulation of corporate accounting systems, just as state utility and insurance commissions have found that pursuit of the goal of fair rate regulation has inexorably transformed them into legislatures of accountancy and tribunals of bookkeeping. Without the development of a jurisprudence of accounting to support the statutory legal capital scheme, the system is inherently incomplete and haphazard in its operation.

2. To the extent that the purpose of the legal capital scheme is to protect creditors from transactions that benefit share-

holders but prejudice creditors, it is at least odd that the statutes should hand over all the control switches and levers to the shareholders and those whom the shareholders elect, the board of directors. The statutes are detailed and explicit about the procedures and steps to be taken in order to effect changes in the capital structure of a corporation, but the decision-making power is always vested in the board or the shareholders, or the two together; in no case do the statutes provide for participation by the creditors, consultation with the creditors, or even notice to the creditors.

3. A corporation's "legal capital" is a wholly arbitrary number, unrelated in any way to any economic facts that are relevant to a creditor. No one who is considering whether to lend money today to General Motors Corporation is interested in knowing what, or whether, a shareholder paid for his shares 50 years ago, or what was the par value that was stamped on the stock certificate that he received at that time. Given the existence of the legal capital system, the creditor would prefer to see a high stated capital figure rather than a low one, but from his standpoint the stated capital is simply a fortuitously-derived number that could as well have been taken from a telephone directory as from a series of unconnected and irrelevant historical events.

4. Similar to the next preceding point is the fact that the entire system has no fundamental "why" to it. There is no reason why a reasonable man would take the number called stated capital and use it as a measure for limiting distributions to equity investors. At the same time, the kinds of things the creditor is interested to know and does want to police . . . are left unasked and unattended by the legal capital system.

(i) CONTRACTUAL RESTRICTIONS ON THE PAYMENT OF DIVIDENDS

FORM OF BOND INDENTURE PROVISION RESTRICTING DIVIDENDS

[See Statutory Supplement]

BACKGROUND NOTE

It should be obvious by now that the dividend statutes provide little protection to creditors beyond that already afforded by the law of fraudulent conveyances. Involuntary creditors, trade creditors, and short-term lenders must normally take the protection of dividend law as they find it. Institutional lenders, however, who provide large amounts of money over a long period of time, have the power to impose contractual restrictions on dividends beyond the weak limits imposed by corporation law, and normally do so. Similar restrictions are often extracted by underwriters in connection with bonds and preferred stock issued to the public. Indeed, as a practical matter, it may be said that much of the modern law of dividends is contractual rather than statutory. There are relatively few instances (except among recently formed companies) where at least some retained earnings do not appear on the balance sheets. Furthermore, corporation statutes are so liberal in allowing capital surplus to be created, either when stock is originally issued through the use of no-par or low-par capitalization, or thereafter through a reduction of capital, that resourceful counsel should be able to make a distribution legal even in the absence of retained earnings. Thus the real question is usually not whether a dividend is prohibited by statute, but whether it is prohibited by arrangements with lending institutions, or provisions agreed upon in connection with bond or preferred stock financing.

———

(j) THE NEW STATUTES

———

CAL. CORP. CODE §§ 114, 166, 500–502, 507

[See Statutory Supplement]

———

NOTE ON CALIFORNIA'S DIVIDEND PROVISIONS

California's dividend provisions, enacted in 1977, marked a sweeping break with traditional dividend statutes. Until that time, the foundation of most statutes was a legal concept—stated capital. In contrast, the foundation of the California statute is a set of economic realities: retained earnings, asset-liability ratios, liquidation preferences, and an insolvency test.

———

REV. MODEL BUS. CORP. ACT §§ 1.40(6), 6.40

[See Statutory Supplement]

———

**KUMMERT, STATE STATUTORY RESTRICTIONS ON FINAN-
CIAL DISTRIBUTIONS BY CORPORATIONS TO SHAREHOLDERS**
(pt. II), 59 Wash.L.Rev. 185, 282–84 (1984). "[The California and
Revised Model Business Corporation Act approaches] have some
remarkable similarities. [Both] proceed from a common assessment of the inadequacies of the concept of legal capital to abolish
not only the statutory underpinnings of the concept (the notion of
par value and accounting rules for consideration received for
shares), but also the series of exceptions (nimble dividends, depletion dividends, and special repurchases of shares) and fictions
(treasury shares) erected because of the existence of the concept.
[Both] subject transfers of cash or property, or incurrences of
indebtedness, by a corporation without consideration to its shareholders to a single set of restrictions, regardless of the form in
which the transfer, or incurrence, occurs. [Both] address applications of the restrictions to such transfers, or incurrences, where the
transferor, or obligor, is either the parent, or the subsidiary, of
another corporation. Finally, drafters of each of the systems based
their efforts on the premise that statutory systems founded on legal
capital were essentially misleading insofar as they led creditors and
senior security holders to believe that such systems operated to
protect their interests.

"[D]espite these similarities, the [California and RMBCA] systems can be clearly distinguished on the basis of their respective
responses to that possible misrepresentation. The California series
attempts to rectify the misrepresentation by promulgating rules that
will provide creditors and senior shareholders with the type of
protection they *thought* they were getting from the legal capital
system. On the other hand, the Amended Model Act [attempts] to
rectify the misrepresentation by promulgating rules that will provide
creditors and senior shareholders with the level of protection that
the drafters perceived such groups *actually received* from the legal
capital system. This variance in fundamental goals in turn produces
the significant differences between the Acts on such issues as the
relative freedom directors have and the status in the event of
financial difficulty of debt issued on repurchase of shares."

———

Another difference between the California and RMBCA approaches is that the California statute is in effect an economic

counterpart of the earned surplus test, while the RMBCA is in effect an economic counterpart of the balance sheet test.

————

B. MANNING & J. HANKS, LEGAL CAPITAL 195 (3d ed. 1990). "[A]n interesting question is just how the legal and accounting professions—and ultimately the courts—will adapt to the Revised Model Act where it is enacted into law. The Revised Model Act cannot prevent lawyers, accountants and corporate financial officers—and courts—from thinking in traditional terms of 'stated capital.' Many will find it difficult to take seriously mere statutory efforts to obliterate their doctrinal learning at a stroke. . . .

"To many experienced readers of corporate balance sheets, it will come as a distinct shock to discover suddenly that as a legal matter the southeast corner may henceforth carry only an entry for shareholders' equity—with no distinctions drawn between 'stated capital' accounts and surpluses of myriad kinds, and with no elaborate entries for 'treasury shares.' Indeed, one may predict with some confidence that many practitioners will simply keep on in their old ways for years to come—their commitment to ancient doctrine unwavering."

————

(k) JUDICIAL REVIEW OF DIVIDEND POLICY

————

SINCLAIR OIL CORP. v. LEVIEN

[See p. 496, supra]

————

SECTION 3. THE REPURCHASE BY A CORPORATION OF ITS OWN STOCK

————

N.Y. BUS. CORP. LAW §§ 513, 515, 517

[See Statutory Supplement]

————

DEL. GEN. CORP. LAW § 160(a)

[See Statutory Supplement]

REV. MODEL BUS. CORP. ACT § 6.31(a)

[See Statutory Supplement]

CAL. CORP. CODE § 510(a)

[See Statutory Supplement]

NOTE ON FINANCIAL LIMITATIONS OF A REPURCHASE BY A CORPORATION OF ITS OWN STOCK

When a corporation purchases shares of its own stock, corporate assets flow out to shareholders. Accordingly, from the perspective of creditors a repurchase of stock is economically indistinguishable from a dividend on stock, and from the perspective of preferred a repurchase of common is economically indistinguishable from a dividend on common. Ideally, therefore, repurchases should be treated like dividends for legal purposes. The California statute and the Revised Model Business Corporation Act do just that, by treating repurchases and dividends together under the heading of "distributions." Most other statutes go a long way toward that end, by providing that (with specified exceptions) a corporation can expend funds to purchase its own stock only if it could pay a dividend in the same amount. However, the treatment of repurchases and dividends is not fully parallel under most statutes, since a dividend irreversibly decreases surplus, while a repurchase may not. This is because under most statutes repurchased stock is known as "Treasury Stock"—i.e., stock held in the corporation's own treasury—and retains the status of issued stock until it is cancelled or disposed of. The rationale of this treatment is that repurchased shares resemble an asset, since they can be resold. (Indeed, at one time treasury stock was frequently shown on the asset side of the balance sheet.) This rationale might make a little sense if a corporation had no capacity to issue any shares unless it first repurchased shares already outstanding. In modern corporations, however, authorized shares normally far exceed issued shares, or can easily be made to do so by certificate amendment, so that a repurchase of its own stock normally enables a corporation to do nothing more than it could have done without the repurchase.   Economically, therefore, repurchased shares are no more of an asset than authorized but unissued shares.

In recognition of this economic reality, both the new California statute and the Revised Model Business Corporation Act eliminate the concept of treasury stock, by providing that reacquired shares revert to the status of authorized but unissued stock.   Cal.Corp. Code § 510(a); RMBCA § 6.31(a).   For an excellent discussion of the effect that a repurchase has on capital and surplus under traditional statutes, as well as the effects of a resale or cancellation of treasury stock under such statutes, see T. Fiflis, Accounting Issues for Lawyers 413–21 (4th ed. 1991).

Chapter XIII

THE PUBLIC DISTRIBUTION
OF SECURITIES

SECTION 1. INTRODUCTION

(a) SECURITIES ACT TERMINOLOGY

SECURITIES ACT §§ 2(1), 2(4), 2(10), 2(11), 2(12); SECURITIES ACT RULE 405

[See Statutory Supplement]

NOTE ON SECURITIES ACT TERMINOLOGY

The purpose of this chapter is to provide an introduction to the law concerning the public distribution of securities, which is governed principally by the Securities Act of 1933 and (to a lesser extent) by state Blue Sky laws. It is useful to begin by introducing some of the terminology employed in the Securities Act, particularly because the Act defines many key terms in a way that differs from ordinary business usage. Bear in mind that the following discussion is very broad. Many of the terms that are briefly discussed below will be considered in much greater depth later in this Chapter, and certain exceptions to the Securities Act's definitions are omitted at this stage for purposes of clarity.

Security. In ordinary usage, a "security" is a corporate stock or bond. Under section 2(1) of the Securities Act, however, the term security is defined to include "any note, stock, ... bond, debenture, evidence of indebtedness, certificate of interest or participation in any profit-sharing agreement, investment contract, ... or, in general, any interest or instrument commonly known as a 'security'."

Issuer. For most practical purposes, an "issuer" is a corporation that issues (that is, sells) its own stock or bonds. This usage is reflected in section 2(4) of the Securities Act, which defines "issuer" to mean "every person who issues or proposes to issue any security." Under section 2(11) of the Securities Act, however, for certain purposes the term issuer includes "an issuer, any person directly or

902

indirectly controlling or controlled by the issuer, or any person under direct or indirect common control with the issuer."

Controlling person. Under Securities Act Rule 405, "[t]he term 'control' (including the terms 'controlling,' 'controlled by' and 'under common control with') means the possession, direct or indirect, of the power to direct or cause the direction of the management and policies of a person, whether through the owner-ship of voting securities, by contract, or otherwise."

Underwriter. In ordinary usage, an "underwriter" is a firm that markets securities on behalf of an issuer or controlling person. Under section 2(11) of the Securities Act, however, the term under-writer is defined to include "any person who has purchased from an issuer with a view to, or offers or sells for an issuer in connection with, the distribution of any security."

Dealer. In ordinary usage, a "dealer" is a person who buys and sells securities on his own behalf, taking title to the securities until sale. Under section 2(12) of the Securities Act, however, a dealer is defined as "any person who engages either for all or part of his time, directly or indirectly, as agent, broker, or principal, in the business of offering, buying, selling, or otherwise dealing or trading in securities issued by another person."

Broker. In ordinary usage, a "broker" is a person who buys and sells securities on behalf of others, never taking title to the securities. This usage is reflected in section 3(4) of the Securities Exchange Act of 1934, which defines a broker as "any person engaged in the business of effecting transactions in securities for the account of others." Under section 2(12) of the Securities Act, however, the term dealer is defined to include brokers.

Registration statement. The Securities Act requires that under certain circumstances securities must be registered with the Securi-ties and Exchange Commission before they can be sold. To register securities under the Act it is necessary to file a registration statement that sets forth certain business and financial information concerning the issuer and the securities.

Prospectus. In ordinary usage, a prospectus is a document, prepared for distribution to the investment community and the public, that describes the issuer, the securities that are proposed to be sold, and the terms of the offering. Under section 2(10) of the Securities Act, however, a prospectus is defined much more broadly as "any prospectus, notice, circular, advertisement, letter, or com-munication, written or by radio or television, which offers any security for sale or confirms the sale of any security."

(b) AN OVERVIEW OF THE SECURITIES MARKETS

ROSS, WESTERFIELD, & JORDAN, FUNDAMENTALS OF CORPORATE FINANCE

See pp. 224–225, supra.

(c) AN OVERVIEW OF THE SECURITIES ACT

SECURITIES AND EXCHANGE COMMISSION, THE WORK OF THE SEC

p. 7, 1992.

Securities Act of 1933

This "truth in securities" law has two basic objectives:

- To require that investors be provided with material information concerning securities offered for public sale; and
- To prevent misrepresentation, deceit, and other fraud in the sale of securities.

A primary means of accomplishing these objectives is disclosure of financial information by registering offers and sales of securities. Securities transactions subject to registration are most offerings of debt and equity securities issued by corporations, limited partnerships, trusts and other issuers. Federal government debt securities are not. Certain securities and transactions qualify for exemptions from registration provisions; these exemptions are discussed below.

PURPOSE OF REGISTRATION

Registration is intended to provide adequate and accurate disclosure of material facts concerning the company and the securities it proposes to sell. Thus, investors may make a realistic appraisal of the merits of the securities and then exercise informed judgment in determining whether or not to purchase them.

Registration requires, but does not guarantee, the accuracy of the facts represented in the registration statement and prospectus. However, the law does prohibit false and misleading statements under penalty of fine, imprisonment, or both. And, investors who purchase securities and suffer losses have important recovery rights under the law if they can prove that there was incomplete or inaccurate disclosure of material facts in the registration statement or prospectus. If such misstatements are proven, the following could be liable for investor losses sustained in the securities purchase: the issuing company, its responsible directors and officers, the underwriters, controlling interests, the sellers of the securities, and others. These rights must be asserted in an appropriate federal or state court (not before the Commission, which has no power to award damages).

Registration of securities does not preclude the sale of stock in risky, poorly managed, or unprofitable companies. Nor does the Commission approve or disapprove securities on their merits; it is unlawful to represent otherwise in the sale of securities. The only standard which must be met when registering securities is adequate and accurate disclosure of required material facts concerning the company and the securities it proposes to sell. The fairness of the terms, the issuing company's prospects for successful operation, and other factors affecting the merits of investing in the securities (whether price, promoters' or underwriters' profits, or otherwise) have no bearing on the question of whether or not securities may be registered.

THE REGISTRATION PROCESS

To facilitate registration by different types of companies, the Commission has special forms. These vary in their disclosure requirements but generally provide essential facts while minimizing the burden and expense of complying with the law. In general, registration forms call for disclosure of information such as:

- Description of the registrant's properties and business;
- Description of the significant provisions of the security to be offered for sale and its relationship to the registrant's other capital securities;
- Information about the management of the registrant; and
- Financial statements certified by independent public accountants.

Registration statements and prospectuses on securities become public immediately upon filing with the Commission. After the registration statement is filed, securities may be offered orally or by certain summaries of the information in the registration statement as permitted by Commission rules. However, it is unlawful to sell the securities until the effective date. The act provides that most registration statements shall become effective on the 20th day after filing (or on the 20th day after filing the last amendment). At its discretion, the Commission may advance the effective date if deemed appropriate considering the interests of investors and the public, the adequacy of publicly available information, and the ease with which the facts about the new offering can be disseminated and understood.

Registration statements are subject to examination for compliance with disclosure requirements. If a statement appears to be materially incomplete or inaccurate, the registrant usually is informed by letter and given an opportunity to file correcting or clarifying amendments. The Commission, however, has authority to refuse or suspend the effectiveness of any registration statement if it finds that material representations are misleading, inaccurate, or incomplete.

The Commission may conclude that material deficiencies in some registration statements appear to stem from a deliberate attempt to conceal or mislead, or that the deficiencies do not lend themselves to correction through the informal letter process. In these cases, the Commission may decide that it is in the public interest to conduct a hearing to develop the facts by evidence. This [hearing] determines if a "stop order" should be issued to refuse or suspend effectiveness of the statement. The Commission may issue stop orders after the sale of securities has been commenced or completed. A stop order is not a permanent bar to the effectiveness of the registration statement or to the sale of the securities. If amendments are filed correcting the statement in accordance with the stop order decision, the order must be lifted and the statement declared effective.

Although losses which may have been suffered in the purchase of securities are not restored to investors by the stop order, the Commission's order precludes future public sales. Also, the decision and the evidence on which it is based may serve to notify investors of their rights and aid them in their own recovery suits.

EXEMPTIONS FROM REGISTRATION

In general, registration requirements apply to securities of both domestic and foreign issuers, and to securities of foreign governments (or their instrumentalities) sold in domestic securities markets. There are, however, certain exemptions. Among these are:

- Private offerings to a limited number of persons or institutions who have access to the kind of information that registration would disclose and who do not propose to redistribute the securities;
- Offerings restricted to residents of the state in which the issuing company is organized and doing business;
- Securities of municipal, state, federal, and other governmental instrumentalities as well as charitable institutions, banks, and carriers subject to the Interstate Commerce Act;
- Offerings not exceeding certain specified amounts made in compliance with regulations of the Commission; and
- Offerings of "small business investment companies" made in accordance with rules and regulations of the Commission.

Whether or not the securities are exempt from registration, antifraud provisions apply to all sales of securities involving interstate commerce or the mails.

Among the special exemptions from the registration requirement, the "small issue exemption" was adopted by Congress primarily as an aid to small business. The law provides that offerings of securities under $5 million may be exempt from the full registration, subject to conditions the Commission prescribes to protect investors. The Commission's Regulation A permits certain domestic and Canadian companies to make exempt offerings. A similar regulation is available for offerings under $5 million by small business investment companies licensed by the Small Business Administration. The Commission's Regulation D permits certain companies to make exempt offerings under $1 million with only minimal federal restrictions; more extensive disclosure requirements and other conditions apply for offerings exceeding that amount.

Exemptions are available when certain specified conditions are met. These conditions include the prior filing of a notification with the appropriate SEC regional office and the use of an offering circular containing certain basic information in the sale of the securities. . . .

SEC, Q & A: SMALL BUSINESS AND THE SEC
pp. 8–9, 1993.

How does my small business "go public"?

Section 5 of the Securities Act requires that a registration statement be filed with the SEC before securities are offered for sale to the public. It also prohibits the sale of those securities until the registration statement becomes "effective." (Although registration statements become public immediately upon filing with the Commission, it is illegal to sell the securities until the effective date.) The basic registration statement consists of two principal parts:

- Part I is the prospectus (the legal offering or "selling" document), which must be furnished to all purchasers of the securities. Your company—the "issuer" of the securities—is required to put in the printed prospectus the essential facts regarding its business operations, financial condition, and management. The prospectus must be made available to everyone who buys the new issue, and also to anyone who is made an offer to purchase the securities.

- Part II contains additional information available at the SEC for inspection by the public. (Copies of all disclosure documents filed with the SEC may be obtained by mail, for a nominal copying charge.)

Basic Registration of Securities

The basic registration form is Form S–1. It requires companies to disclose, among other things:

- A description of the company's business;
- Its properties;

- Material transactions between the company and its officers and directors;
- Competition;
- Identification of officers and directors and their remuneration;
- Certain pending legal proceedings;
- The plan for distributing the securities; and
- The intended use of the proceeds.

It is not prepared as a fill-in-the-blank form like a tax return but is similar to a brochure, with information provided in a narrative format. There are also detailed requirements concerning financial statements, including the requirement that such statements be audited by an independent certified public accountant.

In addition to the information expressly required by the form, the company must also provide any other information necessary to make the statements complete and not misleading. If sufficient adverse or risk factors exist concerning the offering and the issuer, they must also be set forth prominently in the prospectus, usually in the beginning. Examples of these factors are:

- Lack of business operating history;
- Adverse economic conditions in a particular industry;
- Lack of market for the securities offered; and
- Dependence upon key personnel.

———

(d) AN OVERVIEW OF THE UNDERWRITING PROCESS

———

L. LOSS, FUNDAMENTALS OF SECURITIES REGULATION 75–86

2d ed. 1988 & 1993 Supp.

A.   DISTRIBUTION TECHNIQUES

The registration and prospectus provisions of the Securities Act of 1933 can be understood—and their effectiveness evaluated—only on the background of the techniques by which securities are distributed in the United States. With a healthy obeisance in honor of the still new "shelf registration" technique, there are three basic types of so-called underwriting that are in common use, sometimes with variations.

1.   STRICT OR "OLD-FASHIONED" UNDERWRITING

Under the traditional English system of distribution—which is no longer common in that country—the issuer did not sell to an investment banking house for resale to the public, either directly or through a group of dealers. Instead a designated "issuing house" advertised the issue and received applications and subscriptions from the public on the issuer's behalf after an announced date. When sufficient applications had been received, an announcement was made that "the lists are closed," and the issuer proceeded to allot the securities directly to the applicants or subscribers, using various methods of proration in the event of an oversubscription. Securities firms normally subscribed to new issues not for their own accounts with a view to resale at a profit, but only as brokers for the accounts of their customers. Before the public offering was thus made, the issue was "underwritten" in order to ensure that the company would obtain the amount of funds it required.

This was underwriting in the strict insurance sense. For a fee or premium, the underwriter agreed to take up whatever portion of the issue was not purchased by the public within a specified time. And, just as insurance companies frequently reinsure large underwritings with other companies in order to distribute the risk, so the initial underwriter often protected himself by agreements with sub-underwriters, to which the issuer was not a party. The typical underwriting syndicate was not limited to investment bankers or so-called issuing houses. It included or might consist entirely of insurance companies or investment trusts or other institutions, or even large individual investors, who thus obtained large blocks of securities at less than the issue price. Accordingly, the underwriters planned to hold for investment any securities they might be required to take. Even the issuing houses that found themselves required to take up unsubscribed portions of issues were included to hold them temporarily until they found a buyer on favorable terms, instead of trying to resell them immediately, at a loss if necessary, as underwriters generally do in this country when issues get "sticky."

This method of distribution is called in the United States "strict" or "old-fashioned" or "standby" underwriting. It is seldom if ever used here except in connection with offerings to existing stockholders by means of warrants or rights. . . .

2. FIRM-COMMITMENT UNDERWRITING

"Firm-commitment" underwriting is not technically underwriting in the classic insurance sense. But its purpose and effect are much the same in that it assures the issuer of a specified amount of money at a certain time (subject frequently to specified conditions precedent in the underwriting contract) and shifts the risk of the market (at least in part) to the investment bankers. Traditionally the issuer would simply sell the entire issue outright to a group of securities firms, represented by one or several "managers" or "principal underwriters" or "representatives"; they in turn would sell at a price differential to a larger "selling group" of dealers; and they would sell at another differential to the public. In a very limited sense the process is comparable to the merchandising of beans or automobiles or baby rattles. The issuer is the manufacturer of the securities; the members of the underwriting group are the wholesalers; and the members of the selling group are the retailers. But it is not quite so simple. Except in the case of open-end investment companies, securities of particular issuers are distributed not continually but once in a long time, and then in a large batch. And the securities market is quite a different animal from the market for canned beans.

Before the Securities Act of 1933—particularly during the period of tremendous industrial and business expansion that began roughly in 1900—the procedure underwent an elaborate development. The risk of handling the increasingly large securities offerings of the Nation's industrial units had to be spread, and methods had to be developed to merchandise the securities among the ever-growing numbers of investors spread across the continent.

Jay Cooke is credited with having introduced the "underwriting syndicate" into this country in the sale of a $2 million bond issue by the Pennsylvania Railroad in 1870. By the turn of the century it was common in the case of large offerings for a single investment banker to do the "origination"—that is, carry on the preliminary negotiations with the issuer, make the investigations deemed necessary, and then purchase the issue from the issuer. The banker was chosen (and still is to a large extent except when the law requires competitive bidding) on the basis of his past relationships with the issuer and his past performance. The "origination" stage was followed by the process of "syndication": In order to spread the commitment, the originating banker would immediately sell the issue to a small "original purchase group." And that group would in turn sell to a larger "banking group"; or the members of the latter group might occupy the status of "old-fashioned underwriters." The originating banker would become a member of the purchase group; the members of that group would likewise become members of the banking group; and the originating banker would manage both groups. When the issue was not too large, the intermediate group might be omitted. In either event, the two or three steps followed each other very closely. The function of both groups was to spread the risk—although the process also permitted the originating banker to make participations available on favorable terms to large distributors, to those firms that had reciprocated in the past or might do so in the future, to those he might count on in less favorable times, and to those suggested by the issuer. In any event, these groups were not designed primarily to do the actual distributing; often the members of the groups were not organized for retailing purposes. The public sale would be effected, for the account of whichever group last bought the issue, by the manager (the originating banker) through an organization of employees and agents, which would sometimes include those members of the purchase and banking groups who were geared for retail distribution.

With the increase in the number and size of securities issues during World War I, as well as the development of coast-to-coast telephone and wire systems, both groups tended to grow in membership and, in order to facilitate the actual mechanics of distribution, it became customary to add still another step to the elaborate process: Instead of the originating banker's selling through agents and employees, a much larger and more dispersed "selling group" or "selling syndicate" would take the issue from the banking group; those members of the earlier group or groups with distributive facilities would join this new group; and it, too, would be managed by the originating banker. These developments also tended to speed up the distribution process and shorten the lives of the several groups.

The passage of the Securities Act of 1933, as well as the new federal securities transfer taxes that were imposed in 1932 [later repealed], made for a simplification of this system. Under the statute only negotiations between the issuer and "underwriters" are permitted before the filing of the registration statement. Until then the securities may not be offered to the public or even to dealers who are not "underwriters" within the statutory definition. And until the actual effective date of the registration statement, no sales or contracts may be made except with underwriters. This, in practice, means that today the interval between the signing of the underwriting contract and the effectiveness of the registration statement, during which whoever is committed to purchase at a fixed price cannot legally shift his liability against a decline in a frequently volatile market, has been reduced to an hour or two.

One result of this has been the development of the "market out" clause in the underwriting contract. Although the use of this clause is by no means universal and in practice it is not considered "cricket" to take advantage of it, it typically provides that the manager of the underwriting group (or the representatives of the group) may terminate the agreement if before the date of public offering (or before the date of the closing or settlement between underwriters and issuer) the issuer or any subsidiary sustains a material adverse change, or trading in the securities is suspended, or minimum or maximum prices or government restrictions on securities trading are put into effect, or a general banking moratorium is declared, or in the judgment of the managing underwriter (or, alternatively, the representatives of the underwriters or a majority in interests of the several underwriters) material changes in "general economic, political, or financial conditions" or the effect of international conditions on financial markets in the United States makes it impracticable or inadvisable to market the securities at specified public offering price. This clause is much broader than the traditional *force majeure* provision. In Walk–In Medical Centers, Inc. v. Breuer Capital Corp., 818 F.2d 260 (2d Cir.1987), the court conceded that the interpretation of "adverse market condition * * * remains an open issue," but held that the firm's president had desired to cancel the underwriting not because of general market conditions but because of a drop in the after-market price of the securities.

Another result of the Securities Act and the former transfer taxes has been a tendency to reduce the number of transfers between groups and to enlarge the number of "underwriters" who bear the initial risk. In effect, the originating banker and the purchase and banking groups have all been combined into a single "underwriting syndicate or group."

It is difficult to generalize about the practice today, because it may vary substantially from issue to issue. Each of the prominent banking houses tends to develop variations of its own. Nevertheless, certain patterns are familiar. Quite early the underwriter, specifically negativing any obligation, gives the issuer sufficient assurance, either orally or by a "letter of intent" to warrant the issuer's going ahead with the extensive work and expenses that are necessary. The single underwriting group is then created by a contract among its members (usually called the "agreement among purchasers" or the "agreement among underwriters") whereby they agree to be represented in their negotiations with the issuer by one or two or three of their number, whom it is currently the style to call merely the "representatives of the underwriters." It is the latter who, as successors to the old originating bankers, take the initiative and run the show. Through them all the underwriters enter into a "purchase contract" directly with the issuer. In order to limit exposure under § 11 of the 1933 Act, the liability of each underwriter to the issuer is several rather than joint. The trend has been toward larger underwriting groups, whose members are more and more able to do their own distributing. For that reason, and because of the tremendous expansion of the retail capability of many of the underwriting houses, there has also been a tendency to deemphasize formal "selling groups."

Typically the underwriters authorize their representatives to reserve out of the syndicate account (the "pot") whatever amount of the issue the latter choose for sale to selling-group dealers— sometimes termed simply "selected dealers"—as well as institutional investors. The dealers are usually selected by the representatives, or in any event approved by them if suggested by other members of the underwriting group. The degree of formality that surrounds the organization of the selling group (if there is one) or the selection of the "selected dealers" depends largely on the predilections of the representatives. Usually the dealers sign some sort of uniform "dealer offering letter" that is sent to them by the representatives.

The method of determining the [participations] of the several underwriters is by no means fixed. How much a particular house gets is apt to depend on its prestige, its capital, its distributing capacity, its geographical location, whether it has any special outlets (perhaps connections with large pension funds or the like), and frequently the issuer's wishes. The participation of a given house is not necessarily related to the amount it can distribute. Some houses join the group primarily as underwriters, with a view to making a profit out of assuming their shares of the risk, and they may give up most or all of their participations for sale by the representatives, for their account, to institutions and dealers. In other words, the amount reserved for such sale is not always prorated among the accounts of all the underwriters. Sometimes it is, but sometimes each member of the group indicates to the representatives what proportion of its share it would like to have for its own retail distribution. The portion that particular houses thus distribute at retail usually varies between 25 and 75 percent. Those underwriters who want more for their own retail distribution become "selected dealers." Not infrequently, too, the representatives reserve the right, in checking on the progress of the distribution, to take securities away from those underwriters that are slow and allocate them to members of the selling group whose distribution has been more successful. In any event the representatives are obligated under the "agreement among purchasers" to notify each underwriter, on or before the public offering date, of the amount of its securities that has not been reserved for offering to institutions and dealers, so that the several underwriters will know how much they have to distribute....

[A recent trend] will bear watching....

... The entire syndication procedure may be going the way of the elaborate pre–1933 system. Although 98 percent of common stock issues (measured in dollars) were syndicated as recently as 1981, by 1985 more than 30 percent were sold entirely by the managing underwriters. With 50–85 percent of even a syndicated deal going to institutional investors in the light of the increasing institutionalization of the market, syndication does not buy much extra distribution....

3. BEST-EFFORTS UNDERWRITING

Companies that are not well established are not apt to find an underwriter that will give a firm commitment and assume the risk of distribution. Of necessity, therefore, they customarily distribute their securities through firms that merely undertake to use their best efforts. Paradoxically, this type of distribution is also preferred on occasion by companies that are so well established that they can do without any underwriting commitment, thus saving on cost of distribution. The securities house, instead of *buying* the issue *from* the company and reselling it as principal, *sells* it *for* the company as agent; and its compensation takes the form of an agent's commission rather than a merchant's or dealer's profit. There may still be a selling group to help in the merchandising. But its members likewise do not buy from the issuer; they are subagents. This, of course, is not really underwriting; it is simply merchandising....

SECTION 2. WHAT CONSTITUTES A "SECURITY"

SECURITIES ACT § 4(1)

[See Statutory Supplement]

McGINTY, WHAT IS A SECURITY?

1993 Wisc.L.Rev. 1033, 1037–39.

In drafting the definition of security, Congress faced two opposing problems. On the one hand, if it defined "security" to include only arrangements with the same names as instruments traded on securities exchanges (like "stock" and "bonds"), shady promoters could escape the securities laws simply by labeling their investment schemes with unusual names. On the other hand, if Congress defined "security" overbroadly (for example, to include "any . . . evidence of indebtedness"), the securities laws could apply to I.O.U.s given between friends or to notes given by parents to a private school for the duration of their child's enrollment. The former approach would exclude arrangements that should be included, thus frustrating Congress's purpose of protecting investors. The latter approach would include arrangements that should not be included, impose significant unnecessary transaction costs, burden the federal judiciary and federalize numerous issues better left to state law. Congress, for its part, drafted the definition of "security" broadly enough to sweep in devious investment schemes bearing innocuous titles. The courts, for their part, have attempted to construe "security" broadly enough to include such schemes, and yet narrowly enough to exclude arrangements whose names fortuitously suggest a security but whose economic realities do not. . . .

Some of the terms that Congress used to define security—such as "investment contract"—lack an established meaning outside judicial opinions and so create elasticity. Other more standard terms such as "stock" or "notes" have accepted meanings within the securities industry, but can also be used in circumstances where one would rationally think no security exists. Because the definitional paragraph begins with the proclamation, "The term 'security' means *any* note, stock . . ." and the other included instruments, the unqualified "any" suggests that all instruments bearing a name listed in the definitional paragraph should be covered, even a note given by one neighbor to another.

Some courts and commentators have argued that the context clause [that is, the introductory clause to Section 2, which provides that "unless the context otherwise requires" the terms in Section 2 have the meanings given in that Section] permits courts to exclude arrangements that possess the standard names but that are not really securities. Yet the statute nowhere defines or even suggests the scope of the context clause's qualification. Thus, construing the definitional section presents two unappetizing choices. If courts restrict the definitional section to the definitional paragraph alone, the logical result is over-inclusiveness and mindless literalism. If the definitional section includes the context clause, the statute is threatened with unbounded judicial discretion. ...

REVES v. ERNST & YOUNG

Supreme Court of the United States, 1990.
494 U.S. 56, 110 S.Ct. 945, 108 L.Ed.2d 47.

Justice MARSHALL delivered the opinion of the Court.

This case presents the question whether certain demand notes issued by the Farmer's Cooperative of Arkansas and Oklahoma are "securities" within the meaning of § 3(a)(10) of the Securities Exchange Act of 1934. We conclude that they are.

I

The Co–Op is an agricultural cooperative that, at the time relevant here, had approximately 23,000 members. In order to raise money to support its general business operations, the Co–Op sold promissory notes payable on demand by the holder. Although the notes were uncollateralized and uninsured, they paid a variable rate of interest that was adjusted monthly to keep it higher than the rate paid by local financial institutions. The Co–Op offered the notes to both members and non-members, marketing the scheme as an "Investment Program." Advertisements for the notes, which appeared in each Co–Op newsletter, read in part: "YOUR CO–OP has more than $11,000,000 in assets to stand behind your investments. The Investment is not Federal [sic] insured but it is ... Safe ... Secure ... and available when you need it." App. 5 (ellipses in original). Despite these assurances, the Co–Op filed for bankruptcy in 1984. At the time of the filing, over 1,600 people held notes worth a total of $10 million.

After the Co–Op filed for bankruptcy, petitioners, a class of holders of the notes, filed suit against Arthur Young & Co., the firm that had audited the Co–Op's financial statements (and the predecessor to respondent Ernst & Young). Petitioners alleged, *inter alia,* that Arthur Young had intentionally failed to follow generally accepted accounting principles in its audit, specifically with respect to the valuation of one of the Co–Op's major assets, a gasohol plant. Petitioners claimed that Arthur Young violated these principles in an effort to inflate the assets and net worth of the Co–Op. Petitioners maintained that, had Arthur Young properly treated the plant in its audits, they would not have purchased demand notes because the

Co–Op's insolvency would have been apparent. On the basis of these allegations, petitioners claimed that Arthur Young had violated the antifraud provisions of the 1934 Act as well as Arkansas' securities laws.

Petitioners prevailed at trial on both their federal and state claims, receiving a $6.1 million judgment. Arthur Young appealed, claiming that the demand notes were not "securities" under either the 1934 Act or Arkansas law, and that the statutes' antifraud provisions therefore did not apply. A panel of the Eighth Circuit, agreeing with Arthur Young on both the state and federal issues, reversed. Arthur Young & Co. v. Reves, 856 F.2d 52 (1988). We granted certiorari to address the federal issue, 490 U.S. ——, 109 S.Ct. 3154, 104 L.Ed.2d 1018 (1989), and now reverse the judgment of the Court of Appeals.

II

A

This case requires us to decide whether the note issued by the Co–Op is a "security" within the meaning of the 1934 Act. Section 3(a)(10) of that Act is our starting point:

> "The term 'security' means any note, stock, treasury stock, bond, debenture, certificate of interest or participation in any profit-sharing agreement or in any oil, gas, or other mineral royalty or lease, any collateral-trust certificate, preorganization certificate or subscription, transferable share, investment contract, voting-trust certificate, certificate of deposit, for a security, any put, call, straddle, option, or privilege on any security, certificate of deposit, or group or index of securities (including any interest therein or based on the value thereof), or any put, call, straddle, option, or privilege entered into on a national securities exchange relating to foreign currency, or in general, any instrument commonly known as a 'security'; or any certificate of interest or participation in, temporary or interim certificate for, receipt for, or warrant or right to subscribe to or purchase, any of the foregoing; but shall not include currency or any note, draft, bill of exchange, or banker's acceptance which has a maturity at the time of issuance of not exceeding nine months, exclusive of days of grace, or any renewal thereof the maturity of which is likewise limited." 48 Stat. 884, as amended, 15 U.S.C. § 78c(a)(10).

The fundamental purpose undergirding the Securities Acts is "to eliminate serious abuses in a largely unregulated securities market." United Housing Foundation, Inc. v. Forman, 421 U.S. 837, 849, 95 S.Ct. 2051, 2059, 44 L.Ed.2d 621 (1975). In defining the scope of the market that it wished to regulate, Congress painted with a broad brush. It recognized the virtually limitless scope of human ingenuity, especially in the creation of "countless and variable schemes devised by those who seek the use of the money of others on the promise of profits," SEC v. W.J. Howey Co., 328 U.S.

293, 299, 66 S.Ct. 1100, 1103, 90 L.Ed. 1244 (1946), and determined that the best way to achieve its goal of protecting investors was "to define 'the term "security" in sufficiently broad and general terms so as to include within that definition the many types of instruments that in our commercial world fall within the ordinary concept of a security.'" Forman, supra, 421 U.S., at 847–848, 95 S.Ct., at 2058–2059 (quoting H.R.Rep. No. 85, 73d Cong., 1st Sess., 11 (1933)). Congress therefore did not attempt precisely to cabin the scope of the Securities Act.[1] Rather, it enacted a definition of "security" sufficiently broad to encompass virtually any instrument that might be sold as an investment.

Congress did not, however, "intend to provide a broad federal remedy for all fraud." Marine Bank v. Weaver, 455 U.S. 551, 556, 102 S.Ct. 1220, 1223, 71 L.Ed.2d 409 (1982). Accordingly, "[t]he task has fallen to the Securities and Exchange Commission (SEC), the body charged with administering the Securities Acts, and ultimately to the federal courts to decide which of the myriad financial transactions in our society come within the coverage of these statutes." Forman, supra, 421 U.S., at 848, 95 S.Ct., at 2059. In discharging our duty, we are not bound by legal formalisms, but instead take account of the economics of the transaction under investigation. See, e.g., Tcherepnin v. Knight, 389 U.S. 332, 336, 88 S.Ct. 548, 553, 19 L.Ed.2d 564 (1967) (in interpreting the term "security," "form should be disregarded for substance and the emphasis should be on economic reality"). Congress' purpose in enacting the securities laws was to regulate *investments,* in whatever form they are made and by whatever name they are called.

A commitment to an examination of the economic realities of a transaction does not necessarily entail a case-by-case analysis of every instrument, however. Some instruments are obviously within the class Congress intended to regulate because they are by their nature investments. In Landreth Timber Co. v. Landreth, 471 U.S. 681, 105 S.Ct. 2297, 85 L.Ed.2d 692 (1985), we held that an instrument bearing the name "stock" that, among other things, is negotiable, offers the possibility of capital appreciation, and carries the right to dividends contingent on the profits of a business enterprise is plainly within the class of instruments Congress intended the securities laws to cover. *Landreth Timber* does not signify a lack of concern with economic reality; rather, it signals a recognition that stock is, as a practical matter, always an investment if it has the economic characteristics traditionally associated with stock. Even if sparse exceptions to this generalization can be found, the public perception of common stock as the paradigm of a security suggests that stock, in whatever context it is sold, should be treated

---

1. We have consistently held that "[t]he definition of a security in § 3(a)(10) of the 1934 Act, is virtually identical [to the 1933 Act's definition] and, for present purposes, the coverage of the two Acts may be considered the same." United Housing Foundation, Inc. v. Forman, 421 U.S. 837, 847, n. 12, 95 S.Ct. 2051, 2058, n. 12, 44 L.Ed.2d 621 (1975) (citations omitted). We reaffirm that principle here.

as within the ambit of the Acts. Id., at 687, 693, 105 S.Ct., at 2302, 2305.

We made clear in Landreth Timber that stock was a special case, explicitly limiting our holding to that sort of instrument. Id., at 694, 105 S.Ct., at 2304. Although we refused finally to rule out a similar *per se* rule for notes, we intimated that such a rule would be unjustified. Unlike "stock," we said, " 'note' may now be viewed as a relatively broad term that encompasses instruments with widely varying characteristics, depending on whether issued in a consumer context, as commercial paper, or in some other investment context." Ibid. (citing Securities Industry Assn. v. Board of Governors, FRS, 468 U.S. 137, 149–153, 104 S.Ct. 2979, 2985–88, 82 L.Ed.2d 107 (1984)). While common stock is the quintessence of a security, *Landreth Timber,* supra, 471 U.S., at 693, 105 S.Ct., at 2305, and investors therefore justifiably assume that a sale of stock is covered by the Securities Acts, the same simply cannot be said of notes, which are used in a variety of settings, not all of which involve investments. Thus, the phrase "any note" should not be interpreted to mean literally "any note," but must be understood against the backdrop of what Congress was attempting to accomplish in enacting the Securities Acts.[2]

Because the *Landreth Timber* formula cannot sensibly be applied to notes, some other principle must be developed to define the term "note." A majority of the Courts of Appeals that have considered the issue have adopted, in varying forms, "investment versus commercial" approaches that distinguish, on the basis of all of the circumstances surrounding the transactions, notes issued in an investment context (which are "securities") from notes issued in a commercial or consumer context (which are not). See, e.g., Futura Development Corp. v. Centex Corp., 761 F.2d 33, 40–41 (CA1 1985); McClure v. First Nat. Bank of Lubbock, Texas, 497 F.2d 490, 492–494 (CA5 1974); Hunssinger v. Rockford Business Credits, Inc., 745 F.2d 484, 488 (CA7 1984); Holloway v. Peat, Marwick, Mitchell & Co., 879 F.2d 772, 778–779 (CA10 1989), cert. pending sub nom. Peat Marwick Main & Co., No. 89–532.

The Second Circuit's "family resemblance" approach begins with a presumption that *any* note with a term of more than nine months is a "security." See, e.g., Exchange Nat'l Bank of Chicago v. Touche Ross & Co., 544 F.2d 1126, 1137 (CA2 1976). Recognizing that not all notes are securities, however, the Second Circuit has also devised a list of notes that it has decided are obviously not securities. Accordingly, the "family resemblance" test permits an

---

2. An approach founded on economic reality rather than on a set of *per se* rules is subject to the criticism that whether a particular note is a "security" may not be entirely clear at the time it is issued. Such an approach has the corresponding advantage, though, of permitting the SEC and the courts sufficient flexibility to ensure that those who market investments are not able to escape the coverage of the Securities Acts by creating new instruments that would not be covered by a more determinate definition. One could question whether, at the expense of the goal of clarity, Congress overvalued the goal of avoiding manipulation by the clever and dishonest. If Congress erred, however, it is for that body, and not this Court, to correct its mistake.

issuer to rebut the presumption that a note is a security if it can show that the note in question "bear[s] a strong family resemblance" to an item on the judicially crafted list of exceptions, id., at 1137–1138, or convinces the court to add a new instrument to the list. See, e.g., Chemical Bank v. Arthur Andersen & Co., 726 F.2d 930, 939 (CA2 1984).

In contrast, the Eighth and District of Columbia Circuits apply the test we created in SEC v. W.J. Howey Co., 328 U.S. 293, 66 S.Ct. 1100, 90 L.Ed. 1244 (1946), to determine whether an instrument is an "investment contract" to the determination whether an instrument is a "note." Under this test, a note is a security only if it evidences "(1) an investment; (2) in a common enterprise; (3) with a reasonable expectation of profits; (4) to be derived from the entrepreneurial or managerial efforts of others." Arthur Young & Co. v. Reves, 856 F.2d at 54. Accord Baurer v. Planning Group, Inc., 215 U.S.App.D.C. 384, 391–393, 669 F.2d 770, 777–779 (1981). See also Underhill v. Royal, 769 F.2d 1426, 1431 (CA9 1985) (setting forth what it terms a "risk capital" approach that is virtually identical to the *Howey* test).

We reject the approaches of those courts that have applied the Howey test to notes; *Howey* provides a mechanism for determining whether an instrument is an "investment contract." The demand notes here may well not be "investment contracts," but that does not mean they are not "notes." To hold that a "note" is not a "security" unless it meets a test designed for an entirely different variety of instrument "would make the Acts' enumeration of many types of instruments superfluous," Landreth Timber, 471 U.S., at 692, 105 S.Ct., at 2305, and would be inconsistent with Congress' intent to regulate the entire body of instruments sold as investments. . . .

The other two contenders—the "family resemblance" and "investment versus commercial" tests—are really two ways of formulating the same general approach. Because we think the "family resemblance" test provides a more promising framework for analysis, however, we adopt it. The test begins with the language of the statute; because the Securities Acts define "security" to include "any note," we begin with a presumption that every note is a security.[3] We nonetheless recognize that this presumption cannot be irrebuttable. As we have said ... Congress was concerned with regulating the investment market, not with creating a general federal cause of action for fraud. In an attempt to give more content to that dividing line, the Second Circuit has identified a list of instruments commonly denominated "notes" that nonetheless fall with-

---

3. The Second Circuit's version of the family resemblance test provided that only notes *with a term of more than nine months* are presumed to be "securities". See supra, at 950. No presumption of any kind attached to notes of less than nine months duration. The Second Circuit's refusal to extend the presumption to *all* notes was apparently founded on its interpretation of the statutory exception for notes with a maturity of nine months or less. Because we do not reach the question of how to interpret that exception ... we likewise express no view on how that exception might affect the presumption that a note is a "security."

out the "security" category. See *Exchange Nat. Bank,* supra, at 1138 (types of notes that are not "securities" include "the note delivered in consumer financing, the note secured by a mortgage on a home, the short-term note secured by a lien on a small business or some of its assets, the note evidencing a 'character' loan to a bank customer, short-term notes secured by an assignment of accounts receivable, or a note which simply formalizes an open-account debt incurred in the ordinary course of business (particularly if, as in the case of the customer of a broker, it is collateralized)"); *Chemical Bank,* supra, at 939 (adding to list "notes evidencing loans by commercial banks for current operations").

We agree that the items identified by the Second Circuit are not properly viewed as "securities." More guidance, though, is needed. It is impossible to make any meaningful inquiry into whether an instrument bears a "resemblance" to one of the instruments identified by the Second Circuit without specifying what it is about *those* instruments that makes *them* non-"securities." Moreover, as the Second Circuit itself has noted, its list is "not graven in stone," ibid., and is therefore capable of expansion. Thus, some standards must be developed for determining when an item should be added to the list.

An examination of the list itself makes clear what those standards should be. In creating its list, the Second Circuit was applying the same factors that this Court has held apply in deciding whether a transaction involves a "security." First, we examine the transaction to assess the motivations that would prompt a reasonable seller and buyer to enter into it. If the seller's purpose is to raise money for the general use of a business enterprise or to finance substantial investments and the buyer is interested primarily in the profit the note is expected to generate, the instrument is likely to be a "security." If the note is exchanged to facilitate the purchase and sale of a minor asset or consumer good, to correct for the seller's cash-flow difficulties, or to advance some other commercial or consumer purpose, on the other hand, the note is less sensibly described as a "security." See, e.g., Forman, 421 U.S., at 851, 95 S.Ct., at 2060 (share of "stock" carrying a right to subsidized housing not a security because "the inducement to purchase was solely to acquire subsidized low-cost living space; it was not to invest for profit"). Second, we examine the "plan of distribution" of the instrument, SEC v. C.M. Joiner Leasing Corp., 320 U.S. 344, 353, 64 S.Ct. 120, 124, 88 L.Ed. 88 (1943), to determine whether it is an instrument in which there is "common trading for speculation or investment," id., at 351, 64 S.Ct., at 123. Third, we examine the reasonable expectations of the investing public: The Court will consider instruments to be "securities" on the basis of such public expectations, even where an economic analysis of the circumstances of the particular transaction might suggest that the instruments are not "securities" as used in that transaction. Compare Landreth Timber, 471 U.S., at 687, 693, 105 S.Ct., at 2302, 2305 (relying on public expectations in holding that common stock is always a security) with id., at 697–700, 105 S.Ct., at 2307–2308 (STEVENS, J., dissenting) (arguing that sale of business to single informed purchaser through stock is not within the purview of the Acts under the economic reality test). See also *Forman,* supra, at 851, 95 S.Ct., at 2060. Finally, we examine whether some factor such as the existence of another regulatory scheme significantly reduces the risk of the instrument, thereby rendering application of the Securities Acts unnecessary. See, e.g., Marine Bank, 455 U.S., at 557–559, and n. 7, 102 S.Ct., at 1224–1225, and n. 7.

We conclude, then, that in determining whether an instrument denominated a "note" is a "security," courts are to apply the version of the "family resemblance" test that we have articulated here: a note is presumed to be a "security," and that presumption may be rebutted only by a showing that the note bears a strong resemblance (in terms of the four factors we have identified) to one of the enumerated categories of instrument. If an instrument is not sufficiently similar to an item on the list, the decision whether another category should be added is to be made by examining the same factors.

B

Applying the family resemblance approach to this case, we have little difficulty in concluding that the notes at issue here are "securities." Ernst & Young admits that "a demand note does not closely resemble any of the Second Circuit's family resemblance examples." Brief for Respondent 43. Nor does an examination of the four factors we have identified as being relevant to our inquiry suggest that the demand notes here are not "securities" despite their lack of similarity to any of the enumerated categories. The Co–Op sold the notes in an effort to raise capital for its general business operations, and purchasers bought them in order to earn a profit in the form of interest.[4] Indeed, one of the primary inducements offered purchasers was an interest rate constantly revised to keep it slightly above the rate paid by local banks and savings and loans. From both sides, then, the transaction is most naturally conceived as an investment in a business enterprise rather than as a purely commercial or consumer transaction.

As to the plan of distribution, the Co–Op offered the notes over an extended period to its 23,000 members, as well as to nonmembers, and more than 1,600 people held notes when the Co–Op filed for bankruptcy. To be sure, the notes were not traded on an

4. We emphasize that by "profit" in the context of notes, we mean "a valuable return on an investment," which undoubtedly includes interest. We have, of course, defined "profit" more restrictively in applying the *Howey* test to what are claimed to be "investment contracts." See, e.g., Forman, 421 U.S., at 852, 95 S.Ct., at 2060 ("[P]rofit" under the *Howey* test means either "capital appreciation" or "a participation in earnings"). To apply this restrictive defini-tion to the determination whether an instrument is a "note" would be to suggest that notes paying a rate of interest not keyed to the earning of the enterprise are not "notes" within the meaning of the Securities Acts. Because the *Howey* test is irrelevant to the issue before us today, . . . we decline to extend its definition of "profit" beyond the realm in which that definition applies.

exchange. They were, however, offered and sold to a broad segment of the public, and that is all we have held to be necessary to establish the requisite "common trading" in an instrument. See, e.g., *Landreth Timber,* supra (stock of closely held corporation not traded on any exchange held to be a "security"); *Tcherepnin,* 389 U.S., at 337, 88 S.Ct., at 553 (nonnegotiable but transferable "withdrawable capital shares" in savings and loan association held to be a "security"); *Howey,* 328 U.S., at 295, 66 S.Ct., at 1101 (units of citrus grove and maintenance contract "securities" although not traded on exchange).

The third factor—the public's reasonable perceptions—also supports a finding that the notes in this case are "securities". We have consistently identified the fundamental essence of a "security" to be its character as an "investment." . . . The advertisements for the notes here characterized them as "investments," . . . and there were no countervailing factors that would have led a reasonable person to question this characterization. In these circumstances, it would be reasonable for a prospective purchaser to take the Co–Op at its word.

Finally, we find no risk-reducing factor to suggest that these instruments are not in fact securities. The notes are uncollateralized and uninsured. Moreover, unlike the certificates of deposit in *Marine Bank,* . . . which were insured by the Federal Deposit Insurance Corporation and subject to substantial regulation under the federal banking laws, and unlike the pension plan in Teamsters v. Daniel, 439 U.S. 551, 569–570, 99 S.Ct. 790, 801–802, 58 L.Ed.2d 808 (1979), which was comprehensively regulated under the Employee Retirement Income Security Act of 1974, 88 Stat. 829, 29 U.S.C. § 1001 et seq., the notes here would escape federal regulation entirely if the Acts were held not to apply.

The court below found that "[t]he demand nature of the notes is very uncharacteristic of a security," 856 F.2d, at 54, on the theory that the virtually instant liquidity associated with demand notes is inconsistent with the risk ordinarily associated with "securities." This argument is unpersuasive. Common stock traded on a national exchange is the paradigm of a security, and it is as readily convertible into cash as is a demand note. The same is true of publicly traded corporate bonds, debentures, and any number of other instruments that are plainly within the purview of the Acts. The demand feature of a note does permit a holder to eliminate risk quickly by making a demand, but just as with publicly traded stock, the liquidity of the instrument does not eliminate risk [altogether]. Indeed, publicly traded stock is even more readily liquid than are demand notes, in that a demand only eliminates risk when and if payment is made, whereas the sale of a share of stock through a national exchange and the receipt of the proceeds usually occur simultaneously.

We therefore hold that the notes at issue here are within the term "note" in § 3(a)(10).

III

[In Part III of its opinion, the Court held that whether notes have a maturity not exceeding nine months for purposes of the exclusion for short-term instruments at the end of Section 3(a)(10) is a question of federal law, and that as a matter of federal law the demand notes at issue in *Reves* did not fall within that exclusion.]

IV

For the foregoing reasons, we conclude that the demand notes at issue here fall under the "note" category of instruments that are "securities" under the 1933 and 1934 Acts. We also conclude that, ... these demand notes do not fall within the exclusion [for short-term notes]. Accordingly, we reverse the judgment of the Court of Appeals and remand the case for further proceedings consistent with this opinion.

So ordered.

[Justice Stevens concurred in the Court's opinion. Chief Justice Rehnquist and Justices White, O'Connor, and Scalia concurred in Part II of the Court's opinion, but dissented from Part III on the ground that the notes at issue fell within the short-term exclusion.]

SECTION 3.   WHAT CONSTITUTES A "SALE" AND AN "OFFER TO SELL"

SECURITIES ACT §§ 2(3), 3(a)(9); SECURITIES ACT RULE 145

[See Statutory Supplement]

NOTE ON THE MEANING OF "SALE" AND "OFFER TO SELL"

The term "sale" or "sell" is defined in section 2(3) of the Securities Act to include "every contract of sale or disposition of a security or interest in a security, for value." The term "offer to sell," "offer for sale," or "offer" is defined to include "every attempt or offer to dispose of, or solicitation of an offer to buy, a security or interest in a security, for value." The use of the word "includes" rather than "means" emphasizes the breadth of these definitions, and the courts have also interpreted the terms broadly "to include ingenious methods employed to obtain money from members of the public to finance ventures." S.E.C. v. Addison, 194 F.Supp. 709, 722 (N.D.Tex.1961)

A transfer of securities need not be voluntary to be a sale under the Securities Act. For example, most mergers and stock-for-assets combinations, and certain reclassifications, are sales under Rule 145.

Section 3(a)(9) of the Securities Act provides that "the provisions of this title shall not apply to.... any security exchanged by the issuer with its existing security holders exclusively where no commission or other remuneration is paid or given directly or indirectly for soliciting such exchange." There is an overlap between section 3(a)(9) and Rule 145, because both cover reclassifications. The SEC's position is that Rule 145 is applicable only if no exemption is available, so that if section 3(a)(9) is applicable to a reclassification, Rule 145 is not. See Securities Act Release No. 5463.

Rule 145 does not cover business combinations achieved through a stock-for-stock exchange. However, such an exchange is clearly a sale, and is not covered by Rule 145 only because Rule 145 was adopted to reverse a prior SEC interpretation under which mergers and other stock-for-assets transactions were not deemed to be sales. This interpretation had not affected stock-for-stock exchange offers, which therefore did not need to be covered by Rule 145. Both the transactions specified in Rule 145 and stock-for-stock exchange offers are registered under the same registration form, Form S-4.

Under Rubin v. United States, 449 U.S. 424, 101 S.Ct. 698, 66 L.Ed.2d 633 (1981), a pledge is an offer or a sale for purposes of the 1933 Act.

SECTION 4. THE REQUIREMENT OF REGISTRATION

(a) THE BROAD SWEEP OF SECTION 5

SECURITIES ACT §§ 2(10), 5

[See Statutory Supplement]

NOTE ON SECTION 5

The structure of the Securities Act is exceptionally intricate. The key provision is section 5. Section 5(a) provides:

Unless a registration statement is in effect as to a security, it shall be unlawful for any person, directly or indirectly—

(1) to make use of any means or instruments of transportation or communication in interstate commerce or of the mails

to sell such security through the use or medium of any prospectus or otherwise; or

(2) to carry or cause to be carried through the mails or in interstate commerce, by any means or instruments of transportation, any such security for the purpose of sale or for delivery after sale.

Section 5(c) provides:

It shall be unlawful for any person, directly or indirectly, to make use of any means or instruments of transportation or communication in interstate commerce or of the mails to offer to sell or offer to buy through the use or medium of any prospectus or otherwise any security, unless a registration statement has been filed as to such security. . . .

Section 2(10) defines a "prospectus" to mean "any prospectus, notice, circular, advertisement, letter, or communication, written or by radio or television, which offers any security for sale or confirms the sale of any security," subject to certain exceptions. Putting section 2(10) together with section 5(a) and (c), if any person proposes to sell a security by any means of communication in interstate commerce or by mail, or sends a security through the mail for purposes of sale, or offers to buy or sell a security by a letter, the security must be registered, unless an exemption applies. On its face, therefore, section 5 prohibits virtually every sale of securities, no matter how trivial and no matter who the seller, unless the securities are registered under the Act. Other provisions of the Act, however, carve out a variety of exemptions for large classes of securities and transactions. By virtue of the exemptions, these securities and transactions do not require registration despite the sweeping language of section 5. The balance of this Section will consider exemptions based on the number and character of the offerees, on the size of the offering, on the intrastate nature of an offering, and on the absence of an issuer, underwriter, or dealer.

(b) PRIVATE PLACEMENTS

SECURITIES ACT § 4(2)

4. The provisions of section 5 shall not apply to . . .

(2) transactions by an issuer not involving any public offering.

S.E.C. v. RALSTON PURINA CO.

Supreme Court of the United States, 1953.
346 U.S. 119, 73 S.Ct. 981, 97 L.Ed. 1494.

Mr. Justice CLARK delivered the opinion of the Court.

Section 4(1) of the Securities Act of 1933 exempts "transactions by an issuer not involving any public offering" [1] from the registration requirements of § 5. We must decide whether Ralston Purina's offerings of treasury stock to its "key employees" are within this exemption. On a complaint brought by the Commission under § 20(b) of the Act seeking to enjoin respondent's unregistered offerings, the District Court held the exemption applicable and dismissed the suit. The Court of Appeals affirmed. The question has arisen many times since the Act was passed; an apparent need to define the scope of the private offering exemption prompted certiorari. 345 U.S. 903, 73 S.Ct. 643.

Ralston Purina manufactures and distributes various feed and cereal products. Its processing and distribution facilities are scattered throughout the United States and Canada, staffed by some 7,000 employees. At least since 1911 the company has had a policy of encouraging stock ownership among its employees; more particularly, since 1942 it has made authorized but unissued common shares available to some of them. Between 1947 and 1951, the period covered by the record in this case, Ralston Purina sold nearly $2,000,000 of stock to employees without registration and in so doing made use of the mails.

In each of these years, a corporate resolution authorized the sale of common stock "to employees . . . who shall, without any solicitation by the Company or its officers or employees, inquire of any of them as to how to purchase common stock of Ralston Purina Company." A memorandum sent to branch and store managers after the resolution was adopted, advised that "The only employees to whom this stock will be available will be those who take the initiative and are interested in buying stock at present market prices." Among those responding to these offers were employees with the duties of artist, bakeshop foreman, chow loading foreman, clerical assistant, copywriter, electrician, stock clerk, mill office clerk, order credit trainee, production trainee, stenographer, and veterinarian. The buyers lived in over fifty widely separated communities scattered from Garland, Texas, to Nashua, New Hampshire and Visalia, California. The lowest salary bracket of those purchasing was $2,700 in 1949, $2,435 in 1950 and $3,107 in 1951. The record shows that in 1947, 243 employees bought stock, 20 in 1948, 414 in 1949, 411 in 1950, and the 1951 offer, interrupted by this litigation, produced 165 applications to purchase. No records were

---

1. 48 Stat. 77, as amended, 48 Stat. 906,   This is now § 4(2).]
15 U.S.C. § 77d, 15 U.S.C.A. § 77d. [Ed.

kept of those to whom the offers were made; the estimated number in 1951 was 500.

The company bottoms its exemption claim on the classification of all offerees as "key employees" in its organization. Its position on trial was that "A key employee ... is not confined to an organization chart. It would include an individual who is eligible for promotion, an individual who especially influences others or who advises others, a person whom the employees look to in some special way, an individual, of course, who carries some special responsibility, who is sympathetic to management and who is ambitious and who the management feels is likely to be promoted to a greater responsibility." That an offering to all of its employees would be public is conceded.

The Securities Act nowhere defines the scope of § 4(1)'s private offering exemption. Nor is the legislative history of much help in staking out its boundaries. The problem was first dealt with in § 4(1) of the House Bill, H.R. 5480, 73d Cong., 1st Sess., which exempted "transactions by an issuer not with or through an underwriter; ..." The bill, as reported by the House Committee, added "and not involving any public offering." H.R.Rep. No. 85, 73d Cong., 1st Sess. 1. This was thought to be one of those transactions "where there is no practical need for [the bill's] application or where the public benefits are too remote." Id., at 5.[5] The exemption as thus delimited became law.[6] It assumed its present shape with the deletion of "not with or through an underwriter" by § 203(a) of the Securities Exchange Act of 1934, 48 Stat. 906, a change regarded as the elimination of superfluous language. H.R.Rep. No. 1838, 73d Cong., 2d Sess. 41.

Decisions under comparable exemptions in the English Companies Acts and state "blue sky" laws, the statutory antecedents of federal securities legislation, have made one thing clear—to be public, an offer need not be open to the whole world. In Securities and Exchange Comm'n v. Sunbeam Gold Mines Co., 95 F.2d 699 (9th Cir.1938), this point was made in dealing with an offering to the stockholders of two corporations about to be merged. Judge Denman observed that:

> "In its broadest meaning the term 'public' distinguishes the populace at large from groups of individual members of the public segregated because of some common interest or characteristic. Yet such a distinction is inadequate for practical

---

5. " * * * the bill does not affect transactions beyond the need of public protection in order to prevent recurrences of demonstrated abuses." Id., at 7. In a somewhat different tenor, the report spoke of this as an exemption of "transactions by an issuer unless made by or through an underwriter so as to permit an issuer to make a specific or an isolated sale of its securities to a particular person, but insisting that if a sale of the issuer's securities should be made generally to the public that that transaction shall come within the purview of the Act." Id., at 15, 16.

6. The only subsequent reference was an oblique one in the statement of the House Managers on the Conference Report: "Sales of stock to stockholders become subject to the act unless the stockholders are so small in number that the sale to them does not constitute a public offering." H.R.Rep. No. 152, 73d Cong., 1st Sess. 25.

purposes; manifestly, an offering of securities to all redheaded men, to all residents of Chicago or San Francisco, to all existing stockholders of the General Motors Corporation or the American Telephone & Telegraph Company, is no less 'public', in every realistic sense of the word, than an unrestricted offering to the world at large. Such an offering, though not open to everyone who may choose to apply, is none the less 'public' in character, for the means used to select the particular individuals to whom the offering is to be made bear no sensible relation to the purposes for which the selection is made.... To determine the distinction between 'public' and 'private' in any particular context, it is essential to examine the circumstances under which the distinction is sought to be established and to consider the purposes sought to be achieved by such distinction." 95 F.2d at 701.

The courts below purported to apply this test. The District Court held, in the language of the *Sunbeam* decision, that "The purpose of the selection bears a 'sensible relation' to the class chosen," finding that "The sole purpose of the 'selection' is to keep part stock ownership of the business within the operating personnel of the business and to spread ownership throughout all departments and activities of the business." The Court of Appeals treated the case as involving "an offering, without solicitation, of common stock to a selected group of key employees of the issuer, most of whom are already stockholders when the offering is made, with the sole purpose of enabling them to secure a proprietary interest in the company or to increase the interest already held by them."

Exemption from the registration requirements of the Securities Act is the question. The design of the statute is to protect investors by promoting full disclosure of information thought necessary to informed investment decisions. The natural way to interpret the private offering exemption is in light of the statutory purpose. Since exempt transactions are those as to which "there is no practical need for [the bill's] application," the applicability of § 4(1) should turn on whether the particular class of persons affected need the protection of the Act. An offering to those who are shown to be able to fend for themselves is a transaction "not involving any public offering."

The Commission would have us go one step further and hold that "an offering to a substantial number of the public" is not exempt under § 4(1). We are advised that "whatever the special circumstances, the Commission has consistently interpreted the exemption as being inapplicable when a large number of offerees is involved." But the statute would seem to apply to a "public offering" whether to few or many.[11] It may well be that offerings to

---

11. See Viscount Sumner's frequently quoted dictum in Nash v. Lynde, " 'The public' ... is of course a general word. No particular numbers are prescribed. Any-thing from two to infinity may serve: perhaps even one, if he is intended to be the first of a series of subscribers, but makes further proceedings needless by himself

a substantial number of persons would rarely be exempt. Indeed nothing prevents the commission, in enforcing the statute, from using some kind of numerical test in deciding when to investigate particular exemption claims. But there is no warrant for superimposing a quantity limit on private offerings as a matter of statutory interpretation.

The exemption, as we construe it, does not deprive corporate employees, as a class, of the safeguards of the Act. We agree that some employee offerings may come within § 4(1), e.g., one made to executive personnel who because of their position have access to the same kind of information that the act would make available in the form of a registration statement. Absent such a showing of special circumstances, employees are just as much members of the investing "public" as any of their neighbors in the community. Although we do not rely on it, the rejection in 1934 of an amendment which would have specifically exempted employee stock offerings supports this conclusion. The House Managers, commenting on the Conference Report, said that "the participants in employees' stock-investment plans may be in as great need of the protection afforded by availability of information concerning the issuer for which they work as are most other members of the public." H.R.Rep. No. 1838, 73d Cong., 2d Sess. 41.

Keeping in mind the broadly remedial purposes of federal securities legislation, imposition of the burden of proof on an issuer who would plead the exemption seems to us fair and reasonable. Schlemmer v. Buffalo, R. & P.R. Co., 1907, 205 U.S. 1, 10, 27 S.Ct. 407, 408, 51 L.Ed. 681. Agreeing, the court below thought the burden met primarily because of the respondent's purpose in singling out its key employees for stock offerings. But once it is seen that the exemption question turns on the knowledge of the offerees, the issuer's motives, laudable though they may be, fade into irrelevance. The focus of inquiry should be on the need of the offerees for the protections afforded by registration. The employees here were not shown to have access to the kind of information which registration would disclose. The obvious opportunities for pressure and imposition make it advisable that they be entitled to compliance with § 5.

Reversed.

The CHIEF JUSTICE and Mr. Justice BURTON dissent.

Mr. Justice JACKSON took no part in the consideration or decision of this case.

---

subscribing the whole." [1929] A.C. 158, 169.

SEC, Q & A: SMALL BUSINESS AND THE SEC
pp. 14–15, 1993.

Private Offering Exemption

Section 4(2) of the Securities Act provides exemption from registration for "transactions by an issuer not involving any public offering." There has been much uncertainty as to the precise limits of this private offering exemption. Generally, sales to persons who have access to information about the company and are able to fend for themselves (such as those directly managing the business) fall within the intended scope of the exemption. These are known as "sophisticated investors." As the number of purchasers increase and their relationship to the company and its management becomes more remote, however, it becomes more difficult for an issuer to demonstrate that the transaction does, in fact, qualify for the exemption.

To qualify the offering under this exemption, it is necessary that the persons to whom your company sells the security:

- Have sufficient knowledge and experience in financial and business matters that they are capable of evaluating the risks and merits of the investment (the "sophisticated investor"), or are able to bear the economic risk of the investment;

- Have access to the type of information normally provided in a prospectus; and

- Agree not to resell or distribute the securities.

In addition, your offering may not be made by any form of public solicitation or general advertising.

You should be aware that if the security is offered for sale to even one person who does not meet the necessary conditions, the entire offering may be in violation of the Securities Act.

The SEC has adopted Rule 506, another "safe harbor" rule, which provides objective standards upon which business people may rely in order to be certain they meet the requirements of this exemption. [Rule 506 is a part of Regulation D, which is described more fully below—ed.]

(c) LIMITED OFFERINGS

SECURITIES ACT §§ 2(15), 3(b), 4(2), 4(6)

SECURITIES ACT RULE 215; REGULATION D (RULES 501–508)

[See Statutory Supplement]

D. RATNER, SECURITIES REGULATION IN A NUTSHELL 57–58

4th ed. 1992.

[Securities Act] § 3(b) authorizes the SEC, "by rules and regulations," to exempt offerings, not exceeding a specified dollar amount, when it finds that registration is not necessary "by reason of the small amount involved or the limited character of the public offering." The dollar limit has been periodically raised by Congress from its initial level of $100,000, the most recent increase coming in 1980 and raising the limit from $2 million to the present level of $5 million. Under this authority, the Commission has adopted a number of rules providing exemptions for certain specialized kinds of offerings, as well as the general exemption in Regulation A. . . .

Also in 1980, Congress added a new § 4(6) to the 1933 Act, exempting any offering of not more than $5 million made solely to "accredited investors" (defined to include specified types of institutions and other classes of investors that the SEC might specify by rule).

These developments set the stage for the coordination of the private offering and small offering exemptions in a new Regulation D. . . .

SEC, Q & A: SMALL BUSINESS AND THE SEC

pp. 16–21, 1993.

Regulation D

Under Sections 4(2) and 3(b) of the Securities Act, the SEC in March, 1982, adopted Regulation D to coordinate the various limited offering exemptions and to streamline the existing requirements applicable to private offers and sales of securities. The Regulation establishes three exemptions from registration in Rules 504, 505, and 506.

Rule 504

Rule 504, which provides an exemption for non-reporting companies unless they are "blank check" issuers, for sales of securities up to $1,000,000, stipulates that:

- The sale of up to $1,000,000 of securities in a 12–month period is permitted;
- No limitation is placed on the number of persons purchasing securities;
- The offering may be made with general solicitation or general advertising;
- The securities received in the offering are not "restricted securities"; and

- A Form D notice be filed with SEC headquarters within 15 days after the first sale of securities under the Rule.

Unlike Rules 505 and 506, Rule 504 does not mandate that specified disclosure be provided to purchasers. Nonetheless, the businessperson should take care that sufficient information is provided to meet the full disclosure obligations which exist under the antifraud provisions of the securities laws.

Rule 505

Rule 505 was adopted by the SEC to provide small businesses more flexibility in raising capital than under Rule 504—but without the uncertainty of determining the quality of the purchasers that generally is involved in using Rule 506. Rule 505 provides issuers a limited offering exemption for sales of securities totaling up to $5 million in any 12–month period.

Rule 505 contains certain restrictions regarding "accredited investors" and non-accredited persons. The term "accredited investor" includes:

- Banks, insurance companies, registered investment companies, business development companies, or small business investment companies;

- Certain employee benefit plans for which investment decisions are made by a bank, insurance company, or registered investment adviser;

- Any employee benefit plan (within the meaning of Title 1 of the Employee Retirement Income Security Act) with total assets in excess of $5 million;

- Charitable organizations, corporations or partnerships with assets in excess of $5 million;

- Directors, executive officers, and general partners of the issuer;

- Any entity in which all the equity owners are accredited investors;

- Natural persons with a net worth of at least $1 million;

- Any natural person with an income in excess of $200,000 in each of the two most recent years or joint income with a spouse in excess of $300,000 for those years and a reasonable expectation of the same income level in the current year; and

- Trusts with assets of at least $5 million, not formed to acquire the securities offered, and whose purchases are directed by a sophisticated person.

There is no specific information the issuer must furnish to accredited investors. However, non-accredited investors must be advised of and furnished, upon request, all material information furnished to accredited investors, as well as certain specified information.* ...

- The issuer must also be available to answer questions by prospective purchasers about the issuer or the offering.

Further restrictions under Rule 505 include:

- The total offering price of each issue of securities may not exceed $5 million.

- The offering may not be made by means of general solicitation or general advertising.

- The issuer may sell the securities to an unlimited number of "accredited investors" and to 35 non-accredited persons. There are no requirements of "sophistication" or "wealth" for persons to whom the securities are sold.

- A company must take any necessary steps to ensure that the purchasers are acquiring securities for investment only, not for resale. The securities are thus "restricted" and investors must be informed that they may not be able to sell for at least two years.

- The issuer is not required to file any offering materials with the Commission. Fifteen days after the first sale in the offering, the issuer must file a notice of sales on Form D. The notice also contains an undertaking under this Rule for the issuer to furnish the Commission, upon its staff's request, any information given to non-accredited purchasers in connection with the offering.

Rule 506

Offers and sales of securities by an issuer that satisfy the conditions stated below are deemed transactions not involving any public offering within the meaning of Section 4(2) of the Securities Act. For an offering to be considered exempt from the registration requirements, Rule 506 stipulates:

- There is no ceiling on the amount of money which may be raised.

- No general solicitation or general advertising is permitted.

- The issuer may sell its securities to an unlimited number of accredited investors and 35 non-accredited purchasers. Unlike Rule 505, all non-accredited purchasers (either alone or with a purchaser representative) must be sophisticated—that is, have sufficient knowledge and experience in financial and business matters to render them capable of evaluating the merits and risks of the prospective investment.

---

* The Commission has under consideration proposed rule revisions which would change information and financial statement requirements for purposes of Rules 505 and 506 of Regulation D. These changes had not been adopted as of the publication date of this brochure. (Footnote by SEC.)

- The term "accredited investor" is defined as above under Rule 505.

- There is no specific information which the issuer must furnish to accredited investors. However, non-accredited investors must be advised of and furnished, upon request, all material information furnished to accredited investors, as well as certain specified information.

- The information requirements are generally the same as those on the registration form the issuer would be entitled to use. If the issuer cannot obtain audited financial statements without unreasonable effort or expense, then financial statements may be provided in accordance with the special treatment described under Rule 505 above.

- The securities sold are "restricted" under the same stipulations in Rule 505.

- A company is required to file a notice of the offering on Form D at SEC headquarters within 15 days after the first sale in the offering. There is no requirement to file the offering memorandum with the Commission.

Accredited Investor Exemption: Section 4(6)

The Small Business Investment Incentive Act of 1980 created a new statutory exemption from registration under the Securities Act for transactions involving offers and sales of securities by any issuer solely to one or more "accredited investors." Under Section 4(6):

- The total offering price of each issue of securities under the exemption may not exceed the limit on small offerings set by Section 3(b) the Securities Act, which currently is $5 million per issue.

- The offering may not be made by means of any form of advertising or public solicitation.

- The term "accredited investor" is defined to include the same individuals and entities as included for purposes of Rules 505 and 506.

- The issuer is required to file a notice of sales on Form D with the Commission 15 days after the initial sale is made in reliance on the exemption.

- The Section 4(6) exemption does not contain any specific disclosure requirements. The issuer is cautioned however, that, as in the case of the other exemptions, Section 4(6) does not exempt the issuer from the antifraud provisions of the securities laws.

———

D. RATNER, SECURITIES REGULATION IN A NUTSHELL 63 (4th ed. 1992). "Offerings complying with the terms of Rule 504 or

505 are deemed to be exempt under [Securities Act] § 3(b); offerings pursuant to Rule 506, since they may exceed $5 million, cannot be exempt under § 3(b) and are considered to be non-public offerings under § 4(2). Rule 506 is not the exclusive means of making a non-public offering; the Preliminary Note to Regulation D states specifically that failure to satisfy all the terms and conditions of Rule 506 shall not raise any presumption that the exemption provided by § 4(2) is not available."

NOTE ON THE SIGNIFICANCE OF EXEMPTIONS

It's important to keep in mind that a provision exempting securities from registration under Section 5 does not necessarily mean that a seller or offeror of those securities is not required to provide the buyers with information. Some exemptions explicitly require the seller to provide information very much like that required in a registration statement. For example, Regulation A (discussed below in Section (e)) requires an elaborate Offering Circular, and Regulation D requires the provision of registration-like information in certain cases. Other exemptions implicitly require the provision of information. For example, a distribution is unlikely to qualify as a private placement unless the offerees have had access to the kind of information that would have been disclosed under a registration statement. Accordingly, when sales are made under Section 4(2) or Rule 506 through investment bankers, the issuer typically supplies an information statement that provides prospectus-like disclosure.

If an offeror of securities has to provide information comparable to that in a registration statement, what is the benefit of an exemption? First, *comparable* information may cost less to assemble and provide than the full information required in a registration statement. Second, an information statement may not require clearance by the SEC, as does a registration statement. Third, certain liability provisions of the Securities Act are keyed into registration, and therefore do not apply to an information statement. See Section 7, *infra*.

(d) REGULATION A

SECURITIES ACT § 3(b); SECURITIES ACT REG. A [RULES 251–263]

[See Statutory Supplement]

SECURITIES ACT RELEASE NO. 33–6949 (1992)

[Small Business Initiatives] . . .

A. *Regulation A*

As adopted, the dollar ceiling for a Regulation A offering is now $5 million in any 12–month period, including no more than $1.5 million in non-issuer resales. . . .

B. *"Testing the Waters"*

As discussed in the [Proposing] Release, one of the major impediments to a Regulation A financing for a small start-up or developing company with no established market for its securities, is the cost of preparing the mandated offering statement. The full costs of compliance would be incurred without knowing whether there will be any investor interest in the company.

To remedy this situation, the Commission proposed for the first time to permit companies relying on the Regulation A exemption to "test the waters" for potential interest in the company prior to filing and delivery of the mandated offering statement. All test the water documents are required to be submitted to the Commission at the time of first use. The proposal was enthusiastically endorsed by private sector commenters as a necessary and appropriate solution to a significant regulatory impediment to small business financing, and, as drafted, is consistent with investor protection interests.

A number of refinements have been included in the test the water provisions in response to public comment. First, while the Regulation continues to require that the "testing of the waters" begin with a written solicitation of interest submitted to the Commission at the time of first use, the rules have been revised to make clear that submission of the document is not a condition to the exemption. Failure to comply with the requirement is a grounds for Commission suspension of the exemption.

As proposed, the written test the water document was a free writing subject to the inclusion of two mandated statements—first, that no funds were being solicited or would be accepted, and secondly that a detailed offering document would follow. Some commenters suggested that even these few items should be deleted, while others suggested additional requirements or specific prescription of the content.

The rule as adopted continues to provide for free writing with the inclusion of the following items:

1. a statement that no money is being solicited, or will be accepted; that no sales can be made until delivery and qualification of the offering circular, and that indications of interest involve no obligation or commitment of any kind; and

2. a brief, general identification of the company's business, products and chief executive officer.

The rule has been revised to make clear that inclusion of these statements in the soliciting document is not a condition to the exemption, but failure to include the statements is a basis for Commission suspension of the exemption. . . .

Once the offering statement required by Regulation A is filed with the Commission, the issuer may not continue to use its written "test the waters" solicitation materials. The rule requires that at least 20 calendar days elapse between the last use of the solicitation of interest document or broadcast and any sale of securities in the Regulation A offering. Compliance with the rules limiting the use of the test the water documents after filing of the offering statement is not a condition to the exemption, but [noncompliance] is a violation of the rule and is a basis for Commission suspension of the exemption. . . .

SEC, Q & A: SMALL BUSINESS AND THE SEC
pp. 15–16, 1993.

. . . Regulation A

Section 3(b) of the Securities Act gives the SEC authority to exempt from registration certain offerings where the securities to be offered involve relatively small dollar amounts. Under this provision, the SEC has adopted Regulation A, a conditional exemption for certain public offerings not exceeding $5 million in any 12–month period. An offering statement (consisting of a notification, offering circular, and exhibits) must be filed with the SEC Regional Office in the region where the company's principal business activities are conducted. Although Regulation A is technically an exemption from the registration requirements of the Securities Act, it is often referred to as a "short form" of registration since the offering circular (similar in content to a prospectus) must be supplied to each purchaser and the securities issued are freely tradeable in an after-market. The principal advantages of Regulation A offerings, as opposed to full registration on either Form S–1 or SB–2, are

- Required financial statements are simpler and need not be audited; and

- There are no periodic SEC reporting requirements (other than sales reports following the sale of the securities) unless the issuer has more than $5 million in total assets and more than 500 shareholders.

- There are three permitted offering circular formats under Regulation A, one of which is a simplified question-and-answer document. This style of disclosure is useful to potential investors and may offer significant benefits to the issuer in the time expended and the costs of preparation.

All types of companies which are not reporting under the Exchange Act may use Regulation A, except "blank check" companies (i.e., those with the business of seeking an unspecified business) and investment companies registered or required to be registered under the Investment Company Act of 1940. In most cases, Regulation A may also be used by shareholders for the resale of up to $1.5 million of securities.

———

(e) SMALL BUSINESS ISSUERS

———

REGULATION S–B

[See Statutory Supplement]

———

SECURITIES ACT FORM SB–2

[See Statutory Supplement]

———

SEC, Q & A: SMALL BUSINESS AND THE SEC
pp. 9–10, 1993.

... Alternative Registration Forms for Small Business Issuers

In August 1992, the SEC adopted a simplified form (Form SB–2) for use by small business issuers. A small business issuer is a United States or Canadian issuer that had less than $25 million in revenues in its last fiscal year, provided that the value of its outstanding securities in the hands of the public is no more than $25 million.

An alternative to Form S–1, Form SB–2 permits the offering of an unlimited dollar amount of securities by any small business issuer. The form may be used again and again as long as the issuer meets the definition of small business issuer. Form SB–2 offers certain advantages, including the location of all disclosure requirements in a central repository, Regulation S–B. These disclosure requirements are presented in simple, non-legalistic terminology.

Form SB–2 also permits the issuer to

- Provide audited financial statements, prepared in accordance with generally accepted accounting principles, for two fiscal years (Form S–1 requires the issuer to provide audited financial statements, prepared in accordance with more detailed SEC regulations, for three fiscal years);

- Include less extensive narrative disclosure, particularly in the areas of the description of business, and executive compensation, than that required by Form S–1; and

- File its initial public offering with either the SEC Regional Office nearest to where the company conducts its principal business operations or with the SEC Division of Corporation Finance in Washington DC. The primary advantage of regional filing is that regional office personnel may be more familiar with local economic conditions, the business community, the financial environment, and, in some cases, the background and history of the company....

(f) THE INTRASTATE EXEMPTION

SECURITIES ACT § 3(a)(11); SECURITIES ACT RULE 147

[See Statutory Supplement]

SEC, Q & A: SMALL BUSINESS AND THE SEC

pp. 13–14, 1993.

Intrastate Offering Exemption

Section 3(a)(11) of the Securities Act is generally known as the "intrastate offering exemption." It exempts from registration any security which is part of an issue offered and sold only to residents of a single state or territory and the issuer is both a resident of and doing business within that state or territory. This exemption is intended to facilitate the local financing of local business operations. In order to qualify for the intrastate offering exemption, your company must:

- Be incorporated in the state where it is making the offering;

- Carry out a significant amount of its business in that state; and

- Make offers and sales only to residents of that state.

Although there is no fixed limit on the size of the offering or the number of purchasers, your company has the obligation to determine the residence of each purchaser. If any of the securities are offered or sold to one out-of-state purchaser, the exemption may be lost. In addition, if any of the securities are resold by an original resident purchaser to a person resident outside the state within nine months after the offering by the issuer is completed, the entire transaction may be in violation of the Securities Act. Therefore, there is usually no significant after-market for any securities issued in an intrastate offering during the nine-month period following the initial sale. Consequently, they must normally be sold at a discount.

It is difficult for you as an issuer to rely on the intrastate exemption unless your company knows the purchasers and the sale is directly negotiated with them. A company with some of its assets outside the state, or deriving a substantial portion of its revenues outside the state where it proposes to offer its securities, will probably have a difficult time justifying the exemption.

The SEC has adopted Rule 147, a "safe harbor" rule, which may be followed by companies to be certain they meet the requirements for this exemption. It is possible, however, that transactions not meeting all requirements of Rule 147 may still qualify for the exemption.

NOTE ON THE INTRASTATE EXEMPTION

1. Section 3(a)(11) is restricted to cases where the corporation is both doing business *and* incorporated in the relevant state. For example, a corporation incorporated in Delaware cannot make use of the exemption unless it is doing business in Delaware and restricts the offer to Delaware residents.

2. Rule 147 offers a safe harbor for determining whether the requirements of section 3(a)(11) are satisfied, but it is not exclusive. An issuer may show that it satisfied section 3(a)(11) even though it failed to satisfy Rule 147.

(g) TRANSACTIONS NOT INVOLVING AN ISSUER, UNDERWRITER, OR DEALER

SECURITIES ACT §§ 2(11), 4(1), 4(3)

[See Statutory Supplement]

INTRODUCTORY NOTE

Section 4(1) of the Securities Act provides that "The provisions of section 5 shall not apply to ... transactions by any person other than an issuer, underwriter, or dealer." Requiring registration for *issuer* transactions is fairly straightforward, and section 4(3) exempts most transactions by *dealers.* Accordingly, the difficult problems under § 4(1) concern the meaning of the term "underwriter."

The paradigm case of an underwriter is an investment professional who distributes stock on behalf of an issuer. Section 2(11), however, defines "underwriter" so as to pick up transactions that don't look anything like that paradigm:

> The term "underwriter" means any person who has purchased from an issuer with a view to, or offers or sells for an issuer in connection with, the distribution of any security, or participates or has a direct or indirect participation in any such undertaking, or participates or has a participation in the direct or indirect underwriting of any such undertaking; but such term shall not include a person whose interest is limited to a commission from an underwriter or dealer not in excess of the usual and customary distributors' or sellers' commission. As used in this paragraph the term "issuer" shall include, in addition to an issuer, any person directly or indirectly controlling or controlled by the issuer, or any person under direct or indirect common control with the issuer.

This balance of this Section will focus on the meaning and implications of three terms in section 2(11): (i) "offers or sells for an issuer in connection with . . . the distribution of any security"; (ii) "any person directly or indirectly controlling . . . the issuer"; and (iii) "purchased from an issuer with a view to . . . the distribution of any security."

---

(1) "Offers or sells for an issuer in connection with . . . the distribution of any security"

NOTE ON SEC v. CHINESE BENEVOLENT ASS'N

The language in section 2(11), "offers or sells for an issuer in connection with . . . the distribution of any security," picks up the paradigm case of an investment banker distributing securities on an issuer's behalf. This language has also been broadly construed to encompass other situations. Perhaps the most notable case is SEC v. Chinese Consolidated Benevolent Ass'n., 120 F.2d 738 (2d Cir. 1941), cert. denied 314 U.S. 618, 62 S.Ct. 106, 86 L.Ed. 497. There, persons loyal to the Republic of China, who sold Chinese government bonds in the United States without recompense at the beginning of World War II, were held to be underwriters, within the meaning of section 2(11), and therefore subject to the registration requirements of the Securities Act. The court said:

> Under section 4(1) the defendant is not exempt from registration requirements if it is "an underwriter". The court

below reasons that it is not to be regarded as an underwriter since it does not sell or solicit offers to buy "for an issuer in connection with, the distribution" of securities. In other words, it seems to have been held that only solicitation authorized by the issuer in connection with the distribution of the Chinese bonds would satisfy the definition of underwriter contained in Section 2(11) and that defendant's activities were never for the Chinese government but only for the purchasers of the bonds. Though the defendant solicited the orders, obtained the cash from the purchasers and caused both to be forwarded so as to procure the bonds, it is nevertheless contended that its acts could not have been for the Chinese government because it had no contractual arrangement or even understanding with the latter. But the aim of the Securities Act is to have information available for investors. This objective will be defeated if buying orders can be solicited which result in uninformed and improvident purchasers. It can make no difference as regards the policy of the act whether an issuer has solicited orders through an agent, or has merely taken advantage of the services of a person interested for patriotic reasons in securing offers to buy. The aim of the issuer is to promote the distribution of the securities, and of the Securities Act is to protect the public by requiring that it be furnished with adequate information upon which to make investments. Accordingly the words "[sell] for an issuer in connection with the distribution of any security" ought to be read as covering continual solicitations, such as the defendant was engaged in, which normally would result in a distribution of issues of unregistered securities within the United States. Here a series of events were set in motion by the solicitation of offers to buy which culminated in a distribution that was initiated by the defendant. We hold that the defendant acted as an underwriter.

120 F.2d at 740–41.

———

(2) "Any person directly or indirectly controlling the issuer"; What constitutes a "distribution"; The broker's exemption

———

NOTE ON OFFERS OR SALES FOR CONTROLLING PERSONS

Under the last sentence of section 2(11), a person is an "underwriter" if he offers or sells securities for a person who *controls* the issuer, "in connection with . . . the distribution of any security." This rule is particularly important in cases where brokers or dealers sell stock, without registration, on behalf of a controlling person. The applicability of this rule is often complicated by two issues: whether a particular sale on behalf of a controlling person is a "distribution," and whether the sale comes within the exemption in section 4(4) for "brokers' transactions executed upon customers' orders on any exchange or in the over-the-counter market but not the solicitation of such orders."

In In the Matter of Ira Haupt & Co., 23 S.E.C. 589 (1946), Ira Haupt & Company, a brokerage firm, sold approximately 93,000 shares of the unregistered common stock of Park & Tilford, Inc. for the accounts of David A. Schulte and a corporation and trust controlled by him. The sales were made in small lots over the course of approximately six months pursuant to Schulte's instructions to sell 200–share blocks from his personal holdings at "59 and every quarter up," and up to 73,000 shares for the trust "at $80 per share or better." The price of the stock rose sharply from $57 to $98 per share during this period because of the announcement that a whiskey dividend would be distributed in kind to the shareholders of Park & Tilford. (It should be borne in mind that a dividend in liquor was especially welcome during the wartime shortage.) Schulte was aware of the planned dividend at the time he placed his order to sell with Ira Haupt.

The Schulte interests initially held over 90 percent of the common stock of Park & Tilford, and it was therefore conceded that they controlled Park & Tilford. It was thus clear that Ira Haupt was selling the securities for a person "controlling the issuer" as contemplated by the last sentence of section 2(11). Ira Haupt nevertheless denied that it was a statutory underwriter for purposes of the transactions, claiming that such sales were not effected "in connection with . . . the distribution of any security."

At the outset, the Commission noted that although the term "distribution" is not defined in the Act, it had previously been held to comprise "the entire process by which in the course of a public offering the block of securities is dispersed and ultimately comes to rest in the hands of the investing public." The Commission further remarked:

> We find no validity in the argument that a predetermination of the precise number of shares which are to be publicly dispersed is an essential element of a distribution. Nor do we think that a "distribution" loses its character as such merely because the extent of the offering may depend on certain conditions such as the market price. . . . Such offerings are not any less a "distribution" merely because their precise extent cannot be predetermined.

The Commission concluded that

> . . . respondent was selling for the Schulte interests, controlling shareholders of Park & Tilford, in connection with the distribution of their holdings in the stock and was, therefore, an "underwriter" within the meaning of the Act.

Thus, the exemption of section 4(1) was not applicable to the transactions.

---

(3) "Any person who has purchased from an issuer with a view to ... distribution"

NOTE ON GILLIGAN, WILL & CO. v. S.E.C.

Section 2(11) includes within the term "underwriter" a person "who has purchased from an issuer with a view to ... distribution." Even a person who is not an underwriter in the normal usage of that term may be a statutory underwriter under this provision. Assume that A has purchased securities from an issuer. If A purchased the securities with the intent to offer or resell them through a distribution—as opposed to having purchased with an "investment intent"—he is an underwriter under section 2(11) and therefore cannot claim the section 4(1) exemption from registration. The classic case is that in which A has purchased unregistered securities under the private-placement exemption and then turns around and reoffers the securities to a number of buyers. In Gilligan, Will & Co. v. S.E.C., 267 F.2d 461 (2d Cir.1959), cert. denied 361 U.S. 896, 80 S.Ct. 200, 4 L.Ed.2d 152, Gilligan, a partner in Gilligan, Will, purchased $100,000 of a $3,000,000 private placement of Crowell–Collier convertible debentures for his own account, representing that he purchased for investment. Notwithstanding these representations, Gilligan quickly sold $45,000 of the debentures to Louis Alter, made offers to two other potential purchasers, selling $5,000 of debentures to one of them, and placed the remaining debentures in a Gilligan, Will trading account. Ten months later, Gilligan, Alter, and the Gilligan, Will firm converted their debentures into common stock and sold the stock at a profit on the American Stock Exchange. Gilligan and Alter later subscribed to an additional $200,000 of debentures, which they similarly converted to common stock. Gilligan, Will also was active in selling $200,000 of the debentures to a mutual fund, and as a result of this transaction other parties received warrants to purchase Crowell–Collier stock.

Gilligan and Gilligan, Will argued that since the conversion and sales occurred more than ten months after the purchase of the debentures, the Commission was bound to find that the debentures so converted had been held for investment, and were not purchased with a view to distribution. In answer to this contention the court noted that

> ... Petitioners concede that if such sales were intended at the time of purchase, the debentures would not then have been held as investments; but [they argue] that the stipulation

reveals that the sales were undertaken only after a change of the issuer's circumstances as a result of which petitioners, acting as prudent investors, thought it wise to sell. The catalytic circumstances were the failure, noted by Gilligan, of Crowell–Collier to increase its advertising space as he had anticipated it would. We agree with the Commission that in the circumstances here presented the intention to retain the debentures only if Crowell–Collier continued to operate profitably was equivalent to a "purchase ... with a view to ... distribution" within the statutory definition of underwriters in § 2(11). To hold otherwise would be to permit a dealer who speculatively purchases an unregistered security in the hope that the financially weak issuer had, as is stipulated here, "turned the corner," to unload on the unadvised public what he later determines to be an unsound investment without the disclosure sought by the securities laws, although it is in precisely such circumstances that disclosure is most necessary and desirable. . . .

(4) Rules 144 and 144A

SECURITIES ACT RULE 144

[See Statutory Supplement]

SECURITIES ACT RELEASE NO. 5223 (1973)

NOTICE OF ADOPTION OF RULE 144. . . .

. . . [T]he Commission is of the view that "distribution" is the significant concept in interpreting the statutory term "underwriter." In determining when a person is deemed not to be engaged in a distribution several factors must be considered.

First, the purpose and underlying policy of the Act to protect investors requires, in the Commission's opinion, that there be adequate current information concerning the issuer, whether the resales of securities by persons result in a distribution or are effected in trading transactions. Accordingly, the availability of the rule is conditioned on the existence of adequate current public information.

Secondly, a holding period prior to resale is essential, among other reasons, to assure that those persons who buy under a claim of a Section 4(2) exemption have assumed the economic risks of investment, and therefore, are not acting as conduits for sale to the public of unregistered securities, directly or indirectly, on behalf of an issuer. It should be noted that there is nothing in Section 2(11) which places a time limit on a person's status as an underwriter. The public has the same need for protection afforded by registration whether the securities are distributed shortly after their purchase or after a considerable length of time.

A third factor, which must be considered in determining what is deemed not to constitute a "distribution," is the impact of the particular transaction or transactions on the trading markets. It is consistent with the rationale of the Act that Section 4(1) be interpreted to permit only routine trading transactions as distinguished from distributions. Therefore, a person reselling securities under Section 4(1) of the Act must sell the securities in such limited quantities and in such a manner so as not to disrupt the trading markets. The larger the amount of securities involved, the more likely it is that such resales may involve methods of offering and amounts of compensation usually associated with a distribution rather than routine trading transactions. Thus, solicitation of buy orders or the payment of extra compensation are not permitted by the rule.

In summary, if the sale in question is made in accordance with all the provisions of the rule, ... any person who sells restricted securities shall be deemed not to be engaged in a distribution of such securities and therefore not an underwriter thereof. The rule also provides that any person who sells restricted or other securities on behalf of a person in a control relationship with the issuer shall be deemed not to be engaged in a distribution of such securities and therefore not to be an underwriter thereof, if the sale is made in accordance with all the conditions of the rule.

———

D. RATNER, SECURITIES REGULATION IN A NUTSHELL 75 (4th ed. 1992). "One unresolved question is whether a person who has purchased securities from the issuer in a non-public transaction can resell those securities in another *private* transaction, and, if so, what limitations apply to such resales. Since this situation is not technically covered by either § 4(1) or § 4(2), it is sometimes said to be covered by the '§ 4(1½) exemption.' See Ackerberg v. Johnson, 892 F.2d 1328 (8th Cir.1989)."

———

RULE 144A

[See Statutory Supplement]

———

NOTE ON EXEMPTED SECURITIES

The exemptions considered in this Section relate to types of *transactions,* and for the most part provide an exemption only from section 5. The Securities Act also exempts certain types of *securities* from the provisions of *the entire Act.* These exemptions are to be found in sections 3(a)(1)–(a)(8). They include U.S. government, state, and municipal securities (section 3(a)(2)), certain short-term paper (section 3(a)(3)), and bankruptcy trustee certificates (section 3(a)(7)).

SECTION 5. MECHANICS OF REGISTRATION

SECURITIES ACT FORMS S–1, S–2, AND S–3

[See Statutory Supplement]

NOTE ON THE MECHANICS OF REGISTRATION

Assuming that securities must be registered, the registration process is begun by filing with the SEC a registration statement on the applicable form. The basic forms are S–1, S–2, and S–3, but there are many other forms for special situations.

In general, the registration statement must describe such matters as the characteristics of the securities; the character and size of the business enterprise; its capital structure, financial history, and earnings; underwriters' commissions; the names of persons who participate in the direction, management, or control of the business; their security holdings and remuneration, including options; payments to promoters made within two years or intended to be made in the near future; acquisitions of property not in the ordinary course of business, and the interests of directors, officers, and principal stockholders therein; pending or threatened legal proceedings; and the purpose to which the proceeds of the offering are to be applied. The registration statement must include the issuer's financial statements, certified by independent accountants.

The Commission is empowered to prevent the sale of securities to the public on the basis of statements that contain inaccurate or incomplete information. The Staff of the Division of Corporate Finance usually notifies the registrant, by an informal letter of comment, of respects in which the registration statement apparently fails to conform to these requirements. The registrant is afforded an opportunity to file an amendment before the statement becomes effective. However, in certain cases, such as where the deficiencies in a registration statement appear to stem from careless disregard of applicable requirements or a deliberate attempt to conceal or mislead, the Commission either institutes an investigation to determine whether "stop-order" proceedings should be instituted or immediately issues such an order.

The minimum period between the time of filing the registration statement and the time it may become effective is twenty days. This waiting period is designed to provide investors with an opportunity to become familiar with the proposed offering. Information disclosed in the registration statements is disseminated during the waiting period by means of the preliminary prospectus, which presents in summary form the more important of the required disclosures.

————

NOTE ON THE INTEGRATION OF DISCLOSURE UNDER THE 1933 AND 1934 ACTS

Within recent years, the content of the registration forms has been dramatically affected by the concept of integration. The Securities Exchange Act of 1934 requires *periodic disclosure* by issuers whose stock is registered under that Act. For example, such issuers must file an annual 10–K report, which includes financial statements and various other information; must annually distribute a proxy statement, or the equivalent, containing information on such matters as remuneration of directors and officers and conflict-of-interest transactions; and must file timely 8–K reports whenever certain material events have occurred. In contrast, the Securities Act of 1933 requires only *transactional disclosure*—that is, disclosure only in connection with specific public distributions. Until the late 1970's, the disclosure schemes of the two Acts proceeded on separate courses. At that time, however, the Commission undertook a program of integrating the two disclosure schemes. Partly, this was accomplished by a uniform Regulation, S–K, which provides equivalent definitions and disclosure requirements for comparable issues under the two Acts. Partly, it was accomplished by stratifying issuers into three classes, and reducing the amount of disclosure required in registration statements under the 1933 Act filed for issuers that are already making periodic disclosure under the 1934 Act, and issuers as to whom a great deal of information is likely to be publicly available even apart from the 1934 Act's disclosure requirements.

————

SECURITIES ACT RELEASE NO. 6331 (1981)

[REGISTRATION FORMS]

. . . II.   Overview

Under the proposed registration statement framework, registrants would be classified into three categories: (1) companies which are widely followed by professional analysts; (2) companies which have been subject to the periodic reporting system of the Exchange Act for three or more years, but which are not widely followed; and (3) companies which have been in the Exchange Act reporting system for less than three years.   The first category would be eligible to use proposed Form S–3, which relies on incorporation by reference of Exchange Act reports and contains minimal disclosure in the prospectus.   This form is predicated on the Commission's belief that the market operates efficiently for these companies, i.e., that the disclosure in Exchange Act reports and other communications by the registrant, such as press releases, has already been disseminated and accounted for by the market place. The second category would be eligible for Form S–2, which represents a combination of incorporation by reference of Exchange Act reports and presentation in the prospectus or in an annual report to security holders of certain information.   The third category would use Form S–1, which requires complete disclosure of information in the prospectus and does not permit incorporation by reference. . . .

Proposed Form S–3 recognizes the applicability of the efficient market theory to the registration statement framework with respect to those registrants which usually provide high quality corporate reports, including Exchange Act reports, and whose corporate information is broadly disseminated, because such companies are widely followed by professional analysts and investors in the market place. Because these registrants are widely followed, the disclosure set forth in the prospectus may appropriately be limited, without the loss of investor protection, to information concerning the offering and material facts which have not been disclosed previously.   The abbreviated disclosure is made possible by the use of incorporation by reference of the registrant's Exchange Act information into the prospectus.   Because of the abbreviated disclosure, the utility of proposed Form S–3 is limited to widely followed companies. . . . The proposed float requirement is designed to correlate the use of abbreviated Form S–3 to widely followed registrants.

. . . [P]roposed Form S–2 is designed for improved readability by streamlining disclosure requirements and allowing certain disclosure obligations to be satisfied either through the delivery of the annual report to security holders or by presentation of comparable updated information in the prospectus.   More specifically, the financial statements, management's discussion and analysis and the brief business description required by proposed Form S–2 are identical to those already presented in the annual report to security holders. . . .

Finally, proposed Form S–1 ... would be used to register securities when no other form is authorized or prescribed and would be used by companies in the Exchange Act reporting system for less than three years, such as new issuers. To ensure that adequate information concerning these registrants is readily available to investors, proposed Form S–1 requires delivery of a more lengthy and comprehensive prospectus than either proposed Form S–2 or Form S–3....

III. Synopsis ...

A. *Eligibility Rules for Use of Forms S–3, S–2 and S–1* ...

1. *Form S–3*

The eligibility requirements for use of Form S–3 are broken down into two classifications, "Registrant Requirements" and "Transaction Requirements." A registrant first must meet the Registrant Requirements (which are identical for Forms S–3 and S–2) and then must meet at least one of the Transaction Requirements before it can use Form S–3. ...

2. *Form S–2*

... [T]he Registrant Requirements of Form S–3 also constitute virtually the entire eligibility requirements for the use of Form S–2....

3. *Form S–1*

... [T]his more comprehensive form must be used by first time filers and others who have only been filing reports for a short period of time....

c. *Disclosure Provisions*

In proposed Forms S–1, S–2 and S–3, the Commission has developed a Securities Act registration system which identifies the information material to investment decisions in the context of all public offerings and then determines in what form and to whom issuers must disseminate such information. The material information will be required to be part of all Securities Act registration statements, regardless of the form used, through incorporation by reference in some cases. Differences among the forms primarily involve dissemination, i.e., the extent to which the required information must be presented in the prospectus, or may be presented in other documents delivered with the prospectus and incorporated by reference, or may be simply incorporated by reference from information contained in the Exchange Act continuous reporting system.

Generally, it is the issuer-oriented part of the information material to a public offering, as opposed to the transaction-specific information, which, depending on the form available, may be satisfied otherwise than through full prospectus presentation. This information includes the basic package of information about the issuer which the Commission believes is material to investment decisions in all contexts and thus is also required to be presented in annual reports to the Commission on Form 10–K and in annual reports to security holders. Information about the offering will not have been reported on in any other disclosure document or otherwise have been publicly disseminated and thus will be required to be presented in all cases. . . .

2. *Incorporation by Reference*

The technique of incorporation by reference of Exchange Act disclosure documents is central to the integrated Securities Act registration system represented by proposed Forms S–1, S–2 and S–3. Proposed Form S–3 relies on incorporation by reference to replace prospectus presentation of information about the issuer of the securities being registered. Proposed Form S–2 uses incorporation by reference to allow streamlining of the prospectus presentation of issuer-specific information. Proposed Form S–1 uses no incorporation by reference and instead requires full disclosure about the issuer of the securities to be presented in the prospectus. . . .

3. *Disclosure Requirements by Form*

a. *Form S–3*

Proposed Form S–3 provides the shortest form for Securities Act registration. The prospectus would be required to present [certain] items calling for information about the offering. . . .

Information concerning the registrant would be incorporated by reference from Exchange Act reports, which would be available to investors on request. The documents required to be incorporated are the latest annual report on Form 10–K and all other reports filed pursuant to Section 13(a) or 15(d) of the Exchange Act since the end of the fiscal year covered by the Form 10–K, including all Section 13(d) or 15(d) reports filed subsequent to effectiveness of the registration statement and prior to termination of the offering. Unless there has been a material change in the registrant's affairs which has not been reported in an Exchange Act filing, the prospectus would not be required to present any information concerning the registrant. . . .

b. *Form S–2*

Proposed Form S–2 provides a simplified form for registration by certain registrants. While it requires delivery of information about the registrant in addition to delivery of the same information about the offering as required by Form S–3, proposed Form S–2 significantly streamlines the registrant-specific disclosure by making the required level of disclosure delivered to investors that of the annual report to security holders pursuant to Rule 14a–3 rather than that of the annual report on Form 10–K. Required information about the registrant includes the basic information package components (market price and dividend data, selected financial data, financial statements and management's discussion and analysis) and such other items (brief descriptions of business, segments, supplementary financial information) as are required to be included in the annual report to security holders pursuant to Rule 14a–3. Moreover, registrants are granted the option of providing this information either by presenting it in the prospectus or by delivering the latest annual report to security holders along with the prospectus. Finally, the registrant's latest annual report on Form 10–K and periodic reports on Form 10–Q and Form 8–K must be incorporated by reference into the prospectus, and made available upon request, to round out the information provided about the registrant. . . .

If the Form S–2 registrant elects the alternative of delivering its annual report, it must incorporate certain information in that document by reference and describe in the prospectus any material changes in its affairs since the end of the latest fiscal year reported in the delivered annual report. In addition, it must provide updating information but may avoid duplication of previously reported quarterly information because updating may be accomplished by any one of three means: (1) including in the prospectus such financial and other information as would be required to be reported in a report on Form 10–Q; (2) delivering a copy of the latest Form 10–Q with the prospectus and annual report; (3) delivering a copy of the latest informal quarterly report to shareholders if such report contained the same required information. . . .

c. *Form S–1*

Proposed Form S–1 presents a simple format. Full disclosure of all material information about the offering and the registrant is required to be presented in the prospectus itself. No incorporation by reference to any Exchange Act documents is allowed. Proposed Form S–1 looks entirely to Regulation S–K for its non-financial substantive disclosure provisions. First, like proposed Forms S–2 and S–3, proposed Form S–1 requires prospectus presentation of the offering-oriented items of § 229.500 of Regulation S–K and the description of securities (proposed Item 202 of Regulation S–K). In addition, the proposed Form S–1 prospectus must include the same information about the registrant as is required to be reported in an annual report on Form 10–K. This information includes, in addition to the basic information package with respect to the registrant, the full Regulation S–K descriptions of business, properties and legal proceedings as well as the Regulation S–K disclosures with respect to management and security holders. . . .

SECURITIES ACT RULE 415

[See Statutory Supplement]

SECTION 6.   DUTIES AND PROHIBITIONS WHEN A SECURITY IS IN REGISTRATION

SECURITIES ACT RELEASE NO. 4697 (1964)

OFFERS AND SALES OF SECURITIES BY UNDERWRITERS AND DEALERS

In view of recent comments in the press concerning the rights and obligations of, and limitations on, dealers in connection with distributions of registered securities, the Commission takes this opportunity to explain the operation of section 5 of the Securities Act of 1933 with particular reference to the limitations upon, and responsibilities of, underwriters and dealers in the offer and sale of an issue of securities prior to and after the filing of a registration statement.

The discussion below assumes that the offering is not exempt from the registration requirements of the Act and, unless otherwise stated, that the mails or facilities of interstate or foreign commerce are used.

The Period Before the Filing of a Registration Statement

Section 5 of the Securities Act prohibits both offers to sell and offers to buy a security before a registration statement is filed. Section 2(3) of the Act, however, exempts preliminary negotiations or agreements between the issuer or other person on whose behalf the distribution is to be made and any underwriter or among underwriters. Thus, negotiation of the financing can proceed during this period but neither the issuer nor the underwriter may offer the security either to investors or to dealers, and dealers are prohibited from offering to buy the securities during this period.[1] Consequently, not only may no steps be taken to form a selling group but also dealers may not seek inclusion in the selling group prior to the filing.

It should be borne in mind that publicity about an issuer, its securities or the proposed offering prior to the filing of a registration statement may constitute an illegal offer to sell. Thus, announcement of the underwriter's identity should be avoided during this period. Experience shows that such announcements are very likely to lead to illegal offers to buy. This subject will not be further

---

1. The reason for this provision was stated in the House Report on the bill as originally enacted as follows:

"... Otherwise, the underwriter ... could accept them in the order of their priority and thus bring pressure upon dealers, who wish to avail themselves of a particular security offering, to rush their orders to buy without adequate consideration of the nature of the security being offered." H.R.Report No. 85, 73rd Cong., 1st Sess. (1933), p. 11.

discussed in this release since it has been extensively considered elsewhere.[2]

These principles, however, are not intended to restrict the normal communications between an issuer and its stockholders or the announcement to the public generally of information with respect to important business and financial developments. Such announcements are required in the listing agreements used by stock exchanges, and the Commission is sensitive to the importance of encouraging this type of communication. In recognition of this requirement of certain stock exchanges, the Commission adopted Rule 135, which permits a brief announcement of proposed rights offerings, proposed exchange offerings, and proposed offerings to employees as not constituting an offer of a security for the purposes of section 5 of the Act.

The Period After the Filing and Before the Effective Date

After the registration statement is filed, and before its effective date, offers to sell the securities are permitted but no written offer may be made except by means of a statutory prospectus. For this purpose the statutory prospectus includes the preliminary prospectus provided for in Rule 433 as well as the summary prospectus provided for in Rules 434 and 434A. In addition the so-called "tombstone" advertisement permitted by Rule 134 may be used.

During the period after the filing of a registration statement, the freedom of an underwriter or dealer expecting to participate in the distribution, to communicate with his customers is limited only by the antifraud provisions of the Securities Act and the Securities Exchange Act, and by the fact that written offering material other than a statutory prospectus or tombstone advertisement may not be used. In other words, during this period "free writing" is illegal. The dealer, therefore, can orally solicit indications of interest or offers to buy and may discuss the securities with his customers and advise them whether or not in his opinion the securities are desirable or suitable for them. In this connection a dealer proposing to discuss an issue of securities with his customers should obtain copies of the preliminary prospectus in order to have a reliable source of information. This is particularly important where he proposes to recommend the securities, or where information concerning them has not been generally available. The corollary of the dealer's obligation to secure the copy is the obligation of the issuer and managing underwriters to make it readily available. Rule 460 provides that as a condition to acceleration of the effective date of a registration statement, the Commission will consider whether the persons making the offering have taken reasonable steps to make the information contained in the registration statement available to dealers who may participate in the distribution.

---

2. See Securities Act Release No. 3844 (1957); Carl M. Loeb, Rhoades & Co., 38 S.E.C. 843 (1959); First Maine Corporation, 38 S.E.C. 882 (1959).

It is a principal purpose of the so-called "waiting period" between the filing date and the effective date to enable dealers and, through them, investors to become acquainted with the information contained in the registration statement and to arrive at an unhurried decision concerning the merits of the securities. Consistently with this purpose, no contracts of sale can be made during this period, the purchase price may not be paid or received and offers to buy may be cancelled.

The Period After the Effective Date

When the registration statement becomes effective oral offerings may continue and sales may be made and consummated. A copy of the final statutory prospectus must be delivered in connection with any written offer or confirmation or upon delivery of the security, whichever first occurs. Supplemental sales literature ("free writing") may be used if it is accompanied or preceded by a prospectus. However, care must be taken to see that all such material is at the time of use not false or misleading under the standards of section 17(a) of the Act. If the offering continues over an extended period, the prospectus should be current under the standards of section 10(a)(3). All dealers trading in the registered security must continue to employ the prospectus for the period referred to in section 4.

SECURITIES ACT §§ 2(3), 5

[See Statutory Supplement]

NOTE ON THE PRE-FILING PERIOD

Under section 5(a) of the 1933 Act:

> Unless a registration statement is in effect as to a security, it shall be unlawful for any person, directly or indirectly—(1) to make use of any means or instruments of transportation or communication in interstate commerce or of the mails to sell such security through the use or medium of any prospectus or otherwise; or (2) to carry or cause to be carried through the mails or in interstate commerce, by any means or instruments of transportation, any such security for the purpose of sale or for delivery after sale.

Under section 5(c):

> It shall be unlawful for any person, directly or indirectly, to make use of any means or instruments of transportation or communication in interstate commerce or of the mails to offer to sell or offer to buy through the use or medium of any

prospectus or otherwise any security, unless a registration statement has been filed as to such security. . . .

Under section 2(3):

The term "sale" or "sell" shall include every contract of sale or disposition of a security or interest in a security, for value. The term "offer to sell", "offer for sale", or "offer" shall include every attempt or offer to dispose of, or solicitation of an offer to buy, a security or interest in a security, for value.

There is an important exception to section 2(3):

The terms defined in [§ 2(3)] and the term "offer to buy" as used in subsection (c) of section 5 shall not include preliminary negotiations or agreements between an issuer . . . and any underwriter or among underwriters who are or are to be in privity of contract with an issuer. . . .

Putting together §§ 5(a), 5(c), and 2(3), neither a sale nor an oral or written offer to sell securities to be registered may be made during the prefiling period, except for preliminary negotiations between the issuer and the underwriter and between underwriters. The prohibition against offers in the prefiling period extends not only to formal offers, but to "gun-jumping"—unusual publicity by the issuer or a prospective underwriter that is in effect a preliminary step in the selling effort. On the other hand, if a corporation is already publicly held, blocking the normal flow of information would adversely affect the integrity of the market for the securities that are already outstanding. The cases and rules governing the prefiling period attempt to reconcile the undesirability of gun-jumping with the desirability of maintaining the normal flow of information concerning corporations that are already publicly held.

––––––––––

SECURITIES ACT RULE 135, 137, 139

[See Statutory Supplement]

––––––––––

SECURITIES ACT RELEASE NO. 5180 (1971)

GUIDELINES FOR THE RELEASE OF INFORMATION BY ISSUERS WHOSE SECURITIES ARE IN REGISTRATION

The Commission today took note of situations when issuers whose securities are "in registration" may have refused to answer legitimate inquiries from stockholders, financial analysts, the press or other persons concerning the company or some aspect of its business. The Commission hereby emphasizes that there is no basis in the securities acts or in any policy of the Commission which would justify the practice of non-disclosure of *factual* information by a publicly held company on the grounds that it has securities in registration under the Securities Act of 1933 ("Act"). Neither a company in registration nor its representatives should instigate publicity for the purpose of facilitating the sale of securities in a proposed offering. . . .

. . . It has been asserted that the increasing obligations and incentives of corporations to make timely disclosures concerning their affairs creates a possible conflict with statutory restrictions on publication of information concerning a company which has securities in registration. As the Commission has stated in previously issued releases this conflict may be more apparent than real. Disclosure of factual information in response to inquiries or resulting from a duty to make prompt disclosure under the antifraud provisions of the securities acts or the timely disclosure policies of self-regulatory organizations, at a time when a registered offering of securities is contemplated or in process, can and should be effected in a manner which will not unduly influence the proposed offering.

Statutory Requirements

In order for issuers and their representatives to avoid problems in responding to inquiries, it is essential that such persons be familiar with the statutory requirements governing this area. Generally speaking, Section 5(c) of the Act makes it unlawful for any person directly or indirectly to make use of any means or instruments of interstate commerce or of the mails *to offer to sell* a security unless a registration statement has been filed with the Commission as to such security. Questions arise from time to time because many persons do not realize that the phrase "offer to sell" is broadly defined by the Act and has been liberally construed by the courts and Commission. For example, the publication of information and statements, and publicity efforts, made in advance of a proposed financing which have the effect of conditioning the public mind or arousing public interest in the issuer or in its securities constitutes an offer in violation of the Act. The same holds true with respect to publication of information which is part of a selling effort between the filing date and the effective date of a registration statement. . . .

Guidelines

The Commission strongly suggests that all issuers establish internal procedures designed to avoid problems relating to the release of corporate information when in registration. As stated above, issuers and their representatives should not initiate publicity when in registration, but should nevertheless respond to legitimate inquiries for factual information about the company's financial condition and business operations. Further, care should be exercised so that, for example, predictions, projections, forecasts, estimates and opinions concerning value are not given with respect to such things, among other, as sales and earnings and value of the issuer's securities.

It has been suggested that the Commission promulgate an all inclusive list of permissible and prohibited activities in this area. This is not feasible for the reason that determinations are based upon the particular facts of each case. However, the Commission as a matter of policy encourages the flow of factual information to shareholders and the investing public. Issuers in this regard should:

1. Continue to advertise products and services.

2. Continue to send out customary quarterly, annual and other periodic reports to stockholders.

3. Continue to publish proxy statements and send out dividend notices.

4. Continue to make announcements to the press with respect to factual business and financial developments; *i.e.,* receipt of a contract, the settlement of a strike, the opening of a plant, or similar events of interest to the community in which the business operates.

5. Answer unsolicited telephone inquiries from stockholders, financial analysts, the press and others concerning factual information.

6. Observe an "open door" policy in responding to unsolicited inquiries concerning factual matters from securities analysts, financial analysts, security holders, and participants in the communications field who have a legitimate interest in the corporation's affairs.

7. Continue to hold stockholder meetings as scheduled and to answer shareholders' inquiries at stockholder meetings relating to factual matters.

In order to curtail problems in this area, issuers in this regard should avoid:

1. Issuance of forecasts, projections, or predictions relating but not limited to revenues, income, or earnings per share.

2. Publishing opinions concerning values.

In the event a company publicly releases material information concerning new corporate developments during the period that a registration statement is pending, the registration statement should be amended at or prior to the time the information is released. If this is not done and such information is publicly released through inadvertence, the pending registration statement should be promptly amended to reflect such information. . . .

———

SECTION 7. LIABILITIES UNDER THE SECURITIES ACT

SECURITIES ACT §§ 11, 12, 17; SECURITIES ACT RULES 175, 176

[See Statutory Supplement]

NOTE ON LIABILITIES UNDER THE SECURITIES ACT

The Securities Act contains four basic liability provisions: Sections 11, 12(1), 12(2), and 17(a).

1. *Section 17(a).* Section 17(a) is a general antifraud provision, whose applicability does not turn on whether there has been a violation of section 5, the registration provision. Section 17(a) is highly comparable to rule 10b–5, because rule 10b–5 was modeled on section 17(a). However, rule 10b–5 regulates both sellers and buyers, while section 17(a) regulates only sellers. On the other hand, section 17(a) applies to "offers" while rule 10b–5 does not. There is no private right of action under section 17(a). See, e.g., Finkel v. Stratton Corp., 962 F.2d 169, 174–75 (2d Cir.1992). The Supreme Court has held that scienter is a necessary element of a violation of section 17(a)(1), but not of sections 17(a)(2) or 17(a)(3). Aaron v. S.E.C., 446 U.S. 680, 100 S.Ct. 1945, 64 L.Ed.2d 611 (1980).

2. *Section 12(2).* Section 12(2), like section 17(a), is a general antifraud provision. Unlike section 17(a), section 12(2) explicitly provides for liability to injured buyers.

3. *Section 12(1).* Section 12(1) can be most easily understood by comparing it to section 12(2):

(i) Section 12(2) regulates both sellers and buyers. Section 12(1) regulates only sellers.

(ii) Section 12(2) does not depend on whether there has been a violation of section 5, the registration provision. Section 12(1) does.

(iii) Under both sections 12(1) and 12(2), privity is required—that is, a person who wrongfully sells an unregistered security is liable only to her buyer.

(iv) Under both sections 12(1) and 12(2), the buyer's recovery is limited to the return of the purchase price (with interest, but minus the amount of any income received), unless he has resold the security. If the buyer has resold the security, he is entitled to "damages," which is construed to mean the difference between the price he paid for the security and the price at which he resold the security.

(v) Under both sections 12(1) and 12(2), there is no requirement that the plaintiffs have relied on the misstatement or omission. Johns Hopkins Univ. v. Hutton, 422 F.2d 1124, 1129 (4th Cir.1970).

(vi) Under section 12(1), it's irrelevant whether the seller made any false statements or omitted to state material facts; the buyer need only show that the security was sold in violation of section 5. In contrast, under section 12(2) the buyer must show a false statement or material omission. However, the buyer need not show that the seller was at fault. Once the buyer shows that an omission was material, or that a material statement was false, the seller has the burden of showing that he did not know and "in the exercise of reasonable care could not have known" of the untruth or omission. In effect, therefore, section 12(2) imposes a negligence standard but puts the burden of proof on the seller to prove he was not negligent.

(vii) In Gustafson v. Alloyd Co., ___ U.S. ___, 115 S.Ct. 1061, 131 L.Ed.2d 1 (1995), the Supreme Court held that section 12(2) applies only to securities sold in public offerings by issuers or their controlling shareholders.

4. *Section 11.* Section 11, like Section 12(1), is keyed into registration. Under section 11:

(i) Liability is limited to false statements in the registration statement.

(ii) The buyer normally doesn't have to show that he relied on the false statements.[1]

(iii) Damages are limited under the complicated scheme set forth in subsection (e).

(iv) The *issuer* is strictly liable—liable without fault. Any other *nonexpert* defendant is liable if, but only if, as to the nonexpertised portions "he had, after reasonable investigation, reasonable ground to believe" that the relevant statements were true and that there were no material omissions, and as to the expertised portions, "he had no reasonable ground to believe" that the statements made by the expert were untrue or contained material omissions. This is known as the due diligence defense. Thus section 11, like section 12(2), adopts a negligence standard with the burden of proof on the defendants. However, there is a difference in the formulations of the negligence standards in sections 11 and 12(2), and it is not clear whether this means that there are differences in the investigation required to satisfy the defendant's burden of proof under the two sections. See Sanders v. John Nuveen & Co., Inc., 619 F.2d 1222 (7th Cir.1980), cert. denied 450 U.S. 1005, 101 S.Ct. 1719, 68 L.Ed.2d 210 (1981) (opinion of Powell, dissenting from denial of certiorari).

The express remedy provided in section 11 does not preclude a buyer from bringing suit under Rule 10b–5 on the basis of misrepre-

---

1. If a security is acquired after the issuer has published a financial statement for the twelve-month period beginning at the date of the registration statement, the plaintiff's right of recovery is conditioned upon proof of reliance.

sentations or omissions in a registration statement. Herman & MacLean v. Huddleston, 459 U.S. 375, 103 S.Ct. 683, 74 L.Ed.2d 548 (1983).

SECTION 8.   BLUE SKY LAWS

NOTE ON BLUE SKY LAWS

Prior to the entry of the federal government into the field of securities regulation in 1933, almost all of the states had adopted statutes designed to protect the public from "speculative schemes which have no more basis than so many feet of 'blue sky.' " [1] Since section 18 of the 1933 Act provides that "Nothing in this title shall affect the jurisdiction of the securities commission (or any agency or office performing like functions) of any State . . . over any securities or any person," state and federal regulation have continued side by side.

At the present time, all states have blue sky laws in effect. These laws are of major significance, partly because many securities offerings are not registered under the federal Securities Act by virtue of exemptions, and partly because many of the blue-sky laws go beyond the disclosure requirements of the Securities Act.

The state statutes vary tremendously in coverage, approach and impact. Three basic methods of regulation are employed, which are sometimes referred to as the fraud, dealer-registration, and securities-registration methods. The vast majority of the states have adopted all three methods to varying extents, but the methods are embodied in different forms, and standards and procedures vary widely from state to state.

1. *The fraud method.* The fraud method simply makes certain practices, usually described by some form of the word "fraud," grounds for criminal prosecution, suspension of trading, or both. The blue sky administrator normally has broad investigatory powers, but those powers are unlikely to be exercised in the absence of complaint or suspicious circumstances. Probably for this reason, the fraud method is not thought to be sufficient in itself.

2. *The dealer-registration method.* The dealer-registration method requires dealers (including issuers, brokers, and salesmen) to register as a prerequisite to trading in securities within a state's borders. The amount, detail, and nature of the information that must be submitted varies widely. In a majority of states, registration may be denied or revoked for cause, and the administrator

---

1. Hall v. Geiger–Jones Co., 242 U.S. 539, 550, 37 S.Ct. 217, 220–21, 61 L.Ed. 480, 489 (1917).

sometimes has considerable discretion in determining whether a dealer shall be permitted to do business within the state.

3. *The securities-registration method.* The securities-registration method prohibits dealing in an issue of securities until the issue has been qualified under the statutory standard in accordance with the statutory procedure. This method is sometimes referred to as "merit regulation," because, in contrast to registration under the Securities Act, the blue sky administrator can deny registration on the ground that the securities issue lacks merit, even though full disclosure has been made. The standards adopted and the procedures prescribed exhibit considerable variation from state to state. In general, the standards and procedures are aimed at unseasoned speculative securities being offered to the general public.

Three basic types of approaches fall within the securities-registration or merit-regulation method.

Under the *qualifying* approach, trading in non-exempt securities is permitted only following an affirmative administrative determination that the issue meets a designated statutory standard, such as "fair, just and equitable." More specific standards are usually imposed on the qualification of particularly unsafe issues. Thus "in practically all of the states, promotion stock, 'cheap stock,' and options are limited to stated percentages, or amounts which the administrators may deem reasonable." Mofsky, Blue Sky Restrictions on New Business Promotions, 169 Duke L.J. 273. Also, "39 states ... requires escrow arrangements [for the promotional shares]." Id.

Under the *notification* approach, which is often available for seasoned securities, registration by notification becomes effective after a designated period unless the administrator moves to block it.

The *coordination* approach is similar to the notification approach, but is available only for issues registered under the federal Securities Act. The information submitted to the administrator basically consists of copies of the material filed with the SEC. The state registration "becomes effective at the moment the federal registration statement becomes effective," in the absence of adverse action by the administrator.

The potential for automatic effectiveness under the notification and coordination approaches does not mean that securities offerings will avoid merit review. During the waiting period, the administrator can and often does review an offering in light of the applicable merit criteria.

The bewildering variety of blue sky laws has led to attempts standardization. A Uniform Securities Act, drafted by Professor Loss, was adopted by the National Conference of Commissioners on Uniform State Laws in the 1950's and subsequently adopted by about three-fourths of the states, with varying degrees of amendment. At their 1985 annual meeting, the Commissioners approved a revised act, the Uniform Securities Act (1985). See Titus, Uniform

Securities Act (1985), 19 Review of Securities & Commodities Regulation 81 (1986).

———

AD HOC SUBCOMMITTEE ON MERIT REGULATION OF THE STATE REGULATION OF SECURITIES COMMITTEE, AMERICAN BAR ASSOCIATION, REPORT ON STATE MERIT REGULATION OF SECURITIES OFFERINGS

41 Bus.Law. 785 (1986).

The basic similarity among the laws of the fifty-odd blue sky jurisdictions does not mean ... that blue sky law is a monolith. There are, for example, many differences in the language of the statutes and regulations, in the interpretations of that language, in the substantive conditions for registration and exemption of securities and persons, and in the informed practices of the administrators. More profound differences also distinguish the blue sky laws.

First, some states are more seriously engaged in securities regulation than others. State X may have a statute that gives its administrator the fullest possible range of administrative authority, but if the agency lacks funding, a large and well-trained staff, and support from local prosecutorial and law-enforcement agencies, it will not be able to administer its statute effectively. Conversely, if state Y has all of that support, it will regulate far more actively, even if its statute does not grant the broadest range of regulatory powers. States vary significantly in this regard. The blue sky world thus is divided between those states that have the practical ability to regulate and those that do not.

Second, the states are also divided between those that have merit review authority and those that do not. Some states lack merit authority and review securities filings only on a full-disclosure basis. These are the "disclosure," as distinguished from the "merit," jurisdictions. Other jurisdictions either do not require securities registration at all or exempt the vast majority of offerings. These can be described as nonregulatory jurisdictions.

Third, the ranks of the merit states are divided. Although a majority of the states have merit language in their statutes, at any given time only ten or so states can be regarded as tough merit states—jurisdictions that frequently and systematically raise objections on merit grounds to the offerings presented for their consideration. Among the merit states, furthermore, distinctions must be drawn between leaders and followers, that is, states that draw independent conclusions about offerings and states that tend to follow the lead of others. These distinctions must be drawn in pencil, however, because changes in law, in personnel, and in funding often cause states that were inactive or followers to become leaders, and vice versa. These changes can often be quite sudden and dramatic. Illinois and Louisiana have recently shifted from strong merit to pure disclosure systems of review as a result of legislative changes. Conversely, Massachusetts suddenly became one of the most rigorous merit states after years of relative inactivity, largely as a result of a change in directors.

State securities regulation as a whole, therefore, does not constitute a single, homogenous, uniform system: major states, such as California and Texas, are strong merit jurisdictions; Illinois now reviews on a disclosure basis only; and New York generally applies an antifraud statute while merit regulating a very narrow spectrum of real estate and theatrical syndications. The practical and conceptual complexities of this nonsystematic regulation are compounded by the simultaneous applicability of state and federal regulation to many different kinds of transactions.

Index

INDEX

PAYMENT
Dividends, contractual restrictions, 896, 897

PERIODIC DISCLOSURE
Proxy rules, 230

PHANTOM STOCK
Executive compensation, duty of loyalty, 477

PHRASES
See specific index headings

PIERCING THE CORPORATE VEIL
Generally, 111–135

POLICY
Dividend policy, 882–886
  Judicial review, 899
Insider trading regulation, 569–572

PREEMPTION
Shares and shareholders, preemptive rights, 84, 85
State control share acquisition statutes, Williams Act, 863, 864

PREFERRED STOCK
Corporate finance, 86–88

PREINCORPORATION TRANSACTIONS
Promoters, 90–99

PRESIDENT
Authority, 202–205

PRIVATE ACTIONS
Proxy rules, 232–246
Rule 10b-5, generally. Insider Trading, this index

PRIVATE PLACEMENTS
Securities, registration, 925–930

PRIVATIZATION
Publicly held corporations, 801–803

PROCEEDINGS
Actions and Proceedings, generally, this index

PROFITS
Short-swing trading, computation, 636–638

PROMOTERS
Preincorporation transactions, 90–99

PROPERTY
  See, also, Assets, generally, this index
Partnerships, 44–46

PROPOSALS
Shareholders, proxy rules, 246–255

PROSPECTUS
Defined, securities, 903

PROVISIONAL DIRECTORS
Close corporations, 364

PROXIES
  Generally, 227–268
Close corporations, irrevocable proxies, 293, 294
Contests, 230, 231, 255–268
Irrevocable proxies, close corporations, 293, 294

PUBLIC DISTRIBUTION
Securities, 902–964

PUBLICLY HELD CORPORATIONS
  Generally, 166–174
Composition and committees of board, 194, 195
Going private, 801–803
Weighted voting, 190–192

PURPOSE
Securities, registration, 904, 905
Shareholders, inspection of books and records, 219–221

QUO WARRANTO
Defective incorporation, 111

QUORUM
Board of directors, formalities required for action, 197
Close corporations, shareholder and board levels, 308–314
Shares and shareholders, formalities required for action, 207

RAIDER
Defined, tender offers, 804

RATIFICATION
Agency, liability of principal to third party, 12, 13

RECORDS
Shareholders, inspections, 212–221

REDUCTION OF SURPLUS
Dividends, 894, 895

REFORM
Short-swing trading, 631, 632

REGISTERED CORPORATIONS
Reports, shareholder informational rights, 226, 227

REGISTRATION
Securities, this index

INDEX

†

1-56662-276-x

90000